Handbook of Parenting

Volume 5
Practical Issues in Parenting

Handbook of Parenting

Second Edition

Volume 5
Practical Issues in Parenting

Edited by

Marc H. Bornstein

National Institute of Child Health and Human Development

 LAWRENCE ERLBAUM ASSOCIATES, PUBLISHERS
2002   **Mahwah, New Jersey**   **London**

Editor:	Bill Webber
Editorial Assistant:	Erica Kica
Cover Design:	Kathryn Houghtaling Lacey
Textbook Production Manager:	Paul Smolenski
Full-Service Compositor:	TechBooks
Text and Cover Printer:	Hamilton Printing Company

This book was typeset in 10/11.5 pt. Times, Italic, Bold, Bold Italic.
The heads were typeset in Helvetica, Italic, Bold, Bold Italic.

Lawrence Erlbaum Associates, Inc., Publishers
10 Industrial Avenue
Mahwah, New Jersey 07430

Library of Congress Cataloging-in-Publication Data

Handbook of parenting / edited by Marc H. Bornstein.—2nd ed.
    p. cm.
    Includes bibliographical references and indexes.
    Contents: v. 1. Children and parenting—v. 2. Biology and ecology of parenting—v. 3. Being
and becoming a parent—v. 4. Social conditions and applied parenting—v. 5. practical issues
in parenting.
    ISBN 0-8058-3778-7 (hc : v. 1 : alk. paper)—ISBN 0-8058-3779-5 (hc : v. 2 : alk. paper)—
ISBN 0-8058-3780-9 (hc : v. 3 : alk. paper)—ISBN 0-8058-3781-7 (hc : v. 4 : alk. paper)—
ISBN 0-8058-3782-5 (hc : v. 5 : alk. paper)
    1. Parenting.   2. Parents.   I. Bornstein, Marc H.

HQ755.8.H357   2002
649′.1—dc21   2001058458

Printed in the United States of America
10 9 8 7 6 5 4 3 2

For *Marian* and *Harold Sackrowitz*

Contents of Volume 5:
Practical Issues in Parenting

Preface

This new edition of the *Handbook of Parenting* appears at a time that is momentous in the history of parenting. The family generally, and parenting specifically, are today in a greater state of flux, question, and redefinition than perhaps ever before. We are witnessing the emergence of striking permutations on the theme of parenting: blended families, lesbian and gay parents, teen versus fifties first-time moms and dads. One cannot but be awed on the biological front by technology that now renders postmenopausal women capable of childbearing and with the possibility of designing babies. Similarly, on the sociological front, single parenthood is a modern-day fact of life, adult–child dependency is on the rise, and parents are ever less certain of their roles, even in the face of rising environmental and institutional demands that they take increasing responsibility for their offspring. The *Handbook of Parenting* is concerned with all facets of parenting.

Despite the fact that most people become parents and everyone who has ever lived has had parents, parenting remains a most mystifying subject. Who is ultimately responsible for parenting? Does parenting come naturally, or must we learn how to parent? How do parents conceive of parenting? Of childhood? What does it mean to parent a preterm baby, twins, or a child with a disability? To be a younger or an older parent, or one who is divorced, disabled, or drug abusing? What do theories in psychology (psychoanalysis, personality theory, and behavior genetics, for example) contribute to our understanding of parenting? What are the goals parents have for themselves? For their children? What are the functions of parents' beliefs? Of parents' behaviors? What accounts for parents' believing or behaving in similar ways? What accounts for all the attitudes and actions of parents that differ? How do children influence their parents? How do personality, knowledge, and world view affect parenting? How do social status, culture, and history shape parenthood? How can parents effectively relate to schools, daycare, their children's pediatricians?

These are some of the questions addressed in this second edition of the *Handbook of Parenting* . . . for this is a book on *how to parent* as much as it is one on *what being a parent is all about*.

Put succinctly, parents create people. It is the entrusted and abiding task of parents to prepare their offspring for the physical, psychosocial, and economic conditions in which they will eventually fare and, it is hoped, flourish. Amidst the many influences on child development, parents are the "final common pathway" to children's development and stature, adjustment and success. Human social inquiry—at least since Athenian interest in Spartan childrearing practices—has always, as a matter of course, included reports of parenting. Yet Freud opined that childrearing is one of three "impossible professions"—the other two being governing nations and psychoanalysis. And one encounters as many views as the number of people one asks about the relative merits of being an at-home or a working mother, about whether daycare, family care, or parent care is best for a child, about whether good parenting reflects intuition or experience.

The *Handbook of Parenting* concerns itself with different types of parents—mothers and fathers, single, adolescent, and adoptive parents; with basic characteristics of parenting—behaviors, knowledge, beliefs, and expectations about parenting; with forces that shape parenting—employment, social status, culture, environment, and history; with problems faced by parents—handicaps, marital difficulties, drug addiction; and with practical concerns of parenting—how to promote children's health, foster social adjustment and cognitive competence, and interact with school, legal, and public officials. Contributors to the *Handbook of Parenting* have worked in different ways toward understanding all these diverse aspects of parenting, and all look to the most recent research and thinking in the field to shed light on many topics every parent wonders about.

Parenthood is a job whose primary object of attention and action is the child. But parenting also has consequences for parents. Parenthood is giving and responsibility, but parenting has its own intrinsic pleasures, privileges, and profits as well as frustrations, fears, and failures. Parenthood can enhance psychological development, self-confidence, and sense of well-being, and parenthood also affords opportunities to confront new challenges and to test and display diverse competencies. Parents can derive considerable and continuing pleasure in their relationships and activities with their children. But parenting is also fraught with small and large stresses and disappointments. The transition to parenting is formidable; the onrush of new stages of parenthood is relentless. In the final analysis, however, parents receive a great deal "in kind" for the hard work of parenting—they are often recipients of unconditional love, they gain skills, and they even pretend to immortality. This edition of the *Handbook of Parenting* presents the many positives that accompany parenting and offers solutions for the many challenges.

The *Handbook of Parenting* encompasses the broad themes of who are parents, whom parents parent, the scope of parenting and its many effects, the determinants of parenting, and the nature, structure, and meaning of parenthood for parents. This second edition of the *Handbook of Parenting* is divided into five volumes, each with two parts:

Volume 1 concerns CHILDREN AND PARENTING. Parenthood is, perhaps first and foremost, a functional status in the life cycle: Parents issue as well as protect, care for, and represent their progeny. But human development is too subtle, dynamic, and intricate to admit that parental caregiving alone determines the developmental course and outcome of ontogeny. Volume 1 of the *Handbook of Parenting* begins with chapters concerned with how children influence parenting. The origins of parenting are, of course, complex, but certain factors are of obvious importance. First, children affect parenting: Notable are their more obvious characteristics, like age or developmental stage; but more subtle ones, like gender, physical state, temperament, mental ability, and other individual-differences factors, are also instrumental. The chapters in Part I, on Parenting Children and Older People, discuss the unique rewards and special demands of parenting children of different ages—infants, toddlers, youngsters in middle childhood, and adolescents—as well as the modern notion of parent–child relationships in adulthood and later years. The chapters in Part II, on Parenting Children of Varying Status, discuss the common matters of parenting siblings and girls versus boys as well as more unique situations of parenting twins, adopted and foster children, and children with special needs, such as those born preterm, with mental retardation, or aggressive and withdrawn disorders.

Volume 2 concerns the BIOLOGY AND ECOLOGY OF PARENTING. For parenting to be understood as a whole, psychophysiological and sociological determinants of parenting need to be brought into the picture. Volume 2 of the *Handbook* relates parenting to its biological roots and sets parenting within its ecological framework. Some aspects of parenting are influenced by the biological makeup of human beings, and the chapters in Part I, on the Biology of Parenting, examine the evolution of parenting, hormonal and psychobiological determinants of parenting in nonhumans and in human beings, parenting in primates, and intuitive universals in human parenting. A deep understanding of what it means to parent also depends on the ecologies in which parenting takes place. Beyond the nuclear family, parents are embedded in, influence, and are themselves affected by larger social systems. The chapters in Part II, on the Social Ecology of Parenting, examine employment status and parenting, the socioeconomic, cultural, environmental, and historical contexts of parenting, and provide an overarching developmental contextual perspective on parenting.

Volume 3 concerns BEING AND BECOMING A PARENT. A large cast of characters is responsible for parenting, each has her or his own customs and agenda, and the psychological makeups and social interests of those individuals are revealing of what parenting is. Chapters in Part I, on The Parent, show how rich and multifaceted is the constellation of children's caregivers. Considered successively are mothers, fathers, coparenting, single parenthood, grandparenthood, adolescent parenthood, nonparental caregiving, sibling caregivers, parenting in divorced and remarried families, lesbian and gay parents, and the role of contemporary reproductive technologies in parenting. Parenting also draws on transient and enduring physical, personality, and intellectual characteristics of the individual. The chapters in Part II, on Becoming and Being a Parent, consider the transition to parenting, stages of parental development, personality and parenting, parents' knowledge of, beliefs in, cognitions about, attributions for, and attitudes toward childrearing, as well as relations between psychoanalysis and parenthood. Such parental cognitions serve many functions: They generate and shape parental behaviors, mediate the effectiveness of parenting, and help to organize parenting.

Volume 4 concerns SOCIAL CONDITIONS AND APPLIED PARENTING. Parenting is not uniform in all communities, groups, or cultures; rather, parenting is subject to wide variation. Volume 4 of the *Handbook* describes socially defined groups of parents and social conditions that promote variation in parenting. The chapters in Part I, on Social Conditions of Parenting, include ethnic and minority parenting in general and parenting among Latino, African American, and Asian populations, in particular, as well as parents in poverty and parenting and social networks. Parents are ordinarily the most consistent and caring people in the lives of children. In everyday life, however, parenting does not always go right or well. Information, education, and support programs can remedy these ills. The chapters in Part II, on Applied Issues in Parenting, explore parenting competence, maternal deprivation, marital relationships and conflict, parenting with a sensory or physical disability, parental psychopathology, substance-abusing parents, parental child maltreatment, and parent education.

Volume 5 concerns PRACTICAL ISSUES IN PARENTING. Parents meet the biological, physical, and health requirements of children. Parents interact with children socially. Parents stimulate children to engage and understand the environment and to enter the world of learning. Parents provision, organize, and arrange children's home and local environments and the media to which children are exposed. Parents also manage child development vis-à-vis childcare, school, the worlds of medicine and law, as well as other social institutions through their active citizenship. Volume 5 of the *Handbook* describes the nuts and bolts of parenting as well as the promotion of positive parenting practices. The chapters in Part I, on Practical Parenting, review the ethics of parenting, parenting and attachment, child compliance, the development of children's self-regulation, children's prosocial and moral development, socialization and children's values, maximizing children's cognitive abilities, parenting talented children, play in parent–child interactions, everyday stresses and parenting, parents and children's peer relationships, and health promotion. Such caregiving principles and practices have direct effects on children. Parents indirectly influence children as well, for example, through their relationships with each other and their local or larger community. The chapters in Part II, on Parents and Social Institutions, explore parents and their children's childcare, schools, media, and doctors and delve into relations between parenthood and the law and public policy.

Each chapter in the second edition of the *Handbook of Parenting* addresses a different but central topic in parenting; each is rooted in current thinking and theory as well as in classical and modern research in that topic; each has been written to be read and absorbed in a single sitting. Each chapter in this new *Handbook* follows a standard organization, including an introduction to the chapter as a whole, followed by historical considerations of the topic, a discussion of central issues and theory, a review of classical and modern research, forecasts of future directions of theory and research, and a set of conclusions. Of course, each chapter considers the contributors' own convictions and research, but contributions to this new edition of the *Handbook of Parenting* present all major points of view and central lines of inquiry and interpret them broadly. The *Handbook of Parenting* is intended to be both comprehensive and state of the art. To assert that parenting is complex is to understate the obvious. As the expanded scope of this second edition of the *Handbook of Parenting* amply shows, parenting is naturally and closely allied with many other fields.

The *Handbook of Parenting* is concerned with child outcomes of parenting but also with the nature and dimensions of variations in parenting per se. Beyond an impressive range of information, readers will find *passim* critical discussions of typologies of parenting (e.g., authoritarian–autocratic, indulgent–permissive, indifferent–uninvolved, authoritative–reciprocal), theories of parenting (e.g., ecological, psychoanalytic, behavior genetic, ethological, behavioral, sociobiological), conditions of parenting (e.g., mother versus father, cross cultural, situation-by-age-by-style), recurrent themes in parenting studies (e.g., attachment, transaction, systems), and even aphorisms (e.g., "A child should have strict discipline in order to develop a fine, strong character," "The child is father to the man").

In the course of editing this new edition of the *Handbook*, I set about to extract central messages and critical perspectives expressed in each chapter, fully intending to construct a comprehensive Introduction to these volumes. In the end, I took away two significant impressions from my own efforts and the texts of my many collaborators in this work. First, my notes cumulated to a monograph on parenting ... clearly inappropriate for an Introduction. Second, when all was written and done, I found the chorus of contributors to this new edition of the *Handbook* more eloquent and compelling than one lone voice could ever be. Each chapter in the *Handbook of Parenting* begins with an articulate and persuasive Introduction that lays out, in a clarity, expressiveness, and force (I frankly envy), the meanings and implications of that contribution and that perspective to parenting. In lieu of one Introduction, readers are urged to browse the many Introductions that will lead their way into the *Handbook of Parenting*.

Once upon a time, parenting was a seemingly simple thing: Mothers mothered; Fathers fathered. Today, parenting has many motives, many meanings, and many manifestations. Contemporary parenting is viewed as immensely time consuming and effortful. The perfect mother or father or family is a figment of past imagination. Modern society recognizes "subdivisions" of the call: genetic mother, gestational mother, biological mother, birth mother, social mother. For some, the individual sacrifices that mark parenting arise for the sole and selfish purpose of passing one's genes on to succeeding generations. For others, a second child is conceived to save the life of a first child. A multitude of factors influence the unrelenting advance of events and decisions that surround parenting—biopsychological, dyadic, contextual, historical. Recognizing this complexity is important to informing people's thinking about parenting, especially information-hungry parents themselves. This second edition of the *Handbook of Parenting* explores all these motives, meanings, and manifestations of parenting.

Each day more than three fourths of a million adults around the world experience the rewards and the challenges as well as the joys and the heartaches of becoming parents. The human race succeeds because of parenting. From the start, parenting is a "24/7" job. Parenting formally begins during or before pregnancy and can continue throughout the lifespan: Practically speaking for most, *once a parent, always a parent*. But parenting is a subject about which people hold strong opinions and about which too little solid information or considered reflection exists. Parenting has never come with a *Handbook* ... until now.

ACKNOWLEDGMENTS

I would like to express my sincere gratitude to the staffs at Lawrence Erlbaum Associates, Publishers, and TechBooks who perfectly parented production of the *Handbook of Parenting*: Victoria Danahy, Susan Detwiler, Sheila Johnston, Arthur M. Lizza, Paul Smolenski, and Christopher Thornton.

—Marc H. Bornstein

Contents of Volume 1:
Children and Parenting

Contents of Volume 2:
Biology and Ecology of Parenting

PART II: SOCIAL ECOLOGY OF PARENTING

Contents of Volume 3:
Being and Becoming a Parent

Contents of Volume 4:
Social Conditions and Applied Parenting

PART II: APPLIED ISSUES IN PARENTING

About the Authors in Volume 5

DIANA BAUMRIND is a Research Scientist at the Institute of Human Development at the University of California, Berkeley, where for over 40 years she has directed the Family Socialization and Developmental Competence Project, a longitudinal study of parenting effects on children and adolescents. Baumrind received her A.B. degree from Hunter College of the City of New York and her M.A. and Ph.D. from the University of California, Berkeley. She is a recipient of the G. Stanley Hall Award from the American Psychological Association and a Research Scientist Award from NIMH. Baumrind's research focuses on parenting effects, in particular on how contrasting childrearing patterns (for example, authoritative, authoritarian, permissive, and disengaged) influence the development of character and competence in youth. Baumrind is concerned with social policy applications of research on the family and in particular of the cultural moderators of parent–child relationships. She is the author of *Child Maltreatment and Optimal Caregiving in Social Contexts*.

* * *

MARC H. BORNSTEIN is Senior Investigator and Head of Child and Family Research at the National Institute of Child Health and Human Development. He holds a B.A. from Columbia College and a Ph.D. from Yale University. Bornstein was a Guggenheim Foundation Fellow and received a RCDA from the NICHD, the Ford Cross-Cultural Research Award from the HRAF, the McCandless Young Scientist Award from the APA, the United States PHS Superior Service Award from the NIH, and the Arnold Gesell Prize from the Theodor Hellbrügge Foundation. Bornstein has held faculty positions at Princeton University and New York University as well as visiting academic appointments in Munich, London, Paris, New York, and Tokyo. Bornstein is Editor Emeritus of *Child Development* and Editor of *Parenting: Science and Practice*. He has contributed scientific papers in the areas of human experimental, methodological, comparative, developmental, cross-cultural, neuro-scientific, pediatric, and aesthetic psychology. Bornstein is coauthor of *Development in Infancy* (four editions) and general editor of *The Crosscurrents in Contemporary Psychology Series* (ten volumes) and the *Monographs in Parenting* (four volumes). He also edited the *Handbook of Parenting* (Vols. I-V, two editions), and he coedited *Developmental Psychology: An Advanced Textbook* (four editions) as well as a dozen other volumes. He is the author of several children's books and puzzles in *The Child's World* series.

* * *

ELLEN W. CLAYTON is Professor of Pediatrics, Professor of Law, and Director of the Center for Genetics and Health Policy at Vanderbilt University. A graduate of Yale Law School and Harvard Medical School, Clayton is concerned with the ethical and legal aspects of pediatrics. She has served on the Committee on Bioethics of the American Academy of Pediatrics and as a consultant to the National Institute of Child Health and Human Development and the Food and Drug Administration. She is a general pediatrician and teaches and lectures on many topics regarding the care of children.

* * *

KEITH A. CRNIC is Professor of Psychology and Head of the Department of Psychology at Penn State University. He received his B.A. from the University of Southern California and his Ph.D. from the University of Washington. Crnic was an Associate Professor in the Department of Psychiatry and Behavioral Sciences at the University of Washington. He is a member of American Psychological Association and the Society for Research in Child Development, and his primary research interests involve parent–child relationships, familial contexts, and family and parent contributions to children's competence and psychopathology. He is currently the principal investigator on an NICHD investigation of family influences on the emergence of dual diagnosis in young children with developmental delays, and has published on the topics of parenting stress, parent–child relationships, and children's developmental competence.

* * *

E. MARK CUMMINGS is Professor of Psychology at the University of Notre Dame. He received his B.A. from Johns Hopkins University and M.A. and Ph.D. from UCLA. He has served as a member of the Board of Editors of *Child Development* and on the editorial boards of *Developmental Psychology*, *Journal of Family Psychology*, *Parenting: Science and Practice*, the *Journal of Emotional Abuse*, and *Personal Relationships*. Cummings's research interests focus on social, emotional, and personality development, especially relations between adaptive and maladaptive family functioning and children's normal development and risk for the development of psychopathology. He coedited *Altruism and Aggression, Attachment in the Preschool Years*, and *Life-Span Developmental Psychology: Perspectives on Stress and Coping* and coauthored *Children and Marital Conflict* and *Developmental Psychopathology and Family Process*.

* * *

JENNIFER S. CUMMINGS is a Clinical Psychologist specializing in childhood psychopathology and family functioning. She received her B.A. from Miami of Ohio and M.A. and Ph.D. from the Catholic University of America. She is a coinvestigator on a prospective longitudinal study of relations between family processes and child development. She has been active in teaching and supervising psychology students and doctoral trainees and has served as a consultant to legal professionals on cases involving child abuse, divorce, and other matters concerned with the well-being of children and families.

* * *

AIMÉE DORR is Professor of Education and Dean of the Graduate School of Education & Information Studies at the University of California, Los Angeles. She conducted research for the original Surgeon General's Report on Television and Social Behavior and has since continued study of the social effects of television and of media literacy. She has conducted both formative and summative evaluations of health education materials, television programs, public service announcements, teacher in-service programs on technology integration, and more. Dorr has extensive experience working with those who create educational materials for home and school, including materials designed to promote early literacy and positive racial attitudes.

* * *

NANCY EISENBERG is Regents' Professor of Psychology at Arizona State University. She received her Ph.D. in psychology from the University of California, Berkeley. She holds a National Institute of Mental Health Research Scientist Development Award. She has been an associate editor of *Personality and Social Psychology Bulletin* and *Merrill-Palmer Quarterly* and is the current editor of *Psychological Bulletin*. Her research interests span the domain of social development, including the development of moral behaviors, empathy, and socially competent behavior; emotional and personality development; and gender roles. Her work also is focused on the interface of social and developmental psychology. Her books include *The Caring Child*, *The Roots of Prosocial Behavior in Children*, and *Altruistic Emotion, Cognition, and Behavior*. Eisenberg edited Volume 3 in the *Handbook of Child Psychology: Social, Emotional, and Personality Development* and *Empathy and Its Development*.

* * *

JOYCE L. EPSTEIN is Director of the Center on School, Family, and Community Partnerships and the National Network of Partnership Schools, Principal Research Scientist at the Center for Research on the Education of Students Placed at Risk (CRESPAR), and Professor of Sociology at Johns Hopkins University. Epstein has published extensively on the effects of school, classroom, family, and peer environments on student learning and development, focusing on school and family connections. She is interested in the connections among research, policy, and practice. Epstein is a recipient of the Academy for Educational Development's Alvin C. Eurich Education Award and the *Working Mother* magazine special award for her work on school, family, and community partnerships. She has published *School, Family, and Community Partnerships: Your Handbook for Action* and *School, Family, and Community Partnerships: Preparing Educators and Improving Schools*.

* * *

ANDREA J. ERICKSEN is a graduate student in Developmental Psychology at the University of California, Riverside. She received her education at the University of California, Riverside (B.A., M.A.). Ericksen is a Research Coordinator for the Healthy Families Project at the University of California, Riverside. She is a member of Phi Beta Kappa and the Society for Research in Child Development. Her research interests include the study of family and sociocultural influences on the development of risky behaviors and body satisfaction in childhood and adolescence.

* * *

MELANIE FARKAS is a candidate in Clinical Psychology at Clark University. She received her B.S. from Brandeis University, where she was awarded the Elliot Aronson '54 Prize for Excellence in Psychological Research. She is a member of the American Psychological Association. Her research interests include family interactions, adolescent self-regulation, and behavioral medicine.

* * *

DAVID HENRY FELDMAN is Professor of Child Development and Director of the Developmental Science Group in the Eliot-Pearson Department of Child Development at Tufts University. He has degrees from the University of Rochester (B.A.), Harvard University (Ed.M.), and Stanford University (M.A. and Ph.D.). He previously served on the faculties of the University of Minnesota and Yale University and has also served as a visiting professor at Harvard University, Tel Aviv University, and the University of California, San Diego. Feldman was named Distinguished Scholar of the Year by the National Association of Gifted Children. He is the general editor of a series of volumes on early childhood education from Project Zero at Harvard University. His books include *Beyond Universals in Cognitive Development, Nature's Gambit: Child Prodigies and the Development of Human Potential*, and *Changing the World: A Framework for the Study of Creativity*.

* * *

PHILIP A. FISHER is a Research Psychologist at the Oregon Social Learning Center, Eugene, OR. He received his doctoral degree from the University of Oregon. He is principally interested in preventive interventions with high-risk preschoolers, research in Native American communities, children in the child welfare system, and the integration between research on basic biological systems and applied prevention.

* * *

JAMES GARBARINO is Codirector of the Family Life Development Center and Elizabeth Lee Vincent Professor of Human Development in Cornell University's College of Human Ecology. He received his B.A. from St. Lawrence University and his Ph.D. from Cornell University. Garbarino was President of the Erikson Institute for Advanced Study in Child Development. His research interests include the development and implications of family policy, the etiology and prevention of youth violence, and the role of parents in influencing social development. Garbarino has authored or coauthored 20 books, including *Raising Children in a Socially Toxic Environment*, *Lost Boys: How Our Sons Turn Violent and How We Can Save Them*, and *Parents under Siege*.

* * *

WENDY S. GROLNICK is Associate Professor of Psychology at Clark University. She obtained her B.A. from Cornell University and her M.A. and Ph.D. from the University of Rochester. Grolnick is a member of the American Psychological Association and the Society for Research in Child Development. She has published in the development of children's motivation and self-regulation, and her research has focused on the effects of home and school environments on children's motivation as well as factors affecting the environments that parents and teachers create for their children. She is the author of *Antecedents and Consequences of Parental Control*.

* * *

JOAN E. GRUSEC is Professor in the Department of Psychology and Associate Dean for Research, Faculty of Arts and Science, at the University of Toronto. She received her B.A. from the University of Toronto and her Ph.D. from Stanford University. Her previous academic affiliations include Wesleyan University and the University of Waterloo. Grusec is a Fellow of the American and Canadian Psychological Associations. Her research interests include the socialization of prosocial behavior, parenting cognitions, and parent–adolescent conflict. She is an associate editor of *Developmental Psychology*. Grusec coauthored *Social Development: History, Theory, and Research* and coedited *Parenting and Childrens' Internalization of Values: A Handbook of Contemporary Theory*.

* * *

GERALD B. HICKSON is Professor of Pediatrics at Vanderbilt University School of Medicine and Chief of the Division of General Pediatrics. He received his undergraduate education at the University of Georgia and his M.D. degree from Tulane University School of Medicine. Hickson completed a residency in pediatrics at Vanderbilt and a fellowship in general academic pediatrics with Dr. William Altemeier at Metropolitan Nashville General Hospital and Vanderbilt University Hospital. Hickson has served on the National Association of Children's Hospital and Related Institutions, Quality of Care Committee, and the Committee on Quality Improvement of the American Academy of Pediatrics. His research interests include the identification of unmet needs in private pediatric practices and the identification of noneconomic reasons that prompt people to sue for malpractice. He is the coauthor of *Suing for Medical Malpractice*.

* * *

ALICE STERLING HONIG is Professor Emerita in the Department of Child and Family Studies at Syracuse University. She received her education at Barnard College, Columbia University, and Syracuse University (Ph.D.). Honig is a Fellow of the Society for Research in Child Development and of the American Psychological Association and a member of the International Society for Infant Studies. Her research includes the study of caregiver/child interactions, fathering, Piagetian sensorimotor development, prosocial interactions with peers, iron deficiency anemia, intergenerational and cross-cultural practices in childrearing, gender and the effects of divorce, reading with infants in daycare, and longitudinal effects of quality childcare. Honig is a New York State licensed psychologist specializing in parenting problems and custody cases. Honig is North American editor of *Early Child Development and Care* and author/editor of *Risk Factors in Infancy*, *Behavior Guidance for Infants and Toddlers*, *Attachment: What Teachers and Caregivers Need to Know*, *Playtime Learning Games for Young Children*, and *Parent Involvement in Early Childhood Education*. She is coauthor of *Infant Caregiving: a Design for Training* and *Talking with Your Baby: Family as the First School*.

* * *

SANDRA M. IRLEN is a Ph.D. candidate at the University of California, Los Angeles. She earned a B.S. from Cornell University. Irlen has conducted research on moral reasoning and television viewing in early adolescence and on the thoughtful integration of technology into the classroom environment. Her interests include the development of effective children's television programming to promote socioemotional development.

* * *

KATHLEEN KOSTELNY is a Research Associate at the Erikson Institute for Advanced Study in Child Development. She received her her B.A. from Bethel College, her M.A. from the University of Chicago, and her Ph.D. from Erikson Institute/Loyola University. Kostelny's research interests pertain to the protection of children and families in dangerous environments. She is coauthor of *Children in Danger: Coping with the Consequences of Community Violence* and *No Place to Be a Child: Growing up in a War Zone*.

* * *

ALAN KWASMAN is a board-certified pediatrician in Riverside, CA. Kwasman was trained at the Autonomous University of Guadalajara and completed his residency at Loma Linda University Medical Center. He is an Adjunct Associate Professor at the University of California, Riverside. Kwasman is a member of the American Academy of Pediatrics and the Society for Developmental and Behavioral Pediatrics. He is currently in private practice at the Pediatric Medical Group of Riverside. His research and clinical interests include childhood attention deficit disorder, and he has authored *ADD: Diagnosis by Exclusion*.

* * *

GARY W. LADD is Professor of Human and Family Development and of Psychology at Arizona State University. Ladd is a Fellow of the American Psychological Association and has been a Fellow at the Center for Advanced Study in the Behavioral Sciences at Stanford. He coauthored *Peer Relationships and Child Development* and *Family-Peer Relationships: Modes of Linkage*. Ladd is editor of *Merrill-Palmer Quarterly*, and was associate editor for *Child Development* and *Journal of Social and Personal Relationships*. Ladd conducts research on the contributions of families, peers, and teachers to children's early school adjustment and on linkages between children's family and peer relations.

* * *

CHRISTINE LOW is a doctoral candidate at The Pennsylvania State University. She received her B.A. from the University of California, Los Angeles, and her M.S. from The Pennsylvania State University. She is a member of the American Psychological Association and the Society for Research in Child Development. Her research encompasses parent–child relationships, with specific focus on the emergence of young children's self-regulatory skills and the pathways to developing psychopathology.

* * *

PHILLIP LYONS is Assistant Professor of Criminal Justice and Criminal Justice Liaison to the Forensic Clinical Psychology Program at Sam Houston State University. He received his B.S. from the University of Houston-Clear Lake and his J.D., M.A., and Ph.D. from the University of Nebraska-Lincoln. Lyons is Assistant Director of the Texas Regional Community Policing Institute. His interests revolve largely around the incorporation of social scientific findings into the legal system, particularly the criminal justice system and, especially, policing. Lyons is coauthor of *Ethical and Legal Issues in AIDS Research*, *No Place to Go: The Civil Commitment of Minors*, and *Mental Health Services for Children and Families: Building a System That Works*.

* * *

CHARLOTTE N. MARKEY is a graduate student in Developmental Psychology at the University of California, Riverside. She received her education at Santa Clara University (B.S.) and the University of California, Riverside (M.A.). Markey has been the Research Coordinator and Data Manager for the Healthy Families Project at the University of California, Riverside and has assisted with the Girls' Nutrition, Early

Experience, and Development Study at Pennsylvania State University. She is a member of the Society for Research in Adolescence, the Society for Research in Child Development, and the Society for Personality and Social Psychology. Her research interests include the study of sociocultural influences on the development of eating-related behaviors and the links between personality and health.

* * *

BARBARA G. MELAMED is Professor of Clinical Health Psychology in the Division of Social and Behavioral Sciences at Mercy College. She received her B.A. from the University of Michigan and her M.S. and Ph.D. from the University of Wisconsin. Melamed was previously at Kent State University, Case Western Reserve University, and the University of Florida, and she served as Dean of the Ferkauf Graduate School of Psychology at the Albert Einstein College of Medicine of Yeshiva University. She has been associate editor of the *Journal of Health Psychology*. Melamed received the Distinguished Research Award in Pediatric Psychology from the American Psychological Association and is past President of the Division of Health Psychology. She has held appointments at the Max-Planck Institute for Psychiatry in Munich, Germany, and at the Maudsley Institute for Psychiatry in London. Melamed has directed videotapes used in the health care arena, including *Ethan Has An Operation*. Her current research interests are undiagnosed medical disorders, posttraumatic stress disorders, and anxiety in children and adults. She coauthored *Behavioral Medicine: Practical Applications in Health Care* and *Child Health Psychology*.

* * *

GARY B. MELTON is Professor of Psychology, Adjunct Professor of Family and Youth Development, and Director of the Institute on Family and Neighborhood Life at Clemson University. He received his B.A. from the University of Virginia and his M.A. and Ph.D. from Boston University. Melton is president of Childwatch International (a global network of child research centers) and a past President of the American Psychology-Law Society and the American Psychological Association Division of Child, Youth, and Family Services. He has held faculty appointments at Morehead (Kentucky) State University and the Universities of Hawaii, Minnesota, Nebraska, South Carolina, and Virginia. He is a Research Fellow in the Centre for Behavioural Science at the University of the Free State in South Africa. Melton has received distinguished contribution awards from the American Psychological Association (twice), two of its divisions, Psi Chi, and Prevent Child Abuse America. His published works include books on adolescent abortion, child advocacy, child protection policy, children's competence as decision makers, civil commitment of minors, forensic mental health services, motivation in family relationships, pediatric and adolescent AIDS, research ethics, rural psychology, and social science in the law, including *Mental Health Services for Children and Families: Building a System That Works* and *Children's Law*.

* * *

REBECCA VASQUEZ ORTIZ is a Mexican American researcher in the fields of developmental and health psychology. Ortiz received her B.A., M.A., and Ph.D. at the University of California, Riverside. She has been a researcher collaborator on the Healthy Families Project at the University of California, Riverside. Ortiz is a member of Phi Beta Kappa and the Society for Research in Child Development. Her research interests include family socialization processes in Mexican Americans, cultural influences on family dynamics, childhood health socialization, obesity intervention, and indigenous health belief systems.

* * *

PAULINE M. PAGLIOCCA is Assistant Professor of Psychology at the University of South Carolina. She was educated at the University of Massachusetts (B.A.) and the University of Virginia (M.Ed., Ph.D.). She completed a clinical internship and an advanced fellowship at The Cambridge Hospital/Harvard Medical School and then served as a postdoctoral Research Fellow at the Center on Children, Families, and the Law at the University of Nebraska, Lincoln. Previously, she was Assistant Professor at Tulane University and the Institute for Families in Society. Her general research interests relate to children and the law, and her teaching interests include child and family therapy. She is the coordinator of the Crisis Management in the Schools

Interest Group of the National Association of School Psychologists. Pagliocca is coauthor of *Law and Mental Health Professionals: Louisiana*.

* * *

GERALD R. PATTERSON is a Research Psychologist at the Oregon Social Learning Center (OSLC), Eugene, Oregon. He received his doctoral degree from the University of Minnesota. He founded the OSLC to focus on the family interaction process as it relates to aggressive children, marital conflict, and parent-training therapy as applied to antisocial boys. He was a research scientist at the Oregon Research Institute. Patterson is a past President of the Association for the Advancement of Behavior Therapy. He is the recipient of the Distinguished Professional Contribution Award from the section on Clinical Child Psychology of the American Psychological Association, the Distinguished Scientist Award from the Division of Clinical Psychology of the American Psychological Association, and the Distinguished Scientist Award for the Applications of Psychology from the American Psychological Association.

* * *

GREGORY S. PETTIT is Professor in the Department of Human Development and Family Studies, College of Human Sciences, Auburn University. He received his Ph.D. in interdisciplinary child studies from Indiana University. Pettit is a Fellow of the American Psychological Association and associate editor of *Developmental Psychology*.

* * *

JANE PIIRTO is Trustees' Professor and Director of Talent Development Education at Ashland University in Ashland, OH. She has degrees from Northern Michigan University (B.A.), Kent State University (M.A.), South Dakota State University (M.Ed.), and Bowling Green State University (Ph.D.). She has been a college instructor at Northern Michigan University, a high school teacher, a regional educational consultant in South Dakota, Ohio, and Michigan and was the Principal of the Hunter College Elementary School, a school for gifted children, in New York City. She has won Individual Artist Fellowships in both poetry and fiction from the Ohio Arts Council. Her research interests are creativity in adults and children, the education and psychology of the gifted and talented, and arts-based qualitative research methodologies. Her nonfiction books are *Talented Children and Adults: Their Development and Education*, *Understanding Those Who Create*, *"My Teeming Brain": Understanding Creative Writers*, and *Luovuus*. Her literary books are *A Location in the Upper Peninsula: Collected Poems, Stories, and Essays* and *The Three-Week Trance Diet*.

* * *

BETH E. RABIN is Vice President of Research at Research Communications Ltd. in Braintree, MA. She earned an M.A. and a Ph.D. from the University of California, Los Angeles, and a B.A. from the University of California, Berkeley. She has conducted research involving children and television, including projects investigating the relation of parents and television to children's emotion norm knowledge, children's perceived realism of family television programs, children's understanding of prosocial cartoon messages, and children's understanding of emotional display rules on family television programs. Her interests include the impact of television viewing on socioemotional development and processes for developing effective educational programming for children.

* * *

MAVIS G. SANDERS holds a joint appointment as Research Scientist at the Center for Research on the Education of Students Placed at Risk (CRESPAR) and Assistant Professor in the Graduate Division of Education at Johns Hopkins University. Sanders earned her Ph.D. from Stanford University. She has published papers on the processes and outcomes of school, family, and community connections. Sanders' research and teaching interests include school reform, parent and community involvement—especially the possibilities and limitations of community involvement in education—and African American student achievement. She is coauthor of

School, Family, and Community Partnerships: Your Handbook for Action and *Schooling Students Placed at Risk: Research, Policy, and Practice in the Education of Poor and Minority Adolescents.*

*　*　*

ROBERT J. STERNBERG is IBM Professor of Psychology and Education and Director of the Center for the Psychology of Abilities, Competencies, and Expertise at Yale. He received his Ph.D. from Stanford University and his B.A. from Yale University. He holds an honorary doctorate from the Complutense University of Madrid and has been awarded honorary doctorates by the University of Leuven, Belgium, the University of Cyprus, and the University of Paris V, France. Sternberg is a Fellow of the American Academy of Arts and Sciences, the American Association for the Advancement of Science, the American Psychological Association (in 12 divisions), and the American Psychological Society. He has won the Early Career Award and Boyd R. McCandless Award from APA; the Palmer O. Johnson, Research Review, Outstanding Book, and Sylvia Scribner Awards from AERA; the James McKeen Cattell Award from APS; the Distinguished Lifetime Contribution to Psychology Award from the Connecticut Psychological Association; the International Award of the Association of Portuguese Psychologists; the Cattell Award of the Society for Multivariate Experimental Psychology; the Award for Excellence of the Mensa Education and Research Foundation; the Sidney Siegel Memorial Award of Stanford University; the Wohlenberg Prize of Yale University, and a Guggenheim Fellowship. He has been president of the Divisions of General Psychology, Educational Psychology, Psychology and the Arts, and Theoretical and Philosophical Psychology of the APA and has served as Editor of the *Psychological Bulletin* and is Editor of *Contemporary Psychology*. The central focus of his research is on intelligence and cognitive development. He is most well known for his theory of successful intelligence, investment theory of creativity, theory of mental self-government, balance theory of wisdom, and for his triangular theory of love.

*　*　*

CATHERINE S. TAMIS-LEMONDA is Associate Professor in New York University's Developmental Program, in the Department of Applied Psychology, School of Education. She received her Ph.D. from New York University. Her research focuses on the social and cultural contexts of children's language, play, and cognitive development in the first three years of life.

*　*　*

ROSS A. THOMPSON is Carl A. Happold Distinguished Professor of Psychology at the University of Nebraska. He received his A.B. from Occidental College, his A.M. from the University of Michigan, and his Ph.D. from the University of Michigan. He was a Visiting Scientist at the Max-Planck Institute for Human Development and Education in Berlin, Senior NIMH Fellow in Law and Psychology at Stanford University, and was associate editor of *Child Development*. He has received the Boyd McCandless Young Scientist Award for Early Distinguished Achievement from the American Psychological Association, the Scholarship in Teaching Award and the Outstanding Research and Creative Activity Award from the University of Nebraska, and is a lifetime member of the University of Nebraska Academy of Distinguished Teachers. His research interests include basic topics in developmental psychology (especially infant–parent attachment and parent–child relationships, the growth of conscience and emotional understanding, and emotion regulation), and the applications of developmental research to public policy problems concerning children and families. He has written on divorce and child custody, child maltreatment, grandparent visitation rights, research ethics, and early neurophysiological development and early intervention. His books include *Preventing Child Maltreatment through Social Support: A Critical Analysis, Early Brain Development, the Media, and Public Policy*, and *The Postdivorce Family: Children, Families, and Society*. He also edited *Socioemotional Development* and is coauthor of *Infant-Mother Attachment*.

*　*　*

BARBARA J. TINSLEY is Professor in the Department of Psychology and Chair of the Program in Human Development at the University of California, Riverside. Tinsley was educated at the University of Illinois at Urbana and previously was affiliated with the University of Illinois and the Centers for Disease Control and

Prevention. She is a member of the Society for Research in Child Development and the Society for Developmental and Behavioral Pediatrics. Her research interests include cultural and family influences on children's physical health and risk, and pediatrician–parent communication. Tinsley is the author of *How Children Learn to Be Healthy*.

* * *

INA Č. UŽGIRIS was Professor of Psychology in the Frances L. Hiatt School of Psychology at Clark University. She received her Ph.D. from the University of Illinois, Urbana-Champaign. She was a Fulbright Senior Scholar at Utrecht University in the Netherlands and lectured at the University of Vilnius in Lithuania. Her scholarly interests centered around the relations between cognitive and communicative development in infancy and the nature of early parent–child interactions and the role of cultural values in development. She coauthored *Assessment in Infancy: Ordinal Scales of Psychological Development* and edited *Social Interaction and Communication During Infancy*.

* * *

CARLOS VALIENTE is a graduate student in the Department of Family Resources and Human Development at Arizona State University, where he received his B.A. and M.A. His research interests are in the domain of social and emotional development, especially in the family context.

* * *

JOSEPH A. VORRASI is a developmental psychology doctoral candidate in the Department of Human Development at Cornell University. He is a Graduate Research Assistant in the Family Life Development Center and the College of Human Ecology's Flora Rose Fellow for research in child development. He received his B.S. and M.A. from Cornell University. Vorrasi's research interests include the development of aggression and other problematic adolescent behaviors, the effects of exposure to family violence, and the continuity and discontinuity of personality and behavior through the life course.

* * *

VICTORIA WEISZ is an Associate Research Professor at the Center on Children, Families, and the Law at the University of Nebraska-Lincoln and serves as the Director of the Nebraska Court Improvement Project. She received her B.A. from the University of Rochester, her M.A. and Ph.D. in Clinical Psychology from Washington University in St. Louis, and her M.L.S. from the University of Nebraska. Her research interests include court and legal processes in child maltreatment, family group conferencing, juvenile justice, and psycholegal issues in child bone marrow transplantation.

* * *

WENDY M. WILLIAMS is Associate Professor in the Department of Human Development at Cornell University. She received a B.A. from Columbia University and M.Phil., M.A., and Ph.D. degrees from Yale University. Williams is a Fellow of four divisions of the American Psychological Association and is currently Member-at-Large of the Executive Committee of the Society for General Psychology of APA. Williams has won Senior Research Awards from the Mensa Educational and Research Foundation and the Early Career Contribution Award from the American Psychological Association. She is series editor for *The Lawrence Erlbaum Educational Psychology Series*, and she served on the Editorial Review Boards of the journals *Psychological Bulletin* and *Psychology, Public Policy, and Law*. Her research focuses on the identification, assessment, training, and societal implications of intelligence and related cognitive abilities. Williams is author or coauthor of *The Reluctant Reader, Escaping the Advice Trap, How to Develop Student Creativity, Practical Intelligence for School, Creative Intelligence for School*, and *Educational Psychology*.

* * *

Handbook of Parenting

**Volume 5
Practical Issues in Parenting**

PART I

PRACTICAL PARENTING

1

The Ethics of Parenting

Diana Baumrind
University of California, Berkeley
Ross A. Thompson
University of Nebraska

INTRODUCTION

Ethical parenting above all is responsible caregiving, requiring of parents enduring investment and commitment throughout their children's long period of dependency. The effort people put forth to be responsible parents, as in other areas of their lives, is a function of their self-attributions concerning the relation between their effort and outcome. As Bugental, Blue, and Cruzcosa (1989) have shown, parents who attribute a child's dysfunctional behavior primarily to the child's disposition or to peer influences rather than to their own practices are less likely to attempt to alter their disciplinary style when it is ineffective or developmentally unapt, or to attempt to alter their child's behavior when it is changeworthy. Greenberger and Goldberg (1989) found that high-investment parents, as part of their identity, believed that they could meet their children's needs better than other adults, and therefore willingly sacrificed other personal pleasures to be with their children. Such parents (whom the authors identified as authoritative) had higher maturity expectations, were notably responsive, and viewed their children more positively than did less invested parents The remarkable achievement of native and immigrant Asian children in the United States is often attributed to their parents' high investment in parenting fueled by a Confucian-based belief that original nature is uniform and that phenotypic differences in academic performance are due to childhood experiences constructed largely by parents and teachers.

The ethics of parenting begins, therefore, with the assumption of responsibility for children. This chapter is concerned with unfolding the nature of that responsibility in the context of the reciprocal obligations of parents and offspring, and the responsibility of the state to support ethical parenting. The moral obligations of parents to their children, and of the state to the family, have been long-standing concerns of philosophy, the law, and psychology dating back to ancient times. This short chapter does not attempt to comprehensively review this interesting history, nor to offer guidelines to contemporary parents about specific ethical dilemmas (e.g., Should a parent ever lie to a child?). Instead, we outline a theory of the ethics of parenting, rooted in traditional and modern views in moral and political philosophy, that describes the needs and rights of children and the roles and responsibilities of parents and the state for children's welfare. We argue, in brief, that children's rights are complementary and reciprocal (but not equal) to those of parents, that parental responsibilities to offspring arise from a developmental orientation to children's needs and capabilities, that the state has an important role in supporting parents but not assuming parental responsibilities, and that developmental scientists have an obligation to contribute to public understanding of parenting and its influences. Such a theory can, we hope, offer guidance for the specific dilemmas that parents often face, but can also provide a comprehensive, thoughtful perspective on what parenting is for, and why, in relation to the needs of children.

The first part of the chapter concerns the ethical obligations of parents, with special attention to the rights of children, the moral justification of parental authority, and the contrasting views of protectionist, liberationist, and developmentalist approaches to understanding children's best interests. This section closes with a profile of parents' developmental responsibilities to children, especially in relation to the growth of character and competence. The second part of the chapter focuses on the relation among parents, children, and the state. In this section, we describe the state's interest in the well-being of children and the conditions justifying the state's intervention into family life to promote children's well-being. In doing so, we also seek to profile what the state does well, and poorly, in its efforts to assist its youngest citizens. In the concluding section, we briefly consider the responsibilities of developmental scientists for fostering ethical parenting.

THE ETHICAL OBLIGATIONS OF PARENTS

The Rights of Children

Discussions of parenting often begin with the rights of children. But what are children's rights, and how are they justified? We propose that the moral norms of reciprocity and complimentarity offer a new way of regarding children's rights not as absolute entitlements to self-determination and autonomy, but rather as rights that develop in concert with children's growing capacities to exercise mature judgment.

In 1989, the U.N. Convention on the Rights of the Child (United Nations, 1989) codified children's entitlements in a document that was adopted by the U.N. General Assembly and subsequently endorsed by more than 100 countries, but not by the United States. The survival, protection, development, and self-determination of dependent children were identified as children's rights. It was the inclusion of self-determination rights that accounts, in part, for the reluctance of U.S. legislators to endorse the document. According to the Convention, children have the right to express their views (Article 11), have freedom of thought, conscience, and religion (Article 14), associate freely (Article 15), privacy (Article 16), and be protected from all forms of physical or mental violence (Article 19). The Expert Committee on the Rights of the Child, the organization charged with monitoring and implementing the provisions of the Convention, interpreted Article 19, as well as Article 37 (which protects children against any form of cruel, inhuman, or degrading treatment), as prohibiting all physical punishment.

In the United States, the debate over the ratification of the Convention sharpened fundamental differences between liberals and conservatives concerning the desirable degree of interference by the state in family life (the less the better to conservatives) and the freedom with which a child should be legally endowed (the more the better to liberals). Liberals have urged ratification but criticized the Convention for failing to explicitly proscribe physical punishment. Conservatives, on the other hand, have strongly and successfully opposed ratification, arguing that the document contains unwarranted restrictions on the historical right of parents to regulate the physical, moral, intellectual, and cultural development of their children. This liberal-versus-conservative polarity reflects a broader division in views of the family that contrasts a hierarchical paternalistic authoritarian model that places obedience at the cornerstone in the foundation of character (Dobson, 1992; Hyles, 1972) with a children's rights position, which demands for children the same civil rights as are possessed by adults (Cohen, 1980).

The children's rights movement, which rose to prominence in the 1970s (Farson, 1974; Holt, 1974; Worsfold, 1974), viewed children as the last disempowered segment of society and claimed for children all the rights of adult persons, including the right to determine their own living arrangements, associations, and medical options. In this view, children's rights are entitlements and as such impose complementary ethical obligations on parents and the state. Critics of the children's rights movement pointed out that self-determination rights depend for their exercise on competencies that children do not possess, and therefore would require of parents and the state unusual (and impractical) support and assistance simply to enable children to exercise these rights. Members of parents' rights organizations such as the Concerned Women for America and the Christian Coalition charge that the emphasis on children's self-determination rights violates the legitimate rights and responsibilities of parents to discipline and shape their children's character and behavior. An emphasis on self-determination as the focus of children's rights, therefore, sharpens the perceived conflict between the rights of children and parents within the family and, inappropriately in our view, impedes thoughtful reflection on ethical parenting by polarizing discussion according to whether children's rights or parents' rights should be preeminent. We will argue later that it is much more useful to consider children's rights and needs within a developmental perspective and within the context of the mutual obligations of parents and children.

The Moral Norms of Reciprocity and Complementarity

An overemphasis on children's self-determination rights can also be seen as a violation of the moral norms of reciprocity and complementarity (Baumrind, 1978b). Instantiated by different value hierarchies in different cultures, the cornerstone of all ethical systems is the moral norm of reciprocity, represented in Christian religion by the Golden Rule, "do unto others as you would have them do unto you" and in Buddhist thinking as karma, or the sum of the ethical consequences of one's actions (Baumrind, 1980). *Reciprocity* refers to the balance in an interactive system such that each party has both rights and duties, and the subordinate norm of *complementarity* states that one's rights are the other's obligations. The norm of complementarity implies that if children have a right to be nurtured (and not merely to seek nurturance), then there must be adult caregivers with a complementary obligation to nurture. Children also incur obligations reciprocal to that right, such as returning love and complying with parental directives, that motivate and enable caregivers to nurture satisfactorily. Application of the principle of reciprocity requires, therefore, mutuality of gratification and governs relationships within all stable social systems, including the family. Thus parents and children have reciprocal, not equal, rights. The view that the rights and obligations of youthful status are reciprocal rather than identical to those of their caregivers acknowledges reciprocity as a generalizable moral norm based on the mutually contingent exchange of resources and gratification whose application is likely to produce the greatest good over evil of the greatest number.

Consistent with the principle that children's rights and responsibilities are complementary, not identical, to those of their parents is the view that parents incur a duty to commit themselves to the welfare of their dependent children, who in turn have a duty to conform to parental standards. In other words, because of their dependent status, unemancipated youth may claim from adults the protection and support necessary for their growth and development, but may not claim the full rights to self-determination appropriate to an emancipated, independent person. In practice this means that parents may choose their children's education, religion, abode, and, at least until adolescence, censor their reading, media exposure, friends, and attire. As the child approaches adolescence, however, children gradually relinquish the privileges of childhood and assume the responsibilities and entitlements of adulthood, consistent with their developing capabilities. The remaining restrictions on their freedom provide adolescents with an essential impetus to becoming self-supporting and thus self-determining.

Exploitation or indulgence of the child by the parent interferes with the child's internalization of the norm of reciprocity and the child's acknowledgement that her or his actions have consequences for the self and others. A marked imbalance between what is given gratuitously and what is required of the child disequilibrates the social system of the family. Whereas unconditional commitment to the child's welfare and responsiveness to the child's wishes motivate children to comply with their parents' demands for maturity and obedience (Parpal and Maccoby, 1985), noncontingent acquiescence to children's demands is likely to encourage dependency rather than to reward responsible self-sufficiency.

The reciprocal relations between the rights and obligations of parents and children has enduring philosophical roots and constitutes the basis of Rousseau's (1762/1952, p. 387) social contract:

> The most ancient of all societies, and the only one that is natural, is the family: and even so the children remain attached to the father only as long as they need him for their preservation. As soon as this need ceases, the natural bond is dissolved. The children, released from the obedience they owed to the father, and the father, released from the care he owed his children, return equally to independence.

Radical proponents of liberating rights for children (e.g., Cohen, 1980; Farson, 1974; Holt, 1974) negate the principle of reciprocity by claiming simultaneously that because of their temporary dependence children are entitled to beneficent protection, and yet because of their inherent status as autonomous persons children should exercise equal self-determination, as do adults.

The Moral Case For and Against Equal Rights for Children

The case for equal rights for children appeals largely to deontological universalist premises, which maintain that *what is morally right and obligatory is not contingent on its consequences in promoting the welfare of self, society or the world, but rather on principles (such as justice) that have prima facie validity, independent of whether they promote the common good.* By contrast, the case for reciprocal rights for children appeals largely to rule-utilitarian consequentialist premises intended to maximize welfare (i.e., the welfare of the community and the family as well as of the child) at a given historical time and place (see Frankena, 1973, for a succinct discussion of these and other contrasting theories of ethics).

The justification for children's equal rights is commonly grounded in the universalist theory of justice of Rawls (1971), who believed that in order to prove the validity of ethical principles of just treatment, these principles must be selected in the hypothetical "original position," behind "a veil of ignorance" in which individuals are ignorant of their own specific interests, circumstances, and abilities. The "original position" assumes the priority of equal liberty as the fundamental terms of association of all rational persons. Maximizing liberty in equal distribution is a universal, objective end of human nature. This universalist view is the foundation for Rawls's theory, but it is important to note that giving priority to the ideal of the free, autonomous individual is also a uniquely Western notion that is at variance with the Eastern ideals of collective harmony and individual duty (Markus and Kitayama, 1991; Shweder, 1990; Triandis, 1990).

As interpreted by Worsfold (1974), an advocate for children's equal rights, Rawls's universalist theory claims that "in their fundamental rights children and adults are the same" (p. 33) and indeed that children "have a right to do what they prefer when it conflicts with what their parents and society prefer" (pp. 35–36). This is consistent with, and indeed derives from, the foundational deontological principle of maximizing individual liberty of Rawls's theory. Worsfold supports his case for equal rights for children with two empirical claims and two moral principles. The two empirical claims are: (1) the first motive of everyone is to preserve her or his own personal liberty and (2) children have the same capacity as adults to know what they want and are capable of weighing alternatives and acting on their decisions. The moral principles are: (3) all inequalities of primary goods such as liberty must be justified by relevant differences between the people concerned and (4) people are not to enjoy a special advantage as a result of age, natural ability or social status. If the empirical claims (1) and (2) were both true it might be appropriate to conclude, with Worsfold, that children have the same self-determination rights as do adults—but a developmental analysis raises significant doubts about their validity.

Concerning (1): It is doubtful that most people of any age value absolute liberty above other fundamental values (such as a moderate level of material sustenance and security), and children would be especially unlikely to sacrifice security for liberty. There is an abundance of evidence that children of all ages, although they would like to do as they please, accept parental authority as legitimate even when it is punitive as well as firm and deprives them of liberty (Catron and Masters, 1993; Siegal and Barclay, 1985; Smetana and Asquith, 1994).

Concerning (2): immense differences in knowledge, experience, and power make it impossible to conclude that children have the same capacity as adults to know what they want and to weigh alternatives and act on their choices. To regard young children as capable of self-determination is to fail to take into account, for example, their difficulty in coordinating their behavior with that of others in unfamiliar situations, understanding the complementarity of role performance, or anticipating the perceptions or reactions of others to their own actions. All of these abilities are needed to act rationally in one's self-interest. Although what "is" does not determine "ought," beliefs about what is right should be constrained by beliefs about what is true, because it is fatuous to claim that what cannot be, ought to be. Thus restrictions on children's liberty rights based on their natural, developmental incapacities to exercise those rights cannot be regarded as inequitable in the moral sense of being unjust.

Worsfold states that the two moral principles which justify equal rights for children ([3] and [4] previously described) are based on Rawls's "original position" and "veil of ignorance." In order to be logically secured, the equal rights for children position does require the "veil of ignorance." Age cannot be taken into account, and neither adults nor children may claim any special advantages even if their relevant capacities are shown to differ greatly. However, in the hypothetical "original position," few would choose to don the "veil of ignorance," and without the actual interests, circumstances, and ages of themselves and others obscured by the "veil" these essential facts of life would (and do) determine decisions concerning how rights and responsibilities should be apportioned. Indeed, with regard to age distinctions, Rawls himself (1971) makes the same argument for temporary restrictions on children's liberty from paternalism, as do the major philosophers before him (e.g., Locke, Hegel, Mill, and Rousseau), emphasizing however the priority of liberty as an ultimate goal.

In sum, then, the case for equal rights for children as set forth by Worsfold is not convincing. His two empirical claims are, to say the least, controversial. Indeed, claim (2) is clearly false. His moral claim (3) appeals to a counterfactual empirical assumption (that is, claim [2]) whereas his moral claim (4) assumes that people would agree that they ought to don the "veil of ignorance" in determining how rights and responsibilities are to be allotted, even if they did not already agree that age, circumstances, and abilities should not be taken into consideration in such a determination, which is very doubtful.

By contrast with deontological theorists, rule-utilitarian theories claim that *the right, the obligatory, and the morally good are a function of what is nonmorally good.* On the assumption that morality was made for humankind rather than humankind for morality, rule utilitarians are primarily concerned with the long-range consequences for humankind of acting on the ethical guidelines they espouse. Rule utilitarians (unlike rule deontologists) claim that the rules that are right are determined by their long-range consequences. An act is right if, and only if, it would maximize welfare, that is, if in a particular social context it would be as beneficial to the common good to have a moral code permitting that act as to operate under a rule that would prohibit that act (Brandt, 1998). What is judged to be right in principle is based not on a short-range cost–benefit analysis of individual acts, but rather on the long-range consequences of applying the rule in question. The institutions of liberty are valued highly, for example, as a means to assure the rational pursuit of the progressive interests of humankind. The right of parents to restrict the liberty of their dependent children is based on what constitutes the best interests of the child and the common good of the family and the state.

Unlike act utilitarians, rule utilitarians do not claim that each situation is different and unique, but instead claim that general (not necessarily universalizable) rules and guidelines must be formulated in making moral claims. However, based on particular welfare considerations, a moral code may vary from subgroup to subgroup within society. The principle of utility enters in determining what the rules will be in like contexts, rather than what concrete action should be performed in a given instance, as in situation ethics or other variations of act utilitarianism. So, in deciding whether one should lie or tell the truth, the long-range consequences of lying in general must be considered, not merely whether telling the truth or a lie in this particular instance is more beneficent in its effect. Unlike the deontological injunction against lying in all circumstances, for instance, rule utilitarians would claim that to prevent a greater evil, or to achieve a greater good in the long run, it would be right to lie. The example often given is that one ought to lie to secure the safe haven of a potential holocaust victim.

Frankena (1973, p. 52) developed a "mixed deontological theory of obligation" that takes as basic both the principle of beneficence (to do good and prevent or avoid harm) and the principle of justice (equal treatment), but appears to give precedence to the principle of justice. By contrast, rule utilitarians incorporate the principle of social and distributive justice within the principle of utility (or beneficence) by claiming that what satisfies the principle of utility or beneficence in the long run must also satisfy the requirements of justice—that is, an equitable if not equal distribution of tangible and intangible goods is presumed to maximize total welfare (e.g., to each according to her or his needs, even within the family).

In formulating ethical guidelines for parenting we adopt a modified rule-utilitarian stance, not dissimilar to that which Frankena (1973) proposes, in that it subsumes justice (in the sense of equitable, not equal, treatment) as well as beneficence as underlying and unifying principles of morality. In our view, both principles—beneficence and justice—must be taken into account in determining what constitutes ethical parenting (such as in the case of a disciplinary encounter), but justice does not take precedence over beneficence.

Our "mixed rule-utilitarian theory" emphasizes a welfare-maximizing principle of the greatest good for the greatest number, but in addition requires a separate justification for inequality of distribution of resources and goods. The justification for equitable rather than equal distribution of resources and goods to children within a family, for example, must be based on age, gender, and sibling order differences in needs, preferences, and capabilities. Justice is not conceived simplistically as guaranteeing equal treatment in the short run, but rather as demanding a justification for unequal treatment based on relevant differences between the people concerned. Thus with regard to the relationship between parents and children, unequal treatment with regard to liberty is justified on the ground that it will produce greater good (including equality) in the long run. Children's right to protection, support, and nurturance are greater, and their right to self-determination correspondingly less than their parents. Liberty is recognized as *a* good but not as the *primary* good.

A Mixed Rule-Utilitarian Justification for Restricting Children's Liberty

Until the twentieth century, few questioned the justification for restricting children's liberty in the family. Despite his romantic view of childhood, Rousseau argued for authoritative rule in the family on the basis that parental rule "looks more to the advantage of him who obeys than to that of him who commands" (Rousseau, 1762/1952, p. 357). The proprietary interests of parents in their children's welfare presumes a sovereignty more benevolent than that of a disinterested third party. When parents are exploitative, cruel, or incompetent, their authority is thereby rendered illegitimate. In a similar vein more than 50 years later, Hegel (1821/1952, p. 61) wrote:

The right of the parents over the wishes of their children is determined by the object in view—discipline and education. The punishment of children does not aim at justice as such; the aim is more subjective and moral in character, that is, to deter them from exercising a freedom still in the toils of nature and to lift the universal into their consciousness and will.

Hegel chided elders who by romanticizing the immature child "corrupt and distort his genuine and proper need for something better, and create in him . . . a contempt of his elders because they have posed before him, a child, in a contemptible and childish fashion" (p. 61). Similarly, the rule utilitarian John Stuart Mill (1859/1973) restricted the ideal of self-determination to individuals capable of assuming adult responsibilities, arguing that although the adult generation is not perfectly wise and good with regard to the interests of the next generation, it is wiser and better in its judgments of what would benefit it than the generation is itself.

Parental authority, including the right to speak for their children and to discipline them, is rationally justified by children's dependent status and relative incompetence, imposing on parents the obligation to protect, nurture, and train children, and the right to reward and punish them contingent on parents' standards of desirable behavior. As parents do so, children learn to master the environment and to develop a stable sense of self. Self-determination becomes a conscious predominant value during adolescence, with its constructive expression predicated on competence, an internal locus of control, and an understanding of moral reciprocity, all capacities developed through the socialization process, which includes parental limit setting. Prior to the child's acquisition of the ability to think logically and symbolically, parental authority is legitimated in the child's mind by the fact that the child is weak and the parent is strong, and by the child's strong emotional attachment to the parent. Then and subsequently unequal distribution of liberty is justified in the child's mind, as in the adult's mind, by recognition of the relevant age-related differences between them.

The disciplinary encounter, including the use of reward and punishment, is a necessary part of the socialization process through which parents fulfill their fiduciary obligations to their children. Because children's wishes often conflict with those of their caregivers, the notion that all children's immediate or long-term welfare is served by rearing them without using aversive discipline (e.g., McCord, 1991) is utopian. In families with normally assertive toddlers, scarcity of material resources and time invites frequent aversive disciplinary confrontations. Conflictual interactions between young children and their parents occur from 3 to 15 times an hour, and even more often when children are defiant (Lee and Bates, 1985). Hoffman (1975) reported that, when the child is 2 years old, about 65% of parent–child interactions focus on prohibitions, and in a study by Minton, Kagan, and Levine (1971), parents were observed to interrupt their children an average of every 6 to 8 minutes to induce them to change their behavior. Because it is rare for a disciplinary encounter to extinguish a child's motivated behavior permanently, periodic reinforcement and explanations are necessary. Properly handled, these recurring disciplinary encounters enable children to learn the skills of negotiation, and thus promote their future autonomy as well as immediate compliance.

Because punishment is necessarily aversive it can be justified only when aimed at maximizing the child's long-range welfare. By preventing and reforming children's bad behavior and educating and encouraging their good behavior, mild punishment is intended to advance the welfare of the family and the community as well as of the child. A moderate rather than either a severe or a minimal level of distress facilitates child compliance with parental demands (Larzelere and Merenda, 1994). Arbitrary reliance on aversive discipline, rather than its judicious use, is the critical factor resulting in harm to children or failure to obtain their compliance. If the motive of punishment, physical or otherwise, is primarily to inflict pain or to vent anger, it is not corrective and cannot be justified ethically on either utilitarian or deontological grounds.

These ethical considerations are important because serious challenges to the exercise of parental authority that seek to criminalize ordinary mild spanking as a form of assault and violence have been mounted in Canada and the United States. In the United States it has been argued that spanking is wrong from both a rights and a welfare perspective (Bitensky, 1997). From a rights perspective, children have the same right as adults to freedom from assault and violence, and Bitensky sees spanking as both. From a welfare perspective, basing her argument largely on research by Straus (1994, 1996), Bitensky (1997, p. 432) declares that the "vitality and equilibrium of an individual's psychic life may be distorted and violated by corporal punishment in ways that cause lasting suffering and varying degrees of persistent dysfunction". Based on an acceptance of the validity of the data Straus presents, a case to criminalize spanking was mounted in the Ontario Court of Canada but was defeated, due in part to the testimony (by Baumrind) rebutting the validity of Straus's data. However, the case is expected to be appealed up to Canada's Supreme Court, and the issue of the ethics and consequences of physical punishment remains hotly debated in the United States as well as Canada.

The Child's Best Interest Criterion for Determining Ethical Parenting: Protectionist, Liberationist, and Developmental Perspectives

Another way of understanding alternative constructions of children's needs and rights, and the ethical responsibilities of parents, is to consider how best to define children's "best interests." It is incontrovertible that it is in children's best interests to survive, develop fully, and be protected from harm. But advancing beyond these minima reveals significant differences in views of children's needs and the responsibilities of adults as caregivers.

Protectionists and *liberationists* view children's best interests differently, especially with respect to children's self-determination interests. Children's rights advocates (e.g., Cohen, 1980; Harris, 1982; Purdy, 1972) adopt a liberationist view and claim that it suffices for children to have a rudimentary understanding of basic survival facts to entitle them to make their own decisions, whether or not they can do so wisely. This liberationist argument from justice, based on deontological thinking, gives primacy to the moral right of everyone, including children, to self-determination. By contrast the protectionist argument from consequences encourages children's personal agency not as a moral right, but rather as a developmental need to be weighed against other developmental needs.

Wald (1979) distinguished among four categories of children's rights, two of which may be viewed as protectionist and two as liberationist. The two protectionist rights are: (1) "rights against the world," which pertain to adequate nutrition, housing, medical care, and schooling that should be assured by legislatures, not courts; and (2) "protection from inadequate care" by adults, especially parents, or what are typically regarded as abuse and neglect allegations. The two liberationist rights are: (1) "adult legal status," which would relieve children of status offenses or any other form of coercion that would be unconstitutional if attempted with adults; and (2) "rights against parents"— the most controversial—which would enable unemancipated children to act independently of their parents and against their wishes.

From a justice perspective that requires like cases be treated alike, age must be shown to be morally relevant in apportioning either rights or responsibilities. Wald pointed out that granting children liberation rights is a mixed blessing at best. The disadvantage for children of having greater adult-like legal status has been the increasing tendency of the legal system to treat children as adults in the courts, thus holding them (as well as their parents) responsible for their criminal actions. If distinctions based on age in the granting of liberty rights are thought to be unjustifiable, then so are age-based distinctions granting children freedom from responsibility for criminal conduct based on their developmental limitations. Conversely, if children are to be subject to status offenses, then their age may entitle them to freedom from other kinds of criminal responsibility in the courts.

There is, however, a third perspective to children's best interests that is an alternative to protectionist and liberationist views. From a *developmentalist's* perspective, age is a highly relevant justification for constraining children's liberty. The imposition of authority, even against the child's will, is perceived by most children (as well as by their parents) as age appropriate during the first 6 years, the period that Dubin and Dubin (1963) refer to as the "authority inception period." Parental authority is legitimized in the young child's mind by the charisma associated with the person and the role of the parent. During this period, according to Piaget (1935/1965), children have a "heteronomous" belief in rules, that is, a unilateral respect for adults extending, within limits, to an uncritical acceptance of the legitimacy of adult rules. During the preschool years, adult constraint—expressed as consistent contingent reinforcement and regularity—helps to promote the child's sense of security and her or his belief that the world can be a safe, predictable place. In order to achieve a developmentally appropriate level of behavioral compliance, primary caregivers must supply the predictable reinforcing reactions that children require from their social environment in order to feel secure enough to explore and assert agency. Consequently, the probability that children will repeat either prosocial or antisocial acts is determined to a very large extent by the reinforcing responses of their socializing agents, who may contingently support prosocial behavior, overlook minor transgressions in a generally compliant child, and punish intentional transgressions in a spirited, defiant child. Because the preschooler's social-conventional reasoning is limited, reliance on inductive disciplinary techniques that involve complex explanations may confuse the child and facilitate neither compliance nor prosocial behavior. Toddler compliance is most effective when the adult briefly explains the rule and provides a consequence if the child persists in disobeying, reserving longer explanations for when punishment is over (Blum, Williams, Friman, and Christophersen, 1995).

Under most circumstances, children, unlike adults, regard liberty restrictions as legitimate. Children also view nonabusive physical punishment as a legitimate expression of parental authority. Children from age 6 to 17 have been found to evaluate parents who use physical punishment to reinforce their directives as well as induction to explain their directives more favorably than parents who rely on either love withdrawal or permissiveness, and in no age group was induction evaluated more favorably than physical punishment for all situations (Siegal and Barclay, 1985; Siegal and Cowen, 1984). Preschool children in middle-income American families broadly accepted physical punishment as suitable across behavioral domains (moral, conventional, and prudential), whereas by middle childhood children are more discriminating, viewing spanking for moral transgressions and prudential transgressions as acceptable, but for conventional transgressions as unacceptable (Catron and Masters, 1993).

The importance of using reason to justify caregivers' directives increases with age. By early adolescence, children are more likely to identify with parents who use reason rather than force to justify their decisions and demands (Elder, 1963). As children approach adolescence their unqualified acceptance of parental authority, and in particular of physical punishment, decreases in middle-class American homes but still remains quite high (50%) for prudential and moral offenses. Many adolescents continue to accept rationally justified physical punishment as a legitimate form of discipline, especially in some dangerous urban settings where it is perceived by both parent and adolescent as an expression of concern. However, as the child approaches puberty, violations of privacy, especially uninvited touching as well as hitting, are rightfully resented.

There are, of course, limits to children's respect for parents' moral authority. In hypothetical and largely counterfactual situations, some young children will judge an act that causes harm as wrong (such as hitting another child), even if an adult appears to condone that act (Laupa, Turiel, and Cowan, 1995). With increasing maturity, children distinguish between personal issues (e.g., what clothes to wear) and moral issues (e.g., bullying weaker children) or conventional issues (e.g., table manners), and by adolescence tend to regard parental directives pertaining to moral issues as legitimate; conventional or prudential issues (e.g., dietary injunctions) as somewhat less legitimate; and personal issues (e.g., dress), as not legitimate domains in which parents may assert their authority (Nucci, 1981; Smetana, 1988). As children approach adolescence, their growing need for independence as well as their capacities to think through their own best interests and to empathize with the needs of others entitle them to a vote as well as a voice in matters that intimately affect them in the personal domain, such as custody disputes.

In sum, what constitutes children's best interests depends on one's perspective. The protectionist perspective emphasizes children's need for nurturance and protection from danger, including parental and societal neglect and abuse. The liberationist perspective emphasizes the child's inherent right to self-determination with liberty regarded as the primary "good" to which children and adults are equally entitled. From the developmental perspective that we endorse, however, the child's age or stage of development is a highly relevant justification both for restraining children's liberty and for determining their right to protection and nurturance. Justice, according to natural law, must take into account real differences in ability and need in determining the apportionment of privileges, responsibilities, and rewards. At each childhood stage the duties and rights of parents and children differ, finally approximating the balance that characterizes a mature adult–adult relationship. During the adolescent period the child gradually relinquishes the privileges and limitations of childhood and assumes the responsibilities of adulthood, and is rewarded with self-determination.

Parents' Developmental Responsibilities: Shaping Children's Character and Competence

We have sought in this discussion to clarify the nature of children's rights and parental responsibilities and, in particular, to provide an ethical justification for parental authority that is consistent with a mixed rule-utilitarian perspective and developmental science. But what are the purposes for which parental authority is exercised? What, in other words, are parents' developmental responsibilities to offspring?

The power to shape children's character and competence is an awesome responsibility requiring conscious sustained and systematic commitment by dedicated caregivers. Parents are responsible for contributing substantially to the development of ethical character and competence in their children through their socialization efforts (Baumrind, 1998). Socialization is an adult-initiated process by which young persons through education, training, and imitation acquire their culture, and the habits and values congruent with adaptation to that culture. Children's perspectives shape their understanding of parents' socialization efforts, but their perspectives are strongly influenced by their parents' perspectives, which are grounded in particular cultural contexts and instantiated in adult behavior. In this section, we focus particularly on the development of the dual essentials of socialization—character and competence—and then consider briefly the importance of culture in defining these essentials.

Character. Competency to know right from wrong and to regulate one's own actions led Waddington (1960) to refer to human beings as "the ethical animal." When its moral component is made explicit, character may be thought of as personality evaluated. Character constitutes the ethical estimate of an individual and refers to the aspect of personality that engenders accountability. Character is responsible for persistence in the face of obstacles and inhibits immediate impulses in the service of some more remote or other-oriented goal. Character provides the structure of internal law that governs inner thoughts and volitions subject to the agent's control under the jurisdiction of conscience. Within limits imposed by their competencies (cognitive, affective, and physical), circumstances, and cultures, ethical agents are able to plan their actions and implement their plans, examine and choose among options, eschew certain actions in favor of others, and structure their lives by adopting congenial habits, attitudes, and rules of conduct.

How may parents contribute to the development of a virtuous character in their children? Wilson (1993) contends that children are born with the moral sentiments of fairness, duty, sympathy, and self-control. However, they are also born egocentric, requiring cultivation of their moral sentiments by socializing agents. The child's moral sentiments are cultivated most effectively by caregivers who have a clear sense of purpose, enforce their directives, and convey their messages simply, firmly, and consistently. Through the disciplinary encounter, caregivers attempt to induce children to behave in accord with parental standards of proper conduct, become aware that they have an obligation to comply with legitimate authority, and respect the rights of others. The short-range objective of the exercise of parental authority is to maintain order in the family, but this is subordinated to parents' ultimate objective, which is to further children's development from a dependent infant into a self-determining, socially responsible, and moral adult. For parents who want their children to become autonomous adults, behavioral compliance is not the preeminent long-range childrearing objective. Parents encourage the development of ethical agency in children by distinguishing between unconstructive and constructive noncompliance strategies, and encouraging the latter by negotiating with a child who mounts a rational objection to a parental directive (Goodnow, 1994; Kuczynski and Kochanska, 1990). Providing that firm parental control has been exercised in childhood, far fewer rules will be required in adolescence, and family power can be distributed more symmetrically (Baumrind, 1983, 1987; Baumrind and Moselle, 1985; Kandel and Lesser, 1969; Perry and Perry, 1983).

It is not primarily through disciplinary encounters, however, that parents have their greatest influence on the character development of their children. Of paramount importance is the manner in which caregivers live their own lives by acting in accord with their beliefs, modeling compassion and courage, engaging in physically and mentally healthy behaviors, and creating the family as a just institution (Okin, 1989). As Okin, following in the footsteps of Mill (1869/1988) argued, the family is the first and most influential source of moral development. Justice in the family is modeled by attending carefully to everyone's point of view; distributing resources and tasks equitably by taking into account preference, need, and ability; and deconstructing family life by gender. If home responsibilities are inequitably distributed or distributed on the basis of gender without consideration of personal preferences and abilities, children learn injustice and gender-based inequality in power and access to resources.

Modern Western moralists have generally adopted the view, shared by Dewey (1916), that human consciousness is constituted morally to the extent that actions are determined volitionally and consciously rather than by unreflective conformity to inclination or authority. Persons who are highly developed in their moral reflections and ethical behavior do not merely internalize the rules of society, but also construct personal moral standards to guide the conduct of their lives. Although habit more than reflection governs most ethical behavior, the resolution of complex moral dilemmas that arise in life requires self-conscious moral reflection. Morality as a cognitive structure of restraint is the process by which children come to espouse as well as conform to society's rules even when they are free from external inducements or surveillance, and is inculcated by guiding the child to reflect on, as well as to obey, the laws and rules of the community and the family, that is, to become a moral agent in her or his own right.

The mark of exemplary character differs somewhat in Eastern and Western thought. Personal integrity marks exemplary character in Western thought. Integrity implies both wholeness and honesty. Wholeness means that a person's precepts and practices are consistent, that the same standards are applied to means and ends, and that the dichotomy between self and other is transcended in an understanding of true self-interest. Honesty preserves trust in human relationships. Rule utilitarians place a high premium on truth telling and trust, although unlike Kantian deontologists, they do not claim that truth telling is an unconditional duty that holds in all circumstances, even if a life is forfeited (Kant 1797/1964). From a consequentialist perspective, promise keeping and truth telling are, however, of sufficient utility in maximizing social welfare to justify an initial presumption against lying. Truth telling is such a difficult discipline to acquire, and the principle of veracity has such utility in social life that parents need to act as models especially when it is awkward or uncomfortable to tell their child the truth. (For a differentiated treatment of the subject of lying, see Bok, 1979; for a discussion of rule-utilitarian objections to deception research, see Baumrind, 1971b, 1972b, 1979, 1985, 1992.)

It should be noted, however, that the Eastern perspective on integrity differs from Western thought because the self is construed as context-dependent, so its identity is allowed to change with circumstances and relationships. *Jen*, a cardinal Chinese virtue, is the ability to interact in a polite, decent, and sympathetic fashion, and to flexibly change one's behavior in accord with the requirements of a relationship (Hsu, 1985). Therefore, authenticity that requires people to focus their attention on their own inner feelings and convictions rather than on the reactions of others is not considered as important as not hurting others psychologically or disrupting harmonious interactions with them. In Eastern thought, trust is based on goodwill rather than on telling the whole truth because it is understood that how one acts is a negotiated and shared social enterprise.

Ethical personality evolves by successive forms of reciprocity in which the capacity develops for treating the other as someone like oneself rather than alien from oneself. From a young child's dawning awareness of psychological states in others—called "theory of mind" by contemporary developmental theorists—emerges the earliest moral sensibility in a preschooler's awareness of the feelings, beliefs, and preferences of others (Kochanska and Thompson, 1997). By middle childhood, the child recognizes that stable social relationships, including those within the family, are based on reciprocal maintenance of expectations by social partners as well as on appropriate feelings of gratitude or malevolence. Consequently, children actively solicit approval from adults as well as peers and can understand the reasons for parental directives. Perceiving their peers as like themselves in status and nature, they can better extend toward them genuine concern and comprehend their antithetical position in an altercation. By early adolescence, youth acknowledge reciprocity in their relations with adults and adopt a considered view of existential obligations that embraces an understanding of one's obligations to others, or what is called "reciprocal altruism" (e.g., see Erasmus, 1977). By acts of compassionate regard and respect for the rights of others, one invites reciprocal acts of goodwill in time of need.

As children develop intellectually, socially, and emotionally, their character becomes shaped by parental practices that include: (1) the "scaffolding" of shared activity with the child that leads offspring to new patterns of behavior and thought (Damon and Colby, 1987; Pratt, Kerig, Cowan, and Cowan, 1988); (2) family habits of hospitality, compassion, and generosity that are extended to the larger community; (3) direct training in role taking; (4) parental use of induction and reasoning in preference to power; and (5) the child's opportunities to observe loving adults acting consistently with their expressed moral beliefs (Colby and Damon, 1992; Oliner and Oliner, 1988). As a consequence, children become ethically sound by internalizing adult values of kindness, fairness, and respect, experiencing empathy and sympathy for others, and forming personal standards of right and wrong conduct that result in a sense of obligation to others. Perhaps most important, parental practices focused on the principle of compassionate regard for children will foster in children the ability to make inferences about how others feel and respect for those feelings (Kochanska and Thompson, 1997).

Competence.   Competence is effective human functioning in attainment of desired and valued goals. The goals that are valued in a culture are those that enable individuals to pursue their personal objectives within the constraints imposed by the common good and by their social networks. Competence is not the mere absence of psychopathology. Indeed, the presence of virtuous character, intelligence, creativity, and determination have enabled many people with serious emotional problems to make substantial contributions to society.

It takes virtuous character to will the good, and competence to do good well. Optimum competence as well as good character in Western society requires both highly developed communal and agentic (self-assertive) attributes and skills, the two orthogonal dimensions of instrumental competence (see Baumrind, 1970, 1973; Baumrind and Black, 1967). The use of the term "instrumental competence" derives from Parson's (1951, p. 49) distinction between instrumental and expressive functions. By expressive functions, Parsons referred to activities where "the primary orientation is not to the attainment of a goal anticipated for the future, but the organization of the 'flow' of gratifications (and of course the warding off of threatened deprivations)." Parsons designated as instrumental those agentic functions that were oriented to the achievement of an anticipated future goal requiring self-discipline, and the renunciation of certain immediately potential gratifications in the interest of the larger gains to be derived from the attainment of the goal.

Implied by Koestler's (1967) metaphorical reference to the Roman god Janus is the understanding that humans must function simultaneously as autonomous, self-assertive, independent units and as interdependent, cooperative parts of a larger unit. Within the Cartesian dualistic tradition that characterizes the Western perspective, we may treat agency and communion as the two primary orthogonal drives. Agency is the need for autonomous self-expression that sets the individual apart from the community, and communion is the need to be interdependent and part of an integrated, harmonious whole. In Western psychological literature (e.g., Bakan, 1966), agency refers to the drive for independence, individuality, and self-aggrandizement, whereas communion refers to receptivity, empathy, and the need to be of service and engaged with others. In the early sex-role literature (e.g., Spence and Helmreich, 1978), agency was identified as the masculine principle, whereas communion was identified as the feminine principle. The social dimensions of status (e.g., dominance and power) and love (e.g., solidarity and affiliation) which emerge as the two orthogonal axes from almost all factor analyses of Western human behavior (see, e.g., Baumrind and Black, 1967; Leary, 1957; Lonner, 1980; Schaefer, 1959; Wiggins, 1979) are manifestations of agency and communion. Optimum competence requires a balance of highly developed agentic and communal qualities, and thus this is also a prized goal of childrearing. In practice, the integration of the two modalities is represented by actions that resolve social conflicts in a manner that is both just and compassionate, and that promotes the interests of both one's self and one's community (Baumrind, 1982).

The young child's development of competence is the product of increasingly complex interactions of the developing child with socializing adults—primarily parents—who, during the child's early years, have the power to control these interactions. How parents socialize their children, in part through the disciplinary encounter, predicts crucial aspects of children's positive and negative interpersonal behavior and socioemotional and cognitive development. In the past, most socialization researchers implicitly assumed that internalization of society's rules, represented by parental values, was the prime objective of childrearing. However, today fewer parents and educators make that assumption. Internalization by one generation of the rules of the preceding generation represents the conservative force in society, whereas the impetus to social transformation comes about by the challenges each generation presents to the accepted values, rules, and habits of the previous generation. Behavioral compliance and internalization of parental standards are necessary, but not sufficient, childrearing objectives.

We will not attempt to review here the literature on socialization effects as these contribute to the development of competence of children (see the bibliographic references to Baumrind, 1966, 1968, 1996b, 1997a; and Maccoby and Martin, 1983). Instead, we will describe the authoritative model, which has to date proven to be the most effective childrearing style in generating high levels of both agency and communion in European American children. Authoritative parenting balances warm involvement and psychological autonomy with firm, consistent behavioral control and developmentally high expectations for social maturity and cognitive achievement. By contrast with authoritarian parents who are highly demanding but not responsive, permissive parents who are responsive but not demanding, and unengaged parents who are neither demanding nor responsive, authoritative parents are both highly demanding and highly responsive. On the one hand, they provide firm control and high maturity demands, and on the other hand they offer warmth, responsiveness, and encouragement of autonomy (Baumrind, 1966, 1975, 1978a, 1980). Authoritative parents emphasize the importance of well-timed parental interventions. They minimize intrusions on a toddler's autonomy by proactive caregiving such as childproofing, quality time-in, an abundance of positive attention and active listening, clear instructions, and progressive expectations for self-help. Authoritative parents remain receptive to the child's views but take responsibility for firmly guiding the child's actions by emphasizing reasoning, communication, and rational discussion in interactions that are friendly as well as tutorial and disciplinary.

The balanced perspective of authoritative parents is neither exclusively child centered nor exclusively parent centered, but instead seeks to integrate the needs of the child with those of other family members, treating the rights and responsibilities of children and those of parents as complementary rather than as identical. Authoritative parents endorse the judicious use of aversive consequences when needed in the context of a warm, engaged, rational, and reciprocal parent–child relationship. Because children have their own agendas that include testing the limits of their parents' authority, disciplinary encounters are frequent, even in authoritative homes. At such times direct power assertion that is just sufficient to control the child's behavior and is preceded by an explanation most effectively reinforces parental authority concerning the standards that the child must meet.

Studies that focus on the mechanisms that characterize the authoritative parent show how authoritative parents encourage moral internalization, self-assertive, prosocial behavior, and high cognitive performance. Their strategies include: (1) scaffolding of children's competence, including children's social competence, through shared activity and conversations (Pratt, Green, MacVicar, and Bountrogianni, 1993; Zahn-Waxler, Radke-Yarrow, and King, 1979); (2) reliance on person-centered persuasion rather than on coercion (Applegate, Burke, Burleson, Delia, and Kline, 1985); (3) monitoring of offspring and the use of contingent reinforcement; (4) consistency with the "minimum sufficiency principle" (Lepper, 1983) of using just enough pressure to enlist child compliance; (5) instantiation of the ethical principle of reciprocity (Kochanska, 1997; Parpal and Maccoby, 1985); and (6) involved and engaged participation in the child's life.

Cultural considerations.   Steinberg (2000) concluded that the benefits of authoritative parenting transcend differences of household composition, ethnicity, and socioeconomic status. Converging findings support relations between the authoritative style of childrearing and instrumental competence in European American, middle–socioeconomic status children (for a summary of some of these findings, see Baumrind, 1971a, 1983, 1989, 1991a, 1991b, 1991c, 1993, 1994, 1996a, 1996b, 1998). Although alternative candidates for optimal parenting may exist in diverse cultural contexts, no study has shown authoritative parenting to be harmful or less effective than any of the alternative parenting styles in promoting children's optimal competence and character.

The literature suggests that optimal parenting in any culture will have certain features that characterize authoritative parents: deep and abiding commitment to the parenting role, intimate knowledge of their child and her or his developmental needs, respect for the child's individuality and desires, provision of structure and regimen appropriate to the child's developmental level, readiness to establish and enforce behavioral guidelines, cognitive stimulation, and effective communication and use of reasoning to ensure children's understanding of parents' goals and disciplinary strategies. Just what combination of behavioral control, warmth, and psychological autonomy is optimal in advancing children's competence and character, and how each of these outcomes should be operationally defined, may (as Steinberg suggests) transcend differences of ethnicity, family structure, and socioeconomic status or (as we suspect) are moderated by social context.

Socialization practices that are normative for a culture are generally well accepted by children and effective in accomplishing the childrearing goals of that culture. The customs and laws of a society should be given due respect and consideration before banning or stigmatizing a practice, such as physical punishment, that most members practice and consider useful in accomplishing their goals, provided that there is no ethical objection to these goals. Chao (1994) has shown that the concept of "training" in the Chinese culture has important features beyond the hierarchical authoritarian model that contribute to, rather than detract from, the school success of Chinese children (which is a predominant goal of Chinese parents). The Chinese ideal of training includes high achievement and conformity demands in a context of intrusive control and devoted sacrifice on the part of the mother, who remains supportive and physically close to the child. In that kind of childrearing context, the child typically identifies with its parents' values. Thus, a childrearing pattern that might, from an *etic* (outsider's) European American perspective, be categorized as authoritarian and deemed undesirable is instead, when viewed from an *emic* (insider's) cultural perspective, found to have special features that explain its positive association with high achievement in Chinese American children.

Parental practices that would be deemed overly restrictive or harsh in a benign middle-class environment may provide optimum supervision and support in dangerous, impoverished neighborhoods (Baldwin, Baldwin, and Cole, 1990; Baumrind, 1972a, 1995; Kohn, 1977). Middle-income and blue-collar African Americans are more likely than European Americans to use physical punishment without reservation. In one study (Heffer and Kelley, 1987), two thirds of middle-income and lower-income African American mothers accepted spanking as a disciplinary technique in comparison to only one fourth of middle-income European American mothers. Lower-income African American mothers rated "time-out" (which is recommended by most childrearing authorities) very low as a disciplinary method. In general, African American parents exercise a strong preference for physical punishment, which (in contrast to denigrating and screaming) they do not regard as abuse (Mosby, 1999). Deater-Decker, Dodge, Bates, and Petit (1995) reported that for their African American sample, parents' use of physical punishment was associated positively with warmth and use of reason, which may explain why the correlation between spanking and children's externalizing behavior was negative (although not significant), rather than positive (as in their European American sample).

It is sometimes assumed that because African Americans typically endorse the use of physical punishment they are also more tolerant of harsh discipline and child maltreatment. However, there is evidence to the contrary. In a large-scale study of a demographically representative sample of adults, using 78 vignettes representing a wide variety of situations with potential for child maltreatment, Giovannoni and Becerra (1979) found that African Americans and Hispanic Americans compared to European Americans noted more situations as having the potential for child maltreatment. Members of both minority cultures did not rate "punish by spanking with hand" as having a high potential for maltreatment, although spanking was not a preferred method of punishment for any group.

Cultures differ in their emphasis on the rights of individuals or their responsibilities to the polity (Whiting and Whiting, 1975). The ideals of equality and liberty inherent in the Anglo-American Western tradition, and of social harmony, purity, and collectivity in hierarchical collectivist cultures such as India or Japan, affect the parental attitudes and practices that are deemed desirable and the childrearing goals that parents set forth for themselves and their children. The emphasis on children's rights to self-determination is predominantly a Western ideal. The Eastern sensibility of nonintrusive and harmonious social relationships contrasts markedly with the ethical priorities of rights-oriented competitive societies such as the United States.

In the context, therefore, of cultural diversity in conceptions of human needs, rights and responsibilities, the roles of parents and the goals of childrearing, a developmental orientation to parental responsibilities—especially with respect to the development of character and competence—reveals that the significant hallmarks of authoritative parenting are a consistent contributor to child competence. As a consequence, "the ethics of parenting" embraces both broadly generalizable (consistent with a rule-utilitarian framework) and culturally specific considerations. It could not be otherwise, respecting as we must the constructions of children's needs and parenting responsibilities that characterize cultures and cultural groups. Moreover, the importance of culture becomes additionally important as we proceed to broaden our discussion from parents and children to considerations of parents, children, and the state.

PARENTS, CHILDREN, AND THE STATE

Although the emphasis of moral philosophy is on the reciprocal responsibilities of parents and offspring, the community also assumes a significant role in childrearing. As we have noted, cultural values are significant definers of the valued characteristics that parents seek to foster in offspring, the childrearing practices that parents use, and the mutual obligations defining parent–child relationships from the birth of children to the death of parents. Moreover, communities provide resources that can assist adults in ethically responsible parenting. Material resources include income support, respite child care, and workplace practices that enable workers to be responsible parents. Human resources include access to networks of social support (whether in the formal contexts of social services, parent training programs, or religious institutions) or the informal social support systems characterizing many extended families and neighborhoods (Thompson, 1995). Communities also advance ethical parenting by informally supervising and regulating parental practices to conform them to cultural norms and to ensure child well-being.

That "it takes a village to raise a child" reflects (beyond campaign rhetoric) the view that parenting is interpreted, supported, and monitored by others beyond the family, which raises significant questions about the relations between ethically responsible parenting and an ethically responsible society that are the concern of this section. What is the role of society in promoting ethical parenting? Can the state ensure that parents fulfill their positive obligations toward offspring, or can it only sanction them when they do wrong? What can the state do to ensure that parents act in an ethically responsible manner? What are the justifications for the community's intervention into family life? By addressing these questions we may help explain the complex and often troubled relationship among parents, children, and the state. Although parents bear ultimate responsibility for the care and treatment of their offspring, how the community treats families can make the responsibilities of ethical parenting easier, or more difficult, for adults to fulfill.

The State and the Family

The state[1] has considerable interest in the well-being of children. After all, children are citizens, as are their parents. But children are citizens with different qualities. Children's developmentally limited capacities for thinking, judgment, and reasoning previously described mean that children have different needs, capabilities, and circumstances compared with other citizens. They require special protections that are not offered other citizens, such as laws governing their economic support; restrictions on child labor, drinking, and driving; protections from sexual exploitation, abandonment, and corrupting influences; and alternative judicial procedures for the treatment of juvenile offenders. Developmental limitations in decision making and reasoning also mean that, by comparison with adults as "persons" before the law, children have limited autonomy and self-determination, and many decisions (such as consenting to medical treatment and experimentation, and financial decisions) are made on their behalf. The state adopts, in short, an attitude of beneficent paternalism toward its youngest citizens. Such an attitude neither demeans, disadvantages, nor exploits children (as is sometimes claimed by those adopting a liberationist view of children), but instead, by treating children as a "special" group, affords special protections and restrictions suited to children's unique characteristics and needs.

The state's attitude of beneficent paternalism is deeply rooted in Western philosophical and legal traditions, including the Hegelian (1821/1952) distinction between the obligations of family membership and state citizenship. From these traditions has arisen the doctrine of the state as *parens patriae*—literally, "the state as parent." Originally intended to protect the state's concern for the property interests of dependent children, the doctrine indicates that the state may act *in loco parentis* ("in place of the parent") to protect citizens who are unable to defend their own interests. The *parens patriae* doctrine has become well established in Western law and is invoked particularly in situations when parents are unwilling, or unable, to protect the interests of offspring (Areen, 1975). In these circumstances and others, the *parens patriae* doctrine can justify removing children from the family and warrant other interventions into family life.

The state has other reasons to be interested in the well-being of its youngest citizens besides their dependency needs. In particular, the maintenance of the community depends on children's

---

[1]Consistent with its use in philosophical and legal writing, we use the term *state* to refer to the actions and policies of governments at national, state, and local levels. This is most apparent when we consider the regulatory, enforcement, and punitive features of state action. In other contexts, however, state action may instead involve incentive, enablement, or hortatory action in which formal policies are meant to shape the cultural and community context of family life. In these instances, it is important to consider the state not only as the governing system, but also as the representation of shared community goals, values, and ideals.

internalization of values that are consistent with public goals and ideals. These values may emphasize, as earlier noted, the ideals of individualism, equality, competition, and liberty characteristic of the Western, European American tradition, or alternatively the ideals of social harmony, collectivism, deference to authority, and cooperation more characteristic of certain Eastern traditions. Children are expected to accept the values, customs, and responsibilities of community life and also to acquire the skills necessary to contribute meaningfully to the community. These adaptive skills vary significantly according to historical time and location, but whether they concern mastery of agricultural skills, literary and numerical skills, or technological competence, they constitute some of the essential capabilities valued for citizenship. Because of the state's interest in these facets of early socialization, educational institutions outside of the family have become an almost universal feature of childhood.

Thus the state has significant interests in the well-being of its children citizens and promotes these interests in a variety of ways that intrude on parents' autonomy to rear children as they wish. In light of these important state interests, indeed, are families necessary? This is not a casual or unimportant question (Aiken and LaFollette, 1980; Houlgate, 1988). The ideal civic life envisioned in Plato's *Republic* (1979) divorced procreation from childrearing to ensure that children reared communally would internalize the collective values and ideals necessary for social welfare and promote solidarity of interests among those responsible for collective well-being. More recently, advocacy of rearing children collectively rather than by the family has been found in various places, from the institutional childcare centers of the former Soviet Union to traditional Israeli kibbutzim, and from the Marxist critique of the bourgeois family (Engels, 1884/1962) to Skinner's (1948) utopian vision of the community in *Walden Two*.

If we claim that families are necessary for children's well-being, then describing why they are necessary can help to define the unique features of family life that the state should, above all, be hesitant to violate. In moral philosophy as well as developmental science, three justifications for the family are typically offered (McCarthy, 1988; Wald, 1975).

First, children thrive psychologically in the context of the intimate, unique, and enduring relationships they create with specific caregivers, and these relationships can best be found in family life. This view is a cornerstone of classical psychological theories of early personality development and is supported by a substantial empirical literature (see Thompson, 1998, 2001, for reviews). Although families are often rent by separation and divorce, and family intimacy is threatened by stresses of various kinds, it is rare that collective care (even on thoughtfully designed kibbutzim) is capable of providing children with the kinds of warm, specific, reliable relationships with adults who know the child well that are typical in most families (see Sagi, van IJzendoorn, Aviezer, Donnell, and Mayseless, 1994). In institutional contexts, turnover of caregivers and high staff caseloads typically militate against the development of enduring attachments to children.

Second, most parents are highly motivated by the love they naturally feel for offspring to advance children's well-being (Cowan and Cowan, 1992; Holden, 1995). Children are precious to them because parents regard offspring as extensions of themselves, and, according to some views, the desire to nurture and protect offspring is a biologically based characteristic that is deeply rooted in species evolution (Trivers, 1985). Although caregivers outside of the family can be motivated by strong affectional ties to the children they care for, their motivational bases for childcare are nevertheless different from those of parents and may not be as compelling.

Third, although they are each cultural members, parents rear their offspring with different values and preferences that ensure considerable social diversity in childrearing goals and outcomes. One parent seeks to rear her or his child to be above all conscientious and responsible; another values more highly creativity and imagination; a third seeks primarily to foster individuality and leadership. Within the broad boundaries of acceptable parental conduct, these diverse parental practices ensure plurality in the attributes and characteristics of children that is essential to a democratic society that values and benefits from the individuality of its members. This is what Mill (1859/1973, p. 202) called a "plurality of paths":

What has made the European family of nations an improving, instead of a stationary portion of mankind? Not any superior excellence in them, which, when it exists, exists as the effect not as the cause; but their remarkable diversity of character and culture. Individuals, classes, nations, have been extremely unlike one another: they have struck out a great variety of paths, each leading to something valuable.

By contrast with the consistency in practices and goals that necessarily characterize collective forms of childrearing, families afford societal pluralism in child outcomes that is a desirable feature of a creative, dynamic culture.

These arguments from moral philosophy, supported by the findings of developmental science, confirm the unique contributions that parent–child relationships offer to children and, furthermore, justify special provisions to protect this relationship from outside interference. They underscore that respect for family privacy and parental autonomy in childrearing decisions should be protected by the same state that has considerable interest in children's well-being and their appropriate socialization. This is because the unique qualities of family life—intimate relationships, individuality, self-disclosure, and a plurality of developmental paths—are violated by undue outside intrusions on the family. As Blustein (1982, p. 214) has expressed it, "privacy is a precondition of intimacy." These arguments indicate, therefore, that the state's interest in children's well-being is advanced partly by its protection of family life against unnecessary intrusions from the outside, including intrusions from state authorities who may be motivated by the needs of children. There is thus a delicate balancing between the state's interest in child welfare and the state's interest in family privacy.

This view is the basis for the long-standing legal deference to the preferences of parents in childrearing decisions. In U.S. Supreme Court decisions beginning almost 80 years ago (see *Meyer v. Nebraska*, 1923; *Pierce v. Society of Sisters*, 1925), the Court has been clear that:

> [i]t is cardinal with us that the custody, care and nurture of the child reside first in the parents, whose primary function and freedom include preparation for obligations the state can neither supply nor hinder.... And it is in recognition of this that these decisions have respected the private realm of family life which the state cannot enter. (*Prince v. Massachusetts*, 1944, p. 166)

Absent a compelling state interest, therefore, family life and parental decision making concerning the care of offspring are protected from the state's intervention. Although this legal tradition and its philosophical foundations are commonly interpreted within a deontological universalist framework of parental "rights" (often contrasted with children's rights and the "rights" of the state), a more constructive reading focuses on the long-range consequences for human welfare of consequentialist ethical rules protecting family integity compared to rules permitting substantial intervention by outside authorities. From this mixed rule-utilitarian perspective, children are far more likely to thrive psychologically in families in which parents are permitted significant latitude in their childrearing practices and goals compared to alternative forms of collective care, and society in general (at least a society embracing democratic values) is also likely to be stronger when family privacy is safeguarded.

Such an analysis does not ensure that all outcomes arising from this ethical perspective will necessarily be easy or satisfactory. The U.S. Supreme Court has, for example, struggled with the implications of its decisions concerning parental autonomy, affirming in one case (*Wisconsin v. Yoder*, 1972) the rights of Amish families to deny secondary school education to their offspring based on the adults' religious beliefs and community norms despite a stirring dissent emphasizing the needs of the children for secondary education. Nevertheless, we argue that an ethical rule *protecting family integrity and parental autonomy* provides the greatest benefits in the long run to children, parents, and the society in which they live.

The highly publicized ordeal of Elian Gonzalez, a young Cuban boy who arrived on the shores of the United States after a treacherous ocean crossing from Cuba that killed his mother, sharply illustrates the difficult juxtaposition of the interests of children, parents, and the state under the ethical rule of deference to parental autonomy. Did Elian have the right to claim asylum in the

United States against the wishes of his father? Some advocates argued that he should have been allowed to claim asylum because of the benefits of life in the United States, but deference to respect for parental autonomy means that he would not. Developmental scientists would likely agree with this judgment in light of the conceptual limitations in a 6-year-old child's ability to make long-range judgments concerning his future, as well as his vulnerability to the emotionally charged influences of his extended family members in Miami. Parents are provided significant latitude in making such decisions on behalf of children who cannot make these judgments on their own. For these reasons, U.S. courts were wise to defer to the judgments of Elian's father despite the fact that his father intended to return with the boy to Cuba. But while protecting family integrity and confirming the decision-making autonomy of a fit parent, the courts also permitted Elian's return to a life in Cuba that lacks many of the material advantages that he enjoyed with his extended family in Miami, to the disappointment of Cuban Americans to whom Elian was a symbol of their own abandonment of family in pursuit of freedom.

Public and private ordering of "the best interests of the child." Earlier in this chapter we compared philosophically protectionist, liberationist, and developmental perspectives to determining children's best interests. Significantly, the courts hearing the Elian Gonzalez case did not attempt to make a legal judgment of Elian's "best interests." The nature of the legal decision required of them did not permit them to do so, but even if it were permissible it would have been unwise. For many reasons, the state is not well suited to making the kinds of predictive, relational judgments that are entailed in determining "the best interests of the child," and these reasons also illustrate why deference to parental decision making is warranted.

The state's judgment concerning a child's best interests is required in many legal decisions. Most commonly, these concern the custody of children when parents divorce, but grandparent visitation decisions and other situations affecting children also require judgments of the child's best interests. These judgments differ significantly from the decisions that judges and other authorities are well trained to provide. Most legal disputes focus on the documentation of facts. By contrast, judgments concerning children's best interests entail more abstract and ambiguous assessments of relationships and the quality of adult care. Statutory law, administrative policy, and judicial precedent are each significant resources in state decisions concerning legal and policy problems. By contrast, none of these is helpful in the individualized, family-by-family decisions required in determining a child's best interests. The latter are person-oriented rather than act-oriented, are based on knowledge of the individual child's characteristics and the circumstances of particular families, and require complex predictive judgments involving psychological well-being rather than the determination of past actions. Finally, but perhaps most important, state decision making in a democratic society typically involves the representation of all relevant parties and opportunities for each to express their views. By contrast, judgments concerning a child's best interests entail the inferred but seldom directly expressed interests of the most important party to the case: the child.

In short, the judgments required in determining a child's best interests are different from those which administrative, judicial, or regulatory authorities of the state are well prepared to provide. Thus, it is unsurprising that most judges report that child custody disputes—in which judgments of children's best interests most commonly occur—are among the most difficult cases to resolve (Whobrey, Sales, and Lou, 1987).

As a consequence, when parents cannot agree on the postdivorce custody of their offspring and turn to the court for a resolution, judges often rely on their own value preferences and subjective estimates of the determinants of a child's future well-being (Mnookin, 1975). For example, some judges simply adhere to a maternal presumption—especially with younger children—despite the intended gender neutrality of the best-interests standard (Lowery, 1981; Thompson and Wyatt, 1999). Others may use subjective, intuitive criteria (e.g., each parent's disciplinary style, warmth, and other personality characteristics, as well as relative earning power) as the basis for their judgment, which means that the same family circumstances evaluated by two different judges may result in different outcomes

(Chambers, 1984; Mnookin, 1975). This is contrary to normative principles of justice, of course, and in a society that accords parents considerable latitude in their styles of care and discipline, these criteria may inappropriately penalize parents when child custody decisions are made. Moreover, Mnookin (1974, 1975) and other legal scholars have claimed that the expert testimony of forensic psychologists or developmental scientists rarely adds clarity to child custody decisions, given the difficulties of behavioral science and clinical experience in making precise predictions of individual development. Perhaps this is why expert witnesses can typically be found on both sides of a custody dispute.

Even when statutory language more explicitly defines the basis for determining a child's best interests, significant problems remain in the application of these standards. For example, a legal presumption long advocated by legal scholars and social scientists is to award custody to a fit parent who is the child's "primary caretaker" (Chambers, 1984; Maccoby, 1995, 1999; Scott, 1992). By ensuring the child's continuing contact with the parent who has assumed the predominant role in parenting, it is argued, courts can reliably advance a child's best interests. Although this approach has the appeal of providing a straightforward, valid, and readily assessable means of distinguishing parenting roles, it is nevertheless difficult to define the varied responsibilities of parenting and their evolving relevance to children's changing developmental needs and competencies to determine who is the "primary caretaker" (Thompson, 1986, 1994). Physical care, play, instruction, gender socialization, academic encouragement, role modeling, and other responsibilities of parenting vary in their significance as children mature. Furthermore, determining who is the child's "primary caretaker" is a retrospective approach to a prospective determination: The parent who assumed a predominant role in childrearing in the intact, predivorce family when children were younger may or may not be the best caregiver as a single parent as children mature (Thompson and Wyatt, 1999).

Indeed, because postdivorce family life is flexible and dynamic, it is unclear how well a custody judgment made by a court when parents divorce can ensure the future well-being of offspring. After parents divorce, children often change residence as parental circumstances (including residential relocation and remarriage) change and as children's needs evolve, and these often provoke other changes in visitation and child support arrangements (Maccoby and Mnookin, 1992). Increasingly, families find that courtroom decisions made at the time of a divorce settlement do not accommodate the rapidly changing life circumstances of all family members in postdivorce life.

Parents are, of course, accustomed to making judgments about their children's best interests. They know their children well and are experienced with the kinds of complex considerations involved in planning for the child's future. Perhaps, therefore, the best role for the state in child custody disputes is to provide opportunities, incentives, and structure to foster parents' own resolution of this problem. Even if parents appeal to the state to decide a custody dispute that they have been unable to resolve, the judicial system may nevertheless insist on the private ordering of a decision that parents, not the state, are best capable of making. This can occur through mandatory mediation with a skilled counselor who can lead parents through the decision making needed to thoughtfully plan postdivorce life for themselves and their children (Emery, 1994). It can also include the requirement that adults negotiate a parenting plan that identifies the responsibilities of each parent for maintaining a meaningful relationship with children, providing financial support, and renegotiating other aspects of postdivorce life with the former spouse as family circumstances change (Bruch, 1978; Kelly, 1993).

At the same time, the state can also create new ways of thinking about custody issues that help parents more thoughtfully "bargain in the shadow of the law" as they jointly plan postdivorce family life (Mnookin and Kornhauser, 1979). "Bargaining in the shadow of the law" recognizes that legal regulations are important in defining the options and opportunities within which family members negotiate, even if they never bring their dispute to a courtroom. In recent years, the legal options of joint physical and/or legal custody of offspring have provided one avenue for parents to reconsider their postdivorce parenting options. In the years to come, changes in legal conceptions of postdivorce parenting that reduce the winners-and-losers mentality of identifying "custodial" and "visiting" parents may advance the same goal (Bartlett, 1999; Thompson and Wyatt, 1999). These provisions remind parents that, although divorce may end a marriage, it doesn't end their childrearing responsibilities. Moreover, legal provisions such as these underscore the hortatory, expressive functions of the law outside of its regulatory, coercive functions (Bartlett, 1988). In other words, legal reforms both reflect and advance changing societal conceptions of family relationships that, in the case of divorce, may provide catalysts for divorcing couples to consider how each parent can maintain a meaningful, significant relationship with offspring in postdivorce family life. This reflects the principle that when family life is concerned, the state assists parents and children more by providing opportunities and incentives for family members to make their own decisions, and offering options through policy reform, than trying to create and impose judgments that state authorities are poorly prepared to offer.

Grandparent visitation.   On other occasions, the state may seek to improve family functioning by supporting and protecting relationships that are significant to children. But even in these situations the state can overreach, and doing so may inadvertently harm rather than help families, and children within those families.

One illustration of this is the advent of grandparent visitation statutes (Thompson, Scalora, Castrianno, and Limber, 1992; Thompson, Scalora, Limber, and Castrianno, 1991; Thompson, Tinsley, Scalora, and Parke, 1989). On the face of it, it would appear that there could be little harm to legal reforms enabling children to have greater contact with grandparents, especially when a judge has determined that grandparent visitation is in a child's "best interests." Thus, it is easy to understand why, throughout the United States, legislators in all 50 states quickly approved grandparent visitation statutes during the 1980s that permitted grandparents to petition the court for legally enforced visitation rights, even over the objections of parents.

Despite the good intentions underlying legislators' efforts, however, such changes in family law can alter family functioning in unintended as well as intended ways. When grandparents attain legal standing to compel access to grandchildren over parents' objections, for example, it sharpens family conflict and enhances the probability that parents and grandparents will become legal adversaries. Grandparent visitation disputes are thus likely to occur in a psychological environment of intergenerational conflict in which the child is the center of conflict. And given the difficulties of courts in reliably and validly assessing a child's "best interests," children are unlikely to be significantly helped by making the award of grandparent visitation contingent on a court's determination that doing so serves children's "best interests." Instead, there is evidence that judges, who are likely to be grandparents themselves, may simply assume that enhanced visitation will necessarily benefit grandchildren without considering the problems to children of intergenerational loyalty conflicts surrounding each visit with their grandparents (see Thompson et al., 1992).

Grandparent visitation statutes illustrate that, when the blunt instrument of family law is used to protect relationships within the family, there may be unintended consequences that harm rather than advance children's well-being. This is one reason why the U.S. Supreme Court recently struck down a grandparent visitation statute in the state of Washington that permitted not only grandparents, but other adults with an interest in children, the right to petition for visitation rights (*Troxel v. Granville*, 2000). Central to the Court's judgment was that this "breathtakingly broad" statute did not respect the authority of fit parents to guide the lives of their offspring.

Sadly, the noncoercive incentives the state can offer families to enlist intergenerational support on behalf of children have rarely been considered. As when parents divorce, support and resources for private dispute resolution through mediated settlements are more likely to foster satisfactory intrafamilial resolutions that can better advance children's interests than are judicial decrees. The appointment of a *guardian ad leitem* to speak on behalf of the child can help to ensure that children's interests are reflected in these negotiations. Furthermore, just as parents have rights allied with responsibilities to children, families may find it easier to resolve visitation disputes if positive obligations to the child (e.g., regular contact and financial assistance) accompany grandparent visitation privileges (see Ingulli, 1985).

State Intervention Into Family Life

Our discussion thus far has focused on ethical rules governing the nature of the relations between the state and parents that best fosters children's well-being. Our conclusion underscores an irony in public policy. The state has strong interests in ensuring the character development and health and well-being of its youngest citizens, but in doing so it must respect the boundaries of family privacy and parental autonomy that constitute cornerstones of the child's psychological development. Consequently, the state's coercive power over the family must be secondary to the support, incentives, and structure it provides to enable parents to make wise choices on behalf of offspring while accepting the risk that, as long as parental decisions do not exceed clear thresholds of child harm, those choices may not always be optimal for the child's interests. Nevertheless, in recognizing that family privacy and integrity ultimately create the greatest benefits for children, parents, and society, the community's efforts to promote ethical parenting in family life are primarily a matter of enablement, not coercion.

Family privacy and parental autonomy are not, of course, ends in themselves. They are means to the ultimate objective of advancing children's well-being. As John Locke (1690/1965, Treatise 2, sec. 58) argued several centuries ago: "the Power . . . that Parents have over their Children, arises from that Duty which is incumbent on them, to take care of their Offspring, during the imperfect state of Childhood." Because parental rights arise from the performance of parental duties to children, parental rights erode when parents fail to fulfill their legitimate obligations toward offspring (see Blustein, 1982). No parents who are manifestly abusive or neglectful, for example, can expect that the boundaries of family privacy will remain respected by a community that is concerned about children's well-being. The same Supreme Court that has long deferred to parental preferences in childrearing decisions has also declared that parents are not "free . . . to make martyrs of their children" (*Prince v. Massachusetts*, 1944, p. 170). Although our discussion has focused on defining the boundaries beyond which the state cannot normally intrude into family life, therefore, there are circumstances in which the state must intervene. This section of our discussion is devoted to considering the nature of those conditions and their relevance to ethical parenting.

There are several circumstances, of course, in which the state can legitimately intervene into family life (Wald, 1985). One is when the family itself is disrupted, such as by separation, divorce, or other circumstances that make it impossible for preexisting family relationships to be maintained. In these situations the state must ensure that the renegotiation of family resources and relationships ensures fairness to all family members, especially to children. Even when state authorities strongly encourage the private ordering of these arrangements, parental decisions are regulated in light of laws in whose shadow family members conduct their negotiations, and in light of the judical judgments required to ratify parents' decisions.

Another circumstance warranting the state's intervention into family life is when there are threats to the health, safety, or well-being of children, which is the state's most important commitment to ensuring ethical parenting. This is both a negative obligation—ensuring that children are not harmed—and a positive obligation—ensuring that children receive adequate care and training to become productive members of society. The state may intervene in these circumstances to protect children and remediate their harm, correct parental misconduct, and/or express the consensual value preferences of the community. Thus, the ethical obligations of the state's intervention into family life are both specific (e.g., ending a child's physical abuse and preventing its recurrence) and broad (e.g., prosecuting child sexual exploitation as inappropriate adult conduct regardless of its specific harms to children).

How should the state define the conditions warranting its coercive intervention into family life? The tasks of defining in specific terms the ensurance that children are "not harmed" and that they "receive adequate care and training" are challenging because of the varieties of harms that children can experience, the varieties of care that they may lack, and the need to balance the risks and benefits that children derive when state authorities intervene into family life to protect them. The latter is a particularly important consideration from a utlilitarian analysis. When authorities intervene into the family because of a report of suspected child maltreatment, there is an upheaval in the child's life that can have long-term consequences (Thompson, 1993). At the most extreme, children who are rescued from physically or sexually abusive homes are placed in a temporary foster home for an indefinite period of time, with periodic transitions to other temporary arrangements if a permanent placement is unavailable or cannot be negotiated, which is often the case (Mnookin, 1974). Even if the child remains in the home as social services are provided to address family problems, the child has become the locus of family conflict and disruption, which alters family relationships significantly.

Thus, the costs as well as the potential benefits to children of state intervention into family life are important to consider. An important additional consideration is research raising considerable doubt that foster care, social services, or the other interventions typically provided by child protection agencies can effectively alter the family problems that led to maltreatment or can ensure the child's future well-being, especially given the limited resources of social service agencies in the face of growing numbers of reports of child abuse or neglect (Mnookin, 1974; U.S. Advisory Board on Child Abuse and Neglect, 1990; Wald, Carlsmith, and Leiderman, 1988). Indeed, for children who are left for years in "temporary" foster care placements or who remain in severely troubled families that receive inadequate services, the important question is whether they are helped or hindered by the intervention of state authorities. The troubling ethical problem govening state intervention into family life for purposes of child protection, therefore, is defining the forms of child harm that are sufficiently severe that, on balance, these actions of state authorities are likely to yield greater benefit than harm to children.

Moreover, principles of justice require further that the standards for state intervention in family life are sufficiently clear and explicit that there is no doubt about the parental conduct warranting intrusion into family life. This ensures that parents have fair warning of legally prohibited behavior and guards against subjective, potentially arbitrary judicial judgments about what conduct is abusive or not (this can be a particular problem in defining standards of child neglect). Consequently, a rule-utilitaritarian analysis favors narrowly conceived, explicit standards governing state intervention into family life, with an emphasis on evidence of child harm resulting from parental practices. Doing so ensures that a high threshold for intervention is maintained and, consistent with the costs and benefits that must be considered in permitting state intervention into family life, focuses on the consequences to the child. One such standard has been proposed by Wald (1975, 1982, p. 11):

> . . . coercive intervention should be permissible only when a child has suffered or is likely to suffer serious physical injury as a result of abuse or inadequate care; when a child is suffering from severe emotional damage and his or her parents are unwilling to deal with the problems without coercive intervention; when a child has been sexually abused; when a child is suffering from a serious medical condition and his or her parents are unwilling to provide him with suitable medical treatment; or when a child is committing delinquent acts at the urging or with the help of his or her parents.

Although Wald's standard may be unduly narrow in some respects, it reflects the emphasis on narrowly defined, clear, and child-centered standards that we believe are supported by the mixed rule-utilitarian analysis of this discussion.

Are there are other forms of parental misconduct warranting concern by state authorities? Parents may be psychologically abusive to offspring, for example, by their threats, denigration, isolation, missocialization, or exploitation of offspring. Should not state authorities intervene into such families to protect children's emotional well-being (see Garbarino, Guttman, and Seeley, 1986; Hart, Germain, and Brassard, 1987; McGee and Wolfe, 1991)? Consideration of the risks and benefits of doing so reveals several difficulties (Melton and Thompson, 1987; Thompson and Jacobs, 1991).

The first concerns the lack of clarity of the standard for intervention by terms like "exploiting" and "missocializing" offspring. Can a parent who requires children to help with farm chores expect to be accused of "exploiting" the child? Should a judge interpret "missocialization" to include inculcating unusual religious beliefs in offspring, or no religious values at all? In these and many other situations, there is insufficient clarity concerning what constitutes psychological maltreatment to ensure that judges will be guided less by personal values and subjective judgments than by clear legal guidelines. This is similar to the problems discussed above with respect to the "best interests of the child" standard. Moreover, this conceptual ambiguity exists, in part, because of our democratic society's acceptance of diverse forms of childrearing. This means that some parental practices, like corporal punishment, may be regarded as psychologically (and physically) abusive by some but not by many others (Baumrind and Owens, 2001). In the absence of social consensus concerning the boundaries of acceptable parental conduct in this area, the ambiguity of standards of psychological maltreatment invites judicial unfairness and partiality.

Second, most standards of psychological maltreatment focus on parental behavior rather than child outcomes (Baumrind, 1995). But doing so is the wrong focus because of the complex effects of parental conduct on children. As earlier noted, for example, even physically coercive behavior like corporal punishment has different consequences for children depending on other parental practices with which it is associated and the values of the culture or subculture. Standards of child protection must, therefore, focus on whether and how a child has been harmed.

Finally, because the intervention of state authorities into family life is itself psychologically threatening to children, it is important to weigh these potential costs to children against the expected benefits achieved by actions intended to combat psychological maltreatment. For many children, the costs of intervention are likely to outweigh its benefits. For the state, the cost–benefit analysis also concerns whether intervening into families to prosecute psychological maltreatment is likely to benefit the society as a whole, or instead whether limited resources will be diverted from investigating more serious allegations of child maltreatment and result in greater harm to children.

FAMILY ASSISTANCE

One conclusion arising from the preceding analysis is that, although the state has a significant responsibility to support ethical parenting, the authority of the state is a very blunt instrument for doing so. The standards governing coercive intervention into family life must be narrowly and thoughtfully conceived to avoid unwarranted intrusions into family life. More importantly, the tools the state can use to improve family functioning are imprecise, often ineffective, and risk creating more harm in their implementation to remedy child harm. The problem is both inherent in how state institutions function (recall our earlier comments about how legal, administrative, and regulatory officials are poorly prepared to address the complex, relational considerations of family life) and the limited resources of state agencies concerned with children and families. Both are realistic limitations in the capacity of the state to promote ethical parenting in utilitarian cost–benefit analysis, and, even if the latter constraint were not a reality, the former would always be true. The state can, in short, effectively sanction parents when they clearly do wrong. It is much less clear that the state can effectively compel parents to do good.

There are, however, many ways the state influences family life apart from its coercive or punitive power. Legal and regulatory authorities help to order family life by defining the roles and responsibilities of family members, such as in statutes governing marriage, parenting, procreation, adoption, child custody, and defining the obligations (including financial responsibilities) of spouses and parents. These statutes help to ensure that the reciprocal obligations of adults are clearly understood as they enter into family relationships and that their responsibilities to children are fulfilled. In addition, state regulation of institutions affecting children and families, such as schools and day-care centers, also help to ensure the safety and health of the children who attend. As in the case of parental divorce, moreover, the state is well prepared to intervene to help family members reorder their relationships and responsibilities when the family is disrupted. Furthermore, even in its coercive functions, the state can do some things very well. During the 1990s, for example, in response to public concern about the failure of many fathers to fulfill their child support obligations, legal regulations (including mandatory wage garnishment) significantly improved the collection of child support payments, especially from fathers who were capable of paying but were unwilling to do so.[2] And perhaps the most important indication of how the state can benefit children is public education. Indeed, mandatory education requirements are perhaps the most coercive state regulation on family life because parents are compelled to attend to the education of their children, most often through compulsory school attendance, for a sustained period throughout childhood and early adolescence. Yet the inherent coerciveness of this regulation is not immediately apparent to most families because public education has become institutionalized in national culture and worldwide, and because of the clear benefits of school attendance for most children.

These considerations reveal that when the nature of the state's capabilities are thoughtfully considered, there are many ways that society can support ethical parenting and promote the well-being of children. Although coercive changes in family law (such as prohibiting corporal punishment) have the appeal of instituting straightforward, universally implemented, and clearly enforced solutions to family problems, the diversity of families and the complex relationships of family life make it perhaps inevitable that the "law of unintended consequences" would prevail in the effects of these statutory reforms. Family members and the relationships they share are likely to be influenced directly and indirectly by changes in the law that are intended only to have direct, straightforward effects, and this makes it difficult to accurately predict the impact of coercive legal reforms on family functioning, and thus to ensure that children will be benefited rather than harmed.

There are other noncoercive avenues by which the state can assist families. The state can provide enabling conditions that make it easier for family members to fulfill their responsibilities to each other. There are many such enablements—income support, housing assistance, food subsidies, and other programs—that can either facilitate or undermine ethical parenting in their design and/or implementation. One unfortunate illustration of the latter is welfare reform, in which under Temporary Assistance to Needy Families provisions, parents of young infants must return to work early in the child's life. This has recently caused the Committee on Integrating the Science of Early Childhood Development of the National Research Council (2000) to urge lengthening the exemption period before parents of infants are required to work in recognition of the importance of close, nurturing relationships to early mental health. In addition, through the financial incentives it offers businesses, the state can encourage the development of workplace practices (such as family leave) that make it easier for adults to be better parents, and it can provide economic assistance to childcare programs that are willing to invest significantly in improved facilities, teacher training, and developmentally appropriate programs. In these and many other ways the state can strengthen the support and resources that families can draw on as nurturing environments for children.

In the end, moreover, the hortatory power of the state should not be overlooked. The values that are explicitly recognized in the formal and informal regulations influencing family life, and which the state implements in its provisions for the family, speak volumes. This is because legal, administrative, and regulatory reforms not only reflect the changes that occur in family life but help to express and institutionalize those changes. The expressive function of laws affecting families (Bartlett, 1988) is reflected, for example, in divorce and custody statutory reform that implicitly encourages parents to recognize that although they may end a marriage, they can never end their responsibilities as parents. The law's expressive function is reflected in changes in child protection laws that are explicitly child focused in their assessments of the harms of parental conduct and the remedies the state can implement. The expressive function of the law is, in short, revealed in the

---

[2] As noted by Meyer (1999; Meyer and Bartfeld, 1996), however, the new regime of rigorous child-support enforcement procedures provided little benefit to the children of fathers who are unable to pay, owing to their own economic distress.

extent to which the state clearly regards children as a liability and a burden, or as a social resource of shared responsibility.

CONCLUSIONS

The ethics of parenting begins, we have argued, with the assumption of responsibility for offspring by parents. Although parents do not alone have responsibility for the welfare of children—the state, as we have seen, also has important obligations to children—parental responsibilities are first and foremost. Within our mixed rule-utilitarian, consequentialist framework, children and adults have complementary, not equal, rights that arise from their very different capabilities and the mutual obligations they share within the family. Children's right to self-determination is limited, for example, by the exercise of parental authority that functions legitimately to promote healthy development of offspring. We have described the parental responsibilities that legitimate the exercise of parental authority, particularly the adult practices that shape the development of character and competence in children. As children develop and acquire more mature capacities for reasoning, judgment, and self-control, of course, their autonomy increases and parenting responsibilities subside, consistent with a developmentalist orientation to understanding children's best interests. We argue that a developmentalist orientation is preferable to either liberationist or protectionist approaches because it recognizes the changing mutual obligations shared by parents and children with the growth of children's competencies and judgment.

Our theory of ethical parenting underscores that responsible parenting is not solely a family obligation but a responsibility shared by the community. The community's values, resources, and social supports make it easier (or more difficult) for parents to fulfill their responsibilities to offspring, and we have focused on the role of the state and public policy in fostering ethical parenting. Our analysis has highlighted that the state has significant interests in the well-being of its youngest citizens but that in most cases it promotes children's welfare best by respecting family privacy and parental autonomy in childrearing decisions. From a consequentialist perspective, this protects the features of family life that contribute to children's well-being and minimizes unnecessary intrusions into family life that can undermine children, even when motivated to advance their "best interests." Consequently, we have advocated limited, clear standards warranting the state's coercive intervention into the family to protect children's physical or emotional well-being, and emphasized the value of the support, resources, and structure the state can offer parents to make their own wise decisions on behalf of offspring. This is because public policy is a very blunt instrument for altering family life, and thus the state can best assist children through incentives rather than coercion.

Our analysis of the ethics of parenting has drawn on classic and modern ideas within moral and political philosophy, ethical theory, and developmental science. We close with additional comments about the latter because we are both developmental scientists. The integration of developmental research into arguments drawn from ethics and moral philosophy shows that scientists, whether applied or not, have an important contribution to offer to ethical parenting. Fallible and necessarily evaluative as our knowledge is, we believe that developmental scientists do and should contribute to the resolution of ethically saturated disputes about what constitutes a child's best interests by providing relevant information about the probable psychological and social consequences of contrasting social policies. In doing so, however, the information provided must be unbiased and based on firm empirical evidence. Scientists have a responsibility not only to contribute to public discourse in their professional roles but also to base their recommendations on scientifically derived knowledge.

Scientific knowledge is distinguished from ordinary knowledge by the systematic use of procedures that protect against bias due to personal values, confirmity to received wisdom, or misleading surplus meaning in the measurement of theoretical constructs. The scientific method is intended to provide information that is systematic, public, and replicable. Critical thinking instilled by scientific training consists of asking the right questions and asking them in the right way. Consensual rules of objectivity, exemplified by the double blind experiment, were formulated to protect against subliminal as well as intentional confirmatory biases. Hypotheses make explicit investigators' partiality or research biases so that they may then attempt to probe, not prove, their hypotheses. When policymakers consult with social scientists in an effort to better inform their legislative or judicial efforts to address social problems, they assume that the social scientists whom they consult are objective, impartial reporters of their own and others' findings rather than intentionally biased advocates, motivated by self-interest or a political cause.

Merton (1973) articulated four norms of science that are widely accepted by scientists (Koehler, 1993) and laypersons. Merton's norms require scientific information to be: (1) publicly shared; (2) judged by objective rather than personal criteria; (3) unbiased by personal values or interests; and (4) available to the scientific community to scrutinize through established procedures of peer review, replication, and challenges by rival hypotheses. These canons of scientific inquiry underscore how scientific knowledge is different from other forms of knowledge, and help to ensure confidence in the validity and reliability of scientific reports. Unlike lawyers or politicians, research scientists may not suppress disconfirming data and must acknowledge the existence of alternative hypotheses and explanations of their findings, as well as the degree of certainty that should be attached to their findings. However well intentioned, biased interpretation of research results by social scientists undermines public trust in our perceived objectivity and impartiality (Horowitz, 2000; MacCoun, 1998).

Public debate about the nature and consequences of parenting, as well as policymaking affecting families, requires the thoughtful and informed contributions of scientific experts. Because of their unique expertise, developmental scientists are well qualified to transform scientific knowledge into "usable knowledge" that is thoughtfully and responsibly relevant to the public questions under discussion (Lindblom and Cohen, 1979; Thompson, 1993). But two hazards within the scientific community tend to limit the conscientious application of empirical research to the profound questions about parenting posed by the public. The first is the refusal of some developmental researchers to recognize that when they accept public support for their work, they incur a reciprocal obligation to convey in useful language the findings of their research to the public and its elected representatives. The second hazard is the opposite extreme: scientists who inappropriately interpret or overgeneralize their findings to publicly advocate for positions that are not scientifically well founded, sometimes in the context of campaign journalism (see Thompson and Nelson, 2001). This approach fails to respect the consensual canons of ethical responsibility of scientists and, equally importantly, the danger that scientists—and behavioral science—will consequently lose credibility to the public.

Ethical parenting is the responsibility of parents and the state, and of developmental scientists who seek to understand family life. By appreciating the unique roles and responsibilities of each partner for advancing children's well-being, adults offer children the best opportunities to develop the character and competence that lead to successful adult life.

REFERENCES

Aiken, W., and LaFollette, H. (1980). *Whose child? Children's rights, parental authority, and state power.* Totowa, NJ: Rowman & Littlefield.

Applegate, J., Burke, J., Burleson, B., Delia, J., and Kline, S. (1985). Reflection-enhancing parental communication. In I. E. Siegel (Ed.), *Parental belief systems: The psychological consequences for children* (pp. 107–142). Hillsdale, NJ: Lawrence Erlbaum Associates.

Areen, J. (1975). Intervention between parent and child: A reappraisal of the state's role in child neglect and abuse cases. *The Georgetown Law Journal, 63,* 887–937.

Bakan, D. (1966). *The duality of existence: Isolation and communion in western man.* Boston: Beacon.

Baldwin, A. L., Baldwin, C., and Cole, R. E. (1990). Stress-resistant families and stress-resistant children. In J. Rolf, A. Masten, D. Cicchetti, K. Neuchtherlin and S. Weintraub (Eds.), *Risk and protective factors in the development of psychopathology* (pp. 257–280). Cambridge, England: Cambridge University Press.

Bartlett, K. T. (1988). Re-expressing parenthood. *Yale Law Journal, 98*, 293–340.

Bartlett, K. T. (1999). Improving the law relating to postdivorce arrangements for children. In R. A. Thompson and P. R. Amato (Eds.), *The postdivorce family: Children, parenting, and society* (pp. 71–102). Thousand Oaks, CA: Sage.

Baumrind, D. (1966). Effects of authoritative parental control on child behavior. *Child Development, 37*(4), 887–907.

Baumrind, D. (1968). Authoritarian vs. authoritative parental control. *Adolescence, 3*(2), 255–271.

Baumrind, D. (1970). Socialization and instrumental competence in young children. *Young Children, 26*(2), 104–119.

Baumrind, D. (1971a). Current patterns of parental authority. *Developmental Psychology Monograph* (P. 2, 4) (1), 1–103.

Baumrind, D. (1971b). Principles of ethical conduct in the treatment of subjects: Reaction to the draft report of the Committee on Ethical Standards in Psychological Research. *American Psychologist, 26* (10), 887–896.

Baumrind, D. (1972a). An exploratory study of socialization effects on black children: Some black–white comparisons. *Child Development, 43*, 261–267.

Baumrind, D. (1972b). Reactions to the May 1972 draft report of the Ad Hoc Committee on Ethical Standards in Psychological Research. *American Psychologist, 27*(11), 1083–1086.

Baumrind, D. (1973). The development of instrumental competence through socialization. In A. Pick (Ed.), *Minnesota symposia on child psychology* (Vol. 7, pp. 3–46). Minneapolis: University of Minnesota Press.

Baumrind, D. (1975). Some thoughts about childrearing. In U. Bronfenbrenner (Ed.), *Readings in the development of human behavior* (pp. 396–409). New York: Dryden.

Baumrind, D. (1978a). Parental disciplinary patterns and social competence in children. *Youth and Society, 9*(3), 239–276.

Baumrind, D. (1978b). Reciprocal rights and responsibilities in parent–child relations. *Journal of Social Issues, 34*(2), 179–196.

Baumrind, D. (1979). IRBs and social research: The cost of deception. *IRB: A Review of Human Subjects Research, 1*(6), 1–4.

Baumrind, D. (1980). The principle of reciprocity: Development of prosocial behavior in children. *Educational Perspectives, 19*(4), 3–9.

Baumrind, D. (1982). Are androgynous individuals more effective persons and parents? *Child Development, 53*(1), 44–75.

Baumrind, D. (1983). Rejoinder to Lewis's reinterpretation of parental firm control effects: Are authoritative parents really harmonious? *Psychological Bulletin, 94*, 132–142.

Baumrind, D. (1985). Research using intentional deception: Ethical issues revisited. *American Psychologist, 40*(2), 165–174.

Baumrind, D. (1987). A developmental perspective on adolescent risk-taking behavior in contemporary America. In C. E. Irwin, Jr. (Ed.), *New directions for child development: Adolescent health and social behavior, 37*, 93–126. San Francisco: Jossey-Bass.

Baumrind, D. (1989). Rearing competent children. In W. Damon (Ed.), *Child development, today and tomorrow* (pp. 349–378). San Francisco: Jossey-Bass.

Baumrind, D. (1991a). Effective parenting during the early adolescent transition. In P. E. Cowan and E. M. Hetherington (Eds.), *Advances in family research* (Vol. 2, pp. 111–163). Hillsdale, NJ: Lawrence Erlbaum Associates.

Baumrind, D. (1991b). The influence of parenting style on adolescent competence and substance abuse. *Journal of Early Adolescence, 11*(1), 56–95.

Baumrind, D. (1991c). Parenting styles and adolescent development. In R. Lerner, A. C. Petersen, and J. Brooks-Gunn (Eds.), *The encyclopedia on adolescence* (pp. 746–758). New York: Garland.

Baumrind, D. (1992). Leading an examined life: The moral dimension of daily conduct. In W. Kurtines, M. Azmitia, and J. L. Gewirtz (Eds.), *The role of values in psychology and human development* (pp. 256–280). New York: Wiley.

Baumrind, D. (1993). The average expectable environment is not good enough: A response to Scarr. *Child Development, 64*, 1299–1307.

Baumrind, D. (1994). The social context of child maltreatment. *Family Relations, 43*(4), 360–368.

Baumrind, D. (1995). *Child maltreatment and optimal caregiving in social contexts*. New York and London: Garland.

Baumrind, D. (1996a). A blanket injunction against disciplinary use of spanking is not warranted by the data. *Pediatrics, 98*(2), 828–831.

Baumrind, D. (1996b). The discipline controversy revisited. *Family Relations, 45*(4), 405–414.

Baumrind, D. (1997a). The disciplinary encounter: Contemporary issues. *Aggression and Violent Behavior, 2*(4), 321–335.

Baumrind, D. (1997b). Necessary distinctions. *Psychological Inquiry, 8*(3), 176–229.

Baumrind, D. (1998). Reflections on character and competence. In A. Colby, J. James, and D. Hart (Eds.), *Explorations in the development of competence and character through life* (pp. 1–28). Chicago: University of Chicago Press.

Baumrind, D., and Black, A. (1967). Socialization practices associated with dimensions of competence in preschool boys and girls. *Child Development, 38*(2), 291–327.

Baumrind, D., and Moselle, K. (1985). A developmental perspective on adolescent drug abuse. *Advances in Alcohol and Substance Abuse, 4*, 41–67.

Baumrind, D., and Owens, E. B. (2001). *Does normative physical punishment by parents cause detrimental child outcomes? A prospective longitudinal study*. Manuscript in preparation.

Bitensky, S. H. (1997). Spare the rod, embrace our humanity: Toward a new legal regime prohibiting corporal punishment of children. *University of Michigan Journal of Law Reform, 31*(1), 353–474.

Blum, N. J., Williams, G. E., Friman, P. C., and Christophersen, E. R. (1995). Disciplining young children: The role of verbal instructions and reasoning. *Pediatrics, 96*, 336–341.

Blustein, J. (1982). *Parents and children: The ethics of the family.* New York: Oxford University Press.

Bok, S. (1979). *Lying: Moral choice in public and private life.* New York: Vintage.

Brandt, R. B. (1998). *A theory of the good and the right.* Amherst, NY: Prometheus.

Bruch, C. S. (1978, Summer). Making visitation work: Dual parenting orders. *Family Advocate, 22–26,* 41–42.

Bugental, D., Blue, J., and Cruzcosa, M. (1989). Perceived control over caregiving outcomes: Implications for child abuse. *Developmental Psychology, 25,* 532–539.

Catron, T. F., and Masters, J. C. (1993). Mothers' and children's conceptualization of corporal punishment. *Child Development, 64,* 1815–1828.

Chambers, D. L. (1984). Rethinking the substantive rules for custody disputes in divorce. *Michigan Law Review, 83,* 477–569.

Chao, R. K. (1994). Beyond parental control and authoritarian parenting style: Understanding Chinese parenting through the cultural notion of training. *Child Development, 65,* 1111–1119.

Cohen, H. (1980). *Equal rights for children.* Totowa, NJ: Littlefield, Adams.

Colby, A., and Damon, W. (1992). *Some do care: Contemporary lives of moral commitment.* New York: Free Press.

Committee on Integrating the Science of Early Childhood Development, National Research Council and Institute of Medicine. (2000). *From neurons to neighborhoods: The science of early childhood development.* Washington, DC: National Academy Press.

Cowan, C. P., and Cowan, P. A. (1992). *When partners become parents.* New York: Basic Books.

Damon, W., and Colby, A. (1987). Social influence and moral change. In W. M. Kurtines and J. L. Gerwirtz (Eds.), *Moral development through social interaction* (pp. 3–19). New York: Wiley .

Deater-Deckard, K. D., Dodge, K. A., Bates, J. E., and Pettit, G. S. (1995, March). *Risk factors for the development of externalizing behavior problems: Are there ethnic group differences in process?* Paper presented at the biennial meeting of the Society for Research in Child Development, Indianapolis, IN.

Dewey, J. (1916). *Democracy and education.* New York: Macmillan.

Dobson, J. (1992). *The new dare to discipline.* Wheaton, IL: Tyndale House.

Dubin, E. R., and Dubin, R. (1963). The authority inception period in socialization. *Child Development, 34,* 885–898.

Elder, G. H., Jr. (1963). Parental power legitimation and its effect on the adolescent. *Sociometry, 25,* 50–65.

Emery, R. E. (1994). *Renegotiating family relationships: Divorce, child custody, and mediation.* New York: Guilford.

Engels, F. (1962). The origin of the family, private property and the state. In K. Marx and F. Engels, *Selected works* (Vol. 2). Moscow: Progress Publishers. (Original work published 1884.)

Erasmus, C. J. (1977). *In search of the common good.* New York: Free Press.

Farson, R. (1974). *Birthrights.* New York: Macmillan.

Frankena, W. K. (1973). *Ethics* (2nd ed.). Englewood Cliffs, NJ: Prentice-Hall.

Garbarino, J., Guttman, E., and Seeley, J. W. (1986). *The psychologically battered child.* San Francisco: Jossey-Bass.

Giovannoni, J. M., and Becerra, R. M. (1979). *Defining child abuse.* New York: Free Press.

Goodnow, J. J. (1994). Acceptable disagreement across generations. In J. Smetana (Ed.), *Beliefs about parenting* (pp. 51–64). San Francisco: Jossey-Bass.

Greenberger, E., and Goldberg, W. (1989). Work, parenting, and the socialization of children. *Developmental Psychology, 25*(1), 22–35.

Harris, J. (1982). The political status of children. In K. Graham (Ed.), *Contemporary political philosophy: Radical studies.* Cambridge, England: Cambridge University Press.

Hart, S. N., Germain, R. B., and Brassard, M. R. (1987). The challenge: To better understand and combat psychological maltreatment of children and youth. In M. R. Brassard, R. Germain, and S. N. Hart (Eds.), *Psychological maltreatment of children and youth* (pp. 3–24). New York: Pergamon.

Heffer, R. W., and Kelley, M. L. (1987). Mother's acceptance of behavioral interventions for children: The influence of parent race and income. *Behavior Therapy, 2,* 153–163.

Hegel, G. (1952). *The philosophy of right and the philosopy of history.* Chicago: University of Chicago, Great Books. (Original work published 1821.)

Hoffman, M. L. (1975). Moral internalization, parental power, and the nature of parent–child interaction. *Developmental Psychology, 11,* 228–239.

Holden, G. W. (1995). Parental attitudes toward childrearing. In M. H. Bornstein (Ed.), *Handbook of parenting: Vol. 3. Status and social conditions of parenting.* Hillsdale, NJ: Lawrence Erlbaum Associates.

Holt, J. (1974). *Escape from childhood: The needs and rights of children.* New York: Dutton.

Horowitz, F. D. (2000). Child development and the PITS: Simple questions, complex answers, and developmental theory. *Child Development, 71,* 1–10.

Houlgate, L. D. (1988). *Family and state: The philosophy of family law.* Totowa, NJ: Rowman & Littlefield.

Hsu, F. L. K. (1985). The self in cross-cultural perspective. In A. J. Marsella, G. De Vos, and F. L. K. Hsu (Eds.), *Culture and self* (pp. 24–55). London: Tavistock.

Hyles, J. (1972). *How to rear children*. Hammond, LN: Hyles-Anderson.

Ingulli, E. D. (1985). Grandparent visitation rights: Social policies and legal rights. *West Virginia Law Review*, *87*, 295–334.

Kandel, D., and Lesser, G. S. (1969). Parent–adolescent relationships and adolescent independence in the United States and Denmark. *Journal of Marriage and the Family*, *31*, 348–358.

Kant, I. (1964). *The doctrine of virtue* (M. J. Gregor, Trans.). New York: Harper and Row. (Original work published 1797.)

Kelly, J. B. (1993). Developing and implementing post-divorce parenting plans. In C. Depner and J. Bray (Eds.), *Nonresidential parenting: New vistas in family living* (pp. 136–155). Newbury Park, CA: Sage.

Kochanska, G. (1997). Mutually responsive orientation between mothers and their young children: Implications for early socialization. *Child Development*, *68*, 94–112.

Kochanska, G., and Thompson, R. A. (1997). The emergence and development of conscience in toddlerhood and early childhood. In J. E. Grusec and L. Kuczynski (Eds.), *Parenting and children's internalization of values* (pp. 53–77). New York: Wiley.

Koehler, J. J. (1993). The influence of prior beliefs on scientific judgements of evidence quality. *Organ. Behav. Hum. Decis. Proc.*, *56*, 28–55.

Koestler, A. (1967). *Janus: A summing up*. New York: Random House.

Kohn, M. L. (1977). *Class and conformity: A study in values* (2nd ed.). Chicago: University of Chicago Press.

Kuczynski, L., and Kochanska, G. (1990). Development of children's noncompliance strategies from toddlerhood to age 5. *Developmental Psychology*, *26*, 398–406.

Larzelere, R. E., and Merenda, J. A. (1994). The effectiveness of parental discipline for toddler misbehavior at different levels of child distress. *Family Relations*, *43*, 480–488

Laupa, M., Turiel E., and Cowan, P. A. (1995). Obedience to authority in children and adults. In M. Killen and D. Hart (Eds.), *Morality in everyday life: Developmental perspectives* (pp. 131–165). Cambridge, England: Cambridge University Press.

Leary, T. (1957). *Interpersonal diagnosis of personality: A functional theory and methodology for personality evaluation*. New York: Ronald Press.

Lee, C. L., and Bates, J. E. (1985). Mother–child interactions at age two years and perceived difficult temperament. *Child Development*, *56*, 1314–1325.

Lepper, M. (1983). Social control processes, and the internalization of social values: An attributional perspective. In E. T. Higgins, D. Ruble, and W. W. Hartup (Eds.), *Social cognition and social behavior: Developmental perspectives* (pp. 294–330). New York: Cambridge University Press.

Lindblom, C. E., and Cohen, D. K. (1979). *Usable knowledge: Social science and social problem-solving*. New Haven, CT: Yale University Press.

Locke, J. (1965). *Two treatises of government* (P. Laslett, Ed.). New York: New American Library. (Originally published 1690.)

Lonner, W. J. (1980). The search for psychological universals. In H. C. Triandis and W. W. Lambert (Eds.), *Handbook of cross-cultural psychology* (Vol. 1, pp. 143–204). Newton, MA: Allyn & Bacon.

Lowery, C. R. (1981). Child custody decisions in divorce proceedings: A survey of judges. *Professional Psychology*, *12*, 492–498.

Maccoby, E. E. (1995). Divorce and custody: The rights, needs, and obligations of mothers, fathers, and children. In G. B. Melton (Ed.), *The individual, the family, and social good: Personal fulfillment in times of change*. Lincoln: University of Nebraska Press.

Maccoby, E. E. (1999). The custody of children of divorcing families: Weighing the alternatives. In R. A. Thompson and P. R. Amato (Eds.), *The postdivorce family: Children, parenting, and society* (pp. 51–70). Thousand Oaks, CA: Sage.

Maccoby, E. E., and Martin, J. A. (1983). Socialization in the context of the family: Parent–child interaction. In E. M. Hetherington (Ed.) and P. H. Mussen (Series Ed.), *Handbook of child psychology: Vol 4. Socialization, personality, and social development* (pp. 1–101). New York: Wiley.

Maccoby, E. E., and Mnookin, R. H. (1992). *Dividing the child: Social and legal dilemmas of custody*. Cambridge, MA: Harvard University Press.

MacCoun, R. J. (1998). Biases in the interpretation and use of research results. *Annual Review of Psychology*, *59*, 259–87.

Markus, H. R., and Kitayama, S. (1991). Culture and the self: Implications for cognition, emotion, and motivation. *Psychological Review*, *98*(2), 224–253.

McCarthy, F. B. (1988). The confused constitutional status and meaning of parental rights. *Georgia Law Review*, *4*, 975–1033.

McCord, J. (1991). Questioning the value of punishment. *Social Problems*, *38*, 167–173.

McGee, R. A., and Wolfe, D. A. (1991). Psychological maltreatment: Toward an operational definnition. *Development and Psychopathology*, *3*, 3–18.

Melton, G. B., and Thompson, R. A. (1987). Legislative approaches to psychological maltreatment: A social policy analysis. In M. Brassard, R. Germain, and S. N. Hart (Eds.), *The psychological maltreatment of children and youth* (pp. 203–216). New York: Pergamon.

Merton, R. K. (1973). *The sociology of science*. Chicago: University of Chicago Press.

Meyer v. Nebraska, 262 U.S. 390 (1923).

Meyer, D. R. (1999). Compliance with child support orders in paternity and divorce cases. In R. A. Thompson and P. R. Amato (Eds.), *The postdivorce family: Children, parenting, and society* (pp. 127–157). Thousand Oaks, CA: Sage.

Meyer, D. R., and Bartfeld, J. (1996). Compliance with child support orders in divorce cases. *Journal of Marriage and the Family, 58,* 201–212.

Mill, J. S. (1973). *On Liberty* (C. U. Shields, Ed.). Indianapolis, IN: Bobbs-Merrill. (Original work published 1859.)

Mill, J. S. (1988). *The subjection of women* (S. Okin, Ed.). Indianapolis: Hackett. (Original work published 1869.)

Minton, C., Kagan, J., and Levine, J. (1971). Maternal control and obedience in the two-year-old. *Child Development, 42,* 1873–1894.

Mnookin, R. H. (1974). Foster care: In whose best interest? *Harvard Educational Review, 43*(4), 599–638.

Mnookin, R. H. (1975). Child-custody adjudication: Judicial functions in the face of indeterminacy. *Law and Contemporary Problems, 39,* 226–293.

Mnookin, R. H., and Kornhauser, L. (1979). Bargaining in the shadow of the law: The case of divorce. *Yale Law Journal, 88,* 950–997.

Mosby, L. A. (1999). Troubles in interracial talk about discipline: An examination of African American child rearing narratives. *Journal of Comparative Family Studies, 30*(3), 489–521.

Nucci, L. (1981). The development of personal concepts: A domain distinct from moral or societal concepts. *Child Development, 52,* 114–121.

Okin, S. M. (1989). *Justice, gender and the family.* New York: Basic Books.

Oliner, S., and Oliner, P. (1988). *The altruistic personality.* New York: Free Press.

Parpal, M., and Maccoby, E. E. (1985). Maternal responsiveness and subsequent child compliance. *Child Development, 56,* 1326–1334.

Parsons, T. (1951). *The social system.* New York: Free Press.

Perry, D. G., and Perry, L. C. (1983). Social learning, causal attribution, and moral internalization. In J. Bisanz, G. L. Bisanz, and R. Kail (Eds.), *Learning in children: Progress in cognitive development research* (pp. 105–136). New York: Springer-Verlag.

Piaget, J. (1965). *Moral judgment of the child.* New York: Free Press. (Original work published 1935.)

Pierce v. Society of Sisters, 268 U.S. 510 (1925).

Plato. (1979). *The Republic.* New York: Viking. (Original work written ca. 355 B.C.)

Pratt, M. W., Green, D., MacVicar, J., and Bountrogianni, M. (1993). The mathematical parent: Parental scaffolding, parenting style, and learning outcomes in long-division mathematics homework. *Journal of Applied Developmental Psychology, 13*(1), 17–34.

Pratt, M. W., Kerig, P., Cowan, P. A., and Cowan, C. P. (1988). Mothers and fathers teaching three-year-olds: Authoritative parenting and adult scaffolding of young children's learning. *Developmental Psychology, 24,* 832–839.

Prince v. Massachusetts. 321 U.S. 158 (1944).

Purdy, L. M. (1972). *In their best interest?* Ithaca, NY: Cornell University Press.

Rawls, J. A. (1971). *A theory of justice.* Cambridge, MA: Harvard University, Belknap Press.

Rousseau, J. J. (1952). *The social contract.* University of Chicago: Great Books, Encyclopedia Britannica. (Original work published 1762.)

Sagi, A., van IJzendoorn, M. H., Aviezer, O., Donnell, F., and Mayseless, O. (1994). Sleeping out of home in a kibbutz communal arrangement: It makes a difference for infant–mother attachment. *Child Development, 65,* 992–1004.

Schaefer, E. S. (1959). A circumplex model for maternal behavior. *Journal of Abnormal and Social Psychology, 59,* 226–235.

Scott, E. S. (1992). Pluralism, parental preference, and child custody. *California Law Review, 80,* 615–672.

Shweder, R. A. (1990). Cultural psychology: What is it? In J. W. Stigler, R. A. Shweder, and G. Herdt (Eds.), *Cultural psychology: Essays on comparative human development* (pp. 1–46). Cambridge, England: Cambridge University Press.

Siegal, M., and Barclay, M. S. (1985). Children's evaluations of fathers' socialization behavior. *Developmental Psychology, 21,* 1090–1096.

Siegal, M., and Cowen, J. (1984). Appraisals of intervention: The mother's versus the culprit's behavior as determinants of children's evaluations of discipline techniques. *Child Development, 55,* 1760–1766.

Skinner, B. F. (1948). *Walden two.* New York: Macmillan.

Smetana, J. G. (1988). Adolescents' and parents' conceptions of parental authority. *Child Development, 59,* 321–335.

Smetana, J. G., and Asquith, P. (1994). Adolescents' and parents' conceptions of parental authority and adolescent autonomy. *Child Development, 65,* 1147–1162.

Spence, J. T., and Helmreich, R. L. (1978). *Masculinity and femininity: Their psychological dimensions, correlates, and antecedents.* Austin: University of Texas Press.

Steinberg, L. (2000, April). *We know some things: Parent-adolescent relations in retrospect and prospect.* Presidential address at the Society for Research on Adolescence, Chicago.

Straus, M. A. (1994). *Beating the devil out of them: Corporal punishment in American families.* Lexington, MA: Lexington/Macmillian Books.

Straus, M. A. (1996). Spanking and the making of a violent society. *Pediatrics, 98*(4), 837–842.

Thompson, R. A. (1986). Fathers and the child's "best interests": Judicial decision-making in custody disputes. In M. E. Lamb (Ed.), *The father's role: Applied perspectives* (pp. 61–102). New York: Wiley.

Thompson, R. A. (1993). Developmental research and legal policy: Toward a two-way street. In D. Cicchetti and S. Toth (Eds.), *Child abuse, child development, and social policy* (pp. 75–115). Norwood, NJ: Ablex.

Thompson, R. A. (1994). Fathers and divorce. *The Future of Children, 4*(1), 210–235.

Thompson, R. A. (1995). *Preventing child maltreatment through social support: A critical analysis.* Thousand Oaks, CA: Sage.

Thompson, R. A. (1998). Early sociopersonality development. In W. Damon (Series Ed.) and N. Eisenberg (Vol. Ed.), *Handbook of child psychology: Vol. 3. Social, emotional, and personality development* (5th ed., pp. 25–104). New York: Wiley.

Thompson, R. A. (2001). Sensitive periods in attachment? In D. B. Bailey, J. T. Bruer, F. J. Symons, and J. W. Lichtman (Eds.), *Critical thinking about critical periods* (pp. 83–106). Baltimore, MD: Paul H. Brookes Publishing Co.

Thompson, R. A., and Jacobs, J. (1991). Defining psychological maltreatment: Research and policy perspectives. *Development and Psychopathology, 3*(1), 93–102.

Thompson, R. A., and Nelson, C. A. (2001). Developmental science and the media: Early brain development. *American Psychologist, 56*(1), 5–15.

Thompson, R. A., Scalora, M. J., Castrianno, L., and Limber, S. (1992). Grandparent visitation rights: Emergent psychological and psycholegal issues. In D. K. Kagehiro and W. S. Laufer (Eds.), *Handbook of psychology and law* (pp. 292–317). New York: Springer-Verlag.

Thompson, R. A., Scalora, M. J., Limber, S. P., and Castrianno, L. (1991). Grandparent visitation rights: A psycholegal analysis. *Family and Conciliation Courts Review, 29*(1), 9–25.

Thompson, R. A., Tinsley, B., Scalora, M., and Parke, R. (1989). Grandparents' visitation rights: Legalizing the ties that bind. *American Psychologist, 44*(9), 1217–1222.

Thompson, R. A., and Wyatt, J. (1999). Values, policy, and research on divorce: Seeking fairness for children. In R. A. Thompson and P. R. Amato (Eds.), *The postdivorce family: Children, parenting, and society* (pp. 191–232). Thousand Oaks, CA: Sage.

Triandis, H. C. (1990). Cross-cultural studies of individualism and collectivism. In J. J. Berman (Ed.), *Nebraska Symposium on Motivation: 1989: Vol. 37. Cross-cultural perspectives* (pp. 41–133). Lincoln: University of Nebraska Press.

Trivers, R. L. (1985). *Social evolution.* Menlo Park, CA: Benjamin/Cummings.

Troxel v. Granville, 120 S. Ct. 2054 (2000).

U.S. Advisory Board on Child Abuse and Neglect. (1990). *Child abuse and neglect: Critical first steps in response to a national emergency.* Washington, DC: U.S. Government Printing Office.

United Nations General Assembly. (1989). *Adoption of a convention on the rights of the child* (U.N. Doc. A/Res/44/25). New York: Author.

Waddington, C. H. (1960). *The ethical animal.* Chicago: University of Chicago Press.

Wald, M. S. (1975). State intervention on behalf of "neglected" children: A search for realistic standards. *Stanford Law Review, 27*, 985–1040.

Wald, M. S. (1979). Children's rights: A framework for analysis. *University of California Davis Law Review, 12* (2), 255–282.

Wald, M. S. (1982). State intervention on behalf of endangered children—A proposed legal response. *Child Abuse and Neglect, 6*, 3–45.

Wald, M. S. (1985). Introduction to the Symposium on the Family, the State, and the Law. *University of Michigan Journal of Law Reform, 18*, 799–804.

Wald, M. S., Carlsmith, J. M., and Leiderman, P. H. (1988). *Protecting abused and neglected children.* Stanford, CA: Stanford University Press.

Whiting, J. W. M., and Whiting, B. B. (1975). *Children of six cultures: A psychocultural analysis.* Cambridge, MA: Harvard University Press.

Whobrey, L., Sales, B., and Lou, M. (1987). Determining the best interests of the child in custody disputes. In L. Weithorn (Ed.), *Psychology and child custody determinations: Roles, knowledge, and expertise.* Lincoln: University of Nebraska Press.

Wisconsin v. Yoder, 406 U.S. 205 (1972).

Wiggins, J. S. (1979). A psychological taxonomy of trait-descriptive terms: The interpersonal domain. *Journal of Personality and Social Psychology, 37*, 395–412.

Wilson, J. Q. (1993). *The moral sense.* New York: Free Press.

Worsfold, V. L. (1974). A philosophical justification for children's rights. In *The rights of children* (pp. 29–44). Cambridge, MA: Harvard Educational Review.

Zahn-Waxler, C., Radke-Yarrow, M., and King, R. A. (1979). Child rearing and children's prosocial initiations towards victims of distress. *Child Development, 48*, 319–330.

2

Parenting and Attachment

E. Mark Cummings
Jennifer S. Cummings
University of Notre Dame

INTRODUCTION

Attachment is a particular conceptualization of the influence of parents on their children's development in the context of parent–child relationships. Attachment refers to an affective bond between parents and children. The notion is that children form affective bonds with parents that have continuity over time, and that parents form reciprocal relationships with their children. Moreover, relations between attachment and children's and adults' functioning have been repeatedly reported (Ainsworth, Blehar, Waters, and Wall, 1978; Bowlby, 1969; 1973; see reviews in Cassidy and Shaver, 1999; Colin, 1996). It follows that attachment is seminal to the study of parenting. Relatedly, a practical question of some importance for many parents has become: How can we grow a securely attached child?

The theory posits that close relationships between individuals, in particular between parents and their children, are about more than transient variations in interaction patterns over time (Masters and Wellman, 1974). That is, attachments have a substance and continuity that transcend the specifics of day-to-day interactions. Moreover, attachments are held to be formed in Western cultures except under the most unfortunate circumstances of early environment, like the extreme lack of parental care that characterizes conditions of "maternal deprivation" (Ainsworth, 1962; Bowlby, 1951; Rutter, 1995b). Thus, it is expected that the great majority of children living in normal circumstances of Western cultures form attachments to the parents. Accordingly, research on attachment as an investigation into parenting has been primarily concerned with qualitative aspects of interactions between parents and their children rather than with whether or not children form attachments. With regard to qualities of attachment, the security of attachment has been the particular focus of theory and research (Waters and Cummings, 2000).

Thus, attachment is a particular perspective on parenting: a relational perspective on affective ties between children and their parents and the implications of these relationships for a child's development. Moreover, attachments are posited to be pertinent to an individual's functioning across the lifespan (Bowlby, 1969). For example, while the focus of research was initially on infant–parent attachments (Ainsworth et al., 1978), evidence has now accumulated for the significance of attachment to parents for older children (Greenberg, Cicchetti, and Cummings, 1990; Thompson, 1998, 1999), adolescents (Allen and Land, 1999), and adults (Hesse, 1999; Main and Goldwyn, 1984). Moreover, attachments typify other close relationships, including romantic and marital relationships, with implications for the individual's functioning (Ainsworth, 1982; Crowell, Fraley, and Shaver, 1999; Hazan and Shaver, 1987). Furthermore, although much thoughtful discussion has been published with regard to the limitations of attachment research (Dunn, 1993; Goldsmith and Alansky, 1987; Lamb, Thompson, Gardner, and Charnov, 1985; Rutter, 1995a), support for this perspective on close relationships is impressive, including frequent publication and citation in selective and prestigious journals. Accordingly, Thompson (2000, p. 145) commented, "Attachment theory has become the dominant approach to understanding early socioemotional and personality development during the past quarter century of research."

Attachment research and other directions in the study of parenting have common concerns with the effects of parenting on children's development over time. Attachment is posited to be a function of the experiential histories between parents and children (Bowlby, 1969; Waters and Cummings, 2000). Research has been especially concerned with the implications for attachment security of the emotional availability and accessibility of parents to their children (Bowlby, 1973; De Wolff and van IJzendoorn, 1997). Moreover, if continuity of attachment is normally expected, the security of attachment is hypothesized to be subject to change if parenting or ecological contexts of parenting alter substantially over time to challenge the children's existing sense of emotional security. For example, if martial dissolution or dramatic reductions in socioeconomic status significantly reduce the emotional availability or accessibility of parents to their children, attachments may change from secure to insecure (Egeland and Farber, 1984; Lewis, Feiring, and Rosenthal, 2000; Waters, Weinfield, and Hamilton, 2000). Thus, findings of continuity or "lawful discontinuity," that is, changes in attachment status that predictably follow from changes in children's experiences, are both consistent with attachment theory (Thompson, 2000; Waters, Hamilton, and Weinfield, 2000).

The present chapter begins by examining the history of the notion that an affective bond forms between infants and parents that has implications for children's development. After outlining central issues for the study of attachment as parenting, assumptions and principles of attachment theory are reviewed. Next, selected themes in classical and modern research on attachment and parenting are examined, including: (1) parenting and attachment, (2) cross-cultural perspectives on attachment, (3) fathers and attachment, (4) attachment from a family-wide perspective, (5) processes mediating the effects of attachment, and (6) pathways of development. Finally, we conclude by considering future directions and offering take-home messages for the parents.

HISTORICAL ORIGINS OF ATTACHMENT THEORY

The notion that early affective bonds between parents and children are significant to later development has origins in the psychoanalytic perspective advanced by Freud nearly a century ago (Cohler and Paul, in Vol. 3 of this *Handbook*; Waters and Cummings, 2000). Specifically, Freud proposed a drive reduction model within the context of a psychosexual theory of human development to account for the affective ties that formed between infants and their mothers. Children were seen as developing ties to their parents due to the parents' satisfaction of the child's primary needs (e.g., hunger and thirst). Later, this first relationship was termed dependency by American scholars seeking to translate psychoanalytic notions into concepts amenable to social learning theory, with dependency conceptualized as an acquired drive (Miller and Dollard, 1941). As such, dependency was seen as a generalized drive, not specific to the social interactional characteristics that typified particular parent–child relationships (Ainsworth, 1969). While these notions drew attention to the importance of early parent–child relationships to an individual's later development, these ties were seen as immature, "dependent," a state of affairs to be outgrown. Moreover, the relationship was viewed as secondary to, virtually a residue of, the parents' role in satisfying the infant's biologically based needs.

However, subsequent research cast doubt on these assumptions about the bases for the first parent–child bonds. The satisfaction of primary needs was not observed to be essential for relationships to develop. The evidence suggested that children formed close relationships to primary caregivers for their own sake, regardless of who was responsible for feeding the infants (e.g., Ainsworth, 1967; Schaffer and Emerson, 1964). Similar results were observed in studies of the experiential bases of parent–child ties in nonhuman primates, for example, Harlow's famous studies of infant rhesus monkey's ties to cloth monkey "mothers" (Harlow and Harlow, 1965). Furthermore, groundbreaking work by Ainsworth and her colleagues indicated that qualitative aspects of parent–child relationships developed out of the particular qualities of the interactions between parents and children, that is, *parenting* (Ainsworth, 1967; Ainsworth et al., 1978). Moreover, a substantive body of clinical research on the effects of long-term separations, deprivation of care, and loss provided evidence suggesting the desirability of close relationships between parents and children for children's long-term adjustment and the negative consequences of the absence, loss, or deprivation of these first relationships (Ainsworth, 1962; Bowlby, 1951, 1969; Rutter, 1995b).

Thus, the emergence of empirical study of the functioning of parent–child relationships and their implications for children's development supported conclusions that contradicted earlier perspectives based largely on theory. One conclusion was that the formation and maintenance of emotional bonds between parents and children constituted a desirable state of affairs that fostered children's healthy adjustment rather than a reflection of dependency and possible risk for dysfunction (Bowlby, 1969). For example, close relationships between parents and children in which parents were responsive to children's needs were linked with desirable developmental outcomes, whereas the absence of such relationships or disruptions in relationships (e.g., loss and long-term separations) were related to children's problems (Ainsworth, 1962, 1967). Another conclusion supported by empirical study was that attachments were particular to specific parent–child relationships, challenging the notion that early parent–child ties could properly be characterized as generalized drives. For example, differences, as well as similarities, in the security of children's attachments to mothers and fathers were reported (see review in Colin, 1996).

Accordingly, Bowlby (1958) coined the term *attachment* to distinguish this new perspective on early parent–child emotional ties from the earlier, somewhat pejorative characterizations of the nature and developmental implications of these relationships articulated by psychoanalytic and social learning theories. Based on research with human infants as well as nonhuman primates and other species (Harlow and Harlow, 1965), Bowlby (1969) also argued for the developmental primacy of, and biological bases for, parent–child relationships as significant in their own right, and for their importance to species survival from an evolutionary perspective, particularly in the early origins of the species (i.e., in the "environment of evolutionary adaptiveness"; Belsky, 1999; Polan and Hofer, 1999; Simpson, 1999; Suomi, 1999). Rather than seen as a type of relationship to be outgrown for optimal development, attachments were viewed as providing influential initial models for later close relationships and as being formed to new individuals after infancy, with past attachments also remaining important throughout the lifespan. In particular, attachments were conceptualized as a secure base construct, referring to the use of the parent by the child as secure base from which to explore and as a source of security during everyday or normal circumstances, but particularly in times of stress. The individual's confidence in the availability of the attachment figure as a secure base is therefore central to the security of attachment. Thus, the formation of attachments was seen as normal and desirable, with a critical function to play across the lifespan in the individual's functioning (Sroufe and Waters, 1977; Waters and Cummings, 2000).

As a practicing psychiatrist, Bowlby was interested in attachment theory as a theory of the development of psychopathology as well as a theory pertinent to normal development (Greenberg,

1999; Sroufe, Carlson, Levy, and Egeland, 1999). A substantial body of research has emerged to indicate relations between insecure attachment and children's adjustment problems (Carlson and Sroufe, 1995). Notably, however, attachment insecurity is not in itself a classification of psychopathology, although insecure attachments may contribute, in concert with other family and ecological contexts, to children's risk for adjustment problems (Cummings and Cicchetti, 1990).

In summary, attachment theory preserves Freud's key insight about the importance of close relationships between parent and infants to children's functioning and development. On the other hand, based on Bowlby's theorizing and Ainsworth's initial observational studies of infant attachment, attachment theory broke with earlier perspectives by reconceptualizing early affective ties between parents and infants as being based on qualities of parenting, and as optimally serving to foster children's competency and healthy development, rather than being reflective of children's psychological dependency and possibly their increased risk for dysfunction if relationships continued beyond infancy (Waters and Cummings, 2000).

CENTRAL ISSUES IN THE STUDY OF ATTACHMENT AS PARENTING

A central issue for the study of attachment is to appreciate the rich and unique theory about parenting that serves as a foundation for the "field". Attachment refers to an affective tie between parent and child, not, by definition, to any specific parenting behaviors, practices, or styles (Ainsworth, 1969; Sroufe and Waters, 1977). Moreover, attachment is a relational construct, so that one must appreciate the mutual interaction of child and parent in particular contexts in order to evaluate attachment security (Ainsworth et al., 1978). For example, a child with an emotionally warm parent will not *necessarily* be securely attached, especially if the parent's expressions of warmth are intrusive or insensitive to children's signals, for example, kissing a child that does not want to be kissed. Parental warmth does not constitute a secure attachment. Nonetheless, parental warmth may increase the probability of the occurrence of secure attachment *if* it increases the child's confidence in the availability of the parent as a secure base (Waters and Cummings, 2000). The conceptualization of attachment as a relational construct pertinent to parenting thus merits particular attention.

Although attachment, by definition, is not a parenting style or practice, classical and modern directions in attachment research are fundamentally about parenting. As attachment theory posits that attachment security develops as a function of children's experiential histories of parenting, a central issue is to examine relations between parenting and attachment security. For example, in classical research in the attachment tradition, Ainsworth reported a significant relationship between attachment security and parental sensitivity and insensitivity, acceptance and rejection, cooperation and interference, and accessibility and ignoring (Ainsworth et al., 1978). The relationship between parenting and attachment remains central to the concerns of attachment research (De Wolff and van IJzendoorn, 1997).

Space does not permit exhaustive coverage of all of the themes that have been addressed in attachment research over the past several decades. Moreover, updated treatment of many of the classical directions in attachment research is available elsewhere (see reviews in Cassidy and Shaver, 1999; Colin, 1996). Thus, this review focuses on examining what we consider to be particularly promising, emerging directions that contribute to and advance new, process-oriented perspectives on attachment, parenting, and child development (Cummings, Davies, and Campbell, 2000).

Notably, multiple investigatory approaches may advance a process-oriented level of understanding. For example, the processes underlying the effects of parenting on children are illuminated by broadening the scope of research. Most research has focused on mother–child attachment and attachment relationships in American culture. Thus, it is of interest for tests of concepts about process-relations to examine whether the relations between parenting and attachment hold when father–child attachments (Cowan, 1997) or attachments from a cross-cultural perspective (Waters and Cummings, 2000) are studied.

Moreover, attachment does not affect children's development in isolation from other influences from within the family. The investigation of attachment from a family-wide perspective is thus a particularly exciting emerging direction to better account for children's developmental outcomes (Cummings and Davies, 1996). Relatedly, another important process-oriented direction is to articulate the specific mechanisms by which attachment affects children's functioning. For example, children's emotional regulation and representations of self and family relationships are hypothesized to be affected by attachment, with implications for children's development (Thompson, 1994, 1999, 2000; Vaughn and Bost, 1999). Thus, a central issue is to articulate the processes by which attachment affects child development and the common processes affected by attachment and other aspects of family functioning. For example, marital conflict and insensitive parenting may each serve to increase children's emotional insecurity (Davies and Cummings, 1994). Finally, research must address notions of continuity and change over time. Development is not just about the size of relations or correlations between children's functioning at a first (Time 1) and second (Time 2) time of assessment. Another emerging theme is that it is more informative to articulate developmental process in terms of pathways of development over time (Sroufe, 1997).

In summary, research toward articulating the how, when, why, and for whom relations hold in the context of complex models of causal directions and pathways from a family-wide perspective are the next steps in attachment research (Cummings and Cummings, 1988; Cummings et al., 2000). Accordingly, a focus of this review is on examining principles, and particularly promising new directions, that advance a process-oriented perspective on attachment and parenting.

THEORY IN ATTACHMENT AND PARENTING

As we have noted, the essential element of attachment is the emotional bond, not specific parenting behaviors. The bond is seen as not simply the sum of behaviors, but rather as providing a higher order goal or plan around which behaviors are organized and directed. In this sense, attachment is an organizational construct that motivates and directs a relatively complex and sophisticated behavioral control system in response to the contextual demands of situations faced by the child. Moreover, the behaviors in the service of attachment are flexible and interchangeable based on the moment-to-moment needs of the dyad in the context of the attachment relationship (Sroufe and Waters, 1977). Thus, attachment behaviors are properly interpreted in terms of the meaning they have for the quality of the underlying bond in a situational context, rather than as interpretable in isolation from the broader pattern and context of behavior (Waters, 1978). For example, an infant can indicate a secure response to reunion with the parent after a brief separation by greeting the mother across a distance or, alternatively, by running up to her and giving her a hug.

Interdisciplinary Perspectives

The commitment to an interdisciplinary approach to the study of parenting is embodied in Bowlby's formulation of attachment theory, in which he accomplished the laudable feat of cogently integrating concepts from such diverse disciplines as psychiatry, ethology, control systems theory, cognitive psychology, and developmental psychology (Bowlby, 1969).

Ethology and the observation of parenting in naturalistic settings. A particular emphasis in attachment theory is on the detailed behavioral observation of parent–child interactions in naturalistic environments (i.e., the home), which originated from the European tradition of ethology, which stressed the importance of careful behavioral observation of animal behavior in natural habitats.

The concern with intensive data-collection in naturalistic settings was consistent with Bowlby's formulation that attachments were shaped by experience and that understanding the development of attachment relationships is informed by the day-to-day experience of interactions between parents and children. Remarkably, this emphasis on behavioral observation was not valued by psychoanalytic theorists who emphasized intrapsychic influences that were not necessarily of experiential origin and were decidedly not observable.

In the spirit of ethological methods, Ainsworth's original formulations of the secure base function of parent–child attachments were based on lengthy and meticulous observations of mother–child interactions in natural settings in Uganda (Ainsworth, 1967) and Baltimore (Ainsworth et al., 1978). Subsequent investigators have continued this tradition of naturalistic observation of mother–child interaction over substantial periods of time in the home (e.g., Belsky, Rovine, and Taylor, 1984; Bornstein and Tamis-LeMonda, 1990; Egeland and Farber, 1984; Grossmann, Grossmann, Spangler, Suess, and Unzner, 1985). Moreover, the observation of attachment relationships in the natural environment (i.e., the home) is viewed as an essential point of comparison for other methodologies and contexts for assessing attachment, because the ultimate goal of attachment research is to understand the functioning of parent–child relationships in real life.

Control systems theory: Contextualizing attachment behavior.   Another seminal direction is the stress placed on the importance of context in understanding and interpreting children's functioning. In articulating the role of context in the operation of the attachment behavioral system, Bowlby was influenced by control systems theory, which conceptualized how complex behaviors and systems are organized and directed around fixed set points or goals of the individual. Thus, the infant's attachment behavioral system is not in a state of constant activation, but only becomes activated (i.e., the infant seeks proximity to the mother) when intra- (e.g, illness) or extraorganismic factors (e.g., external dangers) pose a threat, as appraised by the infant, to his or her security. Such appraisals cause the infant's sense of security to be reduced below the desirable set point. As a consequence, the attachment behavioral system becomes activated, and the child engages in behaviors (e.g., seeks proximity to the mother) in order to seek to increase her appraised sense of security, ideally so that she again achieves the desired set point of felt security (Sroufe and Waters, 1977). Thus, during many situations, especially when stress, danger, illness, or other threats were not present, the infant could feel confident to explore, feed, play, or engage in other behaviors not related to attachment, although the attachment relationship can still be seen to support these other behaviors (i.e., serve as a secure base from which to explore).

Patterns of Attachment: Secure Versus Insecure Attachment

Methodologies have been developed to assess attachment patterns throughout the lifespan (e.g., Hazan and Zeifman, 1999; Hesse, 1999), but for the purpose of illustration of the nature of attachments we will focus on how attachment patterns have been assessed in childhood, which was the starting point for the assessment of patterns of attachment and is a heavily researched period of the lifespan. Individual differences in patterns of attachment are assessed in infancy based on the Strange Situation (Ainsworth et al., 1978), which consists of a sequence of eight brief contexts (about 3 minutes each) for observing the infant's functioning in relation to the parent's presence, absence, and return (and certain other conditions, including the presence of a strange adult) in an environment that is unfamiliar (i.e., "strange") to the child. Consistent with theory, patterns of attachment are classified to distinguish parent–child relationships in terms of the strategies for using the parent as a secure base and the coherency of children's attachment behavior. Of the various contexts for the child, separations are typically the most stressful, and thus parent–child interactions on reunion are potentially the most informative with regard to the functioning of the attachment system. Four major classifications (one secure classification and three main types of insecure classification) have been distinguished, based on infant behavior across all eight episodes, with an emphasis on the functioning of the relational system on the infant's reunion with the attachment figure.

The organization of children with *secure attachments* reflects optimal use of the attachment figure as a secure base and as support in the context of the attachment relationship. The child thus demonstrates a coherent strategy for using the parent as a source of security. For example, on the return of the parent after separation the child readily makes an emotional connection with the parent by physically seeking contact, seeking closer physical proximity, or through effective signaling of the parent across a distance (e.g., greeting the parent); then the child returns to a nondistressed state and to exploration or play. This pattern is associated with greater responsivity and warmth by the parents toward the children in the home, consistent with the theoretical proposition that such parent–child interactions foster a secure attachment relationship.

The behavioral pattern exhibited by children with *avoidant attachments* indicates less than optimal secure base use and secure base support in the context of the attachment relationship. Avoidant infants use the particular strategy of diverting their attention from anything that would activate attachment behavior, and therefore do not appear to rely on the attachment figure in times of stress. Thus, on reunion the child conspicuously avoids proximity or contact with the parent. It is inferred that these children are not comfortable turning to the parent in the relatively threatening and stressful context of the Strange Situation. Such an interpretation is supported by evidence that parents of avoidant children are more rejecting, tense and irritable, and avoidant of close bodily contact toward the children in day-to-day interaction in the home, thereby fostering less confidence in the child about the parents as a reliable source of security. Other evidence suggests that mothers of avoidant infants are more intrusive and overstimulating (Belsky et al., 1984).

The organization of *resistant attachment* also reflects relatively ineffective use of the parent as a source of security in times of stress and the particular strategy of extreme dependence. Prior to separation, these infants are often clingy and uninterested in toys. On reunion, resistant children may mix angry behavior (e.g., struggling when held, stiffness, hitting or pushing away) with excessive contact and proximity seeking. These attachment patterns are also associated with problematic histories of parent–child interaction in the home, including parenting that is relatively inept or inconsistent.

In an important sense, each of the above three patterns is indicative of a coherent or organized strategy on the child's part for coping with stress and for relying on the attachment relationship. In a final pattern, termed *disorganized/disoriented* (Main and Solomon, 1990), children have failed to develop a coherent strategy. These children may exhibit a variety of behaviors indicative of disturbance and lack of organization during reunion with the parent, including unusual sequences of behavior, both avoidant and resistant reactions in the context of the same reunion, and/or highly apprehensive or depressive behavior. Disorganized attachments have been found to be particularly evident among maltreated children and children of parents with psychopathology (e.g., depression; Radke-Yarrow, Cummings, Kuczynski, and Chapman, 1985).

These tripartite or quadratic patterns or divisions of attachment have been widely adopted in various forms in multiple directions in research on attachment across the lifespan. At the same time, it should be acknowledged that the measurement or conceptualization of how to assess and understand attachment patterns varies widely, particularly between adult social psychological approaches to the assessment of attachment (Hazan and Zeifman, 1999) and approaches based on the assessment of attachment in infancy and early childhood (Ainsworth et al., 1978) or assessments based on the Adult Attachment Interview (Main and Goldwyn, 1984). Moreover, variation in the meaning and interpretation of attachment is evident among researchers concerned with attachment in childhood, with perspectives ranging from views close to traditional psychoanalytic perspectives to perspectives more closely concerned with observational methodologies and the search for the complex processes that mediate or moderate children's development over time (see reviews in Cassidy and Shaver, 1999). Nonetheless, the various approaches owe a common heritage to Bowlby's original conceptualizations of the importance of close emotional bonds as a level of analysis for understanding the impact of parent–child, and other close relationships, on children's and adults' functioning. Moreover, some evidence has emerged to support the predictive validity of each these approaches to classification, in particular, attachment security to parents based on the Strange Situation (see review in Thompson, 1998). On the other hand, weak, complex or inconsistent findings are reported, and controversies exist with regard to various methodologies' directions in attachment research. These matters are beyond the scope of this chapter to thoroughly examine (see reviews in Cassidy and Shaver, 1999; Colin, 1996). Importantly, this rich diversity of perspectives continues to find identity in the pursuit of common research goals, and provides rich and promising perspectives for future research on an important category of influence on human development.

Nonetheless, the secure base concept is held to be central to the coherence and logic of attachment theory and to understanding its status as an organizational construct. Attachment is not about all dimensions of parent–child relationship, but is especially about the parents' relative effectiveness in the provision of security, particularly in times of stress. Waters and Cummings (2000) have expressed concern that by losing sight of the core definition of attachment as being about the provision of emotional security, some modern research runs the risk of overextending the utility, and ultimately credibility, of the construct. Thus, Waters and Cummings commented (2000, p. 165):

> For both Bowlby and Ainsworth, to be attached is to use someone preferentially as a secure base from which to explore. The term secure attachment refers both to skillful secure-base use over time and contexts in naturalistic settings and to confidence in a caregiver's availability and responsiveness.

In summary, attachment theory provides a rich conceptualization of the emotional and social organization of parent–child relationships, the relations between context and parenting, and individual differences in the organization and functioning of parent–child relationships in everyday circumstances. Moreover, as we will see, the theory of attachment as a secure base relationship provides a foundation for expanding research to include attachment from a family-wide perspective and investigations into the emotional and cognitive processes that mediate effects.

CLASSICAL AND MODERN RESEARCH IN ATTACHMENT AND PARENTING

The selected themes in attachment research reviewed here reflect concerns with the relations between parenting and attachment as well as with processes by which attachment affects a child's development as a dimension of parenting. In particular, emphasis will be placed on cross-cultural perspectives on attachment, attachment and fathers, processes mediating effects, a more comprehensive family-wide model, and understanding pathways of development.

Attachment and Parenting Behaviors

Attachment patterns have been proposed to be systematically related to parenting behaviors and practices and to reflect both historical and current patterns of parenting practices. Ainsworth's studies in Uganda (Ainsworth, 1967) and Baltimore (Ainsworth et al., 1978) provided initial and impressive empirical support, based on naturalistic observation and prospective longitudinal research designs, for the role of parenting practices in the formation of attachment relationships. The findings were consistent with the theoretical predictions of Bowlby (1969, 1973) about the importance of the parent's emotional availability and responsiveness for the development of secure attachments. In particular, the work of Ainsworth et al. (1978) indicated the pertinence of sensitivity, accessibility, acceptance, and cooperation as parenting behaviors relevant to the development of a child's security of attachments to parents, with each held to be indicative of the sensitive responsiveness of the parent to infant communications and signals.

Thus, core prediction of attachment theory from its initial formulation was that the child's sense of emotional security would derive from the responsiveness, warmth, and emotional availability of the parent. Maternal sensitivity was particularly emphasized and defined by Ainsworth as the parent's ability to accurately perceive the child's signals and to respond appropriately and promptly. While the size of the relations reported in Ainsworth's pioneering Baltimore study were particularly strong, dozens of published studies have reported that constructs reflecting maternal sensitivity and emotional availability or related constructs significantly predicted the quality of attachment. A meta-analysis suggests that the support for this relation is much more than convincing from a statistical perspective (De Wolff and van IJzendoorn, 1997). When maternal sensitivity was a significant predictor of attachment, it was not the exclusive factor, however, in accounting for the development of attachment. In fact, aspects of parenting that did not directly index maternal sensitivity (e.g., positive attitude and stimulation) had similar associations with attachment security, as reflected by the results of this meta-analysis. Furthermore, a great deal of the variability in the quality of parent–child attachment was not accounted for by parental acceptance and emotional availability, advocating for a multidimensional approach to identifying the parenting antecedents of attachment. Thus, the authors concluded that other dimensions of the emotional qualities of parenting, and family-wide influences (especially the quality of marital relations), are also likely to factor in the prediction of child attachment security. The authors also noted that parental management and control have rarely been considered in predicting attachment security, which is a particular gap in understanding the relations between attachment and parenting.

Even when parents are trained to be more sensitive and responsive to infants and these response dimensions are shown to predict positive outcomes later in development, the quality of parent–child attachment continues to be an independent predictor of positive aspects of later socioemotional functioning. For example, van den Boom (1994) reported that parents of irritable infants who were trained to be more responsive to infant's signals in the last half of the first year had more securely attached infants at 1 year of age. In subsequent years, parental responsivity and attachment security were interrelated, but each also predicted independent variance in children's functioning at home and school. Attachment security also predicts parent's emotional availability from a relational perspective (i.e., maternal structuring, maternal sensitivity, child responsiveness, and child involvement; Easterbrooks, Biesecker, and Lyons-Ruth, 2000). Thus, the emotionality of the parent–child relationship and the quality of the attachment relationship are not redundant predictors of child outcomes, and the direction of effects does not just go one way; attachment security may account for responsiveness over time as responsiveness predicts attachment.

However, attachment is not orthogonal to other dimensions of parenting. Thus, attachment may influence the likelihood that parental control techniques will be effective in obtaining compliance. For example, Londerville and Main (1981) reported that toddlers who were securely attached to their parents were more compliant to their parent's disciplinary directives (See Stayton, Hogan and Ainsworth, 1971). Lay, Waters, and Park (1989) found that parental warmth elicited positive affect in children, and positive affect, in turn, heightened compliance in comparison with children experiencing negative emotions. Moreover, clinical data from families with conduct problem preschoolers suggest that parent training is more effective if steps are taken to improve the quality of the parent–child attachment relationship as well as the effectiveness of the parent's disciplinary strategies (e.g., Speltz, 1990). Other lines of research also indicate that, when the quality of the emotional relationship between the parent and child is positive, there is an increased likelihood that parental disciplinary techniques will be effective (Grusec and Goodnow, 1994).

Emotional availability and responsiveness may also predict children's functioning in their own right, not necessarily mediated through effects on attachment security. A rich foundation of research has demonstrated that parental acceptance and responsiveness predicts positive child development outcomes (Bornstein, in Vol. 1 of this *Handbook*), including greater sociability (Clarke-Stewart, 1973), self-regulation (Grolnick and Farkas, in Vol. 5 of this *Handbook*), prosocial behavior (Eisenberg and Valiente, in Vol. 5 of this *Handbook*, Rothbaum, 1988), self-esteem (Loeb, Horst, and

Horton, 1980), and constructive play (Alessandri, 1992). Parental behaviors indicative of a lack of responsivity or availability, by contrast, have been prospectively linked with a variety of maladaptive outcomes, including social withdrawal (Bakeman and Brown, 1980), aggression (Egeland, Pianta, and O'Brien, 1993), and attention deficit disorder (Jacobitz and Sroufe, 1987).

Understanding the effects of children's relationships with others on their functioning is not simply a matter of the conditions of immediate interaction, especially when close relationships are involved (e.g., parents, children, spouses, and very close friends). For example, the effects of breaking emotional bonds on individuals are pronounced and painful (Bowlby, 1973, 1980). The effects of loss of a relationship characterized by a close emotional bond may have a persisting and long-lasting impact on an individual's adjustment, whether the loss occurs due to death, departure, or other circumstances. On the other hand context matters, so the availability of alternative attachment figures and other conditions of the situation importantly affect adjustment outcomes for the individual when loss occurs (Bowlby, 1980).

Moreover, examination of parenting practices associated with attachment security has largely been limited to constructs associated with sensitive responsiveness, but the results with regard to the prediction of attachment security suggest no more than moderate relations. Clearly, other family influences must be taken into account in order to more completely predict attachment security. Accordingly, there are increasing calls to broaden the purview of the study of the parenting and family determinants of attachment (Belsky, 1999; Cowan, 1997; DeWolff and van IJzendoorn, 1997; Thompson, 1997).

Cross-cultural Perspectives on Attachment

While many of the clinical observations influencing the development of attachment theory were based on samples from Western cultures (Bowlby, 1969, 1973), observational study of attachment security in naturalistic contexts and initial exploration of the tripartite classification of attachment (i.e., secure, avoidant, and resistant) began with Ainsworth's work among the Ganda in Africa (van IJzendoorn and Sagi, 1999). Thus, an interest in cross-cultural perspectives has characterized attachment research from the beginning. Moreover, the pertinence of cross-cultural perspectives is evident in Bowlby's theorizing. He conceptualized attachment as promoting evolutionary fitness. He also introduced the corresponding notions of the universality of an innate bias by infants to become attached and for parental sensitivity and emotional availability to be predictive of children's confidence in the use of the parents as a secure base.

The extent of attachment research conducted across cultures is impressive, especially in comparison to the modest incidence of cross-cultural research for other dimensions of family functioning. In addition to the extensive research based on predominately European or European American samples, a substantial body of work has been based on cultures from other parts of the world, including Japan, Israel, China, Columbia, Chile, and several African cultures. This cross-cultural data base is an admirable contribution to family research, although the number of cultures that have been studied must be regarded as relatively modest in relation to the worldwide domain of different cultures (van IJzendoorn and Sagi, 1999).

Cross-cultural research can be seen as generally supporting the validity of the basic propositions of attachment theory. Attachment phenomena are readily observed across cultures, for example, the child's use of the parents as a secure base. Moreover, the different patterns of attachment found in Western cultures are generally found elsewhere and appear to as adequately describe the domain of attachments in non-Western cultures as in Western cultures. It would also appear that secure attachments are not just a Western ideal, but are normative and preferred across cultures. Finally, while the evidence to date is relatively scant, parental sensitivity has been linked with secure attachment in virtually all cultures in which statistically significant results are found (van IJzendoorn and Sagi, 1999).

However, cross-cultural research can also been interpreted as raising challenges for attachment theory. For example, the distributions of insecure attachments (i.e., avoidant and resistant), in partic- ular, has been reported to vary across cultures. However, the more significant question for attachment theory is whether variations in attachment patterns follow from variations in parenting consistent with the predictions of attachment theory. This level of analysis has hardly been explored, especially with regard to the prediction of different patterns of insecure attachment (Waters and Cummings, 2000).

Fathers and Attachment

The bulk of research on parenting and attachment is concerned with mother–child attachment, and one of the most important omissions in the field is the relative lack of attention to fathers and attachment (Cowan, 1997). Nonetheless, enough research has been conducted on fathers and attachment to warrant certain conclusions. First, the evidence suggests that children are equally likely to form secure attachments to fathers and mothers. In fact, the distribution of secure, insecure-avoidant and insecure-resistant attachments is remarkably similar for mothers and fathers (Colin, 1996). Second, while most studies fail to find associations between a child's secure versus insecure attachments to mother and father, a different picture emerges when the results of available studies are combined and subjected to meta-analysis, which is a statistical way of attempting to bring order to a large body of findings. Based on data from an earlier meta-analysis conducted by Fox, Kimmerly and Schafer (1991), plus the findings of more recent studies, van IJzendoorn and De Wolff (1997) reported evidence for a modest, but statistically significant, similarity between attachment security to mothers and fathers. Nonetheless, the conclusion supported by these results was that attachment security does not substantially generalize across relationships and that infant security is largely relationship specific (van IJzendoorn and De Wolff, 1997). Third, while most studies individually have not found a significant effect of fathering on the security of infant–father attachments, a different picture emerged when van IJzendoorn and De Wolff (1997) combined the data from all of the available studies on this question and subjected them to a meta-analysis. That is, a small, but statistically significant relation between paternal sensitivity and infant–father attachment was found. Notably, however, this association was weaker than the relation that has been reported in meta-analyses of relations between maternal sensitivity and the security of infant–mother attachment (De Wolff and van IJzendoorn, 1997).

Attachment and Family Functioning

A cornerstone of modern developmental theory is that children's functioning, including their dyadic relationships, are nested within broader contexts, with the family being the most significant (Belsky, 1984). Bowlby (1949) was among the first to call attention to the need to consider the family in understanding children's distress and security. These influences may affect children directly through exposure or through their effects on parenting, including attachment (Davies and Cummings, 1994). Owen and Cox (1997) demonstrated negative effects of marital conflict on parental behaviors that influenced the development of attachment over time (e.g., sensitivity) and effects of exposure to parental conflict behaviors on disorganized/disoriented attachment. Effects of the quality of marital relations on children's functioning, as well as on attachment and other dimensions of parenting, indicate that marital relations merit consideration as an influence on children's emotional security (Cummings, Goeke-Morey and Graham, in press; Davies and Cummings, 1994).

Thus, emphasis has been placed on the need to consider broader family influences to better understand and predict children's development as a function of parenting (Belsky, 1984; Cummings and Davies, 1994). Moreover, evidence of links between attachment and marital functioning, and processes of child and family functioning common to each (e.g., inappropriate caregiving of adults in stressful family contexts and heightened proneness to anxiety and emotional dysregulation regulation in response to family stresses) is accumulating (Belsky, 1999; Cummings and Davies, 1994; Davies and Cummings, 1994, 1998; Harold and Shelton, 2000). The next step is to move to more complex and sophisticated models for the processes and factors that mediate and moderate children's development in terms of a family-wide model of influences (Cummings et al., 2000).

Accordingly, it is important to consider the impact of the quality of marital relations on mediational processes related to attachment security and, more broadly, children's sense of emotional security with regard to family functioning. Byng-Hall (1999) has posited an extension of the notion of emotional security to the family as a whole. Thus, he stressed the importance to children's well-being of a reliable family network and a secure family base, with a shared awareness among family members that attachments should be protected and not undermined. A family-wide perspective on children's emotional security takes into account effects on children's emotional security due to parent–child attachment, the quality of marital relations, and other family factors (see Cummings and Davies, 1996).

A key is to precisely specify and operationalize multiple processes of children's psychological functioning so that family-level analysis of effects is possible (Cummings and Davies, 1994; Cummings et al., 2000). One direction with regard to secure base processes pertinent to attachment has been to characterize children's emotional security as a function of specific and measurable emotional, cognitive, and behavioral regulatory processes in a manner that permits examination of how children's emotional security is simultaneously affected as a function of multiple family influences (e.g., parent–child relationships and marital relations; Davies and Cummings, 1994; Sroufe and Waters, 1977; Waters and Cummings, 2000). For example, in a preliminary test of this model, Davies and Cummings (1998) reported evidence to support emotional reactivity and representations of family relations as subprocesses of emotional security that mediated children's adjustment (see also Harold and Shelton, 2000).

Processes Mediating the Effects of Attachment

Sroufe et al. (1999) have noted that Bowlby's formulation of attachment theory is fundamentally a theory of process rather than a theory of outcome. Bowlby proposed that attachment develops as a function of a dynamic process of daily person by environment interactions that accumulate in their effects over time (Cicchetti and Cohen, 1995).

A logical extension of this perspective for parenting research is to further investigate the emotional, cognitive, and social processes that mediate and moderate children's outcomes over time. Acknowledging the multiplicity of pathways and processes leading to developmental outcomes requires the use of multiple, rather than single, mediator models. For example, emotional reactivity and representations of family relationships have been identified as mediators of the effects of marital conflict on children's development (Davies and Cummings, 1998).

Self-regulatory processes. Exemplifying a process-oriented direction, Bowlby delineated the role of self-regulatory processes toward understanding the mechanisms underlying the effects of attachment on children's functioning. In particular, emotional reactions reflecting children's evaluations of events have been conceptualized as playing a role in organizing and motivating their responses to these events, a point subsequently expanded by later theorists (Carlson and Sroufe, 1995; Davies and Cummings, 1994, 1998; Sroufe and Waters, 1977). Over time, these emotionally based self-regulatory patterns, which reflect the relative security or insecurity afforded by their experiential histories with parents in multiple situations, were seen as characterizing children's functioning in response to current experiences. That is, these processes reflect internal self-regulatory structures derived from experience that serve to guide current responding. As articulated by Carlson and Sroufe (1995, p. 594):

From a developmental perspective, these self-regulatory structures and mechanisms are viewed as characteristic modes of affect regulation and associated expectations, attitudes, and beliefs internalized from patterns of dyadic interaction. . . . These processes, or internalized "models" (Bowlby, 1980), serve not as static traits, but as guides to ongoing social interaction, supporting the maintenance of existing patterns of adaptation. What is incorporated from the caregiving experience are not specific behavioral features, but the quality and patterning of relationships, as mediated by affect. . . . Such processes are of great theoretical and practical importance, not only because they may explain continuity in individual development but also because they may lead to an understanding of pathogenesis itself.

This direction, while not endorsed by all attachment researchers, is consistent with other work that demonstrates that self-regulatory processes may mediate relations between children's emotional experiences with their parents and developmental outcomes (e.g., Campos, Campos, and Barrett, 1989; Cole, Michel, and Teti, 1994; Eisenberg et al., 1996; Thompson, 1994). For example, Eisenberg and her colleagues have stressed the role of children's regulatory capacities in accounting for relations between familial experiences (e.g., parents' positive or negative emotional expressivity toward the child), children's temperament, and children's social competence and risk for adjustment problems (Eisenberg and Valiente, in Vol. 5 of this *Handbook*). Relatedly, there is increasing evidence that children's self-regulatory capacities are influenced by their relationships with parents (Kochanska, Murray, and Coy, 1997).

Finally, with regard to a family-wide perspective on processes associated with emotional security, children's reduced capacities to regulate negative emotionality in the face of family stresses have been linked with histories of marital conflict and attachment security on the one hand, and risk for adjustment problems on the other hand (Davies and Cummings, 1998; Harold and Shelton, 2000). For example, children's emotional regulatory processes have emerged as a consistent correlate of marital conflict histories and as a mediator of relations between marital conflict histories and children's adjustment (Cummings, 1998; Cummings and Davies, 1994). However, these directions in research are in an early stage of investigation in terms of the confirmation of causal pathways based on theoretical models (Cummings and Davies, 1996).

These results from attachment and other parenting research and theory underscore the active role of children in regulating and directing their own development and functioning. Davies and Cummings (1994) proposed that emotional security is a set goal for regulatory processes surrounding the child's appraisals of felt security in the context of everyday functioning. This emotional-security model thus posits that children's affective regulatory processes serve an appraisal and guidance function in directing reactions to everyday events (see also Campos, Mumme, Kermoian, and Campos, 1994). Moreover, children's sense of emotional security is seen as reflecting both past and current contexts of experience (e.g., marital conflict and parenting) and as serving to organize, motivate, and direct children's reactions to immediate contexts of experience (e.g., whether or not the child decides to mediate in an interparental dispute). Furthermore, children's sense of emotional security is the product of multiple family experiences, including exposure to marital interactions and parenting. Accordingly, the construct of emotional security as conceptualized by Davies and Cummings reflects the extension of a core psychological construct based on attachment theory to a family-wide model of the origins and implications of these psychological processes as mediators of children's development over time (Cummings et al., 2000).

Cognitive representation and internal working models.   Another process-oriented direction given emphasis by Bowlby was the cognitive processes, or "internal working models," that mediate relations between experiential histories with caregivers and child outcomes. This direction of attachment theory reflected the impact of cognitive psychology as another eclectic influence on Bowlby's development of attachment theory (Thompson, 1998, 2000). The issue is how children represent and organize their cognitions about themselves and their relationships with others as a function of experience with their parents and other attachment figures, particularly in times of stress, and how expectancies about the availability and responsivity of parents and others affect their ongoing functioning. Bowlby's (1969, 1973) hypothesis was that early relationship experiences with parents would lead over time to generalized expectations about the self, the world, and others. While these "internal working models" were expected to emerge in some form very early in development, they were expected to continue to evolve as a function of attachment-related experiences throughout development.

Accumulating evidence suggests that cognitions that result from children's experiences with attachment figures have considerable promise as another avenue toward understanding mediating processes that underlie children's socioemotional development (Main, Kaplan, and Cassidy, 1985; Oppenheim, Emde, and Warren, 1997; Thompson, 2000). Internal representations may mediate the impact of consistent family circumstances on the continuity of developmental trajectories, or, alternatively, changing internal representations due to changing family circumstances may mediate discontinuity in developmental pathways. For example, whereas attachment may be stable over time, early attachment would not be expected to predict later attachment if family circumstances, and consequently internal representations, changed over time (Sroufe et al., 1999). Moreover, children's positive versus negative representations have been found to relate to the quality of mother–child, father–child, and marital relationships (Shamir, Du Rocher-Schudlich, and Cummings, 2000). Thompson (2000) identified several key questions for future research, including:

(1) What are the relations between children's development of episodic memory, event representation, social cognition, and other cognitive capacities and change over time in internal working models?
(2) When during development are internal working models most susceptible to emergence or change as a function of attachment experiences?
(3) How do other developing systems of thought (e.g., personal beliefs related to ability and competence) affect the development of internal working models of attachment relationships?

Another promising research direction is the identification of social-information processing patterns as explanatory processes in the link between negative parent–child emotionality and children's adjustment. For example, adverse parenting may foster negative attribution styles about parent–child relationships that are subsequently used as a blueprint or lens for processing peer events and relationships. Proclivities toward hostile evaluations and response tendencies by children, in turn, have been proposed to increase children's susceptibility to poor peer relationships, aggression, social isolation, and depression (see Crick and Dodge, 1994, for a review). Notably, explorations of social information processing "steps" as mediators of parenting have largely been confined to more negative parenting practices. Thus, a gap in research is the exploration of these social cognitive processes as possible mediators between positive parenting practices and positive child adjustment, and the extension of these constructs to the study of social cognitive processes as mediators of the effects of marital functioning on children's development.

As we have seen, emotional regulatory and cognitive representational processes arising from parent–child interactions in the context of the attachment relationship have been posited to generalize over time to affect functioning in other contexts. Moreover, with regard to intergenerational transmission, parents' experiential history may affect their parenting, in turn affecting their children (Bowlby, 1973; Bretherton and Munholland, 1999). Cummings and Davies (1996) further explicated the emotional, behavioral, and cognitive regulatory and representational processes that mediate relations between attachment and other family relationships and child outcomes over time, including tests of this multiple process model for mediators of relations between marital functioning and child development (Davies and Cummings, 1998; Harold and Shelton, 2000). Although a theoretical foundation is in place, there is need for further testing of such elaborated process-oriented models in the context of prospective longitudinal research designs, including the explicit consideration of multiple mediators and moderators of children's functioning (Cummings et al., 2000; Sroufe et al., 1999; Waters, Weinfield, and Hamilton, 2000).

PATHWAYS OF DEVELOPMENT

The issue of continuity and change in attachment over time raises core issues for conceptualizing attachment as a parenting influence on children's development. In middle-income homes, relatively high levels of stability have been reported in attachment in infancy in most studies, although there are notable exceptions (Belsky, Campbell, Cohn, and Moore, 1996). Stability is substantially lower in risk samples or samples in which family or other circumstances change significantly, even over relatively short periods of time in infancy (Waters et al., 2000). One explanation is that such cases evidence "lawful discontinuity," or changes that follow predictably based on attachment theory from changes in infants' experiences.

However, it is also possible that instances of continuity reflect stability of environment as well as stability of attachment. The current status of the literature does not permit definitive answers to these questions, although the weight of evidence would appear to support attachment theory predictions at least over short periods of time and during infancy. On the other hand, as we will see below, a variety of conceptual and empirical considerations bear on interpretation, even in the case of tests of short-term stability.

However, aside from matters of documenting continuity or discontinuity in attachment over time, or the bases or explanations for change, a critical issue for process-oriented explanations of the cumulative impact of parenting on children's functioning is to account for *how* development occurs over time. In this regard, attachment theorists have made headway in how to conceptualize complex processes of development, including the interaction among and between multiple intra- and extraorganismic influences on children's development. Bowlby led the way in these conceptualizations, which have been further articulated by Sroufe and Cicchetti, among others (see Cummings et al., 2000).

Human development can be considered in terms of various metaphors (see Bowlby, 1973). Sroufe (1990, 1997) has proposed a branching tree metaphor for the multiple pathways individuals may follow during the course of their development. In terms of this metaphor, one may think of relatively normal development as reflected by continuous growth at or near the trunk of the tree. Pathways involving large groups of individuals are represented as large branches diverging only slightly from the tree trunk and reflecting approximations of "normality." As development proceeds, the growth of ever smaller branches represents more differentiated pathways of progressively smaller groups of individuals. Abnormality is reflected by a succession of branchings away from the main body of the tree so that some distance develops between the tree trunk and the branches. When these branches diverge greatly from the tree, they can be seen as representing substantial deviation from common pathways. However, after initial divergence, secondary branches may actually grow closer to its major branch or other major branches, thus representing the potential of individuals to achieve a common outcome despite following different pathways at the outset.

Several assumptions useful to a process-oriented conceptualization of development are illustrated by this metaphor. One is that the organism and the context that supports the organism are inseparable, just as the growth of a tree cannot be separated from the environmental circumstances that support (or fail to adequately support) its growth. That is, development is a complex function of interrelations between the child and environment over time. Moreover, continuities may be due to stabilities in the organization of the environment that supports continuity over time, or stabilities in the organization processes that support consistency of attachment security within the child, or both.

Thus, attachment theorists have proposed ways of thinking about how human development can be seen as reflecting changes that develop over time (Weinfeld, Sroufe, Egeland, and Carlson, 1999). That is, processes of normal or abnormal functioning do not just appear, just as a branch on a tree does not grow disembodied from the tree. Rather, normal or abnormal growth or development occurs gradually over time as a function of the mutual influences amongst intra- and extraorganismic factors, building on the growth (i.e., development) that has occurred before, but also responding continually to present and future conditions. Thus, for example, when childhood disorder occurs, it typically reflects repeated failures to adapt optimally over time (i.e., maladaptation) with respect to the issues facing children during development. Moreover, in positing a living, growing, and changing organism, the tree metaphor also communicates that one must consider interactional, historical, and contextual factors when assessing the pattern of a child's development. That is, the relative normality or abnormality of the child's development is a function of many past, current, and, ultimately, future transactions between the child and the environment. In addition, there is always the possibility of change, so dysfunctional individuals may begin to function more adaptively over time. Accordingly, the branch may grow back toward the main body of the tree.

A focus on the multidirectionality of development reflects more than a different set of assumptions about the number of possible pathways of development; it also reflects a correspondingly sophisticated conceptualization of the causes of development. For example, unidirectional models proceed on the assumption that there is a single proximal cause to child development. Thus, at its heart, the present direction in the conceptualization of developmental processes emerging from one tradition in attachment theory provides avenues toward more complex models for how to understand human development, rather than more simplistic models of single proximate causes, or template or prototype models. For example, process-oriented models might posit that continuity or change in cognitive representations, emotional regulation, and physiological functioning as a function of complex transactions with experiential contexts during development underlie continuity or change in attachment. By contrast, a unidirectional model might predict, for example, that cognitive representations are the sole determinant of continuity or change in attachment. A template model, for example, might predict that attachment at a first time of assessment (Time 1) necessarily predicts attachment at a second time of assessment (Time 2).

Bowlby's emphasis on the importance of early parent–child attachments is sometimes mistaken to mean that Bowlby viewed early attachments as fixed prototypes that influence later development in the manner similar to that of a personality trait (Waters et al., 2000). On the contrary, current attachment theory and research posit a model for the influence of attachment as a dynamic process over the course of development, which may be characterized by either continuity or change as a function of ongoing and continuing processes of interaction between the individual and context. Thus, Bowlby (1973, p. 364) wrote that the development of the child "turns at each and every stage of the journey on an interaction between the organism as it has developed up to the moment and the environment in which it finds itself." While it is expected that existing structures and organizations of children's functioning, particularly the initial organizations on which later development is built (i.e., infant attachment), will tend to persist (Main et al., 1985), the child will reorganize functioning when confronted with persisting or significant challenges to current organizations. For example, a child with a secure attachment to the parent may later develop an insecure attachment if significant changes occur in the interactional relations between parents and children (e.g., the parent becomes increasingly unavailable emotionally due to the onset of chronic depression).

Considerable research has emerged to support the notion that attachments can be stable over short periods of time, although the evidence is not consistent or always supportive of the proposition (Belsky, 1999). However, given the sophisticated model for human development posited by Bowlby, and further refined and articulated in recent years by Sroufe (1997) and other theorists influenced by attachment theory (Thompson, 1999), this lack of one-to-one correspondence between attachment at Time 1 and Time 2 is not a challenge to the validity of attachment theory. As we have noted, the more significant matter is whether attachment evidences *either* continuity or "lawful discontinuities." Moreover, given the demanding requirements for assessment and research design within the context of prospective longitudinal research directions, the appearance of various apparent failures to show continuity or even lawful discontinuity is by no means conclusive. One cannot support or refute process models by accepting the null hypothesis, that is, interpreting nonfindings as having a deter- minative meaning. Studies have rarely met requirements for adequate examination of the operation of mediating and moderating processes in the context of prospective, longitudinal research designs (see Cummings et al., 2000). Evidence of significant effects that directly contradict the predictions of attachment theory, which is a far more serious challenge to the tenets of developmental models inspired by attachment theory, is rare or nonexistent.

It is informative to consider tests of the continuity of attachment over long periods of time, as such research bears on the interpretation of attachment as a long-term parental influence on children's development. Studies of the development of attachment over the span of childhood have reported both continuity and discontinuity from infancy to adulthood. For example, Waters, Merrick, Treboux, Crowell, and Albersheim (2000) reported that attachment security in infancy predicted attachment security in adulthood. Moreover, negative life events (i.e., parental divorce, parental psychopathology, loss of parent, the life-threatening illness of parent or child, or abuse) were important predictors when change in attachment classification occurred. Thus, 56% of children with negative life events during their childhood evidenced changes in attachment classifications from infancy to early adulthood. On the other hand, only 28% without such events changed classifications (Hamilton, 2000, reported similar findings). By contrast, in a prospective, longitudinal study based on a sample initially chosen because of high family adversity (e.g., poverty and high risk for poor developmental outcome), Weinfield, Sroufe, and Egeland (2000) found no continuity in attachment security between infancy and adulthood. However, lawful discontinuity was reported; that is, changes in attachments were linked with difficulties in family circumstances (e.g., maternal depression and problems in family functioning in early adolescence). Given that many individuals changed from secure to insecure attachment classifications over the span of this study and many faced adverse family environments, the results also support that persistently chaotic and difficult life experiences undermine the possibility of secure attachment.

Although several studies support pathways of development as hypothesized by attachment theory, they only begin to address other elements of this complex framework. In particular, initial longitudinal studies focus primarily on the assessment of attachment at the end points of infancy and adulthood, and on family and life circumstances assessed at a relatively global level of analysis. Thus, we are left with many questions to ponder about the specific *processes* (e.g., emotional or other regulatory processes, and cognitive processes of representation) that mediate continuity or change in pathways of development across childhood. In addition, these and other studies call attention to the importance of family variables other than parent–child interactions to child outcomes (Davies and Cummings, 1994). Thus, it is increasingly evident that it is necessary to examine broader family functioning (e.g., other dimensions of parenting, marital relationships, sibling relationships, relations with extended family members, changes in family constellations, and ethnicity and culture as contexts for family functioning) in order to account more fully for attachment as an important aspect of parenting (Dunn, 1993; Parke and Buriel, 1998; Rutter and O'Connor, 1999).

One long-term prospective study of the course of attachment from infancy to adulthood adds support to this perspective. Lewis et al. (2000) examined attachment patterns at 12 months and 18 years of age, and also other aspects of child and family functioning in the period between 1 and 18 years. Lewis et al. reported no continuity between quality of attachment over this time span, although quality of attachment at 18 years was related to adjustment at 18 years. On the other hand, divorce, which might be expected to influence the quality of family functioning and parent– child relationships, was significantly related to insecure attachment status at 18 years, as well as the relative positivity versus negativity of childhood recollections recorded at 13 years of age. These results underscore the potential significance of broader family relationships, particularly mar- ital relationships, to quality of attachment as well as to other aspects of children's functioning. At the same time, for reasons already described, it cannot be concluded necessarily that attachment was not stable or, alternatively, did not evidence lawful discontinuity over this period.

In summary, classical and modern research has explored relations between parenting behaviors and attachment security, cross-cultural variations in attachment, and fathers and attachment. Exciting emerging directions in research that offer promise for breakthroughs in understanding in the future are also evident. One direction in research is concerned with more fully explicating effects on children's development by taking a family-wide perspective on the origins of children's emotional security and the intersection between attachment and nonattachment-related family influences. Relatedly, researchers are moving beyond documenting bivariate relations between attachment security and child outcomes toward articulating the processes within the child that are set in motion by attachment and attachment-related experiences. Achieving understanding at the level of children's dynamic processes of functioning in day-to-day interaction will significantly advance the articulation of patterns of causal influence. Directions toward specifying children's individual development in terms of pathways of development over time promise to advance further the richness of understanding of patterns of causal influence associated with attachment and attachment-related influences. The upshot is that the diverse and sophisticated directions in research inspired by attachment theory continue to make exciting contributions to understanding of relations between parenting and child development.

FUTURE DIRECTIONS IN ATTACHMENT AND PARENTING

This chapter has focused as much on future directions for research on attachment and parenting as on themes of past research. Thus, the future directions we describe clearly have roots in past and current traditions of attachment theory and research. The present chapter calls attention to the fact that attachment-inspired research is in a dynamic phase of growth and development, with numerous promising directions for advancing understanding (Thompson, 2000; Waters and Cummings, 2000).

A particular matter merits emphasis in the context of the present *Handbook of Parenting*: the fact that little intersection is evident between directions in the study of attachment as parenting and other conceptualizations of parenting styles and practices. This reflects a gap in attachment research but also reflects a gap in the research of those who are *not* attachment researchers. Thus, it is important to encourage both more differentiated and integrative considerations of parenting across multiple approaches to the investigations of parenting as an influence on child development (Cummings et al., 2000).

Two relatively broad dimensions of parenting can be distinguished, one pertaining to parenting as behavioral or psychological control and child management (i.e., control) and the other related to parenting as acceptance, emotional availability, sensitivity, and parent–child emotional bond or attachment (i.e., emotional relationship); Cummings and Davies, 1994; Cummings et al., 2000). Awareness of the distinct nature of these two parenting dimensions, and the need for a more integrative study of these dimensions, can potentially lead to more advanced understanding of the influences of parenting on child development. A gap in attachment research is the need for more study of parenting as psychological control and child management. As Baumrind (1971) has indicated (see also Maccoby and Martin, 1983), one ideally must examine both of these major dimensions of parenting in order to fully understand the effects of either dimension of parenting on child development.

For example, although each of these parenting dimensions shares significant variance in predicting individual differences in children's externalizing problems, internalizing symptoms, and competence, each dimension also has unique effects on child adjustment (e.g., Herman, Dornbusch, Herron, and Herting, 1997). Child internalizing symptoms are the most consistent sequelae of high levels of parental psychological control, whereas high parental behavioral control (e.g., consistent monitoring and firm discipline) is related, most commonly, to lower levels of externalizing symptoms (Barber, 1996, 1997); harsh and inconsistent control are often associated with conduct problems (e.g., Patterson, DeBaryshe, and Ramsey, 1989). Dimensions pertaining to the parent–child emotional relationship have been found to predict a wide range of adjustment problems.

Changing the research landscape about parenting to advance parenting models that are more adequate to the task of contributing to explanations of child development in families also requires examining a multiplicity of influences, developmental pathways, and ecological contexts (Parke and Buriel, 1998). As Clarke-Stewart (1988, p. 65) put it, "we no longer assume that parents' effects on children's development are simple, one-sided, or powerful . . . We have opened up a complexity by demonstrating the contributions of the child and context to development by tapping into an apparent myriad of factors in each of the three categories—parent, child, and context." Attachment research embodies one of the most influential and significant directions in the study of how parent–child relationships affect children's development. A challenge for future attachment research and other directions in parenting research is to construct more complete, inclusive, and integrative models toward more explanatory perspectives on how parents and children's relationships operate and affect each others' well-being and development.

CONCLUSION

In examining the model for parenting presented by attachment theory, we have outlined the historical origins and assumptions of the theory with regard to attachment as parenting, examined key directions in research toward explicating relations between parenting and attachment, and considered the generality of its principles as applied to fathers and attachment, and attachment from a cross-cultural perspective. Returning to the question, "How can parents grow a securely attached child?" we can certainly conclude that parental sensitivity and emotional availability foster attachment security and that such security provides a important foundation for children's healthy psychological development. On the other hand, it remains that parental sensitivity and emotional availability require more precise definition and may yet be better differentiated as they pertain to attachment security (Easterbrooks and Biringen, 2000). Moreover, relations between attachment security and maternal sensitivity are moderate, with apparently weaker associations between attachment security and paternal sensitivity.

Thus, with regard to the goal of communicating to parents how to "grow" a securely attached child, much more needs to be learned. One promising direction is to examine the contributors to attachment security from a systemic perspective. Clearly, high-quality marital relations are likely to improve the odds for the development of secure parent–child attachment and children's sense of emotional security. Moreover, security of attachment to fathers may improve the likelihood of attachment security to the mothers, and vice versa. Greater consideration of children's characteristics and the characteristics of the ecological context beyond the family will improve understanding of how to foster attachment security.

The practice of examining bivariate relations between markers for attachment, parenting, and markers for children's functioning can only advance understanding to a limited extent. Thus, another key for future advances is to articulate the processes that mediate effects of parents on children in the context of sophisticated family models, taking into account multiple elements of family, child, and ecological context. Moreover, it is critical to begin to understand how these processes unfold over time in terms of individual pathways of development.

Attachment researchers and theorists have contributed mightily to the conceptual and methodological tools for advancing process-oriented research on children's development. Given that many of these directions in family research are in a relatively early stage of development, it can hardly be surprising that our understanding of how to grow a securely attached child, while resting on a firm foundation in terms of the parental sensitivity construct, leaves much left to be explained. On the other hand, there is no shortage of exciting leads for future advances.

In closing, perhaps the key question is not how to grow a securely attached child, but how attachment informs our understanding of how to grow healthy, happy, and competent children. Thus, ultimately, it is most important for attachment researchers to contextualize attachment in terms of other parenting and family influences, just as it is critical for family researchers from other parenting traditions to include attachment. The challenges for research and theory are substantial, but the promise for the future welfare of children is well worth the effort.

ACKNOWLEDGMENTS

Preparation of this paper was supported in part by grants HD 36261 from the National Institute of Child Health and Human Development and MH57318 from the National Institute of Mental Health.

REFERENCES

Ainsworth, M. D. S. (1962). The effects of maternal deprivation: A review of findings and controversy in the context of research strategy. In *Deprivation of maternal care: A reassessment of its effect* (Public Health Paper No. 14). Geneva, Switzerland: World Health Organization.

Ainsworth, M. D. S. (1967). *Infancy in Uganda: Infant care and the growth of love*. Baltimore: Johns Hopkins University Press.

Ainsworth, M. D. S. (1969). Object relations, dependency, and attachment: A theoretical review of the infant–mother attachment relationship. *Child Development, 40*, 969–1025.

Ainsworth, M. D. S. (1982). Attachment: Retrospect and prospect. In C. M. Parkes and J. Stevenson-Hinde (Eds.), *The place of attachment in human behavior* (pp. 3–30). New York: Basic Books.

Ainsworth, M. D. S., Blehar, M. C., Waters, E., and Wall, S. (1978). *Patterns of attachment: A psychological study of the Strange Situation*. Hillsdale, NJ: Lawrence Erlbaum Associates.

Alessandri, S. M. (1992). Mother–child interactional correlates of maltreated and nonmaltreated children's play behavior. *Development and Psychopathology, 4*, 257–270.

Allen, J. P., and Land, D. (1999). Attachment in adolescence. In J. Cassidy and P. Shaver (Eds.), *Handbook of attachment* (pp. 319–335). New York: Guilford .

Bakeman, R., and Brown, J. V. (1980). Early interaction: Consequences of social and mental development at three years. *Child Development, 51*, 437–447.

Barber, B. K. (1996). Parental psychological control: Revisiting a neglected construct. *Child Development, 67*, 3296–3319.

Barber, B. K. (1997). Introduction: Adolescent socialization in context—The role of connection, regulation, and autonomy in the family. *Journal of Adolescent Research, 12*, 5–11.

Baumrind, D. (1971). Current patterns of parental authority. *Developmental Psychology Monograph, 4*.

Belsky, J. (1984). The determinants of parenting: A process model. *Child Development, 55*, 83–96.

Belsky, J. (1999). Interactional and contextual determinants of attachment security. In J. Cassidy and P. Shaver (Eds.), *Handbook of attachment* (pp. 249–264). New York: Guilford.

Belsky, J., Campbell, S. B., Cohn, J. F., and Moore, G. (1996). Instability of infant–parent attachment security. *Developmental Psychology, 32*, 921–924.

Belsky, J., Rovine, M., and Taylor, D. G. (1984). The Pennsylvania Infant and Family Development Project, 3: The origins of individual differences in infant–mother attachment: Maternal and infant contributions. *Child Development, 55*, 718–728.

Bornstein, M. H., and Tamis-LeMonda, C. S. (1990). Activities and interactions of mothers and their firstborn infants in the first six months of life: Covariation, stability, continuity, correspondence, and prediction. *Child Development, 61*, 1206–1217.

Bowlby, J. (1949). The study and reduction of group tensions in the family. *Human Relations, 2*, 123–128.

Bowlby, J. (1951). Maternal care and mental health. *Bulletin of the World Health Organization, 3*, 355–533.

Bowlby, J. (1958). The nature of the child's tie to his mother. *International Journal of Psychoanalysis, 39*, 350–373.

Bowlby, J. (1969). *Attachment and loss: Vol. 1. Attachment*. New York: Basic Books.

Bowlby, J. (1973). *Attachment and loss: Vol. 2. Separation*. New York: Basic Books.

Bowlby, J. (1980). *Attachment and loss: Vol. 3. Loss, sadness, and depression*. New York: Basic Books.

Bretheron, I., and Munholland, K. A. (1999). Internal working models in attachment relationships: A construct revisited. In J. Cassidy and P. R. Shaver (Eds.), *Handbook of Attachment* (pp. 89–114). New York: Guilford.

Byng-Hall, J. (1999). Family couple therapy: Toward greater security. In J. Cassidy and P. R. Shaver (Eds.), *Handbook of attachment* (pp. 625–645). New York: Guilford.

Campos, J. J., Campos, R. G., and Barrett, K. C. (1989). Emergent themes in the study of emotional development and emotion regulation. *Developmental Psychology, 25*, 394–402.

Campos, J. J., Mumme, D. L., Kermoian, R., and Campos, R. G. (1994). Commentary: A functionalist perspective on the nature of emotion. In N. Fox (Ed.), The development of emotion regulation: Biological and behavioral considerations, *Monographs of the Society for Research in Child Development, 59* (2–3, Serial No. 240), 284–303.

Carlson, E. A., and Sroufe, L. A. (1995). Contribution of attachment theory to developmental psychopathology. In D. Cicchetti and D. Cohen (Eds.), *Developmental psychopathology: Theory and methods* (Vol. 1, pp. 581–617). New York: Wiley.

Cassidy, J., and Shaver, P. (Eds.). (1999). *Handbook of attachment.* New York: Guilford.

Cicchetti, D., and Cohen, D. J. (1995). Perspectives on developmental psychopathology. In D. Cicchetti and D. J. Cohen (Eds.), *Developmental psychopathology: Vol. 1. Theory and methods* (pp. 3–20). New York: Wiley.

Clarke-Stewart, K. A. (1973). Interactions between mothers and their young children: Characteristics and consequences. *Monographs of the Society for Research in Child Development, 38,* (5–6 Serial No. 153).

Clarke-Stewart, K. A. (1988). Parents' effects on children's development: A decade of progress? *Journal of Applied Developmental Psychology, 9,* 41–84.

Cole, P. M., Michel, M., and Teti, L. (1994). The development of emotion regulation and dysregulation: A clinical perspective. In N. Fox (Ed.), The development of emotion regulation: Biological and behavioral considerations. *Monographs of the Society for Research in Child Development* (2–3, Serial No. 240), 73–102.

Colin, V. L. (1996). *Human attachment.* New York: McGraw-Hill.

Cowan, P. (1997). Beyond meta-analysis: A plea for a family systems view of attachment. *Child Development, 68,* 601–603.

Crick, N. R., and Dodge, K. A. (1994). A review and reformulation of social information-processing mechanisms in children's social adjustment. *Psychological Bulletin, 115,* 74–101.

Crowell, J., Fraley, R. C., and Shaver, P. (1999). Measurement of individual differences in adolescent and adult attachment. In J. Cassidy and P. Shaver (Eds.), *Handbook of attachment* (pp. 434–465). New York: Guilford.

Cummings, E. M., (1998). Children exposed to marital conflict and violence: Conceptual and theoretical directions. In G. Holden, B. Geffner, and E. Jouriles (Eds.), *Children exposed to marital violence: Theory, research, and applied issues* (pp. 55–94). Washington, DC: American Psychological Association.

Cummings, E. M., and Cicchetti, D. (1990). Towards a transactional model of relations between attachment and depression. In M. Greenberg, D. Cicchetti, and E. M. Cummings (Eds.), *Attachment in the preschool years* (pp. 339–372). Chicago: University of Chicago Press.

Cummings, E. M., and Cummings, J. S. (1988). A process-oriented approach to children's coping with adults' angry behavior. *Developmental Review, 3,* 296–321.

Cummings, E. M., and Davies, P. T. (1994). *Children and marital conflict: The impact of family dispute and resolution.* New York: Guilford.

Cummings, E .M., and Davies, P. T. (1996). Emotional security as a regulatory process in normal development and the development of psychopathology. *Development and Psychopathology, 8,* 123–139.

Cummings, E. M., Davies, P. T., and Campbell, S. B. (2000). *Developmental psychopathology and family process.* New York: Guilford.

Cummings, E. M., Goeke-Morey, M. C., and Graham, M. A. (in press). Interparental relations as a dimension of parenting: Parenting and the effects of marital conflict on children. In M. M. Bristol-Power, J. G. Borkowski, and S. L. Landesman (Eds.), *Parenting and the child's world: Multiple influences on intellectual and socio-emotional development.* Mahwah, NJ: Lawrence Erlbaum Associates.

Davies, P. T., and Cummings, E. M. (1994). Marital conflict and child adjustment: An emotional security hypothesis. *Psychological Bulletin, 116,* 387– 411.

Davies, P. T., and Cummings, E. M. (1998). Exploring children's emotional security as a mediator of the link between marital relations and child adjustment. *Child Development, 69,* 124–139.

De Wolff, M., and van IJzendoorn, M. H. (1997). Sensitivity and attachment: A meta-analysis on parental antecedents of infant attachment. *Child Development, 68,* 571–591.

Dunn, J. (1993). *Young children's close relationships: Beyond attachment.* London: Sage.

Easterbrooks, M. A., Biesecker, G., Lyons-Ruth, K. (2000). Infancy predictors of emotional availability in middle childhood: The roles of attachment security and maternal depressive symptomatology. *Attachment and Human Development, 2,* 170–187.

Easterbrooks, M. A., and Biringen, Z. (Eds.). (2000). Mapping the terrain of emotional availability and attachment [Special issue]. *Attachment and Human Development, 2.*

Egeland, B., and Farber, E. (1984). Infant–mother attachment: Factors related to its development and changes over time. *Child Development, 55,* 753–771.

Egeland, B., Pianta, R., and O'Brien, M. A. (1993). Maternal intrusiveness in infancy and child maladaptation in early school years. *Development and Psychopathology, 5,* 359–370.

Eisenberg, N., Fabes, R. A., Guthrie, I. K., Murphy, B. C., Maszk, P., Holmgren, R., and Suh, K. (1996). The relations of regulation and emotionality to problem behavior in elementary school children. *Development and Psychopathology, 8,* 141–162.

Fox, N. A., Kimmerly, N. L., and Schafer, W. D. (1991). Attachment to mother/attachment to father: A meta-analysis. *Child Development, 62,* 210–225.

Goldsmith, H. H., and Alansky, J. A. (1987). Maternal and infant temperamental predictors of attachment: A meta-analytic review. *Journal of Consulting and Clinical Psychology, 55,* 805–816.

Greenberg, M. (1999). Attachment and psychopathology in childhood. In J. Cassidy and P. and P. Shaver (Eds.). *Handbook of attachment* (pp. 469–496). New York: Guildford.

Greenberg, M., Cicchetti, D., and Cummings, E. M. (Eds.). (1990). *Attachment in the preschool years.* Chicago: University of Chicago Press.

Grossmann, K., Grossmann, K. E., Spangler, G., Suess, G., and Unzner, L. (1985). Maternal sensitivity and newborns' orientation responses as related to quality of attachment in northern Germany. In I. Bretherton and E. Waters (Eds.), Growing points in attachment theory and research. *Monographs of the Society for Research in Child Development, 50* (Serial No. 209), 233–257.

Grusec, J. E., and Goodnow, J. J. (1994). Impact of parental discipline methods on the child's internalization of values: A reconceptualization of current points of view. *Developmental Psychology, 30,* 4–19.

Hamilton, C. E. (2000). Continuity and discontinuity of attachment from infancy. *Child Development, 71,* 690–694.

Harlow, H. F., and Harlow, M. K. (1965). The affectional system. In A. M. Schrier, H. F. Harlow, and F. Stollnitz (Eds.), *Behavior of nonhuman primates* (Vol. 2, pp. 287–334). New York: Academic.

Harold, G. T., and Shelton, K. (2000, April). Testing the emotional security hypothesis: An analysis across time, gender, and culture. In G. T. Harold (Chair), Marital conflict, emotional security, and adolescent adjustment: A cross-site investigation. Paper presented at the Eighth Biennial Meeting of the Society for Research on Adolescence, Chicago, IL.

Hazan, C., and Shaver, P. R. (1987). Romantic love conceptualized as attachment process. *Journal of personality and Social Psychology, 52,* 511–524.

Hazan, C., and Shaver, P. R. (1990). Love and work: An attachment-theoretical perspective. *Journal of Personality and Social Psychology, 59,* 270–280.

Hazan, C., and Zeifman, D. (1999). Pair bonds as attachments: Evaluating the evidence. In J. Cassidy and P. Shaver (Eds.), *Handbook of attachment* (pp. 336–354). New York: Guilford.

Herman, M. R., Dornbusch, S. M., Herron, M. C., and Herting, J. R. (1997). The influence of family regulation, connection, and psychological autonomy on six measures of adolescent functioning. *Journal of Adolescent Research, 12,* 34–67.

Hesse, E. (1999). The adult attachment interview: Historical and current perspectives. In J. Cassidy and P. Shaver (Eds.), *Handbook of attachment* (pp. 395–433). New York: Guilford.

Jacobvitz, D., and Sroufe, L. A. (1987). The early caregiver–child relationship and attention deficit disorder with hyperactivity in kindergarten: A prospective study. *Child Development, 58,* 1488–1495.

Kochanska, G., Murray, K., and Coy, K. C. (1997). Inhibitory control as a contributor to conscience in childhood: From toddler to early school age. *Child Development, 68,* 263–277.

Lamb, M. E., Thompson, R. A., Gardner, W. P., and Charnov, E. L. (Eds.). (1985). *Infant–mother attachment.* Hillsdale, NJ: Lawrence Erlbaum Associates.

Lay, K., Waters, E., and Parke, K. A. (1989). Maternal responsiveness and child compliance: The role of mood as a mediator. *Child Development, 60,* 1405–1411.

Lewis, M., Feiring, C., and Rosenthal, S. (2000). Attachment over time. *Child Development, 71,* 707–720.

Loeb, R. C., Horst, L., and Horton, P. (1980). Family interaction patterns associated with self-esteem in preadolescent girls and boys. *Merrill-Palmer Quarterly, 26,* 205–217.

Londerville, S., and Main, M. (1981). Security of attachment, compliance, and maternal training methods in the second year of life. *Developmental Psychology, 17,* 289–299.

Maccoby, E., and Martin, J. (1983). Socialization in contexts of the family: Parent–child interaction. In E. M. Hetherington (Ed.), *Handbook of child psychology: Vol. 4. Socialization, personality, and social development* (4th ed., pp. 1–101). New York: Wiley.

Main, M., and Goldwyn, R. (1984). Predicting rejection of her infant from mother's representation of her own experiences: Implications for the abused–abusing intergenerational cycle. *Child Abuse and Neglect, 8,* 203–217.

Main, M., Kaplan, N., and Cassidy, J. C. (1985). Security in infancy, childhood and adulthood: A move to the level of representation. In I. Bretherton and E. Waters (Eds.), Growing points of attachment theory and research. *Monographs of the Society for Research in Child Development, 50* (1–2, Serial No. 209), 66–104.

Main, M., and Solomon, J. (1990). Procedures for identifying infants as disorganized/disoriented during the Ainsworth Strange Situation. In M. T. Greenberg, D. Cicchetti, and E. M. Cummings (Eds.), *Attachment in the preschool years* (pp. 121–160). Chicago: University of Chicago Press.

Masters, J. C., and Wellman, H. M. (1974). The study of human infant attachment: A procedural critique. *Psychological Bulletin, 81,* 218–237.

Miller, N., and Dollard, J. (1941). *Social learning and imitation.* New Haven, CT: Yale University Press.

Oppenheim, D., Emde, R. N., and Warren, S. (1997). Children's narrative representations of mothers: Their development and associations with child and mother adaptation. *Child Development, 68,* 127–138.

Owen, M. T., and Cox, M. J. (1997). Marital conflict and the development of infant–parent attachment relationships. *Journal of Family Psychology, 11,* 152–164.

Parke, R. D., and Buriel, R. (1998). Socialization in the family: Ethnic and ecological perspectives. In N. Eisenberg (Ed.), *Social, emotional and personality development* (5th ed., Vol. 3, pp. 463–552). *Handbook of child psychology.* New York: Wiley.

Patterson, G. R., DeBaryshe, B., and Ramsey, E. (1989). A developmental perspective on antisocial behavior. *American Psychologist, 44,* 329–335.

Polan, H. J., and Hofer, M. A. (1999). Psychobiological origins of infant attachment and separation responses. In J. Cassidy and P. Shaver (Eds.), *Handbook of attachment* (pp. 162–180). New York: Guilford.

Radke-Yarrow, M., Cummings, E. M., Kuczynski, L., and Chapman, M. (1985). Patterns of attachment in two- and three-year-olds in normal families and families with parental depression. *Child Development, 56,* 884–893.

Rothbaum, F. (1988). Maternal acceptance and child functioning. *Merrill-Palmer Quarterly, 34,* 163–184.

Rutter, M. (1995a). Clinical implications of attachment concepts: Retrospect and prospect. *Journal of Child Psychology and Psychiatry, 36,* 549–571.

Rutter, M. (1995b). Maternal deprivation. In M. H. Bornstein (Ed.), *Handbook of parenting: Vol. 4. Applied and practical parenting* (pp. 3–31). Mahwah, NJ: Lawrence Erlbaum Associates.

Rutter, M., and O'Connor, T. (1999). Implications of attachment theory for child care policies. In J. Cassidy and P. Shaver (Eds.), *Handbook of attachment* (pp. 823–844). New York: Guilford.

Schaffer, H. R., and Emerson, P. E. (1964). The development of social attachments in infancy. *Monographs of the Society for Research in Child Development, 29* (3, Serial No. 94).

Shamir, H., Du Rocher Schudlich, T., and Cummings, E. M. (2000). *Marital conflict and children's representations of family relationships.* Unpublished manuscript.

Simpson, J. A. (1999). Attachment theory in modern evolutionary perspective. In J. Cassidy and P. Shaver (Eds.), *Handbook of attachment* (pp. 115–140). New York: Guilford.

Speltz, M. L. (1990). The treatment of preschool conduct problems. In M. T. Greenberg, D. Cicchetti, and E. M. Cummings (Eds.), *Attachment in the preschool years: Theory, research, and intervention* (pp. 399–426). Chicago: University of Chicago Press.

Sroufe, L. A. (1990). Considering normal and abnormal together: The essence of developmental psychopathology. *Development and Psychopathology, 2,* 335–347.

Sroufe, L. A. (1997). Psychopathology as an outcome of development. *Development and Psychopathology, 9,* 251–268.

Sroufe, L. A., Carlson, E. A., Levy, A. K., and Egeland, B. (1999). Implications of attachment theory for developmental psychopathology. *Development and Psychopathology, 11,* 1–13.

Sroufe, L. A., and Waters, E. (1977). Attachment as an organizational construct. *Child Development, 48,* 1184–1199.

Stayton, D. J., Hogan, R., and Ainsworth, M. D. (1971). Infant obedience and maternal behavior: The origins of socialization reconsidered. *Child Development, 42,* 1057–1069.

Suomi, S. (1999). Attachment in rhesus monkeys. In J. Cassidy and P. Shaver (Eds.), *Handbook of attachment* (pp. 181–197). New York: Guilford.

Thompson, R. A. (1994). Emotion regulation: A theme in search of definition. In N. A. Fox (Ed.), The development of emotion regulation: Biological and behavioral considerations. *Monographs of the Society for Research in Child Development, 59*(2–3. Serial No. 240), 25–52.

Thompson, R. A. (1997). Sensitivity and security: New questions to ponder. *Child Development, 68,* 595–597.

Thompson, R. A. (1998). Early sociopersonality development. In N. Eisenberg (Ed.), *Handbook of child psychology: Vol. 3. Social, emotional and personality development* (pp. 25–104). New York: Wiley.

Thompson, R. A. (1999). Early attachment and later development. In J. Cassidy and P. Shaver (Eds.), *Handbook of attachment* (pp. 265–286). New York: Guilford.

Thompson, R. A. (2000). Legacy of early attachment. *Child Development, 71,* 145–152.

Van den Boom, D. (1994). The influence of temperament and mothering on attachment and exploration: An experimental manipulation of sensitive responsiveness among lower-class mothers with irritable infants. *Child Development, 65,* 1457–1477.

Van IJzendoorn, M. H., and DeWolff, M. S. (1997). In search of the absent father: Meta-analyses on infant–father attachment: A rejoinder to our discussion. *Child Development, 68,* 604–609.

Van IJzendoorn, M. H., and Sagi, A. (1999). Cross-cultural patterns of attachment: Universal and contextual dimensions. In J. Cassidy and P. Shaver (Eds.), *Handbook of attachment* (pp. 713–734). New York: Guilford.

Vaughn, B. E., and Bost, K. K. (1999). Attachment and temperament: Redundant, independent, or interacting influences on interpersonal adaptation and personality development? In J. Cassidy and P. Shaver (Eds.), *Handbook of attachment* (pp. 198–225). New York: Guilford.

Waters, E. (1978). The reliability and stability of individual differences in infant–mother attachment. *Child Development, 49,* 483–494.

Waters, E., and Cummings, E. M. (2000). A secure base from which to explore close relationships. *Child Development, 71,* 164–172.

Waters, E., Hamilton, C. E., and Weinfield, N. S. (2000). The stability of attachment security from infancy to adolescence and early adulthood: General introduction. *Child Development, 71,* 678–683.

Waters, E., Merrick, S., Treboux, D., Crowell, J., and Albersheim, L. (2000). Attachment security in infancy and early adulthood: A 20-year longitudinal study. *Child Development, 71*, 684–689.

Waters, E. Weinfield, N. S., and Hamilton C. (2000). The stability of attachment security from infancy to adolescence and early adulthood. *Child Development, 71*, 703–706.

Weinfield, N., Sroufe, L. A., and Egeland, B. (2000). Attachment from infancy to early adulthood in a high-risk sample. *Child Development, 71*, 695–702.

Weinfield, N., Sroufe, L. A., Egeland, B., and Carlson, E. A. (1999). The nature of individual differences in infant–caregiver attachment. In J. Cassidy and P. Shaver (Eds.), *Handbook of attachment* (pp. 68–88). New York: Guilford.

3

Recent Developments in Our Understanding of Parenting: Bidirectional Effects, Causal Models, and the Search for Parsimony

Gerald R. Patterson
Philip A. Fisher
Oregon Social Learning Center

INTRODUCTION

In the last few decades, the study of parenting practices has acquired many of the characteristics of a growth industry. The situation is exemplified by the huge number of publications appearing in an array of scientific journals and the highly visible four-volume series with the title *Handbook of Parenting* (Bornstein, 1995). The revision of this series is a testament to the demand for scientific information about parenting.

Parenting variables occupy a prominent place in modern empirically based studies ranging in focus from studies of crime (Farrington and Hawkins, 1991; Gottfredson and Hirschi, 1990; Loeber and Dishion, 1983; Patterson, Forgatch, Yoerger, and Stoolmiller, 1998; Sampson and Laub, 1993) to the development of cognitive processes (Fagot and Gauvain, 1997; Sternberg and Williams, 1995) and studies of academic achievement skills (DeBaryshe, Patterson, and Capaldi, 1993; Steinberg, Elman, and Mounts, 1989).

At the present time, studies of parenting practices are in transition; they are moving from a sole reliance upon correlational models to the use of experimental manipulations to test these models. These experiments make it possible to examine parenting variables as possible causal mechanisms for specified child outcomes. In a later section, we will review the studies that have been completed thus far and examine their relevance for theories of parenting.

PARENTING PRACTICES AND THEORY

Everyman as Expert: The Heterogeneity of Parenting Practices

It is difficult to set a boundary that accurately specifies just when the scientific study of parenting began. As individuals, each of us has intensely experienced the parenting process at least once in our life. For many of us, there is also a second experience, in which we fill the role of parent with our own children. In this sense, most of us are experts of a kind. In this role, we have had occasion to observe and to share experiences in such a way that knowledge of parenting is embedded in the conventional wisdom. Most of us also have a reasonably comprehensive picture of what parents do. However, we tend to differ profoundly in our explanations as to why parent practices impact child outcomes.

Researchers who study parenting have been equally divergent in their conceptualizations of the relationship between parenting and child behavior. Interestingly, researchers working from different theoretical perspectives show a surprising consensus in their studies of infant and caregiver interactions—in terms of the preferred assessment procedures and in the categorization of effective, inept parenting practices. Attachment (Ainsworth, 1989; Ainsworth and Bowlby, 1991), social information processing (Dodge, Bates, and Pettit, 1990), and social interaction (Fisher, Ellis, and Chamberlain, 1999; Shaw and Bell, 1993) share an interest in describing what parents do and attempting to explain why certain practices are associated with positive or negative child outcomes.

There are several ways in which studies of parenting practices for older children and adolescents may be a more complicated affair. Much of Baumrind's (1971, 1991) interests focus on the adolescent; therefore, she takes on a very different perspective about effective parenting behaviors. Baumrind's (1991) categories of parenting behaviors involve an emphasis on style (rejecting–neglecting) and on the content (authoritarian, authoritative, and permissive). Her categories of parenting practices fit with what many of us have experienced in our roles as parents. She hypothesizes that the key function of these practices is to contribute differentially to the adolescents' identity formation and cognitive and moral development. Her findings show that some practices facilitate growth (social competency), though others do not.

In a similar vein, the social interactional perspective for older children focuses on parenting behaviors that result in control over reinforcing contingencies (Patterson 1982; Patterson, Reid, and Dishion, 1992). For example, monitoring is thought to control to some extent the availability of positive reinforcers supplied by members of a deviant peer group. Parental discipline is thought to control negative reinforcers supplied by family members for coercive and antisocial behaviors. Family problem solving (Forgatch, 1989) and parent involvement are also thought to control important contingencies in the life of the child. As previously noted, the investigators thought that these specific parenting practices might control the key reinforcing contingencies in the life of the child. By definition, then, the mechanisms explaining how a parent influences the child would involve the positive and negative contingencies supplied by parents, siblings, peers, and teachers for competent and deviant behaviors.

Pressures Toward a More Unified Field

This brief review emphasizes the heterogeneity implied in the term *parenting practices* (e.g., how parenting variables are measured depends to some extent on the age of the child and on the predilections of the investigator). However, there is reason to believe that the field is in transition. Hopefully, this is a prelude to a more coherent position that includes standardized measures and a common set of parenting variables (i.e., the beginnings of a unified field).

There are several contextual and societal changes that signify such a transition. First, there is a growing consensus about the increasing stress and complexity facing families today. These pressures from within (increasing sense of stress) and outside the family (pressure for both parents to be working) require that today's parents must be more skilled in meeting their responsibilities than were preceding generations. Furthermore, during the past two decades, decreasing funding for social programs (child care, education, and child health) has been matched by increasing reports of child maltreatment and the number of children in the foster care system (U.S. General Accounting Office, 1994). The rates of antisocial behavior and violence among children and adolescents seem to be increasing (Greenwood, Model, Rydell, and Chiesa, 1996; World Health Organization, 1992). Put simply, there is a clear and immediate need to develop programs that help to support effective parenting among at-risk populations.

All of the parenting theories listed above can point to findings that demonstrate significant correlations between their definitions of parenting variables and certain child outcome variables. The findings imply that the absence of a particular parenting practice produces the negative child outcomes. The correlational models function as directives for prevention scientists who wish to intervene. Most modern prevention–intervention trials include provision for randomized trials; this in turn implies that whatever parenting model is chosen, it can be subjected to experimental manipulations designed to test the causal status of that particular theory. We will further discuss this issue in a later section.

The practitioner planning a preventive intervention study will be faced with a bewildering array of parenting practices to manipulate. Depending on the age of the subject sample, the practitioner might focus on observed contingent-responsive caregiving (infant and toddler samples) or multimethod, multiagent definitions of such macro categories as Authoritative, Monitoring, Permissiveness, Harsh Discipline, and Rejecting. The practitioner could also choose to manipulate the mechanisms that explain why certain parenting practices alter child outcomes. For example, Lieberman (1992) designed a treatment to alter toddler attachment, whereas Snyder, Schrepferman, and St. Peter (1997) tested the hypothesis that changes in contingencies supplied by family members altered future risk for antisocial behavior.

Finally, recent developments in the field of behavior genetics give additional impetus toward a more unified approach to the study of parenting. Early publications by Scarr (1985, 1992) claimed that a substantial portion of the correlation between parenting variables, such as discipline, and child outcomes could reflect the impact of the child on the parent. Furthermore she pointed to evidence that the child evocative effect reflected genetic rather than environmental variables. Then Rowe (1994), Reiss (1997), and Harris (1998) introduced the startling claim that most (or all) of the variance between parenting practices and child outcome reflected heritable rather than environmental components. Their claims were based on replicated findings, most of them from twin designs, which showed that siblings from the same families shared little or no environmental conditions. As Lykken (1995) notes in his discussion of these findings, children from different families are "fungible" (i.e., completely interchangeable).

These claims rest on two assumptions that must be met before the estimates of shared environment become interpretable. First, one must assume that the environments shared by monozygotic twins (MZ) are no more homogeneous than the environments shared by dizygotic twins (DZ). The extensive literature reviewed by Joseph (1998) and studies such as those by Ainslie, Olmstead, and O'Loughlin (1987), and Leve (1999) strongly suggest that the equal environments assumption (EEA) cannot be met. This being the case, it becomes impossible to interpret the term MZ–DZ. The second assumption is that the samples of twins represent a full range of environments. However, most of the families who volunteer for twin studies tend to be middle income (Patterson and Eddy, 2000). As pointed out by Stoolmiller's (1999) critique of adoption designs, this, in turn, offers a very restricted range for variables that assess the environment. Together, the failure to meet the EEA and the restricted range almost guarantees that one will fail to find significant effects for shared environment variables such as parenting practices.

However, it must be said that behavioral geneticists' strident claims energized the leaders in developmental psychology to carefully examine the findings describing the relation between parenting practices and child outcomes (Collins, Maccoby, Steinberg, Hetherington, and Bornstein, 2000). Clearly, developmental psychologists have been wedded far too long to correlational studies. One of the strongest arguments in support of parent effects presented by this august group drew heavily from the new experimental manipulation studies that we will detail in a later section. Developmental psychologists had spent decades developing correlational models, but they were unable to test their hypothesized causal mechanisms. The lack of experimental studies in turn made them vulnerable to attacks by extremists such as Harris (1998). In the scientific community, being dependent on correlational models also carries with it a well-earned status as second-class citizens.

Toward an Evaluative Framework for Parenting Theories

It is important to note that the above discussion highlights the limitations of correlational evidence when it is the sole support for a theory. As part of a larger evaluative framework in which to consider of the adequacy of parenting theories, correlational evidence may play an important role. Indeed, we propose that the adequacy of theories should be examined within a framework that includes three criteria: (1) whether the explanation is as *parsimonious* as possible, (2) whether there is any *correlational evidence* to support that explanation, and (3) whether there is any evidence derived from *experimental manipulations* of the theoretical constructs.

Parsimony refers to the extent to which a theory adopts the simplest formulation possible. The term is derived from the principle of Ockham's razor, which stipulates that concepts should not be multiplied needlessly and, therefore, that theories providing the most straightforward explanations are preferable. These concepts are of great relevance to modern social science methodology, in which the goal is often to account for the greatest degree of variance among specified outcomes. Given that this variance is related to the number of independent variables, complex theories that incorporate large numbers of variables might be expected to perform better than simpler theories with fewer variables. Indeed, it might be able to explain virtually all of the variance in a dependent variable if enough variables were included. However, applying the criterion of parsimony might lead one to question the adequacy of such a complex theory.

Parsimony relates not only to the number of constructs included in a theory but also to the complexity of those constructs. Constructs that can be readily observed and measured, such as physical aggression and inconsistent discipline, are more parsimonious than constructs that cannot be easily operationalized and that must rely on proxy measures. Within theories of parenting, this lack of parsimony is especially evident in constructs that refer to internal states and representations. Although such constructs may be intriguing and intuitively appealing, they add a degree of complexity that is unnecessary in accounting for outcomes. In sum, parsimonious theories are those that include the fewest number of variables that lend themselves to valid and reliable measurement.

Our second criterion for evaluating a theory involves its supporting correlational evidence. As noted above, correlational evidence is insufficient alone; however, as part of the larger process of developing, revising, and clarifying the relationships among variables in a theory, it may provide invaluable information. For instance, much of the groundwork for parenting theories was laid by researchers examining the relationship between parenting and child outcomes in studies that did not involve the manipulation of variables. In our own research at the Oregon Social Learning Center (OSLC), our initial observational studies of family interaction (in particular, the connection between parental discipline practices and child antisocial behavior) led to the development of Coercion Theory (Patterson, 1982; Patterson et al., 1992). From this initial research, more scientifically robust efforts to validate the theory evolved (e.g., Fisher, Gunnar, Chamberlain, and Reid, 2000; Reid, Eddy, Fetrow, and Stoolmiller, 1999). We propose, therefore, that correlational evidence emerging from research that is exploratory in nature, that is based on keen and accurate observation of the phenomena in question, and that provides the impetus for further investigation may be an important step in the development of a strong theory.

Our third criterion for evaluating theories is whether they have supporting experimental evidence. Several researchers have suggested that randomized controlled experiments—especially those oriented toward the prevention of a particular problem—may provide the ultimate evidence of the adequacy of a particular theory (Forgatch, 1991; Robins, 1992). Typically, this research is confirmatory in nature (i.e., it is conducted after a theory has been developed and supported via correlational research). For example, Chamberlain and colleagues (Chamberlain and Reid, 1998; Eddy and Chamberlain, 2000) have tested a model to prevent recidivism and to foster prosocial outcomes among delinquent adolescents via an intervention model called Multidimensional Treatment Foster Care (MTFC). The intervention was developed after correlational research had revealed that parenting variables, including inconsistent discipline and lack of positive reinforcement, mediate the relationship between delinquent behavior and later negative child outcomes. The MTFC intervention acts directly on these parenting variables. A longitudinal randomized control trial to evaluate the intervention yielded evidence that the parenting variables in question are impacted by the intervention and exert an influence over the outcomes of the youth in the program (Eddy and Chamberlain, 2000). Thus, experimental manipulation of the independent variables (in this case parenting) provided evidence of a causal relationship between parenting and antisocial behavior, which constitutes strong support for the underlying theory.

This chapter outlines some of the considerations involved in moving from a correlation-based science to one that might emphasize parsimony and involve experimental manipulations. In the first section, we examine the process of training for moderate levels of compliance as a basis for understanding why some parenting variables will probably not survive such experimental tests. This is followed by a discussion of various explanations for how parenting activities impact child outcomes. We examine the implications that these mechanisms have for the design of preventive intervention trials. In the last section, we detail some of the characteristics of the new studies that employ experimental designs together with a brief review of the preliminary findings and their implications.

Parenting Practices as Products and as Causal Mechanisms

As noted earlier, knowing what parents do is very much a part of the conventional wisdom. How to make a science of this is not so obvious. What an investigator views as key parenting activities varies enormously as a function of the type of families that they study. For example, those of us who study single-mother families (DeGarmo and Forgatch, 1997; DeGarmo, Forgatch, and Martinez, 1999) or families living in poverty (McLoyd, 1998) often see evidence of irritable parents who ineffectively support socially competent behaviors, supervising, and setting firm limits. Alternatively, investigators who study more middle-income samples often find differences in warmth and control to be the most salient issues (Baumrind, 1971, 1991).

Similarly, investigators who examine interactional processes beginning in infancy will more likely examine the extent to which caregivers appear "tuned in" to the needs of their child (c.f. van den Boom, 1994). Those who examine interaction beginning in the preschool or elementary school years may examine the extent to which parents are able to effectively set limits around aggressive and other antisocial behavior (Shaw, Keenan, and Vondra, 1994; Shaw and Winslow, 1997).

Each group of investigators finds significant, albeit modest, correlations between their preferred measures of parenting and child outcomes. However, we assume that when subjected to experimental manipulation, some of the parenting practices will be shown to serve as causal mechanisms, whereas others will not. The problem results from having two components contained in any measure of parenting. One part reflects how parent behaviors impact the child, and the other part reflects how child behaviors impact the parent. Some parenting practices reflect more of the child impact on parent, though others may reflect more of the parent's impact upon the child. We suspect that harsh or abusive discipline represents a disproportionate impact of child on parent and that (if subjected to an experimental test) a selected reduction in harsh discipline would not be accompanied by a commensurate reduction in child antisocial behavior.

Various manifestations of deviant child behavior (e.g., discipline confrontations and failures in school) have been shown to account for more than half the variance in measures of maternal rejection (Patterson, 1986). Again, the correlation does not tell us about the causal mechanism (e.g., whether the deviant behavior of the child evoked the rejection by the mother or the rejection evoked the deviant child behavior). Of course, the correlations between rejection and child deviancy may reflect both effects. Additionally, these correlations may result from the influence of additional variables, such as parental substance abuse or maternal depression, which may vary greatly depending on the sample under investigation.

We assume that efforts to predict the outcomes of experimental manipulation will produce ambiguous results until we can specify the bidirectional effects between parent and child. Does a given parenting practice reflect the influence of the parent on the child or the child on the parent? To facilitate these studies, we might begin by specifying the mechanism by which the parenting behaviors are thought to impact child outcomes: What explains the effect of a parenting practice on the child? How might one measure the hypothesized mechanism?

If we can subject parenting theories to experimental tests, it should be possible to move the field to a new level of scientific excellence. The experiments would help us to sift through the long list of parenting variables and differentiate between those that simply correlate with child outcomes and those that also serve as causal mechanisms. The ultimate outcome of this process might be to move the field to greater parsimony and integration and to the specification of more accurate models. Simultaneously, this approach might move the field away from arguments about the superiority of one theory over another.

Compliance as a Process

We hypothesize that what we observe as parenting is likely the product of a prior process. It has a history that needs to be understood before we can know exactly what a given parenting practice means. We assume that important components in the development of parenting practices are laid down during the early stages of training child compliance to parent requests. The parenting practices continue to emerge during the infancy and the preschool stage (Martin, 1981; Shaw and Winslow, 1997). Parenting skills evolve out of the myriad microsocial exchanges that occur on a daily basis. The longitudinal study by Martin showed that both the mother and the infant interactions were surprisingly stable, even during the initial stages of the compliance training process. For example, mother manipulativeness versus facilitativeness assessed at 22 months correlated .39 with measures obtained at 42 months. For the same interval, the stability of child coerciveness (noncompliance) was .49. Shaw, Bell, and Gilliom (2000) essentially replicated the design for this study and found a stability correlation of .39 between maternal rejection at 24 and 42 months and a stability correlation of .38 for child noncompliance assessed at 24 and externalizing measured at 42 months.

Attachment investigators have also paid careful attention to the identification of those aspects of early parent-child interactions that contribute to long-term outcomes. The key variable was "responsive or sensitive parenting" (van den Boom, 1994). Parental sensitivity implied that the caregiver was carefully tracking the ongoing behavior of the infant and responding in a fashion that the infant would find supportive (rather than disrupting). Second, it required that the caregiver respond in a supportive manner to infant distress; van den Boom described such caregiver behaviors as "contingent." The behaviorists interested in the study of infant caregiver interactions (e.g., Shaw and Winslow, 1997) agree with this description.

This seems to be another area where attachment and behavioral theories of development overlap. For example, Mineka, Gunnar, and Champoux (1986) observed the rhesus monkey in contingent and in noncontingent environments. The data showed contingent environments produced increased exploratory activity and less fearfulness. They cited studies showing similar results in experiments with rats. S. Levine's (personal communication, September 18, 2000) review of findings from studies of rodents and monkeys showed that being reared in noncontingent environments and environments with low levels of positive reinforcement were associated with atypical patterns of cortisol production. Taken together, the findings emphasize the necessity for a contingent environment as support for normal development.

Developmental (Emde, Biringen, Cluman, and Oppenheim, 1991; Kochanska, 1991; Lytton, 1980) and behavioral theorists (Forehand, King, Peed, and Yoder, 1975; Patterson, 1982) would probably agree that a child's ability to achieve about 70% compliance to parental requests and commands constitutes a major milestone in the socialization process. Moreover, in spite of differences in the

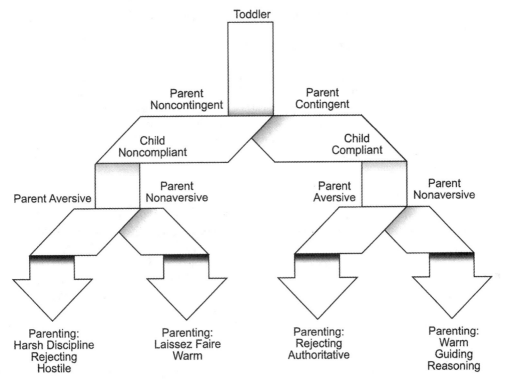

FIGURE 3.1. The compliance process.

specification of causal mechanisms that produce child outcomes, all might also agree that the process begins in infant–caregiver interactions.

As is described in Figure 3.1, toddler compliance (as an outcome) hinges on the exchange between what the caregiver and the child bring to the interaction. The difficult child interacting with a noncontingent parent places the child at risk for compliance failure, as shown in the longitudinal studies by Shaw and Winslow (1997). A failure in this first socialization juncture places the child at dual risk. The noncompliant child becomes at risk both for delayed development of social skills (including language) and for becoming coercive and eventually antisocial in interactions with others. As is shown in the Shaw and Winslow study, the noncompliance quickly expands to include a wide range of aversive child behaviors. The effects are bidirectonal in that the noncompliant child also alters the behavior of the caretaker.

These noncompliant and coercive child behaviors may in turn evoke permissive or negative reactions from the child's primary caregiver. For example, the likelihood of a negative maternal reaction to child coercive behaviors was .18 in a normal sample, .25 in families of problem families, and .30 in abusive families (Patterson, 1982). However, the permissive parent often reacts to child coercive behavior in a neutral or even a positive way (Granic, 2000). For example, the parent simply gives in to whatever it is that the child wants. Our recent clinical studies in Norway suggest that many children brought to the clinic for treatment are accompanied by extremely permissive parents (Askeland, Duckert, and Forgatch, in press).

As shown in an observational study by Snyder and Patterson (1995), a mother's coercive reaction is often successful in terminating a child's coercive behavior. The child provides a (negative) reinforcer for the behavior of the mother. In effect, the child may train the mother to be a harsh disciplinarian.

Notice in Figure 3.1 that some contingent parents, although effective in the training for compliance, continue to react to the child in a punitive and controlling manner. No matter what the child does, the parent reacts with contempt or criticism. We hypothesize that the child outcome is likely to be anxiousness and depression.

In this sense, a large part of what developmentalists and behaviorists label as parenting is a significant byproduct of the compliance training process. Although to many of us child outcomes are the variables of primary importance, the same process encompasses the alteration and shaping of parent practices. We assume that the resulting parenting practices will show a great deal of variability in how well they predict future child outcomes. We also assume that testing for causal status would show that some secondary parental practices are more likely to survive than others. In general, we assume that the more closely the parenting practice reflects contingent behavior, the more likely it will survive both correlational and experimental tests.

Child Compliance Mechanisms

We assume that child compliance is one of the first child outcome variables to significantly predict long-term future adjustment; it has been defined as occurring in instances where the child obeyed immediately after a parental request or after a short (i.e., 15-sec) delay (Roberts, 1988; Whiting and Edwards, 1988). Compliance rates have been empirically defined by dividing the number of instances of compliance plus noncompliance into the frequency of compliances based on data collected during observations of parent–child interactions (Reid, 1978). A number of investigators have examined normative data on compliance rates (e.g., Forehand, Gardner, and Roberts, 1978) and have used rates of child compliance and noncompliance as dependent variables in investigations of the effectiveness of parent-training interventions (e.g., Webster-Stratton and Hammond, 1990).

We assume that a normal toddler would start with high rates of noncompliance because, initially, the child is in the position of failing to understand either a request or the appropriate reaction. In the normal course of events, a 2- or 3-year-old child should be able to understand clearly stated requests and to comply with the majority of them. Whiting and Edwards carried out a landmark cross-cultural study of noncompliance in 2-year-old children. They reported on child compliance rates in 12 cultures and defined compliance as instances where the child obeyed immediately or after an initial short delay. They calculated compliance ratios for different ages and for boys and girls. Across cultures, older children showed more compliance than younger ones: 72% at ages 2 and 3, 79% at ages 4 and 5, and 82% at ages 6 to 8. Girls were observed to be more complaint than boys in 20 out of 28 comparisons by gender.

Comparable rates of child compliance have been found in two laboratory studies with nonclinical samples; both were structured task situations. Children complied with maternal commands 74% and 62% of the time (see Forehand et al., 1978; Lobitz and Johnson, 1975, respectively). Several theories about the onset of child deviant behaviors view high levels of noncompliance during the toddler stage as a significant predictor for various forms of acting out behavior in preschool (Forehand et al., 1975; Kuczynski and Kochanska, 1990; Patterson, 1982; Shaw, Keenan, and Vondra, 1994).

As noted earlier, one of the key questions that must be addressed in parenting theories concerns the specification of the mechanism by which authoritative, warm, responsive parenting, monitoring, or any other parent practice produces change in child outcomes (Patterson, 1997). By the same token, theorists must explain how the child impacts the parent. In this chapter, we use the term developmentalists to refer to investigators who base their studies primarily on attachment and social informational processing models. Behaviorists, on the other hand, focus on contingencies and functional analyses, and place a heavy reliance on observation data as their basic assessment tool.

As is shown in Figure 3.2, developmentalists and behaviorists share several assumptions about the compliance process. Both emphasize the contribution of contextual variables to the caregiver responsiveness. For example, Rutter (1995) views marital quality, stress, and child temperament as playing significant roles in impacting the attachment process. In a similar vein, another attachment theorist (Field, 1995) showed that caretaker depression functioned as a powerful contextual variable in altering caretaker interactions with infants. This, in turn, is similar to a behavioral–mediational

Developmentalist model

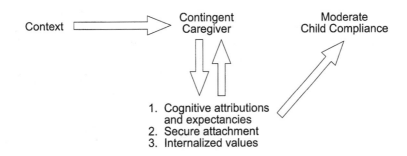

Behavioral model

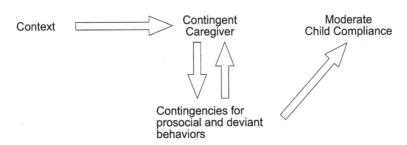

FIGURE 3.2. Mechanisms for compliance.

model for the impact of contextual variables on child outcomes. The behaviorist would assume that the effect of context on child outcomes would be mediated by whether the caregiver–infant exchanges are affected (Patterson, 1982; Patterson, 1983; Patterson et al., 1992).

Both perspectives agree on the centrality of caregiver contingencies (responsiveness) in bringing about child compliance. As noted earlier, the attachment theorist van den Boom's (1994) definition of caregiver contingencies resembles the definition provided by the behaviorists Shaw and Winslow (1997) and Martin (1981). However, two points of view diverge in their explanation of what changes the child's behavior. By the same token they might disagree about how the child changes the caregiver.

We propose to examine behavioral and developmentalist causal mechanisms within the framework provided by the Baron and Kenny (1986) mediational model. Following their procedures, the first requirement is to show that measures of caretaker responsiveness (contingencies) predict later infant compliance. The second requirement is to show that the measures for the assumed causal mechanism correlate significantly with the caretaker responsiveness and with future measures of child compliance. The third requirement is that, when the data specifying the mediating mechanism are introduced, the path from caretaker responsiveness to child outcome becomes nonsignificant.

As suggested in Figure 3.2, there is not necessarily a consensus among developmentalists as to which mechanism might explain how parenting practices influence child outcomes. Nor do they necessarily agree as to how internalized mechanisms are assessed. However, correlational data show that the attachment and the social information processing mechanisms correlate with various child outcomes. The findings suggest that these mechanisms might therefore serve as explanations for how parents impact children and by implication how children impact parents (e.g., De Wolff and van IJzendoorn, 1997; Dodge et al., 1990; MacKinnon, Lamb, Belsky, and Baum, 1990; Yoon, Hughes,

Gaur, and Thompson, 1999). The important implication of these findings is that experimental manipulations that effectively alter the attachment or social information processing mechanisms should be associated with significant reductions in child deviant outcomes. The strongest statement would be based on findings that showed the following: (1) that the interventions altered the mechanisms for the families in the experimental group, (2) that there were no significant changes in the comparison groups, and (3) that the magnitude of change in the mediating mechanisms correlated significantly with the magnitude of changes in the child outcome variables. However, we also refer back to our framework for evaluating theories here, in the sense that despite such evidence, concerns about parsimony remain. Put simply, the question centers on how much is gained when concepts beyond contingency and reinforcement are introduced and whether, because of the added complexity and problems with reliable measurement, what is gained ultimately makes the theory less adequate.

As is shown in Figure 3.2, the behaviorists assume that the measures of caregiver responsiveness used by van den Boom (1994), Martin (1981), and Shaw and Winslow (1997) can also be expressed as relative rate of reinforcement for coercive and for socially competent behaviors. Furthermore, we assume that responsiveness variables account for significant variance in measures of infant prosocial and deviant behaviors.

However, this assumption poses an immediate paradox. A half century of laboratory studies showed a nonlinear relationship between measures of response strength and reinforcement frequency (Herrnstein, 1961). This, in turn, implies that differences in reinforcement could not explain individual differences in child outcomes such as aggression (Patterson, 1982, 1995). As shown in the analyses by Snyder and Patterson (1995), the solution to this problem requires that the data be collected on an intraindividual basis that includes a description of all the child behaviors that occur in a given setting together with an accounting of reinforcement frequency for each of them. From this perspective, it is the relative rates of reinforcement for socially competent and for deviant behavior that account for individual differences. For example, analyses of the relative rates of negative reinforcement supplied by parents for coercive behavior and positive reinforcement supplied by deviant peers for deviant behavior have been shown to be powerful predictors for individual differences in antisocial outcomes for older children (Dishion, Spracklen, Andrews, and Patterson, 1996; Snyder and Patterson, 1995; Snyder et al., 1997).

In the earliest tests of the model in Figure 3.2, behaviorists relied heavily on randomized experiments. Typically, the laboratory studies compared the relative effectiveness of positive reinforcers for cooperation to mild punishments, such as "timeout" for noncompliance. In general, these studies have shown that the most effective means for altering child noncompliance was to use both sets of contingencies. Efforts to use only positive contingencies to bring about compliance often failed (e.g., Eisenstadt, Eyberg, McNeil, Newcomb, and Funderburk, 1993; Roberts, 1985; Wahler, 1969). For example, Eisenstadt et al. (1993) showed that, by itself, praise for cooperation did not reduce noncompliant behavior. However, adding timeout for noncompliance produced dramatic shifts to bring compliance within normal limits. This effect replicates the earlier findings by Roberts, Hazenbuehler, and Bean (1981).

There is some reason to believe that positive reinforcement may play a complex role in the acquisition of compliant behavior. For example, Parpal and Maccoby (1985) showed that introducing an interval of mother-provided frequent support significantly enhanced later efforts to bring about child compliance. Snyder and Huntley (1990) showed that child compliance was significantly correlated with the clarity of parental commands, parent use of positive reinforcement for compliance, and parent use of negative consequences for failure to comply. Taken together, the three variables accounted for 40% of the variance in child compliance.

Martinez and Forgatch (2001) describe a randomized longitudinal design for a prevention trial based on a sample of 238 single mothers and their young sons. Among other things, mothers assigned to the experimental group were trained to alter both sets of contingencies provided specifically for noncompliance. Parenting practices and child compliance were assessed at baseline and at 6, 12, 18, and 30 months. The findings showed that group assignment significantly altered the changes in slope for compliance. In keeping with prior longitudinal studies, the members of the control group became increasingly noncompliant, whereas the members of the experimental group showed no significant changes in slope. When measures of changes in discipline (changes in negative reinforcement and consistency) were introduced, the path from group to outcome became nonsignificant. The set of findings meet the Baron and Kenny (1986) requirements for a mediated model. This in turn suggests that the negative reinforcement variable meets these requirements for consideration as a causal mechanism for child noncompliance.

As previously noted, additional evidence of the centrality of contingencies in the acquisition of behavior can be derived from the seminal research of Levine and colleagues on rats and monkeys, spanning 4 decades. This research (Coe, Stanton, and Levine, 1983; Davis and Levine, 1982; Herrmann, Hurwitz, and Levine, 1984) has shown that activity in the hypothalamic-pituitary-adrenal cortex (HPA) axis of the brain is impacted by the presence or absence of reinforcement and the ability of the organism to predict and control positive and negative experiences (i.e., contingencies). This is significant because the HPA axis is involved in stress reactivity and related to the regulation of emotions. To the extent that atypical patterns of activity are present, organisms can be predisposed to impulsive, disorganized, and aggressive behavior. Moreover, learning can be difficult because hyper-responsivity to stressors can lead to prolonged periods (or even chronic states) in which the organism is in fight or flight mode and is not well predisposed to learning. Levine and colleagues' work showed that the presence of contingencies can increase regulation in the HPA axis (Davis and Levine, 1982; Hennessy, King, McClure, and Levine, 1977) and that reinforcement can decrease activity in the HPA axis, whereas extinction of reinforcement can elevate activity (Coover, Goldman, and Levine, 1971; Goldman, Coover, and Levine, 1973; Herrmann et al., 1984).

Thus, from a physiological perspective, one might argue that the development of child compliance is greatly facilitated by a contingent and positively reinforcing caregiver. It is interesting to note that these assertions support not only the coercion model of what constitutes positive parenting, but also certain elements of what attachment theorists have observed in infancy as contributing to healthy development.

Bidirectional Effects

Bell (1968) and Bell and Harper (1977) were among the first to emphasize the key role that bidirectional effects played in the socialization process. In the decades that followed, developmentalists (Belsky, 1984; Lytton, 1990; Martin, 1981), behaviorists, (Patterson and Bank, 1986), and behavioral geneticists (Scarr, 1985, 1992) shared a consensus about the presence of bidirectional effects in socialization process. The parent and the child both make significant contributions to the process. This concept plays a key role in the present formulation of "parenting as product."

As noted earlier, Harris's (1998) extreme claims for the contributions made by heredity to the socialization process emphasized the importance of child effects on parenting process. Keeping with the emphasis from behavior genetics for evocative effects, observation studies of problem families and normal families showed that, given an aversive child behavior, the odds of the parent responding in kind were about 1 in 6 for normal families and about 1 in 3 for clinical families (Patterson, 1982). Clearly, evocative child behavior has an impact on parents in general, and parents of problem families in particular. An observation study by Snyder and Patterson (1995) showed that the frequency of sons' aversive behavior to mother correlated .55 with the likelihood of the sons' reinforcing of their mothers' aggression. The two variables, frequency of conflict with sons and sons' relative rate of reinforcement for mothers' aggression correlated .73 with mothers' observed rate of aggression a week later. These analyses show that the same mechanisms that produced a coercive and aggressive child also shaped the behavior of a coercive-aggressive mother. The child is an active change agent in this process, a finding very much in keeping with Bell's (1968) early speculations.

Anderson, Lytton, and Romney (1986) were among the first to provide a convincing test of the child evocative effect. When interacting with children with conduct disorder, mothers of normal boys became significantly more aversive than they were observed to be with their own child. Presumably, the evocative effect of the problem child behavior led to the increase in mother aversive behavior.

Barkley and colleagues, who demonstrated that administering stimulant drugs to hyperactive children was followed by a decrease in maternal aversive behavior, provided an equally convincing demonstration of this effect (Barkley, 1981; Barkley and Cunningham, 1979). Barkley, Karlsson, Pollard, and Murphy (1985) strengthened this position by demonstrating a dosage effect in which the greater the increase in the medication, the greater the drop in maternal aversive behavior. There is some reason to believe that mothers who perceive themselves as having little control over life events might be most affected by negative child behavior (Bugental, Caporeal, and Shennum, 1980). For example, a depressed mother confronted with a difficult infant might find herself quickly shaped to avoid the infant.

It is one thing to demonstrate that the child evocative effect exists, but it is quite another matter to specify how to provide a precise estimate of its magnitude. What proportion of the variance in estimates of parenting might be due to child evocative effects? There are only a few studies testing the hypothesis that child level of deviancy at one point in time may account for future levels of parenting. In these studies, the control variable would be the stability of parenting practices across time (Patterson and Bank, 1989). For example, the Patterson, Bank, and Stoolmiller's (1990) study of the Oregon Youth Sample (OYS) showed that boys' antisocial behavior Grade 4 accounted for a significant portion of the stability in parental monitoring and discipline practices. After partialing out the stability in parenting practices, the paths from earlier antisocial were $-.29$ to future monitoring and $-.36$ to future discipline practices. Again, parental disruptions in discipline and monitoring might reflect both a lack of skill and/or the fact that the parents are coping with a particularly difficult child.

One approach to the bidirectional problem is to use structural equation modeling to directly specify the magnitude of both paths. Given a longitudinal data set, it should, in theory, be possible to determine whether the weights for child and parenting effects are of an equal magnitude or the relative weighting varies as a function of gender, age, and child outcome. In an adoption study, the extensive assessment battery employed by Ge et al. (1996) made it possible to estimate the bidirectional path from adolescent outcome to maternal discipline practices. The path coefficient from parenting to antisocial child outcomes was .44, and the path coefficient from child antisocial to discipline practices was .48. The relatively small sample size ($N = 45$) emphasizes the need for caution in assuming that these particular weights are generalizable. Although it is probably coincidental, there is another study where the bidirectional path coefficients between parental discipline and negative sibling exchanges were set to being equal (.42). The a priori model showed an acceptable fit for a structural equation model (SEM) (Patterson, Dishion, and Bank, 1984). The findings from the two pilot studies suggested that structural equation modeling may be a promising, albeit seldom explored, approach to the study of bidirectionality.

The concept of bidirectionality in parenting is not confined to the socialization process. Bornstein, Tamis-LeMonda, and Haynes (1999) conducted research on the development of language in mother–child dyads during the second year of life. They found that between 13 and 20 months of age, there are increases in children's vocabularies, and in the vocabularies of mothers (in speaking to their child) as well. This supports the notion that children are influenced by the language use of their mother and that mothers increase their use of language in response to their child's development (i.e., reciprocal influence). Additionally, children with the most verbally responsive parents were found to have better language development. This supports the idea that contingent responding facilitates development across domains of functioning.

Parenting Practices as Outcomes

In this section, we briefly review some of the implications of viewing parenting practices as an outcome or product of the socialization process rather than as a prime causal mechanism. In the preceding discussion, we examined the potential contribution of child evocative effects on

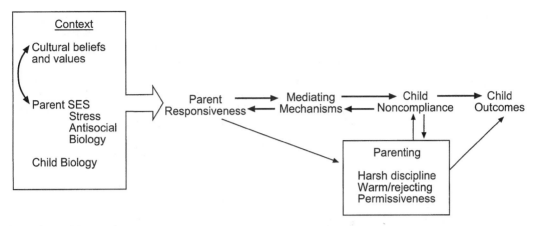

FIGURE 3.3. Parenting as outcome.

parenting practices. We now examine some of the variables that determine what the parent brings to the process. As is shown in Figure 3.3, there is a broad range of contextual variables thought to impact parenting practices ranging from cultural beliefs, to the effects of divorce, and to such parental traits as depression and antisocial behavior. From our perspective, the impact of these contextual factors on child outcome is mediated by their effect on parenting practices. All of the contextual variables shown in Figure 3.3 have been shown to significantly correlate with disruptions in parenting practices (Patterson et al., 1992).

Cultural beliefs.   Culture often defines values and beliefs concerning child rearing and child outcomes. In a review of empirical findings, Darling and Steinberg (1993) concluded that parental beliefs and values were direct determinants for parental practices and indirect determinants for child outcomes. The review by Rubin, Stewart, and Chen (1995) is in general accord with this point of view, as are the findings from the three longitudinal studies carried out at the OSLC (Patterson et al., 1992).

The recent genre of cross-cultural studies contains important findings showing reliable differences in parental beliefs and values among seven different cultures (Bornstein et al., 1998). For example, in one study, pair-wise comparisons of mothers and fathers showed the American mothers ranked themselves as more sensitive and affectionate than did Argentine and French mothers (Bornstein et al., 1996). In the same study, American mothers reported themselves and their husbands as emphasizing the importance of rules and respect for authority more than did Argentine and French parents. Presumably these differences in belief would be reflected in commensurate cross-cultural differences in observed parenting practices.

Parental traits.   It is hypothesized that variables assessing parental stress, depression, and antisocial behavior are all associated with disrupted parenting. The actual mechanisms by which these variables produce disrupted parenting practices are not well understood. For example, Granic (2000) would characterize stressful events as a perturbation that causes some mother–child dyads to shift into a more negative state space. In a similar vein, Patterson (1983) showed that on days characterized by high levels of stress, mothers were observed to be more irritable (e.g., Granic's negative state space). In a longitudinal study of single parents, Patterson and Forgatch (1990) showed that increasing stress was related to increases in irritability, and in turn with increased disruptions in parental discipline practices.

Parental depression seems to relate to disrupted parenting practices in several different ways. On the one hand there are a number of studies that demonstrate that the depressed parent views their children more negatively (Griest, Wells, and Forehand, 1979; Krech and Johnston, 1992; Patterson,

1982). Studies also show that depressed mothers tend to be more negative and punitive in their interactions with the child (Downey and Coyne, 1990; Ghodsian, Zajicek, and Wolkind, 1984).

Our own studies show that a parent's antisocial traits may play a major role in being associated with disruptions in parenting (Bank, Duncan, Patterson, and Reid, 1993; Patterson et al., 1992). Again, we are not at all clear about the exact mechanism that brings this about. Heritability, as is shown in four major adoption studies, may play a role here (Bohman, 1996; Cadoret, Cain, and Crowe, 1983; Cadoret, Leve, and Devor, 1997; Hutchings and Mednick, 1977). Incidentally, contrary to the claims by Harris (1998), each of these adoption designs showed significant contributions for environment, including significant gene–environment interaction terms.

Antisocial parents may tend to be more irritable and to be generally unskilled. From a clinical perspective, it also seems that the antisocial parent often does not perceive stealing, fighting, and similar behaviors as deviant; therefore, this parent tends not to punish occurrences of antisocial behavior. Whatever the mechanism might be, our studies consistently show path coefficients from constructs assessing the antisocial parent to constructs assessing disrupted parenting. In the OYS, the path coefficient was .68. The findings were essentially replicated for families from the Oregon Divorce Study (Bank, Forgatch, Patterson, and Fetrow, 1993).

Clearly, training for the compliance process is complex and reflects contributions from the caregiver and the child. The models summarized in Figure 3.3 imply that experimental manipulations could focus on altering some of the contextual variables. The focus could also be on training caregivers to be more contingent (responsive). Training parents to use more effective strategies might also be useful. In the section that follows, we will briefly examine the feasibility of manipulating a select list of parenting practices.

In passing, it is interesting to note that experimental manipulation of context may also be more feasible than one might think at first glance. For example, one might use medication for maternal depression. There are also programmatic studies by Huston et al. (2001) showing that providing wage supplements effectively raised family income above poverty level (including subsidies for child care and health insurance) and had strong, significant effects on boys' (but not girls') achievement and on classroom behavior reported by teachers. In an exhaustive review of efforts to intervene with families living in poverty, McLoyd (1998) suggests many alternative ways of altering contextual variables.

Harsh and abusive discipline.   Straus (1991, 1994) and the media emphasize the view that abusive parents model aggressive behavior for the child. In this view, parental modeling and the child anger resulting from the abuse combine as causal mechanisms to drive child aggressive behavior in the future. From a social interactional perspective, abusive parenting techniques, such as hitting and threatening, tend to be successful in the short run in terminating child negative behavior. This increases the likelihood that the parent will use abusive practices in the future. However, if the child continues or escalates, these parents tend to back down and terminate the exchange. These reinforcing contingencies operate to increase the likelihood of child deviant behaviors in the future (Patterson, 1982). Thus, in an abusive relationship over time, parent and child behaviors escalate (Reid, Patterson, Lorber, 1981; Reid, Taplin, and Lorber, 1981). This complexity is largely overlooked by theorists who claim that harsh physical punishment and abuse are a direct cause for child aggression.

The idea of parent as model combined with child anger constitutes a powerful image and a close fit to the conventional wisdom about the causes for aggression. When asked to explain the cause for aggression, the average person is likely to point to frustration-based theories. At one level, this is a sensible view in that, when one observes an aggressive incident, anger is frequently a concomitant. However, in our view, an experimental manipulation that focused only on the removal of parental frustration and the accompanying harsh discipline would not be successful. Parent as model in combination with child anger is simply not a viable theory about child aggression. Harsh discipline is a prime example of a parenting practice that reflects the evocative contribution of the child as much as it does the parent as model. Simply reducing harsh discipline would not alter the contingencies supplied by family members and peers for the aggressive behavior.

Alternatively, researchers such as Belsky (1984), Reid (1986), and Knutson and Schartz (1997) see harsh discipline gradually emerging as a function of inept discipline practices. This position is based on intensive observation studies in abusive families carried out in Oregon (Reid, Patterson, and Loeber, 1982) and Washington state (Burgess and Conger, 1978). The findings suggest that each member of the dyad learns that an escalation in amplitude of coercion often "works"—it is consistently followed by the other person backing off (Patterson, 1980; Snyder, Edwards, McGraw, Kilgore, and Holton, 1994). As a result, over time, the mother and the child become increasingly physical. Presumably, there is nothing special about abuse that is not already contained within the context of noncontingent discipline.

McCord (1991) presents her own data and data from Widom (1989) showing that neglect, as a general variable, provides the same criminal and violent outcomes usually associated with abuse. This general view is supported by analyses of data from two different samples (Simons, Johnson, and Conger, 1994; Simons, Wu, Johnson, and Conger, 1995), which showed that, after a general measure of punishment had been partialed out of a rural sample of Iowa families, the contribution of a measure of harsh physical punishment to future child outcomes became trivial. Keeping with this formulation, Greenwald, Bank, Reid, and Knutson (1997) used the OYS data to show that the information contained in measures of abusive parenting is already contained in the more general measure of discipline practices. In their study, the path from the latent construct discipline to the measure abusive parenting was .75. Additional analyses showed that inept disciplinary practices directly predicted abusive outcomes. Thus, we find once more that a concept with intuitive appeal (i.e., that abusive parenting causes noncompliance) should be rejected in favor of a more parsimonious interpretation in which abuse is subsumed within the larger category of noncontingent parenting.

The implication of these findings for prevention trials is straightforward. The findings from the Washington and Oregon observation studies of abusive families (Burgess and Conger, 1978; Reid et al., 1982, respectfully) emphasize the need to teach the parents how to provide an effective set of nonphysical punishments for deviant child behavior. The attachment view and the contingency view would emphasize the need to help the abusive parent become more responsive—in other words, contingent. This would include attending to the child's efforts to be prosocial and providing the parents with some means for setting limits. This was in fact the approach taken when intervening with abusive parents in the Oregon studies, where about one third of the caseload consisted of abused children (Patterson, Dishion, and Chamberlain, 1993).

Permissive parenting. The concept of permissive, laissez-faire parenting has a long and colorful history with rich ties to philosophy (e.g., Rousseau) and psychoanalysis. In the 1940s and 1950s, experts recommended the approach as a childrearing technique. However, in the decades that followed, major longitudinal studies carried out in Norway (Olweus, 1980) and in the United States (Baumrind, 1991) called these recommendations into question. The findings showed that there were significant correlations between permissive parenting and aggressive outcomes. Our own clinical studies in Oregon also identified a small number of extremely permissive parents with antisocial children. Some of them represented a 1960s-style counterculture philosophy that objected vehemently to imposing limits or controls on child behavior.

The pattern of coercion observed for the permissive families did not seem to fit the irritable–coercive pattern we had come to expect and described in our earlier publications (Patterson, 1976). In the permissive families the coercion was initiated by the child in the form of commands and requests for immediate compliance. Both parents acquiesced with startling regularity. Failure of parents to comply was punished, by the child, with temper tantrums.

Lepper (1982) made the interesting point that permissive parenting and harsh discipline practices produce aggressive children. How could it be that seemingly diametric opposites in parenting practices could produce the same outcomes? In the present context, we would suggest that permissive parents and irritable–coercive parents reinforced coercive child behaviors; however, the coercion is initiated by the child in one case and by the parents or siblings in the other case.

A survey study by Palmerus and Scarr (1995) examined the effect on Swedish families of the 1979 law banning corporal punishment and verbal abuse of children. As compared to U.S. parents, Swedish parents reported much less use of physical punishment but more use of physical restraint. Contrary to expectations, there was a fourfold increase in child abuse and a larger increase in teen violence. Norway has developed similar policies. In the last 2 years, staff at the OSLC began training a large cadre of Norwegian therapists to use the parent-training model and adapt it to Norwegian families (Askeland et al., in press). The tape recordings of the treatment sessions show a surprisingly high prevalence of the permissive parenting form of child coercion. In these families, the parents seem often to be immobilized by unreasonable requests made by the child. The parents seem simply unable to say no.

To design an experimental manipulation for permissive families, each of the three developmental theories would need to design an intervention that would significantly change the mechanism that explains how permissiveness leads to antisocial behavior. The attachment theorist could choose to alter the caregiver contingencies or focus on altering the internalized mechanisms. The social-information-processing theorist could suggest a focus on changing the negative attributions or structural changes in the way social information is processed (Dodge et al., 1990). A behavioral theorist could focus on training the parents to be more supportive of socially competent behaviors and then gradually set limits and supply negative consequences for the child's threats and temper tantrums (Askeland et al., in press). In keeping with the mediational model, it would be predicted that the magnitude of changes in mechanisms should then predict the magnitude of changes in child outcome. We will return to this topic in a later section.

Parental rejection and lack of affection.   Even the briefest clinical contact with families of antisocial children leaves one convinced that the child is unloved and rejected by family members. Loeber's and Dishion's (1983) review of the empirical literature showed that rejection was one of the more salient predictors of delinquent outcomes. Our empirical findings and clinical experience suggest that most antisocial children experience rejection by one or more parents and by the normal peer group (Patterson et al., 1992).

This sense of being unloved and unwanted is the focus in the formulation of residential treatment programs as described in Redl's and Wineman's (1952) classic *Controls from Within* and in their description of antisocial boys, *Children Who Hate* (1951). They viewed providing unconditional affection and love as a necessary condition for effective treatment: "In order for ego disturbed children even to begin to function adequately, it is essential that they get a heavy dose of affection" (1952, p. 61). The core assumption was that the therapeutic relationship would serve as a basis for internalizing the values, beliefs, and social behaviors of the adult world.

Rejection and a lack of warmth may constitute maternal dispositions even prior to the birth of the child, as implied in Engfer's and Gavranidou's (1988) studies of abusive parents. We believe that a significant portion of the variance in maternal rejection and lack of warmth are products of the child's behavior. Most adults find it extremely difficult to maintain a warm accepting stance in the face of a rising tide of aversive infant and toddler behavior. During work in a child psychiatry residential treatment center, one of the authors found that the trained nursing staff received the bulk of the medication. Even though the nursing staff members were well-trained professionals, the high rates of abrasive and stressful interactions with these boys exacted its toll, just as it would for a young mother. Longitudinal studies of the toddler stage reviewed in Shaw, Dishion, and Gardner (2000) showed maternal rejection emerging as a significant predictor for later negative child outcomes.

From the perspective of the coercion model, it is assumed that the density of daily hassles with the child contributes significantly to maternal ratings of rejection. Using a composite measure of rejection (child report, interviewer ratings, and parent ratings), Patterson (1986) found that discipline confrontations, child–sibling irritable exchanges, and daily parental reports of conflicts correlated significantly with the composite rejection score. The multiple R was .69, and F value was 12.45 ($p < .001$). The more aversive the child, the greater the likelihood of parental rejection. As expected, the level of antisocial behavior, academic failure, and general lack of social skills also contributed significantly to parental rejection.

There is, of course, nothing in any of these correlations that assigns the rejection variable as product or cause. One of the implications of the Redl and Wineman (1952) approach is that increasing warmth, love, and affection might alleviate antisocial behavior or at least constitute a necessary first stage to treatment. However, two studies using objective measures of treatment outcome and randomized trials have shown no effect for interventions that emphasized a client-centered family approach (Alexander and Parsons, 1973; Bernal, Klinnert, and Schultz, 1980). The client-centered approach typically emphasizes the importance of unconditional positive regard. In passing, it is important to note that the initial phase of almost all parent-training therapy emphasizes dramatic increases in positive reinforcement and general support as a necessary first stage for effective treatment (Forgatch, 2000).

On the other hand, the coercion model would predict that interventions producing reductions in child deviancy would be associated with maternal reports of increased affection from the caregiver and the child, as is shown in the study by Patterson and Reid (1973). However, we also hypothesize that simply increasing parental warmth and affection will fail to bring about clinically significant reductions in antisocial behavior.

Parental monitoring. Our first effort to find a multiagent, multimethod definition of parental efforts to monitor the child's whereabouts proved to be a successful predictor of delinquent behavior (Patterson and Stouthamer-Loeber, 1984). Since the early publication, there has been a great deal of interest in the concept. For example, it was included in the large-scale epidemiological study by Chilcoat, Dishion, and Anthony (1995). Their data showed a clear correlation between parental monitoring and drug use even after age, sex, and minority status were partialed out. In that study, children whose parental monitoring declined over a 1-year interval reported a 16% increase in risk of drug sampling for every unit of decrease in monitoring. The concept is now receiving the careful methodological analyses it deserves. For example, a large-scale Swedish study by Stattin and Kerr (2000) showed that high parental monitoring was related to the child's spontaneous disclosure of information more than to parental tracking per se.

We assume that training parents to increase their supervision and monitoring would have only a borderline impact on such outcomes as delinquency because families at risk for early onset delinquency are ineffective in monitoring and are equally unsuccessful in enforcing limits. The ineffective parent can neither obtain the information necessary to supervise the child nor enforce efforts to set limits even if given accurate information. Changing monitoring without changing contingencies that limit deviant behavior would probably prove ineffective in reducing future delinquency. On the other hand, in the context of the full range of parent-training treatment that is focused on changing contingencies, changes in monitoring are significant predictors for future police arrest and out-of-home placement, as shown in the follow-up study by Patterson and Forgatch (1995).

Summary. We have made a general case against viewing categories of parenting practices as inevitable marker variables for causal mechanisms. Each parenting variable reflects unknown joint contributions of parent and child to the compliance training process. What emerges may or may not prove to be a causal mechanism for child outcomes. The next generation of studies should allow for clarification and integration of concepts derived from various theories of parenting and identify a set of standardized means for their assessment.

SOME CHARACTERISTICS OF THE PARENTING EXPERIMENTS

Recent developments in prevention science have made it possible to carry out Forgatch's (1991) injunction to use intervention trials as experimental manipulations that test theoretical models of parenting. This produces a timely marriage between developmental theory and recent advances in assessment and clinical interventions. In this section, we will review the defining characteristics of the new studies that combine these several themes. We will use this perspective to examine current findings from preventive intervention trials that employ randomized trials to evaluate the causal status of some key parenting variables. We will then discuss how, in spite of widespread acceptance of the need for empirical support in efforts to improve parenting from any theoretical perspective, there continue to be misapplications of parenting theories, which have led to interventions that pose significant risk to children.

Measurement and Design

Related to our concerns about parsimony, we believe that the parenting models most likely to survive will have two characteristics in common. First, they will be based on theoretical constructs that are readily operationalized. Second, the theories will specify an effective means of assessment. In this vein, the bulk of the experimental studies reviewed here are based on data from multiagent measures, which facilitates the use of structural equation growth modeling (Bank, Dishion, Skinner, and Patterson, 1990; Bentler, 1980). The emphasis on multiple indicators means that correlations between parenting variables and child outcomes reflect something more than just shared method variance. Bank et al. (1990) noted that this problem characterizes all studies based on single-agent reports. It must also be said that, at this juncture, the selection of variables that are both reliable and sensitive to change is more art than science. Our greatest successes have followed the use of observation-based measures from either laboratory or natural settings.

At a bare minimum, adequate measures of the parenting model and child outcomes would be taken prior to and following intervention trials. There are now three major prevention studies that employ randomized trials and repeated measures of family processes and child outcomes over long-term follow-up intervals (Forgatch and DeGarmo, 1999; Kellam, Rebok, Ialongo, and Mayer, 1994; Reid et al., 1999). In each case, repeated measures collected for 3 to 5 years following the experimental manipulation show increasing effect sizes. Given that provision is made for the follow-up measures to include assessment of the parenting model, one can actually see the comparison group getting worse, whereas the experimental group remains intact or shows some positive gains. Given that the sample is at risk for negative child outcomes, as in the case of recent divorce or separation (Forgatch and DeGarmo, 1999), the repeated follow-up measures actually trace the development of pathology in the untreated comparison group.

When Forgatch (1991) first proposed the use of preventive intervention trials as experimental tests for correlational models, she added a characteristic that turned out to be a central concern. Preventive intervention trials are complex affairs such that one might well believe that multiple factors are involved in producing a particular child outcome. She suggested, therefore, that testing the correlation between the magnitude of change in the candidate mechanism with the magnitude of change in the child outcome was necessary. She has followed this procedure in prevention trials designed for single-parent families (Forgatch and DeGarmo, 1999).

Specifying the Parenting Model

Needless to say, all parenting models are not equally well developed, nor are they equally parsimonious. For example, Baumrind (1971, 1991) would probably view a model that includes measures of authoritarian, authoritative, and permissive parenting as adequately specified. Others, such as Dodge and colleagues, present a general model that includes measures of discipline (Deater-Deckard and Dodge, 1997), with estimates of social information processing as the causal mechanism (Dodge et al., 1990).

The OSLC coercion model (Patterson, 1995; Patterson et al., 1992) is a hierarchical model with three levels of nested causal mechanisms. The developmental models explain the trajectory for the changes in form of antisocial behavior from age 2 through the young adult years (Reid, Snyder, and Patterson, in press). The model specifies context as the most distal factors affecting development and, therefore, the contextual variables account for the least amount of variance in child outcomes. Presumably, parenting practices (monitoring, discipline, positive involvement, and family problem-solving) mediate the impact of contextual variables on child outcomes and, in so doing, account for 20% to 30% of the variance in outcomes. Observation-based studies show that the analyses of contingencies supplied by family members account for from 40% to 60% of the variance in child antisocial outcomes (Snyder and Patterson, 1995, Snyder et al., 1997). Information about contingencies would be the most proximal and would account for the most variance in child outcomes. Snyder and colleagues are now collecting data in Kansas that will permit multivariate analyses that include estimates of parenting practices, contingencies, social information processing, and negative emotion.

Some Preliminary Findings

To date, three studies have employed randomized trials and measures of parenting practices. The first study, designed as an experimental manipulation, included 129 young adolescents thought to be at risk for later substance abuse (Dishion and Kavanagh, in press). The adolescents and their families were randomly assigned to parent-training, teen-focus, or self-help groups. The findings are summarized in Figure 3.4. The two groups that included parent training were associated with significant reductions in teacher ratings of antisocial behavior. When the parent–child negative engagement variable was introduced into the model, the contribution of group membership to child outcome became nonsignificant. In keeping with a mediational model, the path coefficient from group membership to negative parent–child engagement (observed) was .26, and from the parenting variable to child outcome was .25. The 1-year follow-up data showed that the families who had been in the parent-training group were at significantly reduced risk for tobacco use (Dishion, Kavanagh, and Kiesner, in press). In this study, the high cost of intensive observation data made it impossible to collect data sufficient to define the contributions of contingencies to outcomes.

The second study involved an intervention for chronic offenders that provided for the measurement of parenting skills at mid-treatment (Eddy and Chamberlain, 2000). The adolescents were randomly assigned to group homes that included up to six other adolescent offenders or to treatment foster care (TFC). The foster parents in the TFC condition were carefully screened, intensively trained, and extensively supervised on a weekly basis as they put effective parenting practices to use in working with one or two adolescents. Adolescents, who showed satisfactory adjustment at home and in the public school system, were gradually returned to their biological parents. The biological parents were

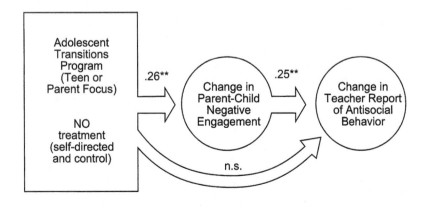

**p < .01

FIGURE 3.4. Changes in parenting predict change in child outcome (from Dishion and Kavanagh, in press).

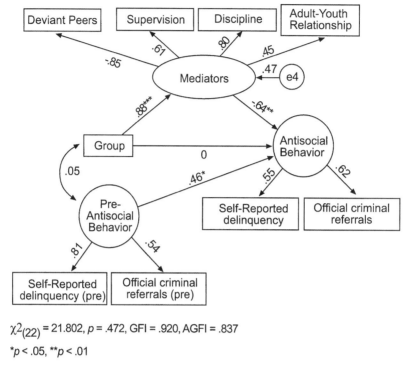

$\chi^2_{(22)}$ = 21.802, p = .472, GFI = .920, AGFI = .837

*p < .05, **p < .01

FIGURE 3.5. Testing a mediational model for parenting (from Eddy and Chamberlain, 2000).

also trained and supervised as they practiced effective parenting skills. The follow-up data showed significant effect sizes for both official and self-report delinquency data.

Parenting practices were assessed for both groups by interviewers/observers who went into the homes during mid-treatment to assess such parenting skills as supervision, discipline, positive support, and deviant peers. Again, the cost of collecting intensive observation data made it impossible to directly assess contingencies. The ratings of parenting skills were based on reports from the foster parents (TFC and group home), on interviews with the adolescents, and on information from three daily telephone calls. The findings from the structural equation model are summarized in Figure 3.5. Being a member of the experimental group was associated with significantly better parenting practices and with significant reductions in delinquent outcomes (Eddy and Chamberlain, 2000). When the mediating variables (parenting, reduced contact with deviant peers, and quality of relationship to foster parents) were introduced, the path from group to delinquency became 0. Notice that future delinquency was more heavily associated with the mediating variables ($-.64$) than it was to prior history of delinquency (.46). The findings showed an acceptable fit between the a priori model and the data set χ^2 value of 21.6 (p = .43).

The third study, a prevention design for single mothers, has completed 3 years of follow-up data (Forgatch and DeGarmo, 1999). Its provision for an intensive assessment of parenting and outcomes, including changes in contingencies, makes it ideally suited as an example of the new developmental-clinical look. The sample consisted of 238 recently separated, single mothers and their sons (ages 6 to 10). Families were randomly assigned to a parent-training group or a comparison group; the mothers in the experimental group received 14 hours of parenting training in a group setting. The families in both groups were assessed at baseline and at 6, 12, 18, and 30 months. Forgatch and DeGarmo (2000) have found significant changes in parenting for three negative aspects of parenting (negative reinforcement, negative reciprocity, and inept discipline) and in four aspects of positive parenting (positive involvement, skill encouragement, monitoring, and family problem solving). The analyses by Martinez and Forgatch (2001) detail the effect of the prevention trials in producing changes in child noncompliance. Changes in coercive discipline were significantly correlated with changes in child noncompliance (.33; $p < .001$); changes in positive parenting were significantly correlated to changes in child noncompliance ($-.59; p < .001$).

The Forgatch and DeGarmo (2000) analyses take the findings one step further in examining the hypothesized path from child noncompliance to child aggression. Correlational models would lead one to expect to find reduced child noncompliance associated with reduced child aggression. At baseline, parenting practices showed the expected relation ($-.51$) to noncompliance and were correlated, in turn, to child aggression (teacher ratings). Group assignment was significantly related to changes in parenting (combined coercive and positive). Changes in parenting covaried (.20) with changes in noncompliance, which is consistent with the assumption that parenting functions as a causal mechanism for compliance. Their earlier publication showed that much of the change resulted from changes in the parental contingencies and that these changes accounted for 50% of the variance in the measures of noncompliance (Martinez and Forgatch, 2001).

Given the design of the study, we cannot say that changes in noncompliance functions as a causal mechanism in producing changes in aggression. Clearly, however, the two child outcome variables are correlated. Notice, too, that the starting levels for parenting and noncompliance significantly predict the magnitude of changes in child behavior.

As is shown in Figure 3.6, the χ^2 value of 7.01, with its p value of .22 and a CFI of .99, is consistent with the idea that the a priori model provides a reasonable fit to the data set. The Forgatch and DeGarmo (2000) analyses covered a variety of outcome variables, such as child achievement, caretaker depression and support groups, delinquency, and shift from poverty.

The findings from these three studies consistently support the idea that changes in positive parenting (skill encouragement, involvement, and monitoring) covary with increases in positive child outcomes. Similarly, reductions in negative parenting (negative reinforcement and inconsistent discipline) covary with increases in positive child outcomes. This is encouraging, as it sets the stage for the more difficult task of determining which changes in parenting are critical for which changes in child outcomes. Given the aforementioned empirical evidence, we can now begin to say that parenting practices may function as causal mechanisms.

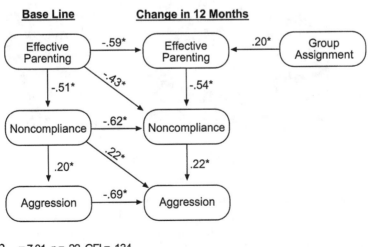

$\chi^2_{(5)} = 7.01, p = .22, GFI = .134$

$*p < .05$

FIGURE 3.6. Changes in parenting and changes in noncompliance and aggression (from Forgatch and DeGarmo, 2000).

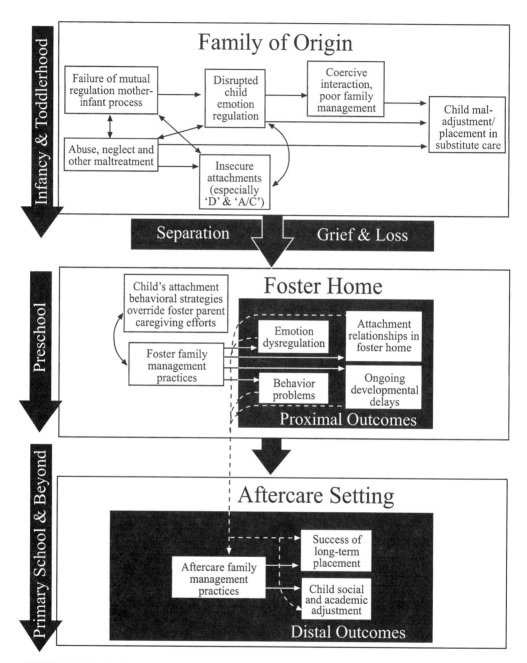

FIGURE 3.7. Hypothesized developmental model for high-risk preschoolers in foster care.

Studies designed to test causal mechanisms and incorporate concepts from attachment and social learning theory are on the horizon (Fisher, Ellis, and Chamberlain, 1999). An example of a theoretical model for this research is shown in Figure 3.7. Based on a successful pilot evaluation of a preventive intervention for maltreated preschoolers in the foster care system (Fisher, Gunnar, Chamberlain, and Reid, 2000), Fisher and colleagues are conducting a longitudinal randomized trial. The intervention employs behavioral and parent management training techniques that have been found in the above cited studies to produce changes in parenting and child outcomes. However, we are interested in testing child outcomes in domains of both behavior and attachment. Dozier and Albus (2000) have found that under the right conditions, intervention with foster children has the potential to change attachment status. We hypothesize that the type of contingent responding that produces prosocial behavior may also produce changes in attachment status. The design permits a comparison of the relative contributions of both mechanisms to the same child outcome.

Misapplication of Parenting Theories in Interventions Without Empirical Support

As noted, in spite of the progress in research on parenting and the widespread acceptance that interventions should be supported by empirical evidence, some researchers continually adhere to approaches that have not been tested empirically. Some of these approaches may produce positive change—whether such change is specific to individuals with certain characteristics or more generalized remains unknown without investigation under controlled conditions. Of further concern, these approaches may produce no change or may place recipients at risk for harm. Such is the case, for instance, for a particular set of intervention techniques for children with reactive attachment disorder.

Reactive attachment disorder is a psychological diagnosis given to children who are characterized by a failure of basic social interactional skills and a basic inability to develop meaningful relationships with others (Knutson and Schartz, 1997). To be diagnosed as such, children must have experienced severe maltreatment, which must be considered to be the cause of the symptoms. Children with this set of symptoms have been difficult to treat using traditional methods of psychotherapy. As an alternative, some clinicians have embraced an approach called holding therapy, which was originally developed to treat autism (Myeroff, Mertlich, and Gross, 1999). Holding therapy involves prolonged and involuntary restraint of the child for reasons other than protection; it may include prolonged noxious stimulation and interference with bodily functions, such as vision and breathing (James, 2000). Proponents of the approach argue that such coercive measures are necessary because children with the disorder are unreachable by more mild means. Despite the fact that no scientific evidence of the effectiveness of holding therapy exists via either correlational or experimental research, many parents with very difficult to manage children have embraced this approach. Indeed, it appears particularly common with adoptive parents who have failed to develop a relationship with their adopted child.

However, a well-publicized case of a child who died during the administration of particular technique, "rebirthing," brought holding therapy to the attention of the general public in the last year (Pertman, 2000). This case is illuminating in several regards. First, although holding therapy is used to treat a failure of a child's attachment system, it does not appear that researchers familiar with attachment theory developed the approach. In fact, treatments that are more substantively based on attachment theory do exist and have received empirical support (Dozier and Albus, 2000; Lieberman, 1992; Lieberman and Pawl, 1993). Second, and perhaps more important, it is striking how willingly the general public adopts psychological interventions that are only superficially connected to established, empirically supported theories of parenting. For these reasons, the scientific community must continue to question parenting interventions that merely adopt a particular set of accepted terms or techniques to appear legitimate, though the application of such techniques may create significant risk for harm. A related example is derived from a discussion by Dishion and colleagues on iatrogenic effects of certain interventions (Dishion, McCord, and Poulin, 1999). Dishion et al. describe a group treatment for adolescents at risk for substance abuse. Though this treatment has been found to increase rates of substance use for participants, it continues to be used on a widespread basis (owing, perhaps, to cost-effectiveness or intuitive appeal).

Our argument here is straightforward. A clear process exists for developing and evaluating the adequacy of parenting theories. A variety of interventions are connected to this process as empirical methods for experimental validation and as applications of the theory. To the extent that researchers adhere to a process that attempts to create parsimony and moves from the correlational to the experimental, the outlook is quite promising for further clarification of issues such as variation in outcomes as a function of culture, age of child, and family structure. However, as the scientific work proceeds, other approaches will continue to emerge that have inherent risks but that prove popular with both providers and recipients and continue to be utilized. It is important that researchers not ignore these activities but rather make attempts to bring them into scientific scrutiny.

CONCLUSIONS

In this chapter we have endeavored to provide insight into the current state of research on parenting. We have focused on the theoretical perspectives with the greatest amount of research—social learning theory, attachment theory, and social information processing. Furthermore, we have attempted to provide a framework for evaluating the adequacy of elements of these and other theories, arriving at the conclusion that processes previously considered mainly within the attachment framework (sensitive caregiving and maternal warmth) are highly compatible with concepts within social learning theory (contingency and positive reinforcement). These twin processes may set the stage for positive development; their absence may connote high risk for psychological maladjustment.

Our review of the research on parenting highlighted the extent to which concepts of bidirectionality between parent and child must be considered. In particular, we examined how compliance training is influenced not only by how a parent interacts with his or her child but also by how the child—via temperament, behavior, and other factors—shapes the parent. We drew attention to the statistical analytic tools of structural equation modeling that are increasingly commonplace in parenting research, in part because they allow for consideration of the directionality of relations within a model.

We then examined certain variables that determine what the parent brings to the process of parenting. These contextual variables, including culture, divorce, and such parental traits as depression and antisocial behavior, were described as acting on child outcome through their effect on parenting practices. We then presented the results of studies that incorporated this model into experimental tests of interventions, and we demonstrated how such tests could provide strong support for a theory. We also described how theories of parenting could be misapplied, thus creating interventions that pose significant risk to recipients.

In spite of issues of misapplication, the future of research on parenting is encouraging. Methodological advances in the past 2 decades and the integration of previously disparate perspectives allow for progress that previously was not possible. As we move toward causal models that are supported by empirical research, the potential exists to develop powerful parenting interventions that may help to move children off of trajectories of risk to more promising paths.

ACKNOWLEDGMENTS

We would like to acknowledge the contributions made in discussion with Marion Forgatch to the general formulation presented here. Support for this project was provided by Grant No. R37 MH 37940 from the Antisocial and Other Personality Disorders Program; the Prevention, Early Intervention and Epidemiology Branch, National Institute of Mental Health (NIMH), U.S. Public Health Service (PHS); Grant No. RO1 MH 47458 from the Center for Studies of Violent Behavior and Traumatic Stress, NIMH, U.S. PHS; Grant No. 90CW0994 from the Administration for Children, Youth, and Families, Child Welfare Services, HDS, Department of Health and Human Services; Grant No. P30 MH 46690 from the Prevention Research Branch, NIMH, U.S. PHS; Grant No. MH 38318 from the Mood, Anxiety, and Personality Disorders Branch, NIMH, U.S. PHS; Grant No. RO1 MH 59780 from the Child and Adolescent Treatment and Preventive Intervention Branch, NIMH, U.S. PHS; and Grant No. RO1 DA 12231 from the Prevention Research Branch, National Institute on Drug Abuse (NIDA), U.S. PHS.

REFERENCES

Ainslie, R. C., Olmstead, K. M., and O'Loughlin, D. D. (1987). The early development context of twinship: Some limitations of the equal environments hypothesis. *American Journal of Orthopsychiatry, 57*, 120–124.

Ainsworth, M. D. S. (1989). Attachments beyond infancy. *American Psychologist, 44*, 709–716.

Ainsworth, M. D. S., and Bowlby, J. (1991). An ethological approach to personality development. *American Psychologist, 46*, 333–341.

Alexander, J. F., and Parsons, B. V. (1973). Short-term behavioral intervention with delinquent families: Impact on family process and recidivism. *Journal of Abnormal Psychology, 81*, 219–225.

Anderson, K. E., Lytton, H., and Romney, D. N. (1986). Mother's interactions with normal and conduct disordered boys: Who affects whom? *Developmental Psychology, 22*, 604–609.

Askeland, E., Duckert, M., and Forgatch, M. S. (in press). A family to learn from: The first Norwegian PMT case. *Cognitive and Behavioral Practice*. [Special issue: Exceptional cases in child psychotherapy: Testing the limits of empirically based protocols].

Bank, L., Dishion, T. J., Skinner, M. L., and Patterson, G. R. (1990). Method variance in structural equation modeling: Living with "glop." In G. R. Patterson (Ed.), *Depression and aggression in family interaction* (pp. 247–279). Hillsdale, NJ: Lawrence Erlbaum Associates.

Bank, L., Duncan, T., Patterson, G. R., and Reid, J. B. (1993). Parent and teacher ratings in the assessment and prediction of antisocial and delinquent behaviors. *Journal of Personality, 61*, 693–709.

Bank, L., Forgatch, M. S., Patterson, G. R., and Fetrow, R. A. (1993). Parenting practices of single mothers: Mediators of negative contextual factors. *Journal of Marriage and the Family, 55*, 371–384.

Barkley, R. A. (1981). The use of psychopharmacology to study reciprocal influences in parent–child interaction. *Journal of Abnormal Child Psychology, 9*, 303–310.

Barkley, R. A., and Cunningham, C. E. (1979). The effects of methylphenidate on the mother–child interactions of hyperactive children. *Archives of General Psychiatry, 36*, 201–208.

Barkley, R. A., Karlsson, J., Pollard, S., and Murphy, J. V. (1985). Developmental changes in the mother–child interactions of hyperactive boys: Effects of two dose levels of Ritalin. *Journal of Child Psychology and Psychiatry, 26*, 705–715.

Baron, R. M., and Kenny, D. A. (1986). The moderator–mediator variable distinction in social psychological research: Conceptual, strategic, and statistical considerations. *Journal of Personality and Social Psychology, 51*, 1173–1182.

Baumrind, D. (1971). Current patterns of parental authority. *Developmental Psychology Monographs, 4*(No. 1, Pt. 2).

Baumrind, D. (1991). Effective parenting during the early adolescent transition. In P. A. Cowan and E. M. Hetherington (Eds.), *Family transitions* (pp. 111–163). Hillsdale, NJ: Lawrence Erlbaum Associates.

Bell, R. Q. (1968). A reinterpretation of the direction of effects in studies of socialization. *Psychological Review, 75*, 81–95.

Bell, R. Q., and Harper, L. V. (1977). *Child effects on adults*. Hillsdale, NJ: Lawrence Erlbaum Associates.

Belsky, J. (1984). The Pennsylvania infant and family development project: Stability and change in mother–infant and father–infant interaction in a family setting at one, three, and nine months. *Child Development, 55*, 692–705.

Bentler, P. M. (1980). Multivariate analysis with latent variables: Causal modeling. *Annual Review of Psychology, 31*, 419–436.

Bernal, M. E., Klinnert, M. D., and Schultz, L. A. (1980). Outcome evaluation of behavioral parent training and client-centered parent counseling for children with conduct problems. *Journal of Applied Behavior Analysis, 13*, 677–691.

Bohman, N. (1996). Predispositions to criminality: Swedish adoption studies in retrospect. In G. Bock and J. A. Goode (Eds.), *Genetics of criminal and antisocial behavior* (pp. 99–114). Chichester, England: Wiley.

Bornstein, M. H. (1995). *Handbook of parenting: Vol. 4. Applied and practical parenting*. Mahwah, NJ: Lawrence Erlbaum Associates.

Bornstein, M. H., Haynes, O. M., Azuma, H., Galperin, C., Maital, S., Ogino, M., Painter, K., Pascual, L., Pecheux, M.-G., Rahn, C., Toda, S., Venuti, P., Vyt, A., and Wright, B. (1998). A cross-national study of self-evaluations and attributions in parenting: Argentina, Belgium, France, Israel, Italy, Japan, and the United States. *Developmental Psychology, 34*, 662–676.

Bornstein, M. H., Tamis-LeMonda, C. S., and Haynes, O. M. (1999). First words in the second year: Continuity, stability, and models of concurrent and predictive correspondence in vocabulary and verbal responsiveness across age and context. *Infant Behavior and Development, 22*, 65–85.

Bornstein, M. H., Tamis-LeMonda, C. S., Pascual, L., Maurice, H. O., Painter, K. M., Galperin, C. Z., and Pecheux, M.-G. (1996). Ideas about parenting in Argentina, France, and the United States. *International Journal of Behavioral Development, 19*, 347–367.

Bugental, D. B., Caporeal, L., and Shennum, W. A. (1980). Experimentally produced child uncontrollability: Effects on the potency of adult communication patterns. *Child Development, 51*, 520–528.

Burgess, R. L., and Conger, R. D. (1978). Family interaction in abusive, neglectful and normal families. *Child Development, 49*, 1163–1173.

Cadoret, R. J., Cain, C. A., and Crowe, R. R. (1983). Evidence for gene–environment interaction in the development of adolescent antisocial behavior. *Behavior Genetics, 13*, 301–310.

Cadoret, R. M., Leve, L. D., and Devor, E. (1997). Genetics of aggressive and violent behavior [Special issue: Anger, Aggression, and Violence]. *Psychiatric Clinics of North America, 20*, 301–322.

Chamberlain, P., and Reid, J. (1998). Comparison of two community alternatives to incarceration for chronic juvenile offenders. *Journal of Consulting and Clinical Psychology, 6*, 624–633.

Chilcoat, H. D., Dishion, T. J., and Anthony, J. C. (1995). Parent monitoring and the incidence of drug sampling in urban elementary school children. *American Journal of Epidemiology, 141*, 25–31.

Coe, C. L., Stanton, M. E., and Levine, S. (1 983). Adrenal responses to reinforcement and extinction: Role of expectancy versus instrumental responding. *Behavioral Neuroscience, 97*, 654–657.

Collins, W. A., Maccoby, E. E., Steinberg, L., Hetherington, E. M., and Bornstein, M. (2000). Contemporary research on parenting: The case for nature *and* nurture. *American Psychologist, 55*, 218–232.

Coover, G. D., Goldman, L., and Levine, S. (1971). Plasma corticosterone increases produced by extinction of operant behavior in rats. *Physiology and Behavior, 6*, 261–263.

Darling, N., and Steinberg, L. (1993). Parenting styles as context: An integrative model. *Psychological Bulletin, 113*, 487–496.

Davis, H., and Levine, S. (1982). Predictability, control, and the pituitary–adrenal response in rats. *Journal of Comparative and Physiological Psychology, 96*, 393–404.

Deater-Deckard, K., and Dodge, K. A. (1997). Externalizing behavior problems and discipline revisited: Nonlinear effects and variation by culture, context, and gender. *Psychological Inquiry, 8*, 161–175.

DeBaryshe, B. D., Patterson, G. R., and Capaldi, D. M. (1993). A performance model for academic achievement in early adolescent boys. *Developmental Psychology, 29*, 795–804.

DeGarmo, D., and Forgatch, M. S. (1997). Determinants of observed confidant support for divorced mothers. *Journal of Personality and Social Psychology, 72*, 336–345.

DeGarmo, D. S., Forgatch, M. S., and Martinez, C. R., Jr. (1999). Parenting of divorced mothers as a link between social status and boys' academic outcomes: Unpacking the effects of SES. *Child Development, 70*, 1231–1245.

De Wolff, M. S., and van IJzendoorn, M. H. (1997). Sensitivity and attachment: A meta-analysis on parental antecedents of infant attachment. *Child Development, 68*, 571–591.

Dishion, T. J., and Kavanagh, K. (in press). *Adolescent problem behavior: Theory and intervention.* New York: Guilford.

Dishion, T. J., Kavanagh, K., and Kiesner, J. (in press). Prevention of early adolescent substance use among high-risk youth: A multiple gating approach to parent intervention. In R. S. Ashery (Ed.), *Research meeting on drug abuse prevention through family interventions.* (NIDA Research Monograph).

Dishion, T. J., McCord, J., and Poulin, F. (1999). When interventions harm: Peer groups and problem behavior. *American Psychologist, 54*, 755–764.

Dishion, T. J., Spracklen, K. M., Andrews, D. W., and Patterson, G. R. (1996). Deviancy training in male adolescent friendships. *Behavior Therapy, 27*, 373–390.

Dodge, K. A., Bates, J. E., and Pettit, G. S. (1990). Mechanisms in the cycle of violence. *Science, 250*, 1678–1683.

Downey, G., and Coyne, J. C. (1990). Children of depressed parents: An integrative review. *Psychological Bulletin, 108*, 50–76.

Dozier, M., and Albus, K. E. (2000). Attachment issues for adopted infants. In R. P. Barth, M. Freundlich, and D. Brodzinsky (Eds.), *Adoption and prenatal alcohol and drug exposure: The research policy, practice and challenges* (pp. 171–197). Washington, DC: Child Welfare League of America, The Evan B. Donaldson Adoption Institute.

Eddy, J. M., and Chamberlain, P. (2000). Family management and deviant peer association as mediators of the impact of treatment condition on youth antisocial behavior. *Journal of Consulting and Clinical Psychology, 5*, 857–863.

Eisenstadt, T. H., Eyberg, S., McNeil, C. B., Newcomb, K., and Funderburk, B. (1993). Parent–child interaction therapy with behavior problem children: Relative effectiveness of two stages and overall treatment outcome. *Journal of Clinical Child Psychology, 22*, 42–51.

Emde, R. N., Biringen, Z., Cluman, R. B., and Oppenheim, D. (1991). The moral self of infancy: Affective core and procedural knowledge. *Developmental Review, 11*, 251–270.

Engfer, A., and Gavranidou, M. (1988, June). *Prospective identification of violent mother–child relationships.* Paper presented at the Third European Conference on Developmental Research, Budapest, Hungary.

Fagot, B. I., and Gauvain, M. (1997). Mother–child problem solving: Continuity through the early childhood years. *Developmental Psychology, 33*, 480–488.

Farrington, D. P., and Hawkins, J. D. (1991). Predicting participation, early onset and later persistence in officially recorded offending. *Criminal Behaviour and Mental Health, 1*, 1–33.

Field, T. (1995). Infants of depressed mothers. *Infant Behavior and Development, 18*, 1–13.

Fisher, P. A., Ellis, B. H., and Chamberlain, P. (1999). Early Intervention Foster Care: A model for preventing risk in young children who have been maltreated. *Children's Services: Social Policy, Research, and Practice, 2*, 159–182.

Fisher, P. A., Gunnar, M. R., Chamberlain, P., and Reid, J. B. (2000). Preventive intervention for maltreated preschoolers: Impact on children's behavior, neuroendocrine activity, and foster parent functioning. *Journal of the American Academy of Child and Adolescent Psychiatry, 39*, 1356–1364.

Forehand, R., Gardner, H., and Roberts, N. (1978, Summer). Maternal response to child compliance and noncompliance: Some normative data. *Journal of Clinical Child Psychology*, 121–124.

Forehand, R., King, H. E., Peed, S., and Yoder, P. (1975). Mother–child interactions: Comparisons of a noncompliant clinic group and a nonclinic group. *American Journal of Sociology, 13*, 79–84.

Forgatch, M. S. (1989). Patterns and outcome in family problem solving: The disrupting effect of negative emotion. *Journal of Marriage and the Family, 5*, 115–124.

Forgatch, M. S. (1991). The clinical science vortex: A developing theory of antisocial behavior. In D. J. Pepler and K. H. Rubin (Eds.), *The development and treatment of childhood aggression* (pp. 291–316). Hillsdale, NJ: Lawrence Erlbaum Associates.

Forgatch, M. S. (2000). *Parenting through change*. Unpublished training manual, Oregon Social Learning Center, Eugene.

Forgatch, M. S., and DeGarmo, D. S. (1999). Parenting through change: An effective prevention program for single mothers. *Journal of Consulting and Clinical Psychology, 67*, 711–724.

Forgatch, M. S., and DeGarmo, D. S. (2000). *Extending and testing the social interactional learning model with divorce samples*. Manuscript in preparation.

Ge, X., Conger, R. D., Cadoret, R. J., Neiderhiser, J. M., Yates, W., Troughton, E., and Stewart, M. A. (1996). The developmental interface between nature and nurture: A mutual influence model of child antisocial behavior and parent behaviors. *Developmental Psychology, 32*, 574–589.

Ghodsian, M., Zajicek, E., and Wolkind, S. (1984). A longitudinal study of maternal depression and child behaviour problems. *Journal of Child Psychology and Psychiatry and Allied Disciplines, 25*, 91–109.

Goldman, L., Coover, G. D., and Levine, S. (1973). Bidirectional effects of reinforcement shifts on pituitary adrenal activity. *Physiology and Behavior, 10*, 209–214.

Gottfredson, M. R., and Hirschi, T. (1990). *A general theory of crime*. Stanford, CA: Stanford University Press.

Granic, I. (2000). *A dynamic systems analysis of heterogeneous family processes underlying childhood aggression*. Unpublished doctoral thesis, University of Toronto, Ontario, Canada.

Greenwald, R. L., Bank, L., Reid, J. B., and Knutson, J. F. (1997). A discipline-mediated model of excessively punitive parenting. *Aggressive Behavior, 23*, 259–280.

Greenwood, P. W., Model, K. E., Rydell, C. P., and Chiesa, J. (1996). *Diverting children from a life of crime: Measuring costs and benefits* (Rep. No. 0-8330-2383-7, prepared for the University of California, Berkeley, James Irvine Foundation). Santa Monica, CA: RAND.

Griest, D., Wells, K. C., and Forehand, R. (1979). An examination of predictors of maternal perceptions of maladjustment in clinic-referred children. *Journal of Abnormal Psychology, 88*, 277–281.

Harris, J. R. (1998). *The nurture assumption: Why children turn out the way they do*. New York: Free Press.

Hennessy, J. W., King, M. G., McClure, T. A., and Levine, S. (1977). Uncertainty, as defined by the contingency between environmental events, and the adrenocortical response of the rat to electric shock. *Journal of Comparative and Physiological Psychology, 91*, 1447–1460.

Herrmann, T. F., Hurwitz, H. M., and Levine, S. (1984). Behavioral control, aversive stimulus frequency, and pituitary–adrenal response. *Behavioral Neuroscience, 98*, 1094–1099.

Herrnstein, R. J. (1961). Relative and absolute strength of response as a function of frequency or reinforcement. *Journal of Experimental Analysis of Behavior, 4*, 267–272.

Huston, A. C., Duncan, G. J., Granger, R., Bos, J., McLloyd, V., Mistry, R., Crosby, D., Gibson, C., Magnuson, K., Romich, J., and Ventura, A. (2001). Work-based anti-poverty programs for parents can enhance the school performance and social behavior of children. *Child Development, 72*, 318–336.

Hutchings, B., and Mednick, S. A. (1977). Criminality in adoptees and their adoptive and biological parents: A pilot study. In S. Mednick and K. O. Christiansen (Eds.), *Biosocial bases of criminal behavior* (pp. 127–141). New York: Gardner.

James, B. (2000). *Handbook for treatment of attachment-trauma problems in children*. New York: Lexington.

Joseph, J. (1998). The equal environment assumption of the classical twin method: A critical analysis. *The Journal of Mind and Behavior, 19*, 325–358.

Kellam, S. G., Rebok, G. W., Ialongo, N., and Mayer, L. S. (1994). The course and malleability of aggressive behavior from early first grade into middle school: Results of a developmental epidemiologically based preventive trial. *Journal of Child Psychology and Psychiatry, 35*, 259–281.

Knutson, J. F., and Schartz, H. A. (1997) Evidence pertaining to physical abuse and neglect of children as parent–child relational diagnoses. In T. A. Widiger, A. F. Frances, H. A. Pincus, R. Ross, M. First, and W. Davis (Eds.), *DSM IV Sourcebook* (Vol. 3, pp. 713–804). Washington, DC: American Psychiatric Association.

Kochanska, G. (1991). Socialization and temperament in the development of guilt and conscience. *Child Development, 62*, 1379–1392.

Krech, K. H., and Johnston, C. (1992). The relationship of depressed mood and life stress to maternal perceptions of child behavior. *Journal of Clinical Child Psychology, 21*, 115–122.

Kuczynski, L., and Kochanska, G. (1990). Development of children's noncompliance strategies from toddlerhood to age 5. *Developmental Psychology, 26*, 398–408.

Lepper, M. R. (1982). Social control processes, attributions of motivation and internalization of social value. In E. T. Higgins, D. N. Ruble, and W. W. Hartuk (Eds.), *Social cognition and social behavior: Developmental processes.* New York: Cambridge University Press.

Leve, L. D. (1999). *Gene–environment correlation in twin studies: A test of the equal environment assumption* (Grant submitted to the National Science Foundation). Eugene: Oregon Social Learning Center.

Lieberman, A. F. (1992). Infant–parent psychotherapy with toddlers. *Development and Psychopathology, 4*, 559–574.

Lieberman, A. F., and Pawl, J. H. (1993). Infant–parent psychotherapy. In J. C. H. Zeanah (Ed.), *Handbook for infant mental health* (pp. 427–442). New York: Guilford.

Lobitz, W. C., and Johnson, S. M. (1975). Parental manipulation of the behavior of normal and deviant children. *Child Development, 46*, 719–726.

Loeber, R., and Dishion, T. (1983). Early predictors of male delinquency: A review. *Psychological Bulletin, 94*, 68–99.

Lykken, D. T. (1995). *The antisocial personalities.* Mahwah, NJ: Lawrence Erlbaum Associates.

Lytton, H. (1980). *Parent–child interaction: The socialization process observed in twin and singleton families.* New York: Plenum.

Lytton, H. (1990). Child and parent effects in boys' conduct disorder: A reinterpretation. *Developmental Psychology, 26*, 683–697.

MacKinnon, C. E., Lamb, M. E., Belsky, J., and Baum, C. (1990). An affective–cognitive model of mother–child aggression. *Development and Psychopathology, 2*, 1–13.

Martin, J. A. (1981). A longitudinal study of the consequences of early mother infant interaction: A microanalytic approach. *Monograph of the Society for Research in Child Development, 46* (3, Serial No. 190).

Martinez, C. R., Jr., and Forgatch, M. S. (2001). Preventing problems with boys' noncompliance: Effects of a parent training intervention for divorcing mothers. *Journal of Consulting and Clinical Psychology, 69*, 416–428.

McCord, J. (1991). Questioning the value of punishment. *Social Problems, 38*, 167–179.

McLoyd, V. C. (1998). Socioeconomic disadvantage and child development. *American Psychologist, 53*, 185–204.

Meyeroff, R., Mertlich, G., and Gross, J. (1999). Comparative effectiveness of holding therapy with aggressive children. *Child Psychiatry and Human Development, 29*, 303–313.

Mineka, S., Gunnar, M., and Champoux, M. (1986). Control in early socioemotional development: Infant rhesus monkeys reared in controllable vs. uncontrollable environments. *Child Development, 57*, 1241–1256.

Olweus, D. (1980). Familial and temperamental determinants of aggressive behavior in adolescent boys: A causal analysis. *Developmental Psychology, 16*, 644–660.

Palmerus, K. E., and Scarr, S. W. (1995, April). *How Swedish parents discipline young children: Cultural comparisons and individual differences.* Paper presented at the meeting of Society for Research in Child Development, Indianapolis, IN.

Parpal, M., and Maccoby, E. E. (1985). Maternal responsiveness and subsequent child compliance. *Child Development, 56*, 1326–1334.

Patterson, G. R. (1976). The aggressive child: Victim and architect of a coercive system. In E. J. Mash, L. A. Hamerlynck, and L. C. Handy (Eds.), *Behavior modification and families* (pp. 267–316). New York: Brunner/Mazel.

Patterson, G. R. (1980). Mothers: The unacknowledged victims. *Monographs of the Society for Research in Child Development, 45* (5, Serial No. 186).

Patterson, G. R. (1982). *A social learning approach: Vol. 3. Coercive family process.* Eugene, OR: Castalia.

Patterson, G. R. (1983). Stress: A change agent for family process. In N. Garmezy and M. Rutter (Eds.), *Stress, coping, and development in children* (pp. 235–264). New York: McGraw-Hill.

Patterson, G. R. (1986). Performance models for antisocial boys. *American Psychologist, 41*, 432–444.

Patterson, G. R. (1995). Coercion as a basis for early age of onset for arrest. In J. McCord (Ed.), *Coercion and punishment in long-term perspective* (pp. 81–105). New York: Cambridge University Press.

Patterson, G. R. (1997). Performance models for parenting: A social interactional perspective. In J. E. Grusec and L. Kuczynski (Eds.), *Parenting and children's internalization of values: A handbook of contemporary theory* (pp. 193–235). New York: Wiley.

Patterson, G. R., and Bank, L. (1986). Bootstrapping your way in the nomological thicket. *Behavioral Assessment, 8*, 49–73.

Patterson, G. R., and Bank, L. I. (1989). Some amplifying mechanisms for pathologic processes in families. In M. R. Gunnar and E. Thelen (Eds.), *Systems and development: The Minnesota symposia on child psychology* (pp. 167–209). Hillsdale, NJ: Lawrence Erlbaum Associates.

Patterson, G. R., Bank, L., and Stoolmiller, M. (1990). The preadolescent's contributions to disrupted family process. In R. Montemayor, G. R. Adams, and T. P. Gullotta (Eds.), *From childhood to adolescence: A transitional period?* (pp. 107–133). Newbury Park, CA: Sage.

Patterson, G. R., Dishion, T. J., and Bank, L. (1984). Family interaction: A process model of deviancy training. *Aggressive Behavior, 10*, 253–267.

Patterson, G. R., Dishion, T. J., and Chamberlain, P. (1993). Outcomes and methodological issues relating to treatment of antisocial children. In T. R. Giles (Ed.), *Effective psychotherapy: A handbook of comparative research* (pp. 43–88). New York: Plenum.

Patterson, G. R., and Eddy, J. M. (2000). *Recent news concerning the demise of parenting may be a bit premature.* Unpublished manuscript. Oregon Social Learning Center, Eugene.

Patterson, G. R., and Forgatch, M. S. (1990). Initiation and maintenance of processes disrupting single-mother families. In G. R. Patterson (Ed.), *Depression and aggression in family interaction* (pp. 209–245). Hillsdale, NJ: Lawrence Erlbaum Associates.

Patterson, G. R., and Forgatch, M. S. (1995). Predicting future clinical adjustment from treatment outcome and process variables. *Psychological Assessment, 7*, 275–285.

Patterson, G. R., Forgatch, M. S., Yoerger, K., and Stoolmiller, M. (1998). Variables that initiate and maintain an early-onset trajectory for juvenile offending. *Development and Psychopathology, 10*, 541–547.

Patterson, G. R., and Reid, J. B. (1973). Intervention for families of aggressive boys: A replication study. *Behaviour Research and Therapy, 11*, 383–394.

Patterson, G. R., Reid, J. B., and Dishion, T. J. (1992). *A social interactional approach: Vol. 4: Antisocial boys.* Eugene, OR: Castalia.

Patterson, G. R., and Stouthamer-Loeber, M. (1984). The correlation of family management practices and delinquency. *Child Development, 55*, 1299–1307.

Pertman, A. (2000, June). Girl's death exposes bizarre treatment for attachment disorder [Online]. Available: http://www.psycport.com/news/2000/06/06/medic/5827-0010-pat_nytimes.html

Redl, F., and Wineman, D. (1951). *Children who hate: The disorganization and breakdown of behavior controls.* Glencoe, IL: Free Press.

Redl, F., and Wineman, D. (1952). *Controls from within: Techniques for the treatment of the aggressive child.* Glencoe, IL: Free Press.

Reid, J. B. (1978). *A social learning approach to family intervention: Vol. 2. Observation in home settings.* Eugene, OR: Castalia.

Reid, J. B. (1986). Social-interactional patterns in families of abused and nonabused children. In C. Zahn-Waxler, E. M. Cummings, and R. Iannotti (Eds.), *Altruism and aggression: Biological and social origins* (pp. 238–255). New York: Cambridge University Press.

Reid, J. B., Eddy, J. M., Fetrow, R. A., and Stoolmiller, M. (1999). Description and immediate impacts of a preventive intervention for conduct problems. *American Journal of Community Psychology, 27*, 483–517.

Reid, J. B., Patterson, G. R., and Loeber, R. (1982). The abused child: Victim, instigator, or innocent bystander? In D. Bernstein (Ed.), *Response structure and organization* (pp. 47–68). Lincoln, NE: University of Nebraska Press.

Reid, J. B., Patterson, G. R., and Lorber, R. (1981). The treatment of multiple-offending young adolescents using family treatment based on social learning principles. In N. Berlin (Ed.), *Children and our future.* Albuquerque, NM: University of New Mexico Press.

Reid, J. B., Snyder, J. J., and Patterson, G. R. (Eds.). (in press). Antisocial behavior in children: Developmental theories and models for intervention. Washington, DC: American Psychological Association.

Reid, J. B., Taplin, P. S., and Lorber, R. (1981). A social interactional approach to the treatment of abusive families. In R. B. Stuart (Ed.), *Violent behavior: Social learning approaches to prediction, management, and treatment* (pp. 83–101). New York: Brunner/Mazel.

Reiss, D. (1997). Mechanisms linking genetic and social influences in adolescent development: Beginning a collaborative search. *Current Directions in Psychological Science, 6*, 1–6.

Roberts, M. W. (1985). Praising child compliance: Reinforcement or ritual? *Journal of Abnormal Child Psychology, 13*, 611–629.

Roberts, M. W. (1988). Enforcing chair timeouts with room timeouts. *Behavior Modification, 12*, 353–370.

Roberts, M. W., Hatzenbuehler, L. C., and Bean, A. W. (1981). The effects of differential attention and timeout on child noncompliance. *Behavior Therapy, 12*, 93–99.

Robins, L. N. (1992). The role of prevention experiments in discovering causes of children's antisocial behavior. In J. McCord and R. E. Tremblay (Eds.), *Preventing antisocial behavior* (pp. 3–18). New York: Guilford.

Rowe, D. C. (1994). *The limits of family influence: Genes, experience, and behavior.* New York: Guilford.

Rubin, K. H., Stewart, S. L., and Chen, X. (1995). Parents of aggressive and withdrawn children. In M. H. Bornstein (Ed.), *Handbook of parenting: Vol. 1. Children and parenting* (pp. 255–288). Mahwah, NJ: Lawrence Erlbaum Associates.

Rutter, M. (1995). Maternal deprivation. In M. H. Bornstein (Ed.), *Handbook of Parenting. Vol. 4: Applied and practical parenting* (pp. 3–32). Mahwah, NJ: Lawrence Erlbaum Associates.

Sampson, R. J., and Laub, J. H. (1993). *Crime in the making: Pathways and turning points through life.* Cambridge, MA: Harvard University Press.

Scarr, S. (1985). Constructing psychology: Making facts and fables for our times. *American Psychologist, 40*, 499–512.

Scarr, S. (1992). Developmental theories for the 1990s: Development and individual differences. *Child Development, 63*, 1–19.

Shaw, D. S., and Bell, R. Q. (1993). Developmental theories of parental contributors to antisocial behavior. *Journal of Abnormal Child Psychology, 21*, 493–518.

Shaw, D. S., Bell, R. Q., and Gilliom, M. (2000). A truly early starter model of antisocial behavior revisited. *Clinical Child and Family Psychology Review, 3*, 155–117.

Shaw, D. S., Dishion, T., and Gardner, F. (2000). *A family-based prevention for early conduct problems.* NIMH grant application, University of Pittsburgh, PA.

Shaw, D. S., Keenan, K., and Vondra, J. I. (1994). Developmental precursors of externalizing behavior: Ages 1 to 3. *Developmental Psychology, 30*, 355–364.

Shaw, D. S., and Winslow, E. B. (1997). Precursors and correlates of antisocial behavior from infancy to preschool. In D. M. Stoff, J. Breiling, and J. D. Maser (Eds.), *Handbook of antisocial behavior* (pp. 148–158). New York: Wiley.

Simons, R. L., Johnson, C., and Conger, R. D. (1994). Harsh corporal punishment versus quality of parental involvement as an explanation of adolescent maladjustment. *Journal of Marriage and the Family, 56*, 591–607.

Simons, R. L., Wu, C.-I., Johnson, C., and Conger, R. D. (1995). A test of various perspectives on the intergenerational transmission of domestic violence. *Criminology, 33*, 141–172.

Snyder, J., Edwards, P., McGraw, K., Kilgore, K., and Holton, A. (1994). Escalation and reinforcement in mother–child conflict: Social processes associated with the development of physical aggression. *Development and Psychopathology, 6*, 305–321.

Snyder, J. J., and Huntley, D. (1990). Troubled families and troubled youth: The development of antisocial behavior and depression in children. In P. E. Leone (Ed.), *Understanding troubled and troubling youth* (pp. 194–225). Newbury Park, CA: Sage.

Snyder, J. J., and Patterson, G. R. (1995). Individual differences in social aggression: A test of a reinforcement model of socialization in the natural environment. *Behavior Therapy, 26*, 371–391.

Snyder, J., Schrepferman, L., and St. Peter, C. (1997). Origins of antisocial behavior: Negative reinforcement and affect dysregulation of behavior as socialization mechanisms in family interaction. *Behavior Modification, 21*, 187–215.

Stattin, H., and Kerr, M. (2000). Parental monitoring: A reinterpretation. *Child Development, 71*, 1072–1085.

Steinberg, L., Elmen, J. E., and Mounts, N. S. (1989). Authoritative parenting, psychosocial maturity, and academic success among adolescents. *Child Development, 60*, 1424–1436.

Sternberg, R. J., and Williams, W. M. (1995). Parenting toward cognitive competence. In M. H. Bornstein (Ed.), *Handbook of parenting: Vol. 4. Applied and practical parenting* (pp. 259–276). Mahwah, NJ: Lawrence Erlbaum Associates.

Stoolmiller, M. (1999). Implications of the restricted range of family environments for estimates of heritability and nonshared environment in behavior genetic adoption studies. *Psychological Bulletin, 125*, 392–407.

Straus, M. A. (1991). Discipline and deviance: Physical punishment of children and violence and other crime in adulthood. *Social Problems, 38*, 133–154.

Straus, M. A. (Ed.). (1994). *Beating the devil out of them: Corporal punishment in American families and its effects on children:* New York: Lexington.

U.S. General Accounting Office. (1994). *Foster care: Parental drug abuse has alarming impact on young children* (Rep. No. GAO/HEHS-94-89). Washington, DC: Author.

van den Boom, D. C. (1994). The influence of temperament and mothering on attachment and exploration: An experimental manipulation of sensitive responsiveness among lower-class mothers with irritable infants. *Child Development, 65*, 1457–1477.

Wahler, R. G. (1969). Oppositional children: A quest for parental reinforcement control. *Journal of Applied Behavior Analysis, 2*, 159–170.

Webster-Stratton, C., and Hammond, M. (1990). Predictors of treatment outcome in parent training for families and conduct problem children. *Behavior Therapy, 21*, 319–337.

Whiting, B. B., and Edwards, C. P. (1988). *Children of different worlds: The formation of social behavior.* Cambridge, MA: Harvard University Press.

Widom, C. S. (1989). Child abuse, neglect, and adult behavior: Research design and findings on criminality, violence, and child abuse. *American Journal of Orthopsychiatry, 59*, 355–367.

World Health Organization. (1992). *Annual report on homicide.* Geneva, Switzerland: World Health Organization.

Yoon, J., Hughes, J., Gaur, A., and Thompson, B. (1999). Social cognition in aggressive children: A meta-analytic review. *Cognitive and Behavioral Practice, 6*, 320–331.

4

Parenting and the Development of Children's Self-Regulation

Wendy S. Grolnick
Melanie Farkas
Clark University

INTRODUCTION

This chapter concerns the ways in which parenting facilitates self-regulation in children. What is self-regulation? We address this question in our chapter from a motivational perspective. From such a motivational viewpoint, concern is with who or what initiates behavior. From this perspective, self-regulated behaviors are those that are initiated by the person, and include a feeling or experience of self-determination or choice. Thus, a hallmark of self-regulation is the experience of volition, of feeling that one has willingly or choicefully engaged in the behavior rather than being coerced or controlled (Deci and Ryan, 1985). In this use of the term, "self" refers not just to the physical body, but to the experiential self and actions that are perceived as one's own.

One way to delineate the area of self-regulation is to distinguish it from other domains reflecting positive child outcomes, the most relevant being compliance. First, consider a widely accepted definition of child compliance. According to Whiting and Edwards (1988), compliance can be defined as the extent to which the child obeys immediately or after a short-delay. Whereas compliance thus concerns adherence to a specific directive, request, or rule to be followed, self-regulation concerns whether children engage in appropriate behaviors when not explicitly asked. For example, does a child clean her or his room without being asked? Does a child spontaneously help another child who is hurt? Second, compliance occurs in situations where someone is present to require adherence to the rule or request, for example, a mother asking her child to clean up her or his room or do her or his homework, or a teacher asking a child to refrain from talking to a classmate. In contrast, self-regulation implies behavior in the absence of adult supervision. Does, for example, a child refrain from engaging in antisocial behavior with peers when there are no adults monitoring her or his behavior? Does a child refrain from eating another cookie when she or he knows it is almost dinnertime? Third, in considering whether a child is compliant, there is no need to attend to the child's experience of the behavior—the evidence for compliance is in the behavior itself and can be objectively determined. Whether a behavior is self-regulated often cannot be determined by observing the behavior itself.

The experience of the person (e.g., whether she or he experiences choice or volition or an internal sense of pressure or coercion) must be taken into account.

Clearly, the identification of parenting factors that facilitate compliance in children is an important task. However, in considering the socialization of children, many of the goals parents have for them bear only indirect relation to compliance. One of the major goals of socialization is for children to take onto themselves the regulation of their own behavior and to act without explicit directives or demands, to engage in socially prescribed behaviors in the absence of adult supervision, and to do all of this in a flexible, nonconflictual manner. Thus the socialization of self-regulation is a major goal of parenting.

Do the same factors facilitate compliance and self-regulation? There is evidence that they may not. For example, both Baumrind (e.g., 1967) and Steinberg and his colleagues (e.g., Steinberg, Elmen, and Mounts, 1989) have found that, whereas children of authoritarian parents may be competent on certain outcomes (e.g., academic achievement) and conforming (i.e., they show low levels of deviant behavior), they also lack self-reliance and initiative, factors more related to self-regulation. Thus, a chapter that specifically focuses on parenting and self-regulation has much to offer.

In this chapter, we explore the literature on the effects of parenting styles and strategies on the development of self-regulation. First, we discuss definitions of self-regulation from various theoretical perspectives. Then we provide a motivational framework for understanding the development of self-regulation. In particular, we discuss three needs (autonomy, competence, and relatedness) that are hypothesized to underlie the intrinsically motivated movement toward more autonomous self-regulation. Next, environments that support these needs, namely those that provide autonomy support, involvement and structure, are discussed. We then use this motivational framework to organize research on three areas of self-regulation in children and adolescents: emotional self-regulation, behavioral self-regulation, and susceptibility to peer influence. We describe why each of these issues comes under the heading of self-regulation and what kinds of parenting have been associated with the development of effective self-regulation in each of these areas. Finally, we discuss several challenges in the study of parenting and the development of self-regulation, such as the problem of specifying the direction of causality.

SELF-REGULATION DEFINED

Self-regulation has been defined in many ways. For social-cognitive theorists, children are self-regulated when they actively participate in their own learning rather than relying on teachers, parents, or other agents of instruction (e.g., Zimmerman, 1989). Sociocultural theorists have discussed self-regulated behavior as occurring when children monitor, plan, guide, and control their behavior to attain challenging personal or situational goals (e.g., Campbell, 1997; Diaz, Neal, and Amay-Williams, 1990). This regulation involves a collection of higher order psychological functions that have their origins in social interaction. That is, these functions are presumed to emerge from the history of the child's interaction with her or his caregivers. Sociocultural theorists emphasize the shift from caregiver to child in responsibility for the initiation or regulation of activities (Diaz, Neal, and Vachio, 1991). Related concepts of emotion regulation (e.g., Eisenberg and Fabes, 1992; Fox, 1994) and delay of gratification (Mischel, 1974) have been conceptualized as aspects of self-regulation. Clearly, self-regulation is a multidimensional construct with motivational, cognitive, behavioral, and affective components.

What unites these various conceptualizations of self-regulation? We suggest that all involve the child's initiating role in enacting behaviors. Self-regulation is a broad rubric used to refer to actions that are initiated by the self and are thus experienced as choiceful or autonomous. A key construct that can be used to describe the regulation of behavior is that of locus of causality. Heider (1958) suggested that all behaviors can be characterized as personally or intentionally caused or impersonally or unintentionally caused. deCharms (1968), building on this work, suggested that some intentionally caused behaviors have a true sense of personal causation whereas others do not. Thus, although one might intend to do one's schoolwork, one can still feel coerced into doing it because of the threat of punishment. deCharms thus further distinguished between behaviors that have an internal and those that have an external perceived locus of causality. Both behaviors with an internal and those with an external locus of causality represent types of personal causation (i.e., both are intended). The distinction lies in the fact that behaviors that have an internal locus of causality are experienced as self-initiated, whereas those that have an external locus of causality are experienced as propelled from without.

One way to conceptualize self-regulated behaviors are those that have an internal locus of causality. There are two types of motivated behaviors that fit this bill—those that are intrinsically motivated and those that are extrinsically motivated. We discuss each of these types of motivated action below.

Intrinsic and Extrinsic Motivation

Intrinsically motivated activity refers to activity that requires no prompts or external contingencies (Deci and Ryan, 1985). It is activity that is autotelic, or conducted for its own sake (Csikszentmihalyi, 1975). Thus, intrinsically motivated activity is that which is done for the inherent enjoyment of the activity itself, the pleasure or positive feedback one gets from doing the activity. Play, exploration, and curious behaviors clearly fall into the domain of intrinsic motivation.

From a self-determination perspective, underlying intrinsically motivated activity are three innate needs common to human beings. These needs are for autonomy, competence, and relatedness to others (Deci and Ryan, 1985). The need for autonomy is a need to experience oneself as an agent or initiator of action. The need for competence concerns the need to feel effective in interacting with one's environment. Finally, the need for relatedness is the need to feel connected to important others. As individuals interact with their surroundings, they engage the world and attempt to master it to fulfill these three needs.

A second class of behaviors are those that are extrinsically motivated. Such behaviors are those oriented to some goal or outcome that is separable from the activity itself. Thus, when children do their homework because they will not be able to go out to recess if they don't, they are extrinsically regulated in their homework activity. The children are regulating their behavior according to the contingency imposed by the parent or teacher. However, there are many types of extrinsic motivation. For example, other children may do their homework because they believe it is important for understanding the particular subject. In this case, the children are not intrinsically motivated to pursue the work because they are not doing it for the inherent pleasure of the activity, but rather the goal of learning the material. However, clearly there is a sense of self-initiation behind this extrinsically motivated behavior.

One way of evaluating extrinsically motivated behaviors is in the degree to which these behaviors are autonomous, or experienced as self-regulated or self-initiated. Several different types of self-regulation are specified, each lying along a continuum of autonomy. Extrinsically motivated behaviors can be highly *external*, as when children regulate their behavior around contingencies in the environment such as rewards and punishments. For example, a child might clean her or his room because she or he would get in trouble if she or he didn't. External regulation is at the lower extreme on the continuum of autonomy because it lacks a sense of personal volition. Further along the continuum of autonomy is *introjected regulation*. At this point, the person is regulating around a contingency, yet this time the contingency is administered by the self rather than some outside agent. When children clean their rooms because they would feel guilty or bad about themselves if they do not, they are regulating through introjection. Still further along the autonomy continuum is *identified regulation*, a true form of self-regulation. At this point, the child identifies with or takes on the value of the behavior or regulation and behaves in accord with it. No longer is there a perceived conflict between the regulation and the self. Children who clean their rooms because they like them neat so they can find their things are regulating through identification. At the final point on the continuum, identifications have been integrated or assimilated with other aspects of the self into a coherent system of values, goals, and motives. Because this form of self-regulation is developmentally advanced and therefore not characteristic of children and adolescents, we do not focus on *integrated regulation* in this chapter.

How do children move along the continuum toward a greater sense of autonomy, or self-regulation for behaviors that are originally externally regulated? According to self-determination theory, individuals move along the autonomy continuum through the process of internalization. Internalization is the process through which originally externally regulated action becomes increasingly taken in by the person and made a part of the self (Ryan, Connell, and Deci, 1985). The process of internalization is proposed to be a natural one that children actively engage in. It is a process whereby children overtake and master both their external and internal worlds. Thus, provided the environment does not interfere too much, children naturally and spontaneously take on regulations, values, and behaviors around them as part of their intrinsically motivated growth and development. A corollary of the theory is that, as an intrinsically motivated process, internalization itself is energized by the same three needs as intrinsic motivation: to feel autonomous, competent, and related to others. Furthermore, factors that facilitate intrinsic motivation should also facilitate the active process of internalization. We now turn to research on environments facilitative of self-regulation.

Facilitative Environments

According to self-determination theory, three needs underlie intrinsic motivation and movement toward autonomy for extrinsically motivated behavior. Although engaging in intrinsically motivated behaviors and internalizing the regulation of action are natural, spontaneous processes, they can be thwarted by environments that prevent the needs from being satisfied or facilitated through environments supportive of the needs. In fact, growth and development are seen as occurring through a dialectic between an individual striving to satisfy her or his needs and an environment that either supports or undermines this striving.

What environmental factors are important facilitators of self-regulation? Self-determination theory has suggested that factors that facilitate the fulfillment of the three needs, that is those that provide for a sense of autonomy rather than controlling behavior, support a sense of competence, and promote a sense of relatedness, should facilitate intrinsic motivation and autonomous self-regulation. We will now explicate each of these factors, beginning with support for autonomy.

Initial studies of factors related to the experience of autonomy focused on the imposition of rewards. These laboratory studies demonstrated that, when individuals were rewarded for activities that they found intrinsically motivating, their subsequent intrinsic motivation to pursue those activities decreased (e.g., Deci, 1971). Deci suggested that, although initially the locus of causality for the behavior was internal, the rewards changed the locus of causality to external thereby undermining motivation. The same effect was found for a number of external controls, such as deadlines, evaluation, and surveillance. All of these external factors undermine intrinsic motivation. Deci concluded that each of these factors is controlling in that each pressures individuals toward specified outcomes, thus diminishing a sense of autonomy.

Further studies focused not on external events per se, but the interpersonal styles of others in the environment, which are arguably the most salient aspects of individuals' environments. Deci and his colleagues (e.g., Deci, Schwartz, Sheinman, and Ryan, 1981) first addressed this issue in studies of teachers. They argued that teachers have different styles of interacting with children that could be evaluated in terms of whether they tend to support the children's autonomy or control their behavior. In other words, do they pressure children to behave in particular ways and solve problems for them, or do they allow children to lead interactions and to solve problems for themselves, supporting their initiations and actions? Deci et al. (1981) showed that one can measure school teachers' orientations along this continuum of control versus support of autonomy. In one study, these authors showed that elementary school students with more autonomy-supportive teachers were more intrinsically motivated and showed greater perceived competence than children in classrooms of more control-oriented teachers. Grolnick and Ryan (1989) examined changes in the degree of autonomy in children's regulation of their school activities. Self-regulation was measured by children's reasons for engaging in school activities. More external and introjected reasons were contrasted with more identified and intrinsic reasons to create a relative autonomy index. This index reflects the degree of autonomy in children's school-related self-regulation. These authors showed that children in classrooms of more autonomy-oriented teachers moved in the direction of greater autonomy over the first five months of school, whereas those of control-oriented teachers did not.

Support of autonomy, however, is not the only environmental dimension that is important for self-regulation. If children are to internalize regulations and move toward autonomy, the environment must support their competence by specifying guidelines and rules so that children can follow them. Children need to have a clear understanding of how their actions are connected to outcomes in order to be motivated to act. Furthermore, the environment must provide a rationale, or meaning, to the behaviors to be internalized. Only when such meaning is available will the child have something to take on as her or his own. For example, a meaningful rationale for keeping a clean room might be that one's possessions will be more easily found. Guidelines, expectations, rationales, and other information in the environment can be conceived of as environmental structure (Grolnick and Ryan, 1989).

Finally, internalization will be most likely when the environment provides a backdrop of warmth, involvement, and caring that facilitates a sense of relatedness. When this sense of security and caring is present, the child will be most likely to want to take on the values and behaviors modeled and valued by those around them (Grolnick, Deci, and Ryan, 1997). We conceptualize this dimension as positive involvement.

Throughout this chapter we use self-determination theory and the three dimensions of parenting (autonomy support to control, involvement, and structure) to organize our review of the literature on parenting and self-regulation. Although we rely on this conceptualization, it is important to note that the framework coincides well with other dimensionalizations of parenting.

Baumrind's typology (1967, 1971), for example, differentiates mainly three types of parents. The authoritative parent encourages verbal give and take, provides rationales for actions, and solicits input into decisions. This parent also firmly enforces rules and demands mature behavior from children. The authoritarian parent, similar to the authoritative, has rules and guidelines for action. However, in contrast, this parent discourages individuality and independence. Finally, the permissive parent imposes few demands and accepts the child's impulses. Similar to the authoritative parent, the permissive parent encourages independence. Seen from a motivational framework, the authoritative parent would be high on autonomy support and structure, the authoritarian parent high on control and structure, and the permissive parent low on structure and high on autonomy support.

Similar to theoretical arguments underlying self-determination theory, Baumrind suggested that both the authoritarian and the permissive styles would undermine children's internalization because both shield children from opportunities to struggle with and assume responsibility for their own behavior. The authoritarian parent does so by preventing the child from taking initiative. Thus the child does not have the opportunity to be responsible for her or his own behavior. Permissive parents shield children by not demanding that they confront the consequences of their own actions (Baumrind, 1973). Children of each of these types of parents should, then, be lower in self-regulation than those of authoritative parents.

The self-determination framework parallels other researchers' work as well. Steinberg's work on parenting (e.g., Steinberg et al., 1989) has focused on authoritative parenting. He and his colleagues have suggested that authoritative parenting combines three components: acceptance, firm control, and psychological autonomy. These dimensions correspond, respectively, to our dimensions of involvement, structure, and autonomy support. Barber (1996) focused on the psychological autonomy to control dimension. He defined this dimension as the extent to which the parent intrudes into the psychological and emotional development of the child. He contrasts the psychological control dimension with a behavioral control dimension. Behavioral control involves monitoring and managing the child's life. As such it corresponds most closely to our structure dimension.

PARENTING AND SELF-REGULATION: DOMAINS OF APPLICABILITY

There is no contained literature on self-regulation. Rather, this dimension underlies work in several separate literatures. The topics we have identified are: (1) emotion regulation, (2) self-regulation of behavior in young and older children, and (3) lack of susceptibility to peer influence. In each of these areas, the issue is whether the child regulates her or his behavior voluntarily or through choice, without a sense of conflict. For each of these issues, we briefly spell out how the issue is one of self-regulation. We then discuss how parenting variables have been related to outcomes in the domain.

Emotion Regulation

Functionalist conceptualizations of emotions (e.g., Campos, Campos, and Barrett, 1989) stress that emotions are adaptive and communicate important messages to those around us. For example, joy signals to maintain interaction. Anger has the function of alerting the self to try to overcome an obstacle and for others to submit to the individual. Although adaptive, emotions, especially strong negative ones, can interfere with short-term goals. Furthermore, the inability to curtail strong emotions in the service of one's goals or of situational demands for appropriate expression of emotion can interfere with social and intellectual development. Because of this, there is a need to both express and manage emotions. Emotion management, or emotion regulation, has been considered a hallmark of early development.

Emotion regulation can be differentiated from emotion suppression or emotion control. Roberts and Strayer (1987) discussed the importance of children experiencing negative affect. According to these authors, if affect is dissipated before the cognitive component of the communication is integrated, the child's ability to learn from the experience is lessened. Affect will be stored in memory but without the cognitive component being integrated. Similarly, Grolnick, McMenamy, and Kurowski (1999) suggested that the energy invested in suppressing emotion will likely interfere with adaptive behavior. The flexible management of emotions allows the child both to experience the emotion (and take in the information it provides to the self and others) as well as to engage the environment. This flexible, adaptive management may be considered emotional self-regulation.

Self-regulation of emotion is thus the child's active regulation of emotional processes. One can conceptualize the development of emotional self-regulation as movement from reliance on outside sources or control-related processes to a growing capacity for autonomous, flexible, smooth, and adaptive regulation (Grolnick, Bridges, and Connell, 1996). Thus, emotional self-regulation is one type of self-regulation. It's development is hypothesized to be subject to the influences of the three aspects of the environment discussed earlier.

How do children develop the capacity to flexibly and autonomously regulate emotions? Consistent with the motivational theory outlined earlier, parents and other caregivers must first expose children to adaptive strategies (e.g., actively engaging in alternative activities during a waiting period; Grolnick, Bridges, and Connell, 1996). Thus, the environment must provide effective strategies to be internalized, such as through adult guidance and modeling. The provision of such strategies can be seen as an aspect of the structure within the environment. Next, children need to be able to practice these strategies, first with the support of these caregivers and later on their own under conditions in which emotions are mildly or moderately strong. The modulation of very strong affect without assistance is an excessively difficult task for young children. Children must thus have the opportunity to autonomously modulate affect, and this can only take place when the regulatory task is within the capacity of the child. In other words, an autonomy-supportive, structured, and involved environment should facilitate the internalization of the regulation of emotion.

Most relevant to the dimension of relatedness, there is much theory and research emphasizing that a responsive, involved parental environment is important for the development of emotion regulation (Greenspan, 1981; Tronick, 1989). One way of conceptualizing this responsiveness is that parents are available to help their children when distress becomes unmanageable, resulting in maladaptive functioning. Keeping affect within tolerable limits allows the child to take steps toward self-regulation. One way parents facilitate their children's emotion regulation is by acting as resources for their children. This is the assumption of work on social referencing (Sorce and Emde, 1981). In this work, it is posited that regulation involves an appraisal process in which primary emotional reactions are modulated by the meaning ascribed to the situation. Caregivers' facial and vocal expressions are important sources of meaning in ambiguous situations. Several studies have found that, when mothers are available for referencing in fear-inducing situations (versus unavailable such as reading a newspaper), children show less distress and more engagement with the stimulus than when she is unavailable (e.g., Diener, Mangelsdorf, Fosnot, and Kienstra, 1997; Sorce and Emde, 1981). Kogan and Carter (1995) found that emotionally available, empathic, and contingent responsiveness to child emotion was associated with less avoidance and resistance on maternal reengagement after a still-face task, indicating good ability to regulate emotion. Raver (1996; Raver and Leadbetter, 1995) conceptualized parental responsiveness as periods of social contingency or collaborative joint attention. More time in such bouts during free play was associated with more successful emotion regulation strategies (less time seeking comfort from mothers and more time distracting themselves with other objects) during a delay task.

Several studies have related parenting along dimensions similar to that of autonomy support to control to the development of emotion regulation capacities in children. In two studies, Calkins (1997; Calkins and Johnson, 1998) examined parents' styles of interacting with their children in play situations. From these interactions, parents' behaviors were coded for the extent to which they used positive guidance, which included praise, affection, and encouragement, and negative control, which included scolding, restricting, and directing the child. Children's use of three strategies in situations requiring emotion regulation (e.g., delay), were coded: orienting to the task, distraction, and aggression. In a study of 24-month-old children, mothers who engaged in more negative control had children who spent more time orienting to the focal object, used less distraction, and had lower levels of vagal suppression, a physiological index of emotion regulation. Interestingly, maternal styles were not correlated with children's level of reactivity (i.e., distress) to the situations—only the strategies children used to modulate emotion. Because reactivity likely has a strong temperamental component (Calkins and Johnson, 1998), it is less likely to be subject to socialization styles. Rather, the modulation of emotion, as indexed by emotion regulation strategies, is the component of emotion regulation that is amenable to and vulnerable to parental styles. In a study of 18-month-old children, positive guidance was associated with greater use of distraction and constructive coping in emotion-inducing situations. Furthermore, an additional maternal variable, preemptive interference, defined as mothers' actions that precluded the child from doing an activity her- or himself, was associated with more use of anger as a regulatory strategy. Thus, in Calkins's work with toddlers, effective emotion regulation was associated with maternal styles that were positive and not overly intrusive or controlling.

Grolnick, Kurowski, McMenamy, Rivkin, and Bridges (1998) examined the ways mothers helped their children regulate mild distress. Twelve-, 18-, 24-, and 32-month-old children waited to obtain a present or eat some goldfish crackers. In one of these situations (parent active), the mother was allowed to be active in helping her child. In the other (parent passive), she was asked to refrain from initiating interaction with her child (though she could respond). Of interest were relations between the ways mothers interacted with their children in the parent-active situation and the children's abilities to modulate distress on their own (in the parent-passive situation).

Six strategies used by mothers were coded; active engagement, redirecting attention, reassurance, following the child, physical comfort, and focus on the desired object. In addition, the authors coded whether the strategy was mother initiated, child initiated, or ongoing from a previous episode. The results showed that mothers who used more ongoing active engagement in the parent-active situation had children who were more distressed in the parent-passive situation (controlling for distress in the parent-active situation). This finding did not occur for mother-initiated active engagement, indicating that it is not mothers' responses per se (which tend to be reactions to child distress), but the maintenance of activity despite decreases in distress that appears to undermine children's active self-regulation. Thus, mothers who take responsibility for regulating children's distress above and beyond what is called for by their distress levels appear to undermine children's abilities to regulate on their own.

A similar result has been found with fear as the emotion to be regulated. Nachmias, Gunnar, Manglesdorf, Parritz, and Buss (1996) examined the strategies that mothers used to help their wary children deal with a mildly fear-inducing stimulus. Mothers who forced their children to focus on a novel event had children with higher postsession cortisol levels, indicating less-effective regulation and possible interference with the children's own attempts to regulate proximity and contact with the arousing stimulus.

With older children, Gottman, Katz, and Hooven (1996) showed that parents who dismiss negative emotions have children who have difficulty managing emotions on their own. Children of parents who are aware of their children's emotions and support their expression themselves show more well-regulated physiological reactions. These authors have also described parents' beliefs and thoughts about their own and their children's emotions as their "meta-emotion philosophy" (Gottman, Katz, and Hooven, 1997). Two philosophies have been identified. Parents who have an emotion-coaching philosophy are aware of their own and their children's emotions. They see emotional expressions as opportunities for teaching and attempt to assist their children with emotions of anger and sadness, much like an emotion coach. By contrast, parents who subscribe to an emotion-dismissing philosophy deny and ignore emotions in themselves and their children. They try to get rid of emotions and convey to their children that emotions are not important and will not last. They view their job as trying to change and minimize emotions. Gottman, Katz, and Hooven (1997) demonstrated that children from homes with an emotion-coaching philosophy were better regulated physiologically and had a greater ability to focus attention and better social skills than those from homes with an emotion-dismissing philosophy.

Similarly, Eisenberg et al. (1999) examined parents' reactions to children's negative emotion. Parents who were more punitive and minimizing of emotion had children who, in the short-term, decreased in emotion expression but in the long-term were more externalizing in their emotion. In this study, Eisenberg was also able to identify bidirectional patterns in which externalizing negative emotion (as perceived by parents) predicted parental reports of more punitive negative reactions. Roberts (1999) examined parents' childrearing practices, children's competence in preschool, and parents' emotional socialization practices. Parents' comforting and nonpunitive reactions to emotional distress were related to boys' resourceful active engagement in preschool and friendly, nonaggressive relationships with peers. There was evidence, however, that emotion control, including pressure for control of emotion expression, was also positively associated with friendly behavior with peers in the preschool. These findings held even controlling for general parenting style (e.g., authoritarian versus authoritative). Tolerant and nonpunitive responses to emotion at 4 years also predicted increases in friendliness and resourcefulness at age 7. Parent practices that emphasized control of emotions were uncorrelated or negatively correlated with resourcefulness at 7. These results suggest that, in the short run, there may be some positive effects of pressuring children to suppress emotion. However, in the long-term, tolerant responses that help children work through their emotions facilitate adaptive self-regulated behavior.

In both Eisenberg's and Roberts's work, one strategy parents used was to ignore or dismiss emotion. How can this strategy be categorized in terms of an autonomy support to control dimension?

Some might say that this strategy allows emotion to run its course and so is not controlling. Roberts and Strayer (1987) provided another perspective. These authors suggested that parents who ignore emotion make clear their demand for control because access to the caregiver is denied at a time when approach tendencies are high. The message to the child is that expression of emotions is not acceptable. As such, this strategy would be categorized as controlling of emotion.

In sum, there is strong evidence that emotional self-regulation is facilitated by involved, responsive parenting but also by styles that tolerate and support emotional expression and allow the child opportunities to autonomously regulate emotions.

Behavioral Self-Regulation

The development of self-regulation in toddlerhood and the early precursors of more internalized responding in older children have been a foci of interest for Kochanska and her colleagues, as well as others. These authors conceptualized self-regulation as a developmental process. Kopp (1982), for example, discussed stages of regulation of behavior. In the neurophysiological stage (2 to 3 months), behavior is regulated largely by arousal states aided by the caregiver. In the sensorimotor stage (3 to 9 months), the child is able to adjust behavior in accord with immediate environmental events and stimuli. The child between 9 and 18 months exhibits control by showing awareness of social and task demands and acting accordingly. However, it is not until the middle of the second year that the child can act in accord with social expectations in the absence of external monitoring or can display self-control. Kopp postulated a final stage of self-regulation (36 months plus) in which a more flexible and adaptive control of behavior is possible, largely because of increasing capacities for representation and symbolic functioning. Several studies have supported the increasing capacity of children between 18 and 48 months to delay (e.g., Golden, Montare, and Bridger, 1977; Vaughn, Kopp, and Krakow, 1984) and use adaptive strategies while waiting (e.g., Van Lieshout, 1975), supporting a developmental model of behavioral self-regulation.

In their developmental conceptualization, Kochanska, Aksan, and Koenig (1995) differentiated situational compliance from committed compliance and suggested that committed compliance is a precursor to internalization. In situational compliance, the child is cooperative and complies but lacks a sincere commitment to the compliance behavior. To sustain the compliance, the child requires reminders and parental control techniques. By contrast, committed compliance is more self-regulated. Here, the child appears to embrace, endorse, and accept the parent's agendum as her or his own. The child does not require prompts or reminders to maintain the behavior and does so enthusiastically. Committed compliance thus compares with our earlier definition of self-regulation.

Supporting the developmental nature of committed compliance, Kochanska and Aksan (1995) found that committed compliance increases with age. Supporting the hypothesis that it is a precursor to internalization, these authors found that committed compliance in the toddler years was associated with indices of internalization in the preschool years, such as doing a requested activity in the absence of the mother and an unwillingness to succumb to enticements to cheat. Situational compliance was not so related to internalization.

What parental qualities would facilitate committed compliance? Kochanska and Aksan (1995) argued that one possibility is shared positive affect between parent and child, a factor that we suggest would facilitate relatedness. Such positive affect, they suggested, would result in an eagerness to engage in shared maternal values and goals. In one study, Kochanska and Aksan (1995) rated positive affect between children and mothers during free play. These authors found positive relations between positive affect in free play and committed compliance in a clean-up task as well as in a dull sorting task. This finding was replicated by Kochanska, Aksan, and Koenig (1995).

Taking the concept of shared positive affect even further, Kochanska (1997) suggested that an atmosphere of "mutual responsiveness" between parents and their young children should set the stage for children to embrace and internalize parental values and goals. Following Maccoby's lead, Kochanska argued that when children find their parents concerned and responsive to their needs, the children will respond in kind, developing a desire to be helpful and cooperative and a readiness to internalize parental goals. It is under these circumstances that children begin to feel an internal rather than only an external obligation to comply with parental wishes. In an experimentally manipulated test of this hypothesis, Parpal and Maccoby (1985) found that children whose mothers were instructed to allow the child to lead the interaction during a play period were subsequently more likely to comply when the mother asked the child to pick up the toys.

Kochanska (1997) assessed the degree of mutually responsive orientation that existed between toddlers and their parents when the children were $2^{1}/_{2}$ and $4^{1}/_{2}$ years old. To create this index, she coded mothers and their toddlers at play for maternal responsiveness and committed compliance of the child and aggregated these indices. Also coded was mothers' use of power assertion, both physical (e.g., taking toy away) and verbal (e.g., direct commands). Finally, the outcome of interest was children's internalization. Internalization was indexed by compliance to mothers' prohibitions in the mother's absence, reluctance to violate rules, and mothers' reports of whether the child complies at home on her or his own. Results showed that mothers in dyads high on mutually responsive orientation used less power assertion both contemporaneously and two years later than did those from dyads lower on this orientation. This suggests a child-to-parent effect in that mothers in dyads that are mutually responsive have less need to exert power because the children are working with their parents rather than against them. Further, mutually responsive orientation at age $2^{1}/_{2}$ predicted more internalization in the child at age $4^{1}/_{2}$.

The results of this study suggest ongoing cycles. It is possible that these cycles begin with either responsive parenting and/or temperamentally easy children who do not resist socialization. When parents are responsive and/or children are easy, there are likely to be more cooperative and positive interchanges between parents and their children. These positive experiences both render children more likely to take on the goals of their parents and make for less need for parents to push and prod children. This mutual responsiveness creates a setting in which socialization efforts are more easily internalized and the child becomes more self-regulated. This conceptualization is consistent with the fact that over the preschool years both mothers and children decrease in aversive behavior and increase in positive behaviors (Kalpidou, Rothbaum, and Rosen, 1998). However, even within these developmental trajectories, there remain individual differences between dyads, with mother-aversive behavior correlated with child-aversive behavior, and child-positive behavior correlated with mothers' positive behavior.

Self-regulation from a sociocultural perspective.   For sociocultural theorists (e.g., Vygotsky, 1978), the growth of self-regulation involves children developing higher order psychological functions, such as self-monitoring, language, private speech, and impulse control. These processes are the result of the gradual internalization of strategies and functions experienced in interaction with parents or other adults. Thus, there is a gradual transfer of the strategies, or "cultural tools," associated with self-regulation from caregiver to child.

Wood (1980) described the parenting strategy that facilitates the internalization process as "scaffolding." Scaffolding is an interactive process in which the adult sensitively modulates the difficulty of the task for the child by tailoring her or his level of assistance and involvement to the child's skills. Thus, when the child is beginning a task or has difficulty with it, the adult may be highly involved. The adult gradually withdraws as the child is able to take more responsibility for the task. Verbal methods are used to facilitate the child taking increasing responsibility for the task. Diaz et al. (1991) pointed out that the concept of scaffolding has much in common with that of an authoritative style or autonomy-supportive behavior. By adjusting the help provided to the child's current level of performance, parents support children's independent mastery of the task. In fact, by definition, autonomy-supportive parents take children's perspectives and allow children to initiate. At the same time, such parents provide structure to facilitate competence.

Pratt, Kerig, Cowan, and Cowan (1988) had mothers and fathers work with their preschoolers on block, matrix, and story tasks. Parents who provided more appropriate scaffolding had children who performed substantially better on the tasks. In addition, parents rated as more authoritative by observers used more appropriate scaffolding. Thus, the connection between autonomy supportive parenting and scaffolding discussed above was supported in this study.

Winsler, Diaz, McCarthy, Atencio, and Chabay (1999) examined a group of behaviorally at-risk preschool children (i.e., those rated by teachers as high on impulsivity, inattention, and hyperactivity) and a matched control group. Children and their mothers completed collaborative tasks in the laboratory. Mother–child interaction in the at-risk children was characterized by more other-regulation, more negative control, and less withdrawal over time (i.e., as children attained increasing competence at the task). Thus, the interaction of dyads with at-risk children was characterized by less scaffolding. For the control children, the more other regulation and negative control mothers exhibited in the collaborative interaction, the lower was children's task performance when on their own. Thus, controlling interactions and those characterized by less scaffolding appear to undermine children's ability to regulate their task behavior when on their own.

Berk and Spuhl (1995) examined whether private speech might be the mechanism through which controlling interactions are related to children's lower task performance. These authors looked at how mothers assisted their preschool children in two challenging tasks. Task sessions were coded for global parenting style (i.e., authoritarian or authoritative) and degree of scaffolding. In subsequent sessions, children's private speech and performance on tasks on their own was measured. Findings suggested that authoritative parenting was associated with more mature forms of private speech (i.e., less muttering and more task-relevant speech). Furthermore, private speech served as a link between authoritative parenting, and task success, such that an authoritative parenting style led to more mature forms of private speech that then led to greater task accomplishment. A similar finding was reported by Behrend, Rosengren, and Permutter (1989) who found that a global rating of scaffolding was positively associated with 3-year-old children's private speech when they worked alone. Furthermore, use of private speech was associated with puzzle solving ability.

These and other studies within the sociocultural tradition appear to mesh easily with those from a motivational perspective. Parents who sensitively tailor their assistance to their child's needs and, while providing support, do not intrude where they are not needed appear to facilitate the child's self-regulation.

Behavioral self-regulation in older children. There have been many different indices of behavioral self-regulation that have been the focus of research studies. One key outcome is children's reports of their reasons for engaging in various behaviors that, because they are not naturally "fun," would need to be internalized. The reasons children endorse for engaging in behaviors such as doing homework, brushing their teeth, and going to bed on time provide a window into the level of autonomy children exhibit in their everyday behaviors. In one study (Grolnick and Ryan, 1989), autonomous regulation in school was the outcome of interest. Children filled out the Self-regulation Questionnaire (Ryan and Connell, 1989), which provides a number of reasons why children might engage in homework, classwork, and other activities. Reasons represent the four types of self-regulation: external (e.g., because I don't want the teacher to yell at me); introjected (e.g., I'd feel guilty if I didn't do my homework); identified (e.g., I want to learn the material); and intrinsic (e.g., because It's fun). Subscale scores are weighted and combined to form a Relative Autonomy Index, which represents the degree of autonomy in children's self-regulation. Grolnick and Ryan (1989) interviewed 114 mothers and fathers of third- through sixth-grade children (8 to 11 years old) regarding the ways in which they motivate their children to engage in school-related activities like homework. Interviews were rated for the degree of parental autonomy support to control, structure, and involvement. Parental autonomy support was associated with children's reports of more autonomous regulation of their school-related activities as well as with teacher ratings of students' competence and adjustment and children's school grades. Furthermore, parents who were more autonomy supportive had children who were less likely, by teacher report, to both act out in school and to exhibit learning difficulties, each of which might be considered indices of poor behavioral self-regulation. Both involvement and structure were associated with children's reports of understanding why success and failure outcomes occur in school and involvement was associated with achievement levels.

In another study, Grolnick et al. (1991) conceptualized motivation as the process through which parenting affects children's school competence. In particular, using structural modeling, these authors examined links among children's perceptions of parental autonomy support and involvement, motivational qualities of autonomous regulation of school activities, perceived competence and perceptions of control, and children's school performance. These techniques supported a model in which parents who are perceived as involved and providing support for autonomy facilitate children feeling autonomous, competent, and in control, and these motivational qualities in turn lead to greater competence. A feedback loop between school outcomes and involvement showed that mothers become more involved with their children's schooling when the children are doing more poorly in school.

A similar role for self-regulation was examined in a study by Steinberg et al. (1989). These authors examined the role of psychosocial maturity as a mediator between authoritative parenting and children's school performance. Controlling for previous school performance, children whose parents were more accepting, provided more psychological autonomy, and implemented higher levels of behavioral control (i.e., rules and guidelines) were higher on dimensions of psychosocial maturity, including self-reliance, identity, and work orientation. These aspects of psychosocial maturity or self-regulation then led to higher school performance.

Both Baumrind's and Steinberg's work illustrate that parenting that facilitates compliance may not facilitate self-regulation. Baumrind (1991), in a follow-up of her longitudinal sample of children followed from preschool, divided parents into several categories reflecting their balance of demandingness (akin to firm control) and responsiveness (akin to support for independence). Authoritative families were highly demanding and highly responsive. Democratic families were highly responsive but not as demanding as the authoritative families. Directive families were highly demanding but not responsive. Good enough families were medium in both demandingness and responsiveness. Nondirective families were very nonrestrictive and medium in responsiveness. Finally, unengaged families were neither demanding nor responsive. As adolescents, offspring of these groups of parents showed different behavioral patterns. First, as expected, children of the unengaged families were lowest in competence and showed the most symptomatology of all the children. Children of authoritative and democratic parents were highly competent and prosocial. They were also motivated in school and were described as self-regulated and socially responsible. However, in contrast to the children from authoritative homes, children from the democratic homes were higher in drug use. Children of the directive parents showed some characteristics in common with those of the authoritative parents; they were also low in drug use and other externalizing behaviors. However, they were also lower in the internalization of prosocial values and lower on indices of individuation. They appeared to be more concerned with eliciting adult approval than acting on their own beliefs and values. Children from nondirective homes were less achievement oriented, less competent, and more likely to use drugs than those from authoritative homes.

In an attempt to replicate Baumrind's findings, Lamborn, Mounts, Steinberg, and Dornbusch (1991) focused on four of these family types: authoritative, neglectful, authoritarian, and indulgent (comparable to Baumrind's democratic). These groups were formed on the basis of adolescents' reports of their parents on two dimensions: acceptance/involvement and strictness. As found by Baumrind, children of authoritative parents showed high levels of competence and low levels of both symptomatology and problem behavior. By contrast, children from neglectful homes were least competent, most distressed, and most likely to get into trouble. Adolescents from authoritarian homes scored reasonably well on achievement indices and measures of deviant activities. At the same time, they were low in self-reliance and less confident in their own abilities than those from authoritative homes. Finally, children from indulgent homes had a high frequency of involvement in deviant activities, including drug and alcohol use (although they were not higher on indices of serious delinquency).

Both Baumrind's and Lamborn's studies illustrate clearly the need for both parental structure and autonomy support for the growth of self-regulation and competence. In highly structured homes that do not support autonomy (directive), children may outwardly conform but do not show the initiative or endorsement of behavior of children whose parents both provide structure and support autonomy. Conversely, when there is a value for freedom but no structures around which children can orient, they fail to develop the internal regulations that allow them to make good decisions and ward off temptations to engage in problem behavior.

Susceptibility to Peer Influence

There is much interest in the literature in the role that peers play in children's antisocial behaviors. Research clearly indicates that children who interact with peers who engage in antisocial behavior are more likely themselves to engage in such behavior (Farrell and White, 1998; Frauenglass, Routh, Pantin, and Mason, 1997). Keenan, Loeber, Zhang, Stouthamer-Loeber, and Van Kammen (1995), for example, found that interaction with peers engaging in deviant behavior patterns was predictive of future (rather than prior) deviance. Furthermore, there is strong evidence that parenting relates to adolescents' association with deviant peers. The focus of much of this research is on the structure provided within the home, including such issues as supervision, monitoring, and discipline (Crouter and Head, in Vol. 3 of this *Handbook*). Patterson and Dishion (1985) examined such issues under the rubric of parental family management. Poor parental skills were indexed by a failure to monitor their children and the children's perceptions of their parents as emotionally uninvolved in their lives. Children from families designated as providing poor management, for example, reported that it was not important to their parents to know where the children were. Poor family management skills were associated with adolescents' engagement with deviant peers. Engagement with deviant peers was, in turn, associated with antisocial behavior. Taking a similar focus on supervision and involvement, Dishion, Patterson, Stoolmiller, and Skinner (1991) showed that children's reports of low supervision, lack of accessibility of parents, and limited communication regarding the children's activities and daily plans was associated with engagement with antisocial peers and higher levels of antisocial behavior.

Such research suggests that failure to monitor children and lack of interest in the children's whereabouts and activities appear to be parental qualities associated with children's engagement in antisocial behavior. Of interest, however, is how self-regulation may be a mechanism through which parenting relates to deviant outcomes. One way to conceptualize this issue is that children are surrounded by opportunities to engage in problematic behavior (more so, of course, in some environmental circumstances than others). Children are regularly faced with situations in which their peers suggest or model antisocial actions. Children need to be able to counter these influences and regulate their own behavior rather than be subject to peers' influences. Thus, one mechanism through which parenting might affect children is in influencing how susceptible children are to peer pressure to engage in deviant activities.

To what degree do children rely on their own decisions and choices versus conform to their friends? We suggest that susceptibility to peer pressure is a matter of internalizing the values of parents and other adults. Such internalizations will allow children to resist peer pressure and regulate their own behavior.

Consistent with this view, Steinberg and Silverberg (1986) conceptualized resistance to peer pressure as one of three indices of adolescent autonomy, the others being emotional autonomy from parents and self-reliance. Resistance to peer pressure was measured using Berndt's (1979) questionnaire, which asks respondents to choose between two courses of action: one suggested by the child's "best friends" and the other what the child "really thinks." Children's subjective sense of self-reliance was indexed by responses to questions such as "In a group, I prefer to let other people make decisions" (reverse scored). The emotional-autonomy measure included subscales such as deidealization, nondependency on parents, and individuation. Although there was the predicted positive relation between resistance to peer pressure and self-reliance, there was a negative relation between resistance and emotional autonomy. This indicated that the adolescents who were most emotionally autonomous from their parents were more susceptible to peer influence than those who were less autonomous. This seemingly anomalous finding was interpreted by Ryan and Lynch (1989). For these authors, the construct of emotional autonomy, as measured in the Steinberg study, was an index of detachment from parents rather than autonomy per se. Supporting this argument, Ryan and Lynch (1989) demonstrated that emotional autonomy was positively associated with perceived parental rejection. If this is the case, the Steinberg and Silverberg finding (1986) suggests that children who tend to be resistant to peer pressure are those who are attached to, rather than detached from, their parents and use them as a base of emotional support and guidance. This finding echoes the conclusions of the large body of literature on deviant behavior per se showing that parental support and positive interaction are negatively related to engagement in deviant activities (e.g., Patterson and Dishion, 1985; Weatherburn and Lind, 1997). This study suggests that connectedness, or relatedness, to parents is important to children's ability to resist peer pressure. When children feel related to their parents, they are most likely to consider their parents' wishes in difficult situations. In addition, as argued earlier, relatedness is likely to facilitate the process of internalizing parental values and goals.

An indirect assessment of this hypothesis is provided in a study by Frauenglass et al. (1997). In this study, adolescents' perceptions of the support provided to them by their parents was assessed, as was their level of engagement with deviant peers and their own drug use and delinquency. As would be expected, adolescents who associated with deviant peers were more likely to engage in problem behaviors themselves than those who associated less with such peers. Furthermore, family support was associated with lower substance use in children. Of interest here, however, were several interactions between family support and peer use of tobacco and drugs. When peer tobacco and marijuana use were low, family support was not predictive of drug use. However, when peer use was high, greater family support was associated with decreased use of tobacco and drug use by the adolescents. Thus, this study suggests that when the youths experienced their parents as supporting and caring about them they were able to stay away from illicit substances despite substance availability and exposure to peer usage. Similarly, Farrell and White (1998) showed that, although there was a strong association between peer models of drug use and peer pressure to engage in drug use with adolescent drug use, the magnitude of the relation varied with parent–child relationships. In particular, the relation between peer pressure and reported drug use was stronger among adolescents with problematic relationships with their parents (i.e., low communication, perceived hostility from parent). This study highlights the role of warmth and active parental involvement in children's abilities to refrain from problem behavior when their peers are modeling it—an issue that we believe is an aspect of self-regulation.

More direct assessments of parenting and susceptibility to peer influence have been undertaken. These studies have focused mainly on two dimensions of our three-dimensional scheme: relatedness and structure. Bixenstine, DeCorte, and Bixenstine (1976) asked adolescents to rate proposed acts of misbehavior on the extent to which the adolescents perceived them as wrong. Adolescents then reported on their likelihood of participating with peers in the events. Participants either believed responses were private, were going to be evaluated by peers, or would be reviewed by parents. Additionally, the children's attitudes toward themselves, their parents, peers, and adults were assessed. Adolescents were more likely to report resistance when parents would be reviewing the results and less likely when their results were to be peer reviewed. Thus, resistance to peer pressure was enhanced in situations of active parental monitoring. In addition, however, children who perceived their relationships with their parents as positive and those with a high regard for the adults in their lives were more likely to say that antisocial acts were "wrong" and more likely to say that they would resist engaging in these acts. In this study, both a sense of relatedness to parents as well as monitoring were important to resistance to peer pressure.

Steinberg (1986) studied the effects of varying degrees of adult supervision of children after school hours on their resistance to peer pressure and delinquent behavior patterns. Children exposed to the least adult presence after school were most likely to engage in antisocial behavior when pressured to do so by peers. This effect differed depending on parents' style of monitoring and the parent–child relationship. When involvement, caring, and availability at a distance were evident, latchkey status was not associated with susceptibility. This study was one of the first to suggest that it is not monitoring per se that is the key element in resistance to peer pressure, but the perception and interpretation of that monitoring by the adolescents. When parents are emotionally available and give the message to the children that they are important and cared about, their physical presence may not be crucial. This finding is in support of a model in which internalization is the mechanism through which parenting impacts on susceptibility to peer pressure. It is quite possible that physical monitoring without a sense of connection and caring would only go so far.

In a second study, Steinberg (1987) examined whether single-parent family status would make children vulnerable to peer influence. In a simple analysis of this issue, he found that adolescents from single-parent homes reported greater susceptibility to negative peer influence than those from two-parent homes. However, further analysis showed that it was not the presence of another adult that was key, but rather having a second biological parent, as indicated by the fact that children from stepfamilies were similar in susceptibility to those from single-parent homes. Furthermore, parental permissiveness had an independent effect on susceptibility, with children of more permissive homes showing greater susceptibility. This study suggests that the nature of relationships in the family may be more important than the presence of adults per se.

Few studies have examined the impact of controlling versus autonomy-supportive styles on children's susceptibility to peer influence. Steinberg (1986) examined the effects of parenting style on susceptibility, and particularly whether parenting style would influence the effects of self-care status on levels of susceptibility. First, there were main effects for parenting style—children from authoritiative homes were more likely to report resistance to peer pressure, whereas children from permissive homes were more likely to succumb. In addition, the negative effects of self-care were buffered when the home was perceived as authoritative. In other words, children from authoritative homes were less susceptible to peer influence than their counterparts from permissive or authoritarian homes, even if they were not supervised by adults after school.

We leave this section with a final issue. In the work described above, it is assumed that children who resist peer pressure exhibit greater self-regulation than those who succumb. The measures used in research typically pit the adolescents' tendency to make the decision sanctioned by the self versus that by peers. Those who decide to act on their decisions are said to be more self-regulated. However, as we argued at the start of this chapter, self-regulation concerns not just whether the action comes from the self or from external sources but whether the action is experienced as autonomous, or, in other words, has an internal causality for action. Self-regulation involves an inner endorsement of action. Not all internally decided actions are autonomous. A child can resist peer pressure and take the socially approved path for many reasons. Some of these reasons suggest an internal locus of causality and others an external one. For example, a child can resist peer pressure because she or he is scared of being caught and getting into trouble. This would be an example of the "right" decision, but one that is externally regulated. Conversely, she or he may refrain from the behavior because of inner feelings of guilt or anxiety, and this would represent introjected regulation. Finally, the child can resist because she or he has more fully internalized the value of the behavior. For example, the child might refrain from studying from the teacher's test because she or he feels that would be wrong and values the teacher's trust. A more differentiated analysis, including the reasons that children resist or succumb to peer pressure, is necessary if we are to understand how parenting affects children's susceptibility to peer influence.

CHALLENGES IN THE STUDY OF SELF-REGULATION

The research cited above provides a rather consistent picture of the parenting characteristics associated with self-regulation in children, but the study of parenting and self-regulation holds a number of challenges. We discuss three of these below.

Specifying Directionality

A key challenge and one that has been evoked by many of the theorists who argue that "parents don't matter" (e.g., Harris, 1998) is that the directionality of work on parenting and self-regulation cannot be definitively established. It is certainly the case that children who initiate their own behavior and who take responsibility for themselves elicit less control from their parents and make it less likely that the parents have to resort to power-assertive techniques. Furthermore, such children increase the likelihood that interactions with parents will be pleasant and satisfying.

There is strong evidence for the child-to-parent hypothesis. Clearly, temperament plays a role in how controlling versus autonomy-supportive parents are. Lee and Bates (1985), for example, found that toddlers with difficult temperaments were more resistant to maternal attempts to exert authority, and their negative behavior was more likely to be met with coercive responses by their mothers. Rutter and Quinton (1984), in their 4-year longitudinal study of children of parents with mental illness, showed that children who have difficult temperamental characteristics, including negative mood and low malleability, were more likely to elicit parental criticism and hostility. Our own work with adolescents (Grolnick, Weiss, McKenzie, and Wrightman, 1996) showed that mothers who saw their adolescents as more difficult were rated by observers as more controlling with them than those who saw their adolescents as easier. This result did not hold for fathers; fathers who saw their adolescents as difficult tended to withdraw from interactions with them rather than becoming controlling. It is likely that this differential response is due to the greater latitude fathers have in becoming involved with their adolescents. Work in behavioral genetics (e.g., Ge, Conger, and Stewart, 1996; Lytton and Gallagher, in Vol. 1 of this *Handbook*; Plomin, Reiss, Hetherington, and Howe, 1994) has suggested that the level of control provided by parents is at least partially due to genetic factors.

The researchers cited in this chapter have attempted to address the issue of directionality in a number of ways. First, the concept of bidirectionality and transactional processes is inherent in many of the concepts being explored. For example, Kochanska's concept of mutual reciprocity is a relational concept that involves the attitudes and behaviors of both parents and children. Studies of scaffolding (e.g., Pratt et al., 1988) assess the coordination of parents' with children's behavior.

Another strategy involves the use of longitudinal data. Particularly compelling are several studies that suggest that the short- and long-term consequences of parental behaviors can be at odds. For example, Roberts and Strayer's (1987) data, reviewed in the section on emotion regulation, showed that pressure to control emotions can have short-term consequence of greater social success but a long-term consequence of lower resourcefulness.

Additional methods of demonstrating that the development of children's self-regulation is influenced by parenting practices involves the use of statistical techniques to attempt to account for children's behavior in understanding parents' actions and their repercussions. For example, Grolnick, Kurowski, McMenamy, Rivkin, and Bridges (1998) controlled for children's levels of distress in asking about parent strategies that facilitate the development of children's self-regulation.

No doubt, the study of parenting and children's self-regulation will require these and other creative approaches to address the issue of directionality.

Specifying the Roles of Mothers and Fathers

Though most research in child development has focused on mothers (Phares, 1992), there is increased emphasis on the differential roles of mothers and fathers in facilitating children's development. The researchers whose work was reviewed earlier have taken different approaches to their studies of parenting effects on children. With some exceptions (e.g., Eisenberg et al., 1999), most of the studies of emotion regulation included only mothers. This strategy is consistent with work in other areas involving very young children. Within the areas of behavior regulation and susceptibility to peer influence the studies vary; some included only mothers, some mothers and fathers (e.g., Grolnick and Ryan, 1989; Pratt et al., 1988), and some focused on parents more generally (e.g., Lamborn et al., 1991; Steinberg et al., 1989). Because of the dearth of studies, conclusions on the differential roles of mothers and fathers in facilitating self-regulation cannot be made at this time.

Research in the area of children's behavior problems more generally has included fathers and gives reason to believe that it is crucial to include fathers in studies of children's self-regulation. Research supports focusing on both quantitative and qualitative measures of fathering. For example, on the quantitative side, children of more-involved fathers have been found to display more positive affect and task orientation during problem solving (Easterbrooks and Goldberg, 1984) and less acting-out behavior (McCabe, Clark, and Barnett, 1999). On the qualitative end, more-sensitive father–child interactions have been associated with positive task behavior and better socialization skills (e.g., Easterbrooks and Goldberg, 1984; Kelly, Smith, Green, Berndt, and Rogers, 1998). More restrictive, harsh, and punitive styles in fathers have been associated with low cognitive and social development and low academic performance (e.g., Feldman and Wentzel, 1993; Kelly et al., 1998; Pettit, Bates, and Dodge, 1993).

The studies of self-regulation reviewed, which included mothers and fathers, support the above findings. While there are mean level differences in fathers' levels of involvement as compared with mothers' (e.g., Grolnick and Ryan, 1989), fathers' styles do appear to be associated with outcomes in similar ways to those of mothers (e.g., Pratt et al., 1988). As we work toward inclusion of fathers in all studies, the questions we ask in our research will need to become more complex. For example, do fathers make independent contributions to the development of self-regulation? Do mothers and fathers play different roles in the onset versus maintainance of self-regulation difficulties (see DeKlyen, Biernbaum, Speltz, and Greenberg, 1998, for support of this hypothesis). Does the role of fathers differ for sons and daughters? These and other questions await answers in the field of self-regulation.

Conceptualizing the Role of Parents in Cultural and Ethnic Groups

Are the patterns we described supporting the importance of autonomy support, structure, and involvement for the growth of self-regulation applicable to all cultural groups? As with the issue of mother–father differences, there is not enough work on specific cultural groups to answer this question for self-regulation per se. However, work in other areas of parenting suggests that this is a promising question to pursue.

The general question of whether "positive parenting" is culture-specific or universal is certainly a controversial one. While some studies suggest similar relations between parenting characteristics and child outcomes across groups, others suggest somewhat different relationships. For example, Baldwin, Baldwin, and Cole (1990) found that, for adolescents living in disadvantaged circumstances, greater parental demandingness (i.e., more rules and regulations) was associated with better child outcomes, whereas for those living in more advantaged circumstances a lower level of demandingness was more adaptive. However, in both types of families, more democratic administration of rules was associated with greater child competence. Lamborn, Dornbusch, and Steinberg (1996) found stronger relations between nondemocratic decision making and poor adjustment in European American than in African American adolescents. On the other hand, autonomy supportive parenting has been found to be associated with positive child outcomes in both Chinese (Chen, Dong, and Zhou, 1997) and Russian (Chirkov and Ryan, 2000) samples.

The exploration of ways in which parenting influences self-regulation will clearly need to consider the ways in which parenting behaviors are interpreted by children given work by Chao (1994), Fuligni, Tseng, and Lam (1999) and others suggesting that the same behaviors may be interpreted as more or less controlling by children. The exploration of ways in which parenting facilitates self-regulation within cultural groups is clearly an area meriting further study.

CONCLUSION

The goals of socialization are more than simply to have children comply with their parents' wishes (see Grusec, in Vol. 5 of this *Handbook*). Growth toward maturity requires children to take an active role in initiating and regulating their own behavior. Self-determination theory provides a framework for understanding how children develop toward increasingly autonomous self-regulation. This theory suggests that internalization of values, behaviors, and attitudes in the social surround is a natural and spontaneous process, part of the organism's innate propensity toward mastery. However, the process is also subject to the facilitating or undermining effects of the social context. Three contextual dimensions—autonomy support, structure, and involvement—have been identified as key facilitators of intrinsic motivation and the internalization process.

In this chapter, this three-dimensional social contextual framework was used to organize data on three issues relevant to self-regulation: emotion regulation, behavioral regulation, and susceptibility to peer influence. In each of these areas, parenting research that corresponded to this dimensional framework was identified. Within different areas, the parenting dimensions have received different levels of attention. Within work on emotion regulation, parental responsiveness has been stressed. Within work on susceptibility to peer influence, researchers start with the concept of monitoring that maps onto the structure dimension. Clearly, this focus is in part a function of the age range of the children being included in the research. However, it is interesting to consider whether the three dimensions have differential salience or centrality for different self-regulatory issues as well.

Despite emphasizing different dimensions, there is consensus across areas of self-regulation that all three dimensions are important. In emotion regulation, the presence of a responsive parent who tailors her or his interventions to the child and actively models regulatory strategies in a nonintrusive way appears to facilitate self-regulation. Clearly, tolerating and working through, rather than dismissing, emotions is key. Work in behavior regulation, although widely divergent in focus, supports the notion that involved parents who provide rules and guidelines, and who foster individuality by involving children in decisions and helping them to solve problems tend to be higher not just on measures of compliance but also on self-regulation. Finally, research on susceptibility to peer influence stresses that not only monitoring but a close and involved relationship with children and support for their autonomy are important.

This chapter focused on parenting, but it is clear that parents are not the only individuals who play a role in children's development of self-regulation. Clearly, teachers vary in their involvement, autonomy support, and structure, and are likely to have a major influence on children. Peers, of course, cannot be ignored. Piaget originally hypothesized that peers, not parents, play the major role in children's moral development. Recent research, however, gives parents an important role in helping children to deal with moral issues (e.g., Walker and Taylor, 1991). In the self-regulation literature, it is assumed that parents play the major role. However, it is likely that peers determine opportunities for self-regulation and present some of the regulatory challenges children need to negotiate. The joint roles of parents, teachers, and peers is clearly an area for future research.

What are the implications of this work for professionals working with parents? One is clearly that it is not enough to help parents to learn to increase child compliance. When socialization is successful, desired behaviors will not merely be undertaken in response to direct communications, but autonomously, as a result of a personal endorsement of an activity, value, or belief. The development of self-regulation is a goal that necessitates different parenting strategies. Professionals in parenting and child development need to go beyond teaching about rewards and contingencies to a broader curriculum of socialization efforts that impact children's self-regulation.

ACKNOWLEDGMENTS

This chapter was supported in part by a grant from the Spencer Foundation to the first author. We would like to thank Marc Bornstein for his excellent editorial advice and support through the writing of the chapter.

REFERENCES

Baldwin, A. L., Baldwin, C., and Cole, R. E. (1990). Stress resistant families and stress resistent children. In J. E. Rolf, A. S. Masten, D. Cicchetti, K. H. Nuechterlein, and S. Weintraub (Eds.), *Risk and protective factors in the development of psychopathology* (pp. 257–280). New York: Cambridge University Press.

Barber, B. K. (1996). Parental psychological control: Revisiting a neglected construct. *Child Development, 67*, 3296–3319.

Baumrind, D. (1967). Child care practices anteceding three patterns of preschool behavior. *Genetic Psychology Monographs 75*, 43–88.

Baumrind, D. (1971). Current patterns in parental authority. *Developmental Psychology Monographs, 4*, 1–102.

Baumrind, D. (1973). The development of instrumental competence through socialization. In S. D. Pick (Ed.), *Minnesota symposium on child psychology* (Vol. 7, pp. 3–46). Minneapolis: University of Minnesota Press.

Baumrind, D. (1991). *Relation of authoritative upbringing to adolescent outcomes.* Paper presented at the Society for Research in Child Development, Seattle, WA.

Behrend, D. A., Rosengren, K. S., and Permutter, M. (1989). A new look at children's private speech: The effects of age, task difficulty, and parent presence. *International Journal of Behavioral Development, 12*, 305–320.

Berk, L., and Spuhl, S. (1995). Maternal interaction, private speech, and task performance in preschool children. *Early Childhood Research Quarterly, 10*, 145–169.

Berndt, T. (1979). Developmental changes in conformity to peers and parents. *Developmental Psychology, 15*, 608–616.

Bixenstine, V., DeCorte, M., and Bixenstine, B. (1976). Conformity to peer-sponsored misconduct at four grade levels. *Developmental Psychology, 12*, 226–236.

Calkins, S. D. (1997). *Maternal interactive style and emotional, behavioral, and physiological regulation in toddlerhood.* Paper presented at the biennial meeting of the Society for Research in Child Development, Washington, DC.

Calkins, S. D., and Johnson, M. C. (1998). Toddler regulation of distress to frustrating events: Temperamental and maternal correlates. *Infant Behavior and Development, 21*, 379–395.

Campbell, S. B. (1997). Behavior problems in preschool children: Development and family issues. *Advances in Clinical Child Psychology, 19*, 1–26.

Campos, J. J., Campos, R., and Barrett, K. C. (1989). Emergent themes in the study of emotional development and emotion regulation. *Developmental Psychology, 25*, 394–402.

Chao, R. K. (1994). Beyond parental control and authoritative parenting style: Understanding Chinese parenting through the cultural notion of training. *Child Development, 65*, 1111–1119.

Chen, X., Dong, Q., and Zhou, H. (1997). Authoritative and authoritarian parenting practices and social and school performance in Chinese children. *International Journal of Behavioral Development, 21*, 855–873.

Chirkov, V. I., and Ryan, R. M. (2000). Control versus autonomy support in Russia and the U.S.: Effects on well-being and academic motivation. Unpublished manuscript, University of Rochester, Rochester, NY.

Csikszentmihalyi, M. (1975). *Beyond boredom and anxiety.* San Francisco: Jossey-Bass.

deCharms, R. (1968). *Personal causation.* New York: Academic.

Deci, E. L. (1971). Effects of externally mediated rewards on intrinsic motivation. *Journal of Personality and Social Psychology, 18*, 105–115.

Deci, E. L., and Ryan, R. M. (1985). *Intrinsic motivation and self-determination in human behavior.* New York: Plenum.

Deci, E. L., Schwartz, A. J., Sheinman, L., and Ryan, R. M. (1981). An instrument to assess adults' orientations toward control versus autonomy with children: Reflections on intrinsic motivation and perceived competence. *Journal of Educational Psychology, 73*, 642–650.

DeKlyen, M., Biernbaum, M. A., Speltz, M. L., and Greenberg, M. T. (1998). Fathers and preschool behavior problems. *Developmental Psychology, 34*, 264–275.

Diaz, R., Neal, C., and Amay-Williams, M. (1990). The social origins of self-regulation. In L. C. Moll (Ed.), *Vygotsky and education: Instructional implications and applications of sociohistorical psychology* (pp. 127–154). New York: Cambridge University Press.

Diaz, R., Neal, C., and Vachio, A. (1991). Maternal teaching in the zone of proximal development: A comparison of low- and high-risk dyads. *Merrill-Palmer Quarterly, 37*, 83–107.

Diener, M., Mangelsdorf, S. C., Fosnot, K., and Kienstra, M. (1997). *Effects of maternal involvement on toddlers' emotion regulation strategies.* Paper presented at the biennial meeting of the Society for Research in Child Development, Washington, DC.

Dishion, T., Patterson, G., Stoolmiller, M., and Skinner, M. (1991). Family, school, and behavior antecedents to early adolescent involvement with antisocial peers. *Developmental Psychology, 27*, 172–180.

Easterbrooks, M. A., and Goldberg, W. A. (1984). Toddler development in the family: Impact of father involvement and parenting characteristics. *Child Development, 55*, 740–752.

Eisenberg, N., and Fabes, R. A. (1992). *Emotion and its regulation in early development: New directions for child development* (Vol. 5). San Francisco: Jossey-Bass.

Eisenberg, N., Fabes, R., Shepard, S., Guthrie, I., Murphy, B., and Reiser, M. (1999). Parental reactions to children's negative emotions: Longitudinal relations to quality of children's social functioning. *Child Development, 70*, 513–534.

Farrell, A., and White, K. (1998). Peer influences and drug use among urban adolescents: Family structure and parent—adolescent relationship as protective factors. *Journal of Counseling and Clinical Psychology, 66*, 248–258.

Feldman, S. S., and Wentzel, K. R. (1993). Parental predictors of boys' self-restraint and motivation to achieve at school: A longitudinal study. *Journal of Early Adolescence, 13*, 193–203.

Fox, N. A. (Ed.). (1994). The development of emotion regulation: Biological and behavioral considerations. *Monographs of the Society for Research in Child Development, 59*, (2–3, Serial No. 240), 152–166.

Frauenglass, S., Routh, D., Pantin, H., and Mason, C. (1997). Family support decreases influence of deviant peers on Hispanic adolescents' substance use. *Journal of Clinical Child Psychology, 26*, 15–23.

Fuligni, A. J., Tseng, V., and Lam, M. (1999). Attitudes toward family obligations among American adolescents with Asian, Latin American and European backgrounds. *Child Development, 70*, 1030–1044.

Ge, X., Conger, R. D., and Stewart, M. A. (1996). The developmental interface between nature and nurture: A mutual influence model of child antisocial behavior and parent behaviors. *Developmental Psychology, 32*, 574–584.

Golden, M., Montare, A., and Bridger, W. (1977). Verbal control of delay behavior in two-year-old boys as a function of social class. *Child Development, 48*, 1107–1111.

Gottman, J. M., Katz, L. F., and Hooven, C. (1996). Parental meta-emotion philosophy and the emotional life of families: Theoretical models and preliminary data. *Journal of Family Psychology, 10*, 243–268.

Gottman, J. M., Katz, L. F., and Hooven, C. (1997). *Meta-emotion: How families communicate emotionally.* Mahwah, NJ: Lawrence Erlbaum Associates.

Greenspan, S. I. (1981). *Psychopathology and adaptation in infancy and early childhood: Principles of clinical diagnosis and early intervention.* New York: International Universities Press.

Grolnick, W. S., Bridges, L. J., and Connell, J. P. (1996). Emotion regulation in two-year-olds: Strategies and emotional expression in four contexts. *Child Development, 67*, 928–941.

Grolnick, W. S., Deci, E. L., and Ryan, R. M. (1997). Internalization within the family: The self-determination theory perspective. In J. E. Grusec and L. Kuczynski (Eds.), *Parenting and the internalization of values* (pp. 135–161). New York: Wiley.

Grolnick, W. S., Kurowski, C. O., McMenamy, J. M., Rivkin, I., and Bridges, L. (1998). Mothers' strategies for regulating their toddlers' distress. *Infant Behavior and Development, 21*, 437–450.

Grolnick, W. S., McMenamy, J., and Kurowski, C. (1999). Emotional self-regulation in infancy and toddlerhood. In L. Balter and C. S. Tamas-LeMonda (Eds.), *Child psychology: A handbook of contemporary issues* (pp. 3–22). Philadelphia: Psychology Press.

Grolnick, W. S., and Ryan, R. M. (1989). Parent styles associated with children's self-regulation and competence in school. *Journal of Educational Psychology, 81*, 143–154.

Grolnick, W. S., Ryan, R. M., and Deci, E. L. (1991). The inner resources for school achievement: Motivational mediators of children's perceptions of their parents. *Journal of Educational Psychology, 83*, 508–517.

Grolnick, W. S., Weiss, L., McKenzie, L., and Wrightman, J. (1996). Contextual, cognitive, and adolescent factors associated with parenting in adolescence. *Journal of Youth and Adolescence, 12*, 332–345.

Harris, J. R. (1998). *The nurture assumption.* New York: Free Press.

Heider, F. (1958). *The psychology of interpersonal relations.* New York: Wiley.

Kalpidou, M. D., Rothbaum, F., and Rosen, K. (1998). A longitudinal study of mothers' and preschool children's aversive behaviors during dyadic interaction. *Journal of Genetic Psychology, 159*, 103–116.

Keenan, K., Loeber, R., Zhang, Q., Stouthamer-Loeber, M., and Van Kammen, W. (1995). The influence of deviant peers on the development of boys' disruptive and delinquent behavior: A temporal analysis. *Development and Psychopathology, 7,* 715–726.

Kelley, M. L., Smith, T. S., Green, A. P., Berndt, A. E., and Rogers, M. C. (1998). Importance of fathers' parenting to African-American toddler's social and cognitive development. *Infant Behavior and Development, 21,* 733–744.

Kochanska, G. (1997). Multiple pathways to conscience for children with different temperaments: From toddlerhood to age 5. *Developmental Psychology, 64,* 325–347.

Kochanska, G., and Aksan, N. (1995). Mother–child mutually positive affect, the quality of child compliance to requests and prohibitions, and maternal control as correlates of early internalization. *Child Development, 66,* 236–254.

Kochanska, G., Aksan, N., and Koenig, A. L. (1995). A longitudinal study of the roots of preschoolers' conscience: Committed compliance and emerging internalization. *Child Development, 66,* 1752–1769.

Kogan, N., and Carter, A. (1995). Mother–infant reengagement following the still-face: The role of maternal emotional availability in infant affect regulation. *Infant Behavior and Development, 18,* 359–369.

Kopp, C. B. (1982). Antecedents of self-regulation: A developmental view. *Developmental Psychology, 18,* 199–214.

Lamborn, S. D., Dornbusch, S. M., and Steinberg, L. (1996). Ethnicity and community context as moderators of the relations between family decision making and adolescent adjustment. *Child Development, 67,* 283–301.

Lamborn, S. D., Mounts, N. S., Steinberg, L., and Dornbusch, S. M. (1991). Patterns of competence and adjustment among adolescents from authoritative, authoritarian, indulgent, and neglectful families. *Child Development, 62,* 1049–1065.

Lee, C. L., and Bates, J. E. (1985). Mother–child interaction at age two years and perceived difficult temperament. *Child Development, 56,* 1314–1325.

McCabe, K. M., Clark, R., and Barnett, D. (1999). Family protective factors among urban African American youth. *Journal of Clinical Child Psychology, 28,* 137–150.

Mischel, W. (1974). Processes in delay of gratification. In L. Berkowitz (Ed.), *Progress in experimental personality research* (Vol. 3, pp. 249–292). New York: Academic.

Nachmias, M., Gunnar, M., Mangelsdorf, S., Parritz, R. H., and Buss, K. (1996). Behavioral inhibition and stress reactivity: The moderating role of attachment security. *Child Development, 67,* 508–522.

Parpal, M., and Maccoby, E. E. (1985). Maternal responsiveness and subsequent child compliance. *Child Development, 56,* 1326–1334.

Patterson, G., and Dishion, T. (1985). Contributions of families and peers to delinquency. *Criminology, 23,* 63–79.

Pettit, G. S., Bates, J. E., and Dodge, K. A. (1993). Family interaction patterns and children's conduct problems at home and school: A longitudinal perspective. *School Psychology Review, 22,* 403–420.

Plomin, R., Reiss, D., Hetherington, E. M., and Howe, G. W. (1994). Nature and nurture: Genetic contributions to measures of the family environment. *Developmental Psychology, 30,* 32–43.

Pratt, M., Kerig, P., Cowan, P., and Cowan, C. (1988). Mothers and fathers teaching 3-year-olds: Authoritative parenting and adult scaffolding of young children's learning. *Developmental Psychology, 24,* 832–839.

Raver, C. (1996). Relations between social contingency in mother–child interaction and 2-year-olds' social competence. *Developmental Psychology, 32,* 850–859.

Raver, C., and Leadbetter, B. J. (1995). Factors influencing joint attention between socioeconomically disadvantaged adolescent mothers and their infants. In C. Moore and P. Dunham (Eds.), *Joint attentions: Its origins and role in development.* Hillsdale, NJ: Lawrence Erlbaum Associates.

Roberts, W. (1999). The socialization of emotional expression: Relations with prosocial behaviour and competence in five samples. *Canadian Journal of Behavioural Science, 31,* 72–85.

Roberts, W., and Strayer, J. (1987). Parents' responses to the emotional distress of their children: Relations with children's competence. *Developmental Psychology, 23,* 415–422.

Rutter, M., and Quinton, D. (1984). Long-term follow-up of women institutionalized in childhood: Factors promoting good functioning adult life. *British Journal of Developmental Psychology, 18,* 225–234.

Ryan, R., and Connell, J. (1989). Perceived locus of causality and internalization: Examining reasons for acting in two domains. *Journal of Personality and Social Psychology, 57,* 749–761.

Ryan, R. M., Connell, J. P., and Deci, E. L. (1985). A motivational analysis of self-determination and self-regulation in education. In C. Ames and R. E. Ames (Eds.), *Research on motivation in education: The classroom milieu* (pp. 13–51). New York: Academic.

Ryan, R. M., and Lynch, J. (1989). Emotional autonomy versus detachment: Revisiting the vicissitudes of adolescence and young adulthood. *Child Development, 60,* 340–356.

Sorce, J. F., and Emde, R. N. (1981). Mother's presence is not enough: Effect of emotional availability on infant exploration. *Developmental Psychology, 17,* 737–745.

Steinberg, L. (1986). Latchkey children and susceptibility to peer pressure: An ecological analysis. *Developmental Psychology, 22,* 433–439.

Steinberg, L. (1987). Single parents, stepparents, and the susceptibility of adolescents to antisocial peer pressure. *Child Development, 58,* 269–275.

Steinberg, L., Elmen, J. D., and Mounts, N. S. (1989). Authoritative parenting, psychosocial maturity, and academic success among adolescents. *Child Development, 60*, 1424–1436.

Steinberg, L., and Silverberg, S. (1986). The vicissitudes of autonomy in early adolescence. *Child Development, 57*, 841–851.

Tronick, E. Z. (1989). Emotions and emotional communication in infants. *American Psychologist, 44*, 112–119.

Van Lieshout, C. F. M. (1975). Young children's reactions to barriers placed by their mothers. *Child Development, 46*, 879–886.

Vaughn, B., Kopp, C., and Krakow, J. B. (1984). The emergence and consolidation of self-control from eighteen to thirty months of age: Normative trends and individual differences. *Child Development, 55*, 990–1004.

Vygotsky, L. S. (1978). *Mind in society: The development of higher psychological processes.* Cambridge, MA: Harvard University Press.

Walker, L., and Taylor, J. (1991). Family interactions and the development of moral reasoning. *Child Development, 62*, 264–283.

Weatherburn, D., and Lind, B. (1997). On the epidemiology of offender populations. *Australian Journal of Psychology, 49*, 169–175.

Whiting, B. B., and Edwards, C. P. (1988). *Children of different worlds: The formation of social behavior.* Cambridge, MA: Harvard University Press.

Winsler, A., Diaz, R., McCarthy, E., Atencio, D., and Chabay, L. (1999). Mother–child interaction, private speech, and task performance in preschool children with behavior problems. *Journal of Child Psychology and Psychiatry, 40*, 891–904.

Wood, D. (1980). Teaching the young child: Some relationships between social interaction, language, and thought. In D. Olson (Ed.), *The social foundations of language and thought* (pp. 280–296). New York: Norton.

Zimmerman, B. J. (1989). A social cognitive view of self-regulated academic learning. *Journal of Educational Psychology, 81*, 329–339.

5

Parenting and Children's Prosocial and Moral Development

Nancy Eisenberg
Carlos Valiente
Arizona State University

INTRODUCTION

The topic of this chapter is the relation of parental characteristics and behaviors to children's moral development, including positive (e.g., sharing and guilt) as well as negative aspects (e.g., aggression and other antisocial behaviors) of morality. In addition, because children's motives for their morally relevant behaviors determine whether their actions are truly moral, socialization correlates of moral reasoning also are discussed.

The role of parents in the socialization process has been a topic of considerable debate for decades. Various psychological theories emphasize different mechanisms of socialization and place differing emphasis on the role of the parent versus the child in development (Maccoby, 1992). Moreover, because none of the major theories of development has adequately explained socialization, a number of mini-theories (i.e., a theory designed to deal with one specific issue rather than many aspects of development) have emerged to explain the socialization of morality.

In the first section of this chapter, theories related to the socialization of moral behavior and reasoning are briefly presented. Next, empirical findings regarding the relations of parental practices and characteristics to a variety of morally relevant behaviors are reviewed. In general, we focus on the patterning of findings rather than the specifics of the many studies. Given the large amount of research on some of these topics, our review is not exhaustive; rather, we try to highlight the most recent, consistent, and interesting findings.

THEORETICAL PERSPECTIVES ON PARENTING AND PROSOCIAL AND MORAL DEVELOPMENT

Two grand theories have been central in the literature on socialization: psychoanalytic theory and behaviorism (from which social learning theory evolved; Maccoby, 1992). In addition, two theoretical perspectives have been very influential in research and conceptualizations of the socialization of morality; these are Kohlberg's (1969, 1984) cognitive developmental theory and Hoffman's (1970b, 1983) moral socialization theory. Each of these perspectives is briefly reviewed, with an emphasis on mechanisms relevant to moral development.

Psychoanalytic Theory

Psychoanalytic theory was introduced early in the twentieth century by Sigmund Freud and has been critiqued and modified in various ways ever since. In the classic versions of this theory, early childhood is a time of plasticity, and, consequently, parent–child interactions have profound effects on children's later functioning (see Cohler and Paul, in Vol. 3 of this *Handbook*). According to Freud, children are driven by two major intrapsychic forces, sexuality (libido) and aggression, and parents and other socializers must impose unwanted restrictions on the child. In addition, children experience very intense conflict because they love their parents and need parental nurturance while at the same time they feel anger toward their parents and desire them sexually. If children express their anger and sexual feelings, they are likely to lose the parent's love and support, and may even engender intense parental anger and aggression; thus, children are emotionally engulfed by conflict. Although descriptions of this conflict vary considerably in the writings of Freud and his disciples, the conflict generally is viewed as being resolved (at least to a fair degree) in childhood (e.g., at age 4 to 6 years, according to Freud) through the mechanism of identification. As is described by Maccoby (1992, p. 1007):

> Children "internalize" their parents and "introject" their values, forming a superego or conscience that is an internal representation of the parents (primarily in their regulatory capacity). Because the children's incestuous wishes are directed primarily toward the opposite-sex parent, there is greater risk of retaliation or rejection by the same-sex parent, and conflict resolution therefore takes the form of identification primarily with the same-sex parent. This identification carries with it an adoption of appropriately sex-typed behaviors and attitudes, along with an adoption of a more general set of prosocial values.

As a consequence of identification, the child develops a conscience (i.e., superego) and guilt feelings, which are feelings of resentment and hostility formerly directed toward the same-sex parent now turned inward (see Freud, 1925, 1959).

Most traditional psychoanalytic theorists view parents as agents of control in the early years and sources of moral values on identification. Thus, parents play a major role in shaping children's morality, albeit sometimes unintentionally. Although psychoanalytic conceptions play a minor role in current theory in developmental psychology (but see Emde, Johnson, and Easterbrooks, 1987), the psychoanalytic notion of identification has been modified by some less behavioral social learning theorists to refer to children's internalization of parents' norms, values, and standards as a consequence of a positive parent–child relationship (Mussen, Rutherford, Harris, and Keasey, 1970).

Behaviorism and Social Learning Theory

In psychoanalytic theory, the child is an emotionally driven, egocentric, irrational being driven to morality only by emotions such as fear and anxiety, and later, guilt. In early behaviorism, the child also was conceptualized in nonrational terms—as a passive being to be shaped by socializers. The child learned through mechanisms such as classical and operant conditioning, particularly through parental contingencies. Behaviors that were reinforced (rewarded) continued; those that were punished dropped out of the child's repertoire.

There are numerous modern learning and social learning theories, all derived from behaviorism. In probably all versions of current thinking, mechanisms of reinforcement and punishment still are important. For example, according to Gewirtz and Pelaez-Nogueras (1991, p. 162), "much of what is termed moral behavior involves responses (including verbal ones) that have been shaped and maintained by positive consequences (e.g., approval, acceptance, praise) or responses that avoid or eliminate aversive consequences (e.g., disapproval, rejection, punishment)." Moreover, the contingencies need not actually occur; people learn through observation and verbal behavior the likely consequences of a behavior. Of course, parents are likely to be among those who provide reinforcements and aversive consequences to the child.

In modern social learning theory, imitation is central to the learning of new behaviors (Bandura, 1986). Indeed, some psychologists have even reframed the psychoanalytic construct of identification into pervasive imitative, as a "selective process whereby a child acquires a range of the behavior repertory of a parent (usually the parent of the same gender as the child), including behaviors connoting moral values, attitudes, and standards" (Gewirtz and Pelaez-Nogueras, 1991, pp. 163–164). Viewed either narrowly or broadly, the process of imitating others in the child's environment, including parents, is deemed as an important source of morality.

In Bandura's view (1986, 1991), the process is even more complex. Moral rules or standards of behavior are fashioned from information from a variety of social sources including tuition, others' evaluative social reactions, and models. Based on experiences, people learn what factors are morally relevant and how much value to attach to each. Moral decision making is an intricate process, and many factors must be weighed in each situation (Eisenberg, 1986; Staub, 1978). In addition, over time people change their conceptions due to experience with the social consequences of their actions.

According to Bandura (1986, 1991), affect also plays a vital regulatory role in moral behavior. Transgressions are controlled by two major types of sanctions: social sanctions (e.g., social disapproval) and internalized self-sanctions. People frequently behave in moral ways to avoid social censure and externally imposed punishments; they may fear the shame, loneliness, or other costs associated with social sanctions. In regard to self-sanctions, people behave morally because to do so produces self-satisfaction and self-respect, whereas immoral conduct results in self-reproof. Anticipation of these self-administered consequences provides the motivational force by which standards regulate behavior. Of course, people may possess self-regulatory capabilities but may not use them consistently or effectively in all circumstances, particularly if they do not perceive themselves as able to effectively exercise control over their own motivation, thoughts, and actions.

Thus, according to contemporary social learning theory, parents play a multifaceted role in their child's moral development. They provide information about behavioral alternatives, expectations, and possible contingencies for various courses of action, model relevant behaviors, and reinforce and punish the child for different actions. In addition, they may play a role in children's development of self-evaluative reactions (e.g., guilt) and in children's perceptions of, and actual ability to control, their own thoughts and actions.

Cognitive Developmental Theory

Children play a very active role in their own moral development in cognitive developmental theory. According to Kohlberg (1969, 1984), the most influential proponent of a cognitive developmental perspective on morality, children actively interpret their environment and construct their own understanding of morality.

In normal environments, children's thinking about moral dilemmas proceeds through a predictable series of stages (although individuals may stop at different points in development). These stages emerge on account of children's increasing capacity to understand and interpret their social environment; particularly important are changes with age in children's ability to take the perspectives of other individuals and, later, of the broader society. The stages progress from externally oriented preconventional or heteronomous morality (based on avoidance of punishment and the superior power of authorities and a concrete, self-interested perspective) to conventional morality (based on considerations of mutual interpersonal expectations, relationships, and interpersonal conformity, or concern with keeping the social system going and the imperatives of conscience) to postconventional morality (based on concerns with social contracts, the greatest good, individual rights, and self-chosen universal ethical principals; see Colby and Kohlberg, 1987). Each stage is considered to represent an organized way of thinking, with movement to the next stage requiring a qualitative reorganization of the individual's pattern of thinking rather than merely the learning of new content. Each higher stage is viewed as more adequate and involves a broader perspective than that achieved at lower stages. At each stage, the child possesses a better understanding and can integrate more diverse points of view regarding moral conflicts (Colby and Kohlberg, 1987). Although many of Kohlberg's specific assertions have been challenged and alternative schema for conceptualizing moral reasoning have been proposed (e.g., Eisenberg, 1986; Gilligan, 1982), his theory dominated the field of morality for decades.

In cognitive developmental theory, advances in cognition are necessary for advances in moral judgment. Such advances are likely to occur when children are ready cognitively and when they are exposed to morally relevant information that is more sophisticated than their current level and at a level that is optimally higher than their current level of functioning (i.e., just a little above their current level). In such circumstances, cognitive disequilibrium occurs, and the child seeks to better understand the moral conflict. Experiences that broaden the individual's perspective, such as negotiation with others, participation in decision-making processes of groups or institutions, and role-taking opportunities in which the child can learn about others' perspectives are viewed as promoting development (Mason and Gibbs, 1993; Walker and Hennig, 1999).

Given the general emphasis on cognition and the child's active role in promoting her or his own development, it is not surprising that socialization, particularly in the home, has been given relatively little attention by cognitive developmentalists (Walker and Hennig, 1999). Generally, parents are viewed as bystanders in the process of moral development; they are involved to the degree that they provide opportunities for cognitive conflict, discussion of issues of fairness and morality, perspective taking, participation in decision making, and exposure to reasoning above their own stage (Walker and Hennig, 1999). According to Kohlberg (1969, p. 399), "family participation is not unique or critically necessary for moral development." Schools and other settings could provide the same opportunities as families, and have been studied more than have families.

Hoffman's Theory of Moral Internalization

In his theory, Hoffman (1983, 1988, 2000) tries to address the question of how societal norms or rules, which are initially external (e.g., based on fear of sanctions), acquire an internal motivational force (i.e., acquire an obligatory, compelling quality experienced as derived from oneself with little or no collection of their origins). According to Hoffman (1983, 2000), although learning relevant to moral development can occur outside the disciplinary context and in interactions with other people, disciplinary encounters with parents are central to moral internalization. In disciplinary encounters, the child acts or is tempted to act in a manner that will adversely affect another. The parent intervenes and tries to change the child's behavior in a manner that is in accordance with the victim's (or potential victim's) needs. Disciplinary situations are similar to a range of moral encounters in which the child is tempted to act in a way that has negative consequences for others. Thus, what is learned in the disciplinary encounter is likely to influence whether or not children internalize norms and act in a manner consistent with these norms in subsequent moral encounters.

Hoffman (1970b, 1983) identified several categories of discipline. Inductive techniques point out the effect of the child's behavior on others. They vary in complexity; early inductions are likely to be very simple (e.g., "If you push him, he'll fall and cry"), whereas with older children parents may refer to more subtle psychological effects or processes (e.g., "Don't yell at him. He was only trying to help" or "He feels bad because he was proud of his tower and you knocked it down"; Hoffman, 1983,

p. 247). In many inductions, reparative actions are suggested by the parent. Hoffman has argued that a moral orientation characterized by independence of external sanctions and by high levels of guilt is associated with frequent parental use of inductions.

In contrast to inductions, power-assertive discipline involves the use of physical force, deprivation of possessions or privileges, direct commands, or threats. Hoffman (1970b, 1983) has asserted that consistent and predominant use of power assertion is associated with a moral orientation in children based on fear of external detection and punishment.

In the third category of discipline discussed by Hoffman (1983, p. 247), love-withdrawal techniques, "the parent simply gives direct, but nonphysical, expressions of anger or disapproval of the child for engaging in some undesirable behavior (e.g., ignores the child, turns his or her back on the child, refuses to speak or listen to the child, explicitly states a dislike for the child, isolates or threatens to leave the child)." Hoffman argued that such techniques are not systematically related to moral internalization.

According to Hoffman (1970b, 1983), inductions promote internalization for a variety of reasons. First, they induce an optimal (i.e., moderate) level of arousal for learning. Inductions are arousing enough to elicit the child's attention, but are unlikely to produce high levels of anxiety or anger. Thus, the child is likely to attend to and process the information embedded in the parent's inductive statement. In addition, because of the information provided in the explanation, the parent's discipline efforts may seem less arbitrary and, consequently, may be unlikely to induce reactance (i.e., the discipline may not be perceived as a threat to the child's freedom). Furthermore, inductions focus children's attention on consequences of their behavior for others and capitalize on children's capacity to *feel* another's negative emotion (i.e., to empathize) and guilt based on the awareness of causing harm to another. Feelings of empathy and concern have been associated with altruistic motivation, and feelings of guilt motivate reparation.

In contrast, power-assertive and love-withdrawal techniques may elicit too much arousal due to fear of punishment or anxiety about loss of the parent's love. In either case, the children's attention is likely to be directed to the consequences of the deviant act for the self rather than for other people; moreover, these techniques heighten the child's view that the relevant moral standard is external to the self.

Hoffman also has tried to explain how, over time, inductive practices result in children's experiencing moral norms as originating from within themselves (i.e., as internalized). He hypothesized that the informational component of inductions is semantically organized, encoded in memory, and modified and integrated with similar information extracted by inductions in other disciplinary encounters. Important features of the process are: (1) that the child plays an active role in processing the information and (2) that inductions focus on the child's action and its consequences rather than on the parent as the disciplinary agent. Consequently, over time children are likely to remember the causal link between their actions and consequences for others rather than the external pressure or the specific disciplinary context. Thus, the inductive message, not the external source of the moral norm in the disciplinary context, is remembered at a later time. Furthermore, when the stored information is recalled at a later time in a similar situation, the child is likely to experience the emotions of empathy and guilt associated with those memories. These emotions may serve as motives for acting in accordance with moral norms at the later point in time. In contrast, in situations involving strong power-assertion or love-withdrawal, the child is unlikely to store or later recall reasons for avoiding the course of action in question; nor is the child likely to experience empathy for a potential victim or anticipate guilt for transgressing against others.

Many researchers examining parents' role in moral development have studied the types of discipline discussed by Hoffman. However, Hoffman has not discussed in any detail how parents influence children's moral development outside of the disciplinary context. Impetus for studying other parental practices such as modeling and parental stimulation of children's thinking about moral conflicts has come primarily from social learning and cognitive developmental theories.

METHODOLOGICAL ISSUES

Prior to reviewing the literature, it is important to start with a discussion of some of the limitations of the existing empirical research. One important limitation in the existing research is the frequent dependence of researchers on parents for information about both the child's moral proclivities and the parents' own behavior (Holden and Buck, in Vol. 3 of this *Handbook*). Ideally, measures of the child's moral behavior or reasoning would be obtained from observation of children's behavior or from moral reasoning interviews, and measures of parental characteristics and practices would be based on observations of the parents. However, it often is difficult or impossible to observe parents or children, especially for extended periods of time or in a variety of settings. Moreover, parents and older children may not act normally when they know they are being observed (Zegiob, Arnold, and Forehand, 1975). Consequently, interviewers frequently have interviewed parents about their childrearing practices, used questionnaire measures designed to assess variables such as parental warmth or discipline, and have questioned parents about their children's moral development or obtained one-time assessments of moral behavior in a laboratory setting.

Thus, the data base on which conclusions are drawn is far from ideal. However, methods vary considerably across studies; therefore, if findings are similar across studies, they are not likely to be attributable to any particular methodological flaw. Moreover, sometimes data are available from more than one Western nation or ethnic or racial group. When this is the case, we can have greater confidence in the data and are safer in generalizing from the research findings to other groups of people. In general, however, we must be cautious about assuming that the conclusions from research based on middle-class Euro–North Americans or Europeans apply to other groups of people.

Another caveat concerns conclusions regarding cause-and-effect relations between parental variables and children's moral development. Implicit in the notions of socialization and childrearing practices is the assumption that it is the adult who is influencing the child. However, it is also likely that children, on account of differences in their characteristics and behaviors, influence how adults treat them (see Bell and Harper, 1977). Much of the research on socialization of moral behavior and moral reasoning is correlational in nature, and correlations tell one nothing about the direction of causality. Indeed, there is evidence that children's behaviors and temperament influence adults' socialization efforts (see Keller and Bell, 1979; Kuczynski and Kochanska, 1990; Maccoby and Martin, 1983; Patterson, 1982), that relations between socialization and child behaviors are bidirectional (Eisenberg et al., 1999), and that temperament and parental practices may interact in their effects (Bates, Petit, Dodge, and Ridge, 1998; Kochanska, 1995). Indeed, there is little doubt that heredity contributes to some of the associations found between parental characteristics or behaviors and children's behavior (see Collins, Maccoby, Steinberg, Hetherington, and Bornstein, 2000). Parent and child behaviors are interwoven; partners regulate each other's behavior, and coherent expectations about each other's behavior, joint goals, and shared meanings may emerge (Maccoby, 1992). Thus, the processes underlying the socialization of children's morality are probably much more complex than the available research indicates.

THE RELATIONS OF PARENTAL CHARACTERISTICS AND BEHAVIORS TO CHILDREN'S MORAL DEVELOPMENT

In this section of the chapter we briefly summarize empirical findings on parental variables associated with different aspects of moral thinking (i.e., moral judgment) and behavior.

Moral Judgment

Socializers typically have been assigned a circumscribed role in moral development by cognitive developmental theorists. Thus, it is not surprising that the contributions of parenting to the development of moral reasoning have received relatively little attention. Those that do typically pertain to aspects of the environment that Kohlberg deemed important: opportunities for perspective taking and for engendering cognitive conflict.

Provision of role-taking opportunities and promotion of autonomous thinking. The research provides some support for Kohlberg's assertion that provision of role-taking opportunities for the autonomous construction of moral ideas fosters children's moral reasoning. For example, Holstein (1972) found that parents who encouraged their children's participation in discussion and decision making are more likely to have children who reason at relatively high levels (see, however, Speicher, 1992). Leahy (1981) found that adolescent males' level of moral judgment was correlated with low maternal punitiveness and control, low maternal emphasis on maintaining boundaries between the child and others, and paternal acceptance and incorporation of the son into the family. Findings for daughters were less consistent. Daughters' higher level reasoning was correlated with low paternal ambivalence about autonomy, low paternal protectiveness, and low maternal intrusiveness, as well as paternal emphasis on control and supervision (see Eisenberg, 1977, for somewhat similar results).

Studies on actual or observed styles of parent–child interactions have produced a mixed pattern of findings. In an early study of mothers' and sons' discussions of moral dilemmas, mothers of higher reasoning boys, in comparison with mothers whose sons exhibited lower moral reasoning, were more dominant and hostile, and less warm and encouraging (Jurkovic and Prentice, 1974). Buck, Walsh, and Rothman (1981) examined the relation of parental practices during a discussion of how to handle sons' aggression with 10- to 13-year-old boys' moral reasoning. They found that boys with higher moral reasoning had parents who considered their son's view, used reasoning themselves, and tended to encourage the expression of the son's view.

Language during parent–child interactions also has been examined. In a study of elementary school girls, Kruger (1992) coded transactive (reasoning about reasoning) statements, questions, and responses in mother–child discussions of moral dilemmas. High use by mother and daughter of transactive statements (spontaneously produced critiques, refinements, extensions, or significant paraphrases of ideas), particularly those that focused on the partner's ideas, was associated with daughters' higher level moral reasoning immediately after the interaction session. Thus, daughters' moral reasoning was associated with egalitarian interactions with their mothers in which both partners were highly involved in a discussion of the moral dilemmas. Similar findings were obtained for fathers' (but not mothers') use of transactive statement with their adolescents (Pratt, Arnold, Pratt, and Diessner, 1999).

Probably the most definitive work on the role of parental emphasis on autonomous thinking and provision of opportunities for critical thinking is that of Walker and colleagues (Walker and Hennig, 1999; Walker and Taylor, 1991). In this work, parents' interaction style during a discussion of moral issues with their first-, fourth-, seventh-, or tenth-grade child, or fifth and tenth graders, was used to predict elementary and high school children's reasoning 2 or 4 years later. During the interaction sessions, parents and their child discussed hypothetical and real-life moral dilemmas (one in the child's life) and attempted to reach a consensus. Parents generally used lower levels of moral reasoning when discussing issues with their children than was evidenced in an individual assessment of the parents' reasoning level, and they used lower level reasoning more with children reasoning at low levels. Children's moral reasoning years later was best predicted by discussions of the real-life rather than hypothetical moral dilemma. Parental behaviors that best predicted children's moral growth were characterized by a Socratic questioning style, supportive interactions, and the presentation of higher level reasoning. A large discrepancy between parents and child (about one stage) was predictive of children's development. Moral growth was associated with parental behaviors such as eliciting the child's opinion, drawing out the child's reasoning with appropriate probing questions, paraphrasing, and checking for understanding, all in the context of emotional support and attentiveness. Parent behaviors such as critiquing and directly challenging the child (especially in a hostile manner), presenting of counterconsiderations, and simply providing information were not associated with children's moral growth. Direct challenges to the child's reasoning may have been viewed as hostile by the child and, consequently, may have been counterproductive, whereas simple provision of information may have been viewed as lecturing. Overall, Walker and his colleagues' findings suggest that parental practices that promote consideration of higher level moral ideas, but do so in a supportive rather than heavy-handed manner, are associated with children's moral growth.

Disciplinary practices. Comprehensive reviews of the relations of various modes of discipline to children's moral development were published by Hoffman (1970b) and Brody and Shaffer (1982). Thus, in this review their findings are cited and updated with discussion of more recent work.

Consistent with Hoffman's theorizing, both Hoffman (1970b) and Brody and Shaffer (1982) found predominantly negative relations between parental power assertive practices and children's moral reasoning, particularly for mothers. Love-withdrawal procedures were for the most part unrelated to children's moral reasoning, although both positive and negative associations were found. Furthermore, the preponderance of studies support the proposed positive relation between mothers' use of inductions and children's moral reasoning; findings for fathers are rare and less consistent, although more positive than negative relations are apparent.

The results of recent studies tend to be similar. In general, inductive parental practices have been associated with higher level moral reasoning in offspring. In a study of Dutch children aged 9 to 13, both mothers' and fathers' use of inductions rather than power assertion was significantly, positively related to level of children's moral reasoning (Janssen, Janssens, and Gerris, 1992), although in a similar sample, maternal, but not paternal, inductions related to Dutch children's moral reasoning about prosocial moral conflicts (Janssens and Gerris, 1992). In yet another study with elementary-school-age Dutch children, mothers' but not fathers' use of victim-oriented inductions was associated with children's internalized moral judgments (de Veer and Janssens, 1992). The positive relation frequently holds for only some children and not others: for upper-middle-socioeconomic status (SES) girls and older boys in India but not other sex, age, and social class groups (Saraswathi and Sundaresan, 1980); for older (15 to 16 years) but not younger upper-middle-SES boys and girls in India (Parikh, 1980); for Israeli fathers' and adolescents' reports of parental induction, but not mothers' reports of their own use of induction (Eisikovits and Sagi, 1982). Thus, although inductive discipline is not related to all measures of moral reasoning for all samples, inductive discipline does seem, in general, to be associated with higher levels of children's moral reasoning.

The style of parenting, more than any one disciplinary practice, may be associated with children's moral reasoning. Consistent with this notion, Janssens and Dekovic (1997) found that children were higher in moral reasoning about helping dilemmas if their parents were supportive, authoritative (e.g., gave explanations or suggestions, or asked child stimulating questions to help find solutions), and used less restrictive control (e.g., fewer commands or orders such as "Don't do that") with their children. Other investigators also have noted relations between authoritative parenting and higher level moral reasoning among adolescents (Boyes and Allen, 1993; Pratt et al., 1999).

Affective environment. Hoffman (1970b) argued that parental warmth provides an optimal environment for socialization because children are more likely to attend to parents and care about pleasing their parents when the relationship generally is supportive. There is some support for the role of parental warmth in fostering children's moral reasoning (e.g., Palmer and Hollin, 1996; Powers, 1988). Recall the Walker and Taylor study (1991); they found that children's moral growth was linked to a supportive, positive environment during family discussion of moral issues. Speicher (1992) and Buck et al. (1981) obtained similar findings. In other studies, researchers have found relations between parental nurturance and moral reasoning for one parent but not the other, one sex but not the other, one age but not others, or for children from middle-class but not lower income families (Eisenberg, Lennon, and Roth, 1983; Hart, 1988; Hoffman and Saltzstein, 1967; Smart and Smart, 1976).

Perhaps parental warmth does not exert a direct effect on children's moral reasoning; it may simply influence the effectiveness of other parental practices in fostering the growth of moral reasoning (i.e., it may be a moderator variable). As suggested by Baumrind's work (1971, 1993), when parental warmth is not combined with appropriate parental disciplinary practices, it may result in a permissive parenting style, one that is not associated with positive child outcomes. This may explain why associations between parental warmth and moral reasoning are mixed in the research literature and why authoritative parenting (which includes support, control, and practices such as induction) has been linked to higher level moral judgment (Boyes and Allen, 1993; Janssens and Dekovic, 1997; Pratt et al., 1999).

Relation between parents' and children's moral reasoning. A number of investigators have examined the correlation between parents' and children's levels of moral reasoning. A positive relation could reflect a number of factors including similarity between parents' and children's cognitive abilities or parents with higher level moral reasoning promoting their children's moral reasoning by stimulating cognitive conflict or using optimal childrearing practices. Findings have been inconsistent. Some researchers have found significant correlations between parents' and children's moral reasoning (Buck et al., 1981; Janssen et al., 1992); others have not (e.g., Walker and Taylor, 1991). In one longitudinal sample, mothers' and fathers' levels of moral judgment were positively related to those of sons and daughters in adolescence and early adulthood; in another sample, only fathers' and sons' reasoning was consistently positively related (Speicher, 1994). Moreover, in some research, the size of the relation varied with the age of the child (Parikh, 1980; c.f. Speicher, 1994). Thus, in general, there appears to be a weak positive relation between children's and parents' moral reasoning, but one that varies across samples, sex of the parent or child, and sometimes the age of the child.

An important question is whether parents at different levels of reasoning evidence different styles of interaction in moral discussions. Walker and Taylor (1991) found no evidence of a relation between parents' moral reasoning and their interaction style. In contrast, Buck et al. (1981) found that parents who reason at higher levels had sons who participated and reasoned more, and who communicated more fully, in family discussion. These findings indirectly support the notion that parents at high levels of moral reasoning create a different family environment than those at lower levels. In fact, Janssen et al. (1992) found that parents' moral reasoning and their use of inductive versus power-assertive discipline were correlated. Thus, the relation between parent and child moral reasoning probably is at least in part because parents who use higher level reasoning also use more inductive and less power-assertive practices. However, children reasoning at higher levels also may elicit different parental reactions.

Summary. Although there is relatively little research on the socialization of moral reasoning, particularly by parents, some tentative conclusions can be drawn. Children with higher level moral reasoning tend to have parents who are supportive and encourage autonomous thinking, who stimulate their children's moral thinking by means of their conversational style and by involving their children in moral discussions, and who use inductive rather than power-assertive modes of reasoning. In addition, there may be a weak relation between parents' and children's moral reasoning, one that is partially mediated by the nature of the parent–child interaction. However, it is unclear if these findings generalize to non-Western countries, as there is little work on the relation of parenting to moral judgment in these countries. Because it is unclear that systems for coding moral judgment developed in the United States by Kohlberg and others appropriately represent the development of moral judgment in non-Western, nonindustrialized countries, the task of determining what aspects of parenting relate to level of moral judgment in these countries is especially complicated.

Lying, Dishonesty, and Resistance to Temptation

Given the importance to parents of children's lying, dishonesty, and failure to resist temptation, it is surprising that there is relatively little research on socialization practices that prevent such behaviors per se independent of aggression or other types of acting-out behaviors (externalizing behavior).

Affective environment.   Several investigators have explored the relation of parental warmth to resistance to temptation and honesty, in part because parental warmth is sometimes presumed to foster identification with parental values. Relevant studies are scarce and often have involved parents' reports of both their own practices and their children's behavior. In other studies, adults other than parents interact with children in laboratory settings (e.g., studies in which an adult experimenter uses either mild or more intense punishment in response to children's attempts to use objects that they were prohibited from touching; see Burton, 1976). In a review of studies pertaining the limited research on dishonesty, Burton (1976) concluded that adults' noncontingent warmth does not foster honesty (cf. Mussen et al., 1970). Similarly, in older studies, the relation of parental warmth to children's resistance to temptation was not consistent (Brody and Shaffer, 1982; Hoffman, 1970b).

However, recent studies using some or all observational measures of parental warmth and/or children's behavior suggest that parental warmth and support are associated with resistance to temptation. Spinrad et al. (1999) found that parents' positive affect and support in interactions with their children were positively related to boys' (but not girls') resistance to cheating when trying to win a game and earn a prize. Similarly, Kochanska and Murray (2000) found that children's cheating in the early school years was inversely associated with a mutually responsive, cooperative, warm parent–child relationship in the toddler and preschool years. When these same children were preschoolers, children's resistance to temptation and compliance with maternal instructions were associated with a mutually responsive, positive mother–child relationship (Kochanska, 1997b). As toddlers, security of attachment to mother also was associated with internalized compliance with maternal commands and resistance to violations of prohibitions for relatively fearless children, not fearful children (Kochanska, 1995). Similar interactions between child temperament and maternal socialization (as toddlers) were found when the children were preschoolers (Kochanska, 1997a). Kochanska (1993) suggested that the socialization basis for the development of conscience for children low in anxiety and fear is the quality of the parent–child relationship; children with warm, reciprocal relationships with their parents are likely to be receptive and positively motivated to respond to parental socialization, identify with the parent, and internalize parental values.

In regard to lying, Stouthamer-Loeber and Loeber (1986) found that maternal rejection correlated with lying in fourth-, seventh-, and tenth-grade boys; paternal rejection was associated with lying in fourth and seventh, but not in tenth graders. Moreover, boys lied more if their parents did not get along well or live together (also see Lewis, 1931).

Modeling.   Although infrequently studied, it is likely that parental modeling of dishonest behavior is associated with children's dishonesty. In laboratory studies, children exposed to dishonest models were more likely to act dishonestly themselves in similar circumstances. However, exposure to honest models is not consistently associated with children's honesty (see Burton, 1976; Hoffman, 1970b). We are not aware of modeling studies with children involving parents. However, Hartshorne and May (1928) found that high parental honesty was associated with children's honesty across situations, and Lewis (1931) found that mothers of liars were more likely to report lying themselves than were mothers of nonliars (see Stouthamer-Loeber, 1986). It seems quite likely that children repeatedly exposed to parental honesty or dishonesty will imitate the behavior their parents model.

Discipline.   There is limited evidence that inconsistency in discipline relates to children's lying (Lewis, 1931; Stouthamer-Loeber, 1986). In addition, Stouthamer-Loeber and Loeber (1986) found that boys who lied were likely to come from families in which mothers poorly supervised and monitored their sons.

In the majority of early studies, parental use of power assertion and love withdrawal was not significantly related to children's resistance to temptation, although power assertion was linked with low resistance to temptation in a few studies (Brody and Shaffer, 1982; Hoffman, 1970b). In addition, parental use of inductions has been associated with higher levels of resistance to temptation slightly more frequently than it has been negatively related (Brody and Shaffer, 1982; de Veer and Janssens, 1992; Hoffman, 1970b). Kochanska (1995, 1997a) found that maternal gentle discipline (deemphasizing power) during the toddler years was related to toddlers' and preschoolers' committed compliance and resistance to violations of prohibitions, but primarily for fearful children. For fearless children, security of attachment and a mutually positive relation were predictive of adherence to prohibitions and rules.

Summary. Overall, it appears that power assertion is negatively related to children's compliance and resistance to temptation in the early years of life, at least for fearful children. The inconsistent pattern of associations between parental socialization and children's resistance to temptation may be due to the fact that this relation is moderated by children's temperament (see Putnam, Sanson, and Rothbart, in Vol. 1 of this *Handbook*). As is discussed later, these findings are similar to those found for aggression and antisocial behavior, more broadly defined.

Guilt and Shame

One indication of moral internalization is if a person experiences guilt after transgressing. Until recently, guilt usually has been assessed by one of two methods: (1) asking parents to report how children behave after a transgression or (2) presenting a child with hypothetical situations in which a child transgresses and asking the child how the story protagonist feels and what he or she did. In the former, reports of children's guilt may be tainted by parental variables (such as the parents' tendencies to view their child in a benign way). In the latter, reports of guilt may be confounded with children's desire to respond in socially desirable ways. Furthermore, often children may be punished less severely if they confess transgressions; thus, confession may be a means of avoiding sanctions. In recent work, however, observational measures of internalization as well as parents' reports have been used, and such measures probably are superior to those used in many early studies.

In the work on internalization, it is important to differentiate among various types of guilt and shame. Many theorists define morally relevant guilt as feelings of discomfort or remorse over violating one's own standards, harm caused, or an untoward behavior; these feelings frequently are accompanied by the desire to make reparation. Furthermore, guilt involves an individual's negative evaluation of particular behaviors enacted by the individual, not a global condemnation of one's entire self. It is a private affair—between one's self and one's internalized standards—in situations involving a breach of those standards (see Hoffman, 1998; Tangney, 1990, 1991). There appear to be at least two types of moral guilt: guilt based on experiencing empathy with victims of one's transgression (Hoffman, 1982) and guilt based on concern with controlling one's own impulses and/or living up to one's own standards (see Eisenberg-Berg, 1979; Hoffman, 1970a). Guilt is conceptually different from fear of punishment for wrongdoing from an external agent.

In contrast to guilt, shame sometimes is defined as "a reaction to public exposure (and disapproval) of some impropriety or personal shortcoming" (Tangney, 1990, p. 102). It involves a negative evaluation of one's entire self; it is a much more global, painful, and devastating experience in which the entire self, not just a particular behavior, is scrutinized and evaluated as fundamentally flawed (Ferguson and Stegge, 1998; Tangney, 1991). The dysfunctional guilt that is emphasized in some clinical work is probably more akin to shame than guilt in that it involves pervasive self-criticism and negative self-evaluations (Koestner, Zuroff, and Powers, 1991). In addition, however, there may be dysfunctional types of guilt that involve an overgeneralized acceptance of responsibility for others' problems (see Zahn-Waxler, Duggal, and Gruber, in Vol. 4 of this *Handbook*). This type of dysfunctional guilt may develop in children with depressed parents (Zahn-Waxler and Kochanska, 1990).

Our discussion focuses on morally relevant, nondysfunctional guilt. However, it frequently is difficult to differentiate between true guilt and anxiety about potential punishment or shame. Thus, in many studies, it is not clear exactly what type of response has been assessed.

Discipline and affective environment.   In most studies on the socialization of children's guilt, parental disciplinary practices have been examined. Based on the early studies reviewed by Hoffman (1970b) and Brody and Shaffer (1982), there appears to be a weak negative relation between parental power assertion and the intensity of children's guilt, and a weak positive association (primarily for mothers; Brody and Shaffer, 1982) between parental use of inductions and intensity of children's guilt. Researchers have replicated the findings pertaining to power assertion and inductions (Abell and Gecas, 1997; Kochanska, Padavich, and Koenig, 1996; Krevans and Gibbs, 1996). For example, Krevans and Gibbs (1996) found that children tended to be high on the combination of empathy and guilt—which is likely to reflect other-oriented, empathy-based guilt—when their parents were relatively high in their use of inductive discipline (see also Ferguson and Stegge, 1995). Inductions were not related to guilt by itself. Moreover, it was found (Laible and Thompson, 1999) that maternal references to feelings, needs, or intentions and moral evaluative statements (e.g., "Good boy," "This was a nice thing to do") during conversations with their 4-year-old children were associated with mothers' reports of children's guilt, remorse, and related reactions to a transgression or mishap, as well as with internalized compliance. Similarly, variables related to guilt and conscience have been associated with maternal affect and childrearing style 2 years earlier. Hastings, Zahn-Waxler, Robinson, Usher, and Bridges (2000) found that mothers who reported experiencing or expressing negative affect with their children (e.g., anger, disappointment, and conflict) and were authoritarian (e.g., used strict supervision, discouraged the expression of affect, used corporal punishment, or issued prohibitions and reprimands) rather than authoritative (used reasoning and guidance, encouraged independence, and supported the open expression of emotion) in their parenting when their children were age 5 had children who, at age 7, were relatively low on a composite score related to guilt (e.g., reparation, confession, apology, concern about others' transgressions, and internalized conduct).

There is little evidence of a consistent association between intensity of guilt and parental love withdrawal (e.g., Abell and Gecas, 1997; Ferguson and Stegge, 1995; Krevans and Gibbs, 1996). Findings in regard to children's confession and acceptance of blame are somewhat clearer; children's confession and acceptance of blame appear to be associated with mothers' (but not fathers') low use of power assertion and high use of induction (Brody and Shaffer, 1982). In addition, maternal use of love withdrawal appears to be weakly linked with children's confession and acceptance of blame (Brody and Shaffer, 1982).

In one study, high levels of both shame and guilt in children were highly associated with both parental induction and parental anger when children transgressed, modestly associated with love withdrawal, and weakly related to high power assertion (Ferguson, Stegge, and Thompson, 1993). The aforementioned findings on love withdrawal, which are contrary to Hoffman's predictions (1970b, 1983), are consistent with Zahn-Waxler and Kochanska's (1990) argument that love withdrawal is associated with inhibition of anger and, consequently, guilt. Zahn-Waxler and Kochanska further suggested that love withdrawal may be effective in fostering guilt only if it is used by parents who usually are affectionate.

As suggested by Zahn-Waxler and Kochanska (1990), love withdrawal and induction may result in different types of guilt. Hoffman (1970a) distinguished between two types of children: humanistic-flexible children who express concern over the harm they do to others and conventional-rigid children who are concerned about the violation of institutionalized norms and laws. Hoffman described the humanistic conscience as oriented outwardly toward the consequences for others, whereas the conventional conscience is oriented inwardly (toward their own impulses). Conventional-rigid children's guilt tends to have a harsh, ego-alien quality; they express more unconscious, intense, and bizarre fears in their guilt themes. Interestingly, Hoffman found evidence indicating that conventional children experience more parental love withdrawal from both parents and more paternal inductions pointing out harm to the parent. In contrast, humanistic children experience more maternal inductions pointing out matter-of-fact requirements of the situation (but not more inductions regarding peers; see however, de Veer and Janssens, 1992). Thus, the combination of high parental love withdrawal in a context conducive to internalization (i.e., high induction and affection, and low power assertion) may lead to an intensified inhibition of hostile impulses. This may occur because such a familial context enhances both children's fears of losing parental love and children's high levels of concern about controlling their impulses. In any case, it appears that love withdrawal is associated with guilt based on impulse control rather than empathy.

In one of the few longitudinal studies on conscience, Kochanska (1991) assessed mothers' disciplinary practices when their children were toddlers (aged $1\frac{1}{2}$ to $3\frac{1}{2}$ years) using both maternal reports and observations of mother–child interaction. These maternal measures were correlated with children's responses at age 8 to 10 years to semiprojective narratives about transgressions (affective/moral orientation, degree of reparation, and reported intensity of feelings if they had been in the situation themselves). Maternal emphasis on power assertion and coercive discipline rather than on democratic, inductive modes of discipline (involving the encouragement of child independence and open communication between parent and child) was associated with low levels of guilt as indexed by level of affective/moral orientation and reparation. However, it is of interest that these relations (as well as the relation between maternal practices and children's reported discomfort feelings) held primarily for children who were prone to anxiety. Recall that Kochanska (1995) obtained a similar pattern of findings when conscience was operationalized as committed, internalized compliance and resistance to temptation. Kochanska suggested that children who are prone to anxiety and fear are likely to be responsive to subtle maternal cues, whereas they may become overaroused in the discipline context (which would be expected to undermine the development of conscience) if exposed to power-assertive modes of discipline.

Summary.   Although research on the socialization of guilt and shame is limited, it appears that children's guilt is fostered by nonpunitive, supportive parental practices and inductive discipline. However, it is likely that empathy-based guilt and more rigid types of guilt based on fear of losing parental love are associated with somewhat different socialization experiences. In addition, children's temperament may influence the degree to which maternal practices are associated with the development of children's guilt.

Prosocial Behavior

Prosocial behavior frequently is defined as voluntary behavior intended to benefit another (Eisenberg and Fabes, 1998). Most parents who desire to foster prosocial behaviors really want to enhance one type of prosocial responding—altruistic behavior. Altruistic behaviors are voluntary, intentional actions that benefit another and are not motivated by the desire to obtain external material or social rewards. They are performed for internalized reasons—empathy and sympathy, the desire to live up to internalized values, or processes such as guilt. Unfortunately, when we observe a prosocial behavior we often cannot ascertain the actor's motives. This makes it difficult to determine which socialization practices are related to the development of altruistic behaviors versus nonaltruistically motivated prosocial behaviors.

Inductions.   There is evidence that parental inductions (e.g., "See, you made Jerry cry"; Hoffman, 1970b) are related to higher empathy in children (Hoffman, 1975a), which in turn is related to children's prosocial behavior (see Eisenberg and Fabes, 1998; Janssens and Gerris, 1992; Krevans and Gibbs, 1996). The effectiveness of inductions has been demonstrated for children as young as $1\frac{1}{2}$ to $2\frac{1}{2}$ years of age if inductions were administered with affective force (i.e., emotion; Zahn-Waxler, Rodke-Yarrow, and King, 1979). Moreover, mothers' explanations to their children for their own sadness in ongoing social interactions (which may or may not have involved disciplinary issues) have been associated with children's prosocial behavior at preschool (Denham and Grout, 1992). Such verbalizations may help children to understand others' emotions.

According to one study, inductions are associated with prosocial development primarily when verbalized by socializers who typically do not use power-assertive (punitive) techniques (Hoffman, 1963) or when children have had a history of inductive discipline (Dlugokinski and Firestone, 1974). When inductions are part of a generally democratic parenting style, democratic parenting has been associated with teachers' and peers' reports of prosocial behavior (Dekovic and Janssens, 1992; Janssens and Dekovic, 1997).

Power-assertive, punitive techniques of discipline.   In general, socializers' use of power-assertive techniques of discipline such as physical punishment or deprivation of privileges has been found to be either unrelated or negatively related to children's prosocial behavior (Brody and Shaffer, 1982; Eisenberg and Fabes, 1998) and negatively related to empathy/sympathy (Krevans and Gibbs, 1996). As suggested by Hoffman (1983), children attribute helping induced by power-assertive techniques to external motives (Dix and Grusec, 1983; Smith, Gelfand, Hartmann, and Partlow, 1979). Nonetheless, as noted by Hoffman (1983), there is a difference between the occasional use of power-assertive techniques in the context of a positive parent–child relationship and the use of punishment as the preferred, predominant mode of discipline. When power-assertive techniques are used in a measured and rational manner by parents who generally are warm and supportive, set high standards, and usually use nonpower-assertive disciplinary techniques such as reasoning, children tend to be socially responsible and positive in their behavior (Baumrind, 1971, 1993). In contrast, it appears that the frequent use of power-assertive techniques, especially by hostile, cold socializers, is negatively related to prosocial development and may hinder the effectiveness of other socialization techniques that usually promote prosocial development (Hoffman, 1963). For example, Dutch parents who use power assertion as part of an authoritarian pattern of discipline have elementary school children who are viewed as low in helpfulness by their peers (although not by their teachers; Dekovic and Janssens, 1992).

Although punishment can induce immediate compliance with socializers' expectations for prosocial behavior if the socializer monitors the child's behavior, there is as yet little evidence that punishment for selfishness has long-term, generalizable effects. It should be emphasized, however, that most mothers infrequently use punishment (especially physical punishment) to induce helping or in response to children's failure to help (Grusec, 1982, 1991; Grusec, Dix, and Mills, 1982; Zahn-Waxler et al., 1979).

Love withdrawal.   There appears to be no consistent relation between parents' use of love withdrawal as discipline and children's prosocial behavior (Brody and Shaffer, 1982; Krevans and Gibbs, 1996). It is likely that the effects of love withdrawal vary with the context and frequency in which it is administered.

The Role of Socializers' Nurturance and Emotional Support

Intuitively, one would expect warm and supportive socializers to rear prosocial children. Consistent with this perspective, in general there seems to be a modest, positive relation between parental warmth (particularly maternal warmth) and children's prosocial development (e.g., Janssens and Gerris, 1992; see Brody and Shaffer, 1982). In addition, there is some evidence that children with a secure attachment to their mother are more prosocial (Iannotti, Cummings, Pierrehumbert, Milano, and Zahn-Waxler, 1992; Kestenbaum, Farber, and Sroufe, 1989). Nonetheless, the relation between parental warmth and children's prosocial behavior is fragile, and the two frequently have been unrelated or inconsistently correlated (e.g., Iannotti et al., 1992; Krevans and Gibbs, 1996; Wentzel and McNamara, 1999; see Eisenberg and Fabes, 1998). However, in many studies, parental nurturance was not assessed directly; rather, measures of parental behaviors were based on parental or child report of socializers' warmth. When socializers' nurturance has been observed or controlled experimentally, the relation of socializers' nurturance and support to children's prosocial behavior has been found to be somewhat stronger and clearer than in the literature involving parental self-report (see Bryant and Crockenberg, 1980; Yarrow, Scott, and Waxler, 1973; Zahn-Waxler et al., 1979).

There is some evidence that parental warmth, support, and sympathy are associated with their children's affective sympathy and empathy (Eisenberg, Fabes et al., 1992; Fabes, Eisenberg, and Miller, 1990; Hastings, Zahn-Waxler, Robinson, Usher, and Bridges, 2000; Spinrad et al., 1999; cf. Iannotti et al., 1992; Koestner, Franz, and Weinberger, 1990). Thus, it is logical to hypothesize that warm, empathic parenting promotes children's prosocial behavior due to its effects on children's perspective taking, empathy, and sympathy. However, Janssens and Gerris (1992) found that Dutch children's empathy did not mediate the effects of parental support on prosocial behavior for either mothers or fathers; for mothers, support had a direct (unmediated) effect on 9- to 12-year-old children's prosocial behavior. In contrast, parents' use of inductions, high demandingness (i.e., parental emphasis on the child's responsibilities and a tendency to say what they expected from the child), and low power assertion (in combination) did appear to affect children's empathy, which in turn was related to children's prosocial behavior.

Although socializers' nurturance and support (especially when measured with observations) do seem to be somewhat positively associated with children's prosocial tendencies, it is likely that the degree of association is moderated by other socialization practices (and characteristics of the child such as dispositional anger or sociability; Carlo, Roesch, and Melby, 1998). Dekovic and Janssens (1992) found that democratic parenting, consisting of a combination of parental warmth and support, combined with inductions, demandingness, and the provision of suggestions, information, and positive comments, was associated with children's prosocial behavior as reported by teachers and peers. In another Dutch sample, parents who were observed and reported themselves to be high on support, authoritative (i.e., giving explanations and suggestions and asking questions to stimulate the child regarding a solution), and nonrestrictive had children viewed by both teachers and peers as prosocial (Janssens and Dekovic, 1997). Similar findings were obtained by Hastings et al. (2000). Nurturance may act as a background or contextual variable that functions to orient the child positively toward the parent and enhances the child's receptivity to parental influence, including parental inductions, preachings, and moral standards (Hoffman, 1970b).

Modeling. Much of the research on modeling of prosocial behavior has taken place in laboratory work where children's imitation of an unfamiliar adult's prosocial behavior or selfishness has been assessed. In general, people (including children) who have viewed a prosocial model are more prosocial themselves than are people who have not viewed a prosocial model or who have viewed a stingy or unhelpful model (see Eisenberg and Fabes, 1998; Radke-Yarrow, Zahn-Waxler, and Chapman, 1983, for reviews). Even in the laboratory, the effects of observing a prosocial model have been found to persist over time (for days or even months; Grusec, Saas-Kortsaak, and Simutis, 1978; Rice and Grusec, 1975; Rushton, 1975) and to generalize to somewhat new and different situations (see Eisenberg and Fabes, 1998).

Despite the preponderance of evidence indicating that children imitate prosocial others, it also is clear that some models are imitated more than others. For example, nurturance by the model is related to children's imitation of prosocial behavior, albeit in a complex manner. It appears that noncontingent nurturance (unconditional constant nurturance) is interpreted by children as indicating permissiveness and, consequently, children do not assist if there is a material cost to doing so (Grusec, 1971; Grusec and Skubiski, 1970; Weissbrod, 1980). However, when adult nurturance is part of an ongoing relationship and is not unconditional (which generally is true in real life), nurturance increases the effectiveness of a model (Yarrow et al., 1973).

Some of the most compelling evidence of the role of modeling in the family in real-life situations comes from studies of people in Europe who saved Jews from the Nazis during World War II. Rescuing activities were often highly dangerous and could result in death if discovered. Two groups of researchers found that rescuers tended to come from families in which parents modeled generosity, helpfulness, and similar behaviors (London, 1970; Oliner and Oliner, 1988). Similar findings were obtained in a study of the "freedom riders" in the late 1950s and early 1960s, a group of young adults (many Euro-American) who engaged in activities designed to increase equal rights and opportunities for African Americans in the southern parts of the United States. Those who were highly committed and involved in the civil rights effort reported that their parents had been excellent models of prosocial behavior and concern for others, working for worthy causes, protesting injustices, and discussing their activities with their children (Rosenhan, 1970). Along the same lines, Hart and Fegley (1995) found that minority youth who were exemplars of caring were more likely than their peers to incorporate aspects of parental related representations (e.g., what their mothers were like or expected of them) in their self-representations. Moreover, Janoski and Wilson (1995) found a positive relation between parents' voluntarism and that of their grown children years later. Thus, there is evidence suggesting that parental modeling of prosocial behavior, which no doubt is often combined with a variety of other parental behaviors that are likely to foster children's prosocial behavior, is associated with adult children's willingness to assist others at a cost to themselves. Of course, hereditary factors also could contribute to similarities in the behavior of parents and children.

Moral preachings. In an attempt to modify or influence children's behaviors, socializers sometimes symbolically model prosocial behavior (say that they are going to act in a prosocial manner) or discuss the merits or consequences of prosocial actions. Such verbalizations frequently have been labeled preachings or exhortations, and represent attempts to influence an individual's future behavior, not a disciplinary response to prior behavior.

Researchers have found that the effectiveness of preachings varies as a function of their content. Children's sharing is enhanced by appeals that provide symbolic modeling, that is, include a description of what the model intends to do (Grusec and Skubiski, 1970; Rice and Grusec, 1975) or include reasons for assisting that are likely to evoke empathy and sympathy (Burleson and Fennelly, 1981; Eisenberg-Berg and Geisheker, 1979; Perry, Bussey, and Freiberg, 1981). In contrast, preachings that are power assertive in content (involve threats of disapproval; Perry et al., 1981) or refer to the norm of sharing (Bryan and Walbek, 1970) or self-oriented reasons for sharing (Burleson and Fennelly, 1981) are relatively ineffective. The effects of preaching with compelling content can be relatively durable; in experimental studies they have lasted over a 3- (Grusec et al., 1978) or even 8- (Rushton, 1975) week period.

It is possible that preachings, even those providing reasons, can backfire if they are viewed by the child as putting pressure on the child to assist. Consistent with findings that children react negatively to attempts to limit their freedom (Brehm, 1981), children may respond negatively and feel unwilling to assist if they feel pressured to comply with an adult's reasoning (see McGrath and Power, 1990; McGrath, Wilson, and Frassetto, 1995). In addition, if preachings are perceived as applying pressure, children may attribute their helping to external causes and, consequently, be less willing to assist at a later time (Lepper, 1983).

Nearly all the studies on preachings have been conducted in laboratory settings. However, it is clear from research on parental use of inductions, verbal demandingness, and other types of verbalizations that parents' verbalizations can influence children's prosocial behavior (e.g., Dekovic and Janssens, 1992). Thus, it is likely that parents' statements about the importance, consequences, or reasons for prosocial action in nondisciplinary settings promote children's tendencies to perform prosocial behaviors.

Assignment of responsibility. Practice performing prosocial behaviors seems to be useful for promoting prosocial tendencies (Barton, 1981; Staub, 1979). Children who were assigned responsibility to teach others or who were induced to participate in prosocial activities subsequently displayed more prosocial behavior (Staub, 1979). Similarly, children who were induced to donate to needy others in one context were more likely to help other people one or two days later (this was true for children in second grade or older, but not kindergartners; Eisenberg, Cialdini, McCreath, and Shell, l987). Furthermore, assigning a specific child responsibility for others seems to enhance prosocial behavior (Maruyama, Fraser, and Miller, 1982; Peterson, 1983). In cross-cultural research, Whiting and Whiting (1975) found that children from non-Western cultures in which youngsters are routinely assigned responsibilities for assisting others (e.g., caregiving activities) were more prosocial than children from other cultures. Finally, participation in voluntary community service sometimes has been linked to greater commitment to helping others in the future (Yates and Youniss, 1996).

Reinforcement. Although both material (Warren, Warren-Rogers, and Bayer, 1976) and social reinforcement (Gelfand, Hartmann, Cromer, Smith, and Page, 1975; Grusec and Redler, 1980) in the laboratory have been found to increase the frequency of prosocial behavior immediately subsequent to the reinforcement, it is not clear whether the effects of material reinforcement are enduring and generalize to new situations. In most research in which reinforced prosocial behaviors have generalized to new settings or have been enduring, reinforcement was used in combination with modeling and other techniques (e.g., Barton, 1981; Rushton, 1975; see Eisenberg and Fabes, 1998). It is likely that the receipt of concrete rewards for a prosocial action leads to the child perceiving that the performance of the prosocial behavior reflected external, and not internal, motivational factors (Lepper, 1983; Szynal-Brown and Morgan, 1983). If this is true, the child would be expected to repeat the prosocial behavior only in settings in which she or he believes that rewards might be forthcoming.

Evidence of the negative effects of rewards on the development of altruism was obtained in one of the few studies concerning parents' use of rewards for prosocial behaviors. Fabes, Fultz, Eisenberg, May-Plumlee, and Christopher (1989) found that second graders to fifth graders who believed that there would be a reward for helping assisted more in that context than did other children. However, the promise of a reward led to *less* helping when the children were given a second opportunity to assist in a context in which rewards were not mentioned and the children were alone. However, the promise of a reward was detrimental only for children whose mothers valued and used rewards relatively frequently. Moreover, mothers who felt relatively positive about using rewards reported that their children were lower in prosocial behavior than did other mothers. Thus, children who were frequently exposed to rewards at home seemed to be less intrinsically motivated to help when there were no rewards for doing so.

It is also possible that parental reinforcement of children's prosocial behavior varies as a function of characteristics of the child. Eisenberg, Wolchik, Goldberg, and Engel (1992) found that mothers and fathers used more social reinforcement (i.e., positive affect) after children engaged in prosocial acts requested by the parent if their children were low in the tendency to perform such prosocial behaviors. It is likely that these parents administered more reinforcement to relatively noncompliant children in an attempt to increase the frequency of their prosocial behavior. Consistent with this notion, Grusec (1991) found that preschoolers who were prosocial were somewhat less likely to receive a response from their mother when they were helpful than were less prosocial children.

Emotion socialization. Children's sympathy and prosocial behavior seem to be related to how parents respond to children's expression of emotion in the home. Parents who help their children to cope with emotions in a constructive manner generally appear to be more sympathetic and prosocial than other children.

For example, in one study, parents of elementary school children who emphasized the need for their sons to control their negative emotions that are not harmful to others tended to experience self-focused distressed responses rather than sympathy when confronted with another's distress. In contrast, same-sex parental restrictiveness in regard to the expression of emotion that might hurt another's feelings was associated with sympathy (Eisenberg, Fabes, Schaller, Carlo, and Miller, 1991). However, such restrictiveness may backfire with younger children if it is not age appropriate (Eisenberg, Fabes et al., 1992).

Parents who encourage their sons to try to take action to deal with stressful situations tend to have sons who are prosocial and sympathetic (Eisenberg, Fabes, and Murphy, 1996; Eisenberg, Fabes, Schaller, Carlos, and Miller, 1991). Moreover, mothers' discussion of their own and their children's emotions with their children sometimes has been associated with sympathy and empathy (e.g., Denham and Grout, 1992; Eisenberg, Fabes et al., 1992). However, focusing too much on children's distress in stressful situations sometimes has been associated with children experiencing less empathy or sympathy, perhaps because some parents talk more about emotion with children who are prone to overarousal or too much empathy (so they experience self-focused personal distress; Trommsdorff, 1995). Alternatively, parents who focus on emotions with children who cannot cope with the emotion may overarouse their children, with the consequence that their children do not learn to regulate their own distress. Indeed, mothers of younger children often try to buffer their children from experiencing too much negative emotion when dealing with empathy-inducing information, and doing so is associated with more sympathy and helpfulness (Fabes et al., 1994).

There also appears to be some relation between emotion expressed in the home and children's prosocial tendencies, although this relation is quite complex (see Eisenberg and Fabes, 1998). Sometimes, but not always, parental expression of positive emotion has been linked to children's prosocial behavior (e.g., Denham and Grout, 1992; Eisenberg, Fabes, Schaller, Miller et al., 1991; Garner, Jones, and Miner, 1994). Conversely, the expression of negative hostile emotion in the home generally has been linked to low levels of sympathy (e.g., Crockenberg, 1985; Denham and Grout, 1992; Eisenberg, Fabes, Carlo et al., 1992), at least outside of the conflict situation (see Eisenberg and Fabes, 1998, for further review and discussion). What is probably most important is whether the emotion is expressed in a manner in which the child does not feel threatened or overwhelmed and can learn about emotions and how to regulate them.

Summary.   A variety of parenting dimensions has been examined in relation to children's prosocial behavior. However, the configuration of a number of parenting behaviors, not any single behavior, appears to have the greatest impact on children's prosocial behavior. Authoritative parents who are generally warm and supportive, but who also encourage and respect the child's autonomy, use constructive disciplinary techniques such as inductions, and set and enforce high standards of behavior (Baumrind, 1971, 1993) are likely to rear prosocial children. Moreover, the effects of authoritative parenting are likely to be augmented if parents also model prosocial actions, discuss the effects of helping on others, and involve children in helping activities without coercing their participation.

Aggression and Related Antisocial Behaviors

The extant literature defines aggression in a number of different ways (see Coie and Dodge, 1998). In the present paper, *aggression* is defined as "behavior that is aimed at harming or injuring another person or persons" (Parke and Slaby, 1983, p. 550). It is now widely acknowledged that aggressive behaviors tend to be a stable across time, often continuing into adulthood (Coie and Dodge, 1998; Olweus, 1979), even over 22 years, from age 8 to age 30 (Huesmann, Eron, Lefkowitz, and Walder, 1984). Based on the stability and social consequences associated with aggressive and delinquent behavior, a large literature on its etiology, including socialization, has emerged in the past decade. Thus, in our review of this literature, we highlight some of the parenting practices receiving the most attention and cite representative studies; a review of the literature prior to 1997 is available in Coie and Dodge (1998).

Monitoring.   Parental monitoring has been, and continues to be, the focus of considerable attention in the parenting literature. Monitoring refers to parents' knowledge of where their children are, with whom, and/or what they are doing. Low levels of monitoring are hypothesized to be negatively related to antisocial behavior, in part because unmonitored children are able to be spend considerable time with deviant peers from whom they can learn and share aggressive and delinquent activities (Patterson, 1995). In addition to being examined as a causal variable, monitoring has been viewed as a mediator of the effects of other variables and as interacting with children's temperament or personality when predicting offsprings' antisocial behavior. A well-established body of literature clearly demonstrates that low levels of monitoring are related to aggression, delinquency, stealing, and conflict with authorities over behaviors such as skipping school and lying (Keenan, Loeber, Zhang, Stouthamer-Loeber, and Van Kammen, 1995; Patterson, Reid, and Dishion, 1992). Moreover, well-supervised Canadian children are less apt to engage in fighting with peers (Haapasalo and Tremblay, 1994). Levels of parental monitoring also have discriminated between delinquent and nondelinquent youths (Gorman-Smith, Tolan, Zelli, and Huesmann, 1996). The lack of a father or an involved father seems to contribute to lax supervision of Euro-American adolescents (Forgatch and Stoolmiller, 1994).

Investigators have also examined more complex models (see Crouter and Head, in Vol. 3 of this *Handbook*). For example, monitoring by adolescents' closest parenting figure has been shown to mediate the relation between sex (being male) and aggression (Carlo, Raffaelli, Laible, and Meyer, 1999). Moreover, low parental monitoring partially mediated the relation between high acculturation among Mexican American adolescents and their delinquent behavior (Samaniego and Gonzales, 1999). Moderational models also have been examined. For example, adolescents' reports of low parental monitoring (mothers and fathers combined) were related to delinquency for boys, but only if their mothers worked part time; it related to girls' delinquency when mothers were not employed (Jacobson and Crockett, 2000). In addition, the negative relation between monitoring and delinquency increased across the grade level (seventh to twelfth grade) for boys and decreased for girls (Jacobson and Crockett, 2000). Moreover, Colder, Lochman, and Wells (1997) noted that poor parental monitoring was significantly related to boys' aggression, but only for boys who were highly active (rather than low or moderate in activity level).

Consistency of discipline. Inconsistent discipline is believed to encourage aggression and delinquency because, when parents give in or do not follow through on disciplinary efforts (a component of the coercive cycle; see below), they reinforce their child's noncompliant behavior (Patterson et al., 1992). The data support this view. For example, low levels of consistent discipline correlate with aggression and antisocial behaviors in children (Stormshak, Bierman, McMahon, Lengua, and the Conduct Problems Prevention Research Group [CPPRG], 2000), and disrupted discipline relates to antisocial behavior in boys (Patterson, DeGarmo, and Knutson, 2000). The relation between inconsistent discipline and conduct problems may be especially strong for clinic-referred adolescents (Frick, Christian, and Wootton, 1999). Inconsistent discipline operates as a partial mediator between family risk (including variables such as minority status, mother never married, low parental education, frequent moves, economic problems, many children in the family, and parental psychological problems) and children's externalizing problem behaviors (Dumka, Roosa, and Jackson, 1997). Finally, evidence suggests that a reciprocal relation exists between ineffective discipline and child antisocial behavior (Vuchinich, Bank, and Patterson, 1992). Consequently, both the child and parent's behaviors may need to be altered in order to produce lasting change.

Coercive parenting. Coercive parent–child interactions are predictive of children's aggressive and delinquent behaviors (Patterson et al., 1992). Because the coercive process has been described in detail elsewhere (Patterson et al., 1992), it is only briefly outlined here. In step 1 of the cycle, the parent makes a request of the child; in step 2, the child engages in negative behaviors (e.g. whining, yelling and/or complaining). Importantly, in step 3 the parent withdraws the request and negatively reinforces the aversive behavior. In the final step, the child terminates the negative behavior. Parents who are inconsistent with discipline or unskilled are particularly apt to engage in coercive interactions, and these interactions perpetuate ineffective discipline.

Empirical support of the coercive process was produced by Snyder and Patterson (1995; see also Patterson, 1982). In this study, mothers of the aggressive boys, compared with mothers of nonaggressive boys, were more likely to negatively reinforce their son's aversive behavior. Additionally, nonaggressive boys were reinforced more for their prosocial behavior than were aggressive boys. A second study by Snyder, Schrepferman, and St. Peter (1997) obtained similar results. Additionally, while controlling for initial levels of aggression, high levels of coercive interactions (only the first two steps of the coercive process) were associated with high levels of aggression for boys (McFadyen-Ketchum, Bates, Dodge, and Pettit, 1996). However, mother–daughter coercion (only the first two steps) was related to decreases in aggression. Future work on how the coercive process operates for females is needed. Additionally, studies that examine how individual characteristics such as the parent's and child's emotionality, regulation, and antisocial behavior contribute to the coercive process should be particularly helpful. Initial work suggests, for example, that children's antisocial characteristics mediate the relation between a coercive style of parenting (defined as coercive, inconsistent, and abusive parenting) and arrests at age 10 to 14 (but not at age 14 to 17; Coughlin and Vuchinich, 1996).

Warmth and negativity. Parental warmth and negativity have long been identified as playing a role in children's antisocial behavior (Martin, 1975). Developmental researchers posit that high levels of parental warmth promote children's conflict resolution skills and help them to improve their interpersonal relations through socially appropriate methods. According to social learning theory, lack of parental warmth is important because a cold parent is not rewarding for the child and provides a hostile and sometimes aggressive model. In contrast, in a positive parent–child relationship, the child may be more likely to attend to and internalize the parent's attitudes.

In general, low levels of warmth and high parental anger or hostility differentiate aggressive children from those with low levels of problem behaviors (Denham et al., 2000; Stormshak et al., 2000; see Coie and Dodge, 1998). Further, supportive parenting seems to reduce the relation between family adversity and high levels of externalizing problems (Pettit, Bates, and Dodge, 1997; cf. Denham et al., 2000). In a longitudinal study, parental negativity was linked to behavior problems; maternal warmth measured when children were 4 years old was negatively related to children's externalizing problems 4 years later (Booth, Rosen-Krasnor, McKinnon, and Rubin, 1994). Similarly, Rubin, Hastings, Chen, Stewart, and McNichol (1998) found that mothers' negative dominance (i.e., unnecessarily controlling, directly commanding, physically intrusive parental behavior, and hostile parental affect) was positively correlated with toddlers', particularly girls', aggressive behaviors. Moreover, observed aggression and mothers' reports of children's externalizing problems were associated with boys' dysregulated temperament only when their mothers displayed high levels of negative dominance. Although it is likely that both maternal and paternal negativity are related to children's aggression, there are fewer data for fathers and some suggests weaker relations for fathers (Forgatch and Stoolmiller, 1994).

Punishment and physical discipline. A number of authors have argued that physical discipline (e.g., spanking or hitting) plays a role in the development of aggression through modeling and/or escape conditioning (Rothbaum and Weisz, 1994). Bandura (1977) suggested that spanking socializes children to use aggression in order to change others' behaviors.

Spanking and physically aggressive parenting generally are related to children's aggressive behavior (Stormshak et al., 2000; Strassberg, Dodge, Pettit, and Bates, 1994). For example, Strassberg, Dodge, Pettit, and Bates (1994) found that spanked children were more aggressive than those who were not spanked. Additionally, children who were exposed to violent discipline (e.g., hitting) were more prone to aggression than those who were spanked. When spanking is implemented impulsively, compared to in a controlled manner, the relation between spanking and aggression may be more robust (Straus and Mouradian, 1998). The use of more severe physical punishment has been associated with behavior problems, even after controlling for various demographic variables (Brenner and Fox, 1998).

Cross-cultural support of punitive discipline comes from a study of Russian children (Hart, Nelson, Robinson, Olsen, and McNeilly-Choque, 1998). However, physical discipline, as well as abusive verbal discipline, may relate to externalizing problems more strongly for European Americans than African Americans (Deater-Deckard, Dodge, Bates, and Pettit, 1996; Spieker, Larson, Lewis, Keller, and Gilchrist, 1999). African-American parents may be more likely to combine warmth with physical punishment, and a warm parent–child relationship may buffer the relation of physical discipline to externalizing problems (Deater-Deckard and Dodge, 1997).

In contrast to parental use of physical punishment that is not abusive, abusive punishment is likely to be associated with the development of antisocial tendencies, regardless of ethnicity or race (Deater-Deckard, Dodge, Bates, and Pettit, 1995; Luntz and Widom, 1994; Weiss, Dodge, Bates, and Pettit, 1992). Dodge, Pettit, and Bates (1997) controlled for 10 factors known to be related to conduct problems (e.g., SES, temperament, exposure to violence, and so forth). Physical harm in the first 5 years of life remained a significant predictor of subsequent peer-reported aggression after covarying those constructs with predictive power. Additionally, the gender of the abuser and whether or not the abuser was a biologically related relative did not diminish the risk for externalizing problems, thereby suggesting that externalizing problems are not totally due to genetic causes (indirect effects of heredity are, as the authors noted, still possible). Further analyses suggested that the relation of physical harm to externalizing problems was mediated by deficits in children's social information processing such as not attending to relevant social cues, attributing hostile intentions to others, and believing that aggression leads to successful instrumental and interpersonal outcomes (see also Weiss et al., 1992).

Contextual factors and parenting as a moderator and/or mediator.   The role of contextual factors such as low SES and community violence in children's aggression has been noted by numerous investigators (e.g., Bolger, Patterson, Thompson, and Kupersmidt, 1995). Low SES has been consistently associated with childhood conduct problems (Patterson, Kupersmidt, and Vaden, 1990) and exposure to community violence is hypothesized to place children at risk for a myriad of psychological problems, including aggression and delinquency (Gorman-Smith and Tolan, 1998). Despite the relatively clear empirical associations obtained in research, the mechanisms by which SES or community violence affect children's aggression are not clear (Dodge, Pettit, and Bates, 1994; Gorman-Smith and Tolan, 1998).

Researchers have begun to examine the hypothesis that various parenting variables either mediate or moderate the relation of SES with children's aggression. Dodge et al. (1994) proposed a model in which the effects of SES on children's conduct problems are mediated by parenting variables. They found that SES when children were preschoolers was predictive of teacher-rated and peer-nominated child behavior problems in grades 1, 2, and 3, and was related to parenting (lack of warmth, harsh discipline, and so forth). Importantly, the socialization variables partially mediated the relation of SES to externalizing problem behaviors. In at least two other studies (Bolger et al., 1995; Sampson and Laub, 1994), parental processes (e.g., parental involvement) partially mediated the relations between SES (and other risk factors) and externalizing problem behaviors.

Interparental conflict.   It is relatively clear that interparental conflict is associated with a variety of children's externalizing behaviors (Davies and Cummings, 1994). What is less clear is why this association exists. In fact, it has been only recently that comprehensive theoretical models have been proposed (Davies and Cummings, 1994; Wilson and Gottman, in Vol. 4 of this *Handbook*).

Davies and Cummings (1994) posited that children's emotional security acts as a mediator between parental conflict and adjustment problems. In empirical work, they found that the relation of interparental conflict to children's externalizing problem behaviors was partially mediated by children's emotional reactivity (a component of emotional security; Davies and Cummings, 1998; cf. Ingoldsby, Shaw, Owens, and Winslow, 1999, who did not find this relation).

Researchers examining the mediating role of coping in the relation between marital conflict and children's adjustment have noted that coping processes may be different for boys and girls (Cummings, Davies, and Simpson, 1994). Boys with high perceptions of control were rated as having fewer externalizing behaviors as interparental conflict increased (Kerig, 1998), and for boys, but not girls, problem- and emotion-focused efficacious coping related negatively to externalizing problems (Cummings et al., 1994). Other data suggest that the type of interparental conflict may be more important than the frequency of conflict in predicting externalizing behaviors (Buehler et al., 1998). Katz and Gottman (1993) found that mutually hostile parental interactions when the child was 5 were predictive of externalizing problems at age 8. Cummings and colleagues found that negative effects of adults' conflict are minimized or absent when the conflict is resolved (Cummings, Simpson, and Wilson, 1993; Davies and Cummings, 1994). In spite of the clear and consistent relation between adult conflict and negative outcomes for children, as noted by Cummings and Davies (1994), it is important to recognize that most children exposed to interparental conflict do not exhibit significant psychological problems.

Parental antisocial behavior and psychopathology.   Children's aggressive and delinquent behaviors are associated with parents' antisocial behavior, leading many to posit that aggression is heritable (Frick et al., 1992; Lahey, Russo, Walker, and Piacentini, 1989; see Coie and Dodge, 1998). However, the presence of these associations also could be due to innate dysfunctional neuroregulatory mechanisms (which affect children's emotion regulation) from adverse prenatal influences, contextual factors also associated with the development of antisocial behavior in the parent, and/or a diminished capacity to parent effectively and provide a positive model (Goodman and Gotlib, 1999). Increasingly, evidence suggests that genetics are important in the development of externalizing problems (Miles and Carey, 1997), although methodological problems are present in this literature (Pam, 1995; Patterson, 1998).

There is empirical support for the hypothesis that the relations between children's antisocial behavior and parental depression or antisocial behavior are at least partly mediated by negative parent–child interactions. Capaldi and Patterson (1991) found that maternal antisocial behavior was related to low parental involvement (i.e., low supervision and shared activities), and this breakdown in parenting predicted children's adjustment (including antisocial behavior, poor peer relationships, low academic skills, and low self-esteem). In research on depressed mothers, Harnish, Dodge, Valente, and the CPPRG (1995) found that the relation between maternal depression and children's disruptive behavior was partly mediated by the absence of a warm and gratifying parent–child interaction (based on ratings of both mothers and children). This association was present for Euro-American boys and girls, but did not hold for African-American families (maternal depression was not related to mothers' interactions with their children). In two different samples, Conger and colleagues demonstrated that acute stress predicted maternal depression and subsequently poor discipline (Conger, Patterson, and Ge, 1995). Additionally, the effects of depression on boys' deviancy were mediated by poor discipline. The relations for fathers were consistent, albeit somewhat weaker.

Summary.   A number of parenting dimensions play an important role in the development and maintenance of children's delinquent and aggressive behaviors. Although most studies have examined specific parenting characteristics, it should be noted that many of the reviewed parenting practices are significantly related (Stormshak et al., 2000). Researchers are beginning to focus on how specific parenting practices relate to specific forms of aggression and delinquency (see Stormshak et al., 2000). Moreover, although much of this review has focused on parenting variables, individual characteristics are predictive of aggression (Coie and Dodge, 1998; Lytton, 1990). In the future it will be important to simultaneously examine various aspects of parenting in conjunction with child characteristics known to be related to different types of antisocial behavior and to test for differential prediction of various types of antisocial behaviors.

PARENT TRAINING PROGRAMS

A number of prevention and intervention programs have been designed and implemented with the goal of decreasing aggressive and delinquent behaviors (McCord and Tremblay, 1992). Most have not produced lasting results (Kazdin, 1987, 1993). Consistent with Kazdin's (1987) recommendations, interventions are increasingly multidimensional and delivered from a developmental perspective. Three such programs will be briefly reviewed (see also McCord and Tremblay, 1992).

The Fast Track Program utilizes a mulitcomponent longitudinal design to assess the effects of the program's seven components, including parent training and parent–child relationship enhancement (CPPRG, 1992). The Fast Track program offers a universal intervention, beginning at Grade 1 and continuing through Grade 6. The 10% of children displaying the highest level of conduct problems were selected to participate in an additional series of interventions. Initial results of the program are promising. Parents in the intervention group reported more warmth, more consistent discipline, and less harsh discipline (CPPRG, 1999a). Children in classrooms where the intervention was delivered showed decreased levels of aggression (CPPRG, 1999b), and parents and teachers credit children in the intervention group with making positive changes in their behaviors (CPPRG, 1999a). Although modest in size, the results of this program are promising and have occurred after a short period of intervention.

The Metropolitan Area Child Study is a longitudinal study of a prevention field trial meant to evaluate the impact of a school-wide, peer and family intervention designed to prevent antisocial behavior in urban children (second to fifth graders) living in poor neighborhoods. Importantly, the program was designed to address how much intervention is necessary and how the process of the intervention affects children's behaviors (Guerra, Eron, Huesmann, Tolan, and Van Acker, 1997). Findings indicate that the alteration of parenting practices is associated with decreases in children's aggressive behavior (Tolan, Hanish, and McKay, 2000).

The Oregon Social Learning Center recently has been testing a universal prevention program for conduct disorder for first graders and fifth graders. The multicomponent program is delivered in the home and school (Reid, Eddy, Fetrow, and Stoolmiller, 1999). Teachers are exposed to new ways of managing off-task students, and parents complete a parent training program. Findings suggest that the most aggressive children experience the most improvement (Stoolmiller, Eddy, and Reid, 2000). Additionally, mothers in the intervention group who used the most aversive behaviors initially experienced the most change (Reid et al., 1999). Although modest in size, the results of this program are promising and have occurred after a short period of intervention.

The three programs reviewed all show promise for reducing children's aggressive behaviors. As more data emerge, it will be important to examine the cost-effectiveness of delivering large-scale interventions.

CONCLUSIONS

Both theory and the empirical data support the conclusion that parents play an important role in their children's moral development. This is not surprising because children learn much about relationships and ways of treating other people in the familial context. However, children are not simply passive recipients of moral values and behaviors; they appear to be active participants in the process of moral socialization. Children's cognitive abilities influence what they understand, and their temperament and style of interaction affect how parents react to them and discipline them. Styles of parent–child interaction evolve as a consequence of characteristics and behaviors of both participants.

Our understanding of the role of parents in moral development of children is more complete in regard to some aspects of moral functioning than others. We know quite a bit about parental contributions to the development of children's prosocial and aggressive behavior, and much less about their role in the development of guilt, dishonesty and lying, and moral reasoning. Furthermore, mothers have been studied much more frequently than fathers, with the consequence that we know much more about mothers' than fathers' roles in moral socialization. In addition, as noted previously, much of the available information comes from studies of middle–SES Euro-American children; it is quite possible that parental practices and characteristics have different meanings and consequences in different socioeconomic and cultural groups (Bornstein, 1995).

Nonetheless, it is possible to draw some tentative conclusions regarding the role of parents' behaviors and characteristics in children's moral development. In general, moral children tend to have parents who are warm and supportive rather than punitive, use inductive discipline, provide opportunities for children to learn about others' perspectives and feelings, and involve children in family decision making and in the process of thinking about moral decisions. Parents of moral children also are likely to model moral behaviors and thinking themselves, and provide opportunities for their children to do so. Parents who exhibit this configuration of behaviors appear to foster the development of concern and caring about others, and create a positive parent–child relationship that the child is invested in maintaining. In addition, these parents provide information about what behaviors are expected of the child and why, and foster an internal rather than external sense of morality. Children who develop internal motives for acting in moral ways based on moral principles and caring for others are likely to act in a moral manner in diverse settings, particularly if their level of moral reasoning is relatively mature.

Although research has provided us with some information regarding the correlates of children's morality, there is much to learn about the processes involved in the socialization of children's moral behavior and reasoning. It is one thing to know that a given parental characteristic or practice is associated with children's moral functioning; it is another to know why this is so. There is a need for research examining how parents and children jointly influence children's moral development. In addition, there is much to learn about the variables that moderate the relation of quality and type of parenting to moral outcomes, including sex of the child, cultural and socioeconomic status, children's temperament, and factors that buffer the negative effects of poor quality parenting.

ACKNOWLEDGMENTS

Work on this chapter, as well as some of the research reported therein, were supported by grants from the National Institutes of Mental Health (1 R01 HH55052 and 1 R01 MH 60838) and a Research Scientist Award (K05 M801321) from the National Institute of Mental Health to the first author, and a minority graduate student supplement on a grant (1 R01 HH55052) from the National Institutes of Mental Health to Carlos Valiente.

REFERENCES

Abell, E., and Gecas, V. (1997). Guilt, shame, and family socialization: A retrospective study. *Journal of Family Issues, 18*, 99–123.

Bandura, A. (1977). *Social learning theory*. Englewood Cliffs, NJ: Prentice-Hall.

Bandura, A. (1986). *Social foundations of thought and action: A social cognitive theory*. Englewood Cliffs, NJ: Prentice-Hall.

Bandura, A. (1991). Social cognitive theory of moral thought and action. In W. M. Kurtines and J. L. Gewirtz (Eds.), *Handbook of moral behavior and development* (Vol. 1, pp. 45–103). Hillsdale, NJ: Lawrence Erlbaum Associates.

Barton, E. J. (1981). Developing sharing: An analysis of modeling and other behavioral techniques. *Behavior Modification, 5*, 386–398.

Bates, J. E., Pettit, G. S., Dodge, K. A., and Ridge, B. (1998). Interaction of temperamental resistance to control and restrictive parenting in the development of externalizing behavior. *Developmental Psychology, 34*, 982–995.

Baumrind, D. (1971). Current patterns of parental authority. *Developmental Psychology Monographs, 4*, 1–103.

Baumrind, D. (1993). The average expectable environment is not good enough: A response to Scarr. *Child Development, 64,* 1299–1317.

Bell, R. Q., and Harper, L. V. (1977). *Child effects on adults.* Hillsdale: Lawrence Erlbaum Associates.

Bolger, K. E., Patterson, C. J., Thompson, W., and Kupersmidt, J. B. (1995). Psychosocial adjustment among children experiencing persistent and intermittent family economic hardship. *Child Development, 66,* 1107–1129.

Booth, C. L., Rosen-Krasnor, L., McKinnon, J. A., and Rubin, K. H. (1994). Predicting social adjustment in middle childhood: The role of preschool attachment security and maternal style. From family to peer group: Relations between relationship systems. *Social Development, 3,* 189–204.

Bornstein, M. H. (1995). Form and function: Implications for studies of culture and human development. *Culture and Psychology, 1,* 123–137.

Boyes, M. C., and Allen, S. G. (1993). Styles of parent–child interaction and moral reasoning in adolescence. *Merrill-Palmer Quarterly, 39,* 551–570.

Brehm, S. S. (1981). Oppositional behavior in children: A reactance theory approach. In S. S. Brehm, S. M. Kassin, and F. X. Gibbons (Eds.), *Developmental social psychology: Theory and research* (pp. 96–121). New York: Oxford University Press.

Brenner, V., and Fox, R. A. (1998). Parental discipline and behavior problems in young children. *The Journal of Genetic Psychology, 159,* 251–256.

Brody, G. H., and Shaffer, D. R. (1982). Contributions of parents and peers to children's moral socialization. *Developmental Review, 2,* 31–75.

Bryan, J. H., and Walbek, N. H. (1970). The impact of words and deeds concerning altruism upon children. *Child Development, 41,* 747–757.

Bryant, B. K., and Crockenberg, S. B. (1980). Correlates and dimensions of prosocial behavior: A study of female siblings with their mothers. *Child Development, 51,* 529–544.

Buck, L. Z., Walsh, W. F., and Rothman, G. (1981). Relationship between parental moral judgment and socialization. *Youth and Society, 13,* 91–116.

Buehler, C., Krishnakumar, A., Stone, G., Anthony, C., Pemberton, S., Gerard, J., and Barber, B. K. (1998). Interparental conflict styles and youth problem behaviors: A two-sample replication study. *Journal of Marriage and the Family, 60,* 119–132.

Burleson, B. R., and Fennelly, D. A. (1981). The effects of persuasive appeal form and cognitive complexity on children's sharing behavior. *Child Study Journal, 11,* 75–90.

Burton, R. V. (1976). Honesty and dishonesty. In T. Lickona (Ed.), *Moral development and behavior: Theory, research, and social issues* (pp. 173–197). New York: Holt, Rinehart, and Winston.

Capaldi, D. M., and Patterson, G. R. (1991). Relation of parental transitions to boys' adjustment problems: I. A linear hypothesis. II. Mothers at risk for transitions and unskilled parenting. *Developmental Psychology, 27,* 489–504.

Carlo, G., Raffaelli, M., Laible, D. J., and Meyer, K. A. (1999). Why are girls less physically aggressive than boys? Personality and parenting mediators of physical aggression. *Sex Roles, 40,* 711–729.

Carlo, G., Roesch, S. C., and Melby, J. (1998). The multiplicative relations of parenting and temperament to prosocial and antisocial behaviors in adolescence. *Journal of Early Adolescence, 18,* 266–290.

Coie, J. D., and Dodge, K. A. (1998). Aggression and antisocial behavior. In N. Eisenberg (Ed.), *Handbook of child psychology: Vol. 3. Social, emotional and personality development* (5th ed., pp. 779–862). New York: Wiley.

Colby, A., and Kohlberg, L. (1987). *The measurement of moral judgment.* Cambridge, England: Cambridge University Press.

Colder, C. R., Lochman, J. E., and Wells, K. C. (1997). The moderating effects of children's fear and activity level on relations between parenting practices and childhood symptomatology. *Journal of Abnormal Child Psychology, 25,* 251–263.

Collins, W. A., Maccoby, E. E., Steinberg, L., Hetherington, E. M., and Bornstein, M. H. (2000). Contemporary research on parenting: The case nature and nurture. *American Psychologist, 55,* 218–232.

Conduct Problems Prevention Research Group. (1992). A developmental and clinical model for the prevention of conduct disorder: The FAST Track Program. *Development and Psychopathology, 4,* 509–527.

Conduct Problems Prevention Research Group. (1999a). Initial impact of the Fast Track Prevention Trial for conduct problems. I. The high-risk sample. *Journal of Consulting and Clinical Psychology, 67,* 631–647.

Conduct Problems Prevention Research Group. (1999b). Initial impact of the Fast Track Prevention Trial for conduct problems. II. Classroom effects. *Journal of Consulting and Clinical Psychology, 67,* 648–657.

Conger, R. D., Patterson, G. R., and Ge, X. (1995). It takes two to replicate: A mediational model for the impact of parents' stress on adolescent adjustment. *Child Development, 66,* 80–97.

Coughlin, C., and Vuchinich, S. (1996). Family experience in preadolescence and the development of male delinquency. *Journal of Marriage and the Family, 58,* 491–501.

Crockenberg, S. (1985). Toddlers' reactions to maternal anger. *Merrill-Palmer Quarterly, 31,* 361–373.

Cummings, E. M., and Davies, P. (1994). *Children and marital conflict: The impact of family dispute and resolution.* New York: Guilford.

Cummings, E. M., Davies, P. T., and Simpson, K. S. (1994). Marital conflict, gender, and children's appraisals and coping efficacy as mediators of child adjustment. *Journal of Family Psychology, 8*, 141–149.

Cummings, E. M., Simpson, K. S., and Wilson, A. (1993). Children's responses to interadult anger as a function of information about resolution. *Developmental Psychology, 29*, 978–985.

Davies, P. T., and Cummings, E. M. (1994). Marital conflict and child adjustment: An emotional security hypothesis. *Psychological Bulletin, 116*, 387–411.

Davies, P. T., and Cummings, E. M. (1998). Exploring children's emotional security as a mediator of the link between marital relations and child adjustment. *Child Development, 69*, 124–139.

Deater-Deckard, K., and Dodge, K. A. (1997). Externalizing behavior problems and discipline revisited: Nonlinear effects and variation by culture, context, and gender. *Psychological Inquiry, 8*, 161–175.

Deater-Deckard, K., Dodge, K. A., Bates, J. E., and Pettit, G. S. (1995, March/April). *Risk factors for the development of externalizing behavior problems: Are there ethnic group differences in process?* Paper presented at the biennial meeting of the Society for Research in Child Development, Indianapolis, IN.

Deater-Deckard, K., Dodge, K. A., Bates, J. E., and Pettit, G. S. (1996). Physical discipline among African American and European American mothers: Links to children's externalizing behaviors. *Developmental Psychology, 32*, 1065–1072.

Dekovic, M., and Janssens, J. M. A. M. (1992). Parents' child-rearing style and child's sociometric status. *Developmental Psychology, 28*, 925–932.

Denham, S., and Grout, L. (1992). Mothers' emotional expressiveness and coping: Relations with preschoolers' social-emotional competence. *Genetic, Social, and General Psychology Monographs, 118*, 73–101.

Denham, S. A., and Grout, L. (1993). Socialization of emotion: Pathway to preschoolers' emotional and social competence. *Journal of Nonverbal Behavior, 17*, 205–227.

Denham, S. A., Workman, E., Cole, P. M., Weissbrod, C., Kendziora, K. T., and Zahn-Waxler, C. (2000). Prediction of externalizing behavior problems from early to middle childhood: The role of parental socialization and emotion expression. *Development and Psychopathology, 12*, 23–45.

De Veer, A. J. E., and Janssens, J. M. A. M. (1992). Victim-oriented discipline and the child's internalization of norms. In J. M. A. M. Janssens and J. R. M. Gerris (Eds.), *Child rearing: Influence on prosocial and moral development* (pp. 145–168). Amsterdam: Swets and Zeitlinger.

Dix, T., and Grusec, J. E. (1983). Parental influence techniques: An attributional analysis. *Child Development, 54*, 645–652.

Dlugokinski, E. L., and Firestone, I. J. (1974). Other centeredness and susceptibility to charitable appeals: Effects of perceived discipline. *Developmental Psychology, 10*, 21–28.

Dodge, K. A., Pettit, G. S., and Bates, J. E. (1994). Socialization mediators of the relation between socioeconomic status and child conduct problems. *Child Development, 65*, 649–665.

Dodge, K. A., Pettit, G. S., and Bates, J. E. (1997). How the experience of early physical abuse leads children to become chronically aggressive. In D. Cicchetti and S. L. Toth (Eds.), *Developmental perspectives on trauma: Theory, research, and intervention* (pp. 263–288). Rochester, NY: University of Rochester Press.

Dumka, L. E., Roosa, M. W., and Jackson, K. M. (1997). Risk, conflict, mothers' parenting, and children's adjustment in low-income, Mexican immigrant, and Mexican American families. *Journal of Marriage and the Family, 59*, 309–323.

Eisenberg, N. (1977). *The development of prosocial moral judgment and its correlates.* Unpublished doctoral Dissertation, University of California, Berkeley. (*Dissertation Abstracts International, 37*, 4753B; University Microfilms No. 77–444).

Eisenberg, N. (1986). *Altruistic emotion, cognition and behavior.* Hillsdale, NJ: Lawrence Erlbaum and Associates.

Eisenberg, N., Cialdini, R. B., McCreath, H., and Shell, R. (1987). Consistency-based compliance: When and why do children become vulnerable? *Journal of Personality and Social Psychology, 52*, 1174–1181.

Eisenberg, N., and Fabes, R. A. (1998). Prosocial development. In W. Damon (Series Ed.) and N. Eisenberg (Vol. Ed.), *Handbook of child psychology: Vol. 3. Social, emotional, and personality development* (5th ed., pp. 701–778). New York: Wiley.

Eisenberg, N., Fabes, R. A., Carlo, G., Troyer, D., Speer, A. L., Karbon, M., and Switzer, G. (1992). The relations of maternal practices and characteristics to children's vicarious emotional responsiveness. *Child Development*, 583–602.

Eisenberg, N., Fabes, R. A., and Murphy, B. C. (1996). Parents' reactions to children's negative emotions: Relations to children's social competence and comforting behavior. *Child Development, 67*, 2227–2247.

Eisenberg, N., Fabes, R. A., Schaller, M., Carlo, G., and Miller, P. A. (1991). The relations of parental characteristics and practices to children's vicarious emotional responding. *Child Development, 62*, 1393–1408.

Eisenberg, N., Fabes, R. A., Schaller, M., Miller, P. A., Carlo, G., Poulin, R., Shea, C., and Shell, R. (1991). Personality and socialization correlates of vicarious emotional responding. *Journal of Personality and Social Psychology, 61*, 459–471.

Eisenberg, N., Fabes, R. A., Shepard, S. A., Guthrie, I. K., Murphy, B. C., and Reiser, M. (1999). Parental reactions to children's negative emotions: Longitudinal relations to quality of children's social functioning. *Child Development, 70*, 513–534.

Eisenberg, N., Lennon, R., and Roth, K. (1983). Prosocial development: A longitudinal study. *Developmental Psychology, 19*, 846–855.

Eisenberg, N., Wolchik, S., Goldberg, L., and Engel, I. (1992). Parental values, reinforcement, and young children's prosocial behavior: A longitudinal study. *Journal of Genetic Psychology, 153,* 19–36.

Eisenberg-Berg, N. (1979). Development of children's prosocial moral judgment. *Developmental Psychology, 15,* 128–137.

Eisenberg-Berg, N., and Geisheker, E. (1979). Content of preachings and power of the model/preacher: The effect on children's generosity. *Developmental Psychology, 15,* 168–175.

Eisikovits, Z., and Sagi, A. (1982). Moral development and discipline encounter in delinquent and nondelinquent adolescents. *Journal of Youth and Adolescence, 11,* 217–246.

Emde, R. N., Johnson, W. F., and Easterbrooks, M. A. (1987). The do's and don'ts of early moral development: Psychoanalytic tradition and current research. In J. Kagan and S. Lamb (Eds.), *The emergence of morality in young children* (pp. 245–276). Chicago: University of Chicago Press.

Fabes, R. A., Eisenberg, N., Karbon, M., Bernzweig, J., Speer, A. L., and Carlo, G. (1994). Socialization of children's vicarious emotional responding and prosocial behavior: Relations with mothers' perceptions of children's emotional reactivity. *Developmental Psychology, 30,* 44–55.

Fabes, R. A., Eisenberg, N., and Miller, P. (1990). Maternal correlates of children's vicarious emotional responsiveness. *Developmental Psychology, 26,* 639–648.

Fabes, R. A., Fultz, J., Eisenberg, N., May-Plumlee, T., and Christopher, F. S. (1989). The effects of reward on children's prosocial motivation: A socialization study. *Developmental Psychology, 25,* 509–515.

Ferguson, T. J., and Stegge, H. (1995). In J. P. Tangney and K. W. Fischer (Eds.), *Self-conscious emotions* (pp. 174–197). New York: Guilford.

Ferguson, T. J., and Stegge, H. (1998). Measuring guilt in children: A rose by any other name still has thorns. In J. Bybee (Ed.), *Guilt and children* (pp. 19–74). San Diego, CA: Academic Press.

Ferguson, T. J., Stegge, H., and Thompson, T. (1993, March). *Socialization antecedents of guilt and shame in young children.* Paper presented at the biennial meeting of the Society for Research in Child Development, New Orleans LA.

Forgatch, M. S., and Stoolmiller, M. (1994). Emotions as contexts for adolescent delinquency. *Journal of Research on Adolescence, 4,* 601–614.

Freud, S. (1925). *Collected papers.* London: Hogarth.

Freud, S. (1959). *The passing of the Oedipus complex: Collected papers* (Vol. 11). New York: Basic Books. (Original work published 1924.)

Frick, P. J., Christian, R. E., and Wootton, J. M. (1999). Age trends in association between parenting practices and conduct problems. *Behavior Modification, 23,* 106–128.

Frick, P. J., Lahey, B. B., Loeber, R., Stouthamer-Loeber, M., Christ, M. G., and Hanson, K. (1992). Familial risk factors to oppositional defiant disorder and conduct disorder: Parental psychopathology and maternal parenting. *Journal of Consulting and Clinical Psychology, 60,* 49–55.

Garner, P. W., Jones, D. C., Miner, J. L. (1994). Social competence among low-income preschoolers: Emotion socialization practices and social cognitive correlates. *Child Development, 65,* 622–637.

Gelfand, D. M., Hartmann, D. P., Cromer, C. C., Smith, C. L., and Page, B. C. (1975). The effects of instructional prompts and praise on children's donation rates. *Child Development, 46,* 980–983.

Gewirtz, J. L., and Pelaez-Nogueras, M. (1991). Proximal mechanisms underlying the acquisition of moral behavior patterns. In W. M. Kurtines and J. L. Gewirtz (Eds.), *Handbook of moral behavior and development* (Vol. 1, pp. 153–182). Hillsdale, NJ: Lawrence Erlbaum Associates.

Gilligan, C. (1982). *In a different voice: Psychological theory and women's development.* Cambridge, MA: Harvard University Press.

Goodman, S. H., and Gotlib, I. H. (1999). Risk for psychopathology in the children of depressed mothers: A developmental model for understanding mechanisms of transmission. *Psychological Review, 106,* 458–490.

Gorman-Smith, D., and Tolan, P. (1998). The role of exposure to community violence and developmental problems among inner-city youth. *Development and Psychopathology, 10,* 101–116.

Gorman-Smith, D., Tolan, P. H., Zelli, A., and Huesmann, L. R. (1996). The relation of family functioning to violence among inner-city minority youths. *Journal of Family Psychology, 10,* 115–129.

Grusec, J. E. (1971). Power and the internalization of self denial. *Child Development, 42,* 93–105.

Grusec, J. E. (1982). The socialization of altruism. In N. Eisenberg (Ed.), *The development of prosocial behavior* (pp. 65–90). New York: Academic.

Grusec, J. E. (1991). Socializing concern for others in home. *Developmental Psychology, 27,* 338–342.

Grusec, J. E., Dix, T., and Mills, R. (1982). The effects of type, severity, and victim of children's transgressions on maternal discipline. *Canadian Journal of Behavioral Science, 14,* 276–289.

Grusec, J. E., and Redler, E. (1980). Attribution, reinforcement, and altruism: A developmental analysis. *Developmental Psychology, 16,* 525–534.

Grusec, J. E., Saas-Kortsaak, P., and Simutis, Z. M. (1978). The role of example and moral exhortation in the training of altruism. *Child Development, 49,* 920–923.

Grusec, J. E, and Skubiski, L. (1970). Model nurturance, demand characteristics of the modeling experiment and altruism. *Journal of Personality and Social Psychology*, *14*, 352–359.

Guerra, N. G., Eron, L. D., Huesmann, L. R., Tolan, P., and Van Acker, R. (1997). A cognitive-ecological approach to the prevention and mitigation of violence and aggression in inner-city youth. In D. P. Fry and K. Bjoerkqvist (Eds.), *Cultural variation in conflict resolution: Alternatives to violence* (pp. 199–213). Mahwah, NJ: Lawrence Erlbaum Associates.

Haapasalo, J., and Tremblay, R. E. (1994). Physically aggressive boys from ages 6 to 12: Family background, parenting behavior, and prediction of delinquency. *Journal of Consulting and Clinical Psychology*, *62*, 1044–1052.

Harnish, J. D., Dodge, K. A., Valente, E., and the Conduct Problems Prevention Research Group. (1995). Mother–child interaction quality as a partial mediator of the roles of maternal depressive symptomatology and socioeconomic status in the development of child behavior problems. *Child Development*, *66*, 739–753.

Hart, C. H., Nelson, D. A., Robinson, C. C., Olsen, S. F., and McNeilly-Choque, M. K. (1998). Overt and relational aggression in Russian nursery-school-age children: Parenting style and marital linkages. *Developmental Psychology*, *34*, 687–697.

Hart, D. (1988). A longitudinal study of adolescents' socialization and identification as predictors of adult moral judgment development. *Merrill-Palmer Quarterly*, *34*, 245–260.

Hart, D., and Fegley, S. (1995). Altruism and caring in adolescence: Relations to self-understanding and social judgment. *Child Development*, *66*, 1346–1359.

Hartshorne, H., and May, M. (1928). *Studies in the nature of character: Vol. I. Studies in deceit.* New York: MacMillan.

Hastings, P. D., Zahn-Waxler, C., Robinson, J., Usher, B., and Bridges, D. (2000). The development of concern for others in children with behavior problems. *Developmental Psychology*, *36*, 531–546.

Hoffman, M. L. (1963). Parent discipline and the child's consideration for others. *Child Development*, *34*, 573–588.

Hoffman, M. L. (1970a). Conscience, personality, and socialization techniques. *Human Development*, *13*, 90–126.

Hoffman, M. L. (1970b). Moral development. In P. H. Mussen (Ed.), *Carmichael's manual of child development* (Vol. 2, pp. 261–359). New York: Wiley.

Hoffman, M. L. (1975a). Altruistic behavior and the parent–child relationship. *Journal of Personality and Social Psychology*, *31*, 937–943.

Hoffman, M. L. (1982). Development of prosocial motivation: Empathy and guilt. In N. Eisenberg (Ed.), *The development of prosocial behavior* (pp. 281–313). New York: Academic Press.

Hoffman, M. L. (1983). Affective and cognitive processes in moral internalization. In E. T. Higgins, D. N. Ruble, and W. W. Hartup (Eds.), *Social cognition and social development* (pp. 236–274). Cambridge, England: Cambridge University Press.

Hoffman, M. L. (1988). Moral development. In M. H. Bornstein and M. E. Lamb (Eds.), *Developmental psychology: An advanced textbook* (2nd ed., pp. 497–548). Hillsdale, NJ: Lawrence Erlbaum Associates.

Hoffman, M. L. (1998). Varieties of empathy-based guilt. In J. Bybee (Ed.), *Guilt and children* (pp. 91–112). Orlando, FL: Academic.

Hoffman, M. L. (2000). *Empathy and moral development: Implications for caring and justice.* Cambridge, England: Cambridge University Press.

Hoffman, M. L., and Saltzstein, H. D. (1967). Parent discipline and the child's moral development. *Journal of Personality and Social Psychology*, *5*, 45–57.

Holstein, C. (1972). The relation of children's moral judgment level to that of their parents and to communication patterns in the family. In R. C. Smart and M. S. Smart (Eds.), *Readings in child development and relationships.* New York: Macmillan.

Huesmann, L. R., Eron, L. D., Lefkowitz, M. M., and Walder, L. O. (1984). Stability of aggression over time and generations. *Developmental Psychology*, *20*, 1120–1134.

Iannotti, R. J., Cummings, E. M., Pierrehumbert, B., Milano, M. J., and Zahn-Waxler, C. (1992). Parental influences on prosocial behavior and empathy in early childhood. In J. M. A. M. Janssens and J. R. M. Gerris (Eds.), *Child rearing: Influence on prosocial and moral development* (pp. 77–100). Amsterdam: Swets and Zeitlinger.

Ingoldsby, E. M., Shaw, D. S., Owens, E. B., and Winslow, E. B. (1999). A longitudinal study of interparental conflict, emotional and behavioral reactivity, and preschoolers' adjustment problems among low-income families. *Journal of Abnormal Child Psychology*, *27*, 343–356.

Jacobson, K. C., and Crockett, L. J. (2000). Parental monitoring and adolescent adjustment: An ecological perspective. *Journal of Research on Adolescence*, *10*, 65–97.

Janssen, A. W. H., Janssens, J. M. A. M., and Gerris, J. R. M. (1992). Parents' and children's levels of moral reasoning: Antecedents and consequences of parental discipline strategies. In J. M. A. M. Janssens and J. R. M. Gerris (Eds.), *Child rearing: Influence on prosocial and moral development* (pp. 169–196). Amsterdam: Swets and Zeitlinger.

Janssens, J. M. A. M., and Gerris, J. R. M. (1992). Child rearing, empathy and prosocial development. In J. M. A. M. Janssens and J. R. M. Gerris (Eds.), *Child rearing: Influence on prosocial and moral development* (pp. 57–75). Amsterdam: Swets and Zeitlinger.

Jannsens, J. M. A. M., and Dekovic, M. (1997). Child rearing, prosocial moral reasoning, and prosocial behavior. *International Journal of Behavioral Development*, *20*, 509–527.

Janoski, T., and Wilson, J. (1995). Pathways to voluntarism: Family socialization and status transmission models. *Social Forces, 74,* 271–292.

Jurkovic, G. J., and Prentice, N. M. (1974). Dimensions of moral interaction and moral judgment in delinquent and nondelinquent families. *Journal of Consulting and Clinical Psychology, 42,* 256–262.

Katz, L. F., and Gottman, J. M. (1993). Patterns of marital conflict predict children's internalizing and externalizing behaviors. *Developmental Psychology, 29,* 940–950.

Kazdin, A. E. (1987). Treatment of antisocial behavior in children: Current status and future directions. *Psychological Bulletin, 102,* 187–203.

Kazdin, A. E. (1993). Treatment of conduct disorder: Progress and directions in psychotherapy research. *Development and Psychopathology, 5,* 277–310.

Keenan, K., Loeber, R., Zhang, Q., Stouthamer-Loeber, M., and Van Kammen, W. B. (1995). The influence of deviant peers on the development of boys' disruptive and delinquent behavior: A temporal analysis. *Development and Psychopathology, 7,* 715–726.

Keller, B. B., and Bell, R. Q. (1979). Child effects on adult's method of eliciting altruistic behavior. *Child Development, 50,* 1004–1009.

Kerig, P. K. (1998). Moderators and mediators of the effects of interparental conflict on children's adjustment. *Journal of Abnormal Child Psychology, 26,* 199–212.

Kestenbaum, R., Farber, E. A., and Sroufe, L. A. (1989). Individual differences in empathy among preschoolers: Relation to attachment history. In N. Eisenberg (Ed.), *New directions for child development: Vol. 44. Empathy and related emotional responses* (pp. 51–64). San Francisco: Jossey-Bass.

Kochanska, G. (1991). Socialization and temperament in the development of guilt and conscience. *Child Development, 62,* 1379–1392.

Kochanska, G. (1993). Toward a synthesis of parental socialization and child temperament in early development of conscience. *Child Development, 64,* 325–347.

Kochanska, G. (1995). Children's temperament, mothers' discipline, and security of attachment: Multiple pathways to emerging internalization. *Child Development, 66,* 597–615.

Kochanska, G. (1997a). Multiple pathways to conscience for children with different temperaments: From toddlerhood to age 5. *Developmental Psychology, 33,* 228–240.

Kochanska, G. (1997b). Mutually responsive orientation between mothers and their young children: Implications for early socialization. *Child Development, 68,* 94–112.

Kochanska, G., and Murray, K. T. (2000). Mother-child mutually responsive orientation and conscience development: From toddler to early school age. *Child Development, 71,* 417–431.

Kochanska, G., Padavich, D. L., and Koenig, A. L. (1996). Children's narratives about hypothetical moral dilemmas and objective measures of their conscience: Mutual relations and socialization antecedents. *Child Development, 67,* 1420–1436.

Koestner, R., Franz, C., and Weinberger, J. (1990). The family origins of empathic concern: A 26-year longitudinal study. *Journal of Personality and Social Psychology, 58,* 709–717.

Koestner, R., Zuroff, D. C., and Powers, T. A. (1991). Family origins of adolescent self-criticism and its continuity into adulthood. *Journal of Abnormal Psychology, 100,* 191–197.

Kohlberg, L. (1969). Stage and sequence: The cognitive-developmental approach to socialization. In D. A. Goslin (Ed.), *Handbook of socialization theory and research* (pp. 325–480). New York: Rand McNally.

Kohlberg, L. (1984). *Essays on moral development: Vol. 2. The psychology of moral development.* San Francisco: Harper & Row.

Krevans, J., and Gibbs, J. C. (1996). Parents' use of inductive discipline: Relations to children's empathy and prosocial behavior. *Child Development, 67,* 3263–3277.

Kruger, A. C. (1992). The effect of peer and adult–child transactive discussions on moral reasoning. *Merrill-Palmer Quarterly, 38,* 191–211.

Kuczynski, L., and Kochanska, G. (1990). Development of children's noncompliance strategies from toddlerhood to age 5. *Developmental Psychology, 26,* 398–408.

Lahey, B. B., Russo, M. F., Walker, J. L. and Piacentini, J. C. (1989). Personality characteristics of the mothers of children with disruptive behavior disorders. *Journal of Consulting and Clinical Psychology, 57,* 512–515.

Laible, D. J., and Thompson, R. A. (1999). *Mother–child discourse, attachment security, shared positive affect, and early conscience.* Paper submitted for review.

Leahy, R. L. (1981). Parental practices and the development of moral judgment and self-image disparity during adolescence. *Developmental Psychology, 17,* 580–594.

Lepper, M. R. (1983). Social-control processes and the internalization of social values: An attributional perspective. In E. T. Higgins, D. N. Ruble, and W. W. Hartup (Eds.), *Social cognition and social development* (pp. 294–330). Cambridge, England: Cambridge University Press.

Lewis, M. (1931). How parental attitudes affect the problem of lying in children. *Smith College Studies in Social Work, 1*, 403–404.

London, P. (1970). The rescuers: Motivational hypotheses about Christians who saved Jews from the Nazis. In J. Macaulay and L. Berkowitz (Eds.), *Altruism and helping behavior* (pp. 241–250). New York: Academic.

Luntz, B. K., and Widom, C. S. (1994). Antisocial personality disorder in abused and neglected children grown up. *American Journal of Psychiatry, 151*, 670–674.

Lytton, H. (1990). Child and parent effects in boys' conduct disorder: A reinterpretation. *Developmental Psychology, 26*, 683–697.

Maccoby, E. E. (1992). The role of parents in the socialization of children: An historical overview. *Developmental Psychology, 28*, 1006–1017.

Maccoby, E. E., and Martin, J. (1983). Socialization in the context of the family: Parent–child interaction. In P. H. Mussen (Ed.), *Handbook of child Psychology: Vol. 4. Socialization, personality, and social development* (E. M. Hetherington, Vol. Ed., pp. 1–101). New York: Wiley.

Martin, B. (1975). Parent–child relations. In F. D. Horowitz (Ed.), *Review of child development research* (Vol. 4, pp. 463–540). Chicago: University of Chicago Press.

Maruyama, G., Fraser, S. C., and Miller, N. (1982). Personal responsibility and altruism in children. *Journal of Personality and Social Psychology, 42*, 658–664.

Mason, M. G., and Gibbs, J. C. (1993). Social perspective taking and moral judgment among college students. *Journal of Adolescent Research, 8*, 109–123.

McCord, J., and Tremblay, R. E. (1992). *Preventing antisocial behavior: Interventions from birth through adolescence*. New York: Guilford.

McFadyen-Ketchum, S. A., Bates, J. E., Dodge, K. A., and Pettit, G. S. (1996). Patterns of change in early childhood aggressive-disruptive behavior: Gender differences in predictions from early coercive and affectionate mother–child interactions. *Child Development, 67*, 2417–2433.

McGrath, M. P., and Power, T. G. (1990). The effects of reasoning and choice on children's prosocial behavior. *International Journal of Behavioral Development, 13*, 345–353.

McGrath, M. P., Wilson, S. R., Frassetto, S. J. (1995). Why some forms of induction are better than others at encouraging prosocial behavior. *Merrill-Palmer Quarterly, 41*, 347–360.

Miles, D. R., and Carey, G. (1997). Genetic and environmental architecture on human aggression. *Journal of Personality and Social Psychology, 72*, 207–217.

Mussen, P., Rutherford, E., Harris, S., and Keasey, C. B. (1970). Honesty and altruism among preadolescents. *Developmental Psychology, 3*, 151–162.

Oliner, S. P., and Oliner, P. M. (1988). *The altruistic personality: Rescuers of Jews in Nazi Europe*. New York: Free Press.

Olweus, D. (1979). Stability of aggressive reaction patterns in males: A review. *Psychological Bulletin, 86*, 852–875.

Palmer, E. J., and Hollin, C. R. (1996). Sociomoral reasoning, perceptions of own parenting, and self-reported delinquency. *Personality and Individual Differences, 21*, 175–182.

Pam, A. (1995). Biological psychiatry: Science of pseudoscience? In C. A. Ross and A. Pam (Eds.), *Pseudoscience in biological psychiatry* (pp. 7–84). New York: Wiley.

Parikh, B. (1980). Development of moral judgment and its relation to family environment factors in Indian and American families. *Child Development, 51*, 1030–1039.

Parke, R. D., and Slaby, R. G. (1983). The development of aggression. In P. Mussen (Series Ed.) and E. M. Hetherington (Ed.), *Handbook of child psychology: Vol. 4. Socialization, personality, and social development* (pp. 547–641). New York: Wiley.

Patterson, C. J., Kupersmidt, J. B., and Vaden, N. A. (1990). Income level, gender, ethnicity, and household composition as predictors of children's school-based competence. *Child Development, 61*, 468–494.

Patterson, G. R. (1982). *Coercive family processes*. Eugene, OR: Castilla.

Patterson, G. R. (1982). *A social learning approach: Vol. 3. Coercive family process*. Eugene, OR: Castalia.

Patterson, G. R. (1995). Coercion as a basis for early age of onset for arrest. In J. McCord (Ed.), *Coercion and punishment in long-term perspectives* (pp. 81–105). New York: Cambridge University Press.

Patterson, G. R. (1998). Continuities—A search for causal mechanisms: Comment on the special section. *Developmental Psychology, 34*, 1263–1268.

Patterson, G. R., DeGarmo, D. S., and Knutson, N. (2000). Hyperactive and antisocial behaviors: Comorbid or two points in the same process? *Development and Psychopathology, 12*, 91–106.

Patterson, G. R., Reid, J. B., and Dishion, T. J. (1992). *A social interactional approach: Vol. 4. Antisocial boys*. Eugene, OR: Castalia.

Perry, D. G., Bussey, K., and Freiberg, K. (1981). Impact of adults' appeals for sharing on the development of altruistic dispositions in children. *Journal of Experimental Child Psychology, 32*, 127–138.

Peterson, L. (1983). Influence of age, task competence, and responsibility focus on children's altruism. *Developmental Psychology, 19*, 141–148.

Pettit, G. S., Bates, J. E., and Dodge, K. A. (1997). Supportive parenting, ecological context, and children's adjustment: A seven-year longitudinal study. *Child Development, 68*, 908–923.

Powers, S. I. (1988). Moral judgment development within the family. *Journal of Moral Education, 17*, 209–219.

Pratt, M. W., Arnold, M. L., Pratt, A. T., and Diessner, R. (1999). Predicting adolescent moral reasoning from family climate: A longitudinal study. *Journal of Early Adolescence, 10*, 148–175.

Radke-Yarrow, M., Zahn-Waxler, C., and Chapman, M. (1983). Prosocial dispositions and behavior. In P. Mussen (Series Ed.) and E. M. Hetherington (Vol. Ed.), *Manual of child psychology: Vol. 4. Socialization, personality, and social development* (pp. 469–545). New York: Wiley.

Reid, J. B., Eddy, J. M., Fetrow, R. A., and Stoolmiller, M. (1999). Description and immediate impacts of a preventive intervention for conduct problems. *American Journal of Community Psychology, 27*, 483–517.

Rice, M. E., and Grusec, J. E. (1975). Saying and doing: Effects on observer performance. *Journal of Personality and Social Psychology, 32*, 584–593.

Rosenhan, D. L. (1970). The natural socialization of altruistic autonomy. In J. Macaulay and L. Berkowitz (Eds.), *Altruism and helping behavior* (pp. 251–268). New York: Academic Press.

Rothbaum, F., and Weisz, J. R. (1994). Parental caregiving and child externalizing behavior in nonclinical samples: A meta-analysis. *Psychological Bulletin, 116*, 55–74.

Rubin, K. H., Hastings, P., Chen, X., Stewart, S., and McNichol, K. (1998). Intrapersonal and maternal correlates of aggression, conflict, and externalizing problems in toddlers. *Child Development, 69*, 1614–1629.

Rushton, J. P. (1975). Generosity in children: Immediate and long-term effects of modeling, preaching, and moral judgment. *Journal of Personality and Social Psychology, 31*, 459–466.

Samaniego, R. Y., and Gonzales, N. A. (1999). Multiple mediators of the effects of acculturation status on delinquency for Mexican American adolescents. *American Journal of Community Psychology, 27*, 189–210.

Sampson, R. J., and Laub, J. H. (1994). Urban poverty and the family context of delinquency: A new look at structure and process in a classic study. *Child Development, 65*, 523–540.

Saraswathi, T. S., and Sundaresan, J. (1980). Perceived maternal disciplinary practices and their relations to development of moral judgment. *International Journal of Behavioral Development, 3*, 91–104.

Smart, R. C., and Smart, M. S. (1976). Preadolescents' perceptions of parents and their relations to a test of responses to moral dilemmas. *Social Behavior and Personality, 4*, 297–308.

Smith, C. L., Gelfand, D. M., Hartmann, D. P., and Partlow, M. P. (1979). Children's causal attributions regarding help-giving. *Child Development, 50*, 203–210.

Snyder, J. J., and Patterson, G. R. (1995). Individual differences in social aggression: A test of a reinforcement model of socialization in the natural environment. *Behavior Therapy, 26*, 371–391.

Snyder, J. J., Schrepferman, L., and St. Peter, C. (1997). Origins of antisocial behavior: Negative reinforcement and affect dysregulation of behavior as socialization mechanisms in family interaction. *Behavior Modification, 21*, 187–215.

Speicher, B. (1992). Adolescent moral judgment and perceptions of family interaction. *Journal of Family Psychology, 6*, 128–138.

Speicher, B. (1994). Family patterns of moral judgment during adolescence and early adulthood. *Developmental Psychology, 30*, 624–632.

Spieker, S. J., Larson, N. C., Lewis, S. M., Keller, T. E., and Gilchrist, L. (1999). Developmental trajectories of disruptive behavior problems in preschool children of adolescent mothers. *Child Development, 70*, 443–458.

Spinrad, T. L., Losoya, S., Eisenberg, N., Fabes, R. A., Shepard, S. A., Cumberland, A., Guthrie, I. K., and Murphy, B. C. (1999). The relation of parental affect and encouragement to children's moral emotions and behaviour. *Journal of Moral Education, 28*, 323–337.

Staub, E. (1978). *Positive social behavior and morality: Vol. 1. Social and personal influences.* New York: Academic.

Staub, E. (1979). *Positive social behavior and morality: Vol. 2. Socialization and development.* New York: Academic.

Stoolmiller, M., Eddy, J. M., and Reid, J. B. (2000). Detecting and describing preventive intervention effects in a universal school-based randomized trial targeting delinquent and violent behavior. *Journal of Consulting and Clinical Psychology, 68*, 296–306.

Stormshak, E. A., Bierman, K. L., McMahon, R. J., Lengua, L. J., and Conduct Problems Prevention Research Group. (2000). Parenting practices and child disruptive behavior problems in early elementary school. *Journal of Clinical Child Psychology, 29*, 17–29.

Stouthamer-Loeber, M. (1986). Lying as a problem behavior in children: A review. *Clinical Psychology Review, 6*, 267–289.

Stouthamer-Loeber, M., and Loeber, R. (1986). Boys who lie. *Journal of Abnormal Child Psychology, 14*, 551–564.

Strassberg, Z., Dodge, K. A., Pettit, G. S., and Bates, J. E. (1994). Spanking in the home and children's subsequent aggression toward kindergarten peers. *Development and Psychopathology, 6*, 445–461.

Straus, M. A., and Mouradian, V. E. (1998). Impulsive corporal punishment by mothers and antisocial behavior and impulsiveness of children. *Behavioral Sciences and the Law, 16*, 353–374.

Szynal-Brown, C., and Morgan, R. R. (1983). The effects of reward on tutor's behaviors in a cross-age tutoring context. *Journal of Experimental Child Psychology, 36*, 196–208.

Tangney, J. P. (1990). Assessing individual differences in proneness to shame and guilt: Development of the self-conscious affect and attribution inventory. *Journal of Personality and Social Psychology, 59*, 102–111.

Tangney, J. P. (1991). Moral affect: The good, the bad, and the ugly. *Journal of Personality and Social Psychology, 61*, 598–607.

Tolan, P. H., Hanish, L. D., and McKay, M. M. (2000). *Measuring process in child and family interventions: An example in prevention of aggression.* Manuscript submitted for publication.

Trommsdorff, G. (1995). Person-context relations as developmental conditions for empathy and prosocial action: A cross-cultural analysis. In T. A. Kindermann and J. Valsiner (Eds.), *Development of person-context relations* (pp. 189–208). Hillsdale, NJ: Lawrence Erlbaum Associates.

Vuchinich, S., Bank, L., and Patterson, G. R. (1992). Parenting, peers, and the stability of antisocial behavior in preadolescent boys. *Developmental Psychology, 28*, 510–521.

Walker, L. J., and Hennig, K. H. (1999). Parenting style and the development of moral reasoning. *Journal of Moral Education, 28*, 359–374.

Walker, L. J., and Taylor, J. H. (1991). Family interactions and the development of moral reasoning. *Child Development, 62*, 264–283.

Warren, S. F., Warren-Rogers, A., and Baer, D. M. (1976). The role of offer rates in controlling sharing by young children. *Journal of Applied Behavior Analysis, 9*, 491–497.

Weiss, B., Dodge, K. A., Bates, J. E., and Pettit, G. S. (1992). Some consequences of early harsh discipline: Child aggression and a maladaptive social information processing style. *Child Development, 63*, 1321–1335.

Weissbrod, C. S. (1980). The impact of warmth and instruction on donation. *Child Development, 51*, 279–281.

Wentzel, K. R., and McNamara, C. C. (1999). Interpersonal relationships, emotional distress, and prosocial behavior in middle school. *Journal of Early Adolesence, 19*, 114–125.

Whiting, B. B., and Whiting, J. W. M. (1975). *Children of six cultures: A psychocultural analysis.* Cambridge, MA: Harvard University Press.

Yarrow, M. R., Scott, P. M., and Waxler, C. Z. (1973). Learning concern for others. *Developmental Psychology, 8*, 240–260.

Yates, M., and Youniss, J. (1996). A developmental perspective on community service in adolescence. *Social Development, 5*, 85–111.

Zahn-Waxler, C., and Kochanska, G. (1990). The origins of guilt. In R. Thompson (Ed.), *The 36th annual Nebraska symposium on motivation: Socioemotional development* (pp. 183–258). Lincoln: University of Nebraska Press.

Zahn-Waxler, C., Radke-Yarrow, M., and King, R. A. (1979). Child rearing and children's prosocial initiations toward victims of distress. *Child Development, 50*, 319–330.

Zegiob, L. E., Arnold, S., and Forehand, R. (1975). An examination of observer effects in parent–child interactions. *Child Development, 46*, 509–512.

6

Parental Socialization and Children's Acquisition of Values

Joan E. Grusec
University of Toronto

INTRODUCTION

The term *socialization* broadly refers to the way in which individuals are assisted in the acquisition of skills necessary to function successfully as members of their social group. Bugental and Goodnow (1998) describe it as the continuous collaboration of elders and novices, of old hands and newcomers, as the latter with the help of the former develop the attitudes, behaviors, values, standards, and motives that enable novices and newcomers to become part of the social community. There is considerable debate about the relative importance of different kinds of elders or old hands. Frequently considered as most important are parents. But other agents of socialization include teachers, older siblings, peers, formal institutions, and the media. This chapter focuses on parents who, for a variety of reasons, can be considered to be primary sources of influence. Thus Kuczynski and Grusec (1997) have argued that parents are most influential in the socialization of children for a number of reasons: socialization, which has evolved as an adaptive evolutionary strategy, is a biosocial system set up to favor the parent's primary influence on the child; society designates parents (or parent surrogates) as primarily responsible for socialization; parents have greater time and opportunity to develop relationships with children, with these relationships essential for successful socialization; and parents also have greater opportunity to monitor their children's actions, another centrally important aspect of successful socialization.

Socialization determines several outcomes in children. One is the development of self-regulation of emotion, thinking, and behavior. The second is the acquisition of a culture's standards, attitudes, and values, including appropriate and willing conformity to and cooperation with the direction of authority figures. The final outcome of socialization is what Kuczynski and Grusec have termed "collateral effects." During the course of helping children develop self-regulation and acquire values and standards, parents also less intentionally teach role-taking skills, strategies for resolving conflicts, and ways of viewing relationships. Their modes of interaction also promote or hinder the development of self-esteem and self-efficacy. The focus of this chapter is on the acquisition of standards and values, with the recognition that the ability to self-regulate is essential for adherence to values and that collateral effects are an inevitable outcome of parenting efforts at imparting values.

It should be noted that values are not equivalent, but rather exist in different domains that have different antecedents, correlates, and outcomes. The social domain approach (see Smetana, 1997, for a review), for example, distinguishes between moral values that involve harm to others, social conventional values that guide social interactions, prudential values having to do with safety, and personal issues that are deemed to be appropriately under the direction of the individual. This approach also suggests that the boundaries between personal and social conventional issues change as a function of the child's developmental status as well as the way in which the child is parented. In another sort of distinction, values have been divided into those that are intrinsic and those that are extrinsic. The former include aspirations for personal growth, meaningful relationships, social responsibility, and physical health, whereas the latter involve goals of financial success, physical attractiveness, and social recognition (Kasser and Ryan, 1996), with intrinsic motives more likely to be associated with happiness and well-being.

This chapter begins with a historical overview of philosophical and scientific perspectives on parenting or childrearing, then moves to a discussion of four central issues for the understanding of parenting and socialization: the interaction between parent and child influence; accounting for similarities and differences between parents and children in their values; children's autonomy from parental influence considered as the ultimate goal of socialization; and some methodological concerns in research on socialization. It then describes three classes of theories that have guided research and thinking about the most effective techniques for achieving children's self-regulation and acquisition of values, moving on to an overview of a very large body of research aimed at documenting the essence of successful parenting techniques and styles, and indicating how this body of research requires some change in traditional ways of viewing the process in order to accommodate individual and cultural differences. Finally, an attempt is made to draw together the various theoretical traditions, both formal and informal, scientific and popular, that have guided thinking and to suggest how these might be organized to provide a consistent picture of effective parenting as well as to direct the path of future research.

HISTORICAL CONSIDERATIONS IN THE STUDY OF PARENTAL SOCIALIZATION

Philosophical Perspectives on Childrearing

At least three ways of viewing children have appeared in Western thought, with each finding some parallels in modern theoretical approaches to the scientific study of socialization. These parallels will be noted as appropriate, and they will be used as a way of attempting to resolve major disagreements about the best way to socialize children that appear currently both in the world of popular advice about childrearing and in the world of scientific study.

One dominant view of the child, linked with Puritan religious views as well as the philosophical views of Hobbes (1651/1885), is of an innately sinful creature needing to be scourged to salvation. Hence the admonition of Susanna Wesley, in the early 1700s, that parents who work to subdue bad actions by breaking children's will, teaching them at an early age to fear the rod, and whipping them to enforce obedience are doing God's work. The parent who indulges children, on the other hand, does the devil's work (Newson and Newson, 1974). In stark contrast is the position of Rousseau (1762/1974). He regarded the child as innately good and believed that parents who intervened in an authoritarian way could only interfere with a naturally positive developmental progression toward becoming a successful member of the social group. Lessons about appropriate behavior should arise from naturally occurring events and those artificially contrived by educators if necessary. But the strict imposition of parental will could lead only to outcomes detrimental to successful socialization. The third view, something of a compromise between these two extreme positions, comes from John Locke (1693/1884), who regarded children as blank slates, waiting for the impact of experience. Locke argued for the importance of parental training and the encouragement of mature behavior. He advocated the use of gentler techniques than did the Puritans, however, emphasizing reasoning rather than physical punishment or material reward.

These three views are reflected in current theories of socialization. For example, in an analysis of theories of childrearing, Kuczynski and Hildebrandt (1997) described what they label as external control, internal control, and relational approaches. The first emphasizes immediate compliance and external contingencies—reward and punishment—as ways of controlling children's behavior. The second, the internal control approach, focuses on the shift from external but subtle control to children's self-regulation. The third, relational approach, emphasizes the fundamental importance of a positive association between parent and child as the foundation of successful socialization. In this perspective, children are not firmly guided or coerced into acceptable behavior but share a common heritage with their caregivers that inclines them to cooperative interaction. Thus, although the overlap is not perfect, the linkages among the external control of a Puritan approach, the internal control of a blank slate approach, and the relational control of an innate goodness approach are evident.

The Scientific Study of Parenting and Socialization

The scientific study of socialization began with Freud. Freud's major contribution to mainstream developmental theory was his analysis of conscience development, with the suggestion that children incorporate or take over the attitudes and standards of their parents through a process of identification. By identifying with or becoming like their parents they develop into functioning members of society. In this way the elders or old hands transmit their ways of behaving to the novices or newcomers.

Freud's ideas about incorporation or identification were the basis of the internal control perspective that has dominated the study of socialization. Thus researchers have conceptualized parenting and socialization as a process whereby children eventually become autonomous from the control of their elders, behaving in accord with social standards because they believe these standards are inherently correct. Internal control theories originated in the combination, in the 1940s and 1950s, of psychoanalytic theory and Hullian learning theory approaches to produce an outcome—social learning theory—that could account for the process of identification or internalization using tested laboratory concepts (see Grusec, 1997, for a review). Thus the actions of parents were viewed as secondarily reinforcing because they were associated with primary drive reduction. Eventually a secondary drive to be like the parent developed, and this accounted for the child's eager willingness to become a conforming member of society. These ideas resulted in a seminal study of the childrearing practices of mothers of preschoolers carried out in Boston (Sears, Maccoby, and Levin, 1957), which demonstrated that mothers who endorsed psychological forms of discipline (reasoning and withdrawal of love), provided they were also warm and nurturant, were more likely to have children who behaved in a prosocial manner than did mothers who endorsed physical discipline such as spanking or withdrawal of rewards.

In an analysis of extant data, Hoffman (1970) moved the thinking of socialization researchers still further by demonstrating that reasoning, particularly reasoning that was other-oriented by focusing on the consequences of misdeeds for others, was more effective than power assertion (punishment) in promoting children's moral development. Warmth he delegated to a somewhat secondary position. As well, he suggested that withdrawal of love held a middle position between reasoning and power assertion in terms of its effectiveness for socialization. Given the far from overwhelming nature of the data, Hoffman tempered his conclusions by noting that power assertion and love withdrawal had some role to play in the acquisition of values in their provision of arousal, but that the accompaniment of reasoning was a necessity. This more moderate conclusion has, in fact, tended to be ignored as a simple distinction between reasoning and power assertion has dominated thinking in the field.

In contrast to this analysis of discipline processes with its origins in social learning theory, social psychology was the source of a second major internal perspective, this one having to do with styles of parenting (Baumrind, e.g., 1971). Maccoby (1992) locates the origins of Baumrind's approach in Lewin's research on group atmospheres (e.g., Lewin, Lippitt, and White, 1938)—research that was generated in reaction to alarm about the growth of totalitarianism in Europe in the 1930s. Lewin's work with groups of boys indicated that authoritarian or autocratic direction led to compliance in the group leader's presence. However, privately, the members expressed dislike of the leader and stopped working in his absence. Moreover, they engaged in wild horseplay, presumably an indication of suppressed tension. In democratic groups, characterized by joint participation in decision making under the guidance of a dispassionate leader, boys worked well even in the absence of the leader, with dispassionate leadership encouraging autonomy and independent thinking. Finally, in the laissez-faire group the members were disorganized and ineffective. This division of leadership styles was ultimately refined by Baumrind, who developed a tripartite division of parenting styles that added to the authoritarian and laissez-faire, or permissive, distinction the authoritative parent, who was not only democratic in tendencies but also imposed rules and demanded mature behavior.

Analyses of discipline and parenting styles comprise the internal perspective on socialization. The external perspective finds its roots in learning theory and, particularly, the work of Skinner and the tradition of behavior modification. Although very far from advocates of severe punishment and without the overlay of a formal religious tradition, those in the behavior modification tradition nevertheless stress the importance of consistent control over a child's behavior. The behavior modification approach was advanced by Patterson and his associates (see Patterson and Fisher, in Vol. 5 of this *Handbook*), who demonstrated in a molecular analysis of family interactions how antisocial or coercive behavior is changed in form as a function of the constant impact of one family member on another.

Interest in a relational perspective, as already discussed, appears in the writings of Sears et al. (1957) and Hoffman (1970). In the social learning tradition, warm and nurturant parents were seen as greater sources of secondary reinforcement than rejecting or cold parents. Already noted is moderate evidence for this assertion. By far, however, the most significant theory about relationships is attachment theory (Bowlby, 1969) whose roots are deep in psychoanalytic theory. Attachment theory (see Cummings and Cummings, in Vol. 5 of this *Handbook*) has been highly influential in developmental psychology for over 30 years, and it is strongly reminiscent of points of view that see the child as inherently good. Thus Stayton, Hogan, and Ainsworth (1971) argued that the human species has evolved to be compliant and that only insensitive and unresponsive parenting, the precursors of insecure attachment, can interfere with this natural proclivity. The study of relationships has become a popular topic in recent years, and substantial parts of this chapter will deal with various features of parent–child relationships and their link to effective socialization.

CENTRAL ISSUES IN THE CONCEPTUALIZATION AND STUDY OF PARENTING AND SOCIALIZATION

A number of general issues arise in the study of parenting and socialization of children's values, and help to set the stage for theory and research. This section addresses four concerns that have been ubiquitous in considerations of socialization processes. They have to do with:

(1) The fact that parent–child influence is bidirectional and that an adequate understanding of socialization requires knowing how parents influence their children, how children influence their parents, and how these directions of influence interact.
(2) The extent to which values are transmitted directly from parent to child during the course of socialization and the extent to which they are constructed by the child.

(3) The extent to which the final product of socialization involves a child who has become autonomous from external control.

(4) The best methodological approaches for understanding socialization processes.

The Interaction Between Parent and Child Influence

The study of parenting and socialization has been driven by an extremely practical and extraordinarily important question, namely, how best to rear children so that they can become happily functioning members of society. It should come as no surprise, then, that the research orientation tends to be unidirectional, in the sense of looking for parenting variables that would have the desired outcomes for children's behavior. This is not to say that there has been lack of awareness of the fact that children's characteristics influence parenting behavior. Indeed, a theory that sees children as innately corrupt or as innately good is clearly acknowledging that child characteristics are directing the parenting process. Sears (1951) made a strong case for the fact that parent and child operate as part of a dyad and as such that they strongly influence each other's actions. Rheingold (1969) noted that infants are biologically prepared to exert influence on their parents. Bell (1968) argued convincingly that many established relations between parenting behavior and child outcomes could be as easily explained in terms of children's effects on their parents' behavior as the reverse. Thus a correlation between coercive punishment and aggression could indicate that parental power assertion produces aggression in children, or that aggressive children elicit strong discipline from their parents because that is the only intervention to which they will respond. Lewis (1981), in a reanalysis of Baumrind's parenting styles, suggested that social competence in authoritative families is a reflection of the child's ability to influence the behavior of the parent, rather than a result of the firm and responsive control imposed by the parent.

Certainly, of course, a good case can be made for parents having greater influence because they have more power, control more resources, have greater knowledge, and are needed by the child for safety and protection. Nevertheless, although the primary goal of many researchers is to answer the practical question of how best to rear children, it is evident that, in order to have an adequate answer, knowledge of how children affect the socialization process is essential.

Child effects come in two different forms. The first involves how child characteristics interact with parenting actions to determine outcomes. Children differ among other things in temperament, mood, developmental period, sex, and history of interaction with their parents. As well, the contexts of parent–child interactions differ, such as in the case of disagreements over moral issues, versus so-called personal issues, where issues of right and wrong are less clearly defined. We know that children actively construct their world. All these features have a demonstrable impact on reactions to parental interventions (Grusec and Goodnow, 1994; Grusec, Goodnow, and Kuczynski, 2000), and they presumably are ones that parents can take into account by tailoring their actions accordingly. It is also very clear, however, that parents are affected by children's actions in ways over which they may have less conscious control, and that some parents are less able than others to manage their affective reactions to their children or process information relevant to their children in an adaptive way (see Bugental and Goodnow, 1998, for a review and Bugental and Happaney, in Vol. 5 of this *Handbook*). This latter is the second way in which child effects can have an impact on parenting behavior.

The chain of interaction, of course, does not stop at child effects. Bidirectionality of influence is uniformly acknowledged by researchers as a primary feature of parent–child interaction, and the challenge is to unpack the interconnections between the impact of parents and children on each other. Longitudinal research and statistical techniques that control for various forms of influence, as well as experimental analyses, have done much in the last decade or more to expand understanding of these complex interactions (for a discussion, see Collins, Maccoby, Steinberg, Hetherington, and Bornstein, 2000).

Accounting for Similarities and Differences Between Parents and Their Children

An oversimplified view of socialization suggests that parental standards are transmitted in their entirety to children. Indeed, psychoanalytic notions of introjection and identification described above do encourage such a view, enabling early debates about whether standards are transmitted or constructed (e.g., Turiel, 1983). It is clear, however, that simple transmission of standards or values is not an apt metaphor for socialization. Nor, indeed, is construction of standards or values. The definition of socialization offered at the beginning of this chapter speaks of "continuous collaboration" and "help" for the novices from the elders—the idea here, then, is that transformation and construction both seem to be essential parts of the socialization process.

It has been argued (e.g., Goodnow, 1994; Kuczynski and Grusec, 1997) that the proper task for researchers is to ask about conditions that determine how closely children match their attitudes and values to their parents, that is, to ascertain when standards are accepted in full and when children add considerable input of their own. One can posit a continuum from total parent transmission to total child construction. Obviously neither end of the continuum can be achieved. Children are likely to have some bias in their perceptions of parental attitudes as a function of such variables as age, mood, temperament, and attributional style. Also, they are subject to input from other sources than their parents. Moreover, parents may not always be anxious to have their own standards and values reproduced exactly, and may therefore encourage some deviation from direct transmission. As well, pure construction is obviously impossible—at least some of the material for construction must come from parental input. Goodnow (1994) proposed that standards, attitudes, and values are more likely to be transmitted when parents care deeply about them. Different positions will not likely be tolerated, and parental consistency will be substantial. On the other hand, a feature of social norms that is not valued highly may be amenable to leeway and construction. Accordingly, research by Devereux (1970) indicates that, when it comes to serious or moral issues, the influence of parents remains dominant, whereas peers may be more important in less serious or nonmoral domains. Also, parents may sometimes not have the energy to wait for children to construct norms through observation of regularities in behavior or differences in expectations across different contexts (Smetana, 1997) and may choose the easier way of simply informing children about proper actions.

Internalization and Autonomy

Internalization and autonomous choice traditionally have been considered to be the essence of effective socialization. This is a primary feature of the internal control perspective, with the developmental process conceived of as a progression from external control of behavior to internal control, or self-regulation. Often internal control is seen as multifaceted and aligned along a continuum of greater degrees of internalization. Hoffman (1970), for example, distinguished between actions that were controlled by neurotic guilt (associated with withdrawal of love) and those controlled by existential guilt (associated with other-oriented induction). More recently, Deci and his colleagues (e.g., Deci and Ryan, 1991) have distinguished among introjected regulation, where external rules have been taken in but not integrated with the self and therefore are seen as coercive and controlling, regulation through identification, which implies greater choice and personal valuing, and, finally, identification where rules have been integrated with a coherent system of values, goals, and motives.

It is this overarching concern with the taking in of social standards that has made external control perspectives less central to developmental researchers. In a parallel fashion, the overarching concern with autonomy or separation has made relational perspectives problematic because the latter imply a continuing emotional link between parents and children. Yet recent research calls the notion into question. Cross-cultural research, for example, suggests a different pattern of thinking with respect to socialization in so-called collectivist as opposed to individualist (Western or European) societies.

In Eastern collectivist cultures, authoritarian parenting practices are more the norm (e.g., Chao, 1994) and the goal is not to see children grow from a state of dependency on adults to one of self-sufficiency and autonomy as it is in individualist cultures. Rather, the goal of socialization is to move children from a state of independence to one of aligning themselves with a larger social group and trusting that the group will work to meet their needs and desires (Markus and Kitayama, 1991). Thus agents of socialization in so-called collectivist cultures want to encourage feelings of interdependence and cooperation in children in order to facilitate their integration into society. Clearly there is some kind of internalization, but it is not the same kind that has characterized the conceptualization of internalization in individualist groups, nor is 'it accomplished in the same way. Grusec et al. (2000) have made one suggestion about the nature of the difference, which has to do with the audiences that agents of socialization emphasize when discussing appropriate actions. In the one case it may be an internal dialogue with one's conscience whereas, in the other case, it may be an internal dialogue with parents or other authority figures.

With respect to autonomy, it is becoming increasingly evident that children do not become autonomous from relationships with their parents. Hill and Holmbeck (1986) have argued that autonomy does not refer to freedom from others but rather freedom to act independently while maintaining social connections. Autonomy is not distancing or separation but, rather, the outcome of self-regulation that develops in concert with interactions with significant others. Thus internalization does not involve separation but, instead, the acquisition of societal standards in the context of relationships that were developed in early infancy and maintain themselves—obviously in altered form—throughout the life course.

Methodological Issues in Research on Parenting and Socialization

Already noted is the importance of a variety of approaches to understanding the processes of socialization. Although cross-sectional correlational studies have dominated the research enterprise, other methodologies are essential to untangle the central issue of direction of effect. Longitudinal studies are becoming more frequent, enabling investigators to control for early levels of a child's behavior and thereby assess the impact of parenting actions on later levels of behavior. Experimental studies are often criticized for their lack of ecological validity, although there is no reason that they cannot be a very useful adjunct in the study of possible mechanisms operating in socialization. As an example, Patterson and his colleagues have made considerable use of prevention trials in which some families receive extended training and supervision in child management skills while others receive a set of placebo procedures, with the impact of training on children's antisocial actions providing useful information about the socialization process (Patterson, 1997).

A particularly critical problem for socialization researchers has been the measurement of parenting behavior. Questionnaires have been a frequent favorite because they are easy to administer. Most frequently, questionnaires have focused on parental warmth and control and comprise a series of short items with which respondents are asked to agree or disagree. Typical items are "Children should always treat adults with respect" and "I enjoy being with my child." Holden and Edwards (1989) discussed a number of limitations of existing questionnaires (see Holden and Buck, in Vol. 3 of this *Handbook*). These include the fact that questions are often very general, making it difficult for parents to express the nuances in their behavior that occur in different contexts. Items are frequently stated in the third person so that it is uncertain whether parents are expressing views they believe are correct or those that actually reflect their own actions. As well, the use of questionnaires makes it difficult to capture the interactive nature of parent–child relationships and the parent's ability to respond adaptively or appropriately moment-by-moment to child behaviors. In response to these limitations, researchers have come to rely more and more on observation of parenting behavior and interviews. The apparent success of their efforts is demonstrated in a meta-analysis in which Rothbaum and Weisz (1994) investigated the relation between parenting variables and children's externalizing behavior (aggression, hostility, and noncompliance) as a function of whether the parenting data had been gathered through questionnaires or by other means (observations or interviews). They found the effect size and percentage of studies finding relations to be significantly greater in the case of observations and interviews than in the case of questionnaires. Sole reliance on observational data, however, is not sufficient. Parke and Buriel (1998), for example, have noted that parental reports, including structured interviews, questionnaires, and focus groups, are underutilized in the study of socialization.

THEORIES IN THE STUDY OF SOCIALIZATION AND PARENTING

The three categories of socialization theories, those emphasizing internal control, those emphasizing external control, and those focusing on the parent–child relationship, will be discussed in turn.

Internal Control Theories

As already noted, internal control theories have focused on two aspects of socialization: parents' discipline practices and the more general characteristics of the emotional and behavioral socialization climate that is referred to as parenting style.

Discipline practices.   The apparent greater effectiveness assumed by internal control theories of one discipline technique, reasoning, over another, power assertion, has been attributed to a number of possibilities. Hoffman (1970) posited that power assertion arouses anger in the child because it directly challenges the child's autonomy and leads to aggressive actions, that it provides a model for antisocial discharge of anger, that it focuses the child's attention on the self rather than the object of harm, that it leads to high levels of arousal that interfere with effective information processing, and that it fails, in contrast to other-oriented induction, to utilize the child's empathic capacities as a way of preventing further wrongdoing.

Another set of explanations has taken its base in attribution theory, suggesting that optimal internal control or internalization occurs when pressure is just sufficient to produce compliance. Pressure that is too strong or too weak will not promote internalization. In the former case, attributions for compliance are made to external demands, whereas in the latter case there is no compliance to explain. In the case of minimally sufficient pressure external forces are discounted, leaving the only possible explanation for compliance as one having to do with self-generation (Lepper, 1983). The notion of pressure, of course, suggests that some minimal level of power assertion is needed. Indeed, this recognition is contained in Hoffman's (1983) suggestion that power assertion captures the child's attention so that the message can be heard although, clearly, the power assertion cannot be too great or information-processing capacities will be seriously diminished. Other formulations hold that power assertion discourages reflection on moral issues, whereas discussion and explanation allow children to elaborate schemas for addressing the psychological experiences of other individuals and thereby develop respect for their rights (Applegate, Burke, Burleson, Delia, and Kline, 1985).

Clearly the opposition of reasoning and power assertion is too simplistic. This fact led Grusec and Goodnow (1994) to posit a more fine-grained analysis of factors that have an impact on discipline effectiveness. First, they noted that many procedures have been included by researchers under the label of reasoning, with no justification for expecting that they would all have similar consequences (compare, for example, other-oriented induction, statements of norms, statement of practical consequences, and unconvincing arguments). Similarly, power assertion has included physical punishment, social isolation, withdrawal of privileges, disapproval, and humiliation, again with no reason to expect that the outcomes would be similar. Additionally, Grusec and Goodnow noted that evidence for the superiority of reasoning over power assertion is not compelling, and that the impact of different discipline techniques depends on a great range of variables including age, sex, mood, and temperament of the child, nature of the misdeed, sex of parent, and socioeconomic class. They argued that, rather than make differentiations in terms of discipline technique, researchers should think of the socialization of standards as involving two aspects, the accurate perception of the parent's message and the child's willingness to accept that message. A child might know what the parent wished to convey but be unwilling to comply with the parental directive. Or a child might be quite willing to comply but misperceive the message. In both cases internalization would not be an outcome.

Accurate perception is facilitated by a number of variables, including clear, frequent, and consistent expression of messages. As well, messages need to accord with the child's cognitive developmental level so they can be understood. Moderate levels of power assertion force attention and underline the importance of the message. Implicit messages (e.g., "This is a house, not a stable") also force attention because they require decoding. Acceptance involves three different sets of variables. The first set involves a feeling by the child that the parent's message is acceptable or reasonable—actions must be appropriate to the nature of the misdeed, arguments must be believable, the parent's behavior must be appropriate for that particular agent of socialization (e.g., to the culture and to the sex of the parent), and the intervention must be matched to the child's temperament, mood, and developmental status. The second set has to do with the child's motivation. Threats to feelings of security, high levels of empathic arousal, the extent to which compliance is seen to be important to the parent, the parent's warmth (which increases the desire to please), a script of mutual compliance that facilitates cooperation, and minimal threats to autonomy are all features of the socialization process that increase acceptance of parental messages. Finally, any condition that leads to feelings that a value or norm has been self-generated (e.g., minimal pressure or the need to decode a parental message) also fosters acceptance.

In this reformulation of how children acquire values, then, Grusec and Goodnow moved from a focus on discipline techniques imposed by parents to a focus on features of the child and the child's perception of parental behavior. This altered perspective leads to more complexity in the analysis of outcomes because it requires consideration of a wide variety of variables. It assesses outcome, however, in a very specific way that can be easily measured—children either comprehend the parent's message or they do not, and they either willingly accept it or they do not. It recognizes that the conditions that promote accurate perception and acceptance differ from one child to another, and it provides some guidelines for establishing what those conditions might be. A position that focuses on specific parental actions does not provide this same level of subtlety.

Parenting styles. According to Baumrind's analysis (e.g., 1971) of styles of parenting, authoritarian parents are rigid, value obedience, restrict the child's autonomy, and discourage expression of emotion. They endorse statements such as "The earlier a child is weaned from its emotional ties to its parents the better it will handle its own problems." Authoritative parents set standards for conduct, value compliance with reasonable rules but respect the child's autonomy and individuality, and are sensitively responsive to the child's needs and desires. They endorse statements such as "Children should be encouraged to tell their parents about it whenever they feel family rules are unreasonable." Permissive parents do not impose restraints and are accepting of the child's actions and benign in their treatment. It is authoritative parents who are most successful in socialization because, Baumrind argues, firm but not restrictive control helps children balance the tendency to comply with rules and consideration for others with autonomy and independent thinking.

In studies of parenting style, two dimensions have frequently emerged, one having to do with whether parents are high or low in control or demandingness and the other with whether they are high or low in responsiveness or warmth to the child. Baumrind's tri-partite classification includes high-control, high-responsive (authoritative) parents, high-control, low-responsive (authoritarian) parents, and low-control, high-responsive (permissive) parents. Not included is the final combination of low-control, low-responsive parents, designated as neglecting or indifferent. Maccoby and Martin (1983) noted that parents in this final combination produce significant deficits in psychological functioning because they neither set controls for their children's behavior nor display any warmth or nurturance toward them.

As with parental discipline, the findings for the impact of parenting style on child outcomes have not always been consistent. Even Baumrind's (1971) original findings were not entirely consistent. In research on parenting styles conducted with lower socioeconomic and with Asian American and African American families, the effects of authoritative parenting have not always been positive. These inconsistencies led to a reanalysis of parenting styles by Darling and Steinberg (1993). In that reanalysis, they distinguished between content and context, that is, between parenting practices and parenting style. Practices refer to specific content and goals for socialization and include such behaviors as spanking, showing an interest in children's activities, and requiring children to do their homework. Style refers to actions that are independent of socialization content, namely, the emotional climate in which parenting takes place, including body language, bursts of temper, tone of voice, inattention to the child, and so on. These latter features of parenting behavior convey how parents feel about the child her- or himself rather than about the child's behavior. An authoritative parent in a Western European context, then, is one who expresses comfort with the child's autonomy and respects the child's wishes and individuality. In summary, parenting practices affect internalization directly, whereas parenting style affects internalization indirectly both by making children more open to socialization attempts and by providing a model of competent social interaction.

Overlap between models of discipline techniques and parenting style.   The Grusec and Goodnow (1994) and Darling and Steinberg (1993) treatments of long-standing models of parenting have much in common. Both attempt to differentiate what is transmitted from the context in which that transmission takes place. For Darling and Steinberg it is socialization goals, and for Grusec and Goodnow it is messages, with an emphasis on the clarity with which those messages are transmitted. Darling and Steinberg emphasize the emotional climate between parent and child as a context in which transmission is facilitated or impeded. Grusec and Goodnow emphasize a number of general features of the way in which socialization takes place, including the emotional climate, although extending it to a number of other mechanisms including feelings of self-generation and judgments of the acceptability of parental actions. Darling and Steinberg also point out the important feature of socialization that involves opportunities for children to learn effective social skills from the actions of their parents.

External Control Theories

The main exemplar of an external control theory is Patterson's formulation of the social interactional perspective (see Patterson and Fisher, in Vol. 5 of this *Handbook*). Patterson's work has been directed toward understanding how aggressive behavior develops in boys. Internalization and discipline practices that involve reasoning play little part in the approach. Instead, the emphasis is on reinforcement contingencies that are embedded in the dyadic interaction between parent and child and that are the primary determinants of children's antisocial actions. Patterson's approach involves both a molar and a molecular analysis of parent–child interactions. In the former, attention is paid to parenting practices that control contingencies. Three practices in particular have been singled out: monitoring, or how well parents keep track of the child's activities (where they are, what they are doing, and who their companions are), discipline or the extent to which parents are consistent and follow through on discipline confrontation, and, finally, family problem solving rated on quality of proposed solutions, extent of resolution, and likelihood of implementation. These features of parenting have been demonstrated to link negatively to children's antisocial behavior.

The molar approach, however, does not clarify processes that guide socialization nor show how child behavior changes its form over time. To achieve this, Patterson and his colleagues have observed interactions between parents and children, focusing on escape conditioning. In this paradigm children select behaviors that are most effective in terminating conflict with other family members. These are usually coercive, antisocial, or unpleasant actions such as noncompliance, yelling, whining, teasing, and hitting that ultimately comprise the actions of an antisocial child. Another feature of the molecular approach is that is sees the child as an active seeker and selector rather than a passive recipient of imposed contingencies. Children select family members (usually mothers and siblings) and actively shape their behaviors. Moreover, behaviors of children and other family members after frequent repetition become overlearned and are exhibited automatically rather than requiring conscious processing.

Relationship Theories

Relationship theories, which emphasize the central role of the quality of the emotional link between parent and child as the foundation of socialization success or failure, come in several different forms. Historically, the first focus on quality of relationships and socialization was in the emphasis of social learning theorists on maternal warmth, nurturance, or noncontingent social and physical reinforcement. Children act in the same way as warm parents because the reproduction of their behavior is secondarily reinforcing. As well, children want to please people who are pleasant to them. In addition to its role in social learning approaches to the socialization process, warmth (or lack of it) is also a major component in parenting styles.

Interest in parental warmth as a feature of relationships has been replaced by one having to do with protection. Thus attachment theory emphasizes the importance of parental sensitivity and responsiveness to children's emotional and physical distress as a central feature of socialization. Children are biologically predisposed to be compliant (Stayton et al., 1971), and it is only in the case of parental insensitivity and nonresponsiveness that this natural tendency to compliance is thwarted. Parents who are insensitive and nonresponsive produce children who are insecurely attached, that is, who do not trust their parents to satisfy their need for protection or to make demands that are in their best interests. A manifestation of this insecurity or lack of trust is noncompliance or superficial compliance that is not willingly given and has an underlay of anger.

Maccoby and Martin (1983) noted the relation between parental behavior and child compliance, but questioned the necessity of secure attachment as a mediator, or link, between parental responsivity and child compliance. Instead, rather than focusing on the necessity of a secure attachment relationship as the precursor of compliance, they argued for a direct route from parenting behavior to child outcome. They suggested that sensitive parents who respond to the needs and desires of their children promote a situation in which their children, in turn, are responsive to the desires of their parents. In an atmosphere of shared goals and reciprocity, mutual scripts develop that facilitate cooperative and receptive compliance. Absent is the idea of conflict in which the needs of parent and child are in opposition. Instead, they are both motivated to please each other and even to postpone their own gratification to meet the needs of the other dyad member.

These three ways of viewing relationships underline the fact that the quality of parent–child relationships is not unidimensional, and that a relationship characterized by warmth need not be one characterized by trust or mutual compliance (see Goldberg, Grusec, and Jenkins, 1999, for a discussion of this point). Moreover, the distinction between aspects of relationships suggests that each of these aspects could play a different role in the facilitation of children's compliance with parental values as well as other socialization outcomes. Grusec et al. (2000), for example, have suggested that warmth and protection both expose children to their parents' values by keeping them in them in the vicinity of their parents and attentive to their behavior. However, warmth may lead to strong identification with all aspects of parental actions, whereas protection may be particularly important in the socialization of emotion regulation, given that attachment processes center around issues of negative affect or distress. Mutual compliance, they suggest, may be particularly important under conditions where compliance requires little self-sacrifice.

CLASSICAL AND MODERN RESEARCH ON PARENTING
AND SOCIALIZATION

There has been considerable research on the various techniques that parents employ in the course of socializing their children. There has also been a substantial amount addressed to the issue of parenting styles and their impact on children's behavior. A significant conclusion that emerges from this research is that the effect of parenting techniques and styles depends on a great many features of the child and the situation in which parent and child find themselves. Modern research clearly indicates that to talk of the impact of parenting techniques and styles is misleading unless one takes into account a wide variety of variables associated with the child and with the situation. After describing general research on techniques and styles, this section will therefore focus on specific variables that affect the outcomes of different techniques and styles.

Parenting Techniques

Parenting techniques include both those that are employed in response to the child's actions and those that occur independent of the child's actions in an attempt to facilitate socially acceptable behavior.

Discipline.   Much of the interest in discipline has been on the contrast between power assertive or punitive techniques and reasoning. Recent interest has focused on mediators, or events that occur as a result of a parenting technique and that, in turn, have an impact on children's actions. Krevans and Gibbs (1996), for example, noted that the link between a form of reasoning that directs children to consider how their behavior has affected others and increased prosocial responding is greater child empathy. A somewhat different perspective on discipline emerges in Patterson's work in its emphasis on contingency (Patterson, 1997; Patterson and Fisher, in Vol. 5 of this *Handbook*). This work demonstrates that effective (that is, contingent) punishment is a substantial positive predictor of compliant behavior, whereas explosive or abusive punishment and what he refers to as "nattering"— scolding or threats not backed up by effective punishment—are substantial negative predictors.

Monitoring.   Many studies have shown that parents who are knowledgeable about their children's activities and whereabouts are successful in promoting positive child behavior. Again, Patterson and his associates (among others) have demonstrated linkages between lack of parental knowledge and antisocial behavior. Presumably, monitoring enables parents to apply appropriate reinforcement and punishment contingencies as well as to protect their children from negative influences of a deviant peer group. Kerr and Statin (2000) have noted that parental monitoring is conceptualized as tracking and surveillance, whereas it is operationalized as knowledge of daily activities. By separating the latter into two components, surveillance and children's spontaneous disclosure of information, they demonstrated that the most powerful predictor of positive adolescent outcomes, including delinquency and school problems, was the willingness of children to inform their parents of their activities. Parental tracking and surveillance predicted positive adjustment only after the child's feelings of being controlled were partialed out. Indeed, children who felt controlled by their parents' monitoring were more likely to score high on indices of maladjustment. These results suggest that a parent–child relationship that facilitates open communication may be a better technique for promoting internalization of values than strict monitoring: They also underline the danger of imposing too much control on a child.

Rewards.   In Patterson's social interactional perspective, rewards for positive behavior have an important role to play in effective socialization. Theorists who focus on internalization, however, have regarded rewards, particularly those of a material nature, with suspicion because they undermine intrinsic motivation. Nevertheless, they are employed by parents. For example, mothers use pocket money to promote children's contributions to household work (Warton and Goodnow, 1995), regarding it as an acceptable, although less than ideal, way to obtain children's cooperation. Moreover, they seem to be able to convey the view that external rewards are and should be temporary: Children change from regarding payment for making a bed as reasonable at age 8 to unnecessary and even strange at age 11 (Warton and Goodnow, 1991). Social reinforcement is another way of responding positively to a child's actions, and it seems to have a less detrimental effect on intrinsic motivation than does material reward (Smith, Gelfand, Hartmann, and Partlow, 1979). Even more effective is attribution of prosocial actions to a child's disposition. This is a technique that, in contrast to social reinforcement, promotes positive behavior across a variety of related situations rather than in the training situation alone (Grusec and Redler, 1980).

Everyday routines. Goodnow (1997) stressed the importance of everyday routines as sources of information about values. Parents who wish to instill a principle of helping others, for example, might make volunteer work a formal part of family life, or enroll their child in a group where such volunteer work was part of the group's function. Reasoning and control would be unnecessary—habits would develop as a function of repetition or routine, with no feeling of coercion. The importance of routine is evident in a study which addressed the issue of children's work around the house. Parents often see household work as a way of teaching children a sense of social responsibility, but the results of studies attempting to link the assignment of household work to positive outcomes have been mixed. In an attempt to clarify the situation, Grusec, Goodnow, and Cohen (1997) compared children who did work around the house either on a routine basis or in response to a request from the parent, as well as those who helped with tasks that benefited the family (e.g., washing the dishes and taking out the garbage) or themselves (e.g., doing their own laundry). Doing family work on a routine basis was the only form of household work that was linked to greater evidence of general concern for others and prosocial action. Thus it may be that practice in assisting others that has become routinized is the combination that leads to habits of being helpful to others.

Prearming. Another socialization technique that parents use involves anticipating difficulties and preparing children for them. Studies of racial socialization provide an example. African American parents who live in racially mixed neighborhoods teach their children about the possibility of discrimination as well as about African American history and tradition. In addition, they talk about actual discrimination and ways of dealing with it (Hughes and Chen, 1997; McAdoo, in Vol. 5 of this *Handbook*; Thornton, Chatters, Taylor, and Allen, 1990).

Parenting Styles

Interest in Baumrind's formulation of styles of parenting continues unabated. Based on self-reports and school records of approximately 4,000 teenagers, Lamborn, Mounts, Steinberg, and Dornbusch (1991) found that those from authoritative families scored high on self-reliance, work orientation, self-esteem, personal competence, and school achievement, and low on substance use, delinquent and antisocial behaviors, anxiety, and depression. Children of authoritarian parents scored reasonably well on school achievement and lack of deviance but poorly on self-reliance and self-conceptions. Those of permissive parents scored poorly on school engagement, drug and alcohol use, and school misconduct, but they did well on social competence and self-confidence. Adolescents most negatively affected were those of neglectful parents, that is, parents who were hostile but who were not controlling. When the adolescents in their study were questioned again a year later, Steinberg, Lamborn, Darling, Mounts, and Dornbusch (1994) found that parenting practices continued to make a difference. Holding initial adjustment scores constant, they reported that differences in adjustment were maintained or increased over time, with the benefits of authoritative parenting largely in the maintenance of previous high levels of adjustment, but with the negative consequences of neglectful parenting continuing to accumulate.

In further work, Baumrind (1989, 1991) identified seven types of parenting style. These included authoritative, democratic, nondirective, authoritarian-directive, nonauthoritarian-directive, unengaged, and good enough. Adolescents from directive homes, where parents were controlling, firm, rejecting, and traditional, were low in social responsibility, conforming, and opposed drug use. Those from authoritarian homes, where parents were highly intrusive and directing, had worse outcomes than those from nonauthoritarian-directive homes. Those whose parents were unengaged had the lowest achievement scores and were the least well adjusted.

A number of studies have asked about the mediators or links between parenting style and child outcomes. Thus authoritativeness appears to be associated with adolescent work orientation, parental involvement in education, and parents' attributions of their children's failure to external causes or lack of ability (the latter predicting less time spent on homework). It appears that this set of variables is then responsible for poor academic performance (Glasgow, Dornbusch, Troyer, Steinberg, and Ritter, 1997; Steinberg, Elmen, and Mounts, 1989; Steinberg, Lamborn, Dornbusch, and Darling, 1992). Parental authoritativeness also seems to promote positive characteristics in adolescents that attract them to (and make them attractive to) well-adjusted peers who, in turn, reinforce their positive attitudes (Fletcher, Darling, Steinberg, and Dornbusch, 1995).

As noted earlier, parenting style can either fit into a category or be seen as lying along a continuum of parenting action. In many studies, then, parents are assessed on the extent to which they are accepting/responsive or rejecting and demanding/controlling or not, and these features are then related to child outcomes. Rothbaum and Weisz (1994) conducted a meta-analysis in which they considered the relations between children's externalizing behavior—aggression, hostility, and noncompliance—and a series of parenting variables that appear to cut across these parenting dimensions. Specifically, they considered a mixture of styles and practices: parental approval (the positive highlighting of desirable child actions); guidance (reasoning, clear messages, demonstrations of desired behaviors); motivational strategies (use of positive and fair incentives); synchrony (acknowledging and cooperating with the child's needs); coercive control (use of force, discouragement of autonomy); and restrictiveness (the placing of limits and constraints on the child's behavior). In a search of studies that have looked for linkages between these variables using factor analytic methods, Rothbaum and Weisz found that approval, guidance, motivational strategies, synchrony, and coercive control loaded on the dimension of acceptance/responsiveness. Restrictiveness (to be differentiated from control) loaded on an orthogonal dimension. Moreover, each of the five variables comprising the acceptance/responsiveness dimension individually related to children's externalizing behavior. Restrictiveness, however, was not related. Of even greater interest is the fact that, when two or more of the five acceptance variables were combined, the effect size and percentage of studies in which significant links between parenting and child outcome were found increased as a function of the number of aggregated variables. Such a finding, of course, underlines the usefulness of a categorical or typology approach to parenting in which combinations of actions appear to be better predictors than individual actions taken alone. (Not to be ignored in the Rothbaum and Weisz meta-analysis is their inclusion of studies that also demonstrated a marked impact of child actions on parenting behaviors, emphasizing once again that socialization is clearly a two-way process.)

Two outcomes of the Rothbaum and Weisz meta-analysis merit emphasis. The first has to do with their definition of parental control. Control has been a difficult concept for socialization theorists because they have disagreed about its importance in effective childrearing. Rothbaum and Weisz suggested that their conceptualization of acceptance/responsiveness captures the positive features of what proponents of high control have emphasized as well as what proponents of low control have emphasized. Those who recommend high control (e.g., Baumrind, 1971) emphasize the clarifying of limits, consistency of limits, and order keeping. Those who recommend low control (e.g., Lewis, 1981) emphasize following the child's lead and absence of force. The first is embodied in Rothbaum and Weisz's variable of guidance, the second in their variable of synchrony, and their results would suggest that both are important. A second outcome of the meta-analysis is its support for the notion that reciprocity and sensitivity to the child's needs are central features of effective parenting, a point made by attachment theorists in the context of the development of secure attachment but clearly extending to other aspects of the relationship between parents and children as well.

Variables Affecting the Impact of Parenting Styles and Discipline

Although, as seen above, there is some evidence for a link between parenting techniques and styles and child outcomes, the effects are far from consistent and generally low in magnitude (Grusec and Goodnow, 1994; Maccoby and Martin, 1983; Rothbaum and Weisz, 1994). The lack of strongly compelling evidence as well as the striking observation that parents are variable in how they react to their children's socialization needs (e.g., Grusec and Kuczynski, 1980; Zahn-Waxler and Chapman, 1982) has encouraged researchers in the last several years to search for variables that differentially affect the impact of parenting strategies and styles on child outcomes. These include the nature of the behavior to be modified, the child's age and sex, whether the parent is a mother or father, the child's temperament, and social class and culture. Each will be discussed in turn.

The nature of the child's misdeed. Mothers vary their discipline style as a function of the misdeed a child has committed. High-arousal behavior, such as rough and tumble play, tends to elicit power assertion alone, whereas violations of social conventions elicit reasoning alone (Trickett and Kuczynski, 1986). Power assertion and reasoning in combination are used in response to antisocial acts (e.g., lying or stealing), but reasoning alone is used in response to failures to show concern for others (Grusec, Dix, and Mills, 1982). Hoffman (1970) noted that different situations seemed to attract a particular form of discipline from parents, particularly mothers of children with a strong moral orientation. Smetana (1995) reported that authoritative mothers make appropriate distinctions among moral, social conventional, and personal issues, whereas authoritarian mothers moralize social conventional acts in their judgments and justifications and treat personal issues as if they were conventional and subject to parental interference. Trickett and Kuczynski (1986) found that physically abusive mothers relied primarily on power assertive interventions regardless of the child's misdeed, whereas nonabusive mothers tailored their interventions to the nature of the misdeed. The natural conclusion is that effective mothers, who show greater flexibility in their responding, may do so because such flexibility promotes better socialization. So far as this writer is aware there is as yet no direct evidence for this contention. However, there is evidence that children evaluate socialization interventions differently depending on the domain of the action in question. Reasoning that is domain-appropriate (e.g., focusing on harm to others in the case of moral transgressions and focusing on rules in the case of violations of social conventions) is more acceptable than that which is not, and punishment is seen as fairer in the case of moral transgressions than it is in the case of failures to be prosocial (Grusec and Pedersen, 1989; Nucci, 1984). If one assumes that perceptions of fairness and acceptability influence children to accept parental standards of behavior, then it would be reasonable to conclude that parental interventions need to be fitted appropriately to the situation in order for them to be effective.

Child's developmental status. A number of studies have demonstrated how children's level of cognitive development has an impact on their understanding of and reactions to different forms of discipline. Abstract reasoning has less effect on behavior suppression in younger than older children (Parke, 1974), and young children, who have a limited ability to decenter, find it difficult to deal with messages delivered in a sarcastic way (Bugental, Kaswan, and Love, 1970). Rothbaum and Weisz (1994), in their meta-analysis, found that the association between parenting behavior and externalizing behavior was greater for older children and adolescents than for toddlers and preschoolers. One explanation for this relation comes from findings that older children evaluate physical punishment from mothers less positively than do younger children, and that they regard increasing numbers of issues as personal ones over which parents do not have a right to exercise control (Siegal and Cowen, 1984; Smetana, 1988). The increase in aggression and noncompliance, then, could be a reflection of an increased unwillingness to see parental power assertion as fair or acceptable. Rothbaum and Weisz offered an explanation that complements this particular observation, suggesting that from preschool to middle childhood there is a shift from externalizing behavior that reflects primarily instrumental and autonomy-seeking motives to behavior that reflects more hostile motives. The latter is more likely to be identified as problematic. Rothbaum and Weisz also hypothesized that the apparent greater impact of negative parenting for older children is a reflection of the fact that, as time passes, the behaviors of parents and children become increasingly interwoven and mutual expectations develop that serve to further strengthen associations. Only further work can untangle the mechanisms operating in this particular case.

Child's sex. Rothbaum and Weisz reported that the link between parenting variables and child externalizing behavior is greater for boys than for girls, but only for preadolescents and only in analyses involving mothers. Their speculations about this outcome include several possibilities. Boys score higher on externalizing behaviors than do girls and, for this reason, may be more likely to become involved in coercive cycles of escalating negative behavior described by Patterson (1982). These coercive cycles are more prevalent with mothers than fathers and more frequent with preadolescents. Second, boys may be more genetically predisposed, given their high externalizing scores, to react negatively to stress such as repeated commands, which are more likely to come from mothers who are the primary caregivers. Finally, there is evidence that mothers react more negatively to sons' than daughters' aggression (Radke-Yarrow, Richters, and Wilson, 1988) and see it as associated with other unfavorable characteristics. Presumably the level of negative parenting behavior increases as a result, leading to greater opportunities for harmful outcomes. Leaper (in Vol. 1 of this *Handbook*) provides an extended discussion of differential parenting of boys and girls.

Parent's sex. Yet another variable that appears to interact with parenting characteristics and child outcomes is parent sex. The findings generally appear more marked for mothers than for fathers. Other-oriented induction is correlated with internalization for middle-income mothers but not fathers (Hoffman and Saltzstein, 1967). Maternal communicativeness about deviation relates to resistance to temptation in adolescent boys, whereas paternal communicativeness does not (LaVoie and Looft, 1973). Similarly, in their meta-analysis, Rothbaum and Weisz (1994) found a much stronger relation between parental responsivity and children's externalizing behavior for mothers than for fathers. (Rothbaum and Weisz noted an opposite effect in a meta-analysis conducted by Loeber and Stouthamer-Loeber, 1986, in a clinic-referred sample, suggesting that normal versus clinic-referred may be another variable that interacts in the socialization equation.) The greater impact of mothers may be simply a function of the fact that they are generally the primary caregivers. It may also be a result of the different styles of mothers and fathers, with mothers being more likely to use explanations, to question the circumstance surrounding their children's actions, and to look for mutually acceptable resolutions (Grusec and Goodnow, 1994). Given the generally more direct and power assertive approach of fathers, children may come to consider power assertion the norm for fathers and find it more acceptable. Indeed, the results of several studies indicate that children consider physical punishment to be more acceptable when it is administered by fathers than by mothers (Dadds, Sheffield, and Holbeck, 1990; Siegel and Barclay, 1985; Siegel and Cowen, 1984).

Child's temperament. Temperament, a constitutionally situated and early appearing feature of a given individual's characteristic emotional, motor, and attentional reactivity and self-regulation, has been linked to a variety of outcomes of interest to socialization theorists. For example, inhibition or fearfulness is linked to later internalizing behavior, whereas early impulsivity or unmanageability and irritability are linked more to externalizing problems. Parenting, however, makes an independent contribution to each of these outcomes. It is becoming clear from research, moreover, that temperament and parenting frequently interact to produce particular child outcomes and that the negative effects of difficult temperament can be modified by particular forms of parenting (Rothbart and Bates, 1998; Putnam, Sanson, and Rothbart, in Vol. 1 of this *Handbook*).

With respect to fearfulness or inhibition, Kochanska (1997a) reported that children who at an early age exhibit discomfort in strange situations, maintaining proximity to their mothers and showing reluctance to explore, show the usual positive relation between maternal use of gentle discipline deemphasizing power and conscience development. Those who are constitutionally fearless, however, do not: Their level of conscience development is better predicted by a mutually cooperative, responsive, and positive orientation with respect to their mothers. Kochanska suggested that gentle discipline for fearless children does not arouse an optimal level of discomfort for internalization, but that greater levels of power assertion (which presumably would be closer to an optimal level) also arouse reactance and hostility and therefore discourage internalization. (Less clear is why a mutually cooperative relationship is not a predictor of conscience in fearful children.) In accord with Kochanska's findings, Colder, Lochman, and Wells (1997) reported that temperamentally fearful boys with parents who used harsh discipline were more aggressive according to their teachers' ratings than either low-fear children with harsh parents or high-fear children with gentle parents.

Bates, Dodge, Pettit, and Ridge (1998) also considered interactions between features of parenting and children's temperament. Specifically, they focused on impulsivity and externalizing problems, operationalizing impulsivity as parental reports of resistance to control or noncompliance. They suggested that resistance to control reflects a relatively strong attraction to rewarding stimuli accompanied by excitement, a relatively weak level of basic social agreeableness, and difficulties in effortful control of attention and vigilance. The parenting variable they assessed was maternal restrictive control, which included prohibitions, warnings, and scoldings. In two separate longitudinal studies, Bates et al. (1998) found that children who were resistant to control as infants and toddlers were also more likely to have externalizing behavior problems in middle childhood, but only when their mothers were low in restrictive control. In the case of children with mothers who were high in restrictive control, early resistance was not predictive of later externalizing behavior problems. Inspection of the scatter plots provided in Bates et al. suggests that in some cases children who were high in resistance and had highly controlling mothers were better behaved than their counterparts who had mothers who were low in control, whereas in other cases they were worse behaved than their counterparts. With resistant children, then, the choice of optimal parenting strategy, in the form of control, may be more complex than it is in the case of children who are less resistant.

Park, Belsky, Putnam, and Crnic (1997) studied inhibition or negative emotional arousal, manifested in outcomes such as fearfulness and shyness. In a sample of boys, they assessed the parenting features of both mothers and fathers, particularly the extent to which parents were insensitive, intrusive, detached, and displayed negative rather than positive affect in their interactions with their children. Early inhibition predicted inhibition at 3 years of age. Moreover, parenting had an impact on 3-year inhibition, after the investigators controlled for extent of inhibition in infancy. However, the relation was strong only for children who were high in negativity, with negative parenting (insensitivity, detachment) negatively correlated with inhibition; that is, parents who were insensitive were more likely to have children who were less inhibited. Aside from demonstrating another temperament by parenting interaction, of course, this finding suggests that sensitive parenting is not always the optimal approach. Park et al. suggest that if parents are sensitive and accepting of inability to cope with stress and novelty they may actually promote the development of inhibition, whereas being less accepting constrains its development. Negative and intrusive parenting, on the other hand, sends the message that change is required. In this sense, then, such parenting can be considered sensitive, if sensitive is now defined not as a willingness to accept and respond positively to a child's actions, but in terms of finding the best way to achieve socialization goals (assuming high levels of inhibition are maladaptive and therefore change worthy). Similarly, we see with the Bates et al. study (1998) that use of prohibitions, warnings, and scoldings may be sensitive parenting for some children in the sense that it achieves more positive outcomes for them. This issue will arise again later in this chapter when an attempt is made to describe the essence of effective parenting.

Child's attachment classification. Previously noted was the fact that relatively fearless children who have a positive relationship with their mothers show higher levels of conscience development. An interaction between attachment and maternal control appears in the work of Allen, Moore, Kuperminc, and Bell (1998). They report that higher levels of actual control by mothers over areas such as friends, intellectual interests, school activities, and sexual behavior are associated with lower levels of externalizing behavior for adolescents who have an autonomous or preoccupied attachment status as assessed by the Adult Attachment Interview. They found no relation for insecure/nonpreoccupied adolescents. Similarly, high maternal control was linked to lower levels of peer-reported delinquency primarily for adolescents who had secure attachment organizations.

Culture and social class. The picture with respect to parenting styles and practices is further complicated when the results of research conducted in different socioeconomic and cultural contexts is considered. Authoritative parenting, although most strongly associated with academic achievement among European American adolescents, is least effective in promoting the academic achievement of Asian American and African American adolescents. Moreover, Asian American and African American parents are more likely to exhibit authoritarian parenting (Dornbusch, Ritter, Leiderman, Roberts, and Fraleigh, 1987; Steinberg, Mounts, Lamborn, and Dornbusch, 1991). Differences have also been observed in the use of power-assertive discipline techniques in lower socioeconomic contexts, with no strong apparent negative impact on children's social and emotional outcomes. In the case of cultural differences, Chao (1994) argued that the observed greater frequency among Asian parents of authoritarian parenting represents a misunderstanding of Asian parenting practices. She demonstrated that, although immigrant Chinese mothers do indeed score higher on standard self-report measures of authoritarianism, this score reflects something different from North American authoritarianism, with its no longer socially acceptable Puritan implications of harshness and breaking of the child's will. In the Chinese culture it reflects a focus on the importance of training children and of parental responsibility for being highly involved, caring, and concerned. Rudy and Grusec (2001) further support the idea that parents who endorse high authoritarianism in different cultures are not always similar in other variables usually related to this form of parenting. They report that, although Egyptian Canadians (who, like Asians, tend to be collectivist rather than individualist in orientation) do indeed endorse authoritarian practices more highly than Anglo-Canadians, they do not exhibit the same pattern of relations between authoritarianism and other variables that are seen among Western individuals. Thus, for Anglo-Canadians, high authoritarianism predicted low warmth and low feelings of control in difficult childrearing situations, both variables that have been associated with negative child outcomes. For the Egyptian Canadians, however, there was no relation between authoritarianism and warmth or relative control.

Brody and Flor (1998) shed further light on the different meanings of controlling or authoritarian parenting in different cultural contexts. In a study of 6- to 9-year-old children from largely poor, single-parent African American families, they identified a form of parenting they labeled "no nonsense"—parenting consisting of highly controlling intervention including physical restraint, accompanied by maternal warmth. This style, seeming to fall between authoritarianism and authoritativeness, was most likely to lead to greater cognitive and social competence and fewer internalizing problems in children, with these outcomes mediated by the child's ability to self-regulate, that is, to plan ahead, stay on task, and think ahead of time about the consequences of actions.

Why do authoritarian parenting and power assertive practices appear more frequently in some cultural contexts than others? It has been argued that in Asian cultures they may reflect greater emphasis on respect for authority. More controlling practices in lower-socioeconomic contexts represent an adaptive response to cultures that are more dangerous and where the opportunities for involvement in antisocial activities are more frequent. It may well be, however, that the association of these practices with a sense of responsibility for teaching children or with warmth and affection may render them less harmful than when they do not appear to the child to reflect parental warmth and concern but rather rejection. The research picture is not entirely consistent, however. Thus, Chen,

Dong, and Zhou (1997) report that children from the People's Republic of China are less socially competent, more aggressive, and do less well in school when their parents are authoritarian, whereas authoritative parenting is linked to positive outcomes.

SOME QUESTIONS ABOUT SOCIALIZATION ANSWERED

Many questions have been raised in the course of this chapter. In this section an attempt is made to answer some of these questions. The questions are: What is the basic nature of children? What is the most effective way to socialize children? Is effective parenting sensitive and responsive parenting? and Which theory of parenting and socialization is the most useful one for guiding parenting behavior?

What is the basic nature of children?   The answer to this is now quite clear from the research on temperament. It is evident that parents begin their task of socialization with children with a variety of basic natures. Some children are more compliant by nature, some are more difficult by nature, and some fall in between. There is no common human basic nature.

What is the most effective way to socialize children?   An answer to this question must take into account substantial basic individual differences and acknowledge that what works for one child will not work for another. Not only does the biologically directed nature of the child need to be considered in an analysis of effective parenting, but so too, as noted above, do a number of other factors having to do with features of the child and of the situation. Thus, Grusec et al. (2000) have argued that effective parenting consists of constant appraisal and flexible behavior in the face of constantly changing features of children and of situations. Parents must be aware of the characteristics of their children and how their children will react, and willing and able to tailor their actions accordingly. In support of this position there is evidence that accurate knowledge of children is related to positive child outcomes. For example, mothers who are high in empathic perspective taking are more likely to have mutually responsive relationships—an antecedent of child compliance—with young children (Kochanska, 1997b) and to be more responsive to adolescents (Gondoli and Silverberg, 1997). Parents who accurately perceive their adolescent's thoughts and feelings during the course of a disagreement experience fewer conflicts overall in the case of fathers and greater satisfaction with the outcome of the disagreement in the case of mothers (Hastings and Grusec, 1997).

Is effective parenting sensitive and responsive parenting?   Current conceptualizations of effective parenting put major emphasis on parental sensitivity and responsiveness to children's needs and an ability to accommodate to those needs as well as to guide children's behavior where appropriate. This is really the essence of Baumrind's authoritative parenting style. As well, it captures the spirit of Rothbaum's and Weisz's (1994) analysis of the parenting literature and is in keeping with the strong emphasis on the importance of relationships in socialization. It could be used as well to characterize Grusec et al.'s (2000) description of the effective parent as appraising and flexible. But the term is vague at best and not clearly operationalized. The importance of caution in its use is evident in a recent comparison by Rothbaum, Weisz, Pott, Miyake, and Morelli (2000) of the essence of sensitive parenting in two different cultures—the American and the Japanese. Rothbaum et al. point out that in Western cultures sensitivity, as described by attachment theory, consists of behaviors that encourage the Western emphasis on autonomy. Thus, sensitive parents are those who avoid imposing their will, who value autonomy in their children, and who encourage feelings of efficacy and value the fact the child has a will of her or his own. Sensitivity in Japan stands in sharp contrast. A sensitive Japanese mother anticipates situations and protects her infant from excessive emotional stress. She does not wait to see what the needs of the infant might be. Thus, for Japanese mothers, sensitivity means responsiveness to the child's need for social engagement whereas, for American mothers, it is responsiveness to needs for individuation.

In a similar vein, Bornstein et al. (1992) note the differential manifestation of mothers' responsiveness to eye-to-eye contact with their infants: Japanese mothers use it to maintain dyadic interaction and to consolidate and strengthen mutual dependence, whereas American mothers use it to promote extradyadic interaction and independence. This confounding of goals with parenting actions is clear as well in the findings of Park et al. (1997) previously described. They noted that parents who were sensitively responsive (in North American terms) to children's fearful behavior were less successful than those who were more intrusive, because this intrusiveness communicated that inhibited behavior was undesirable. In this case, as well as with Japanese parents, sensitive parenting was essentially the ability to optimally achieve desired socialization outcomes. This conclusion mirrors that of Grusec et al. (2000), that effective parenting is sensitive and responsive parenting in the sense that it involves knowledge and understanding of the child and a willingness to apply that knowledge and understanding to accomplish preferred ends.

Which theory of childrearing is most useful in guiding parenting behavior?   If effective parenting is knowing how to achieve what one wants with one's particular child, where do external control, internal control, and relationship theories fit? One suggestion is that the three theoretical approaches may be seen as reflections of three different goals parents might have in mind when dealing with a particular child in a particular situation. Hastings and Grusec (1998) established that parents in fact do have different goals depending on the context. These goals are either parent centered, where parents want their children to change their behavior or to be obedient and respectful; child centered, where parents want to make their children happy or teach them values; or relationship centered, where parents want to build trust and close connections. Importantly, different goals are accompanied by different parenting actions. Thus parent-centered goals are associated more with punishment, child-centered goals with reasoning, and relationship-centered goals with negotiation, compromise, and acceptance of the child's behavior. It may be, then, that theories advocating particular parenting actions do so because they are focused on specific goals. Patterson's emphasis on contingencies and effective use of punishment reflects a focus on behavior change. Hoffman's emphasis on reasoning reflects a focus on the teaching of values. Attachment theory's emphasis on compromise and acceptance reflects a focus on the building of trust and ultimately on the child's belief that parental demands are made in the best interests of the child. Each theory, then, provides a guide for effective parenting depending on the particular goal the parent has in a particular situation.

FUTURE DIRECTIONS IN PARENT SOCIALIZATION

In the last decade researchers have begun to make significant modifications in the theoretical approaches that have guided thinking about socialization as well as employing increasingly sophisticated methodological approaches that enable statements about the role of parenting in socialization to be made with some degree of assuredness. The next generation of research on parenting and socialization will build on these foundations. At the moment, developmentalists are only beginning to understand how biology, context, and environment interact, and the amount of variance explained in studies is generally not large. Studies that have large sample sizes, that consider a number of variables in interaction, and that are longitudinal in design will help to untangle the specific contributions of parent and child to the socialization process. Large samples allow the use of causal modeling techniques that begin to suggest the relative contributions of parent and child at given points in time to various outcomes having to do with socialization.

The problem of direction of causation has been a particularly nagging one in the area of parenting. Increasingly, however, research designs have moved the study of parenting to the point where it is actually possible to talk about the extent to which parents and children both contribute to a particular outcome. Often the point is to demonstrate that parents have an impact once the statistical analysis allows for the control of child characteristics. The time has now come, however, for a more elaborate analysis of how and when children actually do affect parents. Few studies have addressed this issue directly. Several years ago, Lytton (1980) reported that children's impact on parents was substantially greater in the area of attachment than it was in the area of control. Reuter and Conger (1998) demonstrated that nurturant and harsh parenting behavior each affected both flexible and disruptive adolescent problem solving. In turn, however, while disruptive adolescents made their parents less nurturant and more harsh, flexible adolescents had no impact on parental behavior. This finding suggests that, in problem-solving situations, adolescents are affected by all aspects of parental behavior but that parents, while vulnerable to children's negative actions, are seemingly unaffected by their positive ones. These sorts of results have important implications for understanding the socialization process and knowledge in this area needs considerable expansion.

A final event that will have an impact on future research in the area of parenting and socialization involves the significant advances that are being made in the field of molecular genetics and the identification of associations between genes and complex behavioral traits (Plomin and Rutter, 1998). Once researchers interested in parenting and socialization are able to identify the specific genetic features of a particular child, the major developmental task of unraveling the complex interplay between the nature of the child and that child's experience will be able to move forward with unprecedented efficiency.

Clearly, future research will move beyond either/or notions that frequently have characterized ideas about parenting and socialization, and the heated arguments that have taken place about the relative importance of parents, peers, genes, and the wider social context, including the media and school. As Collins et al. (2000) observe, we now know that the impact of parents on children is not as straightforward and unambiguous as early researchers believed. We also know, however, that it is not insubstantial as some current critics claim (e.g., Harris, 1995; Rowe, 1994). People often look for simple answers, but there are no simple answers when it comes to the complexities of parenting and socialization.

CONCLUSIONS

The main conclusion of this chapter is that arguments about the most effective way to assist children in taking on the values and attitudes of society cannot be made in terms of prescribed techniques, actions, or general styles. To characterize effectiveness as the employment of predominantly rational as opposed to power assertive interventions, or of control of environmental contingencies, or of warmth, or of sensitivity to children's emotional distress, or of the exercise of firm control with some degree of responsiveness is to misrepresent the present state of knowledge. If socialization of values involves accurate perception of parental messages and a willingness to accept those messages and act in accord with them (see Grusec and Goodnow, 1994), then it is evident that accurate perception and acceptance depend on interactions between specific parenting approaches and a wide variety of variables. These variables include features of the child, of the parent, and of the situation in which socialization occurs. This is not to say that certain approaches to parenting may not be of universal significance. Human beings, as a result of their biological makeup, may not respond well to coercive control, and they may not function optimally if they do not trust others to protect them from harm and guide them in appropriate directions. The foundation of successful socialization may indeed lie in a secure relationship with the caregiver and in minimization of feelings of forced compliance. But the events that produce feelings of trust and of freely chosen action (with the latter including either a degree of autonomy from the group or interdependence with the group) can vary considerably. Effective parents, then, are those who both understand their children and are able to respond to that understanding in a way that will accomplish the goals they have in mind: obedience and compliance, the long-term acquisition of values, or the negotiation and construction of values that is more likely to come from a goal that emphasizes mutual satisfaction.

The present analysis of socialization, of course, is bidirectional in the sense that it acknowledges the input of the child and the necessity for the parent to accommodate to that input. In addition, it must not be forgotten that parents themselves are reactive to the input of their children, and that this input may either facilitate or interfere with the effective problem solving that good parenting involves.

REFERENCES

Allen, J. P., Moore, C., Kuperminc, G., and Bell, K. (1998). Attachment and adolescent psychosocial functioning. *Child Development, 69*, 1406–1419.

Applegate, J. L., Burke, J. A., Burleson, B. R., Delia, J. G., and Kline, S. L. (1985). Reflection-enhancing parental communication. In I. E. Sigel (Ed.), *Parental belief systems* (pp. 107–142). Hillsdale, NJ: Lawrence Erlbaum Associates.

Bates, J. E., Dodge, K. A., Pettit, G. S., and Ridge, B. (1998). Interaction of temperamental resistance to control and restrictive parenting in the development of externalizing behavior. *Developmental Psychology, 34*, 982–985.

Baumrind, D. (1971). Current patterns of parental authority. *Developmental Psychology Monographs, 4* (1, Pt. 2).

Baumrind, D. (1989). Rearing competent children. In W. Damon (Ed.), *New directions for child development: Child development, today and tomorrow* (pp. 349–378). San Francisco: Jossey-Bass.

Baumrind, D. (1991). Parenting styles and adolescent development. In R. Lerner, A. C. Petersen, and J. Brooks-Gunn (Eds.), *The encyclopedia on adolescence* (pp. 746–758). New York: Garland.

Bell, R. Q. (1968). A reinterpretation of the direction of effects in studies of socialization. *Psychological Review, 75*, 81–95.

Bornstein, M., Tamis-LeMonda, C. S., Tal, J., Ludemann, P., Toda, S., Rahn, C. W., Pecheux, M.-G., Azuma, H., and Vardi, D. (1992). Maternal responsiveness to infants in three societies: The United States, France, and Japan. *Child Development, 63*, 808–821.

Bowlby, J. (1969). *Attachment and loss: Vol. 1. Attachment.* New York: Basic Books.

Brody, G. H., and Flor, D. L. (1998). Maternal resources, parenting practices, and child competence in rural, single-parent African American families. *Child Development, 69*, 803–816.

Bugental, D., and Goodnow, J. J. (1998). Socialization processes: Biological, cognitive, and social-cultural perspectives. In W. Damon (Ed.), *Handbook of child psychology* (Vol. 4, pp. 389–462). New York: Wiley.

Bugental, D. B., Kaswan, J. W., and Love, L. R. (1970). Perceptions of contradictory messages conveyed by verbal and nonverbal channels. *Journal of Personality and Social Psychology, 16*, 647–655.

Chao, R. K. (1994). Beyond parental control and authoritarian parenting style: Understanding Chinese parenting through the cultural notion of training. *Child Development, 65*, 1111–1119.

Chen, X., Dong, Q., and Zhou, H. (1997). Authoritative and authoritarian parenting practices and social and school performance in Chinese children. *International Journal of Behavioural Development, 21*, 855–873.

Collins, W. A., Maccoby, E. E., Steinberg, L., Hetherington, E. M., and Bornstein, M. H. (2000). Contemporary research on parenting: The case for nature and nurture. *American Psychologist, 55*, 218–232.

Colder, C. R., Lochman, J. E., and Wells, K. C. (1997). The moderating effects of children's fear and activity level on relations between parenting practices and childhood symptomatology. *Journal of Abnormal Child Psychology, 25*, 251–263.

Dadds, M. R., Sheffield, J. K., and Holbeck, J. F. (1990). An examination of the differential relationship of marital discord to parents' discipline strategies for boys and girls. *Journal of Abnormal Child Psychology, 18*, 121–129.

Darling, N., and Steinberg, L. (1993). Parenting style as context: An integrative model. *Psychological Bulletin, 113*, 487–496.

Deci, E. L., and Ryan, R. M. (1991). A motivational approach to self: Integration in personality. In R. Dienstbier (Ed.), *Nebraska Symposium on Motivation: Vol. 38. Perspectives on motivation* (pp. 237–288). Lincoln: University of Nebraska Press.

Devereux, E. C. (1970). The role of peer-group experience in moral development. In J. P. Hill (Ed.), *Minnesota symposia on child psychology* (Vol. 4, pp. 94–140). Minneapolis: University of Minnesota Press.

Dornbusch, S., Ritter, P., Leiderman, P., Roberts, D., and Fraleigh, M. (1987). The relation of parenting style to adolescent school performance. *Child Development, 58*, 1244–1257.

Fletcher, A. C., Darling, N. E., Steinberg, L., and Dornbusch, S. M. (1995). The company they keep: Relation of adolescents' adjustment and behavior to their friends' perceptions of authoritative parenting in the social network. *Developmental Psychology, 31*, 300–310.

Glasgow, K. L., Dornbusch, S. M., Troyer, L., Steinberg, L., and Ritter, P. L. (1997). Parenting styles, adolescents' attributions, and educational outcomes in nine heterogeneous high schools. *Child Development, 68*, 507–529.

Goldberg, S., Grusec, J. E., and Jenkins, J. (1999). Confidence in protection: another look at attachment and other components of intimate relationships. *Journal of Family Psychology, 13*, 475–483.

Gondoli, D. M., and Silverberg, S. B. (1997). Maternal emotional distress and diminished responsiveness: the mediating role of parenting efficacy and parental perspective taking. *Developmental Psychology, 33*, 861–868.

Goodnow, J. J. (1994). Acceptable disagreement across generations. In J. Smetana (Ed.), *Beliefs about parenting* (pp. 51–64). San Francisco: Jossey-Bass.

Goodnow, J. J. (1997). Parenting and the transmission and internalization of values: From social-cultural perspectives to within-family analyses. In J. E. Grusec and L. Kuczynski (Eds.), *Handbook of parenting and the transmission of values* (pp. 333–361). New York: Wiley.

Grusec, J. E. (1997). A history of research on parenting strategies and children's internalization of values. In J .E. Grusec and L. Kuczynski (Eds.), *Parenting and the internalization of values: A handbook of contemporary theory* (pp. 3–22). New York: Wiley.

Grusec, J. E., Dix, T., and Mills, R. (1982). The effects of type, severity and victim of children's transgressions on maternal discipline. *Canadian Journal of Behavioural Science, 14*, 276–289.

Grusec, J. E., and Goodnow, J. J. (1994). Impact of parental discipline methods on the child's internalization of values: A reconceptualization of current points of view. *Developmental Psychology, 30*, 4–19.

Grusec, J. E., Goodnow, J. J., and Cohen, L. (1997). Household work and the development of children's concern for others. *Developmental Psychology, 32*, 999–1007.

Grusec, J. E., Goodnow, J. J., and Kuczyniski, L. (2000). New directions in analyses of parenting contributions to children's acquisition of values. *Child Development, 71*, 205–211.

Grusec, J. E., and Kuczynski, L. (1980). Direction of effect in socialization: A comparison of the parent vs. the child's behavior as determinants of disciplinary techniques. *Developmental Psychology, 16*, 1–9.

Grusec, J. E., and Pedersen, L. (1989, April). *Children's thinking about prosocial and moral behavior.* Paper presented at the Biennial Meeting of the Society for Research in Child Development, Kansas City, KS.

Grusec, J. E., and Redler, E. (1980). Attribution, reinforcement, and altruism: A developmental analysis. *Developmental Psychology, 16*, 525–534.

Harris, J. R. (1995). Where is the child's environment? A group socialization theory of development. *Psychological Review, 102*, 458–489.

Hastings, P., and Grusec, J. E. (1997). Conflict outcomes as a function of parental accuracy in perceiving child cognitions and affect. *Social Development, 6*, 76–90.

Hastings, P., and Grusec, J. E. (1998). Parenting goals as organizers of responses to parent–child disagreement. *Developmental Psychology, 34*, 465–479.

Hill, J. P., and Holmbeck, G. N. (1986). Attachment and autonomy during adolescence. *Annals of Child Development, 3*, 145–189.

Hobbes, T. (1885). *Leviathan.* London: Routledge. (Original work published 1651.)

Hoffman, M. L. (1970). Moral development. In P. H. Mussen (Ed.), *Carmichael's manual of child psychology* (Vol. 2, pp. 261–360). New York: Wiley

Hoffman, M. L. (1983). Affective and cognitive processes in moral internalization. In E. T. Higgins, D. Ruble, and W. Hartup (Eds.), *Social cognition and social development: A socio-cultural perspecctive* (pp. 236–274). Cambridge, England: Cambridge University Press.

Hoffman, M. L., and Saltzstein, H. D. (1967). Parent discipline and the child's moral development. *Journal of Personality and Social Psychology, 5*, 45–57.

Holden, G. W., and Edwards, L. A. (1989). Parental attitudes toward child rearing: Instruments, issues, and implications. *Psychological Bulletin, 106*, 1–29.

Hughes, D., and Chen, L. (1997). *When and what parents tell children about race: An examination of race-related socialization in African American families.* Unpublished manuscript, Department of Psychology, New York University.

Kasser, T., and Ryan, R. M. (1996). Further examining the American dream: Differential correlates of intrinsic and extrinsic goals. *Personality and Social Psychology Bulletin, 22*, 281–288.

Kerr, M., and Stattin, H. (2000). What parents know, how they know it, and several forms of adolescent adjustment: Further support for a reinterpretation of monitoring. *Child Development, 36*, 366–380.

Kochanska, G. (1997a). Multiple pathways to conscience for children with different temperaments: From toddlerhood to age 5. *Developmental Psychology, 33*, 228–240.

Kochanska, G. (1997b). Mutually responsive orientation between mothers and their young children: Implications for early socialization. *Child Development, 68*, 94–112.

Krevans, J., and Gibbs, J. C. (1996). Parents' use of inductive discipline: Relations to children's empathy and prosocial behavior. *Child Development, 67*, 3263–3277.

Kuczynski, L., and Grusec, J. E. (1997). Future directions for a theory of parental socialization. In J. E. Grusec and L. Kuczynski (Eds.), *Parenting and the internalization of values: A handbook of contemporary theory* (pp. 399–414). New York: Wiley.

Kuczynski, L., and Hildebrandt, N. (1997). Models of conformity and resistance in socialization theory. In J. E. Grusec and L. Kuczynski (Eds.), *Parenting and the internalization of values: A handbook of contemporary theory* (pp. 227–256). New York: Wiley.

Lamborn, S. D., Mounts, N. S., Steinberg, L., and Dornbusch, S. M. (1991). Patterns of competence and adjustment among adolescents from authoritative, authoritarian, indulgent, and neglectful families. *Child Development, 62*, 1049–1065.

LaVoie, J. C., and Looft, W. R. (1973). Parental antecedents of resistance-to-temptation behavior in adolescents. *Merrill-Palmer Quarterly, 19*, 107–116.

Lepper, M. (1983). Social control processes, attributions of motivation, and the internalization of social values. In E. T. Higgins, D. N. Ruble, and W. W. Hartup (Eds.), *Social cognition and social development: A sociocultural perspective* (pp. 294–330). New York: Cambridge University Press.

Lewin, K., Lippitt, R., and White, R. K. (1938). Patterns of aggressive behavior in experimentally created "social climates." *Journal of Social Psychology, 10*, 271–299.

Lewis, C. C. (1981). The effects of parental firm control: Reinterpretation of findings. *Psychological Bulletin, 90*, 547–563.

Locke, J. (1884). *Some thoughts concerning education.* London: Clay. (Original work published 1693.)

Loeber, R., and Stouthamer-Loeber, J. (1986). Family factors as correlates and predictors of juvenile conduct problems and delinquency. In M. Tonry and N. Morris (Eds.), *Crime and justice* (Vol. 7, pp. 219–339). Chicago: University of Chicago Press.

Lytton, H. (1980). *Parent–child interaction: The socialization process observed in twin and singleton families.* New York: Plenum.

Maccoby, E. E. (1992). Trends in the study of socialization: Is there a Lewinian heritage? *Journal of Social Issues, 48*, 171–185.

Maccoby, E. E., and Martin, J. A. (1983). Socialization in the context of the family: Parent–child interaction. In E. M. Hetherington (Ed.), *Handbook of child psychology* (4th ed., Vol. 4, pp. 1–102). New York: Wiley.

Markus, H. R., and Kitayama, S. (1991). Culture and the self: Implications for cognition, emotion, and motivation. *Psychological Review, 98*, 224–253.

Newson, J., and Newson, E. (1974). Cultural aspects of childrearing in the English-speaking world. In M. P. M. Richards (Ed.), *The integration of a child into a social world* (pp. 53–82). London: Cambridge University Press.

Nucci, L. (1984). Evaluating teachers as social agents: Students' ratings of domain appropriate and domain inappropriate teacher responses to transgression. *American Educational Research Journal, 21*, 367–378.

Park, S.-Y., Belsky, J., Putnam, S., and Crnic, K. (1997). Infant emotionality, parenting, and three-year inhibition: Exploring stability and lawful discontinuity in a male sample. *Developmental Psychology, 33*, 218–227.

Parke, R. D. (1974). Rules, roles, and resistance to deviation: Recent advances in punishment, discipline, and self-control. In A. Pick (Ed.), *Minnesota Symposia on Child Psychology* (Vol. 8, pp. 111–143). Minneapolis: University of Minnesota Press.

Parke, R. D., and Buriel, R. (1998). Socialization in the family: Ethnic and ecological perspectives. In W. Damon and N. Eisenberg (Eds.), *Handbook of child psychology: Social, emotional, and personality development* (Vol. 3, pp. 463–552). New York: Wiley.

Patterson, G. R. (1982). *Coercive family process.* Eugene, OR: Castalia Press.

Patterson, G. R. (1997). Performance models for parenting: A social interactional perspective. In J. E. Grusec and L. Kuczynski (Eds.), *Parenting and the internalization of values: A handbook of contemporary theory* (pp. 193–226). New York: Wiley.

Plomin, R., and Rutter, M. (1998). Child development, molecular genetics, and what to do with genes once they are found. *Child Development, 69*, 1223–1242.

Radke-Yarrow, M., Richters, J., and Wilson, W. E. (1988). Child development in a network of relationships. In R. Hinde and J. Stevenson-Hinde (Eds.), *Relationships within families* (pp. 48–67). Oxford, England: Clarendon.

Reuter, M. A., and Conger, R. D. (1998). Reciprocal influences between parenting and adolescent problem-solving. *Developmental Psychology, 34*, 1470–1482.

Rheingold, H. (1969). The social and socializing infant. In D. A. Goslin (Ed.), *Handbook of socialization theory and research* (pp. 779–790). Chicago: Rand McNally.

Rothbart, M., and Bates, J. (1998). Temperament. In W. Damon and N. Eisenberg (Eds.), *Handbook of child psychology: Social, emotional, and personality development* (Vol. 3, pp. 105–176). New York: Wiley.

Rothbaum, F., and Weisz, J. R. (1994). Parental caregiving and child externalizing behavior in nonclinical samples: A meta-analysis. *Psychological Bulletin, 116*, 55–74.

Rothbaum, F., Weisz, J. R., Pott, M., Miyake, K., and Morelli, G. (2000). Attachment and culture: Security in the United States and Japan. *American Psychologist, 55*, 1093–1104.

Rousseau, J. J. (1974). *Emile, or on education.* London: Dent. (Original work published 1762.)

Rowe, D. (1994). *The limits of family influence: Genes, experience, and behavior.* New York: Guilford.

Rudy, D., and Grusec, J. E. (2001). Correlates of authoritarian parenting in individualist and collectivist cultures and implication for understanding the transmission of values. *Journal of Cross-Cultural Psychology, 32*, 202–212.

Sears, R. R. (1951). A theoretical framework for personality and social behavior. *American Psychologist, 6*, 476–483.

Sears, R. R., Maccoby, E. E., and Levin, H. (1957). Patterns of child rearing. Evanston, IL: Row Peterson.

Siegal, M., and Barclay, M. S. (1985). Children's evaluations of fathers' socialization behavior. *Developmental Psychology, 21*, 1090–1096.

Siegal, M., and Cowen, J. (1984). Appraisals of intervention: The mother's versus the culprit's behavior as determinants of children's evaluations of discipline techniques. *Child Development, 55*, 1760–1766.

Smetana, J. (1988). Adolescents' and parents' conceptions of parental authority. *Child Development, 59*, 321–335.

Smetana, J. (1995). Parenting styles and conceptions of parental authority during adolescence. *Child Development, 66*, 299–316.

Smetana, J. (1997). Parenting and the development of social knowledge reconceptualized: A social domain analysis. In J. E. Grusec and L. Kuczynski (Eds.), *Parenting and the internalization of values: A handbook of contemporary theory* (pp. 162–192). New York: Wiley.

Smith, C. L., Gelfand, D. M., Hartmann, D. P., and Partlow, M. E. P. (1979). Children's causal attributions regarding help giving. *Child Development, 50*, 203–210.

Stayton, D., Hogan, R., and Ainsworth, M. D. S. (1971). Infant obedience and maternal behavior: The origins of socialization reconsidered. *Child Development, 42*, 1057–1070.

Steinberg, L., Elmen, J., and Mounts, N. (1989). Authoritative parenting, psychosocial maturity, and academic success among adolescents. *Child Development, 60*, 1424–1436.

Steinberg, l., Lamborn, S. D., Darling, N., Mounts, N. S., and Dornbusch, S. M. (1994). Over-time changes in adjustment and competence among adolescents from authoritative, authoritarian, indulgent, and neglectful famlies. *Child Development, 65*, 754–770.

Steinberg, L., Lamborn, S., Dornbusch, S., and Darling, N. (1992). Impact of parenting practices on adolescent achievement: Authoritative parenting, school involvement, and encouragement to succeed. *Child Development, 63*, 1266–1281.

Steinberg, L., Mounts, N., Lamborn, S., and Dornbusch, S. (1991). Authoritative parenting and adolescent adjustment across varied ecological niches. *Journal of Research on Adolescence, 1*, 19–36.

Thornton, M. C., Chatters, L. M., Taylor, R. J., and Allen, W. R. (1990). Sociodemographic and environmental correlates of racial socialization by Black parents. *Child Development, 61*, 401–409.

Trickett, P., and Kuczynski, L. (1986). Children's misbehavior and parental discipline in abusive and non-abusive families. *Developmental Psychology, 22*, 115–123.

Turiel, E. (1983). Interaction and development in social cognition. In E. T. Higgins, D. Ruble, and W. Hartup (Eds.), *Social cognition and social development: A socio-cultural perspecctive* (pp. 333–355). Cambridge, England: Cambridge University Press.

Warton, P. M., and Goodnow, J. J. (1991). The nature of responsibility: Children's understanding of "your job." *Child Development, 62*, 156–165.

Warton, P. M., and Goodnow, J. J. (1995). Money and children's household jobs: Parents' views of their interconnections. *International Journal of Behavioral Development, 18*, 235–350.

Zahn-Waxler, C., and Chapman, M. (1982). Immediate antecedents of caretakers' methods of discipline. *Child Psychiatry and Human Development, 12*, 179–192.

7

How Parents Can Maximize Children's Cognitive Abilities

Wendy M. Williams
Cornell University
Robert J. Sternberg
Yale University

INTRODUCTION

I took a good deal o' pains with his eddication, sir; let him run in the streets when he was very young, and shift for hisself. It's the only way to make a boy sharp, sir.

—Charles Dickens, *The Pickwick Papers*, 1836

If children grew up according to early indications, we should have nothing but geniuses.

—Goethe

Too often we give children answers to remember rather than problems to solve.

—Roger Lewin

When I was a kid my parents moved a lot ... but I always found them.

—Rodney Dangerfield

When asked, most parents state that they seek to maximize their children's abilities, whether cognitive, social, emotional, or physical. But how, precisely, can parents accomplish this goal? What actions should be a part of their daily routine? The information parents receive about exactly how to maximize their children's abilities takes many forms and comes from many sources: pediatricians and other medical experts; family members and friends; television shows, books, and magazines; and teachers and other parents. The quality of this information varies widely, and in fact some or even much of what parents hear (and do) may work against the best interests of their children, as the above quote from a Dickens classic well illustrates.

TABLE 7.1
Ten Lessons for Parents for Maximizing their Children's Cognitive Abilities

Lesson *1*:	Recognize what can and cannot be changed in your children.	
Lesson *2*:	Aim to *meaningfully challenge* your children, not bore them and not overwhelm them.	
Lesson *3*:	Teach children that the main limitation on what they *can* do is what they tell themselves they *can't* do.	
Lesson *4*:	Remember that it is more important that children learn what questions to ask, and how to ask them, than that they learn what the answers to questions are.	
Lesson *5*:	Help children find what really excites them, remembering that it may not be what really excites you or what you wish would really excite them.	
Lesson *6*:	Encourage children to take sensible intellectual risks.	
Lesson *7*:	Teach children to take responsibility for themselves—both for their successes *and* for their failures.	
Lesson *8*:	Teach children how to delay gratification—to be able to wait for rewards.	
Lesson *9*:	Teach children to put themselves in another's place.	
Lesson *10*:	Remember that it is *not* the amount of money you spend on your child that matters, but rather the quality of your interactions with your child and the nature of your child's experiences.	

In this chapter we present ten lessons for parents who wish to maximize their children's cognitive potential. These lessons are based on rigorous empirical evidence from a range of disciplines and are designed to be placed into immediate practical use. The science behind the lessons is intriguing, but it is not necessary to become mired in facts and figures to benefit from the lessons we present: Each one can be put into use today to help children make the most of their abilities. Our goal is to cut through the misinformation and disinformation and equip parents with meaningful tools useful in rearing competent and successful children.

We argue in this chapter that there are, in fact, many things parents can do to foster cognitive competence in their children. Consider one example. It is well-known that achievement test scores in this country lag behind those in other countries. However, our educational failings are not due to lack of cognitive competence or underlying genetic deficit. If our children are not performing, it is because we are not teaching them adequately. Indeed, much of what students get in school is review, and review of review: The level at which material is being presented in textbooks has declined 2 years over the past 10 to 15 years, meaning that the level of a fifth-grade textbook now is roughly comparable to the level of a third-grade textbook then (Reis, 1989). Similarly, Hayes (1996) has documented what they term the "dumbing down" of American textbooks at all levels: The typical texts for a third grader in the early 1950s would today be used for sixth graders. (These findings lend credence to the statements many parents make to the their children regarding how much more difficult school was when the parents were young.) Small wonder our children are lagging behind.

As parents, we may or may not have the power to effect changes in schools. Without question, however, we have the power to effect changes in the home. This chapter describes how we can effect meaningful change to encourage and enhance the cognitive development of our children. Our goal is that, after reading this chapter, you will have mastered a number of strategies you can start implementing immediately to improve the cognitive competence of your children. We seek to accomplish this goal through a series of ten lessons for parents. Each lesson makes just one point, illustrated through examples. It is easy to be overwhelmed by a book of strategies, or to understand the strategies but not how to implement them. This is why we present our strategies along with clear take-home messages. First, we describe what not to do, and, second, we describe what to do and how to do it. To provide an overview of all the strategies at the outset, the ten lessons are summarized in Table 7.1.

LESSON 1

Recognize What Can and Cannot Be Changed in Your Children

What __not__ to do.   View your child as if composed of modeling clay that you can shape into anything you wish. Decide what your child will become and accomplish and expect your child to fulfill your vision.

What to do. Watch carefully as your child attempts to acquire new skills and meets new experiences. Be alert for signs of interest and/or talent in a given area or pursuit, and then encourage your child to pursue these skills and explore these areas. Ensure that your child is broadly exposed to many skill areas so that you can identify the full range of her or his interests and natural gifts (even if they do not overlap with yours!).

How much of what children become can parents influence? The nature versus nurture question is a subject of heated and timely debate, particularly as it relates to childrearing. Adding fuel to this already-rich fire was Harris's book *The Nurture Assumption* (1996), which chronicled the evidence for the omnipresent role of genes and peers—as opposed to parents—as the most critical forces in shaping children's development. Harris's book set off a media fenzy, leading to cover stories in major weeklies and top stories on television news magazine shows. The cover of *Newsweek* even asked, "Do Parents Matter?"

Thus, today's parents have seen a phase transition from an emphasis by leading scholars primarily on the role of environmentalism to an emphasis increasingly on the role of genetics. It is an old question and much of the debate is, in fact, an old recipe served on a new platter. Consider that, in 1930, John Watson made the extraordinary claim that, with control over the environment, he could make any infant into anything he wished (Watson, 1930, p. 104):

> Give me a dozen infants, well-formed, and my own specified world to bring them up in and I'll guarantee to take any one at random and train him to become any type of specialist I might select—doctor, lawyer, artist, merchant-chief, and, yes, even into beggar-man and thief, regardless of his penchants, tendencies, abilities, vocations, and race of his ancestors.

Today, most people, psychologists included, would tend to dismiss his claim. Any of us who has tried to shape our children—even down to the level of trying to get them to practice music for a few more minutes per day or to spend just a few minutes more on homework—has seen how hard it can be to effect even small changes, much less large ones. It is understandable that from the practical perspective of daily parenthood we scoff at Watson's claim of the unlimited malleability of human potential.

The emphasis today tends to be on the importance of the genetic control of behavior. Studies reviewed by Plomin (1988, 1997), for example, suggest that at least half and probably more of the variance in general cognitive ability as measured by IQ is due to genetic factors, with the importance of such factors increasing (rather, than, as one might expect, decreasing) with age. Bouchard (1997; Bouchard and McGue, 1981) has estimated heritability as somewhat higher. The heritability of more specific abilities, such as verbal and spatial abilities, appears to be somewhat lower than that of general intelligence as measured by conventional tests. So much, it would appear, for John Watson.

But then again, maybe not. First of all, Watson himself, despite his strong environmentalism, subscribed to the importance of biology; he believed that innate biological tendencies made some things considerably more difficult to effect than others. Watson was surely sophisticated about the importance of biology in the origins of learned behavior; he himself did not believe that "all behavior is learned." In fact, Watson believed that all behavior is based initially on congenitally given, unconditioned responses, consisting of fear, rage, and love. He regarded these as "emotional reactions" (Watson, 1919, pp. 198–202). In the same volume, Chapters 3 and 4, respectively, are titled "The receptors and their stimuli" and "Neuro-physiological basis of action." There is much here about the power of biology in shaping outcomes—Watson was actually well trained in the physiology of the day. He wrote: "Human action as a whole can be divided into hereditary modes of response (emotional and instinctive) and acquired modes of response (habit)," and "... instinctive positive reaction tendencies displayed by the child soon become overlaid with the organized habits of the adult" (p. 194). Thus it is clear that Watson himself, often cited as the ultimate environmentalist, was a firm believer in the balance between the forces of biology and environment in shaping behavior and child development (Lewis P. Lipsitt, personal communication, 2000).

The relative importance of biology and genetics, however, is often misunderstood; people confuse what are actually genetic influences with the ultimate control of genetics over human destiny. It is a myth that, just because a phenomenon is partially genetically based, it is not amenable to environmental interventions. Consider height. The heritability of height (that is, the extent to which individual differences among people are due to genetic factors) is well over 90%. Yet, average heights in Japan have risen close to 4 inches in one generation. The seeming contradiction, as Ceci (1996) noted, is due to the fact that heritability is based on variance (the relative positions of individuals when ranked on an attribute), whereas the impact of the rearing enviornment is documented not by changes in variation but by changes in the mean or average. Thus, everyone can become taller in a second generation (due to better nutrition, for example), but their heights relative to one another can still be the same as were their mothers', thus retaining the high heritability of height: Taller mothers (relative to their peers) still have taller children (relative to their peers).

To take a more extreme example, consider phenylketonuria (PKU), a hereditary disease that results in an inability of the body to metabolize an amino acid, phenylalanine. Susceptibility to this disease is 100% heritable. In the past, sufferers of this disease always became severely mentally retarded, and suffered other ghastly symptoms as well. Today, because we understand the nature of the disease, symptoms can be almost wholly eradicated if phenylalanine is eliminated from the diet of the child immediately upon birth. Thus, a disease that is wholly hereditary can be controlled environmentally (although Diamond, Prevor, Callender, and Druin [1997] have recently shown that some cognitive deficits do linger throughout the lives of PKU individuals despite dietary intervention).

The point is that the existence of a genetic contribution to intelligence does not prevent parents from intervening in their children's cognitive growth or environmental forces, in general, from having powerful effects (Grigorenko, 2000; Grigorenko, and Sternberg, 2001; Sternberg and Grigorenko, 2001). Children can be helped to achieve cognitive competence, regardless of the role of genetics. On the other hand, genetic influences are real. Thus, parents should not view their children as lumps of clay that parents can form into any shape they wish. Rather, parents should work with and not against children's natural gifts, interests, and tendencies, to discover their ultimate potential. Any child can learn and practice and become more proficient in virtually any endeavor, but the room for real and meaningful achievement is greatest when this practice is built on underlying genetic potential. Sampling broadly across a range of interests will help parents determine where their children's talents lie.

LESSON 2

Aim to Meaningfully Challenge Your Children, Not Bore Them and Not Overwhelm Them

What not to do. (1) Keep your children working to learn new and complex things, even if they seem not to understand them. Assume that your children will rise to the occasion and master tough material with enough sustained practice. (2) Be careful not to challenge your children too much—stay within the limits of their understanding so they do not become frustrated.

What to do. Strike a balance by challenging your children meaningfully with tasks that are just beyond their reach and on which they succeed some but not all of the time.

Psychologists who study the development of children's thinking and reasoning have long been fascinated by the question of how to maximize this development. One concept that has proved useful is the *zone of proximal development*, described by Russian psychologist Lev Vygotsky (1978). The zone of proximal development refers to the gap between what children can accomplish independently and what they can accomplish when they are interacting with others who are more competent. The word proximal means that the assistance provided is just beyond the child's current level of competence. This assistance complements and builds on the child's existing abilities rather than directly teaching the child new behaviors. The idea is that the child must learn by stretching herself or himself with the guidance of an adult. The medieval and modern European practices of apprenticeship—in which a child learns a trade working closely under the guidance and supervision of a skilled adult—show how old and enduring is the notion of the zone of proximal development, even if it was not always labeled as such.

The lesson for parents to remember is that inundating children with challenges not coupled with meaningful assistance, and overwhelming them in the process, does little to aid in cognitive development. In fact, the repeated frustration and ongoing lack of understanding created by such a situation may do more harm than good. On the other hand, avoiding opportunities to challenge children and making things easy for them is not the answer, nor is solving problems for them while they watch passively.

Feuerstein (1980) used the term *mediated learning experience* to contrast with the term *direct learning experience*. Direct learning experience, the teaching of facts, may be important, but it is less important than the mediated learning experience, in which adults interpret the environment alongside the child. Thus, a child viewing an exhibit at a planetarium alone or alongside an adult who quietly views the same exhibit is not learning in the same way as a child who has the exhibit actively interpreted and explained by an adult.

One interesting experiment confirmed the importance of parental interactions of this type. In 1978, Riksen-Walraven conducted a study of 100 Dutch mothers' interactions with 9-month-old children. This study looked at parental responsiveness to infants, and especially, at the role of parental stimulation of infants in the infants' development. Mothers were randomly assigned to four groups characterized by different types of interaction; the amounts of interaction were constant across the groups. However, the types of interaction differed in quality and timing. One group of mothers was instructed not to direct the child's activities too much, but rather, to give the child the opportunity to find things out for herself or himself, to praise the child for these efforts, and to respond to the child's initiations of interactions. Basically, these mothers were taught to be responsive to their child (who was in control) and to support the child's initiatives, like a mediated-learning-experience parenting style. Another group of mothers was told to speak often to their infants and to initiate interactions frequently; these mothers controlled the interactions instead of responding to the child. A third group was instructed to do a mixture of what the first two groups were doing. A fourth, control group, was given no instructions.

Three months later the researcher observed and tested all infants. The mothers' behaviors differed significantly from group to group in accord with the instructions they had received. Infants of mothers who had been encouraged to be responsive showed higher levels of exploratory behavior than any other group and preferred novel to familiar objects. These babies also learned more quickly in a contingency task. Thus, infants randomly assigned to a condition of greater maternal responsiveness showed enhanced cognitive functioning. The conclusion was that different styles of parenting caused differential cognitive development in children.

Effective parents challenge their children, within limits. They do not overly inundate and frustrate their children with tough tasks that are well beyond the children's grasp. Effective parents also do not protect their children from all frustration by keeping tasks simple and perfectly achievable—they understand that children need challenges and the meaningful assistance of parents in meeting them.

LESSON 3

Teach Children That the Main Limitation on What They *Can* Do Is What They Tell Themselves They *Can't* Do

What <u>not</u> to do. Tell your children they don't have the ability to do certain kinds of things, or the personality to do other kinds of things, or the motivation to complete something they might start.

What _to_ do. Tell your children they have the ability to meet pretty much any challenge life might offer. What they need to decide is how hard they are willing to work to meet these challenges.

Much—arguably, *most*—of what we can't do in life, we can't do because we tell ourselves we can't (often because others have told us, in the past, that we can't, and because we believed them).

One of the most well-known studies in psychology was conducted by Rosenthal and Jacobson (1968). The investigators told teachers that psychological testing revealed that some of the students in their classes were going to bloom during the next year, and others were not. In fact, the children identified as potential "bloomers" were chosen at random. At the end of the year, the children identified as having exceptional prospects for blooming that year did, in fact, perform better than the rest. This effect is sometimes called the "Pygmalion effect," after Eliza Doolittle (of *My Fair Lady* fame), who discovered that she could do pretty much what she set her mind to do. The author of the play on which this musical was based, George Bernard Shaw, named his work after the ancient mythological king Pygmalion who was able to bring statues to life.

Some investigators have argued over details of the methodology of the Rosenthal and Jacobson experiments (see Snow, 1995, for refutation of original findings), but few would argue with Rosenthal and Jacobson's conclusion that just setting up an expectation is often enough to make it come true. Children can do pretty much what they make up their minds to do, within natural limitations. However, there *are* natural limitations, rendering some things easier to achieve than others, and, in fact, rendering some things impossible to achieve for some children. Very few 12-year-old children have the capacity to bench press 300 pounds with a set of weights, regardless of motivation and practice (skeletal limitations are real). Similarly, people don't have the capacity to swim from New York to London, nor the capacity to multiply two 30-digit numbers in their heads without using paper (save the rare savant or mental calculator who has devised a trick method for doing such calculations). But within the limitations of a given child's capacity, the main thing holding the child back is her or his set of beliefs regarding the limitations on what she or he can do.

As an example of the role of perceptions of ability in subsequent achievement, consider girls' and boys' Scholastic Assessment Test (SAT) math scores as a function of the students' attitudes about their competence in math. Girls and boys tend to have different perceptions about their abilities, with girls believing they are less capable and boys believing they are more capable. Research has shown that students who believe they are quite capable do better than predicted by their ability level, but students who believe they are not capable do less well than predicted by their ability level. In general, children with negative thoughts about their ability become distracted from learning, lose track of the details of their tasks, and sometimes become immobilized from further learning (Brown, Bransford, Ferrara, and Campione, 1983). These children then wind up getting less and less practice in the areas in which they need practice the most.

A program of research by Steele and his associates (Steele and Aronson, 1995) has also looked at the issue of students beliefs about their own competence. This research has focused on minority students' beliefs about their general academic competence and female students' beliefs about their competence in mathematics. Steele has attempted to show that students' negative beliefs lower their performance. Before giving a tough math test to a group of boys and girls, he had the test taker tell one half of the students that girls and boys perform equivalently on the test. The other half of the test takers were given no information related to gender. Steele showed that girls' performance was substantially higher on the same test when they were told beforehand that girls perform the same as boys, compared to when girls were given no information about gender-related performance.

Steele explains the jump in girls' performance by saying that girls hold negative stereotypes about their mathematical ability. These stereotypes depress girls' performance on difficult math tests (only performance on difficult tests was assessed). But when girls are told that past research has shown that on the particular test they are taking that girls perform the same as boys, girls do not suffer from their negative stereotype and their performance shoots up (Steele, 1995). In this situation, Steele believes that because the girls are told that girls do as well as boys, they are not hindered by their negative stereotypes.

Researchers have also looked at the role of perceived competence and control in students' preference for taking on a challenge (Boggiano, Main, and Katz, 1988). They investigated whether students'
perceptions of their academic competence and their beliefs in their level of personal control over
school-related performance affected the students' intrinsic interest and preference for challenge in
an evaluative setting. Students with higher perceptions of their academic competence and personal
control had more intrinsic interest in schoolwork and more preference for challenging school activities. When given an evaluative, controlling directive (such as "Your last three answers are not
correct—try another sample problem and let me check your work before you go on to chapter three"),
students who had high perceptions of their own academic competence and control preferred a greater
challenge than did students who had lower perceptions of their academic competence and control. No
difference between the groups of students in terms of preference for challenge was evident when no
controlling directive was presented. Thus, students' belief in their academic competence is important,
as is their belief in their ability to control their school performance.

Consider three personal examples that serve to illustrate the effects of perceptions of competence
in one's daily life. One of the authors of this paper, like some of the children in the Rosenthal
and Jacobson research, was labeled an ordinary learner in elementary school, due to low scores
on standardized tests of intelligence. The result was that his teachers had low expectations for him
during the first three grades of school. Being the type of student who wished to please his teachers, he
performed at the roughly average level they expected. They were happy because their expectations
were confirmed, and the student was happy because the teachers were happy. In sum, *everyone* was
happy.

Things might have gone on this way indefinitely were it not for the child's fourth-grade teacher.
For whatever reason, she believed that he could perform at a higher level than the level at which he
was currently performing, and at a level higher than the tests predicted he could achieve. In response
to the higher expectations of the teacher, he performed at a higher level, and to his own surprise
he became an A student and remained so thereafter. But he could only become an A student when
he told himself he could, as a result of a teacher who expected nothing less. Had it not been for that
teacher, his whole life would almost certainly have been very different.

Take a second example. One of us always told himself he had very low spatial-visual abilities.
He's the person who can never get the suitcases to fit in the trunk, and who can never find the right
street, despite the use of a map. Indeed, he was once given a map to get to someone's house, which
was practically a stone's throw away, and it nevertheless took him over an hour to find the house.
His spatial-visual test scores were low, and people had always told him that spatial visualization was
one of his weak points.

Then, one day, he was invited to give an evening talk in a school in a deteriorated part of a large
city. He drove to the school in the late afternoon, while it was still light. He was thinking of the
potentially lethal consequences were he to get lost at night, in the dark, on his return. He carefully
observed the complex route that brought him to the school. At the same time, he was deathly afraid
he would forget the route, as he typically had in the past. After the talk was over, late at night, he
retraced his route and had no trouble extricating himself from the threatening neighborhood.

He was amazed with his success, but realized there was a lesson in this success. When he really
set his mind to observing and memorizing the complex route, he was able to do it. In the past, he
had told himself that he would never have been able to do it and therefore didn't try very hard. That
way, he had always set up the situation to confirm his prior low expectation of his spatial abilities.
But when he really put himself to the test he was able to pass it because he felt he had to.

Consider a third example that illustrates in another domain the power of what we tell ourselves we
can do. One of us grew up wishing she could learn to ski, but living in New York City didn't offer many
opportunities. No one she knew skied, and she had no access to the sport. Then, in her late twenties,
she happened to become friends with a ski instructor. He suggested she give skiing a try, but she was
convinced the time to learn had passed. (Older bones aren't as flexible!) But her ski instructor friend
didn't give up, and with encouragement, she began to see herself as someone who could master the

sport. She watched skiing videos and listened to the instructors talking about technique. She realized this was a skill within her grasp, and over two winters became an accomplished skier, able to keep up with the instructor on challenging trails and even earning comments like "You look like a life-long skier!" Developing the skill took time and persistence—she skied three days a week all winter—but once she believed she could conquer the sport, she succeeded. The point is that the major limitations we face are those we place on ourselves.

There is a fascinating footnote to this lesson, one related by the eminent psychologist Seymour Sarason (Sternberg, Wagner, Williams, and Horvath, 1995). Early in his career, Sarason regularly visited institutions for the so-called feeble-minded. On one of his visits, he learned that the "feeble-minded" residents had eluded an elaborate security system and had broken out of the building. Once the residents were rounded up, Sarason proceeded with his task, which among other things involved administering the Porteus Maze Test to the retarded individuals. Their scores were predictably quite low, which is not surprising when one remembers that low scores on tests of intelligence and reasoning were in part responsible for these people being housed in such institutions in the first place. But when it came to eluding the security system and gaining freedom, the residents displayed capabilities no one thought they possessed. Thus, once again, experience shows that people often are capable of far more than they themselves, or others, would predict.

LESSON 4

Remember That It Is More Important That Children Learn What Questions to Ask, and How to Ask Them, Than That They Learn What the Answers to Questions Are

Schools, and most parents as well, tend to make what we believe is a serious pedagogical mistake: They emphasize the *answering* of questions rather than the *asking* of them. The good student is perceived as the one who usually furnishes the right answers, preferably rapidly. The expert in a field thus becomes the extension of the expert student—the one who knows a lot of information and can recite it from memory at will.

Many cognitive and educational psychologists are returning to the thinking of John Dewey (1933), who realized that *how* we think is often more important than *what* we think. We need to stress more the teaching of *how to ask* questions, and how to ask the right questions (good, thought-provoking, and interesting ones), and to stress less the simple retrieval of the correct answers to whatever questions we might pose.

What not to do. Encourage children to view you or their teacher as the one who should ask the questions, and the child as the one to answer them. Perpetuate the belief that the roles of parent and of teacher are ones of teaching children the "facts."

What to do. Realize—and make sure children realize—that what matters most is not the "facts" a child knows, but rather the child's ability to use those facts. Help children learn not only how to answer questions, but how to ask them, and how to formulate the right questions.

Children are natural question askers. They have to be, to learn to adapt to a complex and changing environment. But whether children continue to ask questions—and, especially, to ask good questions—depends in large part on how we, as adults, respond to their questions (Sternberg, 1994). Those who have read the Dickens classic *Oliver Twist* may remember that in Victorian England, children's questions were not tolerated—in fact, children were supposed to be "seen and not heard." The rare child with the gall to ask, "Please, Sir, may I have some more?" at the dinner table was viewed as insolent and in need of strict discipline. Today, many parents share another view of children's question asking. They recognize that the ability to ask good questions and to know how to ask them is an essential part of intelligence and, arguably, the most important part (Arlin, 1990; Getzels and Csikszentmihalyi, 1976; Sternberg, 1985, 1997, 1999). It is an ability we as parents can either foster or stifle. (It is worthwhile to remember, however, that in our era, as always, different religions and cultures have varying tolerances toward children's question asking.)

Russian psychologist Lev Vygotsky (1978) proposed that a primary means by which we develop our intelligence is through *internalization*. We incorporate into ourselves what we absorb as a result of the process of being exposed to and learning from the environment (Vygotsky, 1978). The parent as teacher helps the child make sense of the environment by providing guidance to the child in how to interpret it. As discussed above, Feuerstein (1980) called this guidance *mediated learning experience* and contrasted this kind of learning with *direct learning experience*. Direct learning experience is what happens when a parent or teacher teaches us a fact. It is important in learning, but less important than mediated learning experience, which is the learning children do through adult interpretation of what goes on around the child. Feuerstein has suggested that children who show deficient intellectual skills are often those who have been exposed to insufficient mediation of their learning experiences. On this view, it is not enough just to take the child to a museum or to see interesting sites. What is important is the mediation of the experience for the child by the parent or teacher.

When children seek such mediation through asking questions, we as parents and teachers have several different characteristic ways of responding. We believe that how teachers respond to children's questions is important because types of responses are differentially helpful to children in developing their intelligence. We have proposed a seven-level model of parent–child interaction in the questioning process (Sternberg, 1994). The basic idea is that parents (and other mediators) who respond at higher levels better foster their children's intellectual development. We will briefly review this model to show how the way you handle a child's question can either place the child on the road to intellectual fulfillment or derail him or her.

Consider an example of a question a child might pose while visiting Holland (see Sternberg, 1994), or after seeing a documentary about Holland on television, or after reading a book about Holland. The question is one that occurred to one of us during a recent trip to Holland: Why are people in Holland so tall? Now consider various ways you, as a parent, might respond to this question, or any question your child might ask you. Children will ask you many thousands of questions as they grow up, and you should ask yourself which of these levels best characterizes your typical way of responding. The higher the level, the more you are doing to enhance your child's intellectual development. And notice that it is easily in your power to raise the level at which you respond. It requires no special abilities on your part, just an affirming attitude toward your child and her or his questions.

Level 1: Rejection of questions.   Typical responses of this kind are "Don't ask so many questions!" "Don't bother me!" "Don't ask stupid questions!" and "Be quiet!" When parents respond at this level, the basic message to the child is to shut up. Questions are seen as inappropriate or as irritations. Children should learn to "be seen and not heard" and to keep their place. The result of consistent punishment for question asking, of course, is that children learn not to ask questions, and hence, not to learn.

All of us probably would like to believe that only other people respond to children's questions at such a low and even offensive level. Perhaps we've heard parents on the bus or subway treat children like this, but we never would. Yet it would be the unusual parent indeed who does not occasionally lapse into Level 1 behavior, if only from exhaustion from answering questions or from doing other things. Our children then pay a price for our exhaustion.

Level 2: Restatement of questions as responses.   Typical responses at this level would be "Because they are Dutch, and Dutch people are very tall," or "Because they grow a lot." At this level, we answer our children's questions, but in a wholly empty way. Our response is nothing more than a restatement of the original question. We state redundantly that people from Holland are tall because they are Dutch, or because the Dutch grow a lot. Or we say that a person acts the way he does "because he's human," or acts crazy "because he is insane," or that some people come up with good solutions "because they are high in intelligence." Often we are not even aware we are restating a question because we have a high-falutin' but empty word that hides our ignorance. How many neurotic people do you know? And just what does it explain about a person when we label her or him as "neurotic"?

Level 3: Admission of ignorance or providing direct responses.   Typical responses at this level are "I don't know" or "Because . . . ," followed by a reasonable answer (say, about nutrition or genetics). At this level, we either say we do not know or give a response based on what we do know. Children are given the opportunity to learn something new or to realize that their parents do not know everything. Such answers are quite reasonable in certain situations but do not represent the maximum we can do for our children. (By the way, answering as though you know the answer when you don't is not a response on any of these levels. It is extremely unwise because it gives your children the wrong information and teaches them to pretend to knowledge they don't really have.)

When parents answer at this level, they can do so either with or without "reinforcement." This means that we either can reward kids for asking the question or not reward them. Examples of rewards would be "That's a good question" or "I'm glad you asked that" or "That's a really interesting question." Such a response rewards question-asking and thereby is likely to increase its frequency. And by increasing its frequency, we foster further opportunities for children to learn.

Level 4: Encouragement to seek response through authority.   Typical responses at this level are "I'll look it up in the encyclopedia when we get home" or "Why don't you look it up in the encyclopedia when we get home?" At Level 4, the question-answering process does not just end with an answer or admission of ignorance. Children are taught that information not possessed can and often *should* be sought out.

Notice, though, the difference in the two responses above. In the first, the parent takes responsibility for seeking the information. Children thereby learn that information can be sought, but also that there is someone else to do it for them. Thus, the learning that will ultimately be accomplished is *passive learning*. In the second response, the child is given the responsibility. In this way, the child is asked to take responsibility for learning and, hence, to learn as well as to learn how to learn. This is called *active learning*. As you can probably guess, active learning is better than passive learning. Through active learning, children develop their own information-seeking skills rather than becoming dependent on others.

Level 5: Consideration of alternative explanations.   Here, the parent says she or he doesn't know, but suggests that the child explore some possibilities. Ideally, the child and parent generate possibilities together, such as: People in Holland might be tall because of the food, the weather, genetics, hormone injections, killing of short children, wearing of elevator shoes, and so on. The child thereby comes to realize that even seemingly simple questions can invite hypothesis-formulation and testing.

Level 6: Consideration of explanations plus means of evaluating the explanations.   Here, parents not only encourage alternative explanations, as in Level 5, but discuss ways of evaluating the validity of the alternative explanations. A typical response at this level would be "How might we go about deciding which of these explanations is correct?" For example, if genetics were responsible for the high average height of the Dutch, what might we expect to observe? How might we discern whether food or weather is responsible? How can we quickly rule out the possibility that the Dutch kill short children? Children can learn via the responses of their mediators not only how to generate alternative hypotheses, as in Level 5, but also how to test them.

Level 7: Consideration of explanations, plus means of evaluating them, plus follow-through in evaluations. In Level 7, a typical response might be: "Let's try getting some of the information we need in order to decide among these explanations." Here, the mediator actually encourages the child to perform the experiments by gathering information that could distinguish among the alternative explanations. The child learns not only how to think but how to act on her or his thoughts. Although it may not be possible to test every explanation of a phenomenon, it will often be possible to test several of them. For example, the child can observe whether taller Dutch parents also tend to have taller children, whether there are reports of missing short children, and so forth.

Note how, as we move up the levels, we go from rejecting children's questions, at one extreme, to encouraging hypothesis-formation and testing, at the other. We go from no learning, to passive rote learning, to analytic and creative learning. The higher our level of response, the more we communicate an interest in children's questions. We probably don't have the time or resources always to respond to children's questions in a Level 7 way. Nor are higher levels of response equally appropriate for children of all ages—responses need to be developmentally appropriate to be maximally useful. But, in general and as children grow up, the more we use the higher levels the more we encourage our children to develop their cognitive skills.

Note that we are not advocating rearing children who are little more than "empty-headed" questioners who have acquired the socially acceptable veneer of smartness by asking smart-sounding questions but who do not possess the reservoir of basic knowledge needed to survive in today's world. Children need to learn how to ask questions, and they need also to learn basic facts and information and how to reason effectively with them. Good question-asking skills are an essential foundation of this developmental equation.

LESSON 5

Help Children Find What Really Excites Them, Remembering That It May Not Be What Really Excites You, or What You Wish Would Really Excite Them

People who truly excel in a pursuit in life, whether vocational or avocational, are almost always people who genuinely love what they do. Certainly, the most creative people are intrinsically motivated in their work, meaning that they do their work for internal reasons rather than external ones, for example, because they like it, for self-expression, and for relaxation, and not because they have to do it (Amabile, 1983, 1996; Collins and Amabile, 1999). How many people have you met who followed a career path for the money or prestige, and who, whether or not they attained these goals, loathe what they do? How many don't hate it, but are bored silly? For sure, they are not the people doing the work that makes a difference in their field.

What not to do. Work with your children to find things *you* always hoped they would love to do.

What to do. Work with your children to find things *they* really love to do.

Helping children find what they really love to do isn't always easy. On the contrary, it is often hard and frustrating work, for both parents and children. Yet, unless we are willing to face the frustration now, our children will have to face it later, perhaps for the rest of their lives.

Historically, children often did not have the luxury of choosing how they wished to spend their lives and of doing tasks they enjoyed in pursuit of making a living. The greater economic opportunities of the modern era have allowed us all more choices regarding how we spend our lives. Children today may decide to join a family business or pursue another vocation. The fact that one's parent is a physician does not mean that this is one's only alternative. Our colleges and graduate and professional schools are open to a broader segment of the population today than they were in the pre–World War II era, when wealth and family connections were more salient determiners of who had access to such institutions and who did not (Calvin, 2000). With the growth of the middle class in North America came the growth of leisure time and the increasing access to the luxury of how to spend our lives (Flynn, in press). Our children are deeply fortunate to have the benefit of such choices; it is up to every parent to help her or his children make the most of this opportunity.

We have met any number of college students who, when asked why they are doing what they are doing, reply that they are doing it because it is what their parents want them to do. For example, they might take premed curriculum because their father is a doctor or because their father always wanted to have a doctor in the family. And after all, who's paying? Children who go into a field because their parents want them to may become good at what they do, but they almost certainly won't become great.

Even those of us who preach this message need to remember it when it comes to our own families. For example, the son of one of the authors decided at one point that he wished to play the piano. His father was delighted because he himself was a piano player. His son, therefore, was following in his own footsteps. The son ended up practicing less than regularly, and eventually quit. The father was disappointed, to say the least. A few months later, the son indicated he would like to play the trumpet. The father, disgusted after the son had quit the piano, said he wouldn't even consider the possibility. After all, he had seen what had happened with the piano lessons. But later, he realized that his reluctance had less to do with the fact that the son had quit piano than it had to do with the fact that the father couldn't imagine a child of his playing the trumpet. It just didn't fit his image of his child. Fortunately, the father also realized that his feelings had a lot to do with his image of the son but nothing to do with what was best for the son. The son started trumpet lessons and enjoyed them for several years.

The point of this story, and many others like it, is simple. We need to find what is right for our children, not for our image of what we had hoped they would be. There will be frustrations as we try things that don't work, but the ultimate reward will be their finding the right things that do work.

Although we have emphasized the importance of finding the right activities to do, it is equally important to find the right place to do them. For example, the large majority of people who come to Cornell or Yale universities are happy to be there. But we cannot even count the number of students and faculty we have met at these schools who would have been happier elsewhere. For example, Yale and Cornell are excellent places for students who are independent, who seek high levels of intellectual challenge, and who can cope with an environment where they will probably not be the biggest fish in what might be viewed as a very large pond. A student who needs to be a big fish in a small pond, or who is not up to the intellectual challenge, or who cannot work independently would probably be much happier elsewhere. Similarly, Cornell and Yale are great places for faculty who want to balance teaching and research. But faculty who prefer to teach most of the time and who are not into publishing research definitely would be happier elsewhere.

Some years ago, one of us had an outstanding graduate student who received two very good job offers. One offer was from an extremely prestigious institution and the other from a prestigious institution, but one that could not match the first institution for level of prestige. But there was a problem: The kind of work the student did was a better match to the kind of work done in the somewhat less prestigious place than to the kind of work done in the more prestigious one. Unfortunately, the student took the job at the more prestigious institution. He did well but did not become the great success all had hoped for. His environment just didn't encourage what he had to offer or the kind of work he liked to do.

The lesson to us is clear: What is most important is to find an environment that is compatible with you. For a child, it may not be the most prestigious private school or college (or then again, it may be). For the adult, it may not be the most prestigious job or community (or then again, it may be). The overriding consideration should be to find for your children (and yourself) an environment in which they will thrive as individuals. This environment is not necessarily the same one that will be best for someone else. You need to know your own child. It's not enough just to go with the name—the honors course, the honors school, or the most popular and prestigious alternative. Know your child, and help your child find the environment that is the best fit to her or his abilities, interests, and values.

LESSON 6

Encourage Children to Take Sensible Intellectual Risks

Research on creativity shows that creative children and adults are intellectual risk takers (see Sternberg and Lubart, 1991, 1995, 1999). They are not the people who always play it safe. It is like investing money. If you put all your money in a government-insured passbook savings account, chances are you won't lose it. But you won't make much either, and inflation will chip away at the little interest you gain in any case. To earn more substantial interest or dividends on your money, you have to take some risks with it. This is not to say that all your money should be invested in a risky way. But if you are not willing to take any risks at all, your wealth will scarcely increase. Similarly, not every intellectual activity a child engages in should represent a risk, but if none does, the child will probably not end up doing much, if anything, that is creative and that potentially makes a difference—either to the child or to anyone else.

What not to do.   Always encourage your children to play it safe—with courses, with activities, with teachers, with intellectual challenges.

What to do.   Teach children sometimes to take intellectual risks, and to develop a sense of when to take risks and when not to.

Most creative work goes at least slightly against the established way of doing things, with the result that when children take the risk and do something creative, the reaction to their work is not always positive. Consider an example of what happened to the daughter of one of these authors. Sara was in third grade, and her teacher had a worthwhile idea. The children were studying the planets, and the idea was that the children should pretend to be astronauts about to land on Mars. Such an exercise is called a simulation.

One of the best ways for children (or adults, for that matter) to learn is through simulation. The basic idea of a simulation is that you can often learn more by putting yourself in someone else's place than by simply reading about what the someone else would have done in a given set of circumstances. Thus, children will probably learn more about what it is like for an astronaut to land on another planet if they have to put themselves in the shoes of the astronaut than if they simply read about an astronaut about to land on the Moon (or Mars, for that matter, although obviously most descriptions focus on the Moon because humans have never landed on Mars). Obviously, reading and simulation are not mutually exclusive. After the simulation, children can supplement what they have learned by reading about how their reactions differed from those of, say, professional astronauts.

As the teacher started the lesson, Sara, a mere 8 years old at the time, suggested she might pretend to be a Martian and meet the astronauts as they arrived on Mars. We really like Sara's idea, because it was creative and because it represented a realistic problem people encounter in their lives: How to interact with others who at times seem to act like Martians, whether they are people from another culture, people from another community, or even spouses having an "off day." Thus, we would have hoped the teacher would have received Sara's idea positively.

In fact, what transpired was exactly the opposite. The teacher responded that the idea was unacceptable because we know from space probes and other means that there are no Martians. Hence, including a Martian in the lesson would make it unrealistic and not a science lesson. Well, from one point of view, the teacher was right: Probably there are no Martians, unless they live in the interior of the planet, hidden from the view of space probes and protected from the harsh outer atmosphere of the planet. But from another point of view, the teacher probably did some damage: The lesson Sara learned was that the next time she has a creative idea, she should shut up.

It is easy to feel anger toward the teacher for what seems to have been a thoughtless response. Sara took an intellectual risk in suggesting a change in the lesson plan, and was chastised for the risk. Children often are. They finally screw up the courage to take a difficult course, and receive a bad grade. They write an essay that is provocative and controversial, and the teacher doesn't like it. They do a science project that is a bit offbeat, and don't win any prizes. And failed intellectual risks are not limited to children—almost all of us, at one time or another, have tried taking a risk in our work, and it hasn't worked.

As for ourselves, we have had risky articles and grant proposals turned down. We have tried teaching in innovative ways to our students, and the lessons haven't always worked. Just recently, one of us tried presenting a paper to Montrealers in French, and the result was just short of catastrophic. When you take a risk, you have to be willing to fall flat on your face sometimes.

Then why even encourage children to take risks? Consider the benefits. Practically every major discovery or invention has entailed some amount of risk, but the risks taken by the discoverers and inventors are often forgotten today. Would anyone really want a ballpoint pen when people had fountain pens? Would anyone want to see videos at home on a small television screen when they could go to a movie theater instead? Would anyone find enough use for a home computer to want to spend the money on one? How could the earth revolve around the sun when one only has to look up in the sky to see the sun revolving around the earth? The list is endless. But at all levels, big and small, the people who have contributed most to our world are people who have been willing to take intellectual risks and to see and do things in ways others haven't.

One of our favorite examples is that of an engineer at the 3M company who worked in the adhesives division. Work on adhesives is certainly important (especially given that so many things in the world are falling apart). The job of engineers in such a division is to try to invent ever-stronger adhesives. One engineer came up with a weaker adhesive than those we had at the time. The reaction of the engineer's superiors was that the invention was useless—what we need are stronger, not weaker, adhesives. Indeed, most people in the company reacted in kind. But eventually secretaries (not the high-placed scientists, engineers, and executives) saw a use for the idea, and today we have the yellow Post-it stickers that enable us to leave notes on a piece of paper and then remove them without leaving a mark. The interesting part of the story, of course, is that this very useful and profitable invention came about only because someone was willing to take a risk and actually do the opposite of what he was supposed to do.

Children often learn to avoid intellectual risks. Sometimes, perhaps as a result of their avoidance of intellectual risks, they end up channeling most of the risk taking they do into the social and sexual domains, where the costs of taking a risk are often much higher than in the intellectual domain. A few years ago, the son of one of the authors was in the position of having to make a decision about an intellectual risk. He was choosing between two high schools. Both high schools were good ones. But it was very clear to Seth that the challenge and work load in one high school was substantially greater than in the other. Moreover, the grading system was much tougher in the more challenging high school. From his point of view, it looked like a bad deal: He would probably have to work harder, possibly just to obtain lower grades. His parents supported his taking the risk, and we're happy to say he decided to take it (with the proviso that he could then go to the less challenging high school after a year if things didn't work out in the more challenging one). But he took the risk only with parental encouragement and even prodding. His parents were convinced that he will have a much better educational experience as a result of his decision. If parents don't encourage children to make the most of their abilities, children often won't end up doing so.

One kind of risk for children is the risk of making a mistake, especially in public. Children are often reluctant to make mistakes that might expose them to the ridicule of their teacher, or even worse, their peers. So they start playing it safe in the classroom, responding only when they know they have the correct answer. They may start playing it safe in other situations as well so as not to look stupid. The only problem with this strategy is that the very best way to learn is from our own mistakes. The lessons learned by watching others aren't as powerful as the lessons learned by doing. Smart people are not ones who never make mistakes—on the contrary, smart people *always* make mistakes, because that's how they learn.

Clifford (1988) studied how students' willingness to take academic risks impacted their development and performance. In this research, tolerance for failure at school, which measured how constructively a person responds to failure in school, was highly associated with choosing more difficult and challenging test problems when a choice of problems was offered. Students who tolerated failure well took greater risks and chose harder problems. Tolerance for failure was also associated with higher standardized achievement test scores. However, tolerance for failure decreased with age—it seems that the older children get, the more we teach them to play it safe.

Given the learning opportunities that derive from taking risks and the achievement this learning makes possible, we must ask why so few children are willing to take risks in school. In the school environment, perfect test scores and papers receive praise, and academic failure means extra make-up work. Academic failure is viewed as a result of low ability and motivation rather than a desire to grow. Playing it safe is advocated, particularly as children reach middle-school age. Students are not given choices on assignments, so opportunities to take risks are minimal, and students never develop tolerance for risk taking. Unfortunately, however, risk-averse students (and adults) lose out in the end. The interesting thing is that children are natural risk takers; they feel a certain invulnerability that we as adults no longer feel—until we teach them to feel otherwise. There are many subtle ways parents, teachers, and society at large discourage risk-taking behavior, and we must all become aware of them. We must try to balance the communication of appropriate caution with encouragement of sometimes risky behavior.

We have noted that, often, people's views on intellectual risks are linked to their views on the nature of intelligence. Dweck (1999; Dweck and Bempechat, 1983) has distinguished between two types of conceptions of intelligence in children. One type of conception is that intelligence is a more or less fixed entity with which we are born. On this view, there's not much we can do to increase our intelligence. Children with this point of view often try to minimize and hide their mistakes, and tend to experience debilitation in the face of setbacks. The other type of conception is an incremental one. On this view, we can improve our intelligence as we learn and experience the world. The more we learn, the smarter we become, and setbacks become cues either to increase effort or to vary strategy. Clearly, the conception of intelligence we want to reinforce in our children is the second one. It is also the correct conception of intelligence, because intelligence *can* be increased (Bransford and Stein, 1993; Grotzer and Perkins, 2000; Sternberg, 1986, 1998). To the extent that children believe in this conception, they will be more willing to do what they need to do to increase their intelligence.

Encouraging children to take risks means also teaching them to persevere in the face of difficult tasks and obstacles. Children with the "entity" conception of intelligence often do not like to face such challenges because they are afraid of looking stupid. For children, undertaking difficult tasks endangers both their self-esteem and their esteem in the face of others. But unless they learn to undertake difficult tasks, and to persevere in them even when they become difficult, they cannot make the most of their abilities.

Children (as well as adults) often don't undertake or persevere in difficult tasks because they are afraid to fail. We see this fear especially in subjects such as mathematics and science, and especially for girls. Often, their social milieu has subtly reinforced the message that these pursuits are not for girls. We can help children fight their fear of failure by reassuring them of the content of the third lesson of this chapter: The biggest source of failure is our own belief that we cannot do something.

LESSON 7

Teach Children to Take Responsibility for Themselves—Both for Their Successes *and* for Their Failures

Something sounds a bit trite when we say that we should teach children to take responsibility for themselves: Of course everyone knows this. But sometimes there is a gap between what we know and how we translate what we know into action. In practice, people differ widely in the extent to which they take responsibility for the causes and consequences of their actions.

What not to do. Always look for—or allow children to look for—the outside enemy who is responsible for your children's failures (teachers, other students, illnesses, and so on). Always push kids because they can't do it for themselves.

What to do. Teach children to take responsibility for themselves. Help kids develop their own internal push so you don't have to push them: Enable them to do it for themselves.

Rotter (1966, 1990) distinguished between two personality patterns, which he referred to as "internal" and "external." Internals are people who tend to take responsibility for their lives. When things go well for them, they take credit for their efforts; but when things don't go well, they tend to take responsibility and try to make things go better. Externals, in contrast, tend to place responsibility outside themselves, especially when things do not go well. They are quick to blame circumstances for their failures (and often to attribute their successes to external circumstances as well). Of course, almost no one is purely internal or external. Moreover, all of us know people who accept credit for their successes but who blame others for their failures, or who never credit themselves for their successes but do blame themselves for their failures. The most realistic people recognize that both success and failure come about as an interaction between our own contributions and those of others.

From our standpoint as parents and as researchers studying how to maximize intellectual potential, we have found, as has Rotter, that people who tend toward the internal side of the continuum are better adapted to intellectual success. Because externals are reluctant or even refuse to accept blame, they do not take responsibility for making the most of their lives. They somehow expect others to do for them what they need to do for themselves. We teach at selective universities, and have observed for a number of years which of the young women and men who attend these universities tend to succeed, and which do not. We have found that one of the best predictors of success is the student's willingness to take responsibility for herself or himself. Many of the students who attend these universities are used to success—and wait for something to happen. Usually, little does. The opportunities do not simply come to the students, as they may have in high school. The students who succeed are the ones who *make* their own opportunities—who take responsibility for their lives.

One way to develop this inner sense of responsibility in children is to serve as a role model for it. Children learn more through imitating modeled behaviors than they do through practically any other means: If you want children to behave a certain way, act that way yourself. Don't expect children to take responsibility for themselves if you are always trying to find someone to blame for your own problems—whether it is a boss, a spouse, an ex-spouse, the government, or whomever. That's not to say that these entities may not be in part responsible for whatever problems you face. But it is in your hands to improve your life, not in theirs, just as it is in your hands to set a take-charge example for children.

Recently one of us observed a friend teaching her child precisely how *not* to develop an inner sense of responsibility. The woman was having an in-depth conversation with one of us in her living room, on a topic of much significance to her. Meanwhile, her 3½-year-old child became jealous that his mother was paying more attention to someone else than to him. He shot the adults with a toy gun, hit them with toys, and wailed at the top of his lungs. Finally, he actually hurt his mother with a toy he threw.

She leaned over and said, "Oh, honey, you accidentally hurt Mommy. I know you didn't mean it. Mommy's been ignoring you, I know, and I'm sorry," and so on (you get the picture). The boy answered, "Yes, you've been hurting me, Mommy, but I forgive you!" It was comical, but there was a sobering message being delivered to the child. Later he kicked one of the authors and pulled the family cat's tail, but he was never held accountable for his actions.

This family was headed for a real problem. The mother should have acted as an appropriate role model by taking only the responsibility she deserved and by expecting her son to do the same. He may have been young, but he was not too young to learn to shift blame to others and manipulate the situation to serve his goals. By repeatedly letting him off the hook, his mother was establishing a bad precedent for his later life.

Another way to develop the inner sense of responsibility is to know when to push children, but also when not to. Unfortunately, many young women and men who enroll at Cornell or Yale have been pushed throughout their childhoods. They face a tough problem when they arrive at college: Their parents are no longer there to push them, and they have never learned how to do it for themselves. The children who are most successful are those who were nudged when circumstances required, but who were not constantly pushed. The ones who were constantly pushed are often at a loss when, for the first time in their lives, they have to find the resources to push themselves from within. Because they were always pushed from without, they have never developed these resources.

Nothing is more boring to a teacher than students who always have an excuse for what they should have done that they didn't do. They usually run through several dead grandmothers, family crises, and severe illnesses whose symptoms they do their best to fake. The students do not seem to realize that the teachers have heard it all before. Teachers recognize procrastinators and excuse-invention artists from a mile away. The time and place to teach children not to be procrastinators and excuse makers is in the home. When you give children chores or other tasks to do, expect the children to do them. Moreover, expect them to meet your expectations for the tasks you assign them, not just to get by with the minimum.

Intellectually successful people are never those who just do the minimum needed to get by. As teachers, we see many students pass through our classrooms who do what they think is just the minimum they need to get an A, a B, or whatever grade they set as their goal. They may or may not get the grade, but the person they are fooling is not the teacher, but themselves—these students are not taking responsibility for their lives. Teachers know who these students are and treat them befittingly.

Ask yourself: If you have a special opportunity for someone at work, or in a club where you are an officer, or whatever, to whom will you give that opportunity, the person who does just the minimum to get by, or the person who always tries to meet and even exceed your expectations? Clearly, you will give the choice opportunities to the latter, and so will practically anyone else. People who learn just to get by when they are children behave the same way as adults, and find that it is almost always someone else who gets the choice opportunities in life. When the promotion comes up, or the big salary raise, or the chance to work on a particularly good project, they find that someone else gets the opportunity. Sadly, they rarely understand why. They still think they are fooling people in their attitude of doing the least possible to get by.

At the beginning of this lesson, we mentioned how important it is that parents translate thought into action with regard to teaching their children to take responsibility. But children also need to be taught to translate thought into action. In every line of adult work life, there is potential gap between what we know how to do and what we actually do. As scholars, we see other scholars who have good ideas but who never get around to publishing them. We have seen inventors who have creative ideas, but by the time they get around to trying to put them into practice, someone else has beaten them to it. We have seen managers who know what they need to do in their businesses, but for one reason or another, hesitate to do it until they have driven the company into bankruptcy. And for that matter, we have all seen people in personal relationships who know that changes need to be made but who procrastinate indefinitely. By the time they get around to taking responsibility for making the changes, it is often too late—they've lost the relationship. The point is that to make the most of your children's abilities, it is not enough that they learn what they *can* do—they have to learn to *do* it.

LESSON 8

Teach Children How to Delay Gratification—to Be Able to Wait for Rewards

In a series of studies extending over many years, Mischel has found that children who are better able to delay gratification are more successful in various aspects of their lives, including their academic performance (e.g., Mischel, Shoda, and Rodriguez, 1989). In a typical study, Mischel will place young children in a room and give them a choice between an immediate but smaller reward, and a later but larger reward. He will put various temptations in their paths. For example, it is harder to resist temptation if the immediate reward (e.g., a chocolate bar) is visible than if it is hidden. Children's ability to delay gratification even predicts their scores on the Scholastic Assessment Test (SAT) when they are much older (Goleman, 1995). Rewards for delaying gratification can sometimes surface far down the road.

What not to do. Always reward children immediately. Allow children to expect immediate rewards, to get what they want right away. Emphasize the here and now at the expense of the long term.

What to do. Teach children to wait for rewards. Teach them that the greater rewards are often those that come down the line. Show them examples in your own life and how these examples may apply to them. Emphasize the long term, not just the here and now.

Working hard often does not bring immediate rewards. Children do not become expert baseball players, dancers, musicians, or sculptors right away. And the reward of becoming expert at anything often seems very far away. Often, children succumb to the temptations of the moment—watching mindless programs on television, endlessly playing repetitive video games, or even falling into antisocial groups that seek immediate delights. But the people who make the most of their abilities have to be those who are willing to wait, because there are few challenges that can be met in a moment.

Gruber (1986; Gruber and Wallace, 1999) has studied the careers of great contributors to the world. His findings belie the notion that the great insights in history correspond to the "Eureka!" experience, whereby someone goes from not understanding something to understanding it in a flash. On the contrary, Gruber has found that even the greatest minds had to work hard and long to achieve their major insights and their major works. Of course, there are exceptions. But for the most part, the great accomplishments come after much hard work. Not only do significant accomplishments require hard work, they are often not recognized as significant right away. Creative people have to learn to delay gratification, because their greatest works may be ignored for some period of time before their value is recognized.

One of our children has a tendency to quit on things when they become hard. He is afraid to fail, and thereby look inadequate in his own eyes and those of others. But in many pursuits, the hardest part is the "middle." For example, it is not hard to learn to play tennis or baseball or soccer well enough to get by in gym class. But to become good enough to be on the varsity team often requires a great deal of work and commitment of time. Similarly, to become a really good cellist or pianist or saxophonist requires many, many hours of work and effort.

Ericsson, Krampe, and Tesch-Römer (1993) suggested that probably the most important factor in becoming an expert in anything is sheer hard work and practice. Comparisons of distinguished performers in a number of fields with those who are not so distinguished revealed that the distinguished performers, quite simply, worked much harder than the nondistinguished ones. For the child or adult, such hard work on one pursuit represents a risk. After all, there is no guarantee that all the hard work will yield results. The child may practice for hours and hours and never become a great hockey player, artist, or violinist. But again, the work of Ericsson and his colleagues suggests that nothing pays off better than sheer persistence and determination.

The findings of Ericsson and his colleagues even more strongly show the importance of finding the right pursuits for your children. If they are really going to work to excel at something, it should be something they really like. All of us know how 3 hours doing something we hate can seem like a day, whereas 3 hours spent on something we love can seem like a matter of minutes. So let us help our children find what is right for them and then encourage them really to excel.

Your children may or may not make great contributions to the world, but the chances are that their accomplishments will be better if they learn to delay gratification. It is often hard to see into the distant future and what may lie ahead. But those who do have foresight have the edge in almost all aspects of life. A child may not see in Grade 9, for example, how working hard will benefit him or her later on; but by Grade 12, when the child is ready to apply to colleges, the advantages of hard work and solid academic performance will be obvious.

One of us has a younger brother who suffered significantly because he couldn't delay gratification. As a child, the boy was indulged with toys and rewarded instantly for any positive effort. He never learned patience and perseverance because he just didn't have to. He was naturally gifted academically and never had to work hard and apply himself to do well in school. He always received better-than-average grades for minimal effort, and he never experienced the rewards of working on long-term projects.

This pattern worked for the boy until college. There he found his once-successful approach no longer brought the instant gratification he was accustomed to. Commitments to long-term projects were expected, as were long hours spent studying in the library. Despite his intelligence, the boy did poorly his first semester at college—and so poorly his second semester that he left school. He tried two other colleges for one semester each with the same results.

Finally, he got his act together and learned a tough lesson: Life is work, and rewards often come only with time. He enrolled in a fourth college and applied himself to the difficult tasks entailed in earning a degree. He graduated three years later. The moral of this story is clear: You do your children no favor by providing immediate rewards, because the real world won't follow your example. The older a child gets, the more she or he must be able to accept the delay between performing behaviors and achieving rewards.

When we started working together, we had only short-term funding for our joint projects, and knew we would need to seek some longer-term support. Although we would be fine for three years, we knew that after three years, we would be out of funds. Looking toward the long term, therefore, we started applying for additional funding almost immediately. There is almost nothing we like to do less than write grant proposals. Each of us could have generated endless lists of activities on which we would have rather spent our time. But we did what we needed to do, saving the activities we would have rather done for after we did what we felt we had to do. Actually, we didn't absolutely have to write proposals at the time—after all, we had three full years of support. But we knew that, down the road, we would be sorry if we waited to seek further support. So we took the long view.

Our initial efforts all met with failure. At this point, we really began to ask why we were spending our time on something we didn't like doing when there were other activities that were guaranteed to make us feel better in the short run. Only masochists like to be turned down. But we persevered, and after a losing streak, our fortune changed, and we started winning—we had several proposals accepted. We got more gratification than we had ever imagined possible, but we had to wait for it. That's the way life often is, and children need to know it.

LESSON 9

Teach Children to Put Themselves in Another's Place

Many very bright children never achieve the success in life that could be theirs because they never develop *practical intelligence* (Sternberg, 1985, 1988, 1997; Sternberg et al., 2000). They may do well in school and on tests, but they never learn how to get along with others, and, especially, to see things (and themselves) as others seem them.

What not to do.   Teach children to form a point of view, but not to try to understand the points of view of others.

What to do.   Teach children the importance of understanding, respecting, and responding to the points of view of others.

Some years back, we observed a student at Yale who was academically a great success. He did extremely well in his courses and in all aspects of academic life. His teachers thought that his prospects for success were excellent. We disagreed. Although this student displayed exceptional *academic* intelligence, he displayed a genuine lack of *practical* intelligence. He acted arrogantly toward others—as though he knew everything and they knew nothing. He even acted this way toward his teachers, but the fellow was so damn smart they were willing to overlook it. After all, they were his teachers, and felt a familial concern for him.

The result was that no one ever put the guy in his place. They were doing him no favor. When the fellow went out on the job market, he did not receive a ringing endorsement from his interviewers; in fact, he was a total flop. This individual did not even have the practical intelligence to realize that the day of the job interview, he would have to hide his arrogance. He acted toward the people he met in his interview like he knew it all and they knew nothing. But they knew at least one thing—that this was one person they were not going to hire! Eventually, he received a job, but he later lost it. People without the warm and friendly feelings of family members weren't willing to put up with him.

As parents, we are sometimes willing to overlook the faults of our children that to others are obvious. But in overlooking these faults, we hurt rather than help our children. Others won't have the indulgence for faults that we have in our own kin. Indeed, one of us just had a conversation with his son last night on this issue. When several teachers make the same comment about a student, one has got to start listening carefully to it, whether one agrees with it or not. Of course, the child may feel like he is getting a bum rap. What child doesn't feel this way from time to time? But children need to understand that if people are seeing them in a certain way, whether they are this way or not, they have to take responsibility for changing others' perception.

A few days ago, one of us was told by a subordinate that he had been acting grouchy lately. He then asked others if they had the same perception. He was stunned to find that they did. Were they right? Who knows? But whether or not he was "objectively" grouchy, the perception was there, and the perception was causing problems. He vowed to change the perception, and therefore the behavior that was causing the perception.

For many possible reasons, girls on the average tend to be better able to put themselves in the position of another than do boys. In general, girls tend to be more sensitive to and understanding of feelings than are boys (Hall, 1984); thus, we need to pay special attention to these issues with boys. Of course, we may take the tack of forgiving them because they are boys, adopting the old saw that "Boys will be boys." But again, our forgiveness will only hurt them in later life. The better able a child is to understand the point of view of others, the better that child will adapt not only to the demands of school, but to the demands of life after school.

The lack of ability to see things from another point of view seems almost to be a national weakness in the United States. Many citizens of the United States have had the distressing experience of traveling abroad and of discovering that the perception of the United States and of the people in it is much more negative in many parts of the world than it is here. For whatever reason, we have become used to having our way, and of justifying it in one way or another. For example, we have our Monroe Doctrine, which has been used as an excuse to justify our intervention in Latin America numerous times. But when other countries have intervened outside their borders, we have often been the first to criticize them. Small wonder that people in other countries find our behavior puzzling at best. We often do not see things from their point of view.

But it is not enough just to understand other viewpoints. Children need to learn to act in a way that reflects this understanding, and often to adopt another point of view when it is superior to their own. Probably few things more impede intellectual development in children (and in adults) than does defensiveness against other points of view. Some people just can't accept criticism. They don't want to hear anyone else's point of view, and when they do, they immediately assume it is wrong. Sometimes it is, but it pays to listen.

As scholars, we frequently submit work for publication. When authors submit their work they receive back evaluations of it, sometimes favorable, but more often than not unfavorable. Indeed, sometimes the reviews are scathing. The first reaction to such reviews is natural—it is to assume that the reviewer is an idiot who doesn't know the first thing she or he is talking about. But we have learned to read the reviews, put them away for a few days, and then read them again. Their quality sometimes improves with age. That is, sometimes when we read the reviews for the second time, we are able to see value in the suggestions that we didn't see at first.

When teachers criticize children, the children's first reaction is often that the teachers must be out of their minds. And even we, as teachers, are the first to admit that teachers can be, and frequently are, wrong. But children need to learn to do the same thing we do—think about the criticisms for a while, consider whether they are coming from other places as well, and only then decide whether to reject them categorically. The chances are that they will contain something the child can use to her or his advantage.

Sometimes people are willing to hear other points of view and even process them. But they refuse to consider the possibility that there might be value in adopting the other point of view themselves. A few years ago, we were teaching a class of teachers in a summer course on how to develop thinking skills in one's students. We decided to do a workshop exercise with the teachers. Each teacher was instructed to write on a sheet of paper some view that she or he held especially dear— something that she or he was almost sure was true. The kinds of things the teachers wrote down varied widely. Some dealt with educational practices, others with religion, others with abortion, and still others with social issues. After the teacher had written down the view, she or he was asked to write a defense—of the opposite point of view. The teachers were given about 20 minutes to do so, and were then asked to present the opposite point of view from the one they had written down.

The results were as interesting as they were surprising. The expectation had been that people would be weak in defending the opposing position—that they only would have thought about the arguments on their own side and hence would barely be able to reconstruct the arguments of the opposition. To our surprise, the students generally did excellent work in reproducing the arguments of their opposition. Oftentimes, they knew them cold. In fact, they were so good at repeating the lines of their opponents that the course instructors asked them to defend their own position. And here is where the surprise emerged: Almost everyone was better at defending the opposite point of view than they were at defending their own! Why?

The exercise suggests that often people do not hold their own point of view for rational reasons, nor have they even carefully thought through this point of view. However, they are familiar with the arguments of the opposing point of view, to which they have no particular attachment. As you might expect, despite the fact that people were often better at arguing for the opposite point of view than for arguing their own, no one has yet changed their point of view as a result of the exercise.

In school, children learn through essays, discussions, and debates to defend their point of view. We believe, however, that children (and adults) need at least as much to learn how to falsify their point of view. In other words, they need to learn how to seek evidence that might show them to be wrong. Without learning how to falsify their point of view, they will never grow beyond where they are.

LESSON 10

Remember That It Is Not the Money You Spend on Your Child That Matters,
but Rather the Quality of Your Interactions with Your Child and the Nature of
Your Child's Experiences

What not to do. Worry about the economic resources you are providing your child and spend as much money as possible on toys, camps, special schools, tutors, special lessons, travel, sports, clothes, computers, and so on. Spend all your time earning money to spend on your children.

What to do. Focus on the quality of your interactions with your child, on how you spend your time together, and on the types of experiences your child is having both with and away from you. Remember that material possessions do not in themselves create children's cognitive competence.

It is well-known that middle–socioeconomic status (SES) children have better educational outcomes than inner-SES children (Coleman, 1966; Grissmer, Nataraj, Berends, and Williamson, 1994; Herrnstein and Murray, 1996). Misinterpreting this fact, many parents often act as though there is a perfect causal relation between the money that is spent on children and the children's performance in school and in life. They buy every "smart" toy in the store; birthdays and holidays become an excuse to flood children with expensive and elaborate gifts. They send their children to several specialty camps every summer and enroll them in expensive private schools, hire tutors to work independently with their children, and sign them up for lesson after lesson and sport after sport. These parents believe that the more they spend the more their children will learn.

The omnipresent link between higher social class and children's enhanced performance causes many parents who lack economic resources to feel as though their children do not stand a chance. These parents may focus on the economic resources other children have that their own children do not have. In fact, they may blame their children's failures on a lack of economic resources. These parents are missing an important point: It is not how much money is spent on children that matters, but rather the quality of their experiences both with and apart from their parents. Giving a child every smart toy and computer game in the store and sending her to a ritzy summer camp will not automatically create a budding genius.

Although there is undeniably a relation between reasonable environmental enrichment and cognitive performance, the relationship is complex. Research by Bronfenbrenner and Ceci (1994) showed that the children of wealthier parents tend to perform better cognitively *not* due to anything inherent in the wealth or education associated with middle-class living, but rather with the greater frequency of what those authors termed "proximal processes." Proximal processes are reciprocal, progressively more complex interactions between a parent and child. For example, initially, a 14-month-old child may say the word "Mommy" and thus gain her mother's attention. Her mother will act excited that the child said the word Mommy. The child will thus be reinforced for saying the word. Over time, however, the child simply saying "Mommy" will bring about less and less of a response from the mother—sometimes, if she is busy, she may not even respond right away to the child. At this point the child will elaborate the statement and say, "Mommy, look!" At this new pronouncement the mother will again become excited. Thus the proximal process taking place is one in which the child's language development is proceeding and the parent is causing the child to grow and elaborate on prior learning. Proximal processes are in evidence when parents are responsive to their child's state and level of functioning. As previously discussed, when parents are randomly assigned to behave either in a proximal-process manner or in a nonresponsive manner, the former's children emerge as more cognitively competent, even though both groups of parents may spend similar amounts of time with their children (Riksen-Walraven, 1978).

Thus, wealth may be associated with better cognitive outcomes for children because of the greater frequency of higher quality behavior rich in proximal processes. In general, social class (and its associated wealth) is a complex variable when it comes to understanding parents and their behavior.

For one thing, social-class differences predict parents' perceptions of their efficacy as influencers of their children (Luster, Rhoades, and Haas, 1989). SES also correlates with patterns of parental behavior and particularly discipline—although these patterns and their relation to social class have changed from the time of the World War II to the present, with middle-SES mothers moving from a more rigid and controlling disciplinary style to a more relaxed style over this time period, and lower-SES mothers displaying the reverse trend (Bronfenbrenner, 1985). Any discussion of the importance of proximal processes in rearing cognitively complex children must take into account the fact that parents of different cultural and economic groups have different amounts of time to engage in proximal processes, and differential access to resources with which to enrich their children's cognitive environments.

Despite these factors and their consequences, any parent, regardless of social class and economic resources, has the power to engage in interactions that enhance her or his children's cognitive development. One study by Blau looked at African American inner-city children living in poverty. Blau tried to determine what factors separated the children who succeeded in life from those who did not. She found that the difference consisted of having one educated adult in a child's life who provided mentoring and role modeling; this one adult was able to help these inner-city children escape the cycle of poverty (Blau, 1981). Blau's results showed that the children with better outcomes had at least one adult with an educational orientation in their lives (this adult could be parent, other relative, friend, or other interested individual)—interacting with one person with an educational focus was essential to the child's outcome.

The lesson for all parents is clear—children are not doomed because their parents cannot afford to shower them with elaborate gifts and toys. Parents should not fixate on economic resources. They must remember that it is the nature of a child's experiences and the quality of the child's interactions with parents or other adults that matter most. Many eminent leaders and people who have changed their world as adults have come from humble beginnings. These individuals often mention the role of mentors in their young lives, adults who got and kept them on track and who excited them about their potential. Major achievements are possible for children regardless of the wealth of their parents and the quality of their homes and possessions. What matters is what children experience and what they do with these experiences, not simply what things they possess.

CONCLUSIONS

In this chapter we have presented 10 lessons that parents can use to foster the intellectual development of their children. They are not the only lessons we might have proposed, but we chose these 10 because of their significant impact on children's development and potential for success. They are all things parents can do right away, and they are all things that will make a big difference.

Nearly 2 decades ago, Heath (1983) conducted a study comparing the development of children in three communities. She found that one of the major differences in children's intellectual development stemmed from the involvement of parents in the intellectual upbringing of the children, not only before the children started school, but after as well. The children of parents who quit involving themselves in their children's intellectual development after the children started school—figuring that this had become the teachers' responsibility—fared worse than the children of parents who remained involved.

This study suggests that much of what we can do to foster the intellectual development of our children does not devolve simply from a specific set of behaviors, but rather from an *attitude*. The attitude is one of seeking activities that promote our children's intellectual development and then participating with the children to help them grow. A good model might be that of the athletic coach. The coach watches and helps, but he does not do the activities for the child. Similarly, the parent should watch and guide, remain involved, but not do for the child what the child needs to do for herself or himself. Importantly, the effective coach and parent engineers an environment for which mastery is within the child's potential grasp and yet poses a meaningful developmental challenge.

Unfortunately, some parents believe they are helping their children when they do their children's homework or their science projects, or otherwise take on their children's responsibilities as their own. The parents may be meeting some inner need of their own, but they are not meeting any need of their child. The coach does not play for the team members; he helps each team member be the best she can be. This is what we try to do for our own children, and what we hope you will try to do for yours.

ACKNOWLEDGMENTS

Preparation of this article was supported by Grant REC-9979843 from the National Science Foundation and Grant R206R950001 from the U.S. Office of Educational Research and Improvement. Grantees undertaking such projects are encouraged to express freely their professional judgment. This article, therefore, does not necessarily represent the positions or policies of the government, and no official endorsement should be inferred.

REFERENCES

Amabile, T. M. (1983). *Social psychology of creativity*. New York: Springer-Verlag.

Amabile, T. M. (1996). *The context of creativity*. Boulder, CO: Westview.

Arlin, P. K. (1990). Wisdom: The art of problem finding. In R. J. Sternberg (Ed.), *Wisdom: Its nature, origins, and development* (pp. 230–243). New York: Cambridge University Press.

Blau, Z. S. (1981). *Black children/White children: Competence, socialization, and social structure*. New York: Free Press.

Boggiano, A. K., Main, D. S., and Katz, P. A. (1988). Children's preference for challenge: The role of perceived competence and control. *Journal of Personality and Social Psychology, 54*, 134–141.

Bouchard, T. J., Jr. (1997). IQ similarity in twins reared apart: Findings and responses to critics. In R. J. Sternberg and E. L. Grigorenko (Eds.), *Intelligence, heredity, and environment* (pp. 126–160). New York: Cambridge University Press.

Bouchard, T. J., Jr., and McGue, M. (1981). Familial studies of intelligence. *Science, 212*, 1055–1059.

Bransford, J. D., and Stein, B. S. (1993). *The ideal problem solver: A guide for improving thinking, learning, and creativity* (2nd ed.). New York: Freeman.

Bronfenbrenner, U. (1985). Freedom and discipline across the decades. In G. Becker and L. Huber (Eds.), *Ordnung und Unordnung: Hartmut von Hentig* (pp. 326–339). Weinheim, Germany: Beltz Verlag.

Bronfenbrenner, U., and Ceci, S. J. (1994). Nature-nurture in developmental perspective: A bioecological theory. *Psychological Review, 101*, 568–586.

Brown, A. L., Bransford, J. D., Ferrara, R. A., and Campione, J. C. (1983). Learning, remembering and understanding. In J. Flavell and E. M. Markman (Eds.), *Handbook of child psychology* (4th ed., Vol. 3, pp. 515–629). New York: Wiley.

Calvin, A. (2000). Use of standardized tests in admissions in postsecondary institutions of higher education. *Psychology, Public Policy, and Law, 6*, 20–32.

Ceci, S. J. (1996). *On intelligence*. Cambridge, MA: Harvard University Press.

Clifford, M. M. (1988). Failure tolerance and academic risk taking in ten- to twelve-year-old students. *British Journal of Educational Psychology, 58*, 15–27.

Coleman, J. S. (1966). *Equality of educational opportunity*. Washington, DC: U.S. Government Printing Office.

Collins, M. A., and Amabile, T. M. (1999). Motivation and creativity. In R. J. Sternberg (Ed.), *Handbook of creativity* (pp. 297–312). New York: Cambridge University Press.

Dewey, J. (1933). *How we think*. Boston: Heath.

Diamond, A., Prevor, M., Callender, G., and Druin, D. P. (1997). Prefrontal cortex cognitive deficits in children treated early and continuously for PKU. *Monographs of the Society for Research in Child Development, 62* (Serial No. 252).

Dweck, C. S. (1999). *Self-theories: Their role in personality, motivation, and development*. Philadelphia: Psychology Press.

Dweck, C. S., and Bempechat, J. (1983). Children's theories of intelligence: Consequences for learning. In S. G. Paris, G. M. Olson, and H. W. Stevenson (Eds.), *Learning and motivation in the classroom* (pp. 239–256). Hillsdale, NJ: Lawrence Erlbaum Associates.

Ericsson, K. A., Krampe, R. Th., and Tesch-Römer, C. (1993). The role of deliberate practice in the acquisition of expert performance. *Psychological Review, 100*, 363–406.

Feuerstein, R. (1980). *Instrumental enrichment: An intervention program for cognitive modifiability.* Baltimore: University Park.

Flynn, J. (in press). The history of the American mind in the 20th century. *Intelligence.*

Getzels, J. W., and Csikszentmihalyi, M. (1976). *The creative vision: Problem finding in art.* Chicago: Van Nostrand.

Goleman, D. (1995). *Emotional intelligence.* New York: Bantam.

Grigorenko, E. L. (2000). Heritability and intelligence. In R. J. Sternberg (Ed.), *Handbook of intelligence* (pp. 53–91). New York: Cambridge University Press.

Grigorenko, E. L., and Sternberg, R. J. (Eds.). (2001). *Family environment and intellectual functioning: A life-span perspective.* Mahwah, NJ: Lawrence Erlbaum Associates.

Grissmer, D. W., Nataraj, S. K., Berends, M., and Williamson, S. (1994). Student achievement and the changing American family. Santa Monica, CA: RAND.

Grotzer, T. A., and Perkins, D. N. (2000). Teaching intelligence: A performance conception. In R. J. Sternberg (Ed.), *Handbook of intelligence* (pp. 292–515). New York: Cambridge University Press.

Gruber, H. E. (1986). The self-construction of the extraordinary. In R. J. Sternberg and J. E. Davidson (Eds.), *Conceptions of giftedness* (pp. 247–263). New York: Cambridge University Press.

Gruber, H. E., and Wallace, D. B. (1999). The case study method and evolving systems approach for understanding unique creative people at work. In R. J. Sternberg (Ed.), *Handbook of creativity* (pp. 93–115). New York: Cambridge University Press.

Hall, J. A. (1984). *Nonverbal sex differences.* Baltimore: Johns Hopkins University Press.

Harris, J. R. (1996). *The nurture assumption.* New York: Free Press.

Hayes, D. P. (1996, Summer). Schoolbook simplification and its relation to the decline in SAT-verbal scores. *American Journal of Education Research*, pp. 116–138.

Heath, S. B. (1983). *Ways with words.* New York: Cambridge University Press.

Herrnstein, R. J., and Murray, C. A. (1996). *The Bell curve.* New York: Free Press.

Luster, T., Rhoades, K., and Haas, B. (1989). The relation between parental values and parenting behavior: A test of the Kohn hypothesis. *Journal of Marriage and the Family, 51*, 139–147.

Mischel, W., Shoda, Y., and Rodriguez, M. L. (1989). Delay of gratification in children. *Science, 244*, 933–938.

Plomin, R. (1988). The nature and nurture of cognitive abilities. In R. J. Sternberg (Ed.), *Advances in the psychology of human intelligence* (Vol. 4, pp. 1–33). Hillsdale, NJ: Lawrence Erlbaum Associates.

Plomin, R. (1997). Identifying genes for cognitive abilities and disabilities. In R. J. Sternberg and E. L. Grigarenkoi (Eds.), *Intelligence, heredity, and environment* (pp. 89–104). New York: Cambridge University Press.

Reis, S. M. (1989). Reflections on policy affecting the education of gifted and talented students. *American Psychologist, 44*, 399–408.

Riksen-Walraven, J. M. (1978). Effects of caregiver behavior on habituation rate and self-efficacy in humans. *International Journal of Behavioral Development, 1*, 105–130.

Rosenthal, R. R., and Jacobson, L. (1968). *Pygmalion in the classroom.* New York: Holt, Rinehart and Winston.

Rotter, J. B. (1966). Generalized expectancies for internal versus external control of reinforcement. *Psychological Monographs, 80* (Whole No. 609).

Rotter, J. B. (1990). Internal versus external control of reinforcement: A case history of a variable. *American Psychologist, 45*, 489–493.

Snow, R. E. (1995). Pygmalion and intelligence? *Current Directions in Psychological Science, 4*, 169–171.

Steele, C. M., and Aronson, J. (1995). Stereotype threat and the intellectual test performance of African Americans. *Journal of Personality and Social Psychology, 69*, 797–811.

Sternberg, R. J. (1985). *Beyond IQ: A triarchic theory of human intelligence.* New York: Cambridge University Press.

Sternberg, R. J. (1986). A triarchic theory of intellectual giftedness. In R. J. Sternberg and J. E. Davidson (Eds.), *Conceptions of giftedness* (pp. 223–243). New York: Cambridge University Press.

Sternberg, R. J. (1988). *The triarchic mind: A new theory of human intelligence.* New York: Viking.

Sternberg, R. J. (1994). Answering questions and questioning answers. *Phi Delta Kappan, 76*, 136–138.

Sternberg, R. J. (1997). *Successful intelligence.* New York: Plume.

Sternberg R. J. (1998). Abilities are forms of developing expertise. *Educational Researcher, 27*, 11–20.

Sternberg, R. J. (1999). The theory of successful intelligence. *Review of General Psychology, 3*, 292–316.

Sternberg, R. J., and Grigorenko, E. L. (Eds.). (2001). *Environmental effects on intellectual functioning.* Mahwah, NJ: Lawrence Erlbaum Associates.

Sternberg, R. J., Forsythe, G. B., Hedlund, J., Horvath, J., Snook, S., Williams, W. M., Wagner, R. K., and Grigorenko, E. L. (2000). *Practical intelligence in everyday life.* New York: Cambridge University Press.

Sternberg, R. J., and Lubart, T. I. (1991). An investment theory of creativity and its development. *Human Development, 34*, 1–31.

Sternberg, R. J., and Lubart, T. I. (1995). *Defying the crowd: Cultivating creativity in a culture of conformity.* New York: Free Press.

Sternberg, R. J., and Lubart, T. I. (1999). The concept of creativity: Prospects and paradigms. In R. J. Sternberg (Ed.), *Handbook of creativity* (pp. 3–15). New York: Cambridge University Press.

Sternberg, R. J., Wagner, R. K., Williams, W. M., and Horvath, J. A. (1995). Testing common sense. *American Psychologist, 50*, 912–927.

Vygotsky, L. (1978). *Mind in society*. Cambridge, MA: Harvard University Press.

Watson, J. B. (1919). *Psychology from the standpoint of a behaviorist*. New York: Norton.

Watson, J. B. (1930). *Behaviorism* (Rev. ed.). New York: Norton.

8

Parenting Talented Children

David Henry Feldman
Tufts University
Jane Piirto
Ashland University

INTRODUCTION

Although few would sympathize with parents who find themselves trying to raise a child with exceptional talent, it is in fact one of the most daunting and often discouraging challenges that family life has to offer. It is not simply the fact that parenting at the extremes of ability requires substantially greater resources of all sorts, although that is certainly the case. Contrary to conventional wisdom, which would have it that the more talented the child, the easier it should be to care for her or him, based on recent findings it appears that the reverse is actually the case (Albert, 1990a, 1990b; Bloom, 1981, 1985; Feldman and Goldsmith, 1991; Radford, 1990; Sears, 1979). In addition, rearing children who have extraordinary abilities sometimes engenders negative responses from others in the community, ranging from mild ambivalence to downright hostility.

This chapter discusses some of the issues that confront parents who must try to meet the unique challenges associated with developing the full potential of their talented children. Of course, all parents want to do the best to bring forth and nurture the abilities and interests of their children, but not all parents feel the burden of responsibility that comes from a realization that a child may have exceptional potential. This awareness alone makes the parenting situation quite unlike that which faces most typical parents. Of course, the old saying "All children are gifted" may be true, but those children with outstanding talent demand special efforts from all the systems with which they come into contact: the family, school, and society.

Parents must identify the specific nature of the child's talent and decide how to respond. In some instances, the talents may be multiple, compounding both the identification and the response problems. It may seem obvious that there is not one form of giftedness but several, and that these several kinds of giftedness may have different sorts of implications for parenting (Feldman, 2000; Goldsmith, 2000; Morelock, 2000; Morelock and Feldman, 1991, 1993; Piirto, 1998b, 1999b). And yet, the field that investigates and tries to serve those with exceptional abilities has tended to focus its efforts on one kind of talent, namely the kind that equips a child to do well in a traditional school curriculum. Academic talent is most often identified by using standardized IQ tests or achievement tests.

In fact, the very term *gifted* has come, in the minds of some researchers and to the consternation of others, to be synonymous with having a high IQ (Gagné, 1985; Gardner, 1982, 1983; Piirto, 1999b; Smutny and Eby, 1990; Sternberg, 1985; Tannenbaum, 1983, 1986). In recent years there has been increasing pressure to move toward a more diverse and inclusive notion of *talent*; it is fair to say that the field is currently in a state of transition (Feldman, 1992; Piirto, 1994). The shift from a focus on more general academic talent to an emphasis on multiple specific gifts is a major one and will affect theory, research, and practice with talented children (Feldhusen, 1995; Feldman, 1992; Gardner, 1983; Treffinger, 1991). The field is beginning to see shifts in definitions, policies, and practices aimed at meeting the needs of talented children. For parents, a shift in the underlying conceptualization of the field may well mean a rapidly changing environment within which decisions must be made.

It is beyond the scope of the present chapter to try to provide a review of all of the known forms of talent and giftedness and their consequences for issues of parenting. At best we can provide an overview of the range and variety of the many forms that talents and gifts might take, and then try to suggest what these forms of talent and giftedness might mean for parents and for those who work with parents of talented children.

The chapter is divided into seven main sections. The first deals with general family systems theory and its relationship to talent development. The second deals with parenting children with extreme talent such as that manifested in prodigies and students with very high IQs, more than three standard deviations above the mean (a frequency of fewer than 5 students per 1,000) or students in the top 1% of achievers on the Scholastic Aptitude Test (SAT) and the American College Test (ACT). The third deals with developing talents in young children. The fourth section deals with the kinds of gifts and talents that have received the greatest amount of attention from the scholarly and applied fields during the past half century. These have been of two sorts: general academic talent beyond that of most peers, but not at the far extreme, and some specific kinds of talents. The fifth deals with underachievement as a phenomenon recognized by therapists and educators of academically talented students. The sixth deals with parenting students of different ethnic and economic groups. The seventh section deals with the influence of pressure toward achievement on talent development, with a focus on different parenting styles.

General academic talent means that the child has the ability to do unusually well in standard academic settings embracing traditional curricula and teaching methods. Academic talent of this sort is usually discovered through testing, although other means of identification such as teacher or parent observations, or peer or self nomination, are occasionally used, particularly at younger ages. More specific talents such as artistic or scientific or leadership talent tend to be discovered through children's activities, observations by parents and/or teachers, and performance in organized activities. Occasionally, special testing programs are aimed at the discovery of specific kinds of talent (e.g., the talent searches of Johns Hopkins University, Northwestern University, Duke University and others, or such programs as the Westinghouse Talent Search in science).

There have been more efforts to respond to the needs of academically talented children than to any other form of talent, and so the available options from which parents may choose are both more numerous and better established within most public school systems than are options for the development of extreme academic talent (or very high IQ) or the more specific talent areas. This is not to suggest that resources available are likely to be sufficient, because even in the most active communities with the longest traditions of support for "gifted education," programs are rarely available for children at all age levels; this is especially true for younger children (Alvino, 1985, 1989; Lewis, 1979; Smutney, 1998; Tannenbaum, 1983). Most formal programs begin during the later elementary school years at the earliest. By then, patterns of underachievement may have set in (Piirto, 1999b).

When we turn to the more specific kinds of gifts and talents, we will see that these talents are on the one hand more numerous and on the other hand less systematically served than general academic talent. This means that the challenges facing parents of children with powerful talents that are directed toward more specific domains such as music or dance or sports or computers are at once more difficult to meet and less likely to be met through well-established channels of support, information, or guidance.

THE FAMILY SYSTEM AND THE DEVELOPMENT OF TALENT

There is a saying that talent seems to run in families. Actors breed actors (the Fondas, the Redgraves, the Sheens); professors breed professors (Margaret Mead, Arthur Schlesinger, Jr.); race car drivers breed race car drivers (the Unsers, the Pettys); athletes breed athletes (the Ripkens, the Roses); artists breed artists (the Wyeths, the Renoirs); writers breed writers (the Cheevers, the Updikes); musicians breed musicians (the Graffmans, the Bachs; Albert, 1990a, 1990b; Brophy and Goode, 1988; Goertzel and Goertzel, 1962; Goertzel, Goertzel, and Goertzel, 1978; Simonton, 1984, 1988, 1991, 1994, 1999). Family systems theory has been developed to explain this phenomenon of "like father, like son" (Fine and Carlson, 1992). In family systems theory, a child's talent is viewed as an adaptation of the child to the entire family's interactions. This includes parents, grandparents, and siblings, and takes into account birth order, labeling, and gender (Jenkins-Friedman, 1992). The notion that there is something in the family's interactions that produces talented behaviors takes into account the environment within which a child is reared and that child's responses to the environment (Sulloway, 1996).

Plomin (1997, p. 70) summarized the genetic studies about the relationship between general cognitive ability, heredity, and environment: "Genetic contributions to individual differences in IQ test scores are significant and substantial," he said. Correlations between twins reared apart is greater than for nonrelated siblings reared together. "About half of the IQ differences among individuals in the population can be accounted for by genetic differences among them". Verbal abilities and spatial abilities are more heritable than memory and speed of information processing. As people get older, they show more similarity to their genetic relatives. An interesting finding was that ability (or IQ) test scores and achievement test scores, though they are often similar, reveal differences. "The overlap between intelligence and scholastic achievement is due entirely to genetic factors, whereas the differences between them are environmental in origin" (Plomin, 1997, p. 73). In other words, underachievement (a disparity between achievement test scores and ability test scores) seems to be environmental.

Simonton (1984) found that the age of the parents matters, and younger parents who are able to interest their children in their own passions seem to be better able to excite their children to follow in their footsteps. An example from novelist and essayist Susan Cheever's memoir, *Home Before Dark* (1984, p. 107) illustrates how interest was developed in the children of a writer:

> Every Sunday after dinner, we each recited a poem for the rest of the family. It began with sonnets and short narrative verse, Shakespeare and Tennyson, but soon we were spending whole weekends in competitive feats of memory. My father memorized Dylan Thomas's "Fern Hill," my mother countered with Keats' "Ode to a Nightingale," I did "Barbara Fritchie," my father did "The Charge of the Light Brigade," and so forth. Ben, who was eight, stayed with shorter poems."

Age of parents also takes into account the high level of energy it takes to keep up with a talented child.

There are a number of factors that will determine how parents will react to the presence of great talents in their children. The birth position of the child is one factor (Sulloway, 1996). The last born tends to be more rebellious and perhaps more creative; the firstborn tends to be more conservative and seeks approval more. Simonton (1984, 1988) noted that firstborns tend to reach eminence or to be considered geniuses more often than their younger siblings, but there is some evidence that laterborns whose births have been spaced several years apart have similar opportunities. Much seems to depend on parental will and energy to nurture that talent (Kulieke and Olszewski-Kubilius, 1989).

Family values may place particular importance on certain talents such as music or mathematics, and traditions that provide a context within which the response to talent takes place. For these reasons, children with the same set of talents, manifesting themselves in the same ways but reared in different families, may provoke a strikingly different response depending on one or more of the factors just listed (Benbow, 1992; Feldman, 1992; Feldman and Goldsmith, 1991; Morelock and Feldman, 1991).

A number of studies converge on the idea that a responsive set of parents and a family that values achievement (particularly in the target domain) are critical catalysts in cases of extreme potential (Bloom, 1981, 1985; Feldman and Goldsmith, 1991; Goertzel and Goertzel, 1962; Goertzel et al., 1978; Goldsmith, 1987, 1990; Kulieke and Olszewski-Kubilius, 1989; Radford, 1990; VanTassel-Baska, 1989). This is not to say that children whose homes have been turbulent, fractionated, or even pathological have not sometimes attained eminence or remarkably high achievement, especially achievement in artistic domains (Albert, 1980; Piirto, 1998b).

Many family systems operate on what has been called a dysfunctional level, and these interactions, too, have enhanced talent development. In fact, VanTassel-Baska and Olszewski-Kubilius (1989, p. 8) noted that "some form of adversity or a seemingly inhibiting or detrimental factor which exists within the family structure or happens to the individual can and does somehow work in a beneficial, generative manner." Among such factors are cultural and economic disadvantage, physical deformity, rejection by parents or peers, tension in the family, and parental loss.

Simonton (1988) called the latter "the orphanhood effect." For many children, a parent's death is a provocation for achievement. The mother of Jane and Peter Fonda committed suicide, as did the father of one of Jane's husbands, Ted Turner. So did the mother of the surrealistic painter Magritte. Edgar Allen Poe's mother died, and he and his sister were in the room with her body for several days. Terr (1990) speculated that this precipitated Poe's fascination with death and horror. The poet Robert Frost's father died when he was 11 years old. The writer William Styron's mother died when he was 13, and in his memoir, *Darkness Visible*, he attributed a depression at 60 to "incomplete mourning" (1990, p. 81). This "orphanhood effect" may also have affected Abraham Lincoln, who was an only child whose mother died young.

High achievement after childhood trauma is an area that is not fully explored. The psychoanalyst Miller (1981) postulated that adult achievement in creative domains takes place when there has been childhood trauma with warmth present, whereas childhood trauma without warmth present can produce adult destructive behavior. Albert (1980) called it "wobble," the presence in the families of creative people of tension and dissent. The implications for parents with talented children seem to be that troubles should be faced, dealt with, and the children should be encouraged to express themselves not only in therapy, but through metaphoric media such as the arts (Piirto, 1998b, 1999b). The preponderance of the evidence, however, suggests that the more valued a particular form of talent tends to be within a family, and the greater the amount of support the talent is given, the greater the degree to which those talents will be expressed in significant achievement.

The family's lifestyle is a great influence on a child's and a teenager's talent development and school achievement. Nontraditional lifestyles do not seem to affect achievement as much as one would think. Rather, it is the closeness of the family and the degree to which the family considers itself a family that is important. A 12-year longitudinal study of nontraditional families by Weisner and Garnier (1992, p. 621) showed that academic achievement is not negatively affected when a child is in a one-parent family, a low-income family, a family with "frequent changes in mates or in household composition" if one particular factor was present: if the family chose the lifestyle because it had an intelligible and clear meaning for them, for instance, a religious choice leading to home-schooling. If the nonconventional family emphasized achievement as important, the children did not experience a lowered achievement pattern.

Even though the parents may have been "highly experimental" in such arenas as diet or health care, they saw that their children had inoculations and medical and dental checkups. They thought it was important for their children to do well in school. Indeed, they found that "some nonconventional life-styles can protect children against possible difficulties in school," whereas others can put children at risk. The variable that was important was that the parents were committed to the lifestyle and to the importance of school achievement. One thinks of the "aging hippies," the "bohemian actors," and the "poor struggling artists in garrets" as being in this category. Although poor or in conventional living arrangements, their children are often high achievers who follow in their parents' footsteps, just as children do from families with more conventional lifestyles.

As evidence that family systems have differential effects on genetically similar members, there is some confirmation that siblings reared within the same family often turn out to be remarkably different (e.g., the eminent beat poet Allen Ginsberg and his older brother, Eugene, who was a lawyer; both were sons of a mother who was a schizophrenic and a father who was a high school teacher and poet). Louis Ginsberg, their father, said of Allen's choice of career: "Is he a poet by nature or nurture? I think both" (Miles, 1989, p. 29). The writer Graham Greene was a middle child in a large and nurturing family, and his father was a headmaster. Greene viewed his world with such great sensitivity that he attempted suicide in boarding school during his teenage years; he had to go into psychoanalysis while his older brothers thrived and were school leaders (Sherry, 1989).

Piechowski's interpretation of Dabrowski's "overexcitability" theory may be in operation here; that is, the intensity with which each child perceives events may differ, and what may send one child into extreme reactions may just wash off another child's back (Piechowski, 1979, 1989, 1991). In fact, the children's temperament and personality may be most important in the development of their talents, and even in the case of multitalented children, in the family's choice of which talent to develop. A passive, dreamy personality and temperament may lend itself to the quiet, endless reading that seems to have been evident in the childhoods of most adult writers; an aggressive personality and temperament may lend itself to the cutthroat world of childhood chess or athletics (Piirto, 1994, 1998b, 1999a, 2001).

It is relatively easy for a child to do something his parents approve of and value, and for which they provide teachers, tutors, and materials. The biographical literature is rife with stories of people whose parents pointed them in the right direction and then who stood back and watched them develop. "My son the doctor" is often pointed to medicine by parental desire and will. Sosniak (1985a, in Bloom, 1985), in her study of world-class research neurologists, found that even in college, when some of them thought they would change majors, their parents expressed disapproval and they stayed on the premed track. One said he thought his parents weren't that involved in his choice of career until he threatened not to pursue medicine, and then he found out how adamant they were. This illustrates the strong influence of the family system on a child's interaction with the world.

Other traumas that tear apart the traditionally intact family system are divorce, illness, frequent moving, physical, verbal, and sexual abuse, and the like. Talented youth who become scientists, mathematicians, and classical musicians seem to have come from families that were more stable than the families of actors, writers, popular musicians, visual artists, and dancers–people in the arts (Kulieke and Olszewski-Kubilius, 1989; Piirto, 1992, 1994, 1998b, 1999a). Perhaps the long schooling necessary for functioning as an adult scientist, mathematician, or musician is a result of a family striving together to develop the potential of a talented child.

The fact that many talented adults came from family situations that were less than ideal illustrates that even the most laissez-faire parenting has an impact on talent development. Two interesting phenomena are operant. One is the "stage mother" or "Little League father" situation, where the parent is obsessed, even to the point of destructive narcissism, with the development of a child's talent, whether or not the child wants to have her or his talent developed. The other is the "I don't care what you do just so long as you're happy" situation, where busy parents do what is necessary for safety and health, but little beyond that. Both situations can produce talented adults. Judy Garland is an example of the former; her mother was so obsessed with Judy's career as a child actress that she even permitted the use of amphetamines and tranquilizers so that Judy could work longer hours in the studio (Edwards, 1975). An example of the latter is the mother of the actor and comedian Steve Allen, who permitted him to move, alone, from Chicago to the Southwest at the age of 16 in order to take a job as a radio announcer.

Other parents move with their children to pursue the talent. The mother of the dancer Suzanne Farrell moved Suzanne and her two sisters from Cincinnati to New York City at the offer of an audition with Balanchine; they lived in one room while their mother was a private nurse (Farrell and Bentley, 1990). However, Farrell said her mother was not a "stage mother" because she always worked to support them and never hovered in the practice room antechambers with the other mothers to gossip. The parents of Albert Einstein moved to Italy when he was a teenager, leaving him to board with a local family and attend the gymnasium by himself. He soon quit and went to join his family, never to graduate (Clark, 1971). However, Einstein's father, like Edward Teller's (Blumberg and Panos, 1990), saw his son's mathematical talent and provided him with a college student tutor.

The concert pianist Gary Graffman's father was a violinist, and he frequently sat with Gary while he practiced his lessons (Graffman, 1981). Graffman gave a concert at Carnegie Hall during his early teenage years. The strong influence of family interests is especially operant in the pursuit of musical talent. According to Graffman (1981, p. 47):

> Even though my father was dead set against turning me into a child performer, daily practicing came first: I practiced every morning from 7:20 to 8:20 before school (in addition to two or three hours afterward). Whether or not I wanted to do this was never a consideration. My parents brought me up in a loving, but strict, European manner. I was not consulted in such matters. One went to school, one ate what was set before one; one practiced. It was as simple as that.

Thus, the families of talented children cope with the talent in remarkably different ways; some focus on it and some ignore it. On balance, though, those that focus on their children's talent development are more likely to see the child's talent fulfilled.

Baumrind (1971) indicated that there are three parenting styles: authoritarian, authoritative, and permissive. All three environments have produced talented adults, although the authoritarian style seems to produce resentment and stifling that forces talented students to sneak, hide, and sublimate the expression of their talent so that it takes place outside the home or surfaces later in life. For example, the social reformer Margaret Sanger was forced to leave home in order to gain the freedom to finish school; her mother had had 18 pregnancies and died of cervical cancer at age 49. Margaret's alcoholic father wanted her to be his housekeeper. Gray (1979, p. 25) reported that ". . . she let their run-down house deteriorate even more. Realizing she could never get enough money to return to Claverack to graduate, she decided to leave Corning for good."

Another example is the actor Marlon Brando, who was sent to military school by parents who didn't know what to do with his rebelliousness. He was asked to leave the school and came to New York City to live with his sisters, who were studying the arts. He wanted to study acting, but his father disapproved. As Thomas (1973, p. 20) said, "Marlon would not be dissuaded by his father's scorn." Although he had considered many careers, including the ministry, acting appealed to him. He began to study with Stella Adler at the New School for Social Research.

There is also some evidence that gender of the child and parent influence the development of various kinds of talent. Male writers, for example, seem to have had what Miller (1987, p. 114) called ineffectual fathers: "It would strike me years later how many male writers had fathers who had actually failed or whom the sons had perceived as failures." She noted that this was the case for Faulkner, Fitzgerald, Hemingway, Wolfe, Poe, Steinbeck, Melville, Whitman, Chekhov, Hawthorne, Strindberg, and Dostoevsky. The same is true for women writers (Piirto, 1998a, 2001). Mothers' attitudes toward mathematics have greatly influenced both their sons' and their daughters' achievement.

If mothers say, "Well, I was not any good at math, either," daughters especially might view mathematics as not being a gender-appropriate field to pursue (Eccles and Harold, 1992).

Students with high academic talent who participated in the talent searches conducted among seventh graders also had differential influence by fathers and mothers (Benbow, 1992; Kulieke and Olszewski-Kubilius, 1989; VanTassel-Baska, 1989). Academically talented youth who participated in the talent searches tend to have strong, highly educated fathers as well as mothers who are also highly educated but who do not work full time outside the home. These are tendencies, however. Helson (1983) noted that creative female mathematicians were often only children whose fathers treated them like sons.

PARENTING CHILDREN WITH EXTREME TALENTS

The following types of extreme talents are discussed here: cases of extremely high IQ; cases of extreme talents in specific areas, with or without notable high IQs to go along with them; and genius or eminence, an outcome which has been extensively studied in relation to parenting.

Extremely high IQ has been a topic of study for nearly a century. It began with Terman's massive *Genetic Studies of Genius* in the 1920s (Sears, 1979) and continues to the present day (Tomlinson-Keasey and Little, 1990). Studies of extreme talents in specific areas have been more recent and still more sporadic phenomena, falling into two categories: extreme talent in (usually) mathematical or verbal abilities such as shown by a very high score on the Scholastic Aptitude Tests (e.g., Benbow, 1992; Benbow and Minor, 1990; Hunt, Lunneborg, and Lewis, 1975) or on the American College Tests (Colangelo and Kerr, 1990). One difference found in these extremely high scorers was that high mathematics scorers had superior short-term memory and high verbal scorers had superior long-term memory. High verbal scorers often use their verbal ability in fields that are less specific to their ability than do high mathematics scorers. For example, high verbal talent is necessary in academe, business, leadership and politics, law, and most high-level professions. On the other hand, the lack of high mathematical ability does not mean a person cannot reach eminence. High mathematical ability is much more specific to achievement in science and mathematics (and possibly in invention).

A second area in which extreme talent has been studied is in child prodigies in various specific fields (e.g., Deakin, 1972; Feldman and Goldsmith, 1991; Radford, 1990). Studies of genius and eminence go back at least to Sir Francis Galton (1869) and have been carried on in recent years by Albert (1983, 1990a, 1990b; Albert and Runco, 1986) and Simonton (1984, 1988, 1990, 1992, 1994, 1999), among others. Here, too, family variables have often been found to play a significant role in determining the degree of expression of talent. Biographical studies have produced a substantial amount of information about family influence on the achievement of eminence (Goertzel and Goertzel, 1962; Goertzel et al., 1978).

It should also be noted that, with the exception of Simonton's work (1984, 1988, 1991, 1994, 1999) on historical movements and to some extent Bloom's (1985) on world-class performers, virtually all of the information available from observations of parenting, family structure, and the like is based on the study of individuals or relatively small groups of cases. This means that the data base is quite small on the one hand, but on the other hand such studies often produce rich and extensive information about each situation. There have been few studies of extreme talent that have examined relations among parenting variables and outcomes in children. There have been still fewer studies that attempt to control or manipulate variables, thus limiting the generalizability of findings.

Because the topic of study is so specific to individuals, that is, how their talent was nurtured and developed, this limitation of the research does not look to be easily remedied. Longitudinal studies such as Terman (1925, 1930; Terman and Oden, 1959), Subotnik and Steiner's (1993) study of Westinghouse winners, Arnold's study of Illinois valedictorians (Arnold, 1995; Subotnik and Arnold, 1993), the work by the Study of Mathematically Precocious Youth (SMPY, Benbow, 1993, 2000; Benbow and Lubinski, 1995, 1997) or snapshot studies such as Harris (1990) of the students at the Hollingworth experimental schools in New York City, and the follow-up studies of high-IQ students who attended the Hunter College Campus Schools in New York City (Subotnik, Karp, and Morgan, 1989; Subotnik, Kasson, Summers, and Wasser, 1993) are imperfect but valuable ways of looking at high-IQ and high-achieving students. Most of the students in the Hunter and Hollingworth studies had IQs about three standard deviations above the mean.

Case studies are often the method of choice when an area of investigation is just beginning. This technique is better suited to exploring unknown psychological terrain; Freud's work on the unconscious, Piaget's studies of babies, or Darwin's observations of his son Doddy (Kessen, 1965) were all based on case study research. This should alert the reader to the fact that work in extreme giftedness is still in its early phases, and that whatever patterns of parent behavior have been observed should be taken as provisional.

Those who have studied parenting in cases of extreme giftedness have found that there are many similarities between these situations and the situation of parenting children with handicaps (Albert and Runco, 1986; Bloom, 1982, 1985; Borland, 1989; Clark, 1992; Feldman and Goldsmith, 1991; Goldsmith, 2000; Hall and Skinner, 1980; Morelock, 1995, 2000; Robinson, Zigler, and Gallagher, 2001; Tannenbaum, 1983; Treffert, 1989; Vail, 1987). One difference between the two kinds of extreme situations is that impediments to functioning are quite naturally seen as a higher priority for support, and consequently the allocation of resources tends to be much more substantial, whereas in all but a few countries talents are typically seen as the responsibility of the individual child and her or his family. This makes the likelihood of successfully rearing talented children often as dependent on parents' abilities to generate adequate material resources as on their parenting skills. We consider three issues about parenting extremely talented children: recognizing extreme talents and gifts; responding to identified talents and gifts; and sustaining optimal conditions for the development of talents and gifts.

Recognizing Extreme Gifts and Talents

The first task that faces parents who may think that they have a child of unusual potential is to try to identify what the nature and strength of that talent might be. For some talents this is a relatively straightforward matter, even during the first few year of life. For other talents and gifts, the signs may be more subtle, or not evident until the child is much older.

For the 120 participants in Bloom's (1985) study of world-class performers—mathematicians, research neurologists, concert pianists, sculptors, Olympic swimmers, and tennis champions—the talents that were to lead to such high levels of achievement before age 35 were evident before the age of 5 for some fields, but not others. For research neurologists, mathematicians, and to some extent sculptors, there were few early signs of the children's extreme potential. However, the swimmers and tennis players as well as the pianists were identified as having a special inclination toward the particular field before the age of 5 (Bloom, 1981, 1985; Gustin, 1985; Sloan and Sosniak, 1985; Sosniak, 1985a, 1985b). The identified talent was not always exactly a match for the future field of excellence; for example, a child might have been intensely interested in all ball games before the age of 5 but focused on tennis during the succeeding 5 years.

The research of Bloom, Sosniak, Gustin, and Sloan also revealed that few of the children, across fields, were thought to be child prodigies, that is, to have prodigious talents that leaped full blown into existence. The growth trajectory was more gradual and tended to follow a pattern of expression that depended on the presence of attentive and active parental support, direction, and encouragement. This pattern was also found by Feldman and Goldsmith (1991) and Goldsmith (2000) in child prodigy cases. It was also true that in all fields there was an early need to involve other people who could offer specialized instruction in the target field. In explicit contradiction to the often believed view that extreme talent will somehow express itself, Bloom and his coworkers (1985) found that sustained efforts to identify and nurture talents in their children was a distinguishing feature of the families in the study.

Parenting Children with Extreme Talent: General and Specific

Although the data are less plentiful, it has been found that the more extreme the talents of children, the more extreme will be the qualities and characteristics of their parents (Deakin, 1972; Feldman, 2000; Feldman and Goldsmith, 1991; Goertzel and Goertzel, 1962; Goertzel et al., 1978; Treffert, 1989). For example, in their study of child prodigies, Feldman and Goldsmith found that in each of the six families one or both of the parents essentially devoted their life to providing optimal support for a child's emerging talent. The families also tended to see themselves as different from other families, to isolate themselves from the rest of the community, and to create a kind of cocoon-like structure to nurture their child's early development (Feldman, 1992). These prospective findings tend to be confirmed by the retrospective data on those who have achieved eminence in their lives and careers (Goertzel and Goertzel, 1962; Goertzel et al., 1978).

Parents who were highly opinionated, actively involved in causes or movements, and sometimes unstable were common in the families of those who were to become eminent. On the other hand, it appears that the families in Bloom's (1985) sample of "world-class" performers provided a more stable and tranquil context, albeit one highly focused on the particular domain to be mastered. The cocoon-like quality that Feldman found in the prodigy families seemed to be present as well in the Bloom sample, but with a somewhat different emotional tone. The families of the prodigies seemed more fortresslike, whereas the world-class performers seemed open but protective and focused on the task at hand.

In a longitudinal study of six male child prodigies in fields ranging from chess to music to science to writing, Feldman (Feldman and Goldsmith, 1991; Goldsmith, 2000; Radford, 1990) found that even among these very extreme cases it was not obvious before age 5 for three of the children in what field they would become a prodigy. For one of the musicians and the two chess players in the sample, their talents were strikingly obvious, whereas for the writer, the scientist, and one child whose gifts were so diverse that it was impossible to guess in what direction he would go, the specific focus of talent was not apparent that early.

In a follow-up to the six boy prodigies described by Feldman and Goldsmith (1991), Goldsmith (2000) found that their early adulthood experiences varied from case to case. In two cases, relatively steady progress from early prodigiousness to adult successful careers seemed well under way. A boy who chose violin performance at 10 was establishing himself as an internationally active solo performer, whereas another boy, whose writing interests began at age 3, found himself able to integrate music interests that emerged at about age 8 into a highly successful music journalism career. Another child has become a successful adult, but not in the field of his prodigious activity. By age 10 this child had given up the game of chess and turned his attention to other pursuits. He is currently a lawyer at a large New York firm and seems on his way to a successful career there. A child who was multitalented as well, but who gravitated toward music, has been involved in becoming a more well-rounded person during his early 20s, and it is not clear at this point what direction he will take. Finally, two of the six boys have not been located, one who was strongly focused in natural science, the other a chess player who left chess, but whose academic and professional record was spotty and erratic.

Major differences between and among the family situations of the boys in this study may have accounted for at least some of the variations in how the boys managed the transition from prodigies to young adults. The families that seemed stable and connected to the wider world seemed to have fared better in preparing their talented boys for productive activities as young adults. The more isolated families were at greater risk for disintegration when their boys began to assert their independence, perhaps because so much of their closeness revolved around responding to the child's great talents. The greater the continuity, both in terms of the fields chosen to pursue, and in terms of the family's ability to adapt to changing circumstances, the greater the likelihood that the outcome would be positive for the child, even if the outcome was different from what marked the child as talented earlier (Goldsmith, 2000).

Bloom's, Feldman's, and Goldsmith's research shows that early identification and valuing of talents tend to occur in homes where there is already a tradition of involvement in a relevant field. In other words, if a child with musical talent is born into a family that values and enjoys music and where music is an important part of family life, the chances are better that this talent will be recognized and developed than in a family with different values.

There are few, if any, performers at the top of their fields in classical music or chess who began playing later than age 10, whereas beginning the process by age 3 or 4 confers a distinct advantage. Whether or not there is a critical period in the strict sense of the term (i.e., a period of time during which it is essential to be exposed to a particular kind of stimulation) is not known, but it is true that the later a talent for chess or music is discovered, the less likely it is to be fully expressed. If not discovered and responded to before age 10, the likelihood of full expression of potential is greatly reduced (Feldman and Goldsmith, 1991).

In other fields (such as writing, art, mathematics, dance, and most sports), identifying a strong talent and responding to it can occur several years later. Most writers, artists, and mathematicians, for example, do not begin serious preparation until after age 12, although the interests, predispositions, and predictive behaviors are evident earlier (Piirto, 1999a). For example, the mathematician and philosopher Bertrand Russell and the theoretical physicists Albert Einstein and Edward Teller all demonstrated their passion for mathematics and logical thought before they were 10. Russell (1967, p. 38) wrote:

> At the age of eleven, I began Euclid, with my brother as my tutor. This was one of the great events of my life, as dazzling as first love. I had not imagined that there was anything so delicious in the world. After I had learned the fifth proposition, my brother told me that it was generally considered difficult, but I had found no difficulty whatever. This was the first time it had dawned upon me that I might have some intelligence. From that moment until Whitehead and I finished *Principia Mathematica*, when I was thirty-eight, mathematics was my chief interest, and my chief source of happiness.

For the most part, however, students who pursue natural science and philosophical studies tend to begin later, often well into the teens (Feldman and Goldsmith, 1991; Lehman, 1953).

If a child is a girl, and girls are not encouraged to pursue particular fields, or if a child is later born and only firstborn children tend to be seen as especially talented, the chances of noticing a talent are certainly reduced. Or, if a family's history is focused on one domain, such as theater or medicine or music, but the child's talent happens to be in a different domain, again the chances are diminished that an extraordinary talent will be recognized (Feldman and Goldsmith, 1991). As more is known about the relation between a child's natural areas of talent and a family's match or mismatch with those talents, it may be possible to equip parents to better recognize talent in areas other than those to which they are naturally predisposed. Once recognized and responded to, it then falls to parents to decide how to sustain the development of a talent that has emerged in their child.

When we shift our focus to the more general academic abilities, there are many studies of early identification of high IQ in children. The literature shows that it is difficult to determine the degree of general intellectual giftedness before the child is 3 years old (Roedell, Jackson, and Robinson, 1980; Louis, Lewis, Subotnik, and Breland, 2000). Some studies have used experimental procedures during early infancy to predict IQs at later ages, but these procedures are not available to parents, and are in any case still in the early phases of development (Bornstein, 1989; Rose, 1989). A study of the families of Head Start students who were high achievers showed that the parents had greater education, more income, fewer children, and were probably European American. Contrary to those who did not achieve, these parents rarely suffered from depression and their parents were more attentive, tractable, and promoted the children's autonomy (Robinson, Weinberg, Redden, Ramey, and Ramey, 1998).

SUSTAINING THE DEVELOPMENT OF EXCEPTIONAL TALENTS IN YOUNG CHILDREN

It is now well established that a talent, however extreme it may be, requires sustained, coordinated, and effective support from parents and others for a period of at least 10 years to have a chance of fulfilling its promise (Bloom, 1985; Feldman and Goldsmith, 1991; Hayes, 1981; Morelock and Feldman, 1991; Piirto, 1999b). Having great talent does not guarantee great achievement, nor is talent capable of expressing itself without substantial resources external to the child.

Therefore, the decision to try to develop even an extreme talent has profound implications for every member of the target child's family. It is unlikely that a family will have the resources to sustain more than one process at the same time (Bloom, 1985; Feldman and Goldsmith, 1991; VanTassel-Baska and Olszewski-Kubilius, 1989). This means that siblings of the target child are likely to receive a great deal less, proportionally, of the family's resources, a reality often difficult to accept and live with (Rolfe, 1978). The need to focus or refocus resources makes it in some ways not surprising that there is rarely more than one prodigy in a family and that families historically have tended to concentrate on the first born (usually male) child when it comes to talent development (Feldman and Goldsmith, 1991; Goldsmith, 1990; Radford, 1990). There is also a folk wisdom (however objectionable within contemporary contexts) to withhold support and assistance from talented girls. Because in most cultures the likelihood of a daughter being able to fulfill her talent was less than a son because of lack of opportunity, prejudice, and established networks and institutions, it follows that an investment in her talent would be not as likely to bear full fruit (Goldsmith, 1987, 1990; Greer, 1979; Piirto, 1991b).

How is a parent to know if the sacrifices necessary to develop a child's talent are worth making? This is a question that may seem to have an obvious answer, but in truth does not. Of course, most parents would say that they want to develop a child's talents to their fullest, whatever the cost. But few families have the resources to develop every child's talents to their fullest expression, and that often makes it necessary to choose one child's talents rather than another's, to focus on, or to insist that all the children develop talents in the same domain—the domain valued by the parents. This was the case, for example, with the three Polgar sisters, chess players all. Thus, we have the establishment of salons, dynasties, or teams. "Going into the family business" is a common practice in the development of all talents, not just extreme talent. If a family with a child who has great musical talent, for example, lives in a rural area far from the next level teacher, and the lessons must be taken weekly or semiweekly, the family is faced with a decision: Shall we move to be nearer the teacher? Moves such as this were documented by Feldman and Goldsmith (1991) in the case of one of the prodigies studied, who moved from another city to the Boston area to find a suitable school, but moves to develop the talent are more common in the cases of talented athletes (especially tennis, ice skating, and gymnastics) or musicians. The decision to develop a talent is one that requires reflection as to parents' values, goals, and priorities as well as a realistic assessment of the strength of the child's talent and the effect that developing the talent will have on the family system, especially the siblings.

To help with the decision whether or not to pursue full talent development, it is often wise to consult with individuals who are knowledgeable about the domain in question and who have had experience in what it means to go through a rigorous, protracted training process. This is especially true for parents who find themselves trying to reckon the strength of a child's talent in a field with which they themselves are unfamiliar. Even when parents are experienced in the domain in question, there are reasons to seek advice from outside experts or consultants. First, it is difficult for parents to accurately assess the potential in their own children because of their close attachment to them. And second, coaches, master teachers, trainers, and high-level practitioners generally have much more experience than parents in assessing and developing talent. Parents have themselves and their children to use as a primary basis for judgment. An active coach or teacher may have worked with hundreds of students (Bloom, 1985; Feldman and Goldsmith, 1991).

In most instances, the advice given by experienced people within a domain will not be definitive with respect to the course of the talent's development. This is true for several reasons, the most important of which is that it is not possible to predict with confidence what will happen to a talent over time. There are too many uncertainties in the process to assert with confidence what the course of a child's progress will be. Indeed, parents would be wise to question too positive a prediction, particularly if the person giving that prediction is trying to recruit the child into a program, school, or relationship.

The earlier the prediction about the strength and distinctiveness of a given talent, the less confidence can be placed in its accuracy. This is not so much because it is impossible to detect and assay talent early; in some fields such as chess, music, and certain athletic domains talent can be assessed at very early ages, often younger than 5. The uncertainty in making predictions is that there are many factors, both genetic and environmental, involved in bringing even a very extreme talent to full expression, and these simply cannot be guaranteed to occur. Even if they do occur, they must be sustained over several years as well as be transformed when necessary. The children's chess coach Sunil Weeramantry has indicated that high-IQ children in kindergarten all demonstrate a rudimentary ability to play chess, but that prodigious talent begins to differentiate children as early as age 7, at the end of their primary tournament playing years (S. Weeramantry, personal communication, May 1988).

The kinds of supports that must be put into place and kept there include the right teachers teaching the right kinds of things for child performers, the right integration of the target activity with other priorities for the child and the family, the right level of challenge in terms of competition and public performance, and a context that encourages continued involvement in the activity in question. To summarize, a number of other factors that may be beyond the control of the child and the child's family are also involved in talent development; these are: sufficient financial resources, proximity to appropriate facilities, and the availability of appropriate teachers.

Another less documented but certainly essential component in talent development is freedom from cultural proscriptions against certain activities. Gender proscriptions are the most common. For example, in the United States, young males experience disapproval if they want to use their psychomotor talent in dance, especially classical ballet. Jacques D'Amboise, the former Balanchine dancer who now conducts school-based classes in New York City, is especially eloquent on the topic of attracting psychomotor talented males to dance, and has even set up special classes for them during the school day; but the battle against cultural proscription is an uphill one. Even world-class dancers such as Rudolf Nureyev had to go against a disapproving father in order to seriously pursue dance as a career. Percival (1975, p. 21) wrote that Nureyev's father "was none too pleased to find that his only son had grown up to be interested only in something as 'unmanly' as dancing and told the boy to forget the whole thing." Young females experience disapproval if they want to use their logical–mathematical talent in chess. Few female chess talents continue playing tournament chess beyond the elementary tournament years, even though they have the ability to do so. Reasons given for this are a diversity of other interests and special lessons, a lack of female role models at the higher levels of the chess world, and a lack of understanding of the necessity for constant practice and competition all over the country and the world (S. Weeramantry, personal communication, March 1987).

In some fields where talent development begins early, a phenomenon (perhaps unfortunately) labeled the midlife crisis in musical performers has been observed to occur with some frequency (Bamberger, 1982). Usually occurring some time between 12 and 18, this so-called midlife crisis refers to a breakdown in the child's ability to perform and an accompanying emotional crisis in the child's confidence in being able to perform at a high level. Many promising careers have come to an early end because of the debilitating effects of this crisis. The description of an adolescent crisis for performers has been documented in only one field—music—though informal observations have been made in the field of chess (Feldman and Goldsmith, 1991) and in writing (Piirto, 1998b). It should also be stressed that this phenomenon has been observed only in U.S. culture; it may or may not occur in other cultural contexts. It could also be that the so-called midlife crisis is in part precipitated by the highly professionalized and competition-oriented schools of music where most of the students with extreme talent pursue their chosen field. How such schools are organized, how they respond to and develop talent, and what they see as in their interest in terms of public visibility all play a significant part in how they impact the process of talent development (Subotnik, 2000; van Lieshout and Heymans, 2000).

PARENTING ACADEMICALLY TALENTED CHILDREN AND CHILDREN WITH SPECIFIC HIGH-PRIORITY TALENTS

Alvino (1985) listed common issues faced by parents of gifted and talented students. Some were home related and some were school related. Among the home-related issues were awe and fear of the children and their talents, denial of the children's talents, the burden of supporting the talent (e.g., books, trips, teachers, lessons, equipment), equating verbal maturity with social maturity, sibling issues, stress (both for the child and for the family), friendships and peer relationships, the nature of the interests, and self-esteem. School-related issues included finding programs and schools that supported the child's talent, defining reasonable and unreasonable expectations by the school and the home, apathy of schools to talent development, the potential for social mobility of the child because of the presence of the talent, and being perceived by the school as "pushy."

Shore, Cornell, Robinson, and Ward (1991, p. vii) surveyed recommended practices in gifted education and noted ten commonly cited parenting practices for parents of gifted youth:

(1) Be sensitive to potential sibling adjustment problems.
(2) Avoid excessive emphasis on developing the child's giftedness.
(3) Avoid stereotypes and misconceptions about the gifted label.
(4) Be aware of how personal needs and feelings influence the relationship with the child.
(5) Encourage social as well as academic development.
(6) Foster potential for giftedness through preschool intervention.
(7) Participate in and lobby for programs.
(8) Facilitate social development through ability-peer contact.
(9) Discourage children's perfectionism and excessive self-criticism.
(10) Emotional support from parent groups and counselors should be available.

They found some research support for the first three recommended practices. Numbers 4, 5, and 6 had limited support. Numbers 7, 8, 9, and 10 had been studied little, if at all, in populations of gifted students with suitable comparison groups.

Even though it is apparent that eminent individuals often come from parenting situations that are not ideal, nevertheless, there are many ways that parents can provide optimal environments for the nurture of creative talent. Piirto (1998b) listed twelve:

(1) Provide a private place for creative work to be done.
(2) Provide materials (e.g., musical instruments and sketchbooks).
(3) Encourage and display the child's creative work. Avoid evaluating it overly.
(4) Do your own creative work and let the child see you doing it.
(5) Value the creative work of others. Attend museums, theater, movies. Talk about books and events.
(6) Pay attention to what your family background, your family mythology, your family system is teaching the child.
(7) Avoid emphasizing sex-role stereotypes.
(8) Provide private lessons and special classes.

(9) If hardship comes into your life, use the hardship positively, to encourage the child to express her or himself through the arts.

(10) Emphasize that talent is only a small part of creative production and that discipline and practice are important.

(11) Allow the child to be "odd": avoid emphasizing socialization at the expense of creative expression.

(12) Enjoy your child.

Cornell (1983, 1989) and Cornell and Grossberg (1986, 1987) supplied some evidence in their studies of gifted students and their siblings that how the parents treat the gifted child in relation to siblings is important. Comparisons of siblings should be carefully made, if at all. Parents' reactions to having their children labeled as "gifted" are often problematic within the family system. Some parents develop an especially intense relationship with the labeled child, and are sometimes overinvolved in the child's education and development. Such overinvolvement can lead to underachievement and disabling perfectionism, both widely cited problems of talented students. Underachievement deserves special attention here because it is one of the most common problems for which parents of academically talented youth seek professional help.

PARENTING WHEN ACADEMICALLY TALENTED YOUTH UNDERACHIEVE

Several writers and researchers have made important contributions to our knowledge of under-achievement (Delisle, 1992; Richert, 1991; Rimm, 1986; Supplee, 1990; and Whitmore, 1980). Underachievement continues to plague parents and educators of the talented as one of the most recalcitrant problems that high-IQ youth continue to have. By now we know that each underachiever is different and that each case of underachievement must be looked at individually to determine the reason for the underachievement and thus to be better able to reverse the underachievement.

What is underachievement? The quick answer most people would give is that underachievement is not receiving the grades that the IQ would indicate are possible. Another quick definition is that underachievement is receiving high scores on standardized achievement tests but low grades in school. Another definition of underachievement blames the causes for the underachievement. For example, underachievement is caused by learning disabilities, by the social climate of the school, by affective characteristics in the child, or by passive-aggressive parenting patterns. In a comprehensive survey of research on the underachievement of gifted students, Reis and McCoach (2000, p. 157) defined underachievement thus:

> Underachievers are students who exhibit a severe discrepancy between expected achievement (as mea-sured by standardized achievement test scores or cognitive or intellectual ability assessments) and actual achievement (as measured by class grades and teacher evaluations). Gifted underachievers are under-achievers who exhibit superior scores on measures of expected achievement (i.e., standardized achieve-ment test scores or cognitive or intellectual ability assessments). To be classified as an underachiever, the discrepancy between expected and actual achievement must not be the direct result of a diagnosed learning disability and must persist over an extended period of time.

The emerging paradigm in the field of talent development, as described earlier, features achieve-ment as being predictive for certain manifestations of talent. If a child underachieves, the talent will not be developed: Here is a child with a high IQ who refuses to do the work in the classroom. Here is a child with high achievement test scores who refuses to turn in projects. The educators and parents beg, cajole, compliment, and harangue the child: "You have such potential! You should be doing better! You won't get into a good college with grades like these! You could do so well;

why won't you produce?" The child is a powerful force in these dynamics, both with the parents and with the school, and that is why Rimm (1986) insisted that there must be a tri-focal approach to reversing underachievement, which is that the school, the parents, and the child must all take responsibility for the reversal or the underachievement will continue. The child is the key figure in this triangle. Gallagher (1991, p. 225) said that "until the child essentially agrees" with the parent's and the school's noticing that the child is an underachiever, "it will be very difficult to persuade him/her to change."

It is often assumed that children want to do well in school, and schools and parents are often quick to blame themselves for underachievement. It is often assumed that the evils of the society—racism, classism, prejudice against the handicapped—are to blame for underachievement. It is often assumed that children are feckless victims of "the system." Then why do some children from lower social classes, of various races, with learning disabilities and physical handicaps achieve despite the "system," and others do not? The quality of resiliency that is just beginning to be explored seems operational here.

What are the personality traits of people who underachieve? For underachieving males at least, Terman and Oden (1947) found that those who didn't meet the potential their IQ scores indicated, were: (1) unable to persevere; (2) unable to formulate goals; (3) preferred to drift rather than to take action; and (4) had low self-confidence. These problems were chronic; that is, they continued from childhood to adolescence to adulthood. Underachievement, Delisle (1982, 1992) reminded us, is often in the eyes of the beholder.

Whitmore's book, *Giftedness, Conflict, and Underachievement* (1980), specifically studied children who were put into a special program in 1970 that sought to remedy underachieving behavior. This program was called the Cupertino Project, and it focused on second and third graders who were had very high IQs but who were underachieving. Individualized instruction was offered and results showed that students' achievement generally improved over the long-term.

Rimm (1986) used a behavioral approach to reversing underachievement. She described four different categories of underachievers: (1) the dependent conformers, (2) the dependent nonconformers, (3) the dominant conformers, and (4) the dominant nonconformers. These are children who are outside what she called the "circle of achievers." Underachievers were grouped into dependent children and dominant children, conformers, and nonconformers. Dependent children manipulate adults and others in their environment by such plaintive pleas as "Help me," "Nag me," "Protect me," "Feel sorry for me," "Love me," and "Shelter me." The difficulty is in determining when these pleas are manipulative and when they are genuine. Rimm (1986, p. 148) said parents and teachers "must assure yourselves that these children can build self-confidence and competence only through effort and perseverance, and that it is indeed a true kindness to permit these children to experience some stress."

For each of these groups, there are suggested steps in remediation. Rimm was quick to point out that family patterns often foster or encourage underachievement. Passive–aggressive children often have one passive–aggressive parent and one who is made the bad guy; likewise, with aggressive children, there is often aggression in the family. Patterns in the family can be both positive and negative for achievement. Piirto (1998b) called it the "family mythology." Rimm (1986) said that potentially harmful family models were these: "I didn't like school either"; having a home that is disorganized; having passive aggressive parenting; having parents who are overworked who come home exhausted, complaining, and failing to provide models that work is satisfying, challenging, and life enhancing. Rimm's work was criticized for being too negative to parents (Baum, 1990). However, proponents of clinical interventions utilizing behavioral approaches such as Rimm's would say that drastic measures are often needed in reversing underachievement, which is often entrenched, insidious, and a hallmark of dysfunction in the family or school.

Richert (1991) presented a different definition of underachievement. Pointing out the obvious but often overlooked question: What if the IQ is not a good measure of potential after all? What if the IQ test that puts the child in people's minds into "underachieving status" was inaccurate? Richert noted that "underachievement is most often defined in terms of academic achievement" measured by school-related methods such as grades, standardized test scores, and teacher-made test results. What if these are not good ways of assessing underachievement? What if the tests themselves are the problem?

The children's lives as a whole should be assessed. Do the children who get low grades and who have high test scores have an intense life of achievement at home? Do they read seven books a week? Do they program computers and participate in a wide network of computer friends throughout the area? Do they have sketchbooks and do intensive drawing and artwork? Do they practice their music for seven hours a day? How are these children underachieving? Richert (1991, p. 139) pointed out that "Repeated studies have revealed no correlation, or sometimes even a small negative correlation, between academic achievement (good grades) and adult giftedness in a wide range of fields."

The childhoods of creative people often show that many of them had intense involvements at home, away from school, and that their adult achievements were foreshadowed by their childhood activities, many of which were not school related (Piirto, 1991a, 1998b, 1999b). Many people with arts-related achievements were underachievers in school: Suzanne Farrell (1990), the world-class dancer from Cincinnati, Ohio, never finished high school, and when she did go to school she was too restless to concentrate. The architect Frank Lloyd Wright in his autobiography could not remember a single thing he learned in school in Madison, Wisconsin, but could remember every invention he and his friends made out of school (Wright, 1932/1977). The visual artist Georgia O'Keeffe (Robinson, 1989) called every teacher she had a fool, except for the ones in a convent school in Wisconsin she attended for one year; she consciously got bad grades and disobeyed what she regarded as dumb rules during her last year in high school in Virginia.

Richert (1991) in questioning the definition of underachievement, posed an interesting conundrum: If many high achievers in later life found the schools stifling, boring, and the teachers and rules worse, the role of the schools in talent development in the various domains is diminished and the role of parents and family are probably enhanced. People in the arts do not have the necessity, as do people in mathematics and the sciences, of taking one course following another course in order to make their mark. The attainment of the Ph.D. is de rigueur for mathematicians and scientists, and this means reading many textbooks, conforming, and taking more advanced courses. Such educational attainment is not necessary for visual artists or performers—actors, dancers, or musicians—or for writers, although the schools do encourage writers more than they do other types of creatively talented people.

Supplee (1990) used Abraham Tannenbaum's conception of giftedness to define underachievement. Tannenbaum (1983), in *Gifted Children*, said that giftedness emerges if all five arms in a "starfish" are present. These are the necessary conditions for giftedness to materialize: general intellectual ability (the "g" factor); specific academic abilities (e.g., math ability or reading ability); nonintellective factors (e.g., persistence, self-esteem, or creativity); environmental factors (e.g., family and school); and chance (proximity and knowing the right people). Supplee (1990) noted that the underachievers she studied were missing one or more of the "starfish" arms; some had high IQs but didn't have other factors; some had fantastic special abilities but didn't have persistence; some were very poor, a negative environmental factor, although they had all four other factors; some had physical or learning disabilities, which fall into the chance arm.

Supplee found success in reversing underachievement by beginning with improving the students' self-esteem and proceeding to the improvement of their attitudes, school behaviors, and academic growth. There was also a parent component that helped parents to understand the causes of the student's underachievement, as well as to examine their expectations for their child, to be positive communicators with their child, and to examine familial patterns and familial dynamics. A support group of parents was formed where they could discuss common concerns. Small positive gains in achievement were reported. Nevertheless, underachievement has been and remains a thorny problem for the parents and educators of gifted and talented students.

There are also children of divorce, and talented and gifted children are not immune from this social phenomenon. The family is in many respects in chaos. Karnes and Marquardt (1991a, p. 98), in their consideration of legal issues having to do with gifted children, said, "We were surprised by the number of child custody and child support cases where the giftedness of the child became an issue." Rimm concluded that achievement can continue throughout the divorce, but Wallerstein and Blakeslee, in their longitudinal study of children of divorce, *Second Chances* (1989), and in their 25-year follow-up (Wallerstein, Lewis, and Blakeslee, 2000), noted that underachievement is almost always a by-product of divorce, even years later. Boys who are between the ages of 6 and 8 when their parents get divorced "have a particularly difficult time adjusting to the changes in their lives." They often are unable to concentrate, and may withdraw or "clobber everyone in sight" (Wallerstein and Blakeslee, 1989, p. 77). Wallerstein and Blakeslee attributed this reaction to fears of being overwhelmed by female authority just at the age when the development of strong identification with their fathers and other male figures was crucial. The authors concluded sadly that about one third of the children they studied still lacked ambition 10 years after the divorce, and said that they were "drifting through life with no set goals, limited educations, and a sense of helplessness," and (pp. 148–149):

Many feel discouraged and rejected and . . . cannot close the door to the past, cannot give up the fantasy that history can be changed.

Although only a few dropped out of high school, most have not seriously pursued higher education. They tend to drop out after one or two years of college to take up unskilled jobs—as messenger, delivery truck driver, waitress, physical fitness instructor, video store clerk. They don't make long term plans and are aiming below the intellectual and educational achievements of their fathers and mothers. This discrepancy between life goals and talents is defined as underachievement.

A belief that gifted and talented youth are exempt from the tragic consequences for children of their parents' divorces is certainly a false notion. The sample was from suburban San Francisco, and many attended universities such as Cornell and Stanford. In contrast with a comparison group, the children whose parents divorced indulged in earlier sexual experiences and consumed alcohol and drugs at higher rates. When they reached adulthood, they were reluctant to marry. Forty percent had not married in the 25-year follow-up (Wallerstein et al., 2000) compared to 29% of the people who had grown up in intact families. Most of the single women "had firmly decided against marriage and motherhood" (Wallerstein et al., 2000, p. 289). They often identified themselves as "children of divorce," and they viewed their parents' divorce as "the formative event" in their lives (p. 291). However, at the 25-year follow-up point, many also prided themselves as trusting in their own judgment and in refraining from self-pity.

Falk (1987) in a study that compared the reactions of labelled gifted students with students who were not so designated, said that the gifted students experienced the thought of their parents getting divorced even more intensely than the others. Self-blame was a key theme for the gifted students. Some have theorized that gifted and talented youth may be more vulnerable, because their sensitivities are often higher tuned and deeper felt, as their advanced intellects and intensities cope with the splits in their nuclear families (Morelock, 1992; Piechowski, 1991; Tolan, 1992). In fact, one immutable fact that was found by the Johns Hopkins Study of Mathematically Precocious Youth (SMPY) researchers was that high academic achievers most often came from families that were intact (Benbow, 1992).

Underachievement has been and remains a thorny problem for the parents and educators of gifted and talented students. Reis and McCoach (2000) in their synthesis of research on underachievement noted that family dynamics are crucial in the situation where underachievement happens. Families whose children underachieve show less positive affection; the parents may display a disinterest in education; parenting styles where there was a lot of fighting and arguing seem prevalent; parents are not consistent; the parents may be too indulgent or too exacting; they may treat the children as adults at too young an age; the parents themselves may be underachievers who are frustrated by what life has provided them; there may be more family conflict in the homes. Families who produce high achieving students are often high achieving families that encourage "self-motivation, environmental engagement, and autonomy" (Reis and McCoach, 2000, p. 160).

PARENTING CHILDREN OF DIFFERENT ETHNIC
AND ECONOMIC GROUPS

Recently, some researchers have discussed Baumrind's (1971) widely used labels of parenting styles with regard to parenting in various ethnic groups. Although the authoritative parenting style seems to be related to academic achievement in European American middle– and upper–socioeconomic status students, Chao (2000, p. 234) pointed out that "studies including African American, Hispanic America, and Asian American high school students suggest very weak or inconsistent relations between Baumrind's parenting styles and academic achievement." Chao compared parenting styles of the parents of immigrant Chinese and European Americans. European American parents were more demonstrative in hugs, kisses, and encouragement, whereas the immigrant Chinese mothers seemed to have as a high priority the caretaking and education of their children. Family pride and successful parenting are tied up with a child's achievement in school: The expectations for school success are conveyed to the child as a necessity for a respect from elders and filial piety, in contrast to the typical European American parent's opinion that the child should develop a sense of self. The Chinese immigrant mothers advocated and demonstrated more directive, authoritarian, styles of parenting, especially in the early years. (One must not overgeneralize these findings to all Asian American groups, however, as there are disparities in academic achievement and possibly parenting styles and possibly parenting strifes among subgroups, with Chinese, Japanese, and Koreans achieving higher academically than Southeast Asians and Filipinos.)

The numbers of children of various ethnic groups who are admitted to school programs for the gifted and talented indicate that there may be cultural bias built into selection processes. A National Educational Longitudinal Study (NELS) by Resnick and Goodman (1997) showed that 17.6 percent of Asian students were in programs were Asians, 9% of all European American students, 7.9% of all African American students, 7.7% of all Latin American students, and 2.1% of all Native American students were in programs. Economically disadvantaged students are among the most underserved. In this NELS study, students from the bottom quartile in family income made up only 10% of students in gifted and talented school programs, and 50% of the students in programs were from the top quartile economically.

A document from Texas presented, in English and in Spanish, 10 "tips" for parenting gifted and talented children from minority and economically disadvantaged groups. These tips were probably quite obvious to European American, middle- and upper-income parents, who are perhaps more comfortable in school settings than parents who do not speak English as a first language (Bauer, 1998). The tips were these:

(1) Support your child.
(2) Identify your child's interests.
(3) Request an appropriately challenging curriculum.
(4) Help your child set goals.
(5) Emphasize responsibility.
(6) Provide opportunities (e.g., ask the teachers and the school office about extracurricular clubs and contests).
(7) Look for resources (e.g., go to the public library and ask the librarian for resources).
(8) Encourage your child.
(9) Be an advocate of your child and others.
(10) Do not give up.

The "chance" factors of ethnicity, socioeconomic status, and geographical location can also affect the development of talent. Parents have primary influence on all of these factors. In studying highly academically talented students from disadvantaged backgrounds, Van Tassel-Baska (1989) found that the parents' attitudes toward their situations were primary in the development of talent. If parents viewed their socioeconomic status as temporary, and if they provided enrichment through public libraries, special programs, and involvement in the schools, the students' talents were likely to be developed. Likewise, Ford (1992) noted that academically talented African American youth took their achievement motivation from their parents, but that especially for males in junior high school and high school, the peer group was often a strong deterrent to the development of that talent.

PARENTING CHILDREN OF AFFLUENCE AND PARENTAL SUCCESS

Another situation that merits attention for the parents of talented youth is the influence of affluence and parental success on such children. It is a fact that most students in formal school programs for the gifted and talented have average or above-average socioeconomic status. This discrepancy has led to concerted efforts by the federal government, through the Jacob C. Javits Gifted and Talented Education Act of 1988, to identify and serve students from disadvantaged backgrounds. As Coles (1977) and Elkind (1987), Vail (1987), Brooks (1989), and others have pointed out, children of high-achieving parents often face particular problems such as living up to perhaps unreasonable expectations, living out the dreams of the parents for them instead of finding their own dreams, and fearing that they will disappoint their parents.

Noting that the qualities needed to be a high achiever in the world are sometimes directly opposite to the qualities needed to be a nurturing parent, Brooks (1989, p. 29) pointed out that the difficulties of children with high achieving parents may stem from parents who have succeeded in the workplace, which demands perfection, efficiency, a concern about image, firmness, selfishness, long work hours, and a top priority that success should come first. Children often need to have their errors tolerated, patience and gentleness, special times for family activities, and an understanding that failure promotes growth.

Fast-track, high-achieving parents often made it the hard way, attending public schools and state universities, and they want their children not to have to do it that way, attitudes that may put undue pressure on children to conform to newly acquired lifestyles in affluent surroundings. Brooks (1989) also pointed out that such parents often seek to maintain control to the extent that even their children's achievements should be attributable to the parents' efforts: she cited Henry Ford's behavior with his son Edsel as an example. Whenever Edsel began to achieve on his own, Ford would cut him down and humiliate him, often publicly. The parent who uses connections to get an interview at a prestigious school or an audition with a coveted teacher may thwart a fragile young person's self-esteem, her or his ability to feel proud of accomplishing things by dint of hard work or talent. Such parenting behaviors point out that talented children may be viewed as their parents' products, much like their degrees, prestigious jobs, promotions, and possessions.

Miller (1981) has written extensively about the destructive need for accomplished parents to project themselves within their children's accomplishments. For example, the senior John D. Rockefeller developed the family's fortune through ruthless and cutthroat business methods but insisted that his son, John D. Rockefeller, Jr., and his grandchildren redeem him by creating themselves as good, Baptist Christian philanthropists, devoted to giving most of the money away through the Rockefeller Foundation. His guilt projected on his progeny led to his disapproval of his son's art collecting, his daughter's dabbling with Jungian psychology and exile in Switzerland, and his grandson Nelson's political ambitions (Chernow, 1998).

Amy Tan, in the novel *The Joy-Luck Club* (1989), dramatized this situation among Asian mothers who had immigrated and who had reared American daughters. The mothers competed among themselves for evidence of whose daughter had the most achievements. One forced her daughter to become a chess player; another forced piano lessons on a decidedly uninterested child. Payant (1993, p. 73) stated that in contemporary fiction, as in contemporary life, females especially have difficulty in separating themselves from their mothers, and the mothers have difficulty in seeing their children as whole human beings: "It does not take Freudian-Lacanian theory to tell us of a mother's difficulty in seeing her children as separate people." (Payant, 1993, p. 73).

Parents influence their children's placement in classes in school. A study by Wells and Serna (1996) showed that de facto segregation occurs in integrated schools where European American students are clustered in programs for the gifted and talented, and African American and Latin American students are clustered in regular and remedial programs. Attempts by school officials to change this de facto segregation has often incited parents of the European American students, who threaten to pull their students out of the public schools and start private schools if their children are to be educated with students of color. The classes where European American students are clustered are often fast-paced honors classes, and academically talented African American students are relegated to slower-paced regular classes.

Thus it can be seen that the optimal development of talent is inextricably related to family variables that may or may not be under the control of the parents. Those variables as death, divorce, or other trauma may hit a family unawares, and such events can have minimal or maximal effect on talent development. Other variables such as passive-aggressive parenting, underachievement or perceived underachievement, and providing of opportunities and situations where children's talent can be encouraged are under the control of the parents and awareness of options can enhance talent development.

CONCLUSIONS

To summarize this review of parenting talented children, several points can be made. First, parents often have difficulty in identifying a child's talent and in formulating responses to the presence of talent. The problem is magnified when a child or children have multiple talents or multiple potentialities. Second, general academic talent as identified by having high scores on IQ tests or standardized achievement tests is often developed in the school and in special programs for the gifted and talented; however, outstanding special talent (such as that in athletics, chess, or the arts) needs responses that may not be developed in the school and that may affect the whole family system. Third, talent development is often the product of the whole family's interests, occupations, and heritage. Talent often seems to run in families.

Whether intelligence and the existence of talent and giftedness is mostly heredity or mostly environmental is not the point; the point is that there are families of actors, artists, athletes, business persons, academics, and the like, where the talent is nurtured by the efforts of the whole family system. Fourth, research on children with extremely high IQs or children who are prodigies or savants reveals that there is a cocoon-like quality that the parents engender in the families. The families see themselves as different from the norm, and they often expend extreme amounts of energy in talent development for the prodigy. The talents of siblings are often undernnoticed in such extreme family preoccupations toward a child's talent development. Fifth, underachievement is a phenomenon that affects families with academically talented students. Responses to underachievement ranging from school-based special programs to individual behavioral and family therapy are common. Sixth, a difficult parenting situation for talented children can arise in families of achievement, especially where there is recent affluence, where parents have moved up in social status; these parents often unduly ignore the emotional needs of their children in order to satisfy their own needs.

It should be clear from what has been said that early identification of talent, creating an appropriate response and sustaining an optimal process of talent development are highly complex and subtle matters. Although much more is known about these issues than was true even a decade or so ago, the knowledge base remains spotty, thin, and fragmented.

REFERENCES

Albert, R. S. (1980). Family positions and the attainment of eminence: A study of special family positions and special family experiences. *Gifted Child Quarterly, 24*, 87–95.

Albert, R. S. (1983). *Genius and eminence: The social psychology of creativity and exceptional achievement.* Oxford, England: Pergamon.

Albert, R. S. (1990a). Family position and the attainment of eminence. *Gifted Child Quarterly, 24*, 87–95.

Albert, R. S. (1990b). Identity, experiences, and career choice among the exceptionally gifted and eminent. In M. Runco and R. Albert (Eds.), *Theories of creativity* (pp. 14–34). Newbury Park, CA: Sage.

Albert, R. S., and Runco, M. (1986). The achievement of eminence: A model based on a longitudinal study of exceptionally gifted boys and their families. In R. J. Sternberg and J. E. Davidson (Eds.), *Conceptions of giftedness* (pp. 332–359). New York: Cambridge University Press.

Alvino, J. (1985). *Parents' guide to raising a gifted child.* Boston: Little, Brown.

Alvino, J. (1989). *Parents' guide to raising a gifted toddler.* Boston: Little, Brown.

Arnold, K. D. (1993). The Illinois Valedictorian Project: Academically talented women in the 1980s. In D. T. Schuster and K. D. Hulbert (Eds.), *Women's lives through time: Educated American women of the twentieth century* (pp. 111–145). San Francisco: Jossey-Bass.

Arnold, K. D. (1995). *Lives of promise: What becomes of high school valedictorians: A fourteen-year study of achievement and life choices.* San Francisco: Jossey-Bass.

Bamberger, J. (1982). Growing up prodigies: The midlife crisis. In D. H. Feldman (Ed.), *Developmental approaches to giftedness and creativity* (pp. 61–77). San Francisco: Jossey-Bass.

Bauer, H. (1998). Raising "Will Hunting" 10 tips for parenting gifted and talented children. *Intercultural Development Research Association Newsletter, 25*, 4–5.

Baum, S. (1990). Review of *How to parent so children will learn. Gifted Child Quarterly, 34*, 169–170.

Baumrind, D. (1971). Current patterns of parental authority. *Developmental Psychology Monograph, 4* (1, p. 2).

Benbow, C. P. (1992). Mathematical talent: Its nature and consequences. In N. Colangelo, S. G. Assouline, and D. L. Ambroson (Eds.), *Talent development: Proceedings from the 1991 Henry B. and Jocelyn Wallace national research symposium on talent development* (pp. 95–123). Unionville, NY: Trillium.

Benbow, C. P., and Lubinski, D. (1995). Optimal development of talent: Respond educationally to individual differences in personality. *Educational Forum, 59*, 381–392.

Benbow, C. P., and Lubinski, D. (1997). Intellectually talented children: How can we best meet their needs? In N. Colangelo and G. A. Davis (Eds.), *Handbook of gifted education* (2nd ed., pp. 155–169). Boston: Allyn and Bacon.

Benbow, C. P. (2000, May). *The 25-year follow-up of intellectually talented children in the Talent Searches.* Invited speech at the Wallace Symposium, University of Iowa, Iowa City.

Benbow, C. P., and Minor, L. L. (1990). Cognitive profiles of verbally and mathematically precocious students: Implications for the identification of the gifted. *Gifted Child Quarterly, 34*, 21–26.

Bloom, B. S. (1981). Talent development. *Educational Leadership, 39*, 86–94.

Bloom, B. S. (1982). The master teachers. *Phi Delta Kappan, 63*, 664–667.

Bloom, B. S. (Ed.). (1985). *The development of talent in young people.* New York: Ballantine.

Blumberg, S. A., and Panos, L. G. (1990). *Edward Teller: Giant of the golden age of physics.* New York: Macmillan.

Borland, J. A. (1989). *Planning and implementing programs for the gifted.* New York: Teachers College Press.

Brooks, A. A. (1989). *Children of fast-track parents: Raising self-sufficient and confident children in an achievement-oriented world.* New York: Viking.

Brophy, B., and Goode, E. E. (1988, December 12). Amazing families. *U.S. News and World Report*, 78–87.

Chao, R. K. (2000). The parenting of immigrant Chinese and European American mothers: Relations between parenting styles, socialization goals, and parental practices. *Journal of Applied Developmental Psychology, 21*, 233–248.

Cheever, S. (1984). *Home before dark.* Boston: Houghton Mifflin.

Chernow, R. (1998). *Titan.* New York: Random House.

Clark, B. (1992). *Growing up gifted* (4th ed.). Columbus, OH: Merrill.

Clark, R. (1971). *Einstein: The life and times.* New York: World.

Colangelo, N., and Kerr, B. A. (1990). Extreme academic talent: Profiles of perfect scorers. *Journal of Educational Psychology, 82*, 404–409.

Coles, R. (1977). *Privileged ones. Children of crisis* (Vol. 5). Boston: Little, Brown.

Cornell, D. G. (1983). Gifted children: The impact of positive labeling on the family system. *American Journal of Orthopsychiatry, 53*, 322–335.

Cornell, D. G. (1989). Child adjustment and parent use of the term "gifted." *Gifted Child Quarterly, 33*, 63–64.

Cornell, D. G., and Grossberg, I. N. (1986). Siblings of children in gifted programs. *Journal for the Education of the Gifted, 9*, 253–264.

Cornell, D. G., and Grossberg, I. N. (1987). Family environment and personality adjustment in gifted program children. *Gifted Child Quarterly, 31*, 59–64.

Deakin, M. (1972). *The children on the hill*. Indianapolis, IN: Bobbs-Merrill.

Delisle, J. (1982). Striking out: Suicide and the gifted adolescent. *Gifted/Creative/Talented, 24*, 16–19.

Delisle, J. (1992). *Social and emotional needs of the gifted*. Boston: Longman.

Eccles, J., and Harold, R. D. (1992). Gender differences in educational and occupational patterns among the gifted. In N. Colangelo, S. G. Assouline, and D. L. Ambroson (Eds.), *Talent development: Proceedings from the Henry B. and Jocelyn Wallace National Research Symposium on Talent Development* (pp. 2–30). Unionville, NY: Trillium.

Edwards, A. (1975). *Judy Garland: A biography*. New York: Simon and Schuster.

Elkind, D. (1987). *Miseducation: Preschoolers at risk*. New York: Knopf.

Falk, G. (1987). Gifted children's perception of divorce. *Journal for the Education of the Gifted, 11*, 29–43.

Farrell, S., Bentley, T. (1990). *Holding on to the air*. New York: Summit.

Feldhusen, J. F. (1995). Talent development: The new direction in gifted education. *Roeper Review, 18*, 92.

Feldman, D. H. (1979). The mysterious case of extreme giftedness. In H. Passow (Ed.), *The gifted and the talented* (pp. 335–351). Chicago: University of Chicago Press.

Feldman, D. H. (1992). Has there been a paradigm switch in gifted education? In N. Colangelo, S. G. Assouline, and D. L. Ambroson (Eds.), *Talent development: Proceedings from the 1991 Henry and Jocelyn Wallace national research symposium on talent development* (pp. 89–94). Unionville, NY: Trillium.

Feldman, D. H., and Goldsmith, L. (1991). *Nature's gambit: Child prodigies and the development of human potential*. New York: Teachers College Press.

Fine, M. J., and Carlson, C. (Eds.). (1992). *The handbook of family-school intervention: A systems perspective*. Needham, MA: Allyn and Bacon.

Ford, D. Y. (1992). Determinants of underachievement as perceived by gifted, above-average, and average black students. *Roeper Review, 13*, 130–135.

Gagné, F. (1985). Giftedness and talent: Reexamining a reexamination of the definition. *Gifted Child Quarterly, 29*, 103–112.

Gallagher, J. J. (1991). Personal patterns of underachievement. *Journal for the Education of the Gifted, 14*, 221–233.

Galton, F. (1869). *Hereditary genius: An inquiry into its laws and consequences*. London: Macmillan.

Gardner, H. (1982). *Art, mind, and brain*. New York: Basic Books.

Gardner, H. (1983). *Frames of mind*. New York: Basic Books.

Goertzel, V., and Goertzel, M. G. (1962). *Cradles of eminence*. Boston: Little, Brown.

Goertzel, V., Goertzel, M. G., and Goertzel, T. (1978). *Three hundred eminent personalities: A psychosocial analysis of the famous*. San Francisco: Jossey-Bass.

Goldsmith, L. (1987). Girl prodigies: Some evidence and some speculations. *Roeper Review, 10*, 74–82.

Goldsmith, L. (1990). The timing of talent: The facilitation of early prodigious achievement. In M. J. A. Howe (Ed.), *Encouraging the development of exceptional skills and talents* (pp. 17–31). Leicester, England: British Psychological Society.

Goldsmith, L. T. (2000). Tracking trajectories of talent: child prodigies growing up. In R. C. Friedman and B. M. Shore (Eds.), *Talents unfolding: cognition and development* (pp. 89–117). Washington, DC: American Psychological Association.

Goldsmith, L. T., and Feldman, D. H. (1988). Idiots savants: Thinking about remembering: *New Ideas in Psychology, 6*, 15–23.

Graffman, G. (1981). *I really should be practicing*. New York: Avon.

Gray, M. (1979). *Margaret Sanger: A biography of the champion of birth control*. New York: Marek.

Greer, G. (1979). *The obstacle race: The fortune of women painters and their work*. New York: Farrar, Straus Giroux.

Gustin, W. C. (1985). The development of exceptional research mathematicians. In B. Bloom (Ed.), *Developing talent in young people* (pp. 270–331). New York: Ballantine.

Hall, E. G., and Skinner, N. (1980). *Somewhere to turn: Strategies for parents of the gifted and talented*. New York: Teachers College Press.

Harris, C. R. (1990). The Hollingworth longitudinal study: Follow-up, findings, and implications. *Roeper Review, 12*, 216–221.

Helson, R. (1983). Creative mathematicians. In R. Albert (Ed.), *Genius and eminence: The social psychology of creativity and exceptional achievement* (pp. 211–230). London: Pergamon.

Hunt, E., Lunneborg, C., and Lewis, J. (1975). What does it mean to be high verbal? *Cognitive Psychology, 7*, 194–227.

Jenkins-Friedman, R. (1992). Families of gifted children and youth. In M. J. Fine and C. Carlson (Eds.), *The handbook of family–school intervention: A systems perspective* (pp. 175–186). Needham, MA: Allyn and Bacon.

Karnes, F. A., and Marquardt, R. G. (1991). *Gifted children and legal issues in education: Parents' stories of hope*. Dayton, OH: Ohio Psychology Press.

Kessen, W. (1965). *The child*. New York: Wiley.

Kulieke, M. J., and Olszewski-Kubilius, P. (1989). The influence of family values and climate on the development of talent. In J. Van Tassel-Baska and P. Olszewski-Kubilius (Eds.), *Patterns of influence on gifted learners: The home, the self, and the school* (pp. 40–59). New York: Teachers College Press.

Lehman, H. (1953). *Age and achievement*. Princeton, NJ: Princeton University Press.

Lewis, D. (1979). *How to be a gifted parent*. New York: Norton.

Louis, B., Lewis, M., Subotnik, R., and Breland, P. (2000, April). *Establishing criteria for high ability vs. Selective admission to gifted programs: Implications for policy and practice*. Paper presented at American Educational Research Association Conference. New Orleans, LA.

Miles, B. (1989). *Ginsberg: A biography*. New York: Simon and Schuster.

Miller, A. (1981). *Drama of the gifted child*. New York: Doubleday.

Miller, A. (1987). *Timebends: A life*. New York: Harper & Row.

Miller, A. (1989). *The untouched key: Tracing childhood trauma in creativity and destructiveness*. New York: Doubleday.

Morelock, M. J. (1992). Giftedness: The view from within. *Understanding our gifted, 4*, 11–15.

Morelock, M. J., and Feldman, D. H. (1991). Extreme precocity. In N. Colangelo and G. Davis (Eds.), *Handbook of gifted education* (pp. 347–364). Boston: Allyn and Bacon.

Morelock, M. J., and Feldman, D. H. (1993). Prodigies and savants: What they have to tell us about giftedness and human cognition. In K. Heller, F. Monks, and H. Passow (Eds.), *International handbook for research on giftedness and talent* (pp. 161–181). Oxford, England: Pergamon.

Payant, K. B. (1993). *Becoming and bonding: Contemporary feminism and popular fiction by American women writers*. Westport, CT: Greenwood.

Percival, J. (1975). *Nureyev*. New York: Popular Library.

Piechowski, M. M. (1979). Developmental potential. In N. Colangelo and R. Zaffer (Eds.), *New voices in counseling the gifted* (pp. 25–57). Dubuque, IA: Kendall-Hunt.

Piechowski, M. M. (1989). Developmental potential and the growth of self. In J. VanTassel-Baska and P. Oliszewski-Kubilius (Eds.), *Patterns of influence: The home, the self, and the school* (pp. 87–101). New York: Teachers College Press.

Piechowski, M. M. (1991). Emotional development and emotional giftedness. In N. Colangelo and G. A. Davis (Eds.), *Handbook of gifted education* (pp. 285–306). Needham, MA: Allyn and Bacon.

Piirto, J. (1991a). Encouraging creativity in adolescents. In J. Genshaft and M. Bireley (Eds.), *Understanding gifted adolescents* (pp. 104–122). New York: Teachers College Press.

Piirto, J. (1991b). Why are there so few? Creative women: mathematicians, visual artists, musicians. *Roeper Review, 13*, 142–147.

Piirto, J. (1998a). Themes in the lives of contemporary U.S. women creative writers at midlife [Special issue]. *Roeper Review, 21*, 60–70.

Piirto, J. (1998b). *Understanding those who create* (2nd ed.). Tempe, AZ: Gifted Psychology Press.

Piirto, J. (1999a). Metaphor and image in counseling the talented. *Spotlight: Newsletter of the Visual and Performing Arts Division of the National Association for Gifted Children*, 6–7.

Piirto, J. (1999b). *Talented children and adults: Their development and education* (2nd ed.). Columbus, OH: Prentice-Hall.

Piirto, J. (2001). *My teeming brain: Understanding creative writers*. Cresskill, NJ: Hampton.

Plomin, R. (1997). Genetics and intelligence. In N. Colangelo and G. Davis (Eds.), *Handbook of gifted education* (2nd ed., pp. 67–74). Boston: Allyn and Bacon.

Radford, J. (1990). *Child prodigies and exceptional early achievers*. New York: Macmillan.

Reis, S. M., and McCouch, D. B. (2000). The underachievement of gifted students: What do we know and where do we go? *Gifted Child Quarterly, 44* (3), 152–170.

Resnick, L., and Goodman, J. (1997). *The National Educational Longitudinal Study*. Washington, DC: U.S. Office of Education.

Richert, E. S. (1991). Patterns of underachievement among gifted students. In M. Bireley and J. Genshaft (Eds.), *Understanding the gifted adolescent* (pp. 139–162). New York: Teachers College Press.

Rimm, S. (1986). *The underachievement syndrome*. Apple Valley, WI: Apple Valley Press.

Robinson, N. M., Weinberg, R. A., Redden, D., Ramey, S., and Ramey, C. (1998). Family factors associated with high academic competence among former Head Start children. *Gifted Child Quarterly, 42*, 148–156.

Robinson, N. M., Zigler, E., and Gallagher, J. J. (2001). Two tails of the normal curve: Similarities and differences in the study of mental retardation and giftedness. *American Psychologist, 55*, 1413–1424.

Robinson, R. (1989). *Georgia O'Keeffe: A life*. New York: Harper & Row.

Roedell, W., Jackson, N., and Robinson, H. (1980). *Gifted young children*. New York: Teachers College Press.

Rolfe, L. M. (1978). *The Menuhins: A family odyssey*. San Francisco: Panjandrum/Arts Books.

Rose, S. A. (1989). Measuring infant intelligence: New perspectives. In M. Bornstein and N. A. Krasnegor (Eds.), *Stability and continuity in mental development: Behavioral and biological perspectives* (pp. 171–188). Hillsdale, NJ: Lawrence Erlbaum Associates.

Russel, B. (1967). *The autobiography of Bertrand Russell II, 1872–1914*. Boston: Little-Brown.

Sears, P. S. (1979). The Terman studies of genius, 1922–1972. In A. H. Passow (Ed.), *The gifted and talented: Their education and development* (pp. 75–96). The seventy-eighty yearbook of the national society for the study of education. Chicago: University of Chicago Press.

Sherry, N. (1989). *The life of Graham Greene.* New York: Viking.

Shore, B. M., Cornell, D. G., Robinson, A., and Ward, V. S. (1991). *Recommended practices in gifted education: A critical analysis.* New York: Teachers College Press.

Simonton, D. K. (1984). *Genius, creativity and leadership: Historiometric inquiries.* Cambridge, MA: Harvard University Press.

Simonton, D. K. (1988). *Scientific genius.* Cambridge, MA: Harvard University Press.

Simonton, D. K. (1991). The child parents the adult: On getting genius from giftedness. In N. Colangelo, S. G. Assouline, and D. L. Ambroson (Eds.), *Talent development: Proceedings from the 1991 Henry and Jocelyn Wallace national research symposium on talent development* (pp. 278–297). Unionville, NY: Trillium.

Simonton, D. K. (1994). *Greatness: Who makes history and why.* New York: Guilford.

Simonton, D. K. (1999). *Origins of genius: Darwinian perspectives on creativity.* New York: Oxford University Press.

Sloan, K. D., and Sosniak, L. A. (1985). The development of accomplished sculptors. In B. Bloom (Ed.), *Developing talent in young people* (pp. 298–347). New York: Ballantine.

Smutney, J. (Ed.). (1998). *The young gifted child: Potential and promise, an anthology.* Cresskill, NJ: Hampton.

Smutny, J., and Eby, J. (1990). *A thoughtful overview of gifted education.* New York: Longman.

Sosniak, L. A. (1985a). Becoming an outstanding research neurologist. In B. Bloom (Ed.), *Developing talent in young people* (pp. 348–408). New York: Ballantine.

Sosniak, L. A. (1985b). Learning to be a concert pianist. In B. Bloom (Ed.), *Developing talent in young people* (pp. 19–66). New York: Ballantine.

Stanley, J., and Benbow, C. (1986). Youths who reason exceptionally well mathematically. In R. J. Sternberg and J. E. Davidson (Eds.), *Conceptions of giftedness* (pp. 361–387). New York: Cambridge University Press.

Sternberg, R. (1985). *Beyond IQ: A triarchic theory of human intelligence.* New York: Cambridge University Press.

Styron, W. (1990). *Darkness visible: A memoir of madness.* New York: Random House.

Subotnik, R. F. (2000). The Juilliard model for developing young adolescent performers: an educational prototype. In C. van Lieshout and P. Heymans (Eds.), *Developing talent across the life span* (pp. 249–276). East Sussex, England: Psychology Press.

Subotnik, R. F., and Arnold, K. D. (Eds.). (1993). *Beyond Terman: Longitudinal studies in contemporary gifted education.* Norwood, NJ: Ablex.

Subotnik, R. F., Karp, D. E., and Morgan, E. R. (1989). High IQ children at midlife: An investigation into the generalizability of Terman's *Genetic Studies of Genius. Roeper Review, 11,* 139–145.

Subotnik, R. F., Kasson, L., Summers, E., and Wasser, A. (1993). *Genius revisited: High-IQ children grown up.* Norwood, NJ: Ablex.

Subotnik, R. F., and Steiner, C. (1993). Adult manifestations of adolescent talent in science: A longitudinal study of 1983 Westinghouse Science Talent Search winners. In R. F. Subotnik and K. D. Arnold (Eds.), *Beyond Terman: Longitudinal studies in contemporary gifted education.* Norwood NJ: Ablex.

Sulloway, F. (1996). *Born to rebel: Birth order, family dynamics, and creative lives.* New York: Pantheon.

Supplee, P. (1990). *Reaching the gifted underachiever: Program strategy and design.* New York: Teachers College Press.

Tan, A. (1989). *The Joy-Luck Club.* New York: Putnam's.

Tannenbaum, A. (1983). *Gifted children.* New York: Macmillan.

Tannenbaum, A. (1986). Giftedness: A psychosocial approach. In R. J. Sternberg and J. E. Davidson (Eds.), *Conceptions of giftedness* (pp. 21–51). New York: Cambridge University Press.

Terman, L. M. (1925). *Mental and physical traits of a thousand gifted children* (Vol. 1). Stanford, CA: Stanford University Press.

Terman, L. M. (1930). *The promise of youth, follow-up studies of a thousand gifted children: Genetic studies of genius* (Vol. 3). Stanford, CA: Stanford University Press.

Terman, L. M., and Oden, M. H. (1947). *The gifted child grows up, twenty-five years follow up of a superior group: Genetic studies of genius* (Vol. 4). Stanford, CA: Stanford University Press.

Terman, L. M., and Oden, M. H. (1959). *The gifted group at mid-life, thirty-five years follow-up of the superior child: Genetic studies of genius* (Vol. 3). Stanford, CA: Stanford University Press.

Terman, L. M., and Oden, M. H. (1947). *The gifted child grows up, twenty-five years follow up of a superior group: Genetic studies of genius* (Vol. 3). Stanford, CA: Stanford University Press.

Terr, L. (1990). *Too scared to cry.* New York: Basic Books.

Thomas, B. (1973). *Marlon: Portrait of the rebel as an artist.* New York: Random House.

Tolan, S. (1992). Parents vs. theorists: Dealing with the exceptionally gifted. *Roeper Review, 15,* 14–18.

Tomlinson-Keasey, C., and Little, T. D. (1990). Predicting educational attainment, occupational achievement, intellectual skill, and personal adjustment among gifted men and women. *Journal of Educational Psychology, 82,* 442–455.

Treffinger, D. (1991). Future goals and directions. In N. Colangelo and G. A. Davis (Eds.), *Handbook of gifted education* (pp. 441–449). Needham, MA: Allyn and Bacon.

Vail, P. L. (1987). *Smart kids with school problems: Things to know and ways to help.* New York: Dutton.

van Lieshout, C., and Heymans, P. (Eds.). *Developing talent across the life span*. East Sussex, UK: Psychology Press.

Van Tassel-Baska, J. (1989). The role of the family in the success of disadvantaged gifted learners. In J. Van Tassel-Baska and P. Olszewski-Kubilus (Eds.), *Patterns of influence on gifted learners: The home, the selfs, and the school* (pp. 60–80). New York: Teachers College Press.

Wallerstein, J. S., and Blakeslee, S. (1989). *Second chances: Men, women and children a decade after divorce*. New York: Ticknor and Fields.

Wallerstein, J. S., Lewis, J. M., and Blakeslee, S. (2000). *The unexpected legacy of divorce: A 25-year landmark study*. New York: Hyperion.

Wells, A. S., and Serna, I. (1996). The politics of culture: Understanding local political resistance in detracking in racially mixed schools. *Harvard Educational Review, 66*, 93–118.

Weisner, T. S., and Garnier, H. (1992). Nonconventional family lifestyles and school achievement: A 12-year longitudinal study. *American Educational Research Journal, 29*, 605–632.

Whitmore, J. (1980). *Giftedness, conflict, and underachievement*. Boston: Allyn and Bacon.

Wright, F. L. (1932/1977). *An autobiography*. New York: Horizon.

9

Play in Parent–Child Interactions

Catherine S. Tamis-LeMonda
New York University
Ina Č. Užgiris
Clark University
Marc H. Bornstein
National Institute of Child Health
and Human Development

INTRODUCTION

The oft-quoted saying that "play is children's work" captures some of the implicit notions that make the discussion of play so complex. Play is fun, exciting, and appealing to children of all ages. At the same time, play is serious business, and invoking the image of play as children's work suggests that children accrue some benefits from playing beyond enjoyment of the moment. To the extent that adult involvement in play supports and extends those benefits, parent–child play may be regarded as a meaningful context for children's social and cognitive growth. What functions do specific types of play serve, and what role do parents have in supporting those functions?

In this chapter, we examine the nature and benefits of two forms of parent–child play—interpersonal play and object play—against a background of cultural conceptions of the parent–child relationship. We begin by discussing persistent issues regarding play, including the definitions, characteristics, and developmental trajectories of interpersonal and object play. We then consider the various functions these two major play forms serve, with particular focus on the importance of parents in supporting these functions. We then discuss the role of culture in determining the nature and characteristics of parent–child play and highlight how cultural variation in play reflects distinctive conceptions about children and parents, as well as broader ideologies such as individualism and collectivism. Finally, we attend to the potential educational implications of parent–child play.

CHARACTERIZING CHILD–PARENT PLAY

It is *de rigueur* to initiate a discussion of play by lamenting the difficulties in defining play (e.g., Bornstein and O'Reilly, 1993; Garvey, 1977; MacDonald, 1993b; Millar, 1968; Rubin, Fein, and Vandenberg, 1983). Varied instances of play cannot be identified by means of one characteristic or set of characteristics, although lists of defining characteristics emerge periodically (e.g., Cohen, 1987; Rubin et al., 1983; Smith and Vollstedt, 1985). Some of the most frequently mentioned characteristics include engaging in play for its own sake, its seemingly intrinsic motivation, and its accompaniment by positive affect; the nonliteral quality of play, its pretense, creative, and fantasy aspects; and the repetitive, assimilatory character of play, its direction toward a free refiguration of what is known rather than toward new understanding. The current consensus seems to be that individual instances of play have a "family resemblance" in that they share some, but not all, of the main aspects of what is understood as play. Thus, play is not to be identified with a specific set of activities, but includes any activity that is meaningfully linked with this constellation of defining characteristics.

The difficulty in ascribing a unifying definition to play has led both empirically and conceptually to more differentiated definitions of specific types of play. Some types of play that have been distinguished include interpersonal play, sensorimotor play, pretend play, and rule-governed play. An example of one such taxonomy is Piaget's (1962) distinction of sensorimotor play, symbolic play, and games with rules. By utilizing more specific definitions, it becomes easier to describe the nature of changes in types of play across development, as well as developmental shifts in the prevalence of certain forms of play over others.

The focus on parent–child play faces the same rigor of definition and challenge. One useful classification of parent–child play is to distinguish interpersonal (dyadic) forms of play from object-focused (extradyadic) engagements (e.g., Bornstein and Tamis-LeMonda, 1990). This distinction holds both ecological and practical relevance. The two types of parent–child play are evident from infancy throughout childhood, and each demonstrates patterned developmental change, serves unique functions, and is meaningful in parent–child interactions and child development. This chapter is structured around this dichotomy, with further specification of subtypes of play that characterize these two broad types.

Interpersonal Play

Interpersonal play involves various dyadic exchanges, such as face-to-face interactions, social games or routines, and physical play. By definition, it requires the direct, interactive involvement of the participants in a play episode, and it is typically characterized by high degrees of pleasure on the part of parents and children. Elaborating on Karl Bühler's view of play as a product of children's pleasure in functioning, or *Funktionslust*, Charlotte Bühler (1962) suggested that this pleasure is most characteristic of play during infancy, as in the infamous game of "peek-a-boo," and continues to be prevalent during the first few years of life. Wherever or whenever these episodes take place, they appear to involve a purely social activity with no other goal than to "have fun, to interest and delight and be with one another" (Stern, 1977, p. 71).

Face-to-face play. Stern (1977) was one of the first to describe certain kinds of mother–infant interaction, such as face-to-face engagements, as play. He viewed communication during infancy as basically affective, and parents engage their infants in such interactions so as to enjoy interpersonal engagement.

Face-to-face play is common in the home, where it often occurs within the context of other, more task-oriented activities. For example, feeding a baby may be interrupted by sustained episodes of face-to-face play. An episode of face-to-face play begins when a mother and child establish mutual attention, usually through maternal vocal, tactile, or gestural greeting. To maintain attention, the mother then playfully varies her behavior. For example, she may utilize exaggerated facial expressions as well as elongated and high-pitched vocalizations. As the mother engages her child in this manner, the child's contribution involves signaling interest and expectations through smiling, cooing, or laughing. The mother may then repeat some of her behavior, as well as introduce variations on a theme to maintain the child's attention. Face-to-face engagements are thus composed of a balance between repetitive bouts and creative variations of shared affect; they are framed as playful through specific vocalizations or gestures within the stream of ongoing parent–child interactions. In having fun, both partners adjust and readjust to one another to establish and maintain synchronous exchanges (Tronick, Als, and Adamson, 1979). Imitation is a typical component of early face-to-face play interactions, shown by mothers more often than by infants (e.g., Trevarthen, 1977; Užgiris, 1984).

The Papoušeks (1991, in Vol. 2 of this *Handbook*) view the observed mutuality in such face-to-face play engagements as an integral element of intuitive parenting, an adaptation for mutual interaction by parents and their infants. They described playful interactions as based on preadapted interests and behavioral tendencies to foster learning and positive affective relationships and drew particular attention to vocal play as a central feature of early playful interactions (Papoušek, Papoušek, and Harris, 1987). Negotiations about what can be communicated and what can be included in play are said to be part of later play interactions with parents (Stern, 1985) and to account for some of the individual differences in older children's play.

Social games and routines. Although face-to-face play is common in early infancy, interpersonal play is not confined to this period. As face-to-face play decreases in frequency and duration towards the end of the first year of life (Gustafson, Green, and West, 1979), parents and children often engage one another in social games or routines with differentiated roles, such as "peek-a-boo," "I'm gonna get you," and "pat-a-cake." The child's role often involves motor behaviors that are meaningful within the context of a particular game (Crawley et al., 1978). Through participation in such games, children begin to distinguish set formats of social intercourse as well as optional variations on them (Bruner and Sherwood, 1976).

Longitudinal observations of the coconstruction of social games reveal systematic changes in the participants' roles. For example, Bruner (1983) described changes in the game of peek-a-boo with a toy clown, played by one mother–child pair. When they first began this social routine, the mother was essentially responsible for its various components, and her son assumed the role of a "smiling spectator" (p. 49). As the child paid increasing attention to the game, more sophisticated responses were required of him as his mother asked more questions, as well as more complicated questions about the clown's whereabouts. Over time, the child became increasingly responsible for the vocalizations that accompanied the clown's disappearance and reappearance. Ultimately, he could assume any part in the execution of the game. This description suggests that the parent's role at the inception of social routines is generally one of facilitator; it involves providing opportunities for play by assuming responsibility for the game and by scaffolding. It also allows the child to take on different roles and assume progressively more responsibility for the game.

Physical play. Another prevalent form of interpersonal play is physical play, which is considered particularly salient among fathers and their children (Clarke-Stewart, 1978; Parke, in Vol. 3 of this *Handbook*; Yogman, 1987). A detailed survey in the United States found that physical play occurred with lower frequency during the child's first year, reached a peak between 1 and 4 years, and declined thereafter (MacDonald and Parke, 1986).

Rough-and-tumble play, a form of physical play characterized by coplaying, is less common across cultures, and fathers are not necessarily more likely than mothers to engage in such play with their children (Roopnarine, Talukder, Jain, Joshi, and Srivastav, 1990). Because rough-and-tumble play can easily become too rough, bordering on aggression or even violence, children may learn about the limits of play and what counts as acceptable playful activity by participating in this form of play. The primary role of parents in teaching and providing contexts for appropriate play, however, is tied to Western conceptions of the parent–child relationship that revolve around the establishment and maintenance of friendly and sociable interactions (Whiting and Edwards, 1988). Where the parental role revolves around training children for specific work skills, or controlling their behavior, parents are not viewed as their children's partners in this kind of play.

Object Play

Interpersonal forms of play are typically rooted in social exchanges within the dyad; object play has been characterized as extradyadic, because the play focus is turned outward toward objects and events (Bornstein and Tamis-LeMonda, 1990). In Western cultures, early playful interactions between parents and children expand to include objects by the middle of the first year of life. Trevarthen and Hubley (1978) noted that, once the infant begins to focus attention on interesting objects in the environment, the mother adjusts by starting to create "spectacles" for the child. These kinds of observations show that early playful interactions evolve smoothly into play with objects and change in complexity with children's developing competencies.

To a certain extent, parent–child object play is characterized by less mutual engagement than interpersonal play, especially insofar as toys permit children to remain occupied, and parental participation in such forms of play tends to be more discretionary (Bornstein, in Vol. 1 of this *Handbook*) and subject to cultural influences. In certain cultures, including Mexico, Guatemala, and Indonesia, for example, parents reputedly attach no particular value to play and likewise do not believe that it is important to play with their children (Farver and Howes, 1993; Farver and Wimbarti, 1995; Rogoff, Mistry, Gönçü, and Mosier, 1993). In other cultures, particularly more Westernized societies, parents actively facilitate their children's play through modeling and scaffolding (Teti, Bond, and Gibbs, 1988; Turkheimer, Bakeman, and Adamson, 1989; Zukow, 1986). Like interpersonal play, object play is also subdivided, with categories of object play typically reflecting the developmental progression in children's cognitive competencies. In general, three stages in the development of children's object play have been noted: exploration, nonsymbolic, and symbolic.

Exploration.   The earliest forms of object play can be seen toward the middle of the first year. Until approximately 9 months of age, children's play is predominantly characterized by exploration in the form of sensorimotor manipulation. Infants' actions appear to be aimed at extracting information about objects and their perceivable qualities through mouthing, regard, and palpation. As such, these earlier actions are as much about learning about and practicing with objects as they are about playing. At the same time as infants come to focus on objects, parents increasingly promote and partake in these episodes by introducing novel toys and objects to their infants, showing infants what various objects can do, and repositioning infants so that they might more readily explore objects in their surround (Bornstein and Tamis-LeMonda, 1990).

Nonsymbolic play.   Toward the end of the first year, nonsymbolic play emerges in which children act on objects in appropriate yet concrete ways; active attempts are made to extract information about the unique functions of objects (e.g., pressing buttons on busy boxes). These nonsymbolic activities are first directed to single objects (e.g., squeezing a foam ball) but shortly incorporate combinations of objects; in turn, initially random combinations soon become appropriate (e.g., a nesting block might first be juxtaposed with a busy box, only later to be inserted in its appropriate partner block). As in exploration, parents play an active role in demonstrating the functional and concrete availabilities of objects to their young children. Middle-income parents at play with their infants demonstrate how objects work, and how they might be combined, by shaking rattles, nesting blocks, and the like, and then offering the objects to their infants so as to solicit similar actions from them.

Symbolic play.   In the second year, children's play with objects takes on a "nonliteral" and "generative" quality as children increasingly reenact activities performed by self, others, and objects in simple pretense scenarios. For some investigators, these pretend bouts constitute the first true episodes of object play—that is, terms such as preplay have been used to describe earlier forms of object play, such as exploration and nonsymbolic engagements. Over the course of the second year, symbolic play progresses toward greater decontextualization in at least three ways: (1) play becomes distanced from self, (2) play becomes distanced from the tangible properties of objects, and

(3) play becomes distanced from overt action (Tamis-LeMonda and Bornstein, 1996). Specifically, pretense schemes tend to be applied to self before they are applied to others (e.g., pretending to drink from a cup before feeding a doll); single-scheme pretense often appears before multischeme pretense (e.g., pretending to drink from a cup and later pretending to pour and drink); pretense with actual objects tends to precede pretense with substitution objects (e.g., a telephone will at first represent a telephone, and later a stick might represent a telephone); and substitutions themselves become increasingly distanced from the perceptual qualities of objects (e.g., at first a stick might represent a phone, later a ball might represent a phone). Moreover, in other-directed play, the child first takes the role of agent (e.g., feeding doll) and later enacts vicarious situations in which another is the agent of action (e.g., a doll waves bye-bye). Still later, the child is capable of removing her- or himself from the play scenario completely by enacting interactions between others (e.g., having one doll put another doll to sleep). Finally, emotive play emerges, in which internalized concepts of affect or feeling are expressed (e.g., making a doll cry), but usually after other forms and combinations of symbolic play have been mastered. (For reviews of this literature, see Belsky and Most, 1981; Bornstein and O'Reilly, 1993; Bretherton and Bates, 1984; Fein, 1981; Garvey, 1977; Lowe, 1975; McCune-Nicolich, 1981; Shore, O'Connell, and Bates, 1984; Slade, 1987; Tamis-LeMonda, and Bornstein, 1990, 1991, 1994, 1996; Tamis-LeMonda, Damast, and Bornstein, 1994; Watson and Fischer, 1977.) Importantly, research indicates that lower play levels decrease in their frequency as children become capable of engaging in higher play levels (e.g., Tamis-LeMonda and Bornstein, 1991).

As children develop representational skills, parent–child play begins to include the creation of pretend scenes and the symbolic manipulation of shared meanings (Bretherton, 1984). During joint symbolic play, mothers vary in the extent to which they actively participate, assuming roles of audience and/or facilitator (Dunn, 1986; Fiese, 1990; Haight and Miller, 1992; Miller and Garvey, 1984; Slade, 1987), depending on their children's own activities as well as age. Home observations indicate that mothers are more likely to initiate symbolic play than nonsymbolic play with their 1- to 2-year-old children (Damast, Tamis-LeMonda, and Bornstein, 1996; Dunn and Wooding, 1977; Haight and Miller, 1993) as well as to remain involved in a symbolic play episode until it is completed. Children also are more likely to engage with their mothers during symbolic play. That children tend to seek out maternal involvement, thereby explicitly establishing the play frame, indicates their understanding of symbolic play as a joint activity.

FUNCTIONS OF PARENT–CHILD PLAY

What functions do interpersonal and object play activities serve? Although play is manifestly an activity enjoyable and rewarding in itself, it is viewed as supportive of children's development in diverse ways. Historically, several instinctual and therapeutic functions have been suggested, including the release of surplus energy (Spencer, 1883), presaging and practicing adult roles, instincts, and future relationships (Baldwin, 1902; Bjorklund, Yunger, and Pellegrini, in Vol. 2 of this *Handbook*; Groos, 1901; Stern, 1914), and wish fulfillment without the constraints of reality (Freud, 1959). Stern (1914) suggested that girls' playing with dolls and boys' play fighting were the foundations of a future maternal instinct in women and an aggressive instinct in men. Within the psychoanalytic tradition (Peller, 1954), changes in children's play have been linked to progression in psychosexual development. Play has also been thought to have an affectively restitutive function, as it is a world in which more is possible than in reality. Winnicott (1971) claimed that the mother or mother figure is very important in allowing the child "potential space" (p. 107) to work through subjective feelings during the play relationship. Erikson (1963, 1972) also conceived of play as a way to work through tensions and advanced the use of play for therapeutic purposes. More recent accounts of play have extended beyond instinctual and psychoanalytic functions to include normatively based emotional, cognitive, communicative, social, and cultural functions. For example, play is thought to enable the young of the species to experience and experiment with a full range of emotions by displaying behaviors that might not be safe in real life, as for example mock anger or aggression (Bruner, 1972; Singer, 1995).

The functions of parent–child play parallel those of play more generally. In the great apes, play between the young and their parents or even other adults has been reported (e.g., Bard, in Vol. 2 of this *Handbook*; Fossey, 1983; Goodall, 1986). Such findings prompt the examination of play from an evolutionary perspective (e.g., Bjorklund et al., in Vol. 2 of this *Handbook*; MacDonald, 1993a; Smith, 1982) and certainly support the view that parent-offspring play constitutes a distinct behavioral system characterized by specific functions. Parent-offspring play might be particularly relevant early in development when the young are still too immature to engage in and benefit from play with peers (MacDonald, 1993a; Power, 2000; Tamis-LeMonda, Katz, and Bornstein, in press). In this section, we address the various functions that parent–child play serves in interpersonal as well as object play.

Functions of Parent–Interpersonal Play

Parent–child play serves emotional, communicative, social, and cultural functions in child development.

Emotional functions. Interpersonal play forms a key context for emotional expressivity (e.g., Beckwith, 1986). Children experience and express positive feelings of fun, excitement, and pleasure, as well as negative emotions, such as anger, sadness, and fear in their play (Singer, 1995), and parents may expand these emotional experiences further. From the first days of life, mothers support babies' experience of joy by playing with facial expressions, vocalizations, and touch, and evoking gazing, smiling, and laughing from their infants. According to Stern (1993), the progressive escalation of excitement inherent in mother–infant game rituals boosts infants into higher levels of joy than they can achieve on their own. In typical theme-and-variation play, a caregiver builds predictable sequences of behavior and repeats or varies them based on the infant's response, for example, slowly creeping their fingers up the infant's stomach, waiting for the infant's expectant gaze or smile and then tickling or giving a loud "raspberry." It is the infant's growing awareness of contingency in these interactions that adds to feelings of pleasure, in addition to enabling greater tolerance for higher arousal states (Roggman, 1991). The finding that mothers are more contingent with infants than are siblings or peers (Vandell and Wilson, 1987) suggests that primary caregivers are best able to amplify and prolong the infant's experience of pleasure in the first months of life. Stern (1985) suggested that maternal imitation of infant behavior enables a mother and child to establish and maintain affect congruence or attunement. However, mothers are selective and do not imitate all of their infants' acts (Užgiris, Benson, Kruper, and Vasek, 1989). By selectively imitating acts that they find meaningful, mothers mark them as important, facilitating mutual understanding.

During interpersonal play, children are also supported in their handling of certain aspects of reality in a playful and nonthreatening manner. The game of peek-a-boo, for example, is thought to permit children to enact playfully and exert control over issues related to separation and reunion. It is interesting that across cultures, the disappearance and reappearance of a figure in peek-a-boo games seems to be invariant, although aspects of timing and vocalization differ (Fernald and O'Neill, 1993).

Communicative and verbal functions. Interpersonal play provides children opportunities to construct socially appropriate modes of communication (Bruner, 1983; Hay, Ross, and Davis, 1979; Stern, 1977). Through such playful exchanges children begin practicing critical elements of social interaction, such as engaging another's attention, turn taking, and terminating social encounters. Face-to-face interactions also offer children their earliest opportunities for learning how to participate in framing certain acts as playful. Through the mutual involvement of both partners, face-to-face play allows parents and children to establish, maintain, and constantly construct their relationship by building up common expectations and allowing for creative variations in their exchanges (Lewis, 1979). Through the process of emotional attunement and shared affect, mothers also foster infants' appreciation for the nature of interpersonal communication. In support of this notion, mothers' responsiveness to their 9-month-old children's emotional displays during free play has been shown to predict children's earlier achievement of various language milestones (Nicely, Tamis-LeMonda, and Bornstein, 1999).

However, as Stern (1977) noted, face-to-face play interactions do not always proceed as smoothly as the ideal description implies. For example, a mother may vary her vocalizations or movements too quickly for her child to maintain attention. In response, the child may turn away, indicating a lack of enjoyment. Stern aptly refers to these kinds of sequences as "missteps in the dance," thus emphasizing that both partners must learn how to engage with one another in order to foster positive communications.

Participation in social games also enables children to practice a range of social interactions and communication, including the establishment and maintenance of mutual attention, turn taking, and role reciprocity (Bruner, 1978; Hay et al., 1979). Children learn acts that are meaningful within a particular social context, thereby participating in a common system of meanings and expectations, requisite for further social interaction. Moreover, Bruner (1983) pointed out that many characteristics of such routines are analogous to characteristics of communication generally, implying that not only do these playful interactions change as the child's competence develops, but that they might serve as a context for the child to learn communication skills. Such a description again supports the idea that playful interactions may be described as communicative, only framed by the message "This is play."

Social functions. Certain forms of interpersonal play serve important social functions by establishing the rules and boundaries of social conduct. In one study, 6-month-old children's turn-taking interactions with their parents predicted their turn taking at 9 months with peers (Vandell and Wilson, 1987). Participation in family physical play by preschoolers relates to children's peer interactions (MacDonald and Parke, 1984) as well as to teacher ratings of popularity. However, these social functions were found to be gender-specific: Paternal physical play was correlated with harmonious peer interactions for boys, but with abrasive peer interaction and dominance for girls. If physical interactions are generally considered more appropriate among males in our culture, physical play with fathers may serve as a forum for learning interpretations of interpersonal actions more appropriate to males.

Cultural functions. By providing opportunities to practice culturally appropriate elements of social interaction, games such as peek-a-boo and pat-a-cake set the stage for learning rule-bound conventional behaviors. Patterning behavior to accord with social rules may also be achieved through ritualized parent–child play that is more idiosyncratic and unique to a particular parent–child dyad. Parents and children often create playful routines around a focal topic that initially may have been disciplinary. For example, Duncan and Farley (1990) described the fixed format of a "no wires" game between a father and son. The game begins when the child suddenly crawls toward certain wires, accompanied by laughter. The father then "scoops" the child up and vocalizes "with exaggerated emphasis." The child pauses and may briefly engage in another activity. Then the child starts toward the wires again, and the game is repeated. In addition to helping the child learn social conventions, this form of play contributes to the shared history of a parent–child pair, thus strengthening their affective ties. In terms of affective components of play, routines such as the "no wires" game enable children to grapple with prohibitions and manipulate power relationships characteristic of their culture.

Functions of Object Play

Like interpersonal play, object play with children has multiple functions, including emotional, mastery motivation, symbolic representation, creativity, social functions, language, and cultural functions.

Emotional functions.   By definition, object play focuses on interactions around toys or materials in the environment; consequently, emotional functions of object play have not been considered as often as perceptuocognitive functions. Nonetheless, parent–child interactions during object play provide ample opportunity for the sharing and the extension of emotions as children experience the joys and frustrations of accomplishing and struggling in goal-directed activities. Additionally, object play is a context for parents' labeling and interpreting their children's feelings. Comparisons with sibling symbolic play indicate that parent–child symbolic play involves a greater proportion of inner state discussions (Dunn, 1986). For example, mothers often make attributions about infants' feelings in response to their emotional expressions. Such attributions enable children to learn the verbal labels that are linked to their internal states and possibly to grapple with emotional issues in a nonthreatening way.

Mastery functions.   Over the course of the first two years of life, children increasingly practice emerging skills and attempt multipart tasks with available toys and objects. Infants' exploration and task-directed behaviors are thought to index and fuel mastery motivation and a sense of self-efficacy. Morgan, Maslin-Cole, Biringen, and Harmon (1991) suggested that infants' curiosity and exploration of objects is essentially tantamount to measures of mastery motivation until about 9 months of age. During this developmental period, parents support their children's emerging sense of mastery and exploration by encouraging and sustaining their infants' attention to stimuli (Vandell and Wilson, 1987) and by shifting their infants' attention from interpersonal to object play (Bornstein and Tamis-LeMonda, 1990; Jacobson, 1981; Vandell and Wilson, 1987). Indeed, associations between parenting and mastery motivation in children are developmentally expeditious: Mothers who encourage their 2-month-old children to orient to and explore objects in the environment have infants who explore objects more at 5 months (Bornstein and Tamis-LeMonda, 1990), and parent's stimulation and responsiveness to infants at 6 months is associated with infant persistence on problem solving tasks at 13 months (Yarrow et al., 1984).

During the second year of life, adult play partners continue to foster children's sense of efficacy and persistence on structured tasks. Grolnick and colleagues (Frodi, Bridges, and Grolnick, 1985; Grolnick, Frodi, and Bridges, 1984) found that 12- and 20-month-old children persisted on challenging tasks when mothers were more supportive of their autonomy during play. Similarly, Morgan et al. (1991) reported that mothers who encouraged and physically aided or coached their 18-month-old children when playing had children who persisted on structured tasks.

What mechanisms might underlie these associations? Mothers' early advantage in supporting mastery motivation on structured tasks may be due to their responsiveness to children's initiatives, accuracy in assessing children's need for help, and effectiveness in assistance. Thus, their expert support allows children to perform slightly beyond their independent capacity and within the "zone of proximal development" (Vygotsky, 1978, p. 86). Additionally, the development of attachment between parents and children (Ainsworth, Blehar, Waters, and Wall, 1978; Bowlby, 1969) may foster connections between play and mastery. It has been proposed that emotional security is linked to exploration and that the exploration and play carried on while feeling secure in turn facilitate the growth of competence (Bruner, 1972). The play of children who have a secure emotional attachment to a parent is expected to be venturesome, creative, and contribute to development in other domains (e.g., Pastor, 1981; Singer and Singer, 1990). Empirical studies reveal associations between positive mother–child attachment and child persistence on challenging tasks (e.g., Maslin, Bretherton, and Morgan, 1987; Morgan, Maslin, Ridgeway, and Kang-Park, 1988).

Symbolic functions.   The opportunities created by parents or other adults for pretend play and imaginary situations are important to fostering advances in children's play sophistication per se, as well as for their thinking, representational competence, and problem solving skills more broadly. Piaget (1952, 1962) brought play into the discussion of the context of intellectual development, giving most attention to symbolic play in relation to the attainment of mental representation. Researchers concerned with the sociocultural contexts of development have since highlighted the supportive role of caregivers in such experiences (e.g., Bruner, 1983; Rogoff, 1990; Vygotsky, 1978). Vygotsky (1976, 1978), for example, described two levels of functioning in children: the *actual (intrapsychological) developmental level* represented by a child's level of functioning when solving problems independently; and the *potential (interpsychological) level of development* represented by a child's level of ability when collaborating with more experienced partners. During play with caregivers, children might be expected to exhibit higher levels of play than they would alone, which in turn might engender advances in children's actual developmental abilities. In line with this notion, considerable research has been devoted to comparing children playing alone versus with parents, as well as to examining correspondences between mothers' and children's play sophistication.

Empirical evidence indicates that children's play with mother is more sophisticated, complex, diverse, frequent, and sustained than is their solitary play (e.g., Bornstein et al., 1996; Dunn and Wooding, 1977; Fiese, 1990; Haight and Miller, 1992; O'Connell and Bretherton, 1984; Slade, 1987), and mothers who have been trained to engage in attention-focusing behaviors have toddlers who demonstrate more sophisticated play months later (Belsky, Goode, and Most, 1980). In one study, Vibbert and Bornstein (1989) explored how different modes of parent–child interaction may be reflected in the achievement of increasingly sophisticated levels of solitary play. Using a scale that traced the development of independent play from the manipulation of objects to pretense play, they found that social and didactic interactions between mothers and their 13-month-old children are related to children's achievement of higher levels of play. Similarly, Tamis-LeMonda and Bornstein (1991) assessed levels of maternal and child play when toddlers were 13 and 20 months: Each maternal (and toddler) play act was coded at one of the eight play levels of increasing sophistication, and measures of mothers' and toddlers' total nonsymbolic and total symbolic play were calculated. Findings indicated that mothers' nonsymbolic play relates positively to their toddlers' nonsymbolic play but not to toddlers' symbolic play, and mothers' symbolic play relates positively to toddlers' symbolic play but not to toddlers' nonsymbolic play. Across development, the play of individual mothers and toddlers changed in parallel: Mothers who exhibited increases in the frequency of play at particular levels had toddlers who also increased in the frequency of play at those same levels, and mothers who decreased play had toddlers who decreased play in parallel. Other investigators have demonstrated, through sequential analyses, that episodes of symbolic play are most likely to be preceded by reciprocal play between parent and child.

Creativity functions.   Bruner (1972) highlighted the role of play in the development of creativity and divergent thinking. Taking an ethological perspective, he suggested that the ability and opportunity to "play" with learned behaviors outside of their real context allows the young of a species the freedom to combine actions and objects in novel ways. Bruner speculated that the ability to play engendered the flexible mind-set that made tool use possible. Play has been correlated with success on divergent problem-solving tasks and with some measures of creativity (see Rubin et al., 1983). The opportunity to play freely with materials is associated with an increase in innovative uses of objects, a flexible approach to problem-solving tasks, and better performance on divergent thinking tasks. Imaginative play, in particular, has been causally linked to measures of creativity (i.e., more unique responses on the Rorschach Ink Blot test; Rubin et al., 1983; Singer, 1995). Researchers speculate that the act of pretense fosters flexible and multidimensional thinking because it involves a constant shifting in and out of the play frame from real to imagined identities of people, situations, and objects (Rubin et al., 1983; Rubin and Howe, 1986; Singer, 1995).

Social functions.   Parent–child object play has also been shown to contribute to social domains of children's functioning, particularly with respect to children's relationships with peers. For example, mothers' involvement in symbolic play with children between 21 months and 4 years predicts peer competence at $5\frac{1}{2}$ years (Vandell, Ramanan, and Lederberg, 1991). Children's play with their more competent mothers may serve as a foundation for enhanced peer competence, once peer interactions become prevalent in children's lives (Rubin and Burgess, in Vol. 1 of this *Handbook*).

Language functions.   To the extent that parent–child object play involves communication, it is not surprising that functional connections of play have been associated with development in children's language. At minimum, parent–child play provides children with opportunities to communicate nonverbally and verbally with their parents. Participation in different modes of communication during play with a parent may also afford the child entry into a variety of culturally scripted events. Thus, communication during play provides more than a grasp of symbols; it may allow construction of the meaningful nuances of interpersonal acts.

Play with objects serves as an opportune time for children to acquire language and expand their lexicon. However, which aspects of children's language are supported may depend on toys and play contexts. Research reveals that the particularization of audience and facilitator roles during parent–child object play varies with these factors (Lewis and Gregory, 1987). For example, O'Brien and Nagle (1987) analyzed parental speech to toddlers during parent–child object play involving dolls, vehicles, and shape sorters. During doll play, the total amount and length of parental utterances was highest. Parents tended to label objects, using a variety of words, and they also tended to ask questions. In contrast, while playing with shape sorters, parents tended to use directives and attention-getting tactics. Finally, during vehicle play, parents spoke least, and their vocalizations involved mostly imaginative sounds (e.g., motor noises). This research suggests that, by participating in different kinds of joint play based on different play objects, actual relations to children's language acquisition may vary.

In a series of studies, we have sought to discern the interrelations among parent–child play, child play, and language development (Bornstein, Vibbert, Tal, and O'Donnell, 1992; Tamis-LeMonda, and Bornstein, 1991, 1993; Tamis-LeMonda, Bornstein, Baumwell, 2001; Tamis-LeMonda, Bornstein, Kahana-Kalman, Baumwell, and Cyphers, 1998). Across sequential longitudinal cohorts, we visited families in their homes and provided toys for mothers and children to play with when the children were 9, 13, and 20 months old. At all ages, different aspects of children's language competence were related to mothers' language use during play. Notably, mothers' who appropriately responded to their children's play and communicative initiatives had children who achieved language milestones such as first words, vocabulary spurt, and combinatorial speech sooner in development. Some longitudinal links between language use during mother–child play and children's language development also emerged. These results imply that play that involves the symbolic manipulation of reality and the creation of shared fantasy worlds may relate to achievement of communication skills in ways that extend beyond competencies gained from practice.

Cultural functions.   Symbolic play sequences reveal how parents utilize play to introduce children to conventional practices and to prepare them to assume future social roles and culturally favored patterns of activity. Vygotsky (1976) conceived of play as central to the fundamental transition from having a direct relation to the environment to an indirect one, mediated by culturally constituted signs. As children create imaginary situations in play, in which substitutions are made for everyday objects and actions, they come to appreciate the mediating role of words and gestures, enabling them to subordinate actions to signs and to enter the culturally structured realm of mediated functioning. By actively creating play situations, the child also comes to appreciate the regulatory nature of signs.

Because toys are cultural objects at base, children learn to play with them in particular and conventional ways during play with parents. When engaged in joint object play with young infants, mothers tend to model and perform "conventional play actions" (p. 119) rather than imitating how the infants handle the toys (Užgiris et al., 1989). Fiese (1990) found that 15- to 24-month-old children increased the use of toys in "functionally expected ways" (p. 1650) when playing with mother as compared to when playing alone. However, only certain aspects of adult involvement contributed to the child's level of play; children engaged in their most complex play when their mothers modeled specific ways of playing with the toys. Similarly, Howes (1992) noted that mothers use pretend play to model a "right" way of doing things, for example, by demonstrating how to pour tea with a pretend teapot. Conversely, mothers correct children's pretend actions when they "violate the real world" (p. 15), for example, protesting (seriously or playfully) when youngsters drink tea from the teapot instead of the cup. Dale (1989) also found that mothers of 2-year-old children initiate and sustain pretend play by focusing on objects and their functional use. That is, mothers might engage their toddlers by pretending to talk on a toy telephone and then handing the phone to their child; if the child accepts the bid, coaching would follow: "Daddy wants to talk. Say hello."

In addition to providing information regarding the conventional uses of toys, parent–child play is a forum for practicing cultural scripts concerning prevalent roles and relationships in society (e.g., mother–baby, doctor–patient, grocer–customer). Miller and Garvey (1984) observed mothers and their 2- to 3-year-old children playing together during episodes of mothering play (i.e., the child pretends to be a mother). Overall, children initiated most of the mothering play episodes. Mothers' facilitation consisted mostly of "explicit instruction and direction" (p. 116) regarding the function and appropriateness of various objects, as well as what to say to the "babies." Mothers were also likely to model mothering activities for their 2-year-old children. Because the $2\frac{1}{2}$-year-old children were less dependent on their mothers' directions and demonstrations, their mothers assumed the audience role of "approving spectators" (p. 119). At the same time, however, mothers facilitated their children's play by advising, encouraging, and directing children to engage in more "detailed and realistic motherhood procedures" (e.g., heating the milk; p. 119).

Children's knowledge of cultural activities also contributes to the structure of parent–child play. Lucariello (1987) observed mothers and their 24- to 29-month-old children during novel play (involving a model castle and figures) and during free play (involving common toys such as a tea set and a train). In the novel play situation, mothers were mostly responsible for initiating and organizing pretend play. However, with toys that could represent events, which were familiar to the children, pretend play took on its more usual form, with child initiating and the mother serving as audience and facilitator. The roles assumed during play by children are shown to relate to their knowledge of cultural events and patterns of activity.

ROLE OF PARENTS IN CHILD PLAY ACROSS CULTURES

Playful interactions between young children and their parents are universal as part of human parenting, apparently selected in the course of human evolution, and serve several important developmental functions. Cross-cultural observations, however, raise the possibility that parent–child play may not be universal, but rather it is found only where it is culturally favored. Cultural conceptions of parenting and children's play effectively shape the prevalence and nature of parental play with children. This observation raises the question as to whether early playful interactions between children and older individuals occur universally or only in some cultural groups, for it is possible that the participation of parents is culturally determined, but that other adults or older siblings take on the role of playing with young children when it is deemed inappropriate for parents.

Although play may be ubiquitous among human children, parental involvement in children's play varies historically and across cultures (Power, 2000; Rogoff, 1990). For example, in a study of 12 cultures, middle-income mothers in the United States were found to engage in play with their children most frequently (Whiting and Edwards, 1988). In contrast, in hunting-and-gathering and agricultural village cultures, children tended to be the principal playmates of one another, even in early development (e.g., Edwards and Whiting, 1993; Göncü, Mistry, and Mosier, 1991). In order to place current knowledge about parent–child play in perspective, it is necessary to consider both the cultural context of the observations and the understanding of play that they imply. At the same time, we recognize that parent–child play is but a segment of a larger whole comprising children's and adults' playful activities. In this light consider the role of culture in parent–child interpersonal and object play.

Interpersonal Play Across Cultures

In linking interpersonal play to cultural modes of interaction and communication, it is first useful to consider how interpersonal play is related to cultural conceptions of children and conceptions of the parent–child relationship. Parents and children alike strengthen their emotional attachment to one another through constructions of interpersonal play, which contribute to their shared experiences. Where mutuality and intimacy do not characterize the parent–child relationship, interpersonal play between parents and children may be rare. Additionally, where different conceptions of children or different childcare arrangements prevail, parents may serve otherwise as play partners for their children. Finally, everyday cultural practices may directly affect the prevalence and nature of parent–child play. For example, in many traditional cultures, mothers use devices such as slings to carry infants and to free their hands for work; this practice results in less opportunity for face-to-face interpersonal play (e.g., Brazelton et al., 1969; Goldberg, 1977). Two examples of how cultural practices and ideologies affect characteristics of interpersonal play between parents and children are exemplified in studies of mothers from the Marquesas Islands (Martini and Kirkpatric, 1981) and mothers of the Gussii of southwestern Kenya (Dixon, Tronick, Keefer, and Brazelton, 1981).

On the Marquesas Islands, mothers are the primary caregivers for their children during the first 2 or 3 months of life. They tend to hold their children in a face-to-face position only until they are $3\frac{1}{2}$ months old, after which they direct their children's faces outward. Rather than engaging in face-to-face play interactions, these mothers structure interpersonal games that involve a third person; their own role is to direct the infant's gaze toward others or to hold the infant on a sibling's shoulders. Thus, Marquesas children are introduced to playful interactions that foster multifaceted and complex social connections. Once able to sit up, the Marquesas infant is generally cared for by older children in the household and "caregiving activities are performed while the baby faces outward" (Martini and Kirkpatrick, p. 193). As infants are cared for by a number of older children, they continue to be involved in social interactions with three or more people; one child holds the infant facing a third child, and the infant is instructed to interact with the third child "who patiently tolerates the games" (p. 193). A similar nondyadic structure for interpersonal interaction has been observed amongst the Kaluli of Papua New Guinea (Ochs and Schieffelin, 1984). Thus, although interpersonal games between mothers and infants are rare in some cultures, children engage in such games with other children and have playful interactions that facilitate mastery of modes of communication appropriate to the culture.

As another example, the Gusii of southwestern Kenya impose various restrictions on eye-to-eye gaze during social interaction deriving from cultural beliefs about the dangers of visual contact (Dixon et al., 1981). Although mothers and infants maintain much physical contact, their relationships are "characterized by avoidance of eye-to-eye contact and restraint in playful interactions" (p. 152). Mothers respond to infant demands, but do not engage them in communicative exchanges because infants are not viewed as capable of interpersonal interaction. Parents of this culture may view their role as protecting the child from overexcitement and distress (LeVine et al., 1994), rather than as being a source or partner of playful stimulation. Nevertheless, when the Gusii were asked to engage in face-to-face play, their interactions resembled those of Western mothers and infants in many ways. But they also differed along certain dimensions: The duration of playful interchanges was shorter, and their interactions did not revolve around peaks of stimulation and affect arousal.

Object Play Across Cultures

As with interpersonal play, cultural differences in object play provide insight into how play both reflects cultural ideologies and serves as a forum for learning culturally appropriate patterns of activities. Cultures differ with respect to the frequency with which parents engage in object play with children, as well as in the nature and characteristics of play that are observed. Both sets of differences originate from cultural variation in social structure and practices, as well as distinct cultural ideologies about children's and parents' roles. Within European and U.S. American communities, parental participation in play is widespread, especially during early development when children's cognitive, social, motor, and affective abilities undergo rapid change (e.g., Haight and Miller, 1992). This may be due to the segregation of children from adult activities, and parents' sense of responsibility for their children's learning; as such, parents often teach their children in the context of play (Rogoff et al., 1993). In more traditional cultures, parents do not directly teach their children, but rather provide assistance in the context of shared group activities (Power, 2000; Rogoff et al., 1993). Consequently, play is viewed solely as a child's activity, and children engage in play primarily with peers and siblings. Interestingly, this emphasis on peers and siblings as primary play partners is observed across different patterns of caregiving in traditional societies. For example, Morelli and Tronick (1991) studied two groups in Zaire—the Efe and Lese—and uncovered distinct patterns of caregiving practices in the two: One-year-old children of the Efe were most often cared for by multiple caregivers (including their mothers, other women, and older children) and played mostly with older children. Infants of the Lese were generally under the care of their mothers and other children, but their primary play partners were also older children.

In a comparison of U.S. American and Mexican mother–child pretend object play, Farver (1989) found differences related to both cultural modes of interaction and conceptions of the parent–child relationship. When American mothers encouraged their children's independent activity and praised their children, the children engaged in more complex play. In contrast, the Mexican children engaged in more complex play when their mothers organized and directed their activities. These findings reflect the importance given to encouraging independent and autonomous activity by American vis-à-vis Mexican mothers. Farver (1989) described Mexico as a hierarchically structured culture, in which interdependence and obedience to elders are emphasized. Children's learning is more likely to occur there through observation and explicit instruction. In light of the value of interdependence and social interconnectedness, parent–child play in Mexico may not necessarily include toys, and may more often revolve around interpersonal activities. Rather than viewing the object play situation as a playful one, Mexican mothers may view it as a didactic context where they had to make sure that their children engaged with the objects in particular ways.

Cultural ideologies pertaining to individualism and collectivism may also contribute to cultural differences in parent–child object play. Numerous cross-cultural studies reveal how autonomy is fostered in Western parent–child play, in contrast to the facilitation of social connectedness in non-Western cultures (e.g., Rabain-Jamin, 1989). For example, findings from a comparative study of U.S. and Japanese mother–toddler object play (Tamis-LeMonda, Bornstein, Cyphers, Toda, and Ogino, 1992) indicate how play provides opportunities for the enactment of cultural values and modes of interaction along the dimension of individualism–collectivism. Japanese toddlers were found to engage in more symbolic, other-directed play (e.g., pretending to feed the doll a bottle), and their mothers were more likely to demonstrate other-directed play to them. In contrast, American mothers tended to engage their children more in nonsymbolic, functionally oriented object play (e.g., nesting shapes in shape sorters). These differences in the nature of play suggest that American mothers encourage independent activity with objects during play, whereas Japanese mothers emphasize the importance of interpersonal connectedness in their play.

PEDAGOGICAL APPLICATIONS OF PARENT–CHILD PLAY

In the United States, psychological research that pointed to the importance of play in development was put to practical use early in this century. By the turn of the century, establishment of the Playground Association in 1906 (Curtis, 1917) reflected the increasing attention that was being paid to the welfare of children, particularly poor children, living in America's cities. In providing opportunities for play, social service programs sought to ensure that children spent their time constructively in activities deemed appropriate for children.

Continuing to echo early perspectives on play that highlighted its educational and remedial functions, a variety of intervention programs geared toward enhancing children's cognitive and academic potential have included play as an important element. During the 1960s, concerns that children from lower socioeconomic backgrounds were at risk for poor academic achievement spurred the establishment of such programs as Head Start. Similar concerns also led to home-based intervention programs that included play (e.g., Andrews et al., 1982; Slaughter, 1983). Intervention programs for high-risk infants have also encouraged parent–child play (Field, 1983; Scarr-Salapatek and Williams, 1973). The use of parent–child play in the treatment of children who exhibit problematic or disruptive behavior has been proposed as well (Guerney, 1991).

Levenstein's (1970) Verbal Interaction Project's Mother–Child Home Program serves as a notable example because it revolved around mother–child joint play beginning when children were 2 years old. As Levenstein (1970, p. 427) wrote, "The goal was to make the very young child's own mother the ultimate agent of his cognitive enrichment." A caseworker, known as a Toy Demonstrator, visited participants' homes twice a week for 2 years, bringing toys and books. She modeled activities with the toys and books aimed at fostering maternal verbal play with the child. Assessments after 5 years indicated that the IQ scores of participant children were higher than those of nonparticipants, and this advantage continued throughout the eighth grade (Levenstein and O'Hara, 1993). The academic achievement of participant children was equal to that of their "nondisadvantaged" counterparts. Moreover, the mothers' interaction styles continued to reflect the techniques encouraged by the Toy Demonstrators.

Such intervention programs were designed for children of lower socioeconomic backgrounds, but the relation between class and children's play, especially symbolic play, is unclear (McLoyd, 1982). In Great Britain, Dunn and Wooding (1977) found that middle-income mothers were more involved in reciprocal play with their children than blue-collar mothers. However, ethnographic research in the United States comparing two blue-collar communities and one middle-income group (Heath, 1983) showed that socioeconomic factors are hard to disentangle from the cultural dimension. Although the middle-income group differed from the two blue-collar communities, parent–child interactions in the two blue-collar communities differed as well. Not only were different kinds of objects used as toys with children, but adults structured play interactions in keeping with their values and beliefs. For example, with respect to children's storytelling, in one blue-collar community parents encouraged their children to tell stories based on facts, in keeping with their "commitment to community and Church values" (p. 185), but in the other children were encouraged to tell stories that creatively embellished the facts, reflecting cultural ideals of individuality. As Schwartzman (1984) has pointed out, intervention to encourage particular kinds of play in "disadvantaged children" (Smilansky, 1968) may be no more than an attempt to get children of a different cultural or ethnic background to adopt the play patterns valued by the middle class.

Efforts to promote parent–child play are not made solely for remedial purposes, nor have they been confined to at-risk groups. Encouraging parent–child play as part of customary parent–child relationships has become a trend, but only since the last half of the twentieth century. During the early decades of the twentieth century, as psychology was getting established as a bona fide scientific discipline, childrearing practices characterized by "scientific mothering" (Mintz and Kellogg, 1988, p. 121) were promoted, which undermined the importance of parent–child play. Mothers were generally advised to adhere strictly to regular schedules and not to indulge their children's desires.

As Piagetian views gained ground in the United States, parenting books emphasized the importance of play for child development (e.g., Pulaski, 1978). However, the parental role remained one of stimulating play by providing children with appropriate opportunities, based on an increased understanding of different stages of cognitive advancement. Contemporary parenting books highlight the importance of playing with children not only to facilitate their acquisition of various skills, but also to enjoy interpersonal engagement and establish mutual emotional bonds (Leach and Matthews, 1997; Spock and Parker, 1998). Thus, parent–child play is associated with basic and important psychological functions for both partners.

CONCLUSIONS

Research in Western countries demonstrates that one way in which children become adept at cultural modes of communication and interpersonal interaction is by playing with their parents. In this chapter, we distinguished two forms of play that are prominent in early parent–child play interactions: interpersonal play and object play. We described the character of these forms of play and reviewed the array of functions that are served when children engage in these types of play with their parents. Generally speaking, during play with their parents, children expand and act on their emotional experiences, share affect, learn how to socially negotiate, acquire rules and pragmatics of communication and language, practice social roles, enhance their representational capacities through the symbolic manipulation of reality, and enact culturally specific modes of activity. Although these variegated functions of play characterize both interpersonal and object forms of play, different emphases have been attributed to the social-affective functions of interpersonal play and to the cognitive-representational functions of object play.

Play is shaped and nurtured in the family, primarily through children's participation in play interactions with family members. Studies of parent–child play indicate that parents take varying roles in play, including that of partner, facilitator, or interested observer. Parents' active participation in play has been shown to be especially critical to scaffolding children to higher levels of functioning, as parents expand on play themes new to children and initiate themes and ways of play that extend their children's abilities. By actively playing together, parents and children construct mutually meaningful activities that help fashion and augment their relationship with each other. Parental availability and play facilitation help children to become proficient at symbolic play as well as play with objects in accordance with culturally accepted patterns. However, even more passive forms of parental involvement, such as mere presence during play, may be beneficial to children: By simply acknowledging a play frame, parents recognize and implicitly support their children's activities.

Qualitative changes in parent–child play accompany children's cognitive and social competence advances. Moreover, different forms of parent–child play apparently undergo different transformations. For example, during interpersonal play, children at first pay active attention to their parents, who essentially structure face-to-face play or social games. As they continue to participate in such play and develop in other domains, the play between parents and children becomes reciprocal and symmetrical (where such role relations are supported by cultural beliefs). At the same time, interpersonal play serves as an arena where children practice cultural modes of communication and interaction.

With object play, participant roles undergo somewhat different changes; they start with mutual engagement around objects, focus on more tangible and concrete functions of toys, and then move toward levels of imagination that extend the realm of reality. By participating in play in which parents model typical acts with play objects and guide event-based symbolic scenarios, children become increasingly competent, independent and imaginative players. Their play competence is related to their sophistication in other areas too, including the ability to coordinate different aspects of a situation, linguistic and symbolic representation, knowledge of events and cultural patterns of activity, and social interaction and communication skills. At the same time, achievements in object play contribute to changes in language competence and peer interaction, among other things. Thus, a reciprocal relation seems to obtain between transformations in play and qualitative changes in children's competence. Fruitful research on parent–child play may flow from a theoretical view that highlights the ongoing relations between patterns of play and children's other achievements.

These different sequences for interpersonal play on the one hand, and object and symbolic play on the other, may be associated with Western conceptions of play, as well as with Western conceptions of the parent–child relationship. In support of the position that playful interactions are particularized instantiations of cultural values, cross-cultural studies reveal that play involving parents and children varies around the world. The cultural specificity of parent–child play suggests that some social partners, such as siblings and peers, may serve the functions of parents in other societies. Cultural differences in parent–child play might reflect differences in cultural ideologies about parent–child relationships, as well as larger cultural values, such as individualism and collectivism. Because interpersonal play involves shared understanding and role reciprocity, parent–child coplay may facilitate horizontal egalitarian relationships between parents and children, and thereby complement vertical and hierarchical parent–child relationships. In contrast, object and symbolic play may be viewed as primarily children's activities, as ways for children to practice roles favored by the culture and to remain occupied on their own. Although coplay occurs most readily during interpersonal play, it is not restricted to this context; similarly, not all interpersonal play entails symmetrical roles. Finally, the course of parent–child play beyond early childhood remains largely unaddressed, both theoretically and empirically.

Where a certain equality between parents and children is the cultural ideal, children may learn to be equal players with their parents; where hierarchical relationships between parents and children are the cultural norm, children may explore ways to navigate such relationships through play. Because empirical studies of play in many cultures have been scattered, it is difficult to draw general conclusions about the nature and functions of parent–child play as compared to play with other persons and to specify its relation to cultural values and social organization. More systematic cross-cultural research on play in various interpersonal contexts is needed to further clarify the role of parent–child play in child development.

Where parent–child relationships do not emphasize sociability and a view of children as communicative partners, parent–child play is not necessarily the arena in which children principally develop interaction and symbolic competencies. It cannot be assumed that parents are the primary play partners for their children even in the West, because children are often in the care of other adults such as grandparents (Smith and Drew, in Vol. 3 of this *Handbook*) or daycare workers (Clarke-Stewart and Allthusen, in Vol. 3 of this *Handbook*). However, to the extent that parents organize these care settings, they indirectly fashion their children's play experiences as well. Cross-cultural studies also indicate that where children do not play with their parents' they may play with other more competent persons (e.g., relatives, older siblings; Zukow-Goldring, in Vol. 3 of this *Handbook*); such play can similarly facilitate children's induction into culturally favored modes of activity.

Research on parent–child play is complicated by the fact that cultural understandings pervade both the definition of play and of parental roles in relation to children. The play frame is communicated and enacted differently not only in connection with the competencies of the play participants, but also with cultural understandings of play activities and cultural expectations for children's developmental progress. Nevertheless, because the realm of play gives children their first encounter with a reality distinct from everyday life, we think it is a significant dimension of their experience. Either directly or indirectly, parents participate in ensuring that their children have rich, variegated, and growth-promoting encounters with play. The cognitive representations, communicative formats, and affective expressions inherent in play ensure that through the matrix of play interactions available to them, children work toward becoming adept members of society.

ACKNOWLEDGMENTS

This chapter is dedicated to the memory of Ina Č. Užgiris. We thank Barbara Wright for assistance.

REFERENCES

Ainsworth, M., Blehar, M. C., Waters, E., and Wall, S. (1978). *Patterns of attachment*. Hillsdale, NJ: Lawrence Erlbaum Associates.

Andrews, S. R., Blumenthal, J. B., Johnson, D. L., Kahn, A. J., Ferguson, C. J., Lasater, T. M., Malone, P. E., and Wallace, D. B. (1982). The skills of mothering: A study of parent–child development centers. *Monographs of the Society for Research in Child Development, 47*(6, Serial No. 198).

Baldwin, J. M. (1902). *Social and ethical interpretations in mental development*. New York: MacMillan.

Beckwith, L. (1986). Parent-infant interaction and infants' social-emotional development. In A. W. Gottfried and C. C. Brown (Eds.), *Play interactions* (pp. 279–292). Lexington, MA: Heath.

Beizer, L., and Howes, C. (1992). Mothers and toddlers: Partners in early symbolic play. In C. Howes (Ed.), *The collaborative construction of pretend* (pp. 25–43). Albany: State University of New York Press.

Belsky, J., Goode, M. K., and Most, R. K. (1980). Maternal stimulation, and infant exploratory competence: Cross-sectional, correlational, and experimental analyses. *Child Development, 51*, 1163–1178.

Belsky, J., and Most, R. K. (1981). From exploration to play: A cross-sectional study of infant free play behavior. *Developmental Psychology, 17*, 630–639.

Bornstein, M. H., Haynes, O. M., O'Reilly, A. W., and Painter, K. (1996). Solitary and collaborative pretense play in early childhood: Sources of individual variation in the development of representational competence. *Child Development, 67*, 2910–2929.

Bornstein, M. H., and O'Reilly, A. W. (Eds.). (1993). *The role of play in the development of thought*. San Francisco: Jossey-Bass.

Bornstein, M. H., and Tamis-LeMonda, C. S. (1990). Activities and interactions of mothers and their firstborn infants in the first six months of life: stability, continuity, covariation, correspondence, and prediction. *Child Development, 61*, 1206–1217.

Bornstein, M. H., Vibbert, M., Tal, J., and O'Donnell, K. (1992). Toddler language and play in the second year: Stability, covariation and influences of parenting. *First Language, 12*, 323–338.

Bowlby, J. (1969). *Attachment and loss: Vol. 1. Attachment*. New York: Basic Books.

Brazelton, T. B., Robey, J. S., and Collier, G. A. (1969). Infant development in the Zinacanteco Indians of southern Mexico. *Pediatrics, 44*, 274–290.

Bretherton, I. (1984). *Symbolic play*. Orlando, Florida: Academic Press.

Bretherton, I., and Bates, E. (Ed.). (1984). *Symbolic play*. San Diego, CA: Academic.

Bruner, J. (1972). Nature and uses of immaturity. *American Psychologist, 27*, 687–708.

Bruner, J. (1978). Learning how to do things with words. In J. Bruner and A. Garton (Eds.), *Human growth and development* (pp. 62–84). Oxford, England: Clarendon.

Bruner, J. (1983). *Child's talk*. New York: Norton.

Bruner, J., and Sherwood, V. (1976). Peek-a-boo and the learning of rule structures. In J. Bruner, A. Jolly, and K. Sylva (Eds.), *Play—Its role in development and evolution* (pp. 277–285). New York: Basic Books.

Bühler, C. (1962). *Psychologie im Leben unserer Zeit* [Psychology for contemporary living]. Munich, Germany: Droemer Knaur.

Clarke-Stewart, K. A. (1978). And daddy makes three: The father's impact on mother and young child. *Child Development, 49*, 466–478.

Cohen, D. (1987). *The development of play*. New York: New York University Press.

Crawley, S. B., Rogers, P. P., Friedman, S., Iacobbo, M., Criticos, A., Richardson, L., and Thompson, M. A. (1978). Developmental changes in the structure of mother–infant play. *Developmental Psychology, 14*, 30–36.

Curtis, H. S. (1917). *The play movement and its significance*. New York: MacMillan.

Dale, N. (1989). Pretend play with mothers and siblings: relations between early performance and partners. *Journal of Child Psychiatry, 30*, 751–759.

Damast, A. M., Tamis-LeMonda, C. S., and Bornstein, M. H. (1996). Mother–child play: Sequential interactions and the relation between maternal beliefs and behaviors. *Child Development, 67*, 1752–1766.

Dixon, S., Tronick, E., Keefer, C., and Brazelton, T. B. (1981). Mother–infant interaction among the Gusii of Kenya. In T. M. Field, A. M. Sostek, P. Vietze, and P. M. Leiderman (Eds.), *Culture and early interactions* (pp. 149–168). Hillsdale, NJ: Lawrence Erlbaum Associates.

Duncan, S., Jr., and Farley, A. M. (1990). Achieving parent–child coordination through convention: Fixed- and variable-sequence conventions. *Child Development, 61*, 742–753.

Dunn, J. (1986). Pretend play in the family. In A. W. Gottfried and C. C. Brown (Eds.), *Play interactions* (pp. 149–162). Lexington, MA: Heath.

Dunn, J., and Wooding, C. (1977). Play in the home and its implications for learning. In B. Tizard and D. Harvey (Eds.), *Biology of play* (pp. 45–58). London: Heinemann.

Edwards, C. P., and Whiting, B. B. (1993). "Mother, older sibling, and me": The overlapping roles of caregivers and companions in the social world of two- and three-year-olds in Ngeca, Kenya. In K. MacDonald (Ed.), *Parent–child play: Descriptions and implications* (pp. 305–329). Albany: State University of New York Press.

Erikson, E. H. (1963). *Childhood and society*. New York: Norton.

Erikson, E. H. (1972). Play and actuality. In M. W. Piers (Ed.), *Play and development* (pp. 127–167). New York: Norton.

Farver, J. M. (1989, April). *Cultural differences in American and Mexican mother–child pretend play*. Paper presented at the meeting of the Society for Research in Child Development, Kansas City, MO.

Farver, J. M., and Howes, C. (1993). Cultural differences in American and Mexican mother–child pretend play. *Merrill-Palmer Quarterly*, *39*, 344–358.

Farver, J. M., and Wimbarti, S. (1995). Indonesian children's play with their mothers and older siblings. *Child Development*, *66*, 1493–1503.

Fein, G. G. (1981). Pretend play in childhood: an integrative review. *Child Development*, *52*, 1095–1118.

Fernald, A., and O'Neill, D. K. (1993). Peekaboo across cultures: How mothers and infants play with voices, faces, and expectations. In K. MacDonald (Ed.), *Parent–child play: Descriptions and implications* (pp. 259–285). Albany: State University of New York Press.

Field, T. (1983). Early interactions and interaction coaching of high-risk infants and parents. In M. Perlmutter (Ed.), *Minnesota Symposia on Child Psychology: Vol. 16. Development and policy concerning children with special needs* (pp. 1–33). Hillsdale, NJ: Lawrence Erlbaum Associates.

Fiese, B. H. (1990). Playful relationships: A contextual analysis of mother–toddler interaction and symbolic play. *Child Development*, *61*, 1648–1656.

Fossey, D. (1983). *Gorillas in the mist*. Boston: Houghton Mifflin.

Freud, S. (1959). Creative writers and day-dreaming. In J. Strachey (Ed.), *The standard edition of the complete works of Sigmund Freud* (Vol. 9, pp. 143–153). London: Hogarth. (Original work published 1908.)

Frodi, A., Bridges, L. J., and Grolnick, W. S. (1985). Correlates of mastery-related behavior: A short-term longitudinal study of infants in their second year. *Child Development*, *56*, 1291–1298.

Garvey, C. (1977). *Play*. Cambridge, MA: Harvard University Press.

Goldberg, S. (1977). Infant development and mother–infant interaction in urban Zambia. In P. H. Leiderman, S. R. Tulkin, and A. Rosenfeld (Eds.), *Culture and infancy: Variations in the human experience* (pp. 211–243). New York: Academic.

Göncü, A., Mistry, J., and Mosier, C. (1991, April). *Cultural variations in the play of toddlers*. Paper presented at the Society for Research in Child Development, Seattle, WA.

Goodall, J. (1986). *The chimpanzees of Gombe*. Cambridge, MA: Belknap.

Grolnick, W. S., Frodi, A., and Bridges, L. J. (1984). Maternal control style and the mastery motivation of one-year-olds. *Infant Mental Health Journal*, *5*, 72–82.

Groos, K. (1901). *The play of man* (E. L. Baldwin, Trans.). London: Heinemann. (Original work published 1899.)

Guerney, L. F. (1991). Parents as partners in treating behavior problems in early childhood settings. *Topics in Early Childhood Special Education*, *11*, 74–90.

Gustafson, G. E., Green, J. A., and West, M. (1979). The infant's changing role in mother–infant games: The growth of social skills. *Infant Behavior and Development*, *2*, 301–308.

Haight, W. L., and Miller, P. J. (1992). The development of everyday pretend play: A longitudinal study of mothers' participation. *Merrill-Palmer Quarterly*, *38*, 331–349.

Haight, W. L., and Miller, P. J. (1993). *Pretending at home*. Albany: State University of New York Press.

Hay, D. F., Ross, M. S., and Davis, B. (1979). Social games in infancy. In B. Sutton-Smith (Ed.), *Play and learning* (pp. 83–107). New York: Gardner.

Heath, S. B. (1983). *Ways with words*. Cambridge, MA: Cambridge University Press.

Howes, C. (1992). Mastery of the communication of meaning in social pretend play. In A. Pellegrini (Ed.), *The collaborative construction of pretend* (pp. 13–24). Albany: State University of New York Press.

Jacobson, J. L. (1981). The role of inanimate objects in early peer interaction. *Child Development*, *52*, 618–626.

Leach, P., and Matthews, J. (1997). *Your baby and child*. New York: Knopf.

Levenstein, P. (1970). Cognitive growth in preschoolers through verbal interaction with mothers. *American Journal of Orthopsychiatry*, *40*, 426–432.

Levenstein, P., and O'Hara, J. (1993). The necessary lightness of mother–child play. In K. MacDonald (Ed.), *Parent–child play: Descriptions and implications* (pp. 221–237). Albany: State University of New York Press.

LeVine, R. A., Dixon, S., LeVine S., Richman, A., Leiderman, P. H., Keefer, C. H., and Brazelton, T. B. (1994). *Child care and culture: Lessons from Africa*. Cambridge, England: Cambridge University Press.

Lewis, C., and Gregory, S. (1987). Parents' talk to their infants: The importance of context. *First Language*, *7*, 201–216.

Lewis, M. (1979). The social determination of play. In B. Sutton-Smith (Ed.), *Play and learning* (pp. 23–33). New York: Gardner.

Lowe, M. (1975). Trends in the development of representational play in infants from one to three years: An observational study. *Journal of Child Psychology and Psychiatry*, *16*, 33–47.

Lucariello, J. (1987). Spinning fantasy: Themes, structure, and the knowledge base. *Child Development*, *58*, 434–442.

MacDonald, K. (1993a). Parent–child play: An evolutionary perspective. In K. MacDonald (Ed.), *Parent–child play* (pp. 113–143). Albany: State University of New York Press.

MacDonald, K. (Ed.). (1993b). *Parent–child play*. Albany: State University of New York Press.

MacDonald, K., and Parke, R. D. (1984). Bridging the gap: Parent–child play interaction and peer interactive competence. *Child Development, 55*, 1265–1277.

MacDonald, K. B., and Parke, R. D. (1986). Parent–child physical play: The effects of sex and age of children and parents. *Sex Roles, 15*, 367–378.

Martini, M., and Kirkpatrick, J. (1981). Early interactions in the Marquesas Islands. In T. M. Field, A. M. Sostek, P. Vietze, and P. M. Leiderman (Eds.), *Culture and early interactions* (pp. 189–213). Hillsdale, NJ: Lawrence Erlbaum Associates.

Maslin, C. A., Bretherton, I., and Morgan, G. A. (1987, August). *Toddlers' independent mastery motivation as related to attachment security and quality of maternal scaffolding.* Paper presented at the MacArthur Foundation Research Network Summer Institute, Durango, CO.

McCune-Nicolich, L. (1981). Toward symbolic functioning: Structure of early pretend games and potential parallels with language. *Child Development, 52*, 785–797.

McLoyd, V. C. (1982). Social class differences in sociodramatic play: A critical review. *Developmental Review, 2*, 1–30.

Millar, S. (1968). *The psychology of play*. Harmondsworth, England: Penguin.

Miller, P., and Garvey, C. (1984). Mother–baby role play: Its origins in social support. In I. Bretherton (Ed.), *Symbolic play: The development of social understanding* (pp. 101–130). New York: Academic.

Mintz, S., and Kellogg, S. (1988). *Domestic revolutions*. New York: Free Press.

Morelli, G. A., and Tronick, E. Z. (1991). Parenting and child development in the Efe foragers and Lese farmers of Zaire. In M. H. Bornstein (Ed.), *Cultural approaches to parenting* (pp. 91–113). Hillsdale, NJ: Lawrence Erlbaum Associates.

Morgan, G. A., Maslin-Cole, C. A., Biringen, Z., and Harmon, R. J. (1991). Play assessment of mastery motivation in infants and young children. In. C. E. Schaefer, K. Gitlin, and A. Sandgrund (Eds.), *Play diagnosis and assessment* (pp. 65–86). New York: Wiley.

Morgan, G. A., Maslin-Cole, C. A., Ridgeway, D., and Kang-Park, J. (1988). Toddler mastery motivation and aspects of mother-child affect communication (Summary). *Program and Proceedings of the Developmental Psychobiology Research Group Fifth Biennial Retreat, 5*, 15–16.

Nicely, P., Tamis-LeMonda, C. S., and Bornstein, M. H. (1999). Mothers' attuned responses to infant affect expressivity promote earlier achievement of language milestones. *Infant Behavior and Development, 22*, 557–568.

O'Brien, M., and Nagle, K. J. (1987). Parents's speech to toddlers: The effect of play context. *Journal of Child Language, 14*, 269–279.

Ochs, E., and Schieffelin, B. B. (1984). Language acquisition and socialization: Three developmental stories and their implications. In R. A. Shweder and R. A. LeVine (Eds.), *Culture theory* (pp. 276–320). Cambridge, England: Cambridge University Press.

O'Connell, B., and Bretherton, I. (1984). Toddlers' play alone and with mother: The role of maternal guidance. In I. Bretherton (Ed.), *Symbolic play* (337–369). Orlando, FL: Academic.

Papoušek, H., and Papoušek, M. (1991). Innate and cultural guidance of infants' integrative competencies: China, the Unites States, and Germany. In M. H. Bornstein (Ed.), *Cultural approaches to parenting* (pp. 23–44). Hillsdale, NJ: Lawrence Erlbaum Associates.

Papoušek, M., Papoušek, H., and Harris, J. (1987). The emergence of play in parent–infant interactions. In D. Görlitz and J. F. Wohlwill (Eds.), *Curiosity, imagination, and play* (pp. 214–246). Hillsdale, NJ: Lawrence Erlbaum Associates.

Pastor, D. L. (1981). The quality of mother–infant attachment and its relationship to toddler's initial sociability with peers. *Developmental Psychology, 17*, 326–335.

Peller, L. E. (1954). Libidinal phases, ego development and play. *Psychoanalytic Study of the Child, 9*, 178–198.

Piaget, J. (1952). *The origins of intelligence* (M. Cook, Trans.). New York: Norton. (Original work published 1936.)

Piaget, J. (1962). *Play, dreams and imitation in childhood* (C. Gattegno and F. M. Hodgson, Trans.). New York: Norton. (Original work published 1945.)

Piaget, J. (1965). *The moral judgment of the child* (M. Gabain, Trans.). New York: Free Press. (Original work published 1932.)

Power, T. G. (2000). *Play and exploration in children and animals*. Mahwah, NJ: Lawrence Erlbaum Associates.

Pulaski, M. A. S. (1978). *Your baby's mind and how it grows: Piaget's theory for parents*. New York: Harper and Row.

Rabain-Jamin, J. (1989). Culture and early social interactions: The example of mother–infant object play in African and native French families. *European Journal of Psychology of Education, 4*, 295–305.

Roggman, L. A. (1991). Assessing social interactions of mothers and infants through play. In. C. E. Schaefer, K. Gitlin, and A. Sandgrund (Eds.), *Play diagnosis and assessment* (pp. 427–462). New York: Wiley.

Rogoff, B. (1990). *Apprenticeship in thinking*. New York: Oxford University Press.

Rogoff, B., Mistry, J., Göncü, A., and Mosier C. (1993). Guided participation in cultural activity by toddlers and caregivers. *Monographs of the Society for Research in Child Development, 58*(7, Serial No. 236).

Rubin, K. H., Fein, G., and Vandenberg, B. (1983). Play. In P. Mussen (Ed.), *Handbook of child psychology: Vol. 4. Socialization, personality and social development* (E. M. Hetherington, Vol. Ed., pp. 693–774). New York: Wiley.

Rubin, K. H., and Howe, N. (1986). Social play and perspective-taking. In G. Fein and M. Rivkin (Eds.), *The young child at play* (pp. 113–125), Washington, DC: National Association for the Education of Young Children.

Roopnarine, J. L., Talukder, E., Jain, D., Joshi, P., and Srivastav, P. (1990). Characteristics of holding, patterns of play, and social behaviors between parents and infants in New Delhi, India. *Developmental Psychology, 26*, 667–673.

Scarr-Salapatek, S., and Williams, M. L. (1973). The effects of early stimulation on low-birth-weight infants. *Child Development, 44*, 94–101.

Schwartzman, H. (1984). Imaginative play: Deficit or difference? In T. D. Yawkey and A. D. Pellegrini (Eds.), *Child's play: Developmental and applied*, Hillsdale, NJ: Lawrence Erlbaum Associates.

Shore, C., O'Connell, B., and Bates, E. (1984). First sentences in language and symbolic play. *Developmental Psychology, 20*, 872–880.

Singer, D. G., and Singer, J. L. (1990). *The house of make-believe*. Cambridge, MA: Harvard University Press.

Singer, J. L. (1995). Imaginative play in childhood: precursor of subjunctive thought, daydreaming, and adult pretending games. In A. D. Pellegrini (Ed.), *The future of play theory* (pp. 187–219). Albany: State University of New York Press.

Slade, A. (1987). A longitudinal study of maternal involvement and symbolic play during the toddler period. *Child Development, 58*, 367–375.

Slaughter, D. T. (1983). Early intervention and its effects on maternal and child development. *Monographs of the Society for Research in Child Development, 48*(4, Serial No. 202).

Smilansky, S. (1968). *The effects of sociodramatic play on disadvantaged preschool children*. New York: Wiley.

Smith, P. K. (1982). Does play matter? *The Behavioral and Brain Sciences, 5*, 139–184.

Smith, P. K., and Vollstedt, R. (1985). On defining play: An empirical study of the relationship between play and various play criteria. *Child Development, 56*, 1042–1050.

Spencer, H. (1883). *The principles of psychology* (Vol. 2). New York: Appleton.

Spock, B., and Parker, S. (1998). *Dr. Spock's baby and child care*. New York: Pocket.

Stern, D. N. (1977). *The first relationship*. Cambridge, MA: Harvard University Press.

Stern, D. N. (1985). *The interpersonal world of the infant*. New York: Basic Books.

Stern, D. N. (1993). The role of feelings for an interpersonal self. In U. Neisser (Ed.), *The perceived self* (pp. 205–215). New York: Cambridge University Press.

Stern, W. (1914). *Psychologie der Frühen Kindheit bis zum sechsten Lebensjahre*. [Psychology of early childhood up to the sixth year of age]. Leipzig, Germany: Quelle and Meyer.

Tamis-LeMonda, C. S., and Bornstein, M. H. (1991). Individual variation, correspondence, stability, and change in mother and toddler play. *Infant Behavior and Development, 14*, 143–162.

Tamis-LeMonda, C. S., and Bornstein, M. H. (1994). Specificity in mother–toddler language-play relations across the second year. *Developmental Psychology, 30*, 283–292.

Tamis-LeMonda, C. S., and Bornstein, M. H. (1996). Variation in children's exploratory, nonsymbolic, and symbolic play: an explanatory multidimensional framework. In C. Rovee-Collier and L. Lipsitt (Eds.), *Advances in infancy research* (pp. 37–78). Norwood, NJ: Ablex.

Tamis-LeMonda, C. S., Bornstein, M. H., and Baumwell, L. (2001). Maternal responsiveness and children's achievement of language milestones. *Child Development, 72*, 748–767.

Tamis-LeMonda, C. S., Bornstein, M. H., Cyphers, L., Toda, S., and Ogino, M. (1992). Language and play at one year: A comparison of toddlers and mothers in the United States and Japan. *International Journal of Behavioral Development, 15*, 19–42.

Tamis-LeMonda, C. S., Bornstein, M. H., Kahana-Kalman, Baumwell, L., and Cyphers, L. (1998). Predicting variation in the timing of language milestones in the second year: an events history approach. *Journal of Child Language, 25*, 675–700.

Tamis-LeMonda, C. S., Katz, J. C., and Bornstein, M. H. (in press). Infant play: Functions and partners. In M. Lewis and A. Slater (Eds.), *Introduction to infant development*. New York: Oxford University Press.

Tamis-LeMonda, C. S., Melstein-Damast, A., and Bornstein, M. H. (1994). What do mothers know about the developmental nature of play?, *Infant Behavior and Development, 17*, 341–345.

Teti, D. M., Bond, L. A., and Gibbs, E. D. (1988). Mothers, fathers, and siblings: A comparison of play styles and their influence upon infant cognitive level. *International Journal of Behavioral Development, 11*, 415–432.

Trevarthen, C. (1977). Descriptive analyses of infant communicative behavior. In H. R. Schaffer (Ed.), *Studies in mother-infant interaction* (pp. 227–270). New York: Academic.

Trevarthen, C., and Hubley, P. (1978). Secondary intersubjectivity: Confidence, confiding and acts of meaning in the first year. In A. Lock (Ed.), *Action, gesture and symbol* (pp. 182–229). New York: Academic.

Tronick, E., Als, H., and Adamson, L. (1979). Structure of early face-to-face communicative interactions. In. M. Bullowa (Ed.), *Before speech* (pp. 349–372). New York: Cambridge University Press.

Turkheimer, M., Bakeman, R., and Adamson, L. B. (1989). Do mothers support and peers inhibit skilled object play in infancy? *Infant Behavior and Development, 12*, 37–44.

Užgiris, I. Č. (1984). Imitation in infancy: Its interpersonal aspects. In M. Perlmutter (Ed.), *Minnesota Symposia on Child Psychology: Vol. 17. Parent–child interactions and parent–child relations in child development* (pp. 1–32). Hillsdale, NJ: Lawrence Erlbaum Associates.

Užgiris, I. Č., Benson, J. B., Kruper, J. C., and Vasek, M. E. (1989). Contextual influences on imitative interactions between mothers and infants. In J. J. Lockman and N. L. Hazen (Eds.), *Action in social context* (pp. 103–127). New York: Plenum.

Vandell, D. L., Ramanan, J., and Lederberg, A. R. (1991, April). *Mother–child pretend play and children's later competence with peers*. Paper presented at the meeting of the Society for Research in Child Development, Seattle, WA.

Vandell, D. L., and Wilson, K. S. (1987). Infants' interactions with mother, sibling, and peer: Contrasts and relations between interaction systems. *Child Development, 58*, 176–186.

Vandenberg, B. (1986). Play theory. In G. Fein and M. Rivkin (Eds.), *The young child at play* (pp. 17–27). Washington, DC: National Association for the Education of Young Children.

Vibbert, M., and Bornstein, M. H. (1989). Specific associations between domains of mother–child interaction and toddler referential language and pretend play. *Infant Behavior and Development, 12*, 163–184.

Vygotsky, L. S. (1976). Play and its role in the mental development of the child. In J. S. Bruner, A. Jolly, and K. Sylva (Eds.), *Play—Its role in development and evolution* (pp. 537–554). New York: Basic Books.

Vygotsky, L. S. (1978). *Mind in society*. Cambridge, MA: Harvard University Press.

Watson, M., and Fischer, K. (1977). A developmental sequence of agent use in late infancy. *Child Development, 48*, 828–836.

Whaley, K. K. (1990). The emergence of social play in infancy: A proposed developmental sequence of infant–adult social play. *Early Childhood Research Quarterly, 5*, 347–358.

Whiting, B. B., and Edwards, C. P. (1988). *Children of different worlds*. Cambridge, MA: Harvard University Press.

Winnicott, D. W. (1971). *Playing and reality*. Harmondsworth: Penguin.

Winnicott, D. W. (1977). *The piggle*. New York: International Universities Press.

Yarrow, L. J., MacTurk, R. H., Vietze, P. M., McCarthy, M. E., Klein, R. P., and McQuiston, S. (1984). Developmental course of parental stimulation and its relationship to mastery motivation during infancy. *Developmental Psychology, 20*, 492–503.

Yogman, M. W. (1987). Father–infant caregiving and play with preterm and full-term infants. In P. W. Berman and F. A. Pedersen (Eds.), *Men's transitions to parenthood* (pp. 175–195). Hillsdale, NJ: Lawrence Erlbaum Associates.

Zukow, P. G. (1986). The relationship between interaction with the caregiver and the emergence of play activities during the one-word period. *British Journal of Developmental Psychology, 4*, 223–234.

10

Everyday Stresses and Parenting

Keith Crnic
Christine Low
The Pennsylvania State University

INTRODUCTION

Stress has long played an integral role in understanding parenting processes and families in general. The sheer volume of research has been staggering, both in regard to research that has specifically addressed stress as a construct (see Garmezy and Rutter, 1983), and research that has focused on contextual and events (e.g., poverty, divorce, single parenting, and illness) implicitly assumed to be stressful for families (Cummings, Davies, and Campbell, 2000). The volume of work is surprising, given the fact that no single, clear conceptualization of stress has emerged over the years. In general, stress involves an individual's emotional and behavioral response to some unpleasant event. Typically, the response involves some level of distress that adversely affects subsequent behavior and functioning. Furthermore, the stress response has multiple parameters (emotional, behavioral, and physiological) that affect well-being. Subjective assessment of the response involves an individual's appraisal of the adaptive significance of the stressor (event) that creates the response, whereas objective assessments strictly address the presence of adverse events without seeking individual appraisal.

Over time, the focus of attention in relevant stress research has primarily targeted major life changes or significant problematic circumstances facing parents and families. Yet such a singular conceptualization of the relation between stress and parenting ignored a more direct domain in which stress operates, and one which appears to have substantial effects on parental (and subsequently children's) psychological well-being.

Perhaps nothing characterizes parenting better than the everyday challenges and caregiving demands that involve relationships with the developing child. Certainly, many daily experiences with children are a source of joy or pleasure, and provide parents with a sense of competence and confidence as individual challenges or issues are met and solved. It is also the case, however, that children's behaviors and the daily tasks of parenthood can at times confuse, frustrate, or irritate, and thereby create situations that may easily be perceived as stressful by parents. It is these seemingly everyday minor events, as well as related parent and child processes, that are the focus of this chapter and create a context for understanding parenting stress from a more broadly emerging perspective. From various studies that have addressed this topic, parents describe a myriad of situations and contexts that illustrate these stress processes:

> My child refuses to eat her dinner, or protests against eating what is on the plate. I expect this at times, but when her whining starts to irritate my spouse and then he or she starts to battle with our child and I try to intervene it becomes stressful.

> I find that I get really tense when my son or daughter get upset in public, maybe because they are tired and need a nap. This is especially true for my son, because he is just really sensitive and doesn't adapt very well to changes in his routine. I know why he might be upset and crying, but I think I worry too much about what other people think. This is true even if I am with my parents and they know how my son is. I find I am always justifying to others why my child might be crying.

> Bedtimes make me crazy. Even with a regular nighttime schedule that we try to keep, it is difficult to get our young child to sleep at night, or even to sleep through the night consistently. Bedtime becomes a battle of wills, as they get up numbers of times to ask for a drink, or another story, or just for our company. This takes away from the amount of time we have together as husband and wife, or time to relax and unwind from the day.

> For me it is the lack of time for the small things, for example, after work I have to balance taking the kids to practice or their doctor's appointments, and then getting home to everything, like dinner, laundry, feeding the dogs and helping with homework. I never seem to have the time to sit down and send cards to friends on their birthdays, or even catch up with them on the phone.

> Now that we are parents I feel like I have lost my identity somewhat. There are some friends we no longer see as often. And I cannot remember the last time the two of us were able to go out on our own. Not having this time together is hard, we never seem to have time to work on our relationship or talk to each other about how are day went. We seem to bicker more and I only hear about his day if he is complaining about it when I ask for his help around the house.

> Having children keeps me from being able to pursue some of the things that I am interested in. I still get to do some things, such as go running and work out, but I can't remember the last time I was able to spontaneously meet up with my friends for basketball. Its frustrating sometimes, not having this time to hang out with the guys. It was not something I thought I would miss so much, or rely upon so much to "blow off steam."

> With such a busy schedule I feel guilty, and then upset that I do not have enough time to help with school fundraisers for my children.

> We often complain about having to battle after-work commute traffic. This is compounded by having to time it to pick up the kids from daycare so that they are not left there beyond the pickup time (which upsets the staff), and then be prepared for them to be hungry and quarreling with one another in the back seat.

Obviously, Parenting is a complicated process, made especially difficult by heterogeneity in children's characteristics, complexity of developmental processes, and continual demands for caregiving. Smooth transitions to parenting, and less stress in the parenting role across time, is considered critical to positive parent and child outcomes (Deater-Deckard, 1998). Yet parenting can seem onerous at times, and most parents have experience with being nagged or whined to, being interrupted, continually cleaning up after their children, finding it difficult to secure any privacy, not knowing how to handle a specific situation that arises with their child, running extra errands to meet a child's needs, or any one of a myriad of possible everyday events of a similar nature. These events reflect parenting daily hassles (Crnic and Booth, 1991; Crnic and Greenberg, 1990), and they represent the typical, normal events that characterize some of the everyday transactions that parents have with their children. Generally, these daily stressors tend to involve either the normal challenging behaviors or misbehaviors that children display in their daily activities, or the multiplicity of time-consuming tasks associated with parents' routine caregiving or childrearing responsibilities. In either case, parents' actual experience with, and subjective evaluation of, these events may prove instrumental to their eventual responsiveness to their children and their needs, and to variations in the emergence of parent–child relationships (Deater-Deckard, 1998).

Because parenting daily hassles are common and are shared by families across conditions (e.g., high or low socioeconomic status) and contexts (e.g., home or grocery stores), they are particularly important in understanding qualitative aspects of parenting processes such as responsiveness, sensitivity, and affective interactions. It is critical to note that everyday parental stress, as measured in various ways, is meant to comprise a normative process common to all families; that is, daily parenting stressors are not particular to any high-risk or problematic population, as has been the case with most previous stress research models involving parenting (Crnic and Greenberg, 1990). Thus, it is important to conceptually differentiate parents' perceptions of minor parenting stressors from more general parenting stress notions and ratings of children's behavior problems. There is certainly shared variance between the typical or normal "challenging" behavior of children and perceived behavior problems in children or distress in parents, but the constructs are also independent in their meaning and ability to predict other relevant dimensions of parent and child functioning (Crnic and Greenberg, 1990). That is, children's normally challenging or difficult behavior may be perceived as hassles from time to time, but may not rise to level of identification as "problematic" without substantial considerations of greater intensity, frequency, and consistency in the behaviors. This distinction continues to be an important one in establishing the validity of the minor stress construct for parenting. Furthermore, it is the case that parenting stress is not only a function of children's behavior; parents may be stressed by the everyday tasks specifically associated with parenting (e.g., managing complicated schedules, and arranging childcare).

Notably, there are also contexts outside the family system that may well affect the degree to which parents are stressed and indirectly affect parental perception of the parenting process. Perhaps the most salient of these contexts is the workplace. Repetti and Wood (1997), as well as Windle and Dumenci (1997), suggested that when parents experience stress at work, their patience, sensitivity, and responsiveness toward family members may be reduced. Similarly, high workload (Ostberg and Hagekull, 2000), self-reported feelings of stress after work (Crouter, Perry-Jenkins, Huston, and Crawford, 1989), and high levels of work–family interference are associated with increases in marital conflict (Belsky, Perry-Jenkins, and Crouter, 1985). Research also supports a positive association between satisfaction with the role of employed mother and parenting behavior (Harrell and Ridley, 1975; Lerner and Galambos, 1985; Stuckey, McGhee, and Bell, 1982). Maternal job dissatisfaction has been linked to the use of rejecting parenting behaviors (Lerner and Galambos, 1985) and to greater display of negative affect by parents (Stuckey et al., 1982). Finally, high commitment to both work and parenting has been associated with an authoritative parenting style for mothers (Greenberger and Goldberg, 1989). Likewise, fathers holding jobs that typically require compliance to authority tend to favor physical punishment and stress obedience and conformity in their children (Bronfenbrenner and Crouter, 1982; Kohn and Schooler, 1982). These findings regarding the effects of the workplace on parenting suggest that there may well be important everyday extrafamilial processes that affect mothers' and fathers' perceptions of parenting stress.

Although any one typical daily hassle of parenting may be of little significance in and of itself, the cumulative impact of relatively minor events over time may well present a meaningful source of stress for a parent. Indeed, the chronic experience of these events, and the parental response to them, may eventually have an adverse influence on the quality of parenting, the parent–child relationship, and ultimately child functioning (Belsky, Woodworth, and Crnic, 1996). It is the case, however, that not all parents perceive these events as uniformly stressful. Individual differences factors, such as personality characteristics, marital quality, available social support, and parental beliefs are critical considerations for understanding the nature of parenting stress and may well influence the degree to which parents feel stressed and therby how they respond to these everyday events (Deater-Deckard, 1998). It is therefore important to understand both the complex multivariate processes that influence parents' perceptions of daily stressors, the parental response to them, and the wide range of eventual outcomes that such experiences may influence.

This chapter addresses issues that are central to an understanding of emerging models of parenting stress, and particularly the everyday stresses that are associated with parenthood. To provide a basis for the current state of research and theory, a discussion of the historical development of stress research begins the chapter. Following this brief history, the theoretical base for the importance of everyday stresses associated with parenting is provided, in which the major issues related to such stress processes are set forth and contrasted with general parenting stress considerations. Major issues will again include both the determinants of the stresses of parenting and the consequences ultimately associated with them. As stress has proven a difficult construct to disentangle from coping, the effectiveness of several potential coping mechanisms is detailed. Finally, the chapter concludes with a comment on the developmental salience of children's challenging behavior and the resilience that parents often demonstrate in the face of repetitive stress.

HISTORICAL CONSIDERATIONS IN STRESS RESEARCH

The study of everyday stressors of parenting has only what might best be termed a "brief history" to date. Nevertheless, there are a number of important historical considerations, coming primarily from the general stress literature, that have led the field to its current early state.

From the work of Homes and Rahe (1967), stress was conceptualized as the experience of major life change. From their research with the Social Readjustment Rating Scale, Holmes and Rahe provided evidence connecting the experience of major life change with physical illness and poorer psychological functioning. A wealth of research followed, suggesting a somewhat clouded picture of the relation between major life events (i.e., change) and physical and psychological well-being. Rabkin and Streuning's (1976) review subsequently called into question the validity of the relation between life event stress and physical outcome, although there is clearly more power in the prediction between life event stress and later psychological status.

One of the major developments in stress research involved both a methodological and conceptual redefinition of the stress construct. The notion of individual "appraisal" was added to the conceptualization, as stress researchers began to consider the salience of an individual's cognitive evaluations of the impact of life events (Lazarus, 1984), and measures of life event stress began to ask individual respondents to appraise both the valence (positive or negative) and degree of effect of any one life change event that may have occurred (see Sarason, Johnson, and Siegel, 1978). Cognitive appraisal then became a critical aspect of stress research methodology and theory that recognized individual differences in the nature and degree of stressful experience. To this end, simple frequency counts of events were not sufficient to capture the nature of stressful experience. The perceived intensity of the event, or the degree to which the event was judged to be impactful, became a critical aspect of the conceptual and measurement paradigm. This emphasis has continued into the current contexts of parenting stress (Deater-Deckard, 1998).

A second major development in stress research involved the movement from an exclusive focus on the major life event approach to including the experience of minor daily hassles as a relevant stress domain (Kanner, Coyne, Schaefer, and Lazarus, 1981). Lazarus and his colleagues questioned the utility of the major life events approach and suggested that the cumulative impacts of relatively minor daily hassles may have major adaptational significance for individuals, affecting their basic sense of competence. Indeed, their research supported such considerations as "daily hassles" appraised by the individual were consistently shown to be better predictors of adults' psychological well-being than were major life events. In addition, daily hassles operated independently in the prediction of psychological distress, such as depression and anxiety (DeLongis, Coyne, Dakof, Folkman, and Lazarus, 1982; Kanner et al., 1981; Lazarus, DeLongis, Folkman, and Gruen, 1985). Important for considering the salience of parenting daily hassles, other research supported these early findings and further indicated that interpersonal conflicts with a spouse, child, or other adults may in fact be the most distressing type of daily stress event (Bolger, DeLongis, Kessler, and Schilling, 1989; O'Brien, 1996).

Theoretically, hassles have been conceptualized as the irritating, frustrating, annoying, distressing demands that to some degree characterize everyday transactions with the environment (Kanner et al., 1981). Some hassles may be situational determined and infrequent, whereas others may repeat because the individual remains in the same context with consistent, predictable demands. It is this latter point that best captures the nature of hassles or minor stressors that relate to parenting (Crnic and Greenberg, 1990; O'Brien, 1996), as parental characteristics, children's behavior, and developmental processes often create situations that are at odds with, challenge, or interfere with parental responsibilities and needs.

Nevertheless, the hassles model and the inclusion of cognitive appraisal into the stress research paradigm raise important conceptual problems that have been well delineated by those who favor a more objective life events approach to stress measurement. These concerns, well articulated by Dohrenwend and Shrout (1985), suggest that individual cognitive appraisal of the meaningfulness or impact of life events, as opposed to simply counting the number of occurred events, introduces a potential confound in the measurement paradigm. Because individuals experiencing distress may be more likely to rate life events as having larger negative impacts, the correlations found between appraisal measures of stress and psychological outcomes are confounded. In essence, Dohrenwend and Shrout's argument suggests that nothing correlates with symptoms like other symptoms, and hassles appraised by any individual are simply a proxy for concurrent mood and psychological status.

Although the argument in favor of purely objective measurement of events is compelling in some respects and necessitates careful selection of items in stress measures to avoid mood/pathology confounds, the importance of cognitive appraisal of events has been well established within both major life event and daily hassle approaches to stress research (Lazarus et al., 1985; Sarason et al., 1978). Indeed, Crnic and Greenberg (1990) found that objective ratings of the frequency of parenting hassles were highly correlated with parental appraisals of the impact of those hassles when measurement items were carefully selected to avoid subjective mood states, and Creasey and Reese (1996) likewise showed that independent teacher ratings of child behavior were associated with parent appraised stresses of childrearing.

Research specific to parenting daily hassles remains scarce. In contrast, however, there is a vast literature on relations between major life event stress and parenting, with particular emphases on identified problematic or at-risk populations (Abidin, 1990; Deater-Deckard, 1998). In almost every study, greater parenting stress appears related to poorer outcome regardless of the outcome construct of interest. There is nothing particularly surprising in such findings, although it is also clear that there is vast individual variability in the specific response to stress. Yet, little research has attempted to address issues related to stress and parent, child, and family processes in nonproblem or normal populations (Jarvis and Creasey, 1991). It may well be the case, however, that stress processes in typical families help to create the conditions under which more problematic conditions emerge (Belsky et al., 1996), and continued focus on the normal daily stresses of parenting may help to explicate the relations between stress and maladaptation.

CENTRAL ISSUES AND THEORY OF EVERYDAY
PARENTING STRESSORS

There are a number conceptual issues of importance in understanding the construct of everyday stressors to parenthood. One concerns conceptualization of *parenting stress* and the frameworks from which this construct might be best understood. Another involves identification of the various factors that may serve to determine the nature of parents' experiences of stress. Finally, and in some respects most critically, delineation of the potential causative relations between minor parenting stressors and parent, child, and family outcomes is key.

Historically, there was little agreement on how stress might best be conceptualized and measured, and the same has been true when considering the nature and experience of parenting stress. Applying a general stress model (e.g., Lazarus, 1991), Deater-Deckard (1998) proposed that a conceptualization parenting stress requires four components:

(1) A child and/or the parenting role serves as the causal external agent for the stress experience.
(2) Parents must appraise child behavior or parenting events as stressful.
(3) Parental coping interacts with stress to determine the degree of effect of the stress.
(4) Parenting stress has meaningful consequences to parental and child well-being.

Within this framework, parenting stress is defined as "the aversive psychological reaction to the demands of being a parent" (p. 315), and it is experienced as "negative feelings toward self and toward the child or children, and by definition these negative feelings are directly attributable to the demands of parenthood" (p. 315). These definitional qualities are helpful in setting the stage for empirical work but allow for broad measurement possibilities.

The preponderance of the research with parents and families has included either (1) variations within major life stress formats (e.g., Crnic, Greenberg, and Slough, 1986; Pianta and Egeland, 1990) that are not specific to the parenting context, (2) the study of various correlates to the Parenting Stress Index (PSI; Abidin, 1983; Abidin, 1990; Loyd and Abidin, 1985), an instrument designed to assess stress broadly within the family context, or (3) the study of more specific minor daily hassles of parenting, which is focused more on normative stress contexts (Crnic and Greenberg, 1990). Parenting stress as indexed by the PSI differs both conceptually and methodologically from everyday stressors of parenting from the daily hassles perspective. The PSI, for instance, focuses more on issues of general parental distress and children's difficulties, as well as dysfunctional parent–child relationships. As such, its focus is appropriately more toward the pathological spectrum. Indeed, effect sizes found for PSI predictions to parenting outcomes with normal, nondistressed families are generally significant but small (Deater-Deckard and Scarr, 1996). In contrast, the daily hassles perspective attempts to specifically assess everyday stresses associated with typical parenting events and normative, albeit potentially challenging, child behaviors. Both approaches offer meaningful ways of addressing stresses inherent in the parenting context.

The PSI is a well-developed and extensively used instrument that attempts to address the relative magnitude of stress in the parent–child system. The measure factors into two major scales (a Parent Domain and a Child Domain), each of which contains a number of subscales that describe specific areas thought to promote stress. The subscales describe various child characteristics (adaptability, demandingness, mood, hyperactivity/distractibility) that may present difficulties for the parent, and parent characteristics (sense of competence, depression, attachment) that may operate similarly to create stress in the parent–family system. As noted, scores from this measure reflect more problematic circumstance than normative stressors and can be differentiated from daily parenting stress in that major respect. Nevertheless, a large portion of the research and subsequent knowledge base on parenting stress has come from the extensive work conducted from this paradigm, even across cultures (Ostberg, Hagekull, and Wettergren, 1997), and its contribution is relevant to our understanding of everyday stressors and parenthood (Abidin, 1992).

Belsky (1984) provided a working model for the determinants of parenting that has strong implications for the factors that might influence parents' experience of parenting daily hassles. Other, more specific, conceptual frameworks have been proposed to explicate the potential relations between parenting stress and a wide variety of parenting behaviors and family contests (Abidin, 1992; Mash and Johnston, 1990; Webster-Stratton, 1990). These dynamic multivariate models all point to direct, indirect, and reciprocal links between the various factors that may be involved in the development of stressful parental experience (Abidin, 1992). The various models all suggest that the family can be best understood as an interconnected, interdependent system, in which individual psychological characteristics of each parent, couple characteristics, antecedent factors from each parent's family of origin, child characteristics, and environmental characteristics play a role in determining stressful experience from multiple perspectives (Cowan et al., 1985).

Individual differences in stress susceptibility and experience, especially as considered from a cognitive perspective, suggest that it is critical to develop a model of those factors that determine or predict parental stress. It seems clear that not all parents are likely to find their parenting or children's behavior equally stressful; nor are parents likely necessarily to share perceptions of which behaviors and tasks are most stressful. In this respect, there seems to be a variety of factors that may contribute to parents' experience of everyday stress with their children, and these factors may be grouped into three major categories: (1) parental factors, (2) child factors, and (3) family system factors. Parental factors include prebirth functioning, such as stress levels during pregnancy, parent gender, family history, and vulnerability to stress; personality attributes; parental mood; and beliefs in regard to child development and childrearing. Child factors likely include important individual child characteristics such as temperament, gender, and behavior. However, it is also critical to understand the potential for stage-salient transition periods, such as that from infancy to early childhood or the transition to school age, to affect stressful experience. Natural changes in children's developmental ontogeny seem especially likely to create novel and challenging situations for parents (Belsky, Woodworth, and Crnic, 1996; O'Brien, 1996). Likewise, family-level considerations require greater attention to systems notions that include the impact of the marital relationship and coparenting process as well as complex family and sibling relationships that vary with the number of children in the home (Deater-Deckard, 1998; Gable, Belsky, and Crnic, 1992).

Identifying those factors most relevant to the development of stressful experience with children is an important goal. However, the reason to search for such understanding reflects a more basic concern about stress processes in general—that there is a causative link between stress and adverse outcome. Certainly this concept has been widely addressed in the literature on stress processes in families (Abidin, 1990; Cummings et al., 2000; Deater-Deckard, 1998), and there is strong general support for this proposition.

Patterson (1983) described a particular theoretical concept central to considerations of everyday stressors with children. He suggested that stress, especially in the form of minor everyday experiences, may serve as a change agent for certain microsocial processes within families. Parent–child relationship trajectories may be deflected over time by stress processes, such that relationships become more agonistic or problematic when parents are stressed by minor events. Patterson further suggested that over time this slow process of change in relationships, facilitated by the occurrence of accumulated daily hassles, may contribute to the development of psychopathology in children.

Although Patterson's (1983) concepts were meant to highlight issues germane to socially aggressive children and coercive processes in problematic families, the issues raised have proven applicable to normative stress processes in families with more typically developing children (Belsky, Woodworth, and Crnic, 1996a; 1996b). We have suggested that cumulative daily hassles associated with parenting may, over time, change the nature of parent–child relationships and family functioning. Under conditions in which parents experience more frequent and more intense daily stressors in parenting, once competent relationships may be deflected to become more problematic and conflictual. This dynamic and circular process may eventually result in somewhat less competent, less responsive, and less satisfied parents, as well as children who present more behavioral difficulties (see

Belsky, Woodworth, and Crnic, 1996b). In the extreme, such stress processes may well contribute to the development of psychopathologies in children (Cummings et al., 2000).

Research has begun to emerge that sheds light on these proposed processes, although the sheer quantity of research remains somewhat limited. Nonetheless, we are beginning to better understand the determinants of everyday stressors of parenting, as well as some of the specific outcomes that may be involved with the experience of such stressors. In the sections that follow, we attempt to address the emerging empirical bases of those factors that determine the nature of everyday stressors of parenthood and the major outcomes relevant to such stress processes within a developmental perspective.

DETERMINANTS AND PROCESSES OF EVERYDAY PARENTING STRESS

Multiple developmental and clinical models suggest that parental stress is a function of individual child characteristics, parent characteristics, situations that directly involve being a parent, and parental interactions with a child within a family systems perspective (Abidin, 1995; Burke and Abidin, 1980). Daily experiences of parenting stress may be organized around three major areas of concern: (1) specific factors related to the parent, (2) specific characteristics of the child, and (3) broader, systematic family-level processes. In considering parents, various aspects of prebirth functioning, individual characteristics, and childrearing beliefs are germane to understanding their experience of stress in the parenting context. Recent work also suggests that parental gender may be an important consideration in understanding determinants of parenting stress, as it is apparent that some intriguing differences exist between mothers' and fathers' experiences of stress (Deater-Deckard and Scarr, 1996). Child characteristics bring important contributions to parents' stress experiences and require attention to developmental stage considerations, individual differences, and behavior problems. Finally, more systematic family processes require examination, particularly the influence of marital relationships and transitions across the family life cycle.

In most respects, the research that addresses parenting stress reflects broader stress contexts, rather than only those involving everyday stressors of parenthood. These broader contexts include any number of factors descriptive of parenting stress (major life stressors or problematic family circumstances) that have been elaborated on earlier. In the sections to follow, studies involving these various stress contexts are described to the extent that they are important to understanding the potential significance of everyday stressors to parenthood. Those studies that have specifically addressed issues relevant to everyday stressors of parenting, however, are highlighted throughout.

Parent Factors

Parental characteristics and prebirth processes. With the onset of parenthood, many factors, including social support, self-esteem, mood, psychological investment in parenting, and personality characteristics interact with stress to affect the degree of warmth and sensitivity a new parent exhibits with a child. Research indicates that maternal stress in the first year of parenting is associated with less sensitive caregiving and insecure infant–mother attachment relationships (Crnic, Greenberg, Ragozin, Robinson, and Basham, 1983; Egeland and Farber, 1984; Pianta and Egeland, 1990; Vaughn, Egeland, Sroufe, and Waters, 1979). However, key to considerations of parental stress experience are various prebirth characteristics of parents.

The amount of general parenting stress an individual is likely to experience is determined, in part, by individual, couple, and environmental factors present before the transition to parenthood. High levels of prebirth psychological distress have been found to lead to inadequate or impaired parenting and adverse child outcomes (Conger et al., 1992; McLoyd, 1990), and so it is not surprising to find that there have been suggestions that approximately 50% of general parenting stress during early parenthood can be predicted by variables assessed late in the mother's pregnancy (Grossman, 1988). Predictors of stress, however, appear to differ significantly for men and women (Grossman, 1988; Noppe, Noppe, and Hughes, 1991; Parke and Beitel, 1988). For women, the quality of the marital relationship appears to play a central role and may have the potential to either buffer or increase maternal stress. Whereas some correlates of parenting stress may differ, other research indicates that mothers and fathers may be more similar than different in their specific levels of stress experienced (Creasey and Reese, 1996; Deater-Deckard and Scarr, 1996) and in the associated effects (Deater-Deckard, Scarr, McCartney, and Eisenberg, 1994).

Despite the lack of clarity in the issues surrounding gender differences, there are some gender specific findings of note. For example, if a woman lacks adequate social support during the pregnancy, negative outcomes, such as postpartum depression and insensitive parenting behavior may follow (Crockenberg, 1981; Cutrona, 1984). Women who do receive support during pregnancy have more positive physical and mental health outcomes during the birth and postnatal period (Collins, Dunkel-Schetter, Lobel, and Schrimshaw, 1993). In addition, prenatal stress has been linked to lower birthweight, earlier delivery, and other adverse outcomes (see Lobel, 1994, for review). For women, prenatal mood is also associated with prenatal and postpartum stress. Women who report negative mood also tend to report more stress at both time points (Goldstein, Diener, and Mangelsdorf, 1996). For men, the personal stress levels that were apparent before parenthood and their expectations of parenting stress appear to be the strongest predictors of parenting stress once the child is present (Grossman, 1988).

Stress during pregnancy also predicts men's, but not women's, stress during parenthood; however, such reports have not specifically included indices of daily hassles. Fathers with high levels of prenatal stress tend to report feeling more overwhelmed, tense, inadequate, sad, and discouraged during parenthood (Feldman, 1987). These negative feelings, however, may subsequently be associated with more perceived daily hassles that are experienced as particularly troublesome. In addition to experienced prenatal stress levels, fathers' expectations of parenting stress also predict distress during parenting (Noppe et al., 1991).

In terms of prenatal stress and parenting behaviors, interactions of prenatal stress and support appear to be related to observed parenting behaviors. Specifically, women who reported greater support quantity and lower stress during pregnancy were rated as more sensitive in interactions with their infants at 3 months (Goldstein et al., 1996). However, other researchers have reported nonsignificant associations between prenatal stress and parenting behaviors (Hiester and Sapp, 1991; Noppe et al., 1991). These inconsistencies, as well as the lack of association between womens' prenatal stress, expectations of parenting stress, and mothers' actual parenting stress may result from women's difficulty admitting that they find parenting stressful. Women may find it difficult to admit that parenting can be stressful in light of the cultural expectation that women naturally perform the role of family caregiver (Barnett and Baruch, 1987).

It is apparent that the gender issues involved in parenting stress are complex, and there is no simple way to characterize either mothers or fathers experience. This may especially the case in regard to relevant prebirth correlates. As Deater-Deckard (1998) suggested, both biological and social role factors are potentially important determinants of gender differences, and future research is left to disentangle the gender processes relevant to mothers' and fathers' parenting stress experience.

Transition to parenthood.   There are many developmental and life transitions experienced by couples once they become parents. These include changes in the partners' relationship quality as well as the emergence of new behavioral patterns, responsibilities, and routines (Antonucci and Mikus, 1988; Belsky, Rovine, and Fish, 1989). The birth of a first child can have detrimental effects on a partnership (Belsky and Rovine, 1990; Cowan et al., 1985). This may include a general decrease in partnership quality following a wife's first pregnancy for up to 3 years after birth. These partnership quality decreases result in concommittant decreases in marital satisfaction and feelings of love. The transition to parenthood also appears to have a direct effect on marital activities. Specifically, parenthood increases the amount of time couples pursue activities jointly. While ostensibly a good thing, the increases in joint activity typically involve activities that the wife enjoys but their husbands do not. Parenthood also reduces the amount of time new fathers engage in leisure activities independently (Crawford and Huston, 1993).

The impact of these contextual determinants on the experience of stress during the transition to parenthood appears to be important to the quality of eventual parent–child relationships. Individuals' reports of marital difficulties are related to greater amounts of stress (Lavee, Sharlin, and Katz, 1996; Webster-Stratton, 1990), and there is a demonstrated association between marital relationships and the formation of secure child–mother attachment (Belsky and Isabella, 1988; Gloger-Tippelt and Huerkamp, 1998). High-quality marital relationships, including partners' perceptions of the relationship as more positive and less conflictual, support the formation of a secure child–mother attachment.

Social support networks.   Belsky's (1984) Determinants of Parenting model proposes social support as a key determinant of parenting quality. The sources, quantity, and perceived satisfaction with support are all important main effect considerations. In addition, both the ability of support to act as a buffer, and the potential negative aspects of support affect parenting quality (Goldstein et al., 1996). As social support has been found to be a predictor of parenting, it is important to first differentiate types of support and then their specific relationships to stress. Research suggests a strong relationship between social support and both positive and negative qualities of parenting, including better parent–child interactions (Jennings, Stagg, and Connors, 1991), better child outcomes (Melson, Hsu, and Ladd, 1993), specific attitudes about parenting and feelings of social isolation (Crockenberg, 1988), all of which are stress relevant and may affect the quality of everyday experiences with children.

Dimensions of parental support have been differentially related to parenting outcomes, as parental support has been found to reduce or moderate stress in specific contexts (Melson, Hsu, and Ladd, 1993; Melson, Ladd, and Hsu, 1993). In general, social support has been linked to general feelings of well-being and more positive mental health, and in turn more optimal parenting (Mitchell and Trickett, 1980). However, it is also important to consider the negative side of support networks, such as the effects of aversive social exchanges on well-being. Problematic or nonsupportive relationships can contribute to decreased feelings of well-being and increased negative outcomes, including expression of negative affect (Ingersoll-Dayton, Morgan, and Antonucci, 1997). Relative to parenting, some supportive individuals can in fact increase parents' stress by the timing or amount of advice that may be offered (Cochran and Niego, in Vol. 4 of this *Handbook*) if the timing, amount, and quality are poorly chosen.

Melson, Windecker-Nelson, and Schwarz (1998) explored the specific relations social support has to parenting stress, including a relation to daily parenting hassles (Crnic and Greenberg, 1990) and to perceived parental difficulty in guiding children through normative developmental tasks. In general, their findings suggest that kin support is especially effective in moderating stress from parenting daily hassles and was more consistently related to daily hassles than other aspects of stress, such as perceived difficulty or negative life events. Kin support functioned to actively provide the help to parents that was associated with both fewer daily parenting hassles with young children and for other aspects of the parent's life. This finding held for both mothers and fathers. Furthermore, kin proved a more reliable source of support in its effect on stress than were other relationships, such as those with friends or neighbors.

Support at times may serve as a direct effect, a moderator, or sometimes as a mediator. Moderation and mediation involve indirect processes and are often confused in the nature of the relations they describe among a set of variables. Baron and Kenny (1986) define a moderator as a variable that affects the direction and/or strength of the association between a predictor (independent variable) and a criterion (dependent variable). Moderation reflects an interaction between the predictor and the moderator variables in their effect on the criterion. In contrast, a mediator variable accounts for the relation between a predictor and a criterion. That is, the effect of some predictor on a particular outome actually flows through a third variable, the mediator, such that the relation between the predictor and the criterion attentuates when the mediator is included. Certainly, support is typically considered to have positive main effects on parenting, and sometimes operates to moderate (or buffer) the adverse impact of stress on parenting. But, it is likewise important to bear in mind that support can also contribute to the emergence of stress. The results of the various studies described indicate that the conditions under which support operates to increase or decrease parenting stress require continued attention.

Parental beliefs. Parents' beliefs about childrearing in general, and their children in particular, offer one means for examining child and family functioning, as parental beliefs have established relationships to parents' behavior toward their children (Miller, 1995). In relation to parenting parenting stress, attributions about the sources of children's behavior, particularly difficult or challenging behavior, are critically important to understanding whether or not parents are likely to find them stressful (Deater-Deckard, 1998). Not all parents report the same child behaviors as stressful, which suggests that individual differences in parenting beliefs and attitudes are key contributors to parental stress responses. Indeed, Abidin (1992) noted that parenting stress results from appraisals made by each parent regarding her or his general commitment to the parenting role.

Often parents' perceived difficulty in childrearing may be influenced by the parents' beliefs about the child's characteristics. Melson, Ladd, and Hsu (1993), for example, found that mothers who attributed difficulty in helping their children to attain specific qualities perceived more difficulty than did those mothers who made casual attributions to maternal characteristics or behavior. This may be especially salient for children who have special needs, as parental beliefs and subsequent behaviors may differ significantly from parents of typically developing children, due in part to parents' beliefs about the nature or cause of the disability (Booth, 1999).

Parenting values and beliefs more generally appear to have strong relations to parenting stress. Low parenting confidence and inappropriate parenting values were related to high parenting stress in the prediction of low child acceptance in groups of poor adolescent mothers (East, Matthews, and Felice, 1994). Fathers' sense of the degree to which they have power and control in their caregiving toward their infants was related to their reports of stress (Noppe et al., 1991). Crnic and Booth (1991) reported parenting attitudes or values interact with developmental age at times to influence the degree to which parents feel stressed by daily hassles of childrearing. Parents of younger children were more stressed when they had more complex views of child development, whereas parents of older children were more stressed when their views tended to be more categorical or simple. This suggests that parents may be more stressed with infants when they believe that more is going on with their babies than the babies can communicate. In contrast, parents of difficult to handle older children may be most stressed when they believe that development is relatively simple and child behavior determined by single causes.

There is other evidence as well to support the salience of parent beliefs and attitudes as determinants of the stress they may experience related to parenting. Maternal parenting stress was evaluated within a determinants of parenting framework, and increased stress was found to be associated with patterns of anxiousness, ambivalence, attachment, and insecurity (Scher and Mayseless, 2000). However, rather than implicating any specific characteristics of the child (such as temperament), higher levels of parental stress were considered to be a reflection of mothers' internal tensions about parenting (George and Solomon, 1996, 1999; Mayseless, 1988).

The difficulty with judging the role of beliefs and attitudes as determinants of variations in parenting stress comes from the fact that parenting stress is a subjective perception just the same as the attitudes or values that are being assessed to predict the stress. In this sense, it is difficult to disentangle the independence of the constructs. Nonetheless, the facts that there are clear individual differences apparent in parent report of daily hassles, and their appraisal, is central to the understanding of stressful experience in general, both suggest that more attention to conceptually related parental attitudes and beliefs will prove fruitful in leading to greater understanding of the emergence of parenting stress.

Mother–father differences.   Research suggests there are differences in parenting behavior for mothers and fathers, and that parenting behavior may also differ based on the gender of the child. Recent reviews suggest that parenting behavior of mothers and fathers differ in several important ways (Barnard, in Vol. 3 of this *Handbook*; Parke, in Vol. 3 of this *Handbook*; Stafford and Dainton, 1995). Mothers and fathers differ in the quantity and quality of time spent with their children. Mothers spend more time with their children, and the interactions are characterized by the mother's caregiving and managerial role. In contrast, fathers spend more of their time with their children in play activities. This play is more tactile and physical than that of mothers' play, as mothers' play activities are more verbal, didactic, and toy mediated. Crouter, MacDermid, McHale, and Perry-Jenkins (1990) found that mothers monitor children more closely than do fathers. It is also the case that, depending on the child's gender, involvement by mothers and fathers with their children differs. Fathers tend to show more differential treatment of boys and girls than do mothers (Cowan, Cowan, and Kerig, 1992; Siegel, 1987). Specifically, fathers are more involved with their children when they have sons, are typically less involved with daughters than are mothers, and mothers do not differ in their involvement with sons and daughters (Crouter and McHale, 1993; Starrels, 1994).

Given that there are substantial differences between fathers and mothers, it would not be surprising to find these differences carry over into the degree to which fathers and mothers report differential experience of stress in relation to parenting. However, there is not much support for major differences. Crnic and Booth (1991) reported no differences in the absolute number or intensity of the everyday parenting hassles that mothers and father experiences, and only subtle differences emerged that were related to parents' perspectives on development overall. Deater-Deckard and colleagues reported several studies that addressed differences between mothers and fathers with regards to parenting stress (Deater-Deckard et al., 1994; Deater-Deckard and Scarr, 1996). Like the Crnic and Booth (1991) report, these studies indicated that the levels of parenting stress did not really differ between mothers and fathers. Creasey and Reese (1996) likewise reported similar findings. Despite the lack of difference in the amount of experienced stress, there may yet prove to be important differences in the effects of such stresses across mothers and fathers, and continued attention to such processes is warranted (Deater-Deckard, 1998).

Child Factors

Factors related to children and the various characteristics they bring to the caregiving context continue to be a relevant source of stress for parents. Its unlikely that such characteristics alone are sufficient to lead to stressful experience by parents, as the parent must bring specific vulnerabilities or susceptibilities to the process, as noted above. Nonetheless, there do appear to be a number of relevant child-related factors that merit attention in helping to create the experience of stress.

An expanding literature addresses the stressful effects that various child characteristics can have on mothers and fathers. As was previously the case, most of this work describes various problematic conditions of childhood, such as developmental disabilities (Glidden, 1993; Guralnick, 1997; Hanson and Hanline, 1990; Krauss, 1993), biological vulnerability (Robson, 1997), difficult temperament (Ostberg and Hagekull, 2000), and child psychopathologies (Shaw, Keenan, Vondra, Delliquadri, and Giavannelli, 1997; Shaw, Owens, Giovannelli, and Winslow, 2001). For example, Shaw, Winslow, Owens, and Hood (1998) found that children with behavior problems, both of internalizing and externalizing types, show associations to greater stress in the home.

Problematic situations or characteristics such as those above however, are not necessarily routine aspects of most families' everyday lives. In contrast, children's behavioral and emotional dispositions (i.e., temperament) are characteristics that parents must engage everyday, and do provide a context specifically relevant to everyday stresses of parenting. Temperament is biologically rooted, appears early, is relatively stable, and is comprised of basic, nonreflective motivational and attentional processes that influence children's reactivity to stimuli and self-regulatory skills (Rothbart and Bates, 1998; Rothbart and Derryberry, 1981). Related to issues of determinants of parenting stress, children with more difficult temperament characteristics, such as negative mood, nonadaptability, high reactivity, and strong emotional intensity have been shown to develop emotional and behavioral problems in later development as well as to elicit more negative caregiving environments. Persistent infant crying is another example of a difficult infant behavior with measureable relations to caregiver stress (St. James-Roberts, Conroy, and Wilsher, 1998). It seems well apparent that the experience of parenting stress is partially an outcome of a difficult temperament status in a child and the challenges it poses for parents (Abidin, 1986; Ostberg and Hagekull, 2000).

Family-Level Processes

It is essential to regard an individual as part of an organized family system rather than as a self-contained organism, as individual child and parent development can be best understood in the context of the family system as a whole (Emde, 1991; Minuchin, 1988), and by the processes that characterize them across time (Cummings, Davies, and Campbell, 2000). A family systems perspective recognizes that relationships are formed from continuous interactions between individuals and that over time an interdependence develops within relationships. Potential changes in relationships are expected, especially in times of developmental transition and stress. Considering general process-oriented perspectives within family environments, parenting stress has been related to reports of child misbehavior through a lack of maternal attention to the child, rather than directly to parenting skill deficiency per se (Dumas and LaFreniere, 1993; Wahler and Dumas, 1989). When parents have increased stress and fewer available resources, they may have trouble monitoring a child's activities or in setting clear limits. As Wahler and Dumas (1989) suggest parents of problematic children are expected to react similarly to other parents until stress is introduced. However, given increased parental stress and a drop in attentional resources, parents become less proactive in their parenting and rely on more reactive and punitive strategies of child management (Ritchie and Holden, 1998).

Marital relationship. Men's and women's parenting stress appears to be influenced by both individual and couple dimensions (Grossman, 1988). Studies have found that women's marital satisfaction in late pregnancy is a significant predictor of parenting stress at 6 months (Cowan and Cowan, 1983). Various aspects of marriage, as evaluated by woman or their husbands, appear to be the best predictors of women's parenting stress (Feldman, 1987), and daily parenting hassles seem to be somewhat less stressful or impactful under conditions in which parents support one another (Cowan and Cowan, 1988).

Marital relations are a primary stress factor undermining or supporting parent functioning (Belsky, 1984), and low marital satisfaction is associated with greater parenting stress by both men and women (Webster-Stratton, 1990). Marital conflict, in contrast, can lead to parents feeling more stressed by their childcare responsibilities (Goldberg and Easterbrooks, 1984). Marital satisfaction may also have a different moderating effect for men and woman, as evidenced by stronger associations among parenting stress and discipline for fathers and weaker associations for mothers (Deater-Deckard and Scarr, 1996). Mothers in unhappy marriages may respond more to child cues and show more compensation in their parenting. Fathers who are unhappy with the marriage may be more punitive and critical in parenting or distance themselves from the family (Cowan and Cowan, 1993).

Parents who perceive typical child behaviors as deviant are likely to be more stressed by children's daily behaviors than parents who perceive these child behaviors as normative and support each other in their attempts to manage difficult or challenging behavior. Similarly, inconsistent parenting, because of its failure to manage child behaviors (Patterson, 1983) may be associated with more frequent parent–child conflict (Belsky, Woodworth, and Crnic, 1996b). In turn, these parent–child conflicts are likely to interfere with the routine functioning of the family and increase parents' perceptions of such events as stressful or hassles. This might particularly be a risk for those marital dyads in which there is relatively little support (Belsky, Woodworth, and Crnic, 1996a; Lavigueur, Saucier, and Tremblay, 1995).

Summary

It seems apparent that parenting stresses are multiple determined and are rarely the result of single events or characteristics. Transactional and process-oriented models of development suggest that various aspects of parents, children, and family factors (both intrafamilial and extrafamilial) interact across time in complex ways to create conditions under which parenting can be considered more or less stressful. Certainly, parenting stress is not universal, and not all parents share the same perspectives on what might be considered stressful aspects of child behavior or the parenting role. Nevertheless, it is apparent that everyday stresses of parenting are a relatively common phenomena that represent a meaningful context for understanding adults' responses to parenting demands and have adapational significance within the family system.

CONSEQUENCES OF EVERYDAY PARENTING STRESSES

It is apparent that there are many parent, child, and family factors that are associated with parental perceptions of daily hassles of parenting and various conditions that may serve to increase both the frequency and intensity of this experience. Given that normative stressors of parenting are common-place and often unavoidable, it is critical to detail the impact that such stressful experiences may have on parents, children, and families. From the theoretical perspectives presented earlier in this chapter, parenting stress is suggested to act as a change agent, with cumulative experience producing a greater likelihood of more problematic parenting, child functioning, and family status. To date, there is emerging evidence from the literature to suggest that such processes are operative.

Parenting Functioning

The cumulative impact of parents' perceived stress (from major life events, parenting stress, and daily hassle perspectives) has an adverse impact on parent behavior (Abidin, 1990; Belsky, 1984; Crnic, Greenberg, Ragozin, Robinson, and Basham, 1983; Deater-Deckard, 1998; Pianta and Egeland, 1990). Across a wide range of stressors and diverse groups of parents, the experience of stress is nearly always associated with negative outcome (Deater-Deckard, 1998). Similarly, the range of outcomes affected has been quite broad, including individual parental psychological well-being, attitudes toward parenting and children, and actual behavior in interaction with children. With such concerns in mind, it is not surprising to find that in those studies in which everyday stresses of parenting are involved, such stress is strongly related to less adaptive outcomes for parents.

In relation to parental attitude and self-reported well-being, daily hassles have been associated with both mothers' and fathers' satisfaction with parenting (Crnic and Booth, 1991; Crnic and Greenberg, 1990), parents' negative mood (Bolger et al., 1989), negative affect as an index of well-being (Kanner et al., 1981), and more general indices of low life satisfaction (Crnic and Greenberg, 1990). When demographic variables are controlled, maternal daily stress accounts for a 40% increment in maternal distress, an index of psychological distress (Thompson, Merritt, Keith, Bennett, and Johndrow, 1993). Likewise, a series of related studies (Crnic and Greenberg,1990; Naerde, Tambs, Mathieson, Dalgard, and Samuelson, 2000; Rodgers, 1993) has found strong relations between reported daily hassles and maternal psychological distress. Windle and Dumenci (1997), in a study of 200 dual-career married couples, recently reported that parental stress was predictive of depressive symptoms in husbands as well as wives, indicating that the effects on psychological well-being are not specific to mothers, even though mothers still spend the vast majority of caregiving time with the children. Parenting hassles, then, are not simply a function of time spent with the children or the extent of responsibility for their care. Thus, it seems apparent that hassles, especially those related to parenting, are important contributors to various parameters of parental well-being. These findings suggest the importance of examining indirect pathways of influence in the relation between parents' stress and various child outcomes, a process that is explored later in this chapter.

Two other recent studies raise issues in regard to the function of stress as a change agent in mothers' attitudes or perceptions of childrearing. In a study addressing issues of "earned security" in adult attachment models, Phelps, Belsky, and Crnic (1998) studied attachment perspectives, maternal report of daily hassles of parenting, and observed parenting in 97 mothers of preschool-age children. Earned security reflects a change across time from insecure to secure status. Phelps et al. (1998) reported that stress was a risk factor for parenting, but that parents who had earned secure status were the equal of always secure parents, even under conditions of high daily stress with children. These findings suggest that attachment histories may be a risk factor for stress, but current secure status is more critical than the at-risk history in determining the influence of stress on parenting. In a related study (Aber, Belsky, Slade, and Crnic, 1999), changes in maternal representations of their toddler sons across a 1-year period (15 to 27 months) were apparent. Mothers who reported greater parenting hassles reported increased levels of anger in representations of their sons. These two studies offer supportive evidence that daily stresses represent a meaningful correlate for parental functioning, particularly from longitudinal perspectives.

Beyond concerns regarding parental attitudes and well-being, one critical issue involves the degree to which minor stressors affect the nature of parental behavior during actual interactions with children. Because the sources of hassles or everyday stressors of parenthood are predominantly behavioral in nature, they should have observable effects on the way that parents respond to their children in everyday interactions. Several studies have been conducted that begin to detail such effects, although again there are only a few to give some clues as to the nature of such influences. Crnic and Greenberg (1990) found no relations between mothers' reported parenting hassles and the quality of maternal interactive behavior in a sample of mothers of 5-year-old children. However, the interactions they observed were laboratory based, which may have reduced the variability associated with reported hassles. Home-based interactions were considered more likely to produce the stress-to-behavior effects hypothesized.

In support of this contention, Acevedo (1993) showed that minor daily hassles experienced by mothers and fathers were related to their behavioral responses to child negativity in the home. In assessing the relations among minor parenting stressors, parental behavior, and children's emotion regulation, Acevedo coded 2-hour observations of family interactions. Observations and coding categories attended specifically to parents' attempts at affect socialization and toddlers' abilities to regulate their affective responses. Mothers reporting more minor stressors (assessed immediately prior to the home observations) responded with more negative affect and in ways that involved amplification of their children's negativity. Fathers reporting more hassles, on the other hand, tended more often to show no response to their children. Several other more recent studies have also provided strong evidence that interactions in the home or other naturalistic settings appear to provide a robust relation to daily hassles of parenting (Belsky, Woodworth, and Crnic, 1996a; 1996b; Crnic and Spritz, 1997; Jain, Belsky, and Crnic, 1996; Pett, Vaughncole, and Wampold, 1994). Across these studies, hassles have been associated with more difficult control processes and less positive affective relationships between parents and their children during the toddler and preschool periods. This work provides evidence in support of stress-behavior associations in naturalistic settings in contrast to the findings in laboratory-based settings, and in particular addresses the influence of daily hassles with both mothers and fathers. This latter point is critical, as mothers have tended to be the primary focus of parenting stress research. Fathers have been a focus in more recent general parenting stress research by Deater-Deckard and colleagues (Deater-Deckard et al., 1994; Deater-Deckard and Scarr, 1996), but specific stress effects on fathers' interactive behavior has also been reported by Fagan

(2000). In a study of Head Start fathers and their perceptions of daily hassles, Fagan found that father involvement and play with their children was negatively related to their report of daily hassles. Despite the fact that fathers are typically not the primary-care providers for their children, everyday stresses of parenting are a relevant concern of their parenting.

The research that has addressed the effects of parenting stress on parental functioning provides compelling evidence that across indices of attitudes, reports of psychological well-being, and observed parent–child interaction, stress has potentially damaging effects. Of importance, the longitudinal work that has begun to emerge suggests that stress may be a causative factor, but additional research will be necessary to clarify the nature of such relations.

Child Functioning

There are indications that parental stress has influences on children's functioning. In fact, both parents' and childrens' stress have long been strongly implicated as determinants in the development of psychopathology during childhood (Cummings et al., 2000; Garmezy and Rutter, 1983). The influence of parenting stress on child development may on some occasions be direct, but the best evidence to date suggests that more often the effect is indirect. Several researchers have proposed that the impact of stress on children is moderated by the quality of parents' interactions with their children (Belsky, 1984; Deater-Deckard, 1998; Patterson, 1983; Webster-Stratton, 1990). As discussed earlier, stressors appear to have the power to disrupt parenting practices. In turn, such parenting practices may increase the likelihood that children develop behavior problems that may activate a cycle of negative parent–child interactions and place additional stress on parents (Mash and Johnston, 1990; Patterson, 1983; Short and Johnston, 1997; Webster-Stratton, 1990). Crnic and Greenberg (1990) provided correlational evidence of a link between parenting daily hassles and maternal ratings of children's behavior problems. They suggested, however, that such parental stress may indirectly influence the development and/or maintenance of children's behavior problems through its effect on other levels of parental response to children. Although there are indications that parents' perceived stress may relate to the presence of children's reported behavior problems, the concerns regarding direction of effect are relevant in this context, as well as those noted previously. That is, it is equally possible that children with behavior problems create parental stress and the related more negative parental behavior. Realistically, however, the effects are most likely bidirectional. Parental stress can be affected by and affect children's behavior problems.

Several studies have specifically demonstrated links between parenting stress and child developmental outcome. General parenting stress has been associated with indices of insecure infant attachment (Jarvis and Creasey, 1991; Vaughn et al., 1979), a risk factor for later psychological adjustment in children. Jarvis and Creasy presented a convincing argument that psychological separation resulting from parenting stress has a greater impact on the parent–child relationship than actual physical separation. In a study of very-low birthweight infants, Thompson et al. (1994) reported that maternal appraisals of daily stress accounted for significant changes in cognitive functioning over an 18-month period, over and above any change accounted for by the child's neurobiologic risk.

Some findings also indicate that mothers experiencing high negative life stress perceive their children's behavior as more deviant than do low-stress mothers (Pett, Vaughncole, and Wamplod, 1994; Webster-Stratton, 1990). It appears that, especially when the child's behavior is ambiguous or may be interpreted in various ways, situational stress has an impact on parental perceptions of child behavior, skewing it more toward the negative (Middlebrook and Forehand, 1985). These findings have obvious implications for parenting daily hassles, suggesting that negative life stress may indirectly influence parents' perceptions of the stressfulness of certain child behaviors.

The fact that many studies of the relation between stress and child outcomes have relied solely on parental reports of child behaviors is problematic, as the parents are also the reporters of the stress. Issues of discriminate validity in the measurement schemes become critical. That is, the measures must clearly differentiate the two constructs, rather than have both reflect the same underlying construct. Two studies, however, have used objective assessments of child behavior problems and provide strong evidence that minor daily hassles may have adaptational significance for children. Patterson (1983), using single-case observational methodology, noted that on days that mothers report more minor hassles, they are more likely to show irritability with their children. In turn, the children are more likely to respond with aggressive behavior. Furthermore, Thompson, Merritt, Keith, Bennett, and Johndrown (1993) found that with demographic variables controlled, higher levels of maternal daily stress, but not maternal distress, related to both parent- and child-reported adjustment difficulties. These studies suggest that parental stress and hassles are associated with coercive parent–child interactions and disruptions in children's development. Woodworth, Crnic, and Belsky (1995) also showed that reported daily hassles are not simply a function of maternal mood, but rather predict parent and child behavior in the home above an beyond contributions of mood. This result offers some further validity to the construct and its measurement from an appraisal and self-report perspective.

The research addressing the adverse effects of parenting daily stressors on children's behavior and development seems to indicate that children are indeed adversely affected. It is true, however, that the mechanisms that explain such effects have yet to be clearly articulated. Although there are some findings to indicate that minor stressors function as direct change agents for children's behavior, more frequent interpretations of the research suggest that change occurs within parent–child relationships or more global family level functioning and processes across time (Belsky et al., 1996). As such, daily stresses of parenting seem most likely to have indirect influences on children's development and psychological well-being.

Family System Functioning

The pervasive systemic effects of stress suggest that attention to broader family system-level functioning must also be considered. Just as daily stressors appear to affect the nature of parenting, parent–child interactions, and children's behavior and development, it is likely that such stressors may also adversely impact family-level factors. This would not be particularly surprising, as parents and children compose the family unit, and the evidence reviewed previously provides strong supports for the adverse influence of stress on these family members. Nevertheless, the family "system" is greater than the sum of its parts and merits attention in its own right.

Despite its merit, few studies address issues of daily stress and its effect on the family. Goldberg and Easterbrooks (1984), using a measure termed the *bother scale*, reported poorer marital adjustment (but not marital harmony) in dyads in which parents perceived their toddler to be an interference in their spousal relationship and their household and leisure activities. This was perhaps one of the earliest studies of parental daily stress, even though it was not specifically conceptualized as such. Crnic and Greenberg (1990) found that mothers' rating of the intensity of parenting daily hassles related negatively to the quality of family relationships and the quality with which the family system is maintained. These family indices were drawn from the Family Environment Scale (Moos and Moos, 1981), a questionnaire measure that was completed by the mothers in this study. Although such findings are intriguing and potentially meaningful, it is important to corroborate these results with objective data that are not subject to questions of confounded methods. Such confounds may occur when the same reporter responds to measures that are dependent on appraisal (Dohrenwend and Shrout, 1985) or when there is conceptual overlap in the measures themselves.

More objective evidence for family-level influences is provided in a study of coparenting processes (Belsky, Crnic, and Gable, 1995). Coparenting involves the manner in which parents work together in the service of childrearing and childcare, and can involve either supportive or unsupportive interactions between spouses. In this study of maritally intact families of young toddlers, Belsky et al.

(1995) conducted naturalistic home observations of mother-father-child triads. These investigators found hat parents' cumulative experience of daily hassles did not independently predict coparenting, but did interact with parental differences to significantly account for coparenting processes. Their findings suggest that minor daily stressors amplify differences in parents along dimensions of personality, attachment quality, and childrearing attitudes, significantly predicting fewer supportive coparenting events and more unsupportive events.

Two studies address the nature of parenting daily hassles and its implications for family functioning. In their longitudinal study of stress and conflict in families of toddlers, Belsky et al. (1996a, 1996b) attempted to identify families who could be characterized as "troubled," that is, experiencing more difficulties and more negativity in attempting to manage child behavior during this developmental period. Longitudinal analyses across a 2-year period allowed for determination of those families that were stable in the high degree of troubles that they showed, stable in the low degree of difficulty they had, or unstable in that there was change in one direction or the other across the 2-year period. Mothers' parenting hassles proved to be an important correlate of the troubled families, again indicating the salience of this stress context. Such data also support process-oriented approaches to stress and coping models of family functioning that provide potentially powerful explanations for family and child adjustment (Cummings et al., 2000). Patterson's (1983) notion that it is not children who are directly at risk because of stress; rather, it is the family system remains relevant to our current conceptualizations of stress effects.

Summary

The consequences of parenting stress are not necessarily ubiquitous (see Nitz, Ketterlinus, and Brandt, 1995), but they do provide compelling evidence that everyday stresses of parenting have strong adaptational significance to mothers, fathers, children, and the family system as a whole. These daily stresses appear to directly impact parents' psychological well-being, their attitudes and beliefs, and their behaviors toward their children. In contrast, the adverse effects of everyday parenting stress on children's behavior and well-being appear to be more indirect. That is, it is not the stress itself that affects the child. Rather, stress affects the quality of parenting and functioning of the family system, which in turn influences the quality of the child's developmental functioning across the spectrum of social, affective, and cognitive domains. Elements of the family system, may be either directly affected (such as family cohesion and stability of troubledness) or may be indirectly affected (such as coparenting) by everyday stresses. Although the exact mechanisms that underlie these direct and indirect processes are yet to be fully explicated, it is apparent that for most families everyday stresses of parenting have important adverse implications. As parenting stress research continues to emerge, direction of effect remains an important caveat to be considered. More problematic families may well create stressful conditions, rather than stress creating the problematic functioning. More longitudinal research studies will help to disentangle such directional or causal processes. The relation between stress and more problematic functioning, regardless of direction of effect, is clear. Yet, it is also apparent that many families experience these everyday parenting events but do not show adverse effects. Conditions that moderate these adverse effects of stress must be considered equally relevant to understanding stress processes within families.

COPING WITH PARENTING STRESS

Stress, and especially everyday stressors of parenthood, are multiply determined, individual in nature, complex in function, and have wide-ranging effects on parents, children, and the family system. Their potential for adverse influence across a variety of personal domains continues to be of concern to researchers and applied professionals alike. Identification of those factors that might prevent, moderate, or ameliorate the effects of these cumulative stressful events therefore becomes key in addressing the predictive significance of parenting stress.

There is a voluminous literature on individual adult coping processes that is obviously relevant to the concerns raised here (Folkman and Lazarus, 1988). Coping consists of those various cognitive and behavioral efforts to manage both internal and external demands, as well as the conflicts between them, that an individfual considers to be taxing or exceeding their personal resources (Lazarus, 1991). As such, coping involves those aspects of what a person thinks and does in an attempt to manage an emtional encounter.

Although the general coping literature is vast, few studies particular to parenting stress and coping processes offer some insight into more and less productive ways that parents can cope with such stressors. Sommer et al. (1993) reported that adolescent mothers who were prepared for pregnancy reported lower amounts of parenting stress. Likewise, more problem-focused coping strategies and positive parenting beliefs have been related to reports of less parenting stress (Frey, Greenberg, and Fewell, 1989; Miller, Gordon, Daniele, and Diller, 1992). In reviewing the extant work, Deater-Deckard (1998) concluded that a positive coping style may well be a crucial protective factor against the various adverse effects of parenting stress.

Two studies of parental stress and coping processes have also made a substantive contribution to our understanding of adaptation to parenting stress (Creasey and Jarvis, 1993; Jarvis and Creasey, 1991). In maritally intact families with 18-month-old children, Jarvis and Creasey reported that certain coping strategies were associated with parenting stress. Avoidant coping strategies were associated with increased parenting stress, whereas positive reappraisal strategies were associated with decreased parenting stress. These authors also found that positive reappraisal mediated the relation between parenting stress and a questionnaire index of child attachment for both mothers and fathers, although avoidant strategies did not. In a follow-up study when children were 24 months old (Creasey and Jarvis, 1993), cognitive coping strategies again played a similar role for mothers, but the findings for fathers were less clear-cut than at 18 months, as avoidant strategies for fathers partially mediated the stress appraisals from 18 to 24 months.

Social support systems have been a specific target of much research related to parenting stress and offer a potentially effective coping resource (Belsky et al., 1996a; Olson and Banyard, 1992; Ostberg and Hagekull, 2000). Evidence exists to suggest that some aspects of parent support, especially emotional support from a spouse or partner, moderates the adverse effects of major life stress on mothers' well-being and interactive behavior with their children (Crnic et al., 1983). Social support also shows some buffer effects for daily parenting stressors in relation to mothers' interactive behavior with their 5-year-old children (Crnic and Greenberg, 1990). The interaction of parenting hassles and maternal support predicted both mothers' affect and sensitivity in observed interactions with their children. However, these findings were quite different from those buffer effects with major life stress. Emotional support from friends was more important in buffering mothers from hassles than was emotional support from the spouse. Friends may well be more empathetic to this everyday experience, and perhaps mothers may prefer that fathers offer instrumental support (e.g., taking over the childcare responsibilities for a while) rather than emotional support. Unfortunately, such interpretations are speculative only, as instrumental support was not measured in that research.

It is important to note that buffer or moderator effects are not ubiquitous in stress research. In fact, they are often less than routine in the literature. Social support routinely shows stronger main effects on parental well-being than moderator effects in relation to stressful experience. Indeed, Osterberg and Hagekull (2000) found that low social support in a large population-based sample of Swedish mothers was directly related to parenting stress, but no buffering effects were found. Quittner, Glueckauf, and Jackson (1990) suggested that support may in fact have more of a mediating effect between chronic parenting stressors and outcomes than a moderating effect. Regardless of the exact nature of the role, however, it is apparent that parents' social support systems play an important role in affecting the nature of stressful experiences of parenting.

Although these studies provide only a beginning of systematic research into processes that may help protect parenting against everyday stressful experiences, they do provide some useful suggestions for coping with parenting stress. The findings in regard to specific coping responses, especially those involving positive cognitive reappraisal, suggest the importance of the interaction of parental belief systems and stressful response. Support systems are potentially powerful mechanisms and readily available for many mothers and fathers. Formal support programs continue to be available in many communities as well, and often target those parents and families that are more isolated or are at risk for poor adaptational response. In all, it seems apparent that parenting stresses are amenable to positive coping experience.

CONCLUSIONS

This chapter has presented some issues and empirical research on the salience of parenting stress processes in families of normally developing children. The fact that much of what has been reviewed addresses more normative developmental contexts is worthy of comment. Stress in the parenting context does not seem to be tied only to those families in which particular problematic circumstances exist. Rather, it is inherent in many normative parenting situations, engendered by the natural tendencies of children to present challenging situations to which parents must respond. Stress has been considered to be role specific, and parenting stress would therefore be qualitatively distinct from stress in other domains such adult life hassles or work strain (Creasey and Reese, 1996).

The nature of parental response to the dualism of parenting role and child behavior, whether stressful or not, appears to depend on a variety of factors. Certainly, parental characteristics are a primary source of variation. Some parents cope well with the challenges of parenthood and children's behavior, whereas other experience more difficulties. parents' prebirth expectations and experience, personality, mood, belief, and daily experiences all contribute to the degree to which parents find their children's behavior stressful. Mothers and fathers also seem to differ in some ways on the factors that affect their perceptions of stress, but the degree to which they find parenting stressful does not appear to differ substantially. Child characteristics likewise play a critical role, as children differ widely in the extent or degree to which their behavior is challenging. Actual behavior problems in children, however, present little ambiguity in their stressfulness. The marital relationship, as well as unsupportive coparenting processes, can also contribute. No one normative factor is sufficient to create a highly stressful parenting context. Rather, a multiplicity of interacting factors contribute over time to an individual mother's or father's perception of parenting stress.

Perhaps two of the most important issues raised in relation to everyday stressors of parenthood are the concept of developmental periods and the process-oriented approach to understanding the nature of family influences on children's development. At different points in time, developmentally salient behaviors of children challenge the parenting system. From an organizational perspective in which children's development is viewed as a series of hierarchical reorganizations involving increasingly sophisticated abilities, the natural changes through which children progress at certain periods create conditions that may facilitate parental stress. Similarly, natural developmental transitions through which families proceed create additional needs for novel adaptations that may at times produce stressful circumstances (Cummings et al., 2000). As we gain in further understanding the processes that may be involved in the experience of parenting stress, it will be especially important to note the salience of specific developmental periods, longitudinal processes, and the transitions among periods.

Stress is a construct of importance in that it has been associated with adverse outcomes across a variety of functional domains. It is apparent from the growing research available that similar concerns operate in relation to everyday stressors of parenthood. Minor parenting stressors affect the quality of parenting children receive, and the satisfaction that parents receive from the process of childrearing.

Often, these effects in turn produce direct and indirect influences on children's behavior and psychological well-being, such that children become at risk for specific internalizing and externalizing behavior problems (Shaw et al., 2001). Over time, the cumulative everyday stressful experiences of parenting may change the nature of parent–child relationships, deflecting what might have been growth-promoting relationships into ones in which children and their parents are compromised to varying degrees.

We have addressed the concept of everyday stressors of parenthood from a more problematic of "deficit" perspective, but it might be worthwhile to conclude on a more positive note. Challenging circumstance, and the everyday experiences of parenting in particular, may also provide opportunities for positive growth in parent–child dyads. Certainly, the general stress literature suggests that mild stress can be adaptive in that it maintains an optimal level of arousal and stimulates personal growth (Cohen, 1994). It seems equally important in studies of normative experience to account for the possibility of positive influence and effects as it is to assess more traditional problematic outcomes. Indeed, Abidin (1992) has suggested that parenting stress may have a curvilinear function, facilitative, but only up to a point. Many parents do cope well with their children's oftentimes difficult or challenging behavior. In fact, we have continued to find subgroups of parents who report relatively high frequencies of stressful parenting events, but who also report low intensity or little or no effect of such occurrences. Continuing to focus on aspects of resilient parenting will provide new insights into the complex relations between everyday stressors and parenting processes.

REFERENCES

Aber. J. L., Belsky, J., Slade, A. and Crnic, K. (1999). Stability and change in mothers' representations of their relationship with their toddlers. *Developmental Psychology, 35*, 1038–1047.

Abidin, R. R. (1983). *The parenting stress index.* Charlottesville, VA: Pediatric Psychology Press.

Abidin, R. R. (1986). *Parenting stress index-manual* (2nd ed.). Charlottesville, VA: Pediatric Pyschology Press.

Abidin, R. R. (1990). Introduction to the special issue: The stresses of parenting. *Journal of Clinical Child Psychology, 19,* 298–301.

Abidin, R. R. (1995). *Parenting stress index.* Odessa, FL: Psychological Assessment Resources.

Abidin, R. R. (1992). The determinants of parenting behavior. *Journal of Clinical Child Psychology, 21,* 407–412.

Acevedo, M. C. (1993). *Determinants of variations in parental affect socialization: Implications for the development of emotion regulation.* Unpublished master's thesis, The Pennsylvania State University, University Park.

Antonucci, T. C., and Mikus, K. (1988). The power of parenthood: Personality and attitudinal changes during the transition to parenthood. In G. Y. Michaels and W. A. Goldberg (Eds.), *The transition to parenthood: Current theory and research* (pp. 62–84). Cambridge, England, Cambridge University Press.

Barnett, R. C., and Baruch, G. K. (1987). Social roles, gender, and psychological distress. In R. Barnett, L. Biener, and G. Baruch (Eds.), *Gender and stress* (pp. 122–143). New York: Free Press.

Baron, R. M., and Kenny, D. A. (1986). The moderator–mediator variable distinction in social psychological research: Conceptual, strategic, and statistical considerations. *Journal of Personality and Social Psychology, 51,* 1173–1182.

Belsky, J. (1984). The determinants of parenting: A process model. *Child Development, 55,* 83–96.

Belsky, J., Crnic, K., and Gable S. (1995). The determinants of co-parenting in families with toddler boys: Spousal difference and daily hassles. *Child Development, 66,* 629–642.

Belsky, J., and Isabella, R. A. (1988). Maternal, infant, and social contextual determinants of attachment security. In J. Belsky and T. M. Nezworski (Eds.), *Clinical implications of attachment* (pp. 45–94). Hillsdale, NJ: Lawrence Erlbaum Associates.

Belsky, J., Perry-Jenkins, M., and Crouter, A. C. (1985). The work–family interface and marital change across the transition to parenthood. *Journal of Family Issues, 6,* 205–220.

Belsky, J., and Rovine, M. (1990). Patterns of marital change across the transition to parenthood: Pregnancy to three years postpartum. *Journal of Marriage and the Family, 52,* 5–19.

Belsky, J., Rovine, M., and Fish, M. (1989). The developing family system. In M. R. Gunnar and E. Thelen (Eds.), *Systems and development: The Minnesota symposium on child psychology* (Vol. 22, pp. 119–166). Hillsdale, NJ: Lawrence Erlbaum Associates.

Belsky, J., Woodworth, S., and Crnic, K. (1996a). Trouble in the second year: Three questions about family interaction. *Child Development, 67,* 556–578.

Belsky, J., Woodworth, S., and Crnic, K. (1996b). Troubled family interaction during toddlerhood. *Development and Psychopathology, 8*, 477–495.

Bolger, N., DeLongis, A., Kessler, R. C., and Schilling, E. A. (1989). Effects of daily stress on negative mood. *Journal of Personality and Social Psychology, 57*, 808–818.

Booth, C. L. (1999). Beliefs about social skills among mothers of preschoolers with special needs. *Early Education and Development, 10*, 455–474.

Bronfenbrenner, U., and Crouter, A. C. (1982). Work and family through time and space. In C. Hayes and S. Kamerman (Eds.), *Families that work: Children in a changing world.* Washington, DC: National Academy of Sciences.

Burke, W. T., and Abidin, R. R. (1980). Parenting stress index (PSI): A family system assessment approach. In R. R. Abidin (Ed.), *Parent education and intervention handbook* (pp. 516–527). Springfield, IL: Charles H. Thomas.

Cohen, R. J. (1994). *Psychology and adjustment: Values, culture, and change.* Boston: Allyn and Bacon.

Collins, N. L. Dunkel-Schetter, C., Lobel, M., and Schrimshaw, S. C. M. (1993). Social support in pregnancy: Psychosocial correlates of birth outcomes and postpartum depression. *Journal of Personality and Social Psychology, 65*, 1243–1258.

Conger, R. D., Conger, K. J., Elder, G. H., Jr., Lorenz, F. O., Simons, R. L., and Whitbeck, L. B. (1992). A family process model of economic hardship and adjustment of early adolescent boys. *Child Development, 63*, 526–541.

Cowan, C. P., and Cowan, P. A. (1988). Who does what when partners become parents: Implications for men, women, and marriage. *Marriage and Family Review, 12*, 105–131.

Cowan, C. P., Cowan, P. A., Homing, G., Garrett, E., Coysh, W. S., Curtis-Boles, H., and Boles, A. J., III. (1985). Transition to parenthood: His, hers, and theirs. *Journal of Family Issues, 6*, 451–481.

Cowan, P. A., and Cowan, C. P. (1983, April). *Quality of couple relationships and parenting stress in beginning families.* Paper presented at the meeting of the Society for Research in Child Development, Detroit, MI.

Cowan, P. A., Cowan, C. P., and Kerig, P. (1992). Mothers, fathers, sons, and daughters: Gender difference in family formation and parenting style. In P. A. Cowan, D. Field, D. Hanson, A. Skolnik, and G. E. Swanson (Eds.), *Family, self and society: Toward a new agenda for family research* (pp. 165–195). Hillsdale, NJ: Lawrence Erlbaum Associates.

Crawford and Huston, (1993). The impact of the transition to parenthood on marital leisure. *Personality and Social Psychology Bulletin, 19*, 39–46.

Creasey, G. L., and Jarvis, P. A. (1993, March). *Relationships between parenting stress and developmental functioning among 2-year-olds: A short-term longitudinal investigation.* Paper presented at the biennial meeting of the Society for Research in Child Development, New Orleans, LA.

Creasey, G. L., and Reese, M. (1996). Mothers' and fathers' perceptions of parenting hassles: Associations with psychological symptoms, nonparewnting hassles, and child behavior problems. *Journal of Applied Developmental Psychology, 17*, 393–406.

Crnic, K. A., and Booth, C. L. (1991). Mothers' and fathers' perceptions of daily hassles of parenting across early childhood. *Journal of Marriage and the Family, 53*, 1042–1050.

Crnic, K. A., and Greenberg, M. T. (1990). Minor parenting stresses with young children. *Child Development, 61*, 1628–1637.

Crnic, K. A., Greenberg, M. T., Ragozin, A. S., Robinson, N. M., and Basham, R. B. (1983). The effects of stress and social support on mothers of premature and full-term infants. *Child Development, 45*, 209–217.

Crnic, K. A., Greenberg, M. T., and Slough, N. M. (1986). Early stress and social support influences on mothers' and high risk infants' functioning in late infancy. *Infant Mental Health Journal, 7*, 19–33.

Crnic, K., and Spritz, B. (1997, April). Parenting stress during toddlerhood: Change and prediction across the second and third year of life. Paper presented at the biennial meeting of the society for Research in Child Development, Washington, DC.

Crockenberg, S. (1988). Social support and parenting. In W. Fitzgerald, B. Lester, and M. Yogman (Eds.), *Research on support for parents and infants in the postnatal period* (pp. 67–92). New York: Ablex.

Crockenberg, S., and Litman, C. (1990). Autonomy as competence in 2-year-olds: Maternal correlates of child defiance, compliance and self-assertion. *Development Psychology, 26*, 961–971.

Crouter, A. C., MacDermid, S. M., McHale, S. M., and Perry-Jenkins, M. (1990). Parental monitoring and perceptions of children's school performance and conduct in dual-earner and single-earner families. *Developmental Psychology, 26*, 649–657.

Crouter, A. C., and McHale, S. M. (1993). Temporal rhythms in family life: Seasonal variation in the relation between parental work and family processes. *Developmental Psychology, 29*, 198–205.

Crouter, A. C., Perry-Jenkins, M., Huston, T. L., and Crawford, D. W. (1989). The influence of work-induced psychological states on behavior at home. *Basic and Applied Social Psychology, 10*, 273–292.

Cummings, E. M., Davies, P. T., and Campbell, S. B. (2000). *Developmental Psychopathology and Family Process.* New York: Guilford.

Cutrona, C. E. (1984). Social support and stress in the transition to parenthood. *Journal of Abnormal Psychology, 93*, 378–390.

Deater-Deckard, K. (1998). Parenting stress and child adjustment: Some old hypotheses and new questions. *Clinical Psychology: Science and Practice, 5*, 314–332.

Deater-Deckard, K., and Scarr, S. (1996). Parenting stress among dual earner mothers and fathers: Are there gender differences? *Journal of Family Psychology, 10,* 45–59.

Deater-Deckard, K., Scarr, S., McCartney, K., and Eisenberg, M. (1994). Parental separation anxiety: Relationships with parenting stress, child-rearing attitudes, and maternal anxieties. *Psychological Science, 5,* 341–346.

Delongis, A., Coyne, J. C., Dakof, G., Folkman, S., and Lazarus, R. S. (1982). Relationship of daily hassles, uplifts, and major life events to health status. *Health Psychology, 1,* 119–136.

Dohrenwend, B. P., and Shrout, P. E. (1985). "Hassles" in the conceptualization and measurement of life stress variables. *American Psychologist, 40,* 780–785.

Dumas, J. E., and LaFreniere, P. J. (1993). Mother–child relationships as a source of support or stress: A comparison of competent, average, aggressive, and anxious dyads. *Child Development, 64,* 1732–1754.

East, P. L., Malthaws, K. L., and Felice, M. E. (1994). Qualities of adolescent mothers parenting. *Journal of Adolescent Health, 15,* 163–168.

Egeland, B., and Farber, E. A. (1984). Infant–mother attachment factors related to its development and changes over time. *Child Development, 55,* 753–771.

Emde, R. N. (1991). The wonder of our complex enterprise: Steps enable by attachment and the effects of relationships on relationships. *Infant Mental Health Journal, 12,* 164–173.

Fagan, J. (2000). Head Start fathers' daily hassles and involvement with their children. *Journal of Family Issues, 21,* 329–346.

Feldman, S. S. (1987). Predicting strain in mothers and fathers of 6-month-old infants: A short-term longitudinal study. In P. W. Berman and F. A. Pedersen (Eds.), *Men's transitions to parenthood* (pp. 13–35). Hillsdale, NJ: Lawrence Erlbaum Associates.

Folkman, S., and Lazarus, R. S. (1988). Coping as a mediator of emotion. *Journal of Personality and Social Psychology, 54,* 466–475.

Gable, S., Belsky, J., and Crnic, K. A. (1992). Marriage, parenting and child development: Progress and prospects. *Journal of Family Psychology, 5,* 276–294.

Garmezy, N., and Rutter, M. (1983). *Stress, coping, and development in children.* New York: McGraw-Hill.

George, C., and Solomon, J. (1996). Representational models of relationships: Links between caregiving and attachment. *Infant Mental Health Journal, 17,* 198–216.

Glidden, L. M. (1993). What we do not know about families with children who have developmental disabilities: Questionnaire on resources and stress as a case study. *American Journal on Mental Retardation, 97,* 481–495.

Gloger-Tippelt, G. S., and Huerkamp, M. (1998). Relationship change at the transition to parenthood and security of infant–mother attachment. *International Journal of Behavioral Development, 22,* 633–655.

Goldberg, W. A., and Easterbrooks, M. A. (1984). Role of marital quality in toddler development. *Developmental Psychology, 20,* 504–514.

Goldstein, L. H., Diener, M. L., and Mangelsdorf, S. C. (1996). Maternal characteristics and social support across the transition to motherhood: Associations with maternal behavior. *Journal of Family Psychology, 10,* 60–71.

Greenberger, E., and Goldberg, W. A. (1989). Work, parenting, and the socialization of children. *Developmental Pscyhology, 25,* 22–35.

Grossman, F. K. (1988). Strain in the transition to parenthood. *Marriage and the Family Review, 12,* 85–104.

Guralnick, M. J. (1997). Second-generation research in the field of early intervention. In M. J. Guralnick (Ed.), *The effectiveness of early intervention* (pp. 3–20). Baltimore: Brookes.

Hanson, M. J., and Hanline, M. F. (1990). Parenting a child with a disability: A longitudinal study of parental stress and adaptation. *Journal of Early Intervention, 14,* 234–248.

Harrell, J. E., and Ridley, C. A. (1975). Substitute child care, maternal employment, and the quality of mother–child interaction. *Journal of Marriage and the Family, 37,* 556–564.

Hiester, M., and Sapp, J. (1991, April). *The effects of maternal life stress, changes in life stress, and individual stress factors on quality of attachment.* Paper presented at the biennial meeting of the Society for Research in Child Development, Seattle, WA.

Holmes, T. H., and Rahe, R. H. (1967). The Social Readjustment Rating Scale. *Journal of Psychosomatic Research, 11,* 213–218.

Ingersoll-Dayton, B., Morgan, D., and Antonucci, T. (1997). The effects of positive and negative social exchanges on aging adults. *Journals of Gerontology Series B-Psychological Sciences and Social Sciences, 52B,* 190–199.

Jain, A., Belsky, J., and Crnic, K. (1996). Beyond fathering behaviors: Types of dyads. *Journal of Family Psychology, 10,* 431–442.

Jarvis, P. A., and Creasey, G. L. (1991). Parental stress, coping, and attachment in families with an 18-month-old infant. *Infant Behavior and Development, 14,* 383–395.

Jennings, K. D., Stagg, V., and Connors, R. E. (1991). Social networks and mothers' interactions with their preschool children. *Child Development, 62,* 966–978.

Kanner, A. D., Coyne, J. C., Schaefer, C., and Lazarus, R. S. (1981). Comparison of two modes of stress measurement: Daily hassles and uplifts versus major life events. *Journal of Behavorial Medicine, 4,* 1–25.

Kohn, M. L., and Schooler, C. (1982). Job conditions and personality: A longitudinal assessment of their reciprocal effects. *American Journal of Sociology, 87*, 1257–1286.

Krauss, M. W. (1993). Child-related and parenting stress: Similarities and differences between mothers and fathers of children with disabilities. *American Journal on Mental Retardation, 97*, 393–404.

Lavee, Y., Sharlin, S., and Katz, R. (1996). The effect of parenting stress on marital equality: An integrated mother–father model. *Journal of Family Issues, 17*, 114–135.

Lazarus, R. S. (1984). Puzzles in the study of daily hassles. *Journal of Behavioral Medicine, 7*, 375–389.

Lazarus, R. S. (1991). *Emotion and adaptation*. New York: Oxford University Press.

Lazarus, R. S., DeLongis, A., Folkman, S., and Gruen, R. (1985). Stress and adaptational outcomes: The problem of confounded measures. *American Psychologist, 40*, 770–779.

Lerner, J. V., and Galambos, N. L. (1985). Maternal role satisfaction, mother–child interaction, and child temperament: A process model. *Developmental Psychology, 21*, 1157–1164.

Lobel, M. (1994). Conceptualizations, measurement, and effects of prenatal maternal stress on birth outcomes. *Journal of Behavioral Medicine, 17*, 225–272.

Loyd, B. H., and Abidin, R. R. (1985). Revision of the Parenting Stress Index. *Journal of Pediatric Psychology, 10*, 169–177.

Mash, E. J., and Johnston, C. (1990). Determinants of parenting stress: Illustrations from families of hyperactive children and families of physically abused children. [Special issue: The stresses of parenting]. *Journal of Clinical Child Psychology, 19*, 313–328.

Mayseless, O. (1998). Maternal caregiving strategy: A distinction between the ambivalent and the disorganized profile. *Infant Mental Health Journal, 19*, 20–33.

McLoyd, V. C. (1990). The impact of economic hardship on black families and children: Psychological distress, parenting, and socioeconomic development. *Child Development, 61*, 211–246.

Melson, G. F., Hsu, C.-H., and Ladd, G. W. (1993). The parental support networks of mothers and fathers: A multidimensional approach. *Early Development and Parenting, 2*, 169–182.

Melson, G. F., Ladd, G. W., and Hsu, H.-C. (1993). Maternal support networks, maternal cognitions, and young children's social and cognitive development. *Child Development, 64*, 1401–1417.

Melson, G. F., Windecker-Nelson, E., and Schwarz, R. (1998). Support and stress in mothers and fathers of young children. *Early Education and Development, 9*, 261–281.

Middlebrook, J. L., and Forehand, R. (1985). Maternal perceptions of deviance in child behavior as a function of stress and clinic versus nonclinic status of the child: An analogue study. *Behavior Therapy, 16*, 494–502.

Minuchin, P. (1988). Relationships within the family: A systems perspective on development. In R. A. Hinde and J. Stevenson-Hinde (Eds.), *Relationships within families: Mutual influences* (pp. 7–26). Oxford, England: Clarendon.

Mitchell, R., and Trickett, E. (1980). Task force report: Social networks as mediators of social support. *Community Mental Health Journal, 16*, 27–44.

Moos, R. H., and Moos, B. (1981). *Revised Family Environment Scale*. Palo Alto, CA: Consulting Psychology Press.

Naerde, A., Tambs, K., Mathiesen, K. S., Dalgard, O. S., and Samuelsen, S. O. (2000). *Journal of Affective Disorders, 58*, 181–199.

Nitz, K., Ketterlinus, R. D., and Brandt, L. J. (1995). The role of stress, social support, and family environment in adolescent mothers' parenting. *Journal of Adolescent Research, 10*, 358–382.

Noppe, I. C., Noppe, L. D., and Hughes, F. P. (1991). Stress as a predictor of the quality of parent–infant interactions. *The Journal of Genetic Psychology, 152*, 17–28.

O'Brien, M. (1996). Child rearing difficulties reported by parents of infants and toddlers. *Journal of Pediatric Psychology, 21*, 433–446.

Olson, S. L., and Banyard, V. (1993). Stop the world so I can get off for a while: Sources of daily stress in the lives of low-income single mothers of young children. *Family Relations, 42*, 50–56.

Ostberg, M., and Hagekull, B. (2000). A structural modeling approach to the understanding of parenting stress. *Journal of Clinical Child Psychology, 29*, 615–625.

Ostberg, M., Hagekull, B., and Wettergren, S. (1997). A measure of parental stress in mothers with small children: Dimensionality, stability, and validity. *Scandinavian Journal of Psychology, 38*, 199–208.

Parke, R. D., and Beitel, A. (1988). Disappointment: When things go wrong in the transition to parenthood. *Marriage and Family Review, 12*, 221–265.

Patterson, G. R. (1983). Stress: A change agent for family process. In N. Garmezy and M. Rutter (Eds.), *Stress, coping, and development in children* (pp. 235–264). New York: McGraw-Hill.

Pett, M. A., Vaughncole, B., and Wampold, B. E. (1994). Maternal employment and perceived stress—Their impact on children's adjustment and mother–child interaction in young divorced and married families. *Family Relations, 43*, 151–158.

Phelps, J. L., Belsky, J., and Crnic, K. (1998). Earned security, daily stress, and parenting: A comparison of five alternate models. *Development and Psychopathology, 10*, 21–38.

Pianta, R. C., and Egeland, B. (1990). Life stress and parenting outcomes in a disadvantaged sample: Results of the mother–child interaction project. *Journal of Clinical Child Psychology, 19*, 329–336.

Quittner, A. L., Glueckauf, R. L., and Jackson, R. L. (1990). Chronic parenting stress: Moderating versus mediating effects of social support. *Journal of Clinical and Social Psychology, 59*, 1266–1278.

Rabkin, J. G., and Streuning, E. L. (1976). Life events, stress and illness. *Science, 194*, 1013–1020.

Repetti, R. L., and Wood, J. (1997). Effects of daily stress at work on mothers' interactions with preschoolers. *Journal of Family Psychology, 11*, 90–108.

Ritchie, K. L., and Holden, G. W. (1998). Parenting stress in low income battered and community women: Effects on parenting behavior. *Early Education and Development, 9*, 97–112.

Robson, A. L. (1997). Low birthweight and parenting stress during early childhood. *Journal of Pediatric Psychology, 22*, 297–311.

Rodgers, A. Y. (1993). The assessment of variables related to the parenting behavior of mothers of Young children. *Children and Youth Services Review, 15*, 385–402.

Rothbart, M. K., and Bates, J. E. (1998). Temperament. In W. Damon (Series Ed.) and N. Eisenberg (Vol. Ed.), *Handbook of child psychology: Vol. 3. Social, emotional, and personality development* (5th ed., pp. 105–176). New York: Wiley.

Rothbart, M. K., and Derryberry, D. (1981). Development of individual differences in temperament. In M. E. Lamb and A. L. Brown (Eds.), *Advances in developmental psychology* (Vol. 1) pp. 37–86. Hillsdale, NJ: Lawrence Erlbaum Associates.

Sarason, I. G., Johnson, J. H., and Siegel, J. M. (1978). Assessing the impact of life changes: Development of the Life Experiences Survey. *Journal of Consulting and Clinical Psychology, 46*, 932–946.

Scher, A., and Mayseless, O. (2000). Mothers of anxious/ambivalent infants: Maternal characteristics and child-care context. *Child Development, 71*, 1629–1639.

Shaw, D. S., Keenan, K., Vondra, J. I., Delliquadri, E., and Giovanelli, J. (1997). Antecedents of preschool children's internalizing problems: A longitudinal study of low-income families. *Journal of the American Academy of Child and Adolescent Psychiatry, 36*, 1760–1767.

Shaw, D. S., Owens, E. B., Giovanelli, J., and Winslow, E. B. (2001). Infant and toddler pathways to early externalizing disorders. *Journal of the American Academy of Child and Adolescent Psychiatry, 40*, 36–43.

Shaw, D. S., Winslow, E. B., Owens, E. B., and Hood, N. (1998). Young children's adjustment to chronic family adversity: A longitudinal study of low-income families. *Journal of the American Academy of Child and Adolescent Psychiatry, 37*, 545–553.

Short, K. H., and Johnston, C. (1997). Stress, maternal distress, and children's adjustment following immigration: The buffering role of social support. *Journal of Consulting and Clinical Psychology, 65*, 494–503.

Siegel, M. (1987). Are sons and daughters treated more differentially by fathers than by mothers? *Developmental Review, 7*, 183–209.

Sommer, K., Whetman, T. L., Borkowski, J. G., Schellenbach, C., Maxwell, S., and Keogh, D. (1993). Cognitiue readiness and adolescent parenting. *Development Psychology, 29*, 389–398.

St. James-Roberts, L., Conroy, S. and Wilsher, C. (1998). Stability and outcome of persistent infant crying. *Infant Behavior and Development, 21*, 411–435.

Starrels, M. E. (1994). Gender difference in parent–child relations. *Journal of Family Issues, 15*, 148–165.

Stuckey, M., McGhee, P., and Bell, N. (1982). Parent–child interacton. The influence of maternal employment. *Developmental Psychology, 18*, 635–644.

Thompson, R. J., Merritt, K. A., Keith, B. R., Bennett, L., and Johndrown, D. A. (1993). The role of maternal stress and family functioning in maternal distress and mother-reported and child-reported psychological adjustment of nonreferred children. *Journal of Clinical Child Pscyhology, 22*, 78–84.

Thompson, R. O., Goldstein, R. F., Oehler, J. M., Gustafsm, K. E., Catlett, A. T., and Brazy, J. E. (1994). Developmental outcome of very low birthweight infants as a function of biological risk and psychosocial risk. *Journal of Developmental and Behavioral Pediatrics, 15*, 232–238.

Vaughn, B., Egeland, B., Sroufe, L. A., and Waters, E. (1979). Individual difference in infant–mother attachment at twelve and eighteen months: Stability and change in families under stress. *Child Development, 50*, 971–975.

Wahler, R. G., and Dumas, J. E. (1989). Attentional problems in dysfunctional mother–child interactions: An interbehavioral model. *Psychological Bulletin, 105*, 116–130.

Webster-Stratton, C. (1990). Stress: A potential disruptor of parent perceptions and family interactions. *Journal of Clinical Child Psychology, 19*, 302–312.

Windle, M., and Dumenci, L. (1997). Parental and occupational stress as predictors of depressive symptoms among dual income couples: A multilevel modeling approach. *Journal of Marriage and the Family, 59*, 625–634.

Woodworth, S., Crnic, K., and Belsky, J. (April, 1995). The mediating effect of parent negative mood on the relationship between family stress and child behavior management. Paper presented at the Biennial meeting of the Society for Reasearch in Child Development, Indianapolis, IN.

11

Parenting and the Development
of Children's Peer Relationships

Gary W. Ladd
Arizona State University
Gregory S. Pettit
Auburn University

INTRODUCTION

Before the 1980s, the idea that the family and peer systems might operate as interrelated socialization contexts, each affecting the other, received very little empirical attention. This oversight was, in part, attributable to investigators' tendencies to construe the family and peer systems as separate rather than interlocking domains. However, in the last two decades, a paradigm shift occurred because researchers began to search for the origins of children's peer competence within the family (see Ladd, 1999) and embraced tenets from ecological theory that hold that the family and the peer culture operate as interconnected contexts within larger social systems (see Bronfenbrenner, 1986). Out of this shift grew the hypothesis that families and peer groups are linked via bidirectional pathways such that families influence children's peer relationships and vice versa (Ladd, 1992; Parke and Ladd, 1992).

In addition, researchers began to refine their conceptions of the relationships that children form with parents and peers and, in particular, hypotheses about how these relationships might contribute to children's interpersonal development. An early emerging assumption was that children's relationships with parents and peers differed in the types of provisions (i.e., psychological resources versus barriers or constraints) they conferred on children (Hartup, 1979). Whereas parent–child relationships were construed as "vertical" ties, peer relationships were seen as "horizontal" alliances because they were more symmetrical or egalitarian on dimensions such as power, control, and autonomy. Yet, emerging evidence suggests that the contributions of the two kinds of social systems may complement each other (e.g., each may contribute additively to the same aspects of the child's development) or compensate for each other (i.e., one system's contributions may make up for what the other fails to provide). Moreover, as pointed out by Russell, Pettit, and Mize (1998), relationship features that were thought to be present principally in peer relationships (e.g., "horizontal" features) may also be present in certain kinds of parent–child interactions and relationships, such as parent–child play.

Because of this evolution of ideas, inquiry has shifted away from such basic questions as whether the family and peer systems are linked to more complex agendas such as understanding the processes of relationship learning, the transfer of such learning across contexts, and the conditional nature of parenting–child connections and their effects on child outcomes (see Collins, Maccoby, Steinberg, Hetherington, and Bornstein, 2000). Examples include determining whether particular features of parent–child relationships, or parental management strategies, yield different results for girls versus boys, aggressive versus shy children, or children from different neighborhoods and ethnic and cultural backgrounds. In addition, different explanatory paradigms—such as those founded on the principles of behavior genetics—have invoked a new agenda and challenge prevailing assumptions about the mechanisms responsible for links between the family and peer systems.

One emergent controversy concerns the importance of the family environment as a force in the development of children's social skills and relational competence. Researchers operating from social learning, attachment, and other environmental/organismic perspectives have emphasized relationship learning in the family as the means through which children acquire skills and transfer them to the peer context. Those working from behavior-genetic perspectives (e.g., Reiss, with Neiderhiser, Hetherington, and Plomin, 2000; Rowe, 1994) have tended to downplay the role of relationship learning in the family or view its contributions as spurious (Lamb and Nash, 1989) or limited to functioning within the family (Harris, 2000). Instead, the parents and child's shared gene pool and its interaction with rearing experiences (e.g., shared and nonshared family environments) are assumed to underlie children's sociability and competence with peers (Reiss et al., 2000). Some have gone so far as to question whether parenting has *any* enduring effect on children's social behavior and personality (Harris, 1998). This argument draws partly from evidence of gene–environment correlations, and partly from the view that findings from socialization research show limited cross-context consistency. We return to the cross-context consistency issue in a later section of this chapter.

Researchers whose hypotheses are based on the premise that parents influence children's development have been interested in explicating how family experiences and processes affect children's peer competence and relationships. Although developmental scientists have yet to agree on a definition of childhood social competence (Rubin and Burgess, in Vol. 1 of this *Handbook*), the term is used here to refer to children's abilities to: (1) initiate and sustain positive interactions with peers (i.e., utilize specific peer-related social skills), (2) form affiliative ties (i.e., friendships and peer-group acceptance) and high-quality relationships with peers (e.g., stability, support, security), and (3) avoid debilitating social roles (e.g., victimization, rejection, and social withdrawal) and interpersonal and emotional consequences (e.g., loneliness, anxiety, and wariness).

Assuming that families do impact some, if not all of these forms of children's social competence, it becomes important to distinguish among the types of socialization processes that may be responsible for such outcomes. This is a daunting agenda because families are complex environments in which children are exposed to a wide array of social-psychological experiences, only some of which may "socialize" children in ways that are relevant to the peer milieu (see Ladd, 1992). The framework used to organize the evidence reviewed in this chapter is built on the assumption that two types of family processes may have important implications for the socialization of children's social competence: (1) those that occur as part of family life and most likely derive from relationships and dynamics that are internal to the family system (rather than external to it, such as within the child's peer environment) and (2) those that transpire in the family context or with family members but are predicated on children's actual or anticipated experiences in the peer milieu, or parents' perceptions of the child's needs in this context. Thus, for organizational and heuristic purposes, the mechanisms included in the former category are termed *indirect* because they refer to aspects of family life that may affect children's social competence, but they represent modes of influence that do not provide the child with any explicit connection to the world of peers. In contrast, *direct* modes of influence encompass parents' efforts to socialize or "manage" children's social development, especially as it pertains to the peer context. Also considered are mediating variables, such as learning experiences that children acquire in the family that transfer or generalize to the peer context. Of course, our attempt to distinguish between indirect and direct family influences does not preclude the possibility that both forms of socialization operate simultaneously within children's rearing environments and have combined effects on children's competence with peers.

In the sections that follow, evidence pertaining to indirect influences is reviewed first and is parsed into six domains, including studies of attachment, childrearing and parent–child interaction styles, parental disciplinary styles, parental perceptions, family environment, and family pathology. Next, findings pertaining to direct parental influences are organized around four key constructs: parent as designer, mediator, supervisor, and advisor and consultant. In the final sections, we critique the current status of the discipline including issues such as hypothesized "mechanisms of transmission" and the specificity, generality, and causal priority of family socialization "inputs."

A note of clarification is in order with respect to our discussion of *mediating processes* and *moderated associations*. These are statistical terms that describe ways in which predictor variables (e.g., parenting behaviors) and outcome variables (e.g., children's social competence in peer relations) may be related to one another vis-à-vis a third variable (or set of variables). Statistically speaking, a variable that is associated with both predictor and outcome and that accounts for the association (or a portion of the association) between predictor and outcome is termed a mediator (Baron and Kenny, 1986). Typically, mediators are conceptualized as explanatory variables that shed light on underlying processes responsible for the link between family experience and social behavior and competence with peers. Moderators, on the other hand, are variables that condition or alter the strength (or direction) of the association between predictors and outcomes. Moderators are not explanatory variables; rather, they serve to contextualize (e.g., as when an empirical relation holds only in certain kinds of ecological contexts) and delimit linkages (e.g., as when an empirical relation holds only for mothers, or for girls) between parenting and children's behavior and competencies.

INDIRECT PARENTAL INFLUENCES AND CHILDREN'S PEERS

By definition, indirect parental influences occur when children transfer the behavioral and relationship patterns they have learned in the family to the peer domain. Historically, many of the processes that we define as indirect parental influences have been viewed as distinct research domains that have evolved from differing socialization perspectives. However, our goal is to evaluate evidence from each of these literatures as it pertains to a common premise. This premise is that family environments, and the processes that occur within them, impact the quality of children's social competence and peer relationships.

Attachment

In general, research guided by attachment theory has been based on the proposition that children differ in the degree of emotional security and type of "internal working model" they derive from attachment relationships (see Cummings and Cummings, in Vol. 5 of this *Handbook*), and these developments structure their approach and expectations about other, nonparental relationships (Bowlby, 1973; Elicker, Englund, and Sroufe, 1992; Sroufe and Fleeson, 1986). Children whose caregivers are available and responsive, as compared to those who are not, are expected to develop positive expectations about others and be better equipped to apply relationship principles such as reciprocity (Elicker et al., 1992).

The link between parent–child attachment and children's peer relationships was initially researched with infants, toddlers, and preschoolers (see Elicker et al., 1992; Fagot, 1997; Kerns, 1994). Using the Ainsworth Strange Situation procedure, investigators examined early attachment status as an antecedent of the quality of preschoolers' peer relationships (Erickson, Sroufe, and Egeland, 1985; LaFreniere and Sroufe, 1985; Waters, Wippman, and Sroufe, 1979). In general, infants with secure attachments were found to have higher levels of social competence with preschool peers (Waters et al., 1979) and fewer behavior problems (Erickson et al., 1985) than did infants with insecure attachments. Secure attachments (Kerns, Klepac, and Cole, 1996), or attributes associated with secure attachments (e.g., parent availability; see Lieberman, Doyle, and Markiewicz, 1999) are more closely linked with children's friendships and the quality of those relationships than with other types of relationships in the peer context (e.g., peer acceptance). However, other investigators have found secure attachment to be associated with preschoolers tendencies to possess larger support networks (Bost, Vaughn, Washington, Cielinski, and Bradbard, 1998), display positive affect with peers, and garner higher levels of peer acceptance (LaFreniere and Sroufe, 1985). In contrast, anxious attachment histories have been linked with problems in children's peer relationships, such as peer victimization (e.g., see Perry, Finnegan, Hodges, Kennedy, and Malone, 1993; Troy and Sroufe, 1987). Troy and Sroufe, for example, found that preschoolers who had histories of anxious-resistant or anxious-avoidant attachment with their caregivers tended to be victimized by peers in a play group context (typically the perpetrators were age-mates with anxious-avoidant attachment histories).

Less research has been conducted on the link between attachment status and children's peer relationships during later periods of development, such as middle childhood and adolescence. Interest in these periods has been spurred by the contention that some early attachment patterns may persist over the life cycle, and even be transmitted across generations (Allen, Moore, Kuperminc, and Bell, 1998; Elicker et al., 1992; Waters, Merrick, Albersheim, and Treboux, 1995). Consistent with this premise, Grossman and Grossman (1991) found that infants with secure attachments tend to have high-quality friendships during middle childhood, whereas infants with insecure attachments report greater difficulties with friendship and peer relationships. In a study with 10-year-old children in a summer camp, Elicker et al. (1992) found that security of attachment correlated positively with children's social competence, popularity, and participation in a reciprocated friendship. With adolescents, Allen et al. (1998) found that secure attachment organizations (i.e., characteristic strategies for construing memories and affect about attachment experiences) were associated with higher levels of competence and lower levels of dysfunction in several domains, including peer relationships.

Evidence reflecting on the role that children's relationship representations (i.e., internal working models) play in their peer relationships has begun to accumulate. Although at an early stage, the reported findings are consistent with the premise that children's representations of the parent–child relationship generalize to peers (e.g., Cassidy, Kirsh, Scolton, and Parke, 1996; Rudolph, Hammen, and Burge, 1995). Cassidy et al. (1996), for example, found that children who tended to see their parents as rejecting were more likely to ascribe hostile intentions to familiar and unfamiliar peers. Rudolph et al. (1995) found that children's relationship representations correlated with the quality of their interactional competencies in the peer context. Whether these representations are best construed as "internal working models," as described in attachment theory (see Main, Kaplan, and Cassidy, 1985), or defined as "relational schemes or scripts," as depicted in the social cognition literature, remains to be seen. In the context of attachment theory, the construct of the internal working model has typically been construed as an unconscious representation of early intimate ties (primarily with caregivers) that, once formed, remains relatively invariant over development (see Bretherton, 1985; Waters, Vaughn, Posada, and Kondo-Ikemura, 1995). Concepts such as schemes or scripts have their origins in cognitive and/or social-learning theories (e.g., see Mize and Ladd, 1988), and tend to be seen as entities that children learn and modify based on their accumulating and changing experiences with a broad range of socializers (e.g., caregivers, peers, and teachers). Thus, among the implications that follow from the latter perspective are that developmental change rather than continuity would be found in children's relationship representations, and that the effects of these representations on children's peer competence and relationships would vary as a function of children's maturity and history of social experiences.

The majority of researchers who have evaluated the parent–infant attachment relationship have focused on the mother–child dyad. Investigations of father–infant attachment and its impact on the development of children's competence in peer relationships are rare. Some findings, however, suggest that the quality of the attachment relationship children have with fathers is also linked with the child's peer competence. Patterson, Kupersmidt, and Griesler (1990) found that peer-rejected children, and in particular those who were aggressive, reported lower levels of companionship and affection from fathers. Based on a meta-analysis of the literature on attachment and children's peer relationships, Schneider, Atkinson and Tardif (2000) concluded that reported linkages between father–child attachment and children's competence with peers were not substantially different in magnitude than the associations that have been reported for mother–child attachment, although the number of studies including both mothers and fathers was quite small.

Thus, accumulating findings buttress the notion that attachment security fosters children's relational competence and that insecure ties cause social difficulties. Children with secure attachments appear to nurture peer relationships by being more responsive and less critical, and form ties that are higher in quality, such as friendships that are less negative, more harmonious, and higher in companionship (Kerns et al., 1996; Youngblade and Belsky, 1992). In contrast, children with insecure attachments appear less competent with peers (Cohn, 1990) and more prone to negative peer responses even when they display positive overtures (Fagot, 1997). The premise that such outcomes are attributable to the child's internal working model of relationships has received some support (Cassidy et al., 1996), but indices used to tap internal working models sometimes bear considerable similarity with those used to assess other constructs (i.e., features of social-information processing), raising questions about the validity of these findings (Mize, Pettit, and Meece, 2000). Also perplexing is the fact that evidence contrary to the reported links between attachment status and children's peer competence has also emerged (e.g., see Booth, Rubin, and Rose-Krasnor, 1998; Howes, Matheson, and Hamilton, 1994; Youngblade, Park, and Belsky, 1993). Howes and colleagues, for example, found no predictive relations between mother–child attachment security and preschooler's peer competence, but did find that teacher–child attachment security was linked with peer competence, even over substantial time intervals (Howes, Matheson, and Hamilton, 1994; Howes, Hamilton, and Philipsen, 1998).

Clearly, the hypothesis that early parent–child attachment is a precursor of children's peer relational competence deserves further empirical scrutiny and should be evaluated in relation to competing perspectives. The Schneider et al. (2000) meta-analysis, based on 63 studies, yielded an estimated effect size (ES) of 0.20. In view of this modest association, these researchers concluded that attachment is only one of many factors that may influence children's peer relationships, and that researchers should begin to evaluate the relative and combined contributions of multiple family factors to children's peer relationships. It is also possible that, following early parent–child attachment, continuing or later-emerging qualities of the parent–child relationship or the child–peer relationships shape the course of children's peer competence (e.g., see Freitag, Belsky, Grossmann, Grossmann, and Scheuerer-Englisch, 1996; Lewis, Feiring, and Rosenthal, 2000). For example, attachment's influence on peer competence may be mediated through factors such as children's involvement in social networks or the emotional support children receive in such contexts (e.g., Booth et al., 1998; Bost et al., 1998). Feasible too, is the possibility that linkages observed between attachment and peer competence are largely attributable to heritable family characteristics (e.g., general sociability; see Lamb and Nash, 1989).

Other issues that remain to be addressed include the association between children's peer competence and attachment as manifested in singular or multiple ties with other adults (e.g., fathers and teachers) at later stages development, and for children of both genders. Evidence gathered thus far suggests that children's attachment representations for mothers versus fathers may be linked with different aspects of their social competence (Lieberman et al., 1999; Verschueren and Marcoen, 1999). Verschueren and Marcoen, for example, found that one aspect of children's social competence, anxious-withdrawn behavior, was more closely associated with their representations of father–child rather than mother–child attachment representations. Another important agendum will be to clarify how the concept of internal working models is best defined and investigated. The lack of consistency in attachment classifications over time (Belsky, Campbell, Cohn, and Moore, 1996) and across adult caregivers (Howes et al., 1994) raises important questions about the ways in which models come to be constructed from experience and activated in specific social encounters with peers.

Childrearing Styles, Parenting Behavior, and Parent–Child Interaction

Early research on childrearing styles was guided by efforts to demarcate differences in the affective climate and power structure of parent–child relationships (see Baumrind, 1973; Becker, 1964; Maccoby and Martin, 1983). Constructs such as *parental warmth* (e.g., responsiveness of the parent) and *parental control* (e.g., demandingness of the parent) were used to establish a circumplex model (see Maccoby and Martin, 1983) that contained four types of childrearing styles: *authoritarian* (i.e., highly demanding and low in warmth), *authoritative* (i.e., highly demanding and highly responsive), *indulgent* (i.e., undemanding and highly responsive), and *indifferent–uninvolved* (i.e., low in demandingness and responsiveness). In general, research on these childrearing styles suggested that authoritative parenting provided the best foundation for children's peer competence, including their social-behavioral skills and confidence. However, the mechanisms that may account for these linkages have not been well articulated or investigated. It has been suggested that childrearing styles may serve as models from which children learn about relational interactions and skills. Alternatively, or possibly concomitantly, the warmth and responsiveness experienced in the context of parent–child interaction may influence the extent to which children seek out emotional ties with others (Putallaz and Heflin, 1990).

In recent years, researchers have moved away from global typologies and begun to investigate specific features or qualities of the parent–child *relationship* that are associated with specific aspects of children's peer competence. Children's aggressiveness toward peers has been linked with parent–child relationships that are high in coercion and dominance (e.g., Hart et al., 1998; Rubin, Hastings, Chen, Stewart, and McNichol, 1998), or low in responsiveness (Hart et al., 1998). Mistreatment or peer victimization appears to be more common in children whose parents tend to be intrusive, controlling, or overprotective. Finnegan, Hodges, and Perry (1998) examined the links between children's passivity and several aspects of the mother–child relationship (e.g., coercive control, over protectiveness, responsiveness, and emotional control) and found that, whereas coercive and emotional control and lack of responsiveness were correlated with peer victimization in girls, maternal overprotectiveness was linked to peer victimization among boys. The latter finding, for boys, is consistent with evidence reported by Olweus (1993), who found that boys of overprotective mothers were more likely to be victimized by peers.

Along with the shift toward researching specific features of the parent–child relationship, researchers have begun to move away from frameworks that emphasize the parent's role in parent–child relationships and, instead, develop models and assessment strategies that represent features of the dyad. Hodges, Finnegan, and Perry (1999) used child reports to index degree of connectedness and independence that children perceived in their relationships with mothers. Children whose reports reflected substantial deviations on these dimensions, particularly very high connectedness (i.e., a preoccupied relationship stance) or independence (i.e., an avoidant relationship stance) manifested increasing difficulties in their peer relationships over time. Exploring a similar premise, Clark and Ladd (2000) observed actual parent–child narrative conversations and, using the dyad as the unit of analysis, documented the levels of connectedness, or strength of the emotional bond that existed between the parent and child. Also observed was parental autonomy support, which was defined as behaviors performed by the parent that facilitated "self-initiated expression and action" on the part of the child (Ryan and Solky, 1996). Results showed that connectedness was correlated with children's socioemotional orientations (i.e., inclination toward prosocial-empathic interactions with peers) as well as features of their peer relationships including friendship, friendship quality, and peer acceptance. Moreover, analyses of alternative models yielded findings that were consistent with the interpretation that children's prosocial-empathic orientations mediated the association between connectedness and children's peer relationships. Autonomy support, in contrast, did not account for variation in children's prosocial-empathic orientations or peer relationships after accounting for parent–child connectedness.

A similar approach was adopted by Ladd and Ladd (1998) to investigate the familial correlates of peer victimization in kindergarten children. Dyadic features of the parent–child relationship (i.e., intense-closeness) and specific parenting behaviors (e.g., intrusive-demandingness and responsiveness) were assessed while parents and children engaged in multiple interactional tasks. Measures of peer victimization were obtained as children began kindergarten. Parent–child relationships characterized by mutually intense-closeness were associated with higher levels of peer victimization, but only for boys. Additional links were found between parenting behaviors and victimization in both boys and girls; children whose parents tended to be high in intrusive-demandingness and low in responsiveness were more often victimized by classmates.

Other lines of investigation have been focused more narrowly on the parents' behavior or interaction patterns in socialization exchanges with children. Research in this area has often been guided by social learning principles and has been focused on features of the parents' behaviors, such as emotional and linguistic responsiveness (Black and Logan, 1995; Cassidy, Parke, Bukovsky, and Braungart, 1992), intrusiveness and support (Pettit, Bates, and Dodge, 1997; Pettit, Clawson, Bates, and Dodge, 1996), or tendency to balance interactions as reflected in patterns of reciprocity or synchrony (Pettit and Harrist, 1993). These behaviors have been viewed as important elements in the process through which parents socialize children's interpersonal skills (see Parke and Buriel, 1998; Parke and Ladd, 1992; Pettit et al., 1997).

As an illustration, a number of investigators have suggested that parents' behavior during parent–child play is an important contributor to children's skill learning and development. With samples of young children, Parke and colleagues (MacDonald and Parke, 1984; Parke, MacDonald, Beitel, and Bhavnagri, 1988; Parke et al., 1989) found that mothers' and fathers' directiveness and verbal engagement during parent–child play were associated with children's peer acceptance, but in different ways. Whereas maternal directiveness was positively associated with popularity, paternal directiveness was negatively related to popularity, peer competence, and school adjustment. Parental engagement and the ability to sustain play bouts also were associated with children's peer popularity; this finding was particularly evident for maternal verbal engagement with boys. More recently, Lindsey, Mize, and Pettit (1997) have shown that mutuality in play (i.e., a relative balance in parents' and children's rates of initiating play and complying to these initiations) is associated with peer acceptance and teacher-rated social skills. Sex-differentiated patterns were reported by Lindsey and Mize (2000) and by Pettit, Brown, Mize, and Lindsey (1998) in that mothers' play behaviors were more strongly linked with their daughters' competence, whereas fathers' play behaviors were linked more strongly with their sons' competence.

Additional evidence suggests that parental engagement and affect during parent–child play is linked with children's peer competence. Some investigators have found that the parents' ability to sustain parent–child play interactions was positively related to children's skill at interpreting parental emotional cues (MacDonald, 1987; Parke et al., 1989), and this skill was associated with children's acceptance by peers. Similarly, LaFreniere and Dumas (1992) found that mothers of socially competent children displayed more positive behaviors and affect and were more coherent and contingent in their interactions and discipline techniques. Mothers of children rated as average in social competence, in contrast, were less reciprocal and coherent, and mothers of anxious-withdrawn children engaged in a high degree of negative reciprocity, control, and negative affect.

Isley, O'Neil, Clatfelter, and Parke (1999) expand on these findings by showing that parent's affect and children's peer competence are linked through the child's affective expressions. Results showed that the association between parents' positive affect and children's peer competence were mediated by children's expressed positive affect. Other findings suggest that, even outside the play context, the parent's affect is associated with children's peer relations. Cassidy et al. (1992) found that parents' emotional expressions within the family context, and children's understanding of emotions were linked with the quality of children's peer relations. Such findings are not just limited to mothers;

rather, it appears that the affective tone of father–child interactions may be important too. Children exhibiting more reciprocated negative affect during play with fathers were found to elicit higher levels of negative reciprocity in peer interactions (Fagot, 1997) and tended to be avoidant, aggressive, and less prosocial toward peers (Carson and Parke, 1996). In contrast, children with positive father–child relations have been found to form higher quality friendships (Youngblade and Belsky, 1992).

In addition, how mothers react to children's emotional experiences (e.g., offering help and minimizing child's feelings) has been linked with peer competence. Putallaz (1987) evaluated the potential role of response evocation as a mediating influence between parent–child interaction and children's peer competence and found that parents who encouraged autonomy tended to have children who were more assertive, agreeable, and less self-absorbed in peer interactions. Furthermore, evidence gathered by Eisenberg, Fabes, and Murphy (1996) revealed that children of mothers who minimized their feelings exhibited lower levels of social competence.

Another social learning premise, articulated by Putallaz and colleagues (Putallaz, 1987; Putallaz and Heflin, 1990), is that parents transmit interpersonal skills to children by modeling them in the context of parent–child interaction. Central to this argument is the hypothesis that children learn affect regulation by imitating the form and tone of the emotions that parents use when interacting with their children. Consistent with this contention, Putallaz and colleagues found that mothers' behavior correlated positively with the behaviors children used with peers, and mothers' negative affect correlated with children's relational difficulties (i.e., low peer status; Putallaz, 1987; Putallaz, Costanzo, and Smith, 1991). It has also been shown that when minor disputes occur between mothers and their children, there are individual differences in the way mothers argue with children. Herrera and Dunn (1997) found that children of mothers who tended to use other-oriented reasoning during arguments were more likely to develop constructive ways to manage conflicts with a friend than were children whose mothers tended to focus on their own needs during such disputes.

It would appear that that parent–child play has special significance as a context for children's development of social skills (see Tamis-LeMonda, Bornstein, and Užgiris, in Vol. of this *Handbook*). Play skills are important in children's social repertoires and, in the context of play with their children, parents may more easily adapt an interactional role that is more "horizontal" and more germane to young children's success in peer relationships (see Russell et al., 1998). When parents adopt the role of "playmate" (or "coplayer" role; see O'Reilly and Bornstein, 1993), children are more likely to be provided with opportunities for acquiring interactional skills that may generalize to other play contexts, including those with peers. Among the skills and interaction styles that might be fostered when parents engage in the playmate (coplayer) role are matching of affective states, turn taking, synchronous exchanges, and joint determination (coconstruction) of the content and direction of play (Russell et al., 1998).

In sum, among the trends that have characterized advances in research on childrearing styles, parenting behavior, and parent–child interaction are a movement away from frameworks in which parenting is construed in terms of broad, trait-like typologies (e.g., stable parenting styles), toward models that emphasized specific parenting features, behaviors, and interaction patterns. Included in this progression is a propensity to replace unidimensional, unidirectional conceptions of socialization in the family (e.g., parent or parenting effects) with perspectives that broaden the unit of analysis to include more of the family context (e.g., the parent–child dyad and the family as a social system), and potential modes of influence (e.g., reciprocal, bidirectional, and transactional patterns of influence). Not surprisingly, these trends have expanded the purview of research on family socialization beyond the study of parents (e.g., the study of mothers and mothering, in particular) to incorporate constructs such as parent–child interaction patterns, and mother–child, father–child, and mother–father–child relationships.

Accumulating evidence suggests that parent–child and family–child interaction patterns and relationships are complex, and that multiple aspects of childrearing and family relationships are associated with children's peer competence. It would be beneficial to explore how specific relationships within the family (i.e., beyond the traditional dyadic relationship) or combinations of relationships (i.e., the effects of mother–child and father–child relationships) affect children's social development. Toward this end, it might be useful for researchers to investigate the possible "specialized" versus overlapping aspects of parent–child interaction as precursors of children's peer competence. This approach has been used with some success in research on the potential contributions of differing peer relationships (e.g., friendship quality, peer acceptance, and victimization) to children's well-being and adjustment (e.g., see Bukowski and Hoza, 1989; Ladd, Kochenderfer, and Coleman, 1997; Ladd, Birch, and Buhs, 1999). Kerns and Barth (1995), for example, have shown that parent–child attachment and play are nonredundant in their links with children's peer competence. There is also some evidence to suggest that the strength of the relation between particular forms of parent–child interaction and the quality of children's peer relationships varies with the gender of the child (see Ladd and Ladd, 1998).

Parental Disciplinary Styles

Researchers have also sought to evaluate the potential effects of parents' disciplinary styles on the quality of children's peer relationships (see Cohn, Patterson, and Christopoulos, 1991; Putallaz and Heflin, 1990, for reviews). Much of the evidence gathered on parental discipline comes from studies in which multiple aspects of parenting have been researched (e.g., parent's childrearing styles and parent–child interaction). Thus, many of the findings reviewed in this section have been extracted from previously cited investigations.

Early work in this area showed that power assertive disciplinary styles, in which parents rely on verbal commands and physical power, were associated with children's use of aggression and hostility with peers. Inductive disciplinary styles or strategies that emphasize reasoning were found to be associated with prosocial child behavior (Becker, 1964; Hoffman, 1960; Zahn-Waxler, Radke-Yarrow, and King, 1979). In recent years, more specific hypotheses have been proposed to account for linkages between parent–child disciplinary encounters and the quality of children's interactions with peers. Pettit and colleagues (Pettit, Dodge, and Brown, 1988; Pettit, Harrist, Bates, and Dodge, 1991) proposed that the disciplinary style experienced within the family is transferred by the child from the family to the peer systems; the interactions experienced in the family thus indirectly contribute to the quality of the child's interactions within the peer environment. This hypothesis is grounded in social-information-processing theory, which suggests that the social-cognitive orientations children learn in the family environment are responsible for the behaviors they employ with peers.

Although researchers have attempted to substantiate the mechanisms through which children transfer what they have learned in parental disciplinary encounters to the peer context, the associations detected thus far have been limited in scope and not particularly strong (see Pettit et al., 1991). The specific contention that harsh discipline leads to antisocial behavior by encouraging children to develop maladaptive processing patterns has received some empirical support. Evidence gathered by Nix, Pettit, and their colleagues (Nix et al., 1999; Pettit et al., 1988; Pettit, Bates, and Dodge, 1997) has shown that restrictive and harsh disciplinary styles are linked with children's peer problems; specifically, maternal restrictiveness is correlated with lower levels of peer acceptance and social skill, and higher levels of aggressive behavior (Pettit et al., 1988; Pettit, Clawson, Dodge, and Bates, 1996). Moreover, Weiss, Dodge, Bates, and Pettit (1992) found that the linkages between harsh discipline and antisocial behavior are independent of confounds such as family socioeconomic status (SES) and child temperament, and partially mediated by maladaptive social information processing patterns. Also substantiated was the premise that the antisocial behaviors (e.g., fighting and noncompliance) children acquire from coercive parent–child interactions generalize to peers (see Patterson, Reid, and Dishion, 1992); key elements include the parent's power-assertive tactics (Dishion, 1990; Hart, Ladd, and Burlson, 1990) and children's aggressiveness toward the parent (MacKinnon-Lewis et al., 1994).

Of late, investigators have begun to evaluate more complex models of the contributions of discipline and other parenting processes. McFadyen-Ketchum et al. (1996) found that, among boys, the combination of maternal coercion and nonaffection predicted gains in aggressiveness over the early grade school years—a result consistent with formulations of coercion training theory (Patterson et al., 1992). Among girls, however, only coercion predicted changes in aggressiveness over time, and the direction of this trajectory was negative (declining), suggesting that these parenting processes differentially affected girls' and boys' behavior.

Hart and colleagues (Hart, DeWolf, Wozniak, and Burts, 1992; Hart, Ladd, and Burleson, 1990) have worked from a model in which the effects of parental disciplinary styles are seen as affecting the child's outcome expectations for peer interactions, including those involving conflicts. According to this perspective, parents who employ inductive discipline strategies teach children about interpersonal outcomes, and parents who rely on power assertive techniques draw children's attention to control and compliance themes and, thereby, encourage them to develop outcome expectations that are more instrumental in nature (i.e., focused on achieving or satisfying one's own needs). Hart et al. (1990) reported findings consistent with this contention in that children whose parents tend to rely on power assertive disciplinary strategies exhibit a higher incidence of instrumental rather than relational interaction strategies and are less accepted by their peers.

Negative disciplinary styles might reduce children's peer competence. Pettit and colleagues hypothesized that adverse outcomes may occur when parents' disciplinary styles are harsh or unpredictable (e.g., inconsistent use of rewards or punishment; Harrist, Pettit, Dodge, and Bates, 1994; Pettit et al., 1991). The logic behind this argument is that unpredictable discipline may cause children to feel a lack of control over outcomes which, in turn, may lead them to develop maladaptive social skills. Similarly, Patterson (1982) suggested that unpredictable family environments may predispose children toward aggression, given that aggression may be a means of arresting negative events in the environment. Alternatively, a lack of predictability may also result in social withdrawal, as in the case where children disengage from situations that they perceive as uncontrollable.

Parents who engage in intrusive, psychologically controlling forms of parental discipline may also put their children at risk for poor peer relationships. Barber (1996), for example, found that parental controlling behaviors that are thought to undermine children's autonomy and confidence, such as denigration, guilt induction, and shaming, predict higher levels of delinquent behavior as well as higher levels of anxiety, depression, and associated internalizing problems. Ladd and Ladd (1998) found that inappropriate closeness between mother and child was associated with higher levels of peer victimization in boys. Further, controlling forms of discipline may be even less adaptive when children are experiencing adjustment problems. Pettit et al. (2001) found that the negative impact of parental psychological control is exacerbated among youth who earlier had exhibited signs of maladjustment.

Researchers such as Dishion (1990) also have shown that children's—especially boys'—antisocial interaction patterns with parents are linked with peer relational difficulties, including peer rejection. Recent findings implicate both parents' and children's maladaptive behavior patterns as potential contributors to coercive interactions and subsequent child maladjustment. For example, Rubin et al. (1998) found that the combination of poor emotional regulation in toddlers and high levels of aversive control by mothers was predictive of aggressive behavior, especially in boys. Data gathered with adolescents, in contrast, revealed that parents' propensity toward undercontrolled behavior patterns (i.e., low self-restraint), especially in fathers, was linked with boys' peer problems (D'Angelo, Weinberger, and Feldman, 1995). Other studies show that boys who are coercive toward their mothers during the middle childhood years tend to be more aggressive in their interactions with peers, and that this style of peer interaction may mediate the link between child–parent coercion and peer rejection (MacKinnon et al., 1994). MacKinnon-Lewis, Rabiner, and Starnes (1999) have shown that negative mother–son interactions, in addition to being a potential staging area for aggressive behavior, may also contribute to boys' beliefs about age-mates. Boys whose mother–son interactions tend to be aversive were more likely to develop negative beliefs about peers which, along with other factors (e.g., prior peer experience), predicted aggressive behavior and peer rejection.

Thus far, research on parental discipline styles suggests that in the presence of predictable, negative (i.e., power assertive, harsh, or coercive), or unpredictable (i.e., noncontingent) disciplinary styles, children's peer relational competence may be at risk. Some progress has been made in detecting social-cognitive factors that may explain the process through which children acquire and transfer social skills and knowledge from the family to the peer context. Harsh discipline has been implicated as a potential source of maladaptive processing patterns that, in turn, may motivate children to engage in antisocial peer behavior. Similarly, some findings are consistent with the hypothesis that inductive disciplinary styles focus children on the interpersonal consequences of their misdeeds, and thereby encourage them to learn social principles that guide expectations and beliefs about how their behaviors might affect peer interactions and relationships. However, empirical support for these linkages has been modest in scope, suggesting that other potential mediating mechanisms remain to be identified. Another tenet that has received empirical support is that, when parents and children engage in coercive disciplinary interactions, children learn how to escalate oppositional behaviors (e.g., aggressiveness) and become skilled at perpetuating "coercive" cycles of interaction. Such patterns may generalize, such that children who initially learn coercive behavior patterns in disciplinary encounters with parents recreate them in peer culture as a means of resolving conflicts with peers, or as a means through which to obtain desired outcomes. Extant findings, however, suggest that this pattern of linkage is more characteristic among young boys than among young girls (see McFadyen-Ketchum et al., 1996). Thus, it remains unclear whether this premise applies equally well to older children and both genders. Clearly, further research is needed to broaden the purview of investigation on social-cognitive mechanisms, as well as other potential mediators that may account for the link between parental discipline and peer competence.

Parental Perceptions, Attitudes, and Beliefs

Along with features of the parent–child relationship, such as attachment, childrearing practices, and discipline, investigators have considered the hypothesis that parental cognitions impact children's social development, particularly if these cognitions determine how parents socialize their children's peer relationships (Ladd and Price, 1986; Mize, Pettit, and Brown, 1995; Rubin, Mills, and Rose-Krasnor, 1989). Cognitions that have received the most empirical attention include parents' perceptions of the child's social development (e.g., progress; on-time versus delayed development), their attitudes toward peer socialization tasks and relationships (e.g., importance of peer relationships for children), and their beliefs (e.g., attributions about the heritability of social behavior).

Much of the research on parents' perceptions of children's social development and peer relationships has been conducted with mothers rather than fathers, and with samples of young children (e.g., preschool and grade-school-age participants). Ladd and Price (1986) examined parents' perceptions of the difficulty associated with specific socialization tasks, including helping their child with academics and peer-related interpersonal tasks. Results showed that the level of difficulty parents ascribed to both social and academic socialization tasks correlated positively with actual child competence in these respective domains. Profilet and Ladd (1994) extended this work by investigating the linkages among parents' perceptions of children's progress in peer relationships, their concerns about children's progress, and the practices they used to socialize children's competence with peers. Results indicated that parents who saw their children as delayed in the development of interpersonal skills expressed higher levels of concern than those who rated their child's progress as normative. Moreover, parents who rated children's progress as appropriate and expressed low levels of concern were more likely to encourage their child to participate in play contacts with peers.

Mize et al. (1995) further examined the link between mothers' beliefs and perceptions about their child's peer competence and their involvement in the child's play activities with peers. When mothers saw their child as interpersonally skillful, they were less likely to engage in supervision of the child's peer-play activities. These results were interpreted as consistent with the premise that children who manifest lower levels of peer competence elicit higher levels of supervisory involvement from their mothers, rather than vice versa. Their data also indicated that children who received low-quality supervision tended to be less competent when their mothers had highly involved supervisory styles, suggesting that low-quality supervision may have negative effects on children's social competence if it is applied frequently.

In addition to these lines of investigation, other premises have guided research on the links between parents' cognitions and children's competence with peers. Putallaz et al. (1991) proposed that parents' memories of their own childhood peer experiences create a "strategy frame" or "affective lens" that shapes parental socialization practices and parenting behaviors. These investigators found that this type of influence may be strongest for parents whose memories of their own childhood reflect higher levels of anxiety; parents with anxious memories were most concerned about the need to guide their children's peer experiences. The form this guidance takes may be influenced by the gender of the child—mothers of boys were more interested in promoting positive peer experiences, whereas mothers of girls were more concerned with helping their child avoid negative peer experiences.

Beliefs about childrearing styles have also been linked with features of children's peer relationships. Parent's endorsement of practices associated with authoritative parenting correlated positively with indicators of peer competence, especially for special-needs children (i.e., those with ADHD; Hinshaw, Zupan, Simmel, Nigg, and Melnick, 1997). Rubin and colleagues (Mills and Rubin, 1990; Rubin, Hymel, Mills, and Rose-Krasnor, 1991), working from an information-processing model of parent behavior, have examined several types of parental cognitions, including beliefs about the timing of children's social development (i.e., perceptions of the timing of skill development), causes of social development (i.e., attributions of behavior as stable vs. temporary), and the importance of various socialization tasks and strategies. Efforts to test propositions from the Rubin et al. model have been focused on beliefs that were hypothesized to underlie parents' behavior in proactive and reactive socialization situations. Proactive contexts were defined as those in which parents' socialization strategies are aimed at promoting skilled child behavior or competence, whereas reactive contexts were ones in which parents' efforts are directed at the elimination or modification of inappropriate or problematic child behaviors. In one study of mothers' proactive strategies, Rubin and colleagues (1989) assessed maternal beliefs about preschoolers' skills, such as making friends, sharing, and leading or influencing others, and found that mothers attributed friendship and leadership skills to child-related causes (e.g., disposition of child) and sharing to parents' socialization efforts. Their results also indicated that mothers who tended to value skill development were more likely to have children who were successful at problem solving and peer interaction (i.e., prosocial and assertive skills in preschool classrooms). For reactive socialization contexts, Rubin and colleagues (Mills and Rubin, 1990; Rubin et al., 1989) found that mothers tended to attribute problem behaviors such as aggression and withdrawal to transient factors (e.g., children's moods or a "stage") rather than stable child dispositions. In further research with toddlers, Hastings and Rubin (1999) found that both mothers' and children's characteristics may antecede later maternal beliefs about children's aggressive and withdrawn social behavior. Results showed that mothers of aggressive toddlers who espoused authoritarian childrearing attitudes more often reported high-control and angry reactions and were more likely to blame their children for aggressive behavior.

Other investigators (e.g., Dix and Lochman, 1989; Melson, Ladd, and Hsu, 1993) have suggested that parents possess a "positivity bias" in that they tend to attribute their successes at easier socialization tasks to factors in the child (e.g., child skills) and failures at difficult socialization tasks to unstable causes or factors in the parent (e.g., parental incompetence). This positivity bias may influence parents' reactions to children's social difficulties. Parents who take responsibility for negative child behaviors (i.e., believe child behavior is under the parent's control) are less likely to react to problematic child behaviors in negative or punitive ways (Dix and Lochman, 1989). Conversely, Nix et al. (1999) concluded that mothers who expect negative behavior from children may respond more harshly in discipline situations and, in turn, maintain or exacerbate children's problem behaviors. Similarly, Bugental and colleagues (see Bugental and Happaney, in Vol. 3 of this *Handbook*) have shown that, when adults see themselves as having little control over problematic childrearing encounters and attribute greater control to the child, their responses to the child are more likely to be negative (Bugental, Blue, and Cruzcosa, 1989) or even harsh and punitive (Bugental, Lewis, Lin, Lyon, and Kopeikin, 1999). Bugental, Blue, and Lewis (1990) have also shown that mothers of "difficult" (e.g., unresponsive) children are not only more likely to believe that their child has greater control over problematic childrearing, but also respond to such children with higher levels of dysphoric affect.

Thus, there is a growing body of evidence to suggest that parents' perceptions, attitudes, and beliefs about children's social development, and parents' estimations of their ability to influence children's social competence, are associated with children's success in peer relationships. As might be expected, much of this evidence indicates that parents report higher levels of concern and lower levels of parenting self-efficacy when their children manifest actual or perceived social difficulties, such as delays, deficiencies, or impairments in social competence. It would also appear that the norm may be for parents to "frame" negative child behaviors or explain children's social difficulties in ways that do not impugn the child, or preclude the possibility that children will attain higher levels of social competence through continued development or additional socialization. However, this kind of "positivity bias" may be less apparent in extreme situations, such as when parents have a strong propensity toward debilitating cognitions (e.g., believe that they have little control over their lives or children) or when a child tends to be highly unresponsive to caregiving or have serious and chronic behavior problems.

Interpretation of these empirical associations is hindered by the fact that little is known about how these cognitive constructs come to be linked with observable aspects of children's peer competence and relationships. Extant findings tend to be interpreted as evidence indicating that parents' perceptions, beliefs, and attitudes are determinants of their behavior and socialization practices which, in turn, affect children's social competence (i.e., a parent-effects interpretation). Yet, with few noteable exceptions (see Mize et al., 1995), little evidence has been assembled that supports or refutes the direction of effect implied by these hypotheses, such as data showing that parents' beliefs guide their socialization practices or, conversely, that children's interpersonal ineptitude causes parents to change their childrearing beliefs. Because of this evidentiary deficiency, very little can be inferred about the role of parents' cognitions in the development of children's peer relationships. Thus, a great deal remains to be learned about how parents' cognitions influence their behaviors and how these elements, in turn, influence children's skills and competence with peers.

Family Environment

Of the investigators who have researched the potential effects of the family environment on children's peer competence, many have attempted to explicate the association between stressors in the family environment and children's development (see Crnic and Low, in Vol. 5 of this *Handbook*; Crnic and Greenberg, 1990; Cummings and Cummings, 1988; Weinraub and Wolf, 1983). It has been hypothesized that stressors that impinge on the family environment, and those that occur within this context, may have negative effects on children's development. Stressors impacting parents, for example, have been associated with withdrawal, acting out, and aggression among children (Felner, Stolberg, and Cowen, 1975; Kantor, 1965), and may place them at risk for decreased social competence, antisocial behavior, low academic achievement, and increased likelihood of peer rejection (Cowen, Lotyczewski, and Weissberg, 1984; Garmezy, Masten, and Tellegen, 1984; Sandler and Ramsey, 1980).

Stressors that affect the family environment have been distinguished by duration or length of exposure and have typically been classified as chronic or acute. Chronic stressors imply that families are exposed to negative conditions over substantial periods of time, whereas acute stressors are often construed as negative "life events," or negative experiences that may be intense but of brief or temporary duration. Both forms of stressors have been described as factors that may impact negatively the ability of the family to function as a socializing context for children (Patterson, Griesler, Vaden, and Kupersmidt, 1992). Investigators have also studied "daily hassles" as a third type of stressor that embodies minor, transient negative experiences (i.e., everyday irritants; see Crnic and Greenberg, 1990; Crnic and Low, in Vol. 5 of this *Handbook*). The degree to which parental hassles affect child socialization may be related to both the quantity of hassles that are present in the family environment and the frequency with which they occur, as well as the extent to which they involve the child (e.g., hassles associated with parenting versus everyday adult-related hassles; see Crnic and Acevedo, 1995; Crnic and Low, in Vol. 5 of this *Handbook*).

Chronic stressors.   Research on chronic stressors has focused primarily on economic depriva-tion, which has been viewed as a potential cause of both family dysfunction and children's adjustment problems (see Magnuson and Duncan, in Vol. 4 of this *Handbook*). More extreme forms of poverty, such as homelessness (see Buckner, Bassuk, Weinreb, and Brooks, 1999), have been linked with internalizing problems in children, which may well impair their functioning among peers. Conger and colleagues (Conger et al., 1990; Conger and Elder, 1994), for example, have argued that financial stressors negatively impact family processes and relationships which, in turn, increase the probability of dysfunction in children. There is also evidence to suggest that children from low-income families experience a greater need for group inclusion and are more emotionally vulnerable and sensitive to reactions from peers (Elder, 1974). Consistent with these premises, results from several studies suggest that children from low-income families tend to be less popular with peers (Dishion, 1990; Patterson et al., 1990; Roff, Sells, and Golden, 1972). Results reported by Patterson, Vaden, and Kupersmidt (1991) further revealed that children from low-income families are less likely to have peer companionship in school and are more likely to be socially isolated in activities outside of school. Pettit, Bates, and Dodge (1997) found that three indexes of family adversity (SES, stress, and single-parent status), assessed prior to children's entrance into kindergarten predicted lower levels of social skillfulness in Grade 6 after controlling for kindergarten social skillfulness and adjustment. The negative impact of family adversity was attenuated, however, for children who had supportive (e.g., warm and involved) parents.

   Another consequence of economic deprivation may be restricted mobility, or the inability of the family to provide children with frequent and safe access to peers. Ladd, Hart, Wadsworth, and Golter (1988) investigated the effects of economic stability (i.e., higher income levels and dual-wage-earning families) on preschoolers' peer activities. Children from families with higher incomes were found to spend more time playing in peers' homes, possibly due to safer neighborhoods, higher availability of transportation, or increased parental availability to arrange opportunities for peer contacts.

Acute stressors.   Historically, researchers have attempted to estimate the association between acute stressors and indices of dysfunction in adolescents and adults, such as self-esteem and life sat-isfaction (Greenberg, Seigel, and Leitch, 1983), psychiatric symptomology (Barrera, 1981; Compas, Howell, Phares, Williams, and Ledoux, 1989), and self-destructive tendencies, delinquency, drug abuse, violence, anxiety, depression, and academic performance (Barrera, 1981; Gersten, Langner, Eisenberg, and Orzeck, 1974; Mullins, Seigel, and Hodges, 1985). Increasingly, however, investi-gators have considered the possibility that acute stressors within the family impair children's social development. Holahan and Moos (1987) found that acute stressors correlated with indicators of chil-dren's social and emotional competence, including anxiety, negative affect, emotional difficulties, peer difficulties, and discipline problems at school. Similarly, Crnic and Greenberg (1990) concluded that parental stress contributes significantly to child social competence, with increased stress associ-ated with more behavioral problems and lower social competence. Extending this work, Patterson and colleagues (1991, 1992) evaluated the relation between chronic and acute life stressors and children's peer competence and found that the "effects" were cumulative—the greater the number of stressors, the higher the risk of peer rejection. These findings corroborated research by Garmezy (1985), who found that, as the stressors in children's lives increased, the quality of their peer interactions and classroom behavior decreased.

Among the other acute family stressors that have been investigated are divorce and marital discord (see Wilson and Gottman, in Vol. 4 of this *Handbook*). The accumulated evidence suggests that these stressors affect children's overall psychological health and functioning (see Cummings, Iannotti, and Zahn-Waxler, 1985; Grych and Fincham, 1990; Long, Forehand, Fauber, and Brody, 1987). However, far less is known about how divorce and marital discord may affect children's relationships with peers (see Grych and Fincham, 1990). Data gathered by Hetherington, Cox, and Cox (1979) followed children for two years after their parents were divorced and found that, compared to boys from stable households, those from divorced families were more hostile and aggressive in peer interactions, and more disliked by peers. Girls from divorced families, in contrast, did not differ from their stable-family counterparts in peer competence or liking. Contrary to these findings, Long et al. (1987) found that, among adolescents, both boys and girls from divorced households reported significantly lower perceived social competence. These discrepancies point to possible gender- and age-related differences in children's response to divorce, and further illustrate that the impact of divorce on children's peer relationships is not fully understood.

Findings resembling those reported in the divorce literature are evident in studies designed to explore the effects of marital discord on children's peer relationships (see Block, Block, and Gjerde, 1986). Gottman and Katz (1989) hypothesized that children exposed to marital discord would exhibit higher levels of negative affect and less mature play styles with peers. Initial results suggested that this relation may be mediated, in part, by parenting style, leading the investigators to suggest that couples who were maritally distressed may display an unresponsive and permissive parenting style, which children may respond to with noncompliant behavior, less mature play, and increased negative interactions with peers. Subsequent findings have shown that children who have been exposed to conflictual marital relationships or child abuse tend to be more oppositional in their peer interactions and less successful at forming friendships (Katz and Gottman, 1993; Parker and Herrera, 1996).

Minor stressors.   Researchers have begun to evaluate the effects of minor stressors such as daily hassles (i.e., everyday irritants and problems; see Crnic and Low, in Vol. 5 of this *Handbook*) on child outcomes, and a number of important findings have been obtained. Patterson (1983), for example, found that daily hassles predict maternal irritable behavior during parent–child interaction, which in turn predicts children's use of aggression. Similarly, data gathered by Crnic and Greenberg (1990) revealed that hassles associated with parenting correlate with more frequent child behavior problems and lower levels of child social competence.

Although still far from complete, research on the family environment and children's peer relationships supports the conclusion that family stress may exert a deleterious effect on children's social competence. Moreover, there is some support for the contention that children's social dysfunctions are exacerbated under conditions where they are exposed to chronic or multiple stressors. Alternative hypotheses, especially those that embody the possibility of an opposing direction of effect, have yet to be formulated or investigated. However, it does not seem implausible that children's social difficulties function as stressors for their parents' with the consequence of disrupting parent–child interactions or other family processes.

Other premises that are central to this research domain have been less well investigated. Although it has been hypothesized that external stressors such as poverty may disrupt family functioning in ways that impact children's social competence, the mechanisms through which this may occur are still poorly understood (although, see Conger et al., 1990). Chronic stress may, for example, adversely influence parenting styles and parent–child interactions (Gottman and Katz, 1989), reduce parent involvement in childrearing or play activities (Pettit et al., 1996), cause parents to increase their use of harsh disciplinary practices or impair other aspects of the parent–child relationship (e.g., secure attachment). It is also possible that chronic stress may preclude or alter the quality of many "direct" parental influences on children's social competence, which are reviewed in later sections of this chapter (e.g., parental "management" of children's peer activities).

Also important is the need to understand whether different types of stressors (e.g., chronic versus acute versus minor stressors) are associated with different aspects of parent or family functioning, and whether these distal and proximal processes differentially impact specific facets of children's social competence. Equally important is the question of whether potential stress inhibitors or moderators (i.e., parents' or children's social support systems) buffer the effects of family stressors on children's peer relationships and competence.

Family Pathology

In this section, the potential effects of parental disorders on children's peer competence are considered. Disorders such as depression and child abuse (for reviews see Beardslee, Bemporal, Keller, and Klerman, 1983; Cicchetti, Lynch, Shonk, and Manly, 1992; Downey and Coyne, 1990; Forehand, McCombs, and Brody, 1987; Zahn-Waxler et al., 1992) have received the most empirical attention and, thus, serve as focal points for our review.

Parental depression. Parental depression is a type of affective disorder that has been linked to various forms of child pathology, such as aggressive or withdrawn behavior, and depression (see Rubin and Burgess, in Vol. of this *Handbook*; Zahn-Waxler, Cummings, McKnew, and Radke-Yarrow, 1984; Zahn-Waxler, Duggal, and Gruber, in Vol. 4 of this *Handbook*). A number of investigators have reported links between parental depression and socially withdrawn behavior in children (Baldwin, Cole, and Baldwin, 1982; Billings and Moos, 1985; Neale and Weintraub, 1975; Rolf, 1972; Weintraub, Prinz, and Neale, 1978). Zahn-Waxler et al. (1984) showed that children of manic-depressive parents not only had more difficulty maintaining peer interactions and controlling aggressive behavior, but also exhibited lower levels of prosocial behavior.

The means by which parental depression affects children are still unknown. However, five primary pathways have been suggested (Zahn-Waxler et al., 1984) to account for transmission of depression:

(1) Children may adopt the negative emotion of the parent through continued exposure.
(2) Depressed parents may withdraw from the child, rendering an insecure attachment.
(3) Depressed parents may foster learned helplessness in children as a result of traumatic parent–child interactions.
(4) Depression may be biologically transmitted (yet unspecified).
(5) Depression may impact parents' childrearing styles, causing the parent to employ poor socialization practices.

Moreover, subsequent work by Zahn-Waxler and colleagues (1992) suggests that, in part, the depression-related difficulties children display (e.g., inability to sustain peer interactions) may stem from attentional deficits and social-cognitive dysfunctions in the child (e.g., negative self-concept and negative attributional styles). They have further hypothesized that these child outcomes may be acquired from parents' social-communicative styles, behavioral displays, and spousal relationships, but qualified their hypothesis by arguing that the extent of the parents' impact may depend on risk and protective factors in the child's environment (i.e., child temperament and severity of parents' depression).

Child abuse. Children who are maltreated by parents grow up in a context that is not favorable to peer interaction and relationships (see Garbarino and Gilliam, 1980; Garbarino, Vorrasi, and Kostelny, in Vol. 5 of this *Handbook*; Wolfe, 1987) and is often characterized by high levels of conflict, control, and power assertive discipline (Parke and Collmer, 1975; Trickett and Kuczynski, 1986; Wolfe, 1985). In addition, abused children typically have fewer psychological resources and social supports at their disposal (Cicchetti and Carlson, 1989; Garbarino and Gilliam, 1980; Pelton,

1978; Wolfe, 1985, 1987) and often exhibit signs of emotional disturbance (Cicchetti and Carlson, 1989; Wolfe, 1985).

In the peer context, investigators have found that abused children tend to act aggressively toward peers and, in particular, manifest elevated levels of instrumental aggression (i.e., aggression performed as a means toward and end; see George and Main, 1979; Haskett and Kistner, 1991) or verbal aggression (Troy and Sroufe, 1987). There is also evidence to suggest that abused children respond to peer-initiated interactions in maladaptive ways; compared to nonabused children, they are more likely to aggress against (Howes and Eldredge, 1985; Howes and Espinosa, 1985; Main and George, 1985) or withdraw from peers' friendly overtures (George and Main, 1979).

Children's competence with agemates has been shown to vary with the timing, form, and severity of parental maltreatment. Bolger, Patterson, and Kupersmidt (1998) found that children who were emotionally maltreated, especially early in development, appeared to have difficulty forming friendships. In families where children were physically abused, especially chronically so, children appeared to form close friendships but had difficulty maintaining them over time. In contrast, parental neglect was associated with children's social isolation or infrequent contact with peers. Even more important, however, was the duration of maltreatment. The chronicity of maltreatment was found to predict peer dysfunction independent of the type of abuse.

Other studies suggest that abusive family conditions are linked with another form of child abuse—victimization at the hands of peers. Schwartz, Dodge, Pettit, and Bates (1997) found that aggressive male victims had family histories that included physical harm by family members, harsh disciplinary styles, and exposure to violence between adults in the home. Thus, children's vulnerability to peer victimization, particularly among boys, may stem from parents' use of violent, abusive practices in the home.

The question of how abuse affects the quality of children's peer relationships has not been well investigated, but a number of propositions have been advanced to guide research on this topic. Cicchetti and Rizley (1981) have argued that the behavioral and emotional difficulties experienced by maltreated children are the result of poor parent–child relationships and socialization (e.g., maladaptive parenting style and insecure attachment). Another contention is that abusive parental relationships cause children to develop aberrant "working models" (e.g., dysfunctional relationship expectations, schemes, or self-perceptions; Belsky, 1984; Belsky and Vondra, 1989) that lead them to mistrust peers and decrease their ability to develop and perform competent peer-related behavior (Carlson, Cicchetti, Barnett, and Braunwald, 1989; Cicchetti et al., 1992).

However, it may be the case that the links between abuse and dysfunctional peer relationships are not as general as these formulations suggest. Rather, the mediating processes that account for such linkages may be specific to the form of maltreatment that children have experienced. Bolger et al. (1998), for example, proposed that physical abuse lowers children's self-esteem which, in turn, motivates compensatory reactions such as seeking close ties with friends who are expected to affirm their worth. Emotional maltreatment, because it conveys parental rejection, is thought to promote wariness or defensive reactions toward relationships, causing children to avoid or mistrust close ties with peers. Neglecting parents, who are often socially isolated, may bring about the same consequence for their children because they do little to involve their children in play activities or nurture peer relationships.

In summary, the available evidence suggests that children who are exposed to parental disorders or maltreatment within the family environment are likely to exhibit social difficulties in the peer context. Recent findings contradict the assumption that neither parental dysfunction or maltreatment are unitary constructs; rather, it would appear that both concepts embody a range of processes that may be differentially linked with indicators of children's success in peer relationships. Theoretically, some progress has been made toward identifying the processes that may mediate the links between these features of the family environment and children's peer relationships, but much work remains to be done to elucidate these processes empirically. Among the processes that appear to deserve further attention as potential mediators are parents' peer-socialization practices and children's internal working models of relationships, self-perceptions (e.g., self-esteem), interpersonal schema (e.g., beliefs about peers and rejection sensitivity), and social skills.

Thus far, evidence linking parenting and family processes with children's social competence has been reviewed for one set of constructs that can be conceptualized as *indirect parental influences*. Included among these processes were those that occur as part of family life, and for the most part, derive from relationships and dynamics that are internal to the family system rather than external to it, such as within the child's peer environment. Thus, the constructs (and attendant processes) within each of the foregoing sections (i.e., attachment, childrearing styles, parental perceptions, attitudes and beliefs, family environment, and family pathology) were considered indirect influences on children's peer relationships because they are processes that are specific to the family (they typically occur within the family, involve only family members) and are not motivated by or performed to assist children with contexts or persons that lie outside the family (e.g., the peer culture). Attachment, for example, was considered an indirect parental influence because the construct refers to a relationship that develops between the parent and child, quite independently of peers. Yet, as was seen, developments that were hypothesized to occur within this aspect of the parent–child relationship, such as the emergence of the child's internal working model, were construed as mechanisms that might organize the child's interpersonal actions and reactions in other relational contexts, such the peer group or in friendships with agemates.

Considered next are "direct parental influences," or aspects of parenting that transpire in the family context or with family members but are predicated on children's actual or anticipated experiences in the peer milieu, or parents' perceptions of the child's needs in this context. Thus, direct modes of influence encompass parents' efforts to socialize or "manage" children's social development, especially as it pertains to the peer context.

DIRECT PARENTAL INFLUENCES AND CHILDERN'S PEERS

It has been proposed that parents not only socialize their children's peer relationships indirectly, but also directly as "managers" of children's and adolescents' peer relationships (Hart et al., 1998; Ladd, Le Sieur, and Profilet, 1993; Mounts, 2000). Ladd, Profilet, and Hart (1992) posited that parents "manage" various aspects of their children's social lives whether they intend to or not, and these inputs may have different effects on children's social development. As a heuristic tool, Ladd et al. (1993) classified parents' management behaviors into four "roles": parent as designer, mediator, supervisor, and advisor or consultant. Also considered in this review is the potential confluence of direct parental influences, or the possibility that parents engage in multiple forms of management simultaneously or contingently. In the sections that follow, these roles are defined and the empirical status of each is reviewed.

Parent as Designer

Parents act as designers when they seek to control or influence the settings in which children meet and interact with peers. As designers, parents may influence children's access to peers through their choice of neighborhoods, schools, child care or after-school care arrangements, and community activities.

Choice of neighborhood. Neighborhoods, unless dangerous or bereft of families, provide diverse locations (e.g., yards, vacant lots, and playgrounds) for children to meet and interact with peers (see Bradley, in Vol. 2 of this *Handbook*). Young children spend much of their time in neighborhoods, and their social opportunities are affected by its topography and demographic features (Garbarino and Gilliam, 1980). Friends tend to live near each other (Gallagher, 1958; Segoe, 1939), although this relation appears to be moderated by age changes in children's autonomy and mobility (DeVault, 1957). Contact with peers is more common in neighborhoods with sidewalks and playgrounds, and in flat locales as compared to hilly ones. In contrast, homes that are widely spaced, physically isolated, or inaccessible appear to restrict children's mobility and peer contacts (Berg and Medrich, 1980; Medrich, Roizen, Rubin, and Buckley, 1982).

In densely populated neighborhoods, as compared to rural settings, children have more play contacts and larger peer networks (Medrich et al., 1982; van Vliet, 1981). Similarly, peer contacts are more frequent when children live in safe rather than dangerous neighborhoods (Cochran and Riley, 1988), and neighborhood quality may affect other family inputs (e.g., "indirect" influences; see Garbarino, Vorrasi, and Kostelny, in Vol. 5 of this *Handbook*). Attar, Guerra, and Tolan (1994) and Kupersmidt, Griesler, DeRosier, Patterson, and Davis (1995) found that the negative effects of family stressors on children's peer relationships were exacerbated when families resided in dangerous neighborhoods.

Choice of child care and early schooling. Prior to formal schooling, parents in the United States can choose whether their children attend preschool or childcare programs. Higher quality preschool environments have been linked with gains in peer sociability (Finkelstein, Dent, Gallagher, and Ramey, 1978) and the development of stable friendships (Howes, 1983, 1988). In contrast, Vandell, Henderson, and Wilson (1988) found that children in lower quality programs spent more time in nonsocial behaviors, had lower levels of positive, friendly interactions, and were less adjusted to school. The benefits of preschool experience also appear to vary with the stability of children's enrollment and the consistency of their playmates. Mueller and Brenner (1977) found that boys who became familiar with their playmates developed more sophisticated play skills than boys who did not. Similarly, Howes (1988) found that children who entered preschool at earlier ages and remained in stable contexts developed more sophisticated play skills and had less difficulty with peers.

The potential benefits of preschool are also illustrated in studies of children's adjustment to grade school. Ladd and Price (1987) found that preschoolers' prosocial skills predicted their peer acceptance in kindergarten. Further, Ladd (1990) discovered that children who maintained friendships across the transition from preschool to kindergarten tended to develop more favorable attitudes toward grade school.

After-school care arrangements. As children enter elementary school, many families must rely on nonparental care arrangements—including self-care—in the after-school hours. The extent to which these arrangements forecast subsequent child adjustment has been a topic of increasing interest among researchers and policy makers (Vandell and Posner, 1999). When investigating nonparental care, researchers have tended to focus on children's level of involvement in differing arrangements, or on program quality and time use within particular arrangements. Pettit, Laird, Bates, and Dodge (1997) examined the amount of time children spent in a variety of after-school arrangements and found that higher self-care (i.e., time before and after school without adult supervision) in Grades 1 and 3 was associated with lower teacher-rated peer competence with peers in Grade 6. These relationships were significant after controlling for kindergarten peer competence and socioeconomic status, and were consistent with prior findings linking the amount of unsupervised self-care with children's social-emotional difficulties (e.g., Galambos and Maggs, 1991; Steinberg, 1986).

Time use analyses have shown that how children spend their after-school hours also has implications for their peer relationships and competence. Pierce, Hamm, and Vandell (1999) examined children's experiences in after-school programs and found that program flexibility was positively related to boys' social skills. In a survey of after-school activity patterns and social contacts, Posner and Vandell (1994) reported that school-age children's antisocial behavior increased in self-care arrangements, but decreased in formal, adult-supervised arrangements. Similarly, Pettit, Bates, Dodge, and Meece (1999) found that adolescent's unsupervised peer contact was associated with subsequent externalizing behavior problems, but only when parental monitoring was low and preexisting behavior problems were high. On the one hand, these findings corroborate the inference that developmentally appropriate, adult-supervised after-school experiences foster the development of social competence. On the other hand, it appears that social and behavioral adjustment problems tend to increase when children spend large amounts of unsupervised time with peers after school.

Participation in community activities. A small but growing body of evidence indicates that the extent to which children make use of peer-oriented community settings (e.g., parks, libraries, and pools) and participate in community activities (e.g., clubs, scouting, and sports) is associated with childhood social competence. Ladd and Price (1987) found that preschoolers who regularly met peers in settings such as the library, pool, and church school were less anxious and had fewer absences in kindergarten. Based on an in-depth survey of school-age children's neighborhood supports, Bryant (1985) concluded that unstructured community activities help children develop greater autonomy, control, and mastery, and that these developments tended to foster perspective-taking skills. Similarly, school-age children's participation in extracurricular activities (e.g., scouts, music lessons, and organized sports) has been linked with social and school adjustment (Eccles and Barber, 1999) and appears to serve a protective function for behavior problems and school dropout (Mahoney and Cairns, 1997). Adult-supervised after-school activities may foster a greater commitment or connection to conventional social institutions, as well as provide children with opportunities to expand their social networks. And, for children growing up in dangerous neighborhoods or for families that provide little supervision, involvement in such activities also may lessen the likelihood of getting into trouble because more of children's after-school discretionary time is filled with constructive activity (see Pettit et al., 1997).

Thus, whether through active or passive choices, parents "design" or structure many aspects of their children's physical and social surroundings. To the extent that these ecologies create opportunities for children to meet and engage in constructive activities with age-mates, they may become an important staging areas for the development of social skills, peer relationships, and interpersonal competence. Because much of the evidence gathered on parents as designers of social environments is descriptive, more research is needed to expand our understanding of this role and its contributions to children's social development.

Parent as Mediator

As mediators, parents serve as a "bridge" between the family and the world of peers by helping children meet peers, arrange "play dates," and build a social network. They also influence the parameters of play dates by teaching children how to initiate peer activities, structure the play setting, and regulate the frequency with which children see particular play partners. To date, investigation of this managerial activity has been limited to two mediational roles: parental initiation of informal play contacts and sponsorship of informal play groups.

Initiating informal peer contacts. Evidence gathered with young children suggests that some parents involve their children in informal peer contacts at a very early age. Ladd et al. (1988) surveyed parents' management practices during early childhood and found that parental initiations were common for both toddlers and preschoolers. In families where parents arranged informal peer contacts, children tended to spend more time playing in peers' homes suggesting that young children's social ties are more likely to extend beyond the family when their parents actively initiate peer contacts.

Ladd and Golter (1988) found that children whose parents initiated peer contacts, as compared to those who did not, had a larger number of playmates and more consistent play companions in their preschool peer networks. After the transition to kindergarten, boys from these same families tended to become better liked by their classmates, suggesting that boys benefited more than girls from this form of parental management. In an extension of the Ladd and Golter study, Ladd and Hart (1992) obtained a larger sample of preschoolers and assessed parental initiations over a longer time period. Parents who performed more initiations were found to have children who displayed more prosocial behavior and less nonsocial behavior at school. As before, the frequency of parental initiations correlated positively classroom peer acceptance for boys but not for girls. Similarly, in a study of German families, Krappman (1986) found that grade schoolers whose parents took an active role in arranging and organizing their peer relationships tended to develop more harmonious ties with peers.

By late preschool, it appears that parents share the responsibility for arranging informal peer contacts with their children. Bhavnagri and Parke (1991) and Ladd and Hart (1992) found that older as compared to younger preschoolers initiated more of their own play dates, and Bhavnagri and Parke found that older preschoolers also received a larger number of play overtures from peers. Findings from the Ladd and Hart study (1992) provide some insight into how this transition might occur. Children of parents who involved them in the *process* of arranging informal play activities (e.g., assisting the parent with play arrangements) more often initiated their own play dates. Some parents it would appear do more than simply arrange play activities—they also scaffold, or help children master the interpersonal skills needed to manage their own peer activities. Children who develop this kind of autonomy may be better equipped to succeed with peers in extrafamilial contexts.

Sponsoring or involving children in informal play groups. Parents not only initiate play dates with individual peers they also create opportunities for children to participate in peer groups. In play groups, children may acquire skills that are needed to cope with large-group dynamics, as might be found in classrooms and on playgrounds. With young children, parents may sponsor informal play groups in the home, or arrange for children to participate in play groups that are supervised by other caregivers (e.g., a peer's parent). Although few investigators have researched the extent to which parents sponsor informal play groups, there is some evidence to suggest that play groups enhance children's social competence.

Lieberman (1977) assessed preschooler's experience in informal peer groups during home interviews and found that this experience correlated positively with children's social competence in laboratory play sessions. Other findings (Ladd et al., 1988) suggest that older preschoolers derive greater benefits from play-group experience; in this study, the extent of children's play-group experience and their social competence in preschool were more closely linked for preschoolers than for toddlers.

In sum, it would appear that parents' mediational strategies may be aimed at multiple socialization objectives (see Bhavnagri and Parke, 1991; Ladd and Coleman, 1993; Ladd and Hart, 1992; Lollis, Ross, and Tate, 1992), including helping children to: (1) find playmates and build a peer network, (2) initiate and arrange play opportunities, (3) form and maintain relationships with specific peers, and (4) negotiate differing peer contexts (e.g., dyadic versus group settings). At present, more is known about some aspects of parental mediation (e.g., parental initiation of informal peer contacts) than others. Further research is needed to clarify when children profit from this type of parental assistance and how parental mediation impacts specific forms of child competence (e.g., prosocial skills and friendship formation). Also, too little is known about the antecedents of parents' mediational strategies. Parents' attempts to mediate children's peer relationships may be motivated by factors such as their perceptions of their child's social needs and characteristics, their childrearing goals and beliefs, their perceptions of playmate characteristics, and family policies or values (see Ladd et al., 1992).

Parent as Supervisor

Supervision is defined as parents' efforts to oversee and regulate children's ongoing interactions, activities, and relationships with peers. Thus far, researchers have drawn distinctions between the parent's involvement and participation in children's peer interactions as a means of identifying three basic types of supervision: interactive intervention, directive intervention, and monitoring.

Interactive intervention. Lollis and colleagues (1992) defined interactive intervention as the parent's attempts to proactively supervise children's peer interactions from within the play context (e.g., as active participants in the children's play). Lollis et al. argued that this style of supervision best fits the social novice (e.g., very young children) who must, to some extent, rely on a more skillful partner to help them construct and carry out social interactions with peers. When included as participants in children's play, parents are in a position to "scaffold" even the most basic aspects of social interaction, such as maintaining children's interest in peers, shaping the behaviors children direct toward peers, encouraging synchrony or reciprocity during interactions, and preventing or resolving conflicts.

In an early study, Bhavnagri and Parke (1985) compared toddlers' social skills when mothers were present to facilitate peer-play and when children played alone with a peer. Toddlers social skills were more advanced when mothers were present to guide them, but returned to baseline when mothers withdrew from the play context. Moreover, toddlers' gains in competence correlated positively with mothers' skillfulness as supervisors. Lollis (1990) observed child–peer interactions during brief separation periods (without their mothers) after they had first participated in a play group where mothers were discouraged from providing interactive supervision, or in a group in which mothers were encouraged to interact with children. After their mother's departure, children in the interactive intervention condition were less distressed and spent more time playing with peers. Bhavnagri and Parke (1991) extended these findings by showing that fathers and mothers were equally effective as supervisors and that their influence varied with the age of the child. Toddlers appeared to derive greater benefit from parents' interactive interventions than did preschoolers.

In summary, it would appear that parents' interactive interventions facilitate children's competence at basic interpersonal tasks such as initiating and maintaining interactions with peers. Existing evidence supports the contention that younger children (e.g., infants and toddlers) derive greater benefit from this form of supervision than do older children (e.g., preschoolers).

Directive intervention. This form supervision is less proximal and participatory than interactive intervention because parents typically operate from outside the context of children's play (e.g., as observers rather than as participants) and intervene only sporadically in children's interactions. Lollis and colleagues (1992) contended that directive interventions tend to be reactive (i.e., performed in response to play events) rather than proactive forms of supervision, and arise from parents' assessments of play situations, problem behaviors (e.g., conflict), or children's lack of responsiveness to prior supervision.

Levitt, Weber, Clark, and McDonnell (1985) examined mothers' directive interventions and toddlers' sharing behavior in situations where toddlers could monopolize or share toys with an unfamiliar peer. Mothers were told not to intervene until their child had played with the toys for several minutes, and then only if the child had not spontaneously shared with the peer. None of the children shared toys prior to maternal intervention, but the majority did so following prompts by their mothers. Children who shared in response to their mothers' prompts were more likely to receive similar bids from peers (i.e., reciprocated sharing). Ross, Tesla, Kenyon, and Lollis (1991) observed pairs of unfamiliar toddlers during a series of play sessions in which mothers were encouraged to supervise children's interactions but not participate in their play. Analyses showed that mothers' interventions were often used to deflect children's conflicts and were typically aimed at their child rather than the playmate. In subsequent analyses, Lollis et al. (1992) discovered that, during supervision of older children and boys, mothers' interventions were more verbal and explicit and contained a larger number of goals and strategies. Perlman and Ross (1997) expanded this line of research to young children's fights with siblings to elucidate the conditions under which parents intervene in conflicts and whether children's behavior changed following parental intervention. They found that parents most often intervened during intense and persistent fights (e.g., no sign of deescalation) and that children used fewer power-oriented strategies and more sophisticated forms of negotiation after parental interventions. The latter finding was interpreted as evidence that parental interventions may be an impetus for the development of children's conflict resolution skills.

Research on directive intervention has also been conducted with older preschool samples. Finnie and Russell (1988) paired children with differing peer reputations (e.g., popular, unpopular, and average) with average-status partners for 12-minute play sessions. Mothers were asked to supervise (and intervene with) the children's play as needed. Mothers of low-status children were more likely to avoid the supervisory role and, compared to mothers of high-status children, less likely to implement interventions that might improve the quality of children's play. Using a telephone-log methodology, Ladd and Golter (1988) distinguished between parents of older preschoolers who tended to rely on interactive versus directive interventions. Children whose parents typically used directive interventions tended to develop higher levels of peer acceptance in kindergarten than those whose parents tended to rely on interactive interventions. Based on these findings, Mize and Ladd (1990) speculated that, whereas interactive supervision may benefit toddlers, use of this form of supervision with preschoolers might interfere with their ability to develop autonomous and self-regulated play skills.

Monitoring. As children move beyond the preschool years, parents increasingly rely on distal forms of supervision to assess children's peer activities. The end product of such distal supervision has been termed monitoring, which most researchers have defined in terms of parents' knowledge or awareness of children's whereabouts or activities. There is now an extensive literature linking low levels of parental monitoring with a wide array of social and academic difficulties in childhood and, especially, adolescence (Dishion and McMahon, 1998).

During middle childhood, parental monitoring has been linked with children's social and academic competence. Crouter, MacDermid, McHale, and Perry-Jenkins (1990) found that boys who were not well monitored performed less well in school and exhibited conduct problems. Other evidence suggests that the relation between parental monitoring and children's competence is moderated by contextual factors, such as neighborhood safety (Coley and Hoffman, 1996). In high-crime neighborhoods, children with lower social and academic skills tend to be monitored more closely than children who exhibit higher levels of competence. Perhaps in dangerous contexts, parents must disproportionately monitor children who are at risk versus developing normally. It may also be the case the monitoring serves a stronger protective function for children who evidence greater vulnerability under adverse circumstances (Pettit et al., 1999).

There also is evidence that monitoring-relevant constructs are predictive of adolescents' peer relationships. Dishion (1990) assessed several aspects of parental supervision, including whether the adolescent's activities were supervised by parents', the adolescent's perceptions of parents' supervisory rules, and the time parents and adolescents spent together on a daily basis. Analyses performed on composites formed from these measures revealed that, in two separate cohorts, monitoring correlated positively with children's peer acceptance.

Recently it has been asserted that "monitoring" implies that parents actively seek information as a way of becoming more knowledgeable about their teens' whereabouts and companions (Stattin and Kerr, 2000). Most researchers who have investigated this construct, however, have assessed monitoring strictly in terms of what parents know, not how they came to know it (e.g., Crouter et al., 1990; Fletcher, Darling, and Steinberg, 1995). In an effort to understand how parents get such knowledge, Kerr and Stattin (2000) collected questionnaire data from a large sample of Swedish 14-year-old children and their parents. Included were questions about parents' solicitation of information, parents' implementation of controls and restrictions, and teens' disclosure of information. The latter was most strongly associated with parents' "knowledge" and the teens' adjustment. Of particular interest was the finding that only child disclosure was associated with teens' reports of deviant friendships (i.e., teens with deviant friends were less disclosing).

Additional findings reported by Stattin and Kerr (2000) illuminate the multifaceted nature of the monitoring construct. In one set of results, active parental solicitation of information—a strategy expected to underpin parental awareness and knowledge—was associated with adolescent maladjustment once child disclosure had been controlled. This finding suggests that parents' efforts to extract information from teens about their activities and companions may have the unintended result of encouraging their involvement in antisocial activities. It also is possible, of course, that parents who engaged in high levels of solicitation did so, at least in part, because their teens exhibited adjustment problems. Other findings may further explicate the developmental course of "hands-on" supervision. Although child disclosure and parental knowledge were highly correlated, parental knowledge continued to predict teen adjustment (especially delinquency) once the impact of child disclosure had been controlled. Stattin and Kerr speculate that, among well-adjusted youth, child disclosure may not be required for parental knowledge because parents in such families are more physically present in their teen's social lives. By virtue of their presence, parents have less need to ask (or to be told) of their teen's whereabouts and companions; instead, because the parent and teen are home or engaging in activities together, the parent has direct access to such information. Thus, in some well-functioning families, relatively more proximal and distal supervisory strategies may coexist. In other well-functioning families, parents may need to rely more extensively on child disclosure. It is also likely that children's willingness to inform parents hinges on earlier patterns of family communication and responsiveness (Pettit et al., 2001).

Although available evidence points to age-related differences in parents' supervisory behaviors, additional longitudinal investigations are needed to clarify this relation. As in research on monitoring, the question of whether the impetus for parents' supervisory behaviors lies in the parent or the child (or both) deserves further empirical scrutiny. There has been a productive debate among those who research parental monitoring (see Crouter and Head, in Vol. 3 of this *Handbook*), about whether the construct should be defined as a form of supervision that is initiated by parents to elicit compliance (e.g., surveillance), or, alternatively, as a form of knowledge that parents construct from information that is provided by the adolescent.

Parent as Advisor and Consultant

Parents also advise children about peers when their playmates are not present. It is not uncommon for parents to talk with children after school, in the car, before bedtime, or at other times about how to initiate friendships, manage conflicts, maintain relationships, deflect teasing, repel bullies, and so on (Laird, Pettit, Mize, Brown, and Lindsey, 1994; Lollis et al., 1992). Lollis et al. (1992) refer to this type of management as "decontextualized discussion." Such conversations may be proactive or reactive in nature—that is, aimed at preparing children for future challenges or focused on past or present peer experiences. As consultants, parents may be relatively didactic, such as giving "expert" advice or solutions to peer problems, or they may serve as a "sounding board" by listening to children's self-generated assessments and solutions (Kuczynski, 1984).

In one of the first investigations of consulting, Cohen (1989) found that parental advice correlated positively with adaptive interpersonal outcomes for third-through sixth-grade children, especially when it was administered by supportive, noninterfering mothers. In contrast, advice given by either intrusive or disengaged mothers was associated with children's interpersonal difficulties, such as social withdrawal. In a subsequent study, Russell and Finnie (1990) first asked mothers to advise their child before she or he played with unfamiliar peers, and after mothers observed the session, they asked how else mothers might have advised their child. Mothers' advice varied with children's status in their preschool peer groups. Compared to mothers of average-sociometric status children, mothers of rejected and neglected children seldom recommended group-oriented entry strategies, whereas mothers of neglected children often suggested passive strategies, such as asking a peer's name. Postplay data showed that mothers of popular and neglected children, as compared to mothers of peer-rejected children, were more likely to give advice that was contingent on their child's actual play behavior.

Investigators have also documented mother–child advice in natural rather than experimental settings. Using telephone logs, Laird et al. (1994) found that half of sampled mothers reported discussing peer relationships with their child on an every-other-day basis, and indicated that these conversations tended to be initiated by the child and were more common between mothers and daughters than between mothers and sons. A subsample of the participating mothers and children was also observed in a laboratory play situation where other measures of the mothers' parenting behavior were obtained, including maternal involvement and encouragement of children's play with peers. Conversations about children's emotions and problem solving were the most frequently reported forms of consulting, and these discussions were often centered around larger relationship issues. Children's peer competence correlated positively with the frequency of mothers' consulting even after controlling for other features of parent–child relationship (e.g., maternal involvement and support).

In a series of studies, Mize and Pettit (Mize and Pettit, 1997; Pettit and Mize, 1993) examined mothers' social "coaching" in relation to preschool-age children's social competence and behavior. Mother's coaching was conceptualized in the social skills tradition (e.g., Mize and Ladd, 1990) as providing information, guidance, and feedback on the child's ideas and responses in social situations. Mothers and their children watched videotaped vignettes depicting standard peer relationship conflicts and challenges, and mothers' coaching was scored in terms of mothers' framing of the social events (e.g., extent to which mothers suggested the child adopt a resilient, bounce-back attitude), the quality of the strategies mothers suggested or endorsed, and the extent to which mothers helped the child to attend to relevant social cues. Mothers' social coaching predicted children's peer acceptance and social skills independently of either nonsocial coaching or mother–child interactional style. These findings suggest that the "substance" or content of mothers' social coaching serves an important socialization function that is not accounted for by other aspects of the mother–child relationship.

Consulting, as a parental role, has also been examined with adolescents. Vernberg, Beery, Ewell and Abwender (1993) used semistructured discussions to compare naturally occurring friendship-facilitation strategies that parents and their preadolescent children used following a change of residence (i.e., a cross-community relocation). Results showed that parents, more than adolescents, saw themselves as engaging in consulting strategies such as talking with their children and encouraging them to participate in peer activities. Conversely, adolescents tended to perceive their parents as relying on direct forms of facilitation (i.e., parental "mediation"), such as forging friendships by getting to know the parents of other adolescents. Estimates of the frequency of parents' friendship-facilitation strategies were found to predict adolescents' successes at making new friends and attaining certain friendship features (e.g., intimacy).

Unfortunately, of all the processes that fall within the category of direct parental influences, the linkage between parental consulting and children's peer competence has received the least research attention. Further investigation is needed to clarify how, when, and why parents act as interpersonal advisors with their children, and to explicate the nature of the linkages among the frequency, form, and content of parental consultation and children's social development.

Confluence of Direct Parental Influences

Just as it is possible that many indirect family processes operate simultaneously or contingently, it is likely that parents engage in multiple forms of direct social facilitation to influence their children's peer competence and relationships. Although sparse, findings that are consistent with this assumption have been reported. Especially during middle childhood or adolescence, it would appear that parents use a range of methods to facilitate children's peer relationships (see Vernberg et al., 1993). Yet, when considered in this broader context, it may still be the case that some forms of direct facilitation are better suited to certain socialization goals than are others (e.g., fostering friendships versus mitigating peer influence).

Illustrative of this point are findings from Mounts (2000), who asked mothers of ninth graders questions about different types of direct management practices (e.g., If you try to prevent your child from being influenced by peers, what do you do? What things do you do, if any, to influence your child's selection of friends?). Next, ninth graders and their friends were asked about three aspects of their parents' management: monitoring (e.g., "How much do your parents really know . . . about your activities?"), prohibiting (e.g., "My parents tell me if they don't want me to hang out with other kids"), and guiding (e.g., "My parents tell me that who I have for friends will affect my future"). Concurrently, guiding was associated with lower friend delinquency and drug use and higher GPAs and school attitudes, with prohibiting showing the opposite pattern. Monitoring was essentially unrelated to these friend characteristics. Only guiding predicted these same friend characteristics one year later, controlling for earlier friend characteristics. Mounts interpreted these results as indicating that:

(1) Monitoring played less of a role in peer selection than peer influence.
(2) Prohibitions were triggered by teens' associations with antisocial peers, but did little to deter teens from such associations and, thus, were ineffective for managing adolescents' peer relationships.
(3) Guiding was an optimal strategy for changing peer affiliations—that is, altering the adolescent's selection of friends.

Overall, the findings that have accumulated on direct parental influences suggest that there are sizable differences across families in the extent to which parents manage their children's peer relationships, and in the quality and appropriateness of this management. Much remains to be learned about direct parental influences as possible antecedents and consequences of children's peer competence, the relative importance of differing direct influences for children's social development, and the extent to which direct influences co-occur or are contingent on other family processes (e.g., indirect influences) and sociodemographic factors. In the sections that follow, we consider how research on both direct and indirect parental influences might be elaborated and extended so as to achieve a better understanding of the mechanisms that link the family and peer systems.

FAMILY–PEER RELATIONSHIPS: APPRAISING THE DISCIPLINE

It is important to recognize that the taxonomy employed in this chapter carries with it certain limitations. For example, although family "influences" were partitioned into indirect and direct linkages, it seems unlikely that the two types of processes operate independently of each other in real-world contexts. Yet, it would appear that researchers' efforts to conceptualize and investigate these influences have proceeded exactly along these lines. This issue, and several others delineated below, provide focal points for evaluating the discipline's progress and for identifying areas in need of further investigation.

Conceptualizing Family Influences: Level of Analysis and Links Among Indirect and Direct Influences

In families, many persons (e.g., parents, siblings, and grandparents) and processes (e.g., indirect and direct parental influences) may affect children. The breadth and complexity of this system require that researchers entertain the possibility that, in families, a complex web of influences impinge on children's development. Parke (1992), for example, argued that family influences can be defined at several levels of analysis.

Level of analysis.   Historically, researchers have tended to study family influence at the level of the individual (e.g., mothers' behavior) and, more recently, at the level of the dyad (e.g., parent–child relationship). Within these traditions, some family members (e.g., mothers) and relationships (e.g., attachment) have received more attention than others (e.g., fathers and sibling relationships). Clearly, important avenues through which families influence children's peer relationships are likely to be overlooked if we fail to make fathers, siblings, and other types of family members and relationships a priority in future studies.

Also stressed has been the need to study family influences at broader levels of analysis—that is, beyond the realm of the individual or the dyad (e.g., Kreppner, 1989; Lewis, 1984; Parke, 1992). Influences that may operate at the level of the triad (e.g., mother, father, and child), or overall family system (e.g., group dynamics), remain relatively unexplored. The merits of this proposition are, in part, illustrated by results reported by investigators who have attempted to measure the family as a social system. Gauze, Bukowski, Aquan-Assee, and Sippola (1996), for example, found that parents' perceptions of the overall family system—specifically, processes such as adaptability and cohesion—moderated the association between adolescents' friendships and self-perceived adjustment. In general, stronger linkages were found between the adolescents' friendships and adjustment in families that had lower levels of adaptability and cohesion. These results were interpreted as supporting the contention that the effects of poor family environments on adolescent's adjustment may be partially compensated for by the quality of their friendships.

Linkages among indirect and direct family influences. As previously noted, insufficient attention has been devoted to associations among different types of family influences. Indirect influences (e.g., family environment) may interact not only with other indirect processes (e.g., childrearing style), but also with direct influences, such as parents' management of children's peer activities. Progress toward an understanding of the links between indirect and direct family processes has been aided by findings from several recent investigations. Ladd and colleagues (1988) found that low income—a chronic family stressor—was negatively correlated with the frequency with which parents permitted their children to play in peers' homes. Mize and Pettit (1997) found that a lack of responsiveness in mother–child relationships was associated with boys' aggressiveness, but that unresponsive mothers who provided social coaching (i.e., guidance about how to relate with agemates) tended to have sons who were less aggressive toward peers.

Thus, there is a need to not only identify the types of family processes that impact children's peer competence, but also understand how these processes are orchestrated. Toward this end, Parke (1992) suggested that researchers ascertain the combinations of family influences that yield well-adjusted children.

Mediators of Linkages

Some of the connections between parenting and children's peer relationships are merely structural in the sense that parents act as "designers" of children's peer environments. For such linkages, it seems less crucial to posit underlying or intervening psychological constructs to explain why such parenting actions foster children's interpersonal competence. But when parents serve as models of relationships, or actively coach their children in friendship making skills, or punish their children harshly and inconsistently, then the matter of intervening variables or mediators is of central importance. As previously described, a wide array of psychological—and physiological—constructs has been examined as possible mediators of associations between parenting and children's social behavior. Posited within attachment research is the internal working model—a relationship template that first develops in children's earliest caregiver relationships and then generalizes to subsequent ties, including those with peers. Within social-interactional and cognitive social-learning research, key constructs include problem solving skills and social information-processing patterns. And biosocial psychology has contributed the concepts of vagal tone and associated regulatory mechanisms (Porges, Doussard-Roosevelt, and Maiti, 1994). Within each of these subfields, evidence consistent with the "mediating mechanism" hypothesis has been reported.

At this juncture, however, it may be important to reassess the efficacy of existing mediating-linkage models. Mize et al. (2000) have concluded that few studies provide convincing evidence of mediation. This exigency raises questions about why the mediating-mechanisms hypothesis has not yielded more powerful and pervasive findings, and it invites a reappraisal of contemporary theory about the links between parent–child and child–peer relationships. In some of the studies critiqued by Mize et al. (2000), multiple mediators were tested en masse (as in Dodge, Bates, and Pettit, 1990), whereas in other investigations the targeted mediators were examined individually (as in Pettit et al., 1991). Mize et al. concluded that the former approach often lacked precision concerning the specific processes that might bridge children's family experience and peer competence. The latter approach was criticized as largely exploratory in nature and fraught with potential for Type 1 error. Another criticism was that support for the mediation hypothesis was seldom strong and often qualified. Processes such as emotional regulation (e.g., Davies and Cummings, 1998; Gottman, Katz, and Hooven, 1996) received the most consistent empirical support as mediating processes, followed by factors such as encoding and generation of aggressive strategies (Dodge, Pettit, Bates, and Valente, 1995) and empathy (e.g., Krevans and Gibbs, 1996).

Mize et al. offered several explanations for this dearth of empirical demonstrations of mediating effects. First, it is possible that measurement problems (e.g., low power and collinearity) have obscured mediated effects. Second, it may be that family–peer effects are not mediated, but connected via "direct transfer," as has been hypothesized in some behavioral perspectives (e.g., see Wahler, 1996). Alternatively, factors construed as mediators may derive from children's peer experiences rather than those they have within the family (see Trachtenberg and Viken, 1994). Third, the mediators researchers have targeted may not be as specific to the family context or as influential in affecting children's peer relationships as has been assumed in past theory. For example, children's sociocognitive processes and peer relationships may be affected by a wide range of experiences or by cumulative risks (i.e., it may not be one kind of adverse parenting that is influential, but the accumulation of adversity). A fourth possibility is that mediated links are more specific than is assumed within contemporary theories. Such a possibility would be consistent with differentiated socialization models in which it proposed that the effects of children's family experiences on their peer relationships are transmitted through "specialized" mediators, or even different features of the same mediator. For example, certain family experiences may strengthen only those social information-processing mechanisms that underlie reactive rather than proactive forms of aggression (see Dodge, Lochman, Harsh, Bates, and Pettit, 1997). Fifth, certain forms of parent behavior may affect only those aspects of the child's internal working model that encode anxious rejection expectancies (see Downey, Lebolt, Rincon, and Freitas, 1998) that, in turn, motivate children to become overcompliant rather than resistive or cooperative with peers.

Moderators of Linkages

Developmental science frequently follows cyclical trends, as has been the case for research on the interconnections among parent–child and child–peer relationships. Over 20 years ago, Hartup (1979) drew attention to the interdependencies among parent–child and child–peer social systems. A contrasting perspective has been offered by researchers within the behavior-genetics tradition (e.g., Rowe, 1994), some of whom have argued that that the social forces operating within these systems are essentially independent. Currently, the pendulum seems to hang in-between, as researchers begin to recognize the "conditional" nature of relations among parenting and child behavior and personality (Collins et al., 2000). Inherent in this realization is the challenge of explicating the circumstances and contexts within which parents' may have more or less influence on children's developing social skills and orientations. At present, what is known about such contingencies is limited to two potential moderators: the developmental level of the child and the gender of the parent and child.

Developmental change.   The child's development may be an important moderator of family–peer linkages. The family processes that affect children's peer relationships, and the potency of these processes, may vary with the maturity of the child. In research on direct parental influences

(Bhavnagri and Parke, 1991; Ladd et al., 1993), findings suggest that parents adjust their peer management practices to fit the needs of the child. Evidence suggests that parents tend to shift from interactive supervision with toddlers to directive supervision of preschoolers to monitoring grade schoolers and adolescents. Similarly, it appears that parents give children more responsibility for arranging peer activities as they mature (Bhavnagri and Parke, 1991; Ladd and Hart, 1992). Moreover, the efficacy of particular management strategies appears to differ depending on the child's age or developmental status. Parents of older preschoolers who continue to rely on interactive supervision tend to have children who are less competent with peers (Ladd and Golter, 1988).

Gender of parent and child. Another potential moderator of the link between family processes and children's peer competence is gender. Attention to gender, especially the child's gender, has been relatively neglected in research on family-peer relationships and, in fact, it would appear that the influence of family factors on children's peer relationships is better understood for boys than for girls (see Parke, 1992). Perhaps for this reason, few investigators have sought to determine whether specific family processes are differentially associated with the peer relationships of boys versus girls. Of course, notable exceptions exist; it appears that divorce takes a greater toll on boys' peer relationships (e.g., see Hetherington et al., 1979; Hetherington and Stanley-Hagan, in Vol. 3 of this *Handbook*), and parents' facilitation of preschoolers' play dates appears to benefit boys more than girls (e.g., Ladd and Hart, 1992). However, the mechanisms that account for these gender-moderated links are not well understood.

A similar case can be made for the parents' gender because, historically, researchers have devoted more attention to mothers than fathers. This is a concern given that mothers and fathers appear to play different roles in child socialization (Parke, 1992) and may have distinct effects on children's interpersonal competence. Although scant, extant evidence lends credibility to this hypothesis and, therefore, renders it worthy of further investigation. MacDonald and Parke (1984), for example, were among the first to report differences between maternal and paternal behavior and children's peer competence. Ladd and Golter (1988) found that mothers acted as managers of children's peer activities more often than did fathers. Bhavnagri and Parke (1991) extended these findings by showing that even though children's peer-related activities were managed primarily by mothers, fathers were equally competent in this role.

Direction of Effect

Researchers searching for connections between parenting and children's peer relationships have acknowledged that such connections are likely to be bidirectional (see Ladd, 1992). Even though parents may instigate activities that promote social learning and skill acquisition, they must also react to children's changing behaviors and adjust their efforts to fit children's enduring interpersonal proclivities.

In 1992, Ladd speculated that it "seems probable that the events children encounter in the peer culture will, at times, spill over into family life, and precipitate certain reactions (perhaps some of the same processes we now view as potential causes within the family). In the long run, we may find the greatest explanatory power is achieved with models that permit us to consider both types of pathways, or even bi-directional effects" (p. 5). Similarly, Parke (1992) encouraged investigators to embrace transactional models (e.g., Sameroff and Chandler, 1975) as a guide for the development of research questions and designs. Such models encourage researchers to construct and test hypotheses about mutual influences (e.g., parent vs. child) and effects that may change direction over time or contexts.

Possible shifts in the direction of family–peer influences are not difficult to envision. As children grow older they have greater contact with nonparent caregivers and authority figures (e.g., teachers) and age-mates (e.g., friends and peer groups). Thus, the chances that persons outside the family will modify or supplant parental influences increases, as does the probability that children will play a more casual role in determining parenting practices and policies toward peers. Children may also import developments that are nurtured in nonfamilial contexts into the home. As this occurs, the nature of parent–child interactions and relationships is likely to change. Thus, it will be important for researchers to consider the changing roles that parents and children play in each others' lives and begin to think in terms of cyclical, transactional patterns of influence.

Until recently, the concept of bidirectional pathways was more often acknowledged than investigated. However, the discipline seems poised to alter this tendency by encouraging investigators to dialogue about alternate directions of effect, use longitudinal designs, and consider how individual differences in children's peer relationships may flow from earlier parenting and change subsequent parenting.

CONCLUSIONS

Prevailing models and findings create the impression that families are complex systems that bring multiple processes to bear on the developing child, many of which facilitate or inhibit the growth of children's peer relationships and competencies. Some of these processes have been depicted as indirect influences, or elements that are part of the fabric of everyday family interactions and environments that impinge on children and affect their interpersonal competencies. Others are depicted as direct influences, such as managerial, instructional, and advisory roles that parents perform as a means of preparing their child for the peer culture, or facilitating their competence and success in this domain.

The evidence that has accumulated on potential indirect influences—the family environment, and elements of the relational systems that develop within families—is consistent with the view that family life serves as a staging area for children's interpersonal skills and abilities. Among other features, secure, responsive, nonintrusive, playful parent–child relationships have been linked with children's relational competence, whereas asynchronous, harsh, stressful, and disordered parent– child and parent–parent interactions have been associated with children's peer difficulties. Also consistent with this premise are data indicating that acute stressors such as unemployment, marital discord, and divorce increase children's risk for peer difficulties, and that the likelihood of such difficulties escalates as the number of stressors that impinge on the family increases. Apparently even minor stressors (e.g., daily hassles associated with parenting and family life) can exact a toll on both the parent–child relationship and children's relationships with peers.

Another form of indirect influence includes the attitudes, perceptions, and beliefs that underlie parents' socialization practices. Investigators have proceeded from the assumption that the lens through which parents "see" children affects much of what they "do" with children. Corroboration of such complex mediated linkages is far from complete, but extant findings agree with the premises that parental attitudes, perceptions, and beliefs affect many aspects of the parent–child relationship (e.g., interactions, play, discipline and parenting styles, etc.) and that these developments impact children's interpersonal skills and abilities.

The proposition that parents directly socialize children's peer competence has also received considerable support. Research on children's social ecologies buttresses the argument that parents' choice of residence and neighborhood establishes a context that affects many aspects of children's social experiences, including their proximity to peers and their involvement in different types of peer activities and relationships. Accruing evidence is congruent with the assertion that children from economically disadvantaged households have fewer opportunities to interact with peers, especially if they live in rural neighborhoods. Rather, it appears that children are likely to interact with peers, develop friends, and form larger playmate networks when they live in flat, well-populated neighborhoods that contain amenities such as sidewalks, parks, and playgrounds.

Other findings suggest that, especially during the early childhood years, it is not uncommon for parents to facilitate children's exposure to peers by arranging play groups or after-school activities in their homes, yards, or neighborhoods. Moreover, when interpreted from a parent-effects perspective, it would appear that parents' mediational activities promote several forms of peer competence including prosocial interaction skills and broader friendship networks. A link has also been established between children's social competence and the types of supervisory behaviors parents use to oversee and regulate children's peer interactions and relationships. Experimental research indicates that interactive interventions enhance the quality of toddlers' peer interactions and that both mothers and fathers can be effective in this role. Directive interventions, or less proximate and sporadic forms of supervision, become more common in the late-preschool and early grade-school years and appear to be used by parents both proactively and reactively with differing results. When used in noninterfering ways, this form of supervision has been linked with children's peer competence, especially for boys. On the other hand, it has also been shown that parents of unpopular children intervene less often in their children's play, but when they do, they often provide advice or supervision that is disruptive rather than facilitative of children's peer interactions.

In the early and middle childhood years, one of the most common ways that parents manage children's peer interactions and relationships is by consulting with them before or after social activities. Although this form of parental management is still not well understood, there is evidence to suggest that the frequency of consulting is predictive of children's competence and success in peer relationships and that parents advise children in ways that are consistent with children's behavior patterns and peer reputations.

Less direct styles of supervision, such as monitoring, are more often utilized by parents of preadolescents and adolescents. Although there is evidence to suggest that low levels of monitoring antecede child misconduct and peer rejection, other findings indicate that parents' efforts to monitor (extract information about) teens' activities predict adolescents' involvement in antisocial activities. These seemingly contradictory findings underscore the fact that the definition of monitoring remains a controversial topic. Researchers have yet to resolve the question of whether the impetus for parents' monitoring behaviors should be located in the parent or the adolescent, and whether the construct should be defined as a form of supervision (e.g., surveillance) that is initiated by parents to elicit compliance or, alternatively, as a form of knowledge that parents construct from information provided by the adolescent.

As compelling as many of these findings may be, it is important to recognize that much remains to be learned about the role that families play in the development of children's social competence. As we have seen, a large number of premises about how families influence children's social development have been proposed, and a host of family factors and associated mediating and moderating variables has been implicated in the development of children's social skills and peer relationships. Conceptually, many of the frameworks that researchers have developed to guide their investigations are still under development, and few researchers have investigated combinations of family influences, alternate directions of effect, and processes that occur at differing levels of analysis. Factors such as the gender of the child and of the parent have received insufficient attention, as have many of the mechanisms that might explain how family influences are transmitted "through" children to their interactions and relationships with peers.

Because most of the research conducted in this discipline has been framed from the perspective that families influence children's peer competence and adjustment, much of the evidence that has accumulated is consistent with a socialization perspective and has perpetuated the view that: (1) the antecedents of peer competence can be found largely within the family and (2) the learning children acquire within this context is primarily responsible for their success or difficulties within the peer culture. Such conclusions, however, must be tempered in light of the genetic debate regarding the influences of parenting behaviors on children's social-personality development in general, and children's social skills and competencies in peer relationships in particular. Because genes and environments are correlated, connections between parenting characteristics and children's social outcomes may merely be artifacts of children's and parents' shared genetic make-up (Harris, 1998; Rowe, 1994). There are three forms of gene–environment correlations posited, each of which may provide some insight into the nature of the links between parenting and peer-relationships outcomes, including why such links have not been more pronounced. First, parents may create opportunities and environments relevant for children's peer relationships that are consistent with their own and their children's genetic dispositions. Second, in creating such opportunities and environments (or in failing to do so), parents may be responding to their children's dispositions (i.e., the parenting behavior is "evoked" by the child's characteristics). Third, children with certain dispositions also may seek out those environments that are consistent with those dispositions and interests. Collectively, these three forms of gene–environment association, along with direct genetic factors, have been proposed to account for observed correlations between parenting behaviors and strategies and children's social behavior and outcomes (Harris, 1998). But in a critique of this position, Vandell (2000) points out that these sorts of gene-driven effects do not rule out the possibility of parent-to-child influences, at least with respect to between-family individual differences. Whether parenting behavior has an effect—either positive or negative—on child outcomes appears to hinge on characteristics of the child, the child's history with the parent, as well as family circumstances.

The first two forms of gene–environment correlations necessitate that caution be exercised when drawing conclusions about direction-of-effect in studies of parenting and children's peer relationships. Parents may be following the child's lead, or parents and children may be coconstructing environments that fit with their shared interests and dispositions. The third form of gene–environment correlation—where children seek to find their own comfort zone or niche—may lead to a misestimation of possible parenting effects unless both the parents' efforts and the child's disposition are considered within a transactional perspective (Reiss et al., 2000). For example, when a child is uninterested in peers and a parent is disinclined to push for peer involvement, the result probably will be a lack of peer involvement. Recognition that such processes may be at work enables an appreciation of the current status—and needed next steps—in research on parenting and children's peer relationships.

Finally, the discipline has not reached a stage where some frameworks or paradigms achieve prominence over others because they provide the best fit with extant data patterns. At present, there continues to be a proliferation of models—some offer competing explanations about the origins of peer competence, and others generate contentions that remain unopposed. In nearly every case, model evaluation has been impeded by factors such as insufficient evidence, absence of developmental data or longitudinal designs, inattention to competing explanations, and failure to evaluate opposing directions of effect. Continued investigation, especially systematic evaluation of competing perspectives, may show us that some of the family processes researchers have targeted are more powerful explanatory variables than others, allowing us to narrow the search and concentrate our efforts on a few key linkages. These developments may also allow researchers to devise more encompassing frameworks that represent variation in the conditions under which family processes are most likely to affect children's social competence and peer relationships. Furthermore, the next generation of models that investigators develop should take into account the connections that may exist among seemingly diverse family processes (e.g., relations among indirect and direct influences) and reciprocal effects such as the impact of children's peer relationships on family processes, and vice versa. These conceptual refinements will spawn many new areas of investigation and, undoubtedly, produce a number of important empirical discoveries.

ACKNOWLEDGMENTS

Preparation of this chapter was supported in part by NIH grants MH-49223 to the first author and MH-57095 to the second author.

REFERENCES

Allen, J. P., Moore, C., Kuperminc, G., and Bell, K. (1998). Attachment and psychosocial functioning. *Child Development, 69*, 1406–1419.

Attar, B. K., Guerra, N. G., and Tolan, P. H. (1994). Neighborhood disadvantage, stressful life events, and adjustment in urban elementary school children. *Journal of Clinical Child Psychology, 23*, 391–400.

Baldwin, A. L., Cole, R. E., and Baldwin, C. P. (1982). Parental pathology, family interaction, and the competence of the child in school. *Monographs of the Society for Research in Child Development, 47*(5, Serial No. 197).

Barber, B. K. (1996). Parental psychological control: Revisiting a neglected construct. *Child Development, 67*, 3296–3319.

Baron, R. M., and Kenny, D. (1986). The mediator-moderator distinction in social psychology: Conceptual, strategic, and statistical considerations. *Journal of Personality and Social Psychology, 51*, 1173–1182.

Barrera, M. (1981). Social support in the adjustment of pregnant adolescents: Assessment issues and findings. In B. Gottlieb (Ed.), *Social networks and social support in community mental health* (pp. 69–96). Newbury Park, CA: Sage.

Baumrind, D. (1973). The development of instrumental competence through socialization. In A. D. Pick (Ed.), *Minnesota symposium on child psychology* (Vol. 7, pp. 3–46). Minneapolis: University of Minnesota Press.

Beardslee, W. R., Bemporal. J., Keller, M. B., and Klerman, G. (1983). Children of parents with major affective disorder: A review. *American Journal of Psychiatry, 140*, 825–832.

Becker, W. C. (1964). Consequences of different kinds of parental discipline. In M. L. Hoffman and L. W. Hoffman (Eds.), *Review of child development research* (Vol. 1, pp. 169–208). New York: Russell Sage Foundation.

Belsky, J. (1984). The determinants of parenting: A process model. *Child Development, 55*, 83–96.

Belsky, J., Campbell, S. B., Cohn, J. F., and Moore, G. (1996). Instability of infant–parent attachment security. *Developmental Psychology, 32*, 921–924.

Belsky. J., and Vondra, J. (1989). Lesson from child abuse: The determinants of parenting. In D. Cicchetti and V. Carlson (Eds.), *Child maltreatment: Theory and research on the causes and consequences of child abuse and neglect* (pp. 153–202). New York: Cambridge University Press.

Berg, M., and Medrich, E. A. (1980). Children in four neighborhoods: Physical environments and its effects on play and play patterns. *Environment and Behavior, 12*, 320–348.

Bhavnagri, N., and Parke, R. D. (1985, April). *Parents as facilitators of preschool children's peer relationships.* Paper presented at the biennial meeting of the Society for Research in Child Development, Toronto, Ontario, Canada.

Bhavnagri, N., and Parke, R. D. (1991). Parents as direct facilitators of children's peer relationships: Effects of age of child and sex of parent. *Journal of Social and Personal Relationships, 8*, 423–440.

Billings, A. G., and Moos, R. H. (1985). Children of parents with unipolar depression: A controlled one-year follow-up. *Journal of Abnormal Child Psychology, 14*, 149–166.

Black, B., and Logan, A. (1995). Links between communication patterns in mother–child, father–child, and child–peer interactions and children's social status. *Child Development, 66*, 255–271.

Block, J. H., Block, J., and Gjerde, P. F. (1986). The personality of children prior to divorce: A prospective study. *Child Development, 57*, 827–840.

Bolger, K. E., Patterson, C. J., and Kupersmidt, J. B. (1998). Peer relationships and self-esteem among children who have been maltreated. *Child Development, 69*, 1171–1197.

Booth, C. L., Rubin, K. H., and Rose-Krasnor, L. (1998). Perceptions of emotional support from mother and friend in middle childhood: Links with social-emotional adaptation and preschool attachment security. *Child Development, 69*, 427–442.

Bost, K. K., Vaughn, B. E., Washington, W. N., Cielinski, K. L., and Bradbard, M. R. (1998). Social competence, social support, and attachment: Demarcation of construct domains, measurement, and paths of influence for preschool children attending Head Start. *Child Development, 69*, 192–218.

Bowlby, J. (1973). *Attachment and loss: Vol. 2. Separation.* New York: Basic Books.

Bretherton, I. (1985). Attachment theory: Retrospect and prospect. In I. Bretherton and E. Waters (Eds.), Growing points of attachment theory and research. *Monographs of the Society for Research in Child Development* (50, Serial No. 209).

Bronfenbrenner, U. (1986). Ecology of the family as a context for human development: Research perspectives. *Developmental Psychology, 22*, 723–742.

Bryant, B. (1985). The neighborhood walk: Sources of support in middle childhood. *Monographs of the Society for Research in Child Development, 50*(3, Serial No. 210).

Buckner, J. C., Bassuk, E. L., Weinreb, L. F., and Brooks, M. G. (1999). Homelessness and its relation to the mental health and behavior of low-income schoolchildren. *Developmental Psychology, 35*, 246–257.

Bugental, D. B., Blue, J., and Cruzcosa, M. (1989). Perceived control over caregiving outcomes: Implications for child abuse. *Developmental Psychology, 25*, 532–539.

Bugental, D. B., Blue, J., and Lewis, J. (1990). Caregiver beliefs and dysphoric affect directed to difficult children. *Developmental Psychology, 26*, 631–638.

Bugental, D. B., Lewis, J. C., Lin, E., Lyon, J., and Kopeikin, H. (1999). In charge but not in control: The management of teaching relationships by adults with low perceived power. *Developmental Psychology, 35*, 1367–1378.

Bukowski, W. M., and Hoza, B. (1989). Popularity and friendship: Issues in theory, measurement, and outcome. In T. J. Thomas and G. W. Ladd (Eds.), *Peer relationships in child development* (pp. 15–45). New York: Wiley.

Carson, J. L., and Parke, R. D. (1996). Reciprocal negative affect in parent-child interactions and children's peer competency. *Child Development, 67*, 2217–2226.

Carlson, V., Cicchetti, D., Barnett, D., and Braunwald, K. (1989). Disorganized/disoriented attachment relationships in maltreated infants. *Developmental Psychology, 25*, 525–531.

Cassidy, J. (1988). Child–mother attachment and the self in six-year-olds. *Child Development, 59*, 121–134.

Cassidy, J., Kirsh, S. J., Scolton, K. L., and Parke, R. D. (1996). Attachment and representations of peer relaitonships. *Developmental Psychology, 32*, 892–904.

Cassidy, J., Parke, R., Butkovsky, L., and Braungart, J. M. (1992). Family–peer connections: The roles of emotional expressiveness within the family and children's understanding of emotions. *Child Development, 63*, 603–618.

Cicchetti, D., and Carlson, V. (1989). *Child maltreatment: Theory and research on the causes and consequences of child abuse and neglect.* New York: Cambridge University Press.

Cicchetti, D., Lynch, M., Shonk, S., and Manly, J. T. (1992). An organizational perspective on peer relations in maltreated children. In R. D. Parke and G. W. Ladd (Eds.), *Family–peer relationships: Modes of linkage* (pp. 345–384). Hillsdale, NJ: Lawrence Erlbaum Associates.

Cicchetti, D., and Rizley, R. (1981). Developmental perspectives on the intergenerational transmission, and sequelae of child maltreatment. In R. Rizley and D. Cicchetti (Eds.), *Developmental perspectives on child maltreatment* (pp. 31–56). San Francisco: Jossey-Bass.

Clark, K. E., and Ladd, G. W. (2000). Connectedness and autonomy support in parent–child relationships: Links to children's socioemotional orientation and peer relationships. *Developmental Psychology, 36*, 485–498.

Cochran, M., and Riley, D. (1988). Mothers' reports of children's personal networks: Antecedents, concomitants, and consequences. In S. Salzinger, J. Antrobus, and M. Hammer (Eds.), *Social networks of children, adolescents, and college students* (pp. 113–148). Hillsdale, NJ: Lawrence Erlbaum Associates.

Cohen, J. S. (1989). *Maternal involvement in children's peer relationships during middle childhood.* Unpublished doctoral dissertation, University of Waterloo, Waterloo, Ontario, Canada.

Cohn, D. (1990). Child–mother attachment of 6-year-olds and social competence at school. *Child Development, 61*, 152–177.

Cohn, D., Patterson, C., and Christopoulos, C. (1991). The family and children's peer relations. *Journal of Social and Personal Relationships, 8*, 315–346.

Coley, R. L., and Hoffman, L. W. (1996). Relations of parental supervision and monitoring to children's functioning in various contexts: Moderating effects of families and neighborhoods. *Journal of Applied Developmental Psychology, 17*, 51–68.

Collins, W. A., Maccoby, E. E., Steinberg, L., Hetherington, E. M., and Bornstein, M. H. (2000). Contemporary research on parenting: The case for nature and nurture. *American Psychologist, 55*, 218–232.

Compas, B. E., Howell, D. C., Phares, V., Williams, R. A., and Ledoux, N. (1989). Parent and child stress and symptoms: An integrative analysis. *Developmental Psychology, 25*, 550–559.

Conger, R. D., and Elder, G. H. (1994). *Families in troubled times.* Hawthorne, NY: Aldine de Gruyter.

Conger, R. D., Elder, G. H., Lorenz. F. O., Conger, K. J., Simons, R. L., Whitbeck, L. B., Huck, S., and Melby, J. N. (1990). Linking economic hardship to marital quality and instability. *Journal of Marriage and the Family, 52*, 643–656.

Cowen, E. L., Lotyczewski, B. S., and Weissberg, R. P. (1984). Risk and resource indicators and their relationships to young children's school adjustment. *American Journal of Community Psychology, 12*, 343–367.

Crnic, K. A., and Acevedo, M. (1995). Everyday stresses and parenting. In M. H. Bornstein (Ed.), *Handbook of parenting: Vol. 4. Applied and practical parenting.* (pp. 277–297). Mahwah, NJ: Lawrence Erlbaum Associates.

Crnic, K. A., and Greenberg, M. T. (1990). Minor parenting stresses with young children. *Child Development, 61*, 1628–1637.

Crouter, A. C., MacDermid, S. M., McHale, S. M., and Perry-Jenkins, M. (1990). Parental monitoring and perceptions of children's performance and conduct in dual- and single-earner families. *Developmental Psychology, 26*, 649–657.

Cummings, E. M., and Cummings, J. L. (1988). A process-oriented approach to children's coping with adults' angry behavior. *Developmental Review, 8*, 296–321.

Cummings, E. M., Iannotti, R. J., and Zahn-Waxler, C. (1985). Influence of conflict between adults on the emotions and aggression of young children. *Developmental Psychology, 21*, 495–507.

D'Angelo, L. L., Weinberger, D. A., and Feldman, S. S. (1995). Like father, like son? Predicting mal adolescents adjustment from parents' distress and self restraint. *Developmental Psychology, 31*, 883–896.

Davies, P. T., and Cummings, E. M. (1998). Exploring children's emotional security as a mediator of the link between marital relations and child adjustment. *Child Development, 69*, 124–139.

DeVault, M. V. (1957). Classroom sociometric mutual pairs and residential proximity. *Journal of Educational Research, 50*, 605–610.

Dishion, T. J. (1990). The family ecology of boys' peer relations in middle childhood. *Child Development, 61*, 874–892.

Dishion, T. J., and McMahon, R. J. (1998). Parental monitoring and the prevention of child and adolescent problem behavior: A conceptual and empirical formulation. *Clinical Child and Family Psychology Review, 1*, 61–75.

Dix, T. H., and Lochman, J. (1989). *Social cognition in the mediation of negative reactions to children: A comparison of mothers of aggressive and nonaggressive boys*. Unpublished manuscript.

Dodge, K. A., Bates, J. E., and Pettit, G. S. (1990). Mechanisms in the cycle of violence. *Science, 250*, 1678–1683.

Dodge, K. A., Lochman, J. E., Harsh, J. D., Bates, J. E., and Pettit, G. S. (1997). Reactive and proactive aggression in school children and psychiatrically impaired chronically assaultive youth. *Journal of Abnormal Psychology, 106*, 37–51.

Dodge, K. A., Pettit, G. S., Bates, J. E., and Valente, E. (1995). Social-information-processing patterns partially mediate the effect of early physical abuse on later conduct problems. *Journal of Abnormal Psychology, 104*, 632–643.

Downey, G., and Coyne, J. C. (1990). Children of depressed parents: An integrative review. *Psychological Bulletin, 108*, 50–76.

Downey, G., Lebolt, A., Ricon, C., and Freitas, A. L. (1998). Rejection sensitivity and children's interpersonal difficulties. *Child Development, 69*, 1074–1091.

Eccles, J. S., and Barber, B. L. (1999). Student council, volunteering, basketball, or marching band. What kind of extracurricular involvement matters? *Journal of Adolescent Research, 14*, 10–43.

Eisenberg, N., Fabes, R. A., and Murphy, B. C. (1996). Parent's reactions to children's negative emotions: Relations to children's social competence and comforting behavior. *Child Development, 67*, 2227–2247.

Elder, G. H., Jr. (1974). *Children of the Great Depression*. Chicago: University of Chicago Press.

Elicker, J., Englund, M., and Sroufe, L. A. (1992). Predicting peer competence and peer relations in childhood from early parent–child relationships. In R. D. Parke and G. W. Ladd (Eds.), *Family–peer relationships: Modes of linkage* (pp. 77–106). Hillsdale, NJ: Lawrence Erlbaum Associates.

Erickson, M. F., Sroufe, L. A., and Egeland, B. (1985). The relationship between quality of attachment and behavior problems in a high-risk sample. In I. Bretherton and E. Waters (Eds.), *Growing points in attachment theory and research. Monographs of the Society for Research in Child Development, 50*(Serial No. 209).

Fagot, B. I. (1997). Attachment, parenting, and peer interactions of toddler children. *Developmental Psychology, 33*, 489–499.

Felner, R. D., Stolberg, A., and Cowen, E. L. (1975). Crisis events and school mental health referral patterns of young children. *Journal of Consulting and Clinical Psychology, 43*, 305–310.

Finkelstein, N. W., Dent, C., Gallagher, K., and Ramey, C. T. (1978). Social behavior of infants and toddlers in the day-care environment. *Developmental Psychology, 14*, 257–262.

Finnegan, R. A., Hodges, E. V. E., and Perry, D. G. (1998). Victimization by peers: Associations with children's reports of mother–child interaction. *Journal of Personality and Social Psychology, 75*, 1076–1086.

Finnie, V., and Russell, A. (1988). Preschool children's social status and their mothers' behavior and knowledge in the supervisory role. *Developmental Psychology, 24*, 789–801.

Fletcher, A. C., Darling, N., and Steinberg, L. (1995). Parental monitoring and peer influences on adolescent substance use. In J. McCord (Ed), *Coercion and punishment in long-term perspectives* (pp. 259–271). New York: Cambridge University Press.

Forehand, R., McCombs, A., and Brody, G. H. (1987). The relationship of parental depressive mood states to child functioning: An analysis by type of sample and area of child functioning. *Advances in Behavioral Research and Therapy, 9*, 1–20.

Freitag, M. K., Belsky, J., Grossmann, K., Grossmann, K. E., and Scheurer-Englisch, H. (1996). Continuity in parent–child relationships from infancy to middle childhood and relations with friendship competence. *Child Development, 67*, 1437–1454.

Gallagher, J. J. (1958). Social status of children related to intelligence, propinquity, and social perception. *Elementary School Journal, 59*, 225–231.

Galambos, N. S., and Maggs, J. L. (1991). Out-of-school care of young adolescents and self-reported behavior. *Developmental Psychology, 27*, 644–655.

Garbarino, J., and Gilliam, G. (1980). *Understanding abusive families*. Lexington, MA: Lexington.

Garmezy, N. (1985). Stress-resistant children: The search for protective factors. In J. E. Stevenson (Ed.), *Journal of Child Psychology and Psychiatry Book Supplement No. 4* (pp. 213–233). Oxford, England: Pergamon.

Garmezy, N., Masten, S. A., and Tellegen, A. (1984). The study of stress and competence in children: A building block for developmental psychopathology. *Child Development, 55*, 97–111.

Gauze, C., Bukowski, W. M., Aquan-Assee, J., and Sippola, L. K. (1996). Interactions between family environment and friendship and associations with self-perceived well-being during adolescence. *Child Development, 67*, 2201–2216.

George, C., and Main, M. (1979). Social interactions of young abused children: Approach, avoidance, and aggression. *Child Development, 50*, 306–318.

Gersten, J. C., Langner T. S.. Eisenberg, T. G., and Orzeck, L. (1974). Child behavior and life events: Desirable change or change per se? In B. S. Dohrenwend and B. P. Dohrenwend (Eds.), *Stressful life events. Their nature and effects* (pp. 159–170). New York: Wiley.

Gottman, J. M., and Katz, L. F. (1989). Effects of marital discord on young children's peer interactions and health. *Developmental Psychology, 25*, 373–381.

Gottman, J. M., Katz, L, K., and Hooven, C. (1996). Parental meta-emotion philosophy and the emotional life of families: Theoretical models and preliminary data. *Journal of Family Psychology*, *10*, 243–268.

Greenberg, M. T., Siegel, J. M., and Leitch, C. J. (1983). The nature and importance of attachment relationships to parents and peers during adolescence. *Journal of Youth and Adolescence*, *12*, 373–386.

Grossman, K. E., and Grossman, K. (1991). Attachment quality as an organizer of emotional and behavioral responses in a longitudinal perspective. In C. M. Parkes, J. Stevenson-Hinde, and P. Marris (Eds.), *Attachment across the life cycle* (pp. 93–114). London: Routledge.

Grych, J. H., and Fincham, F. (1990). Marital conflict and children's adjustment: A cognitive-contextual framework. *Psychological Bulletin*, *108*, 267–290.

Harris, J. R. (1998). *The nurture assumption*. New York: Free Press.

Harris, J. R. (2000). Socialization, personality development, and the child's environment: A comment on Vandell (2000). *Developmental Psychology*, *36*, 711–723.

Harrist, A. W., Pettit, G. S., Dodge, K. A., and Bates, J. E. (1994). Dyadic synchrony in mother–child interaction: Relations with children's kindergarten adjustment. *Family Relations*, *43*, 417–424.

Hart, C. H., DeWolf, M., Wozniak, P., and Burts, D. (1992). Maternal and paternal disciplinary styles: Relations with preschoolers' playground behavioral orientations and peer status. *Child Development*, *63*, 879–892.

Hart, C. H., Ladd, G. W., and Burleson, B. R. (1990). Children's expectations of the outcomes of social strategies: Relations with sociometric status and maternal disciplinary styles. *Child Development*, *61*, 127–137.

Hart, C. H., Nelson, D. A., Robinson, C. C., Olsen, S. F., and McNeilly-Choque, M. K. (1998). Overt and relational aggression in Russian nursery-school-age children: Parenting style and marital linkages. *Developmental Psychology*, *34*, 687–697.

Hartup, W. W. (1979). The social worlds of childhood. *American Psychologist*, *34*, 944–950.

Haskett, M., and Kistner, J. A. (1991). Social interactions and peer perceptions of young physically abused children. *Child Development*, *62*, 979–990.

Hastings, P. D., and Rubin, K. H. (1999). Predicting mothers' beliefs about preschool-aged children's social behavior: Evidence for maternal attitudes moderating child effects. *Child Development*, *70*, 722–741.

Herrera, C., and Dunn, J. (1997). Early experiences with family conflict: Implications for arguments with a close friend. *Developmental Psychology*, *33*, 869–881.

Hetherington, E. M., Cox, M., and Cox, R. (1979). Play and social interaction in children following divorce. *Journal of Social Issues*, *35*, 26–49.

Hinshaw, S. P., Zupan, B. A., Simmel, C., Nigg, J. T., and Melnick, S. (1997). Peer status in boys with and without attention-deficit hyperactivity disorder: Predictions from overt and covert antisocial behavior, social isolation, and authoritative parenting beliefs. *Child Development*, *68*, 880–896.

Hodges, E. V. E., Finnegan, R. A., and Perry, D. A. (1999). Skewed autonomy-relatedness in preadolescents' conceptions of their relationships with mother, father, and best friend. *Developmental Psychology*, *35*, 737–748.

Hoffman, M. L. (1960). Power assertion by the parent and its impact on the child. *Child Development*, *31*, 129–143.

Hoffman, M. L. (1988). Moral development. In M. H. Bornstein and M. E. Lamb (Eds.), *Developmental psychology* (2nd ed., pp. 497–548). Hillsdale, NJ: Lawrence Erlbaurn Associates.

Holahan, C. J., and Moos, R. H. (1987). Risk, resistance, and psychological distress: A longitudinal analysis with adults and children. *Journal of Abnormal Psychology*, *96*, 3–13.

Howes, C. (1983). Patterns of friendship. *Child Development*, *54*, 1041–1053.

Howes, C. (1988). Peer interaction of young children. *Monographs of the Society for Research in Child Development* (53, Serial No. 217).

Howes, C., and Eldredge, R. (1985). Responses of abused, neglected, and nonmaltreated children to the behaviors of their peers. *Journal of Applied Developmental Psychology*, *6*, 261–270.

Howes, C., and Espinosa, M. P. (1985). The consequences of child abuse for the formation of relationships with peers. *Child Abuse and Neglect*, *9*, 397–404.

Howes, C., Hamilton, C. E., and Philipsen, L. C. (1998). Stability and continuity of child–caregiver and child–peer relationships. *Child Development*, *69*, 418–426.

Howes, C., Matheson, C., and Hamilton, C. E. (1994). Maternal, teacher, and child-care history correlates of children's relationships with peers. *Child Development*, *65*, 264–273.

Isley, S. L., O'Neil, R., Clatfelter, D., and Parke, R. (1999). Parent and child expressed affect and children's social competence: Modeling direct and indirect pathways. *Developmental Psychology*, *35*, 547–560.

Kantor, M. (1965). *Mobility and mental health*. Springfield, IL: Charles C. Thomas.

Katz, L. F., and Gottman, J. M. (1993). Patterns of marital conflict predict children's internalizing and externalizing behaviors. *Developmental Psychology*, *29*, 940–950.

Kerns, K. A. (1994). A longitudinal examination of links between mother-child attachment and children's friendships in early childhood. *Journal of Social and Personal Relationships*, *11*, 379–381.

Kerns, K. A., and Barth, J. M. (1995). Attachment and play: Convergence across components of parent–child relationships and their relations to peer competence. *Journal of Social and Personal Relationships*, *12*, 243–260.

Kerns, K. A., Klepac, L., and Cole, A. K. (1996). Peer relationships and preadolescents perceptions of security in the child–mother relationship. *Developmental Psychology, 32*, 457–466.

Kerr, M., and Stattin, H. (2000). What parents know, how they know it, and several forms of adolescent adjustment: Further support for a reinterpretation of monitoring. *Developmental Psychology, 36*, 366–380.

Krappman, L. (1986, December). *Family relationships and peer relationships in middle childhood.* Paper presented at the Family Systems and Life-Span Development Conference at the Max Planck Institute, Berlin.

Kreppner, K. (1989). Linking infant development-in-context research to the investigation of life-span development. In K. Kreppner and R. Lerner (Eds.), *Family systems and life-span development* (pp. 33–64). Hillsdale, NJ: Lawrence Erlbaum Associates.

Krevans, J., and Gibbs, J. C. (1996). Parents' use of inductive discipline: Relations to children's empathy and prosocial behavior. *Child Development, 67*, 3263–3277.

Kuczynski, L. (1984). Socialization goals and mother–child interaction: Strategies for long-term and short-term compliance. *Developmental Psychology, 20*, 1061–1073.

Kupersmidt, J. B., Griesler, P. C., DeRosier, M. E., Patterson, C. J., and Davis, P. W. (1995). Childhood aggression and peer relations in the context of family and neighborhood factors. *Child Development, 66*, 360–375.

Ladd, G. W. (1990). Having friends, keeping friends, making friends, and being liked by peers in the classroom: Predictors of children's early school adjustment? *Child Development, 61*, 312–331.

Ladd, G. W. (1992). Themes and theories: Perspectives on processes in family–peer relationships. In R. D. Parke and G. W. Ladd (Eds.), *Family–peer relationships: Modes of linkage* (pp. 1–34). Hillsdale, NJ: Lawrence Erlbaum Associates.

Ladd, G. W. (1999). Peer relationships and social competence during early and middle childhood. *Annual Review of Psychology* (Vol. 50, pp. 333–359), Palo Alto, CA: Annual Reviews.

Ladd, G. W., Birch, S. H., and Buhs, E. (1999). Children's social and scholastic lives in kindergarten: Related spheres of influence? *Child Development, 70*, 1373–1400.

Ladd, G. W., and Coleman, C. (1993). Young children's peer relationships: Forms, features and functions. In B. Spodek (Ed.), *Handbook of research on the education of young children* (2nd ed., pp. 57–76). New York: Macmillan.

Ladd, G. W., and Golter, B. (1988). Parents' management of preschoolers' peer relations: Is it related to children's social competence? *Developmental Psychology, 24*, 109–117.

Ladd, G. W., and Hart, C. H. (1992). Creating informal play opportunities: Are parents' and preschoolers' initiations related to children's competence with peers? *Developmental Psychology, 28*, 1179–1187.

Ladd, G. W., Hart, C. H., Wadsworth, E. M., and Golter, B. S. (1988). Preschoolers' peer networks in nonschool settings: Relationship to family characteristics and school adjustment. In S. Salzinger, J. Antrobus, and M. Hammer (Eds.), *Social networks of children, adolescents, and college students* (pp. 61–92). Hillsdale, NJ: Lawrence Erlbaum Associates.

Ladd, G. W., Kochenderfer, B. J., and Coleman, C. C. (1997). Classroom peer acceptance, friendship, and victimization: Distinct relational systems that contribute uniquely to children's school adjustment? *Child Development, 68*, 1181–1197.

Ladd, G. W., and Ladd, B. J. (1998). Parenting behaviors and the parent–child relationship: Correlates of peer victimization in kindergarten? *Developmental Psychology, 34*, 1450–1458.

Ladd, G. W., Le Sieur, K. D., and Profilet, S. M. (1993). Direct parental influences of young children's peer relations. In S. Duck (Ed.), *Learning about relationships* (pp. 152–183). London: Sage.

Ladd, G. W., and Price, J. M. (1986). Promoting children's cognitive and social competence: The relations between parent's perceptions of task difficulty and children's perceived and actual competence. *Child Development, 57*, 446–460.

Ladd, G. W., and Price, J. (1987). Predicting children's social and school adjustment following the transition from preschool to kindergarten. *Child Development, 57*, 446–460.

Ladd, G. W., Profilet, S. M., and Hart C. H. (1992). Parents' management of children's peer relations: Facilitating and supervising children's activities in the peer culture. In R. D. Parke, and G. W. Ladd (Eds.), *Family–peer relationships: Modes of linkage* (pp. 215–254). Hillsdale, NJ: Lawrence Erlbaum Associates.

LaFreniere, P. J., and Dumas, J. E. (1992). A transactional analysis of early childhood anxiety and social withdrawal. *Development and Psychopathology, 4*, 385–402.

LaFreniere, P., and Sroufe, L. A. (1985). Profiles of peer competence in the preschool: Interrelations between measures, influence of social ecology, and relation to attachment history. *Developmental Psychology, 21*, 56–69.

Laird, R. D., Pettit, G. S., Mize, J. Brown, E. G., and Lindsey, E. (1994). Mother–child conversations about peers: Contributions to competence. *Family Relations, 43*, 425–432.

Lamb, M. E., and Nash, A. (1989). Infant–mother attachment, sociability, and peer competence. In T. J. Berndt and G. W. Ladd (Eds.), *Peer relationships in child development* (pp. 219–245). New York: Wiley.

Levitt, M. J., Weber, R. A., Clark, M. C., and McDonnell, P. (1985). Reciprocity of exchange in toddler sharing behavior. *Developmental Psychology, 21*, 122–123.

Lewis, M. J. (Ed.). (1984). *Beyond the dyad.* New York: Plenum.

Lewis, M. J., Feiring, C., and Rosenthal, S. (2000). Attachment over time. *Child Development, 71*, 707–720.

Lieberman, A. F. (1977). Preschoolers' competence with a peers: Relations with attachment and peer experience. *Child Development, 48*, 1277–1287.

Lieberman, M., Doyle, A. B., and Markiewicz, D. (1999). Developmental patterns in security of attachment to mother and father in late childhood and early adolescence: Associations with peer relations. *Child Development, 70,* 202–213.

Lindsey, E. W., and Mize, J. (2000). Parent–child physical and pretense play: Links to children's social competence. *Merrill-Palmer Quarterly, 46,* 565–591.

Lindsey, E. W., Mize, J., and Pettit, G. S. (1997). Differential play patterns of mothers and fathers of sons and daughters: Implications for children's gender role development. *Sex Roles, 37,* 643–661.

Lollis, S. P. (1990). Maternal influence on children's separation behavior. *Child Development, 61,* 99–103.

Lollis, S. P., Ross, H. S., and Tate, E. (1992). Parents' regulation of children's peer interactions: Direct influences. In R. D. Parke and G. W. Ladd (Eds.), *Family–peer relationships: Modes of linkage* (pp. 255–294). Hillsdale, NJ: Lawrence Erlbaum Associates.

Long, N., Forehand, R., Fauber, R., and Brody, G. (1987). Self-perceived and independently observed competence of young adolescents as a function of parental marital conflict and recent divorce. *Journal of Abnormal Child Psychology, 15,* 1547.

Lytton, H. (1990). Child and parent effects in boys' conduct disorder: A reinterpretation. *Developmental Psychology, 26,* 683–697.

Maccoby, E. E., and Martin, J. A. (1983). Socialization in the context of the family: Parent–child interaction. In P. H. Mussen (Series Ed.) and E. M. Hetherington (Vol. Ed.), *Handbook of child psychology: Vol. 4. Socialization, personality and social development* (pp. 1–102). New York: Wiley.

MacDonald, K. (1987). Parent–child physical play with rejected, neglected, and popular boys. *Developmental Psychology, 23,* 705–711.

MacDonald, K. B., and Parke, R. D. (1984). Bridging the gap: Parent–child play interaction and interactive competence. *Child Development, 55,* 1265–1277.

MacKinnon-Lewis, C., Rabiner, D., and Starnes, R. (1999). Predicting boys' social acceptance and aggression: The role of mother–child interactions and boys' beliefs about peers. *Developmental Psychology, 35,* 632–639.

MacKinnon-Lewis, C., Volling, B. L., Lamb, M., Dechman, K., Rabiner, D., and Curtner, M. E. (1994). A cross-contextual analysis of boys' social competence: From family to school. *Developmental Psychology, 30,* 325–333.

Mahoney, M. J., and Cairns, R. D. (1997). Do extracurricular activities protect against early school dropout? *Developmental Psychology, 33,* 241–253.

Main, M., and George, C. (1985). Response of abused and disadvantaged toddlers to distress in agemates: A study in the day-care setting. *Developmental Psychology, 21,* 407–412.

Main, M., Kaplan, N., and Cassidy, J. (1985). Security in infancy, childhood, and adulthood: A move to the level of representation. In I. Bretherton and E. Waters (Eds.), Growing points of attachment theory and research. *Monographs of the Society for Research in Child Development, 50*(Serial No. 201).

McFadyen-Ketchum, S. A., Bates, J. E., Dodge, K. A., and Pettit, G. S. (1996). Patterns of change in early childhood aggressive-disruptive behavior: Gender differences in predictions from early coercive and affectionate mother-child interactions. *Child Development, 67,* 2417–2433.

Medrich, E. A., Roizen, J. A., Rubin, V., and Buckley, S. (1982). *The serious business of growing up: A study of children's lives outside school.* Berkeley: University of California Press.

Melson, G., Ladd, G. W., and Hsu, H. C. (1993). Maternal support networks, maternal cognitions, and young children's social and cognitive development. *Child Development, 64,* 1401–1417.

Mills, R. S., and Rubin, K. H. (1990). Parental beliefs about problematic social behaviors in early childhood. *Child Development, 61,* 138–151.

Mize, J., and Ladd, G. W. (1988). Predicting preschoolers' peer behavior and status from their interpersonal strategies: A comparison of verbal and enactive responses to hypothetical social dilemmas. *Developmental Psychology, 24,* 782–788.

Mize, J., and Ladd, G. W. (1990). A cognitive-social learning approach to social skill training with low-status preschool children. *Developmental Psychology, 26,* 388–397.

Mize, J., and Pettit, G. S. (1997). Mothers' social coaching, mother–child relationship style, and children's peer competence: Is the medium the message? *Child Development, 68,* 291–311.

Mize, J., Pettit, G. S., and Brown, E. G. (1995). Mothers' supervision of their children's peer play: Relations with beliefs, perceptions, and knowledge. *Developmental Psychology, 31,* 311–321.

Mize, J., Pettit, G. S., and Meece, D. (2000). Explaining the link between parenting behavior and children's peer competence: A critical examination of the "mediating process" hypothesis. In K. A. Kerns, J. W. Contreras, and A. M. Neal-Barnett (Eds.), *Family and peers: Linking two social worlds* (pp. 137–168). New York: Greenwood/Praeger.

Mounts, N. (2000). Parental management of adolescent peer relationships: What are its effects on friend selection? In K. A. Kerns, J. W. Contreras, and A. M. Neal-Barnett (Eds.), *Family and peers: Linking two social worlds* (pp. 169–193). Westport, CT: Praeger.

Mueller, E., and Brenner, J. (1977). The origins of social skills and interaction among playgroup toddlers. *Child Development, 48,* 854–961.

Mullins, L. L., Siegel, L. J., and Hodges, K. (1985). Cognitive problem-solving and life events correlates of depressive symptoms in children. *Journal of Abnormal Child Psychology, 13,* 305–314.

Neale, J. M., and Weintraub, S. (1975). Children vulnerable to psychopathology: The Stoney Brook High Risk Project. *Journal of Abnormal Child Psychology, 3*, 95–103.

Nix, R. L., Pinderhughes, E. E., Dodge, K. A., Bates, J. A., Pettit, G. S., and McFadyen-Ketchum, S. (1999). The relation between mothers' hostile attribution tendencies and children's externalizing behavior problems: The mediating role of mothers' harsh disciplinary practices. *Child Development, 70*, 896–909.

Olweus, D. (1993). Bullies on the playground: The role of victimization. In C. H. Hart (Ed.), *Children on playgrounds: Research perspectives and applications* (pp. 85–128). Albany: State University of New York Press.

O'Reilly, A. W., and Bornstein, M. H. (1993). Caregiver–child interaction in play. *New Directions in Child Development, 59*, 55–56.

Parke, R. D. (1992). Epilogue: Remaining issues and future trends in the study of family–peer relationships. In R. D. Parke and G. W. Ladd (Eds.), *Family–peer relationships: Modes of linkage* (pp. 425–438). Hillsdale, NJ: Lawrence Erlbaum Associates.

Parke, R. D., and Buriel, R. (1998). Socialization in the family: Ethnic and ecological perspectives. In W. Damon (Series Ed.), N. Eisenberg (Vol. Ed.), *Handbook of child psychology* (Vol. 3, pp. 463–552). New York: Wiley.

Parke, R. D., and Collmer, C. W. (1975). Child abuse: An interdisciplinary analysis. In E. M. Hetherington (Ed.), *Review of child development research* (Vol. 5, pp. 509–590). Chicago: University of Chicago Press.

Parke, R. D., and Ladd, G. W. (Eds.). (1992). *Family–peer relationships: Modes of linkage*. Hillsdale, NJ: Lawrence Erlbaum Associates.

Parke, R. D., MacDonald, K., Beitel, A., and Bhavnagri, N. (1988). The role of the family in the development of peer relationships. In R. Peters and R. J. McMahon (Eds.), *Social learning systems approaches to marriage and the family* (pp. 17–44). New York: Bruner/Mazel.

Parke, R. D., MacDonald, K., Burks, V. M., Carson, J., Bhavnagri, N., Barth, J. M., and Beitel, A. (1989). Family and peer linkages: In search of linkages. In K. Kreppner and R. M. Lerner (Eds.), *Family systems and life span development* (pp. 65–92). Hillsdale, NJ: Lawrence Erlbaum Associates.

Parker, J. G., and Herrera, C. (1996). Interpersonal processes in friendship: A comparison of abused and nonabused children's experiences. *Developmental Psychology, 32*, 1025–1038.

Patterson, C. J., Griesler, P. C., Vaden, N. A., and Kupersmidt, J. B. (1992). Family economic circumstances, life transitions, and children's peer relations. In R. D. Parke and G. W. Ladd (Eds.), *Family–peer relationships: Modes of linkage* (pp. 385–424). Hillsdale, NJ: Lawrence Erlbaum Associates.

Patterson, C. J., Kupersmidt, J. B., and Griesler, P. C. (1990). Children's perception of self and of relationships with others as a function of sociometric status. *Child Development, 61*, 1335–1349.

Patterson, C. J., Vaden, N. A., and Kupersmidt, J. B. (1991). Family background, recent life events, and peer rejection during childhood. *Journal of Social and Personal Relationships, 8*, 347–362.

Patterson, G. R. (1982). *Coercive family process*. Eugene, OR: Castalia.

Patterson, G. R. (1983). Stress: A change agent for family process. In N. Garmezy and M. Rutter (Eds.), *Stress, coping, and development in children* (pp. 235–264). New York: McGraw-Hill.

Patterson, G. R., Reid, J. B., and Dishion, T. J. (1992). *Antisocial boys*. Eugene, OR: Castalia.

Pelton, L. (1978). Child abuse and neglect: The myth of classlessness. *American Journal of Orthopsychiatry, 48*, 608–617.

Perlman, M., and Ross, H. S. (1997). The benefits of parent intervention in children's disputes: An examination of concurrent changes in children's fighting styles. *Child Development, 68*, 690–700.

Perry, D. G., Finnegan, R. A., Hodges, E. V. E., Kennedy, E., and Malone, M. (August, 1993). *Aspects of aggressive and victimized children's relationships with parents and peers*. Paper presented at the annual meeting of the American Psychological Association, Toronto, Ontario, Canada.

Pettit, G. S., Bates, J. E., and Dodge, K. A. (1997). Supportive parenting, ecological context, and children's adjustment: A seven-year longitudinal study. *Child Development, 68*, 908–923.

Pettit, G. S., Bates, J. E., Dodge, K. A., and Meece, D. (1999). The impact of after-school peer contact on early adolescent externalizing problems is moderated by parental monitoring, perceived neighborhood safety, and prior adjustment. *Child Development, 70*, 768–778.

Pettit, G. S., Brown, E. G., Mize, J., and Lindsey, E. (1998). Mothers' and fathers' socializing behaviors in three contexts: Links with children's peer competence. *Merrill-Palmer Quarterly, 44*, 173–193.

Pettit, G. S., Clawson, M., Dodge, K. A., and Bates, J. E. (1996). Stability and change in children's peer-rejected status: The role of child behavior, parent–child relations, and family ecology. *Merrill-Palmer Quarterly, 42*, 91–118.

Pettit, G. S., Dodge, K. A., and Brown, M. (1988). Early family experience, social problem-solving patterns, and children's social competence. *Child Development, 59*, 107–120.

Pettit, G. S., and Harrist, A. W. (1993). Children's aggressive and socially unskilled playground behavior with peers: Origins in early family relations. In C. H. Hart (Ed.), *Children on playgrounds: Research perspectives and applications* (pp. 240–270). Albany: State University of New York Press.

Pettit, G. S., Harrist, A. W., Bates, J. E., and Dodge, K. A. (1991). Family interaction, social cognition, and children's subsequent relationships with peers at kindergarten. *Journal of Social and Personal Relationships, 8*, 383–402.

Pettit, G. S., Laird, R. D., Bates, J. E., and Dodge, K. A. (1997). Patterns of after-school care in middle childhood: Risk factors and developmental outcomes. *Merrill-Palmer Quarterly, 43*, 515–538.

Pettit, G. S., Laird, R. D., Bates, J. E., Dodge, K. A., and Criss, M. M. (2001). Antecedents and behavior-problem outcomes of parental monitoring and psychological control in early adolescence. *Child Development, 72*, 583–598.

Pettit, G. S., and Mize, J. (1993). Substance and style: Understanding the ways in which parents teach children about social relationships. In S. Duck (Ed.), *Understanding relationship processes: Vol. 2. Learning about relationships* (pp. 118–151). Newbury Park, CA: Sage.

Pierce, K. M., Hamm, J. V., and Vandell, D. L. (1999). Experiences in after-school programs and children's adjustment in first-grade classrooms. *Child Development, 70*, 756–767.

Porges, S. W., Doussard-Roosevelt, J. A., and Maiti, A. K. (1994). Vagal tone and the physiological regulation of emotion. In N. A. Fox (Ed.), The development of emotion regulation: Biological and behavioral considerations. *Monographs of the Society for Research in Child Development, 59*(Serial No. 240).

Posner, J. K., and Vandell, D. L. (1994). Low-income children's after-school care: Are there beneficial effects of after-school programs? *Child Development, 65*, 440–456.

Profilet, S. M., and Ladd, G. W. (1994). Do mothers' perceptions and concerns about preschoolers' peer competence predict their peer management practices? *Social Development, 3*, 205–221.

Putallaz, M. (1987). Maternal behavior and children's sociometric status. *Child Development, 58*, 324–340.

Putallaz, M., Costanzo, P. R., and Smith, R. (1991). Maternal recollections of childhood peer relationships: Implications for their children's social competence. *Journal of Social and Personal Relationships, 8*, 403–422.

Putallaz, M., and Heflin, A. H. (1990). Parent–child interaction. In S. R. Asher and J. D. Coie (Eds.), *Peer rejection in childhood* (pp. 189–216). New York: Cambridge University Press.

Reiss, D., with Neiderhiser, J. M., Hetherington, E. M., and Plomin, R. (2000). *The relationship code: Deciphering genetic and social influences on adolescent development*. Cambridge, MA: Harvard University Press.

Roff, M., Sells, S. B., and Golden, M. M. (1972). *Social adjustment and personality development in children*. Minneapolis: University of Minnesota Press.

Rolf, J. (1972). The social and academic competence of children vulnerable to schizophrenia and other behavioral pathologies. *Journal of Abnormal Psychology, 80*, 225–245.

Ross, H. S., Tesla, C., Kenyon, B., and Lollis, S. (1991). Maternal intervention in toddler peer conflict: The socialization of principles of justice. *Developmental Psychology, 6*, 994–1003.

Rowe, D. C. (1994). *The limits of family influence: Genes, experience, and behavior*. New York: Guilford.

Rubin, K. H., Hastings, P., Chen, X., Stewart, S., and McNichol, K. (1998). Intrapersonal and maternal correlates of aggression, conflict, and externalizing problems in toddlers. *Child Development, 69*, 1614–1629.

Rubin, K. H., Hymel, S., Mills, R. S. L., and Rose-Krasnor, L. (1991). Conceptualizing different developmental pathways to and from social isolation in childhood. In D. Cicchetti and S. L. Toth (Eds.), *Rochester symposium on developmental psychopathology: Vol. 2. Internalizing and externalizing expressions of dysfunction* (pp. 91–122). Hillsdale, NJ: Lawrence Erlbaum Associates.

Rubin, K. H., Mills, R. S., and Rose-Krasnor, L. (1989). Maternal beliefs and children's social competence. In B. Schneider, J. Nadel, G. Attili, and R. Weissberg (Eds.), *Social competence in developmental perspective* (pp. 313–331), Amsterdam: Klewer.

Rudolph, K. D., Hammen, C., and Burge D. (1995). Cognitive representations of self, family, and peers in school-age children: links with social competence and sociometric status. *Child Development, 66*, 1385–1402.

Russell, A., and Finnie, V. (1990). Preschool children's social status and maternal instruction to assist group entry. *Developmental Psychology, 26*, 603–611.

Russell, A., Pettit, G. S., and Mize, J. (1998). Horizontal qualities in parent–child relationships: Parallels with and possible consequences for children's peer relationships. *Developmental Review, 18*, 313–352.

Ryan, R. M., and Solky, J. A. (1996). What is supportive about social support? On the psychological needs for autonomy and relatedness. In G. R. Pierce and B. R. Sarason (Eds.), *Handbook of social support and the family* (pp. 249–267). New York: Plenum.

Sameroff, A. J., and Chandler, M. J. (1975). Reproductive risk and the continuum of caretaking casualty. In F. D. Horowitz (Ed.), *Review of child development research* (Vol. 4, pp. 197–244). Chicago: University of Chicago Press.

Sandler, I. N., and Ramsey, J. (1980). Dimensional analysis of children's stressful life events. *American Journal of Community Psychology, 8*, 285–302.

Schneider, B. H., Atkinson, L., and Tardif, C. (2000). Child–parent attachment and children's peer relations: A quantitative review. *Developmental Psychology, 37*, 86–100.

Schwartz, D., Dodge, K. A., Pettit, G. S., and Bates, J. E. (1997). The early socialization of aggressive victims of bullying. *Child Development, 68*, 665–675.

Segoe, M. (1939). Factors influencing the selection of associates. *Journal of Educational Research, 27*, 32–40.

Sroufe, L. A., and Fleeson, J. (1986). Attachment and the construction of relationships. In W. Hartup and Z. Rubin (Eds.), *Relationships and development* (pp. 57–71). Hillsdale, NJ: Lawrence Erlbaum Associates.

Stattin, H., and Kerr, M. (2000). Parental monitoring: A reinterpretation. *Child Development, 71*, 1072–1085.

Steinberg, L. (1986). Latchkey children and susceptibility to peer pressure: An ecological analysis. *Developmental Psychology, 22*, 433–439.

Trachtenberg, S., and Viken, R. J. (1994). Aggressive boys in the classroom: Biased attributions or shared perceptions? *Child Development, 65*, 829–835.

Trickett, P. K., and Kuczynski, L. (1986). Children's misbehaviors and parental discipline in abusive and nonabusive families. *Developmental Psychology, 22*, 115–123.

Troy, M., and Sroufe, L. A. (1987). Victimization among preschoolers: The role of attachment and relationship history. *Journal of American Academy of Child Psychiatry, 26*, 166–172.

Vandell, D. L. (2000). Parents, peer groups, and other socializing influences. *Developmental Psychology, 36*, 699–710.

Vandell, D. L., Henderson, V. K., and Wilson, K. S. (1988). A longitudinal study of children with day-care experiences of varying quality. *Child Development, 59*, 1286–1292.

Vandell, D. L., and Posner, J. K. (1999). Conceptualization and measurement of children's after-school environments. In S. L. Friedman and T. D. Wachs (Eds.), *Measuring environment across the life span: Emerging methods and concepts* (pp. 167–196). Washington, DC: American Psychological Association.

Van Vliet, W. C. (1981). The environmental context of children's friendships: An empirical and conceptual examination of the role of child density. In A. E. Osterberg, C. P. Tiernan, and R. A. Findlay (Eds.), *Proceedings from the 12th annual conference of the Environmental Design Research Association* (pp. 216–224). Washington, DC: Environmental Design Research Association.

Vernberg, E. M., Berry, S. H., Ewell, K. K., and Abwender, D. A. (1993). Parents' use of friendship facilitation strategies and the formation of friendships in early adolescence: A prospective study. *Journal of Family Psychology, 7*, 356–359.

Verschueren, K., and Marcoen, A. (1999). Representation of self and socioemotional competence in kindergarteners: Differential and combined effects of attachment to mother and father. *Child Development, 70*, 183–201.

Wahler, R. G. (1996). Chaos and order in the parenting of aggressive children: Personal narratives as guidelines. In C. F. Ferris and T. Grisso (Eds.), *Understanding aggressive behavior in children* (pp. 153–168). New York: New York Academy of Sciences.

Waters, E., Merrick, S. K., Albersheim, L. J., and Treboux, D. (March, 1995). *Attachment security from infancy to early adulthood: A 20-year longitudinal study*. Paper presented at the biennial conference of the Society for Research in Child Development, New Orleans, LA.

Waters, E., Vaughn, B., Posada, G., and Kondo-Ikemura, K. (1995). Caregiving, cultural, and cognitive perspectives on secure-base behavior and working models. *Monographs of the Society for Research in Child Development, 60*(Serial No. 244).

Waters, E., Wippman, J., and Sroufe, L. A. (1979). Attachment, positive affect, and competence in the peer group: Two studies in construct validation. *Child Development, 50*, 821–829.

Weinraub, M., and Wolf, B. (1983). Effects of stress and social supports on mother–child interactions in single- and two-parent families. *Child Development, 54*, 1297–1311.

Weintraub, S., Prinz. R., and Neale, J. M. (1979). Peer evaluations of the competence of children vulnerable to psychopathology. *Journal of Abnormal Child Psychology, 4*, 461–473.

Weiss, B., Dodge, K. A., Bates, J. E., and Pettit, G. S. (1992). Some consequences of early harsh discipline: Child aggression and a maladaptive social information processing style. *Child Development, 63*, 1321–1335.

Wolfe, D. A. (1985). Child abusive parents: An empirical review and analysis. *Psychological Bulletin, 97*, 462–482.

Wolfe, D. A. (1987). *Child abuse*. Newbury Park, CA: Sage.

Youngblade, L. M., and Belsky, J. (1992). Parent–child antecedents of 5-year-olds' close friendships: A longitudinal analysis. *Developmental Psychology, 28*, 700–713.

Youngblade, L. M., Park, K. A., and Belsky, J. (1993). Measurement of young children's close friendship: A comparison of two independent assessment systems and their associations with attachment security. *International Journal of Behavioral Development, 4*, 563–587.

Zahn-Waxler, C., Cummings, E. M., McKnew, D. H., and Radke-Yarrow, M. (1984). Altruism, aggression, and social interactions in young children with a manic-depressive parent. *Child Development, 55*, 112–122.

Zahn-Waxler, C., Denham, S., Iannotti, R. J., and Cummings, E. M. (1992). Peer relations in childhood with a depressed caregiver. In R. D. Parke and G. W. Ladd (Eds.), *Family–peer relationships: Modes of linkage* (pp. 317–344). Hillsdale, NJ: Lawrence Erlbaum Associates.

12

Health Promotion for Parents

Barbara J. Tinsley
Charlotte N. Markey
Andrea J. Ericksen
Rebecca V. Ortiz
University of California, Riverside
Alan Kwasman
University of California, Riverside
Pediatric Medical Group, Riverside

INTRODUCTION

Most parents want their children to be safe and healthy. But implementing that desire can be a difficult and challenging struggle. According to a recent survey of American's health habits, American parents and children are fatter, more stressed, exercise less, and pay less attention to what they eat than ever (Richter et al., 2000). Many of the most serious health and social problems facing us today have their origins, and potential solutions, in health behaviors developed in childhood and adolescence (Spruijt-Metz, 1999). At least eight out of ten of the leading causes of death—heart disease, cancer, strokes, injuries, chronic lung disease, diabetes, liver disease, and atherosclerosis—are strongly related to behaviors such as eating, lack of exercise, smoking, and alcohol consumption. In order to prevent these and other causes of morbidity and mortality, maladaptive health behaviors that begin in childhood need to be understood and modified in the context of children's parenting and family environments.

Heart disease and cancer are the first and second leading causes of death in the United States. Although great strides have been made in reducing deaths from heart disease in the last 20 years, due to improvements in treatment for hypertension and myocardial infarction and changes in diet, smoking levels, and exercise patterns, deaths from many cancers continue to increase. Smoking cigarettes is the major cause of lung cancer, the leading cause in both men and women. We know that 80% of smokers begin to smoke during their adolescence and that attitudes learned in childhood and adolescence are the most powerful predictors of smoking in adulthood (Centers for Disease Control and Prevention, 1998). Imagine how much additional reduction in the numbers of death caused by these two major killers could be achieved if children began to eat healthy diets in childhood, if they never started to smoke cigarettes, and if physical exercise was a natural part of every child's life.

Physicians and other public health professionals now know enough about the biomedical causes of disease to prevent most debilitating illnesses in childhood; such morbidity should be much less frequent than it is in the United States. Yet, in this country, children's health suffers from birth onward. The overall U.S. infant mortality rate ranks twenty-second worldwide. The African American infant mortality rate ranks fortieth when compared with other countries' overall rates (Children's Defense Fund, 1994). Nine out of every 1,000 children in the United States die before age 1, which is twice the infant mortality rate of Japan. Between 30% to 55% of U.S. 2-year-old children are not adequately immunized, with the percentages of unimmunized children being even higher in major U.S. cities. Today, a 2-year-old in Mexico City is more likely to be fully immunized than his or her counterpart in the United States. Healthy young children are threatened by the return of such scourges as measles, mumps, and whooping cough. More than 26,000 measles cases—including 97 deaths—were reported in 1990, compared to just 3,000 cases in 1986. Even many older children are not staying healthy in the United States. Although many parents say they try to limit the salt, caffeine, fat and sugar in their children's diets, many children have very unhealthy diets (Gable and Lutz, 2000; Grundy, 2000). Several recent studies have demonstrated important gaps in the fitness levels of children and measured declines in physical ability over the past decade. Nearly one third of children ages 3 through 17 are overweight for their age and gender (Gable and Lutz, 2000). There appears to be an inadequate U.S. national commitment to prevention and health promotion; our national investment in prevention is estimated at less than 5% of the total annual health cost (Stone et al., 2000), and without this orientation toward prevention, the prospects for children's health and functioning cannot be improved. Money is available to provide expensive hospital care for those with serious illnesses; thousands of preterm and otherwise sick infants are hospitalized for months at a time. But Americans make inadequate attempts to improve children's lives before they get sick, and many of today's children will reach adulthood unhealthy.

The goal of this chapter is to review and integrate research focused on how parents promote children's health. Models of child health care, both historical and contemporary perspectives, are examined. Mechanisms of parent health promotion, and how pathways between parents' beliefs about health and their health behavior influence children's health orientation, are outlined. Next, parents' socialization of children's sick role and wellness behaviors is summarized. Evaluation of the research literature describing parental establishment, training, and enforcement of child health behavior guidelines is provided. Finally, a discussion of how parents function as a health socialization unit, beyond the individual level of analysis, is presented. In the following sections, the dominant models of child health socialization and care are described.

MODELS OF CHILD HEALTH CARE: HISTORICAL
AND CONTEMPORARY PERSPECTIVES

In order to understand the role of parents in the etiology of children's health status, it is important to review the historical and contemporary perspectives utilized in portraying the dynamics of child health. Until recently, the dominant model of children's health was biomedical, simultaneously emphasizing biological models of wellness and illness, and disregarding social, psychological, and behavioral dimensions of health. However, the dominance of the strict biomedical model of disease is lessening, and a model incorporating concern with behavior and the "whole" person is much more prevalent in health research and academic and clinical settings.

Developmental models have also undergone a series of revisions over the past three decades, resulting in increased recognition of biological factors such as wellness and illness as factors in development. Not only are genetic and constitutionally based differences among infants and children more often acknowledged as having an impact on health and development, but the continuing importance of biological factors, such as adequate nutrition for proper cognitive development, is increasingly addressed (Nelson, 2000; Wachs, 2000).

New developmental models that incorporate both biological and experiential components have appeared. These models demonstrate that neither biological nor experiential factors alone yield adequate understanding of development, and only by combining these components can one better understand development. Sameroff's (1989) transactional model of development suggests that two continua—one of reproductive casualty, which includes both genetic constitutional factors as well as birth-related trauma, and one of caretaking casualty, which includes the social, intellectual, and physical environment—are necessary for adequate prediction of developmental outcomes. Other models such as systems theory approaches similarly stress the necessity of considering the complex interplay between biological and experiential factors. These shifts suggest that traditional medical and developmental models have undergone modification, resulting in newer models that incorporate major tenets of each. Within this theoretical context, we now turn to an examination of how parents promote their children's health.

MECHANISMS OF HEALTH PROMOTION

The mechanisms of parents' promotion of children's health-related attitudes and behavior acquisition and socialization have been the focus of theoretical and empirical attention (Lees and Tinsley, in press; Tinsley, 1992, 1997). Two issues have been explored. First, what parental or other social environmental conditions provide the opportunity for the acquisition of attitudes or behaviors that are necessary for child wellness? Second, what are the mechanisms that facilitate the acquisition and socialization of these attitudes and behaviors? The research to date has focused on several possible factors that may be involved in explaining parental childhood health promotion. In studies of child health attitudes and behavior, the explanatory burden has fallen individually and interactively on two categories of variables. Child and parent characteristics (i.e., developmental status, demographics, personality variables, and gender) are important influences on children's health socialization potential and outcomes. Second, both independently and in concert with these characteristics, the direct and indirect effects of the social (e.g., parent and family relational and interactional variables) and the nonsocial parent and family environment in which children are reared have profound consequences for child short-term and long-term health (Lees and Tinsley, in press; Tinsley, 1992, 1997).

The most common and well-researched way in which children learn about health is via parents' models of health attitudes and behavior, articulated through parents' demonstrating, teaching, and reinforcing specific health attitudes and behavior (Lees and Tinsley, in press; Tinsley, 1992, 1997).

Children are hypothesized to learn concepts of health and health skills as a result of repeated opportunities for practice of these behaviors in the home. Evidence suggests that these concepts and skills are utilized by children, as they get older, in other health behavior-eliciting situations, such as with friends and in school. Exposure to these alternate, developmentally later contexts serves to modify these health attitudes and behaviors, but nevertheless, the research indicates that children's health attitudes and behaviors appear to be more similar than dissimilar to those of their parents (Brown and Mann, 1990; Wiehl and Tinsley, 1999).

CHILDREARING: A PATHWAY BETWEEN PARENTAL BELIEFS AND BEHAVIORS AND CHILDREN'S HEALTH ORIENTATION

How do parents promote children's positive health values and attitudes and behaviors? One pathway through which parent and child similarity in health beliefs may occur is through parental childrearing behavior. The classic study relating parent childrearing behavior to child health behavior was accomplished by Pratt (1973). This interview investigation of 273 families (mothers, fathers, and 9- to 13-year-old children) involved assessing the relations between childrearing styles and child health behaviors (e.g., brushing teeth, exercise, and nutrition). Pratt identified a style of parenting she termed the "energized family," which was related to the highest levels of child health practices.

The parents in these "energized families" permitted their children a high degree of autonomy and used reasoning rather than punishment as a discipline strategy. Although most of the correlations were low, Pratt reported that childrearing practices had a significant effect on children's health behavior, even when parents' own health behaviors were controlled. Childrearing attitudes that recognize the child as an individual and foster the child's assumption of responsibility were associated with positive health behavior in children (e.g., toothbrushing, sleep habits, exercise, nutritional practices, and refraining from smoking). In contrast, children reared in families with an autocratic style of childrearing were not as likely to practice such behaviors. The study is weakened by reliance on the children's perceptions of their parents' childrearing practices even when evidence from the parents themselves was available. Moreover, the independent contribution of mothers' childrearing practices, separate from fathers' childrearing practices, was not examined separately. Four more recent studies confirm these relations between general parental childrearing practices, and child health behavior.

Lau and Klepper (1988) investigated the illness orientations of 6- to 12-year-old children by examining parents' childrearing practices. Parental punishment and control (i.e., frequency of spanking, frequency of isolation, strictness, and the importance of discipline) were found to influence children's self-esteem, approaching statistical significance. In turn, child self-esteem was a significant predictor of children's illness orientation.

Further validation of this work is found cross-ethnically as well. A series of studies of nutrition-related motivational strategies of Mexican American mothers of 4- to 8-year-old children indicated that serving and helping children with their food was associated with food consumption compliance, and threats and bribes were negatively associated with healthy food consumption (see Birch et al., 2001; Birch and Fisher, 1998; Olvera-Ezzell, Power, and Cousins, 1990). Yamasaki (1990), in a study of parental childrearing attitudes associated with Type A behaviors (characterized by high scores on time urgency, competitive achievement-striving, and aggressiveness-hostility; identified as one of the factors leading to coronary health disease) in Japanese preschool children, found that mothers of Type A boys were less anxious about them, less affectionate toward them, demanded more compliance of them, and were less concerned about them than mothers of Type B boys. Furthermore, mothers of Type A girls were less anxious about their daughters than were mothers of Type B girls.

Finally, a study by Lees and Tinsley (1998) provide additional evidence for the link between parental childrearing practices and child health behavior. Mothers' parenting behavior and child health behavior were assessed in a sample of 70 preschool children. Warm, nurturant mothers (those who gave higher than average amounts of verbal praise and hugs and kisses as rewards for good behavior) had children who were more independent in a variety of health behaviors, such as toothbrushing, handwashing, exercising, going to bed at a regular time, and avoiding risk by staying away from poisons, as reported by parents. Additional results suggested that children whose mothers reported using monetary rewards and granting special privileges for good behavior had a tendency to make fewer nutritious food choices, as reported by their preschool teachers, than mothers who choose to use warmth and nurturance as strategies for encouraging good behavior in their children. In addition, mothers' general beliefs about childrearing were related to some of their children's safety behaviors. For example, parents who reported that children should get more discipline than they usually receive reported that their children showed less independence in seatbelt use. In contrast, mothers who believed that parents should be more flexible with children reported that their children exercised more independently. These findings seem to indicate some relations between maternal orientations toward more child-oriented mothering styles and autonomous healthy behaviors of their children, with a corresponding possible relation between authoritarian mothering and less independence in risk-preventive behaviors of children.

In support of Pratt's (1973) findings about the value of rewarding children for their good behavior, Lees and Tinsley (1998) found that the total time mothers reported using rewards for good behavior related to independence in taking naps and keeping regular bedtimes. Use of rewards was also related to less risky behavior as reported by preschool teachers. These studies, considered together, suggest that non-health-specific parental childrearing behavior affects child health behavior and illustrates the potential of this path from parental attitudes to parental behavior to child health behavior.

Together, these studies provide support for the hypothesis of parent–child transmission of health attitudes. Additional longitudinal work is necessary to clarify these relations. We now turn from an examination of the way in which parent beliefs affect children's health orientation to another way in which parents influence their children's health attitudes and behavior: parents' health behavior.

Parent Health Behavior

Social-learning theory focuses on the role of observational learning and reinforcement in childhood socialization (Caprara, Barbaranelli, Pastorelli, Bandura, and Zimbardo, 2000). The acquisition of internal health values and overt health behavior determined by parental role models is well documented in the child health behavior literature (Tinsley, 1992). In other words, parents who behave in health-enhancing or health-destructive ways are teaching these behaviors to their children. Children may learn and adopt similar behavior strategies by emulating and imitating the health-related behavior of their caregivers.

Research suggests that modeling health behavior is the most effective technique for socializing children's health behavior (Cullen, Baranowski, Rittenberry, and Olvera, 2000). The strongest support for the modeling effects of parents on children's health behavior comes from U.S. studies of the relations between parents' and children's smoking behavior (Carvajal, Wiatrek, Evans, Knee, and Nash, 2000). Having a parent who models smoking strongly increases the chances that a child will smoke, and conversely, parents who do not smoke are equally if not more likely to have a child who does not smoke. Other examples of health behavior which appear to be taught to children at least partially by parental modeling in studies of Euro-American children include using seat belts in a moving car (Stromsoe, Magnaes, and Nakstad, 2000), eating behavior (Birch and Fisher, 1998; Davison, Markey, and Birch, 2000), exercise (Sallis et al., 2000), alcohol use (Abbey, Pilgrim, Hendrickson, and Buresh, 2000), and Type A behavior patterns (Charron-Prochownik and Kovacs, 2000).

Research with non-Euro-American samples on parental modeling of health behavior as a factor in children's health socialization is somewhat consistent with these findings. In studies of the maternal socialization of Latino children's eating habits, Olvera-Ezzell and colleagues (1990) found that although mothers did report using modeling as a socialization technique for influencing their children's mealtime behavior, this technique was reportedly used much less often than other techniques such as threats, bribes, punishments, and nondirectives such as suggestions, questions, and offering choices. Thus, although modeling appears to be a significant mechanism for understanding the relations between parents' and children's health behavior, cultural differences in maternal health socialization strategies appear to be present. Recently, investigators have begun to examine the role of modeling and reinforcement in childhood health socialization, not only in terms of specific health behaviors, but also with regard to perceptions of health, illness, and coping strategies.

Socialization of Children's Sick Role Behavior

McGrath and colleagues (Dunn-Geier, McGrath, Rourke, Latter, and D'Astous, 1986; McGrath et al., 2000) found adolescents who do not cope well with chronic pain, in comparison to adolescents who cope well with chronic pain, have mothers who are more likely to demonstrate behavior that discourages adolescents' efforts at coping with an exercise task. Others have found that mothers who maintain positive environments for their children's pain, and create observational opportunities for their children with respect to pain, have children who report more pain (Chen, Zelter, Craske, and Katz, 2000; Robinson, Alverez, and Dodge, 1990). Still other research suggests a parental basis for children's sick role behavior. Mechanic (1979) assessed 350 fourth- through eighth-grade children and their mothers in order to investigate how children's health-related behaviors develop. Results indicated moderate relations between the extent to which mothers were attentive to their own illness symptoms and children's illness behavior, with only 31% of mothers being high self-reporters of their own symptomatology and high reporters of child symptomatology. However, in general, mothers tend to be more concerned and responsive with respect to their children's health than their own health. Although a very weak relation was found between mothers' attentiveness to symptoms and children's attentiveness to symptoms, a stronger relation was found between mothers' inclination to go to a doctor when feeling ill and their tendency to take their children to the doctor when the children felt ill (41% of the mothers in the study reported both low inclination to take themselves to a doctor when ill and low inclination to take their children to a doctor when the children were ill). Although Mechanic utilized analytical methods that greatly limited the number of different explanatory variables which could be simultaneously considered, Mechanic was able to demonstrate definite, although at times weak mother–child relations in health attitudes and behaviors. Mechanic (1979) conducted a follow-up investigation in an attempt to examine the stability of the original responses of the children. Although the follow-up assessment items were not entirely comparable to the earlier items, the results indicated some minor relations across the time points in health attitudes and behaviors. Young adults with fewer symptoms remembered their parents as concerned with teaching self-care and the promotion of positive health habits. The mothers of children who grew up to have fewer physical symptoms were positively oriented toward health rather than concerned with seeking medical attention for their children's minor illnesses.

In a similar study, Walker and Zeman (1992) investigated parents' responses to their children's illness behavior (i.e., the extent to which parents' encourage child sick role behavior such as giving children special treatment during times of illness, making medical visits for specific symptoms, and being excused from school, chores and homework due to physical symptoms), finding that mothers encourage their children's illness behavior more than fathers. Furthermore, the results of this study indicated that mothers reported that they encouraged illness behavior related to gastrointestinal symptoms more than for cold symptoms. These studies underscore the effectiveness of parental modeling and reinforcement of children's health behavior.

Not only do parents appear to influence children's experience of symptoms, but they help them to cope with related treatment. Specifically, researchers have explored a variety of questions related to parental competence in facilitating children's health treatments and medical procedures. In general, these studies examine maternal influences on children's fear and coping during inpatient and out-patient pediatric medical visits (Melamed, 1998; Peterson, Oliver, and Saldana, 1997). These studies suggest that a variety of behaviors, including parental use of distraction and low rates of ignoring, are associated with lower child distress and increased levels of child prosocial behavior (Stephens, Barkey, and Hall, 1999). Several specific maternal behaviors appear to be related to the extent of child distress during these procedures, including maternal agitation and reassurance. Other studies have focused exclusively on mothers' behavior during their children's immunizations and help us understand the direction of effects issue in these relations (Cohen, Manimala, and Blout, 2000). Cohen and colleagues (2000) examined the relations among parents' reports of their usual behaviors during their children's immunizations, their observed behavior coded from videotapes, and children's coping and distress during immunization procedures. Results suggest that mothers overestimate the quantity of their soothing behaviors and that no relation exists between mothers' reports of the behavior and their actual behavior during their children's immunization procedures. Furthermore, mothers' reports of their behavior were unrelated to their children's distress or coping. However, parents' behaviors were significantly related to children's distress, with parental agitation negatively related to children's coping and parental soothing positively related to child coping. These findings suggest that maternal behavior (in contrast to maternal reports of their own behavior) should be used to evaluate the necessity for training in how to help children cope with aversive medical treatment like immunizations.

Several researchers have similarly focused their attention on questions of whether parents' presence during their children's minor medical procedures is helpful, or possibly even detrimental. There are two viewpoints on this issue. The first is that children demonstrate more negativity during anxiety-producing medical procedures when their parents are present than when they are absent. Researchers who support this position cite operant conditioning theory, which suggests that most children have a history of having their mother comfort them when they display distress and she eliminates aversive stimuli for them. Therefore, the mother acquires discriminative stimulus value for the child during aversive situations. In other words, the presence of the mother during an unpleasant medical procedure serves as a signal to the child that predicts a favorable outcome (e.g., comforting) if the child shows distress (e.g., crying; Stephens et al., 1999). A second perspective suggests that children are more emotionally aroused when their mothers are present, which accounts for their increased crying during the medical procedures (Phipps, Fairclough, Tye, and Mulhern, 1998).

Other related questions concern whether parents want to be present during their children's medical procedures, and whether medical personnel want parents to be with their children during these procedures. One study addressed both of these questions. Powers and Rubenstein (1999) evaluated the effects on children, parents, and medical personnel of allowing parents to be present during their children's invasive medical procedures. Results suggested that parental presence significantly reduced parental anxiety related to the procedure. Moreover, most of the medical staff perceived that parents' presence during these procedures was helpful to the children and to their parents. Finally, most medical staff believed that allowing parents to observe their children's medical procedures was an appropriate policy.

Parents' presence during children's medical procedures: Jennifer's case.   Jennifer, a 3-year-old girl, had a fever spiking to 104 degrees and other flulike symptoms the night before her mother brought her to a pediatrician's office for an exam. Dr. Clark, Jennifer's pediatrician, was somewhat alarmed to find possible indications of meningitis, including a stiff neck, irritability, confusion, lethargy, and sensitivity to light. She told Jennifer's mother of her concerns and asked her mother to meet her at the local hospital, where she would perform a spinal tap to permit analysis of Jennifer's cerebrospinal fluid and diagnosis. Jennifer's mother seemed shocked at Dr. Clark's suggestion and became tearful, but agreed to meet Dr. Clark at the hospital. When Dr. Clark arrived at the hospital, she found Jennifer and her mother in a treatment room, being attended by a nurse and a nurse assistant. Jennifer had been prepared for the spinal tap by the nursing staff and was lying on her side, drifting in and out of sleep, whimpering occasionally. Jennifer's mother was at her side, appearing very pale and anxious. As soon as Dr. Clark entered the room, Jennifer's mother asked that she be allowed to stay with Jennifer during the procedure. Before Dr. Clark could answer Jennifer's mother, the nurse spoke to Dr. Clark, stating that she had already informed Jennifer's mother that parents were not allowed in treatment rooms during procedures, but could be with their children both before and after. Jennifer's mother spoke to Dr. Clark again, stating that she felt that Jennifer was scared of the procedure and she wanted to be able to comfort her during it. Dr. Clark told the nurse that she felt that Jennifer's mother would be a positive influence during the procedure, and agreed that Jennifer's mother could remain in the treatment room during the spinal tap. The nurse seemed annoyed but did not respond, but thought to herself that in her experience children seem to act out more when the parents were present. After preparing, Dr. Clark approached Jennifer's bed to do the spinal tap, with the needle in her hand. At the sight of the needle, Jennifer's mother gasped loudly. Jennifer then became more alert, and began crying. Jennifer's mother began crying softly herself and tried to hug and hold Jennifer. Dr. Clark asked Jennifer's mother to move away from Jennifer's bed so that she could complete the procedure. Jennifer's mother began arguing with Dr. Clark, and Jennifer cried harder, and twisted her body toward her mother. Dr. Clark asked the nurse and assistant to hold Jennifer tightly to ensure the safety and effectiveness of the spinal tap. As they circled the bed to follow Dr. Clark's request, Jennifer began moving vigorously in her bed, trying to climb into her mothers' arms. The nursing staff were trying to hold Jennifer on the bed. Dr. Clark asked Jennifer's mother to leave the room, to permit the procedure to be completed. Jennifer's mother became very angry and refused, still trying to hold her daughter.

Dr. Clark had seen parents behave this way before and was annoyed with herself for letting it happen. She realized that she had not adequately prepared Jennifer's mother for what would happen. She knew that it would have helped Jennifer's mother cope much more successfully if she had told Jennifer's mother, in more detail, exactly what would occur before she did the spinal tap. She also knew that she should have told Jennifer's mother that the sterile procedure was important, and that even though a parent could talk to the child during the procedure, the parent should not reach or touch the child during it. Dr. Clark knew she hadn't had time to teach Jennifer's mother everything there is to know about spinal taps, but a few words about sterile technique and the purpose of the spinal tap: to rule out meningitis, would have gone a long way. Dr. Clark, who was always committed to having a comforting parent near the child as much and often as possible, understood why so many pediatricians did not allow parents in the room during a lumbar puncture, and was, in the end, forced to abort the procedure.

This case study illustrates the complicated nature of medical professionals' decision making in their efforts to complete complex and anxiety-producing medical procedures on children. Balancing the comfort needs of children with the necessity for sterile and accurate completion of diagnostic and treatment procedures is a difficult and inexact science.

Melamed, in a review of maternal influences on children's coping with medical procedures, suggested that much more research in this area is needed in order to sort out the definition of parental competence in these situations and the developmental trajectories of parental influences on child competence during medical events (Melamed, 1998, in Vol. 5 of this *Handbook*). Research on the impact of parent behavior during medical procedures has focused almost exclusively on the mother. Future research in this area should additionally investigate both maternal and paternal behavior with respect to children's coping with medical procedures, specifically, and to illness more generally. Perhaps these studies should also move beyond examining the effects of parental presence, per se, on children's comfort level during such procedures. Evidence for this perspective comes from a study investigating whether inanimate, noninterfering attachment agents (e.g., children's security "blankies") can sooth children during medical procedures (Ybarra, Passman, and Eisenberg, 2000). Utilizing random assignment to the following conditions: (1) mother present, (2) "blankie" present, (3) mother and "blankie" present, or (4) neither mother nor "blankie" present during the medical procedures, behavior and physiological assessments indicated that mothers and children's security blankets were equally soothing to children undergoing medical procedures compared to the extent to which children with neither their mothers or their "blankies" were distressed. Moreover, having both attachment objects present (mothers and "blankies") did not offer additive soothing effects. The authors conclude that children's security blankets can function as appropriate maternal substitutes during aversive medical procedures.

The above discussion highlights the major issues currently under empirical review with respect to the modifying role of parents in both the socialization of children's sick role behavior and the negative impact of illness on children. Parmelee (1997), however, has argued for examining specific positive ways in which parents socialize their children concerning how to respond to recurring childhood minor illness. In a major departure from others' conceptualizations of children's reactions to illness, Parmelee highlighted parental practices that may be unique to the illness context per se, rather than childrearing in general. He suggested that childhood illness provides unique opportunities for such coping behaviors as the development of empathy, knowledge of self, prosocial behavior patterns, and affective and cognitive development. Parmelee suggested that this growth occurs through children's experiencing of minor illness and the care that they receive from parents and other family members, as well as by observing parents providing care when others are ill. Minor childhood illness experienced in the context of parents and family, as conceptualized by Parmelee, influences children's general social competence, their understanding of wellness and illness, and the physical and social-emotional causes of illness sensations (Parmelee, 1997).

Thus far, we have discussed the more indirect ways in which parents' behaviors affect children's health. Now we examine parents' direct efforts to influence child health orientation through direct tutorial and training.

SOCIALIZATION OF CHILDREN'S WELLNESS BEHAVIOR

Several researchers have studied the influence of parents' physical activity levels on children's physical activity levels. Children's physical activity levels have been an important focus of the research on the effect of parents' behavior on children's health because it is a very significant health-related behavioral factor with regard to chronic disease prevention (e.g., heart disease and diabetes) and health promotion. Adult physical activity is notoriously hard to increase with health promotion programs. A better understanding of the determinants of children's physical activity should permit the development of better prevention and intervention programs designed to increase both children's and adults' physical activity levels. Many studies have found a positive relation between parents' and children's physical activity levels (Sallis et al., 2000). For example, in a study of 4- to 7-year-old children and their parents, Moore and her colleagues (Moore et al., 1991) monitored parents' and children's physical activity with a mechanical device for an average of more than 10 hours per day for about 9 days each over the course of a year. Children of active mothers, were twice as likely to be active as children of inactive mothers, and children of active fathers were almost four times as likely to be active as children of inactive fathers. When both parents were active, children were almost six times as likely to be active as children of two inactive parents. Parents' modeling of physical activity, shared activities by family members, and the support of active parents on their participation in exercise activities are possible explanations of these findings, although genetically transmitted factors may also predispose children to increased levels of physical activity.

These studies suggest the importance of parental modeling and reinforcement on children's health physical activity behavior, but a minority of contradictory studies suggest that we have much more to learn about the ways in which parents socialize this aspect of children's health behavior (Godin and Shephard, 1986). For example, Sallis and his colleagues examined the role in parents in children's physical activity (Sallis et al., 1992). In a prospective study of almost 300 9- to 10-year-old fourth-grade children and their parents, contradictory to the findings of Moore and colleagues (1991) related above, these researchers found that parents had only very limited influence on their children's physical activity. Parents' own physical activity, which was assumed to be modeling, and parents' encouragement of their children to be active were not at all related to their children's level of physical activity. Further research is necessary to better specify the nature of parents' influence, via modeling and reinforcement, on children's physical activity behavior, and on wellness behavior more generally.

PARENTAL ESTABLISHMENT, TRAINING, AND ENFORCEMENT
OF CHILD HEALTH BEHAVIOR

The emergence of young children's ability to control and regulate their own health behavior is a very important aspect of parental promotion of children's health behavior. Researchers who study childhood behavioral socialization believe that children's ability to self-regulate develops as a function of children's emerging abilities to engage in behavior that they understand to be approved as a result of their caregivers' transmission of standards of behavior (Gralinski and Kopp, 1993). Research in childhood socialization has focused on a number of factors influencing the effectiveness of parental socialization of children, including parental factors that mediate its effectiveness (e.g., responsiveness, warmth, and control). Other research has examined the nature of parents' rules, as communicated to their children through the socialization process, and how these rules change developmentally. For example, Gralinski and Kopp (1993), in a longitudinal study of mothers' rules for everyday standards of behavior, demonstrated that mothers' earliest socialization efforts are focused on ensuring children's safety, and as children age (18 to 30 months), mothers move their socialization attention to other issues including children's self-care. Finally, by age $3\frac{1}{2}$ years, mothers elaborate on previously established rules and combine categories of rules about self-care and social norms (e.g., you must be dressed before you go outdoors). Other findings from this study suggest that safety rules are very important to mothers. Interestingly, very young children's compliance with mothers' safety rules is highly advanced, in contrast to children's compliance with other categories of mothers' rules. These findings suggest the early and sustained salience of safety rules for both parents and children, and highlight the importance of further research focused on the description of the developmental pathways associated with parents' socialization of health and safety rules.

Other research evaluates the extent of parents' attempts to socialize children's injury prevention behavior (Cook, Peterson, and DiLillo, 1999; Peterson, Brazeal, Oliver, and Brill, 1997). For example, Peterson and her colleagues (Peterson, Bartelstone, Kern, and Gillies, 1995) studied the ways in which mothers provide lectures and other remedial action following children's injuries. From an examination of children's and mothers' written and oral reports of over 1,000 of 8-year-old children's injuries, these investigators found that parental use of such interventions as environment change, discipline, or restriction of child activity following childhood injury occurred in less than 3% of the child injuries studied, despite the fact that mothers were aware of over 92% of the injuries. Most of the remedial behavior in which the parents did engage was in the form of lectures about safety; however, most of the lectures were not even recognized by the children as such. These findings suggest additional efforts need to be made to teach parents about identifying children's risky behavior and risky environmental situations, and how and when to deliver routine injury preventive intervention.

With respect to the impact of parents' direct training and enforcement of children's health behavior, research suggests that parents' explicitly attempt to train their children in health behavior, and that this is an important channel through which parents socialize their children's behavior. Moreover, this training begins very early. In the United States, parents introduce normative standards of cleanliness to their 2-year-old children very early (Kagan, 1992). This timing appears to depend on the child's sense of self (Douglas, as cited in Wilkinson, 1988).

Youth may rely on a complex network of family and peers for communication about sexuality, but parents represent an important component of this network (Pistella and Bonati, 1998). Parents expect to explicitly train children about sexuality (Simanki, 1998). However, despite the fact that parents appear to be willing to teach their children about sexuality (Berne, Patton, Milton, and Hunt, 2000), parents and children have discrepant beliefs concerning the extent to which they perceive that parents communicate to children about sexuality and the sexual topics covered (Jaccard, Dittus, and Gordon, 1998; King and Lorusso, 1997; Rosenthal and Feldman, 1999). In a survey of parents and adolescents concerning discussions about sexual topics within the home, 60% of parents reported meaningful discussions about sex, whereas more than half of their children reported no such discussion (King and Lorusso, 1997).

Many parents believe that our current societal environment pushes sexual information on children too early, which forces parents to have to address these issues earlier than they would prefer with their children. One mother relates, "We turn the TV on and my four-year-old is saying, 'Well, what's safe sex?' 'What's a condom?'" (Geasler, Dannison, and Edlund, 1995, p. 186).

Other studies of parent–child communication about sexuality suggest that mothers are the predominant agents of sexual socialization for boys and girls, but more so for girls (Rosenthal and Feldman, 1999). Fathers, compared to mothers, are more likely to discuss sexual topics with sons (DiIorio, Kelley, and Hockenberry-Eaton, 1999). The context of conversations of male children appears to be fairly consistent across mothers and fathers, with sexually transmitted diseases, including HIV/AIDS, and condom use the most popular topics (DiIorio et al., 1999). Both mothers and fathers are reported by their children as uncomfortable during these discussions, and these interactions have been characterized, over several studies, as indirect, involving more dominance and unilateral power assertion, less mutuality and turn taking than during conversations about more benign topics. Children are characterized as equally discomfited by these conversations, and their behavior during them is described as involving more contempt, less honesty, and more avoidance than conversations with their parents about other topics (Feldman and Rosenthal, 2000; Kahlbaugh, Lefkowitz, Valdez, and Sigman, 1997; Lefkowitz, Kahlbaugh, and Sigman, 1996; Rosenthal and Feldman, 2000; Yowell, 1997).

Several studies have demonstrated cultural patterns in the way parents talk to their children about sex and sexual risk (Baumeister, Flores, and Marin, 1995). For example, African American 11- to 12-year-old fifth-grade children were more likely to report that their parents had not discussed sex than were children of other ethnicities. Hispanic parents and parents living in large, metropolitan areas (which include large populations of low socioeconomic African American families) also discuss sex less often with their children than do other parents (Centers for Disease Control and Prevention, 1991). Furthermore, a study by Pillado, Romo, and Sigman (2000) suggests that acculturation level may modify these patterns. In a further reminder of the importance of examining sources of intraethnic variance in studies of parent–child communication, Pillado and colleagues examined the range of topics discussed in Latino mother–child conversations about sexuality. Latino girls and their mothers were videotaped discussing dating and sexuality. Considerable variability was found among the Latino mother–child dyads concerning sensitive sexual issues, especially about issues such as dating, pregnancy, HIV, and other dangers associated with sexual behavior, as a function of language preference (i.e., Spanish or English).

One aspect of sexuality socialization that parents appear very concerned with is the desire to improve on the sex education that they received during their own childhood (Berne et al., 2000), which suggests that parental behavior related to sexuality often reflects the tension between parents' conflicting experiences of sexuality when they were young and their contemporary experience of sexuality with their children.

Other research suggests the importance of parents' continuing efforts to socialize their children about sexuality. Engaging in parent–child communication about sexuality appears to make a difference for youths' sexual risk taking. For example, adolescents who reported discussing a greater number of topics about sexuality with their mothers were less likely to have initiated sexual intercourse than other youth (DiIorio et al., 1999). Another study presents similar findings. Sieving, McNeely, and Blum (2000) examined relations among youths' perceptions of their mothers' approval of sexual activity and the extent of the timing of their first intercourse, utilizing data from a national survey of U.S. children in Grades 7 to 12. Results indicated that adolescents' perceptions of high maternal disapproval of sexual activity and high levels of maternal connectedness (measured by both adolescent and mother report) were each independently related to delay in first intercourse. Together, these studies suggest that this particular type of parental socialization of youths' health behavior is related to making personal decisions about sexual behavior characterized by less risk.

In this era of HIV and AIDS, parental socialization of childhood sexual knowledge has become a critical aspect of health socialization. Despite high levels of knowledge concerning the consequences of high-risk sexual behavior among youth, they continue to engage in risky sexual behavior (Halperin, 1999). Sigelman, Derenowski, Mullaney, and Siders (1993) examined parents' propensity to discuss HIV and AIDS with their children in Grades 1 through 12. Although previous research suggested that children learn more about HIV and AIDS from sources other than their parents (Pistella and Bonati, 1998), findings indicated that frequency of parent–child communication about AIDS was positively associated with children's level of knowledge about AIDS.

Education about sexuality may be effective, but parental training of child health behavior is not always successful and, in fact, may produce negative effects. For example, Birch and colleagues (Birch et al., 2001; Birch and Fisher, 1998) found that mothers who attempt to protect their children from obesity may create children who do not know how to stop eating when they have had enough to eat. In a study of 77 children ages 3 to 5, they found that those with the most body fat had the most "controlling" mothers concerning the amount of food eaten. The more control the mother reported using to manage her child's eating behavior, the less food self-regulation the child demonstrated. In contrast, children whose mothers allowed them to be most spontaneous about food (e.g., eating when they were hungry and not necessarily forced to finish all the food given them) displayed a natural instinct for regulating their own food intake. These findings appear to hold cross-culturally as well, as demonstrated in a Japanese study in which mothers of young adolescent girls were found, as reported by mothers and daughters, to contribute to their daughters eating disorder tendencies through control and monitoring (Mukai and McCloskey, 1996). Results such as these suggest a sound basis for the effect of family members' informational exchange on health-related issues on health behavior, and lend support for the importance of parents' health-related teaching for childhood health socialization.

BEYOND THE INDIVIDUAL LEVEL OF ANALYSIS: PARENTS AS A HEALTH SOCIALIZATION UNIT

The above studies are focused on individual levels of analysis; parents have usually been represented by mothers, and in only a few cases by fathers and mothers. However, it is important to consider both a broader range of effects within the family as well as the family as a unit of analysis itself when considering parental influences on children's health orientation. What are the consequences of identifying family-level influences on childhood parental promotion of health? What advantage does this approach give us, in contrast to considering child health from the individual level (e.g., the child affecting her or his own health, or the mother's attitudes and behavior as determinants of child health)?

First, our current models of health suggest that health status is the result of an interaction of biological, social, and environmental factors. An understanding of the social and environmental contexts in which children exist is a critical ingredient of any model of childhood health. Families are the major component of young children's social and environmental contexts, and therefore knowledge of the role which families play in determining childhood health is necessary. Moreover, familial influence on children's health must also be examined from multiple perspectives.

The role of individual family members in affecting children's health is obviously very important. For example, studies indicate that mothers play a pivotal role in determining the health of their children. Mothers have assumed a dominant and pivotal role in performing health-related activities for all family members, and young children in particular (Carpenter, 1990). Studies suggest that although fathers are making modest gains in participating in child care in general (Parke, 1996, in Vol. 3 of this *Handbook*), mothers continue to be assigned child health care responsibilities in the division of household labor. Several studies suggest that a substantial cause of women's work absenteeism is caregiving for ill children (e.g., Carpenter, 1990), with women reporting about three times as many work hours lost as men for this task. Mothers have been demonstrated to take greater responsibility for family health (Hibbard and Pope, 1983). In a study of the extent to which members of almost 700 families with children had similar and interrelated health behavior, Schor, Starfield, Stidley, and Hankin (1987) found that, whereas overall rates of use of health services by children were affected by the utilization rates of both parents, the effect of the mother was 2.3 times that of the father, and only mothers' utilization rates significantly influenced children's rates of visits for nonillness care.

Other studies suggest that women play a predominant role in establishing health behavior of their children, decision making concerning health services utilization, delivering children for pediatric care, and providing home nursing care for ill children (Carpenter, 1990). Mothers appear to engage in most of the needs assessment and access of formal medical services for children, and in addition usually deliver children for these services. In many families, the decision about whether to declare a child sufficiently ill to stay home from daycare or school and in need of medical services if left to the mother (Dallas, Wilson, and Salgado, 2000). Carpenter (1990, p. 1214) eloquently suggests:

> Women are the principal brokers or arrangers of health services for their children. . . . The assignment of family health responsibilities to the female in her role as . . . mother . . . is deeply rooted in cultural norms. These activities are seen as an integral part of the maternal and nurturing role women are expected to assume within the family structure.

Despite the dominant role of mothers in children's health orientation within the family, fathers do contribute to selected aspects of the child's health environment. Wilkinson (1988) reported young children believe that fathers have health knowledge which they pass on to mothers, as though the mothers are the fathers' agent. And some mothers and fathers in Wilkinson's sample trusted in fathers' expertise during their children's medical emergencies (such as unintentional injuries), in comparison to their own perceived competence to care for children during acute and chronic illness.

It is still an empirical question whether the role of other family members or the family as a unit in determining child health attitudes, health behavior and health status can account for additional portions of the variance in these measures of child health orientation. For example, in two-parent families, do both father and mother health attitudes tell us more about child health outcome than mother attitudes alone? Or is there a family-level assessment of health attitudes, health behavior, or health outcome that predicts to child health attitudes, health behavior, or health outcome better than any individual family member's predictors? In our own work (Ortiz, 2000) on parental socialization of children's health beliefs and behaviors in Mexican American families, health constructs concerned with eating and exercise beliefs and behaviors, and their relations to obesity are examined within the context of acculturative status. The health beliefs of 9- to 11-year-old fourth-grade Mexican American children and their parents are significant predictors of child, mother, and father body mass index. Health behaviors, however, significantly predict body mass index only for the mothers in our study. Path analyses of these data suggest that a best fit model includes information from both mothers and fathers in the prediction of their children's body mass index.

Campbell (1975), in a discussion of the validity of intergenerational predictors of illness concepts, suggested that a combination of paternal and maternal influence would probably predict concordance between parents and children rather than the sole use of maternal influence. However, more than 25 years later, research is still needed to clarify these relations. A study of children who come from families in which there is a parent with somatization disorder (i.e., having physical symptoms out of proportion to demonstrable physical disease) suggested that having a somatizing parent was highly predictive of child somatization (Livingston, Witt, and Smith, 1995). Children in families with somatizing children were found to visit the emergency room with greater than normal frequency, exhibit more suicidal behavior, and more disability. Additionally, children in families with a somatization disorder adult had almost 12 times the number of emergency room visits and missed almost 9 times as much school as children in families with a less severely affected somatizing adult. These data demonstrate that family patterns of medical care utilization are influenced by family definitions of illness, as wells as frequency of disease.

Another example of the potential of family members' influence on children's health comes from a recent study of preschool children's ability to identify alcohol by odor as a function of father and mother alcohol consumption (Noll, Zucker, and Greenberg, 1990). Results demonstrated that very young children's (31 to 69 mos) success in identifying alcoholic beverages by smell was positively related to paternal and maternal alcohol usage. This study suggests that the home is the context in which children learn about health-related risk behaviors such as drinking alcohol. Moreover, the study demonstrates that young children's knowledge about this risky health behavior must be obtained from sources other than television (since odors are not part of television programming), despite the proliferation of television portrayals of alcohol consumption (Austin and Johnson, 1997).

In a consideration of family determinants of health behavior (for both adults and children), Sallis, Nader, and their colleagues conducted a series of studies which suggest that one major mechanism for family influence on health is through examination of the similarities and differences in health variables across family members (Broyles, Nader, Sallis, Frank-Spohrer, 1996; Elder et al., 1998; McKenzie, Nader, Strikmiller, and Yang, 1996; Nader, Sellers, Johnson, and Perry, 1996; Perry et al., 1997). For example, with health variables related to cardiovascular disease, there are statistically significant correlations among parent–child, sibling–sibling, and spouse–spouse blood pressures. Although genetic influences account for part of the variance in at least parent–child, and sibling–sibling blood pressure similarities, this is not the case for spouse–spouse blood pressures. Therefore, not all the variance is explained genetically. Similar family patterns are found with serum cholesterol, and lipoproteins, and body fat (obesity). It is apparent that there are environmental family influences on health behavior and risk. Sallis and Nader and their colleagues (Broyles et al., 1996; Elder et al., 1998; McKenzie et al., 1996; Nader et al., 1996; Perry et al., 1997) discussed three such possible influences: smoking, diet, and exercise. There is a great deal of evidence that smoking habits (Scheer, Borden, and Donnermeyer, 2000), health-related dietary habits (Johnson and Birch, 1994), and habits of physical activity (Sallis et al., 2000) aggregate within families. However, many of the studies which provide this evidence are limited in their scope, in terms of their attention to family structure, demographic variables, and the explication of comparative strengths and interactions of various influences (Sallis et al., 2000). These are empirical questions that must be answered in order to fully understand the role of the family in determining children's health attitudes and behavior. The influence of ethnicity and culture on parents' promotion of children's health are examples of such variables requiring additional empirical examination.

Epidemiological studies suggest an overrepresentation of health problems in minority children living in the United States, compared to the population of U.S. children at large (U.S. Department of Health and Human Services, 2000). Among the most vulnerable and dependent members of any community, children reflect the conditions of their communities within the larger societal context. As a result, the health status of children of ethnic origin in the United States mirrors and magnifies that of their families and neighborhoods, as well as the effectiveness of the formal and informal institutional structures entrusted to meet their health needs (Halfon and Newacheck, 1993; Harkness and Keefer, 2000). Children reared in the plethora of culturally diverse families in the United States are exposed to many conflicting health values and orientations, and these shift over time as a function of such changing phenomena as parental and family acculturation, education, geographic dispersion, and household structure and size. For many children reared in the United States, poverty is the main enemy of optimal health and ranks among the most significant factors affecting children's health.

Work on socialization patterns in minority families suggests that there is not a single pattern that characterizes a particular ethnic group, but instead parents adapt their socialization practices in response to sociocultural values (Julian, McKenry, and McKelvey, 1994; Parke and Buriel, 1998). Studies have identified significant variation associated with ethnicity in attitudes about parenting, childrearing goals, types of parenting behaviors, and amount of parental involvement. Culture and ethnicity are also fundamental to health beliefs and behavior, and must be included in relevant theories and empirical investigations of parents' health promotion on behalf of their children (Landrine and Klonoff, 1992). However, to date, with few exceptions, studies have failed to systematically examine cultural and ethnic influences on parents' health promotion efforts.

CONCLUSIONS

Parents unquestionably aim to promote their children's health, but there are many obstacles to successful socialization of children's health and well-being. New models of child health care that incorporate both biological and experiential components of children's health have facilitated attempts to overcome these obstacles. Research suggests that parents' modeling of health attitudes and behaviors has the potential to influence children's health attitudes and behaviors, resulting in greater child well-being. Particular parenting behaviors (e.g., positive reinforcement) have also been linked to children's development of adaptive health behaviors. Furthermore, parents play an important role in helping children cope with illness and medical treatments. Evidence for the utility of explicit education about prevention comes from research addressing parents' role in teaching their children about sexual health. This and other health research is limited, however, in its focus on mothers' role in health promotion. Additional research is needed to help understand the role of fathers in health promotion. Moreover, the influence of entire families, conceptualized as a unit functioning in a greater cultural, ecological context, on children's health promotion needs further investigation.

ACKNOWLEDGMENTS

This research was funded by grant No. HD32465-02 from the National Institute of Child Health and Development awarded to Barbara J. Tinsley.

REFERENCES

Abbey, A., Pilgrim, C., Hendrickson, P., and Buresh, S. (2000). Evaluation of a family-based substance abuse prevention program targeted for the middle school years. *Journal of Drug Education, 30*, 213–28.

Austin, E., W., and Johnson, K. K. (1997). Effects of general and alcohol-specific media literacy training on children's decision making about alcohol. *Journal of Health, 2*, 17–42.

Baumeister, L. M., Flores, E., and Marin, B. V. (1995). Sex information given to Latina adolescents by parents. *Health Education Research, 10*, 233–239.

Berne, L. A., Patton, W., Milton, J., Hunt, L. Y. A. (2000). A qualitative assessment of Australian parents' perceptions of sexuality education and communication. *Journal of Sex Education and Therapy, 25*, 161–168.

Birch, L. L, and Fisher, J. O. (1998). Development of eating behaviors among children and adolescents. *Pediatrics, 101*, 539–549.

Birch, L. L., Fisher, J. O., Grimm-Thomas, K., Markey, C. N., Sawyer, R., and Johnson, S. L. (2001). Confirmatory factor analysis of the child feeding questionnaire: A measure of parental attitudes, beliefs, and practices about child feeding and obesity proneness. *Appetite, 36*, 201–210.

Brown, J. E., and Mann, L. (1990). The relationship between family structure and process variables and adolescent decision making. *Journal of Adolescence, 13*, 25–37.

Broyles, S. L., Nader, P. R., Sallis, J. F., and Frank–Spohrer, G. C. (1996). Cardiovascular disease risk factors in Anglo and Mexican American children and their mothers. *Family and Community Health, 19*, 57–72.

Campbell, J. D. (1975). Illness is a point of view: The development of children's concepts of illness. *Child Development, 46*, 92–100.

Caprara, G. V., Barbaranelli, C., Pastorelli, C., Bandura, A., and Zimbardo, P. G. (2000). Prosocial foundations of children's academic achievement. *Psychological Science, 11*, 302–306.

Carpenter, P. J. (1990). New method for measuring young children's self-report of fear and pain. *Journal of Pain and Symptom Management, 5*, 233–240.

Carvajal, S. C., Wiatrek, D. E., Evans, R., I., Knee, C. R, and Nash, S. G. (2000). Psychosocial determinants of the onset and escalation of smoking: Cross-sectional and prospective findings in multiethnic middle school samples. *Journal of Adolescent Health, 27*, 255–265.

Centers for Disease Control and Prevention. (1991). Effectiveness in disease and injury prevention characteristics of parents who discuss AIDS with their children—United States, 1989. *Morbidity and Mortality Weekly Report, 40*, 789–791.

Centers for Disease Control and Prevention. (1998). *Tobacco use among U.S. racial/ethnic minority groups.* Washington, DC: U.S. Department of Health and Human Services, Centers for Disease Control Office on Smoking and Health.

Charron-Prochownik, D., and Kovacs, M. (2000). Maternal health-related coping patterns and health and adjustment outcomes in children with type 1 diabetes. *Children's Health Care, 29*, 37–45.

Chen, E., Zelter, L. K., Craske, M. G., and Katz, E. R. (2000). Children's memories for painful cancer treatment procedures: Implications for distress. *Child Development, 71*, 933–947.

Children's Defense Fund. (1994). *The state of American's children yearbook, 1994.* New York: Children's Defense Fund.

Cohen, L. L., Manimala, R., and Blount, R. L. (2000). Easier said than done: What parents say they do and what they do during children's immunizations. *Children's Health Care, 29*, 79–86.

Cook, S., Peterson, L., and DiLillo, D. (1999). Fear and exhilaration in response to risk: An extension of a model of injury risk in a real-world context. *Behavior Therapy, 30,* 5–15.

Cullen, K. W., Baranowski, T., Rittenberry, L., and Olvera, N. (2000). Social-environmental influences on children's diets: Results from focus groups with African-, Euro-, and Mexican-American children and their parents. *Health Education Research, 15,* 581–590.

Dallas, C., Wilson, T., and Salgado, V. (2000). Gender differences in teen parents' perceptions of parental responsibilities. *Public Health Nursing, 17,* 423–433.

Davison, K. K., Markey, C. N., and Birch, L. L. (2000). Etiology of body dissatisfaction and weight concerns among 5-year-old girls. *Appetite, 35,* 143–151.

DiIorio, C., Kelley, M., and Hockenberry-Eaton, M. (1999). Communication about sexual issues: Mothers, fathers, and friends. *Journal of Adolescent Health, 24,* 181–189.

Dunn-Geir, J. B., McGrath, P. J., Rourke, B. P., Latter, J., and D'Astous, J. (1986). Adolescent chronic pain: The ability to cope. *Pain, 26,* 23–32.

Elder, J. P., Broyles, S. L., McKenzie, T. L., Sallis, J. F., Berry, C. C., Davis, T. B., Hoy, P. L., and Nader, P. R. (1998). Direct home observations of the promoting of physical activity in sedentary and active Mexican- and Anglo-American children. *Journal of Developmental and Behavioral Pediatrics, 19,* 26–30.

Feldman, S. S., and Rosenthal, D. A. (2000). The effect of communication characteristics on family members' perceptions of parents as sex educators. *Journal of Research on Adolescence, 10,* 119–150.

Gable, S., and Lutz, S. (2000). Household, parent, and child contributions to childhood obesity. Family Relations: *Interdisciplinary Journal of Applied Family Studies, 49,* 293–300.

Geasler, M. J., Dannison, L. L., and Edlund, C. J. (1995). Sexuality education of young children. *Family Relations, 44,* 184–188.

Godin, G., and Shephard, R. J. (1986). Psychosocial factors influencing intentions to exercise of young students from grades 7 to 9. *Research Quarterly for Exercise and Sport, 57,* 501–508.

Gralinski, J. D., and Kopp, C. B. (1993). Everyday rules for behavior: Mothers' requests to young children. *Developmental Psychology, 29,* 573–584.

Grundy, S. M. (2000). Early detection of high cholesterol levels in young adults. *Journal of American Medical Association, 284,* 365–367.

Halfon, N., and Newacheck, P. (1993). Childhood asthma and poverty: Differential impacts of utilization of health services. *Pediatrics, 91,* 56–61.

Halperin, D. T. (1999). Heterosexual anal intercourse: Prevalence, cultural factors, and HIV infection and other health risks, Part I. *AIDS Patient Care and Standards, 13,* 717–730.

Harkness, S., and Keefer, C. H. (2000). Contributions of cross-cultural psychology to research and interventions in education and health. *Journal of Cross-Cultural Psychology, 31,* 92–109.

Hibbard, J. H. and Pope, C. R. (1983). Gender roles, illness orientation and use of medical services. *Social Science and Medicine, 17,* 129–137.

Jaccard, J., Dittus, P. J., and Gordon, V. V. (1998). Parent–adolescent congruency in reports of adolescent sexual behavior and in communication about sexual behavior. *Child Development, 69,* 247–261.

Johnson, S. L., and Birch, L. L. (1994). Parent's and children's adiposity and eating style. *Pediatrics, 94,* 653–661.

Julian, T. W., McKenry, P. C., and McKelvey, M. W. (1994). Cultural variations in parenting. *Family Relations, 3,* 30–37.

Kagan, J. (1992). Behavior, biology, and the meaning of temperamental constructs. *Pediatrics, 3,* 510–513.

Kahlbaugh, P., Lefkowitz, E. S., Valdez, P., and Sigman, M. (1997). The affective nature of mother–adolescent communication concerning sexuality and conflict. *Journal of Research on Adolescence, 7,* 221–239.

King, B. M., and Lorusso, J. (1997). Discussions in the home about sex: Different recollections by parents and children. *Journal of Sex and Marital Therapy, 23,* 52–60.

Landrine, H., and Klonoff, E. A. (1992). Culture and health-related schemas: A review and proposal for interdisciplinary integration. *Health Psychology, 11,* 267–276.

Lau, R. R., and Klepper, S. (1988). The development of illness orientations in children aged 6 through 12. *Journal of Health and Social Behavior, 29,* 149–168.

Lees, N. B., and Tinsley, B. J. (1998). Patterns of parental socialization of the preventive health behavior of young Mexican origin children. *Journal of Applied Developmental Psychology, 19,* 503–525.

Lees, N. B., and Tinsley, B. J. (2001, in press). Maternal socialization of children's preventive health behavior: The role of maternal affect and teaching strategies. *Merrill Palmer Quarterly.*

Lefkowitz, E. S., Kahlbaugh, P. E., and Sigman, M. (1996). Turn-taking in mother-adolescent conversations about sexuality and conflict. *Journal of Youth and Adolescence, 25,* 307–321.

Livingston, R., Witt, A., and Smith, G. R. (1995). Families who somatize. *Journal of Developmental and Behavioral Pediatrics, 16,* 42–46.

McGrath, P. A., Speechley, K. N., Seifert, C. E., Bieh, J. T., Cairney, A. E. L., Gorodzinsky, F. P., Dickie, G. L., McClusker, P. J., and Morrissy, J. R. (2000). A survey of children's acute, recurrent, and chronic pain: Validation of the pain experience interview. *Pain, 87,* 59–73.

McKenzie, T. L., Nader, P. R., Strikmiller, P. K., Yang, M. (1996). School physical education: Effect of the child and adolescent trial for cardiovascular health. *Preventive Medicine: An International Devoted to Practice and Theory, 25,* 423–431.

Mechanic, D. (1979). Correlates of physician utilization: Why do major multivariate studies of physician utilization find trivial psychosocial and organizational effects? *Journal of Health and Social Behavior, 20,* 387–396.

Melamed, B. G. (1998). Preparation for medical procedures. In R. T. Ammerman, J. V. Campo, (Eds.), *Handbook of pediatric psychology and psychiatry: Disease, injury, and illness* (Vol. 2, pp. 16–30). Boston: Allyn and Bacon.

Moore, L. L., Lombardi, D. A., White, M. J., Campbell, J. L., Oliviera, S. A., and Ellison, R. C. (1991). Influence of parents' physical activity levels on activity levels of young children. *Journal of Pediatrics, 118,* 215–219.

Mukai, T., and McCloskey, L. A. (1996). Eating attitudes among Japanese and American elementary school girls. *Journal of Cross-Cultural Psychology, 27,* 424–435.

Nader, P., Sellers, D. E., Johnson, C. C., Perry, C. L. (1996). The effect of adult participation in a school-based family intervention to improve children's diet and physical activity: The child and adolescent trial for cardiovascular health. *Preventive Medicine: An International Journal Devoted to Practice and Theory, 25,* 423–431.

. Nelson, C. A. (Ed.). (2000). *The Minnesota symposia on child psychology* (Vol. 31). Mahwah, NJ: Lawrence Erlbaum Associates.

Noll, R. B., Zucker, R. A., and Greenberg, G. S. (1990). Identification of alcohol by smell among preschoolers: Evidence for early socialization about drugs occurring in the home. *Child Development, 61,* 1520–1527.

Olvera-Ezzell, N., Power, T. G., and Cousins, J. H. (1990). Maternal socialization of children's eating habits: Strategies used by obese Mexican-American mothers. *Child Development, 61,* 395–400.

Ortiz, R. (2000). Health socialization and cultural adaptation: Longitudinal relations among body mass index in Mexican American preadolescent children. Unpublished doctoral dissertation, University of California, Riverside.

Parke, R. D. (1996). *Fatherhood.* Cambridge, MA: Harvard University Press.

Parke, R. D., and Buriel, R. (1998). Socialization in the family: Ethnic and ecological perspectives. In W. Damon and N. Eisenberg (Eds.), Handbook of child psychology, (Vol. 3, 5th ed.). New York: Wiley.

Parmelee, A. H. (1997). Illness and the development of social competence. *Journal of Developmental and Behavioral Pediatrics, 18,* 120–124.

Perry, C. L., Sellers, D. E., Johnson, C., Pedersen, S., Bachman, K. J., Parcel, G. S., Stone, E. J., Luepker, R. V., Wu, M., Nader, P. R., and Cook, K. (1997). The Child and Adolescent Trial for Cardiovascular Health (CATCH): Intervention, implementation, and feasibility for elementary schools in the United Statess. *Health Education and Behavior, 24,* 716–735.

Peterson, L., Bartelstone, J., Kern, T., and Gillies, R. (1995). Parents' socialization of children's injury prevention: Description and some initial parameters. *Child Development, 66,* 224–235.

Peterson, L., Brazeal, T., Oliver, K., and Bull, C. (1997). Gender and developmental patterns of affect, belief, and behavior in simulated injury events. *Journal of Applied Developmental Psychology, 18,* 531–546.

Peterson, L., Oliver, K. K., and Saldana, L. (1997). Children's coping with stressful medical procedures. In S. A. Wolchik and I. N. Sandler, (Eds.), *Handbook of children's coping: Linking theory and intervention* (pp. 333–360). New York: Plenum.

Phipps, S., Fairclough, D. Tye, V., and Mulhern, R. K. (1998). Assessment of coping with invasive procedures in children with cancer: State–trait and approach–avoidance dimensions. *Children's Health Care, 27,* 147–156.

Pillado, O., Romo, L. F., and Sigman, M. (2000, March). The influence of Latino mother characteristics on the content of dating and sexuality talks with their teenagers. Paper presented at the meetings of the Society for Research on Adolescence, Chicago, IL.

Pistella, C. L. Y., and Bonati, F. A. (1998). Communication about sexual behavior among adolescent women, their family and peers. *Families in Society, 79,* 206–211.

Powers, K. S., and Rubenstein, J. S. (1999). Family presence during invasive procedures in the pediatric intensive care unit: A prospective study. *Archives of Pediatrics and Adolescent Medicine, 153,* 955–958.

Pratt, L. (1973). Child-rearing methods and children's health behaviors. *Journal of Health and Social Behavior, 14,* 61–69.

Richter, K. P., Harris, K. J., Paine-Andrews, A., Fawcett, S. B., Schmid, T. L., Lankenau, B. H., and Johnston, J. (2000). Measuring the health environment for physical activity and nutrition among youth: A review of the literature and applications for community initiatives. *Preventive Medicine, 31,* S98–S111.

Robinson, J. O., Alvarez, J. H., and Dodge, J. A. (1990). Life events and family history in children with recurrent abdominal pain. *Journal of Psychosomatic Research, 34,* 171–181.

Rosenthal, D. A., and Feldman, S. S. (1999). The importance of importance: Adolescents' perceptions of parental communication about sexuality. *Journal of Adolescence, 22,* 835–851.

Sallis, J. F., Alcaraz, J. E., McKenzie, T. L., Hovell, M. F., Kolody, B., and Nader, P. R. (1992). Parental behavior in relation to physical activity and fitness in 9-year-old children. *American Journal of Disease of Children, 146,* 1383–1388.

Sallis, J. F., Patrick, K., Frank, E., Pratt, M., Wechsler, H., and Galuska, D. A. (2000). Interventions in health care settings to promote healthful eating and physical activity in children and adolescents. *Preventive Medicine: An International Journal Devoted to Practice and Theory, 31,* S112–S120.

Sameroff, A. J. (1989). General systems and the regulation of development. In M. Gunner and E. Thelen (Eds.), *Systems and development* (pp. 219–236). Hillsdale, NJ: Lawrence Erlbaum Associates.

Scheer, S. D., Borden, L. M., and Donnermeyer, J. F. (2000). The relationship between family factors and adolescent substance use in rural, suburban, and urban settings. *Journal of Child and Family Studies, 9,* 105–115.

Schor, E. L., Starfield, B., Stidley, C. and Hankin, J. (1987). Family health: Utilization and effects of family membership. *Medical Care, 25,* 616–626.

Sieving, R. E., McNeely, C. S., and Blum, R. W. (2000). Maternal expectations, mother–child connectedness, and adolescent sexual debut. *Archives of Pediatrics and Adolescent Medicining, 154,* 809–816.

Sigelman, C. K., Derenowski, E. B., Mullaney, H. A., and Siders, A. T. (1993). Parents' contributions to knowledge and attitudes regarding AIDS. *Journal of Pediatric Psychology, 18,* 221–235.

Simanski, J. W. (1998). The birds and the bees: An analysis of advice given to parents through the popular press. *Adolescence, 33,* 33–45.

Spruijt-Metz, D. (1999). *Adolescence, affect, and health.* Hove, England: Psychology Press.

Stephens, B. K., Barkey, M. E., and Hall, H. R. (1999). Techniques to comfort children during stressful procedures. *Advances in Mind-Body Medicine, 15,* 49–60.

Stone, P. W., Teutsch, S., Chapman, R. H., Bell, C., Goldie, S. J., and Neumann, P. J. (2000). Cost-utility analyses of clinical preventive services: published ratios, 1976–1997. *American Journal of Preventive Medicine, 19,* 15–23.

Stromsoe, K., Magnaes, B., and Nakstad, P. (2000). Open reduction and internal fixation in flexion–distraction injuries to the lower spine in children and adolescents involved in traffic accidents as car occupants. A report and literature review. *Archives of Orthopaedic and Trauma, Surgery, 120,* 96–99.

Tinsley, B. J. (1992). Multiple influences on the acquisition and socialization of children's health attitudes and behavior: An integrative review. *Child Development, 63,* 1043–1069.

Tinsley, B. J. (1997). Health behaviors of young mothers. In D. S. Gochman (Ed.), *Handbook of health behavior research* (Vol. 1, pp. 223–240). New York: Plenum.

U.S. Department of Health and Human Services. (2000). *Healthy People 2010* (Conference Edition, 2 Vols.) Washington, DC: U.S. Government Printing Office.

Wachs, T. D. (2000). Linking nutrition and temperament. In V. J. Molfese, D. L. Molfese (Eds.) *Temperament and personality development across the life span* (pp. 57–84). Mahwah, NJ: Lawrence Erlbaum Associates.

Walker, L. S. and Zeman, J. L. (1992). Parental response to child illness behavior. *Journal of Pediatric Psychology, 17,* 49–71.

Wiehl, L. G., and Tinsley, B. J. (1999). Maternal personality and health communication in the pediatric context. *Health Communication, 11,* 75–96.

Wilkinson, S. R. (1988). *The child's world of illness: The development of health and illness behaviour.* Cambridge, England: Cambridge University Press.

Yamasaki, K. (1990). Parental child-rearing attitudes associated with Type A behaviors in children. *Psychological Reports, 67,* 235–239.

Ybarra, G. L., Passman, R. H., and Eisenberg, C. S. (2000). The presence of security blankets or mothers (or both) affects distress during pediatric examinations. *Journal of Consulting and Clinical Psychology, 68,* 322–330.

13

Parenting the Ill Child

Barbara G. Melamed
Mercy College

INTRODUCTION

There are approximately 10 million chronically ill children in the United States. Chronic childhood diseases are estimated to affect over 10% of the children in the United States, and many of these children develop psychological difficulties including more troubled family and peer relationships (Pless and Nolan, 1991). After the first year of life, death from trauma assumes first rank as the leading cause of death until age 45. Each year, close to 20,000 children and adolescents die, and a great many more are hospitalized as a result of unintentional and intentional injuries (Grossman, 1999). In New York City in 1999, however, AIDS became the most common cause of death in 1- to 4-year old children. Although childhood malignancy is rare, it is an emotionally charged diagnosis, and of the approximately 7,500 children who are diagnosed with cancer each year in the United States, 80% will survive. Furthermore, it is estimated that by 2010, 1 in 250 persons will be a childhood cancer survivor between the ages of 15 and 45 years old (Tao, Seltzer, and Seltzer, 1999).

Asthma is the most prevalent chronic illness of childhood, with approximately 4% to 9% of children having moderate to severe asthma. It is the leading cause of school absences, accounting for 2% to 25% of all absences Geller (1996). It is the most frequent cause of emergency room visits and hospitalizations for children (Karetsky, 1977).

Cystic fibrosis (CF) is the most common life-shortening and autosomal recessive genetic disease of European American children. Its incidence ranges from one in 1,700 live births in Northern Ireland to one in 7,700 in Sweden. CF is lethal because of chronic bronchopulmonary infections. In recent years the prognosis of children with CF has improved. From 1990–1992, the proportion of adult CF patients in the United States was 33%, a fourfold increase since 1969. The median survival age in 1992 was 29.4 years. CF patients are multisymptomatic involving pulmonary and gastrointestinal dysfunctions. The complicated regimen involves enzyme replacement and chest percussions to improve clearance of infected secretions (Schwartz, 1996). Its demands on the family are continuous.

Cerebral palsy is defined as a group of disorders of movement and posture due to a nonprogressive lesion of the developing brain. The prevalence of cerebral palsy has increased 15% over the past 20 years, coinciding with the increased survival rate of infants who are of very low birthweight (Liptak, 1999). Those children may suffer spasticity, dyskinetic and ataxic movements, impaired speech, and/or mental retardation. The interventions required to be implemented to facilitate functioning vary with degree of disability as well as age of the child. Parents must educate themselves as to the use of assistive devices varying from electric motors, to speech synthesizers.

Diabetes mellitus is a chronic disease characterized by insufficiency or a lack of insulin production by the pancreas. Both insulin dependent and nondependent diabetes affect over 5 million persons in the United States and are responsible for 300,000 deaths a year, making diabetes the third largest cause of death by disease (Johnson, 1988). Diabetes in children is one of the most common endocrine disorders, affecting 1 in 800 youngsters below 18 years of age. People with diabetes are 25 times more prone to blindness, 17 times more prone to kidney disease, 5 times more prone to gangrene and lower extremity amputations, and twice as prone to heart disease (Hanson, Henggeler, and Burghen, 1987; Hanson, Henggeler, Burghen, and Moore, 1989). In childhood diabetes type 1, the data indicate that, like adults, the adolescents in the Diabetes Control and Complications Trials (DCCT Research Group, 1994) 9-year-long, multicenter, prospective, randomized, and controlled clinical trial benefited from a tight therapeutic regimen. This regimen included administration of insulin three or more times per day by injection or by external pump, watching dietary intake, and planned exercise, and often involved parental involvement (Orlowski, 1999).

Hemophilia is a congenital hereditary disorder of blood coagulation, transmitted by a female carrier to her male child. The life expectancy of patients with hemophilia is now the same as that of the general male population. It must then be considered a long-term condition where home care programs are complicated. With the discovery of clotting factors, home infusion of the factor replacement, however, should potentially facilitate psychosocial adjustment, increased school and work attendance, and other daily living activities (Varni and Wallander, 1988).

Two other illnesses that involve chronic pain conditions are juvenile rheumatoid arthritis (JRA) and sickle cell disease (SCD). Juvenile arthritis involves intra-articular swelling, pain or tenderness with motion, or unusual warmth (Siegel, 1999). It is often runs in families (high heritability) and has an onset at 16 years old or earlier. Family functioning, school performance, peer relationships, and normal developmental progression can be affected profoundly. Sickle cell disease (SCD) involves numerous aberrations of hemostasis, such as platelet abnormalities, increased thrombin generation, and reduced anticoagulant factors. It is detected early in life and makes the children susceptible to severe infections (Lerner, 1999). SCD is often experienced as recurrent, episodic pain crises requiring hospitalization.

Thus, in treatment of chronic illness, the family becomes an important focus, as patients are living longer and requiring extensive regimens to control symptoms. Family responsibility for the ill person often does not end at adulthood. The United States is not alone in dealing with an ever increasing need to address chronic health problems in children. A British child health statistical review (Staples and Pharoah, 1994) documented the reduction of infectious diseases in children and the increasing role poverty played in affecting child health. These statistics also suggest that, with the increasing births in women in their 30s and early 40s, the frequency of congenital abnormalities and perinatal infant mortality has risen.

This chapter focuses on using theoretical and behavioral models that have been applied to the literature on coping with stress in general to arrive at specific suggestions that may benefit parents' coping with a chronically ill child. The current and past research approaches are depicted by discussion of prototypical research studies. Review of longitudinal evaluation of treatment issues and definition of critical times of stress will yield an educational guide for the pediatrician, psychologist, or health care professional to communicate with the parent and other caregivers involved in the child's management. The chapter limits itself to chronic medical illnesses. It reviews the change in research perspective over the past 3 decades from that of focusing on the disability and psychopathology of the ill family member to an approach based on systems analyses. The conclusions drawn lead to applications for clinical practice and suggestions for measurement issues. A focus on family functioning with an emphasis on evaluating prospective research is taken. The aim of the chapter is to understand both the developmental aspects of chronic childhood illnesses and capabilities that parents and children need to develop to achieve resilience in family functioning.

The concept of *family resilience* is defined as the coping and adaptational process of the family unit as a whole. Parents' distress can lead to inefficiency in keeping equilibrium in family functioning in a variety of ways:

(1) They may not understand what the illness involves.
(2) They may experience overwhelming guilt that they cannot easily make the child well.
(3) They may experience financial strain due to medical procedures and medications.
(4) They may feel inadequate for meeting support needs to each other.
(5) They may feel that they are unable to give their other children the reassurance and support that they need.
(6) It may alter their own vocational responsibilities.
(7) It may interfere with normal recreational and churchgoing activities, thus depriving them of social support networks that are necessary at these times.

Identifying what attributes a resilient family has is the first step toward providing interventions to help families experiencing adaptation and stress when a child has a chronic illness.

In addition to specifying the family characteristics and the specific illness, defining the phase of diagnosis or treatment is critical when examining resilience. The following stages from prediagnostic, through diagnostic, treatment, rehabilitation and recovery, relapse, return to normalcy, or, in the case of a terminal illness, adjustment to the impending losses involved, are briefly described as they call for very different coping strategies.

Prediagnosis may involve the uncertainty and threats involved when there is an underlying disease process that is as yet undiagnosed. Families living with the anxiety may minimize the threat by delay in seeking care or by turning inward and isolating themselves from others. These approaches are unwarranted and may lead to further disruption in dealing with the illness. There are often changes in mood and emotion that may alienate family members from the preclinically "ill" person (Leventhal, Leventhal, and Van Nguyen, 1985).

In the diagnostic stage, the crisis is defined by how each member of the family represents the illness. Even though the medical tests and physician feedback may have described the problem, the members of the family who have previously dealt with a chronic illness may have a different interpretation about what to expect. Decision making is the most difficult part of this stage, and immediate threats of treatment can postpone consideration of the more remote threats of illness. Coping resources may differ depending on adequate communication between the physician and among family members. Young children may be unfamiliar with hospitals and medical treatments and have no ability to form coping representations. Children's illness beliefs about causation vary with developmenal age. Young children may view illness as punishment for misbehavior, whereas by age 11 most children understand germ theory and something about human pathophysiology. Frustration, anger, and conflict among family members is not uncommon. Once a treatment plan is in place the coping resources focus on pain, anxiety, and the financial and family strains of caring for the sick child.

In the phase of rehabilitation or recovery, the attempt to define and return to normalcy may arouse the most family discord. Does the family return to normal roles or is a major alteration in the family's function necessary to deal with the illness? If there is a long recovery period or uncertainty of outcome, this may breakdown the family's resilience. In diseases where relapse occurs, there may be an altering of expectancies regarding what normalcy now becomes. In dealing with the process of disease, it must be recognized that different family members may conceptualize the illness according to their own capacities to cope. Thus, they may not even define these stages in similar terms. Each family member might have their own trajectory of what the course of illness involves in terms of their own adjustments and ability to satisfy the needs of the ill child. It is critical that professionals give attention to where the family member is in terms of their representation of illness and provide emotional support as well as informational guidance. In families with terminally ill children, issues of hospice and bereavement take precedence over most other family activities.

HISTORICAL CONSIDERATIONS IN RESEARCH
ON PARENTING ILL CHILDREN

Historically, the psychosocial literature has not taken an interactive view of patients' adjustment to chronic illness in which the entire family constellation is examined. Complex relationships that develop between family members when a chronic disease occurs in one member have been the focus of family therapy research (Minuchin, 1967). This clinical approach yielded many useful interaction codes based mainly on verbal analyses. Although quantitative analyses were conducted, investigators have typically been less interested in statistical analyses and have used the data to guide the process of psychotherapy.

The literature on parenting the ill child has generally focused exclusively on patient variables. The most popular approaches have been attempts to define specific personality types as associated with diseases. Other studies have looked at specific diseases and compared ill children's adjustment or psychopathology with normal healthy children. According to Johnson (1985, 1988), the literature suggests that (1) specific personality patterns are not associated with specific illnesses and (2) most children facing chronic disease cope reasonably well by accepting the limitations while trying to fit into normal age-relevant activities and school.

Previous research on families with children with health problems and disabilities does not emphasize resilience. Rather, the focus has been on the negative aspects of having a child with a health problem (e.g., Drotar et al., 1989). Typically, studies involved comparing groups of children with chronic illnesses to control groups of healthy children matched on age and gender. These studies led to inaccurate conclusions that there must be maladaptive functioning in ill children. Measures used often confounded the disease-related variables of fatigue with clinical depression. These studies have been reviewed in detail by Drotar (1999). However, in the 1990s, more studies have focused on successful adaptation outcomes and the coping mechanisms by which they are accomplished. Within these studies, the focus has primarily been on individual outcomes of the sick child. Parents and siblings have received much less attention. Family functioning as a system was rarely an outcome of interest. Family functioning consists of examining mutual and reciprocal influences between members. Thus, the resilient family is both a system that has adapted to the chronic stress associated with a child's disability needs, as well as a mediator or cause of the child's psychosocial development or resilience (Patterson, 1991).

Currently, family-systems-based health care is a growing field of practice. The most recent family intervention models are grounded in a stress-diathesis model that addresses the interactive influences of biological vulnerability and environmental stresses. Intervention is aimed at management of the illness, and the family is viewed as an indispensable ally in treatment. Walsh (1998, p. 212) maintains that "reducing the family's stress and strengthening its protective functioning, are inseparable goals of intervention."

Reiss, Steinglass, and Howe (1993), recognizing that modern medicine has extended life (although for many a prolonged life is of uncertain duration and filled with serious pain and disability), suggested that we must look at the family unit across its full span of development. In order to serve immediate and long-term needs of their members families must develop patterns of transaction both among members and between family members and people outside the family. These regulatory structures are: family paradigm and family identity. Family paradigm refers to implicit emotionally charged conceptions shared by members of the same family. These are their conceptions of the order, coherence, and novelty of the world in which they live. Family identity refers to conceptions the family has about itself in relation to that social world: conceptions of its own competence, stature, intactness, and durability. These shared conceptions guide and constrain the behavior patterns of the family. Reiss and his colleagues (1993) noted that, in addition to the family's organization around the illness, the family needed to recognize the impact of a second system, namely the medical team, on the forms of reorganization engaged in by families. Chronic illness brings the family into regular and intimate contact with medical staff, and these members function as structured systems in their own right. Finally, they point out that chronic illness places demands on families that change over time. These demands appeared to fall into three categories: (1) those related to the onset of a medical condition, usually putting families into an initial state of crisis, (2) those related to chronic management of the condition, and (3) those demands during the terminal period of the illness. These transition periods were very disruptive of developmental transition particularly in families where rigidly organized behaviors for management of illness-related duties precluded sharing responsibilities with the ill child.

CENTRAL ISSUES IN THE STUDY OF PARENTING ILL CHILDREN

The psychological impact of chronic illness transcends the individual ill child and affects the entire family, including parents and siblings. Drotar (1999) pointed out that there is a threefold risk of mental health problems in children with physical disabilities and physical illnesses. The siblings of these children have been noted to have a twofold increase in risk for emotional disorders. Despite the fact that mothers bear the greatest share of the child's caregiving burden (Bristol, Gallagher, and Schopler, 1988; Kazak and Marvin, 1984), there is the least research regarding mothers' mental health risks. It is also not clear how the nature of the stress of having a sick child influences mental distress. In other words, do parents who are stressed have children who become dysfunctional, or is the tension and caregiver burden likely to produce a distressed parent? Only a careful evaluation of longitudinal data, which follow parents over the course of their children's illness from time of uncertainty of diagnosis to treatment process, can illuminate the reciprocal nature of these relations.

Categorical Versus Noncategorical Disease Entities

Another issue that confronts researchers in this field is the noncategorical versus disease category approach in illness. Pless (1985) and Stein and Jessop (1982) suggested that it is not the illness per se but factors such as time of onset, prognosis, the kind of care required, and the visibility of the condition that should be the focus of analyses. The assumption here is that illness produces an effect that is more similar across pediatric conditions, and that these differences do not lead to distinctive patterns of adaptation. In addition, the impact of both developmental stage and phase of illness has often been ignored. However, work by Holden, Chmielewski, Nelson, Kager, and Foltz (1997), in which differences in children's self-competence and family functioning were found between asthmatic and diabetic youngsters, argued that gender and disease-specific categories need to be retained in order to understand differences in adjustment required by very different illnesses. Girls rated themselves as more competent than boys. Once family functioning and disease variables were controlled for, the effect of specific disease dissipated.

Quittner, DiGirolamo, Michel, and Eigen (1992) also demonstrated that the ability to predict depression required looking at parental differences as well as situation-specific requirements of an illness. In this investigation of children under the age of 4 years who were born with cystic fibrosis, it was found that mothers had more role strain than fathers. Role strain referred to the division of caregiving responsibilities among the mothers and fathers (e.g., who performs the medical regimen), excess time demands related to childcare, and perceptions of inadequate or constrained role performance. Depression was measured from the subscale of the Symptom Checklist-90 Revised (SCL-90; Derogatis and Clearly, 1977). Mothers reported greater situation-specific stress than fathers and higher levels of role strain. Mothers reported significantly greater depressive symptomatology. Interestingly, mothers who were employed outside the home showed significantly lower levels of role strain and depression than mothers who were not employed. Employment may have allowed these mothers to receive more self-esteem support.

Social Support

A major issue in the area that needs to be addressed is what types of support are perceived as helpful versus unhelpful in supporting parents of chronically ill children (Garwick, Patterson, Bennett, and Blum, 1998). The concept of "misguided helping" (Anderson and Coyne, 1991) has gained interest as researchers have abandoned the myth that all types of help are warranted and instead studied which types of help are desired by family members and from whom and at what point in the course of the illness. Some types of behaviors are "misguided" because they are excessive, untimely, or inappropriate. In adolescents there is the risk that overprotection by the mothers inhibits independence strivings. Young teenagers needs for privacy, peer acceptance, and control play a role in change toward shared responsibility for management of the disease. Unfortunately, in some diseases such as CF or JRA, the parental involvement is unavoidable.

Access to Health Care, Morbidity, and Compliance

One problem of note is the lack of access to mental health care that families receive when they face physical illness with accompanying depression and anxiety. Health inequalities have often been ignored. Reanalysis of the British statistics of the *Health of the Nation* (Judge and Benzeval, 1993), which looked at childhood mortality data, suggested that nonworking single mothers with dependent children were more likely to have children with the worst mortality record of any social group. In fact, across the ages of 1 to 15 years, children were twice at risk for dying in social classes 4 and 5 (including the unemployed), as they were in the more advantaged classes 1 and 2 (p. 679). In the United States, the statistics of children without health coverage are staggering. Children without health insurance coverage were eight times more likely than children from nonpoor, Eastern European families to report not having a usual source of care. Minority children were three times more likely, and poor children four times more likely, to be reported as not having a usual source of care than children from the reference group (Newacheck, Stoddard, Hughes, and Pearl, 1997). A demographic study of the use of children's mental health services, where a diagnosis of mental illness has been determined (Cohen and Hesselbart, 1993), found significant lags in use in youth 18 to 21 years of age. In addition, families living in rural and semirural areas and those in middle-income families tended not to use services. There are several reasons other than lack of insurance coverage that may be responsible for failure to obtain health services. For one, parents may be hesitant to report adjustment problems, as they fear being labeled a poor parent. In addition, the pediatricians who work with these families may be hesitant to label them adding further to their distress. Another problem is the lack of trained mental health professionals who work with children and families with chronic medical conditions.

　　We also know that, when there is stress, the family will be less likely to comply with the appropriate medication, diet, and exercise requirements and that may serve to increase the medical problems (Kovacs et al., 1990). Few studies have explored the process by which parenting behaviors influence compliance with medical requirements.

Sample Representativeness of Illness Populations

Another neglected issue in the research arena is whether or not families who willingly participating in research are representative of most families with chronically ill children or are the neediest. The individuals choosing to participate and their spouses may be ready for input and show less disruption than those of families who refuse participation. In a study of family attrition, Janus and Goldberg (1997) compared response dropout in a questionnaire study of parents of children with cystic fibrosis, heart disease, or matched healthy controls. There was a 35% loss of participation in the course of the 4-year study. The loss of families was largely attributed to situational variables such as moving away or the death of the child. Attrition occurred to a greater extent in a control sample of healthy individuals.

A second problem in investigations in this area is the level of participation, and it was found that mothers of children with cystic fibrosis (CF) and coronary heart disease (CHD) were more likely to participate in research than comparison mothers. The fact that CF families participate to a greater extent than the CHD families may have to do with care patterns, because these families were seen for the study during treatment visits, and the physicians, involved were more likely to stay involved with them. Another problem identified within the study was that fathers chose to participate at a much lower level of course than mothers. Parental well-being as measured by the Rutter Health Questionnaire (Rutter and Tizard, 1970) was the best predictor of participation in research of families with a chronically ill child.

Theories of Family Adaptation

Normalization of routine in the face of illness is a sign of resilience in families. At receiving the diagnosis of a chronic illness, families are said to go through a grieving process. The theoretical position of Bowlby (1978) is relevant in that families must give up the dream of the "perfect child." The process of resolution of the trauma is conceptualized as an integration of (1) cognitive and affective states, which existed prior to the trauma, and (2) conflicting states, which arose following the traumatic event (in this case learning the nature of impact of chronic disease). In a study of this process, Sheeran, Marvin, and Pianta (1997) found that maternal acceptance of the diagnosis was related to lower parenting stress, greater husband marital satisfaction, and level and helpfulness of social support. When mothers accepted the condition they had children who were more secure in their attachment relationships and husbands who reported greater marital satisfaction.

Imbalance in parenting implies that, when a child is sick, one parent (usually the mother) takes more responsibility, excluding the other parent. In such a situation, the parent–child coalition, and the executive functioning of the marital dyad for decision making, may be disrupted and violate relationships and generational boundaries (Leventhal et al., 1985).

Emotional contagion (Escalona, 1953) is a theory in which the expression of feelings, grief, and anxiety is thought to elevate the problem in the family. Research has been done on the negative effects of repressing emotionality. The research studies (e.g., Patterson, McCubbin, and Warwick, 1990) generally show that open expressiveness is associated with better family outcomes in terms of child adjustment. Thus, families given the opportunity to express anger about the impact of the illness, fears about the future, and other concerns have better family outcomes (Bobrow, Avruskin, and Siller, 1985; Daniels, Moos, Billings, and Miller, 1987; Marteau, Bloch, and Baum, 1987).

Uncertainty or lack of diagnosis is one of the main variables that leads to parental anxiety. In a research study of mothers' experience of their young children's illness prior to a diagnosis of asthma, it was found that during prediagnosis mothers felt that "groping in the dark" was their greatest source of stress (Mishel, 1988). In intensive evaluation of interview protocols and parent verification, the processes underlying this feeling were "unending illness" and "searching for answers."

The McCubbin and Patterson (1982) Double ABCX Model of Family adaptation focuses on processes by which families adapt to a crisis, such as diagnosis of childhood chronic illness. This model encompasses both resources within the family and community system as well as the external demands, including financial strain, worry, and the role changes required to adapt to the crisis. The most striking features of this model include the concept of "pile up" of demands on family resources and the identification of family coping strategies. A further adaptation of this Family Adjustment and Adaptation Response Modes (FAAR; Patterson, 1988) identifies the meanings that family members attribute to stresses. Importance is placed on how families define their capabilities in dealing with the illness-related demands. According to this model, families use many resources, financial, personal, and community wide, including as well as family systems (cohesion, organization, and communication). This model predicts which families will be resilient and has received some support in studies of children with cystic fibrosis (Patterson, 1985).

Risk vulnerability models (Thompson and Gustafson, 1996; Wallander et al., 1989) look at disease severity and handicap as major stressors on the ability to deal with chronic illness. Thompson and Gustafson found that risk factors are moderated by three basic types of resistance: stable intrapersonal attributes, stress processing or coping ability, and social-ecological influences such as strength of family relationships and support.

Another model is the risk and resistance model (Wallander et al., 1989), which looks at family environment, social support, family members' adaptation, and utilitarian resources as examples of resistance factors that influence appraisals and coping in response to stresses of chronic conditions.

Rolland (1987, 1994) has discussed the importance of evaluation of when in the life cycle of the family the child's illness first occurs. He suggested the need to follow the trajectory of the illness as to whether it is chronic, stable, relapsing, or in abeyance. An episodic illness like epilepsy would have a very different effect on the family than a persistent illness such as renal failure. In episodic illness, the family must be on constant guard for reoccurrence and carefully monitor any changes required in medication or dosage. In a persistent illness, there is less likelihood for sudden change in course or drug regimen. If an illness has a deteriorating course with a likely fatal outcome, such as some types of cancer, families must prepare themselves for loss while providing their loved one with palliative care and often engagement of hospice care. In a condition that is serious but stable, such as paraplegia from traumatic spinal cord injury, the family needs to maintain their optimism and continue to fully include the disabled member in family activities. Although all families change in response to a crisis, many need help in adjusting their roles, rules, and leadership to achieve a new balance that maximizes their resources and coping skills as the illness enters a more chronic, long-haul phase.

CLASSICAL AND MODERN RESEARCH IN PARENTING ILL CHILDREN

Many of the early publications about parental stresses in this situation are in the nursing journals and are focused on treatment issues. Empirical studies have primarily focused on the negative parenting of the mother who was often labeled as overprotective. The other body of research has grown up around intervention studies. Those studies where parents have been included will be briefly reviewed. Stein and Jessop (1982) argued for considering a noncategorical approach to defining chronic illness. This emphasis is to study core common features such as illness-related demands and challenges rather than view each illness as a separate entity. The context, stage of illness, and/or cognitive level of the child may influence the way stresses are conceived and problems solved.

In the last two decades, there has been increasing professional interest in the relation between parental adaptation and the adjustment of children to chronic illness and its treatment demands. Two levels of analyses have emerged, the "macro" level (household composition, overall familial attitudes and roles, and family environment) and a "micro" level (family interaction and family communication). The macro level has been more intensively studied. These analyses of family functioning include topics of: (1) family structure and home environment, (2) parental attitudes and roles, and (3) family structure. Research at the micro level includes direct observations of families with chronically medically ill children and have been conducted by Minuchin and his colleagues (1978) and Hauser and his colleagues (Hauser, Vierya, Jacobson, and Wertlieb, 1989).

Measurement Issues

Family adaptation. One central research issue is how to measure family adaptation. The Family Adaptation and Cohesion and the Family Crisis Oriented Personal Evaluation Scales (Olson 1985 and Olson, 1986) are typically used to look in-depth at the types of changes families experience during the course of a child's illness. A research scale called the Maternal Worry Scale (DeVet and Ireys, 1998) has demonstrated good internal reliability and validity, and may be a sensitive measure of maternal anxiety as it is related to having a sick child. Its use was sensitive to developmental change with mothers' report of internalizing and externalizing behaviors of their older children being related to greater worry.

One problem has been a lack of definition in what is an adaptive family. Weiss, Marvin, and Pianta (1997) provided a systems analysis in their ethnographic approach to describing families caring for children with cerebral palsy. They identified three types of adjustment patterns: the traditional pattern where the mother is solely responsible for childcare, the team pattern where both parents are highly active in child care, and the extended family pattern where childcare is spread out across biologically related individuals. A formal support pattern is a strategy of distributing a very significant amount of responsibility for childcare to professional and educational providers. Each of these patterns of family care led to good school and home adjustment of the child.

Empowerment. Investigators have used the Family Empowerment Scale (Koren et al., 1997) and found that there was further validation of the empowerment concept. It was also found that a higher sense of parental empowerment is significantly related to children's better adherence to treatment, including metabolic control. Whereas most previous studies have focused on the negative aspects of mothers' coping, one study (Florian and Elad, 1998) defined the construct of "empowerment" to describe the ongoing capacity of individuals or groups to act on their own behalf to achieve a greater measure of control over their lives and destinies. Jones, Garlow, Turnbull, Rutherford, and Barber (1996) defined five ideas in relation to the construct of empowerment: (1) perceived control and efficacy over the course of life events; (2) effectiveness influencing life conditions through problem-solving skills, coping strategies, and effective use of resources; (3) family–professional partnerships; (4) community participation, including leadership in organizations; and (5) situational and temporal variability. Empowerment takes different forms in divergent contexts, differs across individuals in the same context, and may change over time for the same individual.

Observational methodology. An observational approach taken by Hauser and his colleagues (Hauser et al., 1993) has revealed many features of families dealing with the onset of insulin-dependent diabetes in comparison with families facing an acute illness. They examined the micro level, looking in detail at how aspects of family communication and interaction may be linked with child or adolescent vulnerability and resilience. The unit of analysis here was the individual family member in relation to and in interaction with other members of the family. Their descriptions of coping strategies have been operationally defined. Interview material is audiotaped, and trained raters code the verbal statements of family members into categories of appraisal-focused (cognitive processes), problem-focused (behavioral efforts), and emotion management coping strategies (strategies that deal with emotional regulation of problem feelings). Family cohesiveness is addressed by evaluating specific statements of how individual family members see the unit functioning. These studies are longitudinal, so they will yield important information about changes over the course of development of the family and the adolescent. Preliminary findings on 42 diabetic families and 37 acute illness families suggest that mothers of diabetics describe their families as seeking support, pursuing alternative rewards, and trying out new responses compared to acute-illness families, who see their families as being more self-reliant and operating as a consensual unit (e.g., the "we are all in this together" view).

Fathers also describe the acute-illness families as pursuing alternative rewards, seeking support, and trying out new responses. They do not see their families as more self-reliant than those with acute-illness families. The adolescents in diabetic families characterized their families as being less involved in seeking information about their current difficulties. Regarding emotion management strategies, the diabetic families expressed their feelings to others outside the family and described more impulsive expressions of their feelings than those parents of children with acute illnesses. The diabetic youngsters were less likely to minimize their awareness of their own and other family members' feelings. It is evident from the research studies of this group of investigators (e.g., Hauser et al., 1989) that the three domains of protective factors—personality, social life, and family—frequently interact as determinants of resilient developmental outcomes. Garmezy (1984) detailed a series of possibilities regarding how personal attributes and stressful events may interact to determine the quality of adaptation. Stress factors and personal attributes may combine additively in the prediction of outcome. Stress (if not excessive) may enhance competence; this is the "challenge" model. Or, an alternative perspective suggests that personal attributes may modulate, buffer, or exacerbate the impact of stress.

Role of the Father

There has been a lack of research on fathers' role in caring for the chronically ill child (Timko, Baumgartner, Moos, and Miller, 1993). In one study (Rodrigue et al., 1996), fathers of children who were undergoing evaluation for solid organ or bone marrow transplantation completed family function and parenting stress measures. They were found to be more concerned about the family finances and limitations in family activities than parenting stress. The mothers assumed more responsibility for the child's care.

In evaluating maternal and paternal functioning in parents whose children have spina bifida at preadolescence, it was found that the mothers in the spina bifida group reported less perceived parental competence, more social isolation, and less adaptability to change, whereas fathers reported more psychological symptoms (Holmbeck et al., 1997).

In another study conducted by Goldberg, Morris, Simmons, Fowler, and Levison (1990), fathers were found to have a more difficult attachment relationship than mothers with their sick children. This is consistent with most expectations based on the more limited role most fathers play in caregiving. It was also found that maternal distress was higher for mothers who had children with congenital heart disease than CF, although those mothers reported difficulty with child demandingness.

Hauser et al. (1986) looked at transactional father–child relationships in IDDM using direct observation codes; they found differential patterns of interaction for mothers and fathers. Whereas mothers engaged in more enabling behaviors toward their children (e.g., empathy, assurance, and problem solving), fathers engaged in more constraining behaviors (e.g., devaluation, indifference, critical judgment).

Role of Social Class, Ethnicity, Race, and Gender

The influence of social class on parenting behaviors has been evaluated in regard to parents of mildly retarded youngsters (Floyd and Siatzyk, 1992). It has been postulated that the lower-socioeconomic status (SES) occupations may be contrasted with upper-SES in three significant ways: Lower-SES occupations involve manipulating concrete materials as opposed to abstract ideas, performing standardized work rather than engaging in new problem solving, and being closely supervised rather than working independently. Thus they hypothesized that parents in the lower-SES families are more likely to value conformity to external authority in their children in terms of obedience and good manners, whereas parents in higher social positions are more likely to value self-direction, self-control, and responsibility. The Floyd and Siatzyk study was consistent with these expectations. Interestingly, it was the upper-SES families that reported more family problems with negative and controlling interactions with their retarded children. One would expect this if they were hoping for independent behavior in a child who was cognitively deficient and had minimal social skills.

There have been few studies that have specifically focused on racial or religious differences experienced by families with sick children. One study of African American and European American parents (Williams, Lorenzo and Borja, 1993) examined the characteristics of social networks and provision of support in families with a child who has cancer. It found that, whereas social support appears to buffer distress, the types of social support varied. African American parents described support as instrumental actions, whereas European Americans focused more on affective and emotional support. In this study it was noted that the European American families had support networks twice as large as African Americans, although the African American parents perceived their networks as being more supportive. Another study (Rehm, 2000) looked specifically at Mexican Americans' religiosity as an influence on coping with disease; despite the feeling that God is Supreme, there was active coping by the family and collaboration with medical avenues.

Family cohesion appears to have a differential impact on African American boys and girls with sickle-cell disease (Hurtig, Koepke, and Park, 1989). Girls tend to become more aggressive with parental conflict, whereas low cohesiveness leads to increased somatic, uncommunicative, and schizoid problems in boys.

Prospective Research Design

One of the more positive changes in research on parenting ill children has been the adoption of prospective research designs, which follow the family, coping across the various phases of illness. Frank et al. (1998) using growth analyses looked at single family adaptation patterns to two diseases, juvenile rheumatoid arthritis (JRA) and type 1 diabetes (IDDM). They found that across families, maternal dysphoria was highest at time of diagnosis. The parents of children with JRA were more likely to maintain distress and report difficulty in control of the illness than parents of children with IDDM or healthy children (adaptation or maturation over time). It could be that physical disability, which often accompanies JRA, may be more apparent than the life-threatening aspects of IDDM. In evaluating the importance of timing of social support (as it may reduce anxiety in parents) following transplant procedures Rodrigue et al. (1997) revealed that 6 months following the procedure, the extended family had reduced or withdrawn their support. It was just at this time when anxiety increased due to the arrival of medical bills and compliance problems with the use of drugs to prevent rejection.

In another prospective study (Goldberg et al., 1997), parents of healthy and pediatric samples (congenital heart disorder and cystic fibrosis) were studied over 4 years. It showed that the degree of parenting stress was the best predictor of childhood preschool behavior problems even when the severity of childhood illness and parent–child relationships were included as predictors. It also provided evidence that the predictive value of parenting stress increased over time, thus supporting the notion that having to care for a sick child is what leads to maternal and paternal stress.

In a longitudinal 4-year study of adolescents with IDDM, Seiffge-Krenke (1998) evaluated the effects of a highly structured climate in families of adolescents and used a control group of healthy children. She found that those parents with a sick child reported, on average, a significantly worse emotional climate but a higher amount of structure and organization. However, family environment did not predict metabolic control over the course of time. The findings that adolescents with diabetes and their parents have a family climate characterized by a high amount of structure, organization, control, and achievement orientation are consistent with findings of enmeshed patterns of interaction in families dealing with type 1 diabetes. (Hauser and Solomon, 1985). In addition, Hanson et al.

(1995) similarly found a lack of direct effects of family climate on metabolic control but an indirect effect through positive adherence to the medical regimen. Thus, it seems that in order to improve compliance, close monitoring by parents is desirable.

In studies of the caregiving system, Reiss et al. (1993) focused on the challenges of the medical and social routines on severe illness, and found that many variables predicted survival in end-stage renal disease. They also found a paradoxical effect in that the most highly coordinated families who were most focused on compliance had family members who did not survive. The authors explain their result by family members' lack of discrimination in what management strategies would be helpful during an acute medical emergency in which they remain highly engaged with one another and focus heavily on the needs of the chronically ill member, and those times in which the family should respect the independent needs of the ill child and take care of their own needs.

One study (Berenbaum and Hatcher, 1992) examined the level of maternal distress, comparing children in pediatric intensive care unit (PICU) versus less ill children on the general pediatrics floor, and with a group of nonhospitalized ill children attending an outpatient clinic. Mothers who rated their children's illnesses as more severe, whose families had experienced more negative stressors over the past 6 months, and whose child's hospitalization status reflected more serious illness had higher levels of state anxiety. Younger mothers whose child's hospitalization status was more serious tended to have more confusion as measured by the Profile of Mood States. Prior hospital experience predicted mothers' anger, but not depression or distress. This study also demonstrated that there was no difference in maternal distress for hospitalized children in a pediatric ward and nonhospitalized children attending an outpatient clinic. The mothers of children in the PICU were most distressed.

A longitudinal study of parental coping with children with juvenile rheumatoid arthritis represents one of the only studies in which each spouse's functioning was related to the adaptation by the other. Timko, Stovel, Moos and Miller (1992) found that mothers had more depressed mood at 1-year follow-up than fathers, but they also reported more mastery behaviors. As predicted for both mothers and fathers, spousal dysfunction was associated with their own concurrent functioning. The mechanism may be via the partners' reduced support as well as directly through their own dysfunction. Family resources were more consistent predictors of mothers' than of fathers' functioning. The use of avoidance coping strategies led to a greater degree of child impairment. The opposite was also true, in that the more disability and pain children reported, the less effective the parents strategies were in normalizing the childrens' experience in living.

Preadolescent Vulnerability

Several studies have focused on preadolescent children, as this is a unique developmental period in which autonomy and independence compete with parents' concerns for controlling the illness regimen. In addition, change in hormones makes regulation of disease processes more difficult even with excellent compliance.

A study using a wide collection of self-report measures on adolescents and their parents (Kell, Kliewer, Erikson, and Ohene-Frempong, 1998) found that, after controlling for disease severity, sociodemographic, and medical variables, scores on the Self-Report Family Inventory (Beavers and Hampson, 1990) revealed that higher levels of family competence were associated with fewer behavioral and emotional problems. Interestingly, the influence was greater for younger adolescents and in predicting internalizing problems and somatic complaints among girls. Again, this design was correlational, so no causal relations can be concluded.

A study of preadolescents who had been living with chronic illnesses was conducted in which parents were asked what were helpful versus unhelpful types of support. Garwick et al. (1998) found that both mothers and fathers reported that other family members were the primary source of helpful emotional and tangible support, whereas health care providers were the primary source of helpful informational support. They held in-depth in-home evaluations on two occasions 1 year apart. They found that fathers reported more helpful emotional and informational support from family members 1 year later. Regarding unsupportive behaviors, one third attributed them to health care providers and another third to extended family members. The types of things that were unhelpful from health care providers included insensitivity, rudeness, a negative attitude toward the child or family, inadequate information about the child's condition or care, and inadequate services or referrals. Approximately half were related to communication problems. Extended family members were cited as having inadequate contact or involvement with the child or family, providing inadequate emotional support, making insensitive or invasive comments, or blaming the parents for the child's condition. Acquaintances, neighbors, and community persons were faulted for insensitive comments and questions, lack of understanding, and withdrawal of friendship. School providers were also cited for inadequate services, insensitivity to the child's needs, and lacking knowledge about child's condition. It is important to assess social support within the context of the setting in which it is perceived, given that parents have different experiences of what they need from different individuals. Parents appear to expect particular types of support from specific sources.

PRACTICAL INFORMATION ABOUT PARENTING ILL CHILDREN

There are at least ten strategies that would contribute to enhancing resilience for a family with an ill child:

(1) Balance the illness with other family needs. Roles, that is, status and behavioral expectations, are relatively well-defined in families. Therefore, if a child needs special attention or is hospitalized there must be a shift in roles. Attention to sibling needs by including the extended family during crisis periods can alleviate some of the tension. Having outside paid help to shop, clean, and do other chores will free up time for accomplishing basic family commitments to each other.
(2) Maintain clear family boundaries. During an illness crises, the extended family may assist with normal chores or usurp the role of the parents in disciplining the children. It is important to make it clear that the needs will change over the course of the child's illness.
(3) Develop communication competence. Learn how to talk to the physicians about their concerns and how to help the child communicate their disability to others.
(4) Attribute positive meanings to the situation. Some families become closer when adversity of illness occurs, as they show that the family can maintain its coherence during crises.
(5) Maintain family flexibility—less rigidity as to who does what.
(6) Maintain a commitment to the family as a unity.
(7) Engage in active coping efforts.
(8) Model good coping efforts and facilitate approach-oriented problem solving.
(9) Maintain social integration (e.g., participation in church, community and school).
(10) Develop collaborative relationships with professionals.

One of the advances that has been made in research on chronically ill children is the recognition that dealing with the disease needs to be viewed within the stage of the illness. Thus, the prediagnosis phase has been identified as stress elevating and more nurse support during this phase is advisable. The diagnosis and treatment phases may be a time of crises, depending on the seriousness of the threat. Decisions about treatment must often be made and can be difficult. Better outcomes result when the family members are able to retain control over their lives and deal with the added demands associated with meeting illness-related needs. This calls for greater problem-solving skills. It has been demonstrated that families that are better at problem solving and are organized and can resolve conflicts have improved outcomes (Hauser et al., 1986; Newbrough, Simpkins, and Maurer, 1985; Patterson, 1985). In looking at similarities in anxiety state and coping styles of parents whose children had just been diagnosed with cancer, it was found (Dahlquist et al., 1993) that those couples with the greater discrepancies in state anxiety reported the greater amount of marital distress. Whereas the separate parent scores on repression–sensitization coping style scale (Byrne, 1961) did not predict marital distress, their combined score did. Thus, the importance of looking at the marital unit is reaffirmed. In studying the influence of parenting style on compliance with appointment keeping, reporting reactions to treatment and the like, it was found that supportive parenting enhanced compliance (Manne, Jacobsen, Gorkinkle, Gerstein, and Redd, 1993). This included being more nurturing, sensitive to the child's input, and nonrestrictive in parenting (Power, 1989).

The importance of open communication is vital. In a set of studies of adaptation and competence in families with a child with mental retardation, Beavers, Hampson, Hulgus, and Beavers (1986) found that families whose members were able to express a wide range of feelings, including joy as well as sorrow and frustration, had better adaptation in terms of family functioning. They even felt that the presence of a child with a disability may have contributed to their strong mutual support.

The fact that most children spend a portion of their time in hospitals to receive diagnostics and treatment leads to disruption of family roles. Other siblings may feel alienated, especially if treatment requires the mother to be away from the home for periods of time. The sick child is isolated from school friends and family support systems while dealing with often aversive and unpredictable events leading to pain and uncertainty. Melamed and her colleagues (Melamed, 1998; Melamed and Floyd, 1998; Melamed and Ridley-Johnson, 1988) have suggested psychological preparation for parents as well as children. Parents who can provide support and information in age-appropriate language and who can model coping strategies have children with less anxiety. Melamed, Kaplan, and Fogel (2000) discussed the importance of childhood illness as a long-term source of stress for both children and their families. Children with life-threatening illnesses such as asthma and renal transplantations need to adhere to strict regimens. Parents are under a great deal of stress. Depression and lack of social support are significant predictors of compliance failures.

One of the most trying periods for parents caring for a child with a progressive illness is home care. Parents need support from others that is tangible (e.g., providing respite, shopping, and house cleaning) as well as emotional support. Drotar, Agle, Eckl, and Thompson (1997) studied parents who had children with and without HIV infections and were also hemophiliacs. This disease requires a great deal of home management such as replacement of blood factors, treatment of acute bleeding episodes, pain management, and rehabilitation. They used the Wallander et al. (1989) theoretical framework to predict that hemophilia severity and general life stressors would be associated with higher levels of psychological distress among mothers and that supportive family relationships would be associated with lower distress. They found that stressful life events were associated with higher levels of distress, whereas family relationship support was associated with lower levels of distress in the mother. Hemophilia severity did not relate to maternal psychological distress as measured on the Profile of Mood States. As expected, those mothers with HIV-infected children who had more life stressors were more distressed.

Gravelle (1997) used a phenomenological approach to define increasing spirals of anxiety in families managing adversity of progressive muscular diseases. She found that parents could build on past experiences to face the new challenges. When the child needed a wheelchair there was a real mixture of feelings, namely the recognition that their child was extremely limited, with decreased mobility and independence. The strategies used in managing change were: seeking information, planning and preparing, negotiating, and utilizing resources. Normalization was viewing their child as having a disability rather than a progressive life-threatening illness. In another study evaluating differences in coping strategies (Miller, Gordon, Daniele, and Diller, 1992), problem-focused coping strategies were negatively related to psychological distress, whereas emotion focused strategies were related to distress.

In families with a child who has cystic fibrosis, the nature of burden on the parents for the child's care is enormous. Treatment involves close attention to the child's physical condition (e.g., frequency of coughing, energy level, incidence of gastrointestinal complaints, and weight) and diet, the ingestion of medication throughout the day, and the administration of physical therapy or "postural drainage." Parents must also deal with their children's distress in dealing with social demands, extreme thinness, and rigors of the treatment regimen. Moreover, parents must cope with the fact that their child has a limited life expectancy. A review article on CF (Ievers and Drotar, 1996) found that higher levels of parental distress, an avoidant coping style, and low levels of family support put parents at risk for chronic, psychological dysfunction. These families need additional support and referral to psychologists, social workers, or child psychiatrists.

In families with children whose illnesses are painful but not predictable, recommendations for family interventions and training the parents in behavioral management of pain gives them a sense of control in an otherwise frustrating situation.

CONCLUSIONS

A contextual family–systems approach is needed to understand adaptation to chronic illness in children. This means that the health care system must incorporate families in pediatric medicine. There has been an improvement in research approaches in that many more investigators state theory-derived hypotheses. The incorporation of a broader range of measures is also seen. As Kazak (1997) pointed out, there has been a lag between pediatric family research and what is already being clinically applied particularly by nursing. One reason may be the lack of good family measurement strategies. Even though we talk of families as a unit, their subsystems (e.g., parental, parent–child, and sibling–patient relationships) would be important to study. The family unit has been the object of studies by such investigators and Hauser and his colleagues (Hauser et al. 1989). This time-consuming methodology has, however, not been adopted by other investigators despite its theoretical relevance. There also has been a lack of approaches viewing children who enter the medical system at different stages of conceptual and emotional development as having unique needs. Although the type of illness may impose different limitations on family functioning, it is important to assess each family member's experiences with illness and beliefs about health and illness within this developmental lifespan.

Studies of family intervention need to be more replicable. Manual treatment programs, such as those developed by Kaslow and her colleagues (1997), offer a strategy for examining the effective elements of a program. It is important to evaluate individual differences in who benefits from which programs.

Involving fathers as participants and understanding their role in the care of a chronically ill child is of paramount importance. Data reviewed here suggest that father participation requires more active efforts. In a transactional study of families with a child with IDDM (Seiffge-Krenke, 1998), the divergent influence of the disease was noted, with the father becoming more maladjusted with the decline in child's adjustment over the course of 1 year.

Alternative qualitative strategies for understanding the process by which families adjust to illness demands must be sought, and they must be theory driven. One such approach is the family ritual and family storytelling technique, a narrative approach that can be useful in describing changes that take place because of the medical illness (Fiese, 1997).

One problem revealed by the literature reviewed was that the noncategorical hypothesis, which would treat different chronic illnesses on the same dimension, did not receive uniform support. Several studies have shown that the disease state differentiates the amount of distress parents and child alike experience (Drotar et al., 1997).

The change in the direction of research from pathologizing parents in families dealing with medical illness to collaborating in the care of their children has been a very positive one.

Finally, longitudinal research is crucial. We now possess statistical methods, such as path and sequential analysis, which should encourage more complex evaluation of how a system—including social support networks, peers, hospital systems, and schools—operates to aid parents of ill children.

ACKNOWLEDGMENTS

The author appreciates the support of the National Institutes of Nursing Research grant R25-NR05098 for her National Institutes of Health–funded participation in the interdisciplinary workshop (Blending Physiological, Behavioral, and Family Approaches to Research on Chronic Child Illness) held in Cleveland, Ohio, from July 10–14, 2000. The inspiration of the research of Dr. S. Hauser and his continued support in evaluation of the research methods are gratefully acknowledged. The patience of Thomas and Alex Wills during the manuscript preparation was appreciated.

REFERENCES

Abiden, R. (1986). *Parenting Stress Index* (2nd ed.). Charlottsville, NC: Pediatric Psychology.

Anderson, B., and Coyne, J. C. (1991). "Miscarried helping" in the families of children and adolescents with chronic disease. In J. H. Johnson and S. B. Johnson (Eds.), *Advances in child health psychology*. Gainesville: University of Florida Press.

Barbarin, O., Hughes, D., and Chesler, M. (1985). Stress, coping, and marital function among parents children with cancer. *Journal of Marriage and the Family, 47*, 473–480

Beavers, J., Hampson, R., Hulgus, Y., and Beavers, W. R. (1986). Coping with families with retarded children. *Family Process, 25*, 365–378.

Beavers, W. B., and Hampson, R. B. (1990). Successful families: Assessment and intervention. New York: Norton.

Berenbaum, J., and Hatcher, J. (1992). Emotional distress of mothers of hospitalized children. *Journal of Pediatric Psychology, 17*, 359–372.

Bierman, C. W., Pearlman, D. S., Shapiro, G. G., and Busse, W. W. (1996). *Allergy, asthma, and immunology from infancy to adulthood* (3rd ed.). Philadelphia : Saunders.

Bobrow, E., Avruskin, T., and Siller, J. (1985). Mother–daughter interaction and adherence to diabetes regimen. *Diabetes Care, 8*, 146–151.

Bowlby, J. (1978). Attachment theory and its therapeutic inplications. *Adolescent Psychiatry, 6*, 5–33.

Bristol, M., Gallagher, J., and Schopler, E. (1988). Mothers and fathers of young developmentally disabled and nondisabled boys: Adaptation and spousal support. *Developmental Psychology, 24*, 441–451.

Byrne, D. (1961). The repression–sensitization scale: Rationale, reliability and validity. *Journal of Personality, 29*, 334–349.

Cappelli, M., McGrath, P. J., MacDonald, N. E., Katsanis, J., and Lascelles, M. (1989). Parental care and overprotection of children with cystic fibrosis. *British Journal of Medical Psychology, 62*, 281–289.

Cohen, P., and Hesselbart, C. S. (1993). Demographic factors in the use of children's mental health services. *American Journal of Public Health, 83*, 49–52.

Dahlquist, L., Czyzewski, Copeland, K., Jones, C., Taub, E., and Vaughan, J. (1993). Parents of children newly diagnosed with cancer: Anxiety, coping and marital distress. *Journal of Pediatric Psychology, 18*, 365–376.

Daniels, D., Moos, R., Billings, A., and Miller, J. (1987). Psychosocial risk and resistance factors among children with chronic illness, healthy siblings and healthy controls. *Journal of Abnormal Child Psychology, 1987, 15*, 295–308.

Derogatis, L. R., and Clearly, P. A. (1977). Confirmation of the dimensional structure of the SCL-90; A study in construct validation. *Journal of Clinical Psychology, 33*, 981–989.

DeVet, K. A., and Ireys, H. T. (1998). Psychometric properties of the maternal worry scale for children with chronic illness. *Journal of Pediatric Psychology, 23*, 257–266.

Diabetes Control and Complication Trials Research Group. (1994). The effect of intensive diabetes treatment on the development and progression of long-term complications in adolescents with insulin-dependent-diabetes mellitus: Diabetes Control and Complications Trial. *Journal of Pediatrics, 125*, 177–187.

Drotar, D. (1999). Psychological interventions for children with chronic physical illness and their families: Toward integration of research and practice. In S. Russ and M. Ollendick (Eds.), *Handbook of psychotherapies with children and families*. New York: Plenum.

Drotar, D., Agle, D. P., Eckl, C. L., and Thompson, P. A. (1997). Correlates of psychological distress among mothers of children and adolescents with hemophelia and HIV infection. *Journal of Pediatric Psychology, 22*, 1–14.

Drotar, D., Johnson, S., Ionnotti, R., Krasnegor, N., Matthews, K., Melamed, B. G., Millstein, S., Peterson, R., Popiel, D., and Routh, D. (1989). Child health psychology. *Health Psychology, 8*, 781–784.

Dura, J. R., and Kiecolt-Glaser, J. (1991). Family transitions, stress, and health. In P. Cowan and M. Hetherington (Eds.), *Family transitions* (pp. 59–76). Hillsdole, NJ: Lawrence Erlbaum Associates.

Escalona, S. (1953). Emotional development in the first year of life. In M. J. Senn (Ed.), *Problems of infancy and childhood*. NJ: Foundation.

Fiese, B. H. (1997). Family context in pediatric psychology from a transactional perspective: Family rituals ans stories as examples. *Journal of Pediatric Psychhology*, *22*, 183–196.

Florian, V., and Elad, D. (1998). The impact of mothers' sense of empowerment on the metabolic control of their children with juvenile diabetes. *Journal of Pediatric Psychology*, *23*, 239–247.

Floyd, F. J., and Saitzyk, A. R. (1992). Social class and parenting children with mild and moderate mental retardation. *Journal of Pediatric Psychology*, *17*, 607–631.

Frank, R., Thayer, J., Hagglund, K., Vieth, A., Schopp, L., Beck, N., Kashani, J., Goldstein, D., Cassidy, J., Clay, D., Chaney, J., Hewett, J., and Johnson, J. (1998). Trajectories of adaptation in pediatric chronic illness: The importance of the individual. *Journal of Consulting and Clinical Psychology*, *66*, 521–532.

Garmezy, N. (1983). Stressors of childhood. In N. Garmezy and M. Rutter (Eds.), *Stress, coping and development in children* (pp. 43–84). New York: McGraw-Hill.

Garmezy, N. (1984). Stress-resistant children: The search for protective factors. In J. E. Stevenson (Ed.), *Recent research in developmental psychopathology. Journal of Child Psychology and PsychiatryBook Supplemment No. 4*. Oxford England: Pergamon.

Garwick, A., Patterson, J., Bennett, F., and Blum, R. (1998). Parents' perceptions of helpful versus unhelpful types of support in managing the care of preadolescents with chronic conditions. *Archives of Pediatric Adolescent Medicine*, *152*, 665–671.

Geller, M. (1996). Acute management of severe childhood asthma. *AACN Clinical Issues*, *7*, 519–528.

Goldberg, S., Janus, M., Washington, J., Simmons, R., MacLusky., I., and Gowler, R. (1997). Prediction of preschool behavioral problems in healthy and pediatric samples. *Developmental and Behavioral Pediatrics*, *18*, 304–313.

Goldberg, S., Morris, P., Simmons, R., Fowler, and Levison, H. (1990). Chronic illness in infancy and parenting stress: A comparison of three groups of parents. *Journal of Pediatric Psychology*, *25*, 247–358.

Gravelle, A. M. (1997). Caring for a child with a progressive illness during the complex chronic phase: Parents' experience of facing adversity. *Journal of Advanced Nursing*, *25*, 738–745.

Grossman, C. C. (1999). Common acute illnesses, symptoms, trauma, and impaired function. In M. Green, R. J. Haggerty, and M. Weitzman (Eds.), *Ambulatory pediatrics* (5th ed., pp. 152–156). Philadelphia: Saunders.

Hanson, C. L., De Guire, M., Schinkel, A., and Kolterman, O. (1995). Empirical validation for a family-centered model of care. *Diabetes Care*, *18*, 1347–1356.

Hanson, C. L., Henggeler, S. W., and Burghen, G. A. (1987). Social competence and parent support as mediators of the link between stress and metabolic control in adolescents with insulin-dependent diabetes mellitus. *Journal of Consulting and Clinical Psychology*, *55*, 529–533.

Hanson, C. L., Henggeler, S. W., Harris, M., Burghen, G., and Moore, M. (1989). Family system variables and the health status of adolescents with insulin-dependent diabetes mellitus. *Health Psychology*, *8*, 239–253.

Hauser, S., Jacobson, A. M., Bliss, R., Milley, J., Vieyra, M., Willett, J. B., Cole, C., DiPlacido, J., Paul, E., Lavori, P., Wolfsdorf, J. I., Hershkowitz, R. D., and Wertlieb, D. (1993). The family and the onset of its youngster's insulin-dependent diabetes: Ways of coping. In R. E. Cole and D. Reiss (Eds.), *How do families cope with chronic illness*. NJ: Lawrence Erlbaum Associates.

Hauser, S., Jacobson, D. Wertlieb, B. Weiss-Perry, B., Follansbee, D., Wolfshorf, J., Herskowitz, R., Houlihan, J., and Rajapark, D. (1986). Children with recently diagnosed diabetes: Interactions with their families. *Health Psychology*, *5*, 273–296.

Hauser, S., and Solomon, M. (1985). Coping with diabetes: Views from the family. In P. I. Ahmed and N. Ahmed (Eds.), *Coping with juvenile diabetes* (pp. 234–266). Springfield, IL: Thomas.

Hauser, S., Vierya, M., Jacobson, A., and Wertlieb, D. (1989). Family aspects of vulnerability and resilience in adolescence: A theoretical perspective. In T. F. Dugan and R. Coles (Eds.), *The child in our times: Studies in the development of resiliency*. New York: Bruner/Mazel.

Holden, E. W., Chmielewski, D., Nelson, C. C., Kager, V. A., and Foltz, L. (1997). Controlling for general and disease-specific effects in child and family adjustment to chronic illness. *Journal of Pediatric Psychology*, *22*, 15–27.

Holmbeck G. N., Gorey-Ferguson L., Hudson T., Seefeldt T., Shapero, W., Turner, T., and Uhler, J. (1997). Maternal, paternal, and marital functioning in families of preadolescents with spina bifida. *Journal of Pediatric Psychology*. *22*, 167–181.

Horner, S. (1997). Uncertainty in mothers' care for their ill children. *Journal of Advanced Nursing*, *26*, 658–663.

Hurtig, A. L., Koepke D., and Park, K. B. (1989). Relation between severity of chronic illness and adjustment in children and adolescents with sickle cell disease. *Journal of Pediatric Psychology*. *14*, 117–132.

Ievers, C., and Drotar, D. (1996). Family and parental functioning in cystic fibrosis. *Developmental and Behavioral Pediatrics*, *17*, 48–55.

Janus, M., and Goldberg, S. (1997). Factors influencing family participation in a longitudinal study: Comparison of pediatric and healthy samples. *Journal of Pediatric Psychology*, *22*, 245–262.

Johnson, S. (1985). The family and the child with chronic illness. In D. Turk and R. Kerns (Eds.), *Health, illness and families: A life span perspective*. New York: Wiley.

Johnson, S. (1988). Diabetes mellitus in childhood. In D. Routh (Ed.), *Handbook of pediatric psychology* (pp. 9–31). New York: Guilford.

Jones, T., Garlow, J., Turnbull, H., Rutherford III, and Barber, P. (1996). Family empowerment in a family support program. In G. Singer and L. Powers (Eds.), *Redefining family support: Innovations in public–private partnerships* (Vol. 1). Baltimore: Brookes.

Judge, K., and Benzeval, M. (1993). Health inequalities: New concerns about the children of single mothers. *British Medical Journal, 306*, 677–680.

Karetsky, M. (1977). Asthma in the South Bronx: Clinical and epidemiologic characteristics. *Journal of Allergy and Clinical Immunology, 60*, 383–390.

Kaslow N. J., Collins, M. H., Loundy, M. R., Brown, F., Hollins L. D., and Eckman, J. (1997). Empirically validated family interventions for pediatric psychology: Sickle cell disease as an exemplar. *Journal of Pediatric Psychology, 22*, 213–227.

Kazak, A. E. (1997). A contextual family systems approach to pediatrics: Introduction to the special issue. *Journal of Pediatric Psychology, 22*, 141–148.

Kazak, A. E., and Marvin, R. S. (1984). Differences difficulties and adaptation: Stress and social networks in families with a handicapped child. *Family Relations, 33*, 67–77.

Kell, R. S., Kliewer, W., Erikson, M. T., and Ohene-Frempong, K. (1998). Psychological adjustment of adolescents with sickle cell disease: Relations with demographic, medical, and familiy competence variabbles. *Journal of Pediatric Psychology, 23*, 301–312.

Koren, P. E., DeChillo, N., Friesen, B. J., Singh, N., Curtis, W., Ellis, C., Wechsler, H., Best, A., and Cohen, R. (1997). Empowerment status of families whose children have serious emotional disturbance and attention-defecit/hyperactivity disorder. *Journal of Emotional and Behavioral Disorders, 5*, 223–229.

Kovacs, M., Iyengar, S., Goldston, J. D., Obrosky, J., Stewart, D. S., and Marsh, J. (1990). Psychological functioning of children with insulin-dependent diabetes: A longitudinal study. *Journal of Pediatric Psychology, 15*, 619–632.

Lerner, N. (1999). Sickle cell disease. In M. Green, R. J. Haggerty, and M. Weitzman (Eds.), *Ambulatory pediatrics* (5th ed.). Philadelphia: Saunders.

Leventhal, H., Leventhal, E., and Van Nguyen, T. (1985). Reactions of families to illness: Theoretical models and perspectives. In D. C. Turk and R. Kerns (Eds.), *Health, illness and families: A life-span perspective*. New York: Wiley.

Levy, D. M. (1931). Maternal overprotection and rejection. *Archives of Neurology and Psychiatry, 25*, 886–889.

Liptak, G. S. (1999). Cerebral palsy. In M. Green, R. J. Haggerty, and M. Weitzman (Eds.), *Ambulatory pediatrics* (5th ed., pp. 263–266) Philadelphia: Saunders.

Manne, S., Jacobsen, P., Gorfinkle, K., Gerstein, F., and Redd, W. (1993). Treatment adherence difficulties among children with cancer: The role of parenting style. *Journal of Pediatric Psychology, 18*, 47–62.

Marteau, T. M., Bloch, S., and Baum, J. D. (1987). Family life and diabetic control. *Journal of Child Psychology and Psychiatry and Allied Disciplines, 28*, 823–833.

McBride, J. (1999). Asthma. In M. Green, R. J. Haggerty, and M. Weitzman (Eds.), *Ambulatory pediatrics* (5th ed., pp. 280–287). Philadelphia: Saunders.

McCubbin, H., and Patterson, J. (1982). Family adaptation to crises. In H. McCubbin, A. Gauble, and J. Patterson (Eds.), *Family coping and social support*. Glencoe, IL.

McCubbin, H. I., Cauble, A. E., and Patterson, J. M. (1983). *Family Stress, Coping, and Social Support*. Springfield, IL.: Thomas.

Melamed, B. G. (1998). Preparation for medical procedures. In R. Ammerman and J. Campos (Eds.), *Handbook of pediatric psychology and psychiatry*. New York: Allyn and Bacon.

Melamed, B. G., and Floyd, B. G. (1998). Childhood stress. In H. Friedman (Ed.), *Encyclopedia of mental health*. New York: Academic.

Melamed, B. G., Fogel, J., and Roth, B. (2000). Childhood health. In A. Baum and T. Revenson (Eds.), *Handbook of health psychology*. Mahwah, NJ: Plenum.

Melamed, B. G., and Ridley-Johnson, R. (1988). Psychological preparation of families for hospitalization. *Journal of Developmental and Behavioral Pediatrics, 9*, 96–101.

Melamed, B. G., Kaplan, B., and Fogel, J. (2000). Childhood health issues across the life span. In A. Baum and T. Revenson (Eds.), *Handbook of clinical health psychology*. New York: Guilford.

Miller, A. C., Gordon, R. M., Daniele, R. J., and Diller, L. (1992). Stress, appraisal and coping in mothers of disabled children. *Journal of Pediatric Psychology, 17*, 587–605.

Mishel, M. H. (1988). Uncertainty in illness. *Image—The Journal of Nursing Scholarship, 20*, 225–245.

Minuchin, S. (1967). *Families of the slums. New York: Basic Books*.

Minuchin, S., Baker, L., Rosman, B., Liebman, R., Milman, L., and Todd, T. C. (1975). A conceptual model of psychosomatic illness in children. *Archives of General Psychiatry, 32*, 1031–1038.

Minuchin, S., Rosman, B. L., and Baker, L. (1978). *Psychosomatic families: Anorexia nervosa in context*. Cambridge, MA: Harvard University Press.

Newacheck, P. W., Stoddard, J. J., Hughes, D. C., and Pearl, M. (1997). Children's access to health care: The role of social and economic factors. In R. Stein (Ed.), *Health care for children: What's right, what's wrong, what's next.* New York: United Hospital Fund.

Newbrough, J., Simpkins, C., and Maurer, M. (1985). A family development approach to studying factors in the management and control of childhood diabetes. *Diabetes Care, 8,* 83–92.

Noll, R. B., McKellop, J. M., Vannatta, K., and Kalinyak, K. (1998). Child-rearing practices of primary caregivers of children with sickle cell disease: The perspective of professionals and caregivers. *Journal of Pediatric Psychology, 23,* 131–140.

Olson, D. H. (1986). Circumplex Model VII: Validation studies and FACES III. *Family Process, 25,* 337–351.

Olson, D. H., McCubbin, H., Barnes, H., Larsen, A., Muxem, A., and Wilson, M. (1985). *Family inventories:* Inventories used in a national survey of families across the family life cycle, St. Paul, MN: Univ. of MN.

Orlowski, C. C. (1999). Common issues in childhood type 1 diabetes mellitus. In M. Green, R. J. Haggerty, and M. Weitzman, (Eds.), *Ambulatory pediatrics* (5th ed., pp. 273–280). Philadelphia: Saunders.

Patterson, J. M. (1985). Critical factors affecting family compliance with home treatment for children with cystic fibrosis. *Family Relations, 344,* 79–89.

Patterson, J. M. (1988). Families experiencing stress. *Family systems Medicine, 6,* 202–237.

Patterson, J. M. (1991). Family resilience to the challenge of a child's disability. *Pediatric Annals, 20,* 492–499.

Patterson, J. M., McCubbin H. I., and Warwick, W. J. (1990). The impact of family functioning on health changes in children with cystic fibrosis. *Social Science and Medicine, 3,* 159–164.

Perrin, J. (1985). Chronically ill children in America. *Caring, 4,* 19–26.

Pless, I. B. (1985). Introduction. In N. Hobbs and J. Perrin (Eds.), *Issues in the care of children with chronic illness* (pp. 1–10). San Francisco: Jossey-Bass.

Pless I. B., and Nolan, T. (1991). Revision, replication and neglect—Research on maladjustment in chronic illness. *Journal of Child Psychology and Psycyhiatry and Allied Disciplines, 32,* 347–365.

Pless, I. B., and Rohmann, K. J. (1971). Chronic illness and its consequences: Observations based on three epidemiological surveys. *Journal of Pediatrics, 79,* 351–359.

Power, T. (1989). *Parenting Dimensions Inventory: A research manual.* Unpublished manuscript. University of Houston.

Quittner, A., DeíGirolamoi, A., Michel, M., and Eigen, H. (1992). Parental response to cystic fibrosis: A contextual analyses of the diagnosis phase. *Journal of Pediatric Psychology, 17,* 683–704.

Rehm, R. S. (2000). Parental encouragement, protection, and advocacy for Mexican-American children with chronic conditions. *Journal of Pediatric Nursing, 6,* 89–98.

Reiss, D. Steinglass, P., and Howe, G. (1993). The family's organization around the illness. In R. Cole and D. Reiss (Eds.), *How do families cope with chronic illness?* NJ: Lawrence Erlbaum Associates.

Rodrigue, J., MacNaughton, K., Hoffman, R., III, R., Graham-Pole, J., Andres, J., Novak, D., and Fennell, R. (1996). Perceptions of parenting stress and family relations by fathers of children evaluated for organ transplantation. *Psychological Reports, 79,* 723–727.

Rodrigue, J., MacNaughton, B., Hoffman, R., III, Graham-Pole, J., Andres, J., Novak, D., and Fennell, R. (1997). Transplantation in children: A longitudinal assessment of mother's stress. *Psychosomatics, 38,* 478–486.

Rolland, J. S. (1987). Chronic illness and the life cycle. *Family Process, 26,* 203–221.

Rolland, J. S. (1994). *Families, illness, and disability: An integrative treatment model.* New York: Basic Books.

Rutter, M., and Tizard, I. (1970). *Rutter Health Questionare.*

Rutter, M., Tizard, J., and Whitmore, K. (Eds.). (1970). *Education, Health and Behavior.* London: Longmans.

Schwartz, R. H. (1996). Chronic pulmonary diseases in children: Including CF and primary ciliary dyskinesia. In C. Bierman, D. Pearlman, G. Shapiro, and W. Busse (Eds.), *Allergy. asthma and immunology from infancy to adulthood* (pp. 572–591). Philadelphia: Sauders.

Seiffge-Krenke, I. (1998). Chronic disease and perceived developmental progression in adolescence. *Developmental Psychology, 34,* 1073–1084.

Sheeran, T., Marvin, R. S. and Pianta, R. C. (1997). Mothers' resolution of their child's diagnosis and self-reported measure of parenting stress, marital relation, and social support. *Journal of Pediatric Psychology, 22,* 197–212.

Siegel, D. M. (1999). Arthritis. In M. Green, R. J. Haggerty, and M. Weitzman (Eds.), *Ambulatory pediatrics.* (5th ed., pp. 331–335). Philadelphia: Saunders.

Staples, B., and Pharoah, P. (1994). Child health statistical review. *Archives of Diseases in Childhood, 71,* 548–554.

Stehbens, J. A. (1988). Childhood cancer. In D. Routh (ed.), *Handbook of pediatric psychology* (pp. 135–161). New York: Guilford.

Stein, R., and Jessop, D. (1982). A noncategorical approach to chronic illness. *Public Health Reports, 97,* 354–362.

Tao, M. L., Seltzer, P. M., and Seltzer, L. (1999). The primary care clinician's role with the child cancer patient. In M. Green, R. J. Haggerty, and M. Weitzman (Eds.), *Ambulatory pediatrics* (5th ed., pp. 288–294). Philadelphia: Saunders.

Thomasgard, M. and Metz, W. P. (1997). Parental overprotection and its relation to perceived child vulnerability. *American Journal of Orthopsychiatry, 67,* 330–335.

Thompson, R. J., and Gustafson, K. E. (1996). *Adaptation to childhood chronic illness.* Washinghton, DC: American Psychological Association.

Timko, C., Baumgartner, M., Moos, R. H., and Miller, J. J., III. (1993). Parental risk and resistance factors among children with juvenile rheumatic disease: A four-year predictive study. *Journal of Behavioral Medicine. 16,* 571–588.

Timko, C., Stovel, K. W., and Moos, R. H. (1992). Functioning among mothers and fathers of children with juvenile rheumatic disease: A longitudinal study. *Journal of Pediatric Psychology, 17,* 705–724

Varni, J., and Wallander, J. (1988). Pediatric chronic disabilities: Hemophilia and spina bifida. In D. Routh (Ed.), *Handbook of pediatric psychology.* New York: Guilford.

Walker, J., Manion, I., Cloutier, P., and Johnson, S. (1992). Measuring marital distress in couples with chronically ill children: The Dyadic Adjustment Scale. *Journal of Pediatric Psychology, 17,* 435–357.

Wallander, J., Varni, J., Babani, L., De Haan, C., Wilcox, K., and Banis, H. T. (1989). The social environment and the adaptation of mothers of physically handicapped children. *Journal of Pediatric Psychology. 14,* 371–387.

Walsh, F. (1998). *Strengthening family resilience.* New York: Guilford.

Weiss, K. L., Marvin, R. S., and Pianta, R. C. (1997). Ethnographic detection of family strategies for childcare applications to the study of cerebral palsy. *Journal of Pediatric Psychology, 22,* 263–278.

Williams, P., Lorenzo, F. D., and Borja, M. (1993). Pediatric chronic illnesses: Effects on siblings and mothers. *Maternal-Child Nursing Journal, 21,* 115–121.

PART II

PARENTS AND SOCIAL INSTITUTIONS

14

Parenting in a Multimedia Society

Aimée Dorr
University of California, Los Angeles
Beth E. Rabin
Research Communications Ltd.
Sandra Irlen
University of California, Los Angeles

INTRODUCTION

Media and technology are omnipresent in American family life. Virtually every household with children has at least one television set and some print materials. In 1999, nearly all also had at least one VCR, radio, tape player, and CD player. At least two thirds had a computer, videogame player, and a cable or satellite system (Roberts, Foehr, Rideout, and Brodie, 1999). Children use all these media and technology several hours a day and are exposed to them several more hours each day (Roberts et al., 1999). Use starts very young. Infants and toddlers will attend to radio, television, and picture books. Most 2-year-old children have favorite television programs; most 4-year-old children know how to use a computer.

Many Americans are uncomfortable with our multimedia homes. They worry that we all spend too much time with low-brow, popular culture content that is often also violent, sexual, sexist, or racist, that we are not reading enough, that we retreat to solitary relaxation and ignore important community and civic interactions, and that opportunities for growth and development are lost to almost vegetative multimedia alternatives. The content that media and technology bring to the home both represents and shapes our culture. Most of it is created by Americans and so, broadly speaking, reflects our culture. Children can and do learn from what is offered, acquiring, solidifying, and changing their knowledge, attitudes, and behaviors accordingly. Using media and technology also cultivates the skills required to use them. The time given to their use is either taken away from other possible activities or shared with activities that might otherwise receive a child's full attention. Many parents do little or nothing intentionally to influence their children's engagement with media and technology, but such engagement is very much part of the home environment. It is one of many practical matters that U.S. parents must handle, one way or another, as part of their childrearing.

This chapter is about the roles that parents play—or could play—in their children's interactions with media and technology at home and the associated consequences these interactions have for children. It assumes what the literature shows, which is that these interactions matter, but it does not review that literature. We begin by describing the history of various major media and technology in U.S. society, the main topics that have been studied, and the principal theories guiding the research. We then provide a rich description of how children are living at home with media and technology. Following a discussion of the issues the home multimedia ecology raises, we describe, first, the ways in which parents can or do influence children's media and technology use and, then, how parents can or do mediate the potential effects of this use. We conclude by reviewing practical advice for parents and offering prognostications of future directions for theory and research. Throughout the chapter we use the term *children* to refer to those between the ages of about 2 and 18. When finer age distinctions are needed, the text makes them apparent. Because the nature of media and technology varies from culture to culture and their effects may also vary by culture, we have confined our discussion almost exclusively to the American literature.

U.S. MEDIA AND MEDIA RESEARCH IN THE TWENTIETH CENTURY

In the early years of the twentieth century, film and radio joined print as media available to and used by the general public. Television was a curiosity in the 1930s and became commonplace in the 1950s. Since then, technological innovations have greatly expanded the number of over-the-air television channels available in any region, brought cable and satellite distribution systems into play, and provided videocassette recorders (VCRs) and videodisc players (DVDs) as alternative viewing and distribution systems. Near the end of the twentieth century, computer technology reached the general public. By the end of the century, video game players, personal computers, the Internet, and the World Wide Web were in half or more of the American homes with children ages 2 to 18 living in them (Roberts et al., 1999).

As each medium or technology has become popular, those media that had previously been popular have adapted. None has disappeared. Radio, for example, once offered listeners soap operas, dramas, westerns, mysteries, and comedies. Children and families had their favorites and tuned in regularly. Today, television offers this fare. Radio has become a valued source of music, up-to-the-minute news, sports, talk shows, and religious broadcasting. Television, too, has changed as cable and other distribution systems have developed and found their place in American homes. What the home computer and Internet will mean for other, older media is still unfolding, but already there are signs of change. For example, Napster, the Internet software that allowed fans to download popular music free of charge, seriously disturbed the music industry and may well instigate marked changes in distribution and sales methods and perhaps, as a consequence, in content. The twentieth century was an ever changing landscape of media and technology and their content. New media and technology entered the home; older media adapted so that people continued to use them. This process continues in the twenty-first century.

As the number of media and technology used by the public grew in the twentieth century, cross-media interactions proliferated. Production was simultaneously aimed toward several distribution systems. For example, a film would be produced for movie house distribution and later video and DVD distribution, the music would be planned for a CD, and portions would be planned for a video game. Also, a property made popular in one medium, say a book or comic, would be transferred to another, say a film, television series, or video game. Quite a few popular television programs and, very recently, video games have been the source of one or more films. In this way, popular culture has repeated itself and spread out to encompass several distribution systems. Via cross-media relations, the American public, for better or worse, has had and will continue to have multiple opportunities to encounter the same material.

Many have recognized and sought to harness the power of media and technology to educate, inform, and otherwise do good for U.S. youth. Schramm (1977) summarized much of the early research and development efforts for schools, confirming the ability of radio, film, television, and computers to instruct. Radio and film have virtually disappeared from the classroom. Television, video, and cable programs continue to be used to some degree in elementary and secondary schools, colleges, the military, and vocational schools, and for individually guided self-improvement; the Public Broadcasting Service (PBS) has had a well-justified reputation for providing entertaining educational and informational programming, including many offerings for children and teenagers, some of which are also used in schools. Computers and the Internet, including the World Wide Web, became part of schooling late in the twentieth century and continue to be held in high esteem in educational circles. Print has long been the educational medium of choice and continues to be that today.

Because this chapter focuses on out-of-school uses of media and technology, it is important to realize that the vast majority of the content available to and used by children and their parents has been entertainment oriented. Outside of work and school, people have turned to all forms of media and technology for pleasure and relaxation. In the United States, content producers and distributors operate in a system of private enterprise that foregrounds profit making. Whether this accounts for the predominance of low-brow, popular culture is debatable, but such content is the bulk of what media and technology producers make available to the home user. Certainly, it accounts for the presence of advertising, sponsorship, and/or product placement in virtually all media and technology offerings, even when these require purchase or rental fees that also provide income to the producer and distributor.

A long historical view reveals that every mass medium and every form of mass culture have been of concern to child advocates. Writing around 300 BC, the Greek philosopher Plato (1952, Book 2, p. 321) argued that "a young person cannot judge what is allegorical and what is literal; anything that he receives into his mind at that age is likely to become indelible and unalterable; and therefore it is most important that the tales which the young first hear should be models of virtuous thoughts." In the twentieth century, parents, social commentators, and social scientists alike worried that comic books, radio serials, motion pictures, and television would be deleterious for children who were then enjoying them while becoming enculturated into U.S. society (Luke, 1990; Wartella and Reeves, 1985). Recently, worry has turned to video games, computer games, the Internet, and the World Wide Web (e.g., Bremmer and Rausch, 1998; Emes, 1997; Kraut et al., 1998; Price, 1998).

An illustrative example of earlier concerns about what was then a new mass medium is the 1930s Payne Fund Studies of motion pictures (see Dworkin, 1970, for reprints of some of the reports, and Jowett, Jarvie, and Fuller, 1996, for an historical analysis). This set of studies addressed such issues as whether popular films influenced young people's attitudes, "taught" them "information," affected their emotions, or influenced their social conduct. The work was motivated by public concern about film content and its potential negative effects on young people. Each set of studies was extensive, carefully done, and conservatively interpreted. For example, in their study of social attitudes, Peterson and Thurstone (in Dworkin, 1970) worked with sixth- through twelfth-grade children and college undergraduates in several different communities, using 11 different popular films addressing several different attitudinal objects (e.g., Germans, Chinese, gambling, and war). They examined the attitudinal effects of viewing a single film and of viewing one, two, or three films with the same attitudinal perspective; they also examined the persistence of effects for up to 18 months. The expected attitudinal effects were found, effects were greater with more films, and effects persisted.

Jowett et al. (1996) analyzed the life course of the Payne Fund Studies. They argued that the results from these studies were largely ignored for two reasons: (1) The theoretical and methodological perspectives guiding the research lost what had been their central place in the field just at the time the results became available to the public and (2) the film industry put self-restraints in place, thereby reducing public outrage at Hollywood movie content and decreasing public interest in the research findings. Nonetheless, the research is relevant today because popular movies continue to be part of young people's media experience and there are similar concerns about their effects. Moreover, the events and work of this period are in many ways replicated with succeeding popular media and technology.

These same sorts of effects have been investigated in research about television. Because most people in the United States have used television, as they have film, as a mass medium purveying mass culture, a central concern has been television's potential negative effects, particularly for vulnerable audiences such as children. This concern has persisted throughout the period in which television has been the dominant mass medium. In the last 50 years, thousands of research-based articles and books about children and television have been published, and much social and political attention has been given to the topic (for extensive reviews of the research see, for example, Comstock, Chaffee, Katzman, McCombs, and Roberts, 1978; Dorr, 1986; Huston and Wright, 1997; Liebert and Sprafkin, 1988). Overall, they indicate that children can and do learn information, attitudes, and behaviors from television programming, that influence is content specific reflecting a child's viewing diet more than television's viewing menu, that average influence is small rather than large, and that particular characteristics of children and their lives account for variations in social effects. Luke (1990) provided an analysis of the different ways in which the child has been conceptualized in different eras of this research.

In the long view, as new media and technology and their content become popular, we should expect social concerns and social research about them (see Calvert, 1999, for one approach). The growing body of research on video games (and computer games) parallels much of the earlier work on television, particularly work on the social effects of engagement with programs featuring aggression and violence (e.g., Emes, 1997; Greenfield and Cocking, 1996). Some research on children's engagement with the Internet and the World Wide Web also echoes earlier concerns in the investigations of effects of exposure to inappropriate or unhealthy content and of spending too much time with the technology (Kraut et al., 1998; Turow, 1999). Because the newest popular technologies permit much more interactive engagement than did older media, a newer set of research issues is also beginning to receive attention (e.g., Wartella, O'Keefe, and Scantlin, 2000).

A wide range of theoretical perspectives has been adopted by those studying parents, children, media, and technology. Most are directed toward understanding the relations between children and a particular medium or technology, some toward placing children and the medium or technology within a broader cultural context. None is directed primarily at characterizing the parental role in child-medium/technology-culture relations; however, several incorporate parents into the theoretical framework, and most can be used to consider parents' roles. What are and are not principal theories, indeed whether there is much theory at all, would probably be a topic of some debate among scholars. Although the majority were trained in communication, education, or psychology, disciplinary diversity among prominent students of parents, children, media, and technology is great enough that research evidences several different theoretical perspectives and methods. Furthermore, because many researchers in this area are motivated by practical concerns as well as theoretical interests, it is not uncommon to see work with a decidedly atheoretical cast to it.

THEORY IN MULTIMEDIA RESEARCH

Loosening our own disciplinary blinders and recognizing the real-world impetus for much of the research, we have selected six theoretical perspectives as the most prominent in research involving children and media or technology, and sometimes parents. These are usually referred to as social learning theory, the uses and gratifications approach, cognitive and social cognitive theories, sociocultural theories, cultivation theory, and cultural studies or critical theory. Each will be described briefly. The section will end with a short discussion of prominent ethnographic and descriptive work, work that often explicitly eschews a particular theoretical approach.

An early, highly influential, theoretical approach to explaining learning and behavior was social learning theory (e.g., Bandura, 1977). It was designed to account for most human behavior and has been adopted by many researchers concerned with the social effects of media content. Briefly, the theory proposed that learning and social influence for a wide variety of information, attitudes, and behaviors occurred both directly and vicariously from numerous sources, including teachers, parents, and all forms of media and technology. Traditional learning theory constructs, such as reinforcement, punishment, contiguity, and generalization, were all seen as operative. Modeling or observational learning was emphasized. The theory proposed that various capacities of and activities by the user, such as attention, encoding, and physical skills, influenced the amount and kind of effect content would have. Furthermore, it acknowledged the interactive influences of different social agents, experiences, and settings. With regard to parents, it offered and continues to offer numerous roles in the interaction of parents children, media, and technology, including what live and mediated experiences parents make available to their children, how parents influence children's information-processing and sense-making abilities and activities, the positive and negative reinforcement patterns parents employ, and the attitudes and behaviors parents themselves model. Implicitly or explicitly, social learning theory is probably the most frequent theoretical position in research involving parents, children, media, and technology.

The uses and gratifications approach was first formalized by Blumler and Katz (1974). They saw it as a necessary antidote to what many perceived to be the predominant model of the passive viewer affected by mass communications. Blumler and Katz argued that human beings are motivated mass media users who choose what medium and what content to use based on their own needs and on the ability of the medium and/or content to gratify those needs. Several types of gratifications have been identified, among them learning and information acquisition, entertainment, and interpersonal contact. People, including children, are thought to be aware at some level of their own needs and of the opportunities different media and content offer for the gratification of these needs. Most of the time people choose their experiences, including media use, so as to maximize gratification of their needs. Moreover, the reasons for their choices are related to the social effects of the usage. The uses and gratifications approach has never explicitly addressed parents' roles in influencing children's media use; however, it is easy to identify places where the approach could be used. Parents have a role to play in the kinds of gratifications their children seek, the ways in which children learn to gratify them, the sources of gratification available to children, and the extent to which children are allowed to use any particular source of gratification.

In referring to the uses and gratifications tradition, Katz has been quoted as saying, "This is the research tradition which asks not what the media do to people, but what people do with the media" (cited in Lull, 1980, p. 198). Various cognitive approaches make the same claim but offer a different perspective on what people do with media and technology. Fundamentally, cognitive approaches assert that an individual's cognitive capacities and activities account for the meaning she or he attributes to any event, what she or he recalls about it, and how she or he behaves relevant to it. Over the years, the emphasis in Bandura's social learning theory shifted so much in this direction that he renamed his theory "social cognitive theory" (e.g., Bandura, 1986, 1999). Among those studying parents, children, media, and technology, children's more limited abilities and world knowledge lead one to expect that children will construct different understandings of content and behave differently subsequently than would more able and knowledgeable viewers. This means that cognitive-developmental theories, various script, schema, and story grammar approaches, and various information-processing approaches are relevant. Such emphasis on information-processing and cognitive activities has long been part of research about children, media, and technology (for arguments to this effect see Dorr, 1986; Wartella and Reeves, 1985). In research involving parents, children, media, and technology, cognitive and social cognitive theories have informed explorations of parental roles in children's processing of content, in inculcating information-processing abilities and schemas, and in directing children's engagement with content of varying levels of cognitive demand.

Sociocultural theories conceptualize the process of learning and what is learned rather differently. The Russian psychologist Vygotsky (1978) is often viewed as the father of this class of theory. According to sociocultural theories, children are situated in particular activities, within which they learn how to participate at ever increasing levels of skill. They are guided in their participation by other more skilled people (Rogoff, 1990). Novices may be supported by more experienced participants and/or by social structures geared to them. Such scaffolding provides the necessary structure so that novices can participate in activities and learn their structure and content. Learning of culturally valued skills and activities occurs through apprenticeship. In time, the interpersonal will become intrapersonal. These theories also emphasize the role of culturally specific artifacts and tools in carrying out particular activities. Parents have important roles to play in such theoretical systems. They can structure the activities in which children participate, be the one to whom the child is apprenticed, or serve as the more skilled participant in a particular activity. Parents who are sensitive to the child can provide the scaffolding needed to support the child's participation in a given activity and learning in it. They can engage in dialogue, direct attention, provide advice, support inquiry, and modulate their own participation to provide the child appropriate levels of both support and autonomy.

Cultivation theory has been propounded primarily by Gerbner and his colleagues (e.g., Gerbner, Gross, Morgan, and Signorielli, 1986; Signorielli and Morgan, 2001). It describes a process by which media content influences users' information, beliefs, attitudes, and values, and thereby may influence their behavior. According to cultivation theorists, a medium's social effects occur slowly over time, accumulating with repeated involvement with the medium's messages, which represent certain worldviews much more than others. These messages are assumed to conform to dominant cultural beliefs and values, but the ways in which they are communicated may not always correspond to reality. For example, in reality, by the time they reach adolescence, females outnumber males in the United States, but males outnumber females on television. Assuming that appearing on television is prestigious, the overabundance of males on television arguably conveys the message that females are of lower status in the culture. Two cultivation processes are possible. In mainstreaming, heavy users from different demographic groups who would otherwise have quite different views come to share one view similar to that presented by the medium. In resonance, a heavy user's views are amplified because the medium's social reality corresponds to the user's. Depending on the degree of agreement between parental views and those represented in the medium or technology, heavier usage by children could work respectively either in opposition to or in consonance with parental socialization pressures. Parents have not been explicitly included in cultivation theory, but they have an obvious role in influencing the nature of children's live and mediated experiences, out of which come mainstreaming and resonance effects.

Cultural studies or critical theory perspectives (e.g., Carey, 1989; Grossberg, 1987; Hall, 1992; Kellner, 1995) argue that theories such as those so far described—with the possible exception of cultivation theory—all miss the big picture. Here, media and technology are seen as likely to be instruments of the cultural elite, representing a worldview that helps to perpetuate and recreate the inequities of the current social order and serves to maintain the favored status of the cultural elite. In this view, it is important to become aware of the vision media and technology present and to understand the social organization by which that vision is created and controlled. The most frequent types of cultural studies research are interpretive analyses of content that elucidate themes and tie them to larger social issues, efforts to understand and critique industry structures and functions, and endeavors to teach people how to be "good," meaning critical, users of media and technology. Although parents are not central figures in these approaches, they are seen as influential in socializing children's sociopolitical perspectives and children's approaches to the content of media and technology.

Much of the research about parents, children, and media/technology fits to some degree within one of these six principal theoretical perspectives. There is, in addition, a strong tradition of descriptive research, reflecting respected approaches in child development, communication, and education research. A variety of survey methods (questionnaires, interviews) and field methods (participant observation and ethnography) is used. Although many of these studies also employ and test theoretical perspectives, they primarily seek to provide rich description of children's engagement with media and technology or their utilization of elements from them in other aspects of their lives. For example, ethnographic reports in Lull (1988) described a multiplicity of varying roles for television in families in six countries and suggested ways in which other research may miss important phenomena either by oversimplifying setting or measurement or by overly restricting conceptualization of variables and processes. This descriptive tradition clearly constitutes a seventh approach that is evident from the oldest to the newest publications. Taken altogether, description and the six theoretical perspectives previously presented comprise the intellectual approach taken in nearly all the research about parents, children, media, and technology. That work is introduced in the following description of our multimedia homes and what children do in them.

ECOLOGY OF THE HOME MULTIMEDIA ENVIRONMENT

American children grow up today in homes that are full of media and technology. Nearly every household will have at least one television, radio, and VCR. The majority will have several and much other media and technology as well. Children make much use of what is available. In this section, we paint a picture of the media and technology in American homes and of how young people use them. We rely heavily on one remarkable resource—a survey of a large nationally representative sample of U.S. homes with children ages 2 to 18. The work was carried out by Roberts et al. (1999) with support from the Kaiser Family Foundation. Similar findings have been reported in earlier research that addressed selected topics, covered smaller age ranges, and used nonrepresentative or locally representative samples (e.g., Atkin, Greenberg, and Baldwin, 1991; Bianchi and Robinson, 1997; Brown, Childers, Bauman, and Koch, 1990; Christenson, De Benedittis, and Lindlof, 1985; Huston, Wright, Marquis, and Green, 1999; Kubey and Csikszentmihalyi, 1990; Senechal, LeFevre, Thomas, and Daley, 1998; Snow, Burns, and Griffin, 1998; Truglio, Murphy, Oppenheimer, Huston, and Wright, 1996). When such a study is particularly relevant, it will be cited; otherwise, the reader is referred to Roberts et al. (1999), which is the most comprehensive source by far for understanding the home multimedia environment in the United States today.

We begin with a simple recounting of the percentage of all American children's homes having various media and technology in them:

(1) With respect to audiovisual media, 99% of the homes had at least one television, 97% had at least one VCR, 74% had cable or satellite service, and 44% had premium cable.

(2) With respect to audio media, 97% had at least one radio, 94% had at least one tape player, and 90% had at least one CD player.

(3) With respect to computer technology, 70% had at least one video game player, 69% had at least one computer, 59% had at least one CD-ROM drive, and 45% had access to the Internet.

It is clear from these figures that in 1999 nearly all American children had access to audiovisual and audio media, in addition to print, at home. In fact, at least 60% had two or more televisions, VCRs, radios, and/or CD players in their home. The majority also had access to a computer and a videogame player. Almost half had access to the Internet.

Since families began to acquire second pieces of equipment, they have used them to permit family members, particularly parents and children, simultaneously to indulge their separate tastes. In the Roberts et al. sample, many children had media and technology in their bedrooms. At least a quarter of 2- to 4-year-old children had a television set, radio, and/or tape player in their bedrooms; among 8- to 13-year-old children, 50% to 65% had a video game player, CD player, and/or television set, about 75% had a tape player, and about 80% had a radio, all in their bedrooms; and among 14- to 18-year-old youth, the percentages with various audio systems in their bedrooms were even higher. Among children 8 and older, about one fourth even had a computer in their bedrooms. The homes of American children clearly provide ample opportunities to engage with media and technology, with other family members, friends, and alone.

Children take advantage of this access. On average, children 2 to 18 in the Roberts et al. survey spent about 5½ hours a day in their own personal nonschool uses of media and technology at home. Because children were sometimes simultaneously using more than one medium or technology, the total time averaged 6½ hours a day. There was wide variation. About one fourth of the young people spent 3 or fewer hours a day, and one third spent more than 7 hours a day using media and technology. Those who were high users of one medium or technology were also likely to be high users of other media and technologies. Most children were also exposed to others' media use, particularly their television viewing, for about another hour a day; 42% of the sample reported that television was on most of the time in their home, and 58% reported it was on during meals. Usage time was unevenly distributed among the available options. Use of television and television-like media such as VCRs consumed about one half of children's total daily media and technology time (42% and 13% of total time, respectively)—about 3 hours a day. Another 22% was given to use of audio media. Uses of print media (12%), computer technology (5%), and video game players (5%) consumed much smaller proportions of the daily diet of media and technology.

Because audiovisual media account for so much of children's home media use, it is worth knowing just how much is available to them. Most viewers have access to at least 11 over-the-air channels, including several independent stations and stations associated with the three original major networks (ABC, CBS, and NBC), newer networks (Fox, UPN, and Warner Brothers), and PBS. In addition, newer technologies that deliver signals to the home television set have expanded the options that viewers lump together as "television" and increased viewers' opportunities to control what they will watch and when they will watch it. The most popular of these technologies, VCR and cable, are in most U.S. homes with children 2 to 18 (Roberts et al., 1999). At any point in time, they—along with DVD players and satellites—increase viewer options enormously and guarantee that certain content (e.g., children's fare, sports, religion, foreign language, history, and cartoons) can be available. They have dramatically changed the television viewing options that can be made available to children; parents and children have taken advantage of them to increase the presence of child-oriented material at home (Roberts et al., 1999; Wartella, Heintz, Aidman, and Mazzarella, 1990).

Although television viewing was once a rather momentous occasion, now it is very routine. In 1951, Maccoby reported that all other family life virtually stopped when the television was turned on. Today, television viewing is very often part of such other activities as meals, conversation, play, chores, and homework (Anderson, Lorch, Field, Collins, and Nathan, 1986; Kubey and Csikszentmihalyi, 1990; Lull, 1988). In fact, Kubey and Csikszentmihalyi found that only about one third of all television viewing by teen and adult populations occurred unaccompanied by another activity. Television viewing, however, continues to be mostly a family affair, particularly for younger children and particularly in the evening (Roberts et al., 1999). A child's viewing companions are much more likely to be siblings than parents. In fact, in the Roberts et al. report, only for 2- to 7-year-old children and only in the evening were a majority (63%) viewing with their parents. As children got older they were more likely to view alone, less likely to view with parents, and somewhat less likely to view with siblings. Daytime viewing was mostly alone or with siblings or other peers.

In contrast, music listening has been found to be primarily a solitary activity, particularly as children get older, or an activity with siblings when younger, and peers when older (Christenson and De Benedittis, 1986; Christenson et al., 1985; Roberts et al., 1999). Similarly, reading has been found to be primarily a solitary activity, except for the youngest children (Roberts et al., 1999; Snow et al., 1998). Much computer use has also been found to be solitary, except for gaming—the most popular activity—which is done alone and with siblings and friends (Roberts et al., 1999).

In general, all forms of media and technology are most often used for entertainment, not for information, study, or hobbies. For example, studies of content preferences have shown that children most often liked to watch comedy on television and in videos and movies (Roberts et al., 1999), listen to popular music much more than information on the radio (Carroll et al., 1993; Christenson and De Benedittis, 1986), read scary books and stories, comics and cartoons, pop culture magazines, and sports books and magazines (Worthy, Moorman, and Turner, 1999), and use computers and video game players for action, adventure, and sports games (Roberts et al., 1999). Interpersonal communication has been found to be the dominant use of the Internet at home (Kraut et al., 1998). (Note that tool use, information acquisition, and learning are *not* frequent home uses of the computer and Internet.) In addition, music on the radio, tape player, or CD player has been used for mood management (Christenson et al., 1985), although the positive mood can turn sour if the genre is "heavy metal" and parents are around (Thompson and Larson, 1995). Research in the uses and gratifications tradition has revealed that children were more likely to say they were "killing time" when using television than when using computers (Roberts et al., 1999), reading for enjoyment, its value, social interaction, and others' praise (Baker, Scher, and Mackler, 1997), and watching music videos for music appreciation, enjoyment or entertainment, and visual appreciation (Sun and Lull, 1986).

Differences have been found in the availability and/or use of media and technology according to children's age, gender, social class, race, and ethnicity; however, these differences are best understood as variations on a theme rather than different themes. Most children have access to, and devote many hours a day to, media and technology at home. Most children use television and television-like media a lot. Most children turn to media and technology for fun, mostly engaging with popular culture and so-called low-brow fare. Together, these generalizations create the theme. What are the variations? We again rely on Roberts et al. (1999) for the most authoritative data. This report provided comparisons by age (2, 3, or 4 groupings each covering 2 to 18 years), gender, social class (three levels), and race and ethnicity (African American, Latin American, European American). All were single variable comparisons without controlling for the possible influence of other variables (e.g., gender comparisons without consideration of social class or race and ethnicity).

We begin with age, where there are many developmental changes. More households with older than younger children have been found to have audio media and computer technology. Households with 14- to 18-year-old youth were more likely than households with younger children to have three or more televisions, radios, and the like. The availability of media and technology, especially television, video game players, and music media, in the child's bedroom also increased with the child's age. Also, the likelihood of being alone when using media and technology increased with age. Total time given to media use increased into middle childhood and then decreased in later adolescence. At all ages, television was the most frequently used medium by quite a bit. Even in adolescence, a time of heavy music listening, the total time given to radio, tape, and CDs was somewhat less than that given to television.

However, developmental trends in usage were not the same across media and technology. For television, use increased throughout childhood and then dropped off during adolescence. For print (reading), about the same amount of time was spent from age 2 to 13, and then it declined in adolescence. Teenagers (14 to 18) reported they had stopped reading for fun. For music listening, use increased steadily with age, with a dramatic increase during adolescence (Christenson et al., 1985), with younger teens being the more active radio listeners in terms of calling into stations (Carroll et al., 1993). It has been said that "music is the key to how adolescents express their identity" (Seelow, 1996, p. 52). In terms of content preferences, Roberts et al. reported that the general trends were away from children's content (e.g., preschool educational television and cartoons) toward adult fare, particularly comedy and also action. In adolescence, teen culture—particularly as expressed in music—was a focus of attention, and stereotypical gender differences with respect to preferences for sports, aggression, sexual content, and interpersonal interaction became more apparent in choices in music, video and computer games, and television activities (Gailey, 1996; Greenfield and deWinstanley, 1996; Roberts et al., 1999; Sneegas and Plank, 1998).

With respect to gender, there were fewer differences other than the content preferences just described. What media and technology were in the home and how many there were did not vary by gender, except that homes with boys were more likely to have video game players than were homes with girls, and they were more likely to have a player in the child's bedroom as well. Gender differences in video game use began very early, showing up even among preschoolers and growing larger with age (Huston et al., 1999; Roberts et al., 1999). Girls spent slightly less time overall (20 minutes a week) than did boys with media and technology, but boys 8 to 18, compared to girls 8 to 18, spent more time with television, video games, and computers and less time with print, radio, and CDs. In adolescence, compared to boys, girls spent less time with sports content and more time listening to music and reading teen magazines. Girls have been found to be more likely than boys to report using music for mood management (Carroll et al., 1993).

With respect to social class, households in low- (less than $25,000 per year total family income), medium-, and high-income (more than $40,000 per year) neighborhoods in the Roberts et al. (1999) survey did not differ in the percent that had television, cable or satellite, premium cable, radio, or a tape player. There were small but statistically significant differences in the percentage having a VCR (more high- than low-income households had one), CD player (more high- than low- or medium-income households), or video game player (more medium- than high- or low-income households). There were more substantial differences in the percentage of families having a computer, CD-ROM drive, or Internet access, with the percentage decreasing significantly in households from high- to medium- to low-income neighborhoods. Other research has reported substantial differences in home literacy environments (Snow et al., 1998) and found that children from economically disadvantaged families had access to fewer books and print materials in the home (also in school and childcare settings; Neuman, 1999). Households in the Roberts et al. (1999) survey did not differ by neighborhood in the availability of media and technology in a child's bedroom, except for television and videogame players, both of which were less likely to be in the bedrooms of children from high- than from low- and medium-income neighborhoods. This same class difference showed up in the amount of time children gave to watching television and playing video games, and also showed up in time given to taped television shows, movies, CDs, and audiotapes. In contrast, children from households in high-income neighborhoods spent more time with print and the computer (which also relies on text) than did children in low-income neighborhoods.

In terms of content preferences, the Roberts et al. data identified few differences by income and none that spanned the total 2- to 18-year range. Other research has suggested that higher-income people spend somewhat more time with higher-brow fare (e.g., Bower, 1985). The few differences in the Roberts et al. data followed this pattern, with more 2- to 7-year-old children from lower- than higher-income neighborhoods watching comedy, and more 8- to 18-year-old youngsters from lower- than higher-income neighborhoods watching talk shows. In contrast, more 8- to 18-year-old youngsters from higher- than lower-income neighborhoods watched drama.

With respect to race and ethnicity, there were just a few differences in the Roberts et al. findings. A higher percentage of European American than other households had at least one tape player, CD player, computer, CD-ROM drive, and Internet access, whereas a higher percentage of African American than other households had premium cable. African American children were more likely than others to have audiovisual media (including cable and satellite) in their bedrooms; European American children were more likely than others to have audio media in their bedrooms. Latin American children were less likely than others to have a video game player in their bedrooms, and children did not differ by race and ethnicity in the likelihood of having a computer, CD-ROM drive, or Internet access in their bedrooms. There was a substantial difference by race and ethnicity in children's total exposure to media and technology. European American children averaged 6 hours a day; Latin American children 7 hours and 5 minutes and African American children 7 hours and 56 minutes. The differences were accounted for by African American and Latin American children's greater time spent with audiovisual media (television, taped television, and movies) and video games. The only other significant difference was Latin American children's lesser involvement, compared to that of African American and European American children, with print. In terms of content preferences, African American children more than others preferred comedy, reality, and talk shows; European American children more than others preferred drama.

Let us sum up this picture of the media ecology of American homes with children 2 to 18 in them. Media and technology are prevalent in children's lives, audiovisual and audio media more than computer-based technology. Media use is frequent and widespread. Now more than ever it is frequently a private activity. With a few exceptions—the youngest children, reading books to children, and early evening television viewing—parents are not with their children while media and technology are being used. Enjoyment and entertainment are great motivating factors in all media use, including reading. Patterns of availability and use change in many ways as children mature. The most notable are the substantial increase in media and technology availability in the household and the child's bedroom, the decrease in reading, the increase in music listening, and the movement toward more adult-oriented and gender-stereotyped content. Other than boys' greater engagement with video games and a few gender-specific content preferences, there are comparatively few differences by gender. By social class, children in higher- as compared to lower-income neighborhoods are more likely to have and use computers, CD-ROM drives, and the Internet, to spend more time with print, and to spend less time with audiovisual media. The most remarkable difference by race and ethnicity is the total daily engagement of a child with media and technology, moving from an average of about 6 hours per day for a European American child to about 7 hours for a Latin American child to about 8 hours for an African American child, with the differences largely due to increasing time with audiovisual media and video games.

TODAY'S ISSUES AND CONCERNS IN PARENTING AND MEDIA

The home media ecology of American children raises concerns for many. The concerns differ by medium and the predominant uses of it. For print media, the primary concern is that young people of all ages do not spend enough time reading (or writing) or have enough access to books and other print material (Neuman, 1999; Snow et al., 1998). Rarely is content a worry. For audiovisual media, the concerns for all young people are just the opposite—too much time spent with television, videos, DVDs, and movies as the focus of attention or as the background accompaniment and way too much unpalatable, unhealthy, or simply mundane content (Bower, 1985; Sarlo, Jason, and Lonak, 1988; Wartella et al., 1990; see Bryant and Bryant, 2001, for work on television in the family). For audio media, the concerns focus on adolescent engagement with popular music filled with dubious lyrics and equally worrisome visuals (Johnson, Jackson, and Gatto, 1995; Scheel and Westefeld, 1999; Strouse, Buerkel-Rothfuss, and Long, 1995). For computer technology, video games and computer games have always been of concern, largely for boys, who spend much time playing them and prefer games that feature violence and sexuality (Sneegas and Plank, 1998). Since personal computers have become affordable, there has been interest in having them in all children's homes, where they can be used for various learning and information gathering activities (Watt and White, 1999). With the advent of the Internet, there is now concern about privacy, safety, and access to content inappropriate for children (Bremmer and Rauch, 1998). For all media and technology, a concern is that children engage with them with too little parental oversight and interaction (Kraut et al., 1998).

Why do we worry about time spent with various media and content? We assume, and research evidence indicates (see Singer and Singer, 2001, for a compilation of work), that there is some relation between time spent with a medium (e.g., print) and one's skill in processing its content and between time spent with a particular type of content (e.g., aggression) and one's knowledge and valuing of that content. For example, children who read more or are read to more at home tend to be better readers and to do better in school (Neuman, 1999; Snow et al., 1998); young children who watch more educational and informational children's television programs know more about the topics they cover and often display more of the behaviors and attitudes the programs encourage (Fisch and Truglio, 2001). However, for some media—particularly audio and audiovisual media—the processing demands are such that it may require relatively little time to become a skilled user, though not necessarily a skilled interpreter and critic. So, children may not need much time to become reasonably proficient.

Two contrasts have been central in discussions of the processes by which children interact with media and technology and of the consequences of these interactions. One contrast is that of children as powerful or passive participants. Different media and technology typically use different representational systems that seem to require different degrees of active engagement. For example, understanding text clearly requires decoding and meaning making activities, and using a video game player clearly requires high interactivity. Television, videos, and music, on the other hand, seem to require little effort on the part of the user. Think of the proverbial couch potato. Today, it is recognized that all media and technology require at least some processing in order to use them and understand their content (Shannon and Fernie, 1985), but differences in the processing requirements are also acknowledged. Early models of the effects of mass media content characterized people as virtual slaves to media and passive acceptors of their messages, whether presented in print, on television, or any other way. Such models have by and large given way to formulations in which people take the lead in choosing what medium and content they will use, making sense of the content they encounter, and determining whether and how what they encounter will be incorporated into their daily lives. The leader and follower roles and the twists and turns in children's dances with media and technology are often hotly debated. How, if at all, do media messages create the child? How, if at all, does the child effectively create the messages? We would add, what does the parent do to bolster the child's power vis-à-vis the medium or to harness the medium's power vis-à-vis the child?

The second contrast assumes that children's engagement with media and technology content is related to some kinds of social outcomes and then pits a view of media and technology as the creators of culture against a view of media and technology as the creations of culture. If media and technology reflect culture, which they surely do to some extent, then many of the concerns about their social effects are in reality just misplaced concerns about culture. If, however, media and technology cultivate culture, which they surely also do to some extent, then it is worthwhile to identify the processes by which media and technology and the culture create and recreate each other through the interactions of individuals with media, technology, and culture.

Given that media and technology play some role in children's lives, it becomes reasonable to ask how to orchestrate matters to increase positive and decrease negative elements of that role. In this chapter we focus on parents' roles in achieving this goal. Children themselves, the producers and distributors of media and technology and their content, the public, and elected and appointed officials all have roles to play as well. However, we will look only at what research suggests about how parents influence children's use of media and technology and how parents mediate any possible effects of that use.

PARENTAL INFLUENCES ON USE OF MEDIA AND TECHNOLOGY

A frequent retort to complaints about what children are doing with media and technology is that parents should behave responsibly and control their children. This is an obvious remedy, consonant with American views of individual responsibility in general and parental prerogative in particular. An alternative perspective includes the greater society, arguing that many people and agencies share in the responsibility for children's well-being and healthy development. In a study, mothers of third to sixth graders believed that parents were a close second to broadcasters in being responsible for the television programs and advertisements directed to children (Walsh, Laczniak, and Carlson, 1998). No one can deny industry options for doing good and ill, but in keeping with the topic of this chapter, we focus only on a variety of parental influences on children's engagements with media and technology. We will cover parental rules, use of technological tools, encouragement, family demographics, how parents organize the household and activities, parents' own media habits, and the family climate. It will be clear that each can play a small role in influencing the time children spend with particular media and technology and the way the content influences them. It will also be clear that most research has addressed parental influences on either reading or television viewing. When discussing reading research, we will frequently rely on a comprehensive and authoritative research review prepared under the auspices of Snow et al. (1998).

By and large, parents establish few rules about children's non-school-related interactions with media and technology. Much research has been done for rules about television, the most popular and probably least valued medium and one with much devalued content. Rules have been more frequently reported by parents than by children (Albert and Meline, 1958; Greenberg, Ericson, and Vlahos, 1972; Lyle and Hoffman, 1972a; Rossiter and Robertson, 1975). They are also more often reported for girls rather than boys and for younger rather than older children, except that children younger than about 4 years old have tended to have fewer rules about their television viewing (Atkin et al., 1991; Brown et al., 1990; Bybee, Robinson, and Turow, 1982; Gross and Walsh, 1980; Heintz, 1990; Lin and Atkin, 1989; Lyle and Hoffman, 1972a, 1972b; McLeod, Atkin, and Chaffee, 1972a, 1972b; Mohr, 1979; Roberts et al., 1999; Weaver and Barbour, 1992; West, Hausken, and Chandler, 1992; Williams and Boyes, 1986).

Those promoting early reading recommend that parents limit the amount of television viewing by their children (Calkins, 1997). However, research indicates that most families have few truly restrictive rules about television viewing (see above and Luke, 1990, for a review of studies from 1950 on). A comparison of three studies illustrates both the generally low level and the range that have been found. In face-to-face interviews conducted with mothers of first graders about 30 years ago, about 40% set special viewing hours and 30% restricted total hours (Lyle and Hoffman, 1972a). In an intensive longitudinal study about 15 years ago, about half the parents of 9- to 14-year-old children mentioned curtailing viewing because of content, and about one third mentioned some general rule about total viewing hours or contingencies for viewing (Williams and Boyes, 1986). In contrast, in a telephone survey of nearly 14,000 parents of 3- to 8-year-old children about 10 years ago, the percentages of parents reporting they had different kinds of rules were 89% for how early or late their children could watch television, 85% for content, 60% for number of viewing hours on weekdays, and 56% for total number of viewing hours (West et al., 1992). One study indicated that parents monitored music listening even less than they monitored television viewing (Christenson et al., 1985).

Parental rules make a difference. Again, the evidence is primarily about television viewing. Children who reported parental rules about viewing also reported less viewing on weekdays and weekends (Griffore and Phenice, 1996). In other work, young children (3 to 7 years old) were more likely to view both entertainment and child-oriented programs when there were fewer viewing regulations in the household (Truglio et al., 1996). Finally, youngsters whose parents had rules about bedtime, household chores, and homework were better readers in high school than were youngsters without such rules (Siegel and Hanson, 1992).

Recently, technology has made it possible for parents to exert considerable control over the television programs children watch and the Web sites they visit. Rules no longer need to be made and enforced. The V-chip technology allows blockage of particular content automatically. Programs are rated by the broadcasting industry and parents decide whether programs rated as containing some type(s) of content (e.g., violence and sexuality) will be blocked. As yet, few parents have taken advantage of this option. In fact, most parents are still unaware of or confused about V-chip ratings and what they mean (Kaiser Family Foundation, 1999). Moreover, many experts worry that the industry ratings are not sufficiently meaningful and reliable to allow the V-chip system to meet parental expectations (Kunkel et al., 1998; Potter and Warren, 1996). Internet filters allow parents to block access to particular Web sites based on the kind of content one could expect there. Systems available today most often use the same methods for identifying types of Web sites as search engines use. Parents specify whether access to some type(s) of content should be blocked. System designers have decided how such content would be identified in a search. Impressionistic reports suggest that, to date, few parents have adopted Internet filtering systems as a way of regulating their children's access to different types of content, just as few have adopted the V-chip.

Thus far, parental influence has been framed in terms of restrictions and preconditions on use. Alternatively, parents could require—or at least encourage—use. A frequent recommendation is that parents provide guidelines to encourage children of all ages to read and emphasize reading for entertainment, and both have been associated with better reading and more positive attitudes toward reading (Siegel and Hanson, 1992; Snow et al., 1998). Encouragement to view television has not been widely studied, but what evidence there is suggests it is infrequent (Bybee et al., 1982; Mohr,

1979; St. Peters, Fitch, Huston, Wright, and Eakins, 1991). Encouragement is likely to be directed to particular types of programming. For example, parents who were themselves readers encouraged their children to view a PBS reading series (*Reading Rainbow Study*, 1990) and, at least at one time, mothers encouraged their children to view programs featuring families (Barcus, 1969), a type of programming that remains very popular today. As with rule making, encouragement is probably more common with younger than older children (Gross and Walsh, 1980).

There is some evidence that parental encouragement influences children's viewing behaviors. Young children who watched more entertainment programming had more encouragement to view television (Truglio et al., 1996). Parents who encouraged their preschoolers to watch *Sesame Street* (Pinon, Huston, and Wright, 1989) or other children's informational programs (St. Peters et al., 1991) had children who watched these programs more often. In the latter study, parental encouragement and regulation were found to be orthogonal dimensions, suggesting that parents could adopt both types of strategies to guide their children's television viewing.

In addition to rules, technological barriers, and encouragement, family demographics have been shown to be associated with children's usage patterns (see also the previous section, "Ecology of the Home Multimedia Environment"). Presumably, demographic characteristics are associated with such explanatory variables as parental choices, values, and behaviors, and as opportunities available inside and outside the home. Children in lower-income families have been found to have fewer opportunities to engage in literacy activities (Neuman and Roskos, 1993) and parents more likely to emphasize reading for drill and practice rather than for enjoyment (Baker et al., 1997). These children read less at home and have less positive attitudes toward reading. Just the opposite pattern has been found with respect to television, where children's viewing hours decreased with increases in their families' social status (Atkin et al., 1991; Medrich, Rozien, Rubin, and Buckley, 1982; Nielsen Company, 1988; Roberts, 1981; Roberts et al., 1999; Tangney and Feshbach, 1988; Truglio et al., 1996).

Even with possible social status differences controlled as fully as possible, African American children were reported to spend more time watching television than did European American children (Brown et al., 1990; Greenberg and Dervin, 1970; Tangney and Feshbach, 1988). Again controlling for social status, preteens and teens in homes where parents were more often absent because of single parenting or maternal employment also watched more television (Brown et al., 1990; Medrich et al., 1982), but preschool children's viewing of *Sesame Street* was lower if their mothers were employed (which also makes it more likely the children were out of the house in childcare or preschool; Pinon et al., 1989). In addition to how much viewing goes on altogether, family demographics can also affect the kinds of programs that are watched. For example, among 3- to 7-year-old children followed over 2 years, those with older siblings watched *Sesame Street* less than did those with younger siblings (Pinon et al., 1989).

Usage patterns are also related to the physical characteristics of the home (Bradley, in Vol. 2 of this *Handbook*). Parental decisions about what media and technology to have in the home and where to put them clearly influence children's access and parental oversight (see "Ecology of the Home Multimedia Environment" for a description of what is in children's homes generally and in their bedrooms specifically). Such decisions may as well communicate parental values. Parents heading households with three or more sets have been found to have more positive attitudes about their children watching television, and the parents themselves watched more television (Christopher, Fabes, and Wilson, 1989). Those heading households with fewer television sets were more controlling of their children's viewing and discussed television more (Christopher et al., 1989; Gross and Walsh, 1980). Children with a television set in their bedroom have been found to watch more television than children with no set in their bedroom (Atkin et al., 1991). Similarly, physical proximity to books has been related to literacy development (Neuman, 1999; Snow et al., 1998), as was giving children magazines and books as gifts (Siegel and Hanson, 1992; Snow et al., 1998).

The findings are mixed in their conclusions about the consequences of having access to alternative distribution systems. For popular music, research has indicated that teenagers shifted from radio to tapes and CDs, no doubt because they then had greater control over the music they listened to (Roberts et al., 1999). Similarly, children have used cable to diversify the content they viewed, choosing more age-appropriate programming and more special interest programming; very young children have used VCRs to watch more age-appropriate, often educational, programming, and older children used them to watch more theatrical movies (Brown et al., 1990; Morgan, Alexander, Shanahan, and Harris, 1990; Roberts et al., 1999; Truglio et al., 1996; Wartella et al., 1990). Findings are contradictory as to whether these newer television-like technologies will be adopted by those more or less concerned about or restrictive of their children's viewing habits (Atkin, Heeter, and Baldwin, 1989; Atkin et al., 1991; Heintz, 1990).

Usage patterns are also related to daily activity patterns, which again are by and large a matter of parental decision making. Those who are home more—for example, younger children, women, parents of young children, those with lower incomes, and older people—tend to watch more television (Comstock et al., 1978; Roberts et al., 1999). In one study, for example, preschoolers' viewing of *Sesame Street* was lower the more time the children spent in childcare or preschool (Pinon et al., 1989). In another, involving more than 22,000 3- to 8-year-old children, according to parental report, children not in school viewed 3.1 hours a day, children in preschool or kindergarten viewed about 2.5 hours a day, and children in primary school viewed about 2.2 hours a day, a linear decrease in viewing time as hours in school increased (West et al., 1992). Individual viewing patterns also reflect the timing of activities inside and outside the home. For young children, the more television is incorporated into home activities, the more children's and entertainment programs they watch (Truglio et al., 1996). Also, audience size is larger at times when more people are likely to be home and awake (Comstock et al., 1978; Williams and Boyes, 1986). Finally, for reading, taking children to the library has been associated with better reading skills (Siegel and Hanson, 1992; Snow et al., 1998).

In addition to the influence of parents, organization of the household and daily activities, parents' own media habits are related to those of their children. Whether the relation is due to this organization or to other factors such as modeling of parental behaviors is uncertain. What is known is that parents' levels of television viewing overall, their viewing of aggressive programs, PBS programs, and various genres, their levels of reading, and their attitudes toward reading have each been associated with those of their children (Baker et al., 1997; Chaffee and McLeod, 1972; Chaffee, McLeod, and Atkin, 1971; Gross and Walsh, 1980; Lyle and Hoffman, 1972a; McLeod et al., 1972b; McLeod and Brown, 1976; Roberts, 1981; Schramm, Lyle, and Parker, 1961; Snow et al., 1998). The relations were weak rather than strong and decreased as children got older, but they showed some parent–child similarities.

Finally, the family climate appears to be related to both media use and the consequences of that use. Evidence is mixed as to whether the addition of a computer increases solitary time or family togetherness and communication (Kraut et al., 1998; Watt and White, 1999). For boys, liking heavy metal music has been associated with less satisfaction with their family relationships (Arnett, 1991). A very early finding was that when family relationships were stressful, children from upper-middle-income families tended to watch more television, presumably to avoid some of the stress (Maccoby, 1954; Schramm et al., 1961). Since then, there have been several reports of findings that may be explained by this proposition (Chaffee and McLeod, 1972; Gunter and Svennevig, 1987; McLeod et al., 1972a, 1972b; Tangney, 1988; Tangney and Feshbach, 1988) and of some direct tests that have supported it (Henggeler, Cohen, Edwards, Summerville, and Ray, 1991; Rosenblatt and Cunningham, 1976). Although several studies have found little or no relation (Dorr, Doubleday, and Kovaric, 1987; Kubey and Csikszentmihalyi, 1990; Lyle and Hoffman, 1972a), on balance, research suggests that increased television viewing and viewing of more escapist and less challenging programming are likely when children live in more stressful family environments. Also, girls in such unsatisfactory family environments have been found to be more likely to be influenced by the sexually permissive attitudes and behaviors in music videos (Strouse et al., 1995). Moreover, Snow et al. (1998) concluded that the socioemotional contexts surrounding reading were directly related to the motivation to read later on in life, providing yet another bit of evidence that family climate influences both children's engagement with media and technology and the effects of that engagement.

PARENTAL MEDIATION OF THE INFLUENCE OF MEDIA
AND TECHNOLOGY

Mediation occurs when whatever would be the naturally occurring interaction of the child with a medium or technology and its content is somehow altered by another's actions. When effective, mediation changes children's choices, attention, emotions, interaction, understanding, learning, credulity, attitudes, performance, and the like. Mediation can occur before, during, or after use and can be directed toward specific content, a type of content, or the medium or technology itself. For example, a father could watch *Sesame Street* or read a book with his son and ask him to name letters and numbers as they appear, giving feedback each time, or the father could take time at dinner to discuss the undesirable behaviors in a videogame or cartoon series the son likes, or the father could teach his son about the profit motive underlying the production and distribution of popular music and television programs and how the goals are much more entertainment than information (see Messaris, 1983, for other examples for television).

There is ample evidence that active mediation influences children's engagement with media and technology and the consequences of that engagement. Most of it comes from experimental demonstrations. For example, in an experiment in which an adult helped young children to tell the story in a book (so-called dialogic reading) rather than simply listen as the adult read it to them, the dialogic reading children, compared to controls, significantly improved two important precursors of literacy—their language skills and concepts of print (Whitehurst, Arnold, Epstein, and Angell, 1994). In another experiment with third and fourth graders, Robinson (1999) demonstrated that a 6-month classroom curriculum that involved increasing awareness of usage patterns, teaching intelligent engagement, and advocating reduced usage resulted in decreased television viewing and video game playing at home, meals eaten in front of the television, and body fat. In other experimental work, coviewing with older siblings increased preschoolers' enjoyment of and decreased their arousal from a scary program (Wilson and Weiss, 1993) and changed 6- and 7-year-old children's evaluations of characters in two programs (Haefner and Wartella, 1987). Other research has demonstrated that adult coviewers can use questions, commentary, explanation, evaluation, and feedback during television viewing to increase children's understanding of plot and implicit program content, learning from instructional and entertainment programs, and adopting depicted social attitudes and behaviors (e.g., Bandura, Grusec, and Menlove, 1966; Collins, Sobol, and Westby, 1981; Corder-Bolz, 1980; Grusec, 1973; Lefcourt, Barnes, Parke, and Schwartz, 1966; Reiser, Tessmer, and Phelps, 1984; Watkins, Calvert, Huston-Stein, and Wright, 1980).

Despite the evidence that active mediation is effective, parents apparently do little of it. As was true in the previous section about parental influences on use, most research is about parental mediation with print (for which the Snow et al., 1998, report is a major resource) and television (and its near relatives). Much of that is about mediation with younger children. There is very little, if any, information regarding the ways in which parents mediate children's interactions with audio media and computer-based technology. In fact, what research there is suggests that computers, video game players, and audio media are most often used by children when alone and rarely regulated or mediated by parents (Christenson et al., 1985; Roberts et al., 1999). Moreover, it has been suggested that newer media and technology and the proliferation of media and technology in the home provide increasing freedom from adult supervision of or comment about the messages children receive (Roberts et al., 1999).

The outcomes of interest to those studying mediation are fundamentally different for print and television. To a considerable extent they reflect cultural beliefs and values. For print, the outcomes are usually better reading (and sometimes writing) skills—primarily decoding and comprehension skills, liking to read, and spending more time reading. For television, there is little interest in basic decoding and comprehension—which are assumed to be easy—and much interest in goals such as less liking of television, spending less time watching, watching better content, learning more from educational programming, and accepting fewer of the messages of devalued content (e.g., violence and sexuality). In line with these different goals, the types of mediation studied differ for these two media, the only two for which there is enough research to arrive at generalizations.

Most of the work on parental mediation of print has looked at the literacy experiences parents provide very young children (Meyer, Wardrop, Stahl, and Linn, 1994), particularly reading books with them. Studies have indicated that about 80% of the parents of children 3 to 5 years old read or shared a picture book with their children at least three times a week (National Center for Education Statistics, 1998; Nord, Lennon, Liu, and Chandler, 1999; Young, Davis, and Schoen, 1996). It was more likely in homes at or above the poverty level, two-parent homes, and homes where mothers had at least some college education (National Center for Education Statistics, 1998; Nord et al., 1999). Children have been reported to initiate joint reading experiences (Senechal et al., 1998), and parents have been found to be more likely to provide print materials when they believed their children were interested in reading (Hiebert, 1981). Although experts recommend that parents continue to read with older children and in other ways to mediate their reading experiences, there is little research to indicate whether they do (Snow et al., 1998). It is tempting to assume this is because everyday experience suggests that most parents do little to mediate the print literacy experiences of their older children and teenagers.

There is reasonably good evidence that parents reading to young children increases children's motivation to read (Baker et al., 1997; Goldenberg, 1989; Meyer et al., 1994). When parents were enthusiastic about this reading and viewed it as entertainment, children were also likely to feel positively about reading and learning to read (Baker, Serpell, and Sonnenschein, 1995; Baker et al., 1997; Snow and Tabors, 1996). Moreover, children whose parents read to them more often were also likely to read better in school (Goldenberg, 1989; Meyer et al., 1994; Neuman and Roskos, 1993; Snow et al., 1998). However, improved reading probably occurred in many cases because children's oral language improved (Meyer et al., 1994) or because teachers judged children to be more able and placed them in higher reading groups (Goldenberg, 1989) rather than because children were actually reading better. This is because much story book reading apparently does not include the kinds of assisted learning or teaching about print that helps children actually learn to read (Meyer et al., 1994; Senechal et al., 1998).

For all parents, but particularly those from lower social economic backgrounds, the primary interest of researchers is how to encourage parents to read to young children and to do so for pleasure. However, there is also evidence that more learning about reading per se may occur when parents are more active in their mediation, asking questions about the text, engaging the child in the reading, encouraging the child to read along, and the like (Snow et al., 1998). Moreover, Meyer et al. (1994) reported a positive relation between reading achievement and the time children spent engaged with print, but no relation between reading achievement and the time parents spent reading to their children. In addition, parents can support reading development simply by talking often with children, enriching their vocabulary and conceptual knowledge (Calkins, 1997), provided the conversational content is related to that needed for reading.

When parents read to their children, they are functionally mediating between the print material and their children's experience of it. Not so with television. Even very young children can and do watch television—and get something out of it—without the mediation of their parents. However, as with print, parental mediation can make a difference in children's experiences with the medium. In studying mediation of the television experience, researchers have distinguished among three styles of parental mediation: restrictive—setting rules about use of the television; active or evaluative—discussing and/or criticizing the medium and its content; and unfocused—coviewing and/or discussing without evaluation (Abelman and Pettey, 1989; Bybee et al., 1982; Nathanson, 1999; Sarlo et al., 1988; Weaver and Barbour, 1992). Active mediation is sometimes further differentiated according to valence—negative, positive, and neutral. Restrictive mediation was covered in the preceding section. Note that this same conceptualization can be applied to parental mediation of print and other media and technology, but it has not been, nor, in general, have analogous studies been done with these other media and technology.

Coviewing is common and occurs more often with siblings than parents (see "Ecology of the Home Multimedia Environment"). With parents, coviewing is most common with younger children and during the evening. There is some evidence that increased coviewing is associated with positive outcomes such as more attention to and learning from preschool educational programs (e.g., St. Peters et al., 1991; Salomon, 1977). However, coviewing in everyday home life infrequently involves active or evaluative mediation intended to enhance children's experiences with television (Desmond, Singer, and Singer, 1990; Lyle and Hoffman, 1972a; St. Peters et al., 1991; Stoneman and Brody, 1982, 1983), and coviewing at home is rarely associated with the kinds of positive outcomes experts expect from active mediation (Dorr, Kovaric, and Doubleday, 1989; Messaris and Kerr, 1984; Nathanson, 1999; Rothschild and Morgan, 1987; St. Peters et al., 1991).

When parents are not watching television with their children, they can nonetheless mediate that experience not only by restrictive mediation (reviewed in the preceding section) but also by active or evaluative mediation. Talking about television content can be active mediation, but talk is not necessarily mediation. Various studies have reported that from one third to two thirds of parents or children reported at least sometimes talking with each other about television (Bybee et al., 1982; Lyle and Hoffman, 1972a; Ward, Wackman, and Wartella, 1977). The quantity and style of parental talk have been shown to be related by two different pathways to children's evaluations of television content. In the direct pathway, the more parents talk with their children about specific elements of television programming, the more the children's opinions are likely to correspond to those of their parents (Austin, Roberts, and Nass, 1990; Messaris and Kerr, 1984; Nathanson, 1999; Prasad, Rao, and Sheikh, 1978; Ward et al., 1977). In the indirect pathway reported by Austin et al. (1990), parental communicativeness in general affected a child's view of her or his family's warmth, and the degree of mismatch between the child's views of her or his own family's warmth and of the warmth of a very popular television family, predicted the degree of realism attributed to that television family. Although one can imagine, and research outside the home has sometimes identified, other types of active mediation (e.g., media literacy), there is little or no research about their presence in the home. For active mediation to occur, parents and children must converse with each other, something reputed to occur infrequently (Calkins, 1997), and the conversation must address pertinent topics, again something one suspects occurs infrequently in today's families.

PRACTICAL CONSIDERATIONS FOR PARENTS

The preceding review of classical and modern research makes it clear that media and technology are very much part of American children's lives, consuming several hours a day and bringing them into contact with a very wide range of ideas. Research that is only touched on in this chapter has revealed that the time spent with media and technology is associated with skill development and that the content encountered can affect information, attitudes, and behaviors. Research reviewed in this chapter indicates that parents can make some difference in their children's experiences with media and technology and suggests that most parents are not nearly as active as they could be in exerting such an influence.

Based on such research, and also on common sense, numerous researchers and writers have offered practical information and advice to parents. There have been so many publications that we could not begin to catalog them. Instead, we offer a representative sample of excellent materials prepared for parents: For reading, Calkins (1997), Burns, Griffin, and Snow (1999), and the U.S. Department of Education (1999); for the Internet, Bremmer and Rauch (1998); for the V-chip, the Kaiser Family Foundation and the Center for Media Education (Kaiser Family Foundation, 1999); for advertising to children in all media and technology, the Children's Advertising Review Unit (1993); and for television, the Corporation for Public Broadcasting (1988) and the ERIC Digest (1990).

In materials directed to parents, the most frequent content is a recitation of important facts about children's engagement with one or more media or technology and potential consequences of that engagement (or nonengagement in the case of reading) and then various recommendations. Certain types of recommendations are common: Parents should become more informed, participate more with their children in use of the medium or technology, actively promote the outcomes they value while participating, talk with their children about their media and technology experiences and life in general, maintain rules that support what they value vis-à-vis the medium or technology and its content, learn about their children's interests and abilities and adapt experiences with media and technology to them, help children find pleasure in the activities parents value and not in other activities, and generally be much more active with their children and their interactions with media and technology. Specifics are added to illustrate each recommendation for the particular medium or technology and/or content at issue.

Other topics may be added. For reading, for example, there may be information about how to read to one's child and how to engage her or him in activities that will promote literacy, including using dialogic reading, asking questions about text, emphasizing pleasure not instruction, avoiding frustration, selecting slightly challenging materials, selecting books children will enjoy, varying genres, reading aloud to children of all ages, and encouraging independent reading. For television, there may be information about undesirable content on television, sources of alternative content, media literacy, alternatives to television viewing, and public advocacy for better television. For the Internet, there may be information about the kinds of information available, the ways it is organized and may be found, the options for blocking access to certain types of content, and particular concerns about privacy.

In our view, most publications omit three kinds of recommendations that can be drawn from the research literature. One is that parents make sure their own interactions with media and technology exemplify the best they might hope ever to see in their children. "Do as I say not as I do" is not very effective parenting. Another is to organize both the household and the children's daily lives to emphasize and deemphasize, according to parental values, children's engagement with media and technology, for example, organizing matters to emphasize reading and deemphasize videogame playing and television viewing. Engagement should decrease when the medium or technology is not so accessible and inviting and when other activities are incompatible with using it. Moreover, emphasizing other activities may be more effective in promoting positive development than direct regulation and restriction would be. A final recommendation is that parents be vigorous socializers of their children. Children with well established, socially valued skills, knowledge, beliefs, attitudes, and behavioral patterns are more likely both to stick with what they know rather than adopt any alternative perspective that media and technology may present and to use what they know to interact with media and technology and make sense of any content that permits alternative interpretations. When these three rather indirect approaches are combined with the numerous more direct approaches found in most practical advice, parents have a wide range of options for making media and technology positive forces in children's development.

There are also some tools available that may be of use to parents in their efforts to use media and technology wisely with their children. There is a variety of rating systems that indicate the kinds of content presented and/or the appropriate age range. These include, for example, the Motion Picture Association Ratings (see Wilson, Linz, and Randall, 1990, for an analysis and critique), the Informational/Educational rating on some children's television programs, the ratings for video games and television programs, and the advisories for popular music. There is some evidence that television ratings with content descriptors will be put to use by parents who typically discipline through deprivation and believe that television can influence their children (Abelman, in press). Other tools, in addition to ratings, include filters, such as those for the Internet (Price, 1998) and the V-chip (Kaiser Family Foundation, 1999). Moreover, a few experiments have shown that, when parents are targeted with special materials and programs, they are likely to use them to achieve the intended goals. Consider the following three interesting examples. Parents increased their encouragement or discouragement of viewing specific shows when they received guides that identified shows high in antisocial or prosocial behaviors (Heald, 1980). Children in blue-collar families who were very heavy viewers reduced their viewing to about 10 hours a week under a system in which tokens could be exchanged for viewing and rewards were offered for adherence to the token system (Wolfe, Mendes, and Factor, 1984). Parents who were given books by their pediatricians were four times more likely to read and share books with their children (Needlman, Fried, Morley, Taylor, and Zuckerman, 1991). These are hopeful signs that active engagement of parents can lead them to greater mediation of their children's interactions with media and technology.

CONCLUSIONS

There is still much to learn about parents' roles in children's interactions with today's media and technology. Future theory and research about parents, children, media, and technology will pursue them, but future topics will also depend, to some extent, on how media and technology evolve. Most prognosticators expect rapid technological change, including technological improvements on what is now available, decreased costs for purchase and access, and entirely new options. Changes will increase choice and connectivity, provide greater opportunities to individualize experience and to have mass experiences, increase the attractiveness and power of media and technology, undoubtedly make more undesirable—as well as desirable—content available at home, introduce new issues about interactivity, and expand the means for controlling children's experiences with media and technology. Media, and technology and their cultural uses tend to evolve; research about parents, children, media, and technology is evolving in response (e.g., Dorr and Kunkel, 1990; Heeter and Greenberg, 1988; Levy, 1989; Wartella et al., 2000). We can expect these patterns to continue.

Predictions about the future directions of theory and theory-based research about parents, children, media, and technology depend to some extent on one's view of science. Taking a venerable, ideal science perspective, we would predict a continuation of trends already evident in the literature. Conceptual representations of relations among parents, children, media, and technology, should grow more complex, and the view of the child as an active participant in or even determiner of her or his social experience should become more dominant. The interrelation of media, technology, and culture should be better recognized, and there should be more models in which children, parents, media, and technology form systems within their own ecocultural niche, which is itself situated within a larger culture. Some competing views of the nature of science would suggest a change from, rather than continuation of, trends supported by those now in the field. In these competing views, the change could entail either the study of entirely different problems than those that are currently explored vis-à-vis parents, children, media, and technology or the adoption of a radically different theoretical structure for studying the same problems.

The future cannot be known, but two predictions seem safe. First, topics for future theory and research will reflect changes both in the available media and technology and in the cultural uses to which they are put. Second, in the short run, the current trends in theory and theory-related research about parents, children, media, and technology will continue. The issues, methods, and findings are still productive and provocative. There is no suggestion that scholars have yet pushed the paradigm to its limits.

ACKNOWLEDGMENTS

Alison Bailey, Department of Education, University of California, Los Angeles, provided invaluable assistance in identifying relevant resources in the area of early literacy and offering a spirited review of a draft of the chapter. We gratefully acknowledge her contributions and accept responsibility for any continuing weaknesses in the handling of this area.

REFERENCES

Abelman, R. (in press). Parents' use of content-based TV advisories. *Parenting: Science and Practice.*

Abelman, R., and Pettey, G. R. (1989). Child attributes as determinants of parental television-viewing mediation: The role of giftedness. *Journal of Family Issues, 10,* 251–266.

Albert, R. S., and Meline, H. (1958). The influence of social status on the uses of television. *Public Opinion Quarterly, 22,* 145–151.

Anderson, D. R., Lorch, E. P., Field, D. E., Collins, P. A., and Nathan, J. G. (1986). Television viewing at home: Age trends in visual attention and time with TV. *Child Development, 57,* 1024–1033.

Arnett, J. (1991). Heavy metal music and reckless behavior among adolescents. *Journal of Youth and Adolescence, 20,* 573–592.

Atkin, D. J., Greenberg, B. S., and Baldwin, T. F. (1991). The home ecology of children's television viewing: Parental mediation and the new video environment. *Journal of Communication, 41*(3), 40–52.

Atkin, D. J., Heeter, C., and Baldwin, T. (1989). How presence of cable affects parental mediation of TV viewing. *Journalism Quarterly, 66,* 557–563, 578.

Austin, E. W., Roberts, D. F., and Nass, C. I. (1990). Influences of family communication on children's television-interpretation processes. *Communication Research, 17,* 545–564.

Baker, L. Scher, D., and Mackler, K. (1997). Home and family influences on motivations for reading. *Educational Psychologist, 32,* 69–82.

Baker, L., Serpell, R., and Sonnenschein, S. (1995). Opportunities for literacy learning in the homes of urban preschoolers. In L. M. Morrow (Ed.), *Family literacy: Connections in schools and communities* (pp. 236–252). Newark, DE: International Reading Association.

Bandura, A. (1977). *Social learning theory.* Englewood Cliffs, NJ: Prentice-Hall.

Bandura, A. (1986). *Social foundations of thought and action: A social cognitive theory.* Englewood Cliffs, NJ: Prentice-Hall.

Bandura, A. (1999). Socal cognitive theory of personality. In L. A. Pervin and O. P. John (Eds.), *Handbook of personality: Theory and research* (2nd ed., pp. 154–196). New York: Guilford Press.

Bandura, A., Grusec, J. E., and Menlove, F. L. (1966). Observational learning as a function of symbolization and incentive set. *Child Development, 37,* 499–506.

Barcus, E. E. (1969). Parental influence on children's television viewing. *Television Quarterly, 8,* 63–73.

Bianchi, S., and Robinson, J. (1997). What did you do today? Children's use of time, family composition, and the acquisition of social capital. *Journal of Marriage and the Family, 59,* 332–344.

Blumler, J. G., and Katz, E. (Eds.). (1974). *The uses of mass communications.* Beverly Hills, CA: Sage.

Bower, R. T. (1985). *The changing television audience in America.* New York: Columbia University Press.

Bremmer, J., and Rauch, P. K. (1998). Children and computers: Risks and benefits. *Journal of the American Academy of Child and Adolescent Psychiatry, 37,* 559–560.

Brown, J. D., Childers, K. W., Bauman, K. E., and Koch, G. G. (1990). The influence of new media and family structure on young adolescents' television and radio use. *Communication Research, 17,* 65–82.

Bryant, J., and Bryant, J. A. (Eds.). (2001). *Television and the American family* (2nd ed.). Mahwah, NJ: Lawrence Erlbaum Associates.

Burns, M. S., Griffin, P., and Snow, C. E. (Eds.). (1999). *Starting out right: A guide to promoting children's reading success.* Washington, DC: National Academy Press.

Bybee, C., Robinson, D., and Turow, J. (1982). Determinants of parental guidance of children's television viewing for a special subgroup: mass media scholars. *Journal of Broadcasting, 26,* 697–710.

Calkins, L. (1997). *Raising lifelong learners: A parent's guide.* Reading, MA: Addison-Wesley.

Calvert, S. L. (1999). *Children's journeys through the information age.* Boston: McGraw-Hill College.

Carey, J. W. (1989). *Communication as culture: Essays in media and society.* Boston: Unwin Hyman.

Carroll, R., Silbergleid, M., Beachum, C., Perry, S., Pluscht, P., and Pescatore, M. (1993). Meanings of radio to teenagers in a niche-programming era. *Journal of Broadcasting and Electronic Media, 37,* 159–176.

Chaffee, S. H., and McLeod, J. M. (1972). Adolescent television use in the family context. In G. A. Comstock and E. A. Rubinstein (Eds.), *Television and social behavior: Vol. 3. Television and adolescent aggressiveness* (pp. 149–172). Washington, DC: U.S. Government Printing Office.

Chaffee, S. H., McLeod, J. M., and Atkin, C. K. (1971). Parental influence on adolescent media use. *American Behavioral Scientist, 14,* 323–340.

Children's Advertising Review Unit and International Food Information Council. (1993). *Parent's guide to food advertising.* New York: Author.

Christenson, P., and De Benedittis, P. (1986). "Eavesdropping" on the FM band: Children's use of radio. *Journal of Communication, 36*(2), 27–38.

Christenson, P., De Benedittis, P., and Lindlof, T. (1985). Children's use of audio media. *Communication Research, 12,* 327–343.

Christopher, F. S., Fabes, R. A., and Wilson, P. M. (1989). Family television viewing: Implications for family life education. *Family Relations, 38*, 210–214.

Collins, W. A., Sobol, B. L., and Westby, S. (1981). Effects of adult commentary on children's comprehension and inferences about a televised aggressive portrayal. *Child Development, 52*, 158–163.

Comstock, G., Chaffee, S., Katzman, N., McCombs, M., and Roberts, D. (1978). *Television and human behavior*. New York: Columbia University Press.

Corder-Bolz, C. R. (1980). Mediation: The role of significant others. *Journal of Communication, 30*(3), 106–118.

Corporation for Public Broadcasting. (1988). *TV tips for parents: Using television to help your child learn*. Washington, DC: Author. (ERIC Document Reproduction Service No. ED 299 948.)

Desmond, R. J., Singer, J. L., and Singer, D. G. (1990). Family mediation: Parental communication patterns and the influences of television on children. In J. Bryant (Ed.), *Television and the American family* (pp. 293–309). Hillsdale, NJ: Lawrence Erlbaum Associates.

Dorr, A. (1986). *Television and children: A special medium for a special audience*. Beverly Hills, CA: Sage.

Dorr, A., Doubleday, C., and Kovaric, P. (1987, April). *Them that's got shall get: Family satisfaction and television viewing*. Paper presented at the biennial meetings of the Society for Research in Child Development, Baltimore, MD.

Dorr, A., Kovaric, P., and Doubleday, C. (1989). Parent–child coviewing of television. *Journal of Broadcasting and Electronic Media, 33*, 35–51.

Dorr, A., and Kunkel, D. (Eds.). (1990). Children in a changing media environment [Special issue]. *Communication Research, 17*(1).

Dworkin, M. (Ed.). (1970). *The literature of cinema*. New York: Arno Press and the New York Times.

Emes, C. E. (1997). Is Mr. Pac Man eating our children? A review of the effect of video games on children. *Canadian Journal of Psychiatry, 42*, 409–414.

ERIC Digest. (1990). *Guidelines for family television viewing*. Urbana, IL: ERIC Clearinghouse on Elementary and Early Childhood Education. (ERIC Document Reproduction Service No. ED 320 662.)

Fisch, S. M., and Truglio, R. T. (Eds.). (2001). *"G" is for growing: Thirty years of research on children and Sesame Street*. Mahwah, NJ: Lawrence Erlbaum Associates.

Gailey, C. W. (1996). Videogames as cultural artifacts. In P. M. Greenfield and R. R. Cocking (Eds.), *Interacting with video: Vol. 11. Advances in applied developmental psychology* (pp. 85–94). Norwood, NJ: Ablex.

Gerbner, G., Gross, L., Morgan, M., and Signorielli, N. (1986). Living with television: The dynamics of the cultivation process. In J. Bryant and D. Zillmann (Eds.), *Perspectives on media effects* (pp. 17–40). Hillsdale, NJ: Lawrence Erlbaum Associates.

Goldenberg, C. (1989). Parents' effects on academic grouping for reading: Three case studies. *American Educational Research Journal, 26*, 329–352.

Greenberg, B. S., and Dervin, B. (Eds.). (1970). *Use of the mass media by the urban poor*. New York: Praeger.

Greenberg, B. S., Ericson, P. M., and Vlahos, M. (1972). Children's television behavior as perceived by mother and child. In E. A. Rubinstein, G. A. Comstock, and J. P. Murray (Eds.), *Television and social behavior: Vol. 4. Television in day-to-day life: Patterns of use* (pp. 395–409) (1972-6 PO-904/646). Washington, DC: U.S. Government Printing Office.

Greenfield, P. M., and Cocking, R. R. (Vol. Eds.). (1996). *Interacting with video: Vol. 11. Advances in applied developmental psychology*. Norwood, NJ: Ablex.

Greenfield, P. M., and deWinstanley, P. (1996). Action videogames and informal education effects on strategies for dividing visual attention. In P. M. Greenfield and R. R. Cocking (Eds.), *Interacting with video: Vol. 11. Advances in applied developmental psychology* (pp. 187–205). Norwood, NJ: Ablex.

Griffore, R., and Phenice, L. (1996). Rules and television viewing. *Psychological Reports, 78*, 814.

Gross, L. S., and Walsh, R. P. (1980). Factors affecting parental control over children's television viewing: A pilot study. *Journal of Broadcasting, 24*, 411–419.

Grossberg, L. (1987). Critical theory and the politics of empirical research. In M. Gurevitch and M. R. Levy (Eds.), *Mass communication review yearbook* (Vol. 6, pp. 86–106). Beverly Hills, CA: Sage.

Grusec, J. E. (1973). Effects of co-observer evaluations on imitation: A developmental study. *Developmental Psychology, 8*, 141.

Gunter, B., and Svennevig, M. (1987). *Behind and in front of the screen: Television's involvement with family life*. London: Libbey.

Haefner, M. J., and Wartella, E. A. (1987). Effects of sibling coviewing on children's interpretations of television programs. *Journal of Broadcasting and Electronic Media, 31*, 153–168.

Hall, S. (1992). Cultural studies and its theoretical legacies. In L. Grossberg, C. Nelson, and P. A. Treichler (Eds.), *Cultural studies* (pp. 277–294). New York: Routledge.

Heald, G. R. (1980). Television viewing guides and parental recommendations. *Journalism Quarterly, 57*, 141–144.

Heeter, C. J., and Greenberg, B. S. (Eds.). (1988). *Cableviewing*. Norwood, NJ: Ablex.

Heintz, K. E. (1990). VCR libraries: Opportunities for parent control. In J. R. Dobrow (Ed.), *Social and cultural aspects of VCR use* (pp. 147–162). Hillsdale, NJ: Lawrence Erlbaum Associates.

Henggeler, S. W., Cohen, R., Edwards, J. J., Summerville, M. B., and Ray, G. E. (1991). Family stress as a link in the association between television viewing and achievement. *Child Study Journal, 21,* 1–10.

Hiebert, E. (1981). Developmental patterns and interrelationhips of pre-school children's point awareness. *Reading and Research Quarterly, 16,* 236–260.

Huston, A. C., and Wright, J. C. (1997). Mass media and children's development. In W. Damon, I. Sigel, and A. Renniger (Eds.), *Handbook of child psychology* (5th ed., Vol. 4, pp. 999–1058). New York: Wiley.

Huston, A. C., Wright, J. C., Marquis, J., and Green, S. (1999). How young children spend their time: Television and other activities. *Developmental Psychology, 35,* 912–925.

Johnson, J., Jackson, L., and Gatto, L. (1995). Violent attitudes and deferred academic aspirations: Deleterious effects of exposure to rap music. *Basic and Applied Social Psychology, 16,* 27–41.

Jowett, G., Jarvie, K., and Fuller, K. (1996). *Children and the movies: Media influence and the Payne Fund controversy.* New York: Cambridge University Press.

Kaiser Family Foundation. (1999). A parent's guide to the TV rating and V-chip [On-line]. *The V-chip Education Project.* Available: www.vchipeducation.org

Kellner, D. (1995). *Media culture.* London and New York: Routledge.

Kraut, R., Peterson, M., Lundmark, V., Kiesler, S., Mukopadhyay, T., and Scherlis, W. (1998). Internet paradox: A social technology that reduces social involvement and psychological well-being? *American Psychologist, 53,* 1017–1031.

Kubey, R., and Csikszentmihalyi, M. (1990). *Television and the quality of life: How viewing shapes everyday experience.* Hillsdale, NJ: Lawrence Erlbaum Associates.

Kunkel, D., Maynard Farinola, W. J., Cope, K. M., Donnerstein, E., Biely, E., and Zwarun, L. (1998). *Rating the TV ratings, one year out: An assessment of the television industry's use of V-chip ratings.* Menlo Park, CA: Kaiser Family Foundation. (Report to the Kaiser Family Foundation.)

Lefcourt, H. M., Barnes, K., Parke, R., and Schwartz, F. (1966). Anticipated social censure and aggression-conflict as mediators of response to aggression induction. *Journal of Social Psychology, 70,* 251–263.

Levy, M. R. (Ed.). (1989). *The VCR age: Home video and mass communication.* Newbury Park, CA: Sage.

Liebert, R. M., and Sprafkin, J. (1988). *The early window: Effects of television on children and youth* (3rd ed.). New York: Pergamon.

Lin, C. A., and Atkin, D. J. (1989). Parental mediation and rulemaking for adolescent use of TV and VCRs. *Journal of Broadcasting and Electronic Media, 33,* 53–67.

Luke, C. (1990). *Constructing the child viewer: A history of the American discourse on television and children, 1950–1980.* New York: Praeger.

Lull, J. (1980). The social uses of television. *Human Communication Research, 6,* 197–209.

Lull, J. (Ed.). (1988). *World families watch television.* Newbury Park, CA: Sage.

Lyle, J., and Hoffman, H. R. (1972a). Children's use of television and other media. In E. A. Rubinstein, G. A. Comstock, and J. P. Murray (Eds.), *Television and social behavior: Vol. 4. Television in day-to-day life: Patterns of use* (pp. 129–256) (1972-6 PO-904/646). Washington, DC: U.S. Government Printing Office.

Lyle, J., and Hoffman, H. R. (1972b). Explorations in patters of television viewing by preschool-age children. In E. A. Rubinstein, G. A. Comstock, and J. P. Murray (Eds.), *Television and social behavior: Vol. 4. Television in day-to-day life: Patterns of use* (pp. 257–273) (1972-6 PO-904/646). Washington, DC: U.S. Government Printing Office.

Maccoby, E. E. (1954). Why do children watch television? *Public Opinion Quarterly, 18,* 239–244.

McLeod, J. M., Atkin, C. K., and Chaffee, S. H. (1972a). Adolescents, parents, and television use: Adolescent self-report measures from Maryland and Wisconsin samples. In G. A. Comstock and E. A. Rubinstein (Eds.), *Television and social behavior: Vol. 3. Television and adolescent aggressiveness* (pp. 173–238). Washington, DC: U.S. Government Printing Office.

McLeod, J. M., Atkin, C. K., and Chaffee, S. H. (1972b). Adolescents, parents, and television use: Self-report and other report measures from the Wisconsin sample. In G. A. Comstock and E. A. Rubinstein (Eds.), *Television and social behavior: Vol. 3. Television and adolescent aggressiveness* (pp. 239–313). Washington, DC: U.S. Government Printing Office.

McLeod, J. M., and Brown, J. D. (1976). The family environment and adolescent television use. In R. Brown (Ed.), *Children and television* (pp. 199–234). London: Collier Macmillan.

Medrich, E. A., Rozien, J., Rubin, V., and Buckley, S. (1982). *The serious business of growing up.* Berkeley: University of California Press.

Messaris, P. (1983). Family conversations about television. *Journal of Family Issues, 4,* 293–308.

Messaris, P., and Kerr, D. (1984). TV-related mother–child interaction and children's perceptions of TV characters. *Journalism Quarterly, 16,* 662–666.

Meyer, L., Wardrop, J., Stahl, S., and Linn, R. (1994). Effects of reading storybooks aloud to children. *Journal of Educational Research, 88,* 69–85.

Mohr, P. J. (1979). Parental guidance of children's viewing of evening television programs. *Journal of Broadcasting, 23,* 213–228.

Morgan, M., Alexander, A., Shanahan, J., and Harris, C. (1990). Adolescents, VCRs, and the family environment. *Communication Research, 17*, 83–106.

Nathanson, A. (1999). Identifying and explaining the relationhip between parental mediation and children's aggression. *Communication Research, 26*, 124–143.

National Center for Education Statistics. (1998). *Early literacy experiences in the home.* Washington, DC: U.S. Department of Education, Office of Educational Research and Improvement. NCES 1999-003.

Needlman, R., Fried, L., Morley, D., Taylor, S., and Zuckerman, B. (1991). Clinic-based intervention to promote literacy. *American Journal of Diseases of Children, 145*, 881–884.

Neuman, S. (1999). Books make a difference: A study of access to literacy. *Reading Research Quarterly, 34*, 286–311.

Neuman, S., and Roskos, K. (1993). Access to print for children of poverty: Differential effects of adult mediation and literacy-enriched play settings on environmental and functional print tasks. *American Educational Research Journal, 30*, 95–122.

Nielsen Company. (1988, February). *Television viewing among African Americans* (4th ed.). New York: Author.

Nord, C. W., Lennon, J., Liu, B., and Chandler, K. (National Center for Education Statistics). (1999). Home literacy activities and signs of children's emerging literacy, 1993 and 1999. Washington, DC: U.S. Department of Education, Office of Educational Research and Improvement. NCES 2000-026.

Pinon, M. R., Huston, A. C., and Wright, J. C. (1989). Family ecology and child characteristics that predict young children's educational television viewing. *Child Development, 60*, 846–856.

Plato. (1952). *The republic.* In R. M. Hutchins (Ed.), *Great books of the Western world.* Chicago: Encyclopedia Britannica.

Potter, W. J., and Warren, R. (1996). Considering policies to protect children from TV violence. *Journal of Communication, 46*(4), 116–138.

Prasad, V. K., Rao, T. R., and Sheikh, A. A. (1978). Mother vs. commercial. *Journal of Communication, 28*(1), 91–96.

Price, M. E. (1998). *The V-chip debate: Content filtering from television to the Internet.* Mahwah, NJ: Lawrence Erlbaum Associates.

Reading Rainbow Study. Final Report. (1990). MN: NFO Research. (ERIC Document Reproduction No. ED 331 027.)

Reiser, R. A., Tessmer, M. A., and Phelps, P. C. (1984). Adult–child interaction in children's learning from *Sesame Street. Educational Communication and Technology, 32*, 217–223.

Roberts, C. (1981). Parental influences on viewing and perceptions of television content. *Journalism Quarterly, 58*, 31–37.

Roberts, D., Foehr, U., Rideout, V., and Brodie, M. (1999). *Kids, media and the new millennium: A comprehensive national analysis of children's media use* [Online]. Menlo Park, CA: Kaiser Family Foundation. Available: http://www.kff.org

Robinson, T. (1999). Reducing children's television viewing to prevent obesity: A randomized controlled trial. *Journal of the American Medical Association, 282*, 1561–1567.

Rogoff, B. (1990). *Apprenticeship in thinking: Cognitive development in social context.* New York: Oxford University Press.

Rosenblatt, P. C., and Cunningham, M. R. (1976). Television watching and family tensions. *Journal of Marriage and the Family, 38*, 105–111.

Rossiter, J. R., and Robertson, T. S. (1975). Children's television viewing: An examination of parent–child consensus. *Sociometry, 38*, 308–326.

Rothschild, N., and Morgan, M. (1987). Cohesion and control: Adolescents' relationships with parents as mediators of television. *Journal of Early Adolescence, 7*, 299–314.

St. Peters, M., Fitch, M., Huston, A. C., Wright, J. C., and Eakins, D. J. (1991). Television and families: What do young children watch with their parents? *Child Development, 62*, 1409–1423.

Salomon, G. (1977). Effects of encouraging Israeli mothers to co-observe *Sesame Street* with their five-year-olds. *Child Development, 48*, 1146–1151.

Sarlo, G., Jason, L. A., and Lonak, C. (1988). Parents' strategies for limiting children's television viewing. *Psychological Reports, 63*, 435–438.

Scheel, K., and Westefeld, J. (1999). Heavy metal music and adolescent suicidality: An empirical investigation. *Adolescence, 34*, 253–273.

Schramm, W. (1977). *Big media, little media.* Beverly Hills, CA: Sage.

Schramm, W., Lyle, J., and Parker, E. B. (1961). *Television in the lives of our children.* Stanford, CA: Stanford University Press.

Seelow, D. (1996). Listening to youth: Woodstock, music, America, and Kurt Cobain's suicide. *Child and Youth Care Forum, 25*, 49–53.

Senechal, M., LeFevre, J., Thomas, E., and Daley, K. (1998). Differential effects of home literacy experiences on the development of oral and written language. *Reading Research Quarterly, 33*, 96–116.

Shannon, P., and Fernie, D. (1985). Print and television: Children's use of the medium is the message. *Elementary School Journal, 85*, 663–672.

Siegel, D., and Hanson, R. (1992). Prescription for literacy: Providing critical educational experiences. *ERIC Digest.* ED340001. Bloomington, IN: ERIC Clearinghouse on Reading and Communication Skills.

Signorelli, N., and Morgan, M. (2001). Television and the family: The cultivation perspective. In J. Bryant and J. A. Bryant (Eds.), *Television and the American family* (pp. 333–354). Mahwah, NJ: Lawrence Erlbaum Associates.

Singer, D. G., and Singer, J. L. (Eds.). (2001). *Handbook of children and the media.* Thousand Oaks, CA: Sage.

Sneegas, J. E., and Plank, T. A. (1998). Gender differences in pre-adolescent reactance to age-categorized television advisory labels. *Journal of Broadcasting and Electronic Media, 42*, 423–434.

Snow, C. E., Burns, M. S., and Griffin, P. (Eds.). (1998). *Preventing reading difficulties in young children*. Washington, DC: National Academy Press.

Snow, C. E., and Tabors, P. (1996). Intergenerational transfer of literacy. In L. A. Benjamin and J. Lord (Eds.), *Family literacy: Directions in research and implications for practice*. Washington, DC: Office of Educational Research and Improvement.

Stoneman, Z., and Brody, G. H. (1982). An in-home investigation of maternal teaching strategies during *Sesame Street* and a popular situation comedy. *Journal of Applied Developmental Psychology, 3*, 275–284.

Stoneman, Z., and Brody, G. H. (1983). Family interactions during three programs: Contextualist observations. *Journal of Family Relations, 4*, 349–365.

Strouse, J., Buerkel-Rothfuss, N., and Long, E. (1995). Gender and family as moderators of the relationship between music video exposure and adolescent sexual permissiveness. *Adolescence, 30*, 505–521.

Sun, S., and Lull, J. (1986). The adolescent audience for music videos and why they watch. *Journal of Communication, 36*(1), 115–125.

Tangney, J. P. (1988). Aspects of the family and children's television viewing content preferences. *Child Development, 59*, 1070–1079.

Tangney, J. P., and Feshbach, S. (1988). Children's television-viewing frequency: Individual differences and demographic correlates. *Personality and Social Psychology Bulletin, 14*, 145–158.

Thompson, R., and Larson, R. (1995). Social context and the subjective experience of different types of rock music. *Journal of Youth and Adolescence, 24*, 731–744.

Truglio, R., Murphy, K., Oppenheimer, S., Huston, A., and Wright, J. (1996). Predictors of children's entertainment television viewing: Why are they tuning in? *Journal of Applied Developmental Psychology, 17*, 475–493.

Turow, J. (1999). *The Internet and the family: The view from parents. The view from the press* [Rep. Series No. 27, Online]. Philadelphia: The Annenberg Public Policy Center. Available: http://www.appcpenn.org

U.S. Department of Education. (1999). *Start early, finish strong: How to help every child become a reader* [Online]. Available: www.ed.gov/pubs/startearly/

Vygotsky, L. S. (1978). *Mind in society: The development of higher psychological processes*. Cambridge, MA: Harvard University Press.

Walsh, A., Laczniak, R., and Carlson, L. (1998). Mother's preferences for regulation children's television. *Journal of Advertising, 27*, 23–36.

Ward, S., Wackman, D., and Wartella, E. (1977). *Consumer socialization: An information processing approach to consumer learning*. Beverly Hills, CA: Sage.

Wartella, E., Heintz, K. E., Aidman, A. J., and Mazzarella, S. R. (1990). Television and beyond: Children's video media in one community. *Communication Research, 17*, 45–64.

Wartella, E., O'Keefe, B., and Scantlin, R. (2000). *Children and interactive media: A research compendium*. University of Texas, Austin. (Report prepared for the Markle Foundation.)

Wartella, E., and Reeves, R. (1985). Historical trends in research on children and the media: 1900–1960. *Journal of Communication, 35*(2), 118–133.

Watkins, B. A., Calvert, S., Huston-Stein, A., and Wright, J. C. (1980). Children's recall of television material: Effects of presentation mode and adult labeling. *Developmental Psychology, 16*, 672–674.

Watt, D., and White, J. M. (1999). Computers and the family life: A family development perspective. *Journal of Comparative Family Studies, 30*, 1–15.

Weaver, B., and Barbour, N. G. (1992). Mediation of children's televiewing. *Families in Society: The Journal of Contemporary Human Services, 73*, 236–242.

West, J., Hausken, E. G., and Chandler, K. (1992). *Home activities of 3- to 8-year-olds. Statistics in brief*. Washington, DC: National Center for Education Statistics. (ERIC Document Reproduction Service No. ED 341 513.)

Whitehurst, G. J., Arnold, D. S., Epstein, J. N., and Angell, A. L. (1994). A picture book reading intervention in day care and home for children from low-income families. *Developmental Psychology, 30*, 679–689.

Williams, T. M., and Boyes, M. C. (1986). Television-viewing patterns and use of other media. In T. M. Williams (Ed.), *The impact of television: A natural experiment in three communities* (pp. 215–264). Orlando, FL: Academic.

Wilson, B. J., Linz, D., and Randall, B. (1990). Applying social science research to film ratings: A shift from offensiveness to harmful effects. *Journal of Broadcasting and Electronic Media, 34*, 443–468.

Wilson, B. J., and Weiss, A. J. (1993). The effects of sibling coviewing on preschoolers' reactions to a suspenseful movie scene. *Communication Research, 20*, 214–248.

Wolfe, D. A., Mendes, M. G., and Factor, D. (1984). A parent-administered program to reduce children's television viewing. *Journal of Applied Behavior Analysis, 17*, 267–272.

Worthy, J., Moorman, M., and Turner, M. (1999). What Johnny likes to read is hard to find in school. *Reading Research Quarterly, 34*, 12–27.

Young, K. T., Davis, K., and Schoen, C. (1996). *The Commonwealth Fund Survey of Parents with Young Children*. New York: The Commonwealth Fund.

15

Choosing Childcare for Young Children

Alice Sterling Honig
Syracuse University

INTRODUCTION

On the first day of her new part-time job, the 22-year-old mother woke up early, leaving her three children, 4, 2, and 2 months, with her boyfriend of six months, who was unemployed. Soon after the woman left the infant awoke, fussy. She rejected a bottle and couldn't be soothed with holding or music. When the 2-year-old knocked over a pan, the boyfriend screamed at her and the baby cried louder. Enraged, the man shook the baby and threw her on a bed. When the mother returned four hours later, the infant was bluish and her breathing erratic. The baby was rushed to the hospital and died within hours. The emergency-room doctors said the baby showed signs of what is known as shaken-baby syndrome: Massive hemorrhaging in the eyes and brain, causing severe brain damage (Baurac, 1993, p. 8)

This scenario represents an extreme and tragic, and thankfully rare, outcome of the struggle many parents experience as they choose childcare with little time or knowledge for making satisfactory choices. Yet in 1996, 3.1 million children in the United States were reported abused, and helping families to choose high quality and supportive care might well decrease the extent of this social trauma.

Children are a family's most precious treasure. But the problems faced by parents in finding, affording, and keeping childcare providers are often quite stressful. In 1996, almost 40% of the American labor force had children younger than 18 years. Ten million preschoolers of employed mothers required care, and more than half were cared for outside the family. "As of 1997, fully 56% of the mothers of infants less than 1 year old were employed" (Vandell, Dadisman, and Gallagher, 2000, p. 91).

After-school care choices are often scarce for parents; 1 in 5 American children aged 6 to 12 is left alone after school, and 224 million school-age children need care during out-of-school time (Child Care Bureau, 1997). Only about 10% of employers offer childcare for school-age children during vacations (U.S. Department of the Treasury, 1998).

In a study of youth from welfare families, "those randomly selected to be *left out* of a quality after-school program were six times more likely to be convicted of a crime" (Newman, 2000, p. 1).

Workers with children exhibit higher levels of stress than workers without children, and childcare responsibilities have been shown to be one of the causes (U.S. Department of the Treasury, 1998). Nor can initial choice be assumed to guarantee decreased parental stress. The Families and Work Institute reported in 1998 that one fourth of employed parents with children under the age of 13 have experienced a problem with their childcare arrangements during the previous 3 months.

Increase in the proportion of single-parent families (from 1 in 10 in 1960 to 1 in 4 in 1995) has exacerbated the problem of finding childcare (Weinraub, Horvath, and Gringlas, in Vol. 3 of this *Handbook*). The National Conference of State Legislatures found that "lack of access to child care can be a serious impediment to work for single parents leaving welfare" (U.S. Department of the Treasury, 1998, p. 7). This issue became even more salient in 1996, when Congress passed the TANF (Temporary Assistance for Needy Families) to replace AFDC (Aid to Families with Dependent Children), which requires movement from welfare to work.

Three decades of childcare research have been fairly fruitful in elucidating components of high-quality childcare and in testifying to its positive child development outcomes (Clarke-Stewart and Fein, 1983; Honig, 1990, 2000; Lally, Mangione, and Honig, 1988; Lazar, Darlington, Murray, Royce, and Snipper, 1982; Zigler and Gordon, 1982) as well as lower public expenditures later in life, as the reported governmental savings for the Perry Preschool Project—about $25,000 for every $12,000 spent on high-quality preschool care.

But the knowledge base of childcare professionals is largely unavailable to assist families with nonparental care choices. Few parents know about the work of seminal child development stage theorists such as Erikson, Mahler, or Piaget. Nor have many parents read materials on the effectiveness of a "whole language curriculum" for preschoolers or the positive classroom ambience that is provided by "open education techniques," first promoted decades ago in Britain by the Lady Plowden Report. Nor do parents receive media catalogues advertising for sale videos to help them choose (Family and Consumer Sciences, 2000).

Research is scarce on the basis on which parents make a decision: "whether it is handed down from their parents, whether choice is made at a 'gut' level, or whether there is an informed choice" (Long, Wilson, Kutnick, and Telford, 1996, p. 51).

In addition, there is a gap between what theory and research teach are the most important factors comprising high-quality care and what facilities and personnel are actually available to families (Bradbard and Endsley, 1980; Kahn and Kamerman, 1987). Many families are unaware of the importance of their selection, not only for a child's later personal development but for more global impact on the child's growth into the larger society. Quality childcare has been promoted as a firm base for developing the kinds of citizens who will contribute later to social, economic, and community well-being (Booth, 1992; Campbell, 1993; Galinsky and Friedman, 1993; Hofferth and Phillips, 1987).

This chapter will look at the following aspects of the problem of choice: family vulnerabilities in relation to choosing childcare; quality of care as the prime issue in choice; the intersection of multiple structural and process variables in the world of childcare that influence parental choice; the importance of training for caregivers; the impact of family demographic and structural variables, such as cost and location of care; family cultural and belief factors, such as preference for a lay or religious facility or for kin care; child variables that affect choice, such as temperament, age, sex, and health; factors in facilities and caregiver qualities that influence parental choice, such as center size, caregiver/child ratio, staff stability, curricular philosophy, and staff-parent relationships; and political, business, and community supports for parental choice.

FAMILY VULNERABILITIES IN RELATION TO CHILDCARE CHOICE

Limited Income, Knowledge, and Time: Prescriptions for Poor Choice

A survey of childcare costs in the 50 states found that this is one of the biggest expenses for a family. Poverty and stress have been associated with less than adequate childcare choice. The 1997 "poverty threshold" was $16,036 for a family of four. Childcare costs can range from $4,000 to $10,000 per year per child, exceeding the cost of public college tuition (Shulman and Adams, 1998). Because care for infants is the most expensive (Pungello and Kurtz-Costes, 1999), a poor family with an infant and toddler could be in the grotesque position of choosing center care whose cost is more than their annual salary.

In choosing childcare, even parents with valuable insights into the importance of caregiver warmth and provision of language experiences often have limited knowledge of the particular child development qualifications of personnel in facilities available or under consideration. Sometimes families are under stringent time deadlines in finding a facility prior to return to employment or when their caregiver suddenly is no longer available. These time deadliness will be somewhat mitigated as a result of the Family and Medical Leave Act, which took effect in August 1993. This Federal law guarantees workers an additional 12 weeks of unpaid leave for parental childcare. Employers are required to pay health care premiums during the leave and keep a job available. However, 40% of companies (with under 50 employees) do not fall under the law's guidelines, and their employees still have little time to locate satisfactory care.

Compounding deadline and choice problems is the fact that, in the United States, community childcare for children generally ranges from poor to fair (Keyserling, 1972). For the National Child Care Staffing (NCCS) study, quality ratings were each anchored on a 7-point scale by descriptors from inadequate to excellent care (Whitebook, Howes, and Phillips, 1989). Across five major sites, a below-average overall quality of care was recorded for infants by the Infant/Toddler Environment Rating Scale (ITERS), and for preschoolers by the Early Childhood Environment Rating Scale (ECERS). In a follow-up study, only 8% of care for infants was rated adequate (Cost, Quality, and Outcomes Team, 1995).

The critical problems of availability, access to, and affordability of high-quality care and the importance of educating parents to choose such care are highlighted by recent accounts of the growing numbers of families where children are vulnerable to nonoptimal developmental outcomes (Center for the Study of Social Policy, 1993, p. 13):

> Every year this country produces millions of vulnerable new families. In 1990 there were 1.7 million families started with the birth of a new baby. Forty-five percent started out at a disadvantage for one of more of the following reasons: The mother in some of these new families had not finished high school when she had her first baby; the mother and father of the baby were not married at the time of the child's birth; or the mother was a teenager when her first baby was born, thus still a child herself.

These problems are more severe in some states and for single parent families in some ethnic groups (Garcia Coll and Pachter, in Vol. 4 of this *Handbook*). The percent of all births to single teens varies from 4.7% in Utah, for example, to nearly 16% in Mississippi (Center for the Study of Social Policy, 1993). The percent of children reared in single-parent families ranges from 12.4% in North Dakota to 32.6% in Alabama. The U.S. Department of Commerce Census Bureau report in the summer of 1993 noted that births to single women (18 to 44 years) rose from 15% in 1982 to 24% in 1992. Out-of-wedlock births to European Americans, Latin Americans, and African Americans were 17%, 27%, and 67% respectively. Teen pregnancies have increased among the three groups. The report showed that "94% of African-American teens giving birth were unmarried, compared to 60% of Hispanic and 56% of white teen-age mothers" (Missing Fathers, 1993, p. A-12). Optimal childcare choices for teen parents are crucial, because they need childcare in order to complete their education and their infants often have poorer developmental outcomes (Weinraub, Horvath, and Gringlas, in Vol. 3 of this *Handbook*).

Quality of Care: The Prime Issue in Childcare Choice

"Poor quality care, more than any single type of program or arrangement, threatens children's development, especially children from poor and minority families" (Hayes, Palmer, and Zaslow, 1990,

p. 290). And poorer, more-stressed families tend to choose poor-quality care. Canadian families with lower economic and educational resources chose family daycare of poorer quality than higher socio-economic status (SES) families (Goelman and Pence, 1990). Provider characteristics in poor-quality facilities were in turn related to children's poorer performance on measures of early language and literacy. Phillips, McCartney, and Scarr (1987) reported that children from poorer quality day-care were less considerate and less sociable. The National Day Care Study project noted that preschoolers who had better trained teachers were more cooperative with adults, more persistent on tasks assigned, and achieved higher scores on a preschool inventory (Ruopp, Travers, Glantz, and Coelen, 1979). When compared to children from poorer quality daycare, middle-SES 4-year-old children in high-quality care engaged in more friendly and socially competent peer interactions and fewer unfriendly peer interactions in play triads even when possible effects of family social class were ruled out (Vandell, Henderson, and Wilson, 1988). Children in poor-quality centers engaged in fewer positive interactions with adults and in more aimless wandering. These differences showed significant continuity. Children who had spent more time in positive interactions with adults in high-quality daycare at 4 years were rated as more cooperative with adults, more empathic, more socially competent in negotiating conflicts with peers, and more accepted by peers at 8 years.

Quality of childcare has been found the single most important variable associated with positive developmental outcomes for children (Clarke-Stewart and Allhusen, in Vol. 3 of this *Handbook*; Phillips and Howes, 1989). In a meta-analysis of 17 early intervention programs with rigorous experimental designs, Bryant and Ramey (1987) concluded that, when program benefits were measured by IQ scores, the amount and breadth of caregiver contact with a child (an index of quality) was a major determinant of positive intellectual outcomes. In Bermuda, the quality of center care was as predictive of preschoolers' language skills as family background variables (McCartney, 1984; McCartney, Scarr, Phillips, Grajek, and Schwartz, 1982). Disadvantaged children attending government-supported facilities of high overall quality (as measured by the ECERS scale), when compared with more advantaged children attending a variety of childcare facilities, achieved higher scores on intellectual and language development and on task orientation, sociability, and consi-deration for others. The researchers noted that their findings about the importance of high-quality care are "especially convincing because the comparison group consists of children of higher SES" (McCartney, Scarr, Phillips, and Grajek, 1985, p. 251).

The National Household Education Survey has highlighted the importance of looking at parental choices for before- and after-school care. About 61% of children whose mothers work 35 or more hours per week and less than one third of children whose mothers work part time receive after-school care on a weekly basis (Brimhall and Reaney, 1999). Thus, choice of program becomes vital especially for kindergartners through third grade (Sepannen et al., 1993). When caregivers were positive, then first-grade boys were rated as having few internalizing and externalizing emotional problems (Pierce, Hamm, and Vandell, 1999).

TRANSACTIONAL IMPACTS OF PARENT CHOICE OF DAYCARE

Parental choice and quality care have mutual transactional effects. Support offered to families by a high-quality facility works to decrease parental stress, improve mother–child relationships, increase stability of care and parent satisfaction, and thus contributes to the enhanced well-being of children attending such a facility. Some parents fear that if they search for a quality facility, prices are bound to be higher. Yet a study of prices for childcare in Georgia found that tougher standards for staff training and for adult-child ratios "did not drive fees significantly higher" (SECA, 1993, p. 5).

High-quality childcare has proved particularly effective as a support for the development of children born into poor families or families at risk. The Syracuse Family Development Research Program (FDRP) provided home visitation to poor, single teenage parents from pregnancy onward for 5 years and high-quality childcare in the Children's Center from 6 months after birth (Honig, 1999). Ten years later, juvenile delinquency rates for FDRP adolescents were markedly lower for 65 program teens compared with 54 controls (6% versus 22%). Moreover, delinquencies among control youngsters were more severe, and their recidivism rates were higher in comparison with program youngsters. Girls (but not boys) who had attended the Children's Center daycare program for the first 5 years of life were performing better academically in comparison with control girls and were rated more positively by their teachers. Program graduates reported that they liked more of their personality and physical attributes, such as their sense of humor and their appearance (Lally et al., 1988).

Low-SES infants born to tenth-grade education, single teenage mothers, and placed at about 3 months of age into the nurturing and intellectually stimulating North Carolina Abecedarian daycare program differed significantly in IQ at 36 months from control infants reared at home and provided with free formula and pediatric services (Ramey and Gowen, 1990). Mothers of the control infants were less interactive with their babies as they grew. IQ scores of the program infants were normal ($M = 98.1$) at 36 months in comparison with the control infants ($M = 84.7$). In the daycare group, even fetally malnourished infants scored about average ($M = 96.4$). In contrast, fetally malnourished infants in the control group were already performing in the retarded range ($M = 70.6$) by 36 months, despite program provision of free pediatric care and nutritional supplements from birth onward. These enormous cognitive disparities were not solely due to the high quality of daycare, but also surely partly attributable to the quality of mother–infant interaction in these single-parent low-SES families. Of critical importance were the childcare services of the center and the role models that the caregivers provided. Longitudinal results for the program children grown to adulthood reveal that program graduates tend to have higher reading and mathematics achievement scores through age 21 and have their first child about a year later than the control group (19.1 vs. 17.7 years old). The graduates from this high-quality program were more likely than controls (35% vs. 14%) to attend a 4-year college (Ramey, and Ramey, 1999).

The consequences of parental choice are both direct and indirect. Children are directly influenced by the quality care they receive. In turn, the quality of parental relationships with the child is influenced by center support for the family and positive adult role models provided. Both processes enhance child outcomes. Social workers and referral services need to provide parents with such research "success stories" in order to motivate and support parents, particularly those in stressful or disadvantaged life situations, to seek for and choose high quality care.

MULTIPLE INTERSECTING FACTORS IN CHILDCARE CHOICE

Family choices for childcare depend on dozens of factors, many of which are inextricably clustered and confounded in parental decision making. Aspects of childcare that strongly influence parental choice are often measured by structural and demographic variables, which characterize parents and families as well as providers and facilities. *Structural family variables* include geographical residence location (such as urban, suburban, rural, and public housing in inner city), family configuration (single parent, gay parents, and live-in or nearby grandparents available for childcare), ethnicity and sex of child, and disposable family income available to purchase high-quality care. Some variables depend on family beliefs, values, preferences, and culture. *Facility variables* include child/caregiver ratios for children of different ages, number of hours per day that service is provided, time of day during which care is available, stability of personnel, provision for sliding fee scales, group size for children of different ages, single-age groups or multiage grouping, and availability of outdoor safe play space. *Process or interaction variables* pertain both to parents and to facilities. These variables include parental warmth and attention to child, closeness and trust between parents and providers, and quality of caregiver interactions with children. Process variables often require more qualitative or global measurement, whereas structural variables are often easier to assess through counting (as in the caregiver-to-child ratio) or measuring (as in the number of square feet of space per child available in a facility or percent of family budget available for fee-based care). Parent–caregiver relationships comprise a domain where structural specifics, such as the number of parent/caregiver contacts per month, can be counted. *Process variables* such as caregiver warmth, empathy, and affectionate interactions are strongly related to the quality of care provided for children.

The cost and mechanics of carrying out measurements of program quality may be prohibitive. Measurement systems are voluntary, and compliance is not mandated by states or the federal government. Self-study in centers to attain accreditation by the National Academy of Early Childhood Programs of the National Association for the Education of Young Children (NAEYC) involves staff, parents, and a professional validator. Programs for children from birth through 8 years that meet the criteria are awarded a certificate of recognition that is valid for 3 years. In 1987, the National Black Child Development Institute established guidelines suggesting ways in which a productive, effective, and positive learning environment for African American 4-year-old children could be created in early childhood education programs in the public schools. The use of inexpensive checklists, such as the ABC Adult Behaviors in Caregiving checklists for teachers of infants, toddlers, and preschoolers permits caregivers and directors to monitor their own interactions in the classroom with minimal training in use of the checklists (Honig and Lally, 1981).

TRAINING PROVIDERS: THE SECRET OF QUALITY CARE

Researches reveal how tightly linked high-quality care is to specific training in child development (Fosburg, 1981; Howes, 1983; Kontos and Wilcox-Herzog, 2001; Ruopp et al., 1979; Travers, Goodson, Singer, and Connell, 1979). The NCCS study compared teachers with 15 or more hours of specialized in-service training with those (over three fourths of the sample) who had fewer than 15 hours. Teachers with more hours of annual in-service training engaged in "more *appropriate caregiving*, were more *sensitive*, *less harsh*, and *less detached*" (Whitebook et al., 1989, p. 46).

Formal education contributes modestly to caregiver effectiveness. Berk (1985) reported that, in contrast to high-school-educated caregivers, those with at least 2 years of college had more communications with children in centers. One study analyzed the relative importance of (1) caregiver formal education, (2) caregiver number of courses in child development, and (3) number of years of caregiver experience (Honig and Hirallal, 1998). In 25 centers, training in early childhood appeared overwhelmingly important in predicting the quality of teacher facilitation of preschool children's concept and language development and their positive social skills. Caregiver college education and more years of experience also helped to explain teacher promotion of language development. These center-based data support the National Day Care Home Study findings on family day care, where training had positive, strong effects on caregiver teaching, helping, and dramatic play (Fosburg, 1981).

The major policy variables—group size, caregiver/child ratio, and caregiver qualifications—have been dubbed the "iron triangle" in the NDCS study (Ruopp et al., 1979) because they have had "the most consistent and pervasive effects on teacher and child behavior in child care centers and on children's gains on cognitive tests" (Hayes et al., 1990, p. 87). Table 15.1 specifies five variable domains with a significant impact on parental choice and deserving increased parental and research attention: family structural and demographic variables; family beliefs and cultural variables; child factors; provider and facility factors; and political, community, and business supports for parental choice. The following sections address these variables, together with findings that shed light on their importance and relative influence. Research facts reflect effects of clusters of interrelated as well as single variables.

TABLE 15.1
Variables Affecting Family Choice of Childcare

---

(1) Family Demographic and Structural Variables
  - Cost of care in relation to family disposable income
  - Choosing type of setting or mode of care
  - Family geography as a determinant of childcare choice

(2) Family Beliefs and Cultural Variables
  - Parental beliefs and values
  - Culture and faith preferences for auspices of care
  - Family stress: a determinant of child care choice

(3) Child Variables
  - Child temperament
  - Age of child
  - Number of children needing care
  - Sex of child
  - Health of child

(4) Facility and Caregiver Factors
  - Size of facility and group size
  - Caregiver/child ratios
  - Time during which the facility operates
  - Curriculum issues: language emphasis
  - Parent–provider relationships
  - Usefulness of a parent handbook of rules and regulations
  - Caregiver characteristics: reliability, stability, and warmth
  - Working conditions for providers
  - The daycare provider's family

(5) Political, Business, and Community Supports for Parental Choice
  - Legislation and regulatory agencies
  - Businesses and unions: supports for family childcare choice
  - Accreditation and referral agencies

FAMILY DEMOGRAPHIC AND STRUCTURAL VARIABLES

Even with knowledge of factors affecting outcomes for their children, many families choose care primarily under pressure of compelling pragmatic considerations, such as availability of public transportation to a care setting in a family without a car, or the convenience of a neighbor right next door to baby-sit rather than a licensed site several blocks away that provides quality group care at higher fees (see Table 15.1, Section 1). "The arrangement, location, availability, and hours (measures of the convenience of the available care) were cited by 20% of respondents in the National Child Care Survey as the major reasons for having chosen the current arrangement, and another 9% indicated cost as the major reason" (Prosser and McGroder, 1992, p. 49).

Cost of Care in Relation to Family Disposable Income

Disposable income that affords more latitude in choosing childcare is not available to many families. For some parents, affordability of care will be the primary consideration that overrides all others in choosing care (Fuller and Liang, 1993). Research findings of the National Child Care Survey and the Profiles of Child Care Setting Study suggest that when they pay for care, low-income families spend 22% to 25% of their budgets, which represents a larger share for them compared with higher income families (Hofferth, 1992). For low-SES families, childcare costs become an acute problem. For example, in Santa Clara County, California, over one third of parents on the county's waiting list for childcare assistance earn less than $10,100 annually. Yet "only one in ten children who need child care assistance currently receive subsidies to help with the cost of care" (Blank, 1999, p. 3).

Where the optimal development of young children is in jeopardy due to stringent economic need, communities must galvanize means to support a breadth of choices that will guarantee quality care regardless of family economic circumstances.

The cost of care varies impressively across modes of care and SES. Escalations in cost of care can be an acute factor even for middle-SES families. One center in New York City charged well over $1,000 per month for infant care for upper-middle-SES families and tried to pay good wages to staff. Still, that center was forced to close when insurance costs quadrupled within a few years and rent costs rose dramatically. In contrast to such fees, neighbors in some urban low-SES communities may be charging each family well under $100 per week to "baby-sit" several infants full-time. Differences in the amount paid for care reported in the NLSY study suggest that care by relatives was as low as $30 per week, and family daycare cost close to $40 per week (Hofferth and Phillips, 1987).

In general, the price of childcare declines with increasing age of child. Local labor market conditions affect the costs of care. So do state regulations for childcare ratios. Where parents have the luxury of a wide choice of care at varying prices and with short waiting lists as well as assurances of quality of staff, cost may not be as acute a factor. Surprisingly, no association exists between what parents pay and the quality of care their children receive (Waite, Leibowitz, and Witsberger, 1991). On the other hand, parent dissatisfaction with childcare increases instability of arrangements for children (Endsley and Bradbard, 1987). Mothers receiving AFDC funds reported that convenient hours were very important to their decision making (Wolf and Sonenstein, 1990).

For some low-income families, subsidies will be available for family daycare or center group care. Passage of the Family Support Act of 1988 clarified obligations of welfare recipients to undertake activities toward increasing their self-sufficiency. Mothers receiving AFDC (Aid to Families with Dependent Children) participate in education or job training programs under the Job Opportunities and Basic Skills Training (JOB) program if their youngest child is age 3 or older (although states may lower this age to 1 year). The Congressional law authorizing supplemental earned income tax credit (EITC) for families with young children increases the amount of cash available to families but has no direct relation to support for childcare (the EITC percentage of earned income allowable for two or more children was pegged at 15% for 1994). For families whose earned income is under $10,000 annually, the Dependent Care Tax Credit currently authorizes a maximum tax credit of 30% for children who are under 13 years of age or mentally or physically unable to care for themselves. The EITC is applied after the dependent care tax credit has been applied. The maximum limits on allowable costs are $2,400 for one child and $4,800 for two. Thus the maximum benefit is 30% of each sum, or $720 for one child and $1,400 for two (Sugarman, 1991). Therefore, given the current costs of high-quality childcare, current subsidies for families in poverty who need childcare severely limit affordable parental choices. After comparing prices and quality of care in relation to family income, Hofferth and Wissoker (1992) noted that the price of childcare is a critical variable in care choice. Mothers who earn more per hour and families with higher incomes are more likely to select center care.

Choosing Type of Setting or Mode of Care

Parents need to choose a mode of care (Duncan and Hill, 1977). The cost of in-home nanny or baby-sitter care has risen dramatically over the past decade. Some high schools offer courses for youngsters to learn skills and safety tips required of a competent sitter, and there are also far more written materials to help parents choose a baby-sitter wisely. For example, parents need to provide house rules and guidelines for a sitter before leaving their home in order to prevent dangerous situations and to head off potential conflict between the sitter and the children. Guidelines should include lists of emergency telephone numbers, location of flashlights, thermostats, circuit breakers, and water shutoffs as well as information about door and window locks. In-home caregivers preferably should take safety courses, such as those offered by the American Red Cross.

Half-day fee-based nursery school in a university facility may not meet the needs of an employed single, low-income parent. Full-day publicly supported kindergartens may be the most useful economic support for some families as well as an educational booster for their young children. During World War II, publicly supported day nurseries that even provided suppers for employed mothers at pickup time provided a vital support for employed mothers participating in the war effort (Honig, 1992).

Center-based care increased in the 1990s. In 1975 about 12% of children needing care were in group daycare centers (Honig, 1984). In 1990, 26% of preschool children whose mothers were employed were in center-based programs, 19% were in family daycare, and just 4% were primarily cared for at home by a nonrelative. Significantly, of all preschool children with employed mothers, half were primarily cared for either exclusively by their own parents (30%) or by relatives (18%) (Hofferth, 1992). Some parents prefer a center program with a particular philosophy, such as a Montessori program, or a program that emphasizes science and math skills, or one that emphasizes whole language or free play or academics (Honig, 1979).

In-home care by a relative, such as father or grandmother, is a strong choice of many families (Smith and Drew, in Vol. 3 of this *Handbook*). Less preferred is out-of-home relative care, and far more expensive is in-home nanny care. Supports for childcare, such as offers of free babysitting by grandparents or other relatives are not always a clear positive factor, despite economic savings and greater feelings of parental security. When a family chooses care by relatives, emotional or time-demanding reciprocal social obligations may increase stress on the family, even though the economic costs or time convenience may be a plus factor in that choice. In addition, clinical cases (such as the rape of a 3-month-old infant while left in the care of her grandmother by a teen mother away for the weekend) suggest that some trust in relative care may be misplaced.

Family Geography as a Determinant of Childcare Choice

The demographics of childcare choice differ significantly depending on the state and community, whether rural or urban, for example, as well as what the program needs of parents are.

Geographic variations in cost of care are considerable. "Fees charged for care vary widely within and across all types of care and geographic regions. In some areas (e.g., Seattle), family day care is considerably less expensive than center-based care for infants and toddlers. However, in other areas (e.g., Boston and Denver), family day care may be similar in price" (Hayes et al., 1990, p. 162). The range of options for childcare varies widely by region. Parents in rural areas may have far fewer trained personnel available whether for family daycare or center care. Choosing appropriate or needed childcare may be quite different depending on family needs and resources (Hayes and Kamerman, 1983; Kivikink and Schell, 1987). The family receiving AFDC funds and free access to a quality Head Start program part time for their preschooler, or the middle-SES two-parent family with one major breadwinner with a high-quality half-day university nursery school available nearby at modest cost, differ (in need and resources available) from the dual-career or employed single-parent family, where the desperate search for childcare may reach crisis proportions after an infant is born and the employed adult must return to the job or lose employment.

FAMILY BELIEFS AND CULTURAL VARIABLES AFFECT CHOICE

Parental Beliefs and Values

Parental beliefs, preferences, values, ethnicity, and faith communities influence the search for and satisfaction with childcare (see Table 15.1, Section 2). Analysis of the National Household Education Survey (which controlled for parental education and household income) of 4,380 parents of 3- and 4-year old children revealed that parents who chose nonparental care engaged in more academic types of activities (such as reading to children), and their children watched less television than did parents who chose to rear children in parent-only care (Kimmerly, 1998). How the home functioned as a learning environment was related to some extent to the type of child care choice that parents made. Such data make the case that parent education and knowledge about child development, not only about what facilities are available in a community, are critical factors for informed choice.

Culture also influences parental choice. Parents from different cultural backgrounds differ in their implicit beliefs and theories about child development, what tasks young children need to master, and what children need to grow well (Bornstein, 1991). Parental beliefs about appropriate care and education for young children guide their care choices and impact on child school outcomes (Klysz, 1995; Okagaki and Sternberg, 1993). When parents chose less academic preschools for their children, they believed their children needed to learn more independence and initiative rather than academics; parental beliefs were congruent with choice of care facility (Stipek, Milburn, Clements, and Daniels, 1992).

A study of low-income Mexican American, Chinese American, and European American mothers found that all preferred to have their 3-year-old children cared for in their own homes by spouses, relatives, neighbors, or friends (Becerra, 1992). However, when long-term arrangements were necessary, then European American and Chinese American parents preferred formal care, whereas Mexican-American families preferred informal care.

Preferences of urban Zimbabwean mothers in choosing preschools differed by income level. Low-income mothers most frequently reported looking for good food (or a balanced diet), caring teachers, a facility with good physical structure and adequate space, and help in preparing the child for school. Moderate-income mothers mentioned the facility and its convenience of location and child school preparation. The highest income mothers cited hygiene, good food, qualified and loving teachers, and an adequate facility. Regardless of whether their child attended a preschool, 63% of the women felt that a female servant would be their primary choice, but the other respondents preferred sisters, grandmothers, and aunts as a childcare option (Johnson, Dyanda-Marira, and Davimbo, 1997).

Russian mothers, when questioned about childrearing goals most important in influencing their choices, cited conformity to rules, concern with spoiling children, and belief in adult control. These beliefs were stronger for less-educated mothers. More educated mothers were more likely to believe in the importance of talking to infants. It takes time for more democratic goals for childrearing to emerge after a culture has lived for a long period under a totalitarian regime (Ispa, 1995).

Ethnicity is another factor in choice of type of care. Latino parents have been found more likely to select informal child care rather than center-based or preschool arrangements, and they are less likely than European American parents to choose any form of out-of-home care (Fuller et al., 1996). Compared with 75% of African American families and 69% of European American families, only 59% of Latin American families with children age 3 to 5 years choose some form of nonparental care (West, Hausken, and Collins, 1993). African American parents are more supportive of formal centers than other ethnic groups (Mason and Kuhlthau, 1989). They may have more access to subsidized preschools, including Head Start centers (Fuller et al., 1996).

Parents, regardless of ethnicity, may prefer certain types of care more than others. And types of care may differ markedly from maternal care in some locales. Balleyguier (1990) observed that in French daycare centers, time schedules were far more rigid than at home, so that it was frequent "to see a quiet and submissive child in the daycare center become very demanding as soon as the mother arrives" (p. 55). Parents who are aware of such differences in demands for obedience or maturity in the childcare facility can be alerted to possible acting out in emotional release once the child is back in the secure environment of the home. On the other hand, based on such knowledge of children's reactions, parents may decide to search for a facility more respectful of the emotional needs of the very young child.

Care providers have been interviewed regarding their theories about parental choices. Atkinson (1991) surveyed regulated family daycare providers via open-ended questions as to why they thought parents had chosen their facility. Providers responded with the following characteristics: a family-like setting and personal relationship (94% had children of their own), fewer children served than in a center (from 2 to 6 children), lower cost of childcare, greater flexibility of hours, personal characteristics of the provider, and quality of care offered. The providers rated themselves highest in meeting parents' needs by virtue of the reliability and stability of care they provided, their openness for parents to visit, and the longer hours and greater number of days their facility was available to parents. Providers served children from early infancy through third grade, although toddlers comprised the largest age grouping. A wide age range better suits some families' needs for care for several siblings. Family daycare providers identified themselves as professionals, small business owners, teachers, and substitute parents and babysitters. They considered that their experience and liking children were more important than formal training. Reasons for choice of family daycare given by the mothers in this study confirmed the accuracy of providers' estimates. Mothers stated that they wanted personal relationships in a small group with a family atmosphere and in a convenient and low-cost setting. What was interesting was that neither group considered family daycare choice important as an opportunity for parents to meet other parents, to receive help in parenting, or to participate in family daycare activities.

Parents of both groups considered informal training for caregivers as appropriate. Thus, a concerted political effort to obtain more state and federal economic support for professional caregiver training will have to take into account parent and provider satisfaction with informal training and devise ways to accommodate such perceptions. It appears that "baby-sitting" as a caregiver role is acceptable to many families. Indeed, parents overestimate the quality of their children's programs and are "unaware that they are not obtaining high quality with respect to those aspects of quality that they value most highly" (Cryer and Burchinal, 1997, p. 54). These researchers, having contrasted parent ratings of quality of care with those of trained observers, commented that "the concept of parents as consumers who can make informed choices about child care is controversial" (p. 35).

More support for video and written materials directed at low-literacy, low-income families (see, e.g., Honig, 1982, 1996; Honig and Brophy, 1996) is surely needed to increase parent awareness of what constitutes excellence in caregiving interactions. Currently there is a rich supply of such materials written for middle-income, high-literacy parents. Convincing families that professional expertise is strongly related to specific child development training may be a difficult psychological task for social agency and support personnel offering advice on childcare choices to families. Helping parents to monitor ongoing program quality may also be a difficult task, although crucial considering the numbers of facilities that offer low-quality programs (Kisker and Maynard, 1991; Phillipsen, Cryer, and Howes, 1995).

Outreach strategies to increase a school's partnership with parents so that they become more involved in the quality of their children's education and after-school care include early fall mailings, school–parent compacts, home visits, and open houses (Office of Educational Research and Improvement, 2000). The Center for Early Childhood Leadership reports that only 1 in 4 directors of childcare said they were competent in using the Internet, although about two thirds of the directors reported having a computer modem (see the Center for Early Childhood Leadership Web site at http://www.nl.edu/cecl). Computer reach-out to families may, in the future, prove to be good way to inform families about optimizing their choices for care. From 1997, when less than 10% of directors reported using e-mail, nearly half (47%) now report using e-mail "on a daily basis" (Report on Preschool Programs, 2000, p. 165).

Cultural/Faith Preferences for Auspices of Care

Some families choose a facility because it is under particular religious or cultural auspices or includes children of a particular ethnic origin or, conversely, because a particular facility celebrates diversity in a multicultural program. Data suggest that choice of facilities under specific religious auspices may increase rates of prosocial interactions of girls but not boys with peers in comparison with centers under lay auspices (Honig, Douthit, Lee, and Dingler, 1992).

Family Stress: A Determinant of Childcare Choice

Family stress affects choice of quality of childcare. Families described as "restrictive and stressed" chose less adequate care than families described as "nurturing and supportive" (Howes and Stewart, 1987).

Stress affects the family even when the stress is not directly due to structural or process factors such as job loss or spousal abuse. Children's unique needs may increase stress. Focus on the special needs of each individual child may not be primary when families are stressed and struggling to find childcare. Indeed, some parents need supportive help to gain insights into how distressed infants and toddlers can become when "casual and unfeeling plans for baby-sitting" are made (Fraiberg, 1988, p. 112–113):

> When she took part-time work at one point, Mrs. March made hasty and ill-thought-out sitting arrangements for Mary and then was surprised, as was Mr. March, to find that Mary was sometimes "cranky" and "spoiled" and "mean". [The therapist] tried in all tactful ways to help the Marches think about the meaning to Mary of her love for mother and her temporary loss of mother during the day. She met a blank wall. Both parents had known shifting and casual relationships with parents and parent substitutes from their earliest years. The meaning of separation and loss was buried in memory.... One morning... Mary had just lost one sitter and started with another. Mrs. Adelson [the therapist] wondered out loud what this might mean to Mary. Yesterday she had been left, unexpectedly, in a totally new place with a strange woman. She felt alone and frightened without her mother, and did not know what was going to happen.... She was only a baby, with no words to express her serious problem. Somehow, we would have a find a way to understand and to help her with her fears and worries.

CHILD VARIABLES

Children differ in their characteristics and needs, and many families searching for care are often sensitive to these individual differences as well as to developmental needs of children at different stages (see Table 15.1, Section 3).

Child Temperament

One of the sensitive personal characteristics of their child that parents need to consider in choosing childcare is temperament (Putnam, Sanson, and Rothbart, in Vol. 1 of this *Handbook*). Longitudinal research by Thomas, Chess, and Birch revealed marked differences in child temperament styles. Some children are adaptable, easy to socialize, positive in mood, approach the new (whether a caregiver or a first taste of spinach) with curiosity and zest. Others are suspicious, slow to warm up to new people or experiences, and low in activity level. Some are triggery and strongly reactive in their interactions, more prone to express distress intensely, and less likely to have predictable rhythms of feeding, eliminating, or sleeping. Children with more feisty temperaments or those with specific behavioral difficulties such as attention deficit disorder may be particularly in need of highly trained, responsive caregivers who tune into their temperament style with sensitivity and support. Family daycare with few other children in the facility may then be the mode of choice (Baker, 1993). Center caregivers without special training in dealing with inappropriate aggression in stressed children sometimes "re-create" the disapproving negative interactions with which the child is already only too familiar (Wittmer and Honig, 1990).

Age of Child

Age of child will often be a decisive factor in choice of care personnel for many families. Parental considerations in their search for a caregiver for a newborn infant or a toddler may well differ from their assessment of factors in choosing care for a 4-year-old child. Timing of infant entry into care is an important variable that intersects with center quality (Howes and Rubenstein, 1985). Choice of mode of care is most problematical for parents of infants because infants in full-time nonparental care prior to 12 months have been found to be at slightly higher risk of forming insecure attachments with mothers, regardless of mode of care (Belsky, 1988, 1990).

Number of Children Needing Care

The number of children needing care in a family, and how close they are in age to one another, influence parental choice. Parents with three small preschool children may choose an in-home sitter rather than incurring the expense of center care for all three youngsters. The intersection of variables and available options sometimes makes it difficult for families to make an optimal child care choice, and they may end up with an in-home sitter who has no training in child development.

Sex of a Child

The sex of a child is a variable often neglected in considering parental options for childcare, and yet male children may be more vulnerable to poor childcare choices than females (Leaper, in Vol. 1 of this *Handbook*). Boys who began daycare in their first year of life had poorer attention spans and general abilities than did boys in parental care, but the opposite was true for girls (Robinson and Corley, 1989). Honig and Park (1993) found that although boys were rated by daycare teachers on the Preschool Behavior Questionnaire as significantly more aggressive than girls, no differences in ratings of their aggressiveness or affiliativeness could be attributed to whether the preschoolers had entered full-time daycare in either earlier or later infancy or not until after 36 months. Data from the 1986 National Longitudinal Survey of Work Experience of Youth revealed that 3- to 4-year-old boys had lower cognitive scores if their mothers had been employed full-time during the child's first year of life (Blau and Grossberg, 1990). The ongoing longitudinal NICHD national study of parental choices for care from birth onward and their outcomes reveals that at 15 months male infants received less responsive care than females both in centers and in childcare homes (NICHD Early Child Care Research Network, 1997).

A significantly higher proportion of insecure attachments of male babies (but not females) at 12 months to fathers has been reported in families where mothers are employed and infants are in nonparental care (Chase-Lansdale and Owen, 1987). Parents of infants may need special skills to assist them in choosing childcare where caregivers frequently engage in tender, responsive interactions that increase babies' chances for secure attachment to adult caregivers (Honig, 2001).

Child Health

One salient pragmatic factor that increases family concern in seeking care is the physical health of children as affected both by individual child status and by the increasing risks of infection for infants in group care. Infancy group care, formerly in very short supply in many communities, is currently much more available. Yet many infants have experienced increased frequency of respiratory ailments in group care (Aronson, 1991). Health problems can lead to great distress for families when children are excluded from a center because of continued illness and the parent is threatened with job loss if she or he stays home any further days, as in the following case this author encountered:

> A computer analyst came for a clinical consultation in a quandary. Her infant in center care for the past half-year had suffered innumerable bouts of otitis media. Threatened with job loss for taking too much time off to care for her constantly sick baby, the mother felt stressed, torn between her personal needs, family financial needs, and the infant's needs. "Must I leave my job?", she asked tearfully.

In such cases parents may search for baby-sitters, family daycare, or nanny care, even when center care is more readily available. It is often difficult to establish the optimal mesh between family needs and circumstances and the care that would be optimal for the child.

There are few data on how parents choose care for children with handicapping conditions (Hodapp, in Vol. 1 of this *Handbook*). The cost of caring for children with disabilities varies significantly depending on the degree of disability and public support for programs. Sometimes a toddler enrolled in a program for special needs youngsters may have to be bused for more than 1 hour to a program that provides the quality of skilled caregiving that the parents desire. Many parents with young disabled children may choose to forego employment if faced with inadequate choices for childcare. Head Start requires local programs to set aside 10% of spaces for children with disabilities. Federal funds are available to support a variety of childcare services, such as transportation, for children with disabilities. But the dearth of services for the very young is particularly acute, because the Education for the Handicapped Act (P.L. 99-142 and its amendment, P.L. 99-457) leaves decisions concerning service provision of childcare for handicapped infants and toddlers up to each state. The primary intent of the amendments is to provide federal funds to coordinate services through an individualized family service plan (IFSP), which includes identification of family strengths and needs. Thus, parents may identify childcare as a necessary component of their IFSP as a complement to intervention services that are already being provided. States also receive Chapter 1 funds (P.L. 89-313) to educate institutionalized children (including preschool-age children) with disabilities.

As the number of infants and toddlers with AIDS rises, families may face more difficulties in finding childcare choices that meet all the health needs of their children. In the past decade there has been a notable increase in public awareness of the need for, and civic implementation of, collaborative agency efforts to provide appropriate services for integrating atypical with typical infants and young children.

CAREGIVER AND FACILITY FACTORS

Size of Facility and Group Size

If parents are to make optimal choices for their children, they will need to become more aware of factors in a particular facility under consideration that may affect how well their youngster does in that environment (see Table 15.1, Section 4). Group size varies dramatically in childcare. In the National Day Care Study, preschoolers who were in smaller classes attained higher scores on kindergarten and first-grade readiness tests (Ruopp et al., 1979). Larger groups in family daycare are associated with less-positive interaction patterns (Fosburg, 1981). Centers serving over 100 children tend to be more authoritarian than smaller centers, with greater regimentation and lack of personalized interactions between teacher and child (Prescott, 1973). In smaller centers, serving 30 to 60 children, caregivers were more often rated as sensitive and children as enthusiastically involved and highly interested in activities.

Caregiver/Child Ratios

Caregivers in centers with lower caregiver/child ratios for toddlers foster a more positive social and emotional climate for interactions (Howes, 1983). Ratio, regulated by all but one of the states, has been found particularly important in considering the adequacy of infant and toddler care. But state standards vary widely. For infants, Georgia allows 1 to 7; the District of Columbia requires a 1 to 4 ratio. For 3-year-old children, North Dakota specifies a ratio of 1 to 7; Texas permits 1 to 15 (Hayes et al., 1990). In the NDCS study, ratio did not have a widespread effect for preschooler outcomes, but was significant in predicting infant and toddler daily experiences. Infants with poor staff/child ratios showed more apathy and distress, and they were in situations involving potentially more danger. In addition to prolonged distress, observers note "dead eyes"—the lack of sparkle on the cornea that can occur when infants do not have enough responsive, personally attuned care—in centers with insufficient staff for babies. Undoubtedly, when care quality is inadequate, the intersection and cumulative effects of several variables will contribute to unfocused child behaviors, apathy, wild behaviors, and compulsive self-stimulation such as rocking or constant thumb-sucking. Informed parents who visit childcare facilities before choosing one need to become alert to child distress and body behaviors that reflect the effects of poor-quality care.

Time During Which the Facility Operates

Length of care daily provided by a facility and time of day during which care is provided are critical variables for parents who work a night shift or who work on weekends. One fifth of all parents with young children, and one third of dual-earner couples with young children include at least one spouse who works nonstandard hours, such as evenings or nights or rotating schedules (Presser, 1989). Convenient hours were "a key element of mothers' satisfaction with care regardless of the age of their preschool child" (Sonnenstein, 1991, p. 29). Hospital-based facilities often provide 24-hour available care, because nurses and other staff have shifts at all hours.

Some facilities have constrictions on time provision of care that militate against families who are striving to rise out of poverty by taking full-time entry-level job positions. Head Start is a federally funded program that has permitted preschoolers from poverty families to enjoy health and educational benefits that boost child success on school entry. Yet, many Head Start programs provide only half-day care for preschoolers from low-SES families. Nursery schools have traditionally provided half-day, fee-based developmentally enriched experiences for middle-SES children.

Many factors (such as time of availability of facility) intersect in complex ways to influence parental choice. Of a sample of 814 teenage mothers in a Teenage Parent Demonstration program and in local control group families, roughly one third of those interviewed engaged in activities that included evening or weekend hours. Yet center-based care is rarely available during such hours (Kisker and Silverberg, 1991). Additionally, many young mothers believe that a stranger cannot be trusted to take care of their children, partly because they feel that infants are too young to report any abuse by a caregiver. Teenagers' children were twice as likely as local children to receive care from a grandparent. Teens were far less likely than control families to utilize care by the baby's father or by a nonrelative. Thus, age of parent and availability of family supports are important consumer variables that intersect with time during which care is required by families and care is offered by providers.

Caregiver Characteristics: Reliability, Stability, and Warmth

Reliability of provider (in addition to effects on cognitive development) was the feature of childcare valued most highly by dually employed parents surveyed about their attitudes regarding the importance of different features of childcare arrangements (Lein, 1979). Can they count on a provider being available? Parents felt that formal, full-time paid centers or parental care provided the greatest reliability, and informal unpaid arrangements offered the least reliability.

Staff stability is a significant variable in predicting more optimal outcomes for children. Instability, as reflected in high staff turnover rates in a facility, has been found predictive of lower child language development scores (Whitebook et al., 1989). Staff stability in turn depends significantly on wages.

Turnover nationally reaches more than 40% annually, in comparison with a 15% turnover rate a decade ago (Whitebook et al., 1989). Staff who left had less-specialized child development training, and they showed less appropriate caregiving in preschool classrooms and more detachment with children compared with caregivers who stayed. Low-wage facilities had much higher staff turnover. Equally troubling is that "Directors across the country lament that . . . the baseline skills that entry-level caregivers bring to their jobs are not what they used to be" (Rafanello, 2000, p. 1).

Parents concerned about stability of care will want to inquire about the wage structure of the facility they are considering as well as the training of individual caregivers. The Child Care Employee Project follow-up survey of 193 of centers remaining open from the major 1988 National Child Care Staffing Study reports the following disconcerting facts about provider wages (Teacher Compensation Not Improving, 1993, p. 65):

> Real wages for the lowest paid teaching assistants, the fastest growing segment of the child care work force, have declined 1.5% since 1988 to $8,890 per year. Real wages for the highest paid teaching staff, who constitute a small segment of the work force have improved approximately 66 cents an hour in four years to $15,488 per year. In 1992 only 27% of centers provided fully paid health insurance for teaching staff, and, of these, 32% did not cover assistant teachers.

Many family daycare providers offer service for limited periods of time while their own children are very young, or while minding their own preschool-age grandchildren (Atkinson, 1991). Unstable arrangements impel parents to undertake frantic journeys from one source to another to find satisfactory stable care.

Parent dissatisfaction with childcare increases instability of arrangements for children (Wolf and Sonnenstein, 1990). Parents need information on child body "danger" signals that reveal insecure infant attachments due to instability of care arrangements. Insecure attachments to a parent are a poor prognosis for later child ego resiliency and ego control. Thus, parents will want to note signs such as: avoidance rather than greeting the parent at pickup time, stiffening and lack of molding to the parent's body when comfort is needed, anger and even hitting out at the parent who picks up the infant at day's end, and compulsive self-stimulation. It is hard to empathize with infant needs unless you know "who" babies are. Thus, families particularly need to be tuned in to developmental ages and stages. Increased child development training for social workers, nurses, Women, Infants and Childcare (WIC) personnel, as well as childcare providers is one way to increase the number of professionals as prevention specialists who can support infant mental health by generously sharing information with parents searching for childcare (Honig, 1990, 1993).

Empathy and positive discipline techniques.   Parents who are in the process of choosing a facility will want to note caregiver characteristics that predict more positive adaptation, more prosocial relationships with peers, and more ease in adapting to childcare (Honig, 1987). Parents need to observe whether caregivers behave in ways that are empathic, attuned to, and responsive to children's needs. Do caregivers freely offer hugs, smiles, and laps? Do they give genuine focused attention to each individual child? Do they use a variety of *positive* discipline techniques (Honig, 1996) that seem tailored to each particular child's personality, or do they apply a single method, such as "time-out," regardless of the circumstances of the child's inappropriate behavior? Caregiver-watching by astute parents will go far toward helping them make wise choices of a facility based on caregiver emotional strengths as well as experiential or educational expertise.

Curriculum Issues: Language Emphasis

In their search for satisfactory childcare, parents may overlook indices of quality as reflected in curricula, in favor of convenience of location or cost. Yet many facilities lack a developmentally appropriate curriculum. What curricular aspects are critical for parents to look for? Reading with children on a regular basis enhances their language skills and pleasure in books; yet frequency of reading in a childcare facility varies widely. So does the amount of time spent in a reading episode—about 1 minute for some infants and toddlers (Honig and Shin, 2001). So does accessibility to books. In some centers few books are available. One caregiver explained that the 4-year-old children tore them too frequently. Another said they kept books on a locked cabinet shelf and would take them out when there was time. Other centers seem to have a satisfactory supply of children's books. However, in one well-supplied center the block area was located nearby, but blocks scattered about made it impossible for children to choose a book and curl up on a comfortable rug or couch to turn pages and enjoy looking at the books on their own. Availability of reading materials, emphasis on "whole language" so that even toddlers are encouraged to scribble grocery lists and letters to family, frequency of programmed reading times with children, and staff dedication to "hooking" very young children on books vary widely among providers.

In an exploration of family daycare variables that impacted on child development, Carew (1980) reported that "language mastery experiences" rather than other provider qualities, such as ethnicity, made all the difference in intellectual outcomes for the children served. Language-rich interactions are probably one of the most difficult staff qualities to implement. Yet if parents are to have true options to choose excellence in language and intellectual stimulation in childcare as well as safe, healthy, emotionally nurturing environments, then directors must develop innovative ways to enhance staff language skills by embedding language-rich curricula in daily routines as well as providing materials to encourage parental language stimulation, beginning in infancy (Honig, 1985).

The Daycare Provider's Family

Some families prefer a grandmother with no young children of her own who cares for only one or two other children. When a provider has very young children of her own, parent satisfaction is significantly lower; increased jealousy and attention seeking as well as biting has occurred (Powell and Baleen, 1992). Parents choosing family daycare where the provider's toddler considers the new tot to be an unwelcome intruder will need to consider possible positive and negative aspects of such a choice. The support of the family daycare provider's spouse is often perceived positively by parents. Many single employed mothers are particularly gratified when a provider's husband serves as a surrogate father or grandfather for the child; but research on the role of the provider's husband is much needed.

Parent–Provider Relationships

Parent–provider relationships do not always go smoothly. Indeed, there may well be a philosophical tension between different views of childrearing. Such tensions will need to be worked out so that parents and providers can create a mutual support system (Galinsky, 1988). In centers, program administrators articulate definite goals and philosophy for their programs. Their focus is on the well-being of all the children. In contrast, parents have an individualized focus on the well-being of their own child (Lurie and Newman, 1980, p. 71):

> If this dynamic isn't acknowledged, accepted and structured into the operation of the program, it can produce continuing "grinding" between parents and program, parental dissatisfaction and confrontation. However, if a receptivity to individual parent needs is incorporated, this "healthy tension" can help promote parental satisfaction and the continuing development of the program.

Parents and providers have closer or more distant, more frequent or rarer contacts. Hughes (1985) interviewed 73 providers and found that center staff spent an average of 13.7 minutes per week, whereas family daycare providers averaged 54.7 minutes per week with each parent. Yet increased time of contact does not necessarily translate into increased focus on the child's activities or developmental needs. After observing six family daycare providers and their interactions with parents over a 10-month period, Leavitt (1987, p. 12) concluded that "very little information may actually be exchanged about the children."

Some parents feel more constrained about commenting on a family daycare provider's way of organizing her home and routines. They might be more at ease in visiting the facilities in a center, a space where the caregivers themselves do not live. Other parents feel more comfortable in a home setting than in "school-like" settings. Thus, parents with different expectations, anxieties, and relationship histories will be more comfortable in choosing different care settings.

Parents in Canada who used family daycare reported a closer personal relationship with the provider than did those parents who used center care (Pence and Goelman, 1987). Licensed Canadian providers had more professional attitudes toward parents. Despite judging unlicensed providers less positively on aspects of the caregiving facility, parents were more likely to perceive an unlicensed provider as a good friend.

The parent–provider relationship is a system in delicate balance. Comfort and mutual respect between parent and provider represent the outcome of interactive processes that strongly influence parental satisfaction with the provider. Most exchanges occur at transition times—drop-off and pickup. The parent–provider relationship may be difficult to measure but can impact strongly on stability of care for a child. Parents who are satisfied with provider care will be less likely to change providers and consequently provide more stable care for young children. Parents have confided that they deliberately chose group center care because they worry about becoming jealous if their toddler became "too attached" to a family daycare provider. Other families deliberately choose a family daycare provider because they feel reassured when a provider has a similar ethnic or SES background and shares family childrearing style and philosophy. Although caregivers sometimes disapprove of parental lifestyles or childrearing practices, Kontos and Fiene (1987) pointed out that, even when caregivers have judgmental attitudes toward parents, this does not does not necessarily mean that caregiver interactions with mothers are unfriendly or unsupportive. They noted that subjectively parents in their study felt comfortable with the caregiver–parent relationship.

A study of family daycare relations between mothers and caregivers, and child behaviors with adults in each setting, uncovered similarities and differences that mothers and caregivers identified in their perceptions of each other. Mothers described the daycare home as cleaner, neater, larger, better organized and more endowed with play equipment than their own homes. Caregivers were sensitive to the fact that most of the children in their care lived in single-parent families. Caregivers expressed the notion that daycare made up for what home lacked. Mothers identified differences between the two settings in the tempo or pace of the day. They commented that there were more rules at daycare, more organization, and more routines. Mothers saw this structure as beneficial, and many expressed frustration in their own inability to impose some structure or organization in daily routines. For the most part:

> Mothers perceived daycare as expanding children's opportunities and not as compensating for something missing in their homes.... Caregivers, on the other hand, viewed most differences in terms of factors missing from the children's homes rather than as a bonus or benefit of day care.... The caregivers perceived themselves as providing a valuable service to families who did not match the culturally-defined ideal image of a family.... They filled in the gaps by providing a 'traditional' family setting, social and educational experiences, and a secure routine. (Nelson and Garduque, 1991, p. 103)

Mothers and caregivers described differences yet felt that they agreed. As one mother noted: "I think we do things not exactly the same, but the same idea's behind it" (p. 108). One caregiver remarked that the mother "feels comfortable with what I do, how J. feels, not that we've ever had a chance to talk about these things" (p. 108). Family systems theory would suggest a need for more role clarification than this for the parent–provider system to work well. Yet fuzzy and unarticulated boundaries between parent–caregiver goals, beliefs, and practices did not seem to prevent good relationships. After researching the relationship between 115 mothers and 46 family daycare providers, Whitehead (1989) concluded that maternal perception of similarity between her own and the provider's childrearing beliefs and values was the sole predictor of the mother's satisfaction with her childcare choice.

Caregivers in Nelson and Garduque's (1991) study did not see themselves as surrogate mothers, and they recognized the strain that mothers were under. The caregivers were observed to use more positive reinforcements than mothers in initiating interactions with the children, who were observed to behave more negatively at home. There seemed to be a tacit agreement and acceptance of each other's roles so that both sets of adults perceived that differences of setting and organization might not threaten but enhance children's ability to understand and cope with different experiences in both childcare settings. Indeed, when goodwill and compassion for parents prevails, young children learn a wider repertoire of appropriate behaviors in different environments—a boost for early classification skills.

Staff supports for parents occur in informal interactions at the beginnings and ends of days, or via more formal avenues (such as individual and/or group meetings with parents, or visits to the home by a social worker or parent outreach professional) and can influence parental choice. A notebook available at the entry to a facility allows parents to write any concerns they want staff to be alerted to for that day, such as teething or diarrhea. Some parents want the reassurance that either staff will meet regularly with them to discuss the child's experiences in program or that staff will provide written or telephone feedback.

Communication between caregivers and parents is sometimes difficult to arrange and even adversarial. Observational study of parent–staff communication in 16 childcare centers determined that an average such conversation lasted only 12 seconds (Endsley and Minish, 1991). Caregivers of infants and toddlers asked parents more questions and initiated more conversation than parents of preschoolers. Morning drop-off and afternoon pickup were prime conversation times. But parents preferred afternoon talk, and caregivers were more likely to be free early in the morning. No conversation at all was observed in 43% of the cases. One fifth consisted of simple greetings, and the content of most conversations was social and routine, rather than sharing more substantive information about child development or parental concerns.

Other kinds of parental supports make a subtle difference. One middle-SES parent complained that she was not satisfied with the infant program in the center where her baby was enrolled because they did not provide a couch where she could sit for a long time during the first week of care. As a first-time parent, she felt worried and guilty about leaving her young infant and wanted to try to continue to nurse her baby despite enrollment into full-time care. Parental discomfort with staff can be lessened through more open communication. A drop-in, open-door visitation policy in some centers includes a coffee pot and lounge for parents and even a VCR and a videotape library so that parents can watch their child's classroom interactions on tape. In the Syracuse Children's Center, childcare was provided for siblings during evening group meetings for parents (Lally and Honig, 1975).

Usefulness of a Parent Handbook of Rules and Regulations

Providers need to be honest with parents about the services offered in order to facilitate communication and trust building. A handbook of rules for parents can answer many parents' questions about a facility. Will the care facility be willing to include an atypical youngster? Are infants assigned to a primary caregiver or cared for by many different caregivers daily? Does the facility group children by narrow age range or provide multiage "family-style" groupings? Are toddlers moved to an older group together with a friend or rigidly by birthdate? Toddlers moved up with peers they know well will adjust much better as they advance to a new classroom. If a facility accepts only preschoolers, will preschoolers still in diapers be admitted? Are there reductions in cost if more than one child in a family is enrolled with the provider? What is the monetary penalty for a family that picks up a child beyond the time set for the hours the facility operates? Are fees required to be paid in advance by parents or at the end of a set period of services received, such as weekly? A handbook also provides clear guidelines about whether staff will be permitted to administer medicine that a doctor prescribes or whether teachers or aides may accept after-hours jobs with families to care for their children on evenings or weekends. Clarity of communication about policy issues decreases painful surprises for families and increases chances that the parent–provider relationship will support family as well as child needs.

Working Conditions for Providers

Parents who are concerned about the critical importance of staff stability for their very young children may want to make special inquiry about work-related factors in the center they are considering. Such factors affect the stability and quality of providers. Are wage levels consistent with attracting trained personnel? Are health care and retirement plans provided? Do working conditions permit caregivers coffee breaks and paid preparation time with adequate care provided to cover groups? A "floater" staff person is sometimes available during staff breaks at centers, or else a director does part-time substituting when staff have time off. Does the center have sufficient funds for hiring substitute caregivers when necessary? Is professional growth valued so that caregivers are given time off and/or financial support to attend professional training workshops and early childhood professional meetings?

Some parents will be forced to choose and rechoose care because their provider is unable to maintain the facility given the prevailing wage scales in childcare. The low wages for childcare providers can be boosted if governmental grants are provided and if career development ladders are carefully specified. Career development ladders, based on key dimensions of professionalism, including high levels of competency, knowledgeability, and professional practice, involve a continuum (Willer and Bredekamp, 1993). Such ladders will boost morale and are likely to ensure staff stability. Childcare facilities may need to consider tying a menu of professional benefits to providers working up the career ladder (Bloom, 1993, p. 70). If a family childcare worker does not earn sufficient funds to keep in business, then parents who have chosen such care specifically because of the "homey" quality of the environment may find that they are forced to change providers to the detriment of the child's well-being.

POLITICAL, BUSINESS, AND COMMUNITY SUPPORTS FOR PARENTAL CHOICE

How well do current political, business, and community efforts support parental choice of childcare? (See Table 15.1, Section 5.)

Legislation and Regulatory Agencies

Diversity strikingly characterizes childcare legislation across states. The Federal Interagency Day Care Requirements were discarded in 1982 after much bitterness and disagreement nationally. Regulation of childcare services is now reserved to the states, which vary dramatically in regulations, funding, and support for quality childcare. Some form of licensing or registration for family daycare providers is required in 17 states; 13 states offer voluntary registration; 4 states combine these two mechanisms; and 6 states have an approval or certification procedure if a provider receives federal funds (Hayes et al., 1990, p. 183). In addition, states differ in allowing corporal punishment in centers. Some, like Arkansas and North Carolina, permit corporal punishment in centers if parents give permission (Children's Foundation, 1991).

Licensure laws vary widely by state. Caregivers may be required to: (1) be above 18 years of age, (2) take tuberculosis tests or measles shots prior to employment, (3) have an annual chest X ray, and (4) undergo a fingerprint test for possible prior conviction for child abuse. Other state specifications include the minimum number of square feet per child a center provides and required purchase of liability insurance by a facility.

Some demographic variables are rarely the focus of regulatory laws. Wages are unregulated, and in 1987 more than half of childcare workers earned less than $5.00 per hour. At the start of the new millennium, the average salary for staff was "$6 an hour" (Springer, 2000, p. 32).

In 23 states there are no regulations for preservice training for teachers in childcare centers. Other unregulated demographic variables are: (1) the number of years of formal education required of caregivers, (2) availability of support for staff advancement on a career ladder, (3) provision of staff health insurance or paid holidays, and (4) the number of parent–staff conferences held annually. Some of these variables have been emphasized as indicators of quality addressed by professional organizations, such as Head Start, the NAEYC, or the Child Welfare League of America (Meadows, 1991). The number of specific child development/early childhood education (CD/ECE) credits or courses that workers must complete each year to continue employment is unregulated in many states, although they often require some specific number of hours of training, such as 15 to 18 hours annually, which may be satisfied by workshops on fire prevention or mouth-to-mouth resuscitation without any CD/ECE courses either required or offered in some communities.

Estimates of unregulated care cited in Congressional testimony range from 60% to 90%. Care in a child's own home is totally unregulated. Thus, accountability for quality care is neither high nor uniform. On the other hand, if elaborate licensure requirements were implemented, more totally nonregulated care might flourish in an "underground" market, and some high-quality facilities might not be able to afford the additional fees and bureaucratic paperwork required. Professional preparation of caregivers and professional licensure seem a more feasible way to ensure caregiver qualifications, particularly since child-related training has so often been found to be the key quality variable, as in the NDCS national study (Ruopp et al., 1979; Travers et al., 1979) and the National Day Care Home Study (Fosburg, 1981). Some states, such as New York, fund high quality prekindergarten programs with licensed teachers who are specialists in early childhood education. California has been a pioneer in support for quality childcare. Other states put no restrictions on caregiver education level, nor do they provide special training programs.

Theoretically, the Child Care and Development Block Grant (CCDBG), passed by Congress in 1990, earmarked $860 million to states in Fiscal Year 1992 for childcare and should result in an increase in the quality and availability of childcare. However, Miller (1992, pp. 10–11) noted that there are severe restrictions on these funds that work against informed parental choice:

> All states receiving CCDBG money must develop a child care system that provides parents with childcare vouchers or certificates redeemable for whatever provider the parents choose. While most parents would applaud the ability to choose, restrictions on the CCDBG monies limit states' ability to ensure safety at any given site, reducing the benefit of having a range of options. Specifically, proposed federal regulations would prohibit the state from setting health and safety standards for certain categories of care, including school and church-run centers and families caring for fewer than three children. The result would be minimal background checks on those caregivers and few safety reviews of their homes or centers. Without such standards, states cannot ensure the quality of child care among choices available to parents. Ironically, funds to provide adequate information from which parents could make an informed choice are also restricted, leaving parents choices that might all end up to be bad.

Restrictions on CCDBG funds also mean that few dollars can be used to develop new childcare facilities in or near schools that adolescent parents attend. Teen parents' needs—for specialized locales close to schools and for specialized trained workers to care for infants and toddlers—will essentially go unmet. More hopeful predictions may be expected for the first decade of the new millennium, because Congress approved a large federal budget expansion of the CCDBG for fiscal year 2001. In comparison with fiscal year 2000. Congress also approved an 87% increase for after-school care, a 69% increase for childcare, and an 18% increase for Head Start (Fight Crime: Invest in Kids, 2000). But further revenue sources are needed (NAEYC, 2001).

Businesses and Unions: Supports for Family Childcare Choice

Corporations over the last decades have slowly increased their supports for parental ability to find high-quality, convenient childcare. Many large corporations continue to build center-based facilities on their premises in order to keep parents as long-term employees. However, the high cost of subsidizing quality care makes such programs feasible only for large businesses. Hospitals have been pioneers in opening group care facilities. For example, Methodist Hospital in Lubbock, Texas, built a $1.7-million center for 259 children in 1991. They launched an on-site childcare center because of a severe shortage of nurses. In a survey of workers, "11% said that if it were not for the center, they might have left that hospital for employment elsewhere" (Texas Work and Family Clearinghouse, 1992, p. 3). The hospital subsidizes from 40% to 50% of program costs and is a pioneer in including special needs children (such as those with Down syndrome) and accepting sick children.

The Educare Center in Chicago serves as an example of how private dollars can leverage public commitment. The Ounce of Prevention fund added to an initial investment from Chicago business-man Irving B. Harris, with Head Start funds, local government (the Chicago public schools), state government, and other private donors to develop "an island of calm"—a childcare facility resembling an old-fashioned school house—for young children in low-income families (Ounce of Prevention Fund, 2000).

Flex-time offered by some companies assists parents with childcare needs. Companies may supply optional childcare benefits. For example, Prudential Insurance Company provides information kits, seminars, and checklists to help families choose childcare or eldercare. In their program called "Generations: A Family Resource," Prudential assists families with a toll-free 800 number referral service supplying leads to appropriate care. Annually, a Family Festival is held on-site, when employees can talk to representatives from local agencies serving the needs of children and the elderly.

Some corporations have Search-and-Find contracts with community agencies that will locate care for skilled employees relocating into a community. Family daycare, which has not usually been the recipient of corporate attention, has recently benefitted from this business trend. Professional, family care providers are being recruited and trained to care for children through corporate-funded programs that seek to expand the supply and quality of home childcare for working parents (Texas Work and Family Clearinghouse, 1992). Some companies underwrite all or part of the costs of transforming the childcare professional's home into a safe place to care for a small number of the employees' children. The Child Care Company of Dallas has recruited and trained about 80 family, day-home providers in employees' neighborhoods under contracts from IBM and AT&T. The Child Care Company provided 14 hours of training in seven separate 2-hour sessions on child development, nutrition, and operating a home business. They noted (Texas Work and Family Clearinghouse, 1992, p. 1):

> This type of venture benefits all parties involved: the corporations, their working-parent employees, persons in the business of caring for children in their homes, and the children themselves.... From a corporate standpoint, family day home care is both cost-efficient and flexible because it doesn't require the large capital outlay that daycare centers often do.... and is the top choice of employees.

Models to enhance center care quality are supported in some states through public-sector unions. The most extensive such initiative has been established in New York state through collective bar-gaining. The state provides for start-up costs, space, utilities, and maintenance for dozens of centers. However, there is no provision for quality control, and grant support fluctuates yearly with the per-centage of state employees' children enrolled. This leaves centers vulnerable to financial deficits in times of personnel cutbacks. Unions can still assume a more active role in providing workers with in-depth information to facilitate quality choices for care.

Federal involvement is just beginning. Focus groups are now run in federal agencies to find out about family-friendly programs they are implementing, such as flexible work schedules and referral services for child care (U.S. Office of Personnel Management, 1998).

Through the Child Care Technical Assistance Network of the Child Care Bureau, seven projects have been begun to address the needs of states, territories, and tribes through technical assistance and networks of specialists. Their goal is to provide more coordinated partnership delivery systems of care, more training for staff, more tiered reimbursement rates, and more supports for working families, including those seeking care for children with disabilities (Azer and Elliott, 1998). The U.S. Office of Personnel Management is establishing work-site parenting support groups (Office of Workforce Relations, 1999). They encourage employee surveys to "assess the extent to which men and women have parenting responsibilities or concerns and would like help in addressing them" (p. 2).

The U.S. Department of Labor (1998) has created collaborations between business, unions, community groups, and nonprofit organizations to improve the quality and availability of care. Thus, at participating health care facilities in New York state, the AFL-CIO, the National Health and Human Service Employees Union, and 17 health care employers assess union member child care needs, run a child care resource and referral service, select childcare offerings from a menu, and contribute to parent fees through a Child Care Fund in order to improve the quality and availability of care. The Department of Labor (1998) publicizes such consortiums, and encourages them to offer a wide variety of choices, such as 24-hour care and back up emergency care. Many of these collaborations were the result of an initiative by President Bill Clinton "that called upon employers to make concrete changes to improve work for women and their families" (Department of Labor, 1998, Preface).

Private-sector initiatives have arisen because employee surveys have found, for example, at General Motors, that "almost half the workers cited child care as a reason they could not work overtime, and more than one-third missed 2 to 4 days of work over a 3-month period because of child care problems" (U.S. Department of the Treasury, 1998, p. 20). The American Business Collaboration for Quality Dependent Care, headed by 22 major corporations, "is the largest and most comprehensive private-sector initiative specifically designed to improve the quality and expand the supply of dependent care" (U.S. Department of the Treasury, 1998, p. 19). Private-sector support for quality choice has also been advanced by some of the large national corporate childcare organizations, such as Bright Horizons (Mason, 2000), which is committed to building and running centers that serve the needs of the whole family and works toward accreditation of every childcare facility built. Research on private-sector initiatives has been furthered by the survey work of the Family and Work Institute to document the prevalence of work-life support in nationally representative samples of leading companies (Friedman and Galinsky, 2000; Galinsky and Bond, 1998).

Accreditation and Referral Agencies

Federal funds are available for Child Development Associate (CDA) credentialling to support a competency-based model that, since its founding in 1975, graduated over 125,000 caregivers in 25 years (Council News and Views, 2000). The Council for Early Childhood Professional Recognition sets policies and standards. The council awards the CDA Credential, an assurance of skill upgrading among childcare staff working under the supervision of specialists. The number of CDA Credentials increases by more than 10,000 per year.

In some communities, city-supported child care resource and referral (CCR&R) agencies provide parents with names and telephone numbers of all types of childcare services. Fuqua and Labensohn (1986) found that parents did not pursue their choice of childcare from a consumer point of view. CCR&R agencies can help parents become more discriminating consumers of childcare programs. Fuqua and Shieck (1989), controlling for income and education level, found that when parents seeking childcare used CCR&R agency referral, then 91.1% of them visited two or more providers, whereas only 56.8% of parents who did not use such services made two or more visits to choose a care provider. A majority (55.4%) of the CCR&R group spent about 7 hours looking for childcare, compared with 41.2% of parents who had not used the service.

Many CCR&R agencies carefully refrain from giving parents qualitative information about a facility, although some try to educate the parent as consumer about what qualities to look for in choosing care. Fortunately, the NAEYC accreditation procedures make it possible for parents to find out from a director whether or not a center is accredited. As of May 1993 almost 2,500 centers in the United States were NAEYC accredited (Herr, Johnson, and Zimmerman, 1993). By 2001, this had increased to nearly 7,800 NAEYC accredited centers, but this represents only 7% of centers in the United States (National Association for the Education of Young Children, 2001).

In a revisitation of childcare centers involved in the National Child Care Staffing Study, Whitebook et al. (1993) describe the overwhelmingly (95%) positive response of directors seeking NAEYC reaccreditation. Interviews revealed that directors felt accreditation was a "seal of quality" and a model for others. The self-study process required during the accreditation process impelled staff to become more sensitive to the importance of high-quality interactions: "Evaluation processes improved in some programs, communications between staff and parents improved, and parents increased their understanding of what constitutes high-quality childhood programs" (Herr et al., 1993, p. 34).

Directors believed that the accreditation process reflected professionalism, positively affected staff and parent morale, and increased parental pride in having a child attend an accredited center.

CONCLUSIONS

Finding professionals to care for young children when parents are employed can prove even more difficult and frustrating than the search for a reliable car repair person. No single governmental agency or community resource can help improve the supply of high quality childcare nor be responsible for increasing the effectiveness of family choices. Indeed, the National Research Council of the National Academy of Science (Hayes et al., 1990, p. 291), after an in-depth and extensive investigation of childcare in the United States, urged that "responsibility for meeting the nation's child care needs should be widely shared among individuals, families, voluntary organizations, employers, communities, and government at all levels."

Too little is currently known about parental decision making in choice for childcare (Sonnenstein, 1991). Large surveys provide more national information (Hofferth, Shauman, Henke, and West, 1998). Parental knowledge can be increased through more concerted and vigorous efforts to provide information that would promote the likelihood of informed choice. Rarely do public education institutions such as high schools inform young people about quality childcare as they approach the age of childbearing and childrearing. Mandatory high school courses on family issues including child development, and quality childcare can increase adolescent awareness of what kinds of optimal transactions with caring adults young children need in order to flourish in their development. Positive communication techniques offered in such courses can boost young families' ability to cope with the stress of a new baby and other interpersonal stresses in their lives.

Community agency personnel in pregnancy and well-baby clinics, pediatric nurses, WIC personnel, and agencies that serve parents through provision of legal services and housing referrals can become locales for providing information to assist parental choice. Families can plan more thoughtfully for childcare when pediatricians' offices offer easy-to-read pamphlets that alert parents to pitfalls and to the advantages of quality care. Parental childcare decision making may improve when childcare specialists begin to write in appealing ways to "give away" their knowledge to families. This "infrastructure" to informed choice is an essential element of quality care choice and implementation (Kagan and Cohen, 1997).

Professional child development specialists can never shoulder the total job of dissemination of information and provision of supports for optimal decision making in families. Certainly, system reforms in funding early childhood services can increase "collaboration and empowerment" (Kagan, 1994, p. 17). In addition, media specialists in radio, newspapers, and television need to assume a more vigorous, proactive role in assisting consumers to make enlightened childcare choices. Distribution of materials may be a weak link in parent education. Many pamphlets and books are available that alert families to watch for particular practices and conditions that signal high-quality childcare (Honig, 1983, 1984, 1987; Miller and Weissman, 1988; Scarr, 1985). But where can parents find such resources? Prenatal services in the community need to become conduits for alerting families to child development information and to resource materials that can empower them to make optimal childcare choices (Honig, 1987). Employee unions need to offer brochures and a book and video lending library on quality care to improve the consumer skills of working parents who need to choose childcare. NAEYC affiliates disseminate many valuable pamphlets to assist parents with choice. For example, the Chicago AEYC affiliate provides materials in English and also in Spanish that detail a step-by-step procedure to enable parents of special needs children to make an informed choice of an appropriate center. Parents are given detailed information about state licensure and accreditation and even transportation and daily schedules for each facility (Bernstein, Wonderlick, and Madden, 1997).

Both locally and on the state and federal levels, the role of government urgently needs to include economic supports for training quality care providers. Federal funding exclusively earmarked to support caregiver training will provide a far wider supply of quality care and career ladders for providers, which can guarantee more optimal parental choices in communities.

In the National Child Care Survey, researchers asked what type of child care was first considered and why it was not selected (Hofferth and Phillips, 1991). They also asked why the last arrangement ended, whether through parent initiation, perhaps to find more age-appropriate care, or provider-initiated, as when a family daycare worker closes a home facility. Such behavioral research is to be commended, and more such informational resources are needed for specific populations, such as rural parents, teen parents, gay parents, and others. Yet difficulties in research on choice preferences and behaviors will still persist (Prosser and McGroder, 1992, p. 50).

> The child care search and selection process is a dynamic one, consisting of identifying a "preferred" type of care, searching for it, encountering one or more barriers (price, availability, accessibility, etc.), and modifying preferences to accommodate what is available. Surveys that attempt to identify preferences are prone to capturing some degree of constraints in measures of preference, as parents pre-screen their responses to reflect what options are actually feasible. Consequently, researchers may never completely understand what parental preferences are by asking preference-type questions.

Research on childcare choices needs to invent and use more innovative designs and methodology. Perhaps unobtrusive measures such as park bench conversations or participant observation techniques at WIC centers (providing nutritional aid for infants and mothers) and other facilities for parents of new babies can be devised (Honig, 1997).

Research also needs to address the problem of tied variables with more ingenuity. In Britain, Tizard and Hughes (1984) researched the differential effects of structural and process variables on child language outcomes in group care situations. Facilities with more hierarchically rigid staff structuring had higher staff turnover rates and less facilitative staff talk with children. Structural variables, such as more staff autonomy in choosing daily program content and sequence of activities, were indeed associated with higher language scores for young children. But autonomous caregivers also showed richer language interactions with the children. Structure and process variables are often confounded, and clever research designs are needed to untangle the importance and relevance of certain variables.

Sometimes hidden variables interfere with ability to untangle such effects. In a study of the effects of choice of full-time care for infants, whether parents enrolled prior to the birth of their baby or entered the study after the birth may have a strong effect on outcomes of full-time early infancy care. In one study of the effects of full-time versus part-time infant nonparental care on later aggression and cognition among preschoolers, families were located who had placed infants in full-time care prior to 1 year, during the second year, or not until after 36 months (Honig and Park, 1993; Park and Honig,

1991). However, the researchers could find very few families who had chosen full-time infancy care in the first year and part-time care during the second year. Parental choices are sometimes revealed in the *lack* of families who choose certain options.

In summary, empowering parents to make wise choices and to demand options for quality care takes concerted multifaceted efforts. Community-supported resource and referral agencies can upgrade quality through offering parents information and support for choosing quality care. Businesses and community agencies can donate money for brochures and for training workshops for providers. Directors can institute career ladders for staff and initiate accreditation procedures via the NAEYC National Academy of Early Childhood Programs. State and federal lawmakers must legislate monetary grants to support caregiver training and education. High school principals need to implement, for both female and male students, courses in child development and family communication skills. Such coursework should include materials on positive childrearing techniques and responsive caregiver interactions, as well as practica in on-site high-quality centers serving adolescent parents in the school as well as teachers. Media advocacy for quality care needs to be far more prominent in newspaper columns and TV public service spot announcements in order to promote citizen awareness of quality caregiving practices and facilities. Researchers who study the outcomes for children and families of the clusters of variables affecting parent choice can publicize their findings not only in professional journals but in more reader-friendly venues so that families become informed and satisfied finders and consumers of, and advocates for, high-quality childcare.

REFERENCES

Aronson, S. S. (1991). *Health and safety in childcare*. New York: HarperCollins.

Atkinson, A. M. (1991). Providers' evaluations of family day care services. *Early Child Development and Care, 68*, 113–123.

Azer, S., and Elliott, K. (1998, November/December). States move toward systems that encompass training, compensation, and program quality. *Child Care Bulletin, 20*.

Baker, A. C. (1993). New frontiers in family day care: Integrating children with ADHD. *Young Children, 48*, 69–73.

Balleyguier, G. (1990). What is the best mode of day care for young children: A French study. In A. S. Honig (Ed.), *Optimizing early child care and education* (pp. 41–66). London: Gordon and Breach.

Baurac, D. (1993, May 16). Programs try to help parents keep their cool. *Chicago Tribune*, pp. 8–9.

Becerra, R. (1992). Child care preferences among low-income, minority families. *International Social Work, 35*, 35–47.

Belsky, J. (1986). Infant day care: A cause of concern? *Zero to Three, 6*, 1–9.

Belsky, J. (1988). The "effects" of infant day care reconsidered. *Early Childhood Research Quarterly, 3*, 235–272.

Belsky, J. (1990). Parental and nonparental child care and children's socioemotional development: A decade in review. *Journal of Marriage and the Family, 52*, 885–903.

Berk, L. (1985). Relationships of educational attainment, child oriented attitudes, job satisfaction, and career commitment to caregiver behavior toward children. *Child Care Quarterly, 14*, 103–129.

Bernstein, S., Wonderlick, M., and Madden, D. (1997). *Finding an appropriate preschool for your child with special needs*. Chicago, IL: Chicago Metropolitan Association for the Education of Young Children.

Blank, H. (1999, December). *Child Care Action News, 16*, p. 3.

Blau, F. D., and Grossberg, A. J. (1990). *Maternal labor supply and children's cognitive development* (Working Paper No. 3536). Cambridge, MA: National Bureau of Economic Research.

Booth, A. (Ed.). (1992). *Child care in the 1990s: Trends and consequences*. Hillsdale, NJ: Lawrence Erlbaum Associates.

Bornstein, M. (1991). *Cultural approaches to parenting*. Hillsdale, NJ: Lawrence Erlbaum Associates.

Bloom, P. J. (1993). "But I'm worth more than that!" Implementing a comprehensive compensation system. *Young Children, 48*, 67–72.

Bradbard, M., and Endsley, R. (1980). The importance of educating parents to be discriminating day care consumers. In S. Kilmer (Ed.), *Advances in early education and day care* (Vol. 1). Greenwich, CT: JAI.

Brimhall, D. W., and Reaney, L. M. (1999, August). National Center for Education Statistics. Participation of kindergartners through third-graders in before-and-after school care. Washington, DC: U.S. Department of Education, Office of Educational Research and Improvement.

Bryant, D. M., and Ramey, C. T. (1987). An analysis of the effectiveness of early intervention programs for high-risk children.

In M. Guralnick and C. Bennett (Eds.), *The effectiveness of early intervention for at-risk and handicapped children.* New York: Academic Press.

Campbell, R. E. (Ed.). (1993). *Why child care matters: Preparing young children for a more productive America.* New York: Committee for Economic Development.

Carew, J. (1980). Experience and the development of intelligence in young children at home and in day care. *Monographs of the Society for Research in Child Development, 45* (6–7, Serial No. 187).

Center for the Study of Social Policy. (1993). *Kids count data book: State profiles of child well-being.* Washington, DC: Annie E. Casey Foundation.

Chase-Lansdale, P. L., and Owen, M. T. (1987). Maternal employment in a family context: Effects on infant–mother and infant–father attachments. *Child Development, 58,* 1505–1512.

Child Care Bureau. (1997). *School-age care out of school time resource notebook.* Washington, DC: Department of Health and Human Services.

Children's Foundation. (1991). *1991 Day care licensing study.* Washington, DC: The Children's Foundation.

Clarke-Stewart, A., and Fein, G. (1983). Early childhood programs. In P. H. Mussen (Ed.), *Handbook of child psychology* (Vol. 2, pp. 917–999). New York: Wiley.

Cost, Quality, and Outcomes Team. (1995). *Cost, quality, and child outcomes in child care centers.* Denver, CO: University of Colorado at Denver, Department of Economics.

Council News and Views. (2000). Council celebrates the twenty-fifth anniversary of the CDA. *CNV, 17.*

Cryer, D., and Burchinal, M. (1997). Parents as child care consumers. *Early Childhood Research Quarterly, 12,* 35–58.

Duncan, G. J., and Hill, C. R. (1977). The child care mode choices of working mothers. In G. J. Duncan and J. N. Morgan (Eds.), *Five thousand American families; Patterns of economic progress* (Vol. 5, pp. 379–388). Ann Arbor, MI: Institute for Social Research.

Endsley, R. C., and Bradbard, M. (1987). Dissatisfaction with previous child care among current users of proprietary center care. *Child and Youth Quarterly, 16,* 249–262.

Endsley, R. C., and Minish, P. A. (1991). Parent–staff communication in day care centers during morning and afternoon transition. *Early Childhood Research Quarterly, 6,* 119–136.

Family and Consumer Sciences. (2000). *Child care alternatives* (Video No. 2602-MG1, 14 min.) South Charleston, WV: Meridian Education Corporation.

Fight Crime: Invest in Kids. (2000, December). Federal budget for FY 2001 includes over $2 billion in new investment in America's kids! *FCIK Annual Update 2000.*

Fortner-Wood, C., Elicker, J., and Noppe, I. C. (2000). *Social support of family child care and center care providers is related to the quality of the care they provide infants.* Poster presented at the Biennial International Conference on Infant studies, Brighton, England.

Fosburg, S. (1981). *Family day care in the United States: National Day Care Home Study: Vol. 1. Summary of findings* (Pub. No. 80-30282). Washington, DC: U.S. Department of Health and Human Services, Office of Human Development Services.

Fraiberg, S. (1988). Ghosts in the nursery. In L. Fraiberg (Ed.), *Selected writings of Selma Fraiberg* (pp. 100–136). Columbus: Ohio State University Press.

Friedman, S. D., and Galinsky, E. (2000, September). *Private sector initiatives on caring for the young children of working parents.* Paper presented at the Wharton Impact Conference on public–private partnerships to support the working parents of young children. New York: Families and Work Institute.

Fuller, B., Eggers-Pierola, C., Liang, X., Holloway, S., and Rambaud, M. (1996). *Rich culture, poor families: Why do Latino families forgo preschools?* New York: Teachers College Press.

Fuller, B., Holloway, S., and Liang, X. (1996). Family selection of child care centers: The influence of household support, ethnicity, and parental practices. *Child Development, 67,* 3320–3337.

Fuller, B., and Liang, X. (1993). *The unfair search for child care: Working moms, poverty, and the unequal supply of preschools across America.* Cambridge, MA: Harvard University Press.

Fuqua, R. W., and Labenson, P. (1986). Parents as consumers of child care. *Family Relations, 35,* 295–303.

Fuqua, R. W., and Shieck, R. (1989). Childcare resource and referral programs and parents' search for quality child care. *Early Childhood Research Quarterly, 4,* 357–365.

Galinsky, E. (1988). Parents and teacher-caregivers. Sources of tension, sources of support. *Young Children, 43,* 4–12.

Galinsky, E. (1992). The impact of childcare on parents. In A. Booth (Ed.), *Child care in the 1990's: Trends and consequences* (pp. 159–171). Hillsdale, NJ: Lawrence Erlbaum Associates.

Galinsky, E., and Bond, J. T. (1998). The 1998 Business Work-Life Study. New York: Families and Work Institute.

Galinsky, E., and Friedman, D. (1993). *Education before school: Investing in quality child care.* New York: Committee for Economic Development.

Goelman, H., and Pence, A. R. (1990). Children in three types of daycare: Daily experiences, quality of care and developmental outcomes. In A. S. Honig (Ed.), *Optimizing early child care and education* (pp. 67–76). London: Gordon and Breach.

Hayes, C. D., and Kamerman, S. B. (Eds.). (1983). *Children of working parents: Experiences and outcomes.* Washington, DC: National Academy Press.

Hayes, C. D., Palmer, J. L., and Zaslow, M. (1990). *Who cares for America's children: Child care policy for the 1990s.* Washington, DC: National Academy Press.

Herr, J., Johnson, R. D., and Zimmerman, K. (1993). Benefits of accreditation: A study of directors' perceptions. *Young Children, 48,* 32–35.

Hofferth, S. L. (1992). The demand for and supply of child care in the 1990s. In A. Booth (Ed.), *Child care in the 1990s: Trends and consequences* (pp. 3–25). Hillsdale, NJ: Lawrence Erlbaum Associates.

Hofferth, S. L., and Phillips, D. A. (1987). Child care in the United States: 1970–1995. *Journal of Marriage and the Family, 47,* 93–116.

Hofferth, S. L., and Phillips, D. A. (Eds.). (1991). Child care policy research. *Journal of Social Issues, 47,* 1–23.

Hofferth, S. L., Shauman, K., Henke, R., and West, J. (1998). *Characteristics of children's early care and education programs: Data from the 1995 National Household Education Survey* (NCES Pub. No. 98-128). Washington, DC: National Center for Education Statistics.

Hofferth, S. L., and Wissoker, D. (1992). Price, quality, and income in child care choice. *Journal of Human Resources, 27,* 70–111.

Holloway, S. D., and Fuller, B. (1992). The great child-care experiment. What are the lessons for school improvement? *Educational Researcher, 21,* 281–298.

Honig, A. S. (1979). *Parent involvement in early childhood education.* Washington, DC: National Association for the Education of Young Children.

Honig, A. S. (1982). *Playtime learning games for young children.* Syracuse, NY: Syracuse University Press.

Honig, A. S. (1983). Choosing a quality care environment for your young child. In S. Gordon and M. Wollin (Eds.), *Parenting: A guide for young people* (pp. 181–186). New York: Oxford Book Company.

Honig, A. S. (1984). Child care options and decisions: Facts and figurings for families. In K. Borman, D. Quarm, and S. Gideonse (Eds.), *Women in the workplace* (pp. 89–111). Norwood, NJ: Ablex.

Honig, A. S. (1985). The art of talking to a baby. *Working Mother, 8,* 72–78.

Honig, A. S. (1987). How to spot top-notch day care. *Working Mother, 10,* 72–73.

Honig, A. S. (1990). Infant/toddler education: Principles, practices, and promises. In C. Seefeldt (Ed.), *Continuing issues in early childhood education* (pp. 61–115). Columbus, OH: Merrill.

Honig, A. S. (1992). Historical overview of child care. In B. Spodek and O. Saracho (Eds.), *Yearbook in early childhood education* (Vol. 3, pp. 9–30). New York: Teachers College Press.

Honig, A. S. (1993). Mental health for babies: What do theory and research teach us? *Young Children, 48,* 69–76.

Honig, A. S. (1996). Behavior guidance for infants and toddlers. Little Rock, AR: Southern Early Childhood Association.

Honig, A. S. (1997). Evaluation and parents of young children. In B. Spodek and O. N. Saracho (Eds.), *Issues in early childhood educational assessment and evaluation* (pp. 179–197). New York: Teachers College Press.

Honig, A. S. (1999, April). *Longitudinal outcomes from the Family Development Research Program.* Paper presented at the symposium "How High-Quality Early Childhood Programs Enhance Long-Term Development: A Comparison of Findings and Models" at the biennial meetings of the Society for Research in Child Development, Albuquerque, NM.

Honig, A. S. (2000). The Eriksonian approach. In J. L. Roopnarine and J. E. Johnson (Eds.), *Approaches to early childhood education* (3rd ed., pp. 97–122). New York: Merrill.

Honig, A. S. (2001). *Safe and secure: Nurturing healthy infant/toddler attachment.* Washington, DC: National Association for the Education of Young Children.

Honig, A. S., and Brophy, H. (1996). *Talking with your baby: Family as the first school.* Syracuse, NY: Syracuse University Press.

Honig, A. S., Douthit, D., Lee, J., and Dingler, C. (1992). Prosocial and aggressive behaviors of preschoolers at play in secular and church-based day care. *Early Child Development and Care, 83,* 93–101.

Honig, A. S., and Hirallal, A. (1998). Which counts more for excellence in childcare staff: Years in service, education level, or ECE coursework? *Early Child Development and Care, 145,* 31–46.

Honig, A. S., and Lally, J. R. (1981). *Infant caregiving: A design for training.* Syracuse, NY: Syracuse University Press.

Honig, A. S., and Park, K. (1993). Effects of day care on preschool sex-role development. *American Journal of Orthopsychiatry, 63,* 481–486.

Honig, A. S., and Shin, M. (2001). Reading aloud to infants and toddlers in child care settings: An observational study. *Early Childhood Education Journal, 28*(3), 193–197.

Howes, C. (1983). Caregiver behavior in center and family day care. *Journal of Applied Developmental Psychology, 4,* 99–107.

Howes, C., and Rubenstein, J. (1985). Determinants of toddlers' experiences in daycare: Age of entry and quality of setting. *Child Care Quarterly, 14,* 140–151.

Howes, C., and Stewart, P. (1987). Child's play with adults, toys, and peers: An examination of family and child care influence. *Developmental Psychology, 23,* 423–430.

Hughes, R. (1985). The informal help-giving of home and center childcare providers. *Family Relations, 34,* 359–366.

Ispa, J. M. (1995). Ideas about infant and toddler care among Russian child care teachers, mothers, and university students. *Early Childhood Research Quarterly, 10,* 359–379.

Johnson, D. J., Dyanda-Marira, C., and Davimbo, P. K. (1997). Urban Zimbabwean mothers' choices and perception of care for young children. *Early Childhood Research Quarterly, 12*, 199–219.

Kagan, S. L. (1994, February/March). Parent choice in early care and education: Myth or reality? *Zero to Three*, 11–18.

Kagan, S. L., and Cohen, N. E. (1997). *Not by chance: Creating an early care and education system for America' children.* New Haven, CT: The Bush Center in Child Development and Social Policy at Yale University.

Kahn, A. J., and Kamerman, S. B. (1987). *Child care: Facing the hard choices.* Dover, MA: Auburn House.

Keyserling, M. D. (1972). *Windows on day care.* New York: National Council of Jewish Women.

Kimmerly, N. L. (1998). Parental choice of child care: relationship of family characteristics to the type of child care parents use. *Dissertation Abstracts International, 59*, 5621.

Kisker, E. E., and Maynard, R. (1991). Quality, cost, and parental choice of child care. In D. M. Blau (Ed.), *The economics of child care.* New York: Russell Sage Foundation.

Kisker, E. E., and Silverberg, M. (1991). Child care utilization by disadvantaged teenage mothers. *Journal of Social Issues, 47*, 159–177.

Kivikink, R., and Schell, A. (1987). Demographic, satisfaction, and commitment profiles of day care users, nursery school users, and babysitter users in a medium-sized Canadian city. *Child and Youth Care Quarterly, 16*, 116–130.

Klysz, M. (1995). Family characteristics and child care arrangements. *Child and Youth Care Forum, 24*, 175–194.

Kontos, S., and Fiene, R. (1987). Child care quality, compliance with regulations, and children' development: The Pennsylvania Study. In D. A. Phillips (Ed.), *Quality in child care: What does research tell us?* (pp. 57–80). Washington, DC: National Association for the Education of Young Children.

Kontos, S., and Wilcox-Herzog, A. (2001). How do education and experience affect teachers of young children? *Young Children, 56*(4), 85–91.

Lally, J. R., and Honig, A. S. (1975). Education of infants and toddlers from low-income and low-education backgrounds: Support for the family's role and identity. In B. Friedlander, G. Kirk, and G. Sterritt (Eds.), *Exceptional infant: Assessment and observation* (Vol. 3, pp. 285–303). New York: Bruner/Mazel.

Lally, J. R., Mangione, P., and Honig, A. S. (1988). The Syracuse University Family Development Research Program: Long-range impact of an early intervention with low-income children and their families. In D. Powell (Ed.), *Parent education as early childhood intervention: Emerging directions in theory, research, and practice* (pp. 79–104). Norwood, NJ: Ablex.

Lazar, I., Darlington, R. B., Murray, H., Royce, J., and Snipper, A. (1982). Lasting effects of early education: A report of the Consortium for Longitudinal Studies. *Monographs of the Society for Research in Child Development, 47* (2–3, Serial No. 195).

Leavitt, R. L. (1987). *Invisible boundaries: An interpretive study of parent–provider relationships* (ERIC Doc. No. ED 299 035).

Lein, L. (1979). Parental evaluation of child care alternatives. *Urban and Social Change Review, 12*, 11–16.

Long, P., Wilson, P., Kutnick, P., and Telford, L. (1996). Choice and childcare: A survey of parental perceptions and views. *Early Child Development and Care, 119*, 51–63.

Lurie, R., and Newman, K. (1980). A healthy tension—parent and group infant/toddler care. In R. Lurie and R. Neugebauer (Eds.), *Caring for infants and toddlers; What works, what doesn't* (Vol. 2, pp. 71–76). Redmond, WA: Child Care Information Exchange.

Mason, J., and Kuhlthau, B. (1989). Literacy transfer from parents to children in the preschool years. In T. G. Stricht, M. J. Beeler, and B. A. McDonald (Eds.), *Cognition and literacy* (Vol. 1, pp. 49–68). Norwood, NJ: Ablex.

Mason, L. (2000). *Bright Horizons Family Solutions: A caring Community.* Unpublished paper.

McCartney, K. (1984). Effect of quality of day-care environment on children's language development. *Developmental Psychology, 20*, 244–260.

McCartney, K., Scarr, K., Phillips, D., and Grajek, S. (1985). Day care as intervention: Comparisons of varying quality programs. *Journal of Applied Developmental Psychology, 6*, 247–260.

McCartney, K., Scarr, S., Phillips, D., Grajek, S., and Schwartz, C. (1982). Environmental differences among day care centers and their effects on children's levels of intellectual, language, and social development. In E. Zigler and E. Gordon (Eds.), *Day care: Scientific and social policy issues* (pp. 126–151). Boston: Auburn House.

Meadows, A. (1991). *Caring for America's children. Panel on Child Care Policy.* Washington, DC: National Academy Press.

Miller, J., and Weissman, S. (1988). *The parents' guide to day care.* New York: Bantam.

Miller, S. (1992, Summer). Better days for child care? Don't believe everything you hear. *The Ounce of Prevention Fund Quarterly*, 10–12.

Missing Fathers. (1993, August 5). *The Syracuse Post-Standard*, p. A-12.

NAEYC (2001a). Financing the early childhood education system. NAEYC Policy Brief. *Young Children, 56*(4), 54–57.

National Association for the Education of Young Children. (2001b). Private communication from Michael Vaughn. Washington, DC: Author.

Nelson, F., and Garduque, L. (1991). The experience and perception of continuity between home and day care from the perspectives of child, mother, and caregiver. *Early Child Development and Care, 68*, 99–112.

Newman, S. A. (2000). *Funding for after school programs*. Unpublished paper.

NICHD Early Child Care Research Network. (1997). The effects of infant child care on infant–mother attachment security: Results of the NICHD study of early child care. *Child Development, 68*, 860–879.

Number of CDA's passes 50,000. (1993, July). *Competence: News for the CDA Community, 10*, p. 1.

Okagaki, L., and Sternberg, R. (1993). Parental beliefs and children's school performance. *Child Development, 64*, 36–45.

Office of Educational Research and Improvement. (2000). Reaching all families. Creating family-friendly schools. Washington, DC: U.S. Department of Education.

Office of Workforce Relations. (1999, May). *Establishing a work-site parenting support group*. Washington, DC: U.S. Office of Personnel Management.

Ounce of Prevention Fund. (2000). *Delivering early education and childcare*. Chicago, IL: Author.

Park, K., and Honig, A. S. (1991). Infant care patterns and later teacher ratings of preschool behaviors. *Early Child Development and Care, 68*, 89–96.

Pence, A., and Goelman, H. (1987). Silent partners: Parents, children in three types of day care. *Early Childhood Research Quarterly, 2*, 315–334.

Phillips, D., and Howes, C. (1989). Indicators of quality in child care: Review of research. In D. Phillips (Ed.), *Quality in child care: What does research tell us?* (pp. 1–20). Washington, DC: National Association for the Education of Young Children.

Phillips, D., McCartney, K., and Scarr, S. (1987). Child care quality and children's social development. *Developmental Psychology, 23*, 537–543.

Phillipsen, L., Cryer, D., and Howes, C. (1995). Classroom process and classroom structure. In S. Helburn (Ed.), *Cost, quality and child outcomes in child care centers* (Technical Report). Denver: University of Colorado at Denver, Department of Economics, Center for Research in Economics and Social Policy.

Pierce, K. M., Hamm, J. V., and Vandell, D. L. (1999). Experiences in after-school programs and children's adjustment in first-grade classrooms. *Child Development, 70*, 756–767.

Powell, D. R., and Baleen, G. (1992). Dimensions of parent–provider relationships in family day care. In D. L. Peters and A. R. Pence (Eds.), *Family day care: Current research for informed public policy*. New York: Teachers College Press.

Prescott, E. T. (1973, April). *A comparison of three types of day care and nursery-school-home care*. Paper presented at the biennial meetings of the Society for Research in Child Development, Philadelphia.

Presser, H. B. (1989). Can we make time for children: The economy, work schedules, and child care. *Demography, 26*, 523–543.

Prosser, W. R., and McGroder, S. M. (1992). The supply of and demand for child care: Measurement and analytic issues. In A. Booth (Ed.), *Child care in the 1990s: Trends and consequences* (pp. 42–55). Hillsdale, NJ: Lawrence Erlbaum Associates.

Pungello, E. P., and Kurtz-Costes, B. (1999). Why and how working women choose child care: A review with a focus on infancy. *Developmental Review, 19*, 31–96.

Ramey, C. T., and Gowan, J. W. (1990). A general systems approach to modifying risk for retarded development. In A. S. Honig (Ed.), *Risk factors in infancy* (pp. 9–26). London: Gordon and Breach.

Ramey, C. T., and Ramey S. (1999). *Gains from high-quality care persist into adulthood—landmark study* [Online]. Available: http://www.fpg.unc.edu

Rafanello, D. (2000, Winter). Recruiting and retaining high-quality staff: No easy answers. *The Director's Link*.

Report on Preschool Programs. (2000, October 25). Early childhood directors grow more adept at technology use. *Report on School Programs, 32*.

Robinson, J., and Corley, R. (1989). *The effects of day care participation: Sex differences in early and middle childhood*. Poster presented at the biennial meeting of the Society for Research in Child Development, Kansas City, MO.

Ruopp, R., Travers, J., Glantz, F., and Coelen, C. (1979). *Children at the center: Final results of the National Day Care Study*. Boston: ABT Associates.

Scarr, S. (1985). *Mother care: Other care*. New York: Basic Books.

SECA. (1993, Spring). *SECA Reporter*, p. 5.

Seppanen, P. S., Love, J. M., de Vries, D. K., Bernstein, L., Seligson, M., Marx, F., and Kisker, E. E. (1993). *National study of before-and-after school programs: Final report*. Washington, DC: U.S. Department of Education, Office of Policy and Planning.

Schulman, K., and Adams, G. (1998). *Issue brief: The high cost of child care puts quality care out of reach for many families*. Washington, DC: Children's Defense Fund.

Sonnenstein, F. L. (1991). The child care preferences of parents with young children. How little is known. In J. Hyde and M. Essex (Eds.), *Parental leave and child care: Setting a research and policy agenda* (pp. 337–353). Philadelphia: Temple University Press.

Springer, K. (2000, Fall/Winter). What to look for in preschools. *Newsweek, 30, 32*.

Stipek, D., Milburn, S., Clements, D., and Daniels, D. H. (1992). Parents' beliefs about appropriate education for young children. *Journal of Applied Developmental Psychology, 14*, 293–310.

Sugarman, J. (1991). *Building early childhood systems: A resource handbook.* Washington, DC: Child Welfare League of America.

Teacher compensation not improving. (1993, July/August). *Child Care Information Exchange,* pp. 65–66.

Texas Work and Family Clearinghouse. (1992, Fall). *Clearinghouse News, 4.*

Tizard, B., and Hughes, M. (1984). *Young children learning.* London: Fontana.

Travers, J., Goodson, B. D., Singer, J. D., and Connell, D. B. (1979). *Final report to the National Day Care Study: Research results of the National Day Care Study.* Cambridge, MA: ABT Associates.

U.S. Department of Labor. (1998). *Meeting the needs of today's workforce: Child care best practices.* Washington, DC: U.S. Department of Labor.

U.S. Department of the Treasury. (1998). *Investing in child care: Challenges facing working parents and the private sector response.* Washington, DC: Author.

U.S. Office of Personnel Management. (1998, June). *A review of Federal family-friendly workplace arrangements.* Washington, DC: Author.

Vandell, D. L., Dadisman, K., and Gallagher, K. (2000). Another look at the elephant: Child care in the nineties. In R. Taylor (Ed.), *Resiliency across contexts: Family, work, culture, and community.* Hillside, NJ: Lawrence Erlbaum Associates.

Vandell, D. L., Henderson, V. K., and Wilson, K. S. (1988). A longitudinal study of children with day-care experiences of varying quality. *Child Development, 59,* 1286–1292.

Waite, L. J., Leibowitz, A., and Witsberger, C. (1991, April). *What parents pay for: Quality of child care and child care costs.* Paper presented at the annual meeting of the Population Association of America.

West, J., Hausken, E. G., and Collins, M. (1993). *National household educational survey profile of preschool children's childcare and early education program participation. Statistical Analysis Report.* Washington, DC: U.S. Department of Education, National Center for Education Statistics.

Whitebook, M., Howes, C., and Phillips, D. (1989). *Who cares? Child care teachers and the quality of care in America* (Final Report of the National Child Care Staffing Study). Oakland, CA: Child Care Employee Project.

Whitebook, M., Phillips, D., and Howes, C. (1993). *National child care staffing study revisited: Four years in the life of center-based child care.* Oakland, CA: Child Care Employee Project.

Whitehead, L. C. (1989). Predictors of maternal satisfaction with family day care. *Dissertation Abstracts International, 49,* 9011A (University Microfilms No. ADG90-19295).

Willer, B., and Bredekamp, S. (1993). A "new" paradigm of early childhood professional development. *Young Children, 48,* 63–66.

Wittmer, D. S., and Honig, A. S. (1990). Teacher re-recreation of negative interactions with toddlers. In A. S. Honig, (Ed.). *Optimizing early child care and education* (pp. 77–88). London: Gordon and Breach.

Wolf, D. A., and Sonnenstein, F. L. (1990). *References, perceptions, and child care turnover: Patterns among welfare mothers.* Washington, DC: Urban Institute.

Zigler, E. F., and Gordon, E. W. (Eds.). (1982), *Day care: Scientific and social policy issues.* Boston: Auburn House.

16

Family, School, and Community Partnerships

Joyce L. Epstein
Mavis G. Sanders
Johns Hopkins University

INTRODUCTION

Families, schools, and communities play important roles in socializing and educating children. In this chapter, we review the literature on the connections in these contexts that support students' learning and we consider how parents, educators, and community members separately and jointly influence the education and development of children. Two purposes of this work are to encourage researchers who study families and parenting to pay more attention to schools during the years that children are students, and to encourage researchers who study schools and children's learning to examine the influence of families and communities in children's education and development. It is important to recognize that schools and teachers critically influence families, and that families influence educators every year that children attend school. Another purpose is to illustrate how research and development may help schools and families create broader and deeper support for student learning. It is important for educators, policy leaders, counselors, community leaders, and other professionals who work with families and children to understand the inevitable connections of home, school, and community, and to maximize the positive results of those connections for students.

The chapter begins with a short summary of the history of relations between home and school in American education. There has been an interesting evolution from very high control by families and communities of children's education and schools to strict separation of family and school responsibilities for formal education, and to new partnerships based on shared responsibilities of educators, families, and community members for children's learning and development.

The second section summarizes some of the major theories of family–school–community relations and how the theories have changed over time. Theories of separate, nested, and overlapping influences of families and schools have guided research and practice. The different perspectives are reflected in various practical models that define the roles and responsibilities of parents, teachers, and members of the community. Historic fluctuations in practices and the progression of distinct theories and models demonstrate that family–school–community collaborations can be designed and modified.

Although some parents have always guided their own children's learning, many parents have been disconnected from their children's schools and schooling. In order for all parents to become and remain influential in their children's education, schools must take leadership in building good programs and practices of partnership that reach out to and include all families. Research conducted in elementary, middle, and high schools for the past 20 years reveals the usefulness of a framework of six types of involvement that assist educators in developing programs to inform and engage all families and their communities in ways that contribute to student success. The framework also guides researchers to conduct studies of the organization and results of partnerships. The third section of the chapter discusses this framework and the roles and responsibilities of schools and families in conducting activities for the six types of involvement.

Finally, we discuss selected educational issues that are important to parents as their children proceed through school. School reform initiatives often include improving the curriculum, revising instructional approaches, and conducting new assessments of students' work and progress. Parents often are uninformed about these and other organizational and program changes that affect their children's education and experiences in school. Teachers and administrators need to address key questions to inform and involve families in school improvement plans and decisions. Each topic also poses opportunities for researchers to frame new studies that could help educators, parents, and others in the community proceed more effectively as partners in children's education.

This chapter continually refers to school, family, and community connections that influence children's learning and development (Epstein, 1995) rather than only parent–teacher relations. The broader term recognizes that many adults (e.g., parents, guardians, grandparents, clergy, mentors, and others) play major roles in children's lives and in their schools. Although much of the literature focuses on mothers, recent attention has been given to fathers' involvement and influence on children's learning (Nord, Brimhall, and West, 1997; Parke, 1996, and in Vol. 3 of this *Handbook*). Other studies are revealing how community groups and resources contribute to school programs, student learning, and families' well-being (Dryfoos, 1994, 1998; Sanders, 2001; Sanders and Harvey, 2000). It is important to view school, family, and community partnerships broadly to understand how people in different contexts connect and influence the likelihood of students' school success, and the quality of children's and families' lives outside of school.

A LOOK BACK IN TIME AT FAMILY–SCHOOL RELATIONS

This section takes a brief look back in time to identify important trends in home and school connections. The literature on family–school relations in the United States reveals recurring themes of conflict and dissonance. One might think that parents and teachers would be natural allies, as both groups are concerned with children's growth and development. Society places great expectations and serious responsibilities on parents and on educators to do their best for students and for the future of the community. However, ideas differ and have changed over time about how families and schools should fulfill these responsibilities. Thus, the history of periodic conflict and dissonance in parent–teacher relationships is not surprising given the uncertainties generated by changing societal needs and pressures (Finkelstein, 1992). Conflicts and concerns also may result from parents' and teachers' unfamiliarity with each other's goals, beliefs, and efforts, and the tendencies for teachers to blame parents for students' problems (Becker and Epstein, 1982; Epstein and Becker, 1982; Voltz, 1998) and for parents to report they need more and better information from teachers (Epstein, 1986; Hoover-Dempsey and Sandler, 1997).

Until recently, there has been little recognition of how parents and educators can work together to reduce their conflicts and concerns and how they may share responsibilities for socializing and educating children. Here, we examine a few of the changing roles and relationships of families and schools since the colonial period in the United States, identify some sources of conflict, and discuss some reasons why new forms of contact and collaboration have emerged. This short summary provides an historical base for later discussions of theories, research, and practices of partnerships. (For more complete histories of parenting, see Bjorklund, Yunger, and Pelligrini, in Vol. 2, and French, in Vol. 2 of this *Handbook*.)

In colonial days, children's education was conducted mainly in everyday contexts of the family, church, farm, shop, and village. The family was the fundamental institution responsible for creating a healthy, religious, and civil society. Only some children, mainly selected males, attended church-run or private schools for classical education that supplemented the basic knowledge and skills taught by parents and others in the community (Campbell, Cunningham, and McPhee, 1965; Handlin, 1976).

In New England, where public or "common" schools were established and grew in number in the early 1800s, the family, church, town, and school set a common agenda. The primary purposes of education were to instill in students the religious, moral, and political beliefs of their communities, and to prepare children to become young adults with their own families and productive workers in their communities (Grubb, 1995). To limit conflict and build the kind of political consensus needed to support a fledgling democracy, public schools often were governed by the same trustees who governed the church and the town (Campbell et al., 1965; Gutek, 1992; Lutz and Merz, 1992).

Amendments to the nation's constitution specified the rights of citizens, and a series of court challenges later clarified the separation of church and state. Over time, state laws for public schools were supported by laws for school funding and for redirecting the curriculum from the needs of a local religious community to the needs of the broader society. This shift reduced the power of the family, church, and local community over education, and signaled the beginning of a process in which outside institutions assumed some of the functions of families in guiding and educating children, and in preparing them for work (Lewis, 1989).

By the time of the Industrial Revolution in the late eighteenth century, it was well accepted that the family alone could not educate and socialize children for the new occupations that were proliferating in factories and cities. As nondomestic and nonfarm occupations increased and home-based hand manufacturing declined, families had to balance their strong interests and emotions in rearing their children with the need to educate children to qualify for better jobs. The public schools became the major mechanism for most families to improve their own and their children's economic and social standings. Sons of farmers, daughters of immigrants, and children of parents with little or no formal schooling attended public school to improve their chances for success and their status in society (Finkelstein, 1992).

In the early days of this democracy, not all families believed that public schools were important for children's success in society. Middle- and upper-income families resisted sending their children to public schools, which were considered places to serve paupers (Campbell et al., 1965) and to "civilize the lower classes" (Williams, 1989, p. 72). However, by the early 1900s, as a result of laws for compulsory attendance and for public funding of education, most middle-income and some upper-income children attended public schools. As the population of the nation increased and moved westward new communities formed, opened public schools, and were less likely to create as many private schools as were established and attended in the east. Thus, most students from families in all socioeconomic groups attended public schools (Graham, 1976).

Public schools represented this society's great equalizer of opportunities for children from diverse backgrounds. Schools were expected to open their doors to all and foster upward mobility. In reality, however, some schools were segregated, some were of poor quality, and most schools "sorted" children into programs that led to different career paths. Only some students with the highest intellectual skills were assisted to obtain education beyond the elementary grades (Gutek, 1992). As late as 1900, only about 6.4% of all 17-year-olds graduated from high school (Nichols and

Good, 2000). In theory, the sorting policies were an expedient response to the need for a diversified labor force, but in reality, schools' restrictions and selections reflected the discriminatory characteristics of the larger society.

As the most public of all institutions, schools have always mirrored the struggles of sharing power among people of different races, classes, cultures, and genders. For example, since this nation's earliest days, there have been debates and challenges about inequities in the educational opportunities of European Americans and African American children, and of males and females (Graham, 1976; Lutz and Merz, 1992). Throughout history, many families undoubtedly were hostile toward the schools' sorting policies that prevented female children and children of color from enjoying the full benefits of education, and from meeting families' aspirations for their children's educational and occupational success (Lightfoot, 1978).

Over time, schools were viewed as institutions that should compensate for the declining authority of families and communities. Within the past century, schools have been assigned many more responsibilities to "preserve democracy, eliminate poverty, reduce unemployment, ease the assimilation of immigrants to the nation, overcome differences between ethnic groups, advance scientific knowledge and technical progress, prevent traffic accidents, raise health standards, refine oral character, and guide young people into useful occupations" (Ravitch, 1983, cited in Williams, 1989, p. 12).

Conditions that affect the connections of parents and children, and of parents and schools, are very different today from any time in the past. For example, at the start of the twentieth century, 41% of families consisted of two parents living on a farm, and only 20% of women were employed outside the home. By the 1950s, about one third of all women were in the labor force. Currently, the number of two-parent farm families is under 1%, and over 60% of women are employed (Council of Economic Advisors, 2000). These social facts of family life have created a need for new family–school–community relationships that support students, parents, schools, and the economy and quality of communities.

Ironically, the additional demands on schools over the past four decades, the predominance of mothers' employment, and other changing characteristics, needs, and resources of families have helped to redirect relations between parents and schools from conflict toward collaboration. There is a growing recognition that families, schools, and communities will be able to do more to help children reach important educational goals if they work together, combine resources, communicate effectively, and let students know about their collaborations. The need for cooperation is forcing educators and community leaders to shift from criticizing families and trying to make parents meet the demands of schools to changing schools and communities to meet the needs, interests, and goals of families and children.

This short summary followed the trail from the emergence of colonial schools to common schools to the acceptance of public education for all students, and the changing contexts of family life. Advances in education and the economy have necessitated changes in the connections of families and schools in the United States. Similar developments in home-school connections also have occurred in other countries. Researchers and practitioners in some nations, including Australia, Canada, Chile, Cyprus, England, Portugal, Scotland, and Spain, have been working for many years to reduce the separation and conflict between home and school, and to increase cooperation and partnerships (Sanders and Epstein, 1998b). Researchers in other nations have just begun to move from highly separate family and school responsibilities to more collaborative work, as in the new democracies in Poland (Mendel, 1998) and the Czech Republic (Davies and Johnson, 1996). There is growing recognition across borders that just about all parents want their children to succeed in school, but that most families need guidance in how to best assist their children with schoolwork and school decisions across the grades. Importantly, educators across countries are finding that if schools plan and implement good partnership practices, many more parents respond and become more involved (Davies and Johnson, 1996; Sanders and Epstein, 1998a).

THEORIES AND MODELS OF
FAMILY–SCHOOL–COMMUNITY CONNECTIONS

In this section, we explore selected theories of family, school, and community connections, and outline some of the major practical models that translate the different theories into practice.

Theoretical Perspectives

Theoretical frameworks for understanding family–school–community relations are found in socio-logical, psychological, and educational literature on child development and school and classroom organization. Three broad perspectives have guided thinking about these contextual connections. Theories of separate, embedded, and overlapping influences of schools, families, and communities help explain the learning and development of children of all races, cultures, genders, and family backgrounds (see Epstein, 1987, for an extended discussion of these perspectives).

Separate influences. The psychological and sociological literature in the early twentieth cen-tury argued for the separateness of teachers' and parents' roles in schooling. Anna Freud (1935, cited in Lightfoot, 1978) discussed the dangers in teachers becoming too "mother-like," which she believed would result in children becoming too demanding of teachers. Waller (1932) wrote about the necessity of separate roles for parents and teachers in order to successfully train children to assume their responsibilities for their own learning and the demands of work. These views reflected other longstanding sociological theories that organizations are most effective when they set unique missions, clear goals, and fulfill distinct responsibilities (Weber, 1947).

The early view that a child's mind was, in effect, a tabula rasa, directed parents to fill that blank slate with basic skills and social competencies in the early years. Then, parents presented their children to the school for academic skills. The prevailing theories assumed that the separate and sequenced activities of home and school were clear and necessary. Parents and educators were thought to operate in separate settings, had different levels and kinds of professional training, and thought differently about their contributions to child development. These perspectives put the family in charge of the child's initial education and training, and their ongoing social, moral, and religious development, and placed the school in charge of formal education.

Embedded influences. Bronfenbrenner (1979, 1986) introduced a theoretical framework that recognized the multiple and interdependent influences of various social contexts on children's de-velopment. Bronfenbrenner's paradigm suggests that child development is "nested" or embedded in an expanding set of ecological environments. The microsystem refers to relationships in a primary setting (such as the child interacting with parents at home); the macrosystem refers to patterns of cultural or societal beliefs outside the home that may influence parents' and/or children's behavior. Bronfenbrenner's model is depicted as a set of concentric circles of increasingly distal influences on the child, who is at the center of the model. Researchers have used this paradigm to study con-textual effects on individual child development, with attention to the impact on children of maternal employment, daycare, social support, community conditions, and other factors that may influence children's learning, achievement, attitudes, and success (see, e.g., in this *Handbook*, Bradley, in Vol. 2; Cochran and Neigo, in Vol. 4; Harkness and Super, in Vol. 2; and Lerner, Rothbaum, Boulos, and Castellino, in Vol. 2).

Overlapping influences. Epstein (1987) suggested a social organizational perspective of over-lapping spheres of influence to understand and study school, family, and community connections. This model integrates and extends Bronfenbrenner's (1979) ecological model, Leichter's (1974) insights on families as educators, sociological perspectives of the connections of professional and nonprofessional institutions and individuals (Litwak and Meyer, 1974), an emphasis on the shared responsibility for children's education and well-being (Seeley, 1981), and a long line of sociological and psychological studies of school and family environments (Barker and Gump, 1964; Coleman et al., 1966; Epstein and McPartland, 1979; McDill and Rigsby, 1973; Moos and Insel, 1974).

Pictorially, this model is shown as spheres of influence, which can, by design, be pushed together to overlap or pulled apart to increase the separation of home, school, and community. The model identifies an external structure of moving spheres of influence and an internal structure of interpersonal exchanges and interactions among children and others who are at home, in school, and in the community. The full model recognizes the interlocking histories of institutions that motivate, socialize, and educate children. It also represents changes over time in the skills and collaborative activities of parents, teachers, community partners, and students.

The external model assumes that the shared responsibilities of home, school, and community for children's education are affected by forces of time, which accounts for different patterns of interactions that occur at various ages and stages of children's development, and experience, which accounts for family, school, and community background characteristics, philosophies, and practices.

The internal model identifies the interpersonal relationships that occur between and among parents, children, educators, and members of the community, which may positively or negatively influence student learning and development. There are two levels of interaction at the institutional level (e.g., schools invite all families or community groups to an event) and at the individual level (e.g., teachers and parents confer about one student's work). Students are at the center of this model as the main actors in their own education and as the reason for home, school, and community connections.

The interactions of educators, students, parents, and others that occur in the internal structure of the model at the institutional and individual levels represent social ties that may generate "social capital." Social capital (Coleman, 1988; Lin, 2000) refers to resources such as information, attitudes, and behaviors that are the product of relationships and that may be collected or accrued, and then invested or used to benefit students, families, schools, and the community. For example, parents may meet and interact with other parents and other helpful adults and then translate the ideas and information they obtain into involvement at school and at home, and actions to guide and support their children (Sheldon, in press).

Within the overlapping areas of the internal model, connections are made, information is exchanged, respect is built, and ties develop between and among teachers, parents, students, and others in the community. If resulting actions are based on good information and positive connections, students will hear the same messages from home, school, and the community about the importance of learning, attending school, doing homework, and fulfilling their roles and responsibilities as students. This common focus creates "family-like" schools that welcome parents and treat each student as an individual and "school-like" families that help children fulfill their role as students.

The overlap and interactions of home, school, and community are dynamic processes that produce continually changing social interactions and exchanges. These may have positive or negative results, depending on how activities are designed, discussed, and implemented. All three theoretical perspectives—separation of home and school, embedded development, and overlapping spheres of influence—have been applied in practice. Researchers may study the theories and linked practical approaches to better understand their influences on students, families, and schools.

Practical Models of Partnership

Swap (1993) discussed four practical models that schools use to resist or encourage effective home—school partnerships: the *protective model*, the *school-to-home transmission model*, the *curriculum enrichment model*, and the *partnership model*. These educational approaches reflect the theoretical perspectives discussed above.

The protective model takes a business-like view in requiring parents to delegate the responsibility for educating children to the schools and to hold the schools accountable for the results (Swap, 1993,

p. 28). This model represents the theory that home and school have unique missions and goals, and that parents and teachers have separate roles and influences on children's development. When this model is practiced in schools, parents may be infrequently involved, or involved in limited ways, such as fund raising, chaperoning trips, or providing other services. Schools activating this model are unlikely to conduct or support serious two-way parent–teacher communications or activities that recognize parents and teachers as equals in the education of children or school-related decisions.

The school-to-home transmission model recognizes the value and power of the family to influence children's learning, but emphasizes communication in one direction only—from the school to the home. This model assumes that parents should and will agree with the school's goals and programs. Educators may share information on school activities, students' strengths and weaknesses, school policies, the curriculum, and other information. However, the school is unlikely to offer families or others in the community opportunities to share ideas, give reactions, provide input to policies or decisions that affect student work or school programs and practices.

The protective and school-to-home transmission models limit parents' roles in schools and in their children's education. These two models do not integrate family or community knowledge, values, talents, traditions, or cultures into the curriculum or life of the school. Rather, these models protect educators by building figurative fences or walls around the school and by defining teachers and schools as the people and places for formal education.

The curriculum enrichment model recognizes that teachers, parents, and students can learn from and about each other. This model integrates family and community knowledge into the school curriculum and children's learning (Gonzalez, Andrade, Civil, and Moll, 2001; Moll, Amanti, Neff, and Gonzalez, 1992). The focus on the curriculum is important because students' homework, classwork, decisions about courses, and other curriculum-related issues affect every student's success in school.

Studies indicate that, through middle school and high school, parent–child discussions about schoolwork, school programs, and plans for the future are among the measures of parent involvement with the strongest positive effects on student outcomes over time (Lee, 1994; Simon, 2000). However, a curriculum focus alone does not constitute a comprehensive program of school, family, and community partnerships, which must include many types of involvement that are designed to improve student learning and other indicators of student success.

The partnership model activates the theory of overlapping spheres of influence for student success (Epstein, 1987, 1990, 1992). A partnership program is built on "long-term commitments, mutual respect, widespread involvement of families and educators in many levels of activities, and sharing of planning and decision-making responsibilities" (Swap, 1993, p. 47). A comprehensive program of school, family, and community partnerships is represented by a framework of six types of involvement (i.e., parenting, communicating, volunteering, learning at home, decision making, and collaborating with the community, see below), and is realized through an action team approach (Epstein, 1995). In a partnership model, teachers, parents, administrators, and others work together to plan, implement, and evaluate activities that help students reach important learning and behavioral goals. This may include a parenting program on child and adolescent development, two-way communications, volunteer activities, curriculum-related learning at home, decisions about school programs and policies, and connections with the community.

Summary. The three theoretical perspectives and four practical approaches described above are linked. Those who believe that families and schools are separate institutions with specific and distinct missions and different influences on students tend to promote practices that assign teachers and parents dissimilar roles and limit connections of parents and teachers. Those who believe that each student is embedded in a series of expanding social contexts will consider the home influence, the school influence, and society's influence on individual student development. Those who believe that home, school, and community are overlapping and dynamic influences will implement a partnership model that encourages parents, teachers, and others in the community to share ideas and focus on common goals for helping all students succeed. There is a growing awareness that educators and parents need to share their mutual interests, knowledge, experiences, and resources to promote children's learning (American Federation of Teachers, 1999; Comer and Haynes, 1991; Dianda and McClaren, 1996; Epstein, Coates, Salinas, Sanders, and Simon, 1997; National PTA, 2000).

Interpersonal and organizational factors play important roles in how well students learn and in how well families, educators, and community members work together to help students succeed. Schools' philosophies of separate or overlapping spheres of influence determine, in large measure, the nature and extent of interactions of parents, teachers, administrators, students, and others in the community. Most schools and school districts lack an explicit, written philosophy, policy, and plan of whether and how they will inform, invite, and involve all families and the community in the life of the school and in children's education. Educators and parents need to discuss and decide which theoretical perspectives represent their views on how students learn, how adults influence children's education, and which activities for partnerships they will implement to help all students succeed.

FAMILY PARTNERSHIPS WITH SCHOOLS

When parents become involved in their children's education, students tend to do better in school. When schools implement effective parent involvement activities, more parents tend to respond in the ways that they are invited and guided to do. These two major results of research pose an important challenge for educators to design comprehensive partnership programs that reach out to involve all parents and other partners in productive ways. In this section, we explore how some families presently are involved in helping students build literacy skills, complete homework, and plan for postsecondary education. We note the generally weak level of involvement of most families, and discuss, in detail, how parents, educators, and community partners could improve the nature and extent of involvement by implementing partnership activities for six types of involvement.

How Parents Support Children's Education

Numerous studies confirm that some parents are presently involved in their children's education and their schools, whereas other parents are not regularly or productively involved (Dauber and Epstein, 1993; Epstein, 1986; Hoover-Dempsey, Battiato, Walker, Reed, and Jones, 2001; Hoover-Dempsey and Sandler, 1997; Sanders, Epstein, and Connors-Tadros, 1999). This uneven participation is due largely to the fact that involvement traditionally depends more on parents' own initiatives than on schools' systematic outreach to involve all families.

When involvement is left up to parents to figure out own their own, parents with more formal education and school experience are more likely to become and remain involved in their children's education and in the schools, and effectively guide their children through the grades (Baker and Stevenson, 1986; Lareau, 1989; Useem, 1992; and see other chapters in this *Handbook* by Hetheringon and Stanley-Hagan, in Vol. 3; Hoff, Laursen, and Tardif, in Vol. 2; and Goodnow; Gottfried, Gottfried, and Bathurst, in Vol. 3, for overviews of the connections family structure and socioeconomic status with patterns of parenting). Also, parents with younger children are, on average, more frequently involved in their children's education than are parents of students in the upper grades (Eccles and Harold, 1996; Epstein and Lee, 1995; Hoover-Dempsey and Sandler, 1997; Stevenson and Baker, 1987). Parents of older students report feeling increasingly less able to help with homework (Dauber and Epstein, 1993; Grolnick and Slowiaczek, 1994; Simon, 2000).

Studies have shown that, regardless of parent income or formal education, if parents are involved, students tend to do better in their academic work and have more positive school attitudes, higher aspirations, and other positive behaviors (Clark, 1983; Comer, 1980; Epstein, 1991, 2001; Gutman and McLoyd, 2000; Sanders, 1998a; Sanders and Herting, 2000). Even at the middle school and high school levels, analyses indicate that students benefit if their parents remain involved in their education (Catsambis, 1998; Desimone, 1999; Fehrmann, Keith, and Reimers, 1987; Ho and Willms, 1996; Keith et al., 1993; Lee, 1994; Simon, 2000). After family background, parents' education, and students' prior skills are accounted for, students who continue to communicate with their parents about schoolwork and school decisions tend to have better attendance, higher report card grades, and more course credits completed.

Most parents, even those with many years of formal education, say they could use more help to better support their children's learning and development from preschool through high school (Corno, 2000; Dauber and Epstein, 1993; Eccles and Harold, 1996; Hoover-Dempsey and Sandler, 1997; Sanders et al., 1999). New efforts have begun to help educators and parents develop more effective partnership programs and to focus their collaborations on student learning. For example, since 1996, leaders in many schools, school districts, and state departments of education have been working to identify and implement planned programs of interactions among families, schools, and communities that are linked to school improvement goals (Epstein, 1995; Sanders and Epstein, 2000b).

The approaches to increase and improve involvement are needed because studies are accumulating that show that if schools and teachers implement specific practices, parents respond by becoming more involved in those very practices (Ames, DeStefano, Watkins, and Sheldon, 1995; Balli, Demo, and Wedman, 1998; Delgado-Gaitan, 1990; Epstein and Dauber, 1991; Ho and Willms, 1996; Lee, 1994; Sanders et al., 1999; Simon, 2000; Van Voorhis, 2000).

In this section we discuss a few key parenting practices that facilitate students' success in school. These include activities that parents may initiate on their own or that may be part of schools' programs and practices designed to involve all families in ways that have been shown to promote student success.

Parenting for literacy learning. Parents are urged by professionals to establish a rich oral and written language environment in the home from infancy on, and to serve as model readers for and with their children in order to boost children's readiness for reading and their chances for success in school (Gomby, Larner, Stevenson, Lewit, and Behrman, 1995; Morisset, 1993; Wasik and Karweit, 1994; Williams and Sternberg, in Vol. 5 of this *Handbook*).

There is long-standing agreement about the importance of family involvement in student literacy learning. Walberg (1984) reported that "the curriculum of the home" predicts school success twice as well as socioeconomic status. This curriculum includes "informed parent–child conversations about everyday events, encouragement and discussion of leisure reading, and expressions of affection and interest in children's academic and personal growth" (p. 400). Similarly, studies indicated that parents' reading with children and interacting with them verbally are positively related to children's reading performance (Hess, Holloway, Dickson, and Price, 1984; Marjoribanks, 1988).

Topping (1995) identified specific factors that linked parent involvement with children's reading. These are: (1) allowing time for children to practice reading at home, (2) making reading enjoyable and valued, (3) giving children praise for reading and feedback, and (4) modeling reading and writing at home to encourage children to relate to and imitate these behaviors. Others also found significant effects on children's reading skills from close parent–child relationships, reading with and listening to children read, and sharing and exploring books (Snow and Tabors, 1996; Wolfendale, 1985). In Australia, Cairney and Ruge (1997) explored differences in language patterns and practices at home, at school, and in the community. They concluded that schools should better integrate into the curriculum the richness of all families' language experiences, not just those that match the formal language patterns of schools.

When educators assist and guide families in supporting children's literacy development, more families conduct these practices and children's reading skills improve (Epstein, 1991). Moreover, when schools value and incorporate students' home and community language experiences into the school curriculum, literacy instruction and learning are enriched. A number of programs have been designed to help educators organize their work with families on reading (Cairney, Ruge, Buchanan, Lowe, and Munsie, 1995; Goldsmith and Tevlin, 1998; Handel, 1999). Home–school literacy activities include sending books home for parent–child reading, teaching parents how to read aloud effectively to young children, offering literacy classes for adult learners, and organizing opportunities for family and community volunteers to tell traditional stories to students.

Parent involvement with children on homework.   Parents of elementary school children report that they spend more time and feel more capable of helping their children with homework than do parents of students in the middle grades (Dauber and Epstein, 1993). Even though parental involvement in homework declines across the grades, parental involvement still influences the time that middle and high school students spend on homework, the completion of their assignments, and their report card grades (Fehrmann et al., 1987; Keith et al., 1993). As students progress through the grades and the curriculum becomes more difficult, most parents want information from the school on how to help their adolescents with homework (Connors and Epstein, 1994; Sanders et al., 1999).

Teachers expect parents to value, monitor, and assist with homework (Epstein and Dauber, 1991; Scott-Jones, 1995), including providing space, scheduling time, and conducting positive parent–child discussions about important skills and ideas. Teachers often assign homework to help students build independent study skills and to take responsibility for their academic work. Some homework, however, may be designed for students to share their ideas and their work with parents or other family members (Epstein, Salinas, and Jackson, 1995).

It is clear that parents have important roles to play in the homework process (Cooper and Valentine, 2001; Hoover-Dempsey et al., 2001). However, without good guidance from teachers at every grade level, most parents will continue to struggle over whether and how to become involved with their children on learning activities at home. With support and ideas from classroom teachers, more children and parents would have productive conversations and interactions about homework (Epstein and Van Voorhis, 2001).

Studies suggest that teachers can increase parents' understanding, self-confidence about helping on homework, and actual involvement activities (Ames et al., 1995; Dauber and Epstein, 1993; Epstein, 1986; Hoover-Dempsey and Sandler, 1997). Some educators are using new strategies to engage students with their parents in homework discussions and activities. For example, the Teachers Involve Parents in Schoolwork (TIPS) interactive homework process; (Association for Supervision and Curriculum Development [ASCD], 2001; Epstein, Salinas, and Jackson, 1995; and see TIPS at www.partnershipschools.org) and other parent–child approaches (Topping, 1995) enable teachers to assign weekly activities that require students to share their work and ideas with a family partner. TIPS assignments in math, science, and language arts are written so that students conduct the interactions with their parents or other family partners. In this way, all families can assist their children, regardless of the level of parents' formal education. Evaluations of these approaches indicate that parents can effectively interact with their children in language arts (Epstein, Simon, and Salinas, 1997; Epstein, Herrick, and Coates, 1996), math (Balli, 1995; Balli et al., 1998), and science (Van Voorhis, 2000) in the elementary and middle grades.

Parents' influence on students' postsecondary plans for college and careers.   Parents' education levels and expectations for their children's education are significant predictors of students' college attendance and other postsecondary education and training (Davies and Kandel, 1981; Hossler and Stage, 1992; Sorensen and Morgan, 2000) Students are more likely to attend a 4-year college when their parents convey that expectation early and often (Conklin and Dailey, 1981), encourage students to explore options for postsecondary education, and help them prepare for college by succeeding in school (Lavin and Hyllegard, 1996). Jordan and Plank (2000) found that the lack of such guidance and support, in part, explains why many low-income, academically able students fail to attend postsecondary institutions after completing high school. Their analyses indicated that when low-income parents talked with their children about their future plans, encouraged them to prepare for SAT, and communicated with other parents about postsecondary opportunities, students were more likely to set educational goals and attend college regardless of socioeconomic status.

Many students say they want to go to college, but many students do not achieve at high levels or have the course credits they need to meet their aspirations (Connors and Epstein, 1994; Catsambis and Garland, 1997). Many families of these students also have high aspirations for their children but need better information from school teachers, administrators, and counselors on financial aid, course requirements, credits accumulated, PSAT, SAT, and ACT preparation, and other issues about postsecondary planning.

Whether the focus is developing literacy skills, completing homework, or planning postsecondary education, research is accumulating that indicates that well-designed parenting practices help students reach these goals. Ensuring a rich literacy environment begins in infancy and continues across the years of schooling. Establishing strong support for homework and conducting conversations about postsecondary education begin in the elementary grades and continue through high school. Families' influence on student learning occurs at all ages and stages of development on these and other topics in education.

Schools have a great deal of timely information that parents need to effectively guide and influence these and other important activities in their children's school careers. If schools exchanged useful, usable information with more families, more students would meet their learning goals and fulfill their plans for the future. Research on school, family, and community partnerships is showing how all schools and educators may organize programs and practices so that all families can assist their children in reading and other subjects, homework completion, postsecondary planning, and other important goals (Epstein, 2001).

Extent of Family Involvement at School and at Home

The glass is half full and half empty when it comes to family involvement. The National Household Education Surveys (NHES) indicated that over 60% of parents say they attend at least two activities at their children's schools each year. That statistic was stable from 1993 to 1996 (National Center for Educational Statistics, 1996). The NHES surveys showed that most parents are infrequently involved and that many parents in the younger grades (over 25%) and most in the middle school and high school grades (over 66%) are seldom or never involved, not even in one or two basic activities at their children's schools. Using other measures, research based on the National Education Longitudinal Study (NELS:88) surveys found that most parents (over 90%) set rules and try to monitor and guide their children, but few parents (from 30% to 35%) have the information they need from their children's middle schools about the students' academic programs or opportunities to volunteer (Epstein and Lee, 1995). In reality, many parents are isolated from middle schools and high schools and have a hard time understanding and guiding their older children as students.

The more challenges that parents face in their own lives, the less they are involved with their children's schooling. Quantitative and qualitative studies have shown that, on average, single parents, working parents, and parents with less formal education or less income are less frequently involved at school than are other parents, and those with more formal education are more likely to act on their beliefs about the importance of home–school connections (Astone and McLanahan, 1991; Baker and Stevenson, 1986; Delgado-Gaitan, 1990; Lareau, 1989; Xu and Corno, 1998). Importantly, parents' involvement is more strongly influenced by the actions of their children's schools than by their personal family characteristics. That is, schools that welcome parents and guide them in various involvement activities help most or all parents to become involved, including single parents, working parents, and parents with less formal education or less income (Ames et al., 1995; Becker and Epstein, 1982; Epstein and Dauber, 1991; Sanders et al., 1999).

Title I legislation provides federal funds for the education of educationally disadvantaged students. This and other federal funding sources (e.g., Even Start, Safe and Drug Free Schools, and Migrant

Education) require that schools develop programs of school, family, and community partnerships. However, the legislative language and intent have not been translated by most schools into well-planned programs that involve families in ways that help their children succeed in school.

According to one study of over 2,000 parents of educationally disadvantaged students in a poor, urban community, parents reported that they tried to get involved in education but their schools were not always welcoming places and did not often provide good information about how to become involved (Dauber and Epstein, 1993). Importantly, when the schools did so, many parents responded by becoming more involved in exactly the ways that the schools implemented.

Increasingly, schools are recognizing that they need to take more and better responsibility for involving families in productive ways. Educators report that they need training, ongoing support from school administrators and district leaders, and resources to design and implement better partnerships with families and communities. Educators, in collaboration with researchers, are beginning to identify "essential elements" of effective partnership programs (Sanders, 1999). These factors include teamwork, annual written plans, the implementation of planned activities, and support from school colleagues and from state, district, and other external sources.

Shared Responsibilities for Partnerships

To build strong school–family partnerships, researchers have worked to apply the theory of overlapping spheres of influence in research, policy, and practice. The emerging field of study asks: What are the shared responsibilities of families and schools, schools and communities, and families and communities that contribute to strong families, effective schools, and successful students? How can schools organize and implement activities in cooperation with families and communities so that all parents experience many opportunities for involvement and become and remain important influences in their children's education?

Results from many studies led to the formulation of a framework of six types of involvement and the substitution of the term *partnership* for the more limited and less collaborative term *parent involvement* (Epstein, 1992). The framework helps schools develop full programs of school, family, and community partnerships. The six types of involvement have been used in many studies and in the development of state and district policies and school practices (Epstein, 2001).

In this section, the goals of each type of involvement are summarized, along with some basic responsibilities for implementing useful activities for the six types. Parents are central players in activities for the six types of involvement, whether or not their children's schools implement comprehensive programs of partnership. Indeed, by understanding the research-based framework and by becoming involved in various ways, parents can improve their own connections with their children and their partnerships with their children's schools and teachers.

Type 1—Parenting: Basic obligations of families.   Schools that work in partnership with parents provide information to families about children's health and safety, supervision, nutrition, discipline and guidance, and other parenting skills. Schools also provide families with information about building positive home conditions that support student learning and development at each grade level. Some schools help parents with their basic parenting obligations through family support programs, workshops at the school or in other locations, parent-to-parent networks, and other forms of parent education, training, and information sharing.

Families tend to act on their own or seek help from their schools and communities to provide for children's housing, health, nutrition, clothing, and safety. Families also are responsible for teaching their children the attitudes, behaviors, beliefs, customs, traditions, talents, and skills that are unique to and valued by the family, apart from the school curriculum (Rich, 1988). Parents also may help students balance their schedules to allow time for family chores, homework, and leisure activities and fun (Epstein, 1989). By establishing supportive home conditions for healthy child development, families help children define themselves as valued sons or daughters *and* as students. If families need help in organizing their home environments for healthy children, schools should provide useful information at each age level and stage of child and adolescent development. If schools or community groups are not prepared to provide such assistance, families and other community partners should work together to develop and strengthen programs that serve these functions.

Schools are enriched, educators and children are enlightened, and parents gain confidence in their own abilities and approaches when families and the community share their backgrounds, cultures, skills, and interests in school or classroom programs and activities (Collingnon, Men, and Tan, 2001; Duran, Duran, Perry-Romero, and Sanchez, 2001). At the heart of Type 1 activities are the two-way and three-way exchanges that connect home, school, and community. These exchanges include information from schools and from the community to help families understand child and adolescent development and the essentials of home environments to support students at every age level, as well as information from families to help schools understand family life, parents' goals, and students' needs and talents.

If serious problems arise in childhood or adolescence, such as tobacco, drug, or alcohol abuse, suicide threats, violence, and early sexual behavior, solutions will be strongest if home, school, and community work well together. Partnership activities have been shown to prevent children's high-risk behaviors (Benson, 1997; Council of Economic Advisors, 2000). These relationships also make it more likely that, should problems arise, they will be more quickly identified and resolved.

In recent years, a spotlight has been cast on a few unusual incidents of violence at schools where youngsters use weapons and explosives against their classmates and teachers. Many explanations have been offered to explain why such violent episodes occur. One reason that is often overlooked is the absence of ongoing connections and communications between parents and teachers. These incidents emphasize the need for parental monitoring, parent–child interactions, and parent–teacher communications at every grade level. Reports of the incidents revealed that such communications were few or nonexistent. By contrast, the National Study of Adolescent Health has shown that students who feel "connected" to their families, schools, and communities are less likely to engage in high-risk behaviors and more likely to succeed in school (Resnick et al., 1997).

Type 2—Communicating: Basic obligations of schools. Most schools send communications to families about school programs and students' progress. The communications typically include memos, notices, phone calls, newsletters, report cards, conferences, and open-house nights. Increasingly, schools and individual teachers also use voice-mail, e-mail, and Web sites to communicate with students' families. Good information helps families know what programs are offered before school, during the school day, after school, and how their children may take advantage of various opportunities. Schools vary the forms, frequency, and content of their communications with families. These variations may greatly influence which families understand and use the information that comes home and whether parents conduct two-way communications with their children's teachers and the school administration.

Families must work with their children and with educators to improve their interactions. Students deliver many communications from their teachers to their families and from their parents to their teachers. However, students' roles as couriers, mediators, and interpreters of school-to-home and home-to-school communications are not well understood (Montandon and Perrenoud, 1987). In a survey of high school students, about 24% reported that they promptly delivered notices from school to their families (Connors and Epstein, 1994). This percentage can be improved if parents are guided to ask their children whether they have notices from the school and if teachers and parents discuss with students the importance of their roles in successful school, family, and community partnerships. Families also can encourage this process by letting teachers know that they appreciate useful information about their children or school programs.

Schools are aided when educators provide opportunities for families to respond to information that is sent home. Parents have important ideas, reactions, questions, and other contributions that increase the chances that their children will be understood, well served, and successful in school. To obtain reactions from all parents, schools need to communicate clearly in languages and vocabulary that all parents will understand; identify which parents they are reaching and which parents need additional or different kinds of information; and use various two-way communication strategies so that all parents feel comfortable in sharing their suggestions and concerns. All families should have several opportunities each year to ask questions about school programs, share reactions and suggestions to school policies, and provide information about their children to increase teachers' appreciation of their children and the families' goals for student learning and success.

Type 3—Volunteering: Support for the school and for students.   This type of involvement recognizes and organizes the use of parents' and others' talent and time to increase the quality of school programs and the success of students. Parents, family members, and others in the community may volunteer at the school, in classrooms, or in other locations. Volunteers also include those who come to school as audiences to support student performances, sports, and other events. Schools may increase the number of volunteers who assist students, teachers, and others by varying schedules and tasks so that all families feel welcome and are able to participate as volunteers and as audiences.

Volunteers may contribute their time and talents at school, at home, or in other locations. Audiences may be invited during the day, in the evening, on weekends, in the summer, and on holidays, when different family members are available. Activities may be designed that tap parents and others' talents and draw lessons from their occupations, hobbies, interests, and experiences in order to enrich students' classes and expand students' career explorations. Mentoring, coaching, and tutoring activities may be helpful in the younger grades, when assistance can be targeted and guided to help students gain basic skills, and in the upper grades, when students' skills and interests become deeper and more diverse, and individual attention from caring adults may help students cope with and overcome the growing pains of adolescence.

Families can take the initiative to find ways to contribute time and talent to their children's schools. Volunteering at the school building during school hours has become increasingly difficult for many families as the number of mothers in the work force has increased (U.S. Department of Labor, 1999). Other families have transportation and childcare problems that must be solved in order for them to give time to their children's schools.

Epstein (2001) suggested that a "volunteer" is anyone at any time and in any place who supports school goals and children's learning. This is one of many redefinitions of family involvement that are needed to increase the number of parents who participate in their children's education. This redefinition changes the way that schools identify and count the number of families who participate as "volunteers."

All families can help their children's schools by offering to make phone calls or talk with other parents, community groups, and other helpful contacts; or assist the school during early mornings, late afternoons, evenings, vacation days, weekends, or other convenient times. Educators can organize and welcome volunteers for different purposes. This may be done by setting up a "wish list" from teachers and administrators of the kinds of assistance that would help them and their students, or a "talent pool" from families offering specific skills, talents, and time which then could be considered by the educators to match school needs and goals (Epstein, 2001).

Family members also can help educate and influence their employers to support the local schools by encouraging and supporting volunteers. Increasingly, employers are considering the legitimate requests of families of school-age children for release time, compensatory time, or "flex" time to attend parent–teacher conferences or to participate, even occasionally, as volunteers at their children's schools. Parents should take advantage of state or business policies that permit involvement at their children's schools. If such policies do not exist, parents may work together to influence policy makers or business leaders to establish laws that support families in these ways.

Type 4—Learning at home: Involvement in curricular-related activities and decisions.
Teachers can guide parents to monitor, assist, and interact with their children at home on learning

activities that are coordinated with the classroom curriculum. Type 4 activities enable families to become more knowledgeable about the curricula in specific subjects, teachers' instructional methods, the academic and other skills required to pass each grade, the work their children are doing in class, how to support, monitor, discuss, and help with homework, how to help students practice and study for tests, and how to discuss academic decisions about course choices, academic programs, and schools (e.g., selecting a middle or high school within a school district or surrounding area).

Families need to do more than ask their children, "How was school today?" That question rarely elicits information about what students are learning, what skills they have mastered, or their ideas about important topics or issues. Exchanges such as "What did you learn in math today?" or "Read me something you wrote" or "Share an idea that you learned in science today" or other similar requests for shared information on learning are more likely to lead to parent–child conversations about interesting topics, and enable parents to praise their children for their effort and for mastering new skills or gaining new ideas.

In the younger grades, families may support reading and reading-related activities on a daily basis, whether their children's schools guide the process or not. Regardless of their own education or the language spoken at home, all parents can listen to their children read library books or school books, encourage reading for pleasure; ask for short "book reports" to share stories and ideas, go to the library with their children, practice spelling words, talk about new vocabulary words from class lessons, and conduct other easy conversations about reading, listening, and writing. Of course, it helps families if teachers guide these interactions so that the parent–child conversations reinforce information that will be marked or graded in school. Nevertheless, positive, age-appropriate, enjoyable activities around reading are enriching even when conducted independently by parents with children.

In the upper grades, students know more about many topics and have much to share with parents. Older students should be encouraged to lead conversations about schoolwork. Students may show, share, and demonstrate skills they are practicing in homework, read stories and poems they are writing, and conduct science experiments with parents as their science assistants (Epstein et al., 1995; Van Voorhis, 2000). It helps if teachers design homework that guides students in how and when to interact with a parent or family partner, but parents can ask students to show and explain new math skills, new words learned in a foreign language class, or new technology skills without thinking that they are supposed to know or teach these skills. As one mother noted, "Sometimes I knew what it [a science experiment] was about, and sometimes he knew more than I did. That made it interesting" (ASCD, 2001).

Families who interact with their children in these ways learn about classroom activities. They also may begin and sustain conversations that include real-world examples of how math concepts apply to the family budget, purchases, or other things that families do, and how they use reading or math in their own work or home activities. In many ways, all families can help children see that school skills are useful in daily life (Gonzalez et al., 2001; Moll et al., 1992).

Type 5—Decision making: Involvement in school decisions, governance, and advocacy. Schools strengthen parents' participation in school decisions by encouraging the organization of strong parent associations, and by including parents and community representatives on school councils and committees. Parent organizations and councils are more likely to contribute positively to school discussions and decisions if the parent-leaders represent all of the groups or neighborhoods served by the school. Parents and teachers benefit from leadership training and team building so that they learn to respect one another's views and work better together. A strong PTA or PTO includes active parents and teachers and administrators, as the name—parent–teacher association—implies. An effective PTA or PTO focuses its work on helping students reach school goals and working on all other types of involvement.

Some parents take leadership roles and participate actively on school improvement teams, councils, parent organizations, and committees. Other parents do not want to be active, or have little time for those activities, but do wish to be informed about and consulted on school decisions that affect their children (Connors and Epstein, 1994). Type 5 decision making also includes parents who are advocates for education in independent groups in the community and who work to increase funding and support to improve the quality of school and district-wide programs.

Families at all school levels may form, join, and become active members of the PTA, PTO, PTSA, Home and School Association, or other committees. Families can join a parent organization and offer their suggestions for or reactions to school decisions that affect their children. In leadership roles, parents may become important problem solvers for the school, particularly if the parent association's agenda focuses on assisting students, strengthening families, and increasing the overall success of the school.

Whether a school has a formal parent organization or not, parents' concerns and needs should be periodically and systematically addressed, either through school- or parent-initiated procedures. For example, one or a group of parents may gather the views of other parents to discuss in a letter to a principal, district superintendent, or school board; request new programs or policies for their children; or ask teachers about particular classroom practices. A parent organization may organize a series of meetings on parents' goals for children or concerns about the quality of the school's facilities, programs, materials, or climate. In a well-planned program of school, family, and community partnerships, these discussions would be designed to solve problems, not create conflicts. This requires that parents and educators understand their shared goals and have the organizational structures, decision-making skills, and support they need to work together.

Type 6—Collaborating with the community: Involvement to identify, use, and improve community programs and services.   Schools make connections with governmental agencies, businesses, faith-based organizations, cultural associations, senior citizens, and other groups in the community that share an interest in and responsibility for children's education and success (Epstein, 1992; Sanders, 2001). School and parent groups may work to inform students and families about community programs and support services, and may arrange procedures to increase opportunities for families and children to access these programs and services. This includes after-school programs, summer enrichment and remedial activities, health services, cultural events, and other beneficial programs. Presently, schools vary greatly in how much they draw on community resources to strengthen and support other types of family involvement, and in how well they inform all families about the services, deadlines, fees and scholarships, and alternatives that may benefit their children (Sanders and Harvey, 2000).

Parents and other family members can influence whether, how often, and in what ways their children join community activities to extend learning and to develop their talents. It helps families to have good information from the schools or directly from community groups to make these decisions for and with their children. Sometimes schools are the best "brokers" for information to reach all families, not just a few who are individually well positioned to receive the information in the community.

Parents and other volunteers can work with teachers and administrators to identify and disseminate information on community resources and programs to all families (Weiss, 2000). Parents also can draw from their own networks of friends and acquaintances to help schools make productive connections with business, community, fraternal, and other organizations. Collaborations with the community should be designed to assist students and their families to obtain desired services and to assist the school to improve the quality of its curricular or extracurricular programs.

Service learning programs are becoming more common in middle and high schools, Grades 6 to 12, with 83% of high schools and 77% of middle schools guiding students to participate in community service activities recognized or arranged by the school (Kleiner and Chapman, 1999; Shine, 1997; Youniss and Yates, 1997). Students in well-organized community service programs are expected to succeed in school and graduate from high school at high levels, but also to demonstrate and exercise positive personal skills and talents. Service learning programs may strengthen schools' collaborating with the community activities, especially if students' families are well informed about and involved in the program and the work that their children are doing in and for the community.

Family–school–community partnerships for the six types of involvement include many ways for schools to involve parents, and for parents to take responsibility for becoming involved in their children's education. When families become involved they learn more about the schools' programs and goals, become more effective supporters of their children's learning, and continue to influence their children's education, attitudes, and behaviors, across the grades. True partnerships among parents, teachers, and community members and groups occur when all parties engage in conversations and actions that focus on student learning and success.

TALKING POINTS AND STUDY TOPICS: LINKING SCHOOL IMPROVEMENT AND STRONGER PARTNERSHIPS

Across the grades and at each stage of development, parents need information about school programs in order to act as knowledgeable partners in their children's lives (Connors and Epstein, 1995). Educators often have, but do not always share, the information that parents need to participate in decisions about their children's education. For example, as school improvements are made, educators need to consider how new assessments, grading systems, and other reforms may affect family involvement. In turn, when new school initiatives are considered and implemented, families should be able to ask questions and offer suggestions that may help them help their children adjust to and thrive in the new programs.

In this section, we discuss a few talking points that illustrate not only how school improvement topics affect school, family, and community partnerships, but also how these partnerships affect the direction and success of school improvement. We also raise questions for new research and more effective partnership practices.

Talking Point and Study Topic: How Is the School Organized?

Families need to understand how their children's schools are organized and how school structures are being changed to improve the students' experiences (Berends, Kirby, Naftel, and McKelvey, 2001). This includes how grade levels are organized; how students are assigned to classes, grouped within classes or regrouped for specific subjects; and whether and how school-within-a-school structures are used. Many middle and high schools are organizing "schools within schools," "houses," "teams," or "academies" (MacIver, MacIver, Balfanz, Plank, and Ruby, 2000). These divisions may have specific teams of teachers, counselors, assistant principals, or other leaders. Parents need to understand the structures, the reasons for them, and how they affect students learning and directions. For example, students at different grade levels may be asked to choose academies, programs, courses, and other activities that affect their future educational opportunities (Legters, 2000). Families need to be well informed to discuss these programs and choices with their children and to guide the decisions that arise.

Educators need to consider how new organizational plans for schools, grade levels, and teachers' classes enhance or limit the participation of families. Families may have questions about how middle schools differ from junior high schools, why prealgebra or algebra are important courses for students in the middle grades, and how their children relate to counselors, teachers, and administrators in schools that are subdivided in different ways.

Educators need to establish ways for parents to ask questions and obtain answers about school and classroom organization. For example, some schools organize parent-to-parent telephone trees or other networks for easy communications among parents, computerized phone or e-mail systems, newsletter columns for parents' questions, or parent rooms or family centers for parent group discussions (Epstein et al., 1997; Johnson, 1996).

Questions for research and for designing more responsive partnership practices. Researchers and educators may be interested in finding answers to the following questions on school and classroom organization to improve the content, processes, and results of school, family, and community partnerships:

(1) How do different organizational and structural features of schools facilitate or hinder two-way communications of educators and parents?
(2) How do differently organized elementary, middle, and high schools welcome all families and provide time for school staff, families, and community partners to get to know one another?
(3) What information do educators believe should be shared every year or at particular grade levels? What do families want to know? What forms should this information take to reach all families?
(4) How might researchers study the effects of school and classroom organization on school, family, and community partnerships at the elementary, middle, and high school levels, and in diverse communities? Over time, how do family and community involvement activities in differently organized schools affect students?

Talking Point and Study Topic: How Do Schools Welcome and Involve Diverse Families and Enable All Students to Thrive?

Schools are becoming increasingly diverse. They differ, however, in the degree to which they create a positive and healthy climate for diversity (Datnow and Cooper, 2000). Research shows that minority and poor students may attend the same schools as European American and economically advantaged students but have very different experiences (Fine, 1991; Oakes, 1988). These experiences determine the quality of schooling that students receive and their educational opportunities and outcomes.

For example, a case study of a comprehensive high school in California showed that students from different racial and social class backgrounds had different counseling experiences that led to different course selections and schooling outcomes (Yonezawa, 2000). The students' counseling experiences often were influenced by preconceived, stereotypic notions of their abilities and interests. Conversely, Nieto (1993) noted that many schools attempt to be "color blind" and deny "the very identity of . . . students, thereby making them invisible." As an unintended result of such policies, schools deprive some students of affirming educational experiences.

To ensure that students from all racial, ethnic, and socioeconomic backgrounds receive a high-quality education, families must obtain information and be able to ask questions not only about course offerings and extracurricular opportunities, but also about how the school creates an inclusive environment where all students and families feel a sense of belonging (Chavkin, 1993). Families of all linguistic, cultural, and educational backgrounds need to know that teachers will communicate with them, that all students and families are included in school events and activities, how students and families from diverse backgrounds are represented on school councils, committees, and teams, and how topics of diversity and multiculturalism are included in the school's curriculum, programs, and activities (Hidalgo, Bright, Siu, Swap, and Epstein, 1995). With this information, more families would be better positioned to monitor and enhance the quality of their children's school experiences.

Questions for research and for designing more responsive partnership practices. Researchers and educators may be interested in finding answers to the following questions on how to involve multicultural, multilingual, and other groups of parents, and the results for students of specific approaches to diversity.

(1) How can teachers be assisted to create classroom environments that support and build on diversity?
(2) How can students and parents be actively engaged in creating classrooms that accept and respect diversity?
(3) In what ways can culturally homogeneous schools create environments that allow students to become aware and respectful of difference and diversity?
(4) How might researchers study the effects of contrasting approaches to developing and supporting diversity, the involvement and roles of families from diverse backgrounds, and the effects on students of schools' contrasting attitudes and practices concerning diversity?

Talking Point and Study Topic: How Do School, Family, and Community Partnerships Develop and Change at Different Age and Grade Levels?

Partnerships tend to decline as students move across the grades (Catsambis and Garland, 1997; Epstein and Dauber, 1991; Lee, 1994; Simon, 2000; Stevenson and Baker, 1987; Useem, 1992). When children are younger, parents are more likely to volunteer at the school building, attend parent–teacher conferences, and supervise children's homework. Elementary schools are more likely to expect and encourage parental involvement than middle schools or high schools (Sanders and Epstein, 2000a). In part these patterns are developmentally appropriate. That is, younger children need more active parental support and guidance. In part, the average decline in involvement across the grades represents a serious gap in important, age-appropriate communication between parents and teachers at every grade level. That is, most parents are not helped to remain involved in their teens' education by most secondary school administrators and teachers.

As children get older, they need more opportunities to develop their independence, take responsibility for their own learning, and work closely with peers. However, they also continue to need adult guidance and supervision. These simultaneous developmental needs appear to be in conflict, but they may work together. Studies show, for example, that students are *more* independent if their families and other adults remain age-appropriately involved in their education (Epstein, 1983). Data also indicate that early adolescents recognize that their families are supervising their development (Johnson and Farkas, 1997) and want their families to support them in learning activities at home (Connors and Epstein, 1994).

As students go through the grades, their schools and school experiences become more complex, and more difficult for parents to figure out on their own. Middle schools and high schools are usually larger and further from home than were elementary schools. The students may have more teachers, counselors, and administrators in their school lives. The curriculum is more complex, often with more and harder homework. All of these features of secondary schools make it important for educators to communicate effectively with families of middle and high school students.

Data from several studies suggest that early adolescents want and need their families to support them in learning activities at home, and that parents of middle and high school students remain important influences in their children's lives (Catsambis, 1998; Council of Economic Advisors, 2000; Epstein and Lee, 1995; Lee, 1994; Sanders, 1999; Sanders and Epstein, 2000a; Simon, 2000). This means that parents must understand their teens' school experiences, demands, and opportunities. It should be "basic" for parents at all grade levels to attend back-to-school nights, parent–teacher conferences, concerts, plays, athletics, and other events, communicate with teachers, participate in activities with other parents in the PTA or PTO; discuss school and homework, course choices, program decisions, and summer options with their children; and discuss and help solve important personal and school problems (Epstein and Connors, 1995; Sanders, 1998b).

Questions for research and for designing more responsive partnership practices. Researchers and educators may be interested in finding answers to the following questions on the nature and results of developmental patterns of school, family, and community partnerships:

(1) What information do parents need at different grade levels on child and adolescent development and school topics in order to remain "connected" to their children across the grades?
(2) How do parent–child discussions help young children, early adolescents, and later adolescents remain focused on the role of "student?"
(3) What roles can students play at each grade level to contribute to effective family–school–community connections, even as the students are working to become more independent?
(4) How might researchers study the effects of developmentally specific practices of school, family, and community partnerships across the grades and in diverse communities?

Talking Point and Study Topic: When are Young Children Ready for School?

Schools constantly evaluate students' progress. Educators decide whether children are ready to start formal schooling, and when they are ready to proceed to the next group, grade level, or lesson. Parents have many questions about how their very young children are evaluated for "readiness" and how to help their children prepare for school.

Indeed, one of the first experiences many parents have with schools is a "screening" to determine if their children are ready for kindergarten. If parents are anxious about this test, they may delay their child's entry to kindergarten for a year (Lareau, 1992; West, Denton, and Hausken, 2000). There are no clear studies that suggest this is a beneficial strategy, but without good information about the requirements for school entry, parents are left on their own to think about what readiness means and how to prepare their children for school (Meisels, 1996; Shepard and Smith, 1986; West and Hausken, 1993).

In later years, "readiness" refers to whether students are prepared for promotion to each new grade level. Parents of children who are falling behind in skills want to know how to help their children catch up in learning. Parents should be included in decisions with educators if students are not ready to advance. This requires that educators communicate clearly with parents and support their participation in discussions, evaluations, and decisions that affect children's education.

Questions for research and for designing more responsive partnership practices. Researchers and educators may be interested in finding answers to the following questions on school, family, and community partnerships to ensure students' readiness for school:

(1) What information do parents need to know to help their children become ready for school? And ready for each new grade level?
(2) When do parents need information about school readiness in order to prepare their children for successful entry to school? Who can help all parents with these tasks with very young children (e.g., librarians, pediatricians, health providers, local media, and others)? And with children across the grades? How should this information be communicated to enable parents to understand and take appropriate action?
(3) What are the most effective methods for helping individual educators and teams of teachers, counselors, parents, and others develop the information that parents need to help their children prepare for entry to school? For promotion from year to year?
(4) How should kindergarten screenings be organized to set the stage for open, friendly communications and ongoing relationships of parents, teachers, and administrators?

(5) How might researchers study the effects of school, family, and community partnerships on student readiness for kindergarten? Over time, how do family and community involvement activities affect students' promotion from grade to grade?

Talking Point and Study Topic: What Transitions Do Students Experience From Year to Year?

Although most schools assist students in making successful transitions to each new grade level or school level, few schools systematically take time to help families make successful transitions with their children (Epstein and MacIver, 1990). Parents can either help students adjust successfully to their new schools or watch them struggle on their own to make sense of their new experiences and new requirements. This is true for transitions from preschool to elementary school, elementary to middle school, and middle to high school. When changes are made, students may have negative attitudes about school, their teachers, and their classwork (Eccles and Midgely, 1989; Harter, Whitesell, and Kowalski, 1992). Even students' transitions from high school to college or work are smoother if families support and discuss their young adults' decisions about their postsecondary paths and experiences.

Students report that they want their families involved as knowledgeable partners, even in adolescence when students also are taking steps toward independence (Connors and Epstein, 1994; Johnson and Farkas, 1997; Lee, 1994). Educators can help all families gain the knowledge they need about school transitions so that more parents conduct age-appropriate conversations to support their children at times of change. Other families who previously made successful transitions also can help the next group of parents understand their children's new schools, policies, and practices.

Each time their children change schools, families need good information in order to communicate knowledgeably with their children about these important, exciting, and potentially stressful experiences. Elementary, middle, and high schools need to work together as "feeder" and "receiver" systems to inform and involve parents so that they can assist their children to make successful adjustments to new situations. This includes orienting families to the new settings, new grade levels, new relationships with teams of teachers, counselors, and other school staff, and new expectations and requirements for grading and testing students' work. Studies indicate that when schools communicate clearly with families at major transition points, students make more successful academic and behavioral adjustments and families feel more welcome at school and more aware of their children's challenges in education (Jason, Danner, and Kurasaki, 1993). Other data reveal that middle schools that involve families before students make the transition are more likely to continue other parental involvement practices through the middle grades (Epstein and MacIver, 1990).

Importantly, successful adjustment to middle school or high school may have long-term consequences, not only for the students' academic success, but also for the educational experiences of later generations. Kaplan, Liu, and Kaplan (2000) reported that mothers' poor experiences in junior high school are associated with similar negative experiences of their own children when they are in junior high school. This relation is moderated by other variables, including family involvement in school and interest in their children's work and progress. Thus, explicit activities to involve families at points of students' transition may help more parents remain positively involved in their children's education across the grades, regardless of the parents' own school histories.

Questions for research and for designing more responsive partnership practices. Researchers and educators may be interested in finding answers to the following questions on student transitions to improve the content, processes, and results of school, family, and community partnerships:

(1) How can families be prepared to understand and support the transitions that their children make to new schools and to new grade levels?

(2) What are the most useful schedules, forms, and content of information and activities for students and families about students' transitions from elementary to middle and to high school, and about preparing for postsecondary education and training?

(3) How might researchers study the effects of school transitions on school, family, and community partnerships at the elementary, middle, and high school levels, and in diverse communities? Over time, how do family and community involvement activities at times of transition affect students?

Talking Point and Study Topic: How Are Students Grouped for Instruction?

Schools have traditionally responded to student diversity by grouping or "tracking" children in different subjects, classes, and educational programs. These practices usually create homogeneous groups of students by ability level. Tracking practices have been criticized because they often result in fixed placements, derogatory labels, and restricted learning opportunities for lower performing students (Dauber, Alexander, and Entwisle, 1996; Oakes, 1988, 1992; Stevenson, Shiller, and Schneider, 1994).

Increasingly, schools are being encouraged to eliminate tracking based on ability (Wheelock, 1992). Several comprehensive school reform models include strategies to provide a challenging curriculum to all students, as well as extra academic support to help all students master higher order competencies (MacIver et al., 2000). Other school reform efforts encourage heterogeneous grouping of students based on interests rather than ability to better serve all students and prepare them for postsecondary schooling opportunities (Legters, 2000).

Federal legislation requires schools to provide students who have physical or learning disabilities with the least restrictive learning environments possible. This legislation has resulted in the widespread inclusion in regular classes of students with special needs (Turnbull, Turnbull, Shank, and Leal, 1995). Research suggests that parents have important roles to play in reducing ability tracking (Wheelock, 1992) and in ensuring that all students, including those with disabilities, are provided rich, challenging educational opportunities (Sanders, 2000; Stainback and Stainback, 1996).

Of course, not all grouping practices are "bad" for students. When implemented skillfully, grouping is an organizational tool that can help teachers address the learning needs of large and small numbers of children. To limit the negative effects or possibilities of tracking, some schools have initiated new ways to group students heterogeneously in some or all subjects, and within or across grades (Cohen, 2000). Other schools have eliminated tracking but may still use flexible grouping practices that enable teachers to adapt their teaching to the ever changing needs of students. In a national study of middle schools, principals reported that parents could make or break their efforts to reduce or eliminate tracking. Principals emphasized the need to involve families early in the process of planning and implementing heterogeneous grouping procedures so that parents and students are prepared for the actions that are taken (Wheelock, 1992).

Families need to know about the policies and practices that schools use to group their children, the reasons for the practices, and the consequences for their children's success in school. This information may be shared in workshops, meetings, forums, and in other materials that enable families to ask questions, provide ideas, and help their children in their school experiences.

Questions for research and for designing more responsive partnership practices. Researchers and educators may be interested in finding answers to the following questions on how parents and students understand and are engaged in decisions about grouping in schools, and the results of grouping approaches and decisions:

(1) What kinds of information do parents need about grouping, tracking, and untracking in order to understand their children's school programs?

(2) What are students' roles in schools' policies and decisions about placement in instructional groups? What information about these topics do students need?

(3) How can schools include students and families in plans for, choices about, and changes in grouping policies and decisions?

(4) How might researchers study the effects of what families understand and do about schools' tracking, untracking, and grouping practices, and the effects on students of family discussions and decisions with educators about students' instructional groups? How can researchers study these topics at the elementary, middle, and high school levels in diverse communities?

Talking Point and Study Topic: What Do School Tests Measure, and How Are Test Results Used?

States, districts, and schools across the country are developing and administering new tests and assessments in order to increase the accountability of teachers and schools and to better understand children's progress in learning. Although everyone agrees that assessments are important, there are many questions and controversies about new standards for learning and high-stakes tests that are used to determine student success or failure (D'Agostino, 2000). The use of a single measure has been criticized, whether it is a screening test of readiness for school entry, a standardized test for promotion, or an exit exam for high school graduation (Meisels, 1992; Sacks, 2000; Sigel, 1992). Students and parents may be confused by new tests and new assessment procedures such as "portfolios" unless they have been given good explanations about the nature of the tests, the meaning of new national, state, and local standards, and the consequences of the scores.

Parents are interested in knowing how much teaching time is devoted to instruction and how much time is used to prepare children for tests. Parents also need opportunities to question or comment on the tests and their uses (Kohn, 2001). Because children often are nervous about tests, families need to know how to discuss school tests with their children, help them prepare for calm test taking, and address their children's worries.

Researchers and educators are working to design and improve assessments so that school decisions about promotion, placement, and remedial work will be more reliable, and to improve the technologies of reporting results of assessments so that teachers and parents have a better understanding of students' skills and needs (Baker, 1998).

Questions for research and for designing more responsive partnership practices. Researchers and educators may be interested in finding answers to the following questions on how to involve families and communities in decisions about and interpretations and uses of school tests and assessments:

(1) What information will help parents understand how schools interpret and use the results of particular tests, and how to support their children's test taking?

(2) In what ways should families be involved in selecting, designing, or evaluating alternative assessments strategies?

(3) How might researchers study the effects of different approaches and degrees of involvement of families and students in designing, interpreting, using, and improving tests and school assessments? Over time, how does family awareness of and involvement in testing affect student attitudes toward and results of different evaluations?

Talking Point and Study Topic: What Are Effective Methods of Reporting Student Progress?

Report card grades are periodic records of how well students are doing in specific subjects and remain the most common way that parents receive information from teachers about their children's progress.

Although parents generally report satisfaction with the information they receive on report cards, they are more satisfied with their children's schools if they receive additional, supplemental information about their children's work and progress (Olhausen and Powell, 1992). As children progress through school, report card forms and criteria change. Families need to know about the changes in report cards, how to interpret their children's grades, and how to guide their children to do their best work in school. Parents often are unaware of teachers' methods of gauging and reporting student progress, and they are rarely asked for input to the design of reporting systems (Ohlhausen and Powell, 1992; Reid, 1984).

Parent–teacher conferences are another way to help parents understand how their children are progressing at school. One challenge to educators is to design conferences that not only inform parents of their children's achievements but also enable parents to share their views of their children's skills and abilities (Hackman, Kentworthy, and Nibbelink, 1998; Lloyd, 1996). Over time, in order for parents and students to understand their work and progress, schools need to create an integrated system of information about student assessments including report cards, major standardized tests, grouping procedures, and other evaluations and placements.

Questions for research and for designing more responsive partnership practices. Researchers and educators may be interested in finding answers to the following questions on how to effectively report student progress and involve parents and students in the process:

(1) What information do parents want and need about their children's achievement tests, report cards, and daily, weekly, monthly or other periodic reports of progress?
(2) What methods and opportunities (e.g., meetings, conferences, and communications) enable teachers, students, and families to share information, concerns, and achievements?
(3) What roles can students play in developing new methods of reporting progress, conducting self-assessments, sharing their progress or problems with their families, and working to improve their work and behavior in school?
(4) How might researchers study the effects on students of contrasting communications with families about student progress? Over time, what are the most effective communications about student progress at the elementary, middle, and high school levels, and in diverse communities?

Summary

The talking points discussed in this chapter all address one major question: How can all students be helped to do their best to succeed in school and in life? That is, after all, the "bottom line" for parents, teachers, community partners, and for students, themselves.

Research suggests that the answer to that question is found in the interactions and relationships of parents, students, educators, and others on topics that concern student growth, development, and learning. The National Study of Adolescent Health found that teens who say they are "connected" to their parents are less likely to be involved in risky behaviors (Resnick et al., 1997). Yet to remain "connected" to their children, parents need more and better information on child and adolescent development and ongoing communications with educators, other families, and others in the community. Thus, one major message that is emerging from research, policy, and practice on partnerships is: Parents and educators need to talk with each other, and with students, about their mutual concerns, needs, interests, responsibilities, and goals for students' learning and development.

CONCLUSIONS

This chapter began with a review of some of the reasons why family and school connections have been characterized by conflict. Parents and teachers have crossed paths throughout the history of public schooling, but the nature of their interactions evolved as the nation grew and as schooling changed. Because of greater demands on schools to prepare students for diverse occupations and advanced education, and because of greater demands on families' time and resources, new theories and new practices have emerged that guide families and schools to work better together.

This overview of theory, research, and practice suggests that the roles of families and schools have progressed from emphasizing their separate functions to recognizing their shared and overlapping roles and responsibilities for children's learning and development. In educational practice, more educators are moving away from isolation behind classroom doors and toward new models of family–school–community partnerships.

New knowledge and actions are needed from all participants. Studies of teachers and parents indicate that schools must plan programs of partnerships that will enable families to participate in their children's education every year of school. Parents also must take more responsibility to communicate with their children, the teachers and administrators at school, and other parents in order to understand and support their children as students. Students need to be encouraged and assisted to take greater responsibility for their own learning but also to take active roles in school, family, and community partnerships to help parents and teachers communicate successfully. New definitions of parent involvement based on the concept of partnerships show strong potential for reversing some of the serious conflicts among parents and teachers and for reducing serious inequities and inconsistencies in students' education.

ACKNOWLEDGMENTS

This research was supported by grants from the U.S. Department of Education, Office of Educational Research and Improvement, to the Center for Research on the Education of Students Placed at Risk (CRESPAR), and from Disney Learning Partnership and Wallace-Reader's Digest Funds to the Center on School, Family, and Community Partnerships at Johns Hopkins University. The opinions expressed are the authors' and do not represent the policies or positions of the funding sources. Many thanks to Lori Connors Tadros for her contributions to the earlier version of this chapter, which appeared in the first edition of the *Handbook*.

REFERENCES

American Federation of Teachers. (1999). *Parent and family involvement course*. Washington, DC: Educational Research and Dissemination Program.

Ames, C., De Stefano L., Watkins T., and Sheldon S. (1995). *Teachers' school-to-home communications and parent involvement: The role of parent perceptions and beliefs* (Rep. No. 28). Baltimore: Johns Hopkins University, Center on Families, Communities, Schools and Children's Learning.

Association for Supervision and Curriculum Development. (2001). *How to make homework more meaningful by involving parents*. Alexandria, VA: Author.

Astone, N. M., and McLanahan, S. S. (1991). Family structure, parental practices, and high school completion. *American Sociological Review, 56*, 309–320.

Baker, D. P., and Stevenson, D. L. (1986). Mothers' strategies for children's school achievement: Managing the transition to high school. *Sociology of Education, 59*, 156–166.

Baker, E. L. (1998). *Understanding educational quality: Where validity meets technology*. Princeton, NJ: Educational Testing Service. (Fifth Annual William H. Angoff Memorial Lecture.)

Balli, S. J. (1995). *The effects of differential prompts on family involvement with middle-grades homework*. Unpublished doctoral dissertation, University of Missouri, Columbia.

Balli, S. J., Demo, D. H., and Wedman, J. F. (1998). Family involvement with children's homework: An intervention in the middle grades. *Family Relations, 47*, 149–157.

Barker, R. G., and Gump, P. V. (1964). *Big school, small school*. Stanford, CA: Stanford University Press.

Becker, H. J., and Epstein J. L. (1982). Parent involvement: A study of teacher practices. *Elementary School Journal, 83*, 85–102.

Benson, P. L. (1997). *All kids are our kids: What communities must do to raise caring and responsible children and adolescents*. San Francisco: Jossey-Bass.

Berends, M., Kirby, S. N., Naftel, S., and McKelvey, C. (2001). *Implementation and performance in New American Schools: Three years into scale-up*. Santa Monica, CA: Rand.

Bronfenbrenner, U. (1979). *The ecology of human development: Experiment by nature and design*. Cambridge: Harvard University Press.

Bronfenbrenner, U. (1986). Ecology of the family as a context for human development: Research perspectives. *Developmental Psychology, 22*, 723–742.

Cairney, T. H., and Ruge, J. (1997). *Community literacy practices and schooling: Towards effective support for students*. Canberra, Australia: Department of Employment, Education, Training and Youth Affairs.

Cairney, T. H., Ruge, J., Buchanan, J., Lowe, K., and Munsie, L. (1995). *Developing partnerships: The home, school, and community interface* (Vols. 1–3). Canberra, Australia: Department of Employment, Education, and Training.

Campbell, R. F., Cunningham, L. L., and McPhee, R. F. (1965). *The organization and control of American schools*. Columbus, OH: Merrill.

Catsambis, S. (1998). *Expanding knowledge of parental involvement in secondary education: social determinants and effects on high school academic success* (Rep. No. 27). Baltimore: Johns Hopkins University, Center for Research on the Education of Students Placed at Risk.

Catsambis, S., and Garland, J. E. (1997). *Parental involvement in students' education during middle and high school* (Rep. No. 18). Baltimore MD: Johns Hopkins University, Center for Research on the Education of Students Placed at Risk.

Chavkin, N. (Ed.). (1993). *Families and schools in a pluralistic society*. Albany: State University of New York Press.

Clark, R. M. (1983). *Family life and school achievement: Why poor black children succeed or fail*. Chicago: University of Chicago Press.

Cohen, E. G. (2000). Equitable classrooms in a changing society. In M. Hallinan (Ed.), *Handbook of the sociology of education* (pp. 265–283). New York: Plenum.

Coleman, J. S. (1988). Social capital in the creation of human capital. *American Journal of Sociology, 94*, 95–120.

Coleman, J. S., Campbell, E., Mood, A., Weinfeld, E., Hobson, C., York, R., and McPartland, J. (1966). *Equality of educational opportunity*. Washington, DC: U.S. Government Printing Office.

Collingnon, F. F., Men, M., and Tan, S. (2001). Finding ways in: Community-based perspectives on Southeast Asian family involvement with schools. *JESPAR, 6*, 27–44.

Comer, J. P. (1980). *School power: Implications of an intervention program*. New York: Free Press.

Comer, J. P., and Haynes, N. (1991). Parent involvement in schools: An ecological approach. *Elementary School Journal, 91*, 271–277.

Conklin, M. E., and Dailey, A. R. (1981). Does consistency of parental encouragement matter for secondary students? *Sociology of Education, 54*, 254–262.

Connors, L. J., and Epstein, J. L. (1994). *Taking stock: The views of teachers, parents, and students on school, family, and community partnerships in high schools* (Rep. No. 25). Baltimore: Johns Hopkins University, Center on Families, Communities, Schools and Children's Learning.

Connors, L. J., and Epstein, J. L. (1995). Parent and school partnerships. In M. H. Bornstein (Ed.), *Handbook of parenting: Vol. 4. Applied and practical parenting* (pp. 437–458). Mahwah, NJ: Lawrence Erlbaum Associates.

Cooper, H., and Valentine, J. C. (2001). Using research to answer practical questions about homework. *Educational Psychologist, 36*, 143–153.

Corno, L. (2000). Looking at homework differently. *The Elementary School Journal, 100*, 529–548.

Council of Economic Advisors. (2000). *Teens and their parents in the twenty-first century: An examination of trends in teen behavior and the role of parental involvement*. Washington, DC: Author.

D'Agostino, J. V. (2000). Achievement testing in American schools. In T. L. Good (Ed.), *American education: Yesterday, today, and tomorrow* (pp. 313–337). Chicago: University of Chicago Press. (Ninty-ninth yearbook of the National Society for the Study of Education.)

Datnow, A., and Cooper, R. (2000). Creating a climate for diversity? The institutional response of predominantly white independent schools to African-American students. In M. G. Sanders (Ed.), *Schooling students placed at risk: Research, policy, and practice in the education of poor and minority adolescents* (pp. 207–230). Mahwah, NJ: Lawrence Erlbaum Associates.

Dauber, S. L., Alexander, K. L., and Entwisle, D. R. (1996). Tracking and transitions through the middle grades: Channeling educational trajectories. *Sociology of Education, 69*, 290–307.

Dauber, S. L., and Epstein, J. L. (1993). Parents' attitudes and practices of involvement in inner-city elementary and middle schools. In N. Chavkin (Ed.), *Families and schools in a pluralistic society* (pp. 53–71). Albany: State University of New York Press.

Davies, D., and Johnson, V. R. (Eds.). (1996). Crossing boundaries: Family, community, and school partnerships [Special issue]. *International Journal of Educational Research, 25*.

Davies, M., and Kandel, D. (1981). Parental and peer influences on adolescents' educational plans: Some further evidence. *American Journal of Sociology, 87*, 363–387.

Delgado-Gaitan, C. (1990). *Literacy for empowerment*. New York: Falmer.

Desimone, L. (1999). Linking parent involvement with student achievement: Do race and income matter? *Journal of Educational Research, 93*, 11–30.

Dianda, M., and McLaren, A. (1996). *Building partnerships for student learning*. Washington, DC: National Education Association.

Dryfoos, J. (1994). *Full-service schools*. San Francisco: Jossey-Bass.

Dryfoos, J. (1998). *Safe passage: Making it through adolescence in a risky society*. New York: Oxford University Press.

Duran, R., Duran J., Perry-Romero, D., Sanchez, E. (2001). Latino immigrant parents and children learning and publishing together in an after-school setting. *JESPAR, 6*, 95–114.

Eccles, J. S., and Harold, R. D. (1996). Family involvement in children's and adolescents' schooling. In A. Booth and J. Dunn (Eds.), *Family–school links: How do they affect educational outcomes* (pp. 3–34). Hillside, NJ: Lawrence Erlbaum Associates.

Eccles, J. S., and Midgley, C. (1989). Stage–environment fit: Developmentally appropriate classrooms for young adolescents. In C. Ames and A. Ames (Eds.), *Research on motivation in education: Goals and cognitions* (pp. 139–186). New York: Academic.

Epstein, J. L. (1983). Selection of friends in differently organized schools and classrooms. In J. Epstein and N. Karweit (Eds.), *Friends in school: Patterns of selection and influence in secondary schools* (pp. 73–92). New York: Academic.

Epstein, J. L. (1986). Parents' reactions to teacher practices of parent involvement. *Elementary School Journal, 86*, 277–294.

Epstein, J. L. (1987). Toward a theory of family–school connections: Teacher practices and parent involvement. In K. Hurrelman, F. Kaufmann, and F. Losel (Eds.), *Social intervention: Potential and constraints* (pp. 121–136). New York: DeGruyter.

Epstein, J. L. (1989) Family influence and student motivation: A developmental perspective. In C. Ames and R. Ames (Eds.), *Research on motivation in education* (Vol. 3, pp. 259–295). New York: Academic.

Epstein, J. L. (1990). School and family connections: Theory, research, and implications for integrating sociologies of education and family. In D. Unger and M. Sussman (Eds.), *Families in community settings: Interdisciplinary perspectives* (pp. 99–126). New York: Haworth.

Epstein, J. L. (1991). Effects on student achievement of teacher practices of parent involvement. In S. Silvern (Ed.), *Advances in reading/language research: literacy through family, community, and school interaction* (Vol. 5, pp. 261–276). Greenwich, CT: JAI.

Epstein, J. L. (1992). School and family partnerships. In M. Adkin (Ed.), *Encyclopedia of educational research* (6th ed., pp. 1139–1151). New York: MacMillan.

Epstein, J. L. (1995). School/family/community partnerships: Caring for the children we share. *Phi Delta Kappan, 76*, 701–712.

Epstein, J. L. (2001). *School, family, and community partnerships: Preparing educators and improving schools*. Boulder, CO: Westview.

Epstein, J. L., and Becker, H. J. (1982). Teacher practices of parent involvement: Problems and possibilities. *Elementary School Journal, 83*, 103–113.

Epstein, J. L., Coates, L., Salinas, K. C., Sanders, M. G., and Simon, B. S. (1997). *School, family, and community partnerships: Your handbook for action*. Thousand Oaks, CA: Corwin.

Epstein, J. L., and Connors, L. J. (1995). School and family partnerships in the middle grades. In B. Rutherford (Ed.), *Creating family/school partnerships* (pp. 137–166). Columbus, OH: National Middle School Association.

Epstein, J. L., and Dauber, S. L. (1991). School programs and teacher practices of parent involvement in inner-city elementary and middle schools. *Elementary School Journal, 91*, 289–303.

Epstein, J. L., Herrick, S. C., and Coates, L. (1996). Effects of summer home learning packets on student achievement in language arts in the middle grades. *School Effectiveness and School Improvement, 7*, 93–120.

Epstein, J. L., and Lee, S. (1995). National patterns of school and family connections in the middle grades. In B. A. Ryan, G. R. Adams, T. P. Cullota, R. P. Weisberg, and R. L. Hampton (Eds.), *The family–school connection* (pp. 108–154). Thousand Oaks, CA: Sage.

Epstein, J. L., and McPartland, J. M. (1979). Authority structures. In H. Walberg (Ed.), *Educational environments and effects* (pp. 293–310). Berkeley, CA: McCutchan.

Epstein, J. L., and MacIver, D. (1990). *Education in the middle grades: National practices and trends*. Columbus, OH: National Middle School Association.

Epstein, J. L., Salinas, K. C., and Jackson V. (1995). *Manual for teachers: Teachers Involve Parents in Schoolwork (TIPS) interactive homework and prototype activities in the elementary and middle grades*. Baltimore: Johns Hopkins University, Center on School, Family, and Community Partnerships.

Epstein, J. L., Simon, B. S., and Salinas, K. C. (1997, September). *Effects of teachers involve parents in schoolwork (TIPS) language arts interactive homework in the middle grades* (Research Bulletin No. 18). Bloomington, IN: Phi Delta Kappa Center for Evaluation, Development, and Research.

Epstein, J. L., and Van Voorhis, F. L. (2001). More than minutes: Teachers' roles in designing homework. *Educational Psychologist, 36*, 181–193.

Fehrmann, P. G., Keith, T. Z., and Reimers, T. M. (1987). Home influences on school learning: Direct and indirect effects of parental involvement on high school grades. *Journal of Educational Research, 80*, 330–337.

Fine, M. (1991). *Framing dropouts: Notes on the politics of an urban public high school.* Albany: State University of New York Press.

Finkelstein, B. (1992). Education historians as mythmakers. In G. Grant (Ed.), *Review of research in education* (Vol. 18, pp. 255–297). Washington, DC: American Educational Research Association.

Goldsmith, E., and Tevlin, A. (1998). *Reading starts with us.* New York: Scholastic.

Gomby, D. S., Larner, M. B., Stevenson, C. S., Lewit, E. M., and Behrman, R. E. (1995). Long-term outcomes of early childhood programs: Analysis and recommendations. *The Future of Children, 5*, 6–24.

Gonzalez, N., Andrade, R., Civil, M., and Moll, L. (2001). Bridging funds of distributed knowledge: Creating zones of practice in mathematics. *JESPAR, 6*, 115–132.

Gutek, G. L. (1992). *Education and schooling in America.* Boston: Allyn and Bacon.

Graham, P. A. (1976). America's unsystematic education system. In E. H. Grotberg (Ed.), *200 years of children* (pp. 134–148). Washington, DC: U.S. Department of Health, Education, and Welfare.

Grolnick, W. S., and Slowiaczek, M. L. (1994). Parents' involvement in children's schooling: A multidimensional conceptualization and motivational model. *Child Development, 65*, 237–252.

Grubb, W. N. (1995). The old problem of "new students:" Purposes, content, and pedagogy. In E. Flaxman and H. Passow (Eds.), *Changing populations, changing schools* (pp. 4–29). Chicago: University of Chicago Press. (Ninety-fourth yearbook of the National Society for the Study of Education.)

Gutman, L. M., and McLoyd, V. C. (2000). Parents' management of their children's education within the home, at school, and in the community: An examination of African-American families living in poverty. *The Urban Review, 32*, 1–24.

Hackmann, D., Kentworthy, J., and Nibbelink, S. (1998). Student empowerment through student-led conferences. *Middle School Journal, 30*, 35–39.

Handel, R. (1999). *Building family literacy in an urban community.* New York: Teachers College Press.

Handlin, O. (1976). Education and the American society. In E. H. Grotberg (Ed.), *200 years of children* (pp. 125–134). Washington, DC: U.S. Department of Health, Education, and Welfare.

Harter, S., Whitesell, N. R., and Kowalski, P. (1992). Individual differences in the effects of educational transitions on young adolescents' perceptions of competence and motivational orientation. *American Educational Research Journal, 29*, 777–807.

Hess, R., Holloway, S., Dickson, W., and Price, G. (1984). Maternal variables as predictors of children's school readiness and later achievement in vocabulary and mathematics in sixth grade. *Child Development, 55*, 1902–1912.

Hidalgo, N. M., Bright, J., Siu, S., Swap, S., and Epstein, J. (1995). Research on families, schools, and communities: A multicultural perspective. In J. Banks (Ed.), *Handbook of research on multicultural education* (pp. 498–524). New York: MacMillan.

Ho, E. S., and Willms, J. D. (1996). Effects of parental involvement on eighth-grade achievement. *Sociology of Education, 69*, 126–141.

Hoover-Dempsey, K. V., Battiato, A. C., Walker, J. M., Reed, R. P., and Jones, K. P. (2001). Parental involvement in homework. *Educational Psychologist, 36*, 195–209.

Hoover-Dempsey, K. V., and Sandler, H. M. (1997). Why do parents become involved in their children's education? *Review of Educational Research, 67*, 3–42.

Hossler, D., and Stage, F. K. (1992). Family and high school experience influences on the postsecondary educational plans of ninth-grade students. *American Educational Research Journal, 29*, 425–451.

Jason, L. A., Danner, K. E., and Kurasaki, K. S. (Eds.). (1993). *Prevention and school transitions: Prevention in human services.* New York: Haworth.

Johnson, J., and Farkas, S. (1997). *Getting by: What American teenagers really think about their schools.* New York: Public Agenda.

Johnson, V. R. (1996). *Family center guidebook.* Baltimore: Johns Hopkins University, Center on Families, Communities, Schools and Children's Learning.

Jordan, W., and Plank, S. (2000). Talent loss among high-achieving poor students. In M. G. Sanders (Ed.), *Schooling students placed at risk: Research, policy, and practice in the education of poor and minority adolescents* (pp. 83–108). Mahwah, NJ: Lawrence Erlbaum Associates.

Kaplan, D. S., Liu, X., and Kaplan, H. B. (2000). Family structure and parental involvement in the intergenerational parallelism of school adversity. *Journal of Educational Research, 93*, 235–244.

Keith, T. Z., Keith, P. B., Troutman, G. C., Bickley, P. G., Trivette, P. S., and Singh, K. (1993). Does parental involvement affect eighth-grade student achievement? Structural analysis of national data. *School Psychology Review, 22*, 474–496.

Kleiner, B., and Chapman, C. (1999). *Youth service–learning and community service among sixth- to twelfth-grade students in the United States.* Washington, DC: National Center for Education Statistics.

Kohn, A. (2001). Fighting the tests: A practical guide to rescuing our schools. *Phi Delta Kappan, 82*, 348–357.

Lareau, A. (1989). *Home advantage: social class and parental intervention in elementary education.* Philadelphia: Falmer.

Lareau, A. (1992, April). *Red-shirting and retention: Class difference in parent involvement in schooling.* Paper presented at the annual meeting of the American Educational Research Association, San Francisco.

Lavin, D. E., and Hyllegard, D. (1996). *Changing the odds: Open admissions and the life chances of the disadvantaged.* New Haven: Yale University Press.

Lee, S. (1994). *Family–school connections and students' education: Continuity and change of family involvement from the middle grades to high school.* Baltimore: Johns Hopkins University, Department of Sociology.

Leichter, H. J. (1974). *The family as educator.* New York: Teachers College Press.

Letgers, N. (2000). Small learning communities meet school-to-work: Whole school restructuring for urban comprehensive high schools. In M. G. Sanders (Ed.), *Schooling students placed at risk: Research, policy, and practice in the education of poor and minority adolescents* (pp. 309–338). Mahwah, NJ: Lawrence Erlbaum Associates.

Lewis, J. (1989). Mothers as teachers: Reconceptualizing the role of the family as educator. In W. Weston (Ed.), *Education and the American family: A research synthesis* (pp. 122–137). New York: New York University Press.

Lightfoot, S. L. (1978). *Worlds apart: Relationships between families and schools.* New York: Basic Books.

Lin, N. (2000). *Social capital: Theory of structure and action.* Cambridge, England: Cambridge University Press.

Litwak, E., and Meyer, H. J. (1974). *School, family, and neighborhood: The theory and practice of school-community relations.* New York: Columbia University Press.

Lloyd, G. (1996). Research and practical application for school, family, and community partnerships. In A. Booth and J. Dunn (Eds.), *Family–school links: How do they affect educational outcomes?* (pp. 255–264). Hillsdale, NJ: Lawrence Erlbaum Associates.

Lutz, F. W., and Merz, C. (1992). *The politics of school-community relations.* New York: Teachers College Press.

MacIver, D., MacIver, M., Balfanz, R., Plank, S., and Ruby, A. (2000). Talent development middle schools: Blueprints and results for a comprehensive whole-school reform model. In Mavis G. Sanders (Ed.), *Schooling students placed at risk: Research, policy, and practice in the education of poor and minority adolescents* (pp. 261–288). Mahwah, NJ: Lawrence Erlbaum Associates.

Majoribanks, K. (1988). Individual–environment correlates of children's reading performance. *Perceptual and Motor Skills, 67,* 323–332.

McDill, E. L., and Rigsby, L. C. (1973). *Structure and process in secondary schools.* Baltimore: Johns Hopkins University Press.

Meisels, S. J. (1992). Doing harm by doing good: Iatrogenic effects of early childhood enrollment and promotion policies. *Early Childhood Research Quarterly, 7,* 155–174.

Meisels, S. J. (1996). Performance in context: Assessing children's achievement at the outset of school. In A. J. Sameroff and M. M. Haith (Eds.), *The five to seven year shift: The age of reason and responsibility* (pp. 410–431). Chicago: University of Chicago Press.

Mendel, M. (Ed.). (1998). *Parents at school.* Warsaw, Poland: Ministry of Education.

Montandon, C., and Perrenoud, P. (1987). *Entre parents et ensignants un diologue impossible?* Berne, Switzerland: Lang.

Moll, L. C., Amanti, C., Neff, D., and Gonzalez, N. (1992). Funds of knowledge for teaching: Using a qualitative approach to connect homes and classrooms. *Theory Into Practice, 31,* 132–141.

Moos, R. H., and Insel, P. M. (Eds.). (1974). *Issues in social ecology: Human milieus.* Palo Alto, CA: National Press Books.

Morisset, C. E. (1993). *Language and emotional milestones: On the road to readiness* (Rep. No. 18). Baltimore: Johns Hopkins University, Center on Families, Communities, Schools and Children's Learning.

National Center for Educational Statistics. (1996). *Statistics in brief: Parents' reports of school practices to involve families.* Washington, DC: U.S. Department of Education/OERI/NCES 97-327.

National PTA. (2000). *Building successful partnerships: A guide for developing parent and family involvement programs.* Bloomington, IN: National Educational Service.

Nichols, S. L., and Good, T. L. (2000). Education and society, 1900–2000: Selected snapshots of then and now. In T. L. Good (Ed.), *American education: Yesterday, today, and tomorrow* (pp. 1–52). Chicago: University of Chicago Press. Ninety-ninth yearbook of the National Society for the Study of Education.

Nieto, S. (1993). *Affirming diversity: The sociopolitical context of multicultural education.* New York: Longman.

Nord, C. W., Brimhall, D., and West, J. (1997). *Fathers' involvement in their children's schools.* Washington, DC: National Center for Education Statistics. NCES 98-091.

Oakes, J. (1988). Tracking in mathematics and science education: A structural contribution to unequal schooling. In L. Weis (Ed.), *Class, race, and gender in American education* (pp. 106–125). Albany: State University of New York Press.

Oakes, J. (1992). Can tracking research inform practice? Technical, normative, and political considerations. *Educational Researcher, 21,* 12–21.

Ohlhausen, M., and Powell, R. (1992, April). *Parents: What do they think about traditional and alternative reporting systems?* Paper presented at the annual meeting of the American Educational Research Association, San Francisco.

Parke, R. D. (1996). *Fatherhood.* Cambridge, MA: Harvard University Press.

Reid, M. (1984). School reports to parents: A study of policy and practice in the secondary school. *Educational Researcher, 26,* 82–87.

Resnick, M. D., Bearman, P. S., Blum, R. W., Bauman, K. E., Harris, K. M., Jones, J., Tabor, J., Beuhring, T., Sieving, R., Shew, M., Ireland, M., Bearinger, L. H., and Udry, J. R. (1997). Protecting adolescents from harm: Findings from the National Longitudinal Study on Adolescent Health. *Journal of the American Medical Association, 278*, 823–832.

Rich, D. (1988). *Megaskills: How families can help children succeed in school and beyond.* Boston: Houghton Mifflin.

Sacks, P. (2000). *Standardized minds: The high price of America's testing culture and what we can do to change it.* Cambridge, MA: Perseus.

Sanders, M. G. (1998a). The effects of school, family and community support on the academic achievement of African-American adolescents. *Urban Education, 33*, 385–409.

Sanders, M. G. (1998b). School–family–community partnerships: An action team approach. *The High School Magazine, 5*, 38–49.

Sanders, M. G. (1999). Improving school, family and community partnerships in urban middle schools. *Middle School Journal, 31*, 35–41.

Sanders, M. G. (2000). Creating successful school-based partnership programs with families of special needs students. *The School Community Journal, 10*, 37–55.

Sanders, M. G. (2001). A study of the role of "community" in comprehensive school, family, and community partnership programs. *The Elementary School Journal, 102*, 19–34.

Sanders, M. G., and Epstein, J. L. (2000a). Building school, family and community partnerships in secondary schools. In M. G. Sanders (Ed.), *Schooling students placed at risk: Research, policy, and practice in the education of poor and minority adolescents* (pp. 339–362). Mahwah, NJ: Lawrence Erlbaum Associates.

Sanders, M. G., and Epstein, J. L. (2000b). The National Network of Partnership Schools: How research influences educational practice. *Journal of Education for Students Placed at Risk, 5*, 61–76.

Sanders, M. G., and Epstein, J. L. (1998a). School–family–community partnerships and educational change: International perspectives. In A. Hargreaves, A. Lieberman, M. Fullan, and D. Hopkins (Eds.), *International handbook of educational change* (pp. 482–502). Hingham, MA: Kluwer.

Sanders, M. G., and Epstein, J. L. (Eds.). (1998b). International perspectives on school, family and community partnerships. In *Childhood Education, 74.*

Sanders, M. G., Epstein, J. L., and Connors-Tadros, L. C. (1999). *Family partnership with high schools: The parents' perspective* (Report No. 32). Baltimore: Johns Hopkins University, Center for Research on the Education of Students Placed at Risk.

Sanders, M. G., and Harvey, A. (2000, April). *Developing comprehensive programs of school, family, and community partnerships: The community perspective.* Paper presented at the American Educational Research Association Annual Conference, New Orleans, LA.

Sanders, M. G., and Herting, J. R. (2000). Gender and the effects of school, family and church support on the academic achievement of African-American urban adolescents. In M. G. Sanders (Ed.), *Schooling students placed at risk: Research, policy, and practice in the education of poor and minority adolescents* (pp. 141–162). Mahwah, NJ: Lawrence Erlbaum Associates.

Scott-Jones, D. (1995). Parent–child interactions and school achievement. In B. A. Ryan, G. R. Adams, T. P. Gullota, R. P. Weissberg, and R. L. Hampton (Eds.), *The family–school connection: Theory, research, and practice* (pp. 75–107). Thousand Oaks, CA: Sage.

Seeley, D. S. (1981). *Education through partnership: Mediating structures and education.* Cambridge, MA: Ballinger.

Sheldon, S. B. (in press). Beyond beliefs: Parents' social networks and beliefs as predictors of parent involvement. *Elementary School Journal.*

Shepard, L., and Smith, M. (1986). School readiness and kindergarten retention: A policy analysis. *Educational Leadership, 44*, 78–86.

Shine, J. (Ed.). (1997). *Service learning.* Chicago: University of Chicago Press. (Ninety-sixth yearbook of the National Society for the Study of Education.)

Sigel, I. (1992). Viewpoint on school readiness. *ETS Policy Notes, 4*, 1–3.

Simon, B. S. (2000). *Predictors of high school and family partnership and the influence of partnerships on student success.* Unpublished dissertation, Johns Hopkins University, Department of Sociology, Baltimore.

Snow, C. E., and Tabors, P. (1996). Intergenerational transfer of literacy. In L. A. Benjamin and J. Lord (Eds.), *Family literacy: Directions in research and implications for practice* (pp. 73–80). Washington, DC: U.S. Department of Education.

Sorensen, A. B., and Morgan, S. L. (2000). School effects: Theoretical and methodological issues. In M. Hallinan (Ed.), *Handbook of the sociology of education* (pp. 137–160). New York: Plenum.

Stainback, S., and Stainback, W. (1996). Collaboration, support networking, and community building. In S. Stainback and W. Stainback (Eds.), *Inclusion: A guide for educators.* Baltimore: Brookes.

Stevenson, D. L., and Baker, D. P. (1987). The family–school relation and the child's school performance. *Child Development, 58*, 1348–1357.

Stevenson, D. L., Schiller, K. S., and Schneider, B. (1994). Sequences for opportunities for learning. *Sociology of Education, 67*, 184–198.

Swap, S. M. (1993). *Developing home–school partnerships: From concepts to practice.* New York: Teachers College Press.

Topping, K. J. (1995). Cued spelling: A powerful technique for parent and peer tutoring. *The Reading Teacher, 48,* 374–383.

Turnbull, A., Turnbull, H., Shank, M., and Leal, D. (1995). *Exceptional lives: Special education in today's schools.* Englewood Cliffs, NJ: Prentice-Hall.

U.S. Department of Labor. (1999). *Futurework: Trends and challenges for work in the twenty-first century.* Washington, DC: Author. Available: www.dol.gov

Useem, E. L. (1992). Middle school and math groups: Parents' involvement in children's placement. *Sociology of Education, 65,* 263–279.

Van Voorhis, F. L. (2000). *The effects of interactive (TIPS) and non-interactive homework assignments on science achievement and family involvement of middle grade students.* Unpublished doctoral dissertation, University of Florida, Gainesville.

Voltz, D. L. (1998). Challenges and choices in urban education: The perceptions of teachers and principals. *Urban Review, 30,* 211–228.

Walberg, H. (1984). Families as partners in educational productivity. *Phi Delta Kappan, 65,* 397–400.

Waller, W. (1932). *The sociology of teaching.* New York: Russell and Russell.

Wasik, B. A., and Karweit, N. (1994). Off to a good start: Effects of birth-to-three interventions on early school success. In R. Slavin, N. Karweit, and B. Wasik (Eds.), *Preventing early school failure* (pp. 13–57). New York: Longwood.

Weber, M. (1947). *Theory of social and economic organization* (A. M. Henderson and T. Parsons, trans.). New York: Oxford University Press.

Weiss, M. (2000). R and R if needed: Grand Blanc (MI) Community Schools Resource and Referral Book. In K. Salinas and N. Jansorn (Eds.), *Promising partnership practices—2000* (pp. 117–118). Baltimore: Johns Hopkins University, Center on School, Family, and Community Partnerships.

West, J., Denton K., and Hausken, E. G. (2000). *America's kindergartners: Findings from the Early Childhood Longitudinal Study, Kindergarten Class of 1998–99* (NCES 2000-070). Washington, DC: National Center for Education Statistics.

West, J., and Hausken, E. G. (1993). *Readiness for kindergarten: Parent and teacher beliefs.* Washington, DC: National Center for Education Statistics.

Wheelock, A. (1992). *Crossing the tracks: How "untracking" can save America's schools.* New York: New Press.

Williams, M. R. (1989). *Neighborhood organizing for urban school reform.* New York: Teachers College Press.

Wolfendale, S. (1985). An introduction to parent listening. In K. Topping and S. Wolfendale (Eds.), *Parental involvement in children's reading* (pp. 35–41). London: Croom Helm.

Xu, J., and Corno, L. (1998). Case studies of families doing third-grade homework. *Teachers College Record, 100,* 402–436.

Yonezawa, S. (2000). Unpacking the black box of tracking decisions: Critical tales of families navigating the course placement process. In M. G. Sanders (Ed.), *Schooling students placed at risk: Research, policy, and practice in the education of poor and minority adolescents* (pp. 109–140). Mahwah, NJ: Lawrence Erlbaum Associates.

Youniss, J., and Yates, M. (1997). *Community service and social responsibility in youth.* Chicago: University of Chicago Press.

17

Parents and Their Children's Doctors

Gerald B. Hickson
Ellen W. Clayton
Vanderbilt University Medical Center

INTRODUCTION

At face value, a medical encounter involving a parent, child, and physician should be relatively straightforward. A family perceives the need for assistance for an acute illness or health promotion and seeks help. The physician identifies the child's (family's) need and seeks to meet that need. An encounter, however, can be a complex process involving a host of motivations, expectations, and fears. When the process goes well, there is potential for good, but when the process breaks down, harm may occur, affecting the child immediately or making future encounters less productive. The purpose of this chapter is to discuss the complexities of the relationships between parents and their children's physicians. Included is description of a model of how parents, children, and physicians interact and a discussion of the characteristics of parents and physicians that may affect their interactions. The literature concerning patient satisfaction as evidence of how well these relationships work and of the consequences of dissatisfaction is examined next. Finally, some practical advice for parents and physicians that can help promote productive interactions on behalf of children is provided.

HISTORICAL PERSPECTIVES ON HEALTHCARE FOR CHILDREN

George Armstrong is credited as the father of modern pediatrics (Maloney, 1954). After 20 years of general medical practice, he published a text entitled *Essay on the Diseases Most Fatal to Infants to Which Are Added Rules to Be Observed in the Nursing of Children: With a Particular View to Those Who Are Brought Up by Hand* (Armstrong, 1767), and shortly thereafter established in London the first dispensary for the care of sick children. Of his decision to open a clinic for children Armstrong said, "One main duty was thought by some not to have been attended to, viz the care of infants from their birth to their fourth year completed; in which period by London tables one half of all that are born, die" (p. A-2).

Armstrong made many important observations, some of which were contrary to common practices of the day. Like Semmelweis (Larson, 1989), he stressed the need for hygiene. He maintained that, contrary to the common practice of the day, feeding infants large amounts of fat and frequent quantities of ale and strong liquor was harmful. Armstrong asserted that children were hurt by being crowded together in close quarters and emphasized the need to provide children and their parents with access to medical care (Charney, 1974).

Armstrong's clinic flourished through the 1770s, but he found it increasingly difficult to sustain the program financially. He resorted to fundraising but provided for most of the clinic's needs from his own pocket. Predictably his debt grew, and he was arrested in 1780 for nonpayment of a loan. Within the year he suffered a stroke and was forced to stop practice. Shortly thereafter, the first clinic for the infant poor was closed (Charney, 1974).

George Frederick Still, a distinguished pediatrician of the early twentieth century, described Armstrong's clinic as "the most important step ever taken for the care of children . . . " (Still, 1931, p. 502). "Armstrong's book was good, but his magnum opus was his pioneer work in opening the first institution . . . for the treatment of sick children: it was the beginning of a great movement which was to lift the study of diseases of children on to a different plane by the accumulation of special experience which could not be obtained in any other way" (Still, 1931, p. 425).

Abraham Jacobi is generally identified as the father of pediatrics in America (Hall, 1991). In the late 1800s, he emphasized the differences between the treatment of children and adults: "Therapeutics of infancy and childhood are by no means so similar to those of the adult that the rules of the latter can simply be adapted to the former by reducing doses. The differences are many" (U.S. Department of Health, Education, and Welfare, 1976, p. 9).

By the turn of the century, pediatric practice was largely concerned with identifying diseases, often without being able to help, promoting good feeding and nutrition habits, rehydrating infants suffering from epidemic gastroenteritis, and promoting family hygiene and public sanitation (Holt, 1897; Richmond, 1967). By the 1920s, practice began to change. Development of vaccines for smallpox, typhoid, diphtheria, tetanus, and pertussis altered the role of the child health practitioner. Instead of being able only to react to diseases, pediatricians began to have the tools to promote disease prevention. The next advances came with the development of antibiotics, intravenous therapy, physiologic monitoring, and mechanical ventilation. Such progress led Davison to write in 1952, perhaps on an unrealistically optimistic note, "Eventually, children's hospitals should be empty, except for newborn and premature infants, the ill children of working mothers, accidents and unpreventable surgical operations" (p. 538).

Although most pediatricians were focused on the biological and biochemical and on laboratory investigations of the origins and treatment of specific physical disorders, other investigators were developing a growing interest in the social, emotional, and developmental aspects of children and child health (Hall, 1991). As early as the 1930s, Anderson (1930) predicted that interest in childhood behavior and development was the logical progression of medicine's growing triumph over childhood illnesses. Pediatricians had to take notice as more and more families reported their children's school, feeding, sleep, behavioral, and developmental problems. In 1941, Arnold Gesell chaired the American Academy of Pediatrics' first round table on growth and developmental studies of children (Hall, 1991). He boldly declared that "development as well as disease is now a recognized concern of clinical pediatrics" (Senn, 1975, p. 58). Gesell, who set up the Yale Psycho-Clinic (now the Child Study Center) was also instrumental in promoting collaboration among pediatricians, psychologists, and others concerned about all aspects of children's growth and development (Hall, 1991).

Review of the first 200 plus years of pediatric medicine reveals a field that has changed in response to the changing nature of children's health needs, from responding to severe epidemic diseases to problems associated with the new morbidity, a term coined to describe the effects of the "modern" age on children's growth and development. Poverty, poor housing, and inadequate hygiene continue to extract a toll on too many children. To this have been added the effects of the weakening of the extended family, divorce, and the single-parent family. And, as in Armstrong's day, all of these forces are confounded by a lack of financial resources to pay for children's health care needs (Garbarino, Vorrasi, Kostelny in Vol. 5; Hetherington and Stanley-Hagan in Vol. 3; and Weinraub, Horvath and Gringlas, in Vol. 3 of this *Handbook*).

WHO DECIDES ABOUT CHILDREN'S HEALTH?

Decision making is at the center of all parent–physician relationships. Increasingly, when decision making is discussed notions of informed consent are invoked. Patients have the right to make decisions about their medical treatment in light of their own values (Katz, 1984). With rare exceptions, however, this model has no place in pediatric medicine. Children, particularly when they are young, cannot make decisions about their own treatment, and although they often have opinions about what is being done to them—it is the rare 5-year-old child who wants immunizations—their views often are not and should not be determinative (Baumrind and Thompson, in Vol. 5 of this *Handbook*). As children get older, their wishes should receive more deference, but not until individuals reach adulthood or legal emancipation are they legally entitled to make medical decisions according to their own views (Holder, 1985).

Because children do not make their own health care decisions, someone else must. The people most likely to be involved in these decisions are parents and doctors. Often, parents make decisions alone or with the advice of people who are not physicians; they decide to care for a child with an upper respiratory infection or chicken pox themselves and may heed the suggestions of family members or the neighborhood pharmacist. Much more infrequently, physicians take complete charge, as when a 6-week-old baby presents with a femur fracture and a history that strongly suggests child abuse or when a 4-month-old baby presents with the classic picture of meningitis. In those settings, parents' wishes regarding the child's care that differs from the physician's may appropriately be overridden. For the most part, however, parents and physicians collaborate in making decisions about children's health care.

Different models can apply to the decision-making collaboration. In some instances, physicians are paternalistic and act as if they know what is best. At least in the outpatient setting, however, the paternalist may not be fully successful in directing care because the physician's opinions and recommendations can be ignored by parents (Charney et al., 1967; Lima, Nazarian, Charney, and Lahti, 1976). But even more important than the practical limitations of paternalism is the fact that medical ethics increasingly rejects the paternalistic model and instead asserts that parents have a role to play in decision making as well. In part, this deference to parents is a response to the practical recognition that parents cannot be ignored if only because children live in families and decisions about their care affect and must be effected by the parents. On a more philosophical level, society believes, although reminders are sometimes needed, that parents usually try to help their children and that parents need some room for autonomy in childrearing (Silverman, 1992). The challenge within the context of seeking and delivering care, then, is to develop appropriate collaborative relationships that suitably empower parents so that they may act in concert with physicians on behalf of children.

In addition, relationships between physicians and parents are dynamic. Once the encounter is initiated, authority over the process can shift between parent and physician. Within the context of the encounter, some physicians may take a fairly authoritarian stance, which may make parent–doctor communication difficult. Other physicians indicate by word or deed that they are more open, seeking to inform or engage in joint decision making. At the same time, some parents are quite vocal in expressing their wishes, whereas others are more reserved and may be reluctant to verbalize concerns or desires even in response to direct questions (Pichert and Hickson, 2001). A receptive physician may be able to address the needs of verbal parents better than an authoritarian provider will be able to meet the needs of a relatively silent parent. Defining the contours of desirable relationships is difficult because interactions change over time and in different circumstances and vary with different physician–parent dyads. But the first step in setting forth guidelines are to examine the forces that may affect the parent and the physician as they relate to each other and as they seek to provide care.

Selecting a Physician: The First Step in the Relationship

Although some encounters occur by accident, in most cases, parents initiate medical care by choosing a physician. When they choose well, the family can establish a relationship that provides the basis for access to an array of acute care and health promotion services. The methods that parents use to identify physicians are potential determinants of the quality of care they receive. The process also may influence families' ultimate satisfaction with the care delivered. In spite of the importance of this first step, few studies have been directed at examining how patients seek physicians, and even fewer studies assess how families select child health providers.

An early study of provider selection was conducted by Cartwright (1967). He found that most consumers of health services believe that they are not competent to assess the quality of physician performance. As a result, patients limit their evaluations to those areas where they believe they can make appropriate judgments, including physician personality characteristics and the doctor's "art of care." Glassman and Glassman (1981) sought to identify determinants of obstetric care selection. They found that new obstetrical patients consulted only 1.2 sources of information per decision; the primary sources were friends and neighbors. Their findings support the assertions made by Parsons (1951), that most people choose their physicians almost "blindly." All of this is consistent with theoretical arguments and empirical findings in the marketing literature that extensive search behavior is rare if consumers cannot easily obtain or evaluate information (Furse, Punj, and Stewart, 1984; Stewart, Hickson, Pechmann, Koslow, and Altemeier, 1989).

A study aimed at investigating the process by which child health providers are identified and selected also found little evidence of systematic search behavior on the part of parents (Hickson, Stewart, Altemeier, and Perrin, 1988). Families consulted few sources of information, only 1.2 per decision. Parents selecting pediatricians, however, relied on different sources of information than did those selecting family or general practitioners. The former group were more likely to have obtained information in their search process from other physicians (32.3% vs. 12.6%) or from friends (53.5% vs. 36.9%), whereas those selecting family and general practitioners were more likely to rely on their own experiences with their children's future physicians (35.3% vs. 9.4%). This study also sought to identify which provider characteristics parents considered important in their selection. The most consistent priorities were good communication skills, including the willingness to involve parents in decision making, returning phone calls in a timely fashion, and demonstrating concern. Parents appeared to have less concern about issues of convenience and cost. Nonetheless, it is important to recognize that all families may not share the same priorities. Parents who selected family practitioners were more likely to value short in-office waiting time (40.3% vs. 22.2%) and low fees (25.2% vs. 7.1%).

Parents generally adopt relatively unsophisticated search strategies in looking for a physician and make selections based more on chance than any analytical search process. This is not to imply that parents do not have strong feelings about what they want. The most consistent priorities identified are for good physician communication and interpersonal skills. Patients generally limit their search to these issues perhaps because they assume that state licensing boards protect them from unfit practitioners, or more likely because they simply lack the knowledge or means of assessing the physician's technical competence.

Deciding to Seek Care: Parents' Perceptions

Once families have identified a source of care, interactions with providers do not occur automatically. Except following serious accidents, natural disasters, or compulsion by public authorities, families

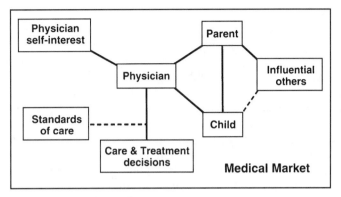

FIGURE 17.1. Model of parent-doctor relationship and medical decision making.

evaluate many factors when deciding to seek care for their children. This process is complex and affected by signs and symptoms of illness, children's demands, families' observation and listening skills, knowledge, past experiences, parents' beliefs about their own health and the health care system, stress, the advice of influential others, and a host of enabling factors including access to care and the means to pay for that care (see Figure 17.1).

Viewed in generic terms, an individual must first perceive need and believe that the need can be met. Second, an individual seeks aid from another person in a direct way (DePaulo, 1983) and as a result may benefit from the assistance provided. Accepting aid, however, may be difficult for some, placing recipients under the authority of others in an asymmetrical power relationship (Whitcher-Alagna, 1983). The acknowledgment of need can cause embarrassment (Shapiro, 1971) and fear of rejection (DePaulo, 1982; Rodin and Janis, 1979). Both may delay decisions to seek help. Like most forms of aid, medical help may represent a mixed blessing, providing benefit but at a cost (Witcher-Alagna, 1983).

The process of seeking medical aid for a child's health is similar, but more complex in that parents are deciding not for themselves but for their children. Having to decide on behalf of a child adds motivations and concerns to the equation, including guilt that they as parents are somehow responsible for their children's condition and the fear that they will somehow make the wrong decision. The process of seeking care can result in fear and ambivalence on the part of parents. Consequently, aid may not be sought unless the parent decides that it is worth it, that is, that the chance of getting assistance outweighs the economic and noneconomic costs of seeking care.

Parents from all walks of life respond to what they recognize as signs and symptoms of illness in their children (Figure 17.1). In most studies of health care utilization, clinical factors are consistently the most important predictors of any medical encounter. Children experience an array of symptoms. Parents recognize that their children are febrile, will not eat, or want to sleep a lot. How they respond depends on a multitude of factors, including knowledge, past experiences, and beliefs about the health care system. Parents may encourage fluids and rest, perhaps administering antipyretics or a number of over-the-counter medications with or without consulting a pharmacist. In most circumstances, this level of intervention is appropriate because most childhood illnesses are self-limited. Many parents are reinforced in the correctness of their decision making because their children eventually stop vomiting or coughing or running a fever, which in turn provides more comfort when dealing with such problems in the future.

At some point, however, symptoms may reach a level that prompts health care–seeking behavior. Hershey, Luft, and Gianaris (1975), in a community survey, asked 1,065 individuals to sort 21 symptoms into three distinct categories: "acute and worrisome," "nonacute and worrisome," and "nonacute nonworrisome." The acute and worrisome symptoms were consistently the most important predictors of decisions to seek care. Perceived seriousness of symptoms was most important in explaining health care use, with the patient's belief in whether or not a physician could actually help as the next most powerful factor.

Parents' perceptions of their children's overall health status also affects use of physician services independent of the influence of signs and symptoms of acute illness. As perceived health status declines, the average number of physician visits per patient rises (Salber, Greene, Feldman, and Hunter, 1976). Freeborn, Pope, Davis, and Mullooly (1977), using a 5% random sampling of Kaiser enrollees including children, found that perceived health status was more important than all sociodemographic variables combined in predicting the use of all medical services except those for preventive health.

Parents' beliefs about children's capacity to tolerate illness affect decisions to seek care. Visits for trivial reasons may be accompanied by the apology: "I really hate to bother you with this but . . . ." The remainder of the message implies a fear that a child is for some reason vulnerable and that, unless intervention is obtained early, a cold will progress into an ear infection, which may progress into pneumonia or something worse. Perceptions of vulnerability are common and may be related to parental difficulty with separation and overprotectiveness (Green and Solnit, 1964). In some cases, parental fears are triggered by previous medical encounters that frightened parents or were misunderstood or that occurred at certain sensitive times of life, as, for example, in the immediate newborn period or when infants are symbolic of a significant person from the past who died prematurely (Altemeier, O'Connor, Sherrod, and Vietze, 1985; Kemper, Forsyth, and McCarthy, 1990). Finally, it is important to recognize that parents' attentiveness to symptoms in their children may relate to their own inclinations to use medical services. Mechanic (1964) identified a direct relation between mothers' tendencies to seek care for themselves and their tendencies to seek care for their children. Mechanic also identified a relation between family stress and maternal reporting of illness symptoms.

Parents' decisions to seek well-child care, by contrast, appear to be influenced by beliefs in the value of general health maintenance services. In 1965, Deisher, Engel, Speilhoiz, and Standfast surveyed a large number of mothers concerning their opinions of pediatric care. As a part of this study, parents were asked why they sought care. Obtaining immunizations was mentioned as very important (by 96% of respondents), followed by having a complete physical examination (85%) and reassurance of normal growth and development (72%). On the other hand, only 29% expressed a desire for information concerning childrearing practices.

Advice of people outside the nuclear family also may influence parents' decisions to seek health care for their children. Members of the extended family serve as advisers, helping parents to identify specific concerns or to weigh the risks and benefits of seeking care. Influential others may accompany the parent and child and even attempt to direct what care is delivered. Even if grandparents advise an appropriate course, their actions may embarrass or promote dependence on the part of young parents and reduce what the young mother hears or accepts.

Babysitters and daycare workers represent another group of powerful others who influence decisions to seek care. The increasing numbers of mothers who work outside the home (Children's Defense Fund, 1990; Hofferth and Phillips, 1987) have created an explosion of demand for childcare services (Clark-Stewart, Allhusen, in Vol. 3 of this *Handbook*). Use of large daycare centers increases the risk of spread of infectious diseases, especially viral upper respiratory infections (Hurwitz, Gunn, Pinsky, and Schonberger, 1991) and gastroenteritis (Alexander, Zinzeleta, Mackenzie, Vernon, and Markowitz, 1990) among enrollees particularly if the center has high child-to-worker ratios or poor hygiene practices (Osterholm, Reves, Murphy, and Pickering, 1992). Workers have responded to the risk of contagion by adopting sound and not so sound local control policies. Many mothers find themselves confronted by daycare workers who urge parents to seek medical care. Furthermore, many go beyond mere counsel by requiring a note from a doctor before a child is allowed to return to the facility. The influence exerted by the worker may create potential conflicts between parents and physicians, especially when workers "know" what children need and physicians fail to meet expectations. It is not uncommon to encounter a child in the office who presents to receive an antibiotic for a green nasal discharge because that is what the daycare worker has already "ordered." Although inadequately studied, childcare workers exert a significant influence on parents' decisions to seek care and on satisfaction with the care delivered.

The media and the Internet have become important sources of medical information for families. Public service announcements, special interest stories, and mass media campaigns have been used to inform individuals about AIDS prevention (Keiser, 1991), the use of child restraint devices (Rivara, 1985), the need to avoid aspirin in children with chickenpox to prevent Reye's syndrome (Arrowsmith, Kennedy, Kuritsky, and Faich, 1987), child physical and sexual abuse, the need for childhood immunization services (National Vaccine Advisory Committee, 1991), and the need to avoid the prone sleeping position in infants (Moon and Biliter, 2000; Moon, Patel, and Shaefer 2000). On the other hand, some media pieces create fear and misunderstanding: Examples include media coverage of chronic fatigue syndrome (Hickson and Clayton, 1993) and the safety of vaccines perhaps contributing to declining immunization rates and to outbreaks of pertussis and measles (Hinman, 1991).

These examples demonstrate that the Internet, just like more conventional media, provides opportunity for both good and bad (Mandl, Feit, Peña, and Kohane, 2000). Increasing access to the Web provides families with availability of almost limitless medical information. But like television, print, and radio, much of the information is not peer reviewed and has the potential to mislead or cause harm (Impicciatore, Pandolfin, Casella, and Bonati, 1992; Mandl, Kohane, and Brandt 1998). Not only can media reports or Internet information influence families' decisions to seek care; they may affect families' perceptions of what physicians should do in response to their complaints. Dissatisfaction may occur when a doctor's advice differs from that offered by a media "experts" (Hickson and Clayton, 1993).

Overall, families make decisions concerning when to seek care in response to their perceptions of the seriousness of their children's symptoms or their children's general health status as influenced by their past experiences, knowledge, belief in the vulnerability of their children, previous interactions with the medical profession, and advice offered by powerful others.

Deciding to Seek Care: Availability of Health Care and Family Resources

Motivations to seek illness-related care or general health maintenance are only one part of the picture, as use of medical services requires certain "enabling factors" (Anderson, 1968). Enabling factors can be subdivided into two distinct groups: *service resources*, including the availability of physician manpower, equipment, and facilities, and *family resources,* including income and third-party coverage in order to pay for services. All of these factors affect families' motivations in seeking care and physicians' motivations in delivering care.

A direct relation exists between availability of physician services and health care consumption. Cross-sectional studies demonstrate that the number of outpatients visits and surgical procedures per capita rise as physician-to-population ratios increase (Fuchs, 1978; Fuchs and Kramer, 1972). The physician-to-population ratio is more important in explaining per capita use of medical services than consumer income, price per visit, or third-party coverage (Andersen and Aday, 1978; Scitovsky 1981). Having a regular source of care also promotes more use of medical services. A continuity relationship may enable physicians to exercise greater influence on families' decisions to seek care. Data from the 1977–1978 National Ambulatory Medical Care Survey revealed a positive correlation between the physician-to-population ratio and the number of per capita visits judged to be provider initiated (Wilensky and Rossiter, 1983).

Per capita use of medical services also is affected by availability of hospital beds (Roemer, 1961a) and new technology. Although physicians order and prescribe services (Rossiter and Wilensky, 1983; Wilensky and Rossiter, 1983), patients may influence their use as well. Through the media, patients become aware of new procedures, diagnostic tools, and therapies almost as fast as members of the medical community. Both patients and physicians ask for, order, and receive new therapies in responding to a "technologic imperative" (Harris, 1990).

Another enabling factor is dollars to pay for care. With the establishment of commercial health insurance (1940s), and passage of Medicare and Medicaid legislation (in the early 1960s), U.S. citizens have increasingly been shielded from the real cost of their health care (Hickson, 1997).

Insurance, whether public or private, has tended to hide the real cost of care from the consumer resulting in increased consumption of all types of health services. As the out-of-pocket price of care falls toward zero, patients and physicians lose motivation to conserve dollars (Newhouse et al., 1982).

Although intended to measure the impact of increasing copayments on patients' use of health services, the Rand Health Insurance Experiment (HIE; Newhouse et al., 1982), if viewed from an alternative perspective, actually illustrated the "subsidy effect" of third-party coverage. Patients of all ages were enrolled in the HIE and randomized to receive traditional indemnity coverage, free care, or to one of several groups of progressively increasing copayments for each service received. A copayment represents an out-of-pocket expenditure for some small percentage of the cost of a service. Copayments are generally instituted to reduce the use of nonessential or discretionary medical services. The HIE revealed that increasing copayments reduced use of inpatient and outpatient services (Newhouse et al., 1982). Conversely, the less patients paid directly, the more services they used.

Using data from the HIE, Leibowitz et al. (1985) examined the effect of cost sharing on families' use of health services and children's health status. Cost sharing reduced children's use of all ambulatory services by one third but did not appear to impact use of inpatient services. Copayments also decreased use of general health maintenance services. Similarly, Lairson and Swint (1978) found that copayments decreased use of general health maintenance visits for children in the Kaiser health system. Whether and how reductions in use of preventive service affect children's overall health status is difficult to assess. Valdez et al. (1985) pointed out that it is difficult to measure the benefits of such interventions, including information transmitted, social support provided, and counseling concerning family psychosocial problems. This study also did not assess how copayments might differentially affect families based on their ability to pay. Financial restraints may cause some families to do without medical screening and immunization services for their children. Others may choose to delay seeking care for acute symptoms until problems escalate, or they may choose to use emergency rooms for acute but nonemergent care.

Deciding to Seek Care: The Influence of the Structure of the Health Care System

The structure and organization of the health care system also influence families and physicians' decisions. It is important to examine the structure of the medical environment in order to understand how the system may affect patients' motivations to seek, and providers' motivations to prescribe care.

Through the early 1960s medicine could be described primarily as a cottage industry of solo and small group physician practices (Hickson, 1997). Physicians completed training and opened offices or chose to associate with a few other colleagues practicing the same kind of medicine, but by and large pediatricians ran service-oriented small businesses delivering high-volume, low-unit-price care. These small businesses varied in efficiency but offered great autonomy for both physicians and patients. Parents were able to select practices as they saw fit, accept or reject recommendations for subspecialty care, seek second opinions directly, and leave practices whenever they were inclined (Grumbach et al., 1999). Physicians and health care institutions needed to be responsive to patients' desires. In consultation with their physician, parents could exercise significant influence over the choice of inpatient versus outpatient care, specialty versus generalist care, as well as selection of specific hospitals if needed. The premanaged care medical market was high in individual freedom but could be low in organization and coordination of care. Payment for care was always the responsibility of the parent, who was expected to pay at the time of service and then perhaps seek reimbursement from a third-party carrier if visits were "covered" expenses. Physicians were generally reimbursed by fee for service. They paid for their office overhead and took home the rest (Friedson, 1963).

Although the cottage industry model was friendly, it was also costly (Hickson, 1997). By the late 1980s health expenditures were growing at such a rate that they threatened government budgets and the bottom lines of business and industry. This health care cost crisis created the will to promote change leading to the growth of a new managed system of care (Iglehart, 1992) focused on prepayment, practice systems development, and greater incentives to provide only the most cost-effective care.

The rise of managed competition has meant that a growing number of physicians and parents have faced a loss of the freedom that was a hallmark of the "old" system. Although parents retain some autonomy over their choice of health care plans and choice of primary providers, they often lose direct access to a subspecialist without prior authorization of their physician "gatekeepers" (Albertson et al., 2000; Grumbach et al., 1999; Iglehart, 1992). Managed plans also subtly change the character of physicians' offices in ways that make them appear less friendly and responsive. As discussed later, many plans reimburse physicians by mechanisms other than fee for service. The physician is no longer able to run a small service-oriented business where every customer represents an opportunity for future business, becoming instead one of many working in someone else's facility or for someone else's plan. Practices may be better organized to coordinate care, but also may be perceived as less welcoming (Albertson et al., 2000).

Influences on Physician Behavior: The Central Role of Autonomy

The next step in developing understanding of the parent–doctor relationship is to consider how physician characteristics and experiences motivate practice behavior. Physicians have always had great autonomy in decision making. Patients tend to invest physicians with far-reaching authority to suggest "required care," that is, the quantity and quality of service to be offered on their behalf. This right to define the care delivered is illustrated in Figure 17.1 by the bold line running from the physician to care and treatment decisions.

The line representing the physician decision-making process is relatively unencumbered. For all practical purposes, medicine is practiced behind closed doors. The practice of an individual physician is effectively screened from the view of others that might have the knowledge and ability to assess and regulate (Eisenberg, 1985). But even if all decisions could be brought to light, assessment would still be difficult because of the general lack of universally accepted standards for quality medical practice. These "standards" are not synonymous with the medicolegal concept of "standard of care," the practice of a reasonably prudent physician, but rather imply the existence of an if-then relationship. If a patient has symptoms A, B, and C, then treatment D should be prescribed because in similar circumstances such treatment clearly results in an improved outcome. This does not mean that no standards exist. There are a few, which is why a dotted line intersects the model between the physician and treatment decisions. An example is the management of a child with fever and stridor who has epiglottitis, an infection of the epiglottis, a connective tissue structure positioned over the vocal cords. When infected with the bacteria *Hemophilus influenza*, the epiglottis swells, risking compromise of the child's airway, potentially resulting in hypoxia (lack of oxygen) and death. Studies demonstrate beyond any reasonable doubt that elective insertion of an artificial airway reduces morbidity and mortality (Margolis, Ingram, and Meyer, 1972) and morbidity (Diaz and Lockhart, 1982). In this setting, the standard for optimal practice and the legal minimum coincide so that the provider's freedom of decision making is constrained by a clear practice standard and the law's mandate.

Such examples, however, are rare; limits of scientific knowledge about most medical conditions do not allow practitioners to define unambiguous relations between decisions and outcomes so precisely. The profession typically has relied on the consensus of its opinion leaders in defining practice standards. Because there is rarely unarguable scientific proof of the optimal method for treatment, the individual physician can still argue that her or his approach to care is most appropriate and tailored for her or his individual patients' needs. This lack of scientific certainty protects physician autonomy over decision making and permits variations in observed practice behavior (Wennberg, McPherson, and Caper, 1984).

Physicians, however, do not make decisions in a vacuum. In fact, decision making is influenced by characteristics of the individual physician, patients, and the medical environment. Such factors may influence decisions independently or may interact with each other in ways that subtly influence the process and outcome of any medical encounter.

Influences on Physician Behavior: A Complex Mixture of Economic and Psychological Factors

Physician motivations in the practice of medicine are complex. One important distinction is whether physicians are acting on their patients' behalf or on their own. First and foremost, physicians serve as their patients' clinical agents. Motivations to serve, deliver quality medical care, and promote health and well-being are probably more important than all other physician characteristics combined. Physicians, like parents, respond to clinical indicators of illness (Figure 17.1). In a busy office setting, physicians may first mentally triage each patient, deciding whether the patient is basically "well" or "sick." They may then direct history taking and the physical examination, focusing on where they think they are most likely to find the answer. Studies of medical practice highlight that the desire to serve and respond to clinical indicators are the greatest predictors of drug prescribing, diagnostic testing, and use of inpatient services (Mcleod, Tamblyn, and Gayton, 1997; Greenfield, Nelson, and Zubkoff, 1992; Hoey, Eisenberg, Spitzer, and Thomas, 1982; Rossiter and Wilensky, 1983; Wennberg et al., 1982; Wilensky and Rossiter, 1983; Zelnio, 1982).

Physicians also serve their patients by responding to patient demand and expectation (Gallagher, Lo, Chesney, and Christensen, 1997). In one study, adult patients presenting for evaluation of abdominal pain were asked by researchers what tests they expected their doctors to order as a part of their evaluations. Results revealed that patients who expected to receive certain tests got what they expected. From a pediatric perspective, there are few practitioners who have not been asked by parents for specific antibiotics for treatment of acute otitis media or a shot of penicillin for streptococcal pharyngitis instead of a 10-day course of oral antibiotics or for a hospital admission after the third day of profuse diarrhea and vomiting. Most physicians will oblige family requests if there are no significant contraindications. Physicians also consider patients' convenience when scheduling visits or diagnostic testing. Considerations of convenience may include physician concerns about costs, transportation difficulties, and time spent away from work (Eisenberg, 1985). In many cases, this responsiveness is desirable.

Although the desire to act on behalf of the patient generally exerts the greatest influence on practice, it is clear that physicians' self-interest and past experiences influence decision making as well. As workers, physicians seek income, certain styles of practice, or leisure time, diagnostic certainty, and protection from the threat of litigation. Physicians may also be influenced by where they were trained, their mentors, previous practice experiences, and adverse outcomes (Eisenberg, 1985).

Many health economists have focused on the physician as an income seeker. A general assumption is that income is sought by any rational person living in a society where money is needed for basic necessities as well as luxuries and social status (Eisenberg, 1985). From their earliest days of the medical education process, students develop a view of what life will be like in the future. This life view coupled perhaps with the need to repay student debt leads to the development of a target income. A target income may promote a student's choice of a high-income specialty rather than a career in general internal medicine, family practice, or pediatrics, which generally are lower paid (Kletke, Emmons, and Gillis, 1996; Sloan, Mitchell, and Cromwell, 1978; Studer-Ellis, Gold, and Jones, 2000). Individual physicians also may express preferences for certain kinds of patients and may prefer to handle certain kinds of medical problems (Hardwick et al., 1975; Williams, Eisenberg, Pascale, and Kitz, 1982). They may prefer certain organizational structures: solo practice, group practice, health maintenance organizations (HMOs) or community versus academic practice environments (Campbell, 1984; Eisenberg, 1979; Reynolds, Rizzo, and Gonzalez, 1987; Rothert et al., 1984).

Educational influences also play a significant role in shaping practice behavior. Few students ever see anything approaching a normal distribution of a patient population. Most education is conducted in major medical centers that attract the most esoteric and complex patient problems. Furthermore, a disproportionate share of clinic education is provided by subspecialists and surgeons who have defined disciplines within which to function. The end result may be a physician who is comfortable ventilating a 700-gram premature infant but is unable to cope with the 14-year-old adolescent who is at risk for becoming pregnant or drug dependant.

Students also leave major teaching centers already fearful of litigation, another major influence on physician decision making. An explosion of medical malpractice claiming began in the early 1960s (Danzon, 1986). The "crisis" created by the growing number of claims, and the publicity surrounding them affected physicians' motivations and practice behaviors. Defensive medicine, the practice of ordering medically unnecessary tests and procedures for the purpose of avoiding litigation, is estimated to add billions a year to the health care bill in the United States (Reynolds et al., 1987).

A closely related but distinct physician characteristic that affects medical decision making is tolerance of ambiguity and the desire for medical certainty (Eisenberg, 1985; Hickson, 1998; Katz, 1984; Wennberg and Gittelsohn, 1982). Medical practice has always been characterized by uncertainty. Sources of uncertainty in the practice of medicine include limitations of knowledge, probability of disease, ambiguities of treatment, and variations in individual patient response (Eddy, 1984; Katz, 1984; Light, 1979; Wennberg et al., 1982).

The effect of intolerance of ambiguity has been studied as a cognitive and emotional personality trait since the late 1940s (Budner, 1962). Norton (1975) defined intolerance of ambiguity as the tendency to perceive unusual, involved, or unclear situations as sources of threat. In medicine, threat to the physician may arise from a less than desirable outcome, such as prolonged illness, failure to recover function, death, or even from patient dissatisfaction, all of which may result in the physician's loss of prestige, income, or self-esteem. In any medical encounter, apprehension or fear generated by potential adverse outcomes has the potential to lead the provider to evaluate, test, or treat more than is absolutely necessary.

In pediatric medicine there are several common situations in which intolerance of ambiguity may impact practice. One of the marks of practice integrity is the ability to gaze into the dark ear canal of a 12-month-old child with fever and a runny nose and correctly declare what is seen, knowing that the child cannot talk, that no one else is likely to check the ear, and that the mother expects an antibiotic. What makes this a dilemma is that the child may in fact develop an ear infection in the next day or so, which no one can predict and at which time the provider may be faced with an unhappy parent. It is too easy to convince oneself that the ear is a "little red" and in "need" of an antibiotic. Intolerance of ambiguity is not limited to outpatient pediatrics but affects prescription of surgical procedures, hospitalizations, and use of new technology, including use of home apnea monitoring (a device to alarm when an infant quits breathing) (Eisenberg, 1985; Hickson, 1998; Wennberg, Barnes, and Zubkoff, 1982).

Just as parents' decisions to seek care may be influenced by the organization of the medical market, physician decision making and response to a patients' demand may be affected as well. Methods of physician reimbursement are critical to the organizational structure of any health system. In turn, the form of payment can powerfully affect physician behavior. In the current health care environment, three methods predominate: fee for service (FFS), salary (S), and capitation; each has its own unique influence on practice behavior.

Fee for service is currently the most common model for reimbursement. Fee for service is characterized by a payment for each unit of service delivered (Roemer, 1961b). The fee may vary with the difficulty of a particular case, the physician's judgment of the patient's affluence, or an insurance company's willingness to pay (Glaser, 1970; Redisch and Gabel, 1979; Roemer, 196lb). In such an FFS system, physician income depends on the number of service units delivered and their assigned difficulty, but not necessarily on how long the physician works.

Inherent in an FFS are several features that influence physician behavior. It has long been argued that FFS encourages the provision of excessive or unnecessary service (Eisenberg, 1985, Hickson, Altemeier, and Perrin, 1987; Luft, 1981; Raskin, Coffey and Farley, 1978; Rossiter and Wilensky, 1983; Wennberg et al., 1982). In general, patients seen by FFS providers use more outpatient services, more hospital bed days, and have more surgery performed than patients seen by physicians reimbursed by other mechanisms (Fuchs and Kramer, 1972; Hickson et al., 1987; Luft, 1981). At the same time, FFS may provide physicians' with incentives to be attentive to their patients' needs and demands. Patient dissatisfaction with any aspect of care may result in loss of patients and revenue. Such responsiveness may not be wholly undesirable.

Salaried reimbursement represents almost the polar opposite from FFS. Salaried physicians receive a predetermined income for a specified work schedule, with compensation independent of the number of patients seen or the complexity of services delivered (Roemer, 1961b). Although traditionally limited to physicians' practicing in institutional or academic settings, the percentage of physicians receiving salaried reimbursement rose significantly in the 1990s due in part to the reorganization of medical practice (Meyers, 1981). Salaried reimbursement is not wholly insensitive to physicians' performance because individual salaries may vary depending on qualifications, experience, and level of responsibility. It boils down to supply and demand for a given type of specialty, experience, and reputation. However, because salary and productivity are not directly linked, several authors suggested that reimbursement motivates physicians to discourage utilization and to be less sensitive in responding to patients' nonurgent needs compared with colleagues paid by other methods (Glaser, 1970; Hickson et al., 1987; Mechanic, 1975; Wolinsky, 1980).

One prospective study compared the influence of S versus FSS reimbursement on pediatric practice behavior (Hickson et al., 1987). Resident physicians who were required to provide comprehensive health care services to a defined panel of patients were randomized to receive either a payment for each patient seen (FFS group) or a monthly salary supplement (S group). Income was calculated and distributed monthly by a research assistant who kept this information blinded from all others and who was not involved in any other aspect of the study. Results revealed that patients seeing FFS physicians scheduled (3.69 vs. 2.83) and completed (2.70 vs. 2.21) more visits per patient than those seeing S physicians during the 9-month study. FFS patients on average completed more well-child visits (1.42 vs. .98), although there was no difference in illness-related visits (.94 vs. .96). These findings are not particularly surprising because parents' perception of their child's ill health will lead them to initiate most of illness care, whereas the pediatrician may influence most the demand for general health maintenance visits. Independent reviewers assessed whether the increased use of well-child care was appropriate as compared to the American Academy of Pediatrics Guidelines (1995–1988) for preventive services. Overall, FFS patients completed more visits judged appropriate, but they also had significantly more visits judged in excess of recommended care. In spite of the differences in per capita use, time with patients, and improved continuity, no differences could be detected in families' satisfaction with the care they received. Finally, when surveyed, the physicians themselves denied that their assigned reimbursement system had any effect on their practice behavior. Methods of reimbursement may affect physician practice motivations in ways that the individual pediatrician never recognizes.

A third method of reimbursement is capitation (Roemer, 1961b). Capitation is often seen in managed care programs. Physicians enroll patients and agree to provide comprehensive health services for a specified period of time for a predetermined amount of money. In some managed programs, physicians bear financial "risk" for prescription of services. Capitation tends to reward physicians for enrolling patients, but may penalize them for excessive use of consultations, laboratory, radiologic, and hospital services, or services outside of their offices. In theory, capitation promotes cost containment through the promotion of health and the use of only the most appropriate health care services. Many argue that capitation provides incentives to skimp on services, although the desire to maintain large patient panels and fear of litigation may prevent flagrant abuse.

In addition of the efforts of reimbursement mechanisms, other organizational and structural characteristics of the health delivery system may affect the doctor–patient relationship and medical decision making. Since the early 1980s, physicians have been subjected to increasing oversight of practice behavior through such mechanisms as preadmission certification, utilization review, and continued hospital stay authorization. The growth of managed care has increased the influence of group discipline. Group discipline is a theoretical process by which a physician organization attempts by subtle or not so subtle means to promote cost-conscious medical practice on the part of its members. Pressure to control spending may translate into reduced responsiveness to patient demand, especially with respect to issues of convenience or preference for referrals or more costly treatment alternatives.

Closer analysis reveals that physicians' and patients' interests and desires can diverge in numerous ways. Differences in philosophical views about the appropriate model of the relationship, clinical factors, physician and patient knowledge, tolerance for ambiguity, past experiences, assertiveness, and preferences, as well as the mundane practice considerations of patient volume, waiting time, time of day, and season of year, may influence any particular encounter. Furthermore, it is likely and perhaps advantageous that relationships between physicians and patients change over time. This is particularly true if participants need to respond to an initially less than optimal relationship. Given the array of pressures and personality characteristics brought to any medical encounter; it is rather remarkable that situations in which physicians and parents cannot work together are the exception rather than rule.

THE OUTCOME OF THE RELATIONSHIP: PATIENT SATISFACTION

Once parents have selected child health providers and have sought care, they walk away with impressions about their experiences. These impressions, coupled with the clinical outcomes, contribute to families' overall view of the medical process. This view defines patient satisfaction. Patient (family) satisfaction has emerged as an important medical outcome in its own right, as well a measure of the quality of care (Cleary and Edgman-Levitan, 1997; Donabedian, 1988; Kenagy, Berwick, and Shore, 1999; Korsch, Gozzi, and Francis, 1968). Satisfaction is important not only in and of itself, but also because of the linkage of this construct with an array of patient behaviors and outcomes. Satisfied patients are more likely to comply with recommended treatment regiment (DiMatteo and DiNicola, 1983; Hulka, Cassell, Kupper, and Burdette, 1976; Raddish, Horn, and Sharkey, 1999; Wartman, Morlock, Malitz, and Palm, 1983), maintain continuity of care (DiMatteo, Prince, and Taranta, 1979; Kasteler, Kane, Olsen, and Thetford, 1976; Love, Mainous, Talbert, and Hager, 2000; Marquis, Davies, and Ware, 1983), and cooperate with physicians in disclosing important although perhaps sensitive medical information (Bartlett et al., 1984; Roter et al., 1997). Furthermore, in certain circumstances, "healing" may occur as a result of patients' perceptions of the medical interaction, as in the placebo effect. Dissatisfied patients, on the other hand, are more likely to miss scheduled appointments, reject recommended actions, turn to nonmedical healers, and sue for medical malpractice (Hickson, Clayton, Githens, and Sloan, 1992; Kasteler et al., 1976; Markson et al., 2001; Ware, 1978).

Conceptualization of Patient Satisfaction

Satisfaction is an evaluation of received services in which patients apply their subjective standards to the health care experience (Pascoe 1983). In conducting such evaluations, Pascoe maintained, patients use either a subjective ideal, a subjective sense of what they feet they deserve, a subjective sense of a minimum, or a subjective expected experience. Such a process contains both cognitively based and emotionally driven responses to care. Fulfillment of expectations and patients' perceptions of equity affect overall satisfaction and predict patients' willingness to use the health care system in the future (Oliver 1989; Swan, 1985).

Dimensions of Patient Satisfaction

Patient satisfaction is a multidimensional concept (Hunt, 1991; Locker and Dunt, 1978; Sitzia and Wood, 1997; Ware, Davis-Avery, and Stewart, 1978). Although authors may classify the constructs slightly differently, there are several recurring themes: technical quality, accessibility, interpersonal aspects of care, outcomes, environment, and organization and finance.

One category as defined by Ware (1978) relates to the way care is organized and financed. Greenley and Schoenherr (1981) found that patients were more satisfied when they received care in practices that had greater autonomy over their organizational structure. Cleary and McNeil (1988) reported that patients in prepaid health care plans, when compared with patients using traditional indemnity coverage, were more satisfied in general with the financial aspects of care. Not all patients, however, were satisfied with the concept of prepayment, especially those with higher incomes and more education. Many such patients tended to be less satisfied because of the perception that they had lost freedom of choice (Bodenheimer, Lo, and Casalino, 1999; Grumbach et al., 1999). Structural aspects of care influence patient satisfaction as well. They include the organization of nursing care, housekeeping, billing operations, quality of food, physical surroundings, and noise (Cleary, Keroy, Karpanos, and McMullen, 1983; Doering, 1983; Lemke, 1987).

All structural, organization, and financial components of health care are important, but they pale in comparison to the contribution of the interpersonal aspects of care in predicting overall patient satisfaction. From the time of William Osler (1904) and before, doctors have recognized the importance of good rapport. Doyle and Ware (1977) identified that patients' perceptions interpersonal conduct accounted for 41% of the variance in patients' overall satisfaction and were more important than availability of services and continuity of care. Other studies support the notion that physicians who established good rapport and provided information are viewed as highly competent (Ben-Sira, 1976, 1980; DiMatteo, Taranta, Friedman, and Prince, 1980). Witcher-Alagna (1983) suggested that the process of establishing rapport and providing information may convey to the patient a sense of personal control allowing patients to feel less dependent.

Rapport is an outcome of the "art of medicine." Osler (1904, p. 279) described this art as "a calling in which your heart will be exercised equally with your head." This art has two main components: nonverbal and verbal communication. A physician's ability to radiate warmth and to convey an empathetic manner is crucial to promoting patient satisfaction with care (DiMatteo et al., 1979; Geersten, Gray, and Ward, 1973). Physicians who are better at expressing emotions nonverbally appear to be more sensitive to patients' nonverbal cues and receive higher ratings on their interpersonal aspects of care (DiMatteo and Hays, 1980; Levinson, Gorawara-Bhat, and Lamb, 2000).

The importance of verbal communication is highlighted by studies that reveal patients' dissatisfaction with the information they receive (Bertakis, 1977; Cartwright, 1967; Jacobs, 1971; Pichert, Miller, Hollo, Gauld-Jaeger, Federspiel, Hickson, 1998; Waitzkin and Stoeckle, 1972; Ware 1978). These authors emphasize that patients appear more dissatisfied with levels of information provided than with other aspects of care. In a study by Cartwright (1967), even though nearly half of the 739 patients surveyed indicated that they viewed physicians as their main source of medical information, over 20% felt that their own physicians clearly were not helpful. Other studies have demonstrated how important or distressing a lack of information can be (Volicer, 1973, 1974). Patients' viewed episodes in which they felt information was not appropriately conveyed, such as inadequate explanations of diagnoses or treatment, as more distressing than not having visitors in the hospital or even pain as a result of treatment.

One possible cause for perceptions of inadequate communication may be that physicians and patients disagree on the amount and type of information that is desirable (Faden, Becker, Lewis, Freeman, and Faden, 1981). In studies of patient preferences, Faden and colleagues found that patients often wanted more detailed disclosures about their medical conditions than are routinely offered. Although only a few physicians felt that detailed information would produce a positive patient response, the majority of patients expressed the belief that complete disclosure significantly increases compliance and confidence in the help being offered. Even if providers who feel that full disclosure is harmful and rely on notions of therapeutic privileges to justify withholding information are becoming fewer, less than full disclosure may continue because physicians view many health problems as routine. Some pediatricians feel that simply providing the appropriate diagnosis and recommended treatment is sufficient. On the other hand, patients take a personal view of their illnesses and desire more information than just name and suggested interventions. A patients' concern about maintaining a sense of self-worth in the face of a stigmatizing disease may heighten the need for detail.

Others have pointed out that what matters most is how the information accompanying medical aid meets recipients' expectations (Korsch et al., 1968; Korsch, Freeman, and Negrette, 1971; Needle and Murray, 1977; Oliver, 1989). Korsch et al. (1968) interviewed 800 parents who sought care for their children in a large metropolitan outpatient facility. Her research team conducted a series of interviews to obtain information about parents' perceptions of their children's illnesses, their expectations for their specific medical encounters, parents' perceptions of interactions with their doctors, parents' satisfaction with the visits, and the extent of their compliance with medical advice. The hypothesis examined was that parents' satisfaction with care was predicted by the extent to which expectations were met. Korsch found that a large proportion of patients had expectations of their physicians that transcended issues of technical competence. Parents told researchers that they expected physicians to be friendly, concerned, sympathetic, and willing to answer questions and provide explanations. Qualitative responses included "He listened to me" and "He answered all my questions." Perhaps an explanation for the importance placed on communication was the finding that parents had intense concerns and needs for explanations about why their children were sick. Korsch suggested this intense concern with causation might be related to a tendency for parents to blame themselves for their children's illnesses. In their follow-up interviews, parents indeed told researchers that they blamed themselves for their children's illnesses. Only a few instances were identified in which physicians actually attempted to deal with these feelings of guilt. It is not suprising, then, that researchers found dissatisfaction among families who wanted and expected an explanation, hoping perhaps for a reprieve from guilt but did not receive one.

On the other hand, parents who get what they expect, including information provided in a caring manner, are likely to be more satisfied with the help they receive (Francis, Korsch, and Morris, 1969; Larsen and Rootman, 1976; Oliver, 1989). Eisenthal and Lazare (1976) found that satisfaction correlated significantly with the extent to which doctors attended to what patients wanted from their interactions, helped patients verbalize their wants, and allowed them to participate in treatment decisions.

Even though patients desire and expect information in connection with receiving medical aid, studies suggest that many patients never spontaneously reveal their greatest concerns to their physicians (Hickson, Altemeier, and O'Connor, 1983; Korsch et al., 1968). Waller and Levitt (1972), in a study conducted in an outpatient facility, found that slightly over 10% of all families offered a chief complaint to office personnel that was unrelated to their motivations in seeking care. Many of the real concerns were related to an unspoken fear that a child might have some dreaded disease, most often a malignancy. Unless providers identify families' concerns and provide appropriate reassurance, parents are likely to go away unsatisfied and perhaps be even less likely to ask for help in the future. Waller also found that parents were particularly reluctant to reveal chief complaints when they involved problems concerning child behavior or educational achievement. Study findings highlight the ambivalence of parents seeking care. Parents may recognize the existence of a problem, decide that they need help, expend energy to seek care, but disguise from the physician the real reason for the visit. Such behavior may be perplexing for the physician who recognizes that the parent is troubled but does not identify why. In this situation both parties may leave the encounter disappointed and dissatisfied.

The magnitude of parents' unspoken concerns was revealed in a study conducted in the waiting rooms of pediatric practices designed to document families' unmet needs for their children (Hickson et al., 1983). Researchers interviewed 207 mothers whose children were waiting to be seen. Parents were asked to indicate all the concerns they had for their children and their single greatest concern. Most of these concerns (70%) were related to behavior, development, adjustment to life changes (divorce, moving, or the death of a family member), and transition to adolescence, and not to issues concerning physical health. Only 30% of parents with psychosocial concerns, however, indicated that they had ever brought or intended to bring their concerns to the attention of their children's doctors even though many indicated that these problems were disruptive to their households. When asked why, parents stated there was simply no time in the confines of a busy pediatric practice to deal with such issues. Others believed that physicians were not interested or qualified to provide assistance, and many indicated that they never recognized that the pediatrician might be a source of help. On the other hand, observation of communication rates concerning families' psychosocial concerns revealed a wide variation among the 20 practices where the study was conducted. An examination of potential predictors of talking about these potentially sensitive issues related in part to the education level of the parent. The greater educational attainment of the parent, the more likely they were to disclose to the pediatrician their greatest concern. Of much greater importance in promoting communication, however, were two physician characteristics: interest and self-perceived competence in managing psychosocial problems. The recognition of the role of physicians' self-perceived competence in promoting communication about behavioral and developmental concerns offers hope that through appropriate training, pediatricians can better meet the needs of young families.

Why Families Change Doctors

Dissatisfaction with a physician sometimes leads parents to break existing relationships and transfer their children's care to new providers. Such transfers may be beneficial if parents can establish relationships with physicians with whom they are comfortable, but may be costly in terms of the energy needed to identify and select another, the inefficient reaccumulation of medical and psychosocial databases, as well as the establishment of new patient–physician relationships. Pediatricians may suffer as well in terms of loss of pride and income.

Young et al. (1985) specifically addressed the question of why families change pediatricians. An anonymous questionnaire was mailed to 170 families who requested transfer of medical records from four pediatric practices in Chittenden County, Vermont. The questionnaires were designed to solicit families' reasons for changing and impressions about the quality of services that the families had received. The authors concluded that parents who were dissatisfied enough to leave one doctor for another did so primarily because of the interpersonal aspects of care and not the organization and structure of the offices. Families who left cited displeasure with the way their pediatricians communicated. They felt explanations were not clear, and they commented negatively on physicians' level of concern and their competence (Young et al., 1985).

Problems with the interpersonal aspects of care are not the only factors that prompt families to leave practitioners. Other studies suggest that parents leave when their expectations concerning the clinical course of specific illnesses are not met. Hickson et al. (1988) found that families most often abandon a provider when they perceive that their child is no better after treatment and hence concludes that the physician does not know what she or he is doing. Just as parents' responses to their children's signs and symptoms drive most decisions to seek care, parents' perceptions of how prescribed treatments affect those illnesses probably play the most significant role in decisions to abandon a provider. Many children, however, develop prolonged illnesses, but few families change providers in response, suggesting that an outcome seen as poor is usually a necessary but insufficient reason to leave the provider. In this setting, the provider's interpersonal skills may often be the determinative factor in decisions to leave or stay.

The impact of dissatisfaction with the physician–patient relationship is even clearer when one looks at families' decisions to sue following adverse events. Most families do not pursue claiming in the face of adverse events, even those caused by medical negligence. Some families may never recognize that a problem with care existed. Some families may recognize a problem existed and exit a relationship, whereas others may choose to "lump it," that is, accept the disappointing results and not complain (May and Stengel, 1990).

By contrast, most families who sue for malpractice appear to be motivated not only by the existence of bad outcomes but also by other factors as well (Entman et al., 1992; Hickson et al., 1992, 1994).

In interviews with families who had filed suit, many indicated that they filed when they decided that the courtroom was the only forum in which they could find out what really happened to cause their adverse outcomes from the physicians who provided care. Even when physicians provided technically adequate care, families expected answers concerning what went wrong. Other families felt misled. In some cases families were correct when they complained that they were not given the whole story concerning why something bad had occurred. No physician likes to share bad news, and some may fear litigation. On the other hand, information may be given but not understood because families do not understand medical terminology or are too anxious and intimidated by discussions with physicians to ask questions. Others may experience denial as a part of grieving and later claim that they were not given information. To point out that families may contribute to misunderstandings is not to imply that families ought to understand better, but to suggest that problems with communication in the face of an adverse outcome may unnecessarily and unfortunately lead to the courtroom (Hickson et al., 1992, 1994).

CONCLUSIONS: WHAT PHYSICIANS AND PARENTS CAN DO TO OPTIMIZE THEIR COLLABORATION ON BEHALF OF CHILDREN

The parent–physician relationship represents the foundation of pediatric medicine. When parents and physicians work in concert the potential exists for good. When strife, misunderstanding, or dissatisfaction characterizes the relationship, children can suffer. What is critical, therefore, is to promote good working relationships among parents and doctors. This process requires concerted effort by all parties.

Physicians must recognize the importance of exemplary verbal and nonverbal communication. They must recognize the existence of hidden agenda, that families may not readily reveal their greatest health care concerns or fears. Physicians cannot rely on the old adage "If the problem is bad enough, families will seek assistance," but must actively seek to identify concerns. Identification of concerns can be accomplished by several approaches. First, physicians should ask at least twice each visit: "What are the concerns you have for your child?" Such an approach has been demonstrated to maximize parental response (Glascoe, 1993; Hickson et al., 1983).

Even if an active approach does not elicit a response at one visit, it may convey a sense of interest that may facilitate a more open exchange during a subsequent visit. A second approach involves the use of preprinted surveys or questionnaires about behavior and development providing parents an opportunity to check off their concerns. Such an approach may reduce parent embarrassment, and the results of the surveys may be used to initiate focused conversations. Problems, however, cannot simply be identified but must be approached in an organized fashion. Many can be dealt with by simple reassurance. Others are more deep-seated and require repeated visits or referrals to appropriate services.

Physicians should also recognize that parents might be predisposed to be unhappy or angry with any medical encounter. Due to conflicts with family members, baby-sitters, teachers, office staff, or to lack of access, means or ability to pay, resentment at being dependent, or adverse outcomes and unmet expectations, families may suddenly and sometimes unexpectedly express anger. Physicians should recognize that it is the parent or family who is angry. If they respond in kind and allow the family to drag them into the fray, the situation may become more volatile. Physicians should deal directly with the issues at hand and acknowledge the family's feelings while trying to deal constructively with the situation. If the focus of a family's anger is a prolonged illness or an adverse outcome, providers must be especially careful because communication difficulties at this point may lead to significant misunderstandings or even to the courtroom.

Finally, physicians should, except in certain circumstances or emergencies, avoid assuming a paternalistic approach in the doctor–parent relationship. The relationship should represent a partnership with both parties maintaining some autonomy and accountability for the well-being of the child. Physicians should work to empower parents so that they see themselves as partners in the relationship. The partnership confirms responsibilities that begin at the moment families recognize that they are going to need the services of a child health care provider.

Parents should invest appropriate energy in identifying and selecting a child health provider. Appropriate search includes consulting sources of information and asking questions likely to provide useful information about practice characteristics that may affect the parent–doctor relationship. Parents, for example, might seek information concerning a physician's willingness to answer questions and involve parents in decision making or at least to outline options. Parents might also inquire about the physician's style of practice and philosophies about treatment, behavior management, nutrition, and other general health maintenance practices. Families should attempt to schedule prenatal visits with potential physicians during which they can explore these same questions and gain insight into the potential personality and expectations fit of parents and doctor. No search process ensures an appropriate fit, but at least the process will bring the parties together prior to the first encounter involving doctor, parent, and sick child. In addition, the process communicates an important message about the family to the physician—that they are concerned, are interested in the well-being of their children, and want to be involved as partners in their children's health delivery.

Parents also must be more forthright with their physicians. Communication represents a partnership, and although busy practices, harried physicians, and short office visits are not particularly conducive to encouraging families to talk, direct communication is always more time efficient than having to search for a hidden agenda. If the family is concerned the physician should be concerned, and although the provider will not be able to address all issues, at least she or he should be able either to schedule a follow-up visit or to direct families to appropriate services. Furthermore, families need to be honest with themselves and their children's providers. If care plans, explanations, or prognosis are unclear, families need to ask for clarifications. Misunderstandings surrounding these issues appear to contribute greatly to families' dissatisfaction with care, especially when an adverse outcome has occurred. Finally, families should recognize that they are a part of the team. And although they do not have the same knowledge or experience as the provider, they are the ones most often responsible for initiating care and ensuring compliance with recommended actions, and they are often the most skilled observers of their own children. Parents working with doctors can promote health and well-being for children.

ACKNOWLEDGMENTS

Preparation of this chapter was supported in part by grant no. 028592 from the Robert Wood Johnson Foundation, the IMPACS program, an early identification and response model of malpractice prevention.

REFERENCES

Albertson, G. A., Lin, C. T., Kutner, J., Schilling, L. M., Anderson, S. N., and Anderson, R. J. (2000). Recognition of patient referral desires in an academic managed care plan frequency, determinants, and outcomes. *Journal of General Internal Medicine, 15,* 242–247.

Alexander, C. S., Zinzeleta, E. M., Mackenzie, E. J., Vernon, A., and Markowitz, R. K. (1990). Acute gastrointestinal illness and child care arrangements. *American Journal of Epidemiology, 131,* 124–131.

Altemeier, W. A., O'Connor, S. M., Sherrod, K. B., and Vietze, P. M. (1985). Prospective study of antecedents for nonorganic failure to thrive. *Journal of Pediatrics, 106,* 360–365.

American Academy of Pediatrics, Committee on Psychosocial Aspects of Child and Family Health. (1985–1988). *Guidelines for health supervision II.* Elk Grove Village, IL: Author.

American Academy of Pediatrics, Task Force on Infant Positioning and SIDS. Positioning and SIDS. (1992). *Pediatrics, 89,* 1120–1126.

Anderson, J. (1930). Pediatrics and child psychology. *Journal of the American Medical Association, 95,* 1015–1019.

Anderson, R. (1968). *A behavioral model of families' use of health services: HSA studies* (Research Series No. 25). Chicago: University of Chicago Press.

Andersen, R., and Aday, L. A. (1978). Access to medical care in the U.S.: Realized and potential. *Medical Care, 16,* 533–546.

Armstrong, G. (1767). *Essay on the diseases most fatal to infants to which are added rules to be observed in the nursing of children.* London: Printed for T. Cadell, in the Strand.

Armstrong, G. (1772). *A general account of the dispensary for the relief of infant poor.* London: Printed for T Cadell, in the Strand.

Arrowsmith, J. B., Kennedy, D. L., Kuritsky, J. D., and Faich, G. A. (1987). National patterns of aspirin use and Reye's syndrome reporting, United States, 1980 to 1985. *Pediatrics, 79,* 858–863.

Bartlett, E. E., Grayson, M., Barker, R., Levine, D. M., Golden, A., and Libber, S. (1984). The effects of physician communication skills on patient satisfaction, recall and adherence. *Journal of Chronic Diseases, 37,* 755–764.

Ben-Sira, Z. (1976). The function of the professional's affective behavior in client satisfaction: A revised approach to social interaction theory. *Journal of Health and Social Behavior, 17,* 3–11.

Ben-Sira, Z. (1980). Affective and instrumental components in the physician–patient relationship: An additional aspect of interaction theory. *Journal of Health and Social Behavior, 21,* 170–180.

Bertakis, K. D. (1977). The communication of information from physician to patient: A method for increasing patient retention and satisfaction. *Journal of Family Practice, 5,* 217–222.

Bodenheimer, T., Lo, B., and Casalino, L. (1999). Primary care physicians should be coordinators, not gatekeepers. *Journal of the American Medical Association, 281,* 2045–2049.

Budner, S. (1962). Intolerance of ambiguity as a personality variable. *Journal of Personality, 30,* 29–50.

Cafferata, G. L., and Kasper, J. D. (1985). Family structure and children's use of ambulatory physician services. *Medical Care, 23,* 350–360.

Campbell, D. M. (1984). Why do physicians in neonatal care units differ in their admission thresholds? *Social Science and Medicine, 18,* 365–374.

Cartwright, A. (1967). *Patients and their doctors.* New York: Atherton.

Charney, E. (1974). George Armstrong: An early activist. *American Journal Diseases of Children, 128,* 824–826.

Charney, E., Bynum, R., Eldredge, D., Frank, D., MacWhinney, J. B., McNabb, N., Scheiner, A., Sumpter, E. A., and Iker, H. (1967). How well do patients take oral penicillin? A collaborative study in private practice. *Pediatrics, 40,* 188–195.

Children's Defense Fund. (1990). *Children 1990: A report card, briefing book and action primer.* Washington, DC: Author.

Cleary, P. D., Keroy, L., Karpanos, G., and McMullen, W. (1983). Patient assessment of hospital care. *Quality Review Bulletin, 9,* 172–179.

Cleary, P. D., and Edgman-Levitan, S. (1997). Health care quality: Incorporating the patients perspective. *Journal of the American Medical Association, 278,* 1608–1612.

Cleary, P. D., and McNeil, B. J. (1988). Patient satisfaction as an indicator of quality of care. *Inquiry, 25,* 25–36.

Danzon, P. M. (1986). The frequency and severity of medical malpractice claims: New evidence. *Law and Contemporary Problems, 49,* 57–84.

Davison, W. C. (1952). The pediatric shift. *The Journal of Pediatrics, 40,* 536–538.

Deisher, R. W., Engel, W. L., Spielhoiz, R., and Standfast, S. J. (1965). Mothers' opinions of their pediatric care. *Pediatrics, 35,* 82–90.

DePaulo, B. M. (1982). Social psychological processes in informal help-seeking. In T. A. Wills (Ed.), *Basic processes in helping relationship.* New York: Academic Press.

DePaulo, B. M. (1983). Perspectives on help-seeking. In A. Nadler, J. D. Fisher, and B. M. DePaulo (Eds.), *New directions in helping.* New York: Academic.

Diaz, J. H., and Lockhart., C. H. (1982). Early diagnosis and airway management of acute epiglottis in children. *Southern Medical Journal, 75,* 399–403.

DiMatteo, M. R., and DiNicola, D. D. (1983). *Achieving patient compliance: The psychology of the medical practitioner's role.* New York: Pergamon.

DiMatteo, M. R., and Hays, R. (1980). The significance of patients' perceptions of physician conduct: A study of patient satisfaction in a family practice center. *Journal of Community Health, 6,* 18–34.

DiMatteo, M. R., Prince, L. M., and Taranta, A. (1979). Patients' perceptions of physicians' behavior: Determinants of patient commitment to the therapeutic relationship. *Journal of Community Health, 4,* 280–290.

DiMatteo, M. R., Taranta, A., Friedman, H. S., and Prince, L. M. (1980). Predicting patient satisfaction from physicians' nonverbal communication skills. *Medical Care, 18,* 376–387.

Doering, E. R. (1983). Factors influencing inpatient satisfaction with care. *Quality Review Bulletin, 9,* 291–299.

Donabedian, A. (1988). The quality of care. How can it be assessed? *Journal of the American Medical Association, 260,* 1743–1748.

Doyle, B. J., and Ware, J. E. (1977). Physician conduct and other factors that affect consumer satisfaction with medical care. *Journal of Medical Education, 52,* 793–801.

Eddy, D. M. (1984). Variations in physician practice: The role of uncertainty. *Health Affairs, 3*, 774–789.

Eisenberg, J. M. (1979). Sociological influences on decision-making by clinicians. *Archives of Internal Medicine, 90*, 957–964.

Eisenberg, J. M. (1985). Physician utilization: The state of research about physician practice patterns. *Medical Care, 23*, 461–483.

Eisenthal, S., and Lazare, A. (1976). Evaluation of the initial interview in a walk-in clinic. *The Journal of Nervous and Mental Diseases, 162*, 169–176.

Entman, S. S., Glass, C. A., Hickson, G, B., Githens, P. B., Whetten-Goldstein, K., and Sloan, F. A. (1994). The relationship between malpractice claims history and subsequent obstetric care. *Journal of the American Medical Association, 272*, 1588–1591.

Faden, R. R., Becker, C., Lewis, C., Freeman, J., and Faden, A. (1981). Disclosure of information to patients in medical care. *Medical Care, 19*, 718–733.

Feldman, D. S., Novack, D. H., and Gracely, E. (1998). Effects of managed care on physician–patient relationships, quality of care and the ethical practice of medicine. *Archives of Internal Medicine, 158*, 1626–1632.

Francis, V., Korsch, B. M., and Morris, M. J. (1969). Gaps in doctor–patient communication II. Patients' response to medical advice. *New England Journal of Medicine, 280*, 535–540.

Freeborn, D. K., Pope, C. R., Davis, M. A., and Mullooly, J. P. (1977). Health status, socioeconomics status, and utilization of outpatient services for members of a prepaid group practice. *Medical Care, 15*, 115–128.

Friedson, E. (1963). The organization of medical practice. In H. A. Freeman, S. Levin, and L. G. Reeder (Eds.), *Handbook of medical sociology*. Englewood Cliffs, NJ: Prentice-Hall.

Fuchs, V. R. (1978). The supply of surgeons and the demand for operations. *Journal of Human Resources, 13*, 35–56.

Fuchs, V. R., and Kramer, M. J. (1972). Determinants of expenditures for physicians' services in the United States 1948–1968. Washington, DC: National Center for Health Services Research and Development.

Furse, D. H., Punj, G. N., and Stewart, D. W. (1984). Typology of individual search strategies among purchasers of new automobiles. *Journal of Consumer Research, 10*, 417–431.

Gallagher, T. H., Lo, B., Chesney, M., and Christensen, K. (1997). How do physicians respond to patients requests for costly, unindicated services? *Journal of General Internal Medicine, 12*, 663–668.

Geersten, H. R., Gray, R. M., and Ward, J. R. (1973). Patient non-compliance within the context of seeking medical help for arthritis. *Journal of Chronic Diseases, 26*, 689–698.

Glascoe, F. P. (1993). The relationship between parents' concerns and children's global delays. *American Journal of Diseases of Children, 147*, 451–452.

Glascoe, F. P. (1995). The role of parents in the detection of developmental and behavioral problems. *Pediatrics, 95*, 829–836.

Glaser, W. A. (1970). *Paying the doctor: Systems of remuneration and their effects*. Baltimore: Johns Hopkins University Press.

Glassman, M., and Glassman, N. (1981). A marketing analysis of physician selection and patient satisfaction. *Journal of Health Care Marketing, 1*, 25–31.

Green, M., and Solnit, A. J. (1964). Reactions to the threatened loss of a child: A vulnerable child syndrome. *Pediatrics, 34*, 58–66.

Greenfield, S., Nelson, E., and Zubkoff, M. (1992). Variations in resource utilization among medical specialties and systems of care: Results from the Medical Outcomes Study. *Journal of the American Medical Association, 267*, 1624–1630.

Greenley, J. R., and Schoenherr, R. A. (1981). Organization effects on client satisfaction with humaneness of services. *Journal of Health and Social Behavior, 22*, 2–18.

Grumbach, K., Selby, J. V., Damberg, C., Bindman, A. B., Quesenberry, C., Truman, A., and Uratsu, C. (1999). Resolving the gatekeeper conundrum: What patients value in primary care and referrals to specialists. *Journal of the American Medical Association, 282*, 261–266.

Hall, N. W. (1991). Pediatrics and child development: A parallel history. In F. S. Kessel, M. H. Bornstein, and A. J. Sameroff (Eds.), *Contemporary constructions of the child: Essays in honor of William Kessen*. Hillsdale, NJ: Lawrence Earlbaum Associates.

Hardwick, D. F., Vertinsky, P., Barth, R. T., Mitchell, V. F., Bornstein, M., and Vertinsky, I. (1975). Clinical styles and motivation: A study of laboratory test use. *Medical Care, 13*, 397–408.

Harris, J. S. (1990). Why doctors do what they do: Determinants of physicians behavior. *Journal of Occupational Medicine, 32*, 1207–1220.

Hershey, J. C., Luft, H. C., and Gianaris, J. M. (1975). Making sense out of utilization data. *Medical Care, 12*, 838–854.

Hickson, G. B., Altemeier, W. A., and O'Connor, S. (1983). Concerns of mothers seeking care in private pediatric offices: Opportunities for expanding services. *Pediatrics, 72*, 619–624.

Hickson, G. B. (1997). Pediatric practice and liability risk in a managed care environment. *Pediatric Annals, 26*, 179–185.

Hickson, G. B., Altemeier, W. A., and Perrin, J. M. (1987). Physician reimbursement by salary or fee-for-service: Effect on physician practice behavior in a randomized prospective study. *Pediatrics, 80*, 344–350.

Hickson, G. B., and Clayton, E. W. (1993). Are you and your waiting room's televised "expert" saying the same thing? *Clinical Pediatrics, 32*, 172–174.

Hickson, G. B., Clayton, E. W., Entman S. S., Miller, C. S., Githens, P. B., Whetten-Goldstein, K., and Sloan, F. A. (1994). Obstetricians' prior malpractice experiences and patients' satisfaction with care. *Journal of the American Medical Association,* *272,*1583–1587.

Hickson, G. B., Cooper, W. O., Campbell, P. W., Atlemeier III, W. A. (1998). Effects of Pediatrician Characteristics on Management Decisions in Simulated Cases Involving Apparent Life-Threatening Events. *Pediatrics & Adolescent Medicine* Volume 152.

Hickson, G. B., Clayton, E. W., Githens, P. B., and Sloan, F. A. (1992). Factors that prompted families to file medical malpractice claims following perinatal injuries. *Journal of the American Medical Association, 267,* 1359–1363.

Hickson, G. B., Stewart, D. W., Altemieier, W. A., and Perrin, J. M. (1988). First step in obtaining child health care: Selecting a physician. *Pediatrics, 81,* 333–338.

Hinman, A. R. (1991). What will it take to fully protect all American children with vaccines? *American Journal of Diseases of Children, 145,* 559–562.

Hoey, J., Eisenberg, J. M., Spitzer, W. O., and Thomas, D. (1982). Physician sensitivity to the price of diagnostic tests: An U.S.–Canadian analysis. *Medical Care, 20,* 302–307.

Hofferth, S., and Phillips, D. (1987). Childcare in the United States 1970–1995. *Journal of Marriage and the Family, 49,* 559–563.

Holder, A. R. (1985). *Legal issues in pediatrics and adolescent Medicine* (2nd ed.). New Haven, CT: Yale University Press.

Holt, L. W. (1897). *Diseases of infancy and childhood.* New York: Appleton.

Hulka, B. S., Cassell, J. C., Kupper, L. L., and Burdette, J. A. (1976). Communication, compliance, and concordance between physicians and patients with prescribed medications. *American Journal of Public Health, 66,* 847–853.

Hunt, C. E., and Shannon, D. C. (1992). Sudden infant death syndrome and sleeping position. *Pediatrics, 90,* 115–118.

Hunt, H. K. (1991). Consumer satisfaction, dissatisfaction and complaining behavior. *Journal of Social Issues, 47,* 107–117.

Hurwitz, E. S., Gunn, W. J., Pinsky, P. F., and Schonberger, L. B. (1991). Risk of respiratory illness associated with day-care attendance: A nationwide study. *Pediatrics, 87,* 62–69.

Iglehart, J. K. (1992). The American health care system: Managed care. *New England Journal of Medicine, 32,* 742–747.

Impicciciatore, P., Pandolfini, C., Casella, N., and Bonati, M. (1997). Reliability of health information for the public on the World Wide Web: Systematic survey of advice on managing fever in children at home. *British Medical Journal, 314,* 1875–1879.

Jacobs, J. (1971). Perplexity, confusion, and suspicion: A study of selected forms of doctor–patient interactions. *Social Science and Medicine, 5,* 151–157.

Kasteler, J., Kane, R. L., Olsen, D. M., and Thettford, C. (1976). Issues underlying prevalence of "doctor-shopping" behavior. *Journal of Health and Social Behavior, 17,* 328–339.

Katz, J. (1984). *The silent world of doctor and patient.* New York: Free Press.

Keiser, N. H. (1991). Strategies of media marketing for "America Responds to AIDS" and applying lessons learned. *Public Health Reports, 106,* 623–627.

Kemper, K. J., Forsyth, B. W., and McCarthy, P. L. (1990). Persistent perceptions of vulnerability following neonatal jaundice. *American Journal of Diseases of Children, 144,* 238–241.

Kenagy, J. W., Berwick, D. M., and Shore, M. F. (1999). Service quality in health care. *Journal of the American Medical Association, 281,* 661–665.

Kletke, P. R., Emmons, D. W., and Gillis, K. (1996). Current trends in physicians' practice arrangements: From owners to employees. *Journal of the American Medical Association, 276,* 555–560.

Korsch, B. M., Freeman, B., and Negrette, V. F. (1971). Pratical implications of doctor–patient interaction: Analysis for pediatric practice. *American Journal of Diseases of Children, 121,* 110–114.

Korsch, B., Gozzi, E., and Francis, V. (1968). Gaps in doctor patient communication: I. Doctor–patient interaction and patient satisfaction. *Pediatrics, 42,* 855–871.

Lairson, D. R., and Swint, J. M. (1978). A multivariate analysis of the likelihood of volume of preventive visit demand in a prepaid group practice. *Medical Care, 16,* 730–739.

Larsen, D. E, and Rootman, I. (1976). Physician role performance and patient satisfaction. *Social Science and Medicine, 10,* 29–32.

Larson, E. (1989). Innovations in health care: Antisepsis as a case study. *American Journal of Public Health, 79,* 92–99.

Leibowitz, A., Manning, W. G., Keeler, E. B., Duan, N., Lohr, K. N., and Newhouse, J. P. (1985). Effect of cost-sharing on the use of medical services by children: Interim results from a randomized controlled trial. *Pediatrics, 75,* 942–951.

Lemke, R. (1987). Identifying consumer satisfaction through patient survey. *Health Care Progress, 66,* 56–59.

Levinson, W., Gorawara-Bhat, R., and Lamb, J. (2000). A study of patient clues and physician responses in primary care and surgical settings. *Journal of the American Medical Association, 284,* 1021–1027.

Light, D. (1979). Uncertainty and control in professional training. *Journal of Health and Social Behavior, 20,* 310–322.

Lima, J., Nazarian, L., Charney, E., and Lahti, C. (1976). Compliance with short-term antimicrobial therapy: Some techniques that help. *Pediatrics, 57,* 383–386.

Locker, D., and Dunt, D. (1978). Theoretical and methodological issues in sociological studies of consumer satisfaction with health care. *Social Science and Medicine,12*, 283–292.

Love, M. M., Mainous, A. G., Talbert, J. C., and Hager, G. L. (2000). Continuity of care and the physician–patient relationship: The importance of continuity for adult patients with asthma. *Journal of Family Practice, 49*, 998–1004.

Luft, H. S. (1981). *Health maintenance organizations: Dimensions of performance*. New York: Wiley.

Maloney, W. J. (1954). *George and John Armstrong of Castleton: Two 18th-century medical pioneers*. Edinburgh, Scotland: Livingstone.

Mandl, K. D., Feit, S., Peña, B., and Kohane, I. (2000). Growth and determinants of access in patient e-mail and Internet use. *Archives of Pediatrics and Adolescent Medicine, 154*, 508–511.

Mandl, K. D., Kohane, I. S., and Brandt, A. M. (1998). Electronic patient–physician communication: Problems and promise. *Annals of Internal Medicine*, 495–500.

Margolis, C. Z., Ingram, D. L., and Meyer, J. H. (1972). Routine tracheotomy in Hemophilus influenza Type B epiglottitis. *Journal of Pediatrics, 81*, 1150–1153.

Markson, L. E., Vollmer, W. M., Fitterman, L., O'Connor, E., Narayanan, S., Berger, M., and Buist, A. S. (2001). Insight into and patient dissatisfaction with asthma treatment. *Archives of Internal Medicine, 161*, 379–384.

Marquis, M. S., Davies, A. R., and Ware, J. E. (1983). Patient satisfaction and change in medical care provider: A longitudinal study. *Medical Care, 21*, 821–829.

May, M. L., and Stengel, D. B. (1990). Who sues their doctors? How patients handle medical grievances. *Law and Society Review, 24*, 105–120.

McLeod, P., Tamblyn, R., and Gayton, D. (1997). Use of standardized patients to assess between physician variation in resource utilization. *Journal of the American Medical Association, 278*, 1164–1168.

Mechanic, D. (1964). The influence of mothers on their children's health attitudes and behavior. *Pediatrics, 33*, 444–453.

Mechanic, D. (1975). The organization of medical practice and practice orientations among physicians in prepaid and non prepaid primary care settings. *Medical Care, 13*, 189–204.

Meyers, S. M. (1981). *Growth in health maintenance organizations. In Health United States—1981*. Hyattsville, MD: U.S. Department of Health and Human Services, Office of Health Research, Statistics and Technology.

Moon, R. Y., and Biliter, W. M. (2000). Infant sleep position policies in licensed childcare centers after back to sleep campaign. *Pediatrics, 106*, 576–580.

Moon, R. Y., Patel, K. M., and Shaefer, S. J. (2000). Sudden infant death syndrome in childcare settings. *Pediatrics, 106*, 295–300.

National Vaccine Advisory Committee. (1991). The measles epidemic: The problems, barriers, and recommendations. *Journal of the American Medical Association, 266*, 1547–1552.

Needle, R. H., and Murray, B. A. (1977). The relationship between race and sex of health provider, the quality of care provided, and levels of satisfaction with gynecological care among Black college women. *Journal of the American College Health Associates, 26*, 127–113.

Newhouse, J., Manning, W., Morris, C., Orr, L. L., Duan, N., Keler, E. B., Leibowitz, A., Marquis, K. H., Marquis, M. S., Phelps, C. E., and Brook, R. H. (1982). *Some interim results from a controlled trial of cost sharing health insurance* (Rand Pub. No. R-2847-HHS). Santa Monica, CA: Rand.

Norton, R. (1975). Measurement of ambiguity tolerance. *Journal of Personality Assessment, 39*, 607–619.

Oliver, R. (1989). Processing of the satisfaction response in consumption: A suggested framework and research propositions. *Journal of Consumer Satisfaction, Dissatisfaction and Complaining Behavior, 2*, 1–16.

Osler, W. (1904). *Aequanimitas with other addresses to medical students nurses, and practitioners of medicine*. Philadelphia: Blakiston.

Osterholm, M. T., Reves, R., Murphy, J. R., and Pickering, L. K. (1992). Infectious diseases and child daycare. *Pediatric Infectious Disease Journal, 11*, 531–541.

Parsons, T. (1951). *The social system*. New York: Free Press.

Pascoe, G. C. (1983). Patient satisfaction in primary health care: A literature review and analysis. *Evaluation and Program Planning,6*, 185–210.

Pichert, J. W., and Hickson, G. B. (2001). Communicating risk to patients and families. In C. Vincent (Ed.), *Clinical risk management* (2nd ed.). BMJ London.

Pichert, J. W., Hickson, G. B., Bledsoe, S., Trotter, T., and Quinn, D. (1997). Understanding the etiology of serious medical events involving children: Implications for Pediatricians and their risk managers. *Pediatric Annals, 26*, 160–172.

Pichert, J. W., Hickson, G. B., and Trotter, T. (1998). Malpractice and communication skill for difficult situations. *Ambulatory Child Health*, 213–221.

Pichert, J. W., Miller, C. S., Hollo, A. H., Gauld-Jaeger, J., Federspiel, C., and Hickson, G. B. (1998). What health professionals can do to identify and resolve patient dissatisfaction. *Joint Commission Journal on Quality Improvement, 24*, 303–312.

Pichert, J. W., Federspiel, C., Hickson, G. B., Miller, C., Gauld-Jaeger, J., and Gray, C. L. (1999). Identifying medical center units with disproportionate shares of patient complaints. *Journal on Quality Improvement, 25*, 288–299.

Raddish, M., Horn, S. D., and Sharkey, P. D. (1999). Continuity of care: Is it cost effective? *American Journal of Managed Care, 5*, 727–734.

Raskin, I. E., Coffey, R. M., and Farley, P. J. (1978). *Cost containment. In Health United States* (DHEW Pub. No. [PHS] 78-1232). Hyattsville, MD: Office of the Assistant Secretary for Health, U.S. Department of Health, Education, and Welfare.

Redisch, M. A., and Gabel, J. R. (1979). Alternative physician prepayment methods: Incentives, efficiency, and national health insurance. *Milbank Memorial Fund Quarterly, 57*, 38–59.

Reynolds, R. A., Rizzo, J. A., and Gonzalez, M. L. (1987). The cost of medical professional liability. *Journal of the American Medical Association, 257*, 2776–2781.

Richmond, J. B. (1967). Child development: A basic science for pediatrics. *Pediatrics, 39*, 649–658.

Rivara, F. P. (1985). Traumatic deaths of children in the United States: Currently available prevention strategies. *Pediatrics, 75*, 456–462.

Rodin, J., and Janis, I. L. (1979). The social power of health-care practitioners as agents of change. *Journal of Social Issues, 35*, 60–68.

Roemer, M. I. (1961a). Bed supply and hospital utilization: A natural experiment. *Hospitals, 35*, 36–42.

Roemer, M. I. (1961b). On paying the doctor and the implications of different methods. *Journal of Health and Human Behavior, 3*, 4–14.

Rossiter, L. F., and Wilensky, G. R. (1983). A reexamination of the use of physician services: The role of physician-initiated demand. *Inquiry, 20*, 162–172.

Roter, D. L., Stewart, M., Putnam, S. M., Lipkin, M., Stiles, W., and Inui, T. S. (1997). The patient–physician relationship: Communication patterns of primary care physicians. *Journal of the American Medical Association, 277*, 350–356.

Rothert, M. L., Rovner, D. R., Elstein, A. S., Holzman, G. B., Holmes, M. M., and Ravitch, M. M. (1984). Differences in medical referral decisions for obesity among family practitioners, general internists, and gynecologists. *Medical Care, 22*, 42–53.

Ryan, M. (1999). Using conjoint analysis to take account of patient preferences and go beyond health outcomes: an applications to in vitro fertilization. *Social Science and Medicine, 48*, 535–546.

Salber, E. J., Greene, S. B., Feldman, J. J., and Hunter, G. (1976). Access to health care in a southern rural community. *Medical Care, 14*, 971–986.

Scitovsky, A. A. (1981). The use of medical services under prepaid and fee-for-service group practice. *Social Science and Medicine,15C*, 107–116.

Senn, M. J. E. (1975). Insights on the child development movement in the United States. *Monographs of the Society for Research in Child Development, 40*(3–4, Serial No. 161).

Shapiro, A. K. (1971). Placebo effects in medicine, psychotherapy and psychoanalysis. In A. Bergen and S. Garfield (Eds.), *Handbook of psychotherapy and behavior change*. New York: Wiley.

Silverman, W. A. (1992). Over treatment of neonates? A personal retrospective. *Pediatrics, 90*, 971–976.

Sitzia, J., and Wood, N. (1997). Patient satisfaction: a review of issues and concepts. *Social Science and Medicine, 45*, 1829–1843.

Sloan, F., Mitchell, J., and Cromwell, J. (1978). Physician participation in state Medicaid programs. *Journal of Human Resources, 13*, 211–245.

Stewart, D. W., Hickson, G. B., Pechmann, C., Koslow, S., and Altemeier, W. A. (1989). Information search and decision making in the selection of family health care. *Journal of Health Care Marketing, 9*, 29–39.

Still, G. F. (1931). *The history of pediatrics*. London: Oxford University Press.

Studers-Ellis, E., Gold, J. S., and Jones, R. F. (2000). Trends in U.S. medical school faculty salaries. *Journal of the American Medical Association, 284*, 1130–1135.

Swan, J. E. (1985). Deepening the understanding of hospital patient satisfaction: Fulfillment and equity effects. *Journal of Health Care Marketing, 5*, 7–18.

U.S. Department of Health, Education, and Welfare. (1976). *Child health in America*. Rockville, MD: Author.

Valdez, R. B., Brook, R. H., Rogers, W. H., Ware, J. E., Keeler, E. B., Sherbourne, C. A., Lohr, K. N., Goldberg, G. A., Carnp, P., and Newhouse, J. P. (1985). Consequences of cost-sharing for children's health. *Pediatrics, 75*, 952–961.

Volicer, B. J. (1973). Perceived stress levels of events associated with the experience of hospitalization: Development and testing of a measurement tool. *Nursing Research, 22*, 491–497.

Volicer, B. J. (1974). Patients' perceptions of stressful events associated with hospitalization. *Nursing Research, 23*, 235–238.

Waitzkin, H., and Stoeckle, J. D. (1972). The communication of information about illness. *Advances in Psychosomatic Medicine, 8*, 180–215.

Waller, D. A., and Levitt, E. E. (1972). Concerns of mothers in a pediatric clinic. *Pediatrics, 50*, 931–934.

Ware, J. E. (1978). Effects of acquiescent response set on patient satisfaction ratings. *Medical Care, 26*, 327–336.

Ware, J. E., Davies-Avery, A., and Stewart, A. L. (1978). The measurement and meaning of patient satisfaction. *Health and Medical Care Services Review, 1*, 1–15.

Wartmian, S. A., Marlock, L. L., Malitz, F. E., and Palm, E. A. (1983). Understanding and satisfaction as predictor of compliance. *Medical Care, 21*, 886–891.

Weiss, G. L., and Ramsey, C. A. (1989). Regular source of primary medical care and patient satisfaction. *Quality Review Bulletin, 5*, 180–184.

Wennberg, J. E., Barnes, B. A., and Zubkoff, M. (1982). Professional uncertainty and the problem of supplier-induced demand. *Social Science and Medicine, 16,* 811–824.

Wennberg, J. E., and Gittelsohn, A. (1982). Variations in medical care among small areas. *Scientific American, 246,* 120–134.

Wennberg, J. E., McPherson, K., and Caper, P. (1984). Will payment based on diagnosis-related groups control hospital costs? *New England Journal of medicine, 311,* 295–300.

Wilensky, G. R., and Rossiter, L. F. (1983). The relative importance of physician-induced demand for medical care. *Milbank Memorial Fund Quarterly, 61,* 252–277.

Williams, S. V., Eisenberg, J. M., Pascale, L. A., and Kitz, D. S. (1982). Physicians' perceptions about unnecessary diagnostic testing. *Inquiry, 19,* 363–370.

Witcher-Alagna, S. (1983). Receiving medical help: A psychosocial perspective on patient reactions. In A. Nadler, J. D. Fisher, and B. M. DePaul (Eds.), *New directions in helping.* New York: Academic Press.

Wolinsky, F. D. (1980). The performance of health maintenance organizations: An analytic review. *Milbank Memorial Fund Quarterly, 58,* 537–587.

Young, P. C., Wasserman, R. C., McAullife, T., Long, J., Hagan, J. F., and Heath, B. (1985). Why families change pediatricians. *American Journal of Diseases of Children, 139,* 683–686.

Zelnio, R. N. (1982). The interaction among the criteria physicians use when prescribing. *Medical Care, 20,* 277–285.

18

Parenting and the Law

Pauline M. Pagliocca
Cambridge Hospital
Gary B. Melton
Clemson University
Phillip M. Lyons, Jr.
Sam Houston State University
Victoria Weisz
University of Nebraska, Lincoln

INTRODUCTION

Although debates may rage as to when other aspects of parenthood begin, one thing is clear: Legal regulation of parenthood begins *before* conception (e.g., reproductive rights) and touches on matters ranging from transporting children (e.g., child safety restraint laws) to income taxation (e.g., deductions for dependents). The scope of regulation is no less than awesome.

Not only is there diversity of activities to which the law is directed, but also diversity of approach undertaken through these laws. Thus, the law may vary both from time to time and from jurisdiction to jurisdiction. This state of affairs renders it impossible to describe definitively and comprehensively what the "law of parenting" is. A comprehensive review of all of the law affecting parenthood is clearly beyond the scope of this chapter. Instead, this chapter describes how the law approaches some of the more salient aspects of parenthood and family life.

This chapter begins by examining legal concepts of parenthood and the family. In doing so, it explores the law's use in various contexts of definitions of *parenthood* that rely on both biological and psychological approaches. Attention then turns to the related notion of the law defining *family* either using a formal or a functional approach. Next, legal interpretations of the different parental roles are explored. These roles include parents functioning as authorities, providers, caregivers, and socializers. The chapter concludes with a discussion of overarching themes that emerge from the bodies of law and policy operative in this context.

Traditionally, American law has viewed relationships between parents and their children from the perspective of the parents. The law has emphasized parents' rights and interests, except when these might conflict with those of the state.[1] At the same time, however, the law frequently purports to act in the best interests of children. That which is in the best interests of parents may not be in the best interests of children. Obviously, it is difficult to ascertain what is in children's best interests when the law views family matters from the perspective of parents. In considering the sometimes competing interests of parents, children, and the state, courts and legislatures have addressed questions concerning definitions, rights, and duties of parenthood.[2]

WHO IS THE PARENT? LEGAL VIEWS OF PARENTS AND FAMILIES

Generally, the law defines parenthood in terms of a relationship—a woman's biological relationship to a child, a man's marital relationship to a child's natural mother, or a nonbiological relationship established by adoption or remarriage. Less commonly, the law may acknowledge an emotional or psychological relationship between people who are otherwise unrelated. Within these various definitions, both legal and social traditions stress the primacy of the nuclear family and the functions it fulfills in the lives of children.

One of the reasons for the complexities regarding the meaning of parent is that parents function in multiple ways in regards to their children. Parents biologically produce children. They provide the economic resources to sustain children. They prepare food for their children, do their laundry, transport them to activities, help them with homework, take care of them when they are ill, and obtain health care for them when needed. Parents form intense affectionate, highly interactive bonds with their children. Parents socialize their children; they inculcate the values of the majority culture— and sometimes minority cultural values as well—in addition to their own unique values, morals, and beliefs. Differing legal definitions of parenthood vary in the way these various aspects of parent–child relationships are taken into account.

Biological Parent

The biological nature of parenthood has legal importance in establishing financial obligations for child support and presumptive rights to custody or visitation. When biological parents are in dispute with nonparents for the custody of children, the traditional view has been that biology is paramount (Craig, 1998; Gregory, 1998). The biological parent always would prevail as long as the parent was considered "fit,"[3] and he or she had not abandoned the child previously (e.g., *LaChapelle v. Mitten*,

---

[1] The use of the term state in this chapter parallels its use in other legal contexts in that it refers to a sovereign government. The term is particularly confusing in the case of republics such as the United States because the federal sovereign comprises relatively independent individual state sovereigns. Consequently, the reader should construe the term generically unless the context clearly indicates that reference is being made to individual states.

[2] Throughout this chapter we refer to various rights and duties parents (and others) possess. Simply put, a duty is an obligation imposed by law on citizens to behave in a certain way or to refrain from behaving in a certain way. A right is an obligation imposed by law on the government to behave in a certain way toward its citizens or to refrain from behaving in a certain way toward its citizens. In the United States, these rights typically take the form of so-called negative rights, which forbid certain government actions (e.g., the Bill of Rights). However, positive rights that compel government action also exist and are increasing in number (e.g., entitlements).

[3] "Suitable or appropriate. Conformable to a duty. Adapted to, designed, prepared. Words 'fit' and 'proper' on issue of custody in divorce cases are usually interpreted as meaning moral fitness" (*Black's Law Dictionary*, 1990, 637 [6th ed.], citations omitted). Definitions of "moral fitness," of course, may vary widely. In one (it is hoped, unrepresentative) early case (*Painter v. Bannister*, 1966, p. 155), the Supreme Court of Iowa decided that custody of a child should be awarded to the child's grandparents because of the unfitness of the biological father. The court commented on the father's fitness:

> Mr. Painter is either an agnostic or atheist and has no concern for formal religious training. He has read a lot of Zen Buddhism and "has been very much influenced by it".... He is a political liberal and got into difficulty in a job at the University of Washington for his support of the activities of the American Civil Liberties Union in the university news bulletin .... There were "two funerals" for his wife. One in the basement of his home in which he alone was present. He conducted the service and wrote her a long letter. The second at a church in Pullman was for the gratification of her friends. He attended in a sport shirt and sweater.

2000). Individual states differ in how far they have drifted from the traditional view. A number of these states continue to maintain a strong presumption in favor of the biological parent (parental rights jurisdictions; e.g., *In re* Ackenhausen, 1963 [Louisiana]). Such states give custody to biological parents as long as they are fit and they have not abandoned the child (occasional birthday cards or gifts are evidence of nonabandonment). Such a presumption may apply, even when the court believes that taking the child from another home and placing him or her with the biological parents will be traumatic or harmful (*In re* Adoption of J.J.B., 1995; Smith, 1978).

Intermediate jurisdictions—so called because they consider neither the child's interests nor the parents' interests to be dispositive (i.e., determinative of the disposition of the case)—view the biological parent's interests as secondary to the child's, but they do consider parental interests to some degree (e.g., *LaChapelle v. Mitten*, 2000 [Minnesota]; *Wallin v. Wallin*, 1971 [Minnesota]). Courts in these states weigh factors concerning the child's welfare, but also consider the reasons that the parent and the child were separated in determining custody (Smith, 1978). Consequently, if a parent were separated from his or her child for socially valued reasons (e.g., military service), the court might be quite supportive of returning the child to the parent if at all possible.

Finally, a number of jurisdictions focus primarily on the child's interests (e.g., *Rhinehart v. Nowlin*, 1990; see also Gregory, 1998). These states provide for award of custody to an individual who is not a biological parent if doing so is the best way to meet those needs. An Illinois court, for example, denied custody to a biological mother after her children's custodial father died, and instead awarded custody to their stepmother with whom they had been living (*Cebrzynski v. Cebrzynski*, 1978). This decision was reached despite the court's recognition of the biological mother's fitness.

The biological nature of parenthood also is considered in the law's approach to the rights of unwed fathers, particularly whether they can block adoption proceedings instituted by the mother. Although biological ties historically have been given enormous weight in consideration of parental rights, they commonly have been recognized only when the father was married to the mother at the time that the child was born. The marital presumption, which has been accepted uniformly, assumes that a child born to a woman living with her husband is the biological child of the husband (e.g., Uniform Parentage Act, 1973; Uniform Putative and Unknown Fathers Act, 1988; Zinman, 1992). Thus fatherhood status is conferred by means of the marital relationship with the birth mother.

The strength of the marital presumption was evidenced by a 1985 case in New York (*Karin T. v. Michael T.*, 1985). In that case, Karin and Michael were married and Karin twice became pregnant through artificial insemination. The couple separated some 6 years later, and Karin sought child support for the two children born during the marital union. Michael (who also was known as Marlene—but not to the clerk who issued the marriage license) disclaimed any responsibility by asserting that, because she was a woman, she could not be the parent of the children (i.e., because Karin was the mother and Michael was her husband, Michael would have to be the father, a biological impossibility for someone who was, and always had been, a woman). The court rejected Michael's argument and found both (1) that she was a woman and (2) that she was the parent of the child.

It is also worth noting that the definitions of fitness may vary as functions of the legal issue involved and the legal interests of the parties. For example, because prospective adoptive parents have no vested constitutional interest in prospective adoptees (and because the demand for adopted children is high and the supply is low), the threshold for fitness may be quite high. In contrast, because biological parents do have a vested constitutional interest in their children, the threshold for fitness should be much lower. Similarly, as regards visitation, because the scope of responsibilities of noncustodial parents is narrower than the scope of responsibilities of custodial parents, the threshold for fitness in this context may be lower still. The Supreme Court of Wisconsin (*In re* Adoption of Tachick, 1973, p. 872) commented on the "separation trauma" associated with disruption of a child's environment:

At one time, the courts paid less attention to the psychological trauma attendant upon disturbing the continuity of a child's environment than the courts do today. Some courts today have gone to the extreme and have held this factor to be controlling in adoption. It has been said by a noted psychiatrist that the stability of environment is far more crucial than its precise nature and content.

Undoubtedly the fact that such a finding was in the best interest of the children (i.e., because of the additional source of support) carried considerable weight. The fact that Michael, pursuant to the artificial insemination contract, had agreed to be the father also was persuasive.

Because legal fatherhood arises from the marital relationship with the birth mother, the traditional view has been that unwed fathers have no rights whatsoever regarding their offspring (e.g., *Michael H. v. Gerald D.*, 1989; *Shoecraft v. Catholic Social Services Bureau, Inc.*, 1986; *Stanley v. Illinois*, 1972). Before 1972, an unwed father could not stop the termination of his parental rights if the mother placed her child for adoption (Zinman, 1992). In *Stanley v. Illinois* (1972), however, the U.S. Supreme Court held that unwed fathers did have some parental rights protected by the due process clause of the Fourteenth Amendment. In that case, an unwed father who had participated in the care of his child was held to be entitled to a hearing to determine his parental fitness before his parental rights could be terminated. The biological relationship is not sufficient, however, to sustain parental rights of an unwed father. An unwed father has to show that he has had an actual parental relationship with the child in order to obtain legal recognition of his interest in the preservation of that relationship (*Lehr v. Robertson*, 1983; Zinman, 1992).

This "biology plus" requirement obviously cannot be met by unwed fathers of babies who are given up for adoption at birth. Some jurisdictions are moving to give unwed fathers greater protections even when they do not have an existing relationship with their child (Meyer, 1999). In 1990, a New York court (*In re* Raquel Marie X) held that an unwed father who is willing to assume custody of his infant and who demonstrates parental responsibility can veto a proposed adoption, whether or not he had lived with the child or the child's mother prior to the proposed adoption.

The law regarding unwed fathers' rights is still unsettled. The Supreme Court has not ruled yet on the scope of the parental rights of an unwed father and the steps that he can take to protect them. Some argue that, unless unwed fathers are given temporary custody of their infants while their parental rights are adjudicated, a father's rights to rear his child likely will not be vindicated (Zinman, 1992). The initial placement of children with prospective adoptive parents creates a situation in which it generally will be in the children's best interests to remain with them rather than be placed with their fathers with whom they have had little, if any, contact.

Other unsettled areas of law regarding biological relationships between parents and children are artificial insemination, surrogate motherhood (Behm, 1999), and posthumously conceived children (Sutton, 1999). According to the Uniform Parentage Act (1973; a model act crafted by legal scholars and adopted by many jurisdictions), the donor of semen in artificial insemination of a married woman is not considered to be the biological father of the child. Rather, relying on the marital presumption, the husband of the mother is considered to be the father. Where there is no husband, however, the donor presumably would be the father.

Consequently, unmarried women who seek artificial insemination are having difficulty keeping the sperm donor from retaining parental rights and obligations (Bartlett, 1988). In *Jhordan C. v. Mary K.* (1986), a California statute provided that the donor of semen provided to a licensed physician for artificial insemination was not the father of the child. Jhordan C. (the donor and biological father), however, asserted paternal rights on the ground that the statute was not effective where, as in their case, the sperm was provided directly without the involvement of a physician (Mary K. was a nurse). Because the statute at issue severed an important constitutional right (i.e., the right to one's child), the court construed the statute strictly and found that it was not operative in the case because it had not been complied with fully.

Similar uncertainties regarding whether statutory and constitutional protections of parental rights can be waived before the birth of one's child cloud the law relating to surrogate motherhood. If such parental rights cannot be waived before birth, surrogacy contracts are unlikely to be enforceable (e.g., *Doe v. Attorney General*, 1990; but see *In re* Adoption of Baby A and Baby B, 1994; *In re* Adoption of Paul, 1990). Moreover, questions may arise concerning events not only before the birth of a child, but also after the death of a parent. For example, in order to qualify as an heir, a child often must be born within 300 days of the death of the father (e.g., Cal. Fam. Code § 7611;

Tex. Fam. Code § 151.003). Obviously, offspring conceived long after the death of the father (e.g., through sperm banking, postmortem sperm harvesting, and so forth) will not be born within the requisite time frame. Thus the law either will have to change to accommodate these technological changes, or it will treat some children differently from others in probate matters.

Although legal and social traditions are based on a presumption of biology in most determinations of parenthood, biotechnological advances have introduced perplexing questions for which the law still is developing answers. Courts soon may have to fashion a "presumption of maternity" as an analogue to the presumption of paternity. Is the mother the wife of the biological father (e.g., in which a man provides his sperm to a surrogate mother)? Is the mother the donor of the egg (e.g., in which a gestational surrogate mother is involved)? Or is the mother the person from whom the child is delivered? As Hill (1991, p. 355) has asked, "Where various parties have made distinct contributions to the procreative process [i.e., coitus, conception, and gestation], who should be recognized as parents of the child?" Such questions are not purely theoretical; courts have confronted these issues already (e.g., *Johnson v. Calvert*, 1993; see Halperin-Kaddari, 1999, for a review).

Psychological Parent

The concept of the psychological parent was articulated three decades ago by Goldstein, Freud, and Solnit (1973) as a means of shifting the focus of custody disputes away from the rights of the biological parents to the best interests of the child, as manifested by the child's need for stability and continuity with regard to relationships with significant others in the child's life. The psychological parent may be a biological parent but is not necessarily so. Rather, the psychological parent is the individual who has fulfilled the child's "psychological needs for a parent" (Goldstein et al., 1973, p. 98). Goldstein et al. argued that a child would suffer significant psychological harm from disruption of a relationship with the psychological parent.

Courts most commonly have raised the concept of the psychological parent when they were choosing between custodial arrangements offered by biological and nonbiological parents, particularly if they were attempting to justify refusal to award custody of a child to a biological parent. Some courts have awarded custody to a stepparent rather than to a biological parent if the stepparent has had a prior strong relationship with the child and is seen as more likely to fulfill the child's need for stability and continuity (Hetherington and Stanley-Hagan, in Vol. 3 of this *Handbook*). In an analogous case, a court ordered the guardianship of a child with Down syndrome who had been institutionalized for years and virtually was abandoned emotionally by his biological parents to a couple who had provided familylike relationships for him through their involvement at the institution (*In re* Phillip B., 1983). Thus some jurisdictions place great value on supporting stable and long-lasting attachment relationships for the child, even if those relationships are not with biological parents (e.g., Greben, 1995, reviewing New York cases).

Another area of law involving the concept of psychological parenthood concerns adoption (Brodzinsky, Smith, and Pinderhughes, in Vol. 1 of this *Handbook*). In California, the adoption consent statutes direct courts to consider the extent of bonding by the child with the adopters and the "potential to bond" with the biological parents when birth mothers try to withdraw their consent to the termination of their parental rights (Cal. Fam. Code § 9005(d)). The court then is required to decide whether the child's best interests would be served by a return to the birth mother or by remaining with the adoptive parents. Similarly, although the act does not use the term specifically, the federal Adoption and Safe Families Act of 1997 seeks to facilitate psychological parenthood through its setting of time limits within which termination of parental rights proceedings must occur. The time limits are designed to facilitate stability in order to maximize the child's opportunity to form long-term, loving attachments (see 42 U.S.C. § 675(2000)). Thus, courts and government agencies in California and other child-focused jurisdictions are balancing psychological parenthood and biological ties in their decisions (Dickson, 1991; see also *Duncan v. Howard*, 1996, Utah's focus on potential to bond in custody disputes between biological parents and third parties).

Finally, the statutory establishment of grandparents' rights to petition for visitation with their grandchildren (that may have been prevented by parental divorce or death) reflects a recognition of the psychological value to children of maintaining relationships with their grandparents (Smith and Drew, in Vol. 3 of this *Handbook*). Legislators endorsed these statutes because the lawmakers believed that grandparental relationships were important not only to children but also to grandparents. Many also placed considerable significance on the value of intergenerational supports to children. However, the laws create some difficulties for courts which are required to determine whether psychological parenting relationships exist between particular grandparents and grandchildren, and whether it would be in children's best interests to preserve such relationships (Thompson, Scalora, Castrianno, and Limber, 1992).

The U.S. Supreme Court provided some guidance on the proper scope of third-party visitation statutes (*Troxel v. Granville*, 2000). At issue in the case was a Washington statute which gave "any person" the right to "petition the court for visitation rights at any time, including, but not limited to custody proceedings" (Wash. Rev. Code § 26.10.160(3)). Although the Court struck down the "breathtakingly broad" (p. 67) statute, the concerns revolved mostly around the law's failure to respect parental authority altogether. Thus, the Court seems receptive to grandparental visitation statutes, but only if they sufficiently protect "the interests of parents in the care, custody, and conrol of their children" (p. 67).

Formal Concepts of Family Life

In defining family relationships, courts generally have adopted a formal analysis in which they designate only members of nuclear families as family, spouse, or parent (see, e.g., Brener, 1999; *City of Ladue v. Horn*, 1986). Exceptions to this view arise when tradition (e.g., inclusion of extended family) or the language of specific legislation directs that alternative family compositions be considered (Note, 1991). Such a traditional view of family persists in the law despite the extraordinary shifts in family demographics in the last generation (Loue, 2000).

This formal analysis focuses on the "automatic" ties created by biology (kinship), marriage, and adoption, rather than the question of whether these relationships actually meet society's expectations of the nuclear family. Jurisdictions that follow this approach require a finding that an individual meets a formal criterion for parenthood as a condition for recognition of a legitimate interest in any procedure affecting a child's welfare. Such recognition may occur even if the individual has not fulfilled any traditional parental roles, such as providing for the economic or emotional well-being of the child.

In most cases, legal parents are the same adults who fulfill society's—and the law's—expectations for the nuclear family. Generally, the law holds a presumption of competence regarding the parenting abilities of biological and other legal parents and refrains from interference in the day-to-day functioning of families. When such competence is questioned, however (e.g., in cases of termination of parental rights), or when family members are in dispute with one another (e.g., in custody cases involving two competent parents), the conflict between legal and functional definitions of family may arise.

Functional Concepts

The functional view includes the traditional nuclear family, but also "legitimizes non-nuclear relationships that share the essential characteristics of traditional relationships" (Note, 1991, p. 1641). Rather than focusing on kinship and other legal ties, the functional view stresses the needs and functions that are fulfilled in determining family membership. Criteria include such functions as sharing of wealth, participation in domestic responsibilities, and provision of affection (e.g., *City of Ladue v. Horn*, 1986; *Desiato v. Abbott*, 1992). Under this view, parent status may be granted to a nonrelative who fulfills the roles traditionally met by legal parents. For example, a domestic partner—whether in a heterosexual or same-sex relationship—might be considered a parent for legal purposes in a jurisdiction adopting a functional view of the family.

Minow (1991) has argued that a functional view is consistent with the child's best interests because family is defined from the child's perspective by highlighting the roles (rather than the legal ties) of parents. Utilizing the concept of the psychological parent (Goldstein et al., 1973), Minow (1991, p. 274) described a parent as someone who "has taken care of the child on a daily basis, is known to the child as a parent, and has provided love and financial support." She argued that courts should focus their inquiry on questions of function in determining whether a group of people is a family: ". . . do they share affection and resources, think of one another as family members, and present themselves as such to neighbors and others?" (Minow, 1991, p. 270).

Although broader and more consistent with changing social structures, a functional definition of family presents potential pitfalls on application. First, the functions by which families are judged are derived from examination of the traditional nuclear family; thus, true alternatives to such a prototype may not be recognized legally. As a practical matter, formal and functional definitions may differ little. Second, in making such comparisons, it is not clear which family features should be weighted most heavily. Third, because of an absence of authoritative guidelines, functional criteria must be established on a case by case basis. Such an inquiry necessarily invites intrusion into families' private lives (Note, 1991).

To be sure, legislatures, courts, and commentators from both the legal and social scientific communities have struggled and continue to struggle to define what constitutes a family relationship. As the preceding discussion makes clear, the issues are not merely theoretical; the particular conceptualization that is applicable to a specific situation may have a profound effect on the parties involved (e.g., to whom custody is awarded, who is entitled to visitation, etc.). In some instances deciding "who" is a "what" to "whom" ends the inquiry. In other cases, however, the law delves more deeply into the nature of the relationship by not only declaring who occupies a particular role vis-à-vis other prospective family members, but also by fleshing out the contours of that role.

LEGAL INTERPRETATIONS OF PARENTAL ROLES

Despite the difficulties in defining a parent, doing so is important because legal recognition as a parent determines who may claim both rights and duties under a variety of laws pertaining to parent–child relationships. Although rights and duties vary across legal questions, such legal entitlements and obligations typically can be categorized according to the various roles parents assume under both social and legal custom. Parents may be described as authorities, providers, caregivers, protectors, and socializers. Parental privileges and responsibilities do not necessarily hold equal status across or within each role, however. For example, rights may take precedence over duties when parents function in the role of authority, but the reverse may be true when they function as providers.

Parent as Authority

As with other domestic relationships (e.g., Wadlington, 1990, p. 2), the laws controlling parent–child relationships are primarily matters of particular states rather than the federal government. In both legal and social realms, parents generally are recognized as having primary authority in all aspects of childrearing. Such authority is based on beliefs (Harris, Waldrop, and Waldrop, 1990, p. 700):

> that parents are in the best position to know and care about their children's needs, that giving parents authority encourages them to assume and discharge the responsibilities of parenthood and that diffusing authority over how children will be raised promotes cultural and social diversity.

Accordingly, pursuant to the protection of liberty under the Fourteenth Amendment, parents generally possess a right to rear their children without interference. For example, the Supreme Court has ruled that, absent a contrary compelling state interest, parents have a right to guide their children's education (*Meyer v. Nebraska*, 1923; *Pierce v. Society of Sisters*, 1925; *Wisconsin v. Yoder*, 1972). Even when parents have been shown to be abusive or neglecting, the state bears a high burden in justifying coercive action (Azar, in Vol. 4 of this *Handbook*). In cases involving state attempts to terminate parental rights to their children, the Supreme Court has held that the state must provide notice and a hearing for parents (*Stanley v. Illinois*, 1972) and must present clear and convincing evidence of a parent's lack of fitness (*Santosky v. Kramer*, 1982).

Parent as Provider

As a general matter, simply stated, parents have a legal duty to provide for their children. This duty is based in part on the presumption that most children cannot provide for themselves adequately during their own childhood. The law, of course, is neither general nor simple. Specific questions emerge and the law must answer them. Some of these questions include: (1) Which "parents" owe such a duty? (2) To which "children" is such a duty owed? (3) What should be done when the presumption fails and children never will be able to provide for themselves (e.g., children with certain disabilities)? and (4) What should be done when children will be able to provide for themselves, but only after a period of continued dependency on their parents well into the children's legal adulthood (e.g., adult children attending college)? An overview of the law's answers to these questions follows.

Support for minor[4] children.   Of course, parenthood brings duties as well as rights. The duty to provide financial support and other necessaries, such as food and shelter, for children is rooted in parental rights (French, in Vol. 2 of this *Handbook*; Harris et al., 1990). Historically, parents—especially fathers—have held rights to their children's custody, control, services, and earnings (Johnson, 1987). In return for such considerations, parents are expected to provide children with financial support in order to prevent the community from assuming the burden of financial maintenance (Harris et al., 1990): "The duty is . . . a legal and natural obligation, the consistent enforcement of which is equally essential to the well-being of the state, the morals of the community, and the development of the individual" (Johnson, 1987, p. 184).

Although originally viewed as a moral rather than legal obligation based on the "voluntariness" of having given birth to a child (Schuele, 1988–89), financial support of minor children now is regarded by all American jurisdictions as both a moral and legal responsibility of parents (Johnson, 1987; Mnookin and Weisberg, 1989). Traditionally, this duty pertained only to fathers, with mothers assuming responsibility on a father's death or refusal to pay. The current trend is to hold both parents responsible for financial support and to apportion parents' responsibilities according to their ability to pay, although some states hold each parent equally responsible (Friedman, 1992; Mnookin and Weisberg, 1989).

Adhering to the principle of parental autonomy—that, to the fullest extent possible, parents should be allowed to rear their children without interference—the government usually does not impose standards for parental support on intact families (Harris et al., 1990). While refraining from determining specific types and amounts of support, courts usually have held parents responsible for providing food, clothing, shelter, education, and medical attention for minor and other children not capable of self-support (Johnson, 1987). However, when courts do intervene, mostly in cases of divorce, amounts typically are determined according to the financial and social status, as well as the age and health of both parent and child, and usually extend beyond the provision of basic necessities

---

[4]The term *minor* is used to refer to individuals who are not adults according to the particular jurisdiction whose laws are applicable. Although the precise ages vary from jurisdiction to jurisdiction, each jurisdiction has established an age—the age of majority—(usually 18 years approximately)—at which individuals become legal adults. At that point the legal "disabilities of minority" (e.g., inability to contract, inability to vote, inability to purchase alcoholic beverages, etc.) are removed. The use of the term herein is somewhat oversimplified. Actually, each jurisdiction has established different ages of majority for different purposes. Thus, a person may be considered an adult at the ages of 16, 17, 18, and 21 years for the purposes of driving, criminal liability, contractual capacity, and purchase of alcohol and cigarettes, respectively.

alone, especially where parents can afford more (Hetherington and Stanley-Hagan, in Vol. 3 of this *Handbook*; Johnson, 1987). This approach requires case-by-case analysis and grants considerable discretion to the courts.

Parents' financial responsibility for their children is not without limits. Courts have sustained parental authority to set conditions under which parents may terminate support to their minor children (Brennan, 1999; Friedman, 1992; Harris et al., 1990). For example, a New York court held that a parent could impose reasonable restrictions on the behavior of a child (requiring the daughter to live in a college dormitory rather than in an off-campus apartment) in exchange for continued financial support (*Roe v. Doe*, 1971).

Although allowing parents some discretion in establishing conditions for support, legislatures and courts have dealt harshly with parents who fail to provide support when they are financially capable. Failure to provide the basic necessities to children now is considered a criminal offense in all states. Some forms of neglect are treated as felonies (e.g., Cal. Pen. Code § 273a(b); child endangerment), whereas other forms are treated as misdemeanors (e.g., Cal. Pen. Code § 270 (simple neglect)). Although child neglect statutes are frequently vague, common forms of neglect are related to the same fundamental responsibilities to "support the child, including providing the child with clothing, food, shelter, medical care, and education" (Tex. Fam. Code Ann. § 12.04(3); see also Friedman, 1992).

Divorce is the most common circumstance for establishment of legal standards for child support. Divorce presents the potential for financial responsibilities to be assumed by or imposed on four different parties: the custodial parents, noncustodial parents, stepparents, and the state. In general, custodial parents are viewed as having primary obligation for supporting minor children. Some statutes impose a support duty on custodial parents (Johnson, 1987). Most often, though, their status is comparable to that of parents in intact families. That is, the state usually does not intervene to impose specific financial duties on custodial parents (Harris et al., 1990).

The state's position of nonintervention in the case of custodial parents does not apply to noncustodial parents, however. In divorce, noncustodial parents usually are ordered to pay some level of child support according to their financial ability and social status and the needs of the particular children. Although other debts may be considered by the court, they normally will not exempt a parent from meeting the child support obligation (e.g., *Kost v. Kost*, 1994; *Park v. Park*, 1981), and a noncustodial parent can anticipate an escalation in ordered amounts over time.

In requiring noncustodial parents to contribute to the financial support of their children, courts essentially break the traditional link between parental control and parental duty (Harris et al., 1990). Although they lose all or much of their control, noncustodial parents are not absolved of their duties as parents. In fact, their obligations may be specified more clearly than any control or rights they retain (Clark, 1999). In contrast, custodial parents retain their control rights whereas they remain relatively free of state-imposed standards for support. Thus, for them, the connection between their duty to support and their right to control remains intact.

Stepparents usually are not held legally responsible for the financial support of their step-children. Perhaps in recognition of a moral or social responsibility, however, some states have enacted statutes that impose a limited duty that applies with full force only while the stepparent is married to the child's natural parent (e.g., N.H. Rev. Stat. Ann. § 546-A:2; see also Friedman, 1992).

When biological parenthood is involved, marriage is not a prerequisite to financial responsibility. Under common law, mothers have held a duty to support their children born outside of marriage. Statutes now impose a duty on unwed fathers to contribute to the financial support of their children (e.g., Or. Rev. Stat. § 109.103). This duty does not apply, though, to biological fathers of children born to women who are married to someone else, because the law presumes the woman's husband to be the father.

Support for emancipated and adult children. The responsibility to provide for the support of a child does not persist in perpetuity. Another problem involves the determination of the point at which such responsibility ends. Although this transition typically occurs at the age of majority, it can occur earlier if the child is emancipated or later if the child is disabled.

The duty of parental support is based on a child's inability to support him- or herself. Because complete emancipation relieves a parent of financial obligations, courts and legislatures are generally conservative in determining emancipation of a minor child. Generally accepted criteria include marriage and enlistment in the military. Other circumstances are assessed on a case by case basis, but may include (Katz, Schroeder, and Sidman, 1973, p. 218):

> whether the child is living at home, whether the child is paying room and board if living at home, whether the parents are exercising disciplinary control over the minor, whether the child is independently employed, whether the child has been given the right to retain wages and spend them without parental restraints, whether the child is responsible for debts incurred and the extent of the parents' contributions toward the payment of outstanding bills, whether the child owns a major commodity such as a car, and whether the parent has listed the child as a dependent for tax purposes. Age, of course, is also a critical element. None of these factors, however, is conclusive.

There also is typically no bright line standard to determine whether parents have a financial obligation to their adult child, but such a duty generally applies where an adult child is incapable of self-support because of mental or physical disability (Zarit and Eggebeen, in Vol. 1 of this *Handbook*). However, state statutes may set limitations on the duty or, in the absence of any statute, a parent may have no legal obligation regardless of the adult child's ability to support himself or herself (Johnson, 1987, pp. 89–91).

One area in which the issue of parental obligation for support of a "capable" adult child may come before the court involves payment for postsecondary education. The general rule is that parents are not required to finance education and training for an adult child (e.g., *Blue v. Blue*, 1992; see also Friedman, 1992) but the trend is to view higher education as a necessary for which parents are responsible, considering their means and the aptitude of the particular child (Johnson, 1987).

In divorce, statutes in some states require providing for a college education (e.g., *Childers v. Childers*, 1978; Mo. Ann. Stat. § 452.340.5; Wash. Rev. Code § 26.09.100), but others mandate support for minor children only, regardless of educational level (e.g., Ill. Rev. Stat. ch. 750, para. 5/510(d)). In the absence of statutory specificity regarding age limits, courts have been divided over financial responsibility for the education of adult children, with some courts finding a duty (e.g., *Newburgh v. Arrigo*, 1982) and others holding that none exists (e.g., *Nolfo v. Nolfo*, 1992; see also Harris et al., 1990).

Inheritance. To some degree, parents continue as designated providers even after death. In every state, intestate laws provide for some share of a parent's estate to go to his or her children when that parent has failed to leave a will. In such situations, all siblings receive an equal share, regardless of age or other limitations on earning power. The "natural" distribution thus may be unfair to younger and disabled children, who might have longer need for parental support than older and more able children (Mnookin and Weisberg, 1989).

Although provision of support after the death of a parent may be expected by the law, such support generally is not a duty. When a parent has drawn a will, every state allows parents to disinherit children, making no provision for them after the parent's death. No such mechanism for disinheritance exists for spouses, however, so that some level of protection may remain for children who are not listed as intended beneficiaries in the deceased parent's will.

Parent as Caregiver

Of course, children need more than financial support. The law supports and values the performance by parents of numerous caregiving activities on behalf of their children.

A controversial approach developed in West Virginia has used care for children as the standard for determination of child custody in divorce (Chambers, 1984; *Garska v. McCoy*, 1981; Neely, 1984;

W.Va. Code § 48-2-15). Neely (1984) argued that a presumption in favor of the person who has been the primary caregiver generally will protect mothers from bargaining away their financial settlement in order to retain custody, whereas such a presumption does not penalize fathers with a gender-based maternal preference.

West Virginia law defines the primary caretaker as the parent who takes primary responsibility for:

(1) Preparing and planning of meals;
(2) Bathing, grooming, and dressing;
(3) Purchasing, cleaning, and care of clothes;
(4) medical care, including nursing and trips to physicians;
(5) arranging for social interaction among peers after school, i.e., transporting to friends' houses or, for example, to girl or boy scout meetings;
(6) arranging alternative care, i.e., babysitting, daycare, etc.;
(7) putting child to bed at night, attending to child in the middle of the night, waking child in the morning;
(8) disciplining, i.e., teaching general manners and toilet training;
(9) educating, i.e., religious, cultural, social, etc.;
(10) teaching elementary skills, i.e., reading, writing, and arithmetic (*Garska v. McCoy*, 1981, p. 363).

The parent who performs the majority of these functions is defined as the primary caretaker and will be awarded custody in most cases. West Virginia's reliance on this test indicates both its interest in protecting the economic welfare of divorcing mothers and their children, and its recognition of the importance and value of the everyday care of children by their parents.

The area of law regarding children's health care is illustrative of the law's view of the importance of and limits to the caregiving function of parents. For example, in their role as caregivers of their child's basic needs, parents are given legal authority to make numerous decisions regarding their child's medical care. As noted *supra*, the parental role of caregiver has been viewed to include obtaining and arranging medical care for the child (e.g., Tinsley, Markey, Ericksen, Kwasman, and Ortiz, in Vol. 5 of this *Handbook*): "It is the right and duty of parents under the law of nature as well as the common law and the statutes of many states to protect their children, to care for them in sickness and in health . . ." (Johnson, 1987, § 14).

Parental consent to treatment. Parents' rights in executing their health caregiving authority are established in parental consent requirements for treatment. The general rule giving parents authority over their minor children's health care derives from the common law (i.e., nonstatutory, judge-made, case law). Excepting specific contexts that will be discussed below, parental consent is both a necessary and sufficient requirement for medical treatment of minors (Holder, 1985; Mnookin and Weisberg, 1989; Rozovsky, 1984).

Traditionally, the common law viewed minors as incapable of consenting to medical or surgical treatment. Consent, however, had to be given in order to protect the physician from a legal action for battery. Thus, the law looked to parents to provide the legal consent for treatment for their children.

Weithorn and McCabe (1988) have listed several reasons for reliance on parental consent, rather than direct consent from minor children when health care is at issue. The historical reason is that children were viewed at common law as the property of their parents with no rights of their own (Rodham, 1973). Under current law, however, the Constitution protects parental authority through the doctrine of family privacy, which protects married couples from government intrusion into matters involving their families, including matters related to health care. That doctrine is based in part on the assumption that parents are best able to make decisions promoting their children's interests. Thus, allowing parents decision making authority for health care is viewed as ultimately beneficial to minors.

Most directly, the law has viewed minors as inherently limited in their judgment and reasoning (e.g., Rozovsky, 1984; *Schall v. Martin*, 1984; *Stanford v. Kentucky*, 1989; *Thompson v. Oklahoma*, 1988). The corollary rejection of minors' autonomy typically is based on the assumption that incompetent people are prone to make such self-injurious decisions and that the state has a compelling interest in preventing them from doing so. Some also regard incompetence as a factor negating personhood—membership in the moral community—and therefore making personal interests in autonomy meaningless.

Parental consent is required in most situations involving medical treatment and nonemergency treatment of children, and such treatments that have not been authorized by parents have resulted in successful lawsuits (e.g., *Zoski v. Gaines*, 1935). However, for the past several decades there have been no successful lawsuits by parents for treatment of adolescents over 15 years of age when the adolescent has provided informed consent (Holder, 1985).

Minors' consent to their own treatment.   The failure of parents to prevail in lawsuits is not the only sign of lessening of the stringency of parental consent. As one court observed (*Belcher v. Charleston Area Medical Center*, 1992, p. 835):

> The traditional common law approach to minors and consent to treatment has undergone a number of modifications. Medical emergencies have provided an inroad, permitting treatment without parental consent in certain situations. The "mature minor" and "emancipated minor" rules, in which certain children are considered capable of giving consent, have also gained recognition.

These gradual changes have increased adolescents' autonomy and privacy. Exceptions to the parental consent requirement have been made when minors appear to be able to care for themselves competently or when the treatment needs are such that it has been determined that there is a societal interest in the state's assumption of the role of caregiver from the parents.

The American Law Institute's (1934) *Restatement of the law of torts* (§ 59a) has stated the governing *mature minor rule* as follows:

> If a child . . . is capable of appreciating the nature, extent and consequences of the invasion (of his body) his assent prevents the invasion from creating liability, though the assent of the parent, guardian, or other person is not obtained or is expressly refused.

Recognizing that the public health sometimes requires permitting minors to obtain confidential health care, most states have enacted laws authorizing the treatment of minors for sexually transmitted diseases and substance abuse without parental notification or consent (e.g., Va. Code Ann. § 54.1-2969(E)). The U.S. Supreme Court has recognized a constitutionally protected privacy interest of minors in access to contraception (*Carey v. Population Services International*, 1977) and abortion (*City of Akron v. Akron Center for Reproductive Health, Inc.*, 1983; *Ohio v. Akron Center for Reproductive Health*, 1990), although the Court also has held that minors' privacy can be limited in ways that would be unconstitutional if applied to adult women. Specifically, the Court has upheld state laws requiring parental notification or consent when an alternative confidential opportunity to go before a judge is available (*Bellotti v. Baird*, 1979; *Planned Parenthood of Southeastern Pennsylvania v. Casey*, 1992; *Hodgson v. Minnesota*, 1990).

State-ordered treatment.   States do intervene in specific situations regarding young children (as well as older children) when parents fail to provide necessary medical treatment to a minor child, even if the reason for the failure is the parent's religious beliefs. There is considerable legal authority for states to remove children from the custody of their parents in order to obtain necessary treatment (e.g., Cal. Welf. and Inst. Code § 300(b)). Courts do so through their *parens patriae* power—the authority and duty to act in the place of the parent to protect the interests of the child.

Psychiatric hospitalization.   Another caregiving area in which the rights and the interests of parents and their children may come into conflict involves psychiatric hospitalization. Historically, parents have held the right to seek hospital placement for minor children who exhibit a wide variety of disturbing behaviors. Such commitments, even when taking place over the objections of the children, have been considered "voluntary" because they are initiated and/or sanctioned by parents and regarded as falling within the scope of constitutionally protected rights of parental authority and family privacy.

Until the mid-1970s, parental commitment of children, accompanied by the concurring opinion of an admitting physician or institution director, but without any judicial hearing or other legal review, was permitted in over three fourths of the states (Brakel, 1985). Then, both state statutes and individual case decisions began to adopt procedural protections for minors facing psychiatric hospitalization. For example, the California Supreme Court, in a case of a 14-year-old adolescent committed by his mother for treatment (*In re* Roger S., 1977, p. 1288), held that, although minors' rights may be "less comprehensive" than those of adults, "no interest of the state or of a parent sufficiently outweighs the liberty interest of a minor old enough to independently exercise his right of due process to permit the parent to deprive him of that right" (p. 1292). This is but one example of the trend in strengthening children's rights and due process protections through case law during that time.

Despite this trend at the state level, the U.S. Supreme Court reaffirmed parental authority in the psychiatric commitment of minor children and held that no formal due process hearing was required before a minor's admission to a psychiatric facility, although a postadmission review may be required (*Parham v. J. R.*, 1979). This holding was strikingly out of step with the course being pursued by individual states, as well as with the Supreme Court's own decisions relative to the constitutional rights of minors (e.g., *Carey v. Population Services International*, 1977; *In re* Gault, 1967; *Planned Parenthood of Central Missouri v. Danforth*, 1976; *Tinker v. Des Moines Independent School District*, 1969). Although cited as a "resounding victory for parental authority" (Wald, 1980, p. 18), *Parham* had little impact on actual practice; that is, rather than setting new guidelines, it merely provided constitutional approval for prevailing standards (Levine, Ewing, and Hager, 1987). In states that already had begun to establish more stringent criteria, the *Parham* decision did little to interrupt the legislative development of procedural protections for children involved in civil commitment (Burlingame and Amaya, 1985).

Currently, although few states provide legally for the involuntary commitment of minor children, the process for their commitment to public psychiatric hospitals typically remains essentially the same as that of adults. In some states, the distinction between voluntary and involuntary commitment is difficult to discern; included in "voluntary" statutes are those that require the consent of the child and/or a court hearing if he or she objects. Although current research suggests that adolescents are capable of participating competently in decision making regarding hospitalization (e.g., Weithorn, 1985), they "may perceive no real choice" (Melton, 1984, p. 156) given the stress of the situation and the potential outcomes of such direct conflict with their own parents.

Other statutes provide for an automatic court hearing, whether the child agrees or objects to hospitalization. Such laws are essentially the same as those governing the involuntary commitment of adults. A third category of statutes may come closer to a "true voluntary model" (Brakel, 1985, p. 46) of commitment. These statutes set specific age standards (usually between 12 and 18 years) above which a minor cannot be hospitalized solely on the petition of parents. It should be noted, however, that many states still conduct such "voluntary" commitments as permitted by *Parham* (for a more detailed discussion see Melton, Lyons, and Spaulding, 1998).

The law is replete with contradiction and confusion regarding the psychiatric hospitalization of children—the blurred distinctions between voluntary and involuntary commitment, the differences between the Supreme Court's interpretations and the trend in statutory and case law, the range of statutory requirements and limitations, and the extent to which any of these is understood by clinical and legal professionals, as well as by parents and children involved in psychiatric commitment. As observed by Jackson-Beeck, Schwartz, and Rutherford (1987, p. 164), "For teenagers [and children] admitted by their parents, hospitalization can be a legal twilight zone, inescapable without parental approval yet beyond legal control."

The "legal twilight zone" of confusion and contradiction parallels a social twilight zone for children, particularly adolescents. It seems somehow perverse that an adolescent simultaneously could be considered (1) young enough to need parental consent for an aspirin and (2) old enough to be put to death for wrongdoing (e.g., *Thompson v. Oklahoma*, 1988). Moreover, social expectations change over time—not only for the individuals across their own development but also for adolescents as a group historically. Because children's abilities to care for themselves are the flip side of the same coin as parental obligations for caregiving, both must evolve hand in hand. As they become increasingly capable of managing their own autonomy and independence, a transfer of authority from parents to adolescents themselves must occur if the latter are to be accorded the respect that is commensurate with the responsibilities that they are capable of undertaking.

Parent as Socializer

The concept of parenting is an elusive one. The confusion inherent in the concept is reflected in the laws pertaining to it. Thus, parental responsibilities for providing and caring for children, at times, are complex, confusing, and poorly defined. Conceptually, however, these responsibilities are somewhat more straightforward than are other parental obligations. The parental responsibility for socializing children—the topic turned to next—is one of these especially vague obligations. Although the contours are delineated imprecisely, the following sections address some of the issues that recur frequently in this context.

Parents' educational rights and obligations. From the state's perspective, parents' responsibility to support and care for their children is rooted in the state's interest in the healthy socialization of children as citizens and workers. In performing this socializing function, most parents rarely come into direct contact with the legal system. Socialization of children occurs in the shadow of the law, however, and both parents and children are likely to find themselves under court jurisdiction when socialization is unsuccessful.

Perhaps the most obvious legal duty of parents in that regard is to ensure that children receive at least a minimal level of education (e.g., Epstein and Sanders, in Vol. 5 of this *Handbook*). Every state requires children to participate in some type of schooling. Accordingly, parental authority over school-age children largely is limited as a practical matter to after-school hours, although parents do retain some authority for decisions about their children's education. The state may regulate the ages of mandatory school attendance, requirements for teacher certification, content of instruction, and the standards and procedures for student discipline.

Education is not a right protected by the U.S. Constitution (*San Antonio Independent School District v. Rodriguez*, 1973), although many state constitutions provide such a right. Thus, the federal government has no direct constitutional power over education and schooling, but it has considerable direct involvement in education through "strings" on federal funds and indirect control through statutes and the Fourteenth Amendment that limit state discretion. For example, antidiscrimination laws regulate allocation of funding for school sports programs, and the religion clauses of the First Amendment limit religious exercise in public schools and government regulation of private schools (see, e.g., *Santa Fe Independent School District v. Doe*, 2000, and citations therein).

Because of their right and obligation to direct and safeguard the upbringing of their children, parents generally are seen as sharing the same legal interests as their school-age children (Valente, 1985/1989). For example, the Supreme Court upheld an exception for Amish parents from the law requiring their high-school-age children to attend school (*Wisconsin v. Yoder*, 1972). The majority recognized the success that Amish parents typically have in socializing law-abiding children. In dissent, however, Justice William O. Douglas argued that the Court had missed the key interests:

"... the parents, absent dissent, normally speak for the entire family, the education of the child is a matter on which the child will often have decided views" (*Wisconsin v. Yoder*, 1972, p. 244).

Although *Yoder* was decided in favor of the parents' rights to free exercise of religion under the First Amendment, Justice Douglas's dissent pointed out that the Court had "treated the religious interest of the child as a factor in the analysis" but should have sought actively the children's own religious views, rather than assuming them to be identical to those of the parents (*Wisconsin v. Yoder*, 1972, p. 242). Interestingly, the particular facts of the case may have rendered this impossible. Although the children of Amish parents are inculcated in Amish values, the custom is such that only adults can be Amish—and then, only after taking affirmative, decisive steps to join their ranks. Thus, whereas there are children of the Amish, there are no Amish children. This fact may have precluded the approach espoused by Justice Douglas in that the children could not have chosen to be Amish.

Even the First Amendment–based exception to the state's authority to require school attendance is limited in *Yoder* to high-school-age children. Determination of whether parents may decide *whether* to educate their children does not end the inquiry, however. Parents also have an interest in determining *what* their children will be taught. Parents' rights to oversee the education of their children was recognized by the Supreme Court first in 1923 in a case that questioned the state's policy limiting the teaching of a foreign language to children who had completed eighth grade (*Meyer v. Nebraska*, 1923). Although the Court held that the constitutional protection of a parent's liberty to bring up children applied to the content of the school curriculum, it recognized that such parental rights sometimes must be limited in order to preserve state interests.

More recently, the issue of controlling educational content has focused on free speech and disciplinary practices rather than directly on academic subject matter (Friedman, 1992). For example, in a Baltimore case, the court found that the introduction of sex education into the public school curriculum did not violate the constitutional prohibition against the establishment of religion, but instead could be considered "quite simply as a public health measure" (*Cornwell v. State Board of Education*, 1969, p. 344). By contrast, student-led prayer at a high school football game has been held to be violative of the First Amendment's compulsory separation of church and state (*Santa Fe Independent School District v. Doe*, 2000).

Although parents are required to provide their children with an education, they are allowed some latitude in where that education is provided. The ability of parents to choose private, rather than public, schools for their children has long been settled (*Pierce v. Society of Sisters*, 1925), although questions remain in many states about the nature of "approved" private schools. The debate centers on home schooling (see Baker, 1988) and proposals to allow parents to use public funds (through school vouchers) to purchase education in the setting of their choice (see Tweedie, 1989).

Although the level of parental involvement that is permitted or required in curricular decisions about their children is unsettled as a general matter, the answer is clear in regard to special education (see Hodapp, in Vol. 1 of this *Handbook*). The Education for All Handicapped Children Act of 1975 (originally titled the Education of the Handicapped Act and now known in modified form as the Individuals with Disabilities Education Act [IDEA]) establishes elaborate procedures for parental involvement in establishment of individual educational plans (IEPs) for their children with disabilities and for parental appeals in cases of disputes with school authorities about the content of IEPs.

Appeals are infrequent (Clune and Van Pelt, 1985), however, and the legal structure for parental involvement often does not translate into actual involvement (Tweedie, 1989, pp. 414–415):

> In most cases, parental rights in special education do not significantly change school officials' approaches to decision making . . . . Parental rights "work" only for the small number of children whose parents participate assertively and knowledgeably in IEP meetings and hearings.

In short, in a professionalized, bureaucratized environment, planning and decision making are apt to take place with minimal parental involvement and little generalized change in ways of doing business. The history of IDEA suggests that this principle applies even when there is an elaborate, judicially affirmed statutory scheme for parental involvement, at least when allocation of public resources is affected.

Although parental rights often have been hollow in the enforcement of positive rights (entitlements to government services), the force of parental rights in the educational context may be greater in regard to negative rights (freedom from governmental intrusion). IDEA's statutory and regulatory structure for parental approval of pupil assessments and control of information generated in that process are mimicked by more general provisions in federal law for protection of student and family privacy (see, e.g., *Merriken v. Cressman*, 1973; Family Educational Rights and Privacy Act of 1974 [commonly known as the Buckley amendment] and the Hatch amendment thereto).

Requirements for parental consent to testing and release of personal information probably are honored generally because they require little investment of resources and because they can be actualized in routine bureaucratic procedures (i.e., obtaining parents' signatures on forms). This fact should not be overgeneralized, though. Although some protection of negative rights is operational in education, compulsory school attendance by its nature involves massive (even if justified) restrictions on student and parental liberty and rampant opportunities to pierce the veil of family privacy. Essentially, compulsory attendance laws require parents to submit to state authority as their children are plucked from the family environment and parental influence and subjected to state-controlled indoctrination (or to forfeit their economic interests—if they can—to fund private education). To use a relatively benign example of intrusion into family privacy, consider the potential disclosures of private family matters when students are asked to write essays describing their summer vacations (see Melton, 1992).

The de facto limitations on parental authority in education are rendered stark when one remembers that school staff historically have been viewed as acting in the place of parents (*in loco parentis*) and thus temporarily assuming authority reserved for parents in other contexts. Thus, schools are free to exercise disciplinary practices disapproved by parents as long as such practices are intended to protect an educational environment and not obviously arbitrarily applied (see, e.g., *Goss v. Lopez*, 1975). The Supreme Court has held that even corporal punishment is constitutionally permissible when it "is reasonably necessary for the proper education and discipline of the child" (*Ingraham v. Wright*, 1977, p. 670), even when parents have objected to the practice.

Parental rights and obligations to discipline children.   Outside the public school context, parents have broad discretion in fulfilling their duty to provide guidance and discipline for their children. The law generally is not involved in parents' daily exercise of control over their children, but two separate but related types of "failures" can bring parents into direct confrontation with the legal system. Court jurisdiction can be invoked when parents fail to control either the public behavior of their children or their own behavior in the course of disciplining their children.

In considering juvenile justice, the legal system may become involved with families whose children misbehave even if that misbehavior does not constitute actual crime. Historically, the legal system rendered identical treatment to children whose behavior was considered "criminal," as it did to status offenders whose behavior was considered "illegal" only because of their age (Note, 1974). Minors whose only offense was staying out late, disobeying parents, running away, being truant from school, or being "incorrigible" were subjected to the same juvenile proceedings and subsequent treatment alternatives, including incarceration, as those who had been violent. Although the Juvenile Justice and Delinquency Prevention Act of 1974 limited the use of incarceration as a disposition in status offense cases, status offenders still typically are subject to the jurisdiction of juvenile and family courts.

It is noteworthy that parents themselves often are the complainants in status offense cases. In such instances, parents use the courts to provide additional authority to assist them in their efforts to socialize their children. In effect, parents and state unite against—although in the interests of—the child. The ability of courts to resolve such family problems is questionable, however, and some states have altered their status offense statutes to make use of such jurisdiction a last resort contingent on trials of other family services (e.g., N.J. Rev. Stat. §§ 2A:4A-76–2A:4A-87 [establishing "juvenile–family crisis intervention" system]).

When law violations (delinquent offenses) are alleged, the procedures used in juvenile courts are generally comparable with those in adult criminal cases. Indeed, over the course of the past decade, a sizable majority of states have changed their laws so as to increase the number of juveniles subjected to adult court jurisdiction (Beschle, 1999). However, those children subjected to juvenile court jurisdictions often lack some of the rights available to adult defendants (e.g., the right to a jury trial; see *McKeiver v. Pennsylvania*, 1971), and the role of parents results in some unusual considerations. For example, *Gault* (*In re* Gault, 1966) requires notice of the charge to the juvenile *and* his or her parents.

The significance of parental involvement becomes apparent in the juvenile process, even at the initial points of investigation and interrogation. Although the Fourth Amendment applies to juveniles as well as to adults, juveniles' dependent status raises questions about their authority to exercise control over property in school lockers (see *New Jersey v. T.L.O.*, 1985) and their parent-owned home. Weinreb (1974, p. 60), for example, made the following comment:

> It does not startle us that a parent's consent to a search of the living room in the absence of his minor child is given effect; but we should not allow the police to rely on the consent of the child to bind the parent. The common sense of the matter is that the host or parent has not surrendered his privacy of place in the living room to the discretion of the guest or child; rather, the latter have privacy of place there in the discretion of the former.

After a suspect has been taken into custody, police generally question him or her about the alleged offense. Although the Supreme Court has held that validity of juvenile respondents' waiver of the right to silence must be seen in the light of the totality of the circumstances (*Fare v. Michael C.*, 1979), research has shown juveniles to be both more likely to waive their rights and less likely to do so competently than adults (Grisso, 1980, 1981). Responding to these facts, some courts have treated a juvenile's request to see a parent as tantamount to an adult defendant's request for legal counsel (see, e.g., *People v. Burton*, 1971) and thus as invoking the right to silence under *Miranda v. Arizona* (1966). Others have required or strongly encouraged the presence of a parent during interrogation of juveniles (see Grisso, 1981, pp. 164–165, and citations therein). Such a requirement may be hollow protection, however, in view of evidence that parents often encourage their children to confess and that waivers of rights by juveniles are no less frequent when their parents are present (Grisso, 1981).

Parents also may be de facto adversaries of their children in juvenile court in other ways. For example, juvenile respondents may be kept in detention before an adjudication hearing if parents are unwilling or unable to accept them back into the home. An extreme example occurred in one urban juvenile court in which the practice was to detain status offenders with bail set at $1, payable only by a parent.

Although such power is used infrequently, courts do have authority to hold parents responsible, at least in part, for the misbehavior of their children. Such authority to prosecute parents arises in four ways. First, most juvenile codes give courts authority to order particular parental actions as part of the disposition of a juvenile case (e.g., Tex. Fam. Code Ann. § 54.041(a)(1)). Parents can be held in contempt of court for failure to comply with such an order (e.g., to participate in counseling).

Second, most states permit prosecution of parents for contributing to the delinquency of a minor if their actions caused or tended to cause such misbehavior (e.g., La. Rev. Stat. § 14:92). Such laws may be applied, for example, if parents involve their children in activities (e.g., gambling, consuming alcoholic beverages, or prostitution) that are illegal, at least for minors.

Third, parents may be civilly liable for torts (civil wrongs) committed by their children (e.g., Cal. Civ. Code § 1714.1). Parental liability laws reverse the common-law presumption that children, rather than their parents, are liable for their own torts. The low maximum limits of compensation (sometimes as low as $250) in such statutes serve as evidence that parental liability laws are not intended primarily to provide restitution to the victims, whose losses often far exceed such amounts. Instead, parental liability laws are intended to curb delinquency by holding parents responsible and to place the burden for any losses on the parents rather than directly on the victims of crime (Geis and Binder, 1991). Despite the widespread existence of such laws, they are applied rarely, perhaps because the parents of many young offenders are no more capable than their children of compensating victims for losses.

Fourth, states are attempting to hold parents directly responsible for status and delinquent offenses committed by their children. Unlike civil parental liability laws, whose remedies are confined to financial remuneration, the newer parental responsibility laws criminalize parents' failure to control the conduct of their children, thus subjecting parents to criminal sanction (e.g., Street Terrorism Enforcement and Prevention Act). "Parental responsibility laws rest on the common legal presumption that the child's delinquent behavior . . . is a consequence of poor parenting" (Humm, 1991, p. 1133). In essence, such laws hold that if a child commits a crime, the parent has committed a crime (Geis and Binder, 1991).

Primarily through newspaper accounts, the general public is becoming aware of "statutes [that] do not punish parents *for* their children's acts but *because* of the acts" (Weinstein, 1991, p. 867). We read about parents being fined or incarcerated—or at least threatened with such sanctions—for their children's chronic truancy, unlawful use of a firearm, and participation in gang-related crimes. Reduction of economic benefits as a result of such behavior also has become a plank in some welfare reform platforms.

Unfortunately, although parental responsibility laws may highlight when a parent has not met society's parenting expectations, they do not delineate what a parent should do in carrying out the socializing functions of parenthood. Little recognition is given to the realities of controlling the behavior of children as they grow older and come under the influence of many sources, other than parents (Humm, 1991, p. 1160). Even in the absence of scholarly or research evidence for what constitutes "good parenting," courts may be treading on areas of family privacy and discretion and establishing standards for childrearing when heretofore they have been reluctant to do so.

Parental responsibility laws have been criticized on a variety of additional grounds, including vagueness (Humm, 1991; Parsley, 1991; Weinstein, 1991), imposition of harsher penalties on accessories (parents) than on principals (children) (Humm, 1991; Weinstein, 1991), and disregard for due process rights of parents (Weinstein, 1991). Humm (1991, p. 1160) has attacked the basic premise of the statutes:

> Parental responsibility laws symbolize the frustration of a nation which does not know how to cope with the problems of its youth. Unable to contain juvenile violence and crime, legislators have begun to fashion vaguely written laws which grant sweeping authority to police and prosecutors to intervene in the affairs of the family.

In short, although the law still seldom punishes parents for their children's misdeeds, public discussion of such measures now is commonplace. In effect, juvenile misbehavior is being conceptualized as a family problem—the product of parental irresponsibility—rather than a social one.

There are myriad factors that influence children's development and shape them into adults. The law accords parents a central role in the processes through which these factors are given force. Formal education figures prominently in the lives of most children. Therefore, it is unsurprising that parents retain considerable decision making authority as regards their children's formal education. Informal education (i.e., education of children that occurs in less formal settings) also is important. Thus, parents possess considerable legal latitude in their efforts to rear their children in accordance with the parents' own values. Even when the state *must* intervene—as does the juvenile justice system—parents still occupy a role of relative centrality.

CONCLUSIONS

The state has a compelling interest in the welfare of its youngest citizens. The state is concerned about both the status of children *qua* children and the status of children *qua* future adults. Childhood experience affects directly not only the child but also the adult the child will become. Thus, the laws and policies relating to childhood are oriented at once to the present and to the future.

As important as nurturing "citizens" is, the state cannot rear its children. To do so would intrude excessively into the lives of children and their families. Moreover, however successful such a practice might be in inculcating the values of society as a whole, the individual values and mores of particular families would be lost—and with them much of the richness and diversity that make us who we are as a people. Consequently, the responsibility of parenting is left appropriately to parents. However, because the interests at stake are so stark, it is perhaps unsurprising that government regulates parenthood, childhood, and family life more generally.

Although reference has been made to *parenthood*, *childhood*, and *family* as if they were patently obvious constructs, the law does not leave these matters to chance. Thus, the law defines who are a family and prescribes the corollary rights and obligations that attach to the respective roles (e.g., unwed fathers and noncustodial parents). The law delineates not only who provides support but also who may receive it (e.g., natural children and stepchildren), for how long (e.g., disabled adult offspring), and for what purpose (e.g., postsecondary education). These laws reflect the kind of variability that one would expect to find when canvassing the product of over 50 different sovereigns struggling with and seeking to balance complex, significant, and often competing interests.

Despite the varying permutations of legal interests and approaches thereto that dot the landscape of child and family law, some consistent themes emerge. It is in the interest of the state and arguably everyone involved that children be kept alive and healthy. Consequently, laws that ostensibly maximize the outcome of treatment decision making are in place (e.g., parental consent laws and minor consent laws), and other laws may be invoked when the former fail (e.g., statutes providing for removal from the home for medical neglect). These laws dovetail nicely with statutes that require more generalized care in the form of provision of food, shelter, and clothing.

The provision of education to children is another consistent theme across all jurisdictions. Education is regarded as essential not only to the cultivation of self-sufficient and productive citizens, but also to the promotion of respect for others and the law—all of which are acute concerns of the state and fellow citizens. As a result, governments mandate school attendance but accord some respect to parental decisions regarding what, where, and how long students must learn. This is especially so where parents have demonstrated that alternative educational approaches are equally efficacious in furthering state interests (e.g., *Wisconsin v. Yoder*, 1972).

No educational strategy, however, is guaranteed to further the interests of the state or anyone else. Some individuals either do not learn or do not embrace the values of the larger society. As is the case with treatment decision making, the law has a backup—the juvenile justice system. When parents, for whatever reason, cannot regulate the conduct of their children within certain boundaries, the juvenile justice system stands ready to supplant parental authority with the state's police power and/or the state's own parental powers (i.e., *parens patriae*). And in some states the backup has a backup. If punitive sanctions against children fail, punitive sanctions may be imposed against parents (parental responsibility laws).

Regulation of childhood, parenthood, and family life, as the preceding discussion makes clear, is extensive. However, the law is self-limiting to a considerable degree. Previously we mentioned governments' obligation to refrain from intruding excessively into the private lives of families. Government interests must be weighed against parental autonomy and privacy. The need for good citizens is pitted against "the right to be let alone" (*Olmstead v. U.S.*, 1928, p. 478). What we call "parenting" hangs in the balance.

REFERENCES

Adoption and Safe Families Act of 1997, Pub. L. No. 105-89, 111 Stat. 2115 (1997) (codified in scattered sections of 42 U.S.C. [LEXIS, 2000, through 106–228, with a gap of 106–224]).

American Law Institute. (1934). *Restatement of the law of torts.* St. Paul, MN: American Law Institute Publishers.

Baker, J. S. (1988). Parent-centered education. *Notre Dame Journal of Law, Ethics, and Public Policy, 3,* 535–561.

Bartlett, K. T. (1988). Re-expressing parenthood. *Yale Law Journal, 98,* 293–334.

Behm, L. L. (1999). Legal, moral and international perspectives on surrogate motherhood: The call for a uniform regulatory scheme in the United States. *De Paul Journal of Health Care Law, 2,* 557–603.

Belcher v. Charleston Area Medical Center, 422 S.E.2d 827 (W.Va. 1992).

Bellotti v. Baird, 443 U.S. 622 (1979).

Beschle, D. L. (1999). The juvenile justice counterrevolution: Responding to cognitive dissonance in the law's view of the decision-making capacity of minors. *Emory Law Journal, 48,* 65–105.

Blue v. Blue, 616 A.2d 628 (Pa. 1992).

Brakel, S. J. (1985). Involuntary institutionalization. In S. J. Brakel, J. Parry, and B. A. Weiner (Eds.), *The mentally disabled and the law* (3rd ed., pp. 21–176). Chicago: American Bar Foundation.

Brener, K. (1999). Belle Terre and single-family home ordinances: Judicial perceptions of local government and the presumption of validity. *New York University Law Review, 74,* 447–484.

Brennan, B. C. (1999). Disinheritance of dependent children: Why isn't America fulfilling its moral obligation? *The Quinnipiac Probate Law Journal, 14,* 125–163.

Burlingame, W. V., and Amaya, M. (1985). Psychiatric commitment of children and adolescents: Issues current practices, and clinical impact. In D. H. Schetky and E. P. Benedeek (Eds.), *Emerging issues in child psychiatry and the law* (pp. 229–249). New York: Brunner/Mazel.

Cal. Civ. Code § 1714.1 (Deering, LEXIS through 1999 Sess.).

Cal. Fam. Code § 7611 (Deering, LEXIS through 1999 Sess.).

Cal. Fam. Code § 9005(d) (Deering, LEXIS through 1999 Sess.).

Cal. Pen. Code § 270 (Deering, LEXIS through 1999 Sess.).

Cal. Pen. Code § 273a(b) (Deering, LEXIS through 1999 Sess.).

Cal. Welf. and Inst. Code § 300(b) (Deering, LEXIS through 1999 Sess.).

Carey v. Population Services International, 431 U.S. 678 (1977).

Cebrzynski v. Cebrzynski, 379 N.E.2d 713 (Ill. App. Ct. 1978).

Chambers, D. L. (1984). Rethinking the substantive rules for custody disputes in divorce. *Michigan Law Review, 83,* 477–569.

Childers v. Childers, 575 P. 2d 201 (Wash. 1978).

City of Akron v. Akron Center for Reproductive Health, Inc., 462 U.S. 416 (1983).

City of Ladue v. Horn, 720 S.W.2d 745 (Mo. App. 1986).

Clark, C. M. (1999). Imputing parental income in child support determinations: What price for a child's best interest? *Catholic University Law Review, 49,* 167–200.

Clune, W. H., and Van Pelt, M. H. (1985). A political method of evaluating the Education for all Handicapped Children Act of 1975 and the several gaps of analysis. *Law and Contemporary Problems, 48,* 7–62.

Cornwell v. State Board of Education, 314 F. Supp. 340 (D. Md. 1969).

Craig, T. L. (1998). Establishing the biological rights doctrine to protect unwed fathers in contested adoptions. *Florida State University Law Review, 25,* 391–438.

Desiato v. Abbott, 617 A.2d 678 (N.J. Super. Ct. Ch. Div. 1992).

Dickson, J. H. (1991). The emerging rights of adoptive parents: Substance or specter? *UCLA Law Review, 38,* 917–990.

Doe v. Attorney General, 487 N.W.2d 484 (Mich Ct. App. 1990).

Duncan v. Howard, 918 P.2d 888 (Utah Ct. App. 1996).

Education of All Handicapped Children Act of 1975, Pub. L. No. 94-142, 89 Stat. 773 (1975) (codified as amended at 20 U.S.C.S. §§ 1400–1485 [LEXIS, 2000, through 106–228, with a gap of 106–224]).

Education of the Handicapped Act, Pub. L. No. 91-230, 84 Stat. 121 (1970) (codified as amended at 20 U.S.C. §§ 1400–1491 [LEXIS, 2000, through 106–228, with a gap of 106–224]).

Family Educational Rights and Privacy Act of 1974, 20 U.S.C. § 1232g (LEXIS, 2000, through 106–228, with a gap of 106–224). (See related "Hatch Amendment" infra.).

Fare v. Michael C., 442 U.S. 707 (1979).

Friedman, S. E. (1992). *The law of parent–child relationships: A handbook.* Chicago: American Bar Association.

Garska v. McCoy, 278 S.E.2d 357 (1981).

Geis, G., and Binder, A. (1991). Sins of their children: Parental responsibility for juvenile delinquency. *Notre Dame Journal of Law, Ethics, and Public Policy, 5,* 303–322.

Goldstein, J., Freud, A., and Solnit, A. J. (1973). *Beyond the best interests of the child.* New York: Macmillan.

Goss v. Lopez, 419 U.S. 565 (1975).

Greben, B. L. (1995). Note, determining the role of psychological bonding in New York foster care law. *Cardozo Women's Law Journal, 2,* 173–194.

Gregory, J. D. (1998). Blood ties: A rationale for child visitation by legal strangers. *Washington and Lee Law Review, 55,* 351–402.

Grisso, T. (1980). Juveniles' capacities to waive *Miranda* rights: An empirical analysis. *California Law Review, 68,* 1135–1166.

Grisso, T. (1981). *Juveniles' waiver of rights: Legal and psychological competence.* New York: Plenum.

Halperin-Kaddari, R. (1999). Redefining parenthood. *California Western International Law Journal, 29,* 313–336.

Harris, L. J., Waldrop, K., and Waldrop, L. R. (1990). Making and breaking connections between parents' duty to support and right to control their children. *Oregon Law Review, 69,* 689–739.

Hatch Amendment (to the Family Educational Rights and Privacy Act), 20 U.S.C. § 1232h (LEXIS, 2000, through 106–228, with a gap of 106–224).

Hodgson v. Minnesota, 497 U.S. 417 (1990).

Holder, A. R. (1985). *Legal issues in pediatric and adolescent medicine.* New Haven, CT: Yale University Press.

Humm, S. R. (1991). Criminalizing poor parenting skills as a means to contain violence by and against children. *University of Pennsylvania Law Review, 139,* 1123–1161.

Ill. Rev. Stat. ch. 750, para. 5/510(d) (1999).

Ingraham v. Wright, 430 U.S. 651 (1977).

In re Ackenhausen, 244 La. 730 (1963).

In re Adoption of Baby A and Baby B, 877 P.2d 107 (Or. Ct. App. 1994).

In re Adoption of J.J.B., 894 P.2d 994 (N.M. 1995).

In re Adoption of Paul, 550 N.Y.S.2d 815 (N.Y. Fam. Ct. 1990).

In re Adoption of Tachick, 210 N.W.2d 865 (Wis. 1973).

In re Gault, 387 U.S. 1 (1967).

In re Phillip B., 139 Cal. App.3d 407, 188 Cal. Rptr. 781 (1983).

In re Raquel Marie X., 559 N.E.2d 418 (N.Y. 1990).

In re Roger S., 569 P.2d 1286 (Cal. 1977).

Individuals with Disabilities Education Act, Pub. L. No. 101-476, 104 Stat. 1141 (1990) (codified as amended at 20 U.S.C.S. §§ 1400–1491 [LEXIS, 2000, through 106–228, with a gap of 106–224]).

Jackson-Beeck, M., Schwartz, I. M., and Rutherford, A. (1987). Trends and issues in juvenile confinement for psychiatric and chemical dependency treatment. *International Journal of Law and Psychiatry, 10,* 153–165.

Jhordan C. v. Mary K., 224 Cal. Rptr. 530 (Cal. Ct. App. 1986).

Johnson, S. L. (1987). Parent and child. *American Jurisprudence, 2nd, 59,* 129–279.

Johnson v. Calvert, 851 P.2d 776 (Cal. 1993).

Juvenile Justice and Delinquency Prevention Act of 1974, 42 U.S.C. §§ 5601–5785 (1994 and Supp. 3 1997).

Karin T. v. Michael T., 484 N.Y.S.2d 780 (N.Y. Fam. Ct. 1985).

Katz, S. N., Schroeder, W. A., and Sidman, L. R. (1973). Emancipating our children: Coming of legal age in America. *Family Law Quarterly, 7,* 211–241.

Kost v. Kost, 515 N.W.2d 209 (S.D. 1994).

LaChapelle v. Mitten, 607 N.W. 2d 151 (Minn. App. 2000).

Lehr v. Robertson, 463 U.S. 248 (1983).

Levine, M., Ewing, C. P., and Hager, R. (1987). Juvenile and family mental health law in sociohistorical context. *International Journal of Law and Psychiatry, 10,* 167–184.

Loue, S. (2000). Intimate partner violence: Bridging the gap between law and science. *Journal of Legal Medicine, 21,* 1–34.

La. Rev. Stat. § 14:92 (Westlaw through 1999 Reg. Sess.).

McKeiver v. Pennsylvania, 403 U.S. 528 (1971).

Melton, G. B. (1984). Family and mental hospitals as myths: Civil commitment of minors. In N. D. Reppucci, L. A. Weithorn, E. P. Mulvey, and J. Monahan (Eds.), *Children, mental health, and the law* (pp. 151–167). Beverly Hills, CA: Sage.

Melton, G. B. (1992). Respecting boundaries: Minors, privacy, and behavioral research. In B. Stanley and J. E. Sieber (Eds.), *Social research on children and adolescents* (pp. 65–87). Newbury Park, CA: Sage.

Melton, G. B., Lyons, P. M., Jr., and Spaulding, W. J. (1998). *No place to go: The civil commitment of minors.* Lincoln: University of Nebraska Press.

Merriken v. Cressman, 364 F. Supp. 913 (E.D. Pa. 1973).

Meyer, D. D. (1999). Family ties: Solving the constitutional dilemma of the faultless father. *Arizona Law Review, 41,* 753–846.

Meyer v. Nebraska, 262 U.S. 390 (1923).

Michael H. v. Gerald D., 491 U.S. 110 (1989).

Minow, M. (1991). Redefining families: Who's in and who's out? *Colorado Law Review, 62,* 269–285.

Miranda v. Arizona, 384 U.S. 436 (1966).

Mo. Ann. Stat. § 452.340.5 (LEXIS through all 1999 legislation).

Mnookin, R. H., and Weisberg, D. K. (1989). *Child, family and state: Problems and materials on children and the law* (2nd ed.). Boston: Little, Brown.

Neely, R. (1984). The primary caretaker rule: Child custody and the dynamics of greed. *Yale Law and Policy Review, 3,* 168–186.

Newburgh v. Arrigo, 443 A.2d 1031 (N.J. 1982).

N. H. Rev. Stat. Ann. § 546-A:2 (Westlaw through 1999 Reg. Sess.).

N. J. Rev. Stat. § 2A: 4A-76 (1987).

New Jersey v. T.L.O., 469 U.S. 325 (1985).

Nolfo v. Nolfo, 188 A.D.2d 451 (N.Y. App. Div. 1992).

Note. (1974). Ungovernability: The unjustifiable jurisdiction. *Yale Law Journal, 83,* 1383–1409.

Note. (1991). Looking for a family resemblance: The limits of the functional approach to the legal definition of family. *Harvard Law Review, 104,* 1640–1659.

Ohio v. Akron. Center for Reproductive Health, 497 U.S. 502 (1990).

Olmstead v. U.S., 277 U.S. 438 (1928).

Or. Rev. Stat. § 109.103 (Westlaw through 1997 Sess.).

Painter v. Bannister, 140 N.W.2d 152 (Wis. 1966).

Parham v. J. R., 442 U.S. 584 (1979).

Park v. Park, 309 N.W.2d 827 (S.D. 1981).

Parsley, K. J. (1991). Constitutional limitations on state power to hold parents criminally liable for the delinquent acts of their children. *Vanderbilt Law Review, 44,* 441–472.

People v. Burton, 6 Cal.3d 375 (1971).

Pierce v. Society of Sisters, 268 U.S. 510 (1925).

Planned Parenthood of Central Missouri v. Danforth, 428 U.S. 52 (1976).

Planned Parenthood of Southeastern Pennsylvania v. Casey, 505 U.S. 833 (1992).

Rodham, H. (1973). Children under the law. *Harvard Education Review, 43,* 487–514.

Roe v. Doe, 29 N.Y.2d 188 (1971).

Rhinehart v. Nowlin, 805 P.2d 88, 94 (N.M. Ct. App. 1990).

Rozovsky, F. A. (1984). *Consent to treatment: A practical guide.* Boston: Little, Brown.

San Antonio Independent School District v. Rodriguez, 411 U.S. 1 (1973).

Santa Fe Independent School District v. Doe, 530 U.S. 290 (2000).

Santosky v. Kramer, 455 U.S. 745 (1982).

Schall v. Martin, 467 U.S. 253 (1984).

Schuele, D. (1988–89). Origins and development of the law of parental child support. *Journal of Family Law, 27,* 807–841.

Shoecraft v. Catholic Social Services Bureau, Inc., 385 N.W.2d 448 (Neb. 1986).

Smith, S. H. (1978). Psychological parents versus biological parents: The courts' response to new directions in child custody dispute resolution. *Journal of Family Law, 17,* 545–576.

Stanford v. Kentucky, 492 U.S. 361 (1989).

Stanley v. Illinois, 405 U.S. 645 (1972).

Street Terrorism Enforcement and Prevention Act, Cal. Penal Code §§ 186.20–186.28 (Deering, LEXIS through the 2000 supplement).

Sutton, S. (1999). The real sexual revolution: Posthumously conceived children. *St. John's Law Review, 73,* 857–931.

Tex. Fam. Code Ann. § 12.04(3) (LEXIS through the 2000 supplement).

Tex. Fam. Code Ann. § 54.041(a)(1) (LEXIS through the 2000 supplement).

Tex. Fam. Code Ann. § 151.003 (LEXIS through the 2000 supplement).

Thompson, R. A., Scalora, M. J., Castrianno, L., and Limber, S. P. (1992). Grandparent visitation rights: Emergent psychological and psycholegal issues. In D. K. Kagehiro and D. S. Laufer (Eds.), *Handbook of psychology and law* (pp. 292–317). New York: Springer-Verlag.

Thompson v. Oklahoma, 487 U.S. 815 (1988).

Tinker v. Des Moines Independent School District, 393 U.S. 503 (1969).

Troxel v. Granville, 530 U.S. 57 (2000).

Tweedie, J. (1989). Parental rights and accountability in public education: Special education and choice. *Yale Law and Policy Review, 7,* 396–418.

Uniform Parentage Act, 9B U.L.A. 287, § 4, 298–299 (1973).

Uniform Putative and Unknown Fathers Act, 9B U.L.A. 22 § 1, (1988, Supp. 1990).

Valente, W. D. (1985, Supp. 1989). *Education and law: Public and private* St. Paul, MN: West.

Va. Code Ann. § 54.1-2969(E) (LEXIS through 2000 Reg. Sess.).

Wadlington, W. (1990). *Cases and other materials on domestic relations.* Westbury, NY: Foundation Press.

Wald, P. (1980). Introduction to the juvenile justice process: The rights of children and the rites of passage. In D. H. Schetky and E. P. Benedek (Eds.), *Child psychiatry and the law* (pp. 9–20). New York: Brunner/Mazel.

Wallin v. Wallin, 187 N.W.2d 627 (Minn. 1971).

Wash. Rev. Code § 26.09.100 (LEXIS through Ch. 1 of the 2000 Reg. Sess.).

Wash. Rev. Code § 26.10.160 (3) (LEXIS through Ch. 1 of the 2000 Reg. Sess.).

Weinreb, L. L. (1974). Generalities of the Fourth Amendment. *University of Chicago Law Review, 42*, 47–85.

Weinstein, T. (1991). Visiting the sins of the child on the parent: The legality of criminal parental liability statutes. *Southern California Law Review, 64*, 859–901.

Weithorn, L. A. (1985). Children's capacities for participation in treatment decision-making. In D. H. Schetky and E. P. Benedek (Eds.), *Emerging issues in child psychiatry and the law* (pp. 22–36). New York: Brunner/Mazel.

Weithorn, L. A., and McCabe, M. A. (1988). Legal and other problems in pediatric psychology. In D. K. Routh (Ed.), *Handbook of pediatric psychology* (pp. 567–606). New York: Guilford.

W. Va. Code § 48-2-15 (Westlaw through 1999 2d Ex. Sess.).

Wisconsin v. Yoder, 406 U.S. 205 (1972).

Zinman, D. C. (1992). Father knows best: The unwed father's right to raise his infant surrendered for adoption. *Fordham Law Review, 60*, 971–1001.

Zoski v. Gaines, 260 N.W. 99 (Mich. 1935).

19

Parenting and Public Policy

James Garbarino
Joseph A. Vorrasi
Cornell University
Kathleen Kostelny
Erikson Institute for Advanced Study in Child Development

INTRODUCTION

The quality and character of parenting result in part from the social context in which families operate. One important feature of this social context is public policy. This chapter examines several public policy issues that affect parenting. It does so within an ecological framework that arises from efforts to understand the interaction of human biological and psychological systems with human social and cultural systems. The issues discussed include policies regarding family planning, state responsibility for children, the role of neighborhoods in family support, economic conditions affecting families, and resiliency.

Parents face different opportunities and risks in rearing their children because of parental and child mental and physical makeup and because of the social environment they inhabit as a family (Garbarino and Bedard, 2001). Moreover, the social environment affects parenting through its impact on the very physical makeup of the child (and the parent). These influences constitute one important factor within the human ecology and form one of the root concepts in the ecological perspective, *social biology*. In contrast to sociobiology, which emphasizes a genetic origin for social behavior, social biology concentrates on the social origins of biological phenomena, including the impact of economic conditions and social policy on brain growth and physical development (e.g., environmental lead poisoning of children that leads to mental retardation and/or behavioral problems).

These social biological effects are often negative (e.g., the impact of poverty and famine on children that leads to mental retardation, or the effect of industrial carcinogens that have mutagenic consequences), but they can be positive as well (e.g., intrauterine surgery or nutritional therapy for a fetus with a genetic disorder). When these positive and negative social influences operate in psychological or sociological terms, we refer to them as sociocultural opportunities and risks, and they constitute an important force in shaping the parenting agenda.

Thus, when we refer to "opportunities for development" that affect parenting, we mean interpersonal and institutional relationships (with kith and kin, professionals, neighbors, community authorities, and so forth) in which parents find material, emotional, and social encouragement compatible with their needs and capacities as they exist at a specific point in their parenting career. For each parent (as for each child), the best fit must be worked out through experience, within some very broad guidelines of basic human needs, and then renegotiated as development proceeds and situations change.

This complex pattern of interactions has profound implications for understanding parenting, and research documenting the effects of "accumulated risk" provides a good starting point for understanding these implications. Sameroff, Seifer, Barocas, Zax, and Greenspan (1987) reported that the IQ scores of 4-year-old children are related to the number of familial and social risk factors (e.g., punitive home environment, parental substance abuse, father absence, and poverty) present in their lives. But this research reveals that the relation is not simply additive. The average IQ of children with zero, one, or two risk factors was above 115, and IQ did not differ significantly across these three groups. With the addition of a third and fourth risk factor, however, the average IQ score dropped precipitously to nearly 90, with relatively little further decrement as risk accumulated further (i.e., 5 to 8 risk factors). Additional work by Dunst and Trivetter (1992) underscores the idea that understanding developmental opportunities helps to explain the variance in outcomes left unaccounted for in models that simply address risk. Using an approach similar to that used by Sameroff et al. (1987), these authors included in the developmental equation the counterpart opportunity measure for each of the original eight risk factors (e.g., a present and highly supportive father as the opportunity counterpart to an absent father). This reconceptualization has important implications for research, policy, and practice because it validates an "accumulation of opportunity" model. Such a model suggests that risk factors may be neutralized or at least partially offset by introducing opportunity factors into other realms of the child's life, even when patterns of risk are thought to be impervious to intervention (Vorrasi and Garbarino, 2000). An ecological perspective on parenting makes good sense empirically, theoretically, and programmatically.

"Windows of opportunity" for intervention on behalf of parents appear repeatedly across the life course, and what may be a critical threat at one point may be benign or even developmentally enhancing at another. For example, Elder's (1974) analyses of children of the Great Depression (i.e., the American economic crisis of the 1930s) revealed that the impact was mediated by parents: Children whose families were unaffected by unemployment and significant income loss showed little effect on their social, emotional, and vocational development. But when parents of young children were hit hard by the economic crisis, the development of those children suffered in terms of self-esteem, relationship formation, vocational aspirations, and academic achievement. In contrast, some adolescents—particularly daughters—benefited from the fact that parental unemployment often meant special opportunities for enhanced responsibility and status (e.g., as caregivers and breadwinners) in the family. Consequently, it was not uncommon for these youth to show patterns of greater competence and achievement.

Analyzing research by Rutter and others, Bronfenbrenner (1986) confirmed that the stress of urban life associated with family adversity is most negative and potent for the development of young children (although such adversity may even stimulate some adolescents who have had a positive childhood). One important theme in current and future research seeking to illuminate the impact of public policy on parenting is to improve our understanding of the circumstances and conditions that constitute challenges and adversity that are growth inducing in contrast to those that are debilitating. A second important theme is to recognize that the "interests" of parents and children are not necessarily synonymous.

Risks to parenting can come both from direct threats and from the absence of normal, expectable opportunities. The experience of homelessness is one example of a sociocultural risk factor that has profound implications for parenting. "Home" implies unconditional permanence, a lack of contingency between behavior and acceptance. When you have a home, you have a place to go, no matter what. You have a home when there is a place with which you are connected permanently, a place that endures and represents you. We note here the similarity between this concept of home and the analogous political concept of "homeland" in a sense that one is part of a nation, that one belongs somewhere politically. This essentially ideological phenomenon of having a political home may serve as a powerful force in parenting. For example, Punamaki (1987) reported that a strong sense of being "at home" in the community sustains parenting under extremely stressful circumstances, such as are found among Palestinians living in refugee camps in the midst of chronic political violence.

We need to study the hypothesis that both home and homeland may be important resources in identity formation in childhood and adolescence, and a childhood lack of either or both may lead to mental health problems associated with alienation, conduct disorder, rootlessness, violence, and depression in adolescence—problems that become intergenerational when they extend into adulthood. Gilligan (1991, 1996) explored just such an analysis in his study of the relations between shame (linked to negative personal and social identity) and violence. Individuals and groups who are ashamed of who they are (e.g., made to feel this way because of personal rejection or racism) are likely to express that negative self-definition in self- and socially destructive acts.

Understanding the experience of home may help sort out the divergent psychological impact and character of experiences that appear similar on the surface—such as being an immigrant and a refugee, or having "moved" and being displaced. With millions of families worldwide experiencing homelessness, this is a crucial issue for study (see Garbarino, Kostelny, and Dubrow, 1991a). Understanding this or any other such issue depends on bringing to bear an ecological perspective on development. Outlining such a perspective is our next task.

AN ECOLOGICAL PERSPECTIVE ON PARENTING

An ecological perspective is a systems approach to human development. It examines the environment at four levels beyond the individual organism—from the micro to the macro (Bronfenbrenner, 1979, 1986; Garbarino et al., 1992). Viewing parents only in terms of organismic and interpersonal dynamics precludes an understanding of the many other avenues of influence that might be open to us as helpers, or that might be topics of study for us as scientists. This message provides a crucial guide to research on intervention and program evaluation and reflects the operation of systems of personality, family, community, economy, culture, and ideology. The starting point for this analysis is the microsystem.

Microsystems

Microsystems are the immediate settings in which individuals develop (e.g., family, school, and workplace). The shared experiences that occur in each setting provide a record of the microsystem and offer some clues to its future. Microsystems evolve and develop much as do individuals themselves from forces generated both within and without. The quality of a microsystem depends on its ability to sustain and enhance development and to provide a context that is emotionally validating and developmentally challenging. This, in turn, depends on its capacity to operate in what Vygotsky (1986) called "the zone of proximal development," the distance between what the child can accomplish alone—the level of actual development—and what the child can do when helped—the level of potential development.

Children can handle (and need) more than infants. Adolescents can handle (and need) more than children. We measure the social richness of an individual's life by the availability of enduring, reciprocal, multifaceted relationships that emphasize playing, working, and loving. And we do that measuring over time, because microsystems, like individuals, change over time.

The "same" daycare center is very different in June from what it was in September for the "same" infants who, of course, are themselves not the same as they were at the beginning of the year. The setting of the family, as the firstborn child experiences it, is different from that experienced by subsequent offspring. Naturally, children themselves change and develop, as do others in the setting. It is also important to remember that our definition speaks of the microsystem as a pattern experienced by the developing person. Individuals influence their microsystems, and those microsystems influence them in turn.

Mesosystems

Mesosystems are relationships between microsystems. These links themselves form a system. We measure richness of a mesosystem in the number and quality of its connections. One example is the connection between an infant's daycare group and her or his home. Do staff visit the child at home? Do the child's parents know her or his friends at daycare? Do parents of children at the center know each other?

A second example concerns the connection between the hospital and the home for a chronically ill child. What role do the parents play in the hospital regime? Do the same health care professionals who see the child in the hospital visit the home? Is the child the only one to participate in both? If she or he is the only "linkage," the mesosystem is weak, and that weakness may place the child at risk. Research suggests that the strength of the mesosystem linking the setting in which an intervention is implemented with the settings in which the individual spends the most significant time is crucial to the long-term effectiveness of the intervention and to the maintenance of its effects (Whittaker, Garbarino, and Associates, 1983).

Exosystems

Exosystems are settings that have a bearing on the development of children, but in which children do not play a direct role. For most children, the key exosystems include the workplace of their parents and those centers of power such as school boards, church councils, and planning commissions that make decisions affecting children's day-to-day life. Note that the concept of an exosystem illustrates the projective nature of the ecological perspective, for the same setting that is an exosystem for a child may be a microsystem for the parent, and vice versa. Thus, one form of intervention may aim at transforming exosystems into microsystems, such as by initiating greater participation in important institutions for isolated, disenfranchised, and powerless clients, for example, by getting parents to visit the family daycare facility or by creating on-site daycare at the workplace.

In exosystem terms, both risk and opportunity come about in two ways. The first is when the parents or other significant adults in a child's life are treated in a way that impoverishes (risk) or enhances (opportunity) their behavior in the microsystems they share with children. Examples include elements of the parents' work experience that impoverish or enhance family life, such as unemployment, low pay, long or inflexible hours, traveling, or stress on the one hand, and an adequate income, flexible scheduling, an understanding employer, or subsidies for childcare on the other (Bronfenbrenner and Crouter, 1983).

The second way risk and opportunity flow from the exosystem lies in the orientation and content of decisions made in those settings that affect the day-to-day experience of children and their families. For example, when the state legislature suspends funding for early intervention programs, it jeopardizes children's development. When public officials expand prenatal health services or initiate specialized daycare in high-risk communities, they increase developmental opportunities for children and reduce risk.

Albee (1980) went so far as to identify powerlessness as the primary factor leading to impaired development and mental disability. Powerlessness plays a large role in determining the fate of groups of individuals via public policy and is important when considering individual cases, such as whether or not parents have the "pull" to get a medically vulnerable child enrolled in a special treatment program. In many cases, risk and opportunity at the exosystem level are essentially political matters.

One of the most useful aspects of the ecological approach is its ability to highlight situations in which the actions of people with whom the individual has no direct contact significantly affect their development. The following example illustrates the relation between social policy and individual child development. Because of a leveraged corporate takeover, a board of directors decides to shift operations from one plant to another. Hundreds of families with young children are forced to move to new locations. Local services are underfunded in a period of escalating demand, and many parents lose their jobs and health insurance. The quality of prenatal and well-baby care declines, and infant mortality increases. This is a classic illustration of an exosystem effect, and it highlights the fact that exosystem events may establish much of the agenda for day-to-day early intervention on behalf of children at risk.

At this point, it is worth emphasizing that the ecological perspective forces us to consider the concept of risk beyond the narrow confines of individual personality and family dynamics. In the ecological approach, both are "causes" of the child's developmental patterns and "reflections" of broader sociocultural forces. We can make good use of the aphorism "If the only tool you have is a hammer you tend to treat every problem as if it were a nail." Inflexible loyalty to a specific focus (e.g., the parents) is often a stumbling block to effective intervention. However, the obverse must also be considered: "If you define every problem as a nail, the only tool you will seek is a hammer." Viewing children at risk only in terms of organismic and interpersonal dynamics precludes an understanding of the many other avenues of influence. This message provides a crucial guide to our discussions of early intervention and social policy affecting parenting.

Macrosystems

Meso- and exosystems are set within the broad ideological, demographic, and institutional patterns of a particular culture or subculture. These are the macrosystems that serve as the master "blueprints" for the ecology of human development. These blueprints reflect a people's shared assumptions about how things should be done as well as the institutions that represent those assumptions. Macrosystems are ideology incarnate. Thus, we contrast social blueprints that rest on fundamental institutional expressions, such as a "collective versus individual orientation." Religion provides a classic example of the macrosystem concept because it involves both a definition of the world and a set of institutions reflecting that definition—both a theology and a set of roles, rules, buildings, and programs.

Macrosystems refer to the general organization of the world as it is and as it might be. Historical change demonstrates that the "might be" is quite real, and occurs either through evolution (many individual actions guided by a common reality) or revolution (dramatic change introduced by a small cadre of decision makers). The Iranian revolution of 1978 to 1979, for example, overturned a "modernizing" society and embodied a changed institutional and ideological landscape that shaped the most basic experiences of childhood. Current efforts to "modernize" in China include a massive shift from "collective reward" to "private initiative" as the dominating economic force. More directly relevant still is the one-child policy, which has altered the demography of the Chinese family and appears to be altering the social fabric at each level of the human ecology (Schell, 1982).

In the United States, the increasing concentration of high-risk families in a geographically concentrated underclass (Garbarino, 1999; Lemann, 1986; Wilson, 1987) is exerting dramatic influences on the need and the prognosis for early interventions. Pockets of marked vulnerability show poverty and infant mortality rates many times the average found in unafflicted communities. For early intervention services to be plausible in such high-risk ecological niches, they must target "ecological transformation" as the program goal (Garbarino and Kostelny, 1994a).

For example, the Beethoven Project put forth by Chicago's Center for Successful Child Development is an effort to prevent developmental delays among an entire birth cohort in a public housing project (i.e., all the children born in 1 year who live in the same school district). Employing home health visitors, early developmental screening, prenatal health care and parent education, job training for parents, infant daycare, child abuse prevention programming, Head Start participation, and other transforming and supportive services, this program successfully increased "school readiness" for students entering first grade (Barclay-McLaughlin, 1987). When such comprehensive efforts are conducted in the context of thoughtful evaluation research, they can serve as the kind of transforming experiments that advance an ecologically valid science of early intervention (Bronfenbrenner, 1979).

An ecological perspective has much to contribute to the process of formulating, evaluating, and understanding social policy. It gives us a kind of social map for navigating a path through the complexities of programming. It helps us see the relations—potential and actual—among programs: how, for example, some programs are complementary whereas others may be competitive. It aids us in seeing the full range of alternative conceptualizations of problems affecting children and points us in the direction of multiple strategies for intervention. It provides a framework to use in thinking about what is happening and what to do when faced with developmental problems and social pathologies that afflict children. It does this by asking us always to consider the micro-, meso-, exo-, and macrosystem dimensions of developmental phenomena and interventions. It constantly suggests the possibility that context shapes causal relations. It always tells us "it depends" and stimulates an attmept to find out "on what."

Consider the case of child abuse. We need to look to the community that establishes laws and policies about child abuse as well as to the families that offer a powerful definition of reality for the next generation. We also should look to the culture that defines physical force as an appropriate form of discipline in early childhood. But we must also look within the individual, as a psychological system affected by conscious and changing roles, and unconscious needs and motives, to know why and how each individual adjusts in ways that generate conflict. In addition, we must also look *across* systems to see how the several systems involved (the family, social services, social network, and economy) adjust to new conditions.

FAMILY PLANNING

Public policy affects parenting most fundamentally through its influence on who is born in the first place. Throughout history, all known societies have taken steps to control fertility, whether by controlling the minimum age of marriage, by specifying the number of wives a man can have, by encouraging longer periods of breast feeding, or by implicitly or explicitly permitting abortion (David, 1994). *Pronativist* policies seek to increase the number of births in a given society by providing financial incentives for couples who have large numbers of children and by restricting access to contraception and abortion. *Antinativist* policies seek to limit the number of children born by encouraging abortion, by proliferating contraceptives, and by providing incentives for small families and penalties for large ones. The Chinese one-child policy is an extreme example of an antinativist approach to public policy.

In the 1970s, the Chinese government limited population growth by enforcing a policy of one child per family. This policy was implemented through incentives and penalties. For example, families who made a public commitment to a one-child family were given preferential treatment in social services and economic benefits programs. Conversely, those who gave birth to a second child saw their benefits reduced or taken away. The government mounted massive public information ("propaganda") campaigns to support the policy, and in some cases strong social pressures were brought to bear on women who conceived a second child and did not voluntarily seek an abortion.

The outcomes of this policy are difficult to determine given the secretiveness of Chinese society and the limited demographic data available. It does seem, however, that the bias in favor of males led many families to refuse "wasting" their allocation on girls (Garbarino, 1992b). As a result, significant numbers of female children were either hidden or killed after their birth. The impact of this on parenting is unknown, as is the changed composition of the Chinese population to include predominantly male children. The long-term "nuclearization" of the Chinese family is clear—sibling, cousin, aunt, and uncle roles diminished—but its impact on parenting remains largely unexplored.

Additionally, policies regarding abortion and contraception have a broader impact on parenting. Their clearest effect is to alter the number of "unwanted" and "unplanned" children born, and research suggests that these unwanted children (i.e., those born to mothers who were denied abortions) are born into significant emotional and psychological disadvantage (Dytrych, 1992). A European study tracked the negative developmental outcomes for children whose mothers were denied abortions for policy reasons (David, Dytrych, Matejcek, and Schüller, 1988). This study provides an important resource in any discussion of the effects of abortion and family-planning policy on parenting, because it demonstrates that the impact of being born unwanted intensifies over time, with differences continuing to emerge well into adulthood (David, 1992).

Additional support for the negative effects of being born unwanted comes from studies demonstrating the impact of acceptance and rejection on children. Unwanted children manifest impaired development that extends into adolescence, and it seems these effects are due to the adverse parenting practices of the mothers. Research demonstrates that from culture to culture rejected children are at elevated risk for a whole host of negative behavioral and psychological outcomes, ranging from low-self esteem to stunted moral development to heightened levels of aggressive behavior and violence (Garbarino, Guttman, and Seeley, 1986). Observing this robust association led Rohner (1980) to draw the universal conclusion that rejection is a "psychological malignancy" regardless of cultural context.

Policy can affect nativity through the allocation or denial of resources to those who lack private means to seek abortion. For example, data from Michigan reveal a significant increase in births to young and poor mothers and in "high-risk offspring" in the years immediately following a termination of state funding for abortion in 1988. Examining the data for the period 1987 to 1990 indicates a 27% increase in low-birthweight babies (under 2,500 grams), and a 457% increase in the number of infants born with congenital abnormalities (Garbarino and Kostelny, 1995). In this case, public policy had a direct effect on the number of "medically fragile" children being born, and it seems fair to assume that this combination of high risk, coupled with the presumption that many of these children were unwanted, means a significant increase in the number of families facing very challenging parenting contexts.

PUBLIC RESPONSIBILITY FOR CHILDREN

At the heart of the debate over public responsibility for children is the matter of how and when families are private and how and when they are public (Garbarino, 1996), and this debate is not new. In colonial America, while the family held a central place as society's primary socializing institution, the state played an active role in monitoring and regulating family life. When the surrounding community felt parents were failing to meet their childrearing obligations (i.e., teaching children to read the Bible and preparing them for their adult occupations), they did not hesitate to intervene by placing these children into institutions or foster homes (Moran and Vinovskis, 1992). This became especially true as American ideology embraced individualism and prioritized the rights and needs of individual family members (Chase-Linsdale and Vinovskis, 1992).

Still today, the state plays an important role in setting the parameters for parental responsibility, and in many ways determines the realms in which variation in parenting skill affects child development. For example, state, county, and local governments in the United States bear the responsibility of providing potable water and waste disposal. From a parental perspective, this is *passive prevention* in the sense that it requires no action on the part of parents to protect their children. In contrast, immunization programs are *active prevention* because they require deliberate efforts of parents, typically that they bring the child to a facility that provides the immunization, or at least that they permit the child to be immunized as part of a program at their school or daycare center.

Passive prevention efforts in the form of community water and sewage systems absolve individual parents of the responsibility to provide clean water and dispose of sewage. Thus, variations in child health due to cholera and other water- or sewage-born agents are absent. Requiring immunization for mandatory school enrollment reduces the role of parental initiative, but the fact that less than 100% of young children are immunized attests to the fact that there are costs and casualties associated with anything less than fully passive prevention. The deregulation of television programming aimed at children is another example of how public policy can affect the individual responsibility of parents (Carlsson-Paige and Levin, 1990). Deregulating children's television programming has increased the individual responsibility of parents to monitor and regulate the television viewing of their children, and the growing demand for monitoring technology like the V-chip is evidence that American parents are failing at the task. According to data from the Center for Media Education (1997), by the time the average child completes elementary school, she or he will witness more than 100,000 acts of violence on television, including 8,000 murders, and these numbers double to 200,000 acts of violence and 16,000 murders by the time they complete high school. In many ways *de*regulation has meant *no* regulation.

When government does not assume responsibility for passive prevention measures, we find significant variation in parental behavior linked to a series of predictable family variables (e.g., parents' education, social class, and personal history). Thus, if the government did not assume responsibility for providing potable water and for sewage treatment, we would expect to find substantial variation in child health due to differences in parental skill, motivation, and resources, as we do in the areas of childhood television viewing and to a lesser degree immunization against childhood illnesses.

Variations in state responsibility for children penetrate into many aspects of parenting. For example, in an effort to prevent the international "kidnapping" of children by noncustodial parents, a number of governments now require written consent of both parents prior to issuing a visa for a minor. Australia and Mexico are two examples.

Perhaps the key issue of public responsibility emerges from the following anecdote. A colleague reports that when he moved to the state of Illinois in 1985, he brought with him a 3-year-old daughter and a 3-year-old automobile. The state of Illinois sent a clear message regarding its conception of responsibility. The state required that the car be registered, and it further required that it be inspected on a regular basis and that the driver be licensed to operate it. Illinois also required liability insurance to operate the automobile. The message was clear: Cars are a public matter. With respect to the daughter, however, no messages of public interest were given. She was invisible to the state, at least until she reached the age of 6 and was required to attend school.

Benson, Leffert, Scales, and Blyth (1998) identified three conditions—all of which are influenced by public policy—that contribute to the privatization and isolation of the American family. The first condition pertains to changes in the workforce that undermine the availability of neighborhood adults during the workday. The second includes patterns of social mobility that cause parents and families to enter communities without known or easily accessible support systems. The third and final condition is the national tendency toward civic disengagement. That is, adults are withdrawing from traditional affiliations and memberships that once provided strong networks of support. In the battle between collectivism and individualism, individualism is winning, and social policy reflects this trend. Growing numbers of American families are living in a state of isolated disconnectedness.

POLICIES AFFECTING THE SAFETY OF SOCIAL ENVIRONMENTS FOR PARENTS

Hundreds of thousands of American children face the developmental challenge of living amidst chronic community violence, and evidence suggests that this problem is growing. For example, in the period between 1974 and 1994, the rate of serious assault (potentially lethal assaults with knives and guns) increased 400% in Chicago (and other major metropolitan areas reveal similar patterns). Interviews with families living in public housing projects in Chicago revealed that virtually all the children had a firsthand experience with a shooting by the time they were 5 years old (Garbarino, Dubrow, Kostelny, and Pardo, 1992).

Other surveys found that 30% of the children living in high-crime neighborhoods of Chicago have witnessed a homicide by the time they are 15 years old, and more than 70% have witnessed a serious assault (Bell, 1991). These figures derive in part from the fact that killings are more public now than they were in the past. For example, Chicago has seen a 50% increase in the likelihood that a homicide is committed "in public" versus "in private" in the 10-year period from 1982 to 1992. In 1982, 32% of homicides were committed in public, whereas in 1992 that figure was 49%.

By the age of 14 years, most children living in these environments have personal knowledge of someone who has been killed in an act of violence. These data bear a greater resemblance to the experience of children in the war zones around the world than they do to what we should expect for our own children living in "peace" (Garbarino, Kostelny, and Dubrow, 1991a, 1991b). However, outright community violence is not the whole, or even the primary, issue facing parents, and with which public policy must contend. More broadly, there is the problem of geographic concentration of risk factors and the challenges these risk factors present to parents.

Amidst such a setting, many parents are likely to confront children who experience the symptoms of posttraumatic stress disorder (PTSD), symptoms that include sleep disturbances, re-creating trauma in play, extreme startle responses, diminished expectations for the future, and biochemical changes in the brain that impair social and academic functioning. Research reports a significant correlation between witnessing violence and both PTSD and more general childhood problems (Achenbach, 1991), especially when children are exposed to violence in the family as well (Garbarino, Kostelny, and Grady, 1993; Richters and Martinez, 1993). There is also evidence that young children are more likely than adolescents to experience PTSD when confronted with traumatic events. In one study, 56% of the children 10 years and younger showed signs of PTSD versus only 18% of those 11 years of age or older (Davidson and Smith, 1990).

What is more, one element that contributes to the problem of community crime and violence is the deterioration of the physical environment. The symbolic value of a deteriorating physical community is that it sends negative signals to residents, particularly to marginal members who are particularly prone to antisocial behavior. The cycle is recognized: Graffiti proliferates, trash accumulates, painting and other needed maintenance is delayed or foregone, vacant housing units increase, illicit drug sales and use escalate, and violence surges. Those responsible for the physical quality and security of the community's housing can play an important role in preventing or exacerbating this cycle, as is illustrated at a later point.

The experience of trauma can produce significant psychological problems that interfere with learning and appropriate social behavior in school and that interfere with normal parent–child relationships. It can also make children prime candidates for involvement in gangs, where the violent economy of the illicit drug trade offers a sense of belonging and solidarity as well as a cash income for those with few prosocial alternatives (Vorrasi and Garbarino, 2000). It requires extraordinary parenting (i.e., parenting that is more than normally informed, sensitive, involved, and skilled) to overcome these forces.

Does public policy create or tolerate social environments in which the accumulation of risk factors exceeds the average expectable competence of parents? It takes an extraordinary parent to succeed in a "socially toxic" environment (Garbarino, 1995), and no public policy can be considered humane if it requires extraordinary parenting. For example, there are many similarities between the experiences of children growing up in refugee and "displaced persons" camps in Thailand, Hong Kong, and the Middle East, and some low-income-housing projects in Chicago and other American cities (Garbarino et al., 1992):

(1) In both the camps and the housing projects, there is a proliferation of weapons—a kind of arms race which exacerbates the effects of conflict and violence. It is common for young

people—particularly males—to be heavily armed and to be engaged in armed attacks and reprisals. Substantial numbers of "bystander" injuries are observed.

(2) In both the camps and the housing projects, representatives of "mainstream" society have only partial control over what happens. International relief workers typically leave the camps at the end of the working day, as do the social workers and educators in the public housing projects. Both the camps and the projects are under the control of the local gangs at night. Therefore, no action during the day can succeed unless it is acceptable to the gangs that rule the community at night. For example, there have been cases in housing projects in Chicago in which local gangs have established curfews on their own initiative and in which gangs make the decision about whether or not someone who commits a crime against residents will be identified and punished.

(3) In both the camps and the projects, women—particularly mothers—are in a desperate situation. They are under enormous stress, often are the target of domestic violence, and have few economic or educational resources and prospects. Men play a marginal role in the enduring life of families—being absent for reasons that include participating in the fighting, fleeing to escape enemies, being injured or killed, and (particularly in the case of the American public housing projects) being imprisoned. Largely as a result, there is a major problem of maternal depression. Studies in both settings have reported 50% of the women being seriously depressed (Osofsky, 1997).

(4) In both the camps and the projects, one consequence of maternal depression is child neglect. This connection is well established in research indicating that neglect leads to elevated levels of "accidental injuries" to children (Wilson, Baker, Teret, Shock, and Garbarino, 1991). In many instances, only the most dedicated and highly motivated mothers can overcome the depressive effects of these high-crime, high-stress environments and rally to protect their children effectively. And this effort becomes more difficult as children reach adolescence and become increasingly independent of maternal control and potentially under the influence of gangs in the environment.

(5) In both the camps and the projects, children and youth have diminished prospects for the future. This lack of a positive future orientation produces depression, rage, and disregard for human life—their own and others'. In its most extreme form this disconnection from the future takes on the guise of "terminal thinking," the belief that the inevitable outcome of life in such an environment is early death. When asked "What will you be when you are 30 years old?" many children in these environments respond, "Dead" (Garbarino, 1995, 1999).

These environments are particularly relevant to our discussion of public policy issues affecting parenting because these settings do not arise "naturally." Rather, they result from public policy decisions. They are deliberate social creations—even if their consequences and dynamics were neither intentional nor anticipated. As a case example, one of the authors was involved as an expert witness in a case in California in which residents of a low-income housing project (owned by a group of private investors) sued the owners for liability because of deteriorating security conditions that produced an increase in violence resulting in traumatic stress for child residents. Tax policies and leniency toward white-collar crime permitted owners of this project to make money while neglecting their responsibility to the tenants. Thus, public policy played a major role in creating the social climate necessary for the neighborhood to become a traumatic setting. The report concluded (Garbarino, 1992a, pp. 10–13):

> Significant numbers of the children residing in Kennedy Manor evidence signs of chronic stress and trauma related to the overall level of danger present and their firsthand, specific encounters with threat and violence. Reports from parents suggest children are manifesting signs of posttraumatic stress disorder and more general indicators of anxiety and fear (including rashes, asthma, stomach pains, etc.). Young children are reported to evidence sleep disorders, fearfulness, clinging, and anger that they must live within the restrictions on their day-to-day lives imposed by their parents in an attempt to protect them from the high level of danger in the environment.

Significant numbers of parents and other caregivers responsible for children in Kennedy Manor report serious distress related to the conditions of life, including the pervasive threat and demoralizing conditions. There are numerous reports of stress-related psychosomatic conditions and sleep disturbances, as well as depression, humiliation, and anger for the adults who care for children.

It is not necessary to have daily incidents of violence to create and sustain a social climate of fear and threat. For example, if shooting occurs regularly—several times per month—that is enough to create an atmosphere of imminent danger, affecting the behavior of parents and children. The probability of violence is sufficiently high in Kennedy Manor to produce such effects. The day-to-day life of children in Kennedy Manor reflects a generalized perception of chronic danger. Children and parents are aware of multiple incidents of violence and fully expect such incidents to recur unless a major change in the management of the community addresses security concerns.

The conditions described by residents and observers in the Kennedy Manor Apartments are quite consistent with conditions in situations of chronic community violence observed in other locations around the United States. Our best estimate is that these conditions of life present a serious threat to the development and psychological well-being of the children who live there. The threat includes specific conditions such as Post Traumatic Stress Disorder related to first-hand encounters with violence and more general problems of chronic fear, anxiety, and depression, with resulting adaptations that impair academic, emotional, and social development. Children who live in such an environment are particularly prone for recruitment into gang activity when they reach adolescence.

Furthermore, the management of Kennedy Manor can exert significant influence over the social environment in the complex through policies and practices with respect to the quality of the physical environment (maintenance and rehabilitation of units and common areas), maintaining high standards for continued residence (by screening new tenants and proceeding with evictions as needed), and committing sufficient resources to on-site security to create a safer environment for residents (and as a result a greater sense of security for children).

How could social policy prevent situations like Kennedy Manor from happening? By dissecting the report, several examples of avenues of policy-based prevention and intervention emerge, including:

(1) Mandated psychological services for children and families who witness violence to help them assimilate and move beyond trauma;
(2) Tax incentives for socioeconomic class integration to dilute clusters of high-risk families and neighborhoods;
(3) Assertive gun control laws to disarm the disgruntled and violent sects of high-risk neighborhoods;
(4) Increased community and police surveillance to combat residents' perceptions of insecurity and threat.

THE ECONOMICS OF PARENTHOOD

Economic policies play an important role in shaping the parental landscape, and recent developments in welfare reform demonstrate this link. A primary goal of the welfare reform initiative of 1996 was to move parents "from welfare to work" with the expectation that the economic productivity and ensuing increases in parental self-efficacy, work ethic, and self-esteem would translate into better prospects for their children. This theorizing suggests an indirect effect of economic policy—in this case welfare reform—on child outcomes by way of a direct effect on parental well-being. That is, any positive effect of welfare reform on children is possible if and only if *parents* are first affected positively by welfare reform. Unfortunately, some initial evidence suggests that the expected positive effects on parents may not have been as strong as anticipated. For example, although most ex-recipients do, in fact, find work, the majority find themselves in jobs paying between $5.50 and $7.00 per hour, earning more than minimum wage but still not enough to raise a family out of poverty (Tweedie, Reichart, and O'Connor, 1999). What is more, there is often a significant amount of stress associated with the transition from welfare to work that undermines parenting ability and taxes parents' emotional and psychological resources. Add to this the fact that these low paying jobs often fail to afford parents the flexibility they need to succeed simultaneously in the labor force (e.g., paid family, personal, and sick leave) and at meeting the health and developmental needs of their children (Heymann and Earle, 1999), and the implications for the policy–parenting equation become clear: Economic policy can be, and in fact is, a highly influential determinant of parenting quality.

All this underscores the association between economic factors and parenting and provides evidence that welfare reform may actually be restricting parental performance rather than enhancing it. But correlations between measures of income or socioeconomic status and basic child outcomes are often higher in some societies than others (Bronfenbrenner, 1986). Why? Because in some societies parental income is the principal determinant of access to resources, whereas in other societies there are policies designed to minimize this correlation. For example, low income is a better predictor of developmental deficits in the United States than in virtually all other "modern" societies, in part because American social policies tend to exaggerate rather than minimize the impact of family income on access to preventive and rehabilitative services (Bronfenbrenner, 1986). Thus, one important aspect of policy is providing income transfers and child allowances to guarantee parents a predetermined minimum income level that allows for universal access to services (Plotnick, 1997). Another important aspect of policy is the extent to which crucial supportive services such as home health visitors and childcare are available to everyone (perhaps with a sliding fee schedule) as opposed to on the basis of availability of special grants in response to an assessment of risk.

The human significance of poverty for parenting has both "objective" and "subjective" dimensions. Among the objective dimensions are implications for illness (morbidity) and death (mortality). Both are substantially—but differentially—correlated with poverty in most societies, usually as a function of public policy. That is, in some societies, public health is such a high policy priority that income is actively and assertively combated as a correlate of heath outcomes. Among the important subjective concerns is the experience of *relative deprivation*, because poverty is a contextual judgment rather than an absolute attribute. It is an assessment of one's position in an overarching social order and is less a matter of what a child or family has as it is what that child or family does not have in relation to other children and families (Vorrasi and Garbarino, 2000). The message of poverty is one of difference, exclusion, and inferiority.

Beyond this concern with the developmental impact of poverty is a broader concern with the economic context of parents and parenthood. The economic "miracles" of the last four decades in nations around the world have raised expectations and led to a larger proportion of daily life becoming part of the monetarized economy (Giarini, 1980). This has important implications for families because, in the absence of a "sustainable society," parents (and thus children) are evermore susceptible to the vagaries of the modern economic order (Garbarino, 1992b). Thus, families will be more vulnerable to the periodic recessions, employment dislocations, and overall polarization of the population into "haves" and "have nots," as the rich really do get richer while the poor do indeed get poorer. It is possible for children to cost too much when their caregivers cannot generate enough income to meet popular expectations for participating in the monetarized economy of day-to-day life.

Thus, children are increasingly an economic burden, directly because of what it costs to rear them and indirectly because of what they cost in lost parental income. Conventional economists tell us to assume that "market forces" will produce a positive adaptation on the part of parents because it is in their self-interest to make whatever investment is needed to produce healthy, successful, and productive children. Sustainable economics challenge this glib assumption that the "invisible hand" of capitalism will take care of business, arguing that "business as usual" can lead to social and economic, as well as environmental disaster. We must study this hypothesis in detail across a variety of cultural and political contexts to have a full appreciation for the economics of parenthood. As we do so, we are drawn to the study of neighborhoods as contexts in which social policy translates into concrete influences on parenting.

NEIGHBORHOOD-BASED PROGRAMMING AS PARENT SUPPORT

However we, as a society, define "neighborhood," we must struggle to understand the potential and actual impact of "neighborhood-based programming" on parenting (Garbarino and Kostelny, 1992, 1994a, 1994b; Garbarino, Stocking, and Associates, 1980). The defining characteristics of a neighborhood-based approach to parenting are premised on the notion that deliberately engineered social support, provided during a formative period in child and family development, can (1) buffer the child and family from some of the psychological and social effects of poverty, (2) promote personal development and psychological well-being, and (3) stimulate healthy patterns of interaction both within the family and between the family and the broader environment (Weiss and Halpern, 1991). In starker terms, it may be argued that deliberately engineered social support can be potent enough to alter parenting capacities and styles acquired and reinforced through a lifetime of experience in a particular family and social world. However, social support systems do more than simply offer nurturance. They also offer feedback, validate the individual, and serve a social control function (Caplan and Killilea, 1976).

Analyzing social support as a strategy for enhancing parenting identifies two corollary premises. The first premise is that the support provided can be internalized in some manner, and thus have a lasting effect beyond the period during which it is provided. The second premise is that the support provided can strengthen childrearing enough to have a meaningful effect on child health and development (Weiss and Halpern, 1991). These corollaries reverberate through all analyses of neighborhood-based parent support in the form of two recurrent questions: (1) Can parent support be a "treatment" or must it be a condition of life? (2) Can parent support succeed amidst conditions of high risk? Both call our attention to the limiting factors on neighborhood support: whether it is possible to "synthesize" a neighborhood, and whether neighborhood-based programming is feasible among the neediest families.

One of the origins of the social support "movement" for parents lies in the settlement houses that were created as part of liberal reform movements in the nineteenth century (e.g., Hull House in Chicago; see Halpern, 1990). These settlement houses sought to provide a neighborhood focus and to serve a wide range of needs—ameliorative, preventive, and enabling. Staff lived in the settlement house, and the overall theme was one of establishing a center for promoting the culture, values, and resources of middle-income America among the poor and immigrant populations.

A second origin of the social support approach lies in the early concept of the visiting nurse. By sending nurses into the community, and by defining their role as "holistic," the visiting nurse programs of the nineteenth and early twentieth centuries complemented the settlement house by incorporating the concept of "friendly visitors" into day-to-day practice. Visiting nurses clearly bear a direct conceptual (and often historical) relation with contemporary approaches to parental social support, in which "community nursing" figures prominently (Froland, Pancoast, Chapman, and Kimboko, 1981; Kagan, Powell, Weissbourd, and Zigler, 1987). From the 1930s through the 1950s, other neighborhood-based strategies emerged.

Current approaches include a wide and proliferating variety of programs and organizations designed to establish social support in the environment of parents. These efforts are often called family support and education programs (e.g., the Family Focus Program, developed by Weissbourd and her colleagues), social support networks (Belle, 1989), parent education projects (e.g., the Parents as Teachers Program; Pfannenstiel and Seltzer, 1989), or home health visitor programs (e.g., the Prenatal and Early Infancy Project; Olds and Henderson, 1990; Olds, Henderson, Tatelbaum, and Chamberlain, 1986).

A study by Freudenburg and Jones (1991) of 23 communities experiencing rapid population growth found that all but two communities had a disproportionate increase in crime, and suggested that changes in a community's social structure that accompany rapid growth result in a breakdown of social control. As the "density of acquaintanceship" (i.e., the proportion of a community's residents who know each other) decreases, criminal activity increases. Another issue concerns out-migration from neighborhoods beginning to "turn bad." Such out-migration may have debilitating effects on social networks (Fitchen, 1981). It is not uncommon for influential social players and leaders to depart the neighborhood and leave behind a social void. What is more, the fact that out-migration is not random means that those who choose to stay and those who have no choice but to stay may increasingly constitute a sample unrepresentative of the general population. This can confound any assessment—and therefore any intervention effort.

Beyond even these obvious selection factors, neighborhoods differ on the basis of "ethos." Some areas are more vital and coherent, even among middle-income families (Warren, 1978). There are common problems too. A survey in South Carolina (Melton, 1992) revealed that on a scale of 1 to 7—with 7 indicating high involvement—the average score for neighborhood residents was 2+ in response to the question "How involved are you in other people's children?" The same survey also revealed that most people could not name one human service agency that had been particularly helpful on behalf of children.

Social context is important to parenting and the impact of policy (as is self-selection and the content of "treatment"). For example, research suggests that youth whose families are relocated to subsidized housing in the suburbs are more than twice as likely to attend college (54% vs. 21%) and find employment (75% vs. 41%) as youth who were relocated to subsidized housing in inner-city areas (Rosenbaum and Kaufman, 1991). Assuming that there were no systematic differences in who relocated where (a product of random assignment), this result suggests a powerful social support effect on important life-course events (i.e., attending college and finding employment).

We can derive the role of neighborhood factors in parenting from an understanding of the link between low income and child maltreatment (National Center on Child Abuse and Neglect, 1981; Pelton, 1978, 1981, 1994). National data tell us that the nation's poorest, most socially isolated, and economically frustrated parents are most likely to use family violence as a coping strategy (Wolfner and Gelles, 1993). From this observation flows a twofold conception of risk as applied to neighborhoods and families (Garbarino and Crouter, 1978). The first refers to areas with a high absolute rate of child maltreatment (based on cases per unit of population). In this sense, concentrations of socioeconomically distressed families are most likely to be at high risk for child maltreatment. For example, in Omaha, Nebraska, socioeconomic status accounted for approximately 40% of the variation across neighborhoods in reported rates of child maltreatment (Garbarino and Crouter, 1978). The magnitude of this correlation may reflect a social policy effect. It seems reasonable to hypothesize that, in a society in which low income is not correlated with access to basic human services (e.g., maternal and infant health care), this correlation would be smaller because the equality of services across social classes would promote universal health. In a society devoid of policies to ameliorate the impact of family-level differences in social class, it might be even larger.

It is the second meaning of high risk that is of greater relevance here, however. High risk can also mean that an area has a higher rate of child maltreatment than would be predicted knowing its socioeconomic character. Thus, two areas with similar socioeconomic profiles may have very different rates of child maltreatment. In this sense, one is high risk whereas the other is low risk, although both may have higher rates of child maltreatment than other, more affluent areas. In Figure 19.1, areas A and B have high observed rates of child maltreatment, whereas areas C and D have lower observed rates. However, areas A and C have higher observed rates than predicted rates (10 per 1,000 predicted and 36 per 1,000 observed for A; 7 per 1,000 predicted and 16 per 1,000 observed for C), whereas areas B and D have lower observed than predicted rates (55 per 1,000 predicted and 34 per 1,000 observed for B; 54 per 1,000 predicted and 14 per 1,000 observed for D). In this sense, A and C are both high risk, and B and D are both low risk. Areas

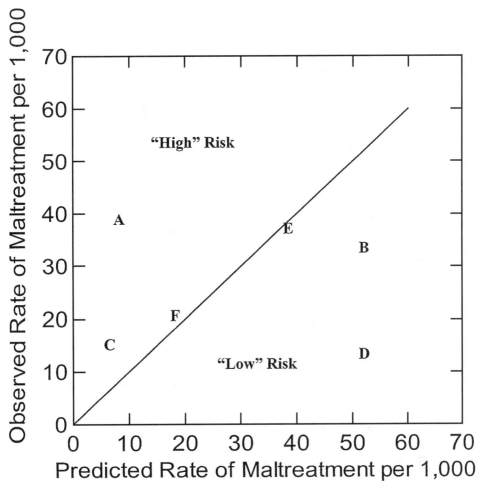

FIGURE 19.1. Two meanings of *Risk* in assessing community areas.

E and F evidence a close approximation between predicted and actual rates. This classification system provides the basis for identifying contrasting social environments. Unfortunately, this sort of community risk analysis is lacking in virtually all programmatic efforts aimed at preventing child maltreatment (indeed, in the areas in which social support programs might be aimed at improved family functioning).

Perhaps the most comprehensive analysis of the human ecology of social pathology to date concerns Chicago neighborhoods (Garbarino and Kostelny, 1992, 1993). It illustrates the challenges that must be faced in order to translate policy into parent support programs in the current context of extremely high levels of socioeconomic deprivation, geographic concentrations of poverty, and community violence. It further illuminates the negative social momentum characterizing many inner-city neighborhoods where child maltreatment is a disproportionately severe problem. Much of the variation among community rates of child maltreatment (using a composite measure that includes all forms, but is largely composed of physical abuse and neglect) is linked to variations in nine socioeconomic and demographic characteristics (with the multiple correlation being 0.89, thus accounting for 79% of the variation).

This is the statistical picture of the context in which prevention programs must operate. One specific piece of evidence communicates the urgency: child deaths due to maltreatment. Such child deaths are a particularly telling indicator of the bottom line in a community. Four Chicago neighborhoods in our statistical analysis reported a total of 19 such deaths during a 3-year period. Eight of these deaths (a rate of one death for each 2,541 children) occurred in a neighborhood identified as high risk. In an area that shared many problems but was identified in the statistical analysis as low risk, the rate was one death for each 5,571 children. The fact that deaths due to child maltreatment were twice as likely in the high-risk area than the low-risk area seems consistent with the overall findings of our statistical analyses and interviews. This is an environment in which there is truly an ecological conspiracy against parents and children (Garbarino and Kostelny, 1993).

FACTORS LEADING TO RESILIENCY AND COPING

Convergent findings from several studies of life course responses to stressful early experience suggest a series of ameliorating factors that lead to prosocial and healthy adaptability (Lösel and Bliesener, 1990): (1) actively trying to cope with stress (rather than just reacting), (2) cognitive competence (at least an average level of intelligence), (3) experiences of self-efficacy and a corresponding self-confidence and positive self-esteem, (4) temperamental characteristics that favor active coping attempts and positive relationships with others (e.g., activity, goal orientation, sociability) rather than passive withdrawal, (5) a stable emotional relationship with at least one parent or other reference person, (6) an open, supportive educational climate and parental model of behavior that encourages constructive coping with problems, and (7) social support from persons outside the family. These factors have been identified as important when the stressors involved are in the "normal" range found in the mainstream of modern industrial societies: poverty, family conflict, childhood physical disability, and parental involvement in substance abuse. They thus provide a starting point for efforts to understand the impact of policy on parenting—and ultimately on children.

Of the seven factors identified in the research on resilience and coping, several are particularly relevant to policy (and some of the others are indirectly relevant). We are particularly interested in three of the factors, and embedded within them is the beginning of an agendum for policy initiatives to enhance parenting—particularly under conditions of high stress and threat:

(1) Social support from persons outside the family: This factor exemplifies the roles of meso- and exosystems within an ecological perspective. We see this as a generic affirmation of the validity of policies designed to promote parental receipt of support efforts. It tells us that the importance of social support increases inversely with the inner resources of the parent: The poorer need more help. Moreover, it is frequently the case that the more troubled and impoverished a parent, the less effective he or she will be in identifying, soliciting, and making effecfive use of resources outside the family. For example, research indicates that neglecting mothers are less ready, willing, and able to see and make use of social support in their neighborhoods and more in need of such support than other mothers (Gaudin and Polansky, 1985).

(2) Open, supportive educational climate and parental models of behavior that encourage constructive coping with problems: This resilience factor explicitly targets the community's institutions. Schools, religious institutions, civic organizations, and other social entities operationalize the concept of "an open, supportive educational climate." Programs and role models that teach and reward the reflective "processing" of experience are an essential feature of social support at the neighborhood and community level.

(3) A stable emotional relationship with at least one parent or other reference person: The significance this factor of resilience has for policies affecting parenting is demonstrated by the recurrent finding that depth—as opposed to mere breadth—is an important feature of social support, not to mention one often neglected in programmatic approaches (Gottlieb, 1981). In addition to having social support effectively available through friends, neighbors, coworkers, and professionals, parents need social support in its most intensive form: You need "someone who is absolutely crazy about

you" (Bronfenbrenner, 1970). It is clear from research on parenting that children must have someone in this role, but it is also important in the healthy development of youth and adults, including those in parenting roles.

The implications of this ecological analysis are quite significant. For example, in his efforts to prevent child maltreatment among malfunctioning parent–child dyads, Wahler (1980) found that the effects of programatic intervention were negligible for mothers who had no close allies who supported revisions in their parenting styles and practices. Only by identifying and incorporating into the preventive intervention a maternal ally—such as her sister or best friend—was Wahler (1980) able to ensure that the preventive strategies he was teaching to mothers would endure. For poor mothers especially, this person is likely to be neighborhood based. This finding parallels other studies emphasizing the importance of social support for the goals of professional intervention (e.g., the congruence of residential treatment goals for youth in the postrelease social environment—see Whittaker et al., 1983).

Social support has at least two distinct dimensions: making the individual feel connected and promoting prosocial behavior (e.g., avoiding child maltreatment even under stressful conditions). Understanding this duality of social support offers an explanation for the finding that, under conditions of social stress, parents whose only social network is kin are more likely to abuse children than families whose network includes nonkin (Gelles and Straus, 1988). Kin-only networks are more likely than more diverse networks to offer consensus support for an interpretation of child behavior and a corresponding rationale for parent behavior. Considering the structure of social support without regard to its value and cultural content is insufficient. We can see further evidence of this by explicitly focusing on socially maladaptive methods of coping.

CONCLUSIONS

Children in conditions of developmental risk need relationships with adults—teaching relationships—to help them process their experiences in ways that prevent developmental harm. Vygotsky (1986) referred to this developmental space between what children can do alone and what they can do with the help of an adult teacher as the "zone of proximal development." Developmentalists have come to recognize that it is this dynamic relation between the child's competence alone and the child's competence in the company of a guiding teacher that leads to forward movement and enhanced development. Children reared by incapable or inaccessible parents are generally denied that processing within the family. Indeed, they receive just the opposite of what they need, particularly in conditions of social risk derived from the social environment outside the home. This is one reason why measures to improve parenting in the context of high-stress social environments deserve the highest priority as a matter of social policy.

Mediation and processing are critical in the case of moral development where the child's moral teachers (be they adults or peers) lead the child toward higher order thinking by presenting positions that are at least one stage above the child's characteristic mode of responding to social events as moral issues. When all this happens in the context of a nurturant-affective system—a warm family, for example—the result is ever advancing moral development, the development of a principled ethic of caring (Gilligan, 1982). What is more, even if the parents create a rigid, noninteractive authoritarian family context (thus blocking moral development), the larger community may compensate: ". . . the child of authoritarian parents may function in a larger more democratic society whose varied patterns provide the requisite experiences for conceptualizing an egalitarian model of distributive justice" (Fields, 1987, p. 5).

If school teachers, neighbors, and other adult representatives of the community are unable or disinclined to model higher order moral reasoning, then the process of moral truncation that is "natural" to situations of family and community violence will proceed unimpeded. This may well be happening in many urban school systems in which teachers are demoralized, parents incapacitated, and students apathetic. The result is to permit the natural socialization of the depleted community to proceed, with its consequences in intergenerational aggression, neighborhood deterioration, and family malfunction (e.g., child maltreatment).

Families can provide the emotional context for the necessary cognitive processing of making positive moral sense of social experience outside the home. But to do so they must be functioning well themselves as systems within the ecology of the child. Thus, in cases of problematic parenting within families, neighbors and professionals in communities usually must take the lead in stimulating higher order moral development and compensatory socialization in children. They do this by presenting a supportive and democratic milieu (e.g., in schools, churches, neighborhood associations, and local political parties). Without these efforts, the result is likely to be impaired social and moral development, particularly among children who are more vulnerable to this consequence of living at risk (Werner, 1990).

Directly and indirectly, policy plays an important role in setting the parameters of parenting, whether it be through social or economic initiatives. The bottom line in our effort to enhance parenting through social policy lies in the degree to which society is able to replace risk with opportunity in the lives of children (or at least compensate for risk by providing compensatory opportunities). The foundation for success in these efforts lies in an ecological perspective, in an appreciation for the role of social context in mediating relations between individuals and the larger society. This recognition that there are multiple systems between the individual and the society is fundamental to our ecological perspective. It focuses attention on the crucial role of policy in stimulating, guiding, and enhancing these intermediary systems (the meso- and exosystems) on behalf of more effective parenting. Social policy decisions influence child development through their effects on parenting. The need for understanding is great, and the stakes are high.

ACKNOWLEDGMENTS

This work was supported, in part, by a grant from Cornell University's College of Human Ecology. Special thanks are due to Brianna Sinnon and Lisa Rose for time spent helping prepare this manuscript for publication.

REFERENCES

Achenbach, T. (1991). *Manual for the child behavior checklist and 1991 profile*. Burlington: University of Vermont, Department of Psychiatry.

Albee, O. (1980). Primary prevention and social problems. In G. Gerbner, C. Ross, and E. Zigler (Eds.), *Child abuse: An agenda for action* (pp. 106–117). New York: Oxford University Press.

Barclay-McLaughlin, C. (1987). *The center for successful child development*. Chicago: The Ounce of Prevention Fund.

Bell, C. (1991). Traumatic stress and children in danger. *Journal of Health Care for the Poor and Underserved, 2*, 175–188.

Belle, D. (Ed.). (1989). *Children's social networks and social supports*. New York: Wiley.

Benson, P. L., Leffert, N., Scales, P. C., and Blyth, D. A. (1998). Beyond the village rhetoric: Creating healthy communities for children and adolescents. *Applied Developmental Science, 2*, 138–159.

Bronfenbrenner, U. (1970). *Two worlds of childhood: U.S. and U.S.S.R.* New York: Russell Sage Foundation.

Bronfenbrenner, U. (1979). *The ecology of human development: Experiments by nature and design*. Cambridge, MA: Harvard University Press.

Bronfenbrenner, U. (1986). Ecology of family as a context for human development. *Developmental Psychology, 22*, 723–742.

Bronfenbrenner, U., and Crouter, A. (1983). The evolution of environmental models in developmental research. In P. Mussen (Ed.), *The handbook of child psychology* (pp. 357–414). New York: Wiley.

Caplan, G., and Killilea, M. (Eds.). (1976). *Support systems and mutual help: Multidisciplinary explorations.* New York: Grune and Stratton.

Carlsson-Paige, N., and Levin, D. (1990). *Who's calling the shots? How to respond effectively to children fascination with war play and war toys.* Philadelphia: New Society.

Center for Media Education. (1997). *Children and television: Frequently asked questions* [Online]. Washington, DC. Available: http://www.cme.org/children/kids_tv/c_and_t.html

Chase-Lansdale, P. L., and Vinovskis, M. A. (1992). Whose responsibility?: A historical analysis of the changing roles of mothers, fathers, and society. In P. L. Chase-Lansdale and J. Brooks-Gunn (Eds.), *Escape from poverty: What makes a difference for children?* New York: Cambridge University Press.

David, H. (1992). Born unwanted: Long-term developmental effects of denied abortion. *Journal of Social Issues, 48,* 163–181.

David, H. (1994). Reproductive rights and reproductive behavior: Clash or convergence of private values and public policies. *American Psychologist, 49,* 343–349.

David, H., Dytrych, Z., Matejcek. Z., and Schüller, V. (1988). *Born unwanted: Developmental effects of denied abortion.* New York: Springer.

Davidson, I., and Smith, R. (1990). Traumatic experiences of psychiatric outpatients. *Journal of Traumatic Stress Studies, 3,* 459–475.

Dunst, C., and Trivetter, C. (1992, November). *Risk and opportunity factors influencing parent and child functioning.* Paper presented at the Ninth Annual Smoky Mountain Winter Institute, Ashville, NC.

Dytrych, Z. (1992). Children born from unwanted pregnancies: Prevention of psychological deprivation. In E. Albee, L. Bond, and T. Munsey (Eds.), *Improving children's lives: Global perspectives on prevention* (pp. 97–105). Newbury Park, CA: Sage.

Elder, C. (1974). *Children of the Great Depression: Social change in life experience.* Chicago: University of Chicago Press.

Fields, R. (1987, October). *Terrorized into terrorist: Sequelae of PTSD in young victims.* Paper presented at the meeting of the Society for Traumatic Stress Studies, New York.

Fitchen, J. (1981). *Poverty in rural America: A case study.* Boulder, CO: Westview.

Freudenburg, W., and Jones, R. (1991). Criminal behavior and rapid community growth: Examining the evidence. *Rural Sociology, 56,* 619–645.

Froland, C., Pancoast, D., Chapman. N., and Kimboko, P. (1981). *Helping networks and human services.* Beverly Hills, CA: Sage.

Garbarino, J. (1992a). *Childhood in Kennedy Manor Apartments: Developmental significance of living in chronic danger.* Chicago: Erikson Institute.

Garbarino, J. (1992b). *Towards a sustainable society: An economic, social and environmental agenda for our children's future.* Chicago: Noble.

Garbarino. J. (1995). *Raising children in a socially toxic environment.* San Francisco: Jossey-Bass.

Garbarino, J. (1996). A vision of family policy for the 21st century. *Journal of Social Issues, 52,* 197–203.

Garbarino, J. (1999). *Lost boys: Why our sons turn violent and how we can save them.* New York: Free Press.

Garbarino, J., and Associates. (1992). *Children and families in the social environment* (2nd ed.). Hawthorne, NY: Aldine de Gruyter.

Garbarino, J., and Bedard, C. (2001). *Parents under siege.* New York: The Free Press.

Garbarino, J., and Crouter, A. (1978). Defining the community context of parent–child relations. *Child Development, 49,* 604–616.

Garbarino, J., Dubrow, N., Kostelny, K., and Pardo, C. (1992). *Children in danger: Coping with the consequences of community violence.* San Francisco: Jossey-Bass.

Garbarino, J., Guttman, E., and Seeley, J. (1986). *The psychologically battered child: Strategies for identification, assessment, and intervention.* San Francisco: Jossey-Bass.

Garbarino, J., and Kostelny, K. (1992). Child maltreatment as a community problem. *Child Abuse and Neglect, 16,* 455–464.

Garbarino, J., and Kostelny, K. (1993). Neighborhood and community influences on parenting. In T. Luster and L. Okagaki (Eds.), *Parenting: An ecological perspective* (pp. 203–226). Hillsdale, NJ: Lawrence Erlbaum Associates.

Garbarino, J., and Kostelny, K. (1994a). Family support and community development. In S. Kagan and B Weissbourd (Eds.), *Putting families first: America's family support movement and the challenge of change* (pp. 297–320). San Francisco: Jossey-Bass.

Garbarino, J., and Kostelny, K. (1994b). *Neighborhood-based programs.* Washington, DC: U.S. Advisory Board on Child Abuse and Neglect.

Garbarino, J., and Kostelny, K. (1995). Parenting and public policy. In M. H. Bornstein (Ed.), *Handbook of parenting: Vol. 3. Status and social conditions of parenting* (pp. 419–436). Mahwah, NJ: Lawrence Erlbaum Associates.

Garbarino, J., Kostelny, K., and Dubrow, N. (1991a). *No place to be a child: Growing up in a war zone.* Lexington, MA: Lexington Books.

Garbarino, J., Kostelny, K., and Dubrow, N. (1991b). What children can tell us about living in danger. *American Psychologist, 46,* 376–383.

Garbarino, J., Kostelny, K., and Grady, N. (1993). Children in dangerous environments: Child maltreatment in the context of community violence. In D. Cicchetti and S. Toth (Eds.), *Child abuse, child development, and social policy* (pp. 167–189). Norwood, NJ: Ablex.

Garbarino, J., Stocking, H., and Associates. (1980). *Protecting children from abuse and neglect: Developing and maintaining effective support systems for families.* San Francisco: Jossey-Bass.

Gaudin, J., and Polansky, N. (1985). Social distancing of the neglectful family: Sex, race, and social class influences. *Social Service Review, 58,* 245–253.

Gelles, R., and Straus, M. (1988). *Intimate violence: The definitive study of the causes and consequences of abuse in the American family.* New York: Simon and Schuster.

Giarini, O. (1980). *Dialogue on wealth and welfare.* New York: Pergamon.

Gilligan, C. (1982). *In a different voice.* Cambridge, MA: Harvard University Press.

Gilligan, J. (1991, May). *Shame and humiliation: The emotions of individual and collective violence.* Paper presented at the Erikson Lectures, Harvard University, Cambridge, MA.

Gilligan, J. (1996) *Violence: Our deadly epidemic and its causes.* New York: Putnam.

Gottlieb, B. H. (Ed.). (1981). *Social networks and social support.* Beverly Hills, CA: Sage Publications.

Halpern, R. (1990). Parent support and education programs. *Children and Youth Services Review, 12,* 285–308.

Heymann, J., and Earle, A. (1999). The impact of welfare reform on parents' ability to care for their children's health. *American Journal of Public Health, 89,* 502–505.

Kagan, S., Powell, D., Weissbourd. B., and Zigler, E. (Eds.). (1987). *America's family support programs: Perspectives and prospects.* New Haven, CT: Yale University Press.

Lemann, N. (1986, June). The origins of the underclass. *Atlantic,* pp. 31–61.

Lösel, F., and Bliesener, T. (1990). Resilience in adolescence: A study on the generalizability of protective factors. In K. Hurrelmann and F. Lösel (Eds.), *Health hazards in adolescence* (pp. 290–320). Berlin: Walter de Gruyter.

Melton, G. (1992). It's time for neighborhood research and action. *Child Abuse and Neglect, 16,* 909–913.

Moran, G., and Vinovskis, M. (1992). *Religion, family, and the life course: Explorations in the social history of America.* Ann Arbor: University of Michigan Press.

National Center on Child Abuse and Neglect. (1981). *The national incidence study of child abuse and neglect: Report of findings.* Washington, DC: NCCAN.

Olds, D., and Henderson, C. (1990). The prevention of maltreatment. In D. Cicchetti and V. Carlson (Eds.), *Child maltreatment* (pp. 722–763). New York: Cambridge University Press.

Olds, D., Henderson, C., Tatelbaum, R., and Chamberlain, R. (1986). Preventing child abuse and neglect: A randomized trial of nurse home visitation. *Pediarrics, 78,* 65–78.

Osofsky, J. (Ed.). (1997). *Children in a violent society.* York, PA: Guilford.

Pelton, L. (1978). Child abuse and neglect: The myth of classlessness. *American Journal of Orthopsychiatry, 48,* 608–617.

Pelton, L. (1981). *The social context of child abuse and neglect.* New York: Human Sciences Press.

Pelton, L. (1994). *The role of material factors in child abuse and neglect.* Washington, DC: U.S. Advisory Board on Child Abuse and Neglect.

Pfannenstiel, J., and Seltzer, D. (1989). New parents as teachers: Evaluation of an early parent education program. *Early Childhood Research Quarterly, 4,* 1–18.

Plotnick, R. D. (1997). Child poverty can be reduced. *Future of Children, 7,* 72–87.

Punamaki, R. (1987). Psychological stress responses of Palestinian mothers and their children in conditions of military occupation and political violence. *Quarterly Newsletter of the Laboratory of Comparative Human Cognition, 9,* 76–84.

Richters J., and Martinez, R. (1993). T'he NIMH community violence project I: Children as victims of and witnesses to violence. *Psychiatry, 56,* 7–21.

Rohner, R. (1980). Worldwide tests of parental acceptance-rejection theory: An overview. *Behavior Science Research, 15,* 1–21.

Rosenbaum, J., and Kaufman, J. (1991, August). *Educational and occupational achievements of low income Black youth in White suburbs.* Paper presented at the annual meetings of the American Sociological Association, Cincinnati, OH.

Sameroff, A., Seifer, R., Barocas, R., Zax, M., and Greenspan, S. (1987). Intelligence quotient scores of 4-year-old children: Social–environmental risk factors. *Pediatrics, 79,* 343–350.

Schell, J. (1982). *The fate of the earth.* New York: Knopf.

Tweedie, J., Reichert, D., and O'Connor, M. (1999). *Tracking recipients after they leave welfare* [Online]. Children and Families Program of the National Conference of State Legistaures. Available: http://www.ncsl.org/statefed/welfare/leavers.htm

Vorrasi, J. A., and Garbarino, J. (2000). Poverty and youth violence: Not all risk factors were created equal. In V. Polakow (Ed.). *The public assault on America's children: Poverty, violence, and juvenile injustice* (pp. 54–72). New York: Teachers College Press.

Vygotsky, L. (1986). *Thought and language.* Cambridge, MA: MIT Press.

Wahler, R. (1980). The insular mother: Her problems in parent–child treatment. *Journal of Applied Behavior Analysis, 13,* 207–219.

Warren, R. (1978). *The community in America*. Boston: Houghton Mifflin.

Weiss, H., and Halpern, R. (1991). *Community-based family support and education programs: Something old or new?* New York: Columbia University, National Center for Children in Poverty.

Werner, E. (1990). Protective factors and individual resilience. In R. Meisells and J. Shonkoff (Eds.), *Handbook of early childhood intervention* (pp. 97–116). Cambridge, England: Cambridge University Press.

Whittaker, J., Garbarino, J., and Associates. (1983). *Social support networks an informal helping in the human services*. Hawthorne, NY: Aldine de Gruyter.

Wilson, M., Baker, S., Teret, S., Shock, S., and Garbarino, J. (1991). *Saving children: A guide to injury prevention*. New York: Oxford University Press.

Wilson, W. (1987). *The truly disadvantaged: The inner city, the underclass, and public policy*. Chicago: University of Chicago Press.

Author Index

W

Subject Index